*Opera Companies and Houses of Western Europe,
Canada, Australia and New Zealand*

Opera Companies and Houses of Western Europe, Canada, Australia and New Zealand

A Comprehensive Illustrated Reference

by
KARYL LYNN ZIETZ

McFarland & Company, Inc., Publishers
Jefferson, North Carolina, and London

Library of Congress Cataloguing-in-Publication Data

Zietz, Karyl Lynn.
    Opera companies and houses of Western Europe, Canada, Australia
and New Zealand : a comprehensive illustrated reference / by Karyl
Lynn Zietz.
       p.   cm.
    Includes bibliographical references and index.
    ISBN 0-7864-0611-9 (library binding : 50# alkaline paper) ∞
    1. Opera companies — Directories.   2. Theaters — Directories.
3. Opera — 20th century — Directories.   I. Title
ML12.Z54   1999
792.5'025 — dc21

                                          98-45854
                                            CIP

British Library Cataloguing-in-Publication data are available

Manufactured in the United States of America

McFarland & Company, Inc., Publishers
  Box 611, Jefferson, North Carolina 28640
    www.mcfarlandpub.com

In memory of Teresa
Amice in vita, in morte

— Inspired by Verdi's "La forza del destino"

Acknowledgments

A book of this kind would not be possible without the cooperation and assistance of a large number of people in many areas. Because of the sizable numbers involved, I have thanked each person individually under the appropriate opera house entry. First there were those who worked at the opera houses and companies, and who graciously responded promptly and offered assistance and provided invaluable information.

There were nonresponsive houses and companies who after three attempts still did not respond, and here I am indebted to a number of European friends, especially in Italy, who prodded the opera houses until they yielded information, and to some very helpful embassy staff in Washington D.C., who both provided information and scolded the houses until they responded.

I am also indebted to the Belgian Tourist Office, the Danish Tourist Office, the Swedish Tourist Office, the Icelandic Tourist Office, the Danish Foreign Ministry, the Economic Development Division of the City of Swansea, Wales, and the South Australian Tourism Commission for providing accommodations and invaluable assistance, and to Icelandair for providing transportation to Iceland and to British Airways for making my journeys to Europe more comfortable.

Table of Contents

List of Photographs

(All photographs are by the author unless specified)

Foreword

When Karyl Lynn Zietz published *Opera Houses and Companies of the United States — A Comprehensive Illustrated Reference* in 1995, I welcomed the book with open arms in the pages of *Opera Now*, the international magazine of which I was privileged then to be the editor.

As a frequent traveller on operatic business to the United States, I always came home laden with the smart, comprehensive publicity kits characteristic of American companies; if I had collected this material over a period of years, and spent countless hours in the historical sections of public libraries and in interviews with opera archivists, general directors and music critics, I could have started my own personal index of opera in America.

To my huge relief, Karyl Lynn Zietz came along and did all this work, and much, much more, in her brilliant book — the product of years of foot-slogging on the American opera trail. The 1995 volume covered over 90 U.S. companies, encompassing their history (including repertory and premiere lists), current programs and artistic policies. It also sorted out, for the first time in a comprehensive survey, the "contradictory and unreliable information" which had been published in various ways over the years. One of the most appealing features of the treatment was that the companies' home theatres were also covered from a historical perspective, and vividly described with Karyl Lynn's keen eye for architectural detail.

The American volume contained wise and objective appraisals of opera politics in the United States today; opera directors themselves were occasionally quoted, mostly but not exclusively to their advantage, and I particularly enjoyed a remark by conductor Kurt Herbert Adler in response to a ticking-off from a San Francisco Opera board member: "If I did not have failures, you could not afford me." Then there was the Sarasota Opera production of Monteverdi's *L'incoronazione di Poppea* trashed by the critics and the subject of board member walkout because it included, appropriately enough for Nero's Rome, "sexual acts of both men with women and men with men" — needless to say, the show became the hottest ticket in town.

In my review of the book in *Opera Now*, I concluded: "In my estimation this is a 300-page book with about 1000 pages of information bursting out of its elegant layout; from now on this will be my *Opernführer* for the USA and I will not get on a plane without it."

In this context I am all the more delighted to introduce Karyl Lynn Zietz's latest work, which fills in the picture of the rest of the known operatic world outside the United States. Its range and scope are ambitious but readers will find they are in the hands of a fellow-traveller whose love for opera is matched by her formidable gifts as a historian and researcher — all of these qualities are channelled into a writing style which laces factual accuracy with wit and liberal helpings of appropriate anecdote. I commend the new vademecum to my airline hand-luggage and, dear reader, to you.

Graeme Kay
Editor, *BBC Music Magazine*
Summer 1999

Preface

Although several books have been written about opera companies and houses in the world, no one book has covered more than a scattered collection of the larger, better known companies and houses, with a sentence or two on some of the smaller ones. These books were often a regurgitation of information skimmed from existing reference books, or propaganda pieces written by the opera companies themselves. Not infrequently, they contained erroneous information which had been taken from previous books without checking for accuracy. And, no book has included lists of world premieres, repertories, and history of company staff. Little has been written in general about the smaller opera houses and companies, and nothing has been written in English about these lesser-known opera establishments in non–English speaking countries, making it all but impossible for the English-speaking researcher or opera aficionado to learn about them.

In a perfect world, every opera house would have a complete entry, but we live in an imperfect world and many smaller, lesser-known opera houses (especially in France, Germany, Italy, and the United Kingdom) never responded to my requests for information. In many cases archives either did not exist or had been destroyed by fire, flood or war, making it impossible to research myself. Each opera house or company was sent three requests (if necessary) in their mother-tongue for information, and I personally visited almost two-thirds of them. But even in person, some opera houses yielded no archives, or historical or background information, and I was limited to personal observations. The only reason why almost every Italian opera house has a fairly complete entry is that I had three persevering friends in Italy who badgered the opera houses until they responded. Also, Italy was the birthplace of opera. Unfortunately, I did not have that assistance in the other countries. If material was not available from any other reliable source, the company received an abbreviated entry, but essentially every professional company and opera house in Western Europe (including Iceland), Canada, Australia and New Zealand has been included.

Space and time considerations prevented as full an entry as I would have liked to write for many of the houses and companies, so I wrote detailed chapters on a few representative houses in a region or country, to give the reader an impression that could be extrapolated to other houses of similar size, status, budget, and mission in the region. For example, I listed the repertory for the first 100 years (1737–1837) for Teatro di San Carlo in Naples, and then noted high points after that time period. I also included the complete repertory for Teatro Comunale in Bologna (northern Italy) from when it opened in 1763 to the present, as well as complete repertories of other Italian opera houses. Repertories of several relatively new companies that would not be available in any other source and did not consume much space were also listed. Otherwise, as far as possible, world premieres, and sometimes country premieres are listed at the end of each entry. For several large houses like the Bayerische Staatsoper (Munich), with hundreds of world premieres, the lists were limited to certain time periods. When a complete premiere listing was not possible, as many premieres as relevant were included in the text. I maintained, as far as space and available information allowed, a uniformity among the chapters for quick comparisons regarding growth and development among houses, cities, regions, and countries. Within these limitations, I included with each entry more substance, facts, figures, and details than are usually found in reference books, especially of this magnitude and scope. To bring the opera houses to life, I added an occasional anecdote or notice of a special event.

In some cases, the smaller and lesser-known houses received longer entries than the larger, more famous houses. This is more the case with houses in non–English speaking countries, since little or no information is available on them in English, and especially because many of the larger and better known theaters, like Opéra National de Paris (Palais Garnier), Staatsoper Wien (Vienna State Opera), Teatro alla Scala (Milan), and Royal Opera (Covent Garden) have entire books in English devoted to them.

The entries concentrate on which works and type of productions are offered at the opera houses, with special attention paid to world and country premieres, because I believe this defines an opera house more than anything else, and also since so little has been published about this aspect of the houses. I have also included the composer next to every opera title, since even though it may be obvious to the researcher or opera lover, I also wanted to make this reference accessible to the novice, who may not know that Verdi composed *La traviata* or Puccini wrote *Madama Butterfly*, and to make it possible to follow individual composers and their works.

Two major problems were encountered in compiling this reference. The first was the Tower of Babel created by the opera titles. Every country translated the original opera title into its own language, regardless of the original title and language in which the opera was performed. Essentially every reference book of this type has left them in the language of the country. This not only made indexing impossible, but was terribly confusing to the reader, who did not know that *Der Bajazzo* was *I pagliacci*; *L'oro del Reno* was *Das Rheingold*; *De jodin* was *La Juive*, or *Ruuvikierre* was *Turn of the*

Screw. Therefore, I translated all titles into their original language applying the grammatical rules of that language, to make all the operas recognizable to the reader, and to permit indexing so the reader can trace performances of individual operas. Russian titles are listed in the standard transliteration, and titles that would be difficult to recognize in the original language (primarily Russian, other Slavic, and Finnish titles) are also translated into English. When there were two versions of the opera in different languages, like Verdi's *Les vêpres siciliennes* and *I vespri siciliani*, *Don Carlos* (French) and *Don Carlo* (Italian), or Donizetti's *La favorite* (French) or *La favorita* (Italian), Rossini's *Guillaume Tell* (French) and *Guglielmo Tell* (Italian), the title used indicates which version was presented.

The second major problem, and the same one I encountered when I wrote *Opera Companies and Houses of the United States,* is the unreliable or conflicting information found in most reference and guide books written in English about European houses, and even in books written in the language of the country in which the opera house is located. For example, one opera house was said to have burned down in 1688 and again in 1692, when it was actually only constructed in 1692. In a book about opera in Italy, it was stated that the theater in Cremona was inspired by a young Mozart's visit in 1747; he did not enter this world until 1756. Incorrect dates and places of inaugural works were also problems frequently encountered. One source stated that the Italian premiere of Fromental Halévy's *La Juive* was in Bologna in 1868, whereas it had already taken place a decade earlier in Genoa. Therefore, I used almost exclusively original source material, and in case of conflicting information, if I could not verify which information was correct, I omitted it or indicated a problem, and that which was included was verified by reliable or archival sources.

A word about funding. In the United States, public funding of opera ranges from approximately zero to 10%; in Canada 10%–50%; in Australia 25%–80%, and in Europe, usually 60% to 100%, although there are some exceptions.

An integral part of a reference book on opera houses and companies is information about visiting the theater and getting tickets to attend a performance, especially those in non–English speaking countries, where it is even difficult for the expert to receive schedules and responses from the opera houses, or to know which hotel is convenient and has connections with the opera house to provide schedules and tickets. Therefore, I have recommended with each opera house (as far as possible) a hotel of which I have personal knowledge that has connections to the opera house, can handle all schedule and ticket requirements, and is convenient to the opera house. Many of these hotels have been in existence as long as the opera houses themselves.

I spent the better part of the last three years visiting these opera houses and attending performances, often several productions, since I am aware of the inherent danger involved in presenting an artistic analysis after seeing only one opera, and interviewing dozens of general and artistic directors (in many different languages) and press officers, to give an accurate and personal portrait of the house, what is often missing in reference books. The reader will be taken on a journey to more than three hundred cities, towns, and villages in Western Europe, Canada, Australia, and New Zealand, ranging from Vaasa, Finland, to Perth, Australia. My intent was to create the quintessential opera reference book.

Australia

The State Opera of South Australia (State Opera)
Adelaide Festival of Arts (Festival)

The State Opera of South Australia

Giacomo Puccini's *La bohème*, staged on August 18, 1975, at Her Majesty's Theatre, was the first production of The State Opera of South Australia, originally called New Opera, South Australia. Domenico Cimarosa's *Il matrimonio segreto* was also on the program that initial season. The State Opera of South Australia was established by Act of Parliament in July 1976. It is the only statutory authority opera company in Australia.

Coppin's English Opera Company presented Vincent Wallace's *Maritana*, Gaetano Donizetti's *Lucia di Lammermoor*, Vincenzo Bellini's *La sonnambula*, and Michael Balfe's *The Bohemian Girl* in 1856, in what could be considered Adelaide's first repertory season of opera and the beginning of the history of opera in South Australia. The arrival of Bianchi's Grand Italian Opera Company in 1861 initiated a "Golden Age" of opera, which Lyster's Royal Italian and English Company continued until William Lyster's death in 1880. Over a three month period, Bianchi's company staged fourteen different operas — Bellini's *Norma* and *La sonnambula*, Donizetti's *Lucrezia Borgia*, *Lucia di Lammermoor*, *L'elisir d'amore*, *La fille du régiment*, and *Don Pasquale*, Giuseppe Verdi's *Attila*, *Il trovatore*, *Rigoletto*, *Ernani*, and *La traviata*, Gioachino Rossini's *Il barbiere di Siviglia*, and Balfe's *The Bohemian Girl*. Not to be outdone, when Lyster's company first arrived in 1865, their four-week season offered 23 different works, including Balfe's *Rose of Castile*, Charles Gounod's

Faust, Julius Benedict's *The Lily of Killarney*, Daniel Auber's *Fra Diavolo* and *La muette de Portici*, Giacomo Meyerbeer's *Les Huguenots* and *Le Prophète*, Carl Maria von Weber's *Der Freischütz*, and Friedrich von Flotow's *Martha*, along with several of the same operas given by Bianchi. Lyster's group returned regularly to Adelaide, always presenting a full repertory schedule. Other companies visited as well — the Simonsen's English Opera Company in 1871, bringing Balfe's *Satanella*, Verdi's *Il trovatore*, Flotow's *Martha*, and von Weber's *Der Freischütz*; the Cagli and Pompei's Royal Italian Opera Company the following year with the popular Italian repertory and a couple of novelites including Giovanni Pacini's *Saffo* and Benedetto Ferrari's *Pipele*; the Royal English Opera Company in 1875 with 15 operas, including Jacques Offenbach's *La Grande Duchesse de Gerolstein*, *Geneviève de Brabant,* and *Barbe Bleue*, Gounod's *Faust*, Verdi's *Il trovatore*, and Balfe's *The Bohemian Girl* and *Satanella*, and Lazar's Royal Italian Company with 21 operas, among which were Filippo Marchetti's *Ruy Blas*, Saverio Mercadante's *La vestale*, Luigi and Federico Ricci's *Ruy Blas*, Carlo Pedrotti's *Tutti in maschera*, Donizetti's *Linda di Chamounix*, Meyerbeer's *Robert le Diable* and *Les Huguenots* and Rossini's *Semiramide*. When Lyster's Royal Italian and English Opera Company arrived in October-November 1880 with ten offerings, including Gilbert and Sullivan's *H. M. S. Pinafore*, they presented a preview of things to come, which was the domination of Gilbert and Sullivan works and other comic operas and operettas during the last couple of

Her Majesty's Theatre (Adelaide, Australia).

decades of the 1800s and the beginning of the 1900s. Prominent in this circuit was J.C. Williamson's English Opera Company. Other companies presenting these works included Pollard's Lilliputian Opera Company, Leumane's English Opera Company, and Kate Howard's Opera Company. As the 20th century progressed, Italian opera (with the odd French work) found favor again. The Gonzales Italian Grand Opera Company and Nellie Melba's company offered this operatic fare.

Around the same time, there were two attempts to establish a resident opera company. The first took place in 1924, when two local businessmen, Mr. Savery and Mr. Uffindell, invited Italian baritone Ercole Filippini to establish a School of Opera Singing and produce grand opera with local talent. Called the South Australian Grand Opera Company, it opened on August 2, 1924, with Verdi's *Il trovatore* at the Prince of Wales Theatre. Verdi's *Rigoletto*, Pietro Mascagni's *Cavalleria rusticana*, and Ruggero Leoncavallo's *I pagliacci* completed the inaugural season. The second season offered Gounod's *Faust*, Bizet's *Carmen*, Verdi's *Rigoletto* and *Il trovatore*, and Puccini's *La bohème*. The company was never heard from again. The second attempt at homegrown opera

emerged with the birth of The State Grand Opera Company on September 23, 1933, with Verdi's *Il trovatore*, followed by Mascagni's *Cavalleria rusticana*, Verdi's *Rigoletto*, and Gounod's *Faust*. This company did not even survive to mount a second season. The Australian Broadcasting Corporation staged a season of eight operas in 1940. Attempts at homegrown opera emerged again in 1955 with the creation of the Adelaide Opera Group, renamed The South Australian National Opera Company two years later to reflect the company's goal — to be a national company. But by 1961, it had floundered, degenerating into a local amateur operetta society.

In 1957, the Intimate Opera Group was founded, from which The State Opera of South Australia would eventually emerge. The strategy of the Intimate Opera Group was to stage both the Australian premieres of contemporary works, like Benjamin Britten's *The Turn of the Screw*, and Australian operas, like Peggy Glanville Hick's *The Glittering Gate* and Margaret Sutherland's *The Young Kabbarli*. The company opened with Anthony Hopkins's *Three's Company* on October 2, 1957, its only offering that season. In 1958, its sole offering was Britten's *Albert Herring*, followed two years later by Gian Carlo Menotti's *The Telephone*,

Lee Hoiby's *The Scarf*, and Ermanno Wolf-Ferrari's *Il segreto di Susanna*. The company went on to perform at the Adelaide Festival of Arts. The active patronage of premier Don Dunstan helped transform the semi-professional Intimate Opera into the resident, professional organization known as New Opera, South Australia. It was a small, flexible music theater ensemble, reflecting the character of its predecessor, with innovative programming of small contemporary masterpieces and mainstream chamber works. It continued its commitment to Australian operas, and employed both experienced and up-and-coming local singers.

After the company was reconstituted as a government statutory authority in 1976 and renamed The State Opera of South Australia, it received its own home in Her Majesty's Theatre, renamed The Opera Theatre, in 1979. This resulted in the company's veering from its founding philosophy of music-theater, and becoming more of a small regional opera company. The repertory became a mix of the smaller standard-fare operas and lesser known 17th, 18th and 20th century pieces, complementing the grander, mainstream repertory performed by the Australian Opera during its Adelaide visits. Works like Jules Massenet's *Werther*, Emilio de Cavalli's *L'Ormindo*, Britten's *Death in Venice*, Pyotr Il'yich Tchaikovsky's *Eugene Onegin*, Georges Bizet's *Les pêcheurs de perles*, Dmitry Shostakovich's *Ledi Makbet Mtsenskovo uyezda* (Lady Macbeth of the Mtsensk District), and Igor Stravinsky's *The Rake's Progress* were on the boards. Eventually the company transformed itself again, away from its "adventurous" (for Adelaide) repertory, regional identity, and commitment to an ensemble of local singers, towards a small mainstream house using contracted singers from around Australia and abroad, with standard late 18th- and 19th-century operas — Bizet's *Carmen*, Verdi's *La traviata* and *Macbeth*, Mozart's *Don Giovanni*, and the like — dominating the repertory. But this re-orientation resulted in an accumulated deficit of A$560,000 by 1988, forcing a reorganization. That year was also the company's last season in the 967-seat Opera Theatre. Various venues (including returning in 1990 to The Opera Theatre for Mozart's *Le nozze di Figaro*) were used until it settled permanently into the Festival Theatre in 1991. The 1990s witnessed a continuation of a mainstream repertory with Puccini's *La bohème*, Verdi's *Falstaff*, Richard Strauss's *Salome*, Rossini's *Il bar-*

biere di Siviglia, among others, in a careful repertory mix of two mainstream works with one lesser known piece. The highpoint of the 1998 season was a staging of the complete Ring Cycle. Recent works include Puccini's *Manon Lescaut*.

Adelaide Festival of Arts

In 1960, John Bishop founded the Adelaide Festival to showcase Australian talent to the world and to import the best of foreign talent to Adelaide. Opera is one of the many components of the festival which includes Music, Drama, Art, and even a Writer's Week. Limiting this discussion to opera, the first festival hosted the Elizabethan Opera Company, which offered Strauss's *Salome*, Verdi's *Rigoletto*, and Puccini's *Il trittico*. The company returned the next year with Strauss's *Ariadne auf Naxos* and Verdi's *La traviata*. In 1964, the repertory was slightly more daring with William Walton's *Troilus and Cressida*, along with Verdi's *Macbeth* and Bizet's *Carmen*. The beginning of the 1970s saw more adventure in the opera offerings with the English Opera Group performing Britten's *The Burning Fiery Furnace* and *The Prodigal Son*, and Intimate Opera Group presenting Maurice Ravel's *L'heure espagnole* and Menotti's *The Old Maid and the Thief*. The Australian Opera appeared in 1972 with Britten's *Rape of Lucretia*, and the Intimate Opera Group gave Giovanni Battista Pergolesi's *La serva padrona*, Holst's *The Wandering Scholar*, and Hick's *The Glittering Gate*. Two years later, the company, now known as New Opera, South Australia, mounted Leoš Janáček's *Výlety Páně Broučkovy* (The Excursions of Mr. Brouček). More novelties followed like Larry Sitsky's *Fiery Tales* and George Dreyfus's *The Lamentable Reign of King Charles the Last*. This remains the festival's philosophy in regards to opera.

Adelaide Festival Theatre

Situated on the banks of the Torrens, the modern Festival Complex was officially opened on March 22, 1977, by Queen Elizabeth. Designed by the architectural firm Colin and John Morphett, the entire complex cost A$25 million, of which A$7 million went for the construction of the large, festival theatre. Premier Steele Hall "turned the first sod" on the site in March 1970

Adelaide Festival Theatre (Adelaide, Australia).

and in June 1973, prime minister Gough Whitlam opened the theater before a distinguished audience, who were treated to the prison scene from Ludwig van Beethoven's *Fidelio*, followed by his Ninth Symphony. The complex appears as massive white tents billowing in the wind. The multipurpose auditorium holds two tiers with boxes jutting out from the side walls, giving an intimate feel to the space. Red seats, white concrete, Australian timber, and Philippine hardwood defines the room, which seats 1,827.

Practical Information. The State Opera of South Australia, GPO Box 1515, Adelaide 5001. Tel: 61 8 212 6644, Fax: 61 8 231 7646. Adelaide Festival Centre, King William Road, Adelaide 5000. Tel: 61 8 216-8600, Fax: 61 8 212 7849. Adelaide Festival of Arts, GPO 1269, Adelaide 5001. Tel: 61 8 216-8600, Fax: 61 8 212-7849. When visiting The State Opera of South Australia, Adelaide Festival Centre, or Adelaide Festival of Arts, contact the South Australian Tourism Commission, 1600 Dove Street, Suite 215, New-

port Beach, CA 92660. Tel: 714-852-2270, Fax: 714-852-2277.

COMPANY STAFF

General Managers (**State Opera of South Australia**). Stephen Phillips (1995–present), Bill Gillespie (1985–95), Ian Campbell (1976–82). **Artistic Director:** Bill Gillespie (1995–present). **General Manager (Adelaide Festival):** Ian Scobie. Artistic Director: Robyn Archer.

Bibliography (**State Opera of South Australia**). Robyn Holmes (ed.), *Through the Opera Glass* (Adelaide, 1991). Harold Love, *The Golden Age of Australian Opera: W.S. Lyster and His Companies 1861–1880* (Sydney, 1981). Interviews with Stephen Phillips, general manager and Bill Gillespie, artistic director, State Opera of South Australia, February 1996. (**Adelaide Festival**): Derek Whitelock, *Festival! The Story of the Adelaide Festival of Arts* (Adelaide, 1980). Interview with Rob Brookman, director Adelaide Festival Centre, February 1996.

Thanks to Jo Peoples, curator, Performing Arts Collection of South Australia Theatre Museum, and Michael Smith and Karyn Guy, South Australian Tourism Commission.

BRISBANE

Opera Queensland (State Opera)

Opera Queensland, formally known as the Lyric Opera of Queensland, was inaugurated on July 31, 1982, with Gilbert and Sullivan's *Iolan-* *the* at Her Majesty's Theatre. The youngest of the state opera companies, it is a small, conservative operation, offering traditional productions of the standard repertory. The company performed at Her Majesty's Theatre until 1985, when it moved to the newly-opened Lyric Theatre in the Queensland Performing Arts Complex, which became its permanent home. Among works performed were Giuseppe Verdi's *Otello*, Engelbert Humperdinck's *Hänsel und Gretel*, Giacomo Puccini's *Turandot*, and Wolfgang Amadeus Mozart's *Don Giovanni*. Recent repertory includes Verdi's *Falstaff*.

Queensland Performing Arts Complex

In 1955, an empty South Bank site was purchased by the Brisbane City Council. The State Development and Public Works Departments took over the land by the Proclamation of 26th May, 1966. Preliminary work began on the complex in 1976 and nine years later, on April 20,

1985, the Duke of Kent officially opened the Performing Arts Complex. The Queensland Performing Arts Trust (QPAT), established by the Queensland Government in 1977, produces, presents and manages the Performing Arts Complex.

Practical Information. Opera Queensland, 12 Merivale Street South Brisbane, QLD, 4101. Tel: 61 7 846 1177, Fax: 61 7 844 5352. If visiting, contact the Australian Tourist Commission, 489 Fifth Avenue, 31st Floor, New York, NY 10017. Tel: 708-296-4900.

COMPANY STAFF

General Managers. Suzannah Conway (1991–present), Rodney Phillips (1988–90), Bill Weston (1984–87), Neil Duncan (1982–83).

Bibliography. Information supplied by the company. Performing Arts Complex information from the Internet.

Thanks to Dale Forrest, Embassy of Australia, Washington D.C., and Julie Cara Geiser, Opera Queensland.

HOBART, TASMANIA

IHOS Opera — Experimental Music Theatre Troupe

IHOS Opera was founded in 1990 by composer Constantine Koukias, using his Greek-Australian background as the basis for the works produced, all of which he composes. It is a very "personal" company. The works explore cross-cultural influences and contemporary problems present in Australia today. The experimental music theater pieces are vast in scale, written in several languages (Greek, Hebrew, Mandarin, and German) and other methods of communication (braille, semaphore, and morse code) and staged with a variety of media and art forms. The company performs in huge, unconventional spaces — warehouses, covered parking lots, wharfs — which accentuate the strangeness of the productions.

The IHOS Opera's first work, Koukias's *Days and Nights with Christ* was based on the composer's personal experience of having a schizophrenic brother and helping his mother care for him. It premiered in Hobart at the 1990 Salamanca Arts Festival at Princes Wharf. Two years later, the work received its Sydney premiere at the Festival of Sydney. The company's next work, Koukias's *To Traverse Water*, based on his mother's

migration experience of arriving in Australia in the 1950s, was staged at the Greek Festival of Sydney, and at the Melbourne International Festival of Arts. Koukias's *Mikrovion*, presented in concert at Elizabeth's St. Pier in November 1995, dealt with the HIV/AIDS problem. Of local interest was *The Pulp,* a work relating to Tasmania and the paper mill in Burnie, seen in 1996. The company's most recent accomplishment has been *Ulysses,* offered in 1998, to coincide with the Tall Ships visit to Hobart.

Practical Information. IHOS Experimental Music Theatre Troupe, R5 Bank Arcade, 1st Floor, 64 Liverpool Street, Hobart, Tasmania 7000. Tel: 61 02 312 219, Fax: 61 02 344 445. When visiting the IHOS Experimental Music Theatre, stay at the Hotel Grand Chancellor, 1 Davey Street, Hobart, Tasmania 7000. Tel: 61 02 35 4535, Fax: 61 02 23 8175. The Hotel Grand Chancellor has a view of the harbor and is near the performance venues. The hotel can assist with opera tickets and schedule.

COMPANY STAFF

Artistic Director. Constantine Koukias (1990–present)

Bibliography. Interview with Constantine Koukias, artistic director, February 1996. Additional information supplied by the company.
Thanks to the IHOS Opera staff.

MELBOURNE

Victoria State Opera
(State Opera)

Jacques Offenbach's *La belle Hélène* inaugurated the Victoria State Opera at the Princess Theatre on March 3, 1977. The other offerings of the company's initial season — Claudio Monteverdi's *La favola d'Orfeo*, Claude Debussy's *Pelléas et Mélisande*, and Béla Bartók's *A Kékszakállú herceg vára* (Duke Bluebeard's Castle) — were unusual for a new company, but in keeping with the policy of its predecessor, the Victorian Opera Company. Verdi's *Don Carlos* welcomed the company into its new home, the Victoria Arts Centre, in May 1984. The Centre, which actually did not officially open until October 29, 1984, was designed by Roy Grounds.

Homegrown opera began in Melbourne around 1943 when the Mont Albert Choral Society presented *The Pirates of Penzance*. The Hawthorne Operatic Society followed, then came the Victorian Opera Society and the Victorian Light Opera Company, whose repertory was limited to Gilbert and Sullivan works. The company then split into the Savoy Opera Company, which continued staging Gilbert and Sullivan pieces, and the Victorian Opera Company. In 1970, the company merged with the Victorian Ballet Guild and received funds from the Australian Council for the Arts. Its philosophy, to walk the thin line between experimental works and traditional works, provided "alternative" opera to that of the Australian Opera, which visited annually. It was an adventurous repertory — Francis Poulenc's *Les Mamelles de Tirésias*, Walton's *Façade*, Claudio Monteverdi's *L'incoronazione di Poppea*, and Gaetano Donizetti's *Maria Stuarda*. The company performed in the National Theatre, a converted movie house with no "atmosphere." Although this company aspired to be professional, lack of money, a poor performance venue, and an inability to have the performances work dramatically as well as musically hindered its development.

After the government approved the new name Victoria State Opera (VSO) and the VSO's move out of the National Theatre, it became an entirely professional organization. Its first few seasons works like Georges Bizet's *Les pêcheurs de perles*, Wolfgang Amadeus Mozart's *La clemenza di Tito* and *Idomeneo*, and Charles Gounod's *Faust* graced the stage. In 1983, it mounted the world premiere of Brian Howard's *Metamorphosis* in the St. Martins Theatre, along with Pyotr Tchaikovsky's *Eugene Onegin*, Verdi's *Rigoletto*, and Johann Strauß's *Die Fledermaus*. After the company moved into the State Theatre, it hosted the world premiere of Barry Conyngham's *Fly*. Other operas in the repertory included Richard Stauss's *Elektra*, Richard Wagner's *Lohengrin* and *Tannhäuser*, and Camille Saint-Saëns's *Samson et Dalila*. Another world premiere took place on October 19, 1996, at the Melbourne Festival — Richard Mills and Peter Goldsworthy's *Summer of the Seventeenth Doll*. The company is also concentrating on musicals to help balance its A$11 million budget, of which it is short by 20–25%. Fifty percent comes from box office receipts, sponsors donate around 15–20%, and around 10% comes from state funds. On the operatic side, it is continuing its philosophy of presenting less well-known operas (for Australia) with the mid–1990s offering Jules Massenet's *Don Quichotte*, Bizet's *Les pêcheurs de perles*, Tchaikovsky's *Eugene Onegin*, Händel's *Semele*, Strauss's *Die Frau ohne Schatten*, and Léo Delibes's *Lakmé*, along with the standard repertory and Gilbert and Sullivan. The productions can be modern, but except for its premieres, the classic 20th century repertory has been neglected, a situation they hope to remedy in the 21st century. Recent repertory includes Puccini's *Madama Butterfly*, Christoph Willibald Gluck's *Iphigénie en Tauride*, Wagner's *Tannhäuser*, Verdi's *Macbeth*, Poulenc's *Dialogues des Carmélites*, and Mozart's *Così fan tutte*. The company performs in the State Theatre.

Victorian Arts Centre (Melbourne, Australia).

Victorian Arts Centre — State Theatre

The history of the Centre goes back to 1946, when the Melbourne South Land Act reserved the site for cultural purposes. Nine years later, a National Art Gallery and Cultural Centre Building Committee was established and in March 1980, the Victorian Arts Centre Trust was founded. Four years later, the Victoria Arts Centre opened.

The Centre is comprised of three main buildings: the spire-topped Theatres, the National Gallery of Victoria, and the Melbourne Concert Hall which includes a Performing Arts Museum. The three theaters cost approximately A$170 million and their spire-top has become Melbourne's most prominent landmark. The Centre's most unique feature is that most of the buildings are below street level. In fact, they reach six levels below St. Kilda Road. Inside, the foyer is filled with black glass ceilings off-set by chrome finishes, and reflecting glass walls. The State Theatre is awash in reds — the seats, the walls, the parapets, and the stage curtain with the Victorian Coat-of-Arms. Seventy-five thousand tiny brass "buttons" decorate an acoustically designed ceiling. The theater accommodates 2,000.

Practical Information. Victorian State Opera, 77 Southbank Boulevard, South Melbourne, Victoria 3205. Tel: 61 3 9685 3777, Fax: 61 3 9686 1441. Victorian Arts Centre, 100 St. Kilda Road, Melbourne 3004. Tel: 61 3 9281 8000; Fax: 61 3 9281 8282. When visiting the Victorian State Opera or the Victorian Arts Centre, stay at the Grand Hyatt Melbourne, 123 Collins Street, Melbourne, Victoria 3000. Tel: 61 3 657-1234 or 1-800-233-1234, Fax: 61 3 650-3491. The Grand Hyatt Melbourne is centrally located near the opera house. The hotel can assist with opera tickets and schedule.

COMPANY STAFF

General Manager. Stephen Dee (1996–present), Ken Mackenzie-Forbes (1976–95).

Bibliography. Victoria State Opera: Tenth Anniversary Season—1987—The First Decade (Melbourne, 1987). VSO News (Melbourne, 1992–95). Michael Kaye (ed.), The Victorian Arts Centre: The Heart of Melbourne (Melbourne, 1990). Interview with Stephen Dee, general manager, and Keith Beecher, finance director, February 1996.

Thanks to John Hay-Mackenzie, Victoria State Opera; Susannah McCosh, Victorian Arts Centre, and Karl Werner Diefenbach.

PERTH

West Australian Opera
(State Opera)

Georges Bizet's *Carmen* inaugurated the West Australian Opera in June 1968 at His Majesty's Theatre. Gian Carlo Menotti's *Amahl and the Night Visitors*, performed at the West Australian Italian Club, completed the inaugural season. His Majesty's Theatre, named after Edward VII, had opened on December 24, 1904, with *The Forty Thieves*. William Wolfe designed the structure.

Perth first witnessed fully-staged grand opera in 1926, when the Italio-Australian Grand Opera Company performed at His Majesty's Theatre. Two years later, the group returned, establishing the West Australian Grand Opera Company, staging four productions that season and five more in 1930. Two years earlier, on October 8, 1928, Dame Nellie Melba Grand Opera Season began with Gaetano Donizetti's *Lucia di Lammermoor*, followed by Giacomo Puccini's *Turandot*, *Tosca*, and *Madama Butterfly*, Gioachino Rossini's *Il barbiere di Siviglia*, Giuseppe Verdi's *Rigoletto*, Jacques Offenbach's *Les contes d'Hoffmann*, and Umberto Giordano's *Andrea Chénier*.

Another grand opera season, organized by J.C. Williamson Theatres Ltd. by arrangement with the Education in Music and Dramatic Society, opened on August 11, 1949, with Puccini's *La bohème*. Puccini's *Tosca* and *Madama Butterfly*, Verdi's *Il trovatore* and *Rigoletto*, Charles Gounod's *Faust*, Rossini's *Il barbiere di Siviglia*, Pietro Mascagni's *Cavalleria rusticana*, Ruggero Leoncavallo's *I pagliacci*, and Georges Bizet's *Carmen* also graced the stage.

In January 1947, a group called the West Australian Opera Society, founded by Hans Briner, staged Engelbert Humperdinck's *Hänsel und Gretel*. The performance was so well received that two operas were given the following year in the Somerville Auditorium — Wolfgang Amadeus Mozart's *Le nozze di Figaro* with local singers and an amateur orchestra led by Briner in February, and Jacques Offenbach's *Les contes d'Hoffmann* in September. In March 1949, Giuseppe Verdi's *La traviata* was on the boards, followed by Johann Strauß's *Die Fledermaus* in November. Then disagreement began to plague the Opera Society. It revolved around the issue of going professional and planning operas based on box office appeal. Briner resigned and A. Rayner was appointed the new music director. The next production, Gaetano Donizetti's *Don Pasquale*, was not successful and bankruptcy forced the Opera Society's dissolution in 1951. Briner, meanwhile, had founded another group called the Studio-Opera and mounted two productions, an operetta *Bless the Bride* and Mozart's *Die Zauberflöte*, before the company folded. In November 1952, the Perth Metropolitan Opera Company was established. Founded by James Penberthy and B.V. Pusenjak, the company mounted Strauß's *Der Zigeunerbaron*, and *Melodies of the Heart*, another Viennese operetta, as its first offerings. Opera was also offered by Rudolf Werther when he was cultural director of the Cottesloe Civic Centre — Claudio Monteverdi's *La favola d'Orfeo* (1952) and Mozart's *Die Entführung aus dem Serail* (1953). Attempts were made to unite all these people and companies to keep homegrown opera alive in Perth, but they proved unsuccessful.

Two years before the West Australian Opera presented its first opera in 1968, Giuseppe Bertinazzo had suggested the formation of an opera company for which he took the role as director of productions. Verdon Williams was named musical director and James Penberthy as artistic director. When Joan Sutherland consented to be the Patron of the new company, its prestige (but not funding) got a boost. The company's budget for the first 18 months was A$34,000 which paid for productions of Giacomo Puccini's *La bohème*, Menotti's *Amahl and the Night Visitors*, and Charles Gounod's *Faust*. The third season's offerings included three operas with popular fare dominating the schedule. The works offered for the Perth Festival, however, were less known, like Benjamin Britten's *Albert Herring* and *The Rape of Lucretia*, and Henry Purcell's *Dido and Aeneas*. The company had performed in His Majesty's Theatre until 1974, when the theater, in a state of disrepair, was closed. Owned by the Edgley Family, the theater was sold to the State Government which refurbished it at a cost of A$13 million. When it reopened on May 28, 1980, it became the permanent home of the West Australian Opera. Verdi's *La traviata* welcomed the company to its new performance venue in June 1980. A decade later, in 1990, the company experienced a financial crisis when the State Government grant was cut and the company could not perform. It reestablished itself the following year with a newly-commissioned opera, *Bride of Fortune*, presented during the Perth Festival.

In the mid–1990s, the West Australia Opera company underwent another crisis — in both direction and funding, and faced the question if it should continue to exist. It appointed a new board and searched for ways to built a more solid financial base, including instituting a subscription series. The budget is around A$1.5 million with money coming from State Government, corporate sponsorship, and box office receipts. It is a small company which primarily fosters and develops local, up-and-coming talent, and tries to bring back ex-patriates of West Australia. The repertory depends on which operas the available singers can perform. The main problem Perth faces is the enormous distance between it and the next "opera" city — more than 1,000 miles. Some local artists which are known internationally include Gregory Yurisich, Bruce Martin, and Glynis Fowles.

The company's production of Georg Friedrich Händel's *Alcina* for the Perth Festival was a clever, innovative, and simple affair. It was performed on a ¾ round stage in the Octagon Festival Theatre with a round island-sandbox acting as the set. The singers, young talent, entered and exited through the audience. The ending, however, was dramatic, with the breaking of Alcina's staff corresponding to huge sparks and a jet gas fire ringing the island-sandbox. Recent repertory includes Mozart's *Don Giovanni* and Donizetti's *Lucia di Lammermoor*.

His Majesty's Theatre

After His Majesty's Theatre opened in 1904, it hosted Nellie Melba, Anna Pavlova, Peter Dawson, Margot Fonteyn, and Yehudi Menuhin among others. The variety of entertainment ranged from boxing matches to political rallies. During the Second World War, it was converted into a movie house, since travel restrictions prevented visits from outside companies. The 1950s and 1960s was the era of the American musical with *Annie Get Your Gun*, *Oklahoma*, *My Fair Lady*, *Pajama Game*, and *Funny Girl* on the boards. During this time the theater was purchased by the Edgley family

His Majesty's Theatre (Perth, Australia).

and sold in the 1970s to the government. Today, the theater hosts musicals like *Les Miserables* and *Cats*, alongside opera.

A large majestic structure, the theater was described in the December 25, 1904, *Western Mail* as follows: "Viewed from the outside, the compact solidarity of the structure is most impressive. The massive grey walls are relieved with long rows of balconies and deep set windows, and are set off with ornamental cement modelling of great variety.... The Italian style of architecture has been followed. Two tiers of balconies, carried out in the Doric order, run round the whole front, while the windows on the top floor have annexed to them balconettes, which form a happy blend with the rest of the facade. Roman columns, piers, and pilasters support the outside fabric. The main pediment bears the Royal crest, while minor pediments, set in a series of segment arches, a carry the models of six lions...."

The auditorium, decorated and painted by the firm of Beeler and Marnes in High Edwardian style, holds two horseshoe-shaped tiers, whose ivory parapets are delicately embellished with gilded garlands. There is a sea of red-burgundy seats. The dome ceiling of ivory, chocolate brown, and orange in geometric shapes, appears as a view through a kaleidoscope. The frieze above the stage is an allegory of Day and Night, painted in the turn-of-the-century style. The theater seats 1,250.

Practical Information. West Australian Opera, His Majesty's Theatre, 825 Hay Street, Perth 6000 Western Australia. Tel: 61 9 321 5869, Fax: 61 9 324 1134. When visiting the West Australian Opera, stay at the Hyatt Regency Perth, 99 Adelaide Terrace, Perth, 6000 Western Australia. Tel: 61 9 225 1234 or 1-800-233-1234, Fax: 61 9 325 8899. The Hyatt Regency Perth is centrally located with views of the Swan River. There is complimentary bus service to the opera house and the hotel can assist with opera tickets and schedule.

COMPANY STAFF, PREMIERES AND REPERTORY

General Managers. Lisa Shilton (1994–present), Terry Craig (1989–93), Vincent Warrener (1976–89)

World Premieres. *Eureka Stockade*, November

His Majesty's Theatre auditorium boxes (Perth, Australia).

1988; *Bride of Fortune*, February 1991; *Heloise and Abelard*, February 1993; *The Burrow*, February 1994.

Repertory. **1968:** Carmen, Amahl and the Night Visitors. **1969:** Faust, La bohème. **1970:** La traviata. **1971:** Madama Butterfly, Un ballo in maschera, Die Fledermaus. **1972:** Der Zigeunerbaron, Madama Butterfly, Il barbiere di Siviglia. **1973:** Albert Herring, Die lustige Witwe. **1974:** Il trovatore, Die Fledermaus, Amahl and the Night Visitors. **1975:** Così fan tutti, Carmen, Orpheus in the Underworld. **1976:** The Medium, Dido and Aeneas, L 'elisir d'amore, Don Pasquale. **1977:** The Mikado, Cavalleria rusticana/I pagliacci. **1978:** The Rape of Lucretia, The Gondoliers, Tosca. **1979:** The Beggar's Opera, Madama Butterfly. **1980:** La traviata, Die Entführung aus dem Serail. **1981:** Les contes d'Hoffmann, La bohème, Die Zauberflöte. **1982:** Rigoletto, Les pêcheurs de perles, Il barbiere di Siviglia. **1983:** Madama Butterfly, Don Giovanni, Carmen. **1984:** Le nozze di Figaro, Lucia de Lammermoor, Die lustige Witwe. **1985:** Nabucco, Così fan tutti, Die Fledermaus. **1986:** Hänsel und Gretel, Falstaff. **1987:** Madama Butterfly, Mignon, La traviata. **1988:** The Mikado, Tosca, Eureka Stockade. **1989:** Countess Maritza, La bohème. **1990:** The Bride of Fortune. **1991:** Le nozze di Figaro. **1992:** Don Pasquale, Carmen. **1993:** Orpheus in the Underworld, Madama Butterfly, Heloise and Abelard. **1994:** Die Zauberflöte, The Burrow. **1995:** L 'elisir d'amore, Don Giovanni. **1996:** Alcina, Falstaff, Die Fledermaus. *Operas in Concert:* **1971:** Fidelio, Everyman's Opera. **1972:** Everyman's Opera. **1973:** Everyman's Opera. **1974:** Everyman's Opera, Music for the People. **1975:** Verdi's Requiem, Music for the People. **1980:** Aida. **1981:** Fidelio. **1983:** Der fliegende Holländer. **1984:** Verdi's Requiem, Everyman's Opera, Music for the People. **1986:** The Gloria. **1991:** Die Fledermaus. **1992:** Madama Butterfly, Il barbiere di Siviglia. **1993:** La traviata. **1994:** Rigoletto, Les pêcheur de perles.

Bibliography. Brian Jenkins, *Art & Aria: Commemorating the Tenth Anniversary of The Western Australian Opera Company 18th July, 1977* (Perth, 1977). Rudolf Werther, *Opera in Australia.* Interviews with Lisa Shelton, general director, and Lindy Hume, former artistic director, February 1996.

Thanks to Judy Reid, West Australian Opera, Ivan King, archivist, Perth Theatre Trust, and George Benney.

SYDNEY

Australian Opera, Sydney (National Opera)

In July 1956, the Australian Opera, known as the Elizabethan Trust Opera Company until 1970, gave its first production sponsored by its original namesake, the Elizabethan Trust. Originally intended as a national touring company, the first season offered four Wolfgang Amadeus Mozart works — *Così fan tutte, Don Giovanni, Die Zauberflöte,* and *Le nozze di Figaro* in the capital cities of the different Australian states. The company traveled more than 8,000 miles.

Australia's first recorded operatic performance, Henry Bishop's *Clari: The Maid of Milan,* took place in 1834. Other "operas" of the era included Isaac Nathan's *The Merry Freaks in Troublous Times* and *Don John of Austria* in the 1840s. That same decade, Signore Carandini founded an Italian opera company with his wife as *prima donna,* and offered many Italian works. Various traveling troupes — Anna Bishop Opera Company, Lyster's Royal Italian and English Company, Simonsen's English Opera Company, and Nellie Melba's company also presented opera during the 1800s and early 1900s. The first part of the 1900s witnessed some Australian operas like Alfred Hill's *Lady Dolly, Teora,* and *The Ship of Heaven,* as well as Melba's farewell tour with Toti dal Monte and Dino Borgioli in 1924. The Imperial Grand Opera Company staged operatic productions between the wars, and in 1952, opera companies in Sydney and Melbourne tried to form a national company. Two years later, their endeavor came closer to reality when the Elizabethan Trust was formed to develop the arts in Australia. Around the same time, Jørn Utzon, a Danish architect, was chosen to design a new opera house in Sydney.

In 1956, the founding of an opera company become a reality with the establishment of the Elizabethan Trust Opera Company (Australian Opera). The company mounted regular seasons in Sydney, Melbourne, Adelaide, and Brisbane, as well as occasional visits to Perth, Canberra, Hobart, and Newcastle. By the second season, the repertory expanded beyond the inaugural Mozart season with Giuseppe Verdi's *Otello,* Giacomo Puccini's *Tosca* and *La bohème,* Jacques Offenbach's *Les contes d'Hoffmann,* Bedřich Smetana's *Prodaná nevěsta* (The Bartered Bride), and John Gay's *The Beggar's Opera* on the schedule. The repertory continued to expand over the next several seasons, with an emphasis on standard fare — Verdi's *Falstaff, La traviata,* and *Rigoletto,* Georges Bizet's *Carmen,* Richard Wagner's *Lohengrin,* Gioachino Rossini's *Il barbieri di Siviglia,* Charles Gounod's *Faust,* Puccini's *Madama Butterfly,* Ludwig van Beethoven's *Fidelio,* Benjamin Britten's

Peter Grimes, and Richard Strauss's *Salome*— along with a few lesser-known pieces, like William Walton's *Troilus and Cressida*, Carl Orff's *Die Kluge*, and Ferdinando Paër's *Il maestro di capella* gracing the stage.

The company got a boost in 1965 when Joan Sutherland and Richard Bonynge returned to Australia and connected with the J.C. Williamson Theatres, creating the Sutherland/Williamson Grand Opera Company. Some of the operas performed over the next five seasons included Verdi's *Don Carlos* and *Il trovatore*, Wagner's *Tannhäuser* and *Der fliegende Holländer*, Modest Mussorgsky's *Boris Godunov*, and a novelty, Ermanno Wolf-Ferrari's *I quattro rusteghi*.

The Australian Opera was incorporated as a separate entity in 1970 and three years later, The Australia Opera's presentation of Sergey Prokofiev's *War and Peace* on September 28 opened (unofficially) the Sydney Opera House, which became the company's permanent home. The combination of these two events saw rapid development in the company, with an expansion of the repertory to around 20 works a season, and the mounting of world premieres, including Peter Sculthorpe's *Rites of Passage*. Less-frequently performed operas also entered the repertory like Leoš Janáček's *Příhody Lišky Bystroušky* (The Cunning Little Vixen) and *Jenůfa*, Léo Delibes's *Lakmé*, Alban Berg's *Wozzeck*, Verdi's *Simon Boccanegra*, and Daniel Auber's *Fra Diavolo*. In 1976, Bonynge became the company's music director, which has been called a "mixed-blessing." He staged a series of operas merely as star vehicles for his wife, Joan Sutherland, and had "shortcomings" as it has been written, as a conductor. It was the latter that finally led to problems with the administration, causing severe financial problems for the company and resulting in an official Australian Council enquiry. The government rescued the company with A$2.5 million.

The mid–1980s were fruitful for world premieres. Four were mounted — Anne Boyd's *Little Mermaid*, Brian Howard's *Metamorphosis* and *Whitsunday*, and Richard Meale's *Voss*, and the repertory continued to expand with Wagner's *Die Walküre* and *Tristan und Isolde*, Kurt Weill's *Der Aufstieg und Fall der Stadt Mahagonny*, Gaetano Donizetti's *Lucrezia Borgia*, Gounod's *Roméo et Juliette*, Rossini's *Semiramide*, Francis Poulenc's *Les dialogues des Carmélites*, Francesco Cilea's *Adriana Lecouvreur*, Verdi's *Nabucco*, and Igor

Stravinsky's *The Rake's Progress*. A similar pattern continued in the 1990s with Meale's *Mer de Glace*, Larry Sitsky's *The Golem*, Alan John & Dennis Watkins's *Eighth Wonder* on the boards for the first time ever, Britten's *Death in Venice*, Jules Massenet's *Werther*, Giacomo Meyerbeer's *Les Huguenots*, Mozart's *La clemenza di Tito*, Donizetti's *Maria Stuarda*, Christoph Willibald Gluck's *Orfeo ed Euridice*, and Hector Berlioz's *Les Troyens* gracing the stage.

The Australian Opera is again an ensemble company, with 22 resident principal singers and full-time chorus. Australian singers from around the globe are brought "home" to sing with the company. It began as an ensemble company, and when Sutherland arrived, it turned into a star vehicle company. When she left, it reverted to its roots. The permanent artistic, administrative, and technical staff number more than 200 with a budget close to A$40 million — 25 percent government funding, 65 percent box office revenue, 10 percent private and corporate sponsorship. The company is on the repertory system, performing eleven months a year, similar to the German opera house system. Although its conductors, directors, and designers might come from around the world, its singers are overwhelmingly Australian.

The company has a philosophy that opera is theater, stressing the theatrical aspect almost as much as the music, hiring many directors from the theater world. There is a diversity of approach to the productions, some of which worked and some which did not. An enchanting and magical *A Midsummer Night's Dream* captured the whimsical quality of the piece with a set comprised of a huge Indian pagoda built over a water grotto and bathed in green light complemented by hundreds of tiny twinkling lights. Genuinely amusing without resorting to slapstick, the Australian cast was well-rehearsed and in fine voice. Two other operas were not as successful. A somber and severe production of *Fidelio*, which originated in Köln, was marred by weak singing and a small orchestral sound. The *Cavalleria rusticana*, updated to Fascist Italy before World War II, and *I pagliacci*, updated to after World War II, were misguided attempts to unite the works and justify the characters's behavior — Alfio was a Fascist, making him a "good catch," "explaining" why Lola married him, and Silvio, made an American G.I., showing why Nedda risked all for him (secure future). Recent repertory includes Verdi's *Macbeth* and *La forza del destino*, Wagner's *Tannhäuser*, Puccini's *Tosca* and *Manon Lescaut*, and Mozart's *Così fan tutte*.

Sydney Opera House

In the mid–1950s, Premier Joseph Cahill heard about a proposal by a group of citizens to build a performing arts complex in Sydney, and he set out to raise the money necessary for construction. Only $900,000 was raised. Undaunted, Cahill introduced what became known as the Opera House lotteries, which earned enough profits to build the opera house and have it paid for by 1975. The site selected for the Opera House, Bennelong Point, was named after the first Aborigine born on the site who could speak English. An international competition was held, supported by the government of New South Wales, for the design of the complex and won by Jørn Utzon, a Danish architect, in January 1957. Construction began in March of 1959 and in 1973, the complex was opened. Those fourteen years were filled with controversy and polemics (as seems to be the case with many large opera house projects). Utzon left the project in 1966, with Peter Hall taking over and subsequent changes made — the

opera theater became the concert hall and the concert hall was made into the opera theater. Meanwhile, the cost skyrocketed to A$120 million. On October 20, 1973, Queen Elizabeth II officially opened the complex, although performances had already taken place.

An architectural landmark, the Sydney Opera House soars above the harbor, its sail-shaped roofs immobile against the persistent sea breezes. A performing arts complex, it houses five theaters — Opera Theatre, Concert Hall, Drama Theater, Playhouse and Broadwalk Studio. It appears that most of the funds were spent on the outside. Not much remained for interior design and decoration. The decor of Opera Theatre gives an inelegant impression with formica seats in imitation white wood, covered with reddish-orange cloth. The three-tier auditorium is steeply graded, ensuring excellent visibility from every seat. Boxes extend out on the sides of the second and third tiers in a zig-zag fashion and the ceiling is arched like the bottom of a boat. The stage curtain is an abstract pattern of brightly-colored Australian wool. There are 1,547 seats.

Practical Information. The Australian Opera, 480 Elizabeth Street, Surry Hills, NSW 2010. Tel: 61 2 699 1099, Fax: 61 2 699 3184. Syd-

Sydney Opera House (Sydney, Australia).

ney Opera House, Bennelong Point, Sydney NSW 2001. When visiting the Sydney Opera House, stay at the Ritz-Carlton at 93 Macquarie Street, Sydney NSW 2000. Tel: 61 2 252-4600 or 1-800-241-3333, Fax: 61 2 252 4286. The hotel, centrally located overlooking The Royal Botanic Gardens, and only steps from the opera house, can assist with opera tickets and schedule.

COMPANY STAFF AND PREMIERES

General Managers. Donald McDonald (1987–present), Patrick Veitch (1980–16), Peter Hem-

mings (1977–80). **Artistic Director:** Moffatt Oxenbould.

World Premieres. P. Sculthorpe's *Rites of Passage*, 1974; A. Boyd's *Little Mermaid*, 1985; B. Howard's *Metamorphosis*, 1985; R. Meale's *Voss*, 1986; B. Howard's *Whitsunday,* 1988; R. Meale's *Mer de Glace*, 1991; L. Sitsky's *The Golem*, 1993; A. John and D. Watkins's *Eighth Wonder*, 1995.

Bibliography. Harold Love, *The Golden Age of Australian Opera: W.S. Lylster and His Companies, 1861–1880* (Sydney, 1981). Ava Hubble, *More than an Opera House* (Sydney, 1978). Additional information supplied by the company.

Thanks to Anthony Clarke, Australian Opera and Kerry Mitruska.

Sydney Metropolitan Opera

In 1989, the Sydney Metropolitan Opera was established by John Wregg for the purpose of staging Australian works with Australian singers of all ages. Wregg described the operas as commissioned works, containing a "political" message, and having a distinctive "contemporary Australian sound." The topics are either based on classic works reinterpreted for a modern theater setting or dealing with Australian problems. The performance venue is frequently the location of the opera. Andrew Ford's *Casanova Confined*, based on Ariosto's *Orlando Furioso*, took place in the Cell Block Theatre.

The company's first production, Andrew Schultz's *Black River*, which involved race relations between the whites and the aborigines, took place in 1989. Raffaello Marcellino's *Remedy* and Michael Whiticker's *The Bamboo Flute* followed the next year. The year 1992 saw Brenton Broadstock's *Fahrenheit 451* and Martin Friedel's *Foxy*, followed by Mark Isaac's *Beach Dreaming*. Martin Wesley Smith's *Quinto* staged in an insane asylum in 1994, dealt with schizophrenia — comparing the invasion of East Timor to the invasion of a boy's body by spirits which caused his mental illness. That same year witnessed Ross Edwards's *Christina's World*, inspired by Andrew Wyeth's famous painting of the same name. Ford's *Casanova Confined* was offered in 1995, Peter

Sculthorpe's *Love Thoughts* the next year, and Andrew Schults's *Going into the Shadows* based on the El AL Hijacking in 1997.

The company mounts one or two productions a year, with up to seven performances of the work and a budget of A$120,000 a production. When it is a co-production or part of a festival, the amount of available money increases. The Australian Council contributes around 80% and the State Government around 18% with box office and corporate funding making up the difference.

Practical Information. Sydney Metropolitan Opera, 31 Tupper Street, Marrickville, Sydney, NSW 2204. Tel & Fax: 61 2 557 5828. When visiting the Metropolitan Opera, stay at the Ritz-Carlton, 93 Macquarie Street, Sydney NSW 2000. Tel: 61 2 252-4600 or 1-800-241-3333, Fax: 61 2 252 4286. The Ritz-Carlton, centrally located overlooking The Royal Botanic Gardens and convenient to the performance venue, can assist with opera tickets and schedule.

BIBLIOGRAPHY

Bibliography. Interview with John Wregg, artistic director, February 1996. Additional information was supplied by the company.

Thanks to the Sydney Metropolitan Opera staff.

Other Australian Companies

Other companies in Australia are noted below by name, address, telephone, and director.

Macclesfield — Co*Opera. P.O. Box 133, Macclesfield, S.A.; Tel: 61 8 388 9428, Fax: 61 8 388 9428. **Artistic Director:** Brian Chatterton.

University of New South Wales Opera. c/o School of Music and Music Education, Sydney, NSW 2052; Tel: 61 2 9385 5407, Fax: 61 2 9313 7338. **Artistic Director:** Roger Covell.

Austria

BREGENZ

Bregenzer Festspiele

The first Bregenz Festival took place on August 5, 1946, with a production of Wolfgang Amadeus Mozart's *Bastien und Bastienne*, staged on two gravel barges, parked on Lake Constance. One barge served as the stage and the other held the orchestra. Mozart's *Eine kleine Nachtmusik* joined his opera on the program that August evening. The concept of a music festival seemed far-fetched at the time, since Bregenz did not even have a theater.

Four years later, in 1950, the first permanent Seebühne (stage on the lake) was constructed on wooden piles anchored to the lake's bottom. The idea was to make the lake an integral part of the stage and the performance, not just a lovely backdrop. Operetta and ballet were the primary fare on the floating stage during the early years. Bregenz received its first theater in 1955, the 700-seat Theater am Kornmarkt. The structure, a converted grain storage place, hosted mainly Italian works of the *opera buffa* and *bel canto* genre — Gioachino Rossini's *Il barbiere di Siviglia*, *Armida*, *L'italiana in Algeri*, *La Cenerentola*, and *Il turco in Italia*, Domenico Cimarosa's *Il maestro di capella* and *Il matrimonio segreto*, Gaetano Donizetti's *Il campanello*, *L'elisir d'amore*, and *Don Pasquale*, Vincenzo Bellini's *La sonnambula*, and Giuseppe Verdi's rarely performed *Un giorno di regno* (Il finto Stanislao). Other forgotten works included Peter Cornelius's *Der Barbier von Bagdad*, Daniel Auber's *Fra diavolo*, and Claudio Monteverdi's *Il combattimento di Tandredi e Clorinda*. Opera graced this stage until the new opera house (Festspielhaus) opened.

Another performance venue for opera began in 1970 — the Gräflicher Palast in Hohenems.

Here operas by Franz Joseph Haydn found a home — *Untreue lohnt sich nicht*, *Der Apotheker*, *List und Liebe*, *Die Fischerinnen*, and *Die Welt auf dem Monde*. The introduction of Haydn's *Unverhofftes Begegnen* in 1981 was the last opera staged at this venue. A few non–Haydn operas were also mounted — Georg Phillipp Telemann's *Pimpinone oder die ungleiche Heirat*, Georg Friedrich Händel's *Xerxes*, and Mozart's *La finta semplice*. The 1972 season was unusual in that there were two different opera productions alternating on the Seebühne — Carl Millöcker's *Der Bettelstudent* and Henry Purcell's *The Fairy Queen*. This experiment lasted only one season.

In 1979, the current floating stage was completed and the following year, a new Festspielhaus opened. With these new performance spaces, the festival was ready to join the other "elaborate" summer festivals. The stage is supported by more than 200 wooden piles, and has a core of concrete to hold everything necessary for the spectacular opera productions, as well as an orchestra pit.

It took five years before Bregenz found its artistic style. A new type of production evolved, characteristic for Bregenz, that of colossal extravaganzas, complete with fireworks, explosions, and dazzling special effects — a popularization of opera for the masses. The emphasis is visual — to present the essence of the opera visually so it is understandable to everyone. The operas are cut to 2–2½ hours, since there are no intermissions at the floating stage presentations. The festival felt with 6,000 spectators, it would not be practical. (This is Austria, not Italy.) For the opera connoisseur, the productions are difficult to accept, but for everyone else, they are good fun. In 1985, with the production of Mozart's *Die Zauberflöte* a new "opulent" direction of the festival was initiated. Each floating stage production remained two seasons, so the elaborate sets were constructed to survive the winter exposed to the elements.

In 1988, or eight years after the Festspielhaus had opened in 1980, it, too, found a specific artistic vision — that of seeking out and staging rarely performed operas to exacting standards — in other words, operas for the opera connoisseur. With the highest artistic level and modern stagings, works that have been unjustly forgotten, like Anton Rubinstein's *The Demon*, Nikolay Rimsky-Korsakov's *Skazaniye o nevidimom grade Kitezhe* (Legend of the Invisible City of Kitezh), and Ernest Chausson's *Le Roi Arthus* have been revived. The dichotic nature of the Bregenz Festival is unusual among opera festivals, and might seem strange to the uninitiated.

Festspielhaus

The festival theaters are part of a large festival and congress center, where the indoor theater and outdoor stage are joined through a large geometrically-shaped, green-trimmed, concrete building. The single-tiered indoor auditorium is rectangular in shape with a steeply raked orchestra level. Mahagony faces the parapet and walls and the proscenium arch is unadorned. Wooded designs embellish the space, contrasting with the blue fabric seats. The ceiling holds gray acoustic panels in geometric shapes. There are approximately 2,000 seats. The outdoor seating area is rustic, with hard, fiberglass seats. It accommodates 7,000.

Practical Information. Bregenzer Festspiele, Platz der Wiener Symphoniker 1, Postfach 311, 6901 Bregenz. Tel: 43 5574 492 0224, Fax: 43 662 492 0228. If visiting the Bregenzer Festspiele, stay at the Messmer Hotel am Kornmarkt, Kornmarktstraße 16, 6901 Bregenz. Tel: 43 5574 423-560, Fax: 43 5574 423-566. It is a comfortable hotel, located in the heart of the old city and near the festival theaters.

COMPANY STAFF AND REPERTORY

Intendant. Franz Salzmann

Festspielhaus (Bregenz, Austria).

Festspielhaus floating stage, *Fidelio* set (Bregenz, Austria).

Repertory (since 1980, Festspielhaus): 1980: Falstaff. 1981: Otello. 1982: Lucia di Lammermoor. 1983: Der Freischütz. 1984: Tosca. 1985: I Puritani. 1986: Anna Bolena. 1987: Ernani. 1988: Samson et Dalila. 1989: Samson et Dalila. 1990: La Wally. 1991: Mazeppa. 1992: La Damnation de Faust. 1993: Fedora. 1994: Francesca da Rimini. 1995: Skazaniye o nevidimom grade Kitezhe (Legend of the Invisible City of Kitezh). 1996: Le Roi Arthus. 1997: The Demon. 1998: L'amore dei tre re. (Seebühne) 1980: Die Entführung aus dem Serail. 1981: West Side Story. 1982: Der Zigeunerbaron. 1983: Kiss Me, Kate. 1984: Der Vogel-händler. 1985: Die Zauberflöte. 1986: Die Zauberflöte. 1987: Les contes d'Hoffmann. 1988: Les contes d'Hoffmann. 1989: Der fliegender Holländer. 1990: Der fliegender Holländer. 1991: Carmen. 1992: Carmen. 1993: Nabucco. 1994: Nabucco. 1995: Fidelio. 1996: Fidelio. 1997: Porgy and Bess. 1998: Porgy and Bess.

Bibliography. Andrea Meuli (ed.), *Die Bregenzer Festspiele* (Salzburg and Vienna, 1995). *Bregenzer Festspiele* (Bregenz, 1993).

Thanks to Evelyn Gmeiner and Bernd Feldmann, Bregenzer Festspiele.

GRAZ

Vereinigte Bühnen Graz

The Vereinigte Bühnen Graz, also known as the Grazer Opernhaus, was inaugurated on September 16, 1899, with Friedrich von Schiller's Wilhelm Tell. Designed by Ferdinand Fellner and Hermann Helmer in the style of Fischer von Erlach, the theater contained both open balconies and boxes in the auditorium.

Opera was first seen in Graz back in 1736 when Pietro Mingotti's Italian opera company visited. The "Nationaltheater" opened in 1776 and the Italian repertory dominated. The operas of Wolfgang Amadeus Mozart were also popular.

Fire destroyed the theater in 1823. Two years later, a Landestheater opened, which served as the opera house until the present building was inaugurated in 1899. Richard Strauss paid a visit and conducted the first Austrian performance of his *Salome* on May 16, 1906, and well-known conductors, like Karl Böhm, Clemens Krauss, and Karl Muck were associated with the house. It also cultivated young talent and was used as a springboard for a larger career. On November 1, 1944, bombs damaged the structure. It was repaired between 1945 and 1948.

Since the 1970s, there has been an emphasis on modern operas and the *bel canto* repertory. Vincenzo Bellini's *I Puritani* and *La sonnambula*, Gaetano Donizetti's *Lucia di Lammermoor*, Gioachino Rossini's *Mosè in Egitto* among others graced the stage. Other works included Amilcare Ponchielli's *La gioconda* and Georges Bizet's *Les pêcheurs de perles*, as well as the Austrian premieres of Ernst Křenek's *Orpheus und Eurydike* on October 20, 1973, Horst Geißler's *Der zerbrochene Krug* on May 27, 1974, Benjamin Britten's *Death in Venice* on October 26, 1974, Wolfgang Rihm's *Jakob Lenz* on October 19, 1980, and Sergey Prokofiev's *Ivan the Terrible*. There is also a predilection toward the avant-garde, and rediscovering forgotten works. In this area are the world premieres of Otto Zykan's *Symphonie aus der heilen Welt* on October 8, 1977, Ivan Eröd's *Orpheus ex machina* on October 14, 1978, and Prokofiev's forgotten *Maddalena*, as well as operas like Ilkka Kuusistos's *Mumin Oper* and Nicholas Maw's *The Rising of the Moon*. International artists have sung on the Graz stage, like Giacomo Aragall, Carlo Bergonzi, José Carreras, Ileana Cotrubas, René Kollo, and Birgit Nilsson.

The opera house was closed for renovation in 1983 and 1984, reopening on January 12, 1985, with Johann Joseph Fux's *Angelica Vincitrice di Alcina*. The 1990s has seen more mainstream repertory with Pietro Mascagni's *Cavalleria rusticana*, Ruggero Leoncavallo's *I pagliacci*, Franz Lehár's *Die lustige Witwe*, Engelbert Humperdinck's *Hänsel und Gretel*, and Puccini's *La bohème*. Recent offerings include Alban Berg's *Wozzeck*, Verdi's *Il trovatore*, and Puccini's *Madama Butterfly*.

Practical Information. Vereinigte Bühnen Graz, Kaiser Josef Platz 10, 8010 Graz: 43 316 8000, Fax: 43 316 800 8565. If visiting the Vereinigte Bühnen Graz, contact the Austrian National Tourist Office, 500 Fifth Avenue, New York, NY 10110; Tel: 212 944-6880.

COMPANY STAFF

Intendanten. Gerhard Brunner, Carl Nemeth, Reinhold Schubert, Karl Heinz Haberland, André Diehl, Fritz Zaun, Alfred Huttig, Helmut Ebbs.

Bibliography. Rudolf List, *Oper und Operette in Graz. Von den Anfängen bis zur Gegenwart. 75 Jahre Grazer Opernhaus* (Graz, 1974). R. Baravelle, *50 Jahre Grazer Opernhaus, 1899–1949* (Graz, 1949).

INNSBRUCK

Tiroler Landestheater
Festwochen–der Alten Musik (Summer Festival)

The Tiroler Landestheater was inaugurated on April 19, 1846, with a mini-festival — Gaetano Donizetti's *Lucrezia Borgia*, Eduard Bauernfeld's *Ein deutscher Krieger*, and Nestroy's *Der Zerrissene*. The theater, designed by Giuseppe Segusini, is located on the same site as the first theater in Innsbruck, the 1653-built Landesfürstliches Comedihaus (Sovereign's Comedy House).

As early as 1622, performances of Italian opera were given on the occasion of a royal wedding. This led to the construction in 1653 of the first "opera house," actually called a Comedy House, which hosted Marcantonio Cesti's *Cleopatra* in 1654. A permanent theater group existed in Innsbruck by 1658, known as the "Erzfürstlichen Hofkomödianten." Opera made an appearance again in 1765, when the royal theater was renovated, reopening with *Romola ed Ersilia*, the libretto by Pietro Metastasio. In 1786, the first subsidy came from Joseph II and the theater was renamed K.K. Nationaltheater. At the dawn of the 19th century, Franz Joseph Haydn's *Schöpfung* and Georg Friedrich Händel's *Messiah* were presented. By 1844, the theater was in such a state of disrepair that it had to be closed. That same year, construction began on a new, Neoclassical-style building, called the Tiroler Landestheater, which opened in 1846. A permanent opera ensemble was founded in 1939, and Richard Strauss journeyed to Innsbruck to conduct his *Salome*. After the war, it reopened during the American occupation with Johann Strauß's *Wiener Blut*. Until 1961, the repertory ranged from works by Gioachino Rossini to Werner Egks's *Christoph Columbus* and Gian Carlo Menotti's *The Consul*. In 1949, a young Leonie Rysanek made her debut.

Tiroler Landestheater (Innsbruck, Austria).

In 1961, after a performance on July 20 of Giacomo Puccini's *Turandot*, the theater had to be closed for reasons of safety. It was totally reconstructed with only the original facade remaining. Erich Boltenstern was responsible for the project. The opera house reopened on November 19, 1967, with Raimund's *Der Alpenkönig und der Menschenfeind*. The first opera staged was Richard Wagner's *Die Meistersinger von Nürnberg* followed by Franz Lehár's *Die lustige Witwe* and Puccini's *Madama Butterfly*. Then "cycles" of works by Richard Wagner, Giuseppe Verdi, and Richard Strauss were mounted. For the 250th birthday of Haydn, there was a "cycle" of his works, beginning with *Apotheker*. A novelty took place in 1987, the staging of Carl Nielsen's *Maskerade*. Other works offered were Gaetano Donizetti's *Don Pasquale*, Carl Maria von Weber's *Der Freischütz*, Pyotr Il'yich Tchaikovsky's *Eugene Onegin*, Sergey Prokofiev's *Lyubov'k tryom apel'sinam* (The Love for Three Oranges). More recently Verdi's *Don Carlo*, Mozart's *La finta giardiniera*, Herbert Willi's *Schlafes Bruder*, Strauß's *Die Fledermaus*, Jacques Offenbach's *Les contes d'Hoffmann*, and Rossini's *La Cenerentola* have been staged. The first Austrian performance of a Danish chamber opera by Tage Nielsen, *Laughing in the Dark*, took place on March 15, 1997. There is a permanent opera ensemble of 20 soloists, 33-member chorus, and 67-musician orchestra. Rossini's *Il barbiere di Siviglia* and Puccini's *Tosca* are recent productions.

Festwochen–der Alten Musik

During the last two weeks in August a festival of Baroque music takes place in the Landestheater. For the 350th anniversary of the death of Claudio Monteverdi, the festival mounted one of the composer's most important operas, *Il ritorno di Ulisse in patria*, along with another early work, Antonio Caldara's *I disingannati*. Opera shares the program with concerts. Recent festival offerings include *La descente d'Orphée*, Georg Friedrich Händel's *Semele*, and Alessandro Scarlatti's *Il primo omicidio*.

Practical Information. Tiroler Landestheater, Rennweg 2, 6020 Innsbruck. Tel: 43 512 520 744, Fax: 43 512 52 074 333. Festwochen–der Alten Musik, Burggraben 3, 6020 Innsbruck. Tel: 43 512 53 56 21, Fax: 43 512 53 56 43. If visiting the Tiroler Landestheater or Festwochen–der Alten Musik, contact the Austrian

National Tourist Office, 500 Fifth Avenue, New York, NY 10110; Tel: 212 944-6880.

Bibliography. F. Hölbing, *Theater in Innsbruck: Überblick über drei Jahrhunderte Festschrift* (Innsburck, 1967).

COMPANY STAFF

Intendanten. Dominique Mentha, Helmut Wlasak, Karl Goritschan, Paul Schmid, Robert Pleß.

KLAGENFURT

Stadttheater Klagenfurt

The Stadttheater, originally known as the Jubiläums-Stadttheater, was inaugurated on September 22, 1910, with Friedrich von Schiller's *Wilhelm Tell.* The 770 seat, Empire-style building was designed by Ferdinand Fellner and Hermann Helmer.

Opera was first heard in 1709 in a *Ballhaus* (dance hall) performed by visiting Italian troupes, traveling between Venice and Vienna. At the end of the 1700s the Theater des Adels was constructed. Italian and Italian-German Singspiele were the primary offerings, a genre which resembled *opera seria.* In 1811, under the reign of Kaiser Franz I, a new theater, the Hoftheater, was built which hosted Wolfgang Amadeus Mozart's *Die Zauberflöte* and *Don Giovanni*, and Domenico Cimarosa's *Il matrimonio segreto.* Gradually, the public was introduced to works by Gaetano Donizetti, Vincenzo Bellini, and Gioachino Rossini as well as Carl Maria von Weber's *Der Freischütz*, Charles Gounod's *Faust*, and several operas by Giacomo Meyerbeer. By the end of the 19th century, the repertory included around 50 different works, like Richard Wagner's *Der fliegende Holländer* and *Tannhäuser.* The beginning of the 20th century saw Giuseppe Verdi's *Aida* and Wagner's *Die Walküre* grace the stage. The last per-

formance in the Hoftheater was Johann Wolfgang Goethe's *Iphigenie* on March 23, 1910.

With the opening of the new theater in September 1910, opera, operetta, and drama all shared the stage, except between 1932 and 1938 when the building was used periodically as a movie house. Closed in July 1944, the theater reopened on August 1, 1945, with Johann Strauß's *Die Fledermaus.* The early 1990s offered interesting repertory with Francis Poulenc's *La voix humaine* and Benjamin Britten's *Death in Venice.* Recent offerings include Beethoven's *Fidelio* and Johann Strauß's *Eine Nacht in Venedig.*

Practical Information. Stadttheater Klagenfurt, Theaterplatz 4, 9020 Klagenfurt. Tel: 43 463 55266, Fax: 43 463 51 69 49. If visiting the Stadttheater Klagenfurt, contact the Austrian National Tourist Office, 500 Fifth Avenue, New York, NY 10110. Tel: 212 944-6880.

COMPANY STAFF

Intendanten. Dieter Pflegerl, Herbert Wochinz, Otto Hans Böhm, Philipp Zeska, Fritz Klingenbeck, Theo Knapp, Walter Sofka, Willy Meyer-Fürst, Gustav Bartelmus, Leopold Schwarz, Karl Krois, Ludwig Gibiser, Hermann Roché, Carl Richter.

LINZ

Landestheater Linz

On October 4, 1803, the 756-seat Landestheater was inaugurated with August von Kotzbue's *Octavia.* Construction had begun on December 7, 1801, and lasted almost two years. Architect Ferdinand Mayr modeled the theater on the Theater an Wien (Vienna).

Opera began to blossom in Linz during the last decade of the 18th century with performances of Wolfgang Amadeus Mozart's *Die Zauberflöte, Die Entführung aus dem Serail, Don Giovanni,* and *Le nozze di Figaro.* After the Landestheater opened, the taste of the Viennese determined the repertory choices, although many works appeared soon after their world premieres, like Daniel Auber's *Le muette de Portici* (1829), and Gaetano Donizetti's *L'elisir d'amore* (1832).

During the Second World War, some noteworthy productions took place, like the Austrian premiere of Ottmar Gersten's *Enoch Arden*, and the world premieres of Bernhard Conz's *Die Nacht der großen Liebe* and Ludwig Schmidseder's *Heimkehr nach Mitterwald*, followed by his *Linzer Torte*. After the hostilities ended, Linz continued to stage the Austrian premieres of unusual operas almost annually until 1955. Among the works introduced were Ernst Křenek's *Leben des Orest*, Jakov Gotovac's *Ero, der Schelm*, Werner Egk's *Die Zaubergeige*, Joseph Haas's *Tobias Wunderlich*, Max Liebermann's *Leonore 40/45*, Antonín Dvořák's *Jakobiner*, and Paul Hindemith's *Mathis der Maler*. In 1958, the original auditorium of boxes and gallery was transformed into an open balcony theater under the supervision of Clemens Holzmeister. Richard Strauss's *Arabella* reopened the theater on December 20, 1958. The end of the 1970s and 1980s saw an infusion of new blood with the return of the world premieres to the Linz stage, including Helmut Eder's *Der Aufstand* and *George Dandlin*, Balduin Sulzer's *In seinem Garten liebt Don Perimplin*, Heinrich Gattermeyer's *Kirbisch*, and Karl Kogler's *Kohlhaas*. There is also an emphasis on presenting contemporary works and to this end, Francis Polenc's *Les dialogues des Carmélites*, Klebe's *Die Fastnachtsbeichte* and *Blood Wedding*, Sandor Szokolay's *Samson*, Gian Carlo Menotti's *The Consul*, Helmut Eder's *Moderner Traum*, Ernst Křenek's *Pallas Athene weint*, and Heinrich Sutermeister's *Romeo und Julia* have graced the stage. Unjustly neglected works have

also found their way into the schedule, including Gioachino Rossini's *Guglielmo Tell*, Arrigo Boito's *Mefistofele*, Carl Maria von Weber's *Oberon*, and Hector Berlioz's *Benvenuto Cellini*. Recent offerings include Rossini's *Il barbiere di Siviglia*, Francis Poulenc's *La voix humaine*, Mozart's *Don Giovanni* and *Le nozze di Figaro*, and Strauss's *Capriccio*.

Practical Information. Landestheater, Promenade 39, 4020 Linz. Tel: 43 732 761-1100, Fax: 43 732 761 1105. If visiting the Landestheater, contact the Austrian National Tourist Office, 500 Fifth Avenue, New York, NY 10110. Tel: 212 944-6880.

COMPANY STAFF AND PREMIERES

Intendanten. Roman Zellinger, Alfred Stögmüller, Adolf Holschan, Kurt Wöss, Karl-Heinz Krahl, Fred Schroer, Askar Walleck, Ignaz Branter, Viktor Pruscha.

World Premieres. Bernhard Conz's *Die Nacht der großen Liebe*, March 5, 1942; Ludwig Schmidseder's *Heimkehr nach Mitterwald*, August 26, 1942; Ludwig Schmidseder's *Linzer Torte*, May 26, 1944; Helmut Eder's *Anamorphose*, June 22, 1963; Helmut Eder's *Der Aufstand*, October 3, 1976; Helmut Eder's *George Dandlin*, October 6, 1979; Balduin Sulzer's *In seinem Garten liebt Don Perimplin*, 1980s; Heinrich Gattermeyer's *Kirbisch*, 1980s; Karl Kogler's *Kohlhaas*, 1980s. **Austrian Premieres:** Ottmar Gersten's *Enoch Arden*, October 26, 1940; Ernst Křenek's *Leben des Orest*, December 6, 1947; Jakov Gotovac's *Ero, der Schelm*, November 23, 1951; Werner Egk's *Die Zaubergeige*, November 8, 1952; Joseph Haas's *Tobias Wunderlich*, December 23, 1952; Max Liebermann's *Leonore 40/45*, April 25, 1953; Antonín Dvořák's *Jakobiner*, June 27, 1954; Paul Hindemith's *Mathis der Maler*, March 1, 1955; Hans Werner Henze's *Undine*, February 3, 1963.

SALZBURG

Salzburger Festspiele

Hugo von Hofmannsthal's *Jedermann*, directed by Max Reinhardt in an open-air platform in Cathedral Square, inaugurated the Salzburger Festspiele on August 22, 1920. Established as a festival to celebrate the operas of Wolfgang Amadeus Mozart, the Salzburg Festival has expanded to include works of many composers. In 1922, the Wiener Staatsoper presented in the Landestheater (see Salzburger Landestheater entry)

Mozart's *Don Giovanni* (August 14), *Così fan tutte* (August 15), *Le nozze di Figaro* (August 16), and *Die Entführung aus dem Serail* (August 17). Richard Strauss conducted the first two and Franz Schalk the latter two. The first festival hall opened in 1925. Originally a 17th-century winter riding school, it was transformed by Eduard Hütter into a provisional theater, and additional restructuring yielded the Kleines Festspielhaus. Johann Bernhard

Großes Festspielhaus (Salzburg, Austria).

Fischer von Erlach's 17th-century Baroque summer riding school was converted into a second theater, known as the Felsenreitschule, and the third theater in the festival complex, the Großes Festspielhaus, was designed by Clemens Holzmeister. Richard Strauss's *Der Rosenkavalier* inaugurated the Large Festival House on July 26, 1960.

The idea of holding a regular Mozart festival was born in 1842 when a statue of Mozart by the sculptor Ludwig Schwanthaler was unveiled in the presence of his two surviving sons. In 1870, Karl Freiherr von Sterneck established the Internationale Mozart-Stiftung, which led to the first Mozart festival seven years later, in 1877. The Festivals were celebrated periodically until 1910. Lilli Lehmann was associated with many of them, singing in 1901 in Mozart's *Le nozze di Figaro* and *Don Giovanni*. Many well-known conductors took part as well, including Hans Richter, Felix von Weingartner, Strauss, Schalk, and Gustav Mahler, who led Mozart's *Le nozze di Figaro* in 1910. The formation in 1917 of the Festspielhausgemeinde by Heinrich Damisch and Friedrich Gehmacher laid a firm foundation for the festival.

Von Hofmannsthal, Reinhardt, Alfred Roller, Schalk, and Strauss were the artistic directors. It seems ironic that the city where Mozart spent several impoverished years gains wealth and world recognition from a festival based on his memory.

Operas were initially hosted at the Landestheater until the first Festspielhaus opened. On August 13, 1927, Ludwig van Beethoven's *Fidelio* with Lotte Lehmann as Leonore, Alfred Jerger as Pizarro, and Alfred Piccaver as Florestan, was the first opera staged inside the new hall. Mozart and Strauss operas graced the stage during the initial seasons, with an occasional Christoph Willibald Gluck piece. In 1929, Strauss conducted his *Der Rosenkavalier*, and Giuseppe Verdi operas joined the repertory in the 1930s. The era of great conductors also began in the 1930s when in 1933 Bruno Walter conducted the first Richard Wagner opera to appear at the festival, *Tristan und Isolde* with Dorothea Manski as Isolde and Hans Grahl as Tristan. Arturo Toscanini led Verdi's *Falstaff*, Beethoven's *Fidelio*, Mozart's *Die Zauberflöte*, and Wagner's *Die Meistersinger von Nürnberg*. When the Nazis came, Walter, Toscanini, Reinhardt, Stefan Zweig, and other talented

Jews and non–Jews associated with the festival had to flee. Those happy to serve the Nazis were richly rewarded by the Third Reich. Clemens Krauss was appointed artistic director, and Wilhelm Fürtwangler, Karl Böhm, Vittorio Gui, and Herbert von Karajan were frequent conductors. "Aryan" works replaced "degenerate modern art," and the festival hit rock bottom. In May 1945, the Americans occupied Salzburg and revived the festival, with Mozart's *Die Entführung aus dem Serail*. The audience consisted primarily of the Occupation Forces. By the next year, three more operas returned to the stage, and tourists were sprinkled in the audience.

Beginning with the 1947 season, Salzburg, feeling competition from other festivals, began hosting world premieres and contemporary works. The first one, Gottfried von Einem's *Dantons Tod*, appeared on stage in 1947, followed six years later by *Der Prozeß*. Carl Orff's *Antigone* was introduced in 1949, Boris Blacher's *Romeo und Julia* in 1950, Werner Egk's *Irische Legende* in 1956, Erbse's *Julietta* in 1959, Strauss's postponed from 1944 *Die Liebe der Danae* in 1952, and Rolf Liebermann's *Penelope* in 1954. Karajan took over leadership of the festival in 1956, remaining at the helm until his death in 1989. His influence on the festival was as pronounced as its founder, Max Reinhardt. (Karajan commissioned the building of the Großes Festspielhaus based on his own ideas.) Karajan's first operatic production was Beethoven's *Fidelio* in 1957, followed by four Giuseppe Verdi works — *Il trovatore* (1962), *Otello* (1971), *Don Carlo* (1976), and *Falstaff* (1981). His last production took place in 1987, Mozart's *Don Giovanni*, two years before his death. He also founded the Easter Festival in 1967. He continued the policy of opera premieres with Hans Werner Henze's *Bassariden*, Orff's *De Temporum Fine Comoedia*, Friedrich Cerha's *Baal*, Luciano Berio's *Un Re in ascolto*, and Krysztof's Penderecki's *Die schwarze Maske*. Karajan turned the festival into a meeting place for the jet-set, and lured opera's greatest voices to perform including Franco Corelli, Leontyne Price, Giulietta Simionato, and Nicolai Ghiaurov. At the same time, Karajan was criticized for increasing the commercialization of the festival, especially regarding the influence of the record companies, who sometimes managed to decide program and casting. In fact, during the Karajan reign, although the ticket prices were (and still are) astronomical, red ink flowed every year. The Austrian government (40%) the province (20%), the city (20%), and the Tourism Promotion Fund (20%) by law passed on July 12, 1950, must pay off any deficit.

Since Gerard Mortier took over the directorship, there are not as many high-priced artists, and the program, which had become inflexible under Karajan, has opened up. Mortier, who previously was *directeur général* of Théâtre Royal de la Monnaie, Brussels (one of the world's leading avant-garde centers), has carried the "revolution" to Salzburg. He has formed a small group of "imaginative radicals" to mount productions which range from creatively outrageous to absurd, from boring to superb. Some examples: Peter Sellers set György Ligeti's *Le grand macabre* in a nuclear catastrophe with lust, hate, love, sexuality as the utopian message. Peter Mussbach set Igor Stravinsky's *The Rake's Progress* with an airplane that looked straight out of a comic-book in some scenes, and symbolic, animalistic throwbacks to the (Nazi) concentration camps in others. Robert Wilson produced Claude Debussy's *Pelléas et Mélisande* as an integral, homogenous whole — music, staging, sets, lights, were all synchronized — along his philosophy that more is less. The problem was, the opera came across as too stylized and too static. A Japanese crew, led by director Keita Asari, made Strauss's *Elektra* Japanese and infinitely boring. A recent *Die Zauberflöte* took place in a modern circus amidst much protest (critical and audience).

There is a clash between Mortier, who is trying to bring the festival into the 21st century with bold, daring operatic concepts, and the old traditionalist of Karajan's ilk, who want it to remain where it had been, in the 19th century, filled with pompousness and elitism, where the rich gathered to show off their wealth, jewels, gowns, and fancy hair styles. Even the cab drivers complain. (They belong to the Karajan group since that group tipped better.) They feel that Salzburg is a traditional city and people come to the festival here to have a reason to go to the hair-dresser and get dressed up. Mortier's reply is that you can go to Monte Carlo if that is what you want. Salzburg should offer something different. He is taking the pompous superficial atmosphere of the festival and turning it into an artistic exploration.

Festival Theaters

The Kleines Festspielhaus was reworked by Holzmeister in the 1930s, refashioned after the *Anschluß* by Benno von Arend, and since the results were still not satisfactory, renovated in 1962-63 by Erich Engels and Hans Hoffmann, resulting in the house's present appearance. The Felsenreitschule initially hosted open-air performances beginning in 1926. After acquiring a convertible roof, stage, and orchestra pit, it hosted its first opera in 1948. Holzmeister remodeled it in 1968-69, when it gained a "removable" auditorium and a waterproof awning. Holzmeister was also responsible for construction of the Großes Festspielhaus, which was begun in 1956 and finished four years later at a cost of AS $210 million. Fifty-five thousand cubic yards of rock were blasted from the face of the mountain to accommodate the stage, reputed to be the largest in Europe.

The three festival halls are under one roof. The steel and concrete building displays a Latin-inscribed façade: *Sacra Camenae Domus / Concitis Carmine Patet / Quo Nos Attonitos / Numen Ad Auras Ferat* (The holy house of the Muse is open for lovers of the arts, may heavenly power inspire us and raise us to the heights). The Großes Festspielhaus, the largest of the three, has a severe, modern auditorium, which exudes a cold, grandiose atmosphere. The orchestra is steeply raked, filled with thinly-padded violet-colored seats with straight, hard wooden backs (which cost upwards of $250 a ticket). The slightly fan-shaped hall holds one tier which gently curves on the sides. Convex and concave wood elements panel the side walls. There are 2,170 seats. The Kleines Festspielhaus auditorium is rectangular with wood panelling and tapestry designed by Slavi Soucek. The room accommodates 1,384. The Felsen-reitschule boasts an arcade of spectator boxes that were cut into the Mönchsberg during the 17th century as its stage backdrop and rows of wooden benches to accommodate the 20th century spectator. A waterproof awning, which can be opened or closed according to the weather's fickleness, protects its 1,549 spectators.

Practical Information. Salzburger Festspiele, Festspielhaus Salzburg, Hofstallgasse 1, 5010 Salzburg. Tel: 43 662 844 501, Fax: 43 662 846 682. If visiting the Salzburger Festspiele, stay at the Goldener Hirsch, Getreidegasse 37, 5020 Salzburg. Tel: 43 662 80-84, Fax: 43 662 84 33 49. It is in the heart of old town and just steps from the festival theaters.

COMPANY STAFF AND PREMIERES

Intendanten. Gerard Mortier (1992–present), Herbert von Karajan (1956–89).

World Premieres. G. von Einem's *Dantons Tod*, August 6, 1947; C. Orff's *Antigone*, August 9, 1949; B. Blacher's *Romeo und Julia*, 1950; R. Strauss's *Die Liebe der Danae*, August 14, 1952; G. von Einem's *Der Prozeß*, August 17, 1953; R. Liebermann's *Penelope*, August 17, 1954. W. Egk's *Irische Legende*, 1956; R. Liebermann's *Schule der Frauen*, 1957; Erbse's *Julietta*, 1959; H. W. Henze's *Bassariden*, August 6, 1966; C. Orff's *De Temporum Fine Comoedia*, 1973. F. Cerha's *Baal*, 1981; L. Berio's *Un Re in ascolto*, 1984; K. Penderecki's *Die schwarze Maske*, 1986.

Bibliography. Edda Fuhrich and Gisela Prossnitz, *Die Salzburger Festspiele: Ihre Geschichte in Daten, Zeitzeugnissen und Bildern 1920–1945,* Band I (1990, Salzburg). *Salzburg Kulturhandbuch: 1997/98* (Salzburg, 1997). *Salzburg Kulturhandbuch: 1996/97* (Salzburg, 1996). Harald Waitzbauer, *Festlicher Sommer: Das gesellschaftliche Ambiente der Festspiele von 1920 bis heute, Festreden seit 1964* (Salzburg, 1997). *Die Salzburger Festspiele und Ihre Spielstätten* (Salzburg, 1990).

Thanks to Hans Widrich, Regina Wohlfarth, and Ulrike Kalchmair, Salzburger Festspiele.

Salzburger Landestheater

The Landestheater was inaugurated on October 1, 1893, with Wolfgang Amadeus Mozart's overture to *La clemenza di Tito* and Ludwig Fulda's *Der Talisman*. The architects of the Neo-Baroque style theater were Hermann Helmer and Ferdinand Fellner.

A traveling Italian troupe brought to Salzburg its first opera performance in 1614, given on the stage of the royal Residenz. The following year, an elaborate stone theater, built in the Italian style in Hellbrunn Castle near Salzburg, hosted more intermezzi and pastoral interludes. The Hellbrunn Castle was the residence of the Archbishop Marcus Sitticus, regarded as the founder of the city's theatrical tradition. Rodolfo Campeggi's *Andromeda* was performed in 1618 and

Salzburger Landestheater (Salzburg, Austria).

Heinrich Biber, better known for his violin playing, wrote an opera, *Arminius*, which was given in 1687, the same year that Georg Muffat's *Le fatali felicità di Plutone* was performed. Two years later, Biber's *Alessandro in Pietra* graced the stage. In 1719, the Heckentheater, located in the gardens of Schloß Mirabell, was inaugurated with Antonio Caldara's *Dafne*. Mozart's *Apollo et Hyacinthus* followed in 1744, *Il sogno di Scipione* in 1772, and *Il Re Pastore* in 1775. That same year, the first "real" theater was erected, very near the present day Landestheater. At the end of 1784, Mozart's *Die Entführung aus dem Serail* and *Le nozze di Figaro* were on the boards. The theater was reconstructed in 1797. During the early 1800s, the operas of Luigi Cherubini, Gasparo Spontini, and Adrien Boieldieu found favor with the Salzburg audience. In 1822, Carl Maria von Weber's *Der Freischütz* was performed for the first time in Salzburg. The first Richard Wagner opera arrived in 1876, *Der fliegende Holländer*, followed by *Lohengrin* in 1877. Construction began on the Landestheater in 1882. Eleven years would pass before it was completed.

The beginning of the 20th century saw the world premiere of Robert Stolz's *Schön-Lorchen*. The theater was used for the first time as part of the Salzburger Festspiele in 1922, when Richard Strauss conducted Mozart's *Don Giovanni* and *Così fan tutte*. In 1949, against strong public protest, the Landestheater did not witness any opera for two years, because of its high cost. In 1963, an unusual production of Claudio Monteverdi's *La favola d'Orfeo*—it was reworked by Carl Orff—graced the stage. Mozart's *Der Schauspieldirektor* followed. Contemporary opera is also in the repertory with works from Benjamin Britten and Ernst Křenek. Some productions are unconventional, like Giacomo Puccini's *Turandot* that found Turandot's "kingdom" on top of a piano. Recent repertory includes Georges Bizet's *Carmen*, Wagner's *Der fliegende Holländer*, Mozart's *Le nozze di Figaro*, Engelbert Humperdinck's *Hänsel und Gretel*, and Igor Stravinsky's *The Rake's Progress*.

Practical Information. Salzburger Landestheater, Schwarzstraße 22, 5020 Salzburg. Tel: 43 662 871 512, Fax: 43 662 87113. If visiting the Salzburger Landestheater, stay at the Goldener Hirsch, Getreidegasse 37, 5020 Salzburg. Tel: 43 662 80 84, Fax: 43 662 84 33 49. It is in the heart of old town and close to the theater.

COMPANY STAFF

Intendanten. Anton Schmidjell, Lutz Hochstraate, Federick Mirdita, Karlheinz Haberland, Gandolf Buschbeck, Fritz Herterich, Helmuth Matiasek, Fritz Klingenbeck, Hans Schulz-Dornburg, Otto Emmerich Groh, Alfred Bernau, Johannes von Hamme, Peter Stanchina, Erwin Kerber.

Bibliography. H. & V. Kutchera, ed. *200 Jahre Landestheater Salzburg 1775–1975* (Salzburg, 1975). *Theater Jahr 1995–96, Salzburger Landestheater* (Salzburg, 1995). *100 Jahre Haus am Marktplatz* (Salzburg, 1995)

Thanks to Edith Schlager and Gaby Bergirt, Salzburger Landestheater.

Salzburger Marionettentheater

On February 27, 1913, Wolfgang Amadeus Mozart's *Bastien und Bastienne* became the first performance of the Salzburg Marionette Theater. Founded by Anton Aicher, the Marionette Theater was originally for his own family's entertainment. After the success achieved at the first performance, the company developed a repertory which not only emphasized the operas of Mozart, but included those of Christoph Willibald Gluck, Jacques Offenbach, Giovanni Battista Pergolesi and even Adolphe Adam. In 1927, Anton gave the company to his son, Hermann Aicher, as a wedding gift.

Originally there were live singers, so the repertory was limited, but when the tape recorders came into play in 1950, the company could expand their repertory. They could take on large operas, since all the singing was prerecorded. The Marionette Theater buys the rights to use the opera recordings and locates the ones with the finest singers. Hermann ran the Marionette Theater for 50 years, until his death in 1977, at which time his daughter, Gretl Aicher took over. She expanded the repertory to include Gioachino Rossini's *Il barbiere di Siviglia*, Offenbach's *Les contes d'Hoffmann*, and Johann Strauß's *Die Fledermaus* among others.

There is a permanent ensemble of 14 people that manipulate the puppets, which are 80 centimeters high. The puppets are carved out of wood. The company does not receive any public subsidy, raising all the money themselves, so they can tour whenever and wherever they want. In 1991, they appeared at Lincoln Center (NY) for the Mozart Festival. The Marionette Theater performs in their own theater, and are part of the Salzburger Festspiele. Recent offerings include Mozart's *Così fan tutte, Le nozze di Figaro, Don Giovanni, Die Entführung aus dem Serail,* and *Die Zauberflöte,* Offenbach's *Les contes d'Hoffmann,* and Johann Strauss's *Die Fledermaus.*

Practical Information. Salzburger Marionettentheater, Schwarzstraße 24, 5024 Salzburg. Tel: 43 662 87 24 04, Fax: 43 662 88 21 41. If visiting the Salzburger Marionettentheater, stay at the Goldener Hirsch, Getreidegasse 37, 5020 Salzburg; Tel: 43 662 8084, Fax: 43 662 84 33 49. It is in the heart of the old town and close to the theater.

COMPANY STAFF AND REPERTORY

Intendanten. Gretl Aicher (1977–present), Hermann Aicher (1927–77), Anton Aicher (1913–27).

Opera Repertory (1913–1966). By year of first performance: **1913:** Bastien und Bastienne. **1923:** Die Nürnberger Puppe. **1924:** Der betrogene Kadi. **1925:** Die Verlobung bei der Laterne. **1926:** Die Zaubergeige. **1928:** Das Mädchen von Elizondo. **1931:** Der Schauspieldirektor. **1935:** Die Maienkönigin. **1937:** La serva padrona. **1946:** Apollo und Hyazinthus. **1948:** La finta giardiniera. **1952:** Die Zauberflöte, Die Entführung aus dem Serail. **1965:** Don Giovanni.

Bibliography. Gottfried Kraus, *The Salzburg Marionette Theatre* (Salzburg, 1966). Interview with Gretl Aicher, June 1995.

Thanks to Christoph Sebastian Schuchter and Ursula Kastinger, Marionettentheater.

—————————————————————————————— VIENNA

Wiener Festwochen (Spring Festival)
Theater an der Wien

The first regular Wiener Festwochen (Vienna Festival Weeks) began in 1927, continuing for a decade. Max Reinhardt, one of the founders of the Salzburger Festspiele, staged the first outdoor performances for the festival in the courtyard of city hall. After World War II, the festival started again in 1951. By the following season, foreign artists were on the program and Bruno Walter conducted the opening concert. Also on the program was Wolfgang Amadeus Mozart's *Le nozze di Figaro*, presented in outdoor performances at the Schloß Schönbrunn. The festival stages both its own operatic productions and invites guest companies to perform.

During the 1960s, some of the festival's own productions included Arnold Schönberg's *Erwartung, Von heute auf Morgen*, and *Die glückliche Hand*, Josef Matthias Hauer's *Die schwarze Spinne*, and Franz Joseph Haydn's *Orfeo et Euridice*. Among the productions from the visiting companies were Leoš Janáček's *Z Mrtvého Domu* (From the House of the Dead) and Bedřich Smetana's *Prodaná nevěsta* (Bartered Bride) (National Theater of Prague), Béla Bartók's *A Kékszakállú herceg vára* (Duke Bluebeard's Castle) and Sándor Szokolay's *Blood Wedding* (Hungarian State Opera), Benjamin Britten's *Peter Grimes* (Sadler Well's Opera, later the English National Opera), and Egk's *La Tentation de St-Antoine* and Paul Dessau's *Puntila* (Staatsoper Berlin). Among the highlights during the 1970s were Nikolaus Harnoncourt conducting Claudio Monteverdi's *Il ritorno di Ulisse in patria*, produced by the festival and Mstislav Rostropowitsch leading Johann Strauß's *Die Fledermaus*. Other festival productions included Gaetano Donizetti's *L'elisir d'amore* and Wolfgang Amadeus Mozart's *La clemenza di Tito*, with guest productions of Jacques Offenbach's *Les contes d'Hoffmann* (Komische Oper Berlin), Rossini's *La Cenerentola* (Teatro alla Scala), Giuseppe Verdi's *La traviata* (Théâtre Royal de la Monnaie), and Mozart's *La finta giardiniera* (Opera de camera del Teatro Colon, Buenos Aires). The 1980s saw Claudio Abbado on the podium for the first staged production of Franz Schubert's *Fierrabras*, Haydn's *Orlando Paladino*, Mozart's *Zaide*, Gottfried von Einem's *Jesu Hochzeit*, Ernst Křenek's *Jonny Spielt auf*, among others. The 1990s offered the world premiere of the avant-garde pieces of Steve Reich's *The Cave*, Jean Genet von Adriana Hölszky's *Die Wände*, and Alfred Schnittke's *Hommage an Schiwago*, with other experimental works like Bruno Maderna's *Hyperio* and Herbert Willi's *Schlafes Bruder*.

The festival concentrates on the modern, avant-garde, and Baroque with recent offerings including the premiere of Tang Xianzu's *Peony Pavilion*, and Salvatore Sciarrino's *Die tödliche Blume* and Monteverdi's *Il ritorno di Ulisse in patria*. A production of Monteverdi's *La favola d'Orfeo* was effectively set on an almost bare stage, and directed with stylized movements which were appropriate for the Baroque piece, rendering the work relevant for today by its emphasis on the emotional impact of loss and death. (There was even a little girl dressed in black and a black poodle running around the stage.) On the other hand, the commissioned work, Franz Hummel's *Beuys* was an avant-garde disaster. A combination of symphonic music, opera and theater, the piece was boring, going nowhere and saying nothing. The set was seven army cots, lined up next to each other where the singers "slept" when they were not singing. Opera performances take place primarily in the Theater an der Wien, but also in other venues.

Theater an der Wien

The Theater an der Wien was inaugurated on June 13, 1801, with Franz Teyber's *Alexander*. Franz Jäger was the architect of the theater, built by Emanuel Schikaneder. Four years after opening, it hosted the world premiere of the original version of Ludwig van Beethoven's *Fidelio* on November 20, 1805. The theater became a home for operetta, introducing Kleist's *Käthchen von Heilbronn*, Nestroy's *Einen Jux will er sich machen*, Franz Schubert's *Rosamunde* and *Die Zauberharfe*

Theater an der Wien (Vienna, Austria).

(1820), Albert Lortzing's *Der Waffenschmied* (1846), Johann Strauß's *Die Fledermaus* (1874) and *Der Zigeunerbaron* (1885), and Franz Lehár's *Die lustige Witwe* (1905). It was reconstructed many times, and most recently restored in the mid–1900s, reopening on May 28, 1962, with Mozart's *Die Zauberflöte.*

The red, gold, and turquoise auditorium holds three tiers, with gilded balustrades. Gilded cornucopia of fruit and groups of putti embellish the space. The ornate proscenium arch has chiaroscuro putti in the spandrels. The seats are deep red velvet and the ceiling displays allegorical figures of the nine Muses.

Practical Information. Wiener Festwochen, Lehárgasse 11, 1060 Vienna. Tel: 43 1 589-220, Fax: 43 1 589-2249. Theater an der Wien, Linke Wienzeile 6, 1060 Vienna. Tel: 43 1 588 300, Fax: 43 222 588 3033. If attending the Weiner Festwochen, stay at the Hotel Bristol, Kärntner Ring 1, 1015 Vienna. Tel: 43 1 51 51 60 or 1 800 223 6800, Fax: 43 1 51 51 6550. It is in the heart of Vienna and convenient to the Wiener Festwochen performance venues.

COMPANY STAFF

Intendant. Wolfgang Wais (General Secretary, 1997–present), Klaus Bachler (1991–96), Ursula Pasterk (1984–87), Gerhard Freund (1978–79), Ulrich Baumgartner (1965–1977), Egon Hilbert (1960–64), Rudolf Gamsjäger (1958).

Bibliography. *Wiener Festwochen 1998* (Vienna, 1998), *Wiener Festwochen 1992–1996: 5 Jahre europäische Theaterarbeit* (Vienna, 1996). Additional information supplied by the company.

Thanks to Judith Kaltenböck.

Wiener Kammeroper
(Regular Season and Summer Festival)

The Wiener Kammeroper was founded in 1953. It is the only permanent, private musical theater in Austria. The company specializes in operas that are not usually performed by the larger companies in Vienna. The genre are *opera buffa*, *Alt-Wiener Singspiele*, and forgotten works of the 18th, 19th, and 20th centuries.

The regular season takes place in a turn-of-the-century building which the company moved into in 1961. The inaugural season saw Claudio Monteverdi's *Arianna*, Orlandini's *I giocatori*, and Bohuslav Martinů's *Ženitba* (The Marriage). The summer performances are given in Schönbrunner Schloßtheater, designed by Ferdinand Hetzendorf von Hohenberg and opened August 28, 1749. The Schloßtheater hosted the world premiere of Wolfgang Amadeus Mozart's *Der Schauspieldirektor* on February 7, 1786. In the area of *Alt-Wiener Singspiele*, the company has performed Dittersdorf's *Doktor und Apotheker*, *Die liebe im Narrenhaus*, and *Betrug durch Aberglauben*. The *opera buffa* has counted among its works, Franz Joseph Haydn's *List und Liebe*, Mozart's *Der Schauspieldirektor* and *Zaide*, Franz Schubert's *Claudine von Villabella* and *Die Zwillingsbrüder*, and Gaetano Donizetti's *Rita, o Le mari battu*. In the modern area, the company has mounted Benjamin Britten's *Turn of the Screw*, Gian Carlo Menotti's *The Telephone*, and Egon Wellesz's *Scherz, List und Rache*. The forgotten 18th-century pieces included Giovanni Battista Pergolesi's *La serva padrona*, Antonio Vivaldi's *Olympiade*, and Martín y Soler's *Una cosa rara*.

Schönbrunner Schloßtheater

The auditorium of the castle theater is a Baroque jewel in red and gold. There is a single tier, a small balcony above it, and center royal box. Red seats match the red drapery on the royal box, which is flanked by gilded ionic columns. The ceiling is embellished with an allegorical painting. There are 306 seats.

Practical Information. Wiener Kammeroper, Fleischmarkt 24, 1010 Vienna. Tel: 43 1 512 0100, Fax: 43 1 512 010-010. If visiting the Weiner Kammeroper, stay at the Hotel Bristol, Kärntner Ring 1, 1015 Vienna. Tel: 43 1 51 51 60 or 1 800 223 6800, Fax: 43 1 51 51 6550. It is in the heart of Vienna, and convenient to the Kammeroper.

COMPANY STAFF

Intendanten. Rudolf Berger, Hans Gabor.

Staatsoper Wien

The Staatsoper Wien, originally known as the Hofoper, reopened on November 5, 1955, with Ludwig van Beethoven's *Fidelio*. Bombs had destroyed the opera house on March 12, 1945, with only the facade and part of the foyer remaining. In 1949, Erich Boltenstern, Otto Prossinger, and Ceno Kosak were entrusted with the reconstruction. This was the second building. Wolfgang Amadeus Mozart's *Don Giovanni* had inaugurated the first Staatsoper on May 25, 1869, with Kaiser Franz Joseph I in attendance. The Hofoper was designed by August Siccard von Siccardsburg and Eduard van der Null.

Opera dates back to the 17th century. With the ascension of Leopold I to the throne in 1658, it became an established form of court entertainment and court architect Johann Burnacini built a three-story wooden opera house. Leopold I, a composer and poet in his own right, wrote *Der verlorene Sohn/Orpheus und Euridike*, and some of the music for Pietro Antonio Cesti's *Il pomo d'oro*. The latter work was written for his marriage to Princess Margaret Theresa of Spain and performed in 1668. A spectacular Baroque court opera, Cesti's *Il pomo d'oro* had 24 settings and required a thousand people for its staging and performance. In 1708, three years after Joseph I ascended the throne, the Kärntnertortheater opened. Renamed the Hofopernhaus in 1792, it staged Carl Maria von Weber's *Euryanthe* (October 25, 1823), Gaetano Donizetti's *Linda di Chamounix* (May 19, 1842), and Friedrich von Flotow's *Martha* (November 25, 1847). During the reign of Maria Theresa, the Theater bei der Hofburg, (better known as the Burgtheater on the Michaelerplatz), was inaugurated on February 5, 1742, with Giuseppe Carcano's *Amleto*. On May 14, 1748, the theater, built by Sellier, offered Christoph Willibald Gluck's *Semiramide riconosciuta*, composed for Empress Maria Theresa's birthday. Gluck was appointed Kapellmeister in 1754, and many of his works received their first performance during the next sixteen years, including *Orfeo ed Euridice* (October 5, 1762), *Alceste* (December 26, 1767), and *Paride ed Elena* (November 3, 1770). The theater also hosted the world premieres of three of Mozart's operas—*Die Entführung aus dem Serail* (July 16, 1782), *Le nozze di Figaro* (May 1, 1786), and *Così fan tutte*

(January 26, 1790), as well as Vincente Martín y Soler's *Una cosa rara* (November 17, 1786), and Domenico Cimarosa's *Il matrimonio segreto* (February 7, 1792). Two other theaters of note were the Theater auf der Wieden (1787–1801), also known as the Freyhaustheater, and the Theater an der Wien (see Wiener Festwochen/Theater an der Wien entry). Auf der Wieden introduced Mozart's *Die Zauberflöte* (September 30, 1791), and an der Wien, which opened on June 13, 1801, with Franz Teyber's *Alexander*, presented the original version of Beethoven's *Fidelio* on November 20, 1805.

The Kärntnertortheater did not pay tribute to Mozart when he died in 1792, so to compensate, a Mozart work was selected to inaugurate Vienna's new opera house. The Hofoper was a director's house, and plagued with problems from its opening. The first director, Franz von Dingelstedt, served less than a year, departing with the comment, "Concerts are superfluous; opera at best a necessary evil!" Johann von Herbeck replaced him, and introduced Karl Goldmark's *Die Königin von Saba* on March 10, 1875. That same year, Franz von Jauner was appointed Intendant, staging the entire Ring Cycle. Jauner had many triumphs, including Giuseppe Verdi conducting his *Aida* and *Messa da Requiem*, but he ran up huge deficits and was dismissed after five years. He committed suicide soon thereafter. The Hofoper was under Wilhelm Jahn's guidance by 1881, and five years later, on November 19, 1886, Goldmark's *Merlin* graced the stage for the first time, followed by *Das Heimchen am Herd* (March 21, 1896), Antonio Smareglia's *Vassallo di Szigeth* (October 4, 1889), and Jules Massenet's *Werther* (February 16, 1892).

The reign of Gustav Mahler started in 1897 and his production of Richard Wagner's *Lohengrin* was a resounding success. Although his choice of repertory was basically conservative, he produced integrated works of operas's masterpieces. The highpoints of Mahler's tenure came in 1903 and 1904, with productions of Wagner's *Tristan und Isolde* and Beethoven's *Fidelio*. The glory was short lived. His experimental production of Mozart's *Don Giovanni* for the 150th anniversary celebration of Mozart's birth, generated such controversy that by the following year, despite a successful *Iphigénie en Aulide*, Mahler resigned. His

Wiener Staatsoper (Vienna, Austria).

uncompromising standards, attacks on tradition (which he called "a blend of convenience and slovenliness"), combined with the revolutionary stage designs of Alfred Roller (the first designer to bring impressionistic techniques to the opera stage), made his position untenable. He said he was forced out by a "revolt of the mediocrities."

Richard Strauss and Franz Schalk shared the directorship duties in 1919, and Strauss's *Die Frau ohne Schatten* received its premiere on October 10, 1919, interpreted by Maria Jeritza and Lotte Lehmann. Despite many successful stagings of Strauss's operas, he left after five years. Clemens Krauss was appointed Intendant in 1929, and he introduced contemporary works. After five years, he departed for Berlin, becoming Hitler's preferred director. Hermann Wilhelm Göring assumed control of the Staatsoper when the Nazis achieved power and with the assistance of compliant directors, transformed the opera house into an Aryan and fascist domain, reducing its quality to that of a provincial opera house. Many of the leading artists and conductors were forced to flee Austria, including Alexander Kipnis, Alfred Piccaver, Friedrich Schorr, Bruno Walter, Richard Tauber, Emanuel List, and Lehmann. The opera house was closed on June 30, 1944, after a performance of Wagner's *Götterdämmerung*. Bombs leveled the building the following year.

The company took up residence at the Volksoper (see Volksoper entry) after the war, opening with Mozart's *Le nozze di Figaro* on May 1, 1945, and also at the Theater an der Wien, opening with Beethoven's *Fidelio* on October 6, 1945. A decade later, the Staatsoper reopened with seven new opera productions in the first three weeks of the inaugural season: Mozart's *Don Giovanni*, with George London and led by Karl Böhm (an abstract production that left much to the audience's imagination), Strauss's *Die Frau ohne Schatten*, Verdi's *Aida*, Wagner's *Die Meistersinger von Nürnberg*, Strauss's *Der Rosenkavalier*, and Alban Berg's *Wozzeck*. In 1956, Herbert von Karajan started his eight-year tenure, one of the most controversial and turbulent in Staatsoper history. His high point was the agreement with Teatro alla Scala (Milan) for joint productions, and many excellent Italian singers performed at the Staatsoper, along side the rising stars of Birgit Nilsson, Leonie Rysanek, and Christa Ludwig. Contemporary works continued with Gottfried von Einem's *Der Besuch der alten Dame* receiving its world premiere on May 23, 1971, and when Egon Seefehlner took the helm for the first time in 1976, a number of 20th-century works entered the repertory, including Hans Werner Henze's *Der junge Lord*, Béla Bartók's *A Kékszakállú herceg vára* (Duke Bluebeard's Castle), Erich Wolfgang Korngold's *Die tote Stadt*, and Arnold Schöenberg's *Erwartung*. The first non–German Intendant, Lorin Maazel, took up his post in 1982. Although his contract was for four years, he survived two. The politics and intrigue that play a major role in the Staatsoper brought him down.

With a repertory covering more than four dozen operas annually, over the decades a wide range of works, especially 20th-century pieces have been on the boards. These have included Einem's *Der Prozeß*, Antonín Dvořák's *Rusalka*, Luciano Berio's *Un re in ascolto*, Hans Pfitzner's *Palestrina*, Igor Stravinsky's *Oedipus*, and Strauss's *Ariadne auf Naxos*, *Salome*, and *Die schweigsame Frau*. But the repertory favorites, like Verdi's *Rigoletto*, *Il trovatore*, *Otello*, and *Don Carlo*, Giacomo Puccini's *Madama Butterfly*, *Turandot*, and *Tosca*, Jules Massenet's *Manon*, Wolfgang Amadeus Mozart's *Le nozze di Figaro*, and Gioachino Rossini's *Il barbiere di Siviglia* still dominate the schedule. The Staatsoper mounts seven operas a week, with results ranging from superb to disastrous. This is partly the result of the three-tier singer system in place at the opera house. The first tier are the stars hired by the performance — the superstars — who receive up to $23,000 per night. The second tier includes middle-quality singers who are on monthly contracts which last from two to four months. The third tier are the yearly contacts for ensemble singers — those at the beginning of their careers. Since both first and second tier singers perform major roles, this can lead to mixed results. A 1995 production of Verdi's *Jérusalem* found Samuel Ramey, José Carreras, and a contract singer in the principal roles. Ramey was superb, Carreras was, at times, in fine voice, and the contract singer was clearly out of her league. The reason for this casting — no one else of higher vocal quality knew the role. The production was a minimalist set of toy buildings that barely changed throughout the opera, although Act I took place in Toulouse and Act II in Jerusalem, and so on. As one disgruntled patron quipped, "At $200 a ticket, we should also get something to look at." That describes the Staatsoper's weakness — productions. Their forte is attracting superstars, especially for the great 19th century repertory. And when all the principal roles are cast with the top artists, as they were in a recent *Die Walküre*, the results can be great. The *Die Walküre* had no staging or sets of any consequence. At least the production did no harm, as it did in a recent

mounting of Meyerbeer's *Le Prophète*. The company's attempt at breaking its traditional bent by hiring director Hans Neuenfels, who updated the work by infusing it with absurd symbolism and irrelevant actions, including a scandalous ballet, was a catastrophe. It not only distracted from the beautiful music and outstanding singing (Plácido Domingo and Agnes Baltsa), but rendered the production irrelevant for all times. This was especially regrettable since it was the first time in sixty years that the work had been performed and first time ever in French at the Staatsoper. On the other hand, a production of Alban Berg's *Wozzeck*, although more appropriately described as a "museum" piece — realistic and traditional — was of the highest quality. As Mahler said, "One great performance a week is pretty good," and that was during the Staatsoper's greatest era.

Recent productions (in one season) include Strauss's *Die schweigsame Frau*, *Salome*, *Ariadne auf Naxos*, *Elektra*, Verdi's *Don Carlo*, *Il trovatore*, *La traviata*, *Rigoletto*, *Jérusalem*, *Stiffelio*, *Un ballo in maschera*, *Otello*, Donizetti's *L'elisir d'amore*, *Linda di Chamounix*, Wagner's *Der Ring des Nibelungen*, *Parsifal*, *Tannhäuser*, *Lohengrin*, *Die Meistersinger von Nürnberg*, *Rienzi*, *Der fliegende Holländer*, Mozart's *Don Giovanni*, Berg's *Wozzeck*, Umberto Giordano's *Fedora*, and Gioachino Rossini's *Il barbiere di Siviglia* for the standard fare, and Alfred Schnittke's *Gesualdo*, George Enescu's *Oedipe*, and Kaiser Leopold I's, *Der verlorene Sohn/Orpheus und Euridike* for rare works.

Staatsoper

Emperor Franz Joseph I had the old Hofopernhaus demolished and ordered a new opera house to be constructed. An architectural competition was held which attracted 35 submissions, with van der Nüll and von Siccardsburg submitting the winning design. In 1861 work began on the project, and eight years passed before it was finished, by which time both architects had died. The Viennese architects who lost the competition had conducted smear campaigns. Van der Nüll hanged himself in April 1863 and two months later, von Siccardsburg died of a stroke and heartbreak. He was only 32. G. Gugitz and J. Stork, oversaw the building's completion. The ultra-conservative Viennese called it "the Waterloo of architecture."

When the Hapsburg Empire collapsed in 1918, the building was renamed Staatsoper. Two decades later, German troops marched on the city and swastika flags flew from the opera house. The Nazis smashed the bust of Gustav Mahler in the opera house vestibule. In 1945, incendiary bombs gutted the theater. It was rebuilt, opening in 1955.

The "French Renaissance" Hofoper is an imposing whitish-gray stone building with arcades, bronze statues by Ernst Julius Hähnel between the loggia arches, and a plaque dedicated to Kaiser Franz Joseph I. The caryatids, garlands, and gallery arches that embellished the original red, cream, and gold horseshoe-shaped auditorium were not reconstructed. The decor of the current five-tier, horseshoe-shaped space is somber and austere. Decorated with ivory, red and gold in the style of the 1950s, the room holds burgundy corduroy seats and huge donut-shaped crystal chandelier. The Staatsoper seats 1,709 with 567 standing.

Practical Information. Wiener Staatsoper, Opernring 2, 1015 Vienna. Tel: 43 1 514 440, Fax: 43 1 514 44 23 30. When visiting the Weiner Staatsoper, stay at the Hotel Bristol, Kärntner Ring 1, 1015 Vienna. Tel: 43 1 51 51 60 or 1-800-223-6800, Fax: 43 1 51 51 6550. It is in the heart of Vienna, across the street from the Staatsoper.

COMPANY STAFF

Intendanten. Ioan Holender (1997–present), Eberhard Wächter (1991–97), Claus Helmut Drese

(1986–91), Egon Seefehlner (1984–86), Lorin Maazel (1982–84), Egon Seefehlner (1976–82), Rudolf Garmsjäger (1972–76), Heinrich Reif-Gintl (1968–72), Egon Hilbert (1964–68), Egon Hilbert & Herbert von Karajan (1963–64), Walter Erich Schäfer & Herbert von Karajan (1962–63), Herbert von Karajan (1956–62), Karl Böhm (1954–56), Karl Böhm (1943–44), Ernst August Schneider (1941–43), Walter Thomas (1941), Heinrich Strohm (1940–41), Erwin Kerber (1936–40), Felix Weingartner (1935–36), Clemens Krauss (1929–34), Franz Schalk (1924–29), Franz Schalk & Richard Strauss (1919–24), Franz Schalk (1918–19), Hans Gregor (1911–18), Felix Weingartner (1908–11), Gustav Mahler (1897–1907), Wilhelm Jahn (1881–97), Franz von Jauner (1875–80), Johann von Herbeck (1870–75), Franz von Dingelstedt (1869–70).

Bibliography. Harald Hoyer, ed., *Chronik der Wiener Staatsoper 1945–1995* (Vienna, 1995). Franz Hadamowsky, *Die Wiener Hoftheater (Staatstheater): 1776–1966; 1966–1975*, 2 Vol. (Vienna, 1966 & 1975). F. Willnauer, *Gustav Mahler und die Wiener Opera* (Vienna, 1979). Marcel Prawy, *The Vienna Opera* (New York, 1987). R. Klein, *Die Wiener Staatsoper: Ein Führer durch das Haus und seine hundertjährige Geschichte* (Vienna, 1967). *Wiener Staatsoper: Die Direktion Claus Helmut Drese* (Vienna, 1991). Österreichischer Bundestheaterverband *Berich 1993/94* (Vienna, 1993). Österreichischer Bundestheaterverband *Berich 1994/95* (Vienna, 1994). *Die Wiener Staatsoper Jahrbuch 1995* (Vienna, 1995).

Thanks to Christoph Wagner-Trenkwitz and Renate Dönch, Staatsoper Wien, and Georg Hochfilzer.

Volksoper Wien

The Volksoper, originally known as Kaiserjubiläumsstadttheater, opened on December 12, 1898, with Franz Wolff's *An der Währinger Linie* and Kleist's *Die Hermannsschlacht*. Taking ten months to construct, the theater was designed by Franz Freiherr von Krauss and Alexander Graf.

The theater's first director, Adam Müller-Guttenbrunn, who had already had problems directing the Raimund-Theaters, failed to build a strong ensemble nor an interesting repertory and the public stayed away from the theater. Rainer Simons took over the theater in 1903, and with it a large deficit. He succeeded, however, in putting the theater on firm ground and entering opera into the repertory. At this time the theater acquired the name it has today, Volksoper. The first

opera performance was Carl Maria von Weber's *Der Freischütz*. During this time, with Alexander Zemlinsky as conductor, many operas graced the stage—*Martha, Undine, Zar und Zimmermann, Frau Diavolo, Il trovatore, La traviata, Rigoletto, Un ballo in maschera, Faust, Il barbiere di Siviglia, La fille du régiment, Carmen,* and *Le nozze di Figaro*. In 1906, the first opera of Richard Wagner was offered, *Tannhäuser,* followed by *Lohengrin,* with a young Maria Jeritza as Elsa. Also, some well-known Hofoper singers, like Emil Schipper and Josef von Manowarda started their careers at the Volksoper. Works that the Hofoper would not or could not stage were given at the Volksoper, like Richard Strauss's *Salome,* and Puccini's *Tosca,* which was first heard in Vienna at the

Volksoper (Vienna, Austria).

Volksoper on February 21, 1907. Even Wagner's *Der Ring des Nibelungen*, *Parsifal*, and *Der Meistersinger von Nürnberg* were staged at the Volksoper. The theater experienced financial problems during and after World War I. Despite some suc-cessful productions — Wagner's *Tristan und Isolde* and *Die Walküre*, and Pietro Mascagni's *Cavalleria rusticana*, conducted by the composer — the theater was closed in 1928. When it reopened in November 1929, it was called Neues Wiener

Schauspielhaus. There was an attempt to turn the opera house into a playhouse again, but without success. By 1931, opera was back in the repertory with one of the high points being Max Reinhardt's production of Jacques Offenbach's *La belle Hélène* the next year. The theater underwent two more name changes during the war period. It was first renamed the Städtische Wiener Volksoper in 1938, and the Opernhaus der Stadt Wien between 1941 and 1944. Closed in the fall of 1944, the theater did duty as a movie house.

The Volksoper reopened on May 1, 1945, with Mozart's *Le nozze di Figaro*. The Staatsoper had been destroyed during the war, so the artists from the Staatsoper performed at the Volksoper, and the orchestra consisted of members from the Vienna Philharmonic. The next year, Hermann Juch took the helm of what was known as "Staatsoper in der Volksoper" and classical operetta graced the stage. Opera was also in the schedule with Franz Schmidt's *Notre Dame*, Sergey Prokofiev's *Lyubov'k tryom apel'sinam* (The Love for Three Oranges), and George Gershwin's *Porgy and Bess*, performed by a visiting American ensemble. The 1950s saw Franz Lehár's *Das Land des Lächelms* and the musical *Kiss Me Kate*, followed in the 1960s by Giuseppe Verdi's *I masnadieri*, Gaetano Donizetti's *La fille du régiment*, Richard Strauss's *Feuersnot*, Maurice Ravel's *L'heure espagnole*, and the world premiere of Robert Stolz's *Frühjahrsparade*, along side the standard operettas and musicals. With the arrival of Karl Dönch in 1973, additional operas and Singspiele graced the stage, like Eugen d'Albert's *Tiefland*, Ralph Benatzky's *Im weissen Rössl*, Kurt Weill's *Der Aufstieg und Fall der Stadt Mahagonny*, Daniel Auber's *Fra Diavolo*, Giacomo Puccini's *Gianni Schicchi* and *Il tabarro*, Leoš Janáček's *Z Mrtvého Domu* (From the House of the Dead), Benjamin Britten's *Albert Herring*, Carl Orff's *Die Kluge*, Ermanno Wolf-Ferrari's *I quattro rusteghi*, and Ambroise Thomas's *Mignon*, the Austrian premiere of Siegfried Matthus's *Die Weise von Liebe und Tod des Cornets Christoph Rilke*, and the world premieres of Marcel Rubin's *Kleider machen Leute* on December 14, 1973, and Franz Alfons Wolpert's *Der eingebildete Kranke* on April 26, 1975.

With the arrival of Klaus Bachler in 1996, the Volksoper, which was sharing its director with the Staatsoper, again had its own Intendant. A new post of musical director was created with Bernand de Billy appointed to the position. Opera is (finally) performed in its original language, although operetta remains in German. The theater's philosophy is to present music theater, with the emphasis on the theatrical aspect of the work, and a production of Charles Gound's *Faust* confirmed this ideology. The staging was clever and uncomplicated, similar to what one might encounter in a musical. Performed in contemporary dress with good voices and strong, solid orchestral sound, the opera (unfortunately) was substantially cut — the popularizing of grand opera for the masses as might be expected in a Volkstheater (People's Theater), and progressed more like a serious musical. Recent repertory includes Albert Lortzing's *Zar und Zimmermann*, Johann Strauß's *Wiener Blut* and *Eine Nacht in Venedig*, Mozart's *Die Zauberflöte*, *Così fan tutte*, *Le nozze di Figaro*, *Don Giovanni*, and *La clemenza di Tito*, Vincenzo Bellini's *Norma*, and Modest Mussorgsky's *Boris Godunov*.

Volksoper

The *fin de siècle* style theater is a large, light yellow concrete structure, trimmed with white. The facade offers two turret-like forms flanking the main entrance, with VOLKSOPER in large gold letters written across it. The U-shaped auditorium holds two center-balcony tiers and four side-box tiers. The plain white parapets with golden stripes relieve the sea of red seats, red curtain, and red decorated boxes. There are 1,472 seats.

Practical Information. Volksoper, Währinger Straße 78, 1090 Vienna. Tel: 43 1 514 44 3318, Fax: 43 1 514 44 3215. When visiting the Volksoper, stay at the Hotel Bristol, Kärntner Ring 1, 1015 Vienna. Tel: 43 1 51 51 60 or 1 800 223 6800, Fax: 43 1 51 51 6550. It is in the heart of Vienna and convenient to the Volksoper.

COMPANY STAFF

Intendanten. Klaus Bachler (1996–present), Ioan Holender (1992–96), Eberhard Wächter (1988–92), Karl Dönch (1973–88), Albert Moser (1963–73), Franz Salmhofer (1955–63), Hermann Juch (1946–55), Alfred Jerger (1945–46), Oskar Jölli (1941–44), Anton Baumann (1938–41), Jean Ernest & Alexander Kowalewsky (1935–38), Karl Lustig-Prean & Jean Ernest (1934–35), Leo Kraus (1931–33), Jakob Feldhammer & Otto Preminger (1929–31),

Hermann Frischler (1925–28), Hugo Gruder-Guntram (1925), August Markowsky & Fritz Stiedry (1924), Felix von Weingartner (1919–24), Raoul Mader (1917–19), Rainer Simons (1903–17), Adam Müller-Guttenbrunn (1898–1903).

Bibliography. Otto Fritz, *95 Jahre Wiener Volksoper: Vom Stadttheater zur Staatsbühne 1898–1993* (Vienna, 1993). *Wiener Volksoper: Die Direktion*

Karl Dönch: 1975–1987 (Vienna, 1987). *Die Volksoper: Geschichte des Hauses* (Vienna, 1973). V. Unterer, *Die Oper in Wien: Eine Überblick* (Vienna, 1970). *Volksopera Wien: Ein Musikalisches Nachrichtenmagazin* (Vienna, May 1998). Interview with Bernard de Billy, musical director, December 1997.

Thanks to Julia Birner, Volksoper Wien.

Other Austrian Companies

Other companies in Austria are noted below by name, address, telephone, and general director (as available).

Stadttheater Baden bei Wein. Theaterplatz 7, 2500 Baden bei Wien. **General Director:** Elisabeth Kales-Wallner.

Sommertheater Bad Ischl. Wiesingerstraße 7, 4820 Bad Oschl. Tel: 43 41 6132 23839, Fax: 43 41 6132 23384. **General Director:** Silvia Müller.

Theater der Landeshauptstadt St. Pölten. Rathausplatz 11, 3100 St. Pölten. Tel: 43 2742 52026,

Fax: 43 2742 541 8326. **General Director:** Peter Wolsdorff.

Studiobühne Villach. Postfach 168, 9500 Villach. Tel: 41 4242 27353, Fax: 41 4242 21 02 50. **General Director:** Michael Weger.

Wiener Operntheater. Myrthengasse 5-11, 1070 Vienna. Tel & Fax: 43 1 526 2136. **General Director:** Sven Hartberger.

Die Wiener Taschenoper. Viktorgasse 22, 1070 Vienna. Tel 43 1 503 1345, Fax: 43 1 503 1346. **Director:** Wolfgang Oswald.

Belgium

ANTWERP/GHENT

De Vlaamse Opera

Giuseppe Verdi's *Simon Boccanegra* inaugurated the newly founded De Vlaamse Opera on October 17, 1989, in Antwerp, with José van Dam, Malcolm King, Marcel Vanaud, Barbara Madra and Barnard Lombardo. Its inaugural season offered eight operas, including Verdi's *Don Carlo*, Claudio Monteverdi's *La favola d'Orfeo*, and a world premiere, Eugeniusz Knapik's *Das Glas im Kopf wird vom Glas*. De Vlaamse Opera fused companies in both Antwerp and Ghent, so one of its first tasks was to restore the Grand Théâtre of Ghent, which had been closed in 1989. The Grand Théâtre, designed by Louis Roelandt, had been inaugurated on August 30, 1840. Humanité-René Philastre and Charles-Antoine Cambon were in charge of the interior decorations. On September 2, 1993, a meticulously restored Grand Théâtre of Ghent reopened with a production of *Die Auferstehung*, the title of Gustav Mahler's second symphony. With the reopening of the Grand Theater in 1993, De Vlaamse Opera (Flanders Opera) began performing in both Antwerp and Ghent with a single orchestra and chorus.

Ghent

Opera was heard as early as 1682, performed in a hall owned by the Guild of St. Sebastian, located on the Kouter. Despite the prohibition of operatic performances by the Bishop of Ghent Albert de Hornes, a certain Mrs. Joanny organized several productions, which the aristocracy, upper classes, and city administration enjoyed. The hall was replaced in 1698 with a real opera house, the Municipal Theatre, inaugurated on May 31 with Jean-Baptiste Lully's *Thésée*. The Municipal Theatre, the predecessor of the "Grand Théâtre," was built on almost the same site as the current opera house. In 1706, the Académie Royale de Musique was founded and it offered opera performances three times a week in Ghent and Bruges. The active operatic life of the Municipal came to an abrupt halt on December 16, 1715, when fire devoured the building. In 1737, the Guild constructed another theater, Saint Sebastian Theatre, designed by Ghent architect Bernard de Wilde. It took forty years for Flemish Opera to play a prominent role. That was the year Ignatius Vitzthumb, a former director at the Théâtre de la Monnaie, took over the Ghent opera. There were two separate companies, one Flemish and one French. In 1837, the Saint Sebastian Theatre, which was owned by the city administration, was demolished. This led to the construction of the current opera house. In 1911, architect Charles van Rysselberghe added an entrance hall to the structure. A decade later, in 1921, the Royal Opera of Ghent was created. Most productions were performed in French until the Germans occupied Belgium and ordered all opera to be sung in Flemish. The practice of performing opera in its original language only came to play at the beginning of the 1960s.

Antwerp

The first Flemish Opera heard in Antwerp dates back to 1661 with the inauguration of the Theatre of the Old Crossbow on the Grote Markt. But not until the end of the 1800s was there a Flemish opera company. There were two companies in existence in 1719, one performed in French, and the other was a traveling Italian troupe. A new theater was built in 1827, commissioned by Pierre Bourla. Inaugurated in 1834, it was called the Théâtre Royal d'Anvers, and offered works from the French repertory.

The Vlaamsche Opera (Flanders Opera), originally called the Nederlands Lyrisch Toneel (Dutch Lyric Theater), was founded in 1893. A well-known bass, Henry Fontaine, ran the company. A new opera house opened on October 18, 1907, with Jan Blockx's *De Herbergprinses*, conducted by the composer himself. On March 17, 1914, Richard Wagner's *Parsifal* was performed, beginning a tradition of a repertory with an emphasis on Wagner works, along with those by Carl Maria von Weber, Albert Lortzing, Heinrich August Marschner, Wolfgang Amadeus Mozart, and Eugen d'Albert. In 1920, the Flanders Opera added "royal" to its name. After 1933, operas from the French and Italian repertories were added to the schedule, but all works were sung in Dutch until the end of the 1970s.

Ghent/Antwerp

The Royal Opera Company of Ghent and of Antwerp were combined in 1982 under the name Opera voor Vlaaderen (Opera for Flanders). Unfortunately, this arrangement improved neither the quality nor the financial situation of the companies, primarily because both opera houses still maintained separate orchestras, chorus, and schedules. This soon led to bankruptcy and the desolving of the two companies.

The Vlaamse Operastichting vzw (Flanders Opera Foundation) was founded in 1988 and asked Gerard Mortier, director of the Théâtre de la Monnaie, to help set up the Flanders Opera. There was a difference of opinion between the Board of Directors and Mortier, and Marc Clémeur was asked to take the helm on December 1, 1989. The company itself is a non-profit private association, as compared to the interurban semi-governmental organization that the Opera voor Vlaanderen had been, giving it more flexibility. Following the innovative trends in European music theater, there are three points of focus for the company: innovative productions of Baroque operas, contemporary works, and a Puccini cycle. The repertory ranges from Erich Wolfgang Korngold's *Die tote Stadt* and Michael Tippett's *King Priam* to Georg Friedrich Händel's *Serse* and Richard Wagner's *Rienzi*. The Baroque operas included *L'infedeltà* and *La favola d'Orfeo, Alcina, Il ritorno di Ulisse in patria, Armide, L'incoronazione di Poppea, Orlando, Serse,* and *Semele*. Since there are a number of well-known Baroque specialists who live in Flanders, among them Philippe Herreweghe, Sigiswald Kuijken, René Jacobs, and Jos van Immerseel, the emphasis of the Flanders Opera on the Baroque repertory gave these artists an opportunity to perform "at home." Emphasis on contemporary works attracted a new and young audience by showing that opera is a living, vibrant art form. To this end, the company has presented three world premieres: Eugeniusz Knapik's *Das Glas im Kopf wird vom Glas* (1989-90 season), Jan Vlijmen's *Un malheureux vêtu de noir* (1990-91 season), and Knapik's *Silent Screams* (1992-93). The company established a new approach to interpreting Puccini works, with a message for our times, by respecting the original story but placing it in timeless surroundings and emphasizing the composers approach to expressing human emotions. Puccini works included *Manon Lescaut, Edgar* (concert), *Tosca, La rondine* (concert), *Turandot, La bohème,* and *Madama Butterfly*. All this has earned the young company an international reputation.

Innovative productions include imaginative sets with great special effects. For Händel's *Orlando*, a fire erupted in the middle of a water-pond — it was staged in a "timeless" setting with a modern interpretation. The approach varies. For a contemporary, lesser-known work like Erich Wolfgang Korngold's *Die tote Stadt*, the staging was more traditional in concept and representation. But even in this production, white clouds of vapor rolled over the water, which flooded the stage at the appropriate time. The company makes use of the excellent technical facilities. The casts are a mixture of established and rising stars, with singing ranging from good to outstanding. It is a versatile and accomplished young company.

Clémeur believes that timeless productions which allow the audience to take home a message from the opera is the most effective approach for opera today. He has no interest in directors who stuff a message down the throat of the audience, nor in updating. For example, his concepts differ from a Paris production at the Théâtre des Champs Élysées of another Baroque opera, Händel's *Ezio*, which was updated to Nazi Germany during World War II — a symbolic concept imposed on the opera with no relation to the work. Clémeur wants to make an opera timeless, relevant for all times and for today's audience. He does not like the use of gimmicks, but prefers to use clever psychological means to accomplish his goals. Clemens took a provincial level opera company and has turned it into a first rate one. Recent repertory includes Mozart's *La clemenza di Tito*, Wagner's *Tristan und Isolde*, Verdi's *Rigoletto*, Richard Strauss's *Daphne*, Benjamin Britten's *Billy Budd*, Jules Massenet's *Cendrillon*, and Puccini's *Turandot*.

Gentse Opera, Ghent

The opera house in Ghent had been closed

Gentse Opera, restored auditorium (Ghent, Belgium).

in 1989 because it was not up to fire code, and a national lottery was held to pay for its restoration. It took five years and 800 million BF to restore the Gentse Opera to its original Neoclassic beauty.

The Neo-Renaissance natural stone facade, with moulding extending almost 270 feet, is subtly interrupted in the middle with a redoubt of pilasters and arches with a carriage entrance beneath. Muses of Music and Dance embellish the facade. The red-and-gold auditorium overflows with medallions, cartouches, painted reliefs and caryatids. Five tiers, the top one hidden from view from below, are horseshoe-shaped. Exquisite decorations ornament their parapets, which hold the names of the composers MEHUL, WEBER, BOIELDIEU, AND BELLINI. Pairs of pillars, embellished with gilded, fluted, engaged columns, separate three levels of boxes from the open balconies. The proscenium boxes are crowned by a broken pediment and muses. Two paintings commemorate Comedy and Tragedy — one with a celebratory procession and the other with a mourning procession. There are 969 seats.

Nieuwen Schouwburg, Antwerp

The Antwerp opera house (Nieuwen Schouwburg), built between 1907 and 1910 by architect Alexis Van Mechelen in an Art Deco style, is sandwiched between two buildings. The ornate facade, embellished with four massive pairs of Ionic columns, a balustrade and rusticated stones, hints at the glorious hall behind the glass and wooden doors. The auditorium holds three balconies, supported by gilded Ionic columns. Gilded festoons ornament the ivory-colored parapets and proscenium boxes. An allegorical mural circles the ceiling outlined by gilded ornamentation. The proscenium arch holds the symbol of the walled city of Antwerp. The seats are deep red velvet.

Practical Information: De Vlaamse Opera, Van Ertbornstraat 8, 2018 Antwerp. Tel: 32 3 233-6808, Fax: 32 3 232-2661. De Vlaamse Opera, Schouwburgstraat 3, 9000 Gent. Tel: 32 9 223 0681, Fax: 32 9 223 8726. When visiting De Vlaamse Opera in Antwerp, stay at the Alfa De Keyser Hotel, De Keyserlei 66-70, 2018 Antwerpen. Tel: 32 3 234-0135, Fax 32 3 232 3970. It is in the center of the city across the street

Nieuwen Schouwburg auditorium entrance (Antwerp, Belgium).

Nieuwen Schouwburg auditorium (Antwerp, Belgium).

from the train station and only a few blocks from the opera house. The hotel can assist with opera tickets and schedule. When visiting the De Vlaamse Opera in Ghent, stay at the Hotel Sofitel, Ghent Belfort, Hoogpcort 63, 9000 Ghent. Tel: 32 9 233 3331, Fax 32 9 233-1102. It is centrally located near the opera house. The hotel can assist with opera tickets and schedules.

COMPANY STAFF, PREMIERES, AND REPERTORY

Intendant. Marc Clémeur.

World Premieres. E. Knapik's *Das Glas im Kopf wird vom Glas* (1989–90); J. Vlijmen's *Un malheureux vêtu de noir* (1990–91); E. Knapik's *Silent Screams* (1992–93).

Repertory. **1989–90:** Simon Boccanegra, Tancredi, Ariadne auf Naxos, L'infedeltà delusa, L'Orfeo, Das Glas im Kopf wird vom Glas, Don Carlo, Eugene Onegin. **1990–91:** Elektra, Macbeth, Un malheureux vêtu, Manon Lescaut, La Cenerentola, Parsifal, Edgar, Alcina. **1991–92:** Der fliegende Hol-

länder, Il ritorno di Ulisse in patria, Tosca, King Priam, Un ballo in maschera, Parsifal, La rondine, Der Rosenkavalier. **1992–93:** Turandot, Armide, Elektra, Falstaff, Parsifal, Attila, Silent Screams, Difficult Dreams, Manon Lescaut. **1993–94:** Otello, Samson et Dalila, La bohème, L'incoronazione di Poppea, La Cenerentola, Lohengrin, Billy Budd, Die Fledermaus. **1995–96:** Le nozze di Figaro, Die tote Stadt, Serse, Tosca, La forza del destino, Parsifal, King Priam, La fanciulla del West. **1997–98:** La clemenza di Tito, Let's Make an Opera, Billy Budd, Rigoletto, Daphne, Semele, Tristan und Isolde, Cendrillon, Turandot.

Bibliography. *De Opera van Gent: Het "Grand Théâtre" van Roelandt, Philastre en Cambon* (Ghent, 1993). *De Vlaamse Opera van de Grondvesten, tot de tempel* (Ghent, 1992). *Op Zoek Naar de Harmonie Tussen Denken en Voelen: Vijf seizoenen Vlaamse Opera* (Antwerp, 1994). *De Vlaamse Opera Magazine* Seizoen 95-96 Nummer 2 Jaargang 7. Interview with Marc Clémeur, Intendant, June 1995.

Thanks to Ingeborg Mertens, De Vlaamse Opera; Liliane Menin-Opsomer, Belgian Tourist Office, New York; Jan Wittouck, Toerisme Vlaanderen, Brussels; and Jacques Konings.

Opéra National/Théâtre Royal de la Monnaie

Fromental Halévy's *Jaguarita l'Indienne* inaugurated the Théâtre Royal de la Monnaie on March 24, 1856. Designed by Joseph Poelaert, it was the third opera house constructed on the site. The first, known as Grand Théâtre sur la Monnoye, or Grand Théâtre de la Monnaie, was opened on November 19, 1700, with Jean-Baptiste Lully's *Atys*. Designed by Paolo and Pietro Bezzi and built by the Italian Gio-Paolo Bombarda, treasurer to Maximilien-Emmanuel of Bavaria, the theater was located on the site of the former Hôtel Ostrevent, where coins were minted. Hence the name *La monniae* (the mint). The second Théâtre de la Monnaie, constructed because of the terrible state of disrepair of the first theater, was inaugurated with André Grétry's *La caravane du Caire* on May 25, 1819. Designed by Louis Damesne, the second La Monnaie was built just behind the first. Fire gutted the theater on January 21, 1855. Only the walls and the peristyle remained. The city rebuilt the opera house and La Monnaie found its niche by becoming a leading avant-garde center.

During the early 1700s, the initial seasons at La Monnaie hosted Lully's *Persée*, *Bellérephon*, *Armide*, and *Amadis*, André Destouches's *Omphale*, André Campra's *Tancrède*, and works by Jean-Philippe Rameau. The Brussels banker Jean-Baptiste Meeus acquired La Monnaie in 1717, which he and his daughters ran until 1763. Domenico Sarri's *Arsace* and Giuseppe Maria Orlandini's *Griselda*, presented in 1727, began three years of staging Italian opera, which was under the artistic direction of Antoine-Marie Peruzzi. When Maurice de Saxe occupied Belgium in 1746, opéra comique entered the repertory. But when the French left three years later, opéra comique went with them. (Note: Maurice de Saxe is the reason Princess de Bouillon sent poisoned violets to Adriana in Francesco Cilea's *Adriana Lecouvreur*.) Around this time the first Belgian opera was staged, Pierre van Maldere's *Le Déguisement pastoral*. The French revolution caused major difficulties at La Monnaie, and although its doors remained open, circus fare — tightrope walkers, ventriloquists, acrobats, and jugglers — provided the entertainment. The first La Monnaie held an elliptically-shaped, five-tier, unheated auditorium, seating 1,200. Although some of the box holders enjoyed the warmth of their own private small stoves, the majority shivered from act to act, thawing out only during intermission in the heated foyer.

In 1810, Napoleon Bonaparte visited the Grand Théâtre. Aghast at its state of disrepair, he promised to build a new opera house. The promise was fulfilled nine years later. A newspaper of the time described the inaugural evening in 1819 as follows: "At 7 o'clock, S.A.R. the prince of Orange, and S.A.I. his esteemed spouse entered their magnificent box; S.M. the king appeared soon thereafter with S.M. the Queen, and S.A.R. Prince Frédéric des Pays-Bas. The audience expressed its satisfaction by repeated applause and calling loudly for the architect, Damesne, in order to pay him a well-deserved tribute for his accomplishment. They honored the royal family by proclaiming *vive le roi! vive la reine! vivent le prince et la princesse! vive le prince grand-maître!* The new opera house held a white and gold auditorium with four box tiers.

Nine years after the opera house opened, Gioachino Rossini's *Il barbiere di Siviglia* received its French premiere, followed by his *Gazza ladra* in 1822 and *Otello* two years later. On August 25, 1830, the course of Belgian history was changed with a performance of Daniel Auber's *La muette de Portici*. The opera concerns the uprising of the Neapolitans against their Spanish oppressors. Belgium was ruled by King William I of the Netherlands, who ordered the opera staged on June 29, 1830. He banned repeat performances because of unrest in the capital. Then the ban was lifted and a performance, scheduled for the evening of August 25, immediately sold out and hundreds more, unable to get tickets, gathered on the square in front of the theater. The opera played without incident until the famous duet, *"Amour sacré de la patrie"* (Sacred love of the fatherland). The audience shouted for an encore and the aria was repeated. Then Masaniello, a Neapolitan fisherman who led the uprising learned that the Spanish Viceroy's son had seduced his helpless mute sister and swore vengeance, shouting *"Aux armes."* The audience charged out of the theater and the Revolution which would give Belgium its independence began. La Monnaie was closed for two weeks, and when it reopened on September 12, 1830, for a benefit performance for the wounded, *Brabançonne*, the Belgian national anthem, was on the program. The constitutional monarchy of Belgium was born and Prince Leopold of Saxe-Coburg ascended the throne as Leopold I, King of Belgium.

In 1845, Giuseppe Verdi's *Ernani* received its French premiere, followed three years later by his *Nabucco*. Beginning in 1850, La Monnaie hosted opera and ballet exclusively, but five years later, while stagehands were erecting scenery for a performance of Giacomo Meyerbeer's *Le Prophète*, fire devoured the theater. Performances continued at the Théâtre du Cirque, which in 1867 (after La Monnaie had opened) hosted one of the first Flemish operas, Benoit's *Isa*. The third La Monnaie experienced a golden age of opera with several world premieres on the boards: Charles Lecocq's *La Fille de Madame Angot* (December 4, 1872) and *Giroflé-Girofla* (1874), Jules Massenet's *Hérodiade* (December 19, 1881), Ernest Reyer's *Sigurd* (January 7, 1884) and *Salammbô* (February 10, 1890), Emmanuel Chabrier's *Gwendoline* (April 10, 1886), Benjamin Godard's *Jocelyn* (1888), Xavier Leroux's *Evangéline* (1895), Vincent d'Indy's *Fervaal* (March 12, 1897) and *L'Étranger* (1901), and Ernest Chausson's *Le roi Arthus* (November 30, 1903). The French premiere of Richard Wagner's *Die Meistersinger von Nürnberg* took place in 1885, followed by his *Die Walküre* two years later. On October 13, 1887, Nellie Melba made her operatic debut as Gilda in Verdi's *Rigoletto* and Enrico Caruso sang Rodolfo in Giacomo Puccini's *La bohème* in 1910. Belgian artists refused to perform during the German occupation of World War I, but opera seasons were mounted by the occupying forces including Richard Strauss conducting his *Der Rosenkavalier*. After the war, a new company, formed by Maurice Kufferath and Corneil de Thoran, reopened the theater on December 21, 1918. Although Kufferath died the following year, de Thoran led La Monnaie until his death in 1953. During his reign, he introduced Darius Milhaud's *Les Malheurs d'Orphée* (May 7, 1926), Arthur Honegger's *Antigone* (December 28, 1927), and Sergei Prokofiev's *Igrok* (The Gambler, April 29, 1929). The French premiere of Alexander Borodin's *Prince Igor* took place in 1924, followed by Strauss's *Ariadne auf Naxos*. After World War II, the city of Brussels gave up ownership of the opera house to the national government and in 1963, *Opéra National* was added to its name.

Gerard Mortier took the helm in 1981, and changed La Monnaie's fame from the role it played in Belgium's fight for freedom to the operas which played on its stage. With a strong commitment to introducing contemporary works, La Monnaie commissioned new operas — Philippe Boesmans's *La Passion de Gilles* (October 18, 1983), André Laporte's *Das Schloß* (December 16, 1986), and John Adams's *The Death of Klinghoffer* (March 19, 1991) and included 20th century works in its repertory. Mortier also initiated an artistic policy of avoiding the "star system" in favor of well-conceived, thoroughly-rehearsed productions. When Bernard Foccroulle assumed the directorship after Mortier departed for Salzburg, the same artistic emphasis continued, which was evident in riveting productions of powerful operas like Leoš Janáček's *Z Mrtvého Domu* (From the House of the Dead) and Béla Bartók's *A Kékszakállú herceg vára* (Duke Bluebeard's Castle). The staging was stripped to its essence, focusing on the dramatic and musical elements. *Z Mrtvého Domu*, recreated, with chilling realism, the grim life in a Siberian prison. A huge broken wing of a tormented eagle, initially lifeless, then symbolically healed and flying to freedom, was set on an almost empty stage focusing the attention on the singers and music. *A Kékszakállú herceg vára* was a mixed media production. Film of macabre dancing, complemented by the masterful acting and singing of the cast, was projected on a stark stage holding only the outlines of locked doors, emphasizing the hidden horror in the work. Benjamin Britten's *Turn of the Screw* was a cleverly-conceived production which through innovative methods explained the story in a straightforward manner, with the numerous scenes flowing seamlessly one after another. It is one of the leading avant-garde opera centers in the world, emphasizing contemporary works in an eclectic repertory.

The repertory spans works from the early 1600s to the 20th century, from Claudio Monteverdi's *La favola d'Orfeo* to Claude Debussy's *Pelléas et Mélisande*. Recent offerings include Verdi's *Otello* and *Rigoletto*, Massenet's *Werther*, Puccini's *Il trittico*, Manuel de Falla's *La vida breve*, Wagner's *Parsifal*, Gioachino Rossini's *Il turco in Italia*, Dmitry Shostakovich's *Ledi Makbet Mtsenskovo uyezda* (Lady Macbeth of the Mtsensk District), and Gaetano Donizetti's *Don Pasquale*.

Théâtre de la Monnaie

In 1958, La Monnaie was condemned as a fire risk. The management appealed and performances continued until 1985, when, after a performance of Richard Wagner's *Die Meistersinger von Nürnberg*, the opera house was closed for 16 months. A group of architects (listed as A.2R.C., Urbat, and Charles Vandenhove) working under the amusing name of *Architecture et Construction entre Rêve et Réalité* (Architecture and Construction Between Dream and Reality) were responsible for the renovation which cost around $25 million. Ludwig van Beethoven's *Ninth Symphony* reopened the theater on November 12, 1986, and Richard Strauss's *Der Rosenkavalier* inaugurated the new opera season seven days later. It is one of the most beautiful opera houses in the world.

La Monnaie presents a dignified, Neoclassic facade with a Grecian-style portico of eight massive Ionic columns and a French stone relief pediment. Designed by Eugène Simonis, the sculpture represents *L'Harmonie des Passions Humaines*. The burgundy and gold horseshoe-shaped auditorium, decorated in the style of Louis XVI, holds four tiers, divided into sections by pairs of massive columns. Large sculpture reliefs ornament the first parapet and a tableaux representing Tragedy, Music, and Dance enhances the second. Two gold genii holding clusters of lights flank the royal stage box. Cherubs and nymphs embellish the space. The ceiling holds allegorical figures of Belgium protecting the Arts. La Monnaie seats 1,140.

Practical Information. Théâtre Royal de la Monnaie, rue Léopold 4, 1000 Brussels. Tel: 32 2 229-1211, Fax: 32 2 229-1384. When visiting Théâtre Royal de la Monnaie, stay at the Hotel Royal Windsor, rue Dusquesnoy 5-7, 1000 Brussels. Tel: 32 2 505-5555 or 1-800-223-6800, Fax 32 2 505-5500. It is located in the center of Brussels, near the opera house. The Royal

Théâtre Royal de la Monnaie (Brussels, Belgium).

Windsor can assist with opera tickets and schedules.

COMPANY STAFF AND SELECT PREMIERES AND REPERTORY

Directeur Général. Bernard Foccroulle (1992–present), Gerárd Mortier (1981–91), Maurice Huisman (1959–81), Joseph Rogatchewsky (1954–58), Corneil de Thoran (1918–53), Maurice Kufferath (1918–19).

***World Premieres*—Mortier Regime (1981–91).** P. Boesmans's *La passion de Gilles*, October 18, 1983; A. Laporte's *Das Schloß*, December 16, 1986.

***Repertory*— Mortier Regime (1981–91). 1981–82:** Don Carlo, Wozzeck, Luisa Miller, Alceste, Cendrillon, La clemenza di Tito, Tosca. **1982–83:** Idomeneo, Simon Boccanegra, Louise, Der Freischütz, Le Comte Ory, Kát'a Kabanová, La Cenerentola, La clemenza di Tito, Centrillon. **1983–84:** Cpariccio, La passion de Gilles, La bohème, Pelléas et Mélisande, Il trovatore, Der fliegende Holländer, Le nozze di Figaro, Così fan tutte, Don Carlo, Idomeneo. **1984–85:** Don Giovanni, Lucio Silla, L'elisir d'amore, Tristan und Isolde, Die Meistersinger von Nürnberg, Le nozze di Figaro, La clemenza di Tito, Capriccio. **1985–86:** Les contes d'Hoffmann, Die Fledermaus, Přihody Lišky Bystroušky (The Cunning Little Vixen), Die lustige Witwe, La finta giardiniera, Boris Godunov, Simon Boccanegra. **1986–87:** Le martyre de Saint-Sébastien, Der Rosenkavalier, Das Schloß, Macbeth, La traviata, Falstaff, Don Carlo, Così fan tutte. **1987–88:** Jenůfa, Otello, Lulu, Elektra, Giulio Cesare in Egitto, Orfeo ed Euridice, Der ferne Klang, Don Giovanni, Les contes d'Hoffmann, Boris Godunov. **1988–89:** Parsifal, Fidelio, L'incoronazione di Poppea, La traviata, Wozzeck, La finta giardiniera. **1989–90:** Die Entführung aus dem Serail, Lohengrin, Z Mrtvého domu (The House of the Dead), Falstaff, Così fan tutte, Der Rosenkavalier. **1990–91:** Simon Boccanegra, Stephen Climax, The Death of Klinghoffer, Die Zauberflöte, Das Rheingold, Die Walküre, Siegfried, Götterdämmerung, Le nozze di Figaro, Jenůfa, L'incoronazione di Poppea.

Bibliography. *Un Théâtre d'Opéra: L'Equipe de Grand Mortier à la Monnaie* (Paris, 1986). *Corriam tutti a festeggiar 1981–1991 La Monnaie * De Munt: Gerárd Mortier* (Brussels, 1992). *Inbel: The Royal Theatre of La Monnaie* Cahier No.5 (Brussels, September 1988). *Opéra National/Théâtre Royal de la Monnaie* *Nationale opera/Koninklijke Muntschouwburg* (Brussels, 1963). Jules Salès, *Théâtre Royal de la Monnaie, 1856–1970* (Nivelles, 1971). Jacques Isnardon and Lionel Renieu, *Histoire des théâtres de Bruxelles depuis leur origine jusqu'à ce jour* 2 Vol. (Paris, 1928). A. de Gers, *Théâtre royal de la Monnaie, 1856–1926* (Brussels, 1926). *De Munt * La Monnaie Magazine* (March-April 1998).

Thanks to Yannick Vermeirsch, De Munt/La Monnaie; Liliane Menin-Opsomer, Belgian Tourist Office, New York; Annette Beautrix, Sabine Rosen and Jan Wittouck, Office de Promotion du Tourisme/Toerisme Vlaanderen, Brussels; and Paul Ch. van Wijk.

—————————————————— LIÈGE

Opéra Royal de Wallonie

The Opéra Royal de Wallonie was created in 1967 from pre-existing opera companies in the Wallonie region. On December 13, 1966, representatives from the cities of Liège, Mons, and Charleroi met to create an opera center in Wallonie to promote opera in the region, with its headquarters in Liège. Maurice Destenay, mayor of Liège, and a former bass at the Théâtre Royal was one of the founders of the Opéra Royal de Wallonie. The company performs in the Théâtre Royal, originally called the Théâtre de Liège, which was inaugurated on November 4, 1820, with André Grétry's *Zémire et Azor*.

The history of opera in Liège dates back to 1702, when Prince Evêque Joseph-Clément of Baviere ordered the construction of a wooden theater in the Grand Market Place building on the pier of the Batte known as Grand Halle aux Blés. Italian troupes arrived, performing Italian farces. When the theater disappeared in 1718, the first of three "La Baraques" was constructed, which stood until 1737. The second arose that same year but survived only three years, to 1740. Then entrepreneurs M. Leroy and M. Defresne constructed Baraque III out of brick in 1740. A decade later, the building was sold to the city for 2,500 florins. In this theater on September 2, 1754, Grétry at the age of 13 years attended his first opera, Giovanni Battista Pergolesi's *La serva padrona*. The theater was demolished in 1760, but on September 19, 1767, another theater opened, known as La Douane. Here Grétry's *Zémire et Azor* was presented for the first time in 1774. A fire destroyed this theater in 1805, when a singer forgot to extinguish the brazier in his box. The following year, at the initiative of the Préfet Impérial Micoud, the Salle Saint-Jacques was created in the church of Saint Jacques where opera was performed until the Théâtre Royal opened in 1820.

Before 1967, there had been five homegrown opera companies in the Wallonie region — in the cities of Verviers, Namur, Charleroi, Mons, and Liège. Each theater was run differently, some by concession, others by communal direction. The productions were semi-professional and mounted with extremely limited budgets. Given the uncertainty of the financing, it was inevitable that these different companies would merge or fold. The inaugural season of the Opéra Royal de Wallonie offered eighteen different operas, including Giuseppe Verdi's *Nabucco*, Gioachino Rossini's *Il barbiere di Siviglia*, Giacomo Puccini's *Tosca*, B. di Vito's *Le logeur*, Charles Gounod's *Faust*, and Darius Milhaud's *Les malheurs d'Orphée*. From the beginning the repertory concentrated on French opera and offered several world and Belgian premieres, including P.M. Dubois's *Les Suisses*, P. Danblon's *Cyrano de Bergerac*, R. Rossel's *Le petit ménestrel*, G. Becaud's *L'opera d'Aran*, Jean-Philippe Rameau's *Les Indes galantes*, and E. Bondeville's *Antoine et Cléopâtre*. Also on the boards were Georges Bizet's *Carmen* and *Les pêcheurs de perles*, Gustav Charpentier's *Louise*, Claude Debussy's *Pelléas et Mélisande*, Léo Delibes's *Lakmé*, Gounod's *Mireille* and *Roméo et Juliette*, Francis Poulenc's *Les dialogues des Carmélites* and *La voix humaine*, Henri Rabaud's *Marouf, savetier du Caire*, Hector Berlioz's *Benvenuto Cellini* and *La Damnation de Faust*, and several operas of Jules Massenet — *Le Cid*, *Don Quichotte*, *Hérodiade*, *Manon*, *Thaïs*, and *Werther* — and Grétry — *L'amant jaloux ou les fausses apparences*, *Zémire et Azor*, *Richard Coeur de Lion*, *Pierre Le Grand*, and *Monsieur Grétry ou les mémoires d'un solitaire*. The most popular composers and mainstream repertory were also on the schedule. Eight works of Wolfgang Amadeus Mozart, including *Così fan tutte*, *Idomeneo*, and *Der Schauspieldirekteur*, nine works of Giacomo Puccini, including *La rondine*, *Manon Lescaut*, and *Turandot*, and 15 of Giuseppe Verdi's operas, including *Nabucco*, *La forza del destino*, and *Simon Boccanegra* have graced the stage. German opera made an appearance with Richard Wagner's *Der fliegende Holländer*, *Lohengrin*, and *Die Walküre*, Paul Hindemith's *Mathias der Mahler*, and Richard Strauss's *Arabella*, *Ariadne auf Naxos*, and *Der Rosenkavalier*. Since 1985, the Opéra Royal de Wallonie has depended upon the French community of Belgium as well as on the region of Wallonie and the city of Liège for a major part of its subsidies. There is a permanent orchestra of 72 musicians, and a chorus of 60.

Although homegrown professional opera is relatively new in Liège, productions are bold and daring. The Opéra Royal de Wallonie offers on the average 12 productions each season, usually from the Italian, German, and French repertory. It is rare to hear an English, Russian, or Spanish opera (although some have been staged, including Modest Mussorgsky's *Boris Godunov* and Manuel de Falla's *La vida breve* and *El retablo de Maese Pedro*). American musical comedies are included in the schedule, like *My Fair Lady* and *Man of La Mancha*. A full schedule of operettas is also part of the season. Recent offerings include Gioachino Rossini's *Guillaume Tell*, Wolfgang Amadeus Mozart's *Die Zauberflöte*, Giuseppe Verdi's *Stiffelio* and *Don Carlo*, Richard Wagner's *Tannhäuser*, Charles Gounod's *Mireille*, and Gottfried von Einem's *Dantons Tod*.

Théâtre Royal de Liège

The first stone for the Théâtre Royal was laid in 1818, and it was opened two years later. The material used for the theater had been recovered from some churches which had been destroyed during the revolution of 1789, primarily the Cathedral Saint Lambert. The columns of the facade came from the Convent of Chartreux. In 1840, the theater was enlarged by enclosing the peristyle, and 20 years later, the amphitheater was expanded, increasing the seating capacity from 1,088 to 1,554 places. During World War I, the Germans requisitioned the theater and converted it into stables, a very unpleasant chapter in the theater's history. A major transformation took place in 1959 when the floor of the auditorium was given an incline and the *baignoires* were removed. The capacity was increased to 1,268 places, but only 17 years later, a "rearrangement" reduced the number of places.

The Théâtre Royal is a Classic building of yellow and grey stone, with arches, a balustrade, and Corinthian columns, crowned by a pediment. The ornately decorated four-tier auditorium holds

Théâtre Royal de Liège (Liège, Belgium).

deep red velvet seats against dark wood walls. The first tier is horseshoe shaped, whereas the second, third, and fourth follow the contour curve of the hall. The ivory and gold parapets are embellished with musical motifs and putti. Two pairs of guilded fluted columns form boxes and divide the tiers into three sections. The theater seats 1037.

Practical Information. Opéra Royal de Wallonie, 1, rue des Dominicains, 4000 Liège. Tel: 32 41 21 47 20, Fax: 32 41 21 02 01. When visiting Opéra Royal de Wallonie, stay at the Hotel Bedford, Quai St. Leonard 36, 4000 Liège. Tel: 32 41 28 81 11, Fax 32 41 27 45 75. It is convenient to the opera house and can assist with opera tickets and schedule.

COMPANY STAFF AND PREMIERES

Directeur Général. Jean-Louis Grinda.

World Premieres. P.M. Dubois's *Les Suisses* (1973); P. Danblon's *Cyrano de Bergerac* (1980); R. Defossez's *Liège-libertés* (1980); A.M. Grétry's *Monsieur Grétry ou les mémoires d'un solitaire* (1980); R. Rossel's *Le petit ménestrel* (1981); R. Rossel's *Le jeu de Saint-Nicolas* (1983). **(Chamber Operas)** R. Defossez's *À chacun son mensonge* (1967); M. Leclerc's *La matrone d'Ephese* (1967); R. Defossez's *La surprise de l'amour* (1971); J. Brumioul's *Sonate à majorque* (1983); R. Schumann's *L'amour et la vie d'une femme* (1984); C. Ledoux & P. Baton's *Ricciolina ou L'amour du masque* (1985). *Belgian Premieres.* B. di Vito's *Bella* (1967); G. Becaud's *L'opera d'Aran* (1968); J.P. Rameau's *Les Indes galantes* (1976); E. Bondeville's *Antoine et Cléopâtre* (1976); P. Daniel-Lesur's *Andrea del Sarto* (1978); G. Menotti's *The Saint of Bleeker Street* (1979); E. Bondeville's *L'ecole des maris* (1982); Daniel-Lesur's *Ondine* (1983); K. Penderecki's *Diably z Loudun* (The Devils of Loudun) (1985).

Bibliography. *Opéra Royal de Wallonie 1967–1987* (Liège, 1987). Additional information supplied by the company.

Thanks to André Dewez, Opéra Royal de Wallonie; Liliane Menin-Opsomer, Belgian Tourist Office, New York; Annette Beautrix and Sabine Rosen, Office de Promotion du Tourisme, Brussels.

Canada

BANFF

The Banff Centre Theatre Arts

In 1952, the Canadian premiere of Henry Purcell's *Dido and Aeneas* became the first opera mounted at The Banff Centre, which had been founded in 1933 by Ned Corbett. Opera productions were the natural offshoot of an opera program begun in 1949 for skilled young professional singers. Since then, operas have been mounted annually.

The second season (1953) offered Gian Carlo Menotti's *The Old Maid and the Thief.* The first decades concentrated on the repertory favorites like Giuseppe Verdi's *La traviata* and *Falstaff*, Giacomo Puccini's *Madama Butterfly* and *Tosca*, and Wolfgang Amadeus Mozart's *Le nozze di Figaro* and *Così fan tutte.* The 1970s signalled an expansion of the repertory. In addition to Gaetano Donizetti's *Don Pasquale* and Mozart's operas, Carlisle Floyd's *Susannah*, Healey Willan's *Deirdre*, and Aaron Copland's *The Tender Land* were staged. The company's first world premiere, David Warrack's *Drummer* welcomed the 1980s, along with Otto Nicolai's *Die lustigen Weiber von Windsor.* Twentieth-century works and novelties dominated the schedule during this era with works like Stephen Foster's *Beautiful Dreamer*, John Beckwith's *The Shivaree*, Benjamin Britten's *Albert Herring*, Igor Stravinsky's *The Rake's Progress* and *Renard*, Francis Poulenc's *Les Mamelles de Tiresias*, Dominick Argento's *Postcard from Morocco*, and the world premieres of Harry Freedman's *Fragments of Alice* and Quenten Doolittle's *Boiler Room Suite.* The same repertory emphasis continued through the 1990s with the Canadian premieres of Harrison Birtwistle's *Punch and Judy* and *Bow Down*, the world premieres of John Metcalf's *Kafka's Chimp* and Christopher Butterfield's *Zürich 1916*, as well as Hans Werner Henze's *El Cimarrón*, Udo Zimmerman's *Die weiße Rose*, and Peter Maxwell Davies's *Miss Donnithorne's Maggot.* The productions tend toward the avant-garde, stretching one's imagination and operatic concepts.

Practical Information. The Banff Centre Theatre Arts, Box 1020, Station 21, Banff, Alberta, T0L 0C0. Tel: 403-762-6365, Fax: 403-762-6334. If visiting, contact the Banff Centre for information.

COMPANY STAFF AND PREMIERES

Directors (of the Centre). Graeme McDonald (1993–present), Paul Fleck (1982–92), David Leighton (1970–82) Donald Cameron (1936–69).

World Premieres. C. Butterfield's *Zürich 1916*, August 5, 1998; M. Daugherty's *Jackie O*, co-production, August 7, 1997; J. Metcalf's *Kafka's Chimp*, 1996; J. Metcalf's *Tornrak*, co-production, 1991; A. Toovey's *Ubu*, co-production, 1992; Doolittle's *Boiler Room Suite*, 1989; H. Freedman's *Fragments of Alice*, 1987; David Warrack's *Drummer*, 1980.

Bibliography. M.J. Thompson, *The Banff Centre Mountain Campus* (Banff, 1993). Additional information supplied by the company.

Thanks to Greg Parry, Theatre Arts, The Banff Centre for the Arts.

EDMONTON

Edmonton Opera

Giacomo Puccini's *Madama Butterfly* inaugurated The Edmonton Opera, originally called the Edmonton Professional Opera Association, on October 11, 1963, in the Jubilee Auditorium. Founded by Jean Létourneau, who conducted the inaugural performance, the company also mounted Pietro Mascagni's *Cavalleria rusticana* and Ruggero Leoncavallo's *I pagliacci* that first season. The Jubilee Auditorium had been opened in 1957 with Georges Bizet's *Carmen*, produced by the Edmonton Civic Opera.

The first opera heard in Edmonton

dates back to 1904 when a group called the Edmonton Operatic Society mounted a production of *The Chimes of Normandie* at the Robertson Hall and Opera House. The population of the city at the time was only 8,350. In 1935, the Edmonton Civic Opera was started as an expansion of the Women's Musical Club. The company survived until the end of the 1950s. Then the Edmonton Opera was established to fill the operatic void.

After the establishment of the Edmonton Opera, Létourneau served as its artistic director until 1966. During his tenure, two works from the standard repertory were mounted each season. For the second season, Giuseppe Verdi's *Rigoletto* and Bizet's *Carmen* were on the boards, followed by Verdi's *La traviata* and Puccini's *La bohème* during the third. Irving Guttman was appointed artistic director in 1966 and expanded the repertory to include works like Gian Carlo Menotti's *The Consul*, Jacques Offenbach's *Les contes d'Hoffmann*, Charles Gounod's *Faust*, and Gaetano Donizetti's *Lucrezia Borgia*. *Lucrezia* featured Joan Sutherland in the title role, with her husband Richard Bonynge conducting. Their combined fee was $10,000. The company has attracted additional well-known artists and launched the careers of others, like Ermanno Mauro, who sang Pinkerton in the inaugural *Madama Butterfly*, and returned many times, including assaying the title role in Gounod's *Faust*, and Maureen Forrester who made her operatic debut as Ulrica in Verdi's *Un ballo in maschera* and returned to sing her first Herodias in Richard Strauss's *Salome*. Other international artists who made their Canadian debut in Edmonton include Beverly Sills in Donizetti's *Lucia di Lammermoor* in January 1969 (for a fee of $2,000), and five years later, José Carreras and Anna Moffo in Verdi's *La traviata*. Also during the 1970s Teresa Stratas and Judith Forst appeared in Puccini's *La bohème*, James Morris in the title

role of Wolfgang Amadeus Mozart's *Don Giovanni*, Carol Neblett in Puccini's *Tosca*, Marilyn Horne in the title role of Ambroise Thomas's *Mignon*, Louis Wuilico in the title role of Verdi's *Macbeth*, and Jerome Hines in the title role of the Canadian premiere of Verdi's *Attila* on April 27, 1978. The 1980s hosted more world class talent with June Anderson in Vincenzo Bellini's *I Puritani*, Marilyn Zschau in Puccini's *La fanciulla del West*, Richard Cassily in Verdi's *Otello*, Stephanie Sundine in Strauss's *Salome*, Richard Margisona in Puccini's *Tosca* and Donizetti's *L'elisir d'amore*, and Diane Soviero in Puccini's *Madama Butterfly*. The decade ended with an impressive *Aida* featuring Neblett, Louis Quilico, and Vladimir Popov, conducted by Eduardo Müller.

Although the seasons offer primarily standard fare, the unusual (for Edmonton) is occasionally mounted — Francis Poulenc's *Les dialogues des Carmélites*, Pyotr Il'yich Tchaikovsky's *Eugene Onegin*, Richard Wagner's *Lohengrin*, and Verdi's *Nabucco* among others. Recent repertory includes Gioachino Rossini's *Il barbiere di Siviglia*, Gounod's *Roméo et Juliette*, and Verdi's *Il trovatore*.

Practical Information. Edmonton Opera, 320-10232 112 Street, Edmonton, Alberta T5K 1M4. Tel: 403 429 1000, Fax: 403-429 0600. If visiting, contact the Canadian Tourist Office for Alberta at 1 800 661 8888.

COMPANY STAFF

General Directors. Nejolla Korris, Richard Mantle. **Artistic Directors.** Irving Guttman (1966– present), Jean Létourneau (1963–66).

Bibliography. *Edmonton Opera 25 Years Silver Celebration: Remembering 25 Years of Edmonton Opera* (Edmonton, 1988).

Thanks to Maureen Eley-Round, Edmonton Opera.

———— HAMILTON

Opera Ontario
(Opera Hamilton and Kitchener-Waterloo Opera)

Opera Ontario was born in late 1995, uniting Opera Hamilton and Kitchener-Waterloo Opera as a single company. This was a result of Opera Hamilton's expansion plan conceived in

March of that same year to provide south and southwestern Ontario with opera productions.

Operatic performances began in Hamilton in the 1960s with the Hamilton Opera Company, an amateur company led by Marty Coughan and Giuseppe Macina. They gave performances at the Mohawk College Auditorium for around a decade. In the mid–1970s, Festitalia was created for the large Italian community in Hamilton. In 1977 and 1978, operatic productions from Catania, Sicily, were imported for the festival and in 1979, the festival mounted is own production, Giacomo Puccini's *La bohème*. Due to the success of the undertaking, a new organization was established the following year, known as Opera Hamilton. Stephen Thomas was its first artistic director with the initial funding coming from Westinghouse Canada and the City of Hamilton. Giuseppe Verdi's *La traviata* was the company's first production in September 1980. Two productions of standard Italian fare followed for each of the first six seasons, including Puccini's *Manon Lescaut* and *Tosca*, Verdi's *Aida* and *Rigoletto*, and Gaetano Donizetti's *Lucia di Lammermoor*. Daniel Lipton assumed the position of artistic director in 1986 and increased the operatic productions to three a season, and expanded the repertory at the same time with Verdi's *I due Foscari*, *Nabucco* and *Simon Boccanegra*, and Charles Gounod's *Faust*

alongside the standard fare. The company has been known for its Verdi operas since 1986 and committed to staging the composer's less known works. Since the company was founded with an Italian base, those works have played the predominate role in the schedule. In the late 1990s the repertory was broadened to add works of Wolfgang Amadeus Mozart and German operas. There are plans to expand the repertory to include early operas and 20th century works as well.

The productions give equal weight to all components to create a complete experience for the audience. Since Kenneth Freeman was appointed the company's first general director, more theatrical elements have been introduced to the productions to bring out the meaning and message of the opera. The singers are a combination of experienced artists and up-and-coming talent. Recent offerings include Wolfgang Amadeus Mozart's *Don Giovanni*, Verdi's *Rigoletto*, and Johann Strauß's *Die Fledermaus*.

Hamilton Place, Great Hall

The performance venue for Opera Ontario

Hamilton Place (Hamilton, Canada).

in Hamilton is the Hamilton Place, a multi-purpose performing arts center which opened on September 22, 1973. Built at a cost of $10.9 million, the structure was designed by Trevor Garwood Jones. Not only are there bricks on the outside, but the walls of the auditorium are red brick arranged in a pyramid fashion to acoustically direct the sound. There are two cantilevered tiers, cedarwood, orange fabric seats, and a black grid ceiling with a row of spotlights. The room accommodates 2,191.

Practical Information. Opera Hamilton, 100 King Street West, Suite 200, Stelco Tower, Hamilton, Ontario L8P 1A2. Tel: 905 527 7627, Fax: 905 527 0014. Hamilton Place, 10 MacNab Street South, Hamilton, Ontario L8P 4Y3. Tel: 905-546-3100, Fax: 905-521-0924. If visiting, contact the Canadian Tourist Office for Ontario at 1 800 ONTARIO (668-2746).

COMPANY STAFF

General Director. Kenneth Freeman (1995–present). **Artistic Directors.** Daniel Lipton (1986–present), Stephen Thomas (1980–86).

Bibliography. Interview with Kenneth Freeman, general director, May 1996. Additional information supplied by the company.

Thanks to Shelley Gadsden, Opera Hamilton.

L'Opéra de Montréal

Giacomo Puccini's *Tosca* inaugurated L'Opéra de Montréal in October 1980. The company had been founded in January 1980 by the Ministère des Affaires Culturelles du Québec with funding from Le Conseil des Arts du Canada and the Ministère des Affaires Culturelles. The company's initial administration was integrated with the Place des Arts complex. It became autonomous in 1983.

The first homegrown opera was staged in 1910, when Albert Clerk-Jeannotte founded the Montreal Opera Company. Presenting 13 operas in its first season, the company ran out of money after three years. One additional season of opera was offered by the National Company of Canada and then traveling troupes provided the operatic entertainment, as they had before 1910. Another attempt at locally produced works came in 1936, when Les Variés Lyriques was founded by Lionel Daunais and Charles Goulet. Surviving until 1955, the company presented primarily operetta. Meanwhile, in 1942, the Canadian soprano Pauline Donalda established the Opera Guild of Montreal and until 1969, mounted 29 operas, mainly repertory favorites with local talent. The Montréal Symphony Orchestra under Zubin Mehta in cooperation with the Place des Arts offered opera between 1964 and 1971, including Giuseppe Verdi's *Otello*, Richard Strauss's *Salome*, and Richard Wagner's *Tristan und Isolde*. Then the provincial government created the Opéra de Québec which performed until 1975 in both Montreal and Quebec City.

The Opéra de Montréal's first season offered two additional works, Wolfgang Amadeus Mozart's *Così fan tutte* and Giuseppe Verdi's *La traviata*. The second season's offerings rose to four works — Puccini's *Madama Butterfly*, Gaetano Donizetti's *L'elisir d'amore*, Jules Massenet's *Werther*, and Verdi's *Il trovatore*. The third season witnessed the first German opera entering the repertory, Ludwig van Beethoven's *Fidelio*, along with Vincenzo Bellini's *Norma*, Donizetti's *Lucia di Lammermoor*, and Verdi's *Macbeth*. It was not until the 1985-86 season that Montreal saw another German opera, Wagner's *Tristan und Isolde*. The repertory included the popular Italian and French repertory, with a few novelties (for the company), like Gounod's *Roméo et Juliette*, Francis Poulenc's *Les dialogues des Carmélites*, and Gioachino Rossini's *Le Comte Ory*. During the 1980s, the company ran up a deficit in excess of $1.2 million. After Bernard Uzan assumed directorship in 1989, he eliminated the red ink through reorganizing, cost-cutting measures such as renting sets and costumes, and introducing bilingual supertitles and operetta to broaden the audience base.

The 1990s were welcomed with Francesco Cilea's *Adriana Lecouvreur*, Offenbach's *Les contes d'Hoffmann*, Strauss's *Der Rosenkavalier*, Puccini's

Gianni Schicchi, Ruggero Leoncavallo's *I pagliacci*, and Franz Lehár's *Die lustige Witwe*. The 1991-92 season offered Puccini's *Tosca*, Verdi's *Rigoletto* and *Nabucco*, Pyotr Il'yich Tchaikovsky's *Eugene Onegin*, and Offenbach's *La belle Hélène*. The mid–1990s were seeing works like Georges Bizet's *Les pêcheurs de perles*, Puccini's *Suor Angelica*, Leoncavallo's *I pagliacci*, Verdi's *Rigoletto*, Leoš Janáček's *Jenůfa*, Carl Orff's *Carmina Burana*, and Puccini's *Turandot*. One recent production of Benjamin Britten's *The Turn of the Screw* was a simple affair with modest props lifted in and out of the set to indicate location change. The singers, young, up-and-coming Canadian singers, were well-cast for the part but their voices sometimes failed to fill the large halls in which the company performs. The dramatic aspect of the work is emphasized along with the musical perspective. Recent repertory includes Puccini's *Manon Lescaut*, Poulenc's *La voix humaine*, Gounod's *Faust*, and Verdi's *Il trovatore*.

Place des Arts

Opened in 1967, the circular-shaped Place des Arts is a glass and concrete structure with sculpted tiles, set on its own plaza, above the hustle and bustle of its busy downtown location. The Salle Wilfried-Pelletier auditorium holds three tiers in a straight-edged U. Brown-hued wood stretches along the sides from the plain proscenium arch. A red curtain matches the red seats. The acoustically transparent ceiling is an open-pattern in white. There are 2,885 seats. The Theatre Maisonneuve holds two tiers with parapets of white geometric forms, which partially jut towards the stage. Tangerine-colored velvet seats contrast with the plain black procenium arch. A black mesh runs across the acoustically transparent ceiling.

Practical Information. L'Opéra de Montréal, 260 boulevard de Maisonneuve Quest, Montréal, Québec H2X 1Y9. Tel: 514-985-2222, Fax: 514-985-2219. Place des Arts, 260 boulevard de Maisonneuve Ouest, Montréal, Québec H2X 1Y9. Tel: 514-285-4270, Fax: 514-285-4272. When visiting the Opéra de Montréal or Place des Arts, stay at Le Meridien Montréal, 4 Complexe Desjardins, Montréal (Québec) H5B 1E5. Tel: 514-285-1450, Fax: 514-285-1243. Le Meridien Montreal is in the city center, across the street from the Place des Arts, and can assist with opera tickets and schedule.

COMPANY STAFF

Directeur Général. Bernard Uzan (1988–present), Bernard Creighton (1986–88, directeur administration), Jacques Langevin (1983–86). **Directeur Artistique.** Bernard Uzan (1989–present). Jean-Paul Jeannotte (1980–89).

Bibliography. *Infoguilde/The Montréal Opera Guild* (vol. 6, no. 1), *L'Opéra de Montréal* (Montréal, 1996–97). Additional information supplied by the company.

Thanks to John Trivisonno and Francine Labelle, L'Opéra de Montréal, and Danielle Champagne, Place des Arts, and Richard McGarr.

— OTTAWA

Opera Lyra Ottawa

Opera Lyra Ottawa was founded in 1984 by Diana Gilchrist with double bill of Wolfgang Amadeus Mozart's *Der Schauspieldirektor* and Georg Philipp Telemann's *Piminone*. It was established to fill the opera void at the Ottawa Festival (see National Arts Centre of Canada entry) caused by the suspension of opera productions. Volunteers, who were amateur opera lovers, started the company. The second season offered Mozart's *Così fan tutte* and a novelty, Burge's *The Master's House*. Gioachino Rossini's *Il barbiere di Siviglia* was mounted in 1986–87 followed by Jules Massenet's *Werther*, and Gaetano Donizetti's *L'elisir d'amore*. A decade late, another premiere graced the stage, Crawley's *Angel Square*. The premiere of Gellman's *Gianni* was given during the 1997-98 season, a work based on the composer Giovanni Battista Pergolesi. However, standard Italian and French operas dominate the repertory. The company is mandated to use 95% Canadian talent. It performs at the National Arts Centre. Recent productions include Giuseppe Verdi's *Aida* and Rossini's *Il barbiere di Siviglia*.

Practical Information. Opera Lyra Ottawa,

Place des Arts, Salle Wilfried Pelletier (Montréal, Canada).

110-2 avenue Daly, Ottawa, Ontario K1N 6E2. Tel: 613-233-9200, Fax: 613-233-5431. When visiting the Opera Lyra Ottawa, stay at the Ramada Hotel & Suites, Ottawa, 111 Cooper Street, Ottawa, K2P 2E3. Tel: 613-238-1331 or 1-800-267-8378, Fax: 613-230-2179. Ramada Hotel & Suites, in a good location and convenient to the opera house, can assist with opera tickets and schedule.

COMPANY STAFF
Artistic Director. Jeannette Aster.

Thanks to Marcus Handman and Gerald Morris, Opera Lyra Ottawa, and Paul Mulcahy.

The National Arts Centre of Canada

On May 31, 1969, the National Arts Centre of Canada opened its doors to the public. Three days later, on June 2, the first performance took place in The Opera House — the National Ballet of Canada presented *Kraanerg*, a world premiere choreographed by Roland Petit with music by Iannis Xenakis. This was part of the opening festival which lasted until June 14 and offered Gabriel Charpentier's *Orphée* as its operatic contribution. Fred Lebensold designed the structure.

At the beginning of the 1960s, Canada's capital still did not possess a proper venue for the performing arts. This prompted the formation of the National Capital Arts Alliance, an association of more than 50 arts groups in the National Capital Region, which joined forces in 1963 to improve the cultural life of Canada's capital by constructing a national center for the performing arts. On December 23, 1963, Canada's then prime minister Lester Pearson approved the project and on July 15, 1966, an Act of Parliament established the Crown Corporation to operate and maintain the future center. From the beginning, there were plans for the center to host a summer festival which included opera and featured Canadian artists.

The first "major" summer festival arrived two years later (1971), and included Wolfgang Amadeus Mozart's *Le nozze di Figaro* with a Canadian cast — Claude Corbeil, Allan Monk, and Judith Forst. Mozart's opera was repeated the following season along with his *Così fan tutte*. In 1973, Jacques Offenbach's *La belle Hélène* joined the two Mozart operas on the program. Mozart's *Die Entführung aus dem Serail* was mounted with his *Don Giovanni* and Gioachino Rossini's *Le Comte Ory* in 1974 followed by Giuseppe Verdi's *La traviata* the next season. The 1976 festival featured Pyotr Il'yich Tchaikovsky's *Pikovaya dama* (The Queen of Spades) with Canadians Jon Vickers and Maureen Forrester. Two years later, Benjamin Britten's *A Midsummer Night's Dream* graced the stage. The 1980s began with Gaetano Donizetti's *La fille du régiment*, Giacomo Puccini's *La bohème*, and Claude Debussy's *Pelléas et Mélisande*, but in-house opera activities were suspended after the 1983 festival, returning five years later with only occasional revivals of previous productions. Until the suspension of in-house opera productions, opera production received 74% of the festival budget, with revenue covering around 30% of the costs. The opera artists were 95% Canadian.

National Arts Centre of Canada

The National Arts Centre of Canada is a massive pink/brown pebble concrete structure perched on the banks of the Rideau Canal on 6.5 acres. A fusion of three hexagonal structures define the building. Hexagonal shapes also permeate the Centre, from the design of the staircase to the form of the ceiling. The auditorium is semi-circular with three suspended tiers displaying white parapets. Lights shower the space amid a sea of red relieved by touches of gold and black. The transparent acoustic ceiling finds a series of golden wood strips and banners as embellishment. There are 2,165 seats.

Practical Information. National Arts Centre of Canada, 53 Elgin Street, Ottawa, Ontario K1P 5W1. Tel: 613-996-5051, Fax: 613-996-9578. When visiting the National Arts Centre of Canada, stay at the Ramada Hotel & Suites, Ottawa, 111 Cooper Street, Ottawa, Ontario K2P 2E3. Tel: 613-238-1331 or 1-800-267-8378, Fax: 613-230-2179. Ramada Hotel & Suites, in a good location and convenient to the opera house, can assist with opera tickets and schedule.

BIBLIOGRAPHY

Bibliography. *The National Arts Centre: A Retrospective* (Ottawa, 1994). Andrée Gingras, *Festival Ottawa History* (Ottawa, 1979). Mark Kristmansion, *Opera Festival* (Ottawa, 1990). Additional information supplied by the archivist, Gerry Grace.

Thanks to Gerry Grace, archivist; Ken Anderson, National Arts Centre, and Paul Mulcahy.

QUÉBEC

Opéra de Québec

Giuseppe Verdi's *La traviata* was the Opéra de Québec's first performance. Established in 1984, the company resulted from the creation of the Fondation de l'Opéra de Québec the previous year. It grew out of the Société Lyrique d'Aubigny, founded in 1968 and in existence until 1984. Meanwhile, the provincial government created L'Opéra du Québec (no connection to the present company) which performed in both Montreal and Quebec City between 1970 and 1975. This company was revived during the Olympics for one production and then permanently disbanded.

The Opéra de Québec, during its first years of existence, was under artistic director Guy Bélanger and concentrated on the French repertory with works like Camille Saint-Saëns's *Samson et Dalila*, Jules Massenet's *Manon*, and Charles Gounod's *Faust*, on the boards. The singers were mainly French-Canadian. Following this path, a huge deficit resulted. When Bernard Labadie took over in 1994, he changed the company's emphasis to the classical works, those from the bel canto era, and the perennial favorites. French

Top: **National Arts Centre (Ottawa, Canada).** *Bottom:* **National Arts Centre auditorium (Ottawa, Canada).**

Canadian singers are "up-and-coming" and fill all the smaller roles. They are in the principal ones only if their voice is suitable. Otherwise, an "outsider" is hired. The company has not staged any contemporary works. It considers itself a provincial opera company with all works sung in French, and a venue for French Canadian singers. The company views itself, as a staff member told me, "as a French outpost in the hostile territory of Canada."

During the mid–1990s, the company produced Wolfgang Amadeus Mozart's *Così fan tutte*, Georges Bizet's *Carmen*, Verdi's *Nabucco*, Gounod's *Roméo et Juliette*, Giacomo Puccini's *La bohème*, and Gioachino Rossini's *La Cenerentola*. The government pays 50% of the $1.5 million budget. The remaining comes from ticket sales (45%) and private donations (5%). Recent repertory includes Gounod's *Faust*, Verdi's *Il trovatore*, and Mozart's *Le nozze di Figaro*. The company performs in the Grand Théâtre de Québec.

Grand Théâtre de Québec

The Grand Théâtre opened on January 16, 1971, with a symphonic program performed by the orchestra of Québec. The theater was designed by Victor Prus, who won the architectural competition. Of special interest is the inside concrete mural wall — actually three separate walls — which occupy 12,000 square feet and have the themes of Death, Space, and Freedom, the work of Jordi Bonet. The square-shaped auditorium, originally conceived as an opera house, holds three concrete tiers that give the space an intimate feeling. The ceiling finds acoustic panels interspersed with 1,800 acrylic tubes, the "chandelier." A sea of azure seats is complemented with a rose-colored carpet and purple/maroon curtain. The hall accommodates 1,892.

Practical Information. Opéra de Québec, 1220 avenue Taché, Québec City, Québec G1R 3B4. Tel: 418-529-4142, Fax: 418-529-3735. Grand Théâtre, 269 boulevard René-Lévesque Est, Québec City, Québec G1R 2B3. Tel: 418-644-3100, Fax: 418 646-7670. When visiting the Opéra de Québec or Grand Théâtre de Québec, stay at the Hotellerie Fleur de Lys, 115 rue Ste-Anne, Québec City, Quebec G1R 3X6. Tel: 418-694-0106; Fax: 418-692-1959. Hotellerie Fleur de Lys is in the old city, close to the opera house, and the opera singers stay in the hotel. Assistance with opera tickets and schedules is available.

COMPANY STAFF

Directeurs Artistique et Musicale. Bernard Labadie (1994–present), Guy Bélanger (1985–94).

Bibliography. Interview with Bernard Labadie, artistic and music director, May 1996. Additional information supplied by the company.

Thanks to Louis Robert, Opéra de Quebec; Michael Côté, Jeannette Martel, and Jérôme Lapointe, Grand Théâtre de Québec, and Solange Plante.

Grand Théâtre de Québec (Quebec, Canada).

Opera Atelier

In April 1985, Georg Friedrich Händel's *Hercules* inaugurated Opera Atelier, founded by two former dancers, Marshall Pynkoski and Jeannette Zingg, to recreate the splendor of the Baroque repertory. The focus of the company is on the neglected works of Jean-Philippe Rameau, Marco da Gagliano, Jean-Jacques Rousseau, Marc-Antoine Charpentier, Henry Purcell, and John Blow, among others. The company used a variety of performance venues, from museums to theaters, until it settled in the Alexandra Theatre (see Canadian Opera Company entry).

Pynkoski explained that "Baroque production style disappeared because it was politically impossible to perform. The works were created to extoll royalty and it was not appropriate in the 19th century to glorify the monarchy which was reviled in political circles. Now we can bring it all back." Some of the Baroque operas unearthed from the past included Rameau's *Pygmalion* and *Myrthis*, Rousseau's *Pygmalion*, Blow's *Dido and Adonis*, Gagliano's *Dafne*, Händel's *Giulio Cesare*, and Charpentier's *Acteon*. The company has also staged authentic period productions of perennial favorites like Wolfgang Amadeus Mozart's *Le nozze di Figaro*, *Don Giovanni*, and *Die Zauberflöte*. Initially the the first violinist led the productions, but since Händel's *Giulio Cesare* was staged, a conductor has been on the podium. The budget approaches a $1 million (Canadian) a year with less than 20% coming from the government. The bulk of the funds come from ticket sales, with 15% donations. Recent repertory includes Gluck's *Orfeo ed Euridice* and Händel's *Acis and Galatea*. The company performs at the Royal Alexandre Theatre.

Practical Information. Opera Atelier, 2 Bloor Street West, Cumberland Terrace, Toronto, Ontario M4W 3E2. Tel: 416-925-3767, Fax: 416 925-4895. Royal Alexandra Theatre, 260 King Street, Toronto, Ontario M5V 1H9. Tel: 416 872-1212. When visiting Opera Atelier, stay at the Royal York, 100 Front Street, Toronto. Tel: 416-368-2511, Fax: 416-368-9040. Royal York, in the center of the city and convenient to the theater, can assist with opera tickets and schedule.

COMPANY STAFF

Artistic Director. Marshall Pynkoski.
Bibliography. Interview with Marshall Pynkoski, director, May 1996. Additional information supplied by the company.

Thanks to Dina Liebermann and Beth Poulter, Opera Atelier.

Canadian Opera Company

On February 3, 1950, Giacomo Puccini's *La bohème* inaugurated the Canadian Opera Company, formally known as the Royal Conservatory Opera Company and then the Opera Festival Company of Toronto, in the Royal Alexandra Theatre. Nicholas Goldschmidt and Herman Geiger-Torel were the company founders. Giuseppe Verdi's *Rigoletto* and Wolfgang Amadeus Mozart's *Don Giovanni* completed the inaugural opera season. The Royal Alexandra Theatre, which had opened in 1907 and restored in 1963, was designed by John Lyle and built by Cawthra.

Opera was first heard in Toronto in 1851 when Adelina Patti and Jenny Lind gave recitals at the newly-opened St. Lawrence Hall. The following year and continuing until 1860, five different troupes visited Toronto — The French Operatic Company, Forme's Italian Company, Curran's Ethiopian Opera Troupe, The Brookhouse Bowler Company, and Cooper's Opera Company. Meanwhile in 1853, the Artist Association Italian Opera Company presented Vincenzo Bellini's *Norma*.

In 1867, George Holman founded the city's first homegrown opera troupe — Holman's Opera Company — at the Royal Lyceum. The repertory included Gaetano Donizetti's *L'elisir d'amore*, and Daniel Auber's *Fra Diavolo*. Six years later in 1873, fire destroyed the Royal Lyceum, but the following year, the Grand Opera House was opened. It hosted the Kellogg, Soldene, and Aimée Opera Troupes. In 1879, the Grand burned down and was rebuilt in 51 days. Charles Gounod's *Faust*, staged by the Holman Opera Company, reopened the opera house. In 1882, the Strakosch English Opera Company presented Auber's *Fra Diavolo*, Michael Balfe's *The Bohemian Girl*, and Georges Bizet's *Carmen* at the Grand. The Abbott Opera Company then offered Donizetti's *Lucia di Lammermoor* with Emma Abbott. The following year (1883), Her Majesty's Opera staged the same work with Canadian soprano Emma Albani in the title role. In 1886, the Toronto Opera House opened and the next year, the National Opera Company of New York mounted Richard Wagner's *Lohengrin* and Karl Goldmark's *Königin von Saba*. The visiting companies continue to the end of the century with Kellogg Opera Company, The Ambroise Thomas Opera Company, Gustav Hinrick's American Opera Company, Melba Operatic Company, San Carlo Opera, International Grand Opera Group. Metropolitan Opera, and Sembrich Opera Company all staging works.

During the first two decades of the 20th century, several recitals were given by leading artists, including Adelina Patti (Farewell Concert), Enrico Caruso, Nellie Melba, Edmund Burke, Louise Homer, and Giovanni Martinelli. The beginning of the 1920s welcomed the Scotti Opera Company, the Russian Opera Company, and the San Carlo Opera. In 1928, Engelbert Humperdinck's *Hänsel und Gretel* inaugurated the Conservatory Opera Company at the Regent Theatre (originally called the Toronto Opera House). The next season, to celebrate the opening of the Royal York Hotel, the company mounted Vaughan Williams's *Hugh the Drover*. Established by Ernest MacMillan, the company survived until 1930. Four years later, the city witnessed a full opera season presented by the San Carlo Opera at Massey Hall — Gounod's *Roméo et Juliette* and *Faust*, Verdi's *La traviata*, *Rigoletto*, and *Aida*, Bizet's *Carmen*, Camille Saint-Saëns's *Samson et Dalila*, and Puccini's *Madama Butterfly*. In 1935, another local company was established, the Toronto Grand Opera Association, which opened with Verdi's *Rigoletto* at the Eaton Auditorium, followed by Bizet's *Carmen* and Puccini's *Tosca*. Later that year, a reorganization resulted in a name change to the Canadian Grand Opera Association, and a second company, the Opera Guild of Toronto was established. Both companies staged operas in 1936 — Canadian Grand Opera Association offered Verdi's *Aida* and *Rigoletto*, and

Bizet's *Carmen* at Massey Hall, and the Opera Guild mounted Puccini's *Tosca*, Pietro Mascagni's *Cavalleria rusticana*, and Ruggero Leoncavallo's *I pagliacci* at the Royal Alexandra. The fall season of the Canadian Grand Opera began with Gounod's *Faust*, but the remainder of the season was cancelled. The Opera Guild mounted its last performance in 1941, Mascagni's *Cavalleria rusticana*. Another company was established in 1938, the Toronto Opera Company, which gave Humperdinck's *Hänsel und Gretel* at the Victoria followed by Robert Planquette's *Les cloches de Corneville*.

The origins of the Canadian Opera Company can be traced to the student performances of the newly-formed Royal Conservatory Opera, founded in 1946 by Arnold Walter. Opera excerpts inaugurated the company, which staged Humperdinck's *Hänsel und Gretel* and Bedřich Smetana's *Prodaná nevěsta* (The Bartered Bride) the following spring. In 1948, several works were mounted, including Christoph Willibald Gluck's *Orfeo ed Euridice* and Giovanni Battista Pergolesi's *La serva padrona*, and the 1951 offerings included Gounod's *Faust*, Puccini's *Madama Butterfly*, and Mozart's *Le nozze di Figaro*. The Canadian premiere of Gian Carlo Menotti's *The Consul* took place in 1953. By 1954, the now fully professional Royal Conservatory Opera Company incorporated as the Opera Festival Company and mounted four works, including Ermanno Wolf-Ferrari's *I quattro rusteghi* and Verdi's *Rigoletto* in the Royal Alexandra Theatre, which had become its home. Standard fare dominated the repertory — Verdi's *La traviata* and *Un ballo in maschera*, Bizet's *Carmen*, Mozart's *Le nozze di Figaro* and *Die Entführung aus dem Serail*, and Jacques Offenbach's *Les contes d'Hoffmann*.

In 1959, the Opera Festival Company became the Canadian Opera Company. Two years later, it moved its home from the 1,479-seat Royal Alexandra Theatre to the 3,167-seat O'Keefe Centre, renamed in 1996 to the Hummingbird Centre. Repertory favorites continued to dominate the schedule, but other works were presented as well. In 1962, Richard Wagner's *Die Walküre* entered the repertory followed by Igor Stravinsky's *Mavra* three years later. The company hosted its first world premiere in 1966, Healey Willan's *Diedre*, followed by Harry Somers's *Louis Riel* and Raymond Pannell's *The Luck of Ginger Coffee*. The 1970s saw more world premieres — Norman

Symonds's *The Spirit of Fundy*, Charles Wilson's *Heloise and Abelard*, and Tibor Polgar's *The Glove*, along with the standard repertory, which was dominated by Italian works, like Verdi's *Macbeth*, *La traviata* and *Aida*, Donizetti's *Lucia di Lammermoor*, Puccini's *Tosca*, and Gioachino Rossini's *Il barbiere di Siviglia*. By the mid–1970s more French, German and Russian works had been staged, including Wagner's *Der fliegende Holländer* and *Götterdämmerung*, Ludwig van Beethoven's *Fidelio*, Richard Strauss's *Salome*, Modest Mussorgsky's *Boris Godunov*, and Pyotr Il'yich Tchaikovsky's *Eugene Onegin*. The 1980s were noted for Joan Sutherland making her debut with the company in Bellini's *Norma* in 1981; the invention of *SURTITLES* (by the company) which were used for the first time in Strauss's *Elektra*, and have since been incorporated in opera houses around the world; the mounting of commissioned works, including Ann Mortifee's *Rose Is a Rose*, Richard Désilets's *Zoé*, and Timothy Sullivan's *Dream Play*, and the staging of several Canadian premieres ranging from the Baroque to the contemporary—Alban Berg's *Lulu*, Leoš Janáček's *Jenůfa* and *Věc Makropulos* (The Makropulos Case), Emilio de Cavalieri's *Rappresentazione di anima e di corpo*, Claudio Monteverdi's *L'incoronazione di Poppea*, Igor Stravinsky's *The Rake's Progress*, Ambroise Thomas's *Hamlet*, and Dmitri Shostakovich's *Ledi Makbet Mtsenskovo uyezda* (Lady Macbeth of the Mtsensk District). During the 1990s, more 20th-century pieces were offered, like the double-bill of Béla Bartók's *A Kékszakállú herceg vára* (Duke Bluebeard's Castle) and Arnold Schönberg's *Erwartung*, Leoš Janáček's *Kát'a Kabanová*, and the world premiers of Randolph Peters's *Nosferatu* and Gary Kulesha's *Red Emma*.

The company is trying to change its traditional image (to get more international recognition) by adopting the philosophy that opera must be exciting visually as well as musically, a new approach which sometimes works but other times does not. The production style of a recent *Rigoletto* lacked consistency and added some distracting activities, but other productions have successfully shed the conventional image, shining with an innovative light. The company, not having the budget to hire singers with large voices, is hampered by the large space in which it must perform. Recent repertory includes Leoš Janáček's *Příhody Lišky Bystroušky* (The Cunning Little Vixen), Ludwig van Beethoven's *Fidelio*, Puccini's *Madama Butterfly* and *Turandot*, and Igor Stravinsky's *Oedipus Rex*. The company performs at the Hummingbird Centre.

Hummingbird Centre for the Performing Arts

The Hummingbird Centre, originally called the O'Keefe Centre after the O'Keefe Brewing Company which built the complex, opened on October 1, 1960, with the musical *Camelot*. Located on a site which had been previously occupied by the Great Western Division of the Grand Trunk Railway, the structure was designed by Earle Morgan and Peter Dickinson (from the firm Page and Steele). It has been owned and run by the municipality of metropolitan Toronto since 1968. Hummingbird Communications donated $5 million to the Centre in 1996, resulting in the new name.

The Centre is a modern building of granite, glass, and limestone. Inside, the main foyer is dominated by York Wilson's mural, *The Seven Lively Arts*. The auditorium is the largest "soft-seat" theater in Canada. Holding a single tier which sweeps across the space, the hall has orange cloth seats, acoustically designed wooden walls, and a white ceiling with rows of spot lights. There are 3,155 places.

Practical Information. Canadian Opera Company, 227 Front Street East, Toronto, Ontario M5A 1E8. Tel: 416-363-6671, Fax: 416 363-5584. The Hummingbird Centre for the Performing Arts, 3 Front Street East, Toronto, Ontario M5E 1B2. Tel: 416 393-7474, Fax: 416-393-7459. When visiting the Canadian Opera Company or Hummingbird Centre, stay at the Royal York, 100 Front Street, Toronto, Ontario. Tel: 416-368-2511, Fax: 416-368-9040. Royal York, in the center of the city near the opera house, can assist with opera tickets and schedule.

COMPANY STAFF AND PREMIERES

General Directors. Brian Dickie (1988–93), Lotfi Mansouri (1976–88), Herman Geiger-Torel (1959–76), Ettore Mazzoleni (1955–59). **Artistic Director:** Richard Bradshaw (1993–present).

World Premieres. H. Willan's *Diedre*, 1966; H. Somers's *Louis Riel*, 1967; R. Pannell's *The Luck of Ginger Coffee*, 1967; N. Symonds's *The Spirit of Fundy*, 1972; C. Wilson's *Heloise and Abelard*, 1973;

Hummingbird Centre (formerly O'Keefe Centre) (Toronto, Canada).

T. Polgar's *The Glove*, 1975; A. Mortifee's *Rose Is a Rose*, 1987; R.M. Schafer's *Patria I* (first complete production, 1987); M.-G. Brégent's *Réalitillusion*, 1988; R. Désilets's *Zoé*, 1988; T. Sullivan's *Dream Play*, 1988; D. Gougeon's *An Expensive Embarrassment*, 1989; P. Koprowski's *Dulcitius: Demise of Innocence*, 1989; A. MacDonald's *The Unbelievable Glory of Mr. Sharp*, 1989; J. Oliver's *Guacamayo's Old Song and Dance*, 1991; H. Somers's *Mario and the Magician*, 1992; R. Peters's *Nosferatu*, 1993; G. Kulesha's *Red Emma*, 1995. **Canadian Premieres:** A. Berg's *Lulu*, 1980; L. Janáček's *Jenůfa*, 1982; R. Strauss's *Capriccio*, 1982; E.de Cavalieri's *Rappresentazione di anima e de corpo*, 1983; C. Monteverdi's *L'incoronazione di Poppea*; G. Donizetti's *Anna Bolena*, 1984; B. Britten's *Death in Venice*, 1984; I. Stravinsky's *The Rake's Progress*, 1985; A. Thomas's *Hamlet*, 1985; F. Poulenc's *Les dialogues des Car-*

mélites, 1986; F. Cilea's *Adriana Lecouvreur*, 1987; D. Shostakovich's *Lady Macbeth of the Mtsensk District*, 1988; L. Janáček's *Věc Makropulos* (The Makropulos Case), 1989; A. Schönberg's *Erwartung*, 1993.

Bibliography. Joan Baillie, *1950–1990: Forty Years of Opera at the COC* (Toronto, 1990). Lofti Mansouri and Aviva Layton, *Lofti Mansouri: An Operatic Life* (Toronto, 1982). Keeneth Peglar, *Opera and the University of Toronto: 1946–1971* (Toronto, 1971). *Remembered Moments of the Canadian Opera Company: 1950–1975* (Toronto, 1976). Hugh Walker, *The O'Keefe Center: Thirty Years of Theatre History* (Toronto, 1991). Interview Elaine Calder, general manager, May 1996.

Thanks to Deborah Knight, Susan Harrington, and Colin Eatock, Canadian Opera Company, and Janelle Hutchison, O'Keefe Centre, and Nancy Hall.

Toronto Operetta Theatre & Opera in Concert

Toronto Operetta Theatre

On September 25, 1985, the Toronto Operetta Threatre was inaugurated with a performance of Franz Lehár's *Der Graf von Luxembourg* in the Bluma Appel Theatre at the St. Lawrence Centre for the Arts. Guillermo Silva-Marin founded the company to produce classical op-

eretta featuring Canadian artists. The company has mounted works like Johann Strauß's *Eine Nacht in Venedig*, *Die Fledermaus*, and *Wiener Blut*, Jacques Offenbach's *La vie parisienne* and *Orphée aux enfers*, Emmerich Kálmán's *Die Csárdásfürstin*, Carl Zeller's *Der Vogelhändler*, Victor Herbert's *Naughtly Marietta*, Geza Dusik's *The Blue Rose*, and Lehár's *Das Land des Lächelns*.

Some of the artists who have appeared with the company include Louis Quilico, Rosemarie Landry, Mark DuBois, Henry Ingram, Susan Haig, and Victor Feldbrill. The one complaint the company has received is that the sets look cheap, which, of course, is due to their limited resources. In fact, the company is experiencing severe financial problems and Silva-Marin is not sure the company will survive. Recent repertory includes Sigmund Romberg's *The New Moon* and Lehár's *Die lustige Witwe*.

Opera in Concert

The company was founded in 1974 by Stuart Hamilton, a vocal coach, to give his students the opportunity to explore operas rarely given in North America, and a stage on which to launch their careers. Hamilton subsidized the first season with his own money. Hamilton had a preference for French operas which included the presentation of nine of Jules Massenet's works — *Cléopâtre, Don Quichotte, Grisélidis, Hérodiade, Manon, La Navarraise, Thaïs, Thérèse,* and *Werther* — along with Georges Bizet's *Djamileh* and *Les pêcheurs de perles*, Francis Poulenc's *La voix humaine*, Camille Saint Saëns's *Samson et Dalila*, Ambroise Thomas's *Hamlet* and *Mignon*, Charles Gounod's *Roméo et Juliette*, Hector Berlioz's *Béatrice et Bénédict*, Jean-Philippe Rameau's *Hippolyte et Aricie*, Claude Debussy's *Pelléas et Mélisande*, and Maurice Ravel's *L'enfant et les sortilèges* and *L'heure espagnole*. Other unusual works included Eugen d'Albert's *Tiefland*, Samuel Barber's *Vanessa*, Saverio Mercadante's *Il giuramento*, Ralph Vaughan Williams's *Riders to the Sea*, Gustav Holst's *Savitri*, and Peter Cornelius's *Der Barbier von Bagdad*. In 1994, after 20 years at the helm, Hamilton retired and Silva-Marin took over as general director of this organization as well. The company receives 12% of its $200,000 budget from the government, 40% from private corporations, and the rest is earned income. Recent repertory includes Alfredo Catalani's *La Wally*, Vincenzo Bellini's *La sonnambula*, and Albert Lortzing's *Zar und Zimmermann*.

Practical Information. Toronto Operetta Theatre & Opera in Concert, 33 West Avenue, Suite 200, Toronto, Ontario M4M 2L7. Tel: & Fax: 416-465-2147. When visiting Toronto Operetta or Opera in Concert, stay at the Royal York, 100 Front Street, Toronto. Tel: 416-368-2511, Fax: 416-368-9040. Royal York, in the center of the city and convenient to the theater, can assist with opera tickets and schedule.

BIBLIOGRAPHY

Bibliography. *Opera in Concert 1974–1984: The First Ten Years* (Toronto, 1984). Additional information supplied by the company. Interview with Guillermo Silva-Marin, general and artistic director, May 1996.

Thanks to Henry Ingram, Toronto Operetta Theatre and Opera in Concert.

VANCOUVER

Opera Breve

Opera Breve is a new professional company dedicated to producing one-act chamber works from the 18th, 19th, and 20th centuries. There is a special interest in Canadian operas. All performances are in English. The well-known singer Judith Forst is associated with the company. Recent repertory includes Georges Bizet's *Le docteur miracle* and Francis Poulenc's *La voix humaine*

Practical Information. Opera Breve, The Ballroom, Listel Vancouver, 1300 Robson Street, Vancouver, BC. Tel: 604 662 7685, Fax: 604-325 9481. When visiting the Opera Breve, contact the Canadian Tourist Office for British Columbia at 1 800 663 6000 (operator #77).

COMPANY STAFF

Artistic Director. Mari Hahn.

Vancouver Opera

Georges Bizet's *Carmen*, with Nan Merriman, Richard Cassilly, and Louis Quilico, inaugurated the Vancouver Opera in April 1960. Irving Guttman, who directed the production, was hired as the artistic director, a position he held until 1974. Guttman was also the artistic director of the Edmonton Opera (see Edmonton Opera entry).

Opera was first heard in the city when Emma Juch English Opera Company offered Richard Wagner's *Lohengrin* for the opening of the Canadian Pacific Railway's Vancouver Opera House on February 9, 1891. Although the seeds were planted, it failed to take root and no homegrown companies blossomed until the birth of the Vancouver Opera, which was established in November 1959.

Some highlights of the early years included Richard Bonyngne conducting Charles Gounod's *Faust*, Joan Sutherland and Marilyn Horne in Vincenzo Bellini's *Norma*, Horne in Gioachino Rossini's *L'italiana in Algeri*, Plácido Domingo in Giacomo Puccini's *Tosca*. In 1973, Opera West was formed, an alliance of the Vancouver Opera, Edmonton Opera, Calgary Opera, and Winnipeg Opera, which resulted in the co-production of Wolfgang Amadeus Mozart's *Don Giovanni*, among others. In 1974, Bonyngne was hired as artistic director. Three years later, the Vancouver Opera Orchestra was formed. Bonyngne conducted Sutherland in Jules Massenet's *Le roi de Lahore* and Mozart's *Don Giovanni*. During the 1980s the "Va pensiero" chorus in Giuseppe Verdi's *Nabucco* was so well-received that a standing ovation resulted — in the middle of the opera. The decade also witnessed the Canadian premiere of Leoš Janáček's *Z Mrtvého Domu* (From the House of the Dead).

The 1990s were welcomed with Georg Friedrich Händel's *Alcina* with Benita Valente as Alcina, Gioachino Rossini's *Il barbiere di Siviglia* with Patrick Raftery as Figaro, Richard Strauss's *Salome* with Stephanie Sundine as Salome, and Giacomo Puccini's *Madama Butterfly* with Hiroko Nishida as Madama Butterfly. The company is committed to developing Canadian talent. It has its own orchestra and chorus which are comprised of local musicians and singers. The lead singers continue to be guest artists with preference shown to Canadian singers. Recent repertory includes Verdi's *Il trovatore*, Puccini's *La bohème*, Jin Xiang's *The Savage Land* (contemporary Chinese opera), and Strauss's *Salome*. The company performs in the 2,821-seat Queen Elizabeth Theatre.

Practical Information. Vancouver Opera, Suite 500, 845 Cambie Street, Vancouver, British Columbia V6B 4Z9. Tel: 604 682-2871, Fax: 604 682-3981. Queen Elizabeth Theatre, 1132 Hamilton Street, Vancouver, BC V6B 2S2. Tel: 604 683-0222, Fax: 604 682 3981. When visiting the Vancouver Opera, contact the Canadian Tourist Office for British Columbia at 1 800 663 6000 (operator #77).

COMPANY STAFF

General Director. Robert Hallam. **Artistic Directors:** Guus Mostart (1989–91), Brian McMaster (1984–89), Irving Guttman (1982–84), Richard Bonygne (1974–77, music director), Irving Guttman (1960–74).

Bibliography. *Tempo Newsletter of the Vancouver Opera*, vol. 6 no. 1, Fall 1990. Additional Information supplied by the company.

Thanks to Nancy Henderson, Vancouver Opera.

Other Canadian Companies

Other Canadian companies are noted below by name, address, telephone, performance venue, recent repertory, and general director (as available).

Calgary Opera. 237-8th Avenue SE, #601, Calgary, Alberta T2G 5C3. Tel: 403 262 7286, Fax: 403 263 5428. **Performance venue:** 2,700-seat Jubilee Auditorium. **Recent Repertory:** Tosca, Il barbiere di Siviglia, Faust. **General Director:** David Speers.

Manitoba Opera. Portage Place, 393 Portage Avenue, Winnipeg, Manitoba R3B 3K9. Tel: 204-927 479, Fax 204-949-0377. **Performance venue:** 2,304-seat Manitoba Centennial Concert Hall. **Recent Repertory:** Don Pasquale, Turn of the Screw, La bohème. **Artistic Director:** Irving Guttman.

Saskatoon Opera Association. 509 Copeland Crescent, Saskatoon, Saskatoon S7H 2Z4. Tel: 306-374-7630, Fax: 306-374-5760. **General Manager:** Marilyn Harrison.

Canada Opera Piccola (Vancouver). 103-3737 Oak Street, Vancouver, British Columbia V6H 2M4. Tel: 604-736-1916, Fax: 604-736-8018. **President:** Elizabeth Eichbauer.

Pacific Opera Victoria. 1316b Government Street, Victoria, British Columbia V5W 1Y8. Tel: 604 382 1641, Fax: 604 382 4944. **Performance venues:** 1,400-seat Royal Theatre, 800-seat McPherson Playhouse. **Recent Repertory:** L'italiana in Algeri, Werther, Rigoletto. **Artistic Director:** Timothy Vernon.

Denmark
—————————————————————————————— ÅRHUS

Den Jyske Opera
(Danish National Opera)

Den Jyske Opera (The Jutland Opera), also called the Danish National Opera, was founded in Århus in 1947 to balance the more conservative Det Kongelige Teater (The Royal Opera) in Copenhagen. The initial repertory offered two operas, performed in the intimate Elsinore Theater. When the Musikhuset Århus opened in 1983, Den Jyske Opera moved to the new theater, becoming one of its resident companies. The 1,477-seat Music House was designed by architects Kjær & Richter.

In 1977, thirty years after its founding, the Jutland Opera formed a national touring company known as Det rejsender Landsteater, which visited all of Denmark in collaboration with five regional symphony orchestras. Det rejsender Landsteater survived a decade. Afterwards, the Jutland Opera received the money directly for touring. The positive impact of the company's touring can be seen from the following statistic. In 1972 only 3% of the population in Denmark had seen opera. By 1994, around 60–70% of the population had seen opera. The success reflects the company's first goal — to perform opera and operetta all over Denmark. Approximately 100 performances a year are currently given around Denmark. The second goal is to present new works and modern operas, usually a world premiere of a Danish opera, in "off-beat" productions. In that area the company has mounted twelve Danish world premieres between 1981 and 1998. The remainder of the opera productions find some traditional and others modern.

Around four operas are in the repertory — one classic, one modern Danish, (frequently a world premiere), one operetta or musical, and since the opening of the Musikhuset in Århus, one Richard Wagner opera (replaced in 1998 by Richard Strauss). Wagner first entered the repertory in 1983 with *Die Walküre*. *Das Rheingold* came the next season followed by *Siegfried* in 1985 and *Götterdämmerung* in 1986. The complete Ring Cycle was mounted in 1987. Two years later, *Tristan und Isolde* was first seen in the Musikhuset Århus followed by *Parsifal*. *Der Ring des Nibelungen* was revived with *Die Walküre* in 1993, *Siegfried* in 1994, *Götterdämmerung* in 1995, and an "adventurous" staging of the complete Ring Cycle in 1996 that attracted international attention. Some of the classic operas included Pietro Mascagni's *Cavalleria rusticana*, Ruggero Leoncavallo's *I pagliacci*, Giacomo Puccini's *Madama Butterfly*, *La bohème*, and *Gianni Schicchi*, Charles Gounod's *Faust*, Giuseppe Verdi's *Rigoletto* and *Otello*, and Gioachino Rossini's *La Cenerentola*. Among the Danish works were Weyse's *Sovedrikken*, Thybo's *Den udødelige historie*, Heise's *Drot og Marsk*, Du Puy's *Ungdom og Galskab*, along with the world premieres of Rovsing Olsen's *Usher*, Karl Åge Rasmussen's *Majakovskij*, *Titanics Undergang*, and *Vores Hoffmann*, Schultz's *Hosekræmmeren*, and Tage Nielsen's *Latter i Mørket*.

With the arrival of Troels Kold as the new *Operachef* in 1996, the works of Richard Strauss replaced those of Wagner in the repertory and a Richard Strauss series began with *Elektra* in 1998, followed by *Salome* in 1999, and will culminate with *Die schweigsame Frau* in the year 2000.

Other works programmed by Kold include Mozart's *Die Zauberflöte*, Tom Johnson's *Four Note Opera*, Giovanni Battista Pergolesi's *La serva padrona*, and the world premiere of Lars Klit's *Anatomisk Opera*. The company has no fixed ensemble, but employs Danish singers and artists from the other Scandanavian countries. All conductors, however, are Danish. The budget is approximately DK 15 million.

Practical Information. Den Jyske Opera, Musikhuset Århus, Thomas Jensens Allé, 8000 Århus. Tel: 45 8931 8260, Fax: 45 8613 3710. When visiting the Den Jyske Opera, contact the Danish Tourist Board, 655 Third Avenue, New York, NY 10017-5617. Tel: 212-949-2333, Fax: 212-983-5260.

COMPANY STAFF AND PREMIERES

Operachefer. Troels Kold (1996–present), Francesco Cristofoli, Torben Wiskum, Per Dreyer, Gerhard Schepelern, Holger Boland, Albeck.

World Premieres. R. Olsen's *Usher* 1981-82; Nørgaard's *The Divine Circus* 1982-83; K. A. Rasmussen's *Majakovskij* 1984-85; Nørholm's *Sandhedens Hævn* 1985-86; Ruders's *Tycho* 1986-87; K. A. Rasmussen's *Vores Hoffmann* 1987-88; Schultz's *Hosekræmmeren* 1989-90; B. Lorentzen's *Den magiske Brillant* (children's opera) 1992-93; K. A. Rasmussen's *Titanics Undergang* 1993-94; T. Nielsen's *Latter i Mørket* 1994-95; A. Pape's *Man behøver ikke være neger for at blive jysk mester i mellemvægt* 1994-95. L. Klit's *Anatomisk Opera* April 23, 1998. **Repertory. 1979-80:** Sovedrikken, Slagen, Dette her er vist noget af Mozart, Der Bettelstudent, Cavalleria rusticana, I pagliacci, La voix humaine, A Kékszakállú herceg vára (Duke Bluebeard's Castle). **1980-81:** La voix humaine, A Kékszakállú herceg vára (Duke Bluebeard's Castle), Die lustige Witwe, Madama Butterfly, The Beggar's Opera. **1981-82:** Il trovatore, The Beggar's Opera, Den udødelige historie, Usher, Les contes d'Hoffmann. **1982-83:** Maskarade, Die lustige Witwe, The Divine Circus, Die Zauberflöte. **1983-84:** Die Walküre, Die Fledermaus, The Lighthouse, Drot og Marsk. **1984-85:** Das Rheingold, Pinafore, Prodaná nevěsta (The Bartered Bride), Majakovskij. **1985-86:** Siegfried, La périchole, Madama Butterfly, Sandhedens Hævn. **1986-87:** Götterdämmerung, Czárdásfürstin, La Cenerentola, Tycho. **1987-88:** Der Ring des Nibelungen, Gianni Schicchi, Farinelli, Vores Hoffmann. **1988-89:** Vores Hoffmann, Otello, The Divine Circus, The Pirates of Penzance. **1989-90:** Tristan und Isolde, The Divine Circus, Eine Nacht in Venedig, Die Entführung aus dem Serail, Hosekræmmeren. **1990-91:** Tristan und Isolde, Paganini, Faust, Hosekræmmeren. **1991-92:** Parsifal, West Side Story, Ungdom og Galskab, Fidelio. **1992-93:** Tristan und Isolde, Parsifal, Farinelli, Rigoletto, Den magiske Brillant (children's opera). **1993-94:** Die Walküre, Die Fledermaus, Die lustigen Weiber von Windsor, Den magiske Brillant, Titanics Undergang. **1994-95:** Siegfried, Orphée aux enfers, La bohème, Latter i Mørket, Man behøver ikke være neger for at blive jysk mester i mellemvægt. **1995-96:** Götterdämmerung, Candide, Le nozze di Figaro, Man behøver ikke være neger for at blive jysk mester i mellemvægt, Das Rheingold. **1996-97:** Der Ring des Nibelungen. **1997-97:** Die Zauberflöte, Four Note Opera, Anatomisk Opera. **1998-99:** Elektra, La serva padrona, Carmen, Der Land des Lächelns.

Bibliography. *Den Jyske Opera 40 År* (Århus, 1986). *Det Rejsende Landsteater 10 År* (Århus, 1987). Additional materials supplied by the company. Interview with Francesco Cristofoli, former general director, November 1995.

Thanks to Jørgen Grunnet, Royal Danish Embassy, Washington D.C., and Bodil Høgh and Karen Sophie Lerhard, Danish Music Information Center, Copenhagen.

Århus Sommer Opera

Århus Sommer Opera is a small company founded in 1988 to perform operas in the Elsinore Theater (the original home of Den Jyske Opera) after Den Jyske Opera moved to the Musikhuset Århus. Preben Bjerkø, one of the founders, was the company's first artistic director, and a member of the singer ensemble. The repertory has included Benjamin Britten's *Rape of Lucretia*, Gioachino Rossini's *Il barbiere di Siviglia*, Gaetano Donizetti's *Don Pasquale*, Giuseppe Verdi's *Macbeth* and *Falstaff* (reduced versions), and Wolfgang Amadeus Mozart's *Così fan tutte* and *Don Giovanni*. In fact, Troels Kold, the current *operachef* of Den Jyske Opera, began his directorial career at the Århus Sommer Opera with *Don Giovanni*, featuring in the title role, the now internationally famous Danish baritone Bo Skovhus. In 1997, the company received a grant from the Danish Ministry of Culture that enabled it to increase its schedule from one to two offerings, allowing both a classical work and a contemporary one. In 1997, Britten's *Turn of the Screw* and Donizetti's *Don Pasquale* were on the schedule. By 1998, the season increased to three works, including the world premiere of John Frandsen's *Tugt og Ut ugt 1* on August 18, 1998. The opera is the first of an opera trilogy which the Århus Sommer Opera has commissioned. Recent repertory includes Lars Klit's *Den sidste Virtuos* and Mozart's *La clemenza di Tito*.

Elsinore Theater

The Elsinore Theater was inaugurated on January 28, 1817, the birthday of the "king of the citizens," Frederik VI, in Elsinore, where it remained for 140 years. Built and paid for by the citizens for their own amusement, it was a theater of the people and as such, had no royal box. During its final 40 years of existence in Elsinore, it was used as a movie house, known as Kosmorama. When the town required a larger cinema, the theater had outlived its usefulness and was slated for demolition. Fortunately, Georg Andrésen, who was associated with the Århus Stiftstidende, thought Århus was the perfect location for the theater and made arrangements with the owners,

Gerda and Haagen (son) Petersen to let the theater be moved. Reconstructed in a newly plastered shell in a large park called Den Gamle By (Old Town), the theater reopened on December 2, 1961. The theater, initially the home to Den Jyske Opera, is now home to the Århus Sommer Opera.

The plain facade of the theater could be mistaken for a large country home. Holding one horseshoe tier, the auditorium is intimate in scale, and the orchestra pit is tiny. Although the orchestra seats are comfortable, the tier holds only wooden benches. It accommodates 260 patrons.

Practical Information. Århus Sommer Opera, Elsinore Theater, Den Gamle By, Århus. Out of season contact Klerkegade 6, Copenhagen 1308. Tel: 45 33 32 30 49, Fax: 45 33 32 29 49. Contact the Danish Tourist Board, 655 Third Avenue, New York, NY 10017-5617; Tel: 212-949-2333, Fax: 212-983-5260.

COMPANY STAFF

Operachef. Kasper Holten (1997–present), Lars Ole Bonde, Troels Kold, Preben Bjerkø.

Bibliography. Information from the Danish Music Information Center and the Internet.

Thanks to Bodil Høgh and Karen Sophie Lerhard, Danish Music Information Center, Copenhagen.

COPENHAGEN

Den Anden Opera

Den Anden Opera (The Other Opera) was officially opened on February 1, 1995, with a guest performance of *Soap Opera* by the Holland House, a Danish music drama company. Founded for *Copenhagen 96 — Cultural Capital of Europe*, the company produced its first opera, Lars Klit's *Den Sidste Virtuos* (The Last Virtuoso) in April 1995, a world premiere of a "horror" opera. The company is located in a building constructed by the Masonic Order in 1805 which houses an auditorium of 200 seats, and a small room which accommodates 40 to 50 visitors.

The Other Opera is a stage for experimental musical drama and small-scale opera, and as Jesper Lützhøft, the company's artistic director put it, "a much needed venue in Copenhagen to produce new contemporary operas by Danish composers." Since cost is a major factor in opera

production, modern and "off-beat" productions are best experimented with on a small scale. Chamber and small scale opera offered at The Other Opera included Karl Åge Rasmusen's *Titanics Undergang*, Michael Mantler's *The School of Languages*, Andy Pape's *Houdini the Great*, and Tage Nielsen's *Latter i Mørket*. The Danish Music Council is supporting the company for a test period, but only with enough money to pay for the organizational structure. All production money is raised from private foundations (no individuals).

For *Titanics Undergang*, a work which explored the inner workings of the minds of the passengers on a sinking ship, the entire theater was transformed into a boat and the audience were part of the sinking ship. The walls were sloped like the sides of a ship, and green lights created the impression of being surrounded by water and ultimately being under water. The orchestra was placed behind the singers.

Practical Information. Den Anden Opera, Kronprinsensgade 7, 1114 Copenhagen. Tel: 45 33 32 38 30. Danish Music Information Center, Graabroedre Torv 16, 1154 Copenhagen. Tel: 45 33 11 20 66, Fax 45 33 32 20 16. When visiting the Den Anden Opera, contact the Danish Tourist Board, 655 Third Avenue, New York, NY 10017-5617. Tel: 212-949-2333, Fax: 212-983-5260.

COMPANY STAFF AND PREMIERES

Operachef. Jesper Lützhøft (1995–present)
World Premieres. L. Klit's *Den Sidste Virtuos*, April 1995.
Bibliography. Den Anden Opera (Copenhagen, 1995). Additional materials supplied by the company and the Danish Music Information Center. Interview with Jesper Lützhøft, artistic director, November 1995.

Thanks to Jørgen Grunnet, Royal Danish Embassy, Washington D.C.; Bodil Høgh and Karen Sophie Lerhard, Danish Music Information Center, Copenhagen, and the Danish Foreign Ministry.

Royal Danish Opera

On October 15, 1874, Det Kongelige Teater (The Royal Theater), also known as the Gamle Scene, was inaugurated with the overture to Frederik Kuhlau's *Elverhøj* and Ludvig Holberg's *Det lykkelige Skibbrud*, among other works. Vilhelm Dahlerup and Ove Petersen designed the structure. An annex, popularly called *Stærekassen* or Nesting Box, but officially known as the Nye Scene, was opened on August 28, 1931, with the overture to Kuhlau's *Elverhøj*, Julius Magnussen's *Fra Fiolstræde til Kongens Nytorv*, and Holberg's *Den Vægelsindede*. Holger Jacobsen designed the Nye Scene annex, which is used for comic opera and spoken theater. The first Royal Theater, which opened on December 18, 1748, was constucted by the court builder, Niels Eigtved.

The first opera in Copenhagen dates back to 1663, with a performance of Caspar Förster's *Il Cadmo*. Paul C. Schindler's *Der vereinigte Götterstreit* (The Feud of the Gods) followed in 1689, and during a performance, the wooden structure caught fire and burned to the ground, killing 180 people. Today, Amalienborg Palace is located on the site. In 1722, the premiere of Reinhard Keiser's *Ulysses* marked Frederick IV's birthday and when he ascended the throne in 1746, he donated land in the Kongens Nytorv to construct the first Kongelige Teater. The rococo-style building, which opened in 1748, offered 800 seats. The following year, it hosted the premiere of Christoph Willibald Gluck's *La contesa dei numi*, presented in honor of the birth of Prince Christian. Scalabrini's *L'amor premiato* (as *Den belønnede Kærlighed*) in 1758, and works by other Italian composers including Giovanni Battista Pergolesi and Niccolò Piccinni, and French composers, like Jean-Baptiste Lully, Jean-Philippe Rameau, François-André Philidor, Pierre-Alexandre Monsigny, and André Grétry graced the stage. Many Danes did not like the rigid and artificial mannerisms of those operas and Johan Herman Wessel wrote a satire about it in 1773, called *Kærlighed uden Strømper* (Love without Stockings). In 1774, King Christian VII commissioned C.F. Harsdorff to enlarge the theater, increasing the seating capacity to 1,375. Five years later, the premiere of Hartmann's Singspiel, *Balders Død*, took place, followed by *Fiskerne* in 1780. Five years later, in 1785, a curious proviso was introduced by the theater's management: curtain calls were prohibited and performers could not bow or curtsy to acknowledge applause, even royal applause.

Danish opera was officially born in 1786, when Johann Gottlieb Naumann's *Orpheus og Euridice* was mounted. The world premiere of F.L.A. Kunzen's *Holger Danske* followed in 1789. With the turn of the century, the operas of Wolfgang Amadeus Mozart, Gaetano Donizetti, Vincenzo Bellini, and Gioachino Rossini were introduced along with Christoph Ernst Weyse's *Sovedrikken* (1809), *Faruk* (1812), *Ludlams Hule* (1816), and *Et Eventyr i Rosenborg Have* (1827). In 1828, the world premiere of Kuhlau's *Elverhøj*, called a "national musical comedy" took place and Jenny Lind made her first appearance at the theater in 1843. Three years later, Hartmann's *Liden Kirsten* received its first performance ever. When King Frederick VII renounced his autocracy in 1849, transforming the country into a constitutional monarchy, the Kongelige Teater became a state institution, with its director accountable to the Minister of Culture.

In 1874, the second Kongelige Teater, was built next to the first. Peter Heise's *Drot og Marsk* was hosted on September 25, 1878, and a decade later, C.F.E. Horneman's *Alladdin* graced the stage. In 1892, August Enna's *Heksen* was mounted followed by *Den lille Pige med Svolvstikkerne* in 1897. Danish opera achieved greater prominence in the beginning of the 20th century with the world premieres of Carl Nielsen's *Saul og David* (1902), his *Maskarade* (1906), and Georg Høeberg's *Et Bryllup i Katakomberne* (1909). The Danish premiere of Richard Wagner's *Der Ring des Nibelungen* (sung in Danish) took place between April 30 and May 5, 1909. Lauritz Melchior made his debut on April 2, 1913, as a baritone singing Silvio in Ruggero Leoncavallo's *I pagliacci* and then made a second debut as a tenor on October 8, 1918, singing the title role in Wagner's *Tannhäuser.* In 1935 a special law known as *Lov om Kulturel Fond* (Cultural Fund Act) was passed, designating the theater as Denmark's national theater and turning it into a heavily subsidized government institution. That same year, Johan Hye-Knudsen, who had assumed the directorship in 1931, reset Giuseppe Verdi's *Un ballo in maschera* in 18th-century Sweden, almost two decades before Stockholm's Kungliga Teater did the same. Then on April 9, 1940, the Nazis occupied Denmark and a dark chapter in Danish history unfolded. Danish national operas were revitalized (to boost morale), and contemporary operas, many of which were banned by the Nazis, were performed during the late afternoon, because of wartime curfews. One such work was the European premiere on March 27, 1943, of George Gershwin's *Porgy and Bess.* Since the war, the most frequently performed works have been comic operas. International stars like Birgit Nilsson, Giuseppe di Stefano, and Victoria de los Angeles have made guest appearances at the theater, but most productions are cast with repertory singers. Elaine Padmore assumed the position of opera director in the early 1990s, and during her reign, the Royal Opera underwent a transformation from a conservative, traditional company, with uninspired productions and limited repertory to a more adventurous company with innovative productions and expanded repertory. By the mid–1990s, works like Richard Strauss's *Ariadne auf Naxos,* Wagner's *Parsifal,* Ludwig van Beethoven's *Fidelio,* Nielsen's *Saul og David,* Mozart's *Die Entführung aus dem Serail,* Puccini's *Madama But-*

terfly, and Verdi's *La forza del destino* were in the repertory. The quality of an opera production depends upon the age of the production. An old production of Rossini's *Il barbiere di Siviglia* was what one might expect from a provincial theater with a tiny budget. The sets were shabby and dated, and the director missed some of the opera's pivotal moments — Rosina never "dropped the note" to Almaviva in the opening act and no ladder was visible in the final scene. This same company, one month later, mounted a timelessly set production of Ambroise Thomas's *Hamlet* that was innovative, well-directed, and well-sung. Padmore explained the problem — that of changing the attitude and fighting the traditionalist. The company must retain its Danish imprint, and that is being done by hiring young, Danish singers. But the (conservative) thinking is so entrenched that the changes have been slow, gentle, and subtle. The outdated productions are being replaced with directors hired from the theater. Productions are also being sung in the original language, to attract guest artists and to integrate the Royal Opera into the international opera community. Previously all works had been sung in Danish by an ensemble of 30 singers. The repertory had been limited by what these artists could sing. Funding is almost all government. The budget of $3.5 million for opera pays for singers, conductors, directors, and designers.

The repertory now spans works from the Baroque to the 20th century, and the Danish premieres of Giacomo Puccini's *Turandot* and Sergei Prokofiev's *Lyubov'k tryom apel'sinam* (The Love for Three Oranges) finally took place in the latter part of the 1990s. Contemporary operas are also on the boards. Recent offerings include Gluck's *Orfeo ed Euridice,* Wagner's *Tristan und Isolde* and *Lohengrin,* Francis Poulenc's *Les dialogues des Carmélites,* Strauss's *Arabella,* Puccini's *Madama Butterfly,* Mozart's *Idomeneo* and *Don Giovanni,* Verdi's *Aida* and *Falstaff,* Benjamin Britten's *Peter Grimes,* Torben Petersen's *Prinsesse Dajli,* and Nielsen's *Maskarade.*

Det Kongelige Teater

Statues of Holberg and Adam Oehlenschläger guard the entrance to the classical Gamle Scene, whose ornate facade is defined by columns, arches, and friezes. The horseshoe-shaped auditorium,

Det Kongelige Teater (Copenhagen, Denmark).

decorated in gold, white, and red velvet, holds four tiers, a canopied royal box, and busts of composers, poets, and philosophers as ornamentation. Over the proscenium the words *"Ei Blot Til Lyst"* (Not Only for Pleasure) are etched. The Gamle Scene seats 1,536. The Nye Scene, which is plain and nondescript, seats 1,091.

Practical Information. Det Kongelige Teater, Kongens Nytorv 9, 1050 Copenhagen. Tel: 45 33 14 10 02, Fax: 45 33 12 36 92. When visiting Det Kongelige Teater, contact the Danish Tourist Board, 655 Third Avenue, New York, NY. Tel: 212-949-2333, Fax: 212-983-5260.

COMPANY STAFF AND WORLD PREMIERES

Operachef. Elaine Padmore.
World Premieres. F.K.Æ. Kunzen's *Holger Danske*, March 31, 1789. J.L. Heiberg's *Elverhøj*, (na-tional musical comedy) November 6, 1828. J.P.E. Hartmann's *Liden Kirsten* (Little Kirsten), May 12, 1846. P. Heise's *Drot og Marsk* (King and Marshal), September 25, 1878. C. Nielsen's *Saul og David* (Saul and David), November 28, 1902. C. Nielsen's *Maskarade,* November 11, 1906. G. Høeberg's *Et Bryllup i Katakomberne*, March 6, 1909. (New Stage) Bent Lorentzen's *Den Stundesløse* (The Fidget), September 16, 1995.

Bibliography. *The Royal Theater: History and Repertory 1995-96* (Copenhagen, 1996). Alf Henriques, *The Royal Theater Past and Present* (Copenhagen, 1967). *Årsberetning 1993, 1994 * Det Kongelige Teater* (Copenhagen, 1993, 1994). Additional information supplied by the Danish Music Information Center. Interviews with Elaine Padmore, director Royal Opera, November 1995, and Michael Christiansen, director Det Kongelige Teater, November 1995.

Thanks to Lillian Hess, Danish Tourist Board, New York; Jørgen Grunnet, Royal Danish Embassy, Washington D.C.; Bodil Høgh and Karen Sophie Lerhard, Danish Music Information Center, Copenhagen, and the Danish Foreign Ministry, Copenhagen.

England

ALDEBURGH

Aldeburgh Festival

The British composer Benjamin Britten established the Aldeburgh Festival in 1948. A native to the region, Britten, along with singer Peter Pears and Eric Crozier, founded the festival to encourage the creation of new British operas on a small to medium scale. Early works and modern British opera dominated the program. The only suitable performing space until the conversion of a disused Maltings in the late 1960s was the local parish church. Here opera found a home and Britten's *Curlew River*, *The Burning Fiery Furnace*, and *The Prodigal Son*, Berkeley's *A Dinner Engagement* and Williamson's *English Eccentrics* were presented.

Britten's *A Midsummer Night's Dream*, performed by the English Opera Group, opened the festival's new performance venue, the Maltings, in 1967. The next year, the Sadler's Wells Opera mounted Britten's *Gloriana*, and Georg Friedrich Händel's *Hercules* was given in concert form. Then fire claimed the performing venue. Two years later, however, it was hosting performances again. The 1970s saw *The Rape of Lucretia*, Henry Purcell's *King Arthur*, the world premiere of Britten's *Death in Venice*, and John Gardner's *The Visitors*. For the 50th festival, two world premieres were offered, a music theater double bill by Mark-Anthony Turnage — *Twice through the Heart* and *The Country of the Blind*.

Practical Information. Aldeburgh Festival, High Street, Aldeburgh, Suffolk 1P15 5AX. Tel: 44 1728 453 543, Fax: 44 1728 452 715. When visiting the Buxton Festival, contact the British Tourist Authority, 40 West 57th Street, New York, NY 10019, 212-581-4700.

BUXTON

Buxton International Arts Festival

In 1903, Frank Marcham designed an Edwardian theater, which, after restoration, found a new life in 1979 as host to the Buxton International Arts Festival. During the festival's early years, it staged neglected operas with a common theme. In 1980, William Shakepeare's plays were the thread, and Ambroise Thomas's *Hamlet* and Hector Berlioz's *Béatrice et Bénédict* were offered. Two years later, Zoltán Kodály's works were the focus with *Háry János* and *The Spinning Room*. Giovanni Boccaccio provided the link in 1983 with the British premiere (professional) of Antonio Vivaldi's *Griselda* and Charles Gounod's *La Colombe*. The following season witnessed a Greek Revival theme inspiring Luigi Cherubini's *Medée* and Pier Francesco Cavalli's *Jason*. In 1985, Baldassare Galuppi's *Il filosofa di campagna* and Niccolò Piccinni's *La Cecchina, ossia La buona figliuola* were joined by a *commedia dell'arte* theme. A King Arthur theme linked Henry Purcell's *King Arthur* and Georg Friedrich Händel's *Ariodante* in 1987, followed by Gioachino Rossini's *L'occasione fa il ladro* and Gaetano Donizetti's *Il pignalione* with Spain as the common bond. The singers are young artists, emerging from the music conservatories. For the 20th festival, Mozart's *La finta semplice* and Pyotr Il'yich Tchaikovsky's *Eugene Onegin* were on the schedule.

Practical Information. Buxton International Arts Festival, Water Street, Buxton SK17 6XN. Tel: 44 1298 70395, Fax: 44 1298 72289. When visiting the Buxton Festival, contact the British Tourist Authority, 40 West 57th Street, New York, NY 10019, 212-581-4700.

COMPANY STAFF

General Manager. Jane Davies. **Artistic Advisor.** Lord Harewood.

Glyndebourne Festival Opera

Wolfgang Amadeus Mozart's *Le nozze di Figaro* inaugurated the Glyndebourne Festival Opera on May 28, 1934. Sir John Christie established the festival at his country estate in Lewes, where his wife, Canadian soprano Audrey Mildmay, sang in the opening night production. A new era at Glyndebourne began on May 28, 1994, when Mozart's *Le nozze di Figaro* opened the new opera house, designed by Michael Hopkins and constructed at a cost of £33 million.

Christie was a frequent visitor to the Salzburger Festspiele (see Salzburger Festspiele entry) and Bayreuther Festspiele (see Bayreuther Festspiele entry), where he got the idea to present a miniature Festspiele himself. The first operatic performances with reduced orchestral scores took place in the early 1920s in the organ room. After marrying Mildmay in 1931, Christie built a small opera house on the estate grounds and began searching for festival leadership. In 1934, Fritz Busch, who had been music director of the Semper Oper (Dresden) until Adolf Hitler's rise to power forced him to escape Nazi Germany, was offered the position of musical director. Carl Ebert, Intendant of the Städtische Oper (Berlin), until Hitler's arrival, was appointed artistic director. With long rehearsal time and total artistic control, and backed by Christie's money, Busch and Ebert created a quality of opera production not seen in the United Kingdom during that era. Even though none of the singers were international-circuit performers, the quality of the ensemble was high, resulting in critical acclaim.

Six performances of Mozart's *Le nozze di Figaro* and six of *Così fan tutte* over a two-week period comprised the first season. Although the opening night performance sold out, only a few dozen people were in the audience for the second and third performances. Then word spread that the Festival Opera offered outstanding opera and the remaining performances played to filled houses. Mozart's *Die Zauberflöte* and *Die Entführung aus dem Serail* joined the repertory in 1935, and Rudolf Bing (former general manager of the Metropolitan Opera, New York) directed the festival's administration. The following year, Mozart's *Don Giovanni* was added to the program,

and by 1938, the season, which had been extended to six weeks, witnessed the first non–Mozart operas — Gaetano Donizetti's *Don Pasquale* and the English premiere of Giuseppe Verdi's *Macbeth*. The festival closed in 1939 because of World War II, reopening on July 12, 1946, with the world premiere of Benjamin Britten's *The Rape of Lucretia*, the season's only offering. The next year introduced Britten's *Albert Herring*, with Christoph Willibald Gluck's *Orfeo ed Euridice* also on the boards. There were no operas during 1948 and 1949, as inflation and taxes made it financially impossible for Christie to support the festival alone. The John Lewis Partnership was established in 1950, the Glyndebourne Festival Society in 1951 (creating subscription series) and the Glyndebourne Arts Trust in 1954 and all combined placed the festival on firm financial footing.

During the 1950s, the repertory dramatically expanded: Richard Strauss's *Ariadne auf Naxos* (1950), Giuseppe Verdi's *La forza del destino* (1951), Mozart's *Idomeneo* (1951), Gioachino Rossini's *La Cenerentola* (1952), Igor Stravinsky's *The Rake's Progress* (1953), Gluck's *Alceste* (1953), Ferruccio Busoni's *Arlecchino* (1954), Rossini's *Le Comte Ory* and *Il barbiere di Siviglia* (1954), Verdi's *Falstaff* (1955), Mozart's *Der Schauspieldirektor* (1957), Rossini's *L'italiana in Algeri* (1957), Ermanno Wolf-Ferrari's *Il segreto di Susanna* (1958), Ludwig van Beethoven's *Fidelio* (1959), Strauss's *Der Rosenkavalier* (1959) all entered the repertory. Christie died in 1962 and his son George took over, continuing the Festival Opera along the same path, presenting outstanding productions in a "court opera" atmosphere. Although several more operas made their Glyndebourne premiere during the 1960s, among them Vincenzo Bellini's *Norma* (1960), Francis Poulenc's *La voix humaine* (1960), Hans Werner Henze's *Elegy for Young Lovers* (1961), Donizetti's *L'elisir d'amore* (1961), Claude Debussy's *Pelléas et Mélisande* (1962), Claudio Monteverdi's *L'incoronazione di Poppea* (1962), Strauss's *Capriccio* (1963), Donizetti's *Anna Bolena* (1965), Georg Friedrich Händel's *Jeptha* (1966), Maurice Ravel's *L'heure espagnole* (1966), Henry Purcell's *Dido and Aeneas*

(1966), Jules Massenet's *Werther* (1966), and Francesco Cavalli's *L'Ormindo* (1967) many works did not remain in the repertory, including those of Bellini, Donizetti, Massenet, Purcell, and Händel.

Each decade, more and more contemporary works were in the season's schedule, so by the dawn of the 1990s, there were four 20th-century works on the boards: Britten's *Albert Herring*, Leoš Janáček's *Kát'a Kabanová*, Michael Tippett's *New Year*, and Strauss's *Capriccio*, along with Verdi's *Falstaff* and Mozart's *Die Zauberflöte*. There were some exceptions to the traditional stagings. Mozart's *Die Zauberflöte*, as conceived by Peter Sellers, was relocated to present day California with photographs of beaches, freeways, residential neighborhoods, and gas stations as backdrops. Tamino was transformed into a contemporary junkie and Sarastro a posthippie cult guru. The Singspiel was performed without spoken dialogue — the words appeared on a screen. A more conventional production in the new opera house was that of Pyotr Il'yich Tchaikovsky's *Eugene Onegin* involving simple, suggestive sets which in part reflected the auditorium's decor. The intimacy from the smaller auditorium has been retained and the high quality of the ensemble — solid singing and acting and cast to type — was still present. Only the convoluted wording of the surtitles (defeating their purpose) could be improved. Recent repertory includes Verdi's *Simon Boccanegra*, Rossini's *Le Comte Ory*, Strauss's *Capriccio*, Janáček's *Kát'a Kabanová*, Mozart's *Così fan tutte*, and Händel's *Rodelinda*.

Festival Opera Auditorium

The construction of the original opera house, completed in 1933, contained up-to-date technical and lighting equipment and a large orchestra pit. The acoustics were tested with performances of three one-act operas. Although Christie wanted a Richard Wagner festival *à la* Bayreuth, the staging of Wagner operas in the small, "cozy" theater was impractical and too expensive. The festival opened as a Mozart opera festival *à la* Salzburg, which also was better suited to Mildmay's voice. During the war, the theater was transformed into an evacuation center for young children caught in London. The theater was enlarged from 300 to 600 seats in 1953, and increased again five years later to 830. This was still inadequate for the high demand for tickets so in the early 1990s a new opera house was constructed. Unlike the original Festival Opera auditorium, which was constructed as an annex to the 700-year-old manor house, a totally new opera house was constructed on the site of the original house, but turned 180°. In other words, the new stage sits where the walled garden once was, and the rear of the auditorium occupies the space where the stage used to be.

The building's exterior is of terracotta brick, lined with promenade decks. The rustic-looking, horseshoe-shaped auditorium holds three tiers and is covered with pine wood — pine walls and pine parapets. A series of intersecting circular shapes define the room. There are midnight-blue fabric seats and a huge center dome circled by lights. The proscenium arch is unadorned and black, topped by acoustic panels. There are 1,200 seats.

Practical Information. Glyndebourne Festival Opera, Glyndebourne Lewes, East Sussex BN8 5UU. Tel: 44 1273 812 321, Fax: 44 1273 812 783. When visiting the Glyndebourne Festival Opera, contact the Lewes District Council Information Office, 32 High Street, Lewes, East Sussex BN7 2NL. Tel: 44 273 471 600.

COMPANY STAFF AND PREMIERES

General Administrators. Anthony Whitworth-Jones (1988–present), Brian Dickie (1981–88), Moran Caplat (1949–81), Rudolf Bing (1935–49). **Music Directors**: Andrew Davis (1980–present), Bernard Haitinik (1978–79), John Pritchard (1964–77), Vittorio Gui (1951–63), Fritz Busch (1934–51).

World Premieres. B. Britten's *The Rape of Lucretia*, July 12, 1946; N. Maw's *The Rising of the Moon*, B. 1970; Britten's *Albert Herring*, June 20, 1985.

Bibliography. *Glyndebourne Festival Programs 1989–1996* (Glyndebourne, 1989–96). Wilfred Blunt, *John Christie of Glyndebourne* (London, 1968). John Julius Norwich, *50 Years of Glyndebourne* (London, 1985). John Higgens (ed.), *Glyndebourne: A Celebration* (London, 1984). Ira Nowinski, *A Season at Glyndebourne* (London, 1986).

Thanks to Press & Public Relations Office, Glyndebourne Festival.

Glyndebourne Festival Opera auditorium (Lewes, England).

——————————————————————————————— LEEDS

Opera North

The inauguration of Opera North in the Grand Theatre with Wolfgang Amadeus Mozart's *Die Zauberflöte* in November 1978 was scheduled to coincide with the centenary of the theater. The company, modeled on the Welsh National Opera and Scottish Opera, was established to provide a professional opera company in northern England. It was a child of the English National Opera. The theater architects were George Corson and James Robertson Watson.

In 1976, the city of Leeds purchased the Grand Theatre, paving the way for the establishment of Opera North. Around the same time, the Arts Council realized that the English National Opera was no longer as suited to touring as it was when it was called the Sadler's Wells Opera. The new company was called the English National Opera North, which soon was shortened to Opera North.

The initial season offered six operas, includ-

ing the opening, which reflected a diversity in repertory that became the company's hallmark: Camille Saint-Saëns's *Samson et Dalila*, Henry Purcell's *Dido and Aeneas*, Giacomo Puccini's *La bohème*, Francis Poulenc's *Les Marmelles de Tiresias*, and Jacques Offenbach's *Orphée aux enfers*. By the second season, the repertory had expanded to ten operas, including Richard Wagner's *Der fliegende Holländer*, Giuseppe Verdi's *La traviata*, and Benjamin Britten's *Peter Grimes*. The third season saw eleven operas on the boards, with some unusual and less performed works among them — Richard Rodney Bennett's *The Mines of Sulphur*, Frederick Delius's *A Village Romeo and Juliet*, Leoš Janáček's *Jenůfa*, and Verdi's *Nabucco*. During the first part of the 1980s, operas like Igor Stravinsky's *Oedipus Rex*, Verdi's *Macbeth*, Alexander Borodin's *Prince Igor*, Bedřich Smetana's *Prodaná nevěsta* (The Bartered Bride), Hector Berlioz's *Béatrice et Bénédict*, Christoph Willibald Gluck's

Orfeo ed Euridice, and the first British performance of Ernst Křenek's *Jonny spielt auf* graced the stage. The second half of the 1980s continued the full, diverse schedules with Berlioz's *Les Troyens*, Janáček's *Kát'a Kabanová*, Stravinsky's *The Rake's Progress*, Strauss's *Intermezzo*, Nikolay Rimsky-Korsakov's *Zolotoy petushok* (The Golden Cockeral), Wilfred Josephs's *Rebecca*, Sergey Prokofiev's *Lyubov'k tryom apel'sinam* (The Love for Three Oranges) among the more interesting offerings.

Gaetano Donizetti's *Don Pasquale* welcomed the 1990s which witnessed Verdi's *Jerusalem*, Maurice Ravel's *L'heure espagnol*, and Carl Nielsen's *Maskarade*, among its less known works. Emmanuel Chabrier's *L'étoile*, Verdi's *Attile*, Michael Tippett's *King Priam* and the company's first world premiere, Robert Saxton's *Caritas* were mounted in 1991. As the 1990s progressed more world premieres graced the stage, including Michael Berkeley's *Baa Baa Black Sheep* in 1993, H.K. Gruber's *Gloria von Jaxberg* in 1994, and Benedict Mason's *Playing Away* in 1995, along with Franz Schreker's *Der ferne Klang*, Ambroise Thomas's *Hamlet*, Sir Walter William's *Troilus and Cressida*, and Britten's *Gloriana*.

General Director Richard Mantle indicated that the repertory is becoming more mainstream to attract greater box office revenue, since grants are flat and costs are rising. Emphasis will continue, however, on presenting the lesser-known works of known composers, and delving more into the Baroque repertory. The artistic approach is eclectic, but with an emphasis on theatrical style. The company is young and still filled with vitality. Productions are updated, but only if it works as an integral part of the opera. The company has given over 2,000 performance of 111 different operas during it first two decades of existence. Its £8.5–£9 million budget comes from the Arts Council (£5 million), Leeds City Council (£1.2 million), private sponsorship (£1 million (£2 million), and box office revenue. The company tours to the other northern English cities, among them Nottingham (Theatre Royal), Hull (New Theatre), Manchester (Palace Theatre), and York (Theatre Royal). The singers are young and mainly British. They have regular commitments but are not on contract. Recent repertory includes Verdi's *Aida* and *Giovanna d'Arco*, Mozart's *Così fan tutte* and *Die Zauberflöte*, Bohuslav Martinů's *Julietta*, Rossini's *Il barbiere di Siviglia*, and Pyotr Il'yich Tchaikovsky's *Eugene Onegin*.

Grand Theatre

The Grand Theatre opened on November 18, 1878, after thirteen months of construction, which cost between £60,000 and £70,000. The inaugural performance was *Much Ado About Nothing*, followed by *The School for Scandal* the next evening and *Money* on the third. Eight years after opening, the Carl Rose Opera Company visited on October 18, 1886, with *Carmen, Don Giovanni, Ruy Blas, Faust, Lohengrin, The Bohemian Girl*, and *Esmeralda*.

The Grand Theatre is a Victorian Gothic building of red brick with turrets, Romanesque arches, and Doric columns. The Italianate auditorium of crimson and gold holds threes tiers which slant towards the stage. Delicate decorations of maroon and gold on a dark green background embellish the parapets. The red velvet seats match the red velvet curtain and harmonize with the red and green wallpaper design. A chandelier is suspended from a salmon-colored dome ceiling. The theater's capacity when it opened in 1878 was 2,600 with 200 more standing. Today, the theater seats 1,554 with 80 standing.

Practical Information. Opera North, Grand Theatre, 46 New Briggate, Leeds LS1 6NU. Tel: 44 113 243 9999, Fax: 44 113 244 0418. When visiting Opera North, stay at the Merrion Centre, Wade Lane, Leeds LS2 8NH. Tel: 44 113 243 9191, Fax: 44 113 242 3527. It is in the heart of the city close to the Grand Theatre and can assist with tickets and schedule.

COMPANY STAFF AND PREMIERES

General Director. Richard Mantle (1993–present), Nicholas Payne (1982–92).

World Premieres. R. Saxton's *Caritas*, 1991; M. Berkeley's *Baa Baa Black Sheep*, 1993; H.K. Gruber's *Gloria von Jaxberg*, 1994; B. Mason's *Playing Away*, 1994.

Bibliography. *Upbeat: The Magazine of Opera North*, Winter 1996-97. Additional information supplied by the company. Interview with Richard Mantle, general director, May 1997.

Thanks to Shona Galletly and Andrew Fairiey, Opera North, and Gillian Evans.

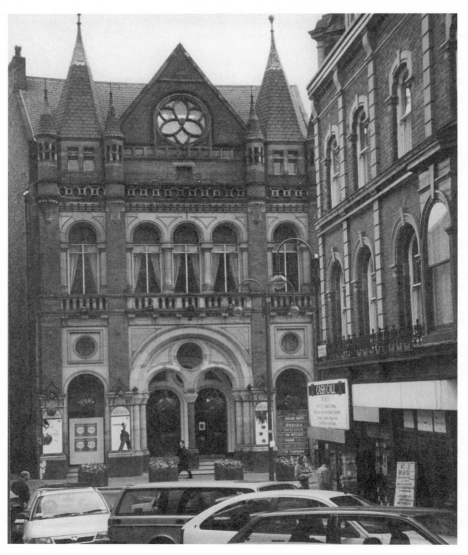

Grand Theatre (Leeds, England).

LONDON

English National Opera

The English National Opera, originally called the Vic-Wells Opera Company, and renamed the Sadler's Wells Opera in 1934, staged its first opera, Georges Bizet's *Carmen*, at the 1,548-seat Sadler's Wells Theatre on January 20, 1931. The theater had opened eight days earlier, on January 12, with William Shakespeare's *Twelfth Night*. Lilian Baylis founded the company and F.M. Chancellor was responsible for the rebuild-ing of the Sadler's Wells Theatre to serve as an opera house.

Back in 1912, Baylis had obtained a license for staged performances and began offering condensed versions of opera. Grand operas were performed with reduced orchestration. Around the same time the Beecham Opera Company ceased operations due to financial problems, and Covent Garden was only offering a short summer season of international quality, with the rest of the year devoted to the Carl Rosa Company and the British National Opera Company. The Sadler's Wells repertory was geared toward attracting the widest possible audience with Giuseppe Verdi and Gaetano Donizetti works dominating the schedule, along with perennial favorites like Bizet's *Carmen*, Charles Gounod's *Faust*, Pietro Mascagni's *Cavalleria rusticana*, Ruggero Leoncavallo's *I pagliacci*, Daniel Auber's *Fra Diavolo*, and Ambroise Thomas's *Mignon*. Other works included Vincent Wallace's *Maritana*, Julius Benedict's *The Lily of Killarney*, and Michael Balfe's *The Bohemian Girl*, and some operas of Richard Wagner —*Lohengrin, Tannhäuser,* and *Tristan und Isolde.* Every Lent, Mendelssohn's *Elijah* was offered. As the 1920s progressed and the audience base expanded, so did the repertory with new British operas like Ethel Smyth's *The Bosun's Mate,* and Nicolas Gatty's *The Tempest* and *Prince Ferelon.* There was no permanent company of singers, but guest artists like Joan Cross, Enid Cruikshank, Edith Coates, Heddle Nash, and Ben Williams were the interpreters. By the mid–1920s, Baylis's opera was attracting enough patrons to open the Sadler's Wells Theatre.

The history of the Sadler's Wells Theatre dates back to 1683 when Dick Sadler constructed a Musikhaus, only to discover that the wells on the land had medicinal uses. So he combined entertainment in this theater with spa services from his waters. The place changed many times, including being the home of the Grimaldi clown and hosting Shakespeare plays in the mid–1800s. Subsequently, the theater was used as a music hall, a movie theater, even a roller-skating rink. The building was in a state of disrepair when it was tapped to be a performance venue for Baylis's opera company, and needed much work to be able to serve as an opera house. A number of fundraising events took place to raise money for the refurbishment, including a 1926 performance of Giacomo Puccini's *La bohème* with Nellie Melba. Baylis developed a repertory spanning more than two dozen operas, with a mission to offer the best performances at the lowest prices.

In the inaugural season, the Sadler's Wells Opera offered 17 different works, including Verdi's *Otello* and *Aida,* and Gounod's *Faust.* By the second season, there were 26 different operas on the boards, with Henry Purcell's *Dido and Aeneas,* Thomas's *Mignon,* Camille Saint-Saëns's *Samson et Dalila,* Verdi's *Rigoletto, La traviata,* and *Un ballo in maschera* among them. By the third season, the company offered its first of several English premieres: Nikolay Rimsky-Korsakov's *Snow Maiden,* which was followed by his *Skazka o Tsare Saltane* (Tale of Tsar Saltan). Other Russian operas entering the repertory included Pyotr Il'yich Tchaikovsky's *Eugene Onegin* and Modest Mussorgsky's *Boris Godunov.* Modern British operas, like Lawrence Collingwood's *Macbeth,* Gustav Holst's *Savitri,* Charles Stanford's *The Travelling Companion,* Vaughan William's *Hugh the Drover,* Arthur Benjamin's *The Devil Take Her,* and Smyth's *The Wreckers* were also on the boards. The company's first world premiere, *Greysteel,* graced the stage on March 23, 1938. There were both regular singers and guest artists. Belonging to the former category were Jeanne Dusseau, Ruth Naylor, Janet Hamilton-Smith, Tudor Davies, Joan Cross, John Wright, Redvers Llewellyn, John Hargreaves, and Henry Wendon, and the guest artists included Florence Easton, David Lloyd, Maggie Teyte, Astra Desmond, Miriam Licette, and Florence Austral. The company was well-received. Sir Hugh Walpole wrote in a letter to *The Times,* after a performance of Wagner's *Die Meistersinger von Nürnburg,* "I have never anywhere seen a performance in which there was so much enjoyment radiating from the stage out to the audience and back from the audience to the stage again. Lilian Baylis has broken down the barriers between two different forces, the performers and the audiences."

Performances stopped at the Sadler's Wells Theatre in September 1940. During the war, the theater was used as a rest center for bombed-out citizens of Finsbury, and the company toured two operas, Verdi's *La traviata* and Mozart's *Le nozze di Figaro* to the northern industrial towns in England. At the end of the war, the successful world premiere of Benjamin Britten's *Peter Grimes* reopened the Sadler's Wells Theatre on June 7, 1945. Other novelties gracing the stage included Williams's *Sir John in Love* and *Two Shepherds of the Delectable Mountains,* Ermanno Wolf-Ferrari's *I quattro rusteghi,* Anthony Hopkins's *Lady Rohesia* (world premiere), and Verdi's *Simon Boccanegra* (British premiere). The primary focus of the expanding repertory remained modern British opera, with the intent, when possible, to mount one new production a year in the field. These included Lennox Berkeley's *Nelson*, Richard Rodney Bennett's *The Mines of Sulphur*, John Gardner's *The Moon and Sixpence*, Francis Burt's *Volpone*, and Malcolm Williamson's *Our Man in Havana*. Some of the revivals were Rutland Boughton's *The Immortal Hour*, Williams's *Riders to the Sea*, and Frederick Delius's *A Village Romeo and Juliet*. The emphasis on modern opera was not limited to British works, but also included Ildebrando Pizetti's *Assassinio nella cattedrale*, Hans Werner Henze's *Boulevard Solitude*, Béla Bartók's *A Kékszakállú herceg vára* (Duke Bluebeard's Castle), Gian Carlo Menotti's *The Consul* and *The Telephone*, Igor Stravinsky's *Oedipus Rex*, *The Rake's Progress*, and *Solovey* (The Nightingale), Sergey Prokofiev's *Lyubov'k tryom apel'sinam* (The Love for Three Oranges), Heinrich Sutermeister's *Romeo und Julia*, and Maurice Ravel's *L'heure Espagnole* and *L'enfant et les sortilèges*.

The beginning of the 1950s saw Leoš Janáček's operas enter the repertory — *Kát'a Kabanová*, *Příhody Lišky Bystroušky* (The Cunning Little Vixen), *Věc Makropulos* (The Makropoulos Affair), *Z Mrtvého Domu* (From the House of the Dead), along with other Czech works, like Bedřich Smetana's *Prodaná nevěsta* (The Bartered Bride), Jaromir Weinberger's *Švanda dudák* (Schwanda the Bagpiper), and Antonín Dvořák's *Rusalka*. By the late 1950s, it was apparent that the Sadler's Wells Opera had outgrown its theater, and this, coupled with the closing of the Carl Rosa Company (touring company) in 1958 due to lack of Arts Council funds, put pressure on the company to continue the tours of the Carl Rosa Company. In 1960, the government announced that it was considering building a National Theatre on the South Bank, but after seven years, it withdrew its support, and the London Coliseum became the company's new performance venue. On August 21, 1968, the Sadler's Wells Opera opened in the Coliseum with Mozart's *Don Giovanni*. It was not as successful as hoped, and not until the company mounted massive works, like Wagner's *Die Meistersinger von Nürnburg*, which took advantage of the vast stage, did the company achieve real success in the Coliseum. Other early productions included Verdi's *La forza del destino* (Colin Graham), Berlioz's *La Damnation de Faust* (Michael Geliot), and Bizet's *Carmen* (John Copley). It was after the company mounted Wagner's Ring Cycle (in English) — *Die Walküre* (1970), *Götterdämmerung* (1971), *Das*

Rheingold (1972), and *Siegfried* (1973), that it gained prestige, along with its presentation of the British stage premiere of Prokofiev's epic work, *Voyna i mir* (War and Peace) on October 11, 1972. Around the same time, it was evident that the public was confused by the two Sadler's Wells (the opera company and the theater) and one of the two had to change its name. Since the powers that be at the theater refused to change the historic name, it was up to the opera company. It was felt that their new name should reflect the national role of the company, especially in fostering British opera and hiring British artists. In January 1974, the company officially became the English National Opera.

Verdi's *La traviata* on August 3, 1974, was the first performance of the company as the English National Opera. Four days later Mozart's *Così fan tutte* was given, followed by Puccini's *Madama Butterfly*, Verdi's *Don Carlos*, Janáček's *Kát'a Kabanová*, and British premiere of Henze's *Bassarids* on October 10, among others. The opening season offered almost two dozen different operas. The company continued to find the unusual and less familiar works to stage, like Gioachino Rossini's *Le Comte Ory*, Carl Maria von Weber's *Euranthe*, Verdi's *I due Foscari*, Smetana's *Dalibor*, and Bohuslav Martinů's *Julietta*. Several of the company's artists went on to international careers like Elizabeth Connell, Josephine Barstow, Richard van Allan, to name a few.

The company's policy is to perform all the operas in English. They feel that the text is an integral part of the opera and with the text translated into good English, combined with good diction, there is a better audience response. They also believe that singing in English also makes the operas accessible to and appreciated by a wider range of people. Most singers are English, or English is their mother tongue. The performances place great emphasis on the theatrical aspect of the work, with stark realism and powerful acting. Actually a performance of Richard Strauss's *Salome* was almost too realistic, with Salome excessively kissing and caressing, with blood-stained hands, a bloody head of John the Baptist. On the other hand, Bizet's *Les pêcheurs de perles* was done in a lithsome, magical mode. Every production has its own special character and message. Among the recent offerings are Puccini's *Tosca*, Wagner's *Der fliegende Holländer*, Janáček's *Z Mrtvého Domu* (From the House of the Dead),

Jules Massenet's *Manon*, Purcell's *The Fairy Queen*, Georg Friedrich Händel's *Serse*, Verdi's *Otello*, Dvořák's *Rusalka*, Donizetti's *Maria Stuarda*, Mussorgsky's *Boris Godunov*, Christoph Willibald Gluck's *Orfeo ed Euridice*, Francis Poulenc's *Les dialogues des Carmélites*, and Arrigo Boïto's *Mefistofele*.

London Coliseum

The London Coliseum opened on December 24, 1904. It was built by Oswald Stoll after the design of Frank Marcham as a high-class variety palace, hosting several of the world's leading artists and companies like Sarah Bernhardt, Ellen Terry, and the Diaghilev Company. Later the Coliseum served as the home of lavish musicals, including *Guys and Dolls*, *White Horse Inn*, *Kiss Me Kate*, and *Annie Get Your Gun*. When those went out of fashion, the Coliseum was transformed into a movie house. When the Sadler's Wells Opera moved in, it underwent major structural alterations to be suitable as an opera house.

The Coliseum is an elaborate Edwardian structure with a detailed terracotta facade. The vast auditorium holds three tiers which undulate around the room and divide into side boxes on two of the levels. An outdoor feeling is accomplished by the high dome, seats of bluish-green, and marble walls which look like the exterior of a structure. The parapets of the boxes and tiers sport a light lavender hue, embellished with faces of maidens, gilded medallions of Roman generals, and electric torches. Gilded Ionic columns support the proscenium boxes, surmounted by gilded chariots pulled by lions. The auditorium seats 2,356.

Practical Information. English National Opera, London Coliseum, St. Martin Lane, London WC2N 4ES. Tel: 44 171 836 0111, Fax: 44 171 836 8379. When visiting the English National Opera, stay at the Four Seasons Inn on the Park, Hamilton Place, Park Lane, London W1A 1AZ, England. Tel: 44 171 499 0888 or 1-800-223-6800, Fax 44 171 493-1895. It is convenient to the London Coliseum, and can assist with tickets and schedule.

London Coliseum (London, England).

London Coliseum auditorium boxes (London, England).

COMPANY STAFF AND PREMIERES

Managing Director. Nicholas Payne (1998–present), Dennis Marks (1993–97), Peter Jonas (1985–93), Lord Harewood 1972–85. **Music Directors**: Paul Daniel 1997–present), Sian Edwards (1993–95), Mark Elder (1979–93), Sir Charles Groves (1978–79), Charles Mackerras (1970–78).

World Premieres. (**English National Opera**): *The Story of Vasco*, March 13, 1974; I. Hamilton's *The Royal Hunt of the Sun*, February 2, 1977; D. Blake's *Toussaint*, September 28, 1977; I. Hamilton's *Anna Karenina*, May 7, 1981; H. Birtwistle's *The Mask of Orpheus*, May 21, 1986; D. Blake's *The Plumber's Gift*, May 25, 1989; R. Holloway's *Clarissa*, May 18, 1990; S. Oliver's *Timon of Athens*, May 17, 1991; J. Buller's *The Bakxai*, May 5, 1992; J. Harvey's *Inquest of Love*, June 5, 1993; J. Weir's *Blond Eckbert*, April 20, 1994; G. Bryars's *Doctor Ox's Experiment*, June 15, 1998. (**Sadler's Wells**): *Greysteel*, March 23, 1938; *Peter Grimes*, June 7, 1945; *Lady Rohesia*, March 17, 1948; *Nelson*, September 22, 1954; *The Moon and the Sixpence*, May 24, 1957; *The Violins of St. Jacques*, November 29, 1966; *A Penny for a Song*, October 31, 1967; *Lucky Peter's Journey*, December 18, 1969. *English Premieres.* (**English National Opera**): *The Bassarids*, October 1974; *Bomarzo*, November 3, 1976 (New Opera Company); *Julietta*, April 5, 1978 (New Opera Company); *The Adventures of Mr. Broucek* (stage premiere), December 28, 1978; *Akhnaten*, June 17, 1985; *Doktor Faust* (stage premiere), April 25, 1986; *The Stone Guest* (stage premiere) April 23, 1987; *Ledi Makbet Mtsenskovo uyezda* (Lady Macbeth of the Mtsenk District) May 22, 1987; *The Making of the Representative for Planet 8*, November 9, 1988; *Lear*, January 24, 1989; (**Sadler's Wells**): *Snow Maiden*, April 12, 1933; *Skazka o Tsare Saltane* (Tale of Tsar Saltan), October 11, 1933; *School for Fathers*, June 7, 1946; *Simon Boccanegra*, October 27, 1948; *Kát'a Kabanová*, April 10, 1951; *Roméo et Juliette*, March 12, 1953; *Voyna i mir* (War and Peace, stage premiere), October 11, 1972; *Diably z Loudun* (The Devils of Loudun), November 1, 1973.

Bibliography. Peter Jonas, Mark Elder, David Poutney, *The English National Opera Experience* (London, 1992). Richard Jarman, *A History of Sadler's Wells Opera* (London, 1974, rev. 1980). Richard Jarman, *A History of the London Coliseum: 1904–1981* (London, 1981). M. Stapleton, *The Sadler's Wells Opera* (London, 1954). Additional information supplied by the company.

Thanks to Oliver Tims, English National Opera.

The Royal Opera

Giacomo Meyerbeer's *Les Huguenots*, sung in Italian, opened the Royal Opera House, originally known as the Royal Italian Opera House, on Saturday, May 15, 1858. It was the third opera house constructed on the site. The inaugural evening, however, was not successful. The start of the performance was delayed because the patrons could not locate their seats and the opera was very long. The result was when Sunday arrived, the management canceled the last act "out of respect for the day of rest." Edward Middleton Barry designed the structure which was built by Charles and Thomas Lucas at the cost of £80,000. The second Theatre Royal had been gutted by fire during the early morning hours of March 5, 1856. It was inaugurated on September 18, 1809, with Shakespeare's *Macbeth*. Robert Smirke was the architect of the opera house, which cost the astronomical sum of £187,888. Fire had destroyed the first Theatre Royal at Covent Garden on September 20, 1808. William Congreve's comedy, *The Way of the World*, had inaugurated the theater on December 7, 1732. Built by John Rich at the cost of £5,650, the theater was designed by Edward Shepherd.

London first heard opera back in 1656, when *The Siege of Rhodes* was presented. Several composers wrote the music. The Drury Lane Theatre, considered London's first opera house, opened in 1674. Sir Christoph Wren was the architect. In 1684, John Blow's *Venus and Adonis* was staged. Five years later Henry Purcell's *Dido and Aeneas* was introduced at Josias Priest's boarding school for girls, and Dorset Garden hosted the premiere of Purcell's *The Fairy Queen* in April 1692. Greber's *Gli amori d'Ergasto*, the first Italian opera performed in London, inaugurated the King's Theatre, also called the Haymarket Opera House, on April 9, 1705. The King's Theatre hosted several of Georg Friedrich Händel's early opera premieres—*Rinaldo* (February 24, 1711), *Il Pastor Fido* (November 22, 1712), *Tesco* (January 10, 1713), *Giulio Cesare in Egitto* (February 20, 1724), *Tamerlano* (October 31, 1724), *Rodelinda* (February 13, 1725), *Sosarme, re di Media* (February 15, 1732), *Orlando* (January 27, 1733), and *Serse* (April 15, 1738). The King's Theatre offered few opera performances after Händel left. Fire destroyed the building in 1789. Reconstructed, it was renamed Her Majesty's Theatre when Queen Victoria ascended the throne in 1837. A decade later, the world premiere of Giuseppe Verdi's *I masnadieri* took place on July 22, 1847, featuring Jenny Lind. Queen Victoria, Prince Albert, the Queen Mother, the Duke of Cambridge, and the Prince of Wales were in attendance.

Meanwhile, John Gay's *The Beggar's Opera* opened at the Lincoln Inn's Fields Theatre on January 29, 1728. It was so successful that Rich built the first Theatre Royal at Covent Garden with the profits. It was an unadorned, fan-shaped auditorium, later reshaped into a horseshoe, with three tiers of boxes, two galleries in the rear, and hard, backless benches in the orchestra. Soon thereafter, Händel, tired of the intrigues by impresarios, composers, and the *castrati*, left the King's Theatre for the newly opened Theatre Royal. For the premieres of his operas, an organ was installed on stage —*Ariodante* (January 8, 1735), *Alcina* (April 16, 1735), *Atalanta* (May 23, 1736), *Arminio* (January 12, 1737), *Berenice* (May 18, 1737), and *Semele* (February 10, 1744). The premieres were so expensive that afterwards Rich presented mainly plays, and Händel had exhausted his own money mounting the works. Although Italian opera disappeared from the repertory, English ballad operas were staged with the world premieres of Thomas Arne's *Artaxerxes* on February 2, 1762, with the famous *castrati*, Giusto Ferdinando Tenducci and Nicolo Peretti, and Arne's *Love in a Village* on December 8, 1762. Although ballad operas continued after the turn of the century, when Charles Dibdin's *The Cabinet* and *Family Quarrels* were mounted in 1802, the theater saw more plays than opera, until it was gutted by fire in 1808, believed to have been caused by hot wadding left in a set from the previous night's performance. Twenty-five people and Georg Friedrich Händel's organ perished in the blaze.

The management decided to rebuild and the second Theatre Royal opened the next year. It was a Greek Revival building with a Doric tetrastyle portico. The red-and-gold auditorium, embellished with mahogany woodwork, held three box tiers topped by two galleries. It was the first centrally-heated theater in Great Britain. Since the new opera house was very expensive, the management raised the price of the tickets. Violent protests, known as the Old Price Riots, followed, and the price increase was dropped. In 1811, Henry Bishop was appointed music director and he adapted some well-known foreign works, including Wolfgang Amadeus Mozart's *Don Giovanni*, and presented it as *The Libertine* in his own arrangement. In 1825, Carl Maria von Weber was commissioned to write a new work for the theater and the following year *Oberon* was premiered on April 12, 1826, with Weber on the podium. The first signs of Covent Garden's future as England's leading opera house appeared in 1843, when Michael Costa, the opera music director at Her Majesty's Theatre, moved his Royal Italian Opera Company to the Theatre Royal. The theater was restructured for grand opera by architect Benedetto Albano, who doubled the number of tiers to six, enlarged the proscenium, and added lavish decorations to the auditorium. Gioachino Rossini's *Semiramide* reopened the 2,800-seat Royal Italian Opera House on April 6, 1847. Although non–Italian operas were also staged, like Weber's *Der Freischütz* and Mozart's *Die Zauberflöte*, all operas were performed in Italian and Italian opera dominated the repertory. The first season witnessed Vincenzo Bellini's *I Puritani* and *Norma*, Gaetano Donizetti's *Anna Bolena* and *Lucia di Lammermoor*, Rossini's *La donna del lago* and *La gazza ladra*, and Verdi's *I due Foscari* and *Ernani* with Marietta Alboni, Luigina Bellini, Giulia Grisi, Guiseppe Mario, Antonio Tamburini, and Luigi Salva, as some of the artists. For the second season, many operas were repeated, with the addition of Francesco Gnecco's *Prova d'un opera seria*, Rossini's *Tancredi*, *La Cenerentola*, and *Guillaume Tell*, Donizetti's *La favorita* and *Lucrezia Borgia*, Bellini's *I Capuletti ed i Montecchi*, and Meyerbeer's *Les Huguenots* to the repertory. There was a fall season of English opera in 1848, including *The Bohemian Girl*, *Maritana*, *Bondman*, and *The Enchantress*.

Frederick Gye took over the management of the theater in 1850 and offered 17 operas during his first season, including Mozart's *Don Giovanni*, Rossini's *Il barbiere di Siviglia*, Verdi's *Nabucco*, Donizetti's *L'elisir d'amore*, Meyerbeer's *Robert le Diable* and *Le Prophète*, and Fromental Halévy's *La Juive*. Soon the operas staged numbered more than 20. Gye's first operatic failure took place in 1853 when Hector Berlioz came to conduct his *Benvenuto Cellini*, which survived only one performance. During a masked ball in 1856, fire gut-

ted the theater. Only the outer walls remained. Lack of funds delayed the reconstruction of the opera house for more than a year. But when the rebuilding began, it proceeded in record time, with around 1,200 workers hired for the last couple of months. Three years after the opera house opened, Adelina Patti, made her Covent Garden debut in Vincenzo Bellini's *La sonnambula* in 1861. Patti also sang in Donizetti's *Lucia di Lammermoor*, Friedrich von Flotow's *Martha*, and Verdi's *La traviata*. She was the reigning diva for 24 years until Nellie Melba became *prima donna assoluta* in 1888, assaying Gilda in Verdi's *Rigoletto* and the title role in *Lucia di Lammermoor*. Melba's reign lasted 38 years, until her farewell concert in 1926. Other renowned artists included Enrico Caruso, Lotte Lehmann, Lauritz Melchoir, and Rosa Ponselle.

Back in 1888, Augustus Harris's tenure as director of the opera house began and he internationalized the Royal Italian Opera House by staging most operas in their original language. "Italian" was not eliminated from its name, however, until Gustav Mahler conducted Richard Wagner's *Der Ring des Nibelungen*. The theater continued presenting world premieres with Herman Bemberg's *Elaine* on July 5, 1892, Jules Massenet's *La Navarraise* on June 20, 1894, and Franco Leoni's *L'oracolo* on June 28, 1905. The theater closed during World War I, reopening on May 12, 1919, with the Grand Opera Syndicate in charge of operations. They presented a three-month season of 20 different operas, including Massenet's *Thaïs* and *Manon*, Puccini's *Tosca*, *La bohème*, and *Madama Butterfly*, Charles Gounod's *Faust* and *Roméo et Juliette*, Verdi's *Un ballo in maschera*, *Aida*, *Rigoletto* and *La traviata*, and Ermanno Wolf-Ferrari's *Il segreto di Susanna*. Opera shared the stage with the circus, cabaret, and films. It became a dance hall for soldiers during the Second World War.

After the war, Pyotr Il'yich Tchaikovsky's ballet *Sleeping Beauty* reopened the opera house on February 20, 1946, the same year it was designated the national home for opera and ballet. Since then, only opera and ballet have graced the stage. In 1947, the Covent Garden Opera Company (renamed The Royal Opera in October 1968), gave its first performance, Georges Bizet's *Carmen* on January 14, 1947. Purcell's *The Fairy Queen*, Massenet's *Manon*, Mozart's *Die Zauberflöte*, Richard Strauss's *Der Rosenkavalier*, Puccini's *Turandot*, and Verdi's

Il trovatore completed the first season schedule. The first world premiere by the Covent Garden Opera Company took place on September 29, 1949, with Arthur Bliss's *The Olympians*, followed by Ralph Vaughan Williams's *The Pilgrim's Progress*, and Benjamin Britten's *Billy Budd*. For Queen Elizabeth II's coronation on June 8, 1953, Covent Garden commissioned Britten's *Gloriana*. Four of Michael Tippett's works were introduced at Covent Garden, including *The Midsummer Marriage*. *Der Ring des Nibelungen* welcomed in the 1980s, along with 16 additional operas, including Verdi's *Luisa Miller*, *Otello*, *Macbeth*, and *Un ballo in maschera*, Alban Berg's *Lulu*, Meyerbeer's *L'Africaine*, and Britten's *Peter Grimes*. Wagner's *Tristan und Isolde* and *Die Miestersinger von Nürnberg* graced the stage the following season, with Verdi's *Simon Boccanegra*, *Falstaff*, and *Il trovatore*, and Claude Debussy's *Pelléas et Mélisande*, among others, also on the boards. The British premiere of Luciano Berio's *Un re in ascolto* took place on February 9, 1989.

Some singing, conducting, and production highlights — Maria Callas made her debut on November 8, 1952, in Bellini's *Norma*, with Joan Sutherland as Clothilde. Sutherland sang the title role in Donizetti's *Lucia di Lammermoor* in 1959, in a production by Franco Zeffirelli. Zeffirelli produced Puccini's *Tosca* on January 21, 1964, with Callas and Tito Gobbi. Luchino Visconti produced Verdi's *Don Carlo* in celebration of the centenary of the opening of the Royal Opera House in May 1958. Otto Klemperer conducted Ludwig van Beethoven's *Fidelio* on February 24, 1961, with Jon Vickers and John Dobson in the cast, and Georg Solti led Arnold Schönberg's *Moses und Aaron* on June 28, 1965. Luciano Pavarotti made his Covent Garden debut as Rodolfo in Puccini's *La bohème* in 1963, followed by Plácido Domingo's debut as Cavaradossi in Puccini's *Tosca* in 1971, and José Carrera's debut as Alfredo in Verdi's *La traviata* in 1974. Carlos Kleiber was on the podium for Verdi's *Otello* on February 5, 1980, with Domingo in the title role.

The 1990s offered two world premieres — Harrison Birtwistle's *Gawain* and Alexander Goehr's *Arianna*. Other 1990s offerings included Paul Hindemith's *Mathias der Maler*, Puccini's *Tosca*, Mozart's *Le nozze di Figaro* and *Die Entführung aus dem Serail*, Verdi's *Aida*, Strauss's *Arabella*, Gounod's *Roméo et Juliette*, and Purcell's *King Arthur*. Some recent operas are Strauss's *Elektra*, Leoš Janáček's *Kát'a Kabanová*, along with the standard Verdi, Puccini, Mozart, and Wagner repertory.

The Royal Opera House has been hosting a June Verdi's Festival, staging both his known and less familiar works albeit with uneven results. The festival presented a mixture of different production styles. The unearthing of his rarely-performed *Giovanni d'Arco* was a great show, if not a great opera, whereas *Nabucco* is a great opera, but their production was a scandalous show. Updated to Nazi Germany with superfluous, distracting activities, horrendous costumes and absurd sets, the production undermined Verdi's work. Whereas Verdi's greatest work, *Don Carlos*, was presented in an unpretentious production which mixed the traditional with the abstract, with some imaginative touches. Big name artists filled the leading roles. As a feature of their 50th anniversary celebration, the Royal Opera, for some inexplicable reason, chose the difficult German work, Hans Pfitzner's *Palestrina*. The work, which tries to put an abstract concept, the question of creativity — who is an artist — against the backdrop of battles and the struggles of the Catholic Church made for a heavy evening, although the interpretation was noteworthy.

The Royal Opera House

The Royal Opera House blends French and Italian classicism. The statues and friezes which survived from the previous opera house embellish a portico, formed by six Corinthian columns. The Victorian-inspired, horseshoe-shaped auditorium is decorated in crimson, gold, and ivory, and originally had three box tiers topped by a gallery. After several remodelings, only the side boxes remain. Electrified candelabra hang from the parapets, decorated with mermaids. Deep crimson velvet seats match a similarly colored curtain. The turquoise dome, ornamented with gold-filigreed spokes in a celestial-like pattern, recreates an open-air theater effect, as was the custom in the Victorian era. The theater accommodates 2,098. The opera house was awarded £78.5 million by the Arts Council of England's National Lottery Board and is undergoing a major redevelopment, preparing it for the next century.

Practical Information. The Royal Opera, Royal Opera House, Covent Garden, London WC2E 9DD. Tel 44 171 240 1200, Fax: 44 171 836 1762. When visiting the Royal Opera, stay at the

Royal Opera House (London, England).

Four Seasons Inn on the Park, Hamilton Place, Park Lane, London W1A 1AZ. Tel: 44 171 499 0888 or 1-800-223-6800, Fax 44 171 493-1895. It is in the heart of the city, convenient to the Royal Opera House and can assist with tickets and schedule.

COMPANY STAFF AND PREMIERES

General Directors. (1946–present) Genista McIntosh (1997–present), Jeremy Issacs (1988–97), John Tooley (1970–88), David Webster (1946–70). **Music Directors**: Bernard Haitink (1987–present), Sir Colin Davis (1971–86), Georg Solti (1961–71), Rafael Kubelik (1955–58), Karl Rankl (1946–51).

World Premieres (1946–present). A. Bliss's *The Olympians*, September 29, 1949; V. Williams's *The Pilgrim's Progress*, April 25, 1951; B. Britten's *Billy Budd*, December 1, 1951; B. Britten's *Gloriana*, June 8, 1953; W. Walton's *Trolius and Cressida*, December 3, 1954; M. Tippett's *The Midsummer Marriage*, January 27, 1955; M. Tippett's *King Priam*, May 29, 1962; R. R. Bennett's *Victory*, April 13, 1970; M. Tippett's *The Knot Garden*, December 2, 1970; P. M. Davies's *Taverner*, July 12, 1972; *We Come to the River*, July 12, 1976; M. Tippett's *The Ice Break*, July 7, 1977; *Therese*, October 1, 1979; H. Birtwistle's *Gawain*, June 30, 1991; A. Goehr's *Arianna*, September 15, 1995.

Bibliography. *A History of the Royal Opera House Covent Garden 1732–1982* (London, 1982). Frances Donaldson, *The Royal Opera House in the Twentieth Century* (London, 1985). Harold Rosenthal, *Opera at Covent Garden: A Short History* (London, 1967). Harold Rosenthal, *Two Centuries of Opera at Covent Garden* (London, 1958).

Thanks to Ann Richards, Helen Anderson, and Francesca Franchi, Royal Opera, and John Stauss and Charlotte Doherty.

Opera Factory

In January 1982, Harrison Birtwistle's *Punch and Judy* inaugurated the Opera Factory in Drill Arts Centre. Gay's *The Beggar's Opera* was also on the schedule that first season. The company was founded by David Freeman.

The repertory spans three centuries from forgotten Baroque works to modern pieces. In this vein, the third season paired Michael Tippett's *The Knot Garden* with Pier Francesco Cavalli's *La Calisto*— performed on roller skates. The 1986 season saw Osborne's *Hell's Angels* paired with *La Calisto*, as well as Birtwistle's *Yan Tan Tethera* and Wolfgang Amadeus Mozart's *Così fan tutte*, the latter set on the beach. The next year presented Peter Maxwell-Davies's *Martyrdom of St. Magnus* and *8 Songs for a Mad King*, and György Ligeti's *Aventures*, followed by Aribert Reimann's *The Ghost Sonata* in 1989. The 1990s began with Mozart's *Don Giovanni* and Bruno Maderna's *Satyricon*, and Keterborn's *Julia* was mounted in 1991. Claudio Monteverdi's *L'incoronazione di Poppea* opened the 1992 season with by Iannis Xenakis's *The Bacchae*, Igor Stravinsky's *The Rake's Progress*, Nigel Osborne's *Sarajevo*, Benjamin Britten's *Curlew River*, and Henry Purcell's *Dido and Aeneas* also on the boards. Standard repertory like Mozart's *Die Zauberflöte* and *Don Giovanni* are presented in non-traditional productions.

One aim of the Opera Factory is to divest opera of its grand and elitist image and re-establish it as a popular art form. The company takes a multi-faceted approach to the relationship of music to theater. The singers improvise to discover their own interpretation, not just a realization of the director's or conductor's concept. The Opera Factory is based at the South Bank Centre in London, but also tours around the United Kingdom — Oxford, Malvern, Reading — and the continent — Zurich (Switzerland), Madrid (Spain), Compiègne (France), and Lisbon (Portugal).

Practical Information. Opera Factory, 9 The Leathermarket, Weston Street, London SE1 3ER. Tel 44 171 378 1029, Fax: 44 171 378 0185. When visiting the Opera Factory, stay at the Four Seasons Inn on the Park, Hamilton Place, Park Lane, London W1A 1AZ, England. Tel: 44 171 499 0888, Fax 44 171 493-1895. It is in the heart of the city, convenient to the Opera Factory and can assist with tickets and schedule.

COMPANY STAFF

Artistic Director. David Freeman (1982–present).

Bibliography. Information supplied by the company.

Thanks to Claire Shovelton, Opera Factory.

--- LINCOLN

Pavilion Opera

Wolfgang Amadeus Mozart's *Così fan tutte* was the inaugural opera of the Pavilion Opera, given during the summer of 1981, in a specially constructed Pavilion. The Pavilion, designed by Francis Johnson, with stained glass windows by John Piper, stood in the garden of Thorpe Tilney.

Freddie Stockdale founded the professional company.

The company offers standard repertory works. Operas most often performed include Giuseppe Verdi's *Rigoletto* and *La traviata*, Mozart's *Die Entführung aus dem Serail, Le nozze di Figaro, Don Giovanni*, and *Die Zauberflöte*, and Gaetano Donizetti's *Don Paquale, Lucia di Lammermoor*, and *L'elisir d'amore*. It is strictly a commercial enterprise which depends completely on its clients for its existence. It receives no grants and plans its repertory to assist these clients whether they are seeking to raise money (60%) or to entertain corporate or private guests (40%). The company has performed in more than 190 different venues in the United Kingdom and around the world. Recent productions include Franz Lehár's *Die lustige Witwe*, Giacomo Puccini's *La bohème*, Donizetti's *Lucia di Lammermoor* and *L'elisir d'amore*, and Jacques Offenbach's *Les contes d'Hoffmann*.

Practical Information. Pavilion Opera, Thorpe Tilney Hall, Thorpe Tilney, nr Lincoln LN4 3SL. Tel 44 1526 378-231, Fax: 44 1526 378 315.

COMPANY STAFF

General Manager. Freddie Stockdale.
Bibliography. Information supplied by the company.

Thanks to the Administration, Pavilion Opera.

Other English Companies

Other companies in England are noted below by name, address, telephone, fax, recent repertory, and general director (as available).

Almeida Opera. Almeida Theatre, Almeida Street, London N1 1TA. Tel: 44 171 226 7432, Fax: 44 171 704 9581. **Recent Repertory:** premieres of newly-commissioned operas: Experimentum Mundi (Giorgio Battistelli), Or the Hapless Landing (Heiner Goebbels), Variété (Mauricio Kagel), Vanitas (Salvatore Sciarrino), Broken Strings (Param Vir), Snatched by the Gods (Param Vir). **Director:** Jonathan Reekie.

City of Birmingham Touring Opera. (Touring Company): 205 The Argent Centre, 60 Frederick St., Birmingham B1 3HS. Tel: 44 121 212 4215, Fax: 44 121 236 6434. **Artistic Director:** Graham Vick.

D'Oyly Carte Opera Company. (Touring Company): 59-65 John Bright Street, Birmingham B1 1GS. Tel: 44 121 643 2021, Fax: 44 121 643 1786. **General Manager:** Ray Brown.

Surrey Opera. 712 Gainsborough Road, Tilgate, Crawley, West Sussex RH10 5LJ. Tel: 44 1293 532 692. **Artistic Director:** Jonathan Butcher.

British Opera Company. The Coach House, 56 Lawrie Park Gardens, London SE26 6XJ. Tel: 44 181 659-5955, Fax: 44 181 659-4582. **Director:** Norman McCann.

English Touring Opera. (Touring Company): 121 West Block, Westminster Business Square, Durham Street, London SE11 5JH. Tel: 44 171 820 1131, Fax: 44 171 735 7008. **Director:** Andrew Greenwood.

European Chamber Opera. (International Touring Company): 60c Kyverdale Road, London N16 7AJ: Tel: 44 181 806 4231, Fax: 44 181 806 4465. **Artistic Director:** Stefan Paul Sanchez.

London Opera Players. (Touring Company): Broadmeade Copse, Westwood Lane, Wanborough, Surrey GU3 2JN. Tel: 44 1483 811 004, Fax: 44 1483 811 721. **Director:** Elizabeth Parry.

Mecklenburgh Opera. (Touring Company): Number Eight, 1 Benjamin Street, London EC 1M 5QL. Tel: 44 171 608 1974, Fax: 44 171 608 2201. **Recent Repertory:** 20th century opera and music theater, including new commissions. **General Manager:** Brian Matcham.

Pocket Opera. (Touring Company): Brixton Opera Center, Wiltshire Road, London SW9 7NE. Tel and Fax: 44 1264 737 351. **Artistic Director:** Michael Armitage.

Spitalfields Market Opera. 4-5 Lamb Street, Spitalfields, London E1 6EA. Tel: 44 171 375 2637, Fax: 44 171 247 6178. **Artistic Director:** Phillip Parr.

Travelling Opera. 114 St. Mary's Road, Market Harborough, Leics LE16 7DX. Tel: 44 1858 434677, Fax: 44 1858 463 617. **Artistic Director:** Peter Knapp.

Finland

Suomen Kansallisooppera
(Finnish National Opera)

The Suomen Kansallisooppera (Finnish National Opera), originally called the Domestic Opera, was born on October 2, 1911, with Ruggero Leoncavallo's *I pagliacci* sung in Swedish, and Jules Massenet's *La Navarraise* sung in Finnish. The Finnish prima donna, Aïno Ackté, assayed the title roll of *La Navarraise*. Finally, five unsuccessful attempts and as the 20th century was drawing to a close, Helsinki received a new Oopperatalo (Opera House), inaugurated on November 30, 1993, with Aulis Sallinen's *Kullervo*, performed by the Finnish National Opera. Architects Eero Hyvämäki, Jukka Karhunen, and Risto Parkkinen designed the structure.

Opera in Finland goes back to 1873, when the Singing Section at the Finnish Theater was founded by Kaarlo Bergbom. They offered Gaetano Donizetti's *Lucia di Lammermoor* in a small provincial house. Insufficient funding forced a long hiatus in performances until 1911, when the Domestic Opera was founded with Ackté as its first artistic director. (It is the custom in Scandinavia for former singers to direct opera companies.) Her "prima donna" attitude, however, resulted in her departure from the company soon thereafter, and the job of holding the fledgling company together fell to Edvard Frazer. Frazer even spent most of his own money on the company. The first name change occurred in 1914, when the company became the Finnish Opera. Initially only six operas a year were mounted in the National Theater, which had opened in 1902. The theater, however, was ill-equipped to handle operatic performances. When the Bolshevik revolution in Russia broke out, Finland seceded from Russia, declaring its independence on December 6, 1917, and the Finnish Opera became the Finnish National Opera. The new Finnish Republic appropriated all of the former Russian Empire's property, including the Aleksanterin teatteri (Alexander Theater). Built in 1879, the small theater was transformed into a new home for opera. On January 19, 1919, with a performance of

Giuseppe Verdi's *Aida*, the company moved into the Aleksanterin teatteri, renamed the Finnish National Opera House. This was the company's permanent home for the next 74 years. Foreign artists filled many posts in the Finnish National Opera, since there were not enough trained Finnish professionals.

As the company's operations were irregular up to this point, World War I did not affect them. After the war, in 1919, the Hungarian-German conductor Franz Mikorey offered a Richard Wagner series, opening with *Tannhäuser*. The organization in the 1920s under Fazer (who stayed at the helm until 1938) offered six to seven premieres a season, with around 20 operas in the repertory and a total of 150 performances. Not infrequently, the performances were international — three languages could be heard in a single performance. By the mid 1920s, the company was almost bankrupt. The Parliment came to the rescue, organizing State run lotteries and football pool funds, money from which was used to support the opera. The 1920s also witnessed the premiere of a "national opera," Leevi Madetoja's *Pohjalaisia* (The Ostrobothnians) and less mainstream works like Leoš Janáček's *Jenůfa* and Ernst Křenek's *Jonny spielt auf*. The next decade saw the complete *Der Ring des Nibelungen* mounted. Opera was very popular during World War II, and although the house was damaged during the air raids, it was not serious. After the war, more 20th-century works entered the repertory including Benjamin Britten's *Peter Grimes*. Tauno Pylkkänen, called a "Finnish Puccini," created several works for the opera stage, including *Mare and His Son*, *Simo Hurtta*, and *Opri and Oleksi*.

In 1956, the Finnish National Opera was converted from a company to a trust with the establishment of the Finnish National Opera Foundation. Afterwards, more modern operas graced the stage, like Alban Berg's *Lulu* and *Wozzeck*, and Dmitry Shostakovich's *Ledi Makbet Mtsenskovo uyezda* (Lady Macbeth of the Mtsensk District).

A forgotten Finnish opera, Aarre Merikanto's *Juha* was also rediscovered. This awoke a Finnish creative chord and the Finnish National Opera presented eight world premieres of Finnish operas during the 1970s — Einojuhani Rautavaara's *Apollo and Marsyas*, Ilkka Kuusisto's *The Moomins*, Joonas Kokkonen's *Viimeiset kiusaukset* (The Last Tempatations), Erkki Salmenhaars's *The Portuguese Woman*, Kuusisto's *Man's Rib*, Jorma Panula's *Jaakko Ilkka*, Sallinen's *Punainen viiva* (The Red Line), and Kalevi Aho's *Avain* (The Key). During this "nationalistic streak," the standard repertory was neglected.

With the opening of the new opera house, the repertory reverted to a more traditional mode, including Wolfgang Amadeus Mozart's *Don Giovanni* and *Die Zauberflöte*, Gioachino Rossini's *Il barbiere di Siviglia*, and Giacomo Puccini's *Tosca*. The intention is to keep one contemporary work, usually Finnish, in the schedule each season. In this vein, Helsinki recently saw Erik Bergman's *The Singing Tree*, Kalevi Aho's *Insect Life*, and Kuusisto's *Come back, Gabriel*. The declining budget has caused the cancellation of some new operas and a limitation on guest artists. There is a "black box" where children's operas and world premieres of experimental works are staged. The repertory is slowly expanding from 12 operas to a goal of 20 a year, but they are moving slowly, since almost no productions could be kept from the old opera house and everything must be created anew for the new house.

The opera company was under the directorship of Walton Grönroos when it moved into its new home. Actually the famous Finnish bass Martti Talvela was slated to become the director, but he died suddenly of a heart attack, so Grönroos was tapped for the position. He explained that a new opera company had to be built up because the old house had no space and only 500 seats, so the situation was very different. His goal was to create a good ensemble of singers, conductors, and directors, so there was not such a great need for guest artists, mainly due to a decrease in funding. There is an ensemble of 30 singers who perform most of the roles, and the schedule is partially determined by what roles they can and cannot sing. Verdi's *Don Carlo* had three guest singers, but Mozart's *Don Giovanni* had none. He was satisfied with the tenors and basses, but the ensemble lacked dramatic sopranos. He also wanted to improve the technical proficiency

of the orchestra. There were two in-house conductors but no stage directors.

The company must raise 25% of their budget, eliminating the possibility of experimental or updating productions. The only new works are Finnish, but the company must steer a traditional course to cater to a traditional audience, since there is a need for box office revenue. Also, the new opera house itself attracts new visitors to every performance and the company wants to keep these newcomers. Corporate sponsorship has also begun and the company recently signed a contract with an insurance company for FM 9 million over 5 years. Corporate sponsorship is a new concept in Finland.

The new productions of Verdi's *Don Carlo* and Mozart's *Don Giovanni* were conventional, lacking inspiration, but the opera house's technical facilities were outstanding. Sets changes were impressive — one set was pulled up as the next was lowered in the matter of a minute or so, or sets turned with a flip of a switch. One could understand the former general director's desire to "build" an ensemble which is uniformly strong. The cast was uneven, even among the guest performers, with some good singing and some that still needed to be worked on. The only singer of international stature was the Finnish bass Matti Salminen, whose sound, stage presence, and Italian diction shone over the others. The orchestra was promising, but also needed work, since at times the beat was off and the notes wrong. The companies recent offerings include Mozart's *Le nozze di Figaro*, Georges Bizet's *Carmen*, Modest Mussorgsky's *Boris Godunov*, Verdi's *La traviata*, and Wagner's *Die Walküre* and *Siegfried*.

Oopperatalo Helsinki

The first proposal for an opera house was made back in 1817, which was very curious since at that time there were no regular opera performances in Finland. The second proposal for an opera house came from architect G. Palmqvist in 1916, after the formation of the Domestic Opera. It would have been located where the University Forestry Faculty building now stands. The third proposal came the following year, to be located on the site where the Parliment House was later constructed. On the 75th anniversary of opera in Finland, in 1948, the City of Helsinki promised a

Oopperatalo Helsinki (Finnish National Opera) (Helsinki, Finland).

site for the opera house but this time the Social Insurance Institution claimed the location. In 1950, the Finnish National Opera petitioned for land along the main thoroughfare in Helsinki, the Mannerheimintie, but two hotels, Inter-Continental and the Hesperia were erected instead. After this last failure, an Opera House Foundation was established which announced an architectural competition on September 3, 1975, attracting 101 entries. More than a year later the results were announced, on January 10, 1977, with architects Eero Hyvämäki, Jukka Karhunen, and Risto Parkkinen submitting the winning entry. Nine more years passed, however, before excavation began. The cornerstone was laid on November 1, 1988, and six years later, construction was completed. The cost approached $190 million (FM 760 million).

The Oopperatalo is a huge white structure of glass, granite and white square tiles, located on the shores of Töölönlahti Bay. Open and airy, the opera house has numerous glass walls which permit commanding views of the bay, Hesperia Park, and the "green-heart" of Helsinki. A pseudo proscenium arch with OOPPERA and OPERAN in large letters welcomes visitors to the Manner-heimintie entrance. The auditorium is in classic opera house style, semi-circular with three un-adorned white tiers, light wood trim, and chrome railings. Black cloth seats, shaped to fit the contour of the back, accommodate the audience. Warm-wood walls, cherry wood floors, and a plain black proscenium arch, with two "crowns" of acoustic panels, ensure good acoustics. The auditorium holds 1365 patrons.

Practical Information. Suomen Kansallisooppera, Helsinginkatu 58, Box 176, 00251 Helsinki. Tel: 358 9 403021, Fax: 358 9 4030 2305. When visiting the Finnish National Opera, stay at the Inter*Continental Hotels Helsinki, Mannerheimintie 46, 00260 Helsinki. Tel: 358 0 40 551 or 1 800 327 0200, Fax 358 0 405 5255. It is across from Hesperia Park, just two blocks from the opera. The hotel can help with opera tickets and schedules.

COMPANY STAFF AND WORLD PREMIERES

General Directors. (Finnish National Opera 1956–present): Juhani Raiskinen (1997–present), Walton Grönroos (1992–96), Ilkka Kuusisto

(1984–92), Juhani Raiskinen (1974–84), Leif Seger-stam (1973–74), Kaj Kauhanen (1972–73), Ulf Söderblom (1971–72), Alfons Almi (1960–71). **(Finnish Opera 1914–56):** Jouko Tolonen (1955–60), Sulo Räikkönen (1952–55), Oiva Soini (1939–52), Aino Ackté (1938–39). **(Domestic Opera 1911–14):** Edvard Fazer (1911–38).

    World Premieres. (Finnish Opera) A. Launis' *The Seven Brothers* 1913; A. Launis's *Kullervo* 1917; O. Merikanto's *Regina von Emmeritz* 1920; L. Madetoja's *Pohjalaisia* (The Ostrobothians) 1924; I. Krohn's *The Deluge* 1928; V. Raitio's *Jefta's Daughter* 1931; L. Madetoja's *Juha* 1935; V. Raitio's *Princess Cecilia* 1936; V. Raitio's *Two Queens* 1944; T. Pylkkänen's *Mare and His Son* 1945; T. Pylkkänen's *Simo Hurtta* 1948; V. Pesola's *The Islanders* 1950; T. Pylkkänen's *Opri and Oleksi* 1958; L. Saikkola's *Ristin* 1959; T. Pylkkänen's *Ikaros* 1960; A. Similä's *Lemmis' Son* 1961; T. Pylkkänen's *The Unknown Soldier* 1967; E. Rautavaara's *Apollo and Marsyas* 1973; I. Kuusisto's *The Moomins* 1974; J. Kokkonen's *Viimeiset kiusauk-*set (The Last Tempatations) 1975; E. Salmenhaars's *The Portuguese Woman* 1976; I. Kuusisto's *Man's Rib* 1978; J. Panula's *Jaakko Ilkka* 1978; A. Sallinen's *Punainen viiva* (The Red Line) 1979; K. Aho's *Avain* (The Key) 1979; I. Kuusisto's *War for Light* 1981; P. Heininnen's *The Damask Drum* 1984; E. Rautavaara's *Vincent* 1990; E. Rautavaara's *The Sunset House* 1991; J. Linkola's *Elina* 1992; E. Bergman's *The Singing Tree* 1995; I. Kuusisto's *Come back, Gabriel* 1998.

    Bibliography. *Oopperatalo Helsinki* * *Opera House Helsinki* (Helsinki, 1995). Lea Venkula Vauraste & Hannu-Iiari Lampila, *Suomen Kansallisooppera* * *Finnish National Opera* (Helsinki, 1994). Lea Venkula-Vauraste (ed.), *Suomen Kansallisoopperan talo* * *The Finnish National Opera House* (Helsinki, 1979). Additional information supplied by the company. Interview with Walton Grönroos, former general director, November 1995.

Thanks to Leena Nivanka, Suomen Kansallisooppera (Finnish National Opera); Anneli Halonen, Embassy of Finland, Washington D.C., and Olof Jurva.

SAVONLINNA

Savonlinnan Oopperajuhlat (Savonlinna Opera Festival)

    The Savonlinnan Oopperajuhlat (Savonlinna Opera Festival) was founded in 1912 by a Finnish diva, Aïno Ackté, with the presentation of Melartin's *Aino.* Four more opera seasons followed, and except for Charles Gounod's *Faust,* offered in 1916 (the last season before its first demise), Finnish operas dominated the schedule: Oskar Merikanto's *Elinan surma* (The Death of Elina), Fredrik Pacius's *Kaarle-kuninkaan metsästys* (The Hunt of Charles the King), and Merikanto's *Pohjan neiti* (The Maid of Pohja). In 1930, there was an attempt to revive the festival offering Leevi Madetoja's *Pohjalaisia* (The Ostrobothnians) and Hannikainen's *Talkootanssit* (The Village Dance), but after the season was over, it disappeared again.

    The current Savonlinnan Oopperajuhlat was inaugurated on July 16, 1967, with Ludwig van Beethoven's *Fidelio,* and a cast which included both Finnish artists and students. The town of Savonlinna organized the festival until 1972, and the repertory slowly became more mainstream, including Giuseppe Verdi's *Il trovatore, Un ballo in maschera* and *Rigoletto,* and Richard Strauss's *Salome,* although Finnish works were not forgot-ten, including Aarre Merikanto's *Juha.* In 1972, an Opera Festival Patron's Association was formed to give the festival financial support, and the famous Finnish bass Martti Talvela became artistic director of the festival. This helped to slowly raise the festival to a more international recognition, although it was hampered by the presentation of the operas in Finnish. This changed when another Finnish opera singer, Timo Mustakallio, took over. With the singing of operas in their original language, more foreign artists began appearing and a more international audience followed. The repertory continued to expand, and by the mid-1990s offered Richard Wagner's *Der fliegende Holländer,* Verdi's *Macbeth,* Wolfgang Amadeus Mozart's *Die Zauberflöte,* Pietro Mascagni's *Cavalleria rusticana,* Ruggero Leoncavallo's *I pagliacci,* along with productions from the Mariinski Theater including Dmitri Shostakovich's *Ledi Makbet Mtsenskovo uyezda* (Lady Macbeth of the Mtsensk District), Giacomo Puccini's *Tosca,* Alexander Borodin's *Prince Igor,* and Wagner's *Parsifal.* The budget is around FM 5–6 million.

    The second half of the 1990s witnessed two Finnish opera world premieres, Aulis Sallinen's

The Palace on July 26, 1995, and, in celebration of the 80th anniversary of the festival, Einojuhani Rautavaara's *Aleksis Kivi* on July 8, 1997. Recent productions include Wagner's *Tannhäuser*, Verdi's *La forza del destino* and *I masnadieri*, Benjamin Britten's *Peter Grimes*, Gaetano Donizetti's *Anna Bolena*, Sallinen's *Kullervo*, and Gioachino Rossini's *Il barbiere di Siviglia*.

Olavinlinna

The greystone Olavinlinna Castle, perched on a small rock islet near the center of Savonlinna, hosts the opera festival. Built in 1475 by the Danish-born knight Erik Axel Tott, the castle offers an auditorium in its courtyard. Massive walls surround the courtyard, which is sheltered from the elements during performances. It accommodates 2,200 people.

Practical Information. Savonlinna Opera Festival, Olavinkatu 35, 57130 Savonlinna. Tel: 358 57 57 67 50, Fax: 358 57 218 66. When visiting Savonlinna Opera Festival, contact the Savonlinna Tourist Service, Puistokatu 1, 57100 Savonlinna, Finland. Tel 358 57 134 92, Fax: 368 57 514 449.

COMPANY STAFF AND
OPERA FESTIVAL PREMIERES

Artistic Directors. Jorma Hynninen (1991–present), Walton Grönroos (1987–91, Ralf Gothóni (1984–87), Timo Mustakallio (1980–84), Martti Talvela (1972–80).

Opera Festival Premieres. 1912: Melartin's *Aino*. 1913: O. Merikanto's *Elinan surma* (The Death of Elina). 1914: F. Pacius's *Kaarle-kuninkaan metsästys* (The Hunt of Charles the King). 1916: O. Merikanto's *Pohjan neiti* (The Maid of Pohja), Gounod's *Faust*. 1930: L. Madetoja's *Pohjalaisia* (The Ostrobothnians), Hannikainen's *Talkootanssit* (The Village Dance). 1967: L. Beethoven's *Fidelio*. 1968: G. Verdi's *Il trovatore*. 1969: R. Strauss's *Salome*. 1970: O. Merikanto's *Juha*. 1971: G. Verdi's *Un ballo in maschera*. 1972: G. Verdi's *Rigoletto*, Twardowski's *The Tragedy*. 1973: W.A. Mozart's *Die Zauberflöte*. 1974: M. Mussorgsky's *Boris Godunov*. 1975: A. Sallinen's *Ratsumies* (The Horseman). 1977: J. Kokkonen's *Viimeiset kiusaukset* (The Last Temptations). 1979: G. Verdi's *Don Carlos*. 1981: R. Wagner's *Der fliegende Holländer*. 1982: A. Sallinen's *Punainen viiva* (The Red Line). 1984: A. Sallinen's *Kuningas lähtee Ranskaan* (The King Goes Forth to France). 1985: G. B. Pergolesi's *La serva padrona*. 1986: G. Verdi's *Aida*, Sibelius's *Myrsky* (The Tempest), K. Aho's *Avain* (The Key), B. Britten's *The Rape of Lucretia*. 1987: G. Bizet's *Carmen*, Mussorgsky's *Khovanshchina*, J. Offenbach's *Orphée aux enfers*. 1988: G. Puccini's *Madama Butterfly*. 1989: P. Heininen's *Veitsi* (The Knife), G. Puccini's *Tosca*, De Frumerie's *Singoalla*. 1990: Miki's *Shunkin-Sho*, Telemann's *Pimpinone*. 1991: B. Smetana's *Prodaná nevěsta* (The Bartered Bride), A. Dvořák's *Rusalka*, W.A. Mozart's *Don Giovanni*. 1992: W.A. Mozart's *Die Entführung aus dem Serail*. 1993: G. Verdi's *Macbeth*. 1995: A. Sallinen's *The Palace*. 1997: E. Rautavaara's *Aleksis Kivi*.

Bibliography. *The Savonlinna Opera Festival: Every Year in July* (1994). Aino Ackté, *Taiteeni taipaleelta* (Helsinki, 1935). Seppe Heikinheimo, *Martti Talvela: Jättiläisen muotokuva* (Helsinki, 1978).

--- TAMPERE

Tampereen Ooppera

Leevi Madetoja's *Pohjalaisia* (The Ostrobothnians, (Finland's national opera) performed in the spring of 1947, inaugurated the Tampereen Ooppera. Georges Bizet's *Carmen* followed in the fall. The company was established as an amateur opera society under the artistic direction of Seppe Silvan with a bank loan of FM 20,000. The humble beginnings of the Tampereen Ooppera are similar to those of regional opera companies in the smaller cities in the United States. (See Zietz's *Opera Companies and Houses of the United States: A Comprehensive, Illustrated Reference*, McFarland, Jefferson N.C. & London, 1995.)

Opera had been heard in Tampere before the founding of the company. As early as 1910, Pietro Mascagni's *Cavalleria rusticana* was presented, followed a decade later by Oskar Merikanto's *Elinan surman* (Elina's Death), three years after the opera had received its world premiere in Helsinki. In 1934, Tampere witnessed Pyotr Il'yich Tchaikovsky's *Eugene Onegin* conducted by Eero Kosonen, who also led Gaetano Donizetti's *La fille du régiment* the following season. On May 24, 1945, an outdoor performance of Friedrich von Flotow's *Martha* was given. The following year, the Tampere Opera was founded. The seeds

Tampere-talo (Tampere, Finland).

for the company were actually planted during World War II, when there was an attempt to form the amateur opera society, but due to the war, it never "got off the ground." The company's first meeting took place on December 8, 1946, and a few months later, their first opera was mounted.

The company's repertory included unusual works. Operas as varied as Daniel Auber's *Fra Diavolo*, Gian Carlo Menotti's *The Consul*, Jules Massenet's *Manon*, Igor Stravinsky's *L'histoire du soldat*, Richard Wagner's *Der fliegende Holländer*, Charles Gounod's *Faust*, and Tchaikovsky's *Iolanta*, *Eugene Onegin* and *Pikovaya dama* (The Queen of Spades) were offered. The company has introduced several operas to Finland as well, among them Leoš Janáček's *Věc Makropulos* (The Makropulos Affair), Kurt Weill's *Der Aufstieg und Fall der Stadt Mahagonny*, and Christoph Willibald Gluck's *Iphigénie en Tauride*, alongside the repertory favorites like Donizetti's *La fille du régiment*, *Don Pasquale*, and the Finnish premiere of *L'elisir d'amore*, Wolfgang Amadeus Mozart's *Die Zauberflöte*, *Le nozze di Figaro*, *Don Giovanni*, and the Finnish premiere of *Bastien und Bastienne*. There

have been several works by Giacomo Puccini — *Madama Butterfly*, *La bohème*, *Il trittico*, *Tosca*, *Manon Lesaut*, *La fanciulla del West*, and Giuseppe Verdi — *Il trovatore*, *La traviata*, *Rigoletto*, *Otello*, *Un ballo in maschera*, including the Finnish premiere of *Macbeth* (1964) on the boards. Several Finnish operas have been given, including Pacius's *Kaarle kuninkaan metsästys* (The Hunt of Charles the King), Merikanto's *Elinan surma* (Elina's Death) and Leevi Madetoja's *Pohjalaisia* (The Ostrobothnians), and the world premieres of Tauno Pylkkänen's *Varjo* (The Shadow) and *Batsheba Saarenmaala*, Sonninen's *Haavruuva*, and Tauno Marttinen's *Faaraon kirje*.

The future points to the establishment of a foundation to ensure the financial security of opera in Tampere. One problem is the large size of the company's performance venue, Tampere Hall, compared to the population of 175,000 in a city where there is no operatic heritage. A foundation would give the company a new beginning and help fulfill their ambition to raise their standards to a fully professional level. The artistic director, Seppe Silvan, has been with the company since its founding in 1946 and will soon step down. The other ambition of the company is to establish a "Winter Savonlinna Festival" in Tampere. They feel that if they can obtain a budget similar to that of the Savonlinna Festival (FM 5-6 million), their goal could be realized. The current budget is FM 1 million with the government contributing around half. Two operas are mounted each year. Recent productions include Gioachino Rossini's *Il barbiere di Siviglia*, Puccini's *Tosca*, Verdi's *Il trovatore*, Tchaikovsky's *Pikovaya dama* (The Queen of Spades), Ruggero Leoncavallo's *I pagliacci* and the Finnish premiere of Luigi Dallapiccola's *Il prigioniero*.

Tampere-Talo

Tampere-talo (Tampere Hall) was inaugurated in 1990. Designed by Sakari Aartelo and Esa Piironen and owned by the city of Tampere, it is part of the largest congress and concert center in Scandanavia. The entire complex cost FM 304.

Located on the edge of Sorsapuisto Park, beside Sorsalampi duck pond, Tampere-talo is a huge free-form structure with a facade of electrically heated glass and white ceramic tiles. The sparkling white auditorium holds one zig-zag tier that floats above the orchestra level which is divided into contoured asymmetrical seating sections. Auditorium walls are of bleached Finnish birch which contrasts with the blue seats. There are 1806 places.

Practical Information. Tampereen Ooppera, Vellamonkatu 2C, 33100 Tampere. Tel: 358 931-212-7726, Fax: 358 931-222-0266. Tampere-talo, Yliopistonkatu 55, 33100 Tampere. Tel: 358 931 243-4111, Fax: 358 931-243-4197. When visiting the Tampereen Ooppera, stay at the Sokos Hotel Ilves, Hatanpäänualtatie 1, 33101 Tampere. Tel: 358 931 212-1212, Fax: 358 931 213-2565. It is centrally located and convenient to the opera house and can assist with opera tickets and schedules.

COMPANY STAFF AND PREMIERES

Artistic Director. Seppo Silvan (1946–present) *World Premieres.* T. Pylkkänen's *Varjo*, fall 1954; T. Pylkkänen's *Batsheba Saarenmaala*, fall 1959; Sonninen's *Haavruuva*, spring 1975; Marttinen's *Faaraon kirje*, fall 1982. *Finnish Premieres.* W. A. Mozart's *Bastien und Bastienne*, autumn 1955; Donizetti's *L'elisir d'amore*, spring 1962; G. Verdi's *Macbeth*, autumn 1964; L. Janáček's *Věc Makropulos* (The Makropulos Affair), spring 1967; K. Weill's *Der Aufstieg und Fall der Stadt Mahagonny*, spring 1968; G. Rossini's *Le Comte Ory*, spring 1969; W. Egk's *Der Revisor* autumn 1978; C. W. Gluck's *Iphigénie en Tauride*, spring 1979; Pasatieri's *Signor Deluso*, spring 1980; P.M. Davies's *The Lighthouse*, spring 1985; R. Kurka's *Good Soldier Schweik*, autumn 1985; A. Schönberg's *Erwartung*, autumn 1984; L. Dallapiccola's *Il prigioniero*, spring 1996.

Bibliography. Käsiohjelmat kertovat: Tampereen Ooppera 1946–1986 (Tampere, 1986). *Blue Line: Tampere Hall.* Additional information supplied by the company. Interview with Jarmo Hakkarainen, head of programming, Tampere-talo, November 1995.

Thanks to Ritva Loimu, Tampereen Ooppera, and Pirjo Ojanperä.

VAASA

Vaasan Ooppera

On April 1, 1958, Leevi Madetojas's *Pohjalaisia* (The Ostrobothnians) (Finland's national opera) inaugurated the Vaasan Ooppera. It was the sole offering of the inaugural season. The Finnish opera diva Irma Rewell had founded the company two years earlier, and she still remains the heart and soul of the operation after more than forty years. Although Rewell had a promising career as a singer, she had married into a wealthy Vaasa family and did not want to travel.

The company's second season also offered only a single work, Johann Strauß's *Der Zigeunerbaron*, but by the third season, the repertory had expanded to two works, Pietro Mascagni's *Cavalleria rusticana* and Georges Bizet's *Carmen*. Rewell feels that in a city of only 56,000, a two-opera season is the maximum a city the size of Vaasa can sustain. During the company's first twenty years, many of the company's productions — Giuseppe Verdi's *Nabucco*, Giacomo Puccini's *Tosca*, Jacques Offenbach's *Les contes d'Hoffmann*, and Amilcare Ponchielli's *La gioconda* — frequently featured Rewell in the leading roll.

It is an adventurous company, best known for commissioning new works, which Rewell feels is important. They include Aaro Kentala's

Tampere-talo auditorium (Tampere, Finland).

Morsiustaivas, Ilkka Kuusisto's *Jääkäri Ståhl* and *Fröken Julie*, Toivo Kuula's *Kuula 1918*, and Atso Almila's *Ameriikka*. Rewell's dream is to turn *Who's Afraid of Virginia Woolf?* into an opera. The company has mounted Scandanavian premieres as well, like Ulo Vinter's *Peppi Pitkätossu* and Lorenzo Ferrero's *Marilyn*, and the European premiere of Scott Joplin's *Treemonisha*. The productions are creative, and the repertory is decided by the roles the singers she finds are able to sing.

Vaasan Ooppera (Vaasa, Finland).

She auditions around 200 singers for her two opera productions. For Ferrero's *Marilyn*, not only did Rewell find a coloratura soprano, Pia Skibdahl, with a good voice, but also the singer looked like Marilyn (Monroe). One of her problems is when she finds good singer, he or she usually gets a contract soon thereafter in Euorpe and she loses them. Probably one of the more interesting stories concerns a 19-year-old tenor, slated for military service. In Finland, however, one can perform civil service in lieu of military, and Rewell convinced the authorities that singing in an opera ompany constituted civil service, so she had the service of this young, promising tenor for two years, for free!

Her budget is FM 1 million. The company's home is a 1906-Jugendstil structure of off-white. In 1992, a modern addition was constructed on the building, and on January 15, 1993, Ferrero's *Marilyn* welcomed the Vaasan Ooppera into its new home. The square-shaped auditorium is black, with bright stripes on the black cloth seats adding the only color to the space. There are 380 seats. The company also performs in a summer festival called the Ohjelma Ilmajoen Musiikkijuhlat.

Practical Information. Vaasan Ooppera, Koulukatu 10, 65100 Vaasa. Tel: 358 961 317 3135, Fax: 358 961 317 9971. When visiting the Vaasan Ooppera, stay at the Hotell Vaakuna, Rewell Center, Vaasa. Tel: & Fax: 358 961 312-7175. It is in the center of the city, convenient to the opera, and can help with tickets and schedules.

COMPANY STAFF AND PREMIERES

Oopperanjohtaja. (general director): Irma Rewell (1956–present)

World Premieres. A. Kentala's *Morsiustaivas*, August 25, 1975; I. Kuusisto's *Jääkäri Ståhl*, June 3, 1982; T. Kuula's *Kuula 1918*, January 15, 1987; A. Almila's *Ameriikka*, June 11, 1992; I. Kuusisto's *Fröken Julie*, January 5, 1994. **European Premieres.** S. Joplin's *Treemonisha*, October 7, 1980. **Scandanavian Premieres.** G. Verdi's *Nabucco*, October 10, 1961; U. Vinter's *Peppi Pitkätossu*, May 3, 1990; L. Ferrero's *Marilyn*, January 15, 1993.

Bibliography. Ilmari Laukkonen, *Pohjalaisista Carmenin: Vaasan Ooppera Historia 1956–96.* (Vaasa, 1995). *Finland Festival— Ohjelma Ilmajoen Musiikkijuhlat* (Ilmajoki, 1995). Interview with Irma Rewell, general director, November 1995. Additional information supplied by the company.

Thanks to the Vaasan Ooppera.

Suomen Oopperaliiton
(Finnish Opera League)

The Finnish Opera League was founded in 1968. There are eleven regional companies in Finland that belong to this league. Each company usually offers one or two operas a year. Two of the companies, Vaasan Ooppera and Tampereen Ooppera are profiled in detail in separate enteries. The remaining nine companies are listed below, including name, address, phone and fax number, date of establishment, director, and recent repertory (as available).

Joensuun Oopperayhdistys (Joensuu Opera Society). Kirkkokatu 10 B 17, 80110 Joensuu; Tel: 358 973-224-563. **Year established:** 1977. **Oopperanjohtaja** (director): Raimo Paltakari. **Repertory:** Emmerich Kálmán's *Gräfin Maritza*, Giacomo Puccini's *La bohème*.

Jyväskylän Ooppera. Pitkäkatu 18-22, 40700 Jyväskylä; Tel: 358 941-618-131, Fax: 358 941-211-803. **Year established:** 1973. **Oopperanjohtaja** (director): Juhani Laurila. **Repertory:** Albert Lortzing's *Undine*.

Kotkan Ooppera. Kottaraisentie 12, 48220 Kotka; Tel: 358 952-610-935, Fax: 358 952-601-936. **Year established:** 1967. **Oopperanjohtaja** (director): Veijo Räsänen. **Repertory:** Ilkka Kuusisto's *Miehen kylkiluu*, Baldassare Galuppi's *Il filosofo di campagna.*

Kuopian Musiikinystavain Yhdistys Ry (Kuopio Society of Music Friends). Vuorikatu 15, 70100 Kuopio; Tel & Fax; 358 971-261-8893. **Year established:** 1988.

Lahden Ooppera. Kuhilaankatu 6, 15900 Lahti; Tel: 358 918-753-5236. **Year established:** 1962. **Oopperanjohtaja** (director): Marja Tikka. **Repertory:** chamber opera.

Mikkelin Oopperayhdistys. (Mikkeli Opera Society). Vuorikatu 3A, 50100 Mikkeli; Tel: 358 955-162-063, Fax: 358 995 191 2323. **Year established:** 1974. **Administrator:** Kimmo Suortamo. **Repertory:** Giuseppe Verdi's *Un ballo in maschera.*

Oulun Ooppera. Oulun kaupunginteatteri, Kaarlenväylä 2, 90100 Oulu; Tel: 358 981-3147-246. **Year established:** 1965. **Oopperanjohtaja** (director): Leena Salonen. **Repertory:** Joonas Kokkonen's *Viimeiset kiusaukset* (The Last Temptation), Gioachino Rossini's *L'italiana in Algeri.*

Porin Opera. Pietniementie 22, 28660 Pori; Tel & Fax: 358 939-637-8125. **Year established:** 1976. **Toiminnanjohtaja** (acting director): Heikki Jylhäsaari. **Repertory:** Bedřich Smetana's *Prodaná nevěsta* (The Bartered Bride).

Turun Oopperayhdistys (Turku Opera Society). Aninkaistenkatu 9, 20110 Turku; Tel: 358 921-231-4563, Fax: 358 921-233-7730. **Year established:** 1964. **Oopperanjohtaja** (director): Seppe Ristilehto. **Repertory:** Georges Bizet's *Les pêcheurs de perles.*

France

AIX-EN-PROVENCE

Festival d'Aix-en-Provence (Summer Festival)

The first Festival d'Aix-en-Provence opened in 1948 with works by Darius Milhaud. Founded by Gabriel Dussurget, the festival also offered Wolfgang Amadeus Mozart's *Don Giovanni* during the inaugural season. Mozart operas became the mainstay of the festival with at least one performed each season. *Così fan tutte* entered the repertory in 1950, *Le nozze di Figaro* in 1952, *Idomeneo* in 1963, and *La clemenza di Tito* in 1974, the same year Bernard Lefort replaced Dussurget as festival director. During Dussurget's tenure, the non–Mozart works offered were primarily from the Baroque and early 19th century: Domenico Cimarosa's *Il matrimonio segreto*, Claudio Monteverdi's *La favola d'Orfeo* and *L'incoronazione di Poppea*, Franz Joseph Haydn's *Il mondo della luna*, Christoph Willibald Gluck's *Orfeo ed Euridice*, André Grétry's *Zemire et Azor*, Jean-Philippe Rameau's *Platée*, and Gioachino Rossini's *L'italiana in Algeri*. Other works included Charles Gounod's *Mireille*, and selections from the contemporary repertory: Henri Sauguet's *Les Caprices de Marianne*, Henri Barraud's *Lavinia*, and Claude Debussy's *Pelléas et Mélisande*. Under Lefort's tenure, the emphasis turned more to big name stars, with at least one or two in each opera. Montserrat Caballé was imported for several seasons, including singing the title role in Rossini's *Semiramide*, in a production conceived by Pier-Luigi Pizzi. The festival also hosted Marilyn Horne and Katia Ricciarelli. When Louis Erlo took over the directorship, big name stars continued with Samuel Ramey, Barbara Hendricks, and Jessye Norman in Richard Strauss's *Ariadne auf Naxos*, and José van Dam in Giuseppe Verdi's *Falstaff*. The festival has been the venue for American singers making their European debut, among which were Thomas Hampson and Dawn Upshaw. The tricentennial of Jean-Baptiste Lully's death was celebrated with an unearthing of his *Psyché*, originally written in 1678. During the 1989 season, the world premiere of Claude Prey's *Le Rouge et la Noir* was staged on July 20.

The 1990s witnessed a Carl Maria von Weber "cycle" with *Euryanthe* and *Oberon*, and the first staged performance in France of Georg Friedrich Händel's *Semele* in 1996. Stéphane Lissner took over in 1998 and the festival, after suffering severe financial problems, reorganized. A European Academy of Music was born in 1998, which, with newly-found talent, offered Henry Purcell's *Dido and Aeneas*, Monteverdi's *La favola d'Orfeo*, and Benjamin Britten's *Curlew River*. The conductors, however, are well known, like Claudio Abbado conducting Mozart's *Don Giovanni* and Pierre Boulez conducting Béla Bartók's *A Kékszakállú herceg vára* (Duke Bluebeard's Castle). The operas are given in the courtyard of the Archbishop's Palace, which was originally designed by Cassandre. The budget is 58 million FF.

Practical Information. Festival d'Aix-en-Provence, Service Location, Palais de l'Ancien Archevêché, 13100 Aix-en-Provence. Tel: 33 442 17 34 00, Fax: 33 442 21 14 40. When visiting Festival d'Aix-en-Provence, contact the Office du Tourisme, 2 place du Général de Gaulle, BP 160, 13605 Aix-en-Provence Cedex. Tel: 33 442 16 11 61.

COMPANY STAFF

Directeur Artistique. Stéphane Lissner (1997–present), Louis Erlo (1981–96), Bernard Lefort (1973–80), Gabriel Dussurget (1948–72).

Bibliography. Robert Aubaniac et al. *Les Opéras du Festival d'Aix* (Aix-en-Provence, 1982), Aix-en-Provence sur l'orbite 2000, *L'Express* (February 6, 1997).

Model of new Festival Théâtre (Aix-en-Provence, France).

——— BORDEAUX

Grand Théâtre de Bordeaux

The Grand Théâtre de Bordeaux was inaugurated on April 7, 1780, with Jean Baptist Racine's *Athalie* set to music by Franz Beck, and Blincourt's *Jugement d'Apollon*. Louis François Armand du Plessis, friend and confident of Louis XV, commissioned the Parisian architect Victor Louis to design the structure. The opening night was delayed because of a group of local nobles were displeased with the architect.

The first opera was heard in Bordeaux in 1688, and Franceour's *Pirame et Thysbé* was seen in 1729. Six years later, an opera house was constructed by Mlle Dujardin for her opera company in the public gardens. Fire destroyed it during the 1750s. The Académie Royale de Musique was founded In 1752, with a company of ten singers. After the Grand Théâtre opened, all opera activity shifted there. Although the theater was damaged during the Revolution, it was restored in 1799. During the 1800s, there was a regular opera company which performed a full program, including such works as Fromental Halévy's *La Juive*, Giacomo Meyerbeer's *L'Africaine*, and Richard Wagner's *Götterdämmerung*. When the works of Wagner premiered in the Teatro Comunale in Bologna (see Teatro Comunale, Bologna, entry) they caused much debate and dissension. A similar situation occurred in Bordeaux, but instead, with the operas of Giuseppe Verdi. After Verdi's *La traviata* was staged at the Grand Théâtre, the ensuing controversy compared Verdi's operas to those of Meyerbeer, with many feeling that Verdi's work was inferior. Jules Massenet's *Manon*, on the other hand, was considered by the Bordeaux inhabitants as unintelligible, and Giacomo Puccini's *Tosca* was criticized for not having a ballet. They were even more hostile to Wagner's Ring Cycle — feeling it should have drowned from its own weight.

In the past, many well-known artists visited Bordeaux, including Fyodor Chaliapin, Tito Schipa, Lilly Pons, Giacomo Lauri-Volpi, Elizabeth Schwartzkopf, Lauritz Melchoir, Martti Talvela,

Thomas Allen, Kiri Te Kanawa, and Samuel Ramey. Now, the theater has few, if any, big names.

The opera company has created almost two dozen works in a little more than a century, including Jean Françaix's *La Main de gloire* (1950), and Tomasi's *Sampiero Corso* (1956), and has hosted more than a dozen French premieres, among them Ruggero Leoncavallo's *I pagliacci* (1894), Massenet's *La Navarraise* (1895), Benjamin Britten's *Gloriana*, Paul Hindemith's *Mathis de Maler* (1963), and Antonio Salieri's *Falstaff*. The company has also mounted some rarely seen works, like Massenet's *Le Jongleur de Notre Dame*, Yumi Narci's *Trois Contes de l'Honorable Fleur*, Landowski's *Montségur*, and Gioachino Rossini's *La pietra del Paragone*. In 1950, the Bordeaux Mai Musical was launched which offers opera as part of its program.

The new administration at the opera participates in regional co-productions, primarily with the Théâtre du Capitole de Toulouse, and Théâtre d'Avignon. Despite the above mentioned novelties, the repertory was overwhelmingly conservative (and boring), but has recently become more interesting. If one could only say that for the productions. Recent offerings include Gounod's *Mireille*, Christoph Willibald Gluck's *Orfeo ed Euridice*, Franz Lehár's *Die lustige Witwe*, Gaetano Donizetti's *Don Pasquale*, Wagner's *Der fliegende Holländer*. Puccini's *La bohème*, Léo Delibes's *Lakmé*, and Franz Joseph Haydn's *L'incontro improvviso*.

Grand Théâtre de Bordeaux

The Grand Théâtre, damaged during the revolution, was restored in 1799. During the 1800s, a Second Empire style was imposed upon the auditorium, giving it a red hue. Then in 1871, during the Franco-Prussian War, when Paris was under siege, the Grand Théâtre did duty as the seat of the French Parliment. Finally in 1990-91, it was restored to its original decor of blue, white, and gold by Bernard Fanquernie. Wolfgang Amadeus Mozart's *Die Zauberflöte* reopened the renovated opera house.

The Grand Théâtre stands like a massive Greek temple on its own island. The main facade is lined with twelve Corinthian columns which form a colonnade extending the length of the building. Surmounting the colonnade is a large terrace enclosed by a balustrade and pedestals which holds twelve statues — nine Muses and three Graces. These are the work of sculptures Berruer and Vandendrix. Twenty-one Corinthian pilasters alternating with rectangular windows over arcades line the side of the building. The bell-shaped auditorium with four tiers of balconies displays its original ivory, gold and blue decor. Massive, fluted, gilded Corinthian columns circle the room, dividing the boxes on the 2nd and 3rd tiers. The allegorical ceiling, painted by Robin, is about the city of Bordeaux. In the center of the ceiling hangs a chandelier with 14,000 pieces of Bohemian crystal. There are 1158 seats.

Practical Information. Grand Théâtre de Bordeaux, place de la Comédie, 33025 Bordeaux. Tel: 33 556 00 85 20, Fax: 33 556 81 93 66. When visiting Grand Théâtre de Bordeaux, contact the Office de Tourisme de Bordeaux, 12 cours du XXX Juillet, 33080 Bordeaux Cedex. Tel: 33 556 44 28 41.

COMPANY STAFF

Directeur Artistique. Thierry Fouquet (1996–present), Alain Lombard (1988–95).

Bibliography. Henri Lagrave, Charles Mazouer, Marc Regaldo, *La vie Théâtrale à Bordeaux* (Paris, 1985). Jacques d'Welles, *Le Grand Théâtre de Bordeaux*. Jean Latreyte, *Le Grand Théâtre de Bordeaux* (Bordeaux, 1977).

Thanks to Catherine Lillet, Opéra de Bordeaux.

LYON

Opéra de Lyon

On July 1, 1831, the Grand Théâtre was inaugurated with Adrien Boieldieu's *La Dame Blanche* and a symphonic overture. The evening ended with the tenor Siran singing *Marseillaise*. Architects Chenavard and Pollet designed the new opera house. More than 160 years later, on May 14, 1993, the Opéra de Lyon inaugurated its "new" opera house with the world premiere of Claude

Debussy's *Rodrigue et Chimène*. Jean Nouvel was the architect responsible for the transformation of the Grand Théâtre.

The debut of the Opéra de Lyon goes back to September 17, 1687, when a young Paris musician, Jean-Pierre Legay obtained from the heirs of Jean-Baptiste Lully the rights to offer opera in Lyon. There were, however, two prohibitions: it was forbidden to stage *tragédies lyriques* before it had been presented in Paris; it was forbidden to engage singers or actors of the Academy of Paris within the six months of their leaving the Academy. The "lease" ran three years at a cost of 2,000 livres annually. Legay formed the troupe and repertory, and rented the Salle de Jeu de Paume located on la rue Pizay on November 23, 1687, as a performance venue. Thus the Académie Royale de Musique was born. The Academy opened its doors on January 3, 1688, with a production of Lully's *Phaëton*. During the next six months, 100 performances of the opera were staged. Lully's *Bellérophon* followed on June 20, then his *Armide* on February 2, 1689, and his *Atys* on August 7, 1689. Then the interest of the music-lovers in Lyon waned and Legay went bankrupt. A fire devoured the "theater" on the evening of November 30, 1689. After Legay recovered financially, he returned in 1695. That year, for the first time, operas other than those by Lully entered the repertory. Lyon saw Desmarets's *Les Amours de Momus* and *Didon*, along side Lully's *Alceste*, *Le temple de la paix*, and *Persée*. The Salle de la Place Bellecour hosted the company until 1711, when flooding from the River Saône caused the building to partially collapse. Opera continued at the Salle de l'Hôtel du Gouvernement from 1711 to 1722, and Desmarets's *Iphigénie* and Destouches's *Omphale* and *Callirohé* were presented. When fire claimed this venue, the Academy moved to the Salle de "la Raquette Royale" which, although regarded as temporary quarters, was used for more than thirty years.

Lyon inaugurated the Grand-Théâtre, its first real opera house, on August 3, 1756, with *Britannicus*. This type of free standing theater, although common in Italy, was a novelty in France at that time. The architect, Germain Soufflot, left Lyon before the completion of the structure, and Melchoir Monet took over supervision of the day-to-day construction. Regarding the style of this theater, Souffle had abandoned the long form of the 17th-century theaters and designed an elliptical-shaped hall like those in Parma and Verona, a form that would triumph in the 19th century opera houses. The auditorium held an orchestra level and three box tiers. Opéra comique by André Grétry, Nicolas Dalayrac, and native-born Nicolas Dezède was very popular at the new opera house. Grétry's works included *La fausse magie*, *L'epreuve villageoise*, *L'amant jaloux*, *Lémire et Azor*, *le magnifique*, *Colinette à la Cour*, *Richard*, *Coeur de Lion*, *L'ami de la maison* and *Panurge dans l'Ile des Lanternes*. Other composers and operas performed were Pierre Alexandre Monsigny's *Rose et Colas* and *Le déserteur*, Antonio Sacchini's *Chimène* and *Renaud*, Bezède's *Blaize et Babet*, Christoph Willibald Gluck's *Iphigénie en Tauride* and *Alceste*, and Niccolò Piccinni's *Didon*, *Atys*, and *Le faux Lord*. As the 19th century dawned, the theater was in a state of advanced disrepair. In 1811, a decree was issued authorizing the city to take back the ancient theater, but either the owners refused to sell or they demanded a prohibitive sum of money for the building. It took fourteen years to reach an agreement and on April 14, 1825, a transfer was signed at the Hôtel de Ville. The cost to the city was 1,200,000 francs. On July 26, 1825, a *Programme Officiel pour la Réparation et la Restauration du Grand-Théâtre* appeared, which became the basis for a public competition. Architects Chenavard and Pollet were selected, but rather than repairing and restoring the old theater, it was demolished and construction of a new one began. Meanwhile, a temporary performance space was constructed, known as the Salle de Farge et Falconne, which was opened on May 21, 1827, with Méhul's *La chasse du jeune Henry* and Molière's *Dépit amoureux*. The opera's temporary home saw many impressive works, including Gioachino Rossini's *Le siège de Corinthe*, *Tancredi* and *Le Comte Ory*, Daniel Auber's *La muette de Portici* and *Fra diavolo*, and Fromental Halévy's *Dilettante d'Avignon*.

After the opening of the Grand Théâtre in 1831, grand-opéra was all the rage, having supplanted the *tragédie lyrique* of the previous century. Rossini's *Guillaume Tell* was offered on September 28, 1831, and his *Semiramide* in 1844. Giacomo Meyerbeer first appeared in Lyon the evening of March 10, 1834, with *Robert le Diable*, with tenor Derancourt (Robert) and his soprano wife (Isabelle). Three years later, on April 3, his *Huguenots* was staged in Lyon for the first time. It was a disaster. Two of the lead singers took ill with catastrophic results with the substitutions. The

Opéra de Lyon facade detail of Muses (Lyon, France).

scenery, however, was opulent and much appreciated by the audience. Meyerbeer's *Le Prophète* premiered in Lyon in 1852, followed by *L'étoile du Nord* in 1854, and *L'Africaine* in 1867. Another grand-opéra composer, Halévy triumphed in Lyon with his *La Juive*, first seen on January 12, 1836, with tenors Sylvain (Eleazar), and Lafond (Léopold), and soprano Mme Derancourt (Rachel). It was an unqualified success with a brilliant production created by Savette. The other operas of Halévy were received just as enthusiastically— *Guido et Ginevra ou la peste à Florence* (1840), *Charles VI* (1845), *Reine de Chypre* (1846), and the comic operas *L'éclair* (1836), *Les mousquetaires de la reine* (1846), and *La val d'Andorre* (1850). Gaetano Donizetti was also applauded in Lyon, with his *Lucia di Lammermoor* given in its (rarely performed) French version Lucie de Lammermoor. Donizetti's *La favorite*, *Les Martyrs*, *Dom Sébastien*, *Don Pasquale*, and *La fille du régiment*, and Louis-Ferdinand Hérold's *Zampa* and *Le Pré au Clers* were also repertory favorites. Giuseppe

Verdi entered the repertory first in 1849 with *Jérusalem* (French adaptation of *I Lombardi alla prima crociata*). *Ernani* (as Il proscritto) followed the next year, with *Nabucco* in 1853, *Il trovatore* in 1857, *Rigoletto* in 1860, *La traviata* (as Violetta) in 1862, and *Aida* in 1879.

The theater was run by a system of concession. Artists were engaged for three weeks, and their reengagement depended upon the amount of applause or hisses and whistles they received. There was also a problem with disorder in the theater when performances did not please. One time in 1865, the disturbance escalated to such a degree that the Place de la Comédie in front of the opera house was transformed into a battlefield. The repertory continued to emphasize French works with Ambroise Thomas's *Mignon* and *Hamlet*, Charles Gounod's *Roméo et Juliette*, *Mireille*, and *Faust*, Georges Bizet's *Carmen* (which provoked a "war"), *La jolie fille de Perth*, and *Les pêcheurs de perles*, and Jules Massenet, considered by many to be the heir of Gounod, with a considerable number of his works being hosted in Lyon—*Marie-Magdeleine, Manon, Hérodiade, Don César de Bazan, Escarmonde, Werther, Le portrait de Manon, Cendrillon, Thaïs, Sapho, Grisélidis, Le jongleur de Notre-Dame, Ariane,* and *Thérèse*. Besides Massenet, other composers's works presented as the century drew to a close included Édouard Lalo's *Le Roi d'Ys,* Camille Saint-Saëns's *Samson et Dalila,* Ernest Reyer's *Sigurd,* and Richard Wagner's *Die Walküre, Lohengrin,* and *Die Meistersinger von Nürnberg.* As the 20th century began, Wagner's *Tristan und Isolde* and Massenet's *Sapho* were premiered in Lyon. Debussy's *Pelléas et Mélisande* was heard first in 1908. Giacomo Puccini had entered the repertory earlier with *Tosca.*

Since its inception, impresarios ran the theater, but between 1902 and 1906, the running of the theater was under the umbrella of the city, which hired a director. This same arrangement returned during World War II. It was only in 1969 that the city permanently took over the administration of the theater, with Louis Erlo as the director. This led to the birth of the "opéra-nouveau" of Opéra de Lyon, a change in the philosophy—instead of grand voices and Lyon premiers, emphasis turned to building an ensemble and creating world premieres. The first evidence appeared on October 21, 1969, with the *création mondiale* of Joseph Kosma's *Les Hussards.* A few weeks later, the world premiere of Claude Prey's *Jonas* took place followed by Antoine Duhamel's *Oiseaux* (1971), Jean Prodromidès's *Passion selon nos doutes,* Maurice Ohana's *Autoclef,* Antoine Duhamel's *Gambara* (1978), and Peter Eötvös's *Trois Sœurs* on March 13, 1998. The world premieres and contemporary operas continue as an integral part of Opéra de Lyon's interesting and unusual repertory. Their budget comes from the city of Lyon, the *région* and the state. The company is also starting to explore private sponsorship. Recent repertory includes Ferruccio Busoni's *Doktor Faust,* Jacques Offenbach's *Orphée aux enfers,* Wolfgang Rihm's *Jakob Lenz,* Claudio Monteverdi's *La favola d'Orfeo,* Gluck's *Orfeo ed Euridice,* Udo Zimmerman's *Rose Blanche,* Benjamin Britten's *A Midsummer Night's Dream,* and Sergey Prokofiev's *Lyubov'k tryom apel'sinam* (The Love for Three Oranges).

Grand Théâtre

Disagreements between the two architects, Chenavard and Pollet, caused four years to pass between the initiation of the work and the completion of the Grand Théâtre. Its Neoclassic facade reflected the original Neoclassic auditorium. Sober in decor with blue as the dominate color, the room offered two box tiers, Italian style, and three balcony tiers with four level of proscenium boxes. An allegorical painting decorated the cupola. There were 1800 places. By 1842, the opera house that met with such approval when it was inaugurated no longer pleased. The primary problem was insufficient seating. Pollet refused to make any changes so René Dardel was hired. First to go were the two box tiers, judged as too small. Pillars of wood were replaced by columns of iron, and the Neoclassic-style auditorium was redecorated in Neo-Baroque fashion, with garlands, medallions, plump angels, and the like, all gilded. The seating was increased to 3,100. The total cost was 4,700,000 FF, which included the demolition of the previous theater, and the temporary "salle." The new theater was completed in 1831, and modifications were done in 1842. The architect and sculpturer Perrache was commissioned to create the eight Muses that line the top of the facade. They were hoisted into place in July 1863. (Urania is missing for lack of space.) In 1895, the day after Christmas, Terpsichore collapsed and fell onto the Place de la comédie. All eight Muses were replaced by new cast-iron Muses hoisted into place on January 3, 1912.

By the 1980s, it was obvious that the opera house could not be adapted for today's technical needs and requirements, and that it did not meet modern safety standards. It was decided to keep the original exterior and public foyer, but to gut everything else. On November 27, 1989, work began which was completed by May 10, 1993. The old body had a new heart—a modern auditorium was "suspended" inside the original shell, and the interior space doubled in size. The cost was 478 million FF.

The facade fuses the original Neoclassic stone with a single, modern glass arch which soars across the top of the structure, mimicking the seven arches on the ground level. Six friezes, with masks of Comedy and Tragedy and embellished by garlands, are above bay windows. A row of eight Muses line the top of the theater. Everything in the horseshoe-shaped auditorium is black. The reason—so the audience is not distracted from the performance by the surroundings. Black wood covers the parapets of all six tiers, and the black folding seats have a tiny circle light that casts an eerie glow on the face of the person seated there. The proscenium arch is plain black. There are 1200 seats.

Practical Information. Opéra de Lyon, place de la Comédie, 69001 Lyon. Tel: 33 72 00 45 00, Fax: 33 72 00 45 43. When visiting Opéra de Lyon, stay at the Grand Hotel des Beaux Arts, 73-75 rue du Président Edouard Herriot, place des Jacobins, 69002 Lyon. Tel: 33 78 38 09 50, Fax 33 78 42 19 19. It is centrally located and convenient to the opera and can assist with opera tickets and schedule.

COMPANY STAFF

Directeur Général. Jean-Pierre Brossmann, Louis Erlo.

Bibliography. *Trois Siècles d'opéra à Lyon: De l'Académie Royale de Musique à l'Opéra-Nouveau* (Lyon, 1982). *Opéra de Lyon* (Lyon, 1993). *Programme de l'Opéra Grand—Théâtre de Lyon Saison 1937-38* (Lyon, 1937). G. Vuillermoz, *Cent ans d'opéra à Lyon: Le centenaire du Grand Théâtre de Lyon, 1831-1931* (Lyon, 1932).

Thanks to Elisa Delorme, Opéra de Lyon.

MARSEILLE

Opéra de Marseille

Marseille's Opéra Minicipale was opened on December 4, 1924, with Ernst Reyer's *Sigurd*. Three architects, Henri Ebrard, Georges Raymond, and Gaston Castel were responsible for the art deco structure. The previous opera house, the Grand Théâtre (originally called Salle Beauveau) was consumed by fire on November 13, 1919, at the conclusion of a rehearsal of Giacomo Meyerbeer's *L'Africaine*. Stanislas Champein's *La mélomaie* had inaugurated the Grand Théâtre on October 31, 1787. The wooden opera house was designed by Charles-Joachim Benard.

Opera dates back to 1685 with the founding of the Académie Royale de Musique by Pierre Gauthier, who had obtained authorization from Jean-Baptiste Lully to produce opera in the city. Gauthier inaugurated the Academy with his *Le triomphe de la paix* on January 28, 1685. The Academy also hosted several of Lully's operas, including *Phaëton*, *Atys*, *Armide*, *Le triomphe de l'amour*, and *Bellérophon*. The Academy experienced financial difficulties which led to a frequent change of directors and theater closings.

On May 27, 1785, King Louis XVI granted architect Benard the right to construct a new opera house, which opened two years later. The inaugural season was impressive, offering Christoph Willibald Gluck's *Iphigénie en Tauride*, *Armide*, and *Alceste*, André Grétry's *La caravane du Caire* and *Panurge dans l'Ile des Lanternes*, Lully's *Atys*, François-André Phildor's *La belle esclave*, and Le Moyne's *Phèdre*. With the arrival of the 1800s, several works by Étienne-Nicolas Méhul entered the repertory—*Irato*, *Hélèna*, *La journée aux aventures*, *Les aveugles de Tolède*, and *Joseph en Egypte*. Adrien Boieldieu was also popular with his *Zoraïne et Zulmar*, *Le basier et la quittance*, *Jean de Paris*, and *La fête du village voisin*, among others, in the schedule. In July 1817, the Grand Théâtre hosted its first world premiere, Bernard's *Les Phocéens*. Four years earlier, in 1813, the theater had received its first public subsidy. The structure was renovated in 1820, and when it reopened, Gioachino Rossini's *Il barbiere di Siviglia* was on the boards. His *Otello* followed in 1824, *Le siège de Corinthe* in 1829, and *La donna del lago* in 1832. Several of Gaetano Donizetti's works were also seen in the opera house, as were those of Vincenzo Bellini. Nevertheless, it was a repertory dominated by French opera. Daniel Auber works first appeared in 1822 when *Emma* was staged, and over the decades, more than twenty of his works were introduced, including *La neige*, *Fra diavolo*, *Le domino noir*, *Le Philtre*, *Le Serment*, *Gustav III*, *Le cheval de bronze*, *Les diamants de la couronne*, *Marco Spada*, and *Le premier jour de bonheur*. Another French composer with several works in the repertory was Adolphe Adam—*Le Dieu et la Boyadère*, *Le postillon de Longjumeau*, *La marquise*, *La reine d'un jour*, and *La fille Berger*. One of the most popular French composers was Fromental Halévy. *L'eclair* was mounted on October 28, 1836, followed by *La Juive* on January 25, 1837. Also presented were his *Guido et Ginevra*, *La Reine de Chypre*, *Charles VI*, *Val d'Andorre*, *La Fée aux Roses*, and *Jaguarita L'Indienne*.

Meyerbeer was also extremely popular with his *Robert le Diable, Marguerite d'Anjou, Les Huguenots, L'Étoile du Nord, Le Pardon de Ploërmerl,* and *L'Africaine* introduced on April 5, 1866, with Adelina Patti making her Marseille debut. Meanwhile, the city first witnessed Charles Gounod's *Faust* on February 16, 1863. Gounod conducted a performance of his opera on March 11. Other Gounod operas staged included *Mireille, Roméo et Juliette, Cinq Mars, Philémon et Baucis,* and *Die Köhigen von Saba.*

The city contributed a large subsidy to the opera house in 1881. The following year, it took control of the building, cutting the price of admission in an attempt to lure back an audience. Around the same time, Jules Massenet operas entered the repertory beginning with *Manon* in 1884 and *Hérodiade* the following season. Eventually seventeen of Massenet's works were given in Marseille, including *Werther, Le Cid, Manon, Sapho, Thaïs, La Navarraise, Le jongleur de Notre-Dame, Le Roi de Lahore, Esclarmonde, Ariane, Thérèse,* and the world premiere of *Don Quichotte* on December 17, 1910. In fact, the Grand Théâtre hosted many *créations mondiaux* during the 19th century into the early part of the 20th century, of which Massenet's opera is the only one that survived the test of time. A. Flégier's *Grognards et Poilus* on January 11, 1919, was the last world premiere to trod the boards for fifty years. By the end of 1919, the opera house lay in ruins, a victim of a fire. The Opéra, as it was known after reconstruction, turned to presenting French premieres, with 21 to its credit. Except for Eugen d'Albert's *Tiefland,* none stood the test of time until Alban Berg's *Lulu* on October 26, 1963. Then world premieres were again presented, with Daniel Lesur's *Andrea del Sarto* on January 24, 1969, Louis Saguer's *Mariana Pineda* on January 16, 1970, and Pascal Bentoiu's *Hamlet* on April 26, 1974.

Meanwhile, in 1945, the Opéra passed under direct control of the city with the first artistic director being appointed, Jean Marny. (Opéra became the Opéra Municipale.) During the 1960s and 1970s, several international guest artists appeared at the Opéra including Gwyneth Jones, Eva Marton, and Luciano Pavarotti.

The quality of the productions can vary, but one production of Reyer's *Sigurd,* despite some powerful moments, was mediocre, with poor quality singing and uninspiring staging and directing.

It was what one might see at a small regional company. Other works have been more successful. The current repertory concentrates on French and Italian operas, with the occasional Russian, German, or Russian work. Recent offerings include Léo Delibes's *Lakmé,* Gounod's *Mireille,* Rossini's *Semiramide* and *Il barbiere di Siviglia,* Giuseppe Verdi's *Rigoletto, Don Carlo,* and *La forza del destino,* Wolfgang Amadeus Mozart's *Don Giovanni,* and Alexander Borodin's *Prince Igor.*

Opéra Municipale

After fire destroyed the Grand Théâtre, only the facade colonnade remained standing. Within a year and a half, the city council approved the rebuilding project on July 26, 1921, and work began shortly thereafter.

The Opéra is a large structure with six massive Ionic columns forming a classic portico on the principal facade. OPÉRA MUNICIPAL in bronze letters rests on the architrave above. Four bas-reliefs of fauns frolicking in Art Deco style decorate the attic level. The auditorium is an Art Deco gem, swimming with pink marble. There are three balcony tiers with undulating parapets — one circular-shaped and the other two lyre-shaped — a split tier of boxes floating about the orchestra level, and four levels of proscenium boxes. Red velvet seats blend with the maroon velvet curtain and lavender-painted ceiling surrounded by scalloped ornamentation. The gilded proscenium arch is crowned by a bas-relief depicting the Birth of Beauty, and surrounded by representations of all the theater arts. Emile-Antoine Bourdelle executed the work. There are approximately 1,800 seats.

Practical Information. Opéra de Marseille, 2 rue Molière, 13001 Marseille. Tel: 33 91 55 00 70, Fax: 33 91 55 21 07. When visiting Opéra de Marseille, stay at the Pullman Beauvau, 4 rue Beauvau, 13001 Marseille. Tel: 33 91 54 91 00, Fax 33 91 54 15 76. It is two blocks from the opera house. The Pullman Beauvau can assist with opera tickets and schedule.

COMPANY STAFF AND PREMIERES

Directeur Général. (since 1945) Elie Bankhalter (1992–present), Jacques Karpo (1975–91), R. Giovaninetti (1972–75), L. Ducreux (1968–72),

Opéra de Marseille facade detail (Marseille, France).

B. Lefort (1965–68), L. Ducreux (1961–65), M. Leduc (1949–61), Jean Marny (1945–49).

World Premieres. Bernard's *Les Phocéens* 1817; Fontmichel's *El Gitano* March 20, 1834; X. Boisselot's *Ne touchez pas à la Reine* April 8, 1847; X. Boisselot's *Mosquita la Sorcière* December 30, 1851; Agnelli's *Léonore de Médicis* March 1855; Morel's *Le Jugement de Dieu* March 7, 1860; Duprat's *Pétrarque* April 19, 1873; Monsigu's *Spartacus* April 30, 1880; Péronnet's *Claudia* April 19, 1882; Paris's *Le secret de Maître Cornille* January 24, 1893; L. Fontagne's *Dramayayti*, May 7, 1895; Grandval's *Mazepa* May 4, 1897; A. Darblay's *Pierre d'Aragon* December 28, 1898; P. Bastide's *L'Idylle à l'Étoile* January 11, 1899; E. Reyer's *Erostrate* October 16, 1899; Desjoyeaux's *Gyptis* October 18, 1899; X. Leroux's *Théodora* March 11, 1909; J. Camondo's *Le Clown* November 30, 1909; J. Massenet's *Don Quichotte* December 17, 1910; D. Bach's *Charlemagne* January 27, 1912; J. Nouguès's *L'Aigle* January 17, 1913; D. Bach's *Annette* February 4, 1913; Gérard's *Le dépit amoureux* March 24, 1914; A. Flégier's *Grognards et Poilus* January 11, 1919; D. Lesur's *Andrea del Sarto* January 24, 1969; L. Saguer's *Mariana Pineda* January 16, 1970; P. Bentoiu's *Hamlet* April 26, 1974. **French Premieres:** I. de Lara's *Les trois masques* February 24, 1912; F. le

Barne's *Néréa* February 25, 1926; G. Hüe's *Dans l'ombre de la Cathédrale* January 12, 1928; D. Bach's *Arlette Bastian* February 2, 1928; H. Fraggi's *A quoi rêvent les jeunes filles* February 23, 1928; D. Polleri's *Taïma* November 17, 1928; F. Alfano's *Resurrezione* November 29, 1928; A. Bachelet's *Quand la cloche sonnera* March 19, 1930; M.F. Gaillard's *La danse pendant le festin* March 27, 1930; F. Bousquet's *Sarrati le Terrible* March 14, 1931; E. d'Albert's *Tiefland* January 21, 1932; V. Puget's *Maître Primasse* April 11, 1933; Peyssies's *La Princesse Imaginaire* March 10, 1940; A. de Lucas's *Vendello* May 16, 1948; A. Dupuis's *La Passion* March 8, 1951; C. Arrieu's *Cadet Roussel* October 2, 1953; B. Pergolèse's *Le Jaloux corrigé* November 23, 1956; H. Sauguet's *La Contrebasse* November 23, 1956; H. Tomasi's *Sampiero Corso* January 16, 1959; A. Berg's *Lulu* October 26, 1963; L. Janáček's *Věc Makropulos* (The Makropulos Affair) October 24, 1968; J.M. Damase's *Madame de...* February 5, 1971; A. Dvořák's *Rusalka*; D. Milhaud's *Christophe Colomb* October 5, 1984.

Bibliography. Emile Spiteri, ed., *Marseille, notre Opéra: Petite Histoire et Grands Événements (1787–1919 et 1924–1987)* (Marseille, 1987). *Divines Divas et vivat l'Opéra: Marseille 1487–1987* (Marseille, 1987).

Thanks to Francine Jouve, Opera de Marseille, and P. Patela.

Opéra de Montpellier

Giacomo Meyerbeer's *Les Huguenots* inaugurated the Grand Théâtre Municipal on October 1, 1888. The evening began at 8 o'clock with a playing of the *Marseillaise*, followed by Meyerbeer's grand opera. This was Montpellier's third opera house. The previous two had burned down. The architect of the opera house was Marie-Joseph Cassien Bernard. A second opera performance venue opened in 1990, the modern, 2,000-seat Opéra Berlioz-Corum, designed by Claude Vasconi.

Operatic tradition had begun in Montpellier more than three hundred years earlier. Initially operas (and other type of performances) were presented in the residences of the wealthy noble families: on December 5, 1655, the town mansion of Gérard de la Treilhe hosted Molière and his troupe performing *Ballet des Incompatibles*; in 1678, the residence of Castries witnessed a work of M. de la Sablière with music by M. Brueys. At the end of the 17th century, Christoph Willibald Gluck's *Alceste*, and Jean-Baptiste Lully's *Armide*, *Bellérophon*, and *Phaëton* were given in a *salle* called "Jeu de Paume des Mignards."

In 1740, the king accorded the rights to Antoine Rey to construct a theater, but Rey died eight years later, without ever having acted upon the patent given him. The project, however did not die with him. Instead, an architect Jacques-Philippe Mareschal was chosen and two years after work began, Montpellier's first theater was inaugurated on December 22, 1755, with Rebel and Francoeur's *Pyrame et Thisbé*. Operas shared the stage with concerts, and the functioning of the theater was under the jurisdiction of the all powerful Académie de Musique de Montpellier. André Grétry was the most popular French composer with several works in the repertory: *Le Jugement de Midas*, *La magnifique*, *L'épreuve villageoise*, and *L'événements imprévus*. Egidio Romualdo Duni was the favorite Italian composer with *Les Moissonneurs*, *Le Milicien*, and *La Fée Urgèle* on the boards. Gluck was also well-liked with his *Orphée*, *Alceste*, and *Iphigénie*. Other operas which were performed included Giovanni Battista Pergolesi's *La serva padrona*, Jean-Philippe Rameau's *Castor et Pollux*, and Jean-Jacques Rousseau's *Le Devin du Village*, and the long forgotten works of Blaise's *Isabelle et Gertrude*, Bruni's *L'isle enchantée*, Champein's *La mélomanie*, Desormery's *Myrtil et Licoris*, D'Herbain's *Nanette et Lucas*, Mondonville's *Daphnis et Alcimadure*, and Monvel's *Julie*. The theater held a U-shaped auditorium. Fire destroyed the building during the night of December 17-18, 1785.

By March of the next year, a provisional theater had been put in place for comedies and opera. It took a year for the theater to be reconstructed, with two city architects, Donnar and Lenoir, responsible for the plans. On October 1, 1787, the *salle* reopened with a piece by André Grétry. Despite political upheavals (revolutions of 1830 and 1848) and a war (Franco-Prussian in 1870), the theater was rarely closed. A permanent troupe guaranteed almost continuous productions. During the revolutionary period, propaganda pieces dominated the stage, like Raynal's *La prière à la liberté* and H. Pradel's *L'instituteur ou le patriote à l'épreuve*. During the Restoration, the theater regained its luster under the impetus of the new prefect, Creuzé de Lesser. During its more than nine decades of existence, the opera house hosted many fine artists, including Rosine Stoltz, Mme Borghèse, Marie Sasse and M. Maury, Mme Galli-Marié, and Louis Nourrit. Between 1787 and 1888, a broadening of the repertory and an expansion of the orchestra took place. There were 26 instruments in 1790, 36 in 1855, and 43 in 1888. During this same time period, more than 150 operas debuted in the city, including Adolphe Adam's *Le Chalet*, Daniel Auber's *La muette de Portici* and *Le cheval de bronze*, Carl Maria von Weber's *Der Freischütz* (as Robin des bois), Vincenzo Bellini's *Il pirata* and *Norma*, Gasparo Spontini's *La vestale*, Adrien Boieldieu's *La Dame Blanche*, Gaetano Donizetti's *L'elisir d'amore* and *Lucia di Lammermoor*, Charles Gounod's *Faust* and *Roméo et Juliette*, Fromental Halévy's *La Juive*, Giacomo Meyerbeer's *Robert le Diable*, *Les Huguenots*, and *L'Africaine*, Wolfgang Amadeus Mozart's *Le nozze di Figaro*, Gioachino Rossini's *Il barbiere di Siviglia*, Ambroise Thomas's *Mignon* and *Hamlet*, Georges Bizet's *Carmen*, Léo Delibes's *Lakmé*, and Giuseppe Verdi's *Il trovatore*, *La traviata, Jérusalem, Un ballo in maschera,* and *I masnadieri.* The two most successful composers in Montpellier were Meyerbeer and Verdi. After Meyerbeer's *Robert la Diable* it was written "one can never see this opera too much because one always discovers beautiful new things." His *L'Africaine* played 51 times between 1867 and 1881. The audience was equally receptive to his *Les Huguenots, Le Prophète,* and *L'Étoile du Nord.* Six of Verdi's operas were in the repertory between 1850 and 1888. Halévy's *La Juive* played almost every season after its initial staging in 1838 and was one of the most popular operas. In April 1881, Montpellier's second opera house was destroyed by fire.

After the new opera house opened in 1888 and until 1914, the operas of Jules Massenet became the most popular with 13 of his works entering the repertory: *Hérodiade, Manon, Le Cid, Marie-Magdeleine, Werther, La Navarraise, Thaïs, Le Roi de Lahore, Sapho, Cendrillon, Le Jongleur de Notre-Dame, Grisélidis,* and *Don Quichotte.* Italian *verismo* was also well-liked with Pietro Mascagni's *Cavalleria rusticana* and Ruggero Leoncavallo's *I pagliacci* receiving many hearings. There were even a few German operas, with Mozart's *Die Zauberflöte* and Richard Wagner's *Lohengrin* and *Tannhäuser* gracing the Montpellier stage for the first time in 1892 and 1896 respectively. During the same time period, the most performed operas were Gounod's *Faust* (182 times), Meyerbeer's *Les Huguenots* (120 times), Massenet's *Werther* (99 times), Halévy's *La Juive* (92 times), and Meyerbeer's *L'Africaine* and Massenet's *Hérodiade* each given 70 times. Despite World War I, the opera house kept its doors open, although with a reduced number of performances. After the war, the emphasis shifted to introducing operettas, with 90% of the works entering the repertory for the first time being of that genre. The dramatic works were limited to Arrigo Boïto's *Mefistofele,* Wagner's *Die Walküre,* Claude Debussy's *Pelléas et Mélisande,* Modest Mussorgsky's *Boris Godunov* and *Khovanshchina,* and Alexander Borodin's *Prince Igor.* The last three Russian operas met with little success. *Boris Godunov* was repeated only once, and the other two disappeared. The German operas did not fare much better. *Lohengrin* was repeated only five times. Between 1915 and 1940, the most popular works were Massenet's *Manon,* Gounod's *Faust,* and Bizet's *Carmen.* Other frequently mounted works included Puccini's *Tosca,* Massenet's *Werther*

and *Thaïs,* Gounod's *Mireille,* Delibes's *Lakmé,* and Verdi's *La traviata* and *Rigoletto.* Two opera long forgotten were given in the period between the wars, Verdier's *Reconnquises* and Busser's *Colomba.*

After 1945 and until 1980, the repertory became less innovative and the permanent ensemble was dissolved, replaced by artists hired for each opera. Nevertheless, a few new works entered the repertory: Maurice Ravel's *L'heure espagnole,* Jacques Ibert's *Angélique,* and Gojac's *Amants de Vérone.* The 1979-80 season of offered eight works of which six were from the 19th century. By the time the 1985-86 season arrived, an equilibrium had been re-established with three from the 19th century, three from the 17th-18th century, and one from the early 20th century and a contemporary work. Since 1985, the Opéra has pursued an adventurous policy of presenting rarely performed works, which have included Luigi Dallapiccola's *Il volo di notte,* Aimé Maillart's *Les Dragons de Villars,* Meyerbeer's *Les Huguenots,* Darius Milhaud's *Le Livre de Christophe Colomb,* Pierre Alexandre Monsigny's *Le cadi dupé,* Hans Pfitzner's *Palestrina,* Ernest Reyer's *Sigurd,* and Georg Philipp Telemann's *Pimpinone.*

After the Opéra Berlioz-Corum opened in 1990, it hosted the grand operas which required a full orchestra and large sets — operas of Wagner, Mussorgsky, Verdi, and Meyerbeer. The operas from the Baroque period, of Mozart, and those better suited to the dimensions of the Grand Théâtre Municipal are staged there. A recent production of Ernest Chausson's *Le Roi Arthus,* a coproduction with the Theater Dortmund (see Theater Dortmund [Germany] entry), bore the minimalist philosophy of Dortmund — at least in regards to the staging of French operas. The set consisted of geometric shapes which were moved around for each act, culminating with a climactic ending. The opera was stripped to its essence, and almost mastered. The singing was good, but the voices lacked nuance and color, but projected with dramatic feeling and powerful acting. Most of Opéra de Montpellier's productions are co-productions with other French and German opera houses. Recent repertory is varied and spans a couple of centuries — from Georg Friedrich Händel's *Arminio* and Gluck's *Iphigénie en Aulide* to Leoš Janáček's *Jenůfa,* with an emphasis on the early and contemporary — Gluck's *La rencontre imprévue,* Händel's *Admeto,* Giovanni Paisiello's

Opéra Berlioz-Corum (Montpellier, France).

Il re Teodoro in Venezia, Mozart's *Die Entführung aus dem Serail*, Igor Stravinsky's *Rake's Progress*, Sergey Prokofiev's *Ognenniy angel* (The Fiery Angel) and *Obrucheniye v monastïre* (Betrothal in a Monastery), and Alban Berg's *Wozzeck*, as well as Camille Saint-Saëns's *Samson et Dalila*.

Grand Théâtre Municipal

After the second opera house was destroyed by fire in 1881, an architectural competition was announced with, among others, Charles Garnier on the jury. By December 5, the architect Cassien-Bernard was chosen. He had been a pupil of arnier. The first stone was laid on July 14, 1884, but slowly the relationship between the architect and the city deteriorated, causing numerous delays and problems. The theater was finally completed in 1888 and opened in October that same year.

It is an imposing structure overlooking the Place de la Comédie. An off-white, the main facade exhibits a modified rusticated ground level punctuated with three glass-and-wood entrance doors. Above this is a trio of arches supported by Ionic columns, flanked by massive Corinthian columns, and crowned by a balustrade. Muses with their "instruments," the work of Antonin Injalbert, embellish the balustrade, behind which sits a recessed attic. The four-tier auditorium is bathed in red burgundy velvet. Musical instruments, gilded fleurs-de-lys, and flowers embellish the parapets. There are medallions with names of composers: BEETHOVEN, MEYERBEER, RAMEAU, MASSENET, GRÉTRY, BERLIOZ in gold letters on a turquoise background crowned by masks of Comedy and Tragedy. More composers names: AUBER, ADAM, GOUNOD, MOZART, flanked by putty are on the ceiling. Guilded Corinthian columns circle around the hall. A huge center chandelier is surrounded by an allegorical mural, the work of Arnaud d'Urbec.

Practical Information. Opéra de Montpellier, 11 Boulevard Victor Hugo, 34000 Montpellier. Tel: 33 467 60 19 80, Fax: 33 467 60 19 90. When visiting Opéra de Montpellier, stay at the Hotel Le Guilhem, 18 rue Jean Jacques Rousseau, 34000 Montpellier. Tel: 33 467 52 90 90, Fax 33

Grande Théâtre Municipal (Montpellier, France).

467 60 67 67. It is in a quiet location in the old city, convenient to the opera house and can assist with tickets and schedules.

COMPANY STAFF AND PREMIERES

Directeur Général. Henri Maier.

Premieres. (1985–97): Frédéric Rzewsky's *Les Perses* 1985–86; Charles Chaynes's *Noces de Sang* March 1988; Pascal Dusapin's *Roméo et Juliette* July 1989; Philippe Hersant's *Le Château des Carpathes* October 27, 1993; René Koering's *Marie de Montpellier* January 25, 1994; Valérie Stephan's *L'Epouse injustement soupçonnée* January 1995; Michael Levinas's *Go-gol* February 1997.

Bibliography. *Le Centenaire Opéra* (Toulouse, 1988). *Les Opéras de Montpellier: 1985–1996* (Montpellier, 1996).

Thanks to Dani Maier, Opéra de Montpellier, and Catherine Charpentier.

Festival de Radio France & Montpellier (Summer Festival)

On July 6, 1985, the Festival de Radio France & Montpellier was opened with a Samba concert. Classical programs of operas and concerts followed. The three opera offerings ranged from the 17th to the 20th century, with Italian, English and French works on the boards: Vincenzo Bellini's *Norma*, Henry Purcell's *Dido and Aeneas*, and Camille Saint-Saëns's *Déjanire*. The festival, founded by René Koering, presents around 125 events a season.

Between 1981 and 1985 Koering led Radio France concerts at the Aix-en-Provence Festival, but opera was broadcast on only one night, so by the mid–1980s, he decided to start his own festival. To distinguish it from the nearby Festival d'Aix and

Chorégies d'Orange, he chose an operatic repertory of rare works, from both the distant and recent past, pieces that would not be given at the other French festivals. With a budget of only 13 million FF, of which 25% is from private sponsors—all French firms—he only has enough funds to stage one production. The other two are done in concert form. Works offered included Oscar Straus's *Die lustigen Nibelungen* (staged), and concert versions of Richard Strauss's *Guntram* and Ernest Bloch's *Macbeth*. To find rare works worthy of another hearing, he reads around 10 to 15 obscure operas a year to choose which to perform. It usually takes around five years from selecting the opera until performance. Part of the delay is that he does not schedule an opera until he finds top quality singers to accept the leading roles. He also discovers young artists, so the final cast is usually a mixture of the important artists with rising stars. Gary Lakes and Hildegard Behrens have performed at the Festival. He views the presentation of Antonio Sacchini's *Oedipe à Colonee* and Luigi Cerebini's *Lodoïska* his only two mistakes. Recent repertory includes Othmar Schoeck's *Penthésilée*, Hector Berlioz's *Roméo et Juliette* (symphonie dramatique), and Ludwig van Beethoven's *Leonore*.

Practical Information. Festival de Radio France & Montpellier, Languedoc-Roussillon, Service Location B.P. 9214 Le Corum, 34043 Montpellier Cedex 1. Tel: 33 467 02 02 01, Fax: 33 467 61 66 82. When visiting Festival de Radio France & Montpellier, stay at the Hôtel Le Guilhem, 18 rue Jean Jacques Rousseau, 34000 Montpellier. Tel: 33 467 52 90 90, Fax 33 467 60 67 67. It is in a quiet location in the old city, convenient to the festival theaters, and can assist with tickets and schedules.

COMPANY STAFF

Directeur Artistique. René Koering (1985–present)

Bibliography. Interview with René Koering, artistic director, July 1997.

Thanks to Fanny Decobert, Festival de Radio France & Montpellier, and Catherine Charpentier.

Outdoor Performance Venue (Montpellier, France).

NANCY

Opéra de Nancy et de Lorraine

The Opéra de Nancy et de Lorraine, originally called the Grand Théâtre de Nancy, was inaugurated in 1919 with Ernst Reyer's *Sigurd*. The previous opera house, Théâtre Municipal, had been consumed by fire in 1906. The delay in reconstruction was first caused by economic and political problems, and then by World War I.

Nancy's first opera house was commissioned by the Grand Duke Leopold in 1709, and inaugurated on November 9 of the same year by Henry Desmarets's *Le Temple de l'Astrée*, a work written especially for the opening. The Municipal, which replaced this structure, hosted a full repertory of operas and operettas by Charles-Simon Favart, Jean-Philippe Rameau, Christoph Willibald Gluck, Jean-Jacques Rousseau, and Giovanni Battista Pergolesi. Thirteen years passed after the Municipal burned to the ground until the Grand Théâtre opened. In 1959, the city took over the running of the 920-seat Grand Théâtre de Nancy, which became the Opéra de Nancy et de Lorraine in 1985. Twentieth century works play a major role in the repertory with Leoš Janáček's *Z Mrtvého Domu* (From the House of the Dead), Michael Tippett's *King Priam*, Richard Strauss's *Der Rosenkavalier*, Claude Debussy's *Pelléas et Mélisande*, and Jean Prochomides's *La noche triste*

on the boards. Other works have included Giuseppe Verdi's *Un ballo in maschera*, Léo Delibes's *Lakmé*, and Wolfgang Amadeus Mozart's *Don Giovanni*. Recent repertory offers Puccini's *Manon Lescaut*, Francis Poulenc's *La voix humaine*, Henri Rabaud's *L'appel de la mer*, and Verdi's *La traviata*.

Practical Information. Opéra de Nancy et de Lorraine, 1 rue Sainte-Catherine, 54000 Nancy. Tel: 33 383 85 33 20, Fax: 33 383 85 30 66. When visiting the Opéra de Nancy et de Lorraine, stay at the Grand Hôtel de la Reine, 2 place Stanislas, 54000 Nancy. Tel: 33 383 35 03 01, Fax: 33 383 32 86 04. It is centrally located and convenient to the opera house and can assist with tickets and schedules.

COMPANY STAFF

Directeur Général. Jean-Marie Blanchard (1996–present), Antoine Bourseiller (1982–95), Jean-Albert Cartier (1979–82), Elie Delfosse (1976–79), Louis Ducreux (1973–76), Jean-Claude Riber (1970–73), Michel Sanduz (1959–70)

Bibliography. Materials supplied by the company

Thanks to Laurence Viriot, Opéra de Nancy et de Lorraine, and Jean Lavalade.

NANTES

Opéra de Nantes et des Pays de Loire

The Théâtre Graslin was inaugurated on May 3, 1813, with André Grétry's *Aline ou la reine de Golgonde*. Designed by Mathurin Crucy, this opera house was the second structure. Fire had devoured the first on August 24, 1796, during a performance of Grétry's *Zémir et Azor*. Named after Jean-Joseph Graslin, the man who had the theater built (earning his money as a tax collector and businessman), the Graslin Theater had been opened on March 23, 1788. Only the vestibule and facade survived the fire. It took the intervention of Napoleon Bonaparte, when he passed

through Nantes in 1808, to get the theater rebuilt. Crucy also designed the original structure.

The Théâtre Graslin was typical of some opera houses during the 19th and early 20th centuries in provincial France that included a resident opera company, which remained in existence until 1935. The French repertory was much better received than the Italian with Adrien Boieldieu's *La Dame Blanche* repeated 27 times, and Giacomo Meyerbeer's *Robert le Diable* and *Le Prophète* both accorded enthusiastic receptions. On the other hand, Wolfgang Amadeus Mozart's *Don Giovanni*,

Gioachino Rossini's *Il barbiere di Siviglia*, and Giuseppe Verdi's *Il trovatore* met with unfavorable responses. Some of the noteworthy performances during the 19th century included Gasparo Spontini's *La vestale* (1807), Étienne-Nicolas Méhul's *Joseph* (1808), and the French premieres of Jules Massenet's *Hérodiade* (1883) and Arigo Boïto's *Mefistofele* (1887). Ernest Reyer's *Sigurd* and Grétry's *Richard Coeur de Lion* were staged in celebration of the theater's centennial, and Richard Wagner's *Lohengrin* arrived in 1891, followed by *Tannhäuser* in 1894, and *Die Walküre* in 1903. The early part of the 20th century also brought the world premiere of Claude Guillon-Verne's *La visionnaire*. In 1945, a performance of Nicolay Rimsky-Korsakov's *Snegurochka* (The Snow Maiden) celebrated the end of World War II, and still in the Russian vein, Modest Mussorgsky's *Khovanshchina* (sung in French) reopened the opera house in 1968 after restoration. The theater was renamed Opéra de Nantes et des Pays de Loire in 1973.

The Opéra de Nantes et des Pays de Loire offers an interesting repertory, through rediscovery of ignored or forgotten French operas and the showcasing of the rich and varied works of the 20th century. In the first category, one finds Gabriel Fauré's *Pénélope*, Léo Delibes's *Le Roi l'a dit*, Boieldieu's *La Dame Blanche*, Louis-Ferdinand Hérold's *Le Pré au Clers*, Emmanuel Chabrier's *Le Roi Malgré lui*, and Adolphe Adam's *Si J'étais Roi*. Other rarely heard works included Spontini's *La vestale* and Saverio Mercadante's *Il giuramento*. In the latter group, composers like Leoš Janáček, Richard Strauss, Dmitry Shostakavich, and Benjamin Britten have had their operas staged in Nantes. The French premieres of Aulis's Sallinen's *Kullervo* and Carlisle Floyd's *Susannah* graced the stage in 1995 and 1996 respectively, and Philippe Boesmans's *Reigen* arrived in 1997. Unfamiliar works by Gian Carlo Menotti and Carl Nielsen have been presented. The company does not shy away from monumental undertakings, like Richard Wagner's The Ring Cycle and *Parsifal*. The artists are a mixture of established and young singers like Donald McIntyre, Natalie Dessay, Mark Baker, Jean-Philippe Lafont, Giuseppe Morino, and Jorma Hynninen. Recent repertory includes Verdi's *Il trovatore*, Jules Massenet's *Don Quichotte*, Claude Debussy's *Pelléas et Mélisande*, Wolfgang Amadeus Mozart's *Idomeneo*, Leoš Janáček's *Z Mrtvého Domu* (From the House of the Dead), Pietro Mascagni's *Cavalleria rusticana*, Ruggero Leoncavallo's *Pagliacci*, and Dmitry

Shostakovich's *Ledi Makbet Mtsenkovo uyezda* (Lady Macbeth of the Mtsensk District).

Théâtre Graslin

Before the construction of the Théâtre Graslin, opera had been performed private palaces. Crucy proposed the plan for the first theater in 1784, but it was only approved in 1787, and was completed by the following year. After fire destroyed it eight years later, nothing was done. Only in 1811, three years after Napoleon decreed it should be rebuilt, was any action taken. Crucy again designed the rebuilt opera house, but with "Italian decor." Only after a 1968 restoration did the auditorium regain its original appearance.

Greek Neoclassicism permeates the facade with eight monumental Corinthian columns forming the portico. Eight Muses crown the structure. The blue, gray, and gold fan-shaped auditorium holds four tiers. The parapets are embellished with medallions, musical motifs, and masks of Comedy and Tragedy. Gilded, fluted, Ionic columns flank the proscenium boxes. In the middle of the proscenium arch is a golden cartouche. The allegorical theme of the painted ceiling is the work of Hippolyte Berteaux. The theater holds 980 seats.

Practical Information. Opéra de Nantes et des Pays de Loire, 1 rue Molière, 44000 Nantes. Tel: 33 240 41 90 60, Fax: 33 240 41 90 77. If visiting, contact the French Government Tourist Office, 444 Madison Avenue, 16th Floor, New York, NY 10022. Tel: 212-838-7800, Fax: 212-838-7855. To speak with a person Tel: 202 659-7779 (Washington D.C.).

COMPANY STAFF AND WORLD PREMIERES

Directeur Général. Philippe Godefroid (1990–present), Marc Soustrot (1986–90), Jean-Louis Simon (1981–86), René Terrasson (1973–81), Lajos Soltesz (1967–72), Jacques Rousseau (1945–67), M. Borelli (1930), Georges Coste (1922–30), Jeanne Gavy-Beledin (1918–22), Etienne Destranges (?–1918).

World Premieres (since 1945). Semenoff's *Sir Halewyn*, May 1974; Jacques Bondon's *1330*, May 1975; Marcel Landowski's *La vieille maison*, February 1988.

Bibliography. Patrick Barbier, *Graslin, Nantes et l'opéra* (Nantes, 1993). Materials supplied by the company.

Thanks to Claire Barbereau, Nantes Opera.

Opéra de Nice

On February 7, 1885, the Opéra de Nice was inaugurated with Giuseppe Verdi's *Aida*, featuring Fanny Rubini Scalisi (Aida), Emma Terrigi (Amneris), Riccardo Petrovick (Radamès) and Emilio de Bernis (Amonasro). Only three more operas were on the boards during the inaugural season: Verdi's *Ernani*, Charles Gounod's *Faust*, and Filippo Marchetti's *Ruy Blas*. Architect François Aune, in collaboration with Charles Garnier, were entrusted with the construction of the opera house.

The history of l'Opéra de Nice goes back to 1776, when the Marquess Alli-Maccarani obtained from Armédée III, king of Sardinia, the authorization to transform his old residence into a theater. (A theater had existed since 1746 in the east wing of the Héraud-Lascaris Palace, but the area had gotten too crowded.) Called the Théâtre Maccarani after its owner, it was a modest wooden structure. In 1787, it went bankrupt and was sold to the Société des Quarante Nobles (Association of Forty Nobles). The theater changed hands again in 1792 when a community of artists and a new Association of Forty took it over until 1815. In 1826, King Charles-Félix bought back the old wooden building and replaced it with a grand Italian opera house, modeled on the Teatro di San Carlo (Naples), but still of wood. Initially, until 1860, it was called Théâtre Royal, then Théâtre Imperial until 1870, and then Théâtre Municipal (or Théâtre Italien). Catastrophe stuck on March 23, 1881. Bianca Donadio had just given her "addio" in Gaetano Donizetti's *Lucia di Lammermoor* when there was an explosion. A horrific fire broke out, spreading so rapidly that 63 spectators perished.

After the new opera house opened, the Opéra de Nice established a regular opera season which lasted from the end of November until the end of March or April. The second season offered all operas in Italian, including Giacomo Meyerbeer's *L'Africaine*. The season also staged Gaetano Donizetti's *Linda di Chamounix*, *Don Pasquale*, *Lucrezia Borgia* and *Poliuto*, Gioachino Rossini's *Il barbiere di Siviglia*, Verdi's *Il trovatore*, *La traviata*, and *Aida*, Luigi and Federico Ricci's *Crispino e la Comare*, and two French premieres, Nicola de Giosa's *Napoli di Carnivale* and Alfredo Catalani's *Dejanice*. The Opéra also welcomed some distinguished singers, including Adelina Patti as Rosina (*Il barbiere di siviglia*) and Violetta (*La traviata*), and Ada Adini as Sélika (*L'Africaine*), Paolina (*Poliuto*), Aida and Lucrezia Borgia. The third season gave the French premiere of Amilcare Ponchielli's *La gioconda*, and a novelty, Errico Petrella's *Ione*, alongside the repertory favorites of Verdi's *Rigoletto*, Donizetti's *Lucia di Lammermoor* and Vincenzo Bellini's *La sonnambula*. A couple of novelties followed the next season, Manzocchi's *Le Comte de Gleichen* and Samara's *Flora Mirabilis*. Ambroise Thomas's *Hamlet* with Emma Calvé as Ophélie was a triumph. Calvé also sang opposite tenor Talazac in Gounod's *Faust*.

It was not until the 1888-89 season, the fifth, that the operas were sung in French and most operas in the schedule were French. One could say that the fifth season gave birth to "l'opéra national à Nice." Fromental Halévy's *La Juive* was the inaugural opera, featuring an excellent tenor, Valentin Duc as Eléazar. Other works included Meyerbeer's *Les Huguenots* (also with Duc as Raoul), *Le Prophète* and *Robert le Diable*, Thomas's *Le songe d'une d'été* and *Mignon*, Adrien Boieldieu's *La Dame Blanche*, Édouard Lalo's *Le Roi d'Ys*, Gioachino Rossini's *Guillaume Tell*, and Donizetti's *La favorite*. During the 1890-91 season the first part of Hector Berlioz's *Les troyens* (La Prise de Troie) was given in France. The season also marked the first appearance of Wolfgang Amadeus Mozart, with *Don Giovanni*. The first appearance of Richard Wagner works came the following year with *Lohengrin*. The brightest star of the season, however, was the appearance of Nellie Melba, who assayed Marguerite (*Faust*), Ophélie (*Hamlet*), Gilda (*Rigoletto*), and Lucia (*Lucia di Lammermoor*), along with other illustrious stars — Emma Nevada and Enrico Tamagno. Before the turn of the century, some novelties graced the stage like Ernst Reyer's *Sigurd* and *Salammbô*, Jules Massenet's *Werther* and *Hérodiade*, Adolph Adam's *Le Chalet*, and Meyerbeer's *Le Pardon de Ploërmel*, and some obscure ones including Messager's *La Basoche*, Gaston Salvayre's

Richard III, Léon Gastinel's *Le Barde*, and André Pollnais's *Mirka l'Enchanteresse* and *Dolorès*. Even the presence of Patti could not save the last work. Puccini's *La bohème* and Wagner's *Tristan und Isolde* arrived in 1899. There were between 20 and 30 operas in the repertory each season.

The arrival of the 20th century marked the French premiere of Richard Wagner's *Das Rheingold*. *Die Walküre* followed in 1902-03, and *Siegfried* the next season. Richard Strauss's *Salome* was first seen during the 1909-10 season. Some novelties before the opera house closed because of World War I — Charles Pons's *L'Epreuve*, Vincent d'Indy's *Etranger*, Poise's *Joli Gilles*, Isidore de Lara's *Sanga*, Massenet's *Thérèse*, and Xavier Leroux's *William Ratcliff*, *Le Chemineau*, and *La Reine Fiammette*. This last work drew much attention, primarily because of the presence of Mary Garden. Unsuccessful operas were Jean Nouguès's *Quo Vadis*, Louis Villemain's *La double Voile*, Léo Blech's *Sous-Scellés*, Félix Fourdrain and Jacques Larmanjat's *Gina*. Closed during World War I, l'Opéra de Nice was back in business on September 20, 1919. Its first season showed that the war had not tarnished its luster, with 27 operas in the schedule. The repertory favorites, like Meyerbeer's *Les Huguenots*, Massenet's *Manon*, *Thaïs*, and *Hérodiade*, Camille Saint-Saëns's *Samson et Dalila*, Reyer's *Sigurd*, and Halévy's *La Juive* joined two novelties, Massenet's *Roma* and Henri Rabaud's *Marouf, Savetier du Caire*. The seasons continued in like fashion, with a full repertory which included several novelties (known and obscure) each season until 1937-38 season, when the emphasis changed from novelties to presenting rare works. War again closed the opera house before the 1939-40 season could begin.

After four years of silence, its doors reopened on December 16, 1944, with 24 works scheduled for the season. (That did not include operetta which the opera house also hosted.) The repertory was similar to that before the war, with Massenet's *Manon*, *Thaïs*, and *Hérodiade*, Camille Saint-Saëns's *Samson et Dalila*, Gounod's *Faust*, *Roméo et Juliette*, and *Mireille*, Verdi's *La traviata* and *Otello*, and Édouard Lalo's *Le Roi d'Ys* among its offerings. In 1948, an Italian troupe presented Verdi's *La forza del destino* for the first time in the Italian version, and the 1953-54 season witnessed Emmanuel Bondeville's *Madame Bovary* with Jacqueline Brumaire, Louis Rialland, and Roger Bourdin. That same season, Régine Crespin assayed Tosca

and Salomé in Massenet's *Hérodiade*. On April 7, 1956, Mario del Monaco interpreted Samson for the first time. There were a couple of novelties — Henri Tomasi's *L'Atlantide* and *Sampiero Corsop* Gian Carlo Menotti's *The Telephone*, and Marcel Landowski's *Le Rire de Nils Halérius*. The opera house was closed for restoration after the 1959-60 season and performances were held at the Palais de la Méditerranée. The late 1960s saw the premiere of George Gershwin's *Porgy and Bess* with Thomas Carey and Joyce Bryant, and Verdi's *Nabucco* graced the Nice opera stage for the first time in the mid–1970s, with Rita Orlandi Malaspina, Gian Piero Mastromei, Silvano Pagliuca, Salvatore d'Amiceo, and Mirna Pecile. The Nice premiere of Berlioz's *Benvenuto Cellini* followed.

In the 1990s, under the tenure of Jean-Albert Cartier, the repertory ranged from the operas of Christoph Willibald Gluck to those of Nino Rota, including Bellini's *I Puritani*, Strauss's *Elektra*, Verdi's *Oberto*, Leoš Janáček's *Z mrtvého domo* (House of the Dead), Puccini's *Turandot*, Nino Rota's *Il cappello di paglia di Firenze*, and a Gluck Cycle: *Alceste*, *Armide*, and *Orfeo ed Euridice* (concert). Recently the company has been plagued by severe financial problems and a more mainstream program of 19th century "war horses" and perennial favorites has graced the stage. Recent repertory includes Rossini's *Il barbiere di Siviglia*, Puccini's *Madama Butterfly*, Gounod's *Faust*, Wagner's *Lohengrin*, Verdi's *Falstaff*, Mascagni's *Cavalleria rusticana* and Ruggero Leoncavallo's *I pagliacci*.

Théâtre Municipal

After fire destroyed the Théâtre Municipal, the city counsel decided to reconstruct immediately. The prestige of the city required a glamourous opera house. Three sites were under consideration: where the destroyed opera house stood, the square of the Phocéens, and the terraces by the sea. The third site was chosen, and the terraces were demolished. (A museum and Palais of Beaux-Arts were constructed where the old theater had been.) Architect Aune submitted his plans in July 1881 and the opera house opened less than four years later.

The large opera house building exhibits a Beaux-Arts facade with four Muses on pedestals on the roof balustrade. Lyres crown the facade.

Corinthian columns of reddish-sand color, with a small lyre embellishment, circle the structure, above which one reads THÉÂTRE MUNICIPAL in gold letters on gray marble. The horseshoe-shaped, ivory, gold, and red auditorium holds four tiers — three box and one gallery — and a center royal box. Gilded angels and portrait medallions embellish the parapets. Lyres and names of composers border the allegorically painted ceiling from which hangs a huge chandelier. There are 1,299 places.

Practical Information. Opéra de Nice, 4 rue St. Françoise de Paule, 06364 Nice. Tel: 33 493 85 67 31, Fax: 33 493 62 69 26. When visiting Opéra de Nice, stay at the Hotel Negresco, 37 Promenade des Anglais, BP 379, 06007 Nice Cedex. Tel: 33 493 16 64 00 or 1 800 223-6800, Fax 33 493 88 35 68. It is located on the famous Promenade and convenient to the opera house. The hotel can assist with opera tickets and schedules.

COMPANY STAFF AND WORLD PREMIERES

Directeur Général. Gian-Carlo Monaco (1996–present), Jean-Albert Cartier (1993–96), Lucien Salles–Pierre Médecin (1982–93), Ferdinand Aymé (1954–82), Ferdinand Aymé–José Luccioni (1950–54), Georges Pogel (1948–50), Raymond Ancel (1946–48), Maurice Carrié (1945–46), Aquistapace–Romette (1944–45), Maurice Carrié (1936–39), Raymond Ancel (1932–36), Constantin Bruni (1931–32), Merle–Forest (1930–31), Paul Cervieres (1927–30), Constantin Bruni (1926–27), Henry Roy (1925–26), Raoul Audier–Maurice Durand (1923–25), Constantin Bruni (1919–23), Auguste Dunet (1919), Thomas Salignac (1913–14), Henri Villefranck (1906–13), Amedée Saugey (1901–06), Baptistin Jauffret (1899–1901), Eugène Lamare (1898–99), Monsieur Campocasso (1897–98), Olive Lafon (1894–97), Santino Costa (1891–94), Raoul Gunsbourg (1889–91), Monsieur Taillefer (1888–89), Edoardo Sonzogno (1887–88), Ercole Bolognini (1885–87).

World Premieres. Manzocchi's *Comte de Gleichen* 1887; Xavier Leroux's *William Ratcliff* 1905; Isidore Lara's *Sanga* 1905; Gabriel Dupond's *Glu* 1910; Témisot's *Auréole* 1910; Félix Fourdrain's *Vercingétorix* 1912; Hirchman's *Danseuse de Tanagra* 1911; Albert Wolff's *Marchand de Masques* 1913; Albert Wolff's *Soeur Béatrice.* **French Premieres:** (select) N. de Giosa's *Napoli di Carnivale* 1885–86; A. Catalani's *Dejanice* 1885–86; A. Ponchielli's *La gioconda* 1886–87; H. Berlioz's *Les Troyens* (La Prise de Troie) 1890–91; P.I. Tchaikovsky's *Eugene Onegin* 1895; R. Leoncavallo's *I pagliacci* 1895; R. Leoncavallo's *La bohème* 1899; R. Wagner's *Das Rheingold* 1901–02; G. Puccini's *Manon Lescaut* 1906. D. Shostakovich's *Ledi Makbet Mtsenskovo uyezda* (Lady Macbeth of the Mtsensk District) 1963; H.W. Henze's *Elegy for Young Lovers* 1965; D. Milhaud's *David*; Sutermeister's *Raskolnikoff* 1967.

Bibliography. *Opéra de Nice: Histoire d'un Centenaire 1885–1985* (Nice, 1985). *D'un siècle à l'autre: Opéra de Nice 1885–1985* (Nice, 1985). Interview with Jean-Albert Cartier, former general director, June 1995.

Thanks to Elisabeth Touraille, Opéra de Nice, and Michel Palmer.

ORANGE

Chorégies d'Orange (Summer Festival)

On August 21, 1869, the Théâtre Antique (Roman amphitheater) in Orange hosted opera for the first time —Étienne-Nicolas Méhul's *Joseph* and the tomb scene from Nicola Vaccai's *Giulietta e Romeo.* The Théâtre Antique, constructed at the beginning of the Common Era, had witnessed Mystery plays during the Middle Ages. The "new" Chorégies d'Orange was inaugurated with Giuseppe Verdi's *Requiem,* conducted by Carlo Maria Giulini in 1971.

Opera continued in the amphitheater in 1874, with Vincenzo Bellini's *Norma,* Victor Massé's *La Chalet,* and Adolphe Adam's *Galan-* *thée.* The operas of Christoph Willibald Gluck were a natural for that setting and in 1900 *Iphigénie en Tauride* was the first to be staged. *Orfeo ed Euridice* followed in 1903, and *Alceste* in 1912. Meanwhile, Camille Saint-Saëns's *Samson et Dalila* made its first appearance in 1902, and three years later Hector Berlioz's *Les Troyens à Carthage* (Les Troyens Part II) arrived, the same year as Arrigo Boïto's *Mefistofele* was staged. The title Chorégies d'Orange became official in 1903. Fourteen opera performances had been given until World War I forced suspension of the seasons.

After the war, opera resumed in 1919, under

the directorship of Victor Magnat. Known as the *Fêtes d'Art* during Magnat's tenure, which lasted until 1924, only four operas were presented: Saint-Saëns's *Samson et Dalila*, Gluck's *Iphigénie en Tauride* and *Armide* and Gabriel Fauré's *Pénélope*, which met with much success. When Alfred Gerson and Eugène Lazard took over in 1925, it was simply called *Fêtes*. During their directorship (until 1929), productions were limited to two Gluck operas, *Orfeo ed Euridice* and *Alceste*. In 1930, René Berton and Hector Jacomet took over, staying until 1933. During this time, it was known as *Représentés nationales*, but curiously included two operas of Richard Wagner, seen for the first time in Orange: *Tannhäuser* and *Die Walküre*. The latter, directed by Pierre Chéreax, included horses for the Valkyries. The first of Charles Gounod's works to enter the repertory, *Mireille*, was given in 1930. The following season there were three operas given, Gluck's *Iphigénie en Tauride*, a condensed version of Berlioz's *Les Troyens* and a novelty, Jean Nouguès's *Quo Vadis*. The directorship passed to Robert Brisacq in 1935. He survived three seasons before declaring bankruptcy. During that time, he introduced four novelties to Orange: Berlioz's *La Damnation de Faust*, Gounod's *Faust*, Édouard Lalo's *Le Roi d'Ys*, and Giuseppe Verdi's *Aida*. The municipality and Ministry of Beaux Arts bailed out the festival and installed J. Rouché and E. Bourdet to run it. They offered Gluck's *Alceste* and *Orfeo ed Euridice*, and Berlioz's *La prise de Troie* (Les Troyens Part I). After the 1939 season, the activities were halted because of the Second World War.

The seasons began again in 1947, with Jean Hervé as artistic director. Gluck continue to be a favorite with *Iphigénie en Tauride*, *Orfeo ed Euridice*, and *Alceste* in the repertory. Other works presented during this time included Lalo's *Le Roi d'Ys*, Saint-Saëns's *Samson et Dalila*, and Wagner's *Die Walküre*. In 1949, there was a single performance of Ernest Reyer's *Sigurd* with José Luccioni in the title role. A couple of contemporary pieces made an appearance: Claude Debussy's *Le Martyre de Saint Sébastien* with Véra Korène (Le Saint), and Arthur Honegger's *Le Roi David*. Maurice Lehmann took over in 1953, followed by G. Hirsch and A.M. Julien. From 1953 until the reorganization in 1971, twenty-one operas were presented, with six by French composers. Gounod was the most popular composer with *Faust*, *Mireille*, and *Roméo et Juliette* on the boards. Saint-

Saëns's *Samson et Dalila* and Berlioz's *La Damnation de Faust* were reprised, and Massenet's *Hérodiade* made its last appearance for 27 years in 1960. The following season, Bizet's *Carmen* with Jane Rhodes in the title role, finally entered the repertory. Grace Bumbry was Carmen in 1962. Bizet was popular with the public with numerous performances of his *L'Arlésienne*. Léo Delibes was not so lucky. His *Lakmé* appeared briefly in 1967, with C. Eda-Pierre in title role, and never returned. Wagner's *Lohengrin* was seen in 1958, with Regine Crespin as Elisabeth. Verdi's *Aida* was well-liked, but his *Rigoletto* was only seen for the first time in 1964, and not repeated until 1980. Only one performance of *Cavalleria rusticana* was mounted, and Giacomo Puccini's *Tosca* with C. Castelli in title role also graced the stage in 1965. In general, the Italian repertory was not well represented. In the contemporary vein, one finds Honegger's *Jeanne d'Arc au bûcher*.

The Chorégies d'Orange was reorganized in 1971 as the Nouvelles Chorégies, to compete on an international level with the other famous summer festivals, like the Arena di Verona, Salzburger Festspiele, and Bayreuther Festspiele. The repertory was expanded and star power was hired. The "new" festival was first under the guidance of Jacques Bourgeois and Jean Darnel. On July 23, 1972, with Montserrat Caballé as Leonora, Verdi's *Il trovatore* graced the stage. Berlioz's *La Damnation de Faust* (as an oratorio) followed with Régine Crespin as Marguerite. The 1973 season presented an historic *Tristan und Isolde* with Birgit Nilsson and Jon Vickers, under the direction of Karl Böhm. The next season saw Richard Strauss's *Salome* with Leonie Rysanek (Salome), Jon Vickers (Herod), Thomas Stewart (Jochanaan) and Ruth Hesse (Herodias). Caballé returned for the title role in Vincenzo Bellini's *Norma* with Vickers as Pollione and Josephine Veasey as Adalgesia, and Nilsson assayed Brünnhilde in Wagner's *Die Walküre*, with Rysanek, Théo Adam, and Richard Cassilly. Verdi's *Otello* was staged for the first time in the Théâtre Antique in 1975, with Vickers and Teresa Zylis-Gara. Gilda Cruz-Romo arrived in 1976 in the title role of *Aida*, with Bumbry, Peter Gougalov, and Ingar Wixell. That same season, James King assayed the title role in Wagner's *Lohengrin*. The 1978 season hosted Plácido Domingo and Elena Obraztsova in the title roles of *Samson et Dalila*, and Bumbry, Siegmund Nimsgern and Paul Plishka in Verdi's *Macbeth*.

Verdi's *Rigoletto* with Renato Bruson, Alfredo Kraus, Barbara Hendricks, and Stefania Toczyska, and Wagner's *Der fliegende Holländer* ushered in the 1980s. Other operas included Amilcare Ponchielli's *La gioconda* with Caballé, Puccini's *Turandot* with Ghena Dimitrova, Verdi's *Don Carlo* with Caballé, Bumbry, Giacomo Aragall, and Renato Bruson, and Bizet's *Carmen* with Toczyska, Hendricks, José Carreras. Verdi's *Simon Boccanegra*, seen for the first time in 1985, with

Caballé, Piero Cappuccilli, and Lando Bartolini, and Modest Mussorgsky's *Boris Godunov* featured Martti Talvela in the title role. Massenet's *Hérodiade* was revived in 1987 and, despite a mistral (cold north wind), was well received. The following season, for the first time in Orange, the complete Ring Cycle took center stage. With the 1990s, Strauss's *Elektra* was presented for the first time, with Gwyneth Jones in the title role and Rysanek as Klytemnestra. Verdi's *La traviata* also receive its first hearing. Recent offerings include Verdi's *Nabucco* and *Requiem*, and Bizet's *Carmen*. Chorégies d'Orange with its opera-air Théâtre Antique seating 10,000, is France's answer to Italy's Arena di Verona.

Théâtre Antique

Orange was founded in 35 B.C. by Roman colonists, former soldiers of the 2nd Gallic Legion. The town, a colony governed by Roman law, was provided with a city wall around 10 B.C. Hexagonal in shape, the wall enclosed part of Saint Eutrope Hill and probably went about 300 feet south of the Triumphal arch. This meant the Théâtre Antique (amphitheater) was located outside of the city, part of a vast complex of monuments most likely related to the worship of the emperors. The amphitheater itself dates back to the end of the Augustian and the beginning of Tiberian reign (A.D. 10–25).

The Théâtre Antique forms a semicircle, ending at the back wall of the stage. Originally ornamented by

Théâtre Antique (Orange, France).

statues, columns, and mosaics, the stone wall was protected by a large, slanting roof which rested on the side walls of the proscenium which jutted out on either side. The sole remaining statue (reconstructed in 1931 from fragments found during excavations) is that of Emperor Augustus. Two Corinthian columns still stand. The stage was a wooden floor which was build on joists and equipped with traps to allow both machinery and actors to appear and disappear. The 10,000 seats are on hard stone.

Practical Information. Chorégies d'Orange, place des Frères Mounet, 84105 Orange. Tel: 33 490 34 24 24, Fax: 33 490 34 15 52.

When visiting the Chorégies d'Orange, contact the Office du Tourisme, 5 cours Aristide Briand, 84100 Orange. Tel: 33 490 34 70 88, Fax: 33 490 34 99 62.

COMPANY STAFF

Directeur Général. (since 1971) Raymond Duffaut (1982–present), Jacques Bourgeois and Jean Darnel (1971–81).

Bibliography. Philippe Chabro, *Chorégies d'Orange* (Avignon, 1995). *Orange: The Roman Theater* (Orange, 1996).

Thanks to Colette Chaunu, Chorégies d'Orange.

PARIS

Opéra National de Paris Bastille

On the eve of Bastille Day, July 13, 1989, the Opéra Bastille was inaugurated with a concert entitled *The Night Before the Day*. Conducted by Georges Prêtre, the program featured Plácido Domingo, Barbara Hendricks, Teresa Berganza, Shirley Verrett, and Ruggiero Raimondi. President François Mitterand invited the heads of state from around the world to the private opening. Hector Berlioz's *Les Troyens* (La prise de Troie and Les Troyens à Carthage) inaugurated the first season on March 17, 1990. Carlos Ott designed the opera house.

The first proposal for a new, state-of-the-art opera house appeared in 1968, when Jean Vilar, Pierre Boulez, and Maurice Béjart published a report recommending the construction of a new opera house. A study was commissioned to investigate the feasibility of the project near the end of 1981. Finally on March 8, 1982, President François Mitterand announced the building of a "modern and popular" theater on the Place de la Bastille, symbolizing a revolution in all ways. In November 1982, an international architectural competition was held which attracted 1,650 entrants, but only 756 projects were received and submitted to the jury, before the May 13, 1983, deadline. The jury declared Ott as the *Lauréat du concours* (winner of the competition) on November 17, 1983, although rumor has it that the jury was convinced that they had chosen Richard Meier. The budget was $400 million and the bi-

centennial of the storming of the Bastille was the target opening date. Controversy and personnel upheavals followed.

On September 1985, Gérard Mortier (then director of Théâtre de la Monnaie, Brussels) was appointed director of the Opéra Bastille project. He planned a season of 200–250 performances in the Grande Salle. Mortier quit only a few months later, in January 1986. The politics and intrigues were not to Mortier's liking. In April 1986 the new Prime Minister Jacques Chirac wanted to abandon the project completely, but François Léotard, the Minister of Culture saved it. But then Edouard Balladur, the Finance Minister suspended construction during the latter half of July, causing losses of 750,000 francs a day until the work resumed. Daniel Barenboïm was appointed artistic and musical director in August 1987 and Pierre Vozlinsky was named general director. In March 1988, the two announced that a Barenboïm/Chéreau production of Wolfgang Amadeus Mozart's *Don Giovanni* would inaugurate the first season on January 10, 1990, with 72 productions planned for 1990, increased to 120 productions by 1991. Barenboïm signed a contract for $1.1 million in May 1988, but Vozlinsky was fired. Pierre Bergé (of Yves Saint Laurent fashion fame) took over in August 1988 and he, in turn fired Barenboïm in January 1989. A short time later, Pierre Boulez quit the planning committee with the statement,

"I cannot work with nonprofessionals." Patrice Chéreau also left with a stronger comment, "the whole thing makes me want to throw up." Their actions set off numerous lawsuits. A new music director, Myung-Whun Chung was appointed in May 1989, and on July 13, 1989, the opera house opened. Then René Gonzalèz resigned as general director in August 1989. The originally scheduled inaugural opera, Mozart's *Don Giovanni*, was cancelled and Berlioz's *Les Troyens* was given instead, with two American artists in the cast—Grace Bumbry (Cassandre), Shirley Verrett (Didon). Chung conducted the production by Pier-Luigi Pizzi. Leoš Janáček's *Kát'a Kabanová* was the only other opera performed that season, which ended two months later. For the 1990-91 season, the opera house launched an eight-opera season with Giuseppe Verdi's *Otello*, Luciano Berio's *Un re in ascolto*, Camille Saint-Saëns's *Samson et Dalila*, Pyotr Il'yich Tchaikovsky's *Pikovaya dama* (The Queen of Spades), Mozart's *Die Zauberflöte*, Janáček's *Kát'a Kabanová*, and Giacomo Puccini's *Manon Lescaut*. The 1993-94 season presented a repertory of 15 works, which ranged from Christoph Willibald Gluck's *Alceste* to Bernd Alois Zimmermann's *Die Soldaten*, and also included Francesco Cilea's *Adriana Lecouvreur*, Jacques Offenbach's *Les Brigands*, Richard Wagner's *Der fliegende Holländer*, Modest Mussorgsky's *Khovanshchina*, and Charles Gound's *Faust*, among others. The 1994-95 season was not as ambitious or interesting as the previous one, and included only nine operas, but the following season ushered in opera performances at both the Bastille and back at Palais Garnier (the opera's original home) with a more mainstream repertory—Puccini's *Tosca* and *Manon Lescaut*, Richard Strauss's *Salome*, and Mozart's *Idomeneo* among others. On May 16, 1998, the Bastille hosted the world premiere of Philippe Fénelon's *Salammbô*.

The scandals, however, continued. After five general directors in less than a decade, Hugues Gall was hired in 1995 from the Grand Théâtre de Genève to run the Bastille and another a power struggle ensued. This one was between Chung and Gall and dealt with who had artistic control of the productions. The result was that on October 14, 1994, Chung was fired after conducting a performance of Verdi's *Simon Boccanegra* and Gall hired James Conlon, music director at Oper der Stadt Köln, to also be music director at the Bastille. Chung, of course, sued and another nasty lawsuit followed. Chung, among other things, claimed discrimination. In the end, Chung got a lot of money and Gall got his way.

When the performances are not cancelled because of labor strikes, they can range from boring, traditional museum pieces, to creative, symbolic productions, and anywhere in the middle. Gall is very conservative and the productions reflect his preference. The 20th century works tend to be more creatively presented than the standard repertory works. One production of Bellini's *I Capuletti ed i Montecchi* took place in a straight-forward unit-type set which twisted and turned for different scenes. The interest lay in the lighting, although the blood red (light) symbolism pervading every scene became tiresome. The quality of the cast ranged from outstanding to "who hired him or her." Recent repertory offerings include Verdi's *Nabucco* and *La traviata*, Kurt Weill's *Der Aufstieg und Fall der Stadt Mahagonny*, Wagner's *Tristan und Isolde*, Puccini's *Turandot* and *Tosca*, and Georges Bizet's *Carmen*, Mozart's *Le nozze di Figaro* and *Così fan tutte*, Claude Debussy's *Pelléas et Mélisande*, Strauss's *Der Rosenkavalier*, Benjamin Britten's *Billy Budd*, Tchaikovsky's *Eugene Onegin*, Vincenzo Bellini's *Norma*, Jules Massenet's *Manon*, Gioachino Rossini's *L'italiana in Algeri*, and Alban Berg's *Lulu*.

Opéra Bastille

The Opéra Bastille is an immense conglomeration of granite, stainless steel, and glass fused together in a striking form. A huge square arch soars in front of the entrance where the "grand staircase for the people" is located. The burgundy and white auditorium holds two steeply raked balconies. The black velvet and pearwood seats blend with the Breton granite walls and oak floors. The fluorescent lights give a cold feeling to the space. The Grande Salle accommodates 2,723.

Practical Information. Opéra National de Paris, 120 rue de Lyon, 75012 Paris. Tel: 33 1 40 01 17 89, Fax: 33 1 44 73 13 00. When visiting the Opéra National de Paris, stay at the Hotel Intercontinental Paris, 3 rue de Castiglione, 75040 Paris Cedex 1. Tel: 33 1 44 77 11 11 or 1 800

Opéra National de Paris Bastille (Paris, France).

327-0200, Fax 33 1 44 77 14 60. It is centrally located and convenient to the opera house and can assist with tickets and schedules.

COMPANY STAFF AND WORLD PREMIERES

Directeur Général. Hugues Gall (1995–present), Jean-Paul Cluzel (1993–95), Dominique Meyer 1990–92), René Gonzalèz (1989), Pierre Vozlinsky (1987–88), Gérard Mortier (1985–86).

Création Mondiale. Philippe Fénelon's *Salammbô*, May 16, 1998.

Bibliography. Garard Charlet, *L'Opéra de la Bastille: Genèse et Réalisation* (Paris, 1989). *Propos d'Opéra — Images de la Bastille* (Paris, 1989).

Thanks to Jean-Pierre Ginoux.

Opéra National de Paris Palais Garnier

On January 5, 1875, the Théatre National de l'Opéra, also known as Palais Garnier, and now called the Opéra National de Paris Palais Garnier, was inaugurated with a program of excerpts from Daniel Auber's *La muette de Portici*, Fromental Halévy's *La Juive*, Gioachino Rossini's *Guillaume Tell*, and Giacomo Meyerbeer's *Les Huguenots*. The opera house, designed by Charles Garnier in the style of and for the Second Empire, was not opened until the Third Republic was in power.

Louis XIV granted Abbé Pierre Perrin, Robert Cambert, and Marquis de Sourdéac the right to establish the Académie Royale de Musique on June 28, 1669. Almost two years later, on March 3, 1671, it was inaugurated with Robert Cambert's *Pomone* at the Salle du Jeu de Paume de la Bouteille. The following year, Lully purchased the patent, ushering in the first great period in French opera. In 1672, Lully's *Les Fêtes de l'Amour et de Bacchus* was premiered, followed in 1673 by *Cadmus et Hermione*. The Academy then moved into the Salle du Palais Royale that same year where they remained until the opera house burned down on April 6, 1763. Lully's operas appeared almost annually until his death — *Alceste, Thésée, Atys, Isis, Psyché, Bellérophon, Proserpine, Persée, Phaëton, Amadis de Gaule, Roland, Armide et Renaud, Acis et Galatée,* and *Achille et Polyxène* (completed by Collasse). A non–Lully opera was also introduced, Marc-Antoine Charpentier's *Médée* on December 4, 1693.

The première of Jean-Phillipe Rameau's *Hippolyte et Aricie* on October 1, 1733, brought in the second great period in French opera. By 1760, 24 operas of Rameau had been produced, including *Les Indes galantes* in 1735, *Castor et Pollux* in 1737, *Dardanus* in 1739, *Platée* in 1745, *Les Fêtes de l'Hymen et de l'Amour* in 1747, *Zoroastre* in 1749, *Acanthe et Céphise* in 1751, *Zephire* and *Anacréon* in 1754, and *Les Paladins* in 1760. Rameau's works were not liked by the followers of the Italian school (Pergolesi and company) which led to the controversy known as the *querelle des bouffons* or *guerre des bouffons* (quarrel or war of the clowns). More than a decade later, Christoph Willibald Gluck came to Paris, and experienced similar hostility from the followers of the Italian school when he tried to produce his *Iphigénie en Aulide*, which premiered on April 19, 1774, followed by *Armide* on September 23, 1777. To settle the dispute, Niccolò Piccinni and Gluck were both commissioned to write an opera based on *Iphigénie en Tauride*. On May 18, 1779, Gluck's work was introduced, and it was so successful that Piccinni tried to withdraw his opera, but could not. His *Iphigénie en Tauride* was presented a short time later, and did not receive as favorable a response as Gluck's opera. Meanwhile, the company had moved into the Salles Machines des Tulleries on January 24, 1764, after their theater, the Salle du Palais Royal burned down in 1763. The Salle du Palais-Royal was rebuilt, reopening on January 26, 1770, with Rameau's *Zoroastre*. The theater was again gutted by fire a decade later, after a performance of Gluck's *Orfeo ed Euridice* on June 8, 1781. The company then performed in the Salle des Menus Plaisirs du Roy until it, too, was a victim of fire in April 1788. Architect Lenoir then designed a new house for the company, known as Salle de la Porte Saint Martin. It burned

down in May 1871, but had actually been declared unsafe soon after it opened.

Back in 1789, the Revolution exploded with the storming of the Bastille and the Academy fell under the control of the city of Paris. In 1791, the "Liberté des Théâtres" was proclaimed, which permitted anyone to build a theater and produce works. During this upheaval, the Royal Academy of Music underwent several name changes. First it became L'Opéra, then Académie de Musique, then got its original name back, Académie Royale de Musique, then was renamed Théâtre des Arts. It also received a new home in 1794, the newly constructed Salle Montansier.

With the dawn of the 19th century, Napoleon took control of the Théâtre des Arts which was then renamed Théâtre de l'Opéra. He instituted major reforms in an attempt to bring back the former glory the company had enjoyed. During the Second Empire, the pomp and grandeur of the regime was reflected in the continuing tradition of grand opera, which required five spectacular acts, huge choruses, and a ballet. Many world premieres were staged. In 1803, Cherubini's *Anacréon* was introduced, followed by Spontini's *La vestale* (December 16, 1807) and *Fernand Cortez* (November 28, 1809), Rossini's *Le siège de Corinthe* (October 9, 1826) and *Le Comte Ory* (August 20, 1828), Auber's *La muette de Portici* (February 29, 1828), and Rossini's *Guillaume Tell* (August 3, 1829). French grand opera blossomed with the world premieres of Meyerbeer's *Robert le Diable* (November 21, 1831), Halévy's *La Juive* (February 23, 1835), Meyerbeer's *Les Huguenots* (February 29, 1836), Hector Berlioz's *Benvenuto Cellini* (September 10, 1838), Gaetano Donizetti's *La favorite* (December 2, 1840), Meyerbeer's *Le Prophète,* (April 16, 1849), Charles Gounod's *Sapho* (April 16, 1851), Giuseppe Verdi's *Les vêpres siciliennes* (June 13, 1855), Meyerbeer's *L'Africaine* (posthumously) (April 28, 1865), Verdi's *Don Carlos* (March 11, 1867), and Ambroise Thomas's *Hamlet* (March 9, 1868).

After the Palais Garnier opened, Mermet's *Jeanne d'Arc au bûcher* was the first complete opera performed on April 5, 1876. Paris's prominent role of introducing new operas continued at the Garnier with Jules Massenet's *Le Roi de Lahore* (April 27, 1877), Camille Saint-Saëns's *Henri VIII* (March 5, 1883), Massenet's *Le Cid* (November 30, 1885) and *Thaïs* (March 16, 1894), Henri Février's *Monna Vanna* (January 13, 1909), Igor Stravinsky's

Solovey (The Nightingale, May 26, 1914), *Mavra* (June 3, 1922), and *Persephone* (April 30, 1934), and Darius Milhaud's *Maximilien* (January 5, 1932). Except for these occasional novelties, and the introduction of the operas of Richard Wagner that caused mini-riots, the programming was conservative with revivals and repeats dominating the repertory. Jacques Rouché, the last director of the Opéra to manage the theater as a concession, had began his 30-year reign in 1915, mounting 71 different operas during that time.

In 1939, all theaters were placed under state supervision, in an organization known as Réunion des Théâtres Lyriques Nationaux. The bureaucratic red tape took its toll, and by 1968, the need for drastic change became evident as the international-circuit singers deserted, resulting in erratic casting and poor attendance. René Nicoly was appointed to reverse this alarming trend, but he died a short time later. Then Rolf Liebermann was hired from the Staatsoper Hamburg in 1973 to restore l'Opéra to its former glory. With a huge budget, he succeeded by staging lavish productions of repertory works in the original language with world-renowned artists. The glory was short-lived. Problems reappeared as soon as Bernard Lefort succeeded Liebermann. Lefort resigned before his contract expired, claiming the position was a "thankless and burdensome task."

In 1958, Maria Callas made her debut singing the first act of Bellini's *Norma*, the second act of *Tosca*, and the third act of Verdi's *Il trovatore*. Twenty-one years later, in 1979, the first complete version of Alban Berg's *Lulu* was mounted with Teresa Stratas in the title role (designed by Patrice Chéreau, conducted by Pierre Boulez). (Berg's widow had prevented the staging of the entire opera.) The world premiere of Olivier Messiaen's *Saint François d'Assise* was presented under the baton of Seiji Ozawa in 1983.

When the Opéra National de Paris Bastille opened in 1989, the intent was that opera would be performed exclusively at the new opera house and that the Palais Garnier would become the home for ballet. But so many problems plagued the new opera house that opera was returned to the Palais Garnier beginning with the 1995-96 season, which offered Mozart's *Così fan tutte*, *Don*

Opéra National de Paris Palais Garnier facade during renovation (Paris, France).

Giovanni, and Rossini's *La Cenerentola*. Recent repertory includes Rameau's *Hippolyte et Aricie*, Claude Debussy's *Pelléas et Mélisande*, Georg Friedrich Händel's *Giulio Cesare*, Wolfgang Amadeus Mozart's *La clemenza di Tito* and *Così fan tutte*, Rossini's *L'italiana in Algeri*, and Franz Lehár's *Die lustige Witwe*.

Opéra National de Paris Palais Garnier

A bomb thrown by the Italian anarchist Felice Orsini the evening of January 14, 1858, at Napoleon III's carriage as he was riding to attend an opera at the Salle Le Peletier resulted in the construction of the Palais Garnier. After the incident, Napoleon ordered Baron Haussmann to clear a site for a new theater, although there were two additional opera houses in Paris at the time, Théâtre Italien and Opéra Comique. An architectural competition was held which attracted 171 entries, from which Garnier's design was selected. Fourteen years passed before the building was completed with problems arising from the start. A subterranean lake was discovered and the soft ground equired a double concrete foundation, and the Second Empire collapsed and the Third Republic replaced it. While all this was going on, the unfinished opera house served as a hospital, a military storage place, and a prison. In 1896, the massive crystal chandelier fell, killing one spectator. (This was recreated in *The Phantom of the Opera*.) In 1995, the stage's technical equipment was updated and the house underwent a major restoration. Jean-Loup Roubert was entrusted with the project. The Palais Garnier remains as a

reminder of the extravagance of Napoleon III's reign.

The Palais Garnier is from the Belle Époque era, with busts and medallions of composers, musical motifs, fluted Corinthian columns, and statues embellishing the facade. The Belle Époque auditorium is crimson and gold. Five levels of boxes and balconies curve around the space, divided into sections by massive gilded Corinthian columns. Golden music motifs embellish the parapets. Marc Chagall's *Bouquet de rêves* decorates the ceiling dome. The theater seats 1,979.

Opéra National de Paris Palais Garnier homage to Charles Garnier, architect (Paris, France).

Practical Information. Opéra National de Paris Palais Garnier, 8 rue Scribe, 75009 Paris. Tel: 33 1 40 01 17 89, Fax: 33 1 40 01 94 01. When visiting the Opéra National de Paris Palais Garnier, stay at the Hotel Intercontinental Paris, 3 rue de Castiglione, 75040 Paris Cedex 1. Tel: 33 1 44 77 11 or 1 800 327 0200, Fax 33 1 44 77 14 60. It is ideally located and convenient to the opera house and can assist with tickets and schedules.

BIBLIOGRAPHY

Bibliography. Christopher Curtis Mead, *Charles Garnier's Paris Opera* (Cambridge, 1991); J. Gourret, *Histoire de l'Opéra de Paris* (Paris, 1978). N. Demuth, *French Opera: Its Development to the Revolution* (Sussex, 1963); Henri Legrave, *Le théâtre et le public à Paris de 1715 à 1750* (Paris, 1972); Stéphane Wolff, *L'Opéra au Palais Garnier (1875–1961)* (Paris, 1962).

Opéra Comique

The Opéra Comique, also known as the Salle Favart, was inaugurated on December 7, 1898, with the President of the Republic Félix Faure in attendance. After the playing of the *Marseillaise* and several overtures, scenes from Ambroise Thomas's *Mignon*, Georges Bizet's *Mireille* and *Carmen*, Léo Delibes's *Lakmé*, and Victor Massé's *Saisons* were staged. This was the third Salle Favart. Fire had claimed the previous two. The structure was designed by Louis Bernier.

The first opéra comique appeared as early as 1640, but the seeds of the opéra comique were planted as a fixed genre around the turn of the century. Opéra comique was born as a parody of the mannerisms of classic grand opera that Jean-Baptiste Lully had imposed on the court of Louis XIV. The *Comédiens Français* were so successful that they were forbidden to use dialogue, so for their monologues, they invented an incomprehensible language which made the public laugh even more. Finally, in 1714, a widowed baron obtained from the Académie the authorization to officially perform opéra comique. The following year *Télémanque,* a parody on the Roman empire by Fénelon, was able to carry the official title of opéra comique. The company joined forces in 1762 with a troupe of Italian comedians and opened in the Théâtre de Bourgogne on February 3, 1762. The first composers of this new genre to find favor with the Parisian public were Charles-Simon Favart, Egidio Romualdo Duni, François André Philidor, Pierre Alexandre Monsigny, and André Grétry. Some of the most popular works included Monsigny's *Rose et Colas*, Philidor's *Déserteur*, and Grétry's *Zémire et Azore*. By 1780, the Opéra Comique had built up a substantial repertory.

Heurtier, architect and building inspector for the king, proposed to the company to build a theater in the garden of Hôtel Duc de Choiseul. In the contract, a box was reserved for Choiseul and his heirs. The new theater, known as the Salle Favart and located where the Opéra Comique stands today, was opened on April 28, 1783. Six majestic columns formed a peristyle that defined the facade. A beautiful golden auditorium offered 900 places. In 1801, the Opéra Comique abandoned the Salle Favart, which needed repairs and joined with a troupe at the Théâtre Feydeau. Except for a brief return to the Salle Favart and a month at the Théâtre Olympique, this arrangement lasted 28 years, until the Théâtre Feydeau threatened to collapse. The players then moved into the Salle Ventadour followed by the Théâtre des Nouveautés. Meanwhile, the Italian troupe moved into the Salle Favart, which became known as the Théâtre Italien, but the Opéra Comique secretly hoped to return to the Salle Favart. The opportunity arose when fire consumed the theater on January 13, 1838. Architect Charpentier was in charge of the rebuilding, and the second Salle Favart was inaugurated on May 16, 1840, by the Opéra Comique performing Ferdinand Hérold's *Le Pré aux Clers*. In the second Salle Favart, the backbone of the opéra comique repertory was premiered with works like Bizet's *Les pêcheurs de perle, Mireille,* and *Carmen,* Thomas's *Mignon,* Jacques Offenbach's *Les contes d'Hoffmann,* Delibes's *Lakmé,* Jules Massenet's *Manon,* and Emmanuel Chabrier's *Le roi malgré lui* which was introduced a week before the theater's destruction. On May 25, 1887, at the beginning of the first act of Thomas's *Mignon* a terrible fire erupted on the stage. Unfortunately, no one thought to lower the fire curtain. Panic erupted among the 700 spectators, and there were many victims. The theater

Top: Opéra Comique facade details (Paris, France). *Bottom:* Opéra Comique proscenium arch details (Paris, France).

lay in ruins. During the eleven years it took to re-build the Salle Favart, the troupe played at the Théâtre des Nations (former second Théâtre Lyrique). Here Édouard Lalo's *Le Roi d'Ys* and Massenet's *Werther* were premiered. The theater was under the guidance of Albert Carré. Under his tenure, diverse styles entered the repertory, with composers like Ludwig van Beethoven, Wolfgang Amadeus Mozart, Christoph Willibald Gluck, Richard Wagner, Manuel de Falla, and Giacomo Puccini. In this theater, Gustave Char-pentier's *Louise*, Claude Debussy's *Pelléas et Mélisande*, Maurice Ravel's *L'heure espagnole*, and Francis Poulenc's *La voix humaine* were intro-duced.

In 1936, Jacques Rouché took the reins and continued the policy of staging a wide-ranging repertory, and works like Claudio Monteverdi's *L'incoronazione di Poppea* were mounted. After the war, operas from 20th century composers played a dominate role with Richard Strass, Béla Bartók, Sergey Prokofiev, Leoš Janáček, Arnold Schöen-berg, Benjamin Britten, Kurt Weill, as well as the contemporary French composers — Darius Mil-haud, André Jolivet, and Francis Poulenc. Even Luigi Dallapiccola's *Il volo di notte*, Marcel Landowski's *Les Adieux*, and Maurice Thiriet's *La Locandiera* have been presented.

The Opéra (National de Paris) and Opéra Comique merged in 1959 and operas went back and forth between the two houses. Bizet's *Carmen* left the Opéra Comique for the stage of the Opéra (Palais Garnier), and Giuseppe Verdi's *La travi-ata* and Charles Gounod's *Roméo et Juliette* re-turned to the Opéra Comique. The permanent troupe was dissolved in 1972, and in 1990, the Opéra Comique became autonomous. It is fol-lowing a mission to reclaim works from the past. Recent offerings include Johann Strauß's *Eine Nacht in Venedig*, Francesco Cavalli's *Didone*, Otto Nicolai's *Die lustigen Weiber von Windsor*, Fabio Vacchi's *Station thermale*, Henry Purcell's *Dido and Aeneus*, Bizet's *Carmen*, and Gaetano Donizetti's *L'elisir d'amore*.

Salle Favart

Debussy called the exterior of the Opéra Comique a Baroque French train station, and that is an accurate description. It is divided into three levels and crowned by masks of Comedy and Tragedy. The facade exhibits a slightly rusticated ground level punctuated by entrance doors alter-nating with lampposts. Two Muses — *Musique* on the left and *Poésie* on the right — inhabit the niches on the second level, which is defined by three arches flanked by attached fluted columns embellished with faces of Comedy and Tragedy. Six caryatids flank small rectangular windows on the top level. The luxurious gold and red, horse-shoe-shaped auditorium holds four tiers. Cary-atids embellished the first and second balcony supports. Lyre ornament the proscenium boxes. The seats are a deep maroon velvet in dark ma-hogany frames. The gilded proscenium arch is decorated with flowers. Muses rest on top. The cupola is surrounded by cherubs which alternate with masks of Comedy and Tragedy. Of the 1,300 places, only 1,000 have good visibility.

Performing Venues of the Opéra Comique. Théâtre de Bourgogne (1762–1815). Salle Favart (1783–1801). Théâtre Feydeau (1801–04). Théâtre Olympique, rue de la Victoire (October 1804). Salle Favart (1804–July 1805). Théâtre Feydeau (1805–April 1829). Salle Ventadour (1829–March 1832). Théâtre des Nouveautés (September 1832–April 1840), Salle Favart (May 1840–June 1852). Salle Ventadour (June 1853–May 1857). Salle Favart (July 1853–May 1887). Théâtre des Na-tions (former second Théâtre Lyrique 1887–1898). Salle Favart (1898–present).

Practical Information. Opéra Comique, 5 rue Favart, 75002 Paris. Tel: 33 1 42 97 58 64, Fax: 33 1 49 26 05 93. When visiting the Opéra Comique, stay at the Hotel Intercontinental Paris, 3 rue de Castiglione, 75040 Paris Cedex 1. Tel: 33 1 44 77 11 11 or 1 800 327 0200, Fax 33 1 44 77 14 60. It is centrally located, convenient to the Opéra Comique, and can assist with tickets and schedules.

COMPANY STAFF AND PREMIERES

Directeur Général. Pierre Meclecin.

World Premieres. A. Boieldieu's *La Dame Blanche* December 10, 1825; D. Auber's *Fra Diavolo*, January 28, 1830; F. Hérold's *Zampa*, May 3, 1831; A. Adam's *Le Chatelet*, 1833; G. Donizetti's *La fille du régiment*, February 11, 1840; G. H. Berlioz's *La Damnation de Faust* (concert version), December 6, 1846; G. Meyerbeer's *L'Étoile du Nord*, February 16, 1854; Bizet's *Les pêcheurs de perle*, September 30, 1863; G. Bizet's *Mireille*, March 19, 1864; A. Thomas's *Mignon*, November 17, 1866; G. Bizet's

Carmen, March 3, 1875; J. Offenbach's *Les contes d'Hoffmann*, February 10, 1881; L. Delibes's *Lakmé*, April 14, 1883; J. Massenet's *Manon*, January 19, 1884; E. Chabrier's *Le Roi malgré lui*, May 18, 1887; É. Lalo's *Le Roi d'Ys*, May 7, 1888; J. Massenet's *Werther*, February 16, 1892; G. Charpentier's *Louise*, February 2, 1900; C. Debussy's *Pelléas et Mélisande*, April 30, 1902; P. Dukas's *Ariane et Barbe-Bleue*, May 10, 1907; M. Ravel's *L'heure espagnole*, May 19, 1911; F. Poulenc's *La voix humaine*, February 6, 1959. **French Premieres:** (select) G. Rossini's *Il barbiere di Siviglia*; G. Puccini's *La bohème*; G. Puccini's *Madama Butterfly*; W.A. Mozart's *Le nozze di Figaro*; G. Puccini's *Tosca*; G. Verdi's *La traviata*; R. Strauss's *Ariadne auf Naxos*; G. Verdi's *Falstaff*.

Bibliography. Albert Soubies and Charles Malherbe, *Histoire de l'Opéra-Comique* (Paris, 1892–93). Stéphane Wolff, *Un demi-siècle d'Opéra-Comique: 1900–1950* (Paris, 1953). Additional information supplied by the company.

Thanks to Edith Frilet and Alice Bloch, Opéra Comique.

Théâtre des Champs-Élysées

On March 31, 1913, Théâtre des Champs-Élysées opened its doors with Hector Berlioz's *Benvenuto Cellini*, a work that had not been performed since 1838. Félix Weingartner conducted. Two days later, an inaugural concert dedicated to French music took place. Camille Saint-Saëns conducted his *Phaeton*, Claude Debussy his *Prélude à l'après-midi d'un faune* and Vincent d'Indy his *Prélude de Wallenstein,* among others. The theater was designed by Roger Bouvard with Emile-Antoine Bourdelle responsible for the facade sculpture.

The inaugural season continued with several operas gracing the stage — Carl Maria von Weber's *Der Freischütz*, Gabriel Fauré's *Pénélope* with Lucienne Bréval, Gioachino Rossini's *Il barbiere di Siviglia*, and Gaetano Donizetti's *Lucia di Lammermoor*. Then a "mini" Russian season followed with Modest Mussorgsky's *Khovanshchina* and *Boris Godunov*. The following season, works of Richard Wagner dominated the repertory with *Tristan und Isolde*, *Die Meistersinger von Nürnberg*, and *Parsifal*, but the Italian repertory was not forgotten with Giuseppe Verdi's *Un ballo in maschera* and *Otello*, Ruggero Leonvacallo's *I pagliacci*, Ermanno Wolf-Ferrari's *Il segreto di Susanna*, and Giacomo Puccini's *Manon Lescaut*. Among the singers were Nellie Melba and Vanni Marcoux. In 1924 there was a "Mozart Festival" with the Wien Staatsoper performing Wolfgang Amadeus Mozart's *Don Giovanni, Die Entführung aus dem Serail*, and *Le nozze di Figaro*, under the direction of Franz Schalk. That same season, a French group also mounted Mozart works — *Così fan tutte, Don Giovanni*, and *Le nozze di Figaro*.

Four years later, Walther Straram took over the directorship of the theater, where he remained until 1933 and the prevalence of Mozart operas continued with Bruno Walter conducting *Die Zauberflöte, Die Entführung aus dem Serail, Così fan tutte*, and *Le nozze di Figaro*. Between 1929 and 1932, the Opéra Russe de Paris, founded by Maria Kouznetzoff-Massenet, offered a few seasons of Russian operas. Besides Mussorgsky's *Boris Godunov*, with Feodor Chaliapin in the title role, the company mounted Nikolay Rimsky-Korsakov's *Sadko*, *Skazka o Tsare Saltane* (The Tale of Tsar Saltan), and *Skazaniye o nevidimom grade Kitezhe* (The Legend of the Invisible City of Kitezh), Mikhail Glinka's *Ruslan and Lyudmila*, Alexander Borodin's *Prince Igor*, and Alexander Dargomyzhsky's *Rusalka*.

The theater had hosted Wagner's complete *Der Ring des Nibelungen* in 1929, given by a troupe from Bayreuth that included Lauritz Melchior as Siegmund and Siegfried, Nancy Larsen-Todsen as Brünnhilde, and Tullio Serafin conducted the Teatro Regio Torino in three Rossini operas — *Il barbiere di Siviglia, La Cenerentola*, and *L'italiana in Algeri*. Staatsoper Berlin arrived in 1937 with Wagner's *Die Walküre* conducted by Wilhelm Furtwängler. The cast included Franz Völker (Siegmund), Rudolf Bockelmann (Wotan), Maria Müller (Sieglinde), and Martha Fuchs (Brünnhilde). Wagner's *Tristan und Isolde* was also on the boards. Richard Strauss conducted two of his operas, *Der Rosenkavalier* and *Ariadne auf Naxos*. The Wien Staatsoper returned after the Second World War in 1947, 1949, and 1951 with Mozart's *Don Giovanni, Die Entführung aus dem Serail, Le nozze di Figaro*, and *Così fan tutte*. Some interpreters included Maria Reining, Elisabeth Schwarzkopf, Irmgard Seefried Sena Jurinac, Hilde Güden, Hans Hotter, and Walther Ludwig. The last year of their visit, in 1951, Ludwig van

Beethoven's *Fidelio* was also presented. Two years later, the Württembergisches Staatstheater Stuttgart offered Wagner's *Tristan und Isolde* and *Die Meistersinger von Nürnberg*. The Staatsoper Berlin returned in 1954, but offered a Mozart repertory — *Don Giovanni*, *Le nozze di Figaro*, and *Così fan tutte*. The following year the Hamburg Staatsoper staged Wagner's *Tristan und Isolde* and also works by Mozart, Arnold Schöenberg, and Luigi Dallapiccola. The 1956 season welcomed the Oper Frankfurt with Strauss's *Der Rosenkavalier*, and Teatro di San Carlo with Puccini's *La bohème* and Rossini's *Il barbiere di Siviglia*. Russian opera returned to the stage the same season with Opera Belgrade staging Borodin's *Prince Igor* and Mussorgsky's *Khovanshchina*.

The first modern execution of Antonio Vivaldi's *La fida ninfa* took place in 1958 by a troupe from Florence. Teatro Massimo di Palermo brought Puccini's *Turandot*, Donizetti's *Don Pasquale*, and Verdi's *Otello* in 1962. Another *Turandot* was mounted nine years later by the Opera Sofia. The company also presented Mussorgsky's *Boris Godunov* and *Khovanshchina*, and Borodin's *Prince Igor*, in 1971. Mozart's *Idomeneo* was staged in 1976 by the Opéra d'Angers, and a decade later, Paris discovered Federico and Luigi Ricci's *Crispino e la comare*, mounted by the Teatro la Fenice. The Opera Sofia returned the same season with a presentation of Sergey Prokofiev's *Voyna i mir* (War and Peace). In 1987, Mozart's *Die Zauberflöte* was in the repertory for the reopening of the theater, after renovation. Recent repertory includes Mussorgsky's *Boris Godunov*, Beethoven's *Fidelio*, and Sergey Prokofiev's *Obrucheniye v monastïre* (Betrothal in a Monastery).

Since its founding, the Théâtre des Champs-Élysées has never received a franc of public money, from the government or any other source. It is privately supported and an excellent example how a modern theater in Europe can function without public money.

Théâtre des Champs-Élysées

The idea to build a theater to welcome contemporary works developed back in 1896 by the city council of Paris. They turned to Gabriel Astruc, Directeur de la Société Musicale, to facilitate the project. Astruc's ideal was a theater with English comfort, German technical facilities, and French taste. Gabriel Thomas, president of the Société financed the project. It was built by Auguste and Gustave Perret. Renovated in 1987, the theater's facilities were updated and it regained its original luster.

The unpretentious white stone facade exhibits three relief panels across the top, the only embellishment on the building's front. Underneath, THÉÂTRE DES CHAMPS-ÉLYSÉES is inscribed in gold letters. The Art Deco auditorium is lyre-shaped, of red, gold, and gray. There are three tiers with deep-red velvet seats. The parapets are of gray marble bordered with gold and match the panels flanking the fluted gold proscenium arch. Allegorical murals by Maurice Denis swirl around the room. There are 2,000 seats.

Practical Information. Théâtre des Champs-Élysées, 15 Ave Montaigne, 75008 Paris. Tel: 33 1 49 52 50 00, Fax: 33 1 49 52 07 41. When visiting Théâtre des Champs-Élysées, stay at the Hotel Intercontinental Paris, 3 rue de Castiglione, 75040 Paris Cedex 1. Tel: 33 1 44 77 11 11 or 1 800 327 0200, Fax 33 1 44 77 14 60. It is ideally located and convenient to the opera house and can assist with tickets and schedules.

COMPANY STAFF AND PREMIERES

Directeur Général. Alain Durel.

World Premieres. G. Bécaud's *L'Opéra d'Aran*, 1962. **French Premieres:** I. Montemezzi's *L'amore dei tre re*, 1914; A. Honegger's *Le Roi David*, 1924 (first stage performance); I. Stravinsky's *L'histoire du soldat*, 1924; E. Křenek's *Jonny spielt auf*, 1928; W. Egk's *Peer Gynt*, 1952; B. Britten's *Billy Budd*, 1952; M. Mihalovici's *Phèdre*, 1953; C. Orff's *Carmina Burana*, 1953; L. Dallapiccola's *Il volo di notte*, 1955 (first stage performance); A. Schöenberg's *Erwartung*, 1952; B. Britten's *The Turn of the Screw*, 1956; A. Schöenberg's *Moses und Aron*, 1961; A. Berg's *Wozzeck*, 1962 (first staged performance).

Bibliography. *Les Cahiers du Théâtre des Champs-Élysées Libre Opéra* (Paris, 1988). Alain Gueullette, *Les riches heures du Théâtre des Champs-Élysées* (Paris, 1987).

Thanks to Nathalie Sergent, Théâtre des Champs-Élysées, and Jean-Pierre Ginoux.

Théâtre du Châtelet

The Théâtre du Châtelet was inaugurated on August 19, 1862, with MM. d'Ennery, Clairville, and Monnier's *Rothomago* in the presence of Empress Eugénie. Designed by architect Gabriel Davioud, it was the largest theater in Paris at the time, with 2,500 seats.

The theater searched for an identity for many years, and its lack of mission was manifest in the frequent turnover of directors. Between 1875 and 1880, there were more than eleven different directors, but it claimed success with the staging of spectacles like *Le tour du monde en quatre-vingts jours* (Around the World in 80 Days) which received 3,707 performances. Finally in 1906, the legendary seasons of Gabriel Astruc began. This artistic reorientation at the beginning of the century helped the Châtelet find its niche. The following year, the French premiere of Richard Strauss's *Salome* took place, with the composer on the podium. Two years later, Diaghilev mounted a season of Russian opera and Paris saw Feodor Chaliapin in the title role of Sergey Rimsky-Korsakov's *Ivan the Terrible*, Mussorgsky's *Boris Godunov* and Alexander Borodin's *Prince Igor*. The following year, Italian opera took center stage. Arturo Toscanini had arrived in Paris with the Metropolitan Opera and mounted Giuseppe Verdi's *Aida*, *Falstaff*, and *Otello*, Pietro Mascagni's *Cavalleria rusticana*, Ruggero Leoncavallo's *I pagliacci*, and Giacomo Puccini's *Manon Lescaut* in its Parisian premiere. The public applauded singers like Emmy Destinn, Louise Homer, and especially Enrico Caruso.

In 1930, Maurice Lehmann took the directorship of the theater, remaining at the helm until 1966. He changed the theater's direction by introducing musicals, like Oscar Hammerstein's *Mississippi Show Boat* and Jerome Kern's *New Moon*. In 1941, Lehmann brought Johann Strauß's *Vienna Waltzes* with much success. The 1950s and 1960s until Lehmann's departure, he offered *L'auberge du cheval blanc*, *Chanteur de Mexico*, *Méditerranée* and *Monsieur Carnaval*, among others. The artists included Georges Guétary, Luis Mariano, Tino Rossi, Francis Lopez, and Jean Richard. When Lehmann left in 1966, the financial situation slowly deteriorated until the city of Paris took over the administration of the theater in 1979. It then became known as the Théâtre Musical de Paris. The city paid for a refurbishment and updating of the theater's facilities. When it reopened in 1980, Jean-Albert Cartier was the new head and it was entirely subsidized by the city of Paris, but with a budget much smaller than that of the Opéra de Paris. Cartier brought several innovations, including introducing unifying themes for the works mounted: "Opéras d'une heure" (Operas of one hour) allowed the staging of contemporary works, from Luciano Berio and Aperghis, among others; "Opéras de jeunesse de Verdi" staged early Verdi operas; "Saison russe," saw Russian works on the boards; "Tricentenaire de Händel" concentrated on Händel's works; "Saison Rossini" welcomed Gioachino Rossini operas; "Saison Mozart" hosted Wolfgang Amadeus Mozart's works, and "L'opéra allemand" emphasized German operas. Operettas, comedies, musicals, ballets, and concerts shared the stage with opera.

Stéphane Lissner took over from Cartier in 1988, and the city once again improved the theater, with better sight-lines for the spectators and improved acoustics. The old curtain was replaced by one created by the painter Gérard Garouste and it took back its original name, Théâtre du Châtelet. Lissner also organized seasons around themes and "cycles": 1988–89: Intégrale Gustav Mahler (Symphonies and Lieder of Gustav Mahler); 1989–90: L'Europe musicale de 1650 à 1750 (European music from 1650–1750); 1990–91: La musique française de Berlioz et Debussy (French Music of Berlioz and Debussy), and included the staging of Berlioz's *La Damnation de Faust* and Debussy's *Pelléas et Mélisande*; 1991–92: Musique de notre siècle (Music of our century); 1992–93: Cycle of Robert Schumann, Igor Stravinsky, and Béla Bartók and featured *A Kékszakállú herceg vára* (Duke Bluebeard's Castle); 1993–94: Cycle of Richard Strauss including *Der Rosenkavalier* and *Die Frau ohne Schatten*, and a new production of *Der Ring des Nibelungen*; 1994–95: Beethoven Cycle; 1996–97: Stravinsky and Arnold Schönberg Cycle, which offered Stravinsky's *The Rake's Progress*, *Oedipus Rex*, and *Solovey* (The Nightingale) and Arnold Schönberg's *Pierrot Lunaire*. Other operas include Claudio Monteverdi's *L'incoronazione di Poppea*, Francis Poulenc's *La voix humaine*, Georg Friedrich Händel's *Alcina*, Jacques Offenbach's *Les contes d'Hoffmann*, Paul Dukas's *Ariane et Barbe-Bleue*, Luigi Dallapiccola's *Il prigioniero*, Philippe Fénelon's

Le Chevalier imaginaire, Alban Berg's *Lulu*, Wolfgang Amadesu Mozart's *Così fan tutte* and *Die Entführung aus dem Serail*, Giuseppe Verdi's *La traviata*, Wagner's *Lohengrin*, Henry Purcell's *King Arthur*, Benjamin Britten's *Peter Grimes*. There was a world premiere during the 1993-94 season, Michael Jarrell's *Cassandre*, followed by the French premiere of Berio's *Outis* at the end of the 1990s. The mid-part of the decade offered Jean-Philippe Rameau's *Zoroastre* (concert version), Richard Wagner's *Götterdämmerung*, Alban Berg's *Wozzeck*, György Ligeti's *Le Grand Macabre* (as part of Hommage à György Ligeti), Wagner's *Parsifal*, and Engelbert Humperdinck's *Hänsel und Gretel*. One recent production of Leoš Janáček's *Příhody Lišky Bystroušky* (The Cunning Little Vixen) was innovative and clever, giving the work a fresh interpretation while not deviating from the "message" of the piece.

In 1998, the theater closed for a 70 million FF renovation, paid for by the city of Paris. It reopened in August 1999, with Christoph Willibald Gluck's *Orfeo ed Euridice* and *Alceste*, Ferruccio Busoni's *Doktor Faust*, and Mozart's *Mitridate, re di Ponto*. "Festival des régions" which includes the Théâtre du Capitole Toulouse presenting Ambroise Thomas's *Hamlet* and Gustave Charpentier's *Louise* also graces the stage.

Théâtre du Châtelet

The plain exterior of the building belies the lavish interior. The red and gold, horseshoe-shaped auditorium holds four tiers, embellished with masks of Comedy and Tragedy, cherubs, and putti. Allegorical figures are painted around a huge cupola.

Practical Information. Théâtre du Châtelet, 2 rue Edouard Colonne, 75001 Paris. Tel: 33 1 40 28 28 28, Fax: 33 1 42 36 89 75. When visiting the Théâtre du Châtelet stay at the Hotel Intercontinental Paris, 3 rue de Castiglione, 75040 Paris Cedex 1. Tel: 33 1 44 77 11 11 or 1 800 327 0200, Fax 33 1 44 77 14 60. It is ideally located and convenient to the opera house and can assist with tickets and schedules.

COMPANY STAFF

Directeur Général. Jean-Pierre Brossmann (1997–present), Stéphane Lissner (1988–96), Jean-Albert Cartier (1980–88), Maurice Lehmann (1930–66).

Bibliography. Châtelet: 1998–1999: Rénovation de la Cage de Scène (Paris, 1998). Additional information supplied by the company.

Thanks to the administration, Théâtre du Châtelet; Stevan Bradley, and Jean-Pierre Ginoux.

REIMS

Grand Théâtre de Reims

The Grand Théâtre de Reims is a small company that concentrates on the French repertory, but includes German and Italian operas as well in its schedule. Recent repertory includes Georges Bizet's *Mireille*, Giacomo Puccini's *Madama Butterfly*, Ludwig von Beethoven's *Fidelio*, Charles Gounod's *Faust*, and Wolfgang Amadeus Mozart's *Die Zauberflöte*.

Practical Information. Grand Théâtre de Reims, 9 rue Chanzy, 51100 Reims. Tel: 33 326 444 43, Fax: 33 326 84 90 02. When visiting the Grand Théâtre de Reims, stay at Les Crayères, 64 boulevard Henry-Vasnier, 51100 Reims. Tel: 33 326 82 80 80, Fax: 326 82 65 52. It is a turn-of-the-century residence, convenient to the opera house. They can assist with schedules and tickets.

COMPANY STAFF

Directeur Général. Jean-Louis Grinda

Bibliography. Materials supplied by the company.

Thanks to Marie-Claire Legrand, Grand Théâtre de Reims.

ROUEN

Opéra de Normandie

Théâtre des Arts was inaugurated on December 11, 1962, with Georges Bizet's *Carmen*. Jean Lecanuet was responsible for the reconstruction of the opera house. The previous building had been destroyed by bombs during World War II. Opéra de Normandie was created in 1991.

Opera in Rouen, however, dates back to the late 17th century, when the Académie Royale de Musique opened with a production of Jean-Baptiste Lully's *Phaëton* on September 15, 1688. Its name was changed to La Comédie in 1696. The 1,600-seat Théâtre de Rouen was inaugurated on June 29, 1776, and in 1793, it received a new name, Théâtre de la Montagne. That same year, the opera house hosted the premiere of Adrien Boieldieu's *La fille coupable* and two years later, in 1795, his *Rosalie et Myrza*. (Boieldieu was born in Rouen.) The opera house acquired its current name, Théâtre des Arts, in 1794, and burned to the ground on April 25, 1876. Reconstructed over the next several years, the 1,500-seat theater was inaugurated on September 30, 1882, with Giacomo Meyerbeer's *Les Huguenots*. In 1890, it hosted the French premieres of Camille Saint-Saëns's *Samson et Dalila* on March 3, 1890 (world premiere in Weimar, Germany, December 2, 1877), and Ernst Reyer's *Salammbô* on November 10, 1890 (world premiere at Théâtre Royal de la Monnaie, Brussels, February 10, 1890). The theater was damaged on June 9, 1940, by a fire caused by shelling, and completely destroyed by bombs on June 4, 1944. The opera seasons were moved to the Théâtre Cirque until 1962, when the Théâtre des Arts was rebuilt and reopened with André Cabourg as the director.

In 1991, Marc Adam became the first appointed general director of the newly created Opéra de Normandie. As he explained, the company has three missions: to stage the "war horse" 19th century repertory to earn box office revenue; to rediscover forgotten works, or those that for some reason had never been staged in Rouen (like Ambroise Thomas's *Hamlet*, given for the first time only a few years ago); and to produce contemporary opera and *créations* (world premieres). (To this end the world premieres of Eugeniusz Knapik's *Silent Screams Difficult Dreams* was given on October 9, 1992, and Charles Chaynes's *Jocaste* on November 5, 1993.) Everyone involved with the opera is young — the singers, directors, conductors, because there is a policy that the artists should be singing the role for the first time, and the conductors leading it for the first time, to ensure a fresh approach to the work. He is trying to find and "touch" different audiences.

Another one of the company's world premieres, Marius Constant's *Teresa*, billed as a *mélodrame fantastique*, was premiered on November 8, 1996. For the production, the 1,350 seat Théâtre des Arts transformed into a 350-seat experimental theater, with all the orchestra seats removed to turn the space into an enormous stage. The work and production were more akin to an Off Off Broadway show, with the abundance of spoken dialogue, strange melodies, and which opened with a huge, white horse trampling across a fog-filled stage (and auditorium). Adam chose works that have something to say to today's audience. *Teresa* dealt with being trapped in life and the saving of a soul. The productions provide a contemporary vision of classic plays. He does not like "museum" pieces. Until the 1960s, world premieres were not uncommon at the theater. Then they ceased. Adam resumed with the world premieres and added rarely-performed works to the repertory. He labels his policies adventurous. The $9 million budget (45 million FF) is 65% financed by the town council, with 6% from the state government in Paris, 6% from the *région* arts board. Only 1% — 2% is from private donations. The culture of private support of the arts is new in France. The remainder must be earned income, with tickets accounting for 10%–12%. With the decrease in government support, the number of performances also decreased — 50% between 1993 and 1996 — from 100 a year to 50 a year. Recent productions include Ruggero Leoncavallo's *I pagliacci*, Leoš Janáček's *Z mrtvého domo* (House of the Dead), Gaetano Donizetti's *Lucia di Lammermoor*, Manfred Gurlitt's *Wozzeck*, and Henri Christiné's *Dédé*.

Théâtre des Arts (Rouen, France).

Théâtre des Arts

The Théâtre is a concrete, box structure, typical of theater architecture of the early 1960s. The lines are severe, with nothing of note on the facade. The auditorium holds three tiers. The parapets are white with geometric indentations, which contrasts with the red seats. The auditorium seats 1,350.

Practical Information. Opéra de Normandie, 7 rue du D'Rambert, BP 1253, 76177 Rouen. Tel: 33 235 98 50 98, Fax: 33 235 15 33 49. When visiting Opéra de Normandie, stay at the Hotel Mercure Rouen Centre, 7 rue Croix de Fer, 76000 Rouen. Tel: 33 235 52 69 52, Fax 33 235 89 41 46. It is in the center of the old city and close to the opera house. The hotel can assist with opera tickets and schedule.

COMPANY STAFF, WORLD PREMIERES, AND REPERTORY

Directeur Général. Marc Adam (1991–present).
World Premieres (Opéra de Normandie).

E. Knapik's *Silent Screams Difficult Dreams* October 9, 1992; C. Chaynes's *Jocaste* November 5, 1993; M. Constant's *Teresa*, November 8, 1996.

Repertory (Opéra de Normandie). **1992–93:** Samson et Dalila (concert version), Silent Screams Difficult Dreams, Tannhäuser, La traviata, Le Cid, Euridice. **1993–94:** Jocaste, La bohème, Il barbiere di Siviglia, Der Freischütz, Capriccio, Hamlet, Die Zauberflöte. **1994–95:** Turn of the Screw, Parsifal, Die lustige Witwe, Die Dreigroschenoper, Faust, Il turco in Italia, La bohème. **1995–96:** Tosca, La vieille Maison, Il barbiere di Siviglia, Die Fledermaus, Un ballo in maschera, La Cenerentola, Carmen; **1996–97:** Teresa, I pagliacci, Z mrtvého domo (House of the Dead), Lucia di Lammermoor, Wozzeck (Gurlitt), Dédé.

Bibliography. Henri Geispitz, *Histoire du Théâtre des Arts de Rouen: 1882–1913* (Rouen, 1913). Robert Etude, *Petite Histoire du Théâtre des Arts* (Rouen, 1963). Interview with Marc Adam, general director, October 1996.

Thanks to Pascale Gruel, Opéra de Normandie, and Cécile Buchard-Leclerc.

STRASBOURG

Festival des Musiques d'Aujourd'hui
(Fall Festival)

The Festival des Musiques d'Aujourd'hui was the brainchild of Laurent Bayle, its initial director and founder. Created in 1983 to showcase contemporary works and opera from the second half of the 20th century, the festival gives promising young composers a chance to have their works performed. The directors and set and costume designers are from the theater and cinema. The productions are modern and relevant, bringing a "message," and the topics dealt with are of concern to today's society. The festival also offers a platform for young singers, since they are the only ones with the time and interest to learn these types of contemporary works. Here you will see the stars of tomorrow.

Each festival concentrates on a different region. In 1995, the festival concentrated on Italy, and their modern composers giving an impression of contemporary Italian repertory. Gualtiero Dazzi's *La rosa de Ariadna*, Luigi Nono's *Intolleranza*, and a reworking by Luciano Berio of Wolfgang Amadeus Mozart's *Zaïde* were on the festival program. Their budget is around 9 million FF. The festival utilizes a variety of performance venues with opera performances often taking place in the Palais des Fêtes and Théâtre National de Strasbourg.

Practical Information. Festival des Musiques d'Aujourd'hui, rue de la Mésange, 67000 Strasbourg. Tel: 33 3 88 32 43 10, Fax: 33 3 88 21 02 88. Palais des Fêtes, 5 rue Sellenick; Théâtre National de Strasbourg, place de la République. When visiting the Festival des Musiques d'Aujourd'hui, stay at the Hôtel Le Régent Contades, 8 avenue de la Liberté, 67000 Strasbourg. Tel: 33 3 88 36 26 26, Fax 33 3 88 37 13 70. It is in a central location near the festival theaters and can assist with opera tickets and schedule.

COMPANY STAFF AND REPERTORY

Directeur Général. Jean-Dominique Marco (1990–present), Laurent Spielmann (1987–90), Laurent Bayle (1983–87).

Repertory (opera and musical spectacles). **1983:** Leoš Janáček's *Zápisník zmizelého* (The Diary of the Young Man Who Disappeared), Françoise Kubler's *Lupe Velez*. **1984:** Denis Cohen's *Ajax*, Zygmunt Krauze's *Fête galante et pastorale*, Dieter Schnebel's *Jowaergli*. **1985:** Robert Ashley's *Atalanta/Acts of God*, Brabant's *M'Kuso*, François-Bernard Mâche's *La Traversée de l'Afrique*. **1986:** Sylvano Bussotti's *Le Racine*. **1987:** Giorgio Battistelli's *Jules Verne*, Mauricio Kagel's *Le tribun*, Claudy Malherbe's *Mobilier urbain*, Iannis Xenakis's *L'Oresteia*. **1988:** Georges Aperghis's *Enumérations*, Heiner Goebbels's *Der Mann im Fahrstuhl*, Bernd Alois Zimmermann's *Die Soldaten*. **1989:** Giorgio Battistelli's *Le combat d'Hector et d'Achille*, Pascal Dusapin's *Roméo & Juliette*, Marc Monnet's *Variations*. **1990:** Georges Aperghis's *La Baraque foraine*, John Cage's *Europeras 3 & 4*, Luc Ferrari's *Labyrinthe Hôtel*, Denis Levaillant's *O.P.A. Mia*, Géradr Pesson's *Beau Soir*, Guedalia Tazartes's *Le Miracles des roses*. **1991:** Marc Monnet's *L'Exercice de la Bataille*. **1992:** Georges Aperghis's *H*, Bernard Cavanna's *La Confession impudique*, Peter Maxwell Davies's *Eight Songs for a Mad King* and *Miss Donnithorne's Maggot*, Iannis Xenakis's *Faust*. **1993:** Marc Monnet's *Fragments*, Yi Xu's *Le Roi des Arbes*, Wolfgang Rihm's *Jakob Lenz*, Georges Aperghis's *Sextuor*. **1994:** Ahmed Essyad's *Le collier des Ruses*, Robert Ashley's *Now Eleanor's Idea*. **1995:** Gualtiero Dazzi's *La rosa de Ariadna*, Luigi Nono's *Intolleranza*, Luciano Berio's *Zaïde*.

Bibliography. *Le Monde de la Musique* (Strasbourg, 1993). *Musica: Festival des Musiques d'Aujourd'hui Strasbourg* (Strasbourg, 1991). *Musica: Festival des Musiques d'Aujourd'hui Strasbourg* (Strasbourg, 1993 & 1994). Additional information supplied by the company. Interview with Jean-Dominique Marco, general director, June 1995.

Thanks to Claire Alby, Festival des Musiques d'Aujourd'hui, and Eddy Marchal.

STRASBOURG/MULHOUSE/COLMAR

Opéra du Rhin

The Théâtre Municipal, originally called Théâtre Napoléon, was inaugurated on May 23, 1821, with Farges-Maricourt's *La promenade du Broglie* followed by André Grétry's *La fausse magie*. The architect was M. Berigny. On September 10, 1870, the theater was in a large part destroyed by German bombardment. Reconstructed by architect Conrathon based on the original plans, it was reinaugurated on September 4, 1873, as the Théâtre d'État (Alsace-Lorraine). Opéra du Rhin was created in 1972.

The first opera recorded in Strasbourg took place on April 20, 1700, performed by a visiting troupe from Nancy and Metz. Around fifty troupes received permission to play in Strasbourg during this time period. There were also comedy and drama companies. The following year, the city transformed the Grange d'Avoine into a performance hall, giving it the name Opernhaus, but despite the German name, French opera was performed. Located at Place Broglie, the Opernhaus was described as a large building with a simple exterior, longer than it was wide. The grand interior held both an amphitheater and boxes, and was beautifully decorated. Nevertheless, the theater never pleased the spectators and underwent numerous transformations until another theater was constructed in 1733. Called the Petite Théâtre or Théâtre des Drapiers, it was built by the Corporation of Drapiers. Here, despite the French name, it was reserved for performances in German. During the 1700s, German companies played regularly at the theater. By the middle of the 18th century, the theater was in dire financial straits, forcing the magistrate to retract the decision regarding German performances and put a French director in charge. Grétry's *Richard, Coeur de Lion* was then staged. On November 9, 1765, Jean-Jacques Rousseau personally attended the general rehearsal of his opera, *Le devin du village*, performed the following day. Fire destroyed the theater on May 31, 1800. Only the sets for Wolfgang Amadeus Mozart's *Die Zauberflöte* escaped the flames. Then the church St. Etienne was converted into a temporary performance venue.

After the new theater opened the city enjoyed numerous operatic activities. The most popular composers of the time at the theater were Fromental Halévy, Giacomo Meyerbeer, and Gaetano Donizetti, with many of their works staged. Pauline Viardot, the sister of Maria Felica Malibran, sang her last triumphs here, in Meyerbeer's *Le Prophète* and Christoph Willibald Gluck's *Orfeo ed Euridice*. Célestine Marié made her debut in Strasbourg, and after marrying the sculpture Galli, became famous as Célestine Galli-Marié. Siegfried Wagner conducted his *Der Bärenhäuter* there on February 23, 1905. Meanwhile, state subsidies for the theater had stopped in 1876, and the city had to bear the financial burden of administering the artistic seasons. There were some good directors of the theater—Alexander Hessler (1872–81), August Aman (1881–84), Hessler (1886–89), Franz Krükl (1892–99), Hans Pfitzner (1910–16), and Anton Otto (1913–17), and an era of illustrious conductors—Otto Lhose (1897–1904), Wilhelm Fürtwangler (1910–11), Otto Klemperer (1914–17), and Georg Szell (1917–18). With the arrival of peace in 1918, Paul Bastide was at the helm and reopened the opera house on March 8, 1919, with Camille Saint-Saëns's *Samson et Dalila*. He re-established the repertory and organized a permanent opera company. Foreign companies were invited to Strasbourg as well and all the musical genres were heard at the theater. During Bastide's tenure, which lasted until 1938, Richard Strauss visited in 1932 to direct his *Die Aegyptische Helena* on December 5, followed by *Elektra* the next day. During the 1932-33 season, Joseph Krips was on the podium for Richard Wagner's *Die Meistersinger von Nürnberg*. Franz von Hösslin and Hermann Scherchen also conducted at the opera house. The theater then closed its doors for some modernization work.

During the German occupation, the theater reopened under the guidance of Hans Rosbaud, who programmed Georges Bizet's *Carmen*, but sung in German. When peace arrived, Bastide returned and on November 16, 1945, opened the season with Bizet's *Carmen*, this time performed in French. In December, the French premiere of Hector Berlioz's *Béatrice et Bénédict* with Bastide conducting, took place. During the late 1950s and early 1960s, the French premieres of Alban Berg's

Wozzeck, Leoš Janáček's *Jenůfa* and Carl Orff's *Carmina Burana* graced the stage. Artists like Astrid Varnay, Wolfgang Eindgassen, Giuseppe Taddei, and Gustav Neidlinger performed at the opera house during the 1960s. Around this time there was a financial crisis in France concerning the opera houses. In 1968, Mulhouse Opera was considering shutting down operations. Strasbourg had to reduce its season to three or four months and Colmar, which received its opera from Mulhouse and Strasbourg, would be without opera entirely. A plan for saving opera in Alsace was born, uniting Strasbourg, Mulhouse, and Colmar as one company. It is the only regional opera company like it in France. Each city brings its own element: Strasbourg is the home of the opera ensemble, chorus, artistic administration, and studios for scenery, costumes, wigs, and accessories; Mulhouse is the home to the Ballet du Rhin; and Colmar is home to L'Atelier du Rhin. The first director of the newly formed Opéra du Rhin was Pierre Barrat, who brought adventurous programming and world premieres of esoteric operas, like Girolamo Arrigo's *Addio Garibaldi*, Yvan Semenoff's *La grande Oreille* and Claude Prey's *Les Liaisons Dangereuses*, and French premieres of Gottfried von Einem's *Der Besuch der alten Dame* and Franz Joseph Haydn's *L'infedelta delusa*. Unfortunately, the programming was too adventurous and esoteric and the audience stayed away, and Barrat was out of a job. Alain Lombard took over in 1974. Not all adventure left, but it was tempered by more mainstream operas, like Bizet's *Carmen*, Giuseppe Verdi's *Don Carlos*, Mozart's *Die Zauberflöte,* Benjamin Britten's *A Midsummer Night's Dream*, Richard Strauss's *Elektra*, and Claudio Monteverdi's *L'incoronazione di Poppea*, which played alongside the European premiere of Alberto Ginastera's *Don Rodrigo*, and the world premiere of Mario Gautherat's *Le chariot d'or*. World premieres continued during the 1980s and 1990s with Georges Aperghis's *Liebestod, Un Opera*, Jean Prodromides's *H.H. Ulysse*, Graciane Pauvre's *Assassin*, and Bernard Cavanna's *La confession impudique*, among others. The repertory of the 1990s spanned works from the Baroque period to the end of the 20th, and included the world premieres of Giorgio Battistelli's *Prova d'orchestra* and Georges Aperghis's *Tristes Tropiques*, Mozart's *Zaïde* and *Die Entführung aus dem Serail*, Gluck's *Alceste*, Leoš Janáček's *Z Mrtvého Domu* (From the House of the Dead),

Domenico Cimarosa's *Il mercato di Malmantile*, Donizetti's *Lucia di Lammermoor* and *L'elisir d'amore*, Strauss's *Der Rosenkavalier* and *Salome*, Benjamin Britten's *Owen Wingrave*, Georg Friedrich Händel's *Orlando*, and Verdi's *Don Carlos*, among others.

Laurent Spielmann, former general director, felt the repertory at Strasbourg was ideal, with a mixture of the popular with the exotic. His philosophy was to ask "why are we doing this opera and what does it have to say." He believed that "opera is not only for entertainment, but to show us how we are. Operas ask questions to get us to think, but they (the operas) do not have the answers." He feels the future of opera rests with attracting the young to the opera house, and he tries to entice them with his innovative and clever productions. Ensemble singers mix with established artists, who come to Strasbourg to try out new roles. The budget is FF 89 million, and the repertory spans from the Baroque to contemporary. Productions are creative with Baroque works often staged in a modern milieu and contemporary pieces in traditional garb. Rudolf Berger was named general director in 1997 and has continued the interesting repertory with the first staged performance in France of Zoltán Kodály's *Háry János*, Francis Poulenc's *Dialogues des Carmélites*, Carl Maria von Weber's *Der Freischütz*, Strauss's *Ariadne auf Naxos*, Verdi's *Simon Boccanegra* and *Macbeth*, Arthur Honegger's *Les aventures du Roi Pausole* (as part of an Opéra-Comédie Cycle), and Britten's *A Midsummer Night's Dream* (as part of a Benjamin Britten Cycle), among others. Recent offerings include the French premiere of Einojuhani Rautavaara's *Aleksis Kivi*, Mozart's *Don Giovanni* and *Die Entführung aus dem Serail*, and Giacomo Puccini's *La bohème*

Théâtre Municipal de Strasbourg

The construction of a new French opera house began in 1804. The city council chose a site at the Place d'Armes and asked the city architect Boudhors for drawings. After the usual problems and delays, the site was moved to Place Broglie and an architectural competition was announced. There were three entries — architects Robin, Boudhors, and Reiner. Robin's plans were selected, but with reservation. Work began under the surveillance of the engineer Kastner, and the

Théâtre Municipal de Strasbourg (Strasbourg, France).

cornerstone was laid on December 2, 1804. The theater was called Théâtre Napoléon, but 17 years passed before the structure was finished. First problems surfaced at the end of 1806, when Robin realized he had made a big mistake, and the chief administrator turned the project over to Boudhors. Robin, not a gracious loser, created "guerrilla warfare" and work on the building was suspended. Finally, in 1811, interest was rekindled in completing the project, and the ministry adapted plans of another architect, Berigny, with M. Villot in charge of the facade and the facade's Muses sculpted by Ohmacht. Thirty-three years after the theater's inauguration, it was redecorated with funds bequeathed to the city by Jean-Guillaume-Louis Apffel.

The facade displays a peristyle of six massive Ionic columns surmounted by a terrace where six Muses — Euterpe, Clio, Thalie, Melpomène, Erato, Terpsichore — looking out over a tree-line *place*. Six pilasters line the facade, flanking five wood-and-glass entrance doors topped by lunettes.

Théâtre Municipal de Strasbourg, detail of auditorium (Strasbourg, France).

The gold-and-red auditorium holds four tiers with bouquets of fruit and putti with musical instruments decorating the parapets. Blood-red velvet seats and a deep maroon curtain complement the gilded auditorium. The ceiling shows an allegorical painting which explores the four art forms in the theater — Dance, Comedy, Opera, and Drama. An empire style, bronze chandelier hangs from the center. There are 1190 places.

Practical Information. Opéra du Rhin, 19 place Broglie, 67008 Strasbourg Cedex. Tel: 33 3 88 75 48 00, Fax: 33 3 88 24 09 34. Opéra du Rhin (Mulhouse), at Théâtre de la Sinne, 39 rue de la Sinne, 68100 Mulhouse. Tel: 33 3 89 45 26 96, Fax: 33 3 89 66 40 17. Opéra du Rhin (Colmar), at Théâtre Municipal, 3 rue des Unterlinden, 68000 Colmar. Tel: 33 3 89 20 29 01, Fax: 33 3 89 20 29 00. It is best to visit the Opéra du Rhin in Strasbourg and stay at the Hôtel Le Régent Contades, 8 avenue de la Liberté, 67000 Strasbourg. Tel: 33 3 88 36 26 26, Fax 33 3 88 37 13 70. It is in a central location near the opera house and can assist with opera tickets and schedule.

COMPANY STAFF AND PREMIERES

Directeur Général **(Opéra du Rhin).** Rudolf Berger (1997–present), Laurent Spielmann (1990–96), René Terrasson (1980–90), Alain Lombard (1974–80), Pierre Barrat (1972–74). **(Théâtre)** Frédéric Adam (1960–72), Ernest Bour & Frédéric Adam (1955–60), Pierre Deloger (1953–55), Roger Lalande (1948–53), Hans Rosbaud (1942–45), Paul Bastide (1919–38 and 1945–48).

World Premieres. G. Arrigo's *Addio Garibaldi* (epopée musicale) 1972; Y. Semenoff's *La grande Oreille* (comédie musicale) 1972; C. Prey's *Les Liaisons Dangereuses* (opéra épistolaire) 1973; G. Delerue's *Medis et Alyssio* (conte lyrique) 1975; M. Gautherat's *Le chariot d'or* (légende lyrique) 1977; J. Valmy, G. Lafarge, J. Ledru's *Le petit café* (comédie musicale) 1980; G. Hasquenoph's *Comme il vous plaira* 1982; G. Aperghis's *Liebestod, Un Opera* 1982; J. Prodromides's *H.H. Ulysse* 1984; R. Koering's *La marche de radetsky* 1988; R.Cagneux's *Orphee* 1989; G. Pauvre's *Assassin* 1992; B. Cavanna's *La confession impudique* 1992. G. Battistelli's *Prova d'orchestra*, 1995; G. Aperghis's *Tristes Tropiques* 1996. **French Premieres:** I. Stravinsky's *The Rake's Progress* 1952; B. Bartók's *A Kékszakállú herceg vára* (Duke Bluebeard's Castle) 1954; S. Prokofiev's *Lyubov'k tryom apel'sinam* (The Love for Three Oranges) 1955; P.I. Tchaikovsky's

Pikovaya dama (Queen of Spades) 1957; G. Bizet's *Don Procopio* 1958; L. Dallapicolla's *Il prigioniero* 1961; J. Ibert's *Le roi d'Yvetot* 1961; L. Janáček's *Jenůfa* 1962; D. Milhaud's *Fiesta* 1965; W.A. Mozart's *La finta giardiniera* 1965; R. Strauss's *Die Frau ohne Schatten* 1965; H.W. Henze's *Der junge Lord* 1967; G. von Einem's *Der Besuch der alten Dame* 1973; F.J. Haydn's *L'infedelta delusa* 1973; A. Ginastera's *Don Rodrigo* (European premiere) 1976; D. Shostakovich's *Nos* (The Nose) 1980; K. Penderecki's *Die schwarze Maske* 1990; P. Boesmans *Reigne* 1993; A. Reimann's *Die Gespenstersonate* 1998; E. Rautavaara's *Aleksis Kivi*, 1998.

Bibliography. Le Théâtre Municipal de Strasbourg et l'Opéra du Rhin: Historique et Presentation (Strasbourg, 1993). Geneviève Levallet-Haug, *Histoire Architecturale du Théâtre de Strasbourg* (Strasbourg, 1935). *Autour de — Opéra du rhin* (Strasbourg, 1996, 1997, 1998). Interview with Laurent Spielmann, former general director, June 1995.

Thanks to Monique Herzog, Opéra du Rhin, and Eddy Marchal.

TOULOUSE

Théâtre du Capitole

The Théâtre du Capitole that we see today was opened on October 1, 1880, with Fromental Halévy's *La Juive*. It was actually the fourth renovation of the Grand Théâtre de Toulouse (original name of the Théâtre du Capitole), which had been inaugurated on October 1, 1818, with *Les Jeux de l'amour et du hasard* and *Le Souper de Madelon*. Architects Cellerier and Gisors were responsible for the Grand Théâtre de Toulouse and architects Dieulafoy and Thillet were in charge of the renovation.

Opera dates back to 1687 with the founding of the Académie Royale de Musique in Toulouse. In 1672, Jean-Baptiste Lully had obtained a monopoly on opera in France. With his death in 1687, it passed to his son-in-law Francine, who granted Toulouse the right to open the Academy in an old Salle du Jeu de Paume, on rue Montardy. The inhabitants did not take kindly to this new genre of music, feeling it was scandalous. The singers were often thrown out of the theater until they received royal protection in 1716. A new theater was constructed in 1736 in the enclosure of the Capitole, known as the Salle du Jeu de Spectacle. Designed by Guillaume Cammas, it held an orchestra level, an amphitheater, and fifteen boxes on three levels, with 667 places. The new opera house opened May 11, 1737, under the direction of Mademoiselle Desjardins, who was also the director of the Royal Academy of Music. Some of the early productions included André Destouches's *Omphale*, Lully's *Atys*, and Marc-Antoine Charpentier's *Médée*. The operas offered were determined by the type of singers available and the troupes. As the 1700s progressed, the repertory was able to expand and between 1786 and 1787,

and 1788 and 1789, more than 90 different lyrical works were presented, including *opéras-bouffons*, *opéras-comiques*, *pastorales*, and *tragédies lyriques*. Among the popular operas were André Grétry's *Jugement de Midas*, *Zémire et Azor*, *Richard Coeur de Lion*, *Le Tableau parlant*, François-André Philidor's *Le Sorcier*, *Tom Jones*, *Sancho Pança*, and *Les Femmes vengées*. There were fewer *tragédies lyriques* on the boards, but Antonio Sacchini's *Oedipe à Colonne*, Niccolò Piccinni's *Didon*, Pierre Alexandre Monsigny's *Le déserteur*, and Christoph Willibald Gluck's *Alceste* were given at the Salle du Jeu de Spectacle.

In 1816, the city counsel voted to construct a new theater with 1,950 places on the same site and in January 1817, the first stone was laid. After the new theater opened in 1818, it gave little satisfaction and was redone many times during the next several years. Often the performances gave little satisfaction as well. Toulouse gained a reputation, almost on a par with Parma (see Teatro Regio, Parma [Italy] entry), of an unruly audience, which whistled, booed, hissed and shouted at anything that displeased them. Even the local papers noted that the problem had reached "crisis" proportions. In fact, one casualty was Mme Saint Clair, who fainted on stage amidst a chorus of boos. Mlle Pouilly handled the rude spectators differently — she walked off stage. One problem was that the singers had to debut in three different roles during their initial season, often in works ill-suited for their voices. Finally in 1834, the police issued a list of ordinances governing audience behavior, threatening jail for those who misbehaved. Around the mid–1800s, the popular composers of *opéra-comique* from the last century were forgotten, replaced by Adrien Boieldieu with his *La Dame Blanche* and *Ma Tante Aurore*, Daniel Auber's *Le Domino noir* and *Fra Diavolo*, Louis-Ferdinand Hérold's *Le Pré au Clers*, Adolphe Adam's *La postillon de Longjumeau* and *Le Chalet*. *Grand opéra à la française* supplanted *tragédie lyrique* with works like Fromental Halévy's *La Juive* and *La Reine de Chypre*, Giacomo Meyerbeer's *Robert le Diable* and *Les Huguenots*, Gioachino Rossini's *Guillaume Tell*, and Gaetano Donizetti's *La favorite*.

When the renovated Théâtre du Capitole reopened, the main goal of the directors was to hire singers who satisfied the public. To this end, three tenors deserve mention, Merritt, Guiot and Tournié. Works from more French composers found favor with the public, like those of Léo Delibes, Jules Massenet, Charles Gounod, Ernst Reyer, Georges Bizet, and Camille Saint-Saëns. In 1885, Carl Maria von Weber's *Der Freischütz* was remounted after a 35 year hiatus in the repertory, and five years later, even a piece by Georg Friedrich Händel was offered, and during the final decade of the 1800s, Wagner fever hit Toulouse. The dawn of the 20th century saw Giacomo Puccini's *Manon Lescaut* before Paris, Umberto Giordano's *Andrea Chénier*, Gustave Charpentier's *Louise*, and Xavier Leroux's *Chemineau*. In 1908, Marie Delna sang in Saint-Saëns's *Samson et Dalila*, and Delmas performed in Massenet's *Thaïs* and in Gounod's *Faust*. Petro Gailhard, a regular at the Opéra in Paris made frequent appearances at the Capitole.

Fire destroyed the theater in 1917. It was reconstructed and on November 6, 1923, the Capitole reopened with Meyerbeer's *Les Huguenots*. During this period, the operas of Wolfgang Amadeus Mozart were rediscovered. The grand repertory of French opera and those of Wagner were particularly popular. Modest Mussorgsky's *Boris Godunov* was staged for the first time in Toulouse in 1926, and five years later, Fyodor Chaliapin came to sing the role. In 1927, Claude Debussy's *Pelléas et Mélisande* was staged, followed three years later by Richard Strauss's *Salome*. Then, because of financial consideration, operetta played a more dominate role in the repertory than opera for several seasons. In 1950, the control of the opera passed directly to the city, and its artistic director, Louis Izar, who had been in the position since 1947, was able to explore the less well-known repertory. Works like Gabriel Fauré's *Pénélope* with Régine Crespin and Raoul Jobin, Marcel Landowski's *Le Fou*, and even the

French premieres of Stanislaw Moniuszko's *Halka* and Sergey Prokofiev's *Igroki* (The Gambler) were presented. The pillars of the repertory remained with works like Meyerbeer's *Les Huguenots*, Massenet's *Manon*, and Gounod's *Faust*. During the 1990s, Charpentier's *Louise*, Jacques Offenbach's *La belle Hélène*, Puccini's *Il trittico*, Mozart's *Die Zauberflöte*, Hans Werner Henze's *Der Prinz von Homburg*, and Giuseppe Verdi's *Rigoletto*, among others, were on the boards.

Despite the traditional bent of the productions and out-dated acting, electricity flowed between the principals in a recent, new production of Massenet's *Werther*. Roberto Alagna and Béatrice Uria-Monzon overcame a too-loud orchestra, mundane scenery, and old-fashioned directing to deliver a mesmerizing performance. Recent offerings include Puccini's *La bohème*, Rossini's *Il barbiere di Siviglia*, Massenet's *Cendrillon*, Richard Strauss's *Ariadne auf Naxos*, and Leoš Janáček's *Věc Makropulos* (The Makropulos Affair).

Théâtre du Capitole

At 2:10 P.M. on August 10, 1917, fire swept through the opera house and in 50 minutes it was gone. The theater was rebuilt by Paul Pujol, who was old and considered by numerous people a poor choice. The result was a Neo-Baroque auditorium that many felt was anachronistic. This was transformed in 1950. Only the bas-reliefs of Paul Gelis remained. A major renovation took place in 1974 which gave the auditorium its appearance today. Architects Yvonnick Corlouër and François Linarès were responsible for the project. The renovation is a *trompe l'oeil* on all the surfaces to allow the splendors of the past to be restored to the auditorium at a cost that was affordable. The work was executed by Richard Peduzzi.

The theater is the right-end corner of a huge terra cotta–colored building which stretches the entire length of the *place* and also holds government offices. White Ionic pilasters break up the long facade and Muses flanking a musical instrument crown the theater portion of the building. The auditorium holds four tiers on the sides but only three in the middle which sweep around in a free-form. The coat-of-arms of the Capitole is reproduced on the undulating parapets. The gilded, fluted columns, and the stucco reliefs on the parapets of cupid with bow and

Théâtre du Capitole (Toulouse, France).

arrow, and mermaids are all painted. The huge light-giving cupola is decorated with a night sky and a gilded proscenium arch frames a deep red curtain which matches the plush red seats. There are 1,158 places.

Practical Information. Théâtre du Capitole, place du Capitole, 31000 Toulouse. Tel: 33 5 61 22 24 30, Fax: 33 5 61 22 31 52. When visiting Théâtre du Capitole, stay at the Mercure Wilson, 7 rue Labéda, 31034 Toulouse. Tel: 33

5 61 21 21 75 or 1 800 637 2873, Fax 33 5 61 22 77 64. It is centrally located near the opera house and can assist with opera tickets and schedule.

COMPANY STAFF

Directeur Général. (since 1947) Nicolas Joël (1990–present), Jacques Doucet (1981–90), Michel Plasson (1973–80), Gabriel Couret (1967–72), Louis Izar. (1947–66).

Bibliography. *Théâtre du Capitole Toulouse* (Toulouse, 1996). *Ouverture du Théâtre du Capitole Rénové* (Toulouse, 1996). *Journal du Capitole* (Toulouse, November 1997).

Thanks to Marie Claire Rettig, Théâtre du Capitole, and Pierre Pons.

TOURS

Grand Théâtre de Tours

The Grand Théâtre de Tours, originally called the Théâtre Municipal, was inaugurated on November 23, 1889, with a diverse program which included selections from operatic and dramatic works. The opera season opened the following day with Edmond Audran's *La Mascotte*. Designed by Jean Hardion, the theater was completed by S. Loison. This was the second Municipal Theater. The first had been inaugurated on August 8, 1872, with *Les Jurons de Cadillac* and Victor Masse's *Les Noces de Jeannette*. Designed by Léon Rohard, the theater was destroyed by fire in 1883.

The first *salle de spectacle* in Tours was the Théâtre de la Place d'Aumont (later named Théâtre de la République), built in 1761. M. Pillerault had received authorization to open the performance venue with 900 places, the majority of which were standing places. Traveling troupes offered opera, vaudeville, comedies, and drama to the inhabitants. The Revolution did not stop the theatrical performances, and operas of the "people" like Giovanni Battista Pergolesi's *La serva padrona* and J.J. Rousseau's *Le Devin du Village*, and works by André Grétry, François-André Philidor, Étienne-Nicolas Méhul, and Gossec trod the boards. During these troubled times, there were many incidents between the performers and spectators, with the authorities frequently closing the theater because of the disorder.

Tours opened its first real theater on December 7, 1796. (This is where the Grand Théâtre is now located.) Known as the Salle Bucheron on rue de la Scellerie, the theater accommodated 800 people. A peristyle formed from a row of Ionic columns defined the facade. The auditorium was an elongated oval shape, making hearing and seeing almost impossible on the sides. The theater was private, belonging to M. Bucheron, who rented it to traveling troupes. Usually at least two operas were performed during an evening — on January 12, 1819, both Grétry's *Richard, Coeur de Lion* and Nicolas Dalayrac's *Les deux Prisonniers* were on the schedule. Other operas offered were Dalayrac's *Nina* and *Les Deux Petits Savoyards*, Grétry's *Zémire et Azor*, Adrien Boieldieu's *Ma Tante Aurore*, *Le Calife de Bagdad*, and *Les Voitures Versées*, and Ferdinand Hérold's *La Clochette* and *Marie*. With the arrival of the 1820s, works like Ferdinando Paër's *La Maître de Chapelle*, Gioachino Rossini's *Il barbiere di Siviglia*, Wolfgang Amadeus Mozart's *Don Giovanni*, Daniel Auber's *La muette de Portici* and *Fra Diavolo*, and Adolphe Adam's *La postillon de Longjumeau* and *Le Chalet* graced the stage. In 1837, the theater was closed for renovation. The auditorium was reshaped into a lyre and the number of places increased to 1,000. Except for performances of Giacomo Meyerbeer's *Robert le Diable*, opera did not reappear on stage until 1841. Three types of operatic works were popular during this time: *grand opéra romantique* of Meyerbeer and Halévy, *opéra-comique* of Auber, Adam, Boieldieu, and Victor Massé, and *bel canto* of Donizetti and Vincenzo Bellini. Works like Auber's *Le Domino Noir*, *Le Cheval de Bronze*, and *Les Diamants de la Couronne*, Fromental Halévy's *La Juive* and *L'Eclair*, Meyerbeer's *Les Huguenots*, and Gaetano Donizetti's *La fille du régiment* and *La favorite* were frequently mounted. With the arrival of Jacques Offenbach the preference changed to operetta, which became very popular. After the French theaters were "liberated" in Tours in 1864, anyone could open a theater, and many appeared. The Cirque-Napoléon, a wood and brick edifice, was inaugurated on August 5,

1865, and held 1,400 spectators, and two years later, the L'Alcazar (later Alhambra) opened.

Construction on the first Théâtre Municipal began in 1869. The first stone was laid on January 4, and the inauguration was planned for the fall of 1870. The Franco-Prussian War caused some delays. The new opera house, which opened late summer 1872, was an impressive building. The theater held a white-and-gold, horseshoe-shaped auditorium with three tiers that accommodated 1,200. The facade sculptures were the work of Frédéric Combarieu. Operetta was very popular, claiming more than 60% of the performances, and included works like *Les Brigands*, *Giroflé-Girofla*, *La mascotte*, and *La Jour et la Nuit*. By 1878, opera had regained a foothold and the program for that season included Donizetti's *Lucia de Lammermoor*, *La favorite*, and *Le fille du régiment*, Gioachino Rossini's *Il barbiere di Siviglia*, Charles Gounod's *Faust*, Boieldieu's *La Dame Blanche*, Adam's *La postillon de Longjumeau* and *Le Chalet*, *Galathée*, *Les dragons de Villars*, Ambroise Thomas's *Mignon* and *Hamlet*, Auber's *La muette de Portici*, Giuseppe Verdi's *La traviata*, and Halévy's *La Juive*. These were all mounted between April 21 and May 20. Then in the early morning hours of August 15, 1883, fire broke out. All that remained of the theater were the four exterior walls.

Two other theaters opened their doors during the six years it took to reconstruct the Municipal. The first was the Théâtre Français, which opened on October 4, 1884, and held a large auditorium, decorated in white, with room for 2,000. Operas like Halévy's *La Juive*, Rossini's *Guillaume Tell*, Meyerbeer's *Les Huguenots* and *L'Africaine*, Verdi's *Jérusalem*, and Georges Bizet's *Carmen* found a home at the Français. Cirque de la Touraine was the second theater, which opened on November 15, 1884, with 1,200 places.

After the opera house opened in 1889, Eugène Aubert was its first director and Aubert organized the seasons with a traditional framework. A typical season might see *Faust*, *Il barbiere di Siviglia*, *Les Mousquetaires de la Reine*, *Le Maître de Chapelle*, *Gillette de Narbonne*, *Carmen*, *Lucia di Lammermoor*, *Le Chalet*, *La Mascotte*, *Si j'étais roi!*, *Mignon*, *La Dame Blanche*, *Les noces de Jeannette*, *Lakmé*, *Miss Helyett*, *Mireille*, *La traviata*, *Manon*, *La fille du régiment*, *La Demoiselle du Téléphone*, *Les Mousquetaires au Couvent*, *Les Dragons de Villars*, *Le Roi d'Ys*, *Rigoletto*, *La fille du Tambour-Major*, *Galathée*, *La favorite*, *Guillaume Tell*, *L'Oncle Célestin*, *Le Rêve*, *Le songe d'une nuit d'été*, *Le Voyage de Suzette*, *Les Huguenots*, *La Juive*, *L'Africaine*, *Robert le Diable*, *Roméo et Juliette*, *Il trovatore*, *Lohengrin*, and *Charles VI*. After Léonce Montel took the helm in 1900, opera played a smaller role in the repertory. In 1910, Viennese operettas first appeared at the Municipal, and were very popular. World War I closed the theater for a short time, but when it reopened, the operatic schedule remained traditional, offering Gounod's *Faust*, Thomas's *Mignon*, Massenet's *Manon* and *Werther* Bizet's *Carmen*, Verdi's *Rigoletto*, Giacomo Puccini's *Tosca*, and Rossini's *Il barbiere di Sivigila*. Finally, in 1918, 37 years after the premiere, Offenbach's *Les contes d'Hoffmann* received its first staging in Tours.

Marcel Morna took over the directorship of the theater on October 1, 1926. He brought a prominence to the theater that it had not previously known. Around 150 lyrical evenings were scheduled each season with operettas performed on Saturday, Sunday, and sometimes Thursdays, and operas given on Tuesdays. There was a permanent troupe which guaranteed the operetta productions. Some of the most popular ones were *Boccace*, *Rip*, *Surcouf*, *Fortunio*, *Le Sire de Vergy*, *Madame Favart*, and *François les Bas Bleus*. The opera repertory expanded its offerings with Modest Mussorgsky's *Boris Godunov* and *Khovanshchina*, Massenet's *La Navarraise*, Verdi's *Aida*, Richard Wagner's *Die Walküre* and *Lohengrin*, and the presentation of little known works — Benjamin's *La Vivandière*, Alfred Bruneau's *L'Attaque du Moulin*, Paul Bastide's *La Vannina*, and Jean Nouguès's *Quo Vadis?* Many popular classic works saw their last light (until recently unearthed) during this time, like Boieldieu's *La Dame Blanche*, Meyerbeer's *L'Africaine*, Rossini's *Guillaume Tell*, and Donizetti's *La favorite*. One sad incident occurred on January 28, 1933, during a performance of *Hans le Joueur de Flûte*. Théo Puget, who was the flute-player, died during the second intermission, but according to theatrical law, the show must continue, and his wife, who was also in the show, had to keep in character until the end.

World premieres began to play a role in the theater's repertory from the end of the 1930s through the 1950s with eleven mounted, including François Perrin's *La Visite à la Crèche*, Marcel Fichefet's *Légende d'Armor* and *Les Caprices de*

Vénus, Henri Beral's *L'Escapade Inachevée* and *Un Seul Amour*, and Henri Lhuis's *Chatterton*, *Atala*, and *Amahura*. Operetta was the dominating lyrical entertainment offered both during and after the war. A group of artists from the Opéra-Comique interpreted Pietro Mascagni's *Cavalleria rusticana* to celebrate the reopening of the theater after the war (although there were some performances during the war). Works like *Andalousie*, *La belle de Cadix*, and *La chanteur de Mexico* were given during the 1940s and 1950s. Some of the singers interpreting the opera performances included Mado Robin in Delibes's *Lakmé* and Rossini's *Il barbiere di Siviglia*, Andréa Guiot and Adrien Legros in Gounod's *Faust*, and Jean Capocci and Renée Doria in Gounod's *Mireille*.

With the arrival of the 1960s and television, combined with economic considerations, the number of presentations fell considerably, but under the leadership of Gil Roland, many works never before seen in Tours appeared in the repertory — Umberto Giordano's *Andrea Chénier*, Francis Poulenc's *Les dialogues des Carmélites*, Gian Carlo Menotti's *The Consul*, and Gilbert Becard's *Opéra d'Aran*. Repertory expansion continued under Francis Balagna with contemporary works like Menotti's *The Medium* and *The Telephone* and Benjamin Britten's *The Turn of the Screw*, and other works that somehow never were staged in Tours, like Verdi's *La forza del destino*, Claude Debussy's *Pelléas et Mélisande*, and Philidor's *Tom Jones*. The Grand Théâtre also embarked on an ambitious program of *créations*, giving new blood to the lyrical theater, which the director felt was important for its continued evolution. These included Adrienne Clostre's *Annapurna*, Claude Prey's *Le rouge et le noir*, Monic Cecconi-Botella's *Il Signait ...Vincent*, Marian Kouzan's *Les Tentations de Saint-Antoine*, Janos Komives's *Le Muet au Couvent*, and Jean Prodromides's *Le Traverse du Temps*. Among the recent offerings are Gounod's *Faust*, Britten's *The Rape of Lucretia*, Donizetti's *Don Pasquale*, Offenbach's *Les contes d'Hoffmann*, and Édouard Lalo's *Le Roi d'Ys*.

Grand Théâtre de Tours, Tours

After the first Municipal theater burned, architect Hardion submitted a project that was ac-

cepted by a jury, but problems arose between the architect and the city, so Loison had to be called in to complete the construction. M. Diosse was responsible for the decorations, except the paintings decorating the grand staircase. The foyer and the ceiling are the work of Clairin. Finally at the end of 1889, the second Municipal opened its doors.

Practical Information. Grand Théâtre de Tours, 34 rue de la Scellerie, 37000 Tours. Tel: 33 247 05 37 87, Fax: 33 247 66 11 92. When visiting the Grand Théâtre de Tours, stay at the Relais et Châteaux "Jean Bardet," 57 rue Groison, 37100 Tours. Tel: 33 247 41 41 11, Fax 33 247 51 68 72. It is a 19th-century residence convenient to the opera house. The "Jean Bardet" can assist with opera tickets and schedule.

COMPANY STAFF AND WORLD PREMIERES

Directeur Général. Michel Jarry (1983–present), Jean-Jacques Etchevery (1973–83), Francis Balagna (1966–73), Gil Roland (1959–66), Marcel Morna (1945–59), Raoul Camp & Marcel Morna (1944–45), Raoul Camp (1943–44), Marcel Morna (1936–43), Raoul Rouge-Bogue (1933–36), Marcel Morna (1926–33), Alphonse Bruinen (1923–26), Pierre Laffond (1908–23), Léonce Montel (1900–08), Joseph Marie Monin (1896–1900), Léonce Montel (1891–96), Victor Bladin (1891–91), Eugène Aubert (1889–91).

World Premieres. E. Lhuillier's *C'est mon Bénéficie* 1884; E. Lhuillier's *Mesdemoiselles de Saint Potin* 1884; E. Lhuillier's *Elle débute ce Soir* 1884; M. Etesse's *Crime d'Amour* 1895; R. Delaunay's *Poisson d'Avril* 1903; F. Perrin's *La Visite à la Crèche* 1938; M. Fichefet's *Légende d'Armor* 1939; H. Lhuis's *Chatterton* 1941; H. Beral's *L'Escapade Inachevée* 1942; H. Lhuis's *Atala* 1944; H. Beral's *Amahura* 1946; H. Beral's *Un Seul Amour* 1947; M Fichefet's *Les Caprices de Vénus* 1951; J. Blumann's *La Légende du Temple* 1952; L. Dubruille's *Le Couronne de Corail* 1952; G. Guy's *Caprice* 1956; E. Damais's *La Dame de l'Aube* 1962; J. Rollin's *Gringoire* 1965; J. Albrespic's *Sotie pour une femme qui fut muette* 1967; J. Bruzdowicz's *La Colonie Pénitentiaire* 1972; A. Clostre's *Le Chant du Cygne* 1974; P. Israel-Meyer's *Anna la Bonne* 1975; C. Arrieu's *La Cabine Téléphonique* 1976; J. Ledru's *La Peur des Coups* 1977; O. Bernard's *La P ... Respectueuse* (Revised version) 1978; P. Sciortino's *L'Affaire F.F.O.P.P.* 1979; B. Videau's *La Corde* 1979; C. Arrieu's *Amour de Don Perlimpin avec Belise en son jardin* 1980; C. Prey's *L'Escalier de Chambord* 1981; J. Ledru's *La Parisienne* 1982; C. Debussy's *La Chute de la Maison Usher* (first staged production) 1982–83; P.M. Dubois's *Comment Causer* (first staged production) 1982–83; A. Duhamel's *Le Scieur de Long* 1984; G. Calvi's *J'aime, j'aime, j'aime* 1984; G. Calvi's *La melodie des Strapontins* 1984–85; C. Prey's *Donna Mobile I* 1985; P. Capdenat's *Sebastien en Martyr* 1986; P. Capdenat's *Croce e Deliza* (first staged production) 1986; A. Clostre's *Annapurna* 1989; C. Prey's *Le rouge et le noir* 1989–90; M. Cecconi-Botella's *Il Signait... Vincent* 1990–91; M.S. Kouzan's *Les Tentations de Saint-Antoine* 1991–92; J. Komives's *Le Muet au Couvent* 1993–94; J. Prodromides's *Le Traverse du Temps* 1994–95.

Bibliography. Jacques Derouet *Le Théâtre Lyriques à Tours des Origines à nos Jours* (Tours, 1989). Additional information supplied by the company.

Thanks to Frédérique Alglave, Grand Théâtre de Tours, and Sophie Bardet.

Other French Companies

Other companies in France are noted below by name, address, telephone, recent repertory, and general director (as available).

Théâtre Musical d'Angers. 7 rue Doboys, 49100 Angers. Tel: 33 41 60 40 40. **Recent Repertory:** Simon Boccanegra, Die Zauberflöte, Il barbiere di Siviglia.

Opéra d'Avignon et de Vaucluse. Place de l'Horloge, 84007 Avignon. Tel: 33 490 82 23 44, Fax: 33 490 85 04 23. **Recent Repertory:** Don Giovanni, Didone, Die Zauberflöte, Eugene Onegin, Il matrimonio segreto, La finta semplice, La Damnation de Faust. **General Director:** Raymond Duffaut.

Théâtre Français de la Musique. Théâtre Imperial, 3 rue Othenin, 60200 Compiègne. Tel: 33 44 40 17 10, Fax: 33 44 40 44 04. **Recent Repertory:** Le nozze di Figaro, La belle Hélène, L'heure espagnole, Tosca. **General Director:** Pierre Jourdan.

L'Opéra de Dijon. 2 rue Longpierre, 2100 Dijon. Tel: 33 380 67 23 23, Fax: 33 380 67 27 82. **Recent Repertory:** Un ballo in maschera, La clemenza di Tito, Manon, Werther, Turandot, Marco Polo (Francis Lopez), Douchka (Charles Aznavour), Le Dragon de Villars (Louise-Aimé Maillart).

Théâtre Draguignan. Boulevard G. Clemenceau, 8300 Draguignan. Tel: 33 94 68 30 98. **Recent Repertory:** Mireille, La traviata.

Opéra de Lille. Théâtre de l'Opéra, 2 rue des Bons Enfants, 59800 Lille. Tel: 33 320 55 48 61, Fax: 33 320 14 99 27. **Recent Repertory:** Le nozze di Figaro, Les contes d'Hoffmann, Eugene Onegin, Zaïde, Lenora (Beethoven), La rosa de Ariadna (Dazzi), Pelléas et Mélisande. **Artistic Director:** Ricardo Szwarcer.

Théâtre de Metz. 4–5 place de la Comédie, 57000 Metz. Tel: 33 387 75 40 50, Fax: 33 387 31 32 37. **Recent Repertory:** Der fliegende Holländer, Don Giovanni, Tosca, Pelléas et Mélisande, La fille du régiment, Turn of the Screw, The Rake's Progress, Samson et Dalila, Rigoletto. **General Director:** D. Ory.

Théâtre de Nîmes. 1 place de la Calade, 3000 Nîmes. Tel: 33 466 36 00 83, Fax: 33 466 36 65 10. **Recent Repertory:** Arminio (Händel), Dédé (Christine), La Cenerentola, Der fliegende Holländer. **General Director:** Marie Collen.

Opéra de Rennes. Place de l'Hôtel de ville, 35000 Rennes. Tel: 33 299 28 40 40, Fax: 33 299 28 58 63. **Recent Repertory:** La traviata, La-Haut (Maurice Yvain), Idomeneo, Orfeo, Let's Make an Opera, Dardanus (Jean-Phillipe Rameau), Briseis (Emmanuel Chabrier).

L'Esplanade Saint-Etienne Opera. Grand Théâtre L'Esplanade, 42013 Saint-Etienne. Tel: 33 77 47 83 47, Fax: 33 77 47 83 69. **Recent Repertory:** Thaïs, Mireille, Otello (Verdi), La Dame Blanche (Boieldieu), Norma, Dialogues des Carmélites, Un ballo in maschera, Il barbiere di Siviglia, Die Zauberflöte. **General Director:** Jean Louis Pichon.

Opéra d'Automne de Semur-en-Auxois. Hôtel de Ville, B.P. 48, 21140 Semur-en-Auxois. Tel: 33 380 97 05 96, Fax: 33 380 97 08 85.

Opéra de Toulon. Boulevard de Strasbourg, Toulon. Tel: 33 494 927 078. **Recent Repertory:** Otello, Lucia di Lammermoor, Tosca, Die Zauberflöte, La gioconda, Les pêcheurs de perles, Aida.

Atelier Lyrique de Tourcoing. Grand Théâtre, 34 rue de la Scellerie, 59200 Tourcoing. Tel: 33 20 26 66 03, Fax: 33 20 70 59 99. **Recent Repertory:** Orfeo ed Euridice (Haydn), Don Giovanni. **General Director:** Jean-Claude Malgloire.

Opéra de Vichy. 1 rue Parc, 03204 Vichy. Tel: 33 70 98 71 94. **Recent Repertory:** King Arthur (Purcell), La Périchole. **General Director:** Diane Polya.

Opéra d'Avignon et de Vaucluse (Avignon, France).

Germany

Stadttheater

Richard Wagner's *Die Meistersinger von Nürnburg* inaugurated the Stadttheater on December 27, 1951. Philipp Kerz was responsible for the reconstruction. The previous theater, the "Neue Schauspielhaus," was destroyed during a bombing raid on July 14, 1943. Built by Peter Cremer, the "Neue Schauspielhaus" had been inaugurated on May 18, 1825, with Louis Spohr's *Jessonda*. Karl Friedrich Schinkel was responsible for the classic portico.

The first theater was built between 1748 and 1751 by Johann Joseph Couven. Here Wolfgang Amadeus Mozart's *Die Entführung aus dem Serail* and *Die Zauberflöte* were offered. After the "Neue Schauspielhaus" opened, works like Ludwig van Beethoven's *Fidelio* graced the stage. The first work of Giuseppe Verdi, *Nabucco*, to appear in Aachen was staged in 1848, and the first performance of Wagner's *Tristan und Isolde* was given in 1898. The complete Ring Cycle had been mounted back in 1883.

After the turn of the century, the opera house was renovated by Heinrich Seeling, turning the original "box" theater into an open balcony theater. Then in 1918, Fritz Busch conducted Richard Strauss's *Salome* and Beethoven's *Fidelio*. Three years later, Wagner's *Parsifal* was given. In the spring of 1934, Herbert von Karajan was hired as the first opera *Kapellmeister* and he conducted Wagner's *Die Walküre* and *Tannhäuser*, and Strauss's *Der Rosenkavalier*. By 1942, another complete Ring Cycle had been mounted, and most of the major works of Mozart and Strauss had been staged.

After the destruction of the theater, opera was performed again in 1947 in the Hall of the Technical High School. During the 1950s, a young Wolfgang Sawallisch was named General Music Director and works like Verdi's *Otello* and *Don Carlo*, Mozart's *Don Giovanni*, Strauss's *Der Rosenkavalier*, and Wagner's *Tristan und Isolde* graced the stage. Between 1962 and 1974, operas from contemporary composers like Alban Berg, Paul Hindemith, Hans Werner Henze, and Ernst Křenek were on the boards, and the 1980s saw Jacques Offenbach's *Les contes d'Hoffmann*, Maurice Ravel's *L'heure espagnole*, Carl Orff's *Die Kluge*, Verdi's *Falstaff*, and Giacomo Puccini's *La bohème*. Recent works include, Verdi's *Il trovatore*, Mozart's *Così fan tutte*, Wagner's *Tannhäuser*, and Gaetano Donizetti's *Don Sebastiano*.

Practical Information. Stadttheater, Theaterplatz, 5100 Aachen. Tel: 49 241-47841, Fax: 49 241 478-4200. If visiting, contact the German National Tourist Office, 747 Third Avenue, 33rd Floor, New York, NY 10017. Tel: 212-308-3300.

COMPANY STAFF

Intendant. Elmar Ottenthal.

AUGSBURG

Städtische Bühnen

The rebuilt, 1,016 seat Städtische Bühnen opened with Wolfgang Amadeus Mozart's *Le nozze di Figaro* on November 10, 1956. The previous theater, the 994-seat Stadttheater, was destroyed during a bombing raid on February 25, 1944. Ludwig van Beethoven's *Fidelio* had inaugurated the Stadttheater in 1877. The theater was designed in a Neo-Renaissance style by Ferdinand Fellner and Hermann Helmer.

The year after the Stadttheater opened, Richard Wagner's *Die Meistersinger von Nürnberg* was staged, but financial problems plagued the theater and the lack of public interest did not help. Then in 1883, Georges Bizet's *Carmen* and Karl Millöcker's *Bettelstudent* graced the stage. The situation improved after the turn of the century when Carl Häusler became director in 1903. The main works of Wagner, Mozart and Giuseppe Verdi were in the repertory, as well as contemporary pieces like Ermanno Wolf-Ferrari's *Le donne curiose*, Giacomo Puccini's *Madama Butterfly* and

Tosca, and Richard Strauss's *Der Rosenkavalier* and *Salome*. Operas of Leoš Janáček, Franz Schreker, Hans Pfitzner, and Ernst Křenek were also prominent in the schedule. Then in November 1928, Siegfried Wagner conducted his opera, *Der Bärenhäuter*, and December 1928 Wilhelm Kienzl conducted his opera, *Der Kuhreigen*. The following year witnessed the first performance in the city of Modest Mussorgsky's *Boris Godunov*, and on January 27, 1932, the German premiere of Verdi's *La battaglia di Legnano* took place. Even during the Third Reich a full opera program was kept until the destruction of the theater.

After the opera house was rebuilt, contemporary works continued to play an important role — Arthur Honegger's *Johanna auf dem Scheiterhaufen*, Francis Poulenc's *Les dialogues des Carmélites*, Alban Berg's *Wozzeck*, Werner Egk's *Die Verlobung in San Domingo*, and Gottfried von Einem's *Der Prozeß* with the composer present. In 1973, the European premiere of Carlisle Floyd's

Of Mice and Men took place. Recent repertory includes Puccini's *Madama Butterfly*, Strauss's *Elektra*, and Wagner's *Das Rheingold*.

Practical Information. Städtische Bühnen, Kasernstraße 4-6, 8900 Augsburg. Tel: 49 821 324-3933, Fax: 49 821 324 4544. If visiting, contact the German National Tourist Office, 747 Third Avenue, 33rd Floor, New York, NY 10017. Tel: 212-308-3300.

COMPANY STAFF

Intendant. Peter Baumgardt.

BAYREUTH

Bayreuther Festspiele

Richard Wagner's *Das Rheingold* inaugurated Bayreuther Festspielhaus on August 13, 1876. The opening opera launched the first complete production of *Der Ring des Nibelungen* ever performed. At the inauguration, Kaiser Wilhelm I, the Emperor of Brazil, and 57 other royals were present along with Franz Liszt, Pyotr Il'yich Tchaikovsky, Edvard Grieg, Charles Gounod, Camille Saint-Saëns, and Gustav Mahler. Designed by Otto Brückwald, the Festspielhaus was built as a shrine to Wagner's art, and the purpose of the Bayreuther Festspiele is the execution of his works. It was one of the earliest summer music festivals that spawned a tradition which the Salzburger Festspiele and Glyndebourne Festival Opera followed.

In 1864, "mad" King Ludwig II commanded an opera house be built for Richard Wagner in Munich with Gottfried Semper drawing up the plans, but the opera house was never built. Wagner then began his search for the ideal location for his "temple to his art." It had to be constructed in a small, out of the way location, so the audience would have no other distractions — thus his journey in April 1870 to Bayreuth, where the magnificent Markgräfliches Opernhaus was located. Although this Baroque theater was not adequate, he decided to construct his festival house in Bayreuth, and on May 22, 1872, laid the cornerstone for the theater. Built to Wagner's specifications, the theater was under construction for four years. The lack of money was a problem until King Ludwig II arranged a state loan to finish the theater and to build Wagner a villa nearby, known as Wahnfried. King Ludwig II came to Bayreuth on August 6, 1876, for the final dress rehearsal of *Das Rheingold*. (His paranoia prevented him from seeing the opera when his subjects were also in the opera house.) On August 13, the first cycle opened with *Das Rheingold*. *Die Walküre* followed the next day, and the world premieres of *Siegfried* and *Götterdämmerung* took place on August 16 and August 17 respectively. The first summer saw three complete Ring Cycles. The reviews of the first *Der Ring des Nibelungen* were not favorable, citing that the orchestra, led by Hans Richter, sounded uninspired and played too fast. (In fact, *Das Rheingold* was completed in 2 hours and 31 minutes, a record until Joseph Keilberth completed the work in 2 hours 30 minutes in 1952.) The staging was also unimpressive and the new gas lighting system failed, causing the stage to go dark during the performance. The singers were good, especially Amalia Materna's Brünnhilde, but no one could show their appreciation since Wagner did not permit curtain calls. The first cycle, the status cycle, sold out, but for the remaining two cycles the theater was half empty — caused by its remote location, expensive tickets, and unfavorable press. The experiment was a financial disaster and the doors of the Festspielhaus remained closed for the next six years, only reopening on July 26, 1882, for the world premiere of *Parsifal*, which was repeated 16 times. It was the only opera on the schedule that season. After Wagner's death in 1883, Cosima took over the festival, believing her mission was to preserve the festival as a memorial to Wagner, and ruling it like a tyrant. The Festspielhaus was transformed into a "temple" and the performances into "religious rites." It was rumored that she even sent notes to the conductor's podium during the performance, if she did not like the conductor's interpretation.

Siegfried Wagner, Richard Wagner's only son, took over the running of the festival in 1908, but during his 22 years at the helm, only ten festivals took place. His influence was beneficial, changing the festival from a "religious rite" to a reexamination and reinterpretation of Wagner's operas. Upon Siegfried's death in 1930, his widow, Winifred Williams Wagner, assumed control. An admirer of Adolf Hitler and his racist policies, she supported Hitler's transforming the festival into a forum for Nazi propaganda and making it the cultural mecca of the Third Reich. Hitler gave the festival large sums of money and granted special dispensation for Jewish artists to perform there. Every summer, Winifred decorated the festival grounds with swastikas. After the war, the taint of Nazism branded the festival until Winifred's sons, Wieland and Wolfgang, were put in charge, reopening it with *Parsifal*. Wieland brought out a new artistic concept, where abstract imagery replaced the nationalistic symbols and that helped remove the stigma of Nazism.

After Wieland died, Wolfgang took sole charge in 1966, inviting well-known directors from different countries to Bayreuth. So began the controversial productions. In 1981, the late Jean-Pierre Ponnelle produced a controversial *Tristan und Isolde*, but the resulting controversy was mild in comparison to the famous (or infamous) centennial Ring created by Patrice Chéreau. Set in the Age of the Industrial Revolution (or capitalist era), the production almost caused a riot. A dozen years later, Harry Kupfer placed the Ring in the aftermath of a nuclear holocaust and the audience almost booed it off the stage.

A recent *Tristan und Isolde*, by the late Heiner Müller, was a bold, daring production that used squares and lighting in an effective symbolic manner to capture the essence of the opera — the consummation of love through death. The current exploration and experimentation of productions at Bayreuth is leading to new paths of visualization through abstract concepts. The quality of performances has improved immeasurably. Only some harsh sounds in Waltrud Meier's top notes and Siegfried Jerusalem's occasional vocal weakness prevented this from being a perfect execution, but their acting and singing, full of feeling and passion, more than compensated for the weaknesses. The ideal pacing by Daniel Baremboim, with the orchestra swelling to unparalleled beauty and force, recreated the passion and ecstasy of love and gave tangible feelings to the gamut of emotions in the work. The repertory is exclusively of Wagner operas. Most summers there is a complete Ring Cycle, along with usually three other works among which are *Die Meistersinger von Nürnberg*, *Der fliegende Holländer*, *Parsifal*, *Lohengrin*, *Tannhäuser*, or *Tristan und Isolde*.

Festspielhaus

The Festspielhaus, located at the top of a hill, is of coral-colored brick with a facade inspired by that of an ancient temple. Tuscan order columns support a balcony, behind which Tuscan order pilasters flank an arch topped by an unadorned tympanum and balustrade. The amphitheater style auditorium is in beige, gold, rose, and turquoise. Lined with rows of gilden Corinthian columns and pillars, the room holds two box levels topped with a balcony-like area with its dark red parapet painted like a curtain. The hard wooden-back seats are of a gold-and-green velveteen. The light gray proscenium arch frames a dark gray stage curtain. With no aisles, extremely long rows, and little leg room, those seated in the middle area could experience claustrophobia. The festival house accommodates 1,925.

Practical Information. Bayreuther Festspiele, 95402 Bayreuth. Tel: 49 921 787 80, Fax: 49 921 787-8130. When visiting the Bayreuther Festspiele, contact the Bayreuth Fremdenverkehrsverein, Postfach 100365, 95403 Bayreuth. Tel: 49 921 885-88, Fax 49 921 885-55.

COMPANY STAFF

Intendanten. (since 1951) Wolfgang Wagner (1951–present), Wieland Wagner (1951–66).

Bibliography. Frederic Spott, *Bayreuth: A History of the Wagner Festival* (New Haven & London, 1994). Geoffrey Skelton, *Wagner at Bayreuth* (London, 1971). Dietrich Mack, *Der Bayreuther Inszenierungsstil 1876 bis 1976* (Munich, 1976). Dietrich Mack, *Bayreuther Festspiele: die Idee, der Bau, die Aufführungen* (Bayreuth, 1983). Friedelind Wagner, *Nacht über Bayreuth* (Cologne, 1994). Stephen Fay & Roger Wood, *The Ring: Anatomy of an Opera* (Somerset, 1984).

Thanks to Peter Emmerich and Friederike Emmerich, Bayreuther Festspiele.

Festspielhaus (Bayreuth, Germany).

BERLIN

Deutsche Oper Berlin

Wolfgang Amadeus Mozart's *Don Giovanni* inaugurated the Deutsche Oper Berlin on September 24, 1961. President Heinrich Lübke, Mayor Willy Brandt, and 21 ambassadors attended the opening. East Berliners, however, who had planned to go could not. The Berlin Wall had been completed six weeks earlier. The new opera house, located on the site of the original Deutsches Opernhaus Charlottenburg, was designed by Fritz Bornemann.

The western part of Berlin did not see opera until 1910, when some prominent citizens of the then-independent city of Charlottenburg raised enough money to build the Deutsches Opernhaus Charlottenburg. Construction began in the summer of 1911, and on November 7, 1912, Ludwig van Beethoven's *Fidelio* inaugurated the Deutsches Opernhaus Charlottenburg. Heinrich Seeling designed the new opera house, which was built on

the corner of Bismarckstraße and Richard-Wagner-Straße on land donated by the city. The Friends of the Charlottenburger Oper financed the operation, which was conceived as a *Volksoper* to cater to middle-class Berliners. The company presented the mainstream repertory in novel productions with good singers. It was so successful that by its second year, there were 11,000 subscribers, and on March 28, 1913, Giacomo Puccini came to Berlin to direct the German premiere of his *La fanciulla del West*. Under the guidance of Georg Hartmann, the company offered several premieres including Kurt Hösel's *Wieland der Schmied*, Ignatz Waghalter's *Mandragola*, Leopold Schmidt's *Die glückliche Insel*, Friedrich E. Koch's *Die Hügelmühle*, Franticek Neumann's *Herbststurm*, and Gustav Scheinpflug's *Das Hofkonzert* on February 3, 1922, which was the last world premiere before the Charlottenburger Oper closed, its glory short-lived. World War I and the defeat of Germany forced Kaiser Wilhelm II's abdication in 1918, and the resulting runaway inflation caused a rapid decline in the value of the deutsche mark. The economic crisis effected the Charlottenburger Oper: subscribers could no longer afford to buy tickets and the audience dwindled. In 1920, Charlottenburg lost its independent city status and became the seventh district in the city of Berlin. Five years later, the Deutsches Opernhaus was taken over by the city of Berlin. The opera house was refurbished and the company renamed Städtische Oper.

The Städtische Oper reopened on September 18, 1925, with Richard Wagner's *Die Meistersinger von Nürnburg*, conducted by Bruno Walter, the company's general music director (until 1929). The Intendant was Heinz Tietjen. Together they staged Ernest Křenek's jazz opera *Jonny spielt auf* in 1927, which caused a scandal, since the main character, Jonny, was a black jazz band leader who stole a violin from the virtuoso Daniello and conquered the world. The opera was ahead of its time. The following year Julius Bittner's *Mondnacht* was premiered. In 1931, Carl Ebert took over the directorship and with Fritz Busch and Fritz Stiedry, changed the philosophy, placing equal emphasis on the dramatic elements of the opera as on the music. Their first production, Giuseppe Verdi's *Macbeth*, created a sensation, and attracted a new audience base — theater-lovers. Contemporary works and premieres continued to play an important role with Kurt Weill's *Die Bürgschaft* and Franz Schreker's *Der Schmied von Gent* gracing the stage. By February 1933, Adolf Hitler and the Nazis were in power, and the advent of the Third Reich had a profound effect on the Städtische Oper. It assumed its birth name, Deutsches Opernhaus, and soon thereafter Ebert staged his last (new) production, Wagner's *Der fliegende Holländer*. In the middle of March, troops stormed the Städtische Oper and Paul Joseph Goebbels took control. Ebert, Busch, and Stiedry, along with other talented Berlin artists, fled Germany. The opera house was transformed into a miniature Reich's Chancellory and used as propaganda for National Socialism. Hitler was a frequent visitor, attending performances of Wagner's *Die Meistersinger von Nürnburg* and Otto Nicolai's *Die lustigen Weiber von Windsor*. The Wagnerian baritone Wilhelm Rode, who had no problem collaborating the with Nazis, was named Intendant, as the

company wallowed in mediocrity. He remained in charge until Allied bombers destroyed the opera house on the night of November 23, 1943. Only the shell of the Deutsches Opernhaus survived.

Four months after the war ended, the Wagnerian bass Michael Bohnen organized a provincial opera company and moved into the Theater des Westens, where he staged Beethoven's *Fidelio*. Against the backdrop of denazification, scandals, and "tainted" artists, seven operas were produced that year. The next year Nazi-banned contemporary operas were revived. Then Frida Leider tried to produce Wagner's *Die Walküre*, and controversy followed the staging of "Nazi Wagner operas" so soon after the surrender. But Tietjen, who was reappointed Intendant in 1948, had no qualms about "Nazi Wagner operas" and proceeded to stage all of them, as well as some world premieres — Werner Egk's *Circe*, Arthur Honegger's *Totentanz*, and Fritz Behrend's *Die lächerlichen Preziösen/Der schwangere Bauer*. In 1954, Ebert, Busch, and Rudolf Bing returned to the Städtische Oper, staging primarily works of Verdi and Mozart, and two years later, Jean-Pierre Ponnelle designed the controversial world premiere of Hans Werner Henze's *König Hirsch*. The well-known singers Dietrich Fischer-Dieskau and Elizabeth Grümmer made their operatic debut with the Städtische Oper.

After the opening of the Deutsche Oper in 1961, the first world premiere, Giselher Klebe's *Alkmene*, took place that same year. Gustav Rudolf Sellner was appointed Intendant in 1961, and during his tenure, modern operas played an important role in the repertory, with several commissions — Roger Sessions's *Montezuma*, Henze's *Der junge Lord*, Roman Haubenstock-Ramati's *Amerika*, Luigi Dallapiccola's *Odysseus*, and Blacher's *200 000 Taler*. When Egon Seefehlner took the helm, the emphasis shifted to gorgeous voices, despite the fact that as a highly subsidized house, the Deutsche Oper is required to stage avant-garde works. There were only a couple — Wolfgang Fortner's *Elizabeth Tudor* and Toshiro Mayuzumi's *Kinkakuyi*. Under the leadership of Siegfried Palm, Plácido Domingo and Luciano Pavarotti made guest appearances, and the world premieres of Wilhelm Dieter Siebert's *Untergang der Titanic* and Mauricio Kagel's *Aus Deutschland* took place.

Götz Friedrich was named Intendant in 1981 and contemporary works again play a dominate role in the repertory. Although several works are from the standard repertory, the productions are unusual. Sometimes Friedrich dresses the productions in avant-garde attire, making the performances challenging and fascinating. The entire Verdi's *Un ballo in maschera* was treated as a masked ball, and opened with a pantomime of Gustav trying on women's clothes. Other times the productions have a more classical bent, including a quintessential interpretation of *Tristan und Isolde*, in which the drama and music fused as a single entity, expressing the essence of the work — consummation of love through death.

Friedrich has a very specific philosophy. He treats opera as music theater, believing that "opera should awaken emotions, and that it should excite." He feels "it is an anachronistic form of art, developed in another era and that it should portray situations that do not exist in our everyday lives. It must say something to the audience, communicate an emotional effect, and have a cathartic function. Since each spectator has had different experiences in life, and holds separate opinions, so each will take home their own message. Opera should be experienced as a fusion of music and theater that form a single unit."

The Deutsche Oper has suffered from budget cuts since the opening of the Berlin Wall. There are now three opera companies in Berlin that vie for government support, and a large amount of money has gone into rebuilding the Staatsoper. It also has the competition of two other opera houses in attracting the public, especially since the Deutsche Oper has more seats to fill in the opera house. The company has 42 singers in its permanent ensemble, which is complemented by around 40 guest singers. The season runs ten and a half months and includes more than 30 different operas in repertory, primarily from the 19th and 20th centuries. Among the recent works are Carl Orff's *Carmina Burana*, Richard Strauss's *Der Rosenkavalier* and *Elektra*, Henze's *Der Prinz von Homburg*, Wagner's Ring Cycle, *Die Meistersinger von Nürnberg*, *Parsifal*, *Tannhäuser*, and *Lohengrin*, Vincenzo Bellini's *Beatrice di Tenda*, Jules Massenet's *Manon* and *Werther*, Verdi's *Rigoletto* and *Nabucco*, and Gaetano Donizetti's *Linda di Chamounix* and *Roberto Devereux*.

Deutsche Oper Berlin

The burned-out ruins of the Deutsches Opernhaus Charlottenburg were demolished in 1957, but a small unscathed section of the building that survived was integrated into the new opera house, which took five years to complete.

It is a stark and modern structure with no resemblance to the opera house it replaced. The concrete, glass, and steel building exhibits a massive stone facade finished in colored mosaic. The east and west exterior walls are of glass. The two-tier auditorium is paneled with cebrano wood and holds mustard-colored tweed seats. The balconies's sides are zigzagged into discrete box-like forms and disk-shaped lights hang from the ceiling. The proscenium arch is plain black. There are 1,885 seats.

Practical Information. Deutsche Oper Berlin, Richard Wagner Straße 10, 10585 Berlin. Tel: 49 30 343 8401, Fax: 49 30 343 8455. When visiting the Deutsche Oper Berlin, stay at the Schlosshotel Vier Jahreszeiten, Brahmsstraße 10, 14193 Berlin. Tel: 49 30 895-840 or 1 800 223 6800, Fax: 49 30 895-84-800. The Schlosshotel Vier Jahreszeiten, built in 1912 as a private mansion that was subsequently converted into a hotel, is convenient to the Deutsche Oper. The hotel can assist with tickets and schedule.

COMPANY STAFF AND PREMIERES

Intendanten. Götz Friedrich (1981–present), Siegfried Palm (1976–81), Egon Seefehlner (1972–76), Gustav Rudolf Sellner (1961–72), Carl Ebert (1954–61), Heinz Tietjen (1948–54), Michael Bohnen (1945–48).

World Premieres **(Charlottenburger Opernhaus):** K. Hösel's *Wieland der Schmied* January 11, 1913; I. Waghalter's *Mandragola* January 23, 1914; F. Weingartner's *Dame Kobold* March 17, 1916; I. Waghalter's *Jugend* February 17, 1917: F.E. Koch's *Die Hügelmühle* May 10, 1918; F. Neumann's *Herbststurm* April 9, 1919; F. Koenneke's *Magdalena* December 8, 1919; P. Scheinpflug's *Das Hofkonzert* February 3, 1922; L. Kreutzer's *Gott und die Bajadere* May 17, 1923; I. Waghalter's *Sataniel* May 31, 1923; E.N. von Reznicek's *Holofernes* October 27, 1923. **(Städtische Oper):** C.R. Maude's *Der letzte Faun* November 22, 1926; J. Bittner's *Mondnacht* November 13, 1928; W. Grosz's *Der arme Reinhold* December 22, 1928; K. Weill's *Die Bürgschaft* March 10, 1932; F. Schreker's *Der Schmied von Gent* October 29, 1932; H. Trantow's *Lärm am Mitternacht* October 16, 1934; P. Mohaupt's *Die Gaunderstreiche der Courasche* August 5, 1936; L. Spie's *Apollo und Daphne* August 5, 1936; L. Spiel's *Der stralauer Fischzug* May 5, 1936; C. Schmalstich's *Wenn der Zarin lächelt* October 28, 1936; K. Stiebitz's *Kinderlied* December 8, 1936;

Deutsche Oper Berlin (Berlin, Germany).

A. Kusterer's *Katarina* May 14, 1939; J. Strauß's *Ein bunter Strauss* October 25, 1939; J. Sobanski's *Die Glasbläser* November 2, 1940; C. Frühauf's *Der Heiratsspiegel* November 2, 1940; L. Spies's *Wenn die Sonne lacht* June 4, 1942. **(Theater des Westens):** W. Egk's *Circe* December 18, 1948; F. Behrend's *Die lächerlichen Preziösen* May 22, 1949; F. Behrend's *Der schwangere Bauer* May 22, 1949; E. Bodart's *Die spanische Nacht* September 17, 1949; B. Blacher's *Chiarina* January 22, 1950; H. Sutermeister's *Die füsse im Feuer* February 12, 1950; H. Sutermeister's *Das Fingerhütchen* February 12, 1950; B. Blacher's *Der erste Ball* June 11, 1950; W. Erg's *Ein Sommertag* June 11, 1950; R. Oboussier's *Amphitryon* March 31, 1951; W. Fortner's *Die weisse Rose* April 28, 1951; B. Blacher's *Lysistrata* September 30, 1951; F. Walter's *Die geraubte Krone* January 12, 1952; B. Blacher's *Preussisches Märchen* September 23, 1952; M. Baumann's *Pelleas und Melisande* September 20, 1954; L. Nono's *Der rote Mantel* September 20, 1954; H.W. Henze's *König Hirsch* September 23, 1956; H.W. Henze's *Maratona di Danza* September 24, 1957; N. Nabakow's *Die letzte Blume* September 24, 1958; G. Klebe's *Die Menagerie* September 24, 1958; H. Searle's *Das Tagebuch eines Irren* October 3, 1958; W. Thärichen's *Anaximanders Ende* October 3, 1958; W. Fortner's *Corinna* October 3, 1958; D. Milhaud's *Fiesta* October 3, 1958; H.F. Martig's *Die schwarze Sonne* September 22, 1959; R. Gassmann & O. Sala's *Paen* May 29, 1960; B. Blacher's *Rosamunde Floris* September 21, 1960. **(Deutsche Oper):** G. Klebe's *Alkmene* September 25, 1961; H.F. Hartig's *Escorial* October 4, 1961; R. Vlad's *Der Doktor aus Glas* October 4, 1961; E. Hartung's *In der Strafkolonie* September 26, 1962; D. Milhaud's *Die Orestie des Aischylos* April 24, 1963; R. Sessions's *Montezuma* April 19, 1964; E. Varèse's *Labyrinth der Wahrheit* October 4, 1964; H.W. Henze's *Der junge Lord* April 7, 1965; I. Yun's *Der Traum des Liu-Tung* September 25, 1965; B. Blacher's *Tristan* October 10, 1965; R. Liebermann's *Capriccio* October 10, 1965; R. Haubenstock-Ramati's *Amerika* October 8, 1966; G. Lampersberg's *Die fahrt zur insel Nantucket* May 18, 1967; B. Martinů's *Anastasia* June 25, 1967; L. Dallapiccola's *Odysseus* September 22, 1968; A. Panufnik's *Kain und Abel* November 1, 1968; B. Blacher's *200 000 Taler* September 25, 1969; B. Britten's *Nocturne* November 5, 1969; M. Subotnick's *When Summoned* November 5, 1969; L. Nono's *Memento* November 5, 1969; F. Zappa's *Susi Cremecheese* November 5, 1969; T. Kessler's *Nationale Feiertage* October 2, 1970; A. Reimann's *Die Vogelscheuchen* October 7, 1970; A. Reimann's *Melusine* April 29, 1971; R. Armbruster & D. Schortemeier's *3 und 16* June 20, 1971; W. Fortner's *Elisabeth Tudor* October 23, 1972; S. Bussotti's *Apology* November 9, 1972; V. Nabokov's *Love's Labour's Lost* February 7, 1973; K. Huber's *Jot* September 27, 1973; E. Varèse *Dèserts* April 5, 1975; M. Subotnick's *Weder Engel Noch Andere Menschen* April 5, 1975; K.H. Wahren's *Fettklösschen* April 24, 1976; T. Mayuzumi's *Kinkakuyi* April 23, 1976; F. Schirren's *Evolutio* December 17, 1977; D. Shostakovich's *Der Idiot* June 26, 1979; W. D. Siebert's *Untergang der Titanic* September 6,

1979; C. Debussy's *La Chute de la Maison Usher* October 5, 1979; M. Kagel's *Aus Deutschland* May 9, 1981; P. Tschaikovsky's *Krieg und Grieden* June 27, 1981; H.J. von Bose's *Die Nacht aus Blei* November 1, 1981; H. Berlioz's *Childe Harold* November 1, 1981; W. Rihm's *Tutuguri* November 12, 1982; R. Kelterborn's *Ophelia* May 2, 1984; A. Madigan's *Carmencita* May 20, 1984; A. Reimann's *Die Gespenstersonate* September 25, 1984; M. Constant's *Der blaue Engel* June 9, 1985; H.W. Henze's *Einhorm* May 3, 1986; B. Blacher's *Habemeajaja* January 29, 1987; H.W. Henze's *Fandango* February 7, 1987; W. Rihm's *Oedipus* October 4, 1987; E. Grosskopf's *Lichtknall* November 15, 1987; M. Neikrug's *Los Alamos* October 1, 1988; H.W. Henze's *Das verratene Meer* May 5, 1990; A. Reimann's *Das Schloß* September 2, 1992; J. Meier's *Dreyfus—Die Affäre* May 8, 1994.

Bibliography. *Dreissig Jahre Deutsche Oper Berlin: Beiträge zum Musiktheater—Band X* (Berlin, 1991). *Deutsche Oper Berlin: Beiträge zum Musiktheater XI* (Berlin, 1992). *Deutsche Oper Berlin: Beiträge zum Musiktheater—Band XII* (Berlin, 1993). *Deutsche Oper Berlin: Beiträge zum Musiktheater—Band XIII* (Berlin, 1994). *Deutsche Oper Berlin: Von Deutschen Opernhaus zur Deutschen Oper Berlin* (Berlin, 1991). *25 Jahre Deutsche Oper Berlin: Ein Documentation der Premieren von 1961 bis 1986* (Berlin, 1986). Detlef Meyer zu Heringdorf, *Das Charlottenburger Opernhaus von 1912 bis 1961 Band I, II* (Berlin, 1988). Interview with Götz Friedrich, Intendant, June 1995.
Thanks to Barbara Hering, Deutsche Oper, and Reto Gaudenzi.

Berliner Kammeroper

The Berliner Kammeroper was founded in 1981 by Henry Akina as the artistic director and Llewelyn Jones as the musical director to produce unknown works from the Baroque era and the 20th century. The company tries to demonstrate the multi-faceted perspective of early opera and 20th-century Musiktheater. Their unusual repertory has included from the early period — Pier Francesco Cavalli's *Il Gastone, L'egisto, La calisto,* Georg Friedrich Händel's *Ezio,* and Giovanni Paisiello's *Il barbiere di Siviglia,* and from the 20th century — Ferruccio Busoni's *Arlecchino,* Hartmann's *Simplicius Simplicissimus,* Hans Werner Henze's *Elegie für junge Liebende,* and Philip Glass's *The Fall of the House of Usher.* The company has also presented several world premieres. The singers are young and talented, interested in performing in rarely performed works. The operas are staged mainly in the Hebbel Theater. They do not have their own venue.

Practical Information. Berliner Kammeroper, Koltbusser Damm 79, 10967 Berlin.

Tel: 49 30 693 1054, Fax: 49 30 692 5201. When visiting the Berliner Kammeroper, stay at the Schlosshotel Vier Jahreszeiten, Brahmsstraße 10, 14193 Berlin. Tel: 49 30 895 840 or 1 800 223 6800, Fax: 49 30 895 84 800. The Schlosshotel Vier Jahreszeiten is in a residential area convenient to the Berliner Kammeroper. The hotel can assist with tickets and schedule.

COMPANY STAFF AND PREMIERES

Künstlerische Leiter (Artistic Director). Henry Akina (1981–present).

World Premieres. G. Lampersberg's *Kleopatra und das Krokodil* 1984; H. Jörns's *Europa und der Stier* 1988; A. Vieru's *Das Gastmahl der Schmarozer* (first staged performance) 1990; C.R. Hirschfeld's *Der satanarchäolügenialkohöllische Wunschpunsch* 1995; M. Constant's *Sade Teresa* 1996.

Bibliography. Information supplied by the company
Thanks to Annette Seimer, Kammeroper.

Komische Oper

The Komische Oper, assuming the name of Hans Gregor's ensemble, opened in the former Metropoltheater (now renamed Komische Oper as well) with Johann Strauß's *Die Fledermaus* on December 23, 1947. Founded by Walter Felsenstein as a music theater company, the Komische

Oper was a place where traditional opera was "reformed" into musical theater — the message of the opera was delivered using both musical and theatrical methods. The understanding of human conflicts and emotions were considered more relevant than top quality voices and refined techniques.

Ferdinand Fellner and Hermann Helmer designed the original theater structure.

The first "Komische Oper," founded by Gregor in 1905, survived only six years. At the time, its music theater orientation was in direct contrast to the vocal emphasis of the Hofoper (see Staatsoper Unter den Linden entry). By retaking the name Komische Oper, Felsenstein wanted to emphasize the company's uniform performance technique which was best described by French popular theater tradition versus that of 19th century grand opera. Under the leadership of Walter Felsenstein, the Komische Oper presented works like Georges Bizet's *Carmen*, Leoš Janáček's *Liška Bystrouška* (The Cunning Little Vixen), Jacques Offenbach's *Les contes d'Hoffmann*, Giuseppe Verdi's *La traviata*, and Wolfgang Amadeus Mozart's *Die Zauberflöte*. The mixed repertory of classical operetta, Singspiele, and opéra comique was meticulously rehearsed, and although the quality of the singers and orchestra was not high, the productions were viewed as theater art at its best.

When Felsenstein died in 1975, the directorship fell to one of his protégés, Joachim Herz, who continued the music theater tradition. Counted among his productions were Alban Berg's *Lulu*, Benjamin Britten's *Peter Grimes*, and Kurt Weill's *Der Augstieg und Fall der Stadt Mahagonny*.

When the helm passed to Harry Kupfer in 1981, a different type of realism — a stark *vérité* — was introduced, which was especially evident in the 1985 world premiere of Siegfried Matthus's *Judith*. Kupfer brought a specific philosophy to the Komische Oper and its productions — emphasizing the "power of the picture," rendered in a clear, concise, understandable manner to the audience, that is relevant for today. He demands a deep concentration from the audience with a focus on the performers. The style is evident in productions of the late 1990s with overacting and over expressing — an exaggeration of emotions and feelings. This, combined with powerful, gripping visual scenes, leaves the audience mesmerized. A production of Jules Massenet's *Werther* (sung in German to a three fourths empty theater despite critical acclaim) had Werther stumble on stage smeared with his own blood and simultaneously a black drop curtain fell to reveal a set of blood-spattered white sheets, a clear but overwhelming expression of the hopeless, doomed love. Sometimes this combination works, like in *Werther*, but sometimes it verges on ludicrous, like in a production of *La bohème*. Kupfer undresses the characters so their inner feelings, emotions, frustrations, and feelings of love are laid bare. He has stated, "I want the spectator in the theater to come along with me (on the journey). They should laugh and cry and not forget the "message." I would like that all the questions of the world play through this beautiful, total art form of opera, which makes suggestions to help mankind live together."

Other productions included Modest Mussorgsky's *Boris Godunov* (original version), Christoph Willibald Gluck's *Orpheus*, Bedřich Smetana's *Prodaná nevěsta* (The Bartered Bride), and a Mozart cycle (*Don Giovanni, Così fan tutte, Le nozze di Figaro, Die Entführung aus dem Serail*). Recent works offered are Georg Friedrich Händel's *Giustino* and *Julius Cesare in Ägypten*, Gluck's *Orfeo ed Euridice*, Verdi's *La traviata* and *Falstaff*, Nikolay Rimsky-Korsakov's *Skazaniye o nevidimom grade Kitezhe* (The Legend of the Invisible City of Kitezh), Ruggero Leoncavallo's *I pagliacci*, Gioachino Rossini's *La Cenerentola*, Georges Bizet's *Carmen*, and several works by Mozart.

Komische Oper

The original theater had been built between 1890 and 1892 as a home for musical revue. Originally called Theater unter den Linden on Behrenstraße, it was renamed Metropoltheater in 1898 and turned into an operetta house where works by Emmerich Kálmán, Franz Lehár, and Leo Fall found a home. In March 1945, bombs severely damaged the building. It was rebuilt, reopening as the Komische Oper in 1947.

The stark beige marble facade, punctuated with rectangular glass windows and arches and topped with bronze cubes, hides an elaborate interior. The rococo auditorium holds two tiers in a semi-circular shape, decorated in ivory and gold, complemented by red velvet seats. Musical shapes embellish the parapets and allegorical sculptures with musical instruments adorn the lower ceiling area. There are around 1,240 places.

Practical Information. Komische Oper, Behrenstraße 55-57, 10117 Berlin. Tel: 49 30 20 260 0, Fax: 49 30 20 260 405. When visiting the Komische Oper stay at the Radisson SAS Hotel Berlin, Karl-Liebknecht-Straße 5, 10178 Berlin.

Tel: 49 30 238 28, Fax: 49 30 23 82 75 90. It is centrally located, and convenient to the Komische Oper. The hotel can assist with opera tickets and schedule.

COMPANY STAFF AND PREMIERES

Intendanten. Albert Kost (1994–present), Werner Rackwitz (1981–93), Joachim Herz (1975–81), Walter Felsenstein (1947–75). **Künstlerische Leiter (Artistic Directors):** Harry Kupfer (1981–present), Joachim Herz (1975–81), Walter Felsenstein (1947–75).

World Premieres. S. Matthus's *Der letzte Schuß* November 7, 1967; S. Matthus's *Noch einen Löffel Gift, Liebling?* April 16, 1972; G. Katzer's *Das Land Bum-Bum* (Der lustige Musikant) September 30, 1978; S. Matthus's *Judith* September 28, 1985; G. Katzer *Antigone oder Die Stadt* November 15, 1991.

Bibliography. Peter Paul Fuchs, ed., *The Music Theater of Walter Felsenstein* (New York, 1975). Clemens Kohl & Ernest Krause, *Felsenstein auf der Probe* (Berlin, 1971). *20 Jahr Komische Oper* (Berlin, 1967). *Vorstellungen von Musiktheater: Ein Almanac auf das 40. Jahr der Komischen Oper* (Berlin, 1987). *Berlins Musiktheater 1995–96* (Berlin, 1995).

Thanks to Anka Großer, Komische Oper, and Alexander Huschka.

Staatsoper Unter den Linden

The Staatsoper Unter den Linden, originally known as the Hofoper Unter den Linden, was inaugurated on December 7, 1742, with Karl Heinrich Graun's *Cleopatra e Cesare*, with lavish sets by Giuseppe Galli-Bibiena. The opera house had been built by Georg Wenzeslaus von Knobelsdorff at the command of Friedrich der Große. Destroyed by fire on August 18, 1843, it was reconstructed by Carl Ferdinand Langhans, reopening on December 7, 1844, with Giacomo Meyerbeer conducting his *Ein Feldlager in Schlesien*. Bombs damaged the structure on April 10, 1941, but it was quickly repaired by Schwiezer, Salexki, and Seydel and reopened with Richard Wagner's *Die Meistersinger von Nürnburg* for the bicentennial in 1942. Another bombing raid destroyed the theater on February 3, 1945. Reconstructed between 1952 and 1955, the Staatsoper was inaugurated on September 4, 1955, with *Die Meistersinger von Nürnberg*. Architect Richard Paulick was responsible for the rebuilding, which was based on the original plans of Knobelsdorff.

Opera first arrived in Berlin in 1700, when Attilio Ariosti's ballet-opera *La festa del Himeneo* was performed on June 1 as court entertainment. During the next decades, the court hosted many opera performances. The first stone for the Hofoper Unter den Linden was laid by Princes Heinrich and Ferdinand on June 22, 1741. When the Hofoper was inaugurated the following year, it was not yet completed. The building was finally finished in 1743 and on October 10, 1743, hosted Johann Adolf Hasse's *La clemenza di Tito*, followed by the first masked ball. The Hofoper was devoted to Italian opera, and Graun was one of the most celebrated composers of the day with more than two dozen world premieres presented to the court, including *Artaserse, Catone in Utica, Alessandro e Poro*, and *Semiramide*. Kaiser Friedrich II contributed to several of Graun's operas, including *Coriolano, Silla*, and *Il re pastore*. The opera house was closed on March 27, 1756, after a performance of Graun's *Merope* due to the Seven Years' War, and the same opera reopened the house on December 20, 1764. The first German prima donna was Elisabeth Schmeling, who made her debut on July 19, 1771, in Hasse's *Piramo e Tisbe*.

After the death of Friedrich II, his nephew Friedrich Wilhelm II took the crown and hired Carl Gotthard Langhans to remodel the opera house, which was reopened on January 11, 1788, with Johann Friedrich Reichardt's *Andromeda*, with Luiza Todi in the title role. After the turn of the century, all the operas given after the carnival season were opened to the public. Since Friedrich Wilhelm II preferred German opera, he opened the Nationaltheater am Gendarmenmarkt and offered Singspiele, including several works by Wolfgang Amadeus Mozart, who came to Berlin on May 19, 1789, for a performance of *Die Entführung aus dem Serail*. Carl Theophil Döbbelin ran the theater. German-language works first entered the repertory of the Hofoper (also called the Lindenoper) a decade later. The most popular composers during this time were Hasse, Reichardt, Felice Alessandri, Johann Gottlieb Naumann, and Friedrich Heinrich Himmel, who all had world premieres of their works given at the Lindenoper. When the French troops under Napoleon occupied Berlin on October 26, 1806, the opera house was used as a bread warehouse. Five years later, the two theaters — Hofoper and Nationaltheater — were united under a single directorship with August Wilhelm Iffland as the "Generalintendant der Königlichen Theaters" (Director of the King's Theaters). He was followed by Graf Karl von Brühl in 1815, who engaged Karl Friedrich Schinkel as set designer at both the Lindenoper and Nationaltheater. The Berlin premiere of Ludwig van Beethoven's *Fidelio* took place on October 11, 1815. Carl Maria von Weber conducted the world premiere of his opera *Der Freischütz* on June 18, 1821, at the new Schauspielhaus am Gendarmenmarkt that ushered in German national opera.

On June 6, 1820, Gasparo Spontini was named general music director, and he supervised lavish productions of his operas, including *Olimpia* on May 14, 1821, with sets designed by Schinkel and for which it was rumored that elephants from the local zoo took part. Giacomo Meyerbeer took the helm on January 1, 1843, but fire destroyed the opera house later that year, with only the facade remaining. Not until the end of 1844 did the Lindenoper reopen with the world premiere of his (Meyerbeer's) opera *Ein Feldlager in Schlesien*, conducted by the composer. Meyerbeer's reign was cut short by his forced resignation. Otto Nicolai conducted the world premiere of his opera, *Die Lustigen Weiber von Windsor*, on March 9, 1849, which was triumphantly received. Unfortunately the composer died a couple of months later. Finally on January 7, 1856, after much controversy between Intendant Botho von Hülsen and Wagner, his *Tannhäuser* was mounted for the first time in Berlin on January 7, 1856, and the first opera of Giuseppe Verdi to grace the stage at the Lindenoper, *Il trovatore*, entered the repertory on March 24, 1857. Three years later, more Verdi operas received their first Berlin performance — *Rigoletto*, *La traviata*, and *Un ballo in maschera*. Wagner works continued with the first performance at the Lindenoper of *Die Meistersinger von Nürnberg* on April 1, 1870, and *Tristan und Isolde* on March 20, 1876. Fourteen years later, Verdi's *Otello* entered the repertory, followed by his *Falstaff* in 1894. Pietro Mascagni's *Cavalleria rusticana* was heard first in 1891 followed by Ruggero Leoncavallo's *I pagliacci* the next year. Wilhelm Kienzl's *Der Evangelimann* received its *Uraufführung* on April 4, 1895. Richard Strauss made his debut on November 5, 1898, conducting Wagner's *Tristan und Isolde*. At the dawn of the 20th century, Strauss led the first performance of his *Feuersnot* on October 28, 1902, but only after much controversy and strife with both the court and Intendant Bolko von Hochberg, which led to his resignation. Enrico Caruso made his debut on October 9, 1906, as the Duke in Verdi's *Rigoletto*, and the same year, Emmy Destinn sang the title role in Strauss's *Salome* on December 5, with the composer conducting. The work received 50 performances within 11 months. *Salome*, conducted by Strauss on November 7, 1918, was also the last opera in the "Royal Theater." One week later, when the curtain rose on *Die Meistersinger von Nürnberg* with Leo Blech on the podium, it was called the Staatsoper Unter den Linden. The following year, Fritz Stiedry conducted the first performance of Hans Pfitzner's *Palestrina*. The most popular composers during this era were Wagner, Giacomo Puccini, Verdi, and Strauss. Several contemporary works were also introduced, including Franz Schreker's *Die Gezeichneten* and *Der Schatzgräber*, Ferruccio Busoni's *Turandot* and *Arlecchino*, Leoš Janáček's *Jenůfa*, Erich Wolfgang Korngold's *Die tote Stadt*, and Ernst Křenek's *Zwingburg*. On May 5, 1930, Darius Milhaud's *Christophe Colomb* received its world premiere with Theodor Scheidl in the title role.

After the National Socialists seized power on January 30, 1933 (Hermann Wilhelm Göring controlled the Staatsoper), all the Jewish ensemble members were dismissed and Otto Klemperer and many top artists went into exile. Wilhelm Furtwängler became opera director. Alban Berg's *Lulu* was world premiered on November 30, 1934, under the baton of Erich Kleiber, and as would be imagined, the Nazis found it scandalous, forcing Kleiber into exile. Furtwängler, in an open letter to Göring, defended his Jewish colleague and resigned. A couple of world premieres followed — Werner Egk's *Peer Gynt* on November 24, 1938, and Rudolf Wagner-Regeny's *Die Bürger von Balais* on January 28, 1939. During the Nazi era, there was no shortage of conductors and singers willing to perform for them, like Herbert van Karajan, Margarete Klose, Frida Leider, Maria Müller, Max Lorenz, Helge Roswänge, Set Svanholm, and Tiana Lemnitz. After the war, with the Staatsoper in ruins, the Admiralspalast became the interim opera house. Renamed the Deutsche Staatsoper Berlin, the company mounted Christoph Willibald Gluck's *Orfeo ed Euridice* as their first opera on September 8, 1945. One of the more important artistic events during this period was the world premiere of the antiwar opera *Die Verurteiling des Lukullus* by Bertold Brecht and Paul Dessau on March 14, 1951, with a new version, *Das Verhör des Lukullus*, given on October 12, 1951. That same year, Kleiber returned to Germany and conducted his first Berlin *Der Rosenkavalier*. On June 14, 1955, the final performance at the Admiralspalast took place, Mozart's *Così fan tutte*.

After the Staatsoper reopened in September 1955, the company embarked upon an ambitious repertory with emphasis in three areas: German opera from Händel and Gluck through Wagner and Strauss; important works from the Italian, Russian, and French repertory; and contemporary opera that included world premieres. This was initially possible since there was a relatively free exchange of talent between East and West for the remainder of the 1950s, and artistic standards remained high. Problems began after the Berlin Wall was constructed. On August 13, 1961, 200 West Berliner Ensemble singers lost their contracts, and severe currency restrictions prevented most Western singers or conductors from appearing at the Staatsoper. Despite some fine voices from the other Eastern Bloc countries, the productions lacked inspiration, with insipid staging and unimaginative direction.

The opening of the Berlin Wall on November 9, 1989, followed by the unification of Germany on October 3, 1990, gave the Staatsoper the opportunity to reclaim its place as one of the leading European opera houses. This became a reality when Georg Quander became Intendant and Daniel Barenboïm the artistic director. In only a few years, the quality went from that of a provincial opera house to that of an international one. Part of Barenboïm's philosophy is to find unconventional solutions for conventional problems. The total budget is 110 million German Marks and the staff numbers around 950, many of whom remained from the old system. It was predominately soloists and directors that were replaced. There are 45 permanent singers plus guest artists, plus a permanent ensemble of young singers.

The Staatsoper is a traditional house with more than a 250-year history, and according to Quander, that plays a role in regards to the repertory. But he is experimenting with directors of different ilks that have resulted in productions from conservative to experimental, realistic to avant-garde. Harry Kupfer's production of *Götterdämmerung* belonged to the experimental category, with a grid of neon lights revealing the emotions and feelings of the characters — red fire, blue ice, and the like, which changed in perfect rhythm and harmony to the music, and the ride down the Rhine was like a trip through the Tunnel of Tomorrow in Chicago's O'Hare Airport, where neon lights are continually changing colors. (Perhaps it inspired the set as the Washington Metro inspired Götz Friedrich's Ring Cycle production.) The singers acted and moved, enough to keep interest, but not too much to distract from the music — a perfect integration of Musiktheater. Kupfer is part of a team that is producing all of Wagner's operas at the Staatsoper through the year 2000.

Contemporary works, like Berg's *Wozzeck* and *Lulu*, and Baroque pieces like Graun's *Cleopatra e Cesare* are finding their way back into the repertory. More than 20 operas are on the boards each season, from Hayden's *Die wüste Insel* and Adolphe Adam's *Le Postillon de Longjumeau* to Albert Lortzing's *Zar und Zimmermann* and Claude Debussy's *Pelléas et Mélisande*, as well as the standard repertory fare, like Verdi's *Aida*, Puccini's *Tosca*, and Wagner's *Lohengrin*.

Kroll Oper

The Krolls Theater, later called the Neues Operntheater, was the second house of the Hofoper. It was inaugurated on August 1, 1895, with Nicolai's *Die lustige Weiber von Windor*. Remodeled and enlarged after World War I, the theater reopened on January 1, 1924, with *Die Meistersinger von Nürnberg*. When the Kroll Oper, also known as the Oper am Platz der Republik, started anew in 1924, it was as a subsidiary of the Staatsoper. Originally founded in 1843, it played an influential role between 1927 and 1931, when on December 19, 1927, it received independent artistic status and staged Beethoven's *Fidelio* with Otto Klemperer on the podium. It also hosted a few world premieres, including Igor Stravinsky's *Oedipus Rex* on February 25, 1928, and Paul Hindemith's *Neues vom Tage* on June 8, 1929. The company attracted attention for its avant-garde productions, many of which caused violent controversy. The conservative opera-goers called it the "Bolshevik Opera" but for the others, it was a healthy remedy for the stuffy traditional productions of the Staatsoper. The experiment lasted only four years. The Prussian legislature decided on March 25, 1931, to closed the Kroll Oper. The last performance, Mozart's *Le nozze di Figaro*, conducted by Fritz Zweig, took place on July 3, 1931.

Staatsoper Unter den Linden

From the fire of 1843, only the facade of the building survived. Langhans added good sightlines and enlarged the auditorium, when he rebuilt the opera house. When the Staatsoper was repaired from the 1941 bombing, it was done in such haste that there was no concern for its historical architecture, but another bombing raid took care of that problem in 1945 by completely destroying the structure. Ten years passed before the Staatsoper was rebuilt. This time, the reconstruction was based on the original 1742 plans.

The Staatsoper has been described as an excellent example of Prussian Classicism, with its "creeping austerity," tempered by "lingering rococo" ornamentation. Extending a city block, the Staatsoper greets its visitors with a six-Corin-

thian-column portico, topped by a pediment of allegorical figures and FRIDERICUS REX APOLLINI ET MUSIS written in gold letters. There are four statues — Sophokles, Aristophanes, Menander, and Euripides, each flanked by engaged columns. The horseshoe-shaped auditorium of coral, ivory, and gold holds three tiers, proscenium boxes and reddish brown velvet seats. The walls surrounding the proscenium boxes display four gilded Corinthian capitals on fluted ivory pilasters. Eight gilded medallions of music motifs, including violins, horns, and flutes ornament the dome ceiling. There are 1,452 seats.

Practical Information. Staatsoper Unter den Linden, Unter den Linden 5-7, 10117 Berlin. Tel: 49 30 20 354 555, Fax: 49 30 20 354 481. When visiting the Staatsoper Unter den Linden, stay at the Radisson SAS Hotel Berlin, Karl-Liebknecht-Straße 5, 10178 Berlin. Tel: 49 30 238 28, Fax: 49 30 23 82 75 90. It is centrally located near the Staatsoper. The hotel can assist with opera tickets and schedule.

COMPANY STAFF AND PREMIERES

Intendanten. Georg Quander (1991–present), Günter Rimkis (1984–91), Hans Pischner (1963–84), Max Burghardt (1954–62), Heinrich Allmeroth

Staatsoper Unter den Linden (Berlin, Germany).

Staatsoper Unter den Linden auditorium (Berlin, Germany).

(1952–54), Ernst Legal (1945–52), Heinz Tietjen (1925–45), Max von Schillings (1919–25), Richard Strauss (1918), Georg Graf von Hülsen-Häseler (1903–18), Bolko Graf von Hochberg (1886–1902), Botho von Hülsen (1851–86), Karl Theodor von Küstner (1842–51), Graf von Redern (1828–42), Graf von Brühl (1815–28), August Wilhelm Iffland (1811–14), Freiherr von der Reck (1788–1806), Baron von Arnim (1776–88), Graf von Zierotin-Lilgenau (1771–75), Freiherr von Pöllnitz (1764–71), Baron von Sweerts (1742–57).

World Premieres. (Italian Hofoper 1742–1805): C.H. Grauen's *Cleopatra e Cesare*, December 7, 1742; C.H. Grauen's *Artaserse*, December 2, 1743; C.H. Grauen's *Catone in Utica*, January 6, 1744; C.H. Grauen's *La festa del Imeneo*, July 15, 1744; C.H. Grauen's *Alessandro e Poro*, December 21, 1744; C.H. Grauen's *Lucio Papirio* January 5, 1745; C.H. Grauen's *Adriano in Siria* December 29, 1745; C.H. Grauen's *Demafonte, re di Tracia* January 17, 1746: C. Nichelmann's *Il sogno di Scipione* March 27, 1746; C.H. Grauen's *Cajo Fabricio* December 2, 1746; C.H. Grauen's *La feste galante*, March 27, 1747; Friedrich II, J.J. Quantz, C. Nichelmann, C.H. Grauen's *Il re pastore* August 4, 1747; C.H. Grauen's *Cinna*, January 1, 1748; C.H. Grauen's *Ifigenis in Aulide* December 13, 1748; C.H. Grauen's *Coriolano*, December 19, 1749; C.H. Grauen's *Fetonte*, March 31,

1750; C.H. Grauen's *Mithridate* December 18, 1750; C.H. Grauen's *Armida*, March 27, 1751; C.H. Grauen's *Britannico* December 17, 1751; C.H. Grauen's *Orfeo e Euridice* March 27, 1752; C.H. Grauen's *Silla* March 27, 1753; J. F. Agricola's *Cleofide* January 1754; C.H. Grauen's *Semiramide* March 27, 1754; C.H. Grauen's *Montezume* January 6, 1755; C.H. Grauen's *Ezio* April 1, 1755; J.F. Agricola's *Il tempio d'amore* September 27, 1755; C.H. Grauen's *I fratelli nemici* January 9, 1756; C.H. Grauen's *Merope* March 27, 1756; J.F. Agricola's *Achille in Scirio* July 16, 1765; J.F. Agricola's *Amor e Psiche* October 5, 1767; J.F. Agricola's *Orest e Pylade* January 6, 1772; J.F. Agricola's *I Greci in Tauride* March 24, 1772; J. A. Hasse's *Artemisia* January 5, 1778; G. Bertoni's *Orpheus* January 31, 1788; J.G. Naumann's *Medea in Colchide* October 16, 1788; J.F. Reichardt's *Protesilao* January 26, 1789; J.F. Reichardt's *Brenno* October 16, 1789; F. Alessandri's *Il ritorno di Ulysse a Penelope* January 25, 1790; F. Alessandri's *Dario* February 14, 1791; J.F. Reichardt's *L'Olympiade* October 3, 1791; several composers *Vasco di gama* January 20, 1792; V. Righini's *Enea nel Lacio* January 7, 1793; J.G. Naumann's *Protesilao* January 21, 1793; V. Righini's *Atalanta e Meleagro* February 15, 1797; V. Righini's *Armida* February 21, 1797; V. Righini's *Tigranes* January 20, 1800; F.H. Himmel's *Vasco di Gama* January 12,

1800; J.F. Reichardt's *Rosmonda's* February 6, 1800. V. Righini's *Der Zauberwald und das befreite Jerusalem* January 21, 1803; J.A. Gürrlich's *Calirrhoe* March 31, 1805. **(Important Operas 1821–1989):** C.M. Weber's *Der Freischütz* June 18, 1821; H. Marschner's *Hans Heiling* May 24, 1833; G. Meyerbeer's *Ein Feldlager in Schlesien* December 7, 1844; O. Nicolai's *Die lustigen Weiber von Windsor* March 9, 1849; F. Mendelssohn-Bartholdy's *Die erste Walpurgisnacht* October 11, 1893; W. Kienzl's *Der Evangelimann* May 4, 1895; A. Lortzing's *Regina oder Die Marodeure* March 21, 1899, R. Leoncavallo's *Der Roland von Berlin* December 13, 1904; E. Křenek's *Zwingburg* October 21, 1924; A. Berg's *Wozzeck* December 14, 1925; K. Weill's *Royal Palace/Der neue Orpheus* March 2, 1927; I. Stravinsky's *Oedipus Rex* February 25, 1928; F. Schreker's *Der singende Teufel* December 10, 1928; P. Hindemith's *Neues vom Tage* June 8, 1929; D. Milhaud's *Christophe Colomb* May 5, 1930; K. Rathaus's *Fremde Erde* December 10, 1931; H. Pfitzner's *Das Herz* November 12, 1931; P. Graener's *Der Prinz von Homburg* March 14, 1935; E. Künneke's *Die große Sünderin* December 31, 1935; P. von Klenau's *Rembrandt van Rijn* January 23, 1937; M. Lothar's *Schneider Wibbel* May 12, 1938; W. Egk's *Peer Gynt* November 24, 1938; R. Wagner-Regency's *Die Bürger von Calais* January 28, 1939; O. Schoeck's *Schloß Dürande* April 1, 1943; P. Dessau's *Die Verurteilung des Lukullus* March 14, 1951; J.K. Forest's *Der arme Konrad* October 4, 1959; P. Dessau's *Puntila* November 15, 1966; P. Dessau's *Lanzelot* December 19, 1969; E.H. Meyer's *Reiter der Nacht* November 17, 1973; P. Dessau's *Einstein* February 16, 1974; J. Werzlau's *Meister Röckle* October 3, 1976; F. Goldmann's *R. Hot bzw. Die Hitze* February 27, 1977; P. Dessau's *Leonce und Lena* November 24, 1979; P.-H.Dittrich's *Die Verwandlung* February 24, 1984; F. Schenker's *Büchner* February 21, 1987; G. Katzer's *Gastmahl oder Über die Liebe* April 30, 1988; S. Matthus's *Graf Mirabeau* July 14, 1989.

Bibliography. Wolfgang Wagner, Daniel Barenboïm, Manfred Haedler, *Portrait der Staatskapelle Berlin* (Berlin, 1995). Manfred Haedler, *Deutsche Staatsoper Berlin: Geschichte und Gegenwart* (Berlin, 1990). Ruth Freydank, *Theater in Berlin von den Anfängen bis 1945* (Berlin, 1988). Hans Curjel, *Experiment Krolloper, 1927–1931* (Munich, 1975). Werner Otto, *Die Lindenoper* (Berlin, 1980). Interview with Georg Quander, Intendant, June 1995.

Thanks to Frank-Rüdiger Berger, Staatsoper Unter den Linden, and Alexander Huschka.

BIELEFELD

Bühnen der Stadt

Wolfgang Amadeus Mozart's *Die Zauberflöte* inaugurated the Bühnen der Stadt on December 1, 1947. The chief city builder Herr Freitag was responsible for the reconstruction. The previous theater, the Stadttheater had been damaged during bombing raids on October 26 and December 6, 1944. Inaugurated on April 3, 1904, with Friedrich von Schiller's *Jungfrau con Orleans*, the Stadttheater had been designed by Bernhard Sehring in a Neo-Baroque style and Jugendstil.

Initially the Stadttheater hosted plays and operettas, since no opera ensemble existed. After World War I, an opera ensemble was in place and Wolfgang Amadeus Mozart's *Die Zauberflöte* was presented, followed by Richard Strauss's *Der Rosenkavalier* and the complete *Der Ring des Nibelungen*. During the Third Reich, Carl Bielefeld saw Maria von Weber's *Oberon*.

After the war, performances continued in temporary quarters where Ludwig van Beethoven's *Fidelio* and Christoph Willibald Gluck's *Iphigénie en Tauride* graced the stage. After the opera house reopened, contemporary operas, like Arthur Honegger's *Johanna auf dem Scheiterhaufen*, Gottfried von Einem's *Dantons Tod*, Igor Stravinsky's *L'histoire du soldat*, Paul Hindemith's *Mathias der Maler*, and Werner Egk's *Zaubergeige*, as well as the world premiere of Marcel Mihalovici's *Krapp oder das letzte Band* and Rudolf Mors's *Vineta*, and the German premiere of Bohuslav Martinů's *Řecké pašije* (The Greek Passion) graced the stage. The early part of the 1970s brought productions of Verdi's *Otello*, von Einem's *Der Besuch der alten Dame* with Martha Mödl, Claude Debussy's *Pelléas et Mélisande*, Mozart's *Die Zauberflöte*, Bedřich Smetana's *Prodaná nevěsta* (The Bartered Bride), and the world premiere of Jolyon Brettingham Smith's *Cuchulains Tod*. Near the end of the decade into the 1980s, Udo Zimmermann's *Der Schuhu und die fliegende Prinzessin*, Heinrich Marschner's *Der Vampyr* and *Templer und Jüdin*, and an early opera, Luigi Cherubini's *Médée,* trod the boards. Recent repertory includes Mozart's *Le nozze di Figaro*, Rossini's *Il barbiere di Siviglia*, Webber's *The Phantom of the Opera*, Puccini's *La bohème*, and Wagner's *Tannhäuser*.

Practical Information. Bühnen der Stadt, Brunnen Straße 3-9, 33602 Bielefeld. Tel: 49 521 512-502, Fax: 49 521 513-430. If visiting, contact the German National Tourist Office, 747 Third Avenue, 33rd Floor, New York, NY 10017. Tel: 212-308-3300.

COMPANY STAFF

Intendant. Heiner Bruns.
Bibliography. P. Schütze (ed.), *75 Jahre Stadttheater Bielefeld 1904–1979* (Bielefeld, 1979).

——— BONN

Oper der Bundesstadt Bonn

The Theater der Stadt Bonn was inaugurated on May 5, 1965, with Aischylos's *Orestie*. Wilfried Beck-Erlang and Klaus Gessler designed the new building. The previous theater, the Theater am Kölntor or the Stadttheater, had been destroyed during World War II. Vincenzo Bellini's *Norma* had inaugurated the Theater am Kölntor on October 29, 1848. It was designed by Herr von der Emden.

As early as 1713, Kurfürst Joseph Clemens, upon his return from exile, wrote to Robert de Cotte, the architect responsible for the rebuilding of the castle, to include a theater "pour représenter des opéras" (to perform operas). From this simple building, his successor Clemens August created a beautiful Baroque theater which hosted Italian operas given by Italian troupes, including Giovanni Battista Pergolesi's *La serva padrona*. The latter part of the 1700s saw Singspiele from Karl Ditters von Dittersdorf and Wolfgang Amadeus Mozart's *Die Entführung aus dem Serail*, as well as his *Le nozze di Figaro* and *Don Giovanni* in the repertory. Max Franz, who was responsible for the theater, had to flee on October 2, 1797, from the approaching troops of the French Revolution. The theater was closed and destroyed in 1830. Four years earlier, in 1826, Bonn had received the Theater am Viereckesplatz which Friedrich Sebald Ringelhardt directed. Four times a week he staged opera, like Gioachino Rossini's *Otello*, Carl Maria von Weber's *Oberon* and *Euryanthe*, Daniel Auber's *La muette di Portici*, and Mozart's *Le nozze di Figaro*. Then in 1844, the surprising news arrived that the theater had been torn down. The reason was not known. Bonn was again without a theater. Then the theater society produced the first Bonn performance of Albert Lortzing's *Der Wildschütz* in the large room of the Lese-und Erholungsgesellschaft.

A new theater, the Theater am Kölntor, opened in 1848, with Wilhelm Löwe as its director. There was a permanent ensemble of 19 singers and actors and an orchestra of 32 musicians. The first year went well, but then there were serious financial problems that led to the liquidation of the theater group in 1859 and the selling of the theater to the city. This is how Bonn received its Stadttheater. Initially, the city leased the theater to the Cologne theater director Eberhard who brought opera and drama to Bonn. Between 1881 and 1902, the well-known Cologne tenor Emil Götze sang often on the Bonn stage, performing in Georges Bizet's *Carmen*, Giacomo Meyerberr's *Le Prophète*, and Richard Wagner's *Lohengrin*. During the 1937-38 season, eleven opera performances took place, including the world premiere of Johanna Kinkel's *Das Malztier*. The Theater am Kölntor had served the performing arts for almost 100 years, when on a night in July 1944, it fell into ruins.

After World War II, the first musical-melodramatic performance took place on July 13, 1945, in the Hofgarten of the Kunstmuseum. Opera performances also took place in the inner court of the Alexander König Museum. During the 1950s and early 1960s, the Bonner Oper had an ambitious schedule. Not only were the familiar works like Mozart's *Don Giovanni, Die Zauberflöte, Idomeneo*, and *Le nozze di Figaro*, Giuseppe Verdi's *Otello, Il trovatore, Aida, Un ballo in maschera*, and *La traviata*, Ludwig van Beethoven's *Fidelio*, Ruggero Leoncavallo's *I pagliacci*, Giacomo Puccini's *Gianni Schicchi, Tosca, La bohème*, and *Madama Butterfly*, Wagner's *Der fliegende Holländer*, and Richard Strauss's *Der Rosenkavalier, Ariadne auf Naxos*, and *Arabella* on the boards, but the unfamiliar and less frequently performed also graced the stage, including Frank Martin's *Der Zaubertrank*, Robert Schumann's *Genoveva*, Antonín Dvořák's *Rusalka*, Christoph Willibald Gluck's *Orfeo ed Euridice*,

Domenico Cimarosa's *Il matrimonio segreto*, Benjamin Britten's *Albert Herring*, Rolf Liebermann's *Die Schule der Frauen*, Peter Cornelius's *Der Barbier von Bagdad*, Luigi Cherubini's *Médée*, Ermanno Wolf-Ferrari's *Die schalkhafte Witwe*, Hermann Goetz's *Der widerspenstigen Zähmung*, Boris Blacher's *Preußisches Märchen*, Daniel Auber's *Fra Diavolo*, Béla Bartók's *A Kékszakállú herceg vára* (Duke Bluebeard's Castle), Hans Werner Henze's *Boulevard Solitude*, Franz Lehner's *Die schlaue Susanne*, Darius Milhaud's *Der arme Matrose*, and Gerhard Wimberger's *Dame Kobold*.

After the opening of the new theater in 1965, unfamiliar works continued in the repertory with Adolphe Adam's *Si j'étais roi*, Maurice Ravel's *L'heure espagnole*, Léo Delibes's *Le Roi l'a dit*, Donizetti's *Maria di Rohan*, Ermano Wolf-Ferrari's *I quattro rusteghi*, Albert Lortzing's *Zar und Zimmermann*, Paul Hindemith's *Cardillac* and *Mathis der Maler*, Carl Orff's *Die Kluge*, and Hans Werner Henze's *Elegy for Young Lovers* and *El Cimarron*. Jean-Claude Riber arrived in 1980 with an interest in attracting an international audience as befitting the capital city of (then) West Germany. He hired "stars" to complement the resident ensemble, including Piero Cappuccilli, Walter Berry, Renata Scotto, and Karl Ridderbusch. The direction of the theater changed again in 1993 with the arrival of Gian-Carlo Monaco. The type of production varies. Puccini's *La rondine* was a co-production with the Washington Opera, and was a luxurious and lavish (traditional) affair, but unimaginative, and ultimately boring. The singers just stood and sang with no expression of feelings or emotions, as though they were afraid to distract from the beautiful sets, and wanted to show off their glittery attire. It was devoid of impact — the antithesis of what, ultimately, opera should do. Other works, however, leave strong impressions and are innovative and creative.

The repertory offers both opera and musicals. Some recent operas include Wagner's *Das Rheingold*, Verdi's *Nabucco* and *Falstaff*, Dmitry Shostakovich's *Ledi Makbet Mtsenskovo uyezda* (Lady Macbeth of the Mtsensk District), Mozart's *Le nozze di Figaro* and *Die Zauberflöte*, and Puccini's *Madama Butterfly*.

Theater der Stadt Bonn

On January 13, 1960, Professor Elermann chose the winning drawings in the architectural competition for the design of the new theater. The construction lasted from 1961 to 1965, when the theater was inaugurated. It is a concrete and glass building, comprised of a series of fused geometric shapes. The modern auditorium is asymmetrically shaped. The single tier, instead of stretching across the room, has a third of itself extending halfway down to the orchestra level in a steeply graded seating arrangement. A single side box is carved out of the wall. The teak-wood walls contrast with the white-marble facing on the parapet. The seats are brown fabric. The plain proscenium arch holds a red velvet curtain and rows of multi-colored spotlights punctuate the black acoustic ceiling. There are 896 seats.

Practical Information. Oper der Bundesstadt Bonn, Am Boselagerhof 1, 53111 Bonn. Tel: 49 228 7281, Fax: 49 228 728-371. When visiting the Oper der Bundesstadt Bonn, stay at the Hotel Königshof, Adenauer Allee 9, 53111 Bonn. Tel: 49 228 26010, Fax: 49 228 260-1529. The Hotel Königshof is centrally located near the opera house. The hotel can assist with tickets and schedule.

COMPANY STAFF

Intendanten. Gian-Carlo Monaco (1993–present), Jean-Claude Riber (1980–92), Hans Joachim Heyse (1970–80), Karl Pempelfort (1951–70).

Bibliography. Hermann-Josef Krämer, *Bonner Theater nach 1950* (Bonn, 1981). W. Detering, C. Fuhrmann, D. Steinbeck, H. Stuckmann, *Theater für eine Stadt: Die siebziger Jahre im Theater der Stadt Bonn* (Cologne, 1981). Additional Information supplied by the company.

Thanks to Andrea Möstl and Cornelia Martens-Sandleben, Oper der Bundesstadt Bonn.

BRAUNSCHWEIG

Stadttheater

Wolfgang Amadeus Mozart's *Don Giovanni* inaugurated the rebuilt Stadttheater on December 25, 1948. Originally called the Hoftheater when it was first constructed in 1861 in *fin de siècle* style, and after World War I renamed Landestheater, the building was destroyed during World War II.

As early as 1650, opera-like performances were seen in the city. Sigmund Johann Kusser was named *Kapellmeister* in 1682 and several of his operas were presented. Next Braunschweig witnessed the works of Reinhard Keiser, before he left for Hamburg. In 1690 an opera house was constructed, supposedly offering works at a level similar to that of Hamburg, Munich, and Dresden. The theater underwent several reconstructions and name changes, from Opernhaus to Nationaltheater to Hoftheater. After the new opera house opened in 1861, opera activity shifted there. When the opera house was reconstructed after World War II, it was called the Stadttheater.

When the Stadttheater reopened, the repertory concentrated on the works of Mozart, Richard Wagner, Giacomo Puccini, and Giuseppe Verdi. Some early operas were performed — Georg Friedrich Händel's *Giulio Caesar, Serses,* and *Rodelinde,* and Christoph Willibald Gluck's *Iphégenie en Aulide.* Contemporary works played an important role, with Benjamin Britten's *Albert Herring,* Giselher Klebe's *Jakobowsky und er Oberst,* Rolf Liebermann's *Penelope* and *Leonore 40/45,* Alban Berg's *Wozzeck,* Ernst Křenek's *Karl V,* Wolfgang Fortner's *Bluthochzeit,* Paul Hindemith's *Mathias der Maler,* Ján Cikker's *Auferstehung* and *Das Erdbeben in Chile,* Paul Dessau's *Lukullus,* Hans Werner Henze's *Boulevard Solitude,* and Aribert Reimann's *Melusine,* all staged at the Stadttheater. Recent repertory includes Ludwig van Beethoven's *Fidelio,* Mozart's *Die Entführung aus dem Serail,* Gioachino Rossini's *Il barbiere di Siviglia,* and Berg's *Wozzeck.*

Practical Information. Stadttheater, Am Theater, 38100 Braunschweig. Tel: 49 531 484 2700, Fax: 49 531 484 2727. If visiting, contact the German National Tourist Office, 747 Third Avenue, 33rd Floor, New York, NY 10017. Tel: 212-308-3300.

COMPANY STAFF

Intendant. Jürgen Flügge.

BREMEN

Bremer Theater (Theater der Freien Hansestadt Bremen)

The Bremer Theater, also known as the Theater der Freien Hansestadt Bremen, opened on August 27, 1950. The president of the Bremer Senate, Wilhelm Kaisen, stated at the inaugural ceremony, "Die Kunst ist der Freude gewidmet, und es gibt keine höhere und ernstere Aufgabe als die Menschen zu beglücken." (Art is dedicated to gladness, and there is no higher and more serious task than to make mankind happy.) The theater was located on the site where the Bremer Schauspielhaus had stood, before its destruction by bombs on October 6, 1944. The new opera house had been designed by Hans Storm.

The first opera performances date back to 1695. Around a century later, two theaters were hosting opera and drama, the Komödienhaus auf dem Reithof and the Schauspielhaus. Opera was more difficult to stage, since the cost was so much higher. However, the 1799-1800 season was successful with 50 operatic performances given. Works of Wolfgang Amadeus Mozart, like *Die Zauberflöte* and Giovanni Paisiello, like *Il barbiere di Siviglia* were especially popular.

On October 16, 1843, the Bremer Stadttheater opened with a gala program, and within a few years, an opera repertory had been established. To prevent competition with the theaters remaining from the late 1700s, they were torn down. Between 1853 and 1860, when L. A. Wohlbrück ran the theater, there was a regular audience for opera and operetta. When Friedrich Feldmann took over the theater, Jenny Lind sang there. Under the tenure of Angelo Neumann, a "Richard-Wagner-Gastspieltheater" was established and presented for the first time in Bremen between October 1 and 5, 1882, Wagner's *Der Ring des Nibelungen.* The first *Tristan und Isolde* in the Hansestadt followed on December 26, 1883. Wagner operas dominated the repertory until after World War I when Mozart, Albert Lortzing, Giacomo Meyerbeer, and Carl Maria von Weber operas became the most popular. Works like

Beethoven's *Fidelio*, Conradin Kreutzer's *Das Nachtlager von Granada*, and Friedrich von Flotow's *Martha* and *Alessandro Stradella* were part of the permanent repertory offerings.

Bremen received a second theater in 1910, when on August 13 the Bremer Schauspielhaus opened, but it was primarily a home for drama. Opera continued as previously in the Stadttheater. On April 22, 1926, Manfred Gurlitt, who was first *Kapellmeister* and then general music director in Bremen saw his opera *Wozzeck* receive its world premiere, four months after Alban Berg's opera by the same name. This sent his opera into oblivion, until it was revived during the 1986-87 season in Bremen. When Hitler seized power, the theaters were turned into propaganda houses of the Third Reich with Nazi ideology permeating all the productions. In January 1943, both the Staatstheater and the Schauspielhaus were placed under a single administration known as "Opernhaus" and used only for opera performances, until September 1, 1944, when all the theaters were closed.

Opera began again in 1947 in the Glockensaal. When the Bremer Theater opened in 1950, opera shared the stage with drama and ballet. Around a decade later, for two seasons—1960 to 1962, Montserrat Caballé assayed the title role in the first German performance of Antonín Dvořák's *Armida*, Giacomo Puccini's *Madama Butterfly*, and Marie in Bedřich Smetana's *Prodaná nevěsta* (The Bartered Bride). Götz Friedrich came to direct Verdi's *Rigoletto* and Richard Strauss's *Ariadne auf Naxos*, and the first German performance of Jean-Philippe Rameau's *Platée* took place. Other works in the repertory included Verdi's *La forza del destino*, Georges Bizet's *Carmen*, Puccini's *Madama Butterfly*, Strauss's *Salome*, Mozart's *Le nozze di Figaro*, and Pyotr Il'yich Tchaikovsky's *Mazzeppa*. Contemporary operas also gracing the stage were Paul Hindemith's *Cardillac*, Kurt Weill's *Der Aufstieg und Fall der Stadt Mahagonny*, and Carl Orff's *Der Kluge*. During the 1979-80 seasons Gottfried von Einem's *Dantons Tod* entered the repertory along with Mozart's *Idomeneo*, and the following season saw the first company performance of Leoš Janáček's *Přihody Lišky Bystroušky* (The Cunning Little Vixen). Bremen's first Modest Mussorgsky's *Boris Godunov* arrived during the 1981-82 season followed by Alban Berg's *Lulu* the next year.

Tobias Richter took the helm in 1985, and within a few years began to stage unknown, rarely performed, and experimental works, like Heusinger's *Der Turm*, Alexander von Zemlinsky's *Der Traumgörge*, Siebert's *Untergang der Titanic*, and Karol Szymanowski's *Król Roger* (King Roger), as well as mount world premieres of the same ilk, and the audience stayed home. Then Hansgünther Heyme took over and he did not care very much about opera and not much attention was given to it, and the audience continued to stay home. In addition, there were political problems and he left after a short time, with the result that there was no director and no audience. Now the company is working to get the audience back, with "easier" repertory. They have no problem filling up the house with Mozart's *Die Entführung aus dem Serail*, or other classic operas. The problem is to get the audience to come to the theater for the 20th century works. There are 18 ensemble singers plus guest artists, and young directors from the theater are hired to stage the productions. The company's music director conducts all the performances. With little money, the staging is tasteful and appropriate. The ensemble singing is good when the works are from the 18th century, like Mozart operas. With the 19th century works from *bel canto* through Richard Wagner, the company does not fare as well. New productions are better than the repeats. The total budget is 40 million German Marks with only 3.5 million a year for opera productions. It was even worse when the Green political party was in power— then they received only 2 million for opera, but it would have meant the death of opera if that continued. (Note black ribbon across the front of the opera house in photo.) Bremen also suffered the largest debt of any city, but with the financial situation improving, the opera company hopes that the budget will also increase.

The repertory is a mixture of experimental and traditional, but even the traditional productions have a taste of the different. Bremen wants to continue to do the unusual and experimental but needs audience approval, and that is one of their goals for the 21st century—to sell out the theater for the experimental works as they do for the classic operas. Then the future will look brighter. Recent works are more mainstream, including Verdi's *Un ballo in maschera* and *Aida*, Bizet's *Carmen*, Gaetano Donizetti's *Don Pasquale*, and Wagner's *Die Meistersinger von Nürnberg*.

Theater am Goetheplatz

The building's massive, white classic facade exhibits THEATER AM GOETHEPLATZ in large letters, and is lined with imposing Doric columns which support an unadorned pediment. The two-tiered, rectangular auditorium is plain and utilitarian, with walls of dark walnut wood and seats of beige corduroy. A red velvet curtain hangs in the plain, black proscenium arch, and rows of spotlights stretch across the white ceiling. There are 989 seats.

Practical Information. Bremer Theater, Goetheplatz, 2800 Bremen. Tel: 49 421 36 53 215, Fax: 49 421 36 53 260. When visiting the Bremer Theater, stay at the Park Hotel, Im Bürgerpark, 28209 Bremen. Tel: 49 421 34080 or 1 800 223 6800, Fax: 49 421 340-8602. Located in a park setting, the Park Hotel is convenient to the opera house. The Park Hotel can assist with tickets and schedule.

COMPANY STAFF AND PREMIERES

Intendanten. Klaus Pierwoß (1994–present), Rolf Rempe Kommissarisch (1993–94), Hansgünther Heyme (1992–93), Tobias Richter (1985–92), Arno Wüstenhüfer (1979–84), Peter Stolzenberg (1973–78), Kurt Hübner (1962–72), Albert Lippert (1956–61), Willi Hanke (1950–55).

World Premieres. (1977–95): Hespos's *Nachtworstellung* 1987–88; Johnson's *Riemannoper* 1988–89; Haupt's *Oh Automobile*, 1990–91; Hiller's *Das Traumfresserchen*, 1990–91; Stäbler's *Sünde, Fall, Beil* 1991–92; N.N. *Drei Wasserspiele*, May 16, 1995. **German Premieres.** (1977–95): N. Maw's *Der Mond geht auf über Irland*, 1977–78; P. Maxwell Davies's *Cinderella*, 1980–81; P. Maxwell Davies's *The Lighthouse*, 1982–83; D. Cimarosa's *L'italiana in Londra*, 1983–84.

Bibliography. *200 Jahre Theater in Bremen* (Bremen, 1993). Interview with Dietmar Schwarz, Musiktheater Dramaturie.

Thanks to Regine Maier, Bremer Theater, and Roberto Klimsh.

Theater am Goetheplatz (Bremen, Germany).

BREMERHAVEN

Stadttheater

Wolfgang Amadeus Mozart's *Don Giovanni* inaugurated the current Stadttheater on April 12, 1952. Walter Unruh and Gerhard Graubner were in charge of the reconstruction. The previous Stadttheater had been destroyed on September 18, 1944, during a bombing raid. It was designed by Oscar Kaufmann and was opened on October 1, 1911, with William Shakespeare's *A Midsummer Night's Dream*. The first opera presented, Carl Maria von Weber's *Der Freischütz*, followed two days later, on October 3, 1911. The inaugural season gave a total of 22 operas, including Richard Wagner's *Lohengrin* and *Tannhäuser*. Wagner works to this day play a major role in the repertory. During the Third Reich, the public stayed away from the opera house and the ensemble was dissolved. After the war, opera was performed in temporary quarters in the *Bürgerhaus*. The repertory improved after the Stadttheater reopened.

During the 1956-57 season Helge Rosvaenge assayed the title role in Ruggero Leoncavallo's *I pagliacci* and in 1963, Verdi's *Attila* was staged. Recent offerings have included Georges Bizet's *Carmen*, Verdi's *Falstaff* and *Nabucco*, and Richard Strauss's *Elektra*.

Practical Information. Stadttheater, Theodor-Heuss-Platz, 27519 Bremerhaven. Tel: 49 471 482 0645, Fax: 49 471 482 0682. If visiting, contact the German National Tourist Office, 747 Third Avenue, 33rd Floor, New York, NY 10017. Tel: 212-308-3300.

COMPANY STAFF

Intendant. Peter Grisebach.

Bibliography. F. Ernst, *Das Bremerhavener Theater. Ein Beitrag zu seiner Geschichte von den Anfängen bis zur Wiederrichtung nach dem Zweiten Weltkrieg* (Bremerhaven, 1981).

COBURG

Landestheater

The Landestheater, originally called the Hoftheater, was inaugurated on September 17, 1840, with *Der Feensee*. Three years under construction, the opera house was designed by Vincenz Fischer-Birnbaum in classic style.

The earliest Hoftheater was opened in 1683. The following year, Christoph Adam Negelein's Singspiel *Der gehorsame Wunderglaube Abrahams in der willigen Opferung seindes Sohnes Isaak* was staged. Wolfgang Amadeus Mozart's *Die Entführung aus dem Serail* and *Die Zauberflöte*, along with works from Karl Ditters von Dittersdorf, were seen in 1794, and the first performance in Coburg of Ludwig van Beethoven's *Fidelio* took place in 1832. Five years later, the first ground stone for a new theater was laid. The theater was inaugurated on September 17, 1840. The following year Albert Lortzing's *Zar und Zimmermann* graced the stage. Beginning in the mid–1850s several of Richard Wagner's operas entered the repertory — *Tannhäuser* in 1854, *Rienzi* six years later,

Der fliegende Holländer in 1864, *Lohengrin* on September 29, 1867, *Die Meistersinger von Nürnberg* in 1889, and during the 1906 and 1907 seasons the Ring Cycle, minus *Die Walküre*. (The complete *Der Ring des Nibelungen* did not take place until November 1925.) After World War I, Richard Strauss visited Coburg to conduct his *Der Rosenkavalier* in 1918. The first performance in Coburg of Wagner's *Parsifal* came two years later. A May Festival in 1924 witnessed Mozart's *Don Giovanni* and Wagner's *Tristan und Isolde*, and the following May saw Franz Schreker's *Schatzgräber*, Strauss's *Der Rosenkavalier*, and Wagner's *Tannhäuser*. Mozart's *Die Entführung aus dem Serail* initiated the opera performances after the World War II on April 21, 1946, followed by Strauss's *Der Rosenkavalier*, Giacomo Puccini's *La bohème*, and Wagner's *Tannhäuser*. The 1980s and 1990s saw works like Carl Maria von Weber's *Der Freischütz*, Mozart's *Le nozze di Figaro*, Georges Bizet's *Carmen*, Eugen d'Albert's *Tiefland*, Lortzing's *Zar und*

Zimmermann and *Der Wildschütz*, Mozart's *Così fan tutte*, Puccini's *Tosca*, Bedřich Smetana's *Prodaná nevěsta* (The Bartered Bride), and Werner Egk's *Die Zaubergeige*. Recent productions include Mozart's *Le nozze di Figaro*, Claude Debussy's *Pelléas et Mélisande*, and Engelbert Humperdinck's *Hänsel und Gretel*.

Practical Information. Landestheater Coburg, Schloßplatz 6, 8630 Coburg. Tel: 49 9561 95021, Fax: 49 9561 99447. If visiting, contact the German National Tourist Office, 747 Third Avenue, 33rd Floor, New York, NY 10017. Tel: 212-308-3300.

COMPANY STAFF

Intendant. Karin Heindl-Lau.
Bibliography. H. Bachmann & J. Erdmann (ed.), *150 Jahre Coburger Landestheater* (Coburg, 1977).

COLOGNE

Oper der Stadt Köln

On May 18, 1957, Carl Maria von Weber's *Oberon* inaugurated the Großes Haus of the Oper der Stadt Köln. Wilhelm Riphahn designed the structure. The previous theater, the Kölner Opernhaus, was destroyed on May 14, 1944. The Cologne Opera House had been inaugurated on September 6, 1902, with Richard Wagner's *Die Meistersinger von Nürnberg*. Located on Barbarossaplatz, the theater was designed by Carl Moritz.

Back in 1768, Cologne received its first permanent theater. Constructed by Joseph von Kurtz on Neumarkt, it was a simple wooden building with four levels. The theater hosted various companies, one of which was led by Johann Heinrich Böhm, who presented more than three dozen operas, including Christoph Willibald Gluck's *Alceste*, Wolfgang Amadeus Mozart's *Die Entführung aus dem Serail*, and works by André Grétry, Antonio Salieri, Niccolò Piccinni, and Giovanni Paisiello, among others. Another theater, constructed by Caspar Rodius, hosted Grétry's *Richard, Coeur de Lion*, Mozart's *Die Zauberflöte* and *Don Giovanni*, and Franz Joseph Haydn's *Ritter Roland*. After the turn of the century, the city commissioned Friedrich Sebald Ringelhardt to build a theater in 1822, which he directed for a decade. Here the city saw Carl Maria von Weber's *Der Freischütz*, Gioachino Rossini's *Il barbiere di Siviglia*, Ludwig van Beethoven's *Fidelio*, and Mozart's *Così fan tutte*. Structural problems caused this opera house to be torn down, but another rose on the same site with almost double the seating capacity—1,500. Several well-known artists appeared on this new theater's stage, including Josef Staudigl, Jenny Lind, and Joseph Tichatschek. Some world premieres were also presented, including Friedrich Krug's *Meister Martin der Küffner und seine Gesellen* on March 18, 1845, and Franz Derckum's *Alda* the following year. Giacomo Meyerbeer's *Robert le Diable* and *Les Huguenots*, and Gaetano Donizetti's *La fille du régiment* also graced the stage. The operas of Richard Wagner were introduced to Cologne under the tenure of Moritz Ernst, with *Der fliegende Holländer*, *Rienzi*, and the first two operas in the Ring Cycle, *Das Rheingold* and *Die Walküre*. Another opera house was opened in 1872, which hosted several international artists — Francesco Tamagno, Nellie Melba, and Fransicso d'Andrade.

When the Kölner Opernhaus opened in 1902, its *fin-de-siècle* style was an architectural curiosity during its almost 42 years of existence. There was an increase in operatic activity, including twelve world premieres within the first decade. The inaugural season offered Beethoven's *Fidelio*, Wagner's *Tristan und Isolde* and *Die Meistersinger von Nürnburg*, Mozart's *Le nozze di Figaro*, and Peter Cornelius's *Der Barbier von Bagdad*. Three years after its inauguration, a summer opera festival was established, which took place, with a few interruptions, until World War I. Some of Cologne's best opera years occurred between 1917 and 1924 under Otto Klemperer, and included the world opera premieres of three important contemporary composers: Erich Wolfgang Korngold's *Die tote Stadt*, Alexander von Zemlinsky's *Der Zwerg*, and Franz Schreker's *Irrelohe*, and the staging of Leoš Janáček's *Kát'a Kabanová*. Other contemporary works entering the repertory included

Claude Debussy's *Pelléas et Mélisande*, Sergey Prokofiev's *Lyubov'k tryom apel'sinam* (The Love for Three Oranges), and Kodály's *Hárry János*. During this time, the opera house hosted singers like Friedrich Schorr, Karl Hammes, Helge Rosvaenge, and Gerhard Hüsch. During the Nazi era, works by "pure" German composers such as Wagner and Hans Pfitzner dominated the repertory, and works by Jewish composers, of course, were forbidden. After World War II, opera performances continued in the Great Hall of the University of Cologne, with Giacomo Puccini's *Madama Butterfly*. Here the first German performances of Benjamin Britten's *The Rape of Lucretia* took place in 1947 followed by a new version of Rolf Liebermann's *Leonore 40/45* in 1952. There were also several world premieres, including Walter Braunfels's *Verkündigung* (April 4, 1948), Bernhard Breuer's *Die fiendlichen Nachbarn* and Friedrich Schmidtmann's *Der Steinbruch* (January 21, 1949), Karl Amadeus Harmann's *Des Simplicius Simplicissiums* (Octo-ber 20, 1949), Herrmann Reutter's *Die Witwe von Ephesus* (June 23, 1954), and Hans Werner Henze's *Ein Landarst* (first staged performance, May 27, 1953). Works by Paul Hindemith, Arnold Schönberg, Gottfried von Einem, and Kurt Weill, among others, were on the schedule.

After the new opera house opened in 1957, the world premieres of Wolfgang Fortner's *Bluthochzeit* and Bernd Alois Zimmermann's *Die Soldaten* were presented on June 8, 1957, and February 15, 1965, respectively. A series of contemporary works were also mounted during the 1970s, including Luigi Nono's *Intolleranza*, Prokofiev's *Ognenniy angel* (The Fiery Angel), Britten's *Billy Budd*, Henze's *Der junge Lord*, Richard Bennett's *Ballade im Moor*, Alban Berg's *Lulu*, Hindemith's *Cardillac*, and Fortner's *Elisabeth Tudor*. In 1980, the 100th anniversary of Jacques Offenbach's death was commemorated with *Les contes d'Hoffmann*, featuring Plácido Domingo in the title role and John Pritchard conducting. During Michael Hampe's tenure, 20th-century operas continued with Henze's *Wie erreichen den Fluß*, Schönberg's *Moses und Aron*, Béla Bartók's *A Kékszakállú herceg vára* (Duke Bluebeard's Castle), Igor Stravinsky's *Oedipus Rex* and *The Rake's Progress*, and Britten's *The Turn of the Screw*. Although the standard repertory was not forgotten, the company was not successful with its productions of popular Italian works like Puccini's *Turandot, Tosca*, and *Manon Lescaut*, Gaetano Donizetti's *Lucia di Lammer-*

moor, and Giuseppe Verdi's *Simon Boccanegra* and *Un ballo in maschera*. The German repertory is better received.

Oper Köln is an ensemble company, with guest directors that have included Harry Kupfer, Hans Neugebauer, and Jean-Pierre Ponelle. The repertory spans a wide operatic spectrum from Claudio Monteverdi and Georg Friedrich Händel to 20th-century composers like Henze and Zimmermann, with some novelties, like Salieri's *Falstaff*, which was executed in a clever manner, although the singing was not memorable. Recently, for budgetary reasons, the repertory has concentrated on operatic favorites like Verdi's *Aida, Macbeth*, and *Falstaff*, Mozart's *Die Zauberflöte* and *Le nozze di Figaro*, Wagner's *Tristan und Isolde*, and Puccini's *Tosca*.

Oper der Stadt Köln

An architectural competition was held after the war for a new opera house, but one of the submissions, from Hermann von Berg, were plans for reconstruction of the old house, which was also considered. Seven sites were reviewed with the Glockengasse area selected, since the new opera house was to be located on its own plaza. On June 17, 1951, it was decided to erect a new opera complex and a second competition was held on March 4, 1952. Riphahn's designs were chosen on September 17, 1952. Work on the opera house started on September 13, 1954, and completed two and a half years later. The functional style was derided as appearing like everything from a "monument to Ramses III" to a "bunker for prelates."

The Oper der Stadt Köln is a concrete, brick, and glass trapeze-shaped building with five protruding balconies. The auditorium holds two tiers of drawer-shaped boxes of black pear wood and silver gray. The seats are gray velvet and the walls are paneled with Persian walnut wood. Numerous butterfly-shaped lights illuminate the space. There are 1,346 seats.

Practical Information. Oper der Stadt Köln, Offenbachplatz, 50505 Cologne. Tel: 49 221 221-8400, Fax 49 221 221-8249. When visiting the Oper der Stadt Köln stay at the Excelsior Hotel Ernst, Domplatz, 50667 Cologne. Tel: 49 221 2701 or 1 800 223 6800, Fax: 49 221 135-150. The Excelsior Hotel Ernst is centrally located

Oper der Stadt Köln (Cologne, Germany).

near the opera house. The hotel can assist with opera tickets and schedule.

COMPANY STAFF AND PREMIERES

Intendanten. Günter Krämer (1996–present), Michael Hampe (1975–95), Claus Helmure Drese (1970–75), Arno Assmann (1965–70), Oscar Fritz Schuh (1959–65), Herbert Maisch (1947–59), Karl Pempelfort (1945–47), Alexander Spring (1933–44), Max Hofmüller (1928–33), Fritz Rémond (1911–28), Max Martersteig (1905–11), Otto Purschian (1903–05).

World Premieres. (1902–1944) E. Moór's *Andreas Hofer*, November 10, 1902; K. Pottgießer's *Die Heimkehr*, November 14, 1903; M. Burghardt's *König Drosselbart*, January 1, 1904; A. Friedheim's *Die Tänzerin*, February 11, 1905; E. Dalcroze's *O. Dazumal*, May 25, 1905; H. Roehr's *Das Vaterunser*, May 25, 1905; G. Keller's *Prinzeß Wäscherin*, December 16, 1905; A. Gorter's *Das süße Gift*, September 1, 1906; P. Cornelius's *Gunlöd*, December 5, 1906; I. de Lara's *Solé*, December 19, 1907; E. Humperdinck's *Die Marketenderin*, May 10, 1914; E. Bossi's *Johanna d'Arc*, January 20, 1914; J. Bittner's *Der Abendteurer*, 1913/14; H. Kempner & J. Siener's *Der lockere Zeisig*, June 1, 1920; E. Korngold's *Die tote Stadt*, December 4, 1920; A. von Zemlinsky's *Der Zwerg*, May 29, 1922; F. Schreker's *Irrelohe*, March 27, 1924; E. Welfsz's *Die Opferung des Gefangenen*, April 10, 1926; J. Künigsberger's *Das Spielzeug ihrer Majestät*, January 9, 1930; W. Braunfels's *Galatea*, January 26, 1930; S. Wagner's *Der Heidenkönig*, December 16, 1933; E. Bodart's *Der abtrünnige Zar*, March 31,

1935; W. Egk's *Georgica*, October 22, 1935; E. von Dohnanyi's *Die heilige Fackel*, October 22, 1935; N. Dostal's *Prinzessin Nofretete*, September 12, 1936; E. Bodart's *Hirtenlegende*, November 26, 1936; E.N. von Reznicek's *Till Eulenspiegel*, June 17, 1937; M.A. Souchay's *Alexander in Olympia*, April 20, 1940; P. Gilson's *Seevolk*, June 28, 1941; P. Graener's *Schwanhild*, January 4, 1942; H. Unger's *Drei Geschichten von Weihnachtsbaum*, December 18, 1943. (1957–1990) W. Fortner's *Bluthochzeit*, May 26, 1957; M. Mihalovici's *Scènes de Thésée*, 1958/59; N. Nabokov's *Der Tod des Grigori Rasputin*, November 23, 1959; K. Stockhausen's *Originale*, October 26, 1961; W. Fortner's *In seinem Garten liebt Don Perlimplin Belisa*, March 19, 1963; W. Haentjes's *Nichts Neues aus Perugia*, June 21, 1964; B.A. Zimmermann's *Die Soldaten*, February 15, 1965; Radermacher's *Tartarin von Tarascon*, July 6, 1965; W. Haentjes's *Gesucht werden Tote*, June 25, 1966; M. Niehaus's *Barthleby*, May 5, 1967; M. Niehaus's *Die Badewanne*, April 16, 1970; Kieselbach, Edmund, Wellershoff, Schünbach's *Hysteria*, October 9, 1971; M. Kagel's *Camera obscura*, June 23, 1978; M. Kagel's *Kantrimusik*, June 23, 1978; S. Matthus's *Omphale* January 31, 1979; J. P. Ostendorf's *Murieta*, October 25, 1984; G. Konzelmann's *Das Gaulermärchen*, September 4, 1988.

Bibliography. Wolfram Hagspiel, *Das Kölner Opernhaus: 1957–1987* (Cologne, 1987). *Oper der Stadt Köln* (Cologne,1991). *Oper der Stadt Köln* (Cologne, 1989). Carl Hiller, *Von Quartermarkt zum Offenbachplatz: Ein Streifzug durch vier Jahrhunderte musiktheatralischer Darbietungen in Köln* (Cologne, n.d.). And additional information supplied by the company.

Thanks to Franz-Peter Kothes, Oper der Stadt Köln, and Charles Roulet.

DARMSTADT

Stadttheater

Ludwig van Beethoven's *Fidelio* inaugurated the 956-seat Stadttheater on October 6, 1972. Rolf Prange was responsible for the modern structure. The previous theater, the Großherzoglichen Hoftheater (Grand Duke's Court Theater), was destroyed by bombs in 1944. Inaugurated on November 7, 1819, with Gasparo Spontini's *Ferdinand Cortez*, the 1,370-seat Großherzoglichen Hoftheater was designed by Georg Moller in a classical style.

The first theater dates back to 1670 when a riding house was converted into a Komödienhaus (Comedy House) and believed to have been opened with Corneille's *Andromède*. After the turn of the century, in 1711, the structure was transformed into an opera house. Two years earlier Christoph Graupner was appointed *Kapellmeister* and three of his works were premiered in the city—*Lucio Vero e Berenice* (1710), *Telemach* (1711), and *La costanza vince l'inganno* (1719). The 1800s witnessed the opening of the Hoftheater, commissioned by the Großherzog (Grand Duke) Ludwig I, in 1819. Here the first German performances of Giuseppe Verdi's *Les vêpres siciliennes* and *Don Carlos*, and Charles Gounod's *Faust* took place on March 14, 1857, March 29, 1868, and February 10, 1861, respectively. In 1871, fire damaged the theater. It reopened with Richard Wagner's *Lohengrin* eight years later. The 20th century welcomed several well-known conductors, including Erich Klieber, Bruno Kettle, Ernst Lert, Felix Weingartner, and Karl Böhm. After World War II, opera continued in temporary quarters, a rebuilt Baroque Orangier, which was inaugurated by Johann Wolfgang Goethe's *Iphigenie auf Tauris* on December 15, 1945. Opera was also performed in a theater in the Schloß. During this period, the German premiere of Sergey Prokofiev's *Igroki* (The Gamblers) was offered in 1956, and well-known artists graced the stage, including Christa Ludwig and Sandor Konya. During the 1980s several contemporary works were in the repertory, including Klebe's *Die Fastnachtsberichte*. Recent repertory includes Wagner's *Tannhäuser*, Engelbert Humperdinck's *Hänsel und Gretel*, Richard Strauss's *Der Rosenkavalier*, Georg Friedrich Händel's *Alcina*, Hans Werner Henze's *Elegy for Young Lovers*, and Mozart's *Die Entführung aus dem Serail*.

Practical Information. Stadttheater, Auf dem Marienplatz, 64229 Darmstadt. Tel: 49 61 51 28111, Fax: 49 61 51 281 1226. If visiting, contact the German National Tourist Office, 747 Third Avenue, 33rd Floor, New York, NY 10017. Tel: 212-308-3300.

COMPANY STAFF

Intendanten. Gerd-Theo Umberg (1997–present), Peter Girth (1991–96), Peter Brenner (1984–90), Kurt Horres (1976–84), Günther Beelitz (1971–76), Gerhard Hering (1961–71), Gustav Rudolf Sellner (1951–60), Siegmund Skraup (1948–51), Walter Jockisch (1946–48), Wihelm Henrich (1945–46).

Bibliography. Hermann Kaiser, *275 Jahre Theater in Darmstadt* (Darmstadt, 1980). Hermann Kaiser, *Modernes Theater in Darmstadt* (Darmstadt, 1955). Hermann Kaiser, *Das Grossherzogliche Hoftheater zu Darmstadt: 1810–1910* (Darmstadt, 1964).

DETMOLD

Landestheater

Albert Lortzing's *Undine* inaugurated the Landestheater on September 28, 1919. Architect Eberhard designed the building in a classic style. The previous theater, the Hoftheater, had been destroyed by fire. Opened in 1825, the theater was designed by Herr Naborp.

Traveling troupes offered the first performances in the early 1700s. A Comedy House was constructed in 1778 which hosted regular shows until its closing in 1825. At which time, a new theater, the Hoftheater, was constructed in less than seven months, opening that same year. The composer Albert Lortzing was engaged by the theater from 1826 to 1833. Then the theater experienced financial problems which negatively affected the performance quality. After the new theater, the Landestheater, opened in 1919, Musiktheater played a more prominent role in the life of the theater, as it does today. During the 1980s, non–German works like Claude Debussy's *Pelléas et Mélisande* and Vincenzo Bellini's *Norma* were offered. Recent repertory includes Franz Lehár's *Die lustige Witwe*, Georg Friedrich Händel's *Agrippina*, Lortzing's *Der Wildschütz*, and Giacomo Puccini's *Madama Butterfly*.

Practical Information. Landestheater, Theaterplatz 1, 32756 Detmold. Tel: 49 5231 97460. If visiting, contact the German National Tourist Office, 747 Third Avenue, 33rd Floor, New York, NY 10017. Tel: 212-308-3300.

BIBLIOGRAPHY

Bibliography. B. Wiesener & O. Röhler, *150 Jahre Theater in Detmold: zum Jubiläum des Landestheater* (Detmold, 1975).

——— DORTMUND

Theater Dortmund

On March 3, 1966, the new Theater Dortmund, previously known as the Städtische Bühnen Dortmund, was inaugurated with Richard Strauss's *Der Rosenkavalier* featuring Elisabeth Grümmer, Teresa Zylis-Gara, and Kurt Böhme in the leading roles and Wilhelm Schüchter on the podium. The architects were Heinrich Rokotten, Josef Clemens, and Edgar Tritthart. The previous theater had been destroyed by bombs on October 6, 1944.

The "National-Theater of the first Gouvernements" hosted the first operatic performances in the Gildenhaus in September and October of 1807. Wolfgang Amadeus Mozart's *Die Zauberflöte* and works by Karl Ditters von Dittersdorf were popular that year, and in April 1826, Carl Maria von Weber's *Der Freischütz* was given. Five years later, a complete opera season with works by Adrien Boieldieu, Gioachino Rossini, Weber, Dittersdorf, Daniel Auber, Étienne Méhul and Mozart was offered. After 1837, the Kühnschen Saal witnessed regular opera performances, which continued until fire destroyed it in 1903. The inhabitants had a strong liking for the operas of Weber, Albert Lortzing, Friedrich von Flotow, Adolphe Adam, Jacques Fromental Halévy, Otto Nicolai, Konrad Kreutzer, Aimé Maillart, and Charles Gounod, which were frequently seen — *Zar und Zimmermann, Waffenschmied, Wildschütz, Die beiden Schützen, Regimentstochters, La muette di Portici, Nachtlager, Fra Diavolo, Il barbiere di Sivilglia, Das Glöckchen des Eremiten*, and

the like. Weber's *Der Freischütz* and Lortzing's *Undine* were given almost every season. In 1866, Giuseppe Verdi operas were seen for the first time in Dortmund — *Il trovatore* and *Rigoletto*, along with Jacques Offenbach's operetta *Orpheus*. One of Mozart's operas from among *Le nozze di Figaro, Die Zauberflöte, Don Giovanni*, or *Die Entführung aus dem Serail* was also staged every opera season.

The city lacked a real theater, which businessman Brügmann built. The theater was originally constructed as a circus that was converted into an opera house, opening on September 28, 1871, with Weber's *Der Freischütz*. From the opening until May 1, 1872, the most spectacular opera season that the city had ever experienced took place — operas of Lortzing, Auber, Flotow, Rossini, Boieldieu, and Gaetano Donizetti, along with Kreutzer's *Nachtlager*, Nicolai's *Die lustigen Weiber von Windsor*, Giacomo Meyerbeer's *Robert le Diable* and *Les Huguenots*, Mozart's *Le nozze di Figaro, Die Zauberflöte*, and *Don Giovanni*, Verdi's *Il trovatore*, and Richard Wagner's *Tannhäuser*. With such success, an Aktiengesellschaft (stock company) was formed which took the official title "Stadttheater." But, when the circus found a home at the Kühnschensaal, the competition caused financial problems for the stock company of the Stadttheater, which was terminated in 1875. Five years later, Ignaz Pollak arrived and produced Wagner's *Lohengrin, Der fliegende Holländer*, and *Tannhäuser* in the Kühnschensaal, which was subsequently destroyed by fire. A new theater was built, which was inaugurated on September 17, 1904, with Wagner's *Tannhäuser*. Designed by Martin Dülfer, it was a fine example of Jugendstil. The auditorium held three tiers and proscenium boxes. After the inaugural *Tannhäuser*, Mozart's *Die Entführung aus dem Serail* and *Die Zauberflöte*, Ludwig van Beethoven's *Fidelio*, Johann Strauß's *Die Fledermaus*, Weber's *Der Freischütz*, Lortzing's *Zar und Zimmermann*, Ambroise Thomas's *Mignon*, Georges Bizet's *Carmen*, and the complete *Der Ring des Nibelungen* graced the stage. Alois Hoffmann arrived in 1907. He had directed the theater in Cologne and intended to raise the level of Dortmund's opera to that of Cologne. To this end, he mounted the complete Ring Cycle several times, offered Verdi's *Aida*, Richard Strauss's *Salome*, and Franz Lehár's *Die lustige Witwe*. On February 25, 1913, Camille Saint-Saëns's *Samson et Dalila* graced the stage, followed by Strauss's *Der Rosenkavalier* on March 2, 1928, and his *Elektra* on June 18, 1934. That same year also witnessed Wagner's *Tannhäuser* on February 16, and Bizet's *Carmen* on October 8, 1934. Two years later, Wagner's *Lohengrin* graced the stage on January 30, followed by Beethoven's *Fidelio* on April 26, 1937. Peter Hoenselaers assumed the directorship in 1937 and stayed until 1944. Despite the war, opera performances continued with the 1940-41 season offering *Der fliegende Holländer*, *Le nozze di Figaro*, *Salome*, *Zar und Zimmermann*, *I quattro rusteghi*, *Rigoletto*, *Ero der Schelm*, *Christelflein*, *Tosca*, *La fille du régiment*, and *Martha*.

With the destruction of the opera house in 1944, different performance venues were used until the new opera house opened in 1966. Performances began again with Mozart's *Die Zauberflöte* on September 17, 1947, at the Städtischen Bühnen Theater in der Lindemannstraße. Engelbert Humperdinck's *Hänsel und Gretel* and Offenbach's *Les contes d'Hoffmann* followed during the 1948-49 season. In 1950, the Schauspielhaus am Hiltropwall became the company's temporary opera house, with Beethoven's *Fidelio* as the inaugural opera on September 12, 1950. The first season saw the remounting of some of Wagner's operas and *Die Meistersinger* opened the following season. Contemporary works were staged, including Ferruccio Busoni's *Doktor Faust*, Hans Pfitzner's *Das Herz*, Alexander von Zemlinsky's *Der Kreiderkreis*, Walter Braunfel's *Don Gil von*

den grünen Hosen, and Felix Weingartner's *Dame Kobold*, but these did not survive in the repertory. A few years later, Alban Berg's *Wozzeck* and works by Werner Egk, Carl Orff, and Gottfried von Einem were on the boards. Other works during this interim period included Modest Mussorgsky's *Boris Godunov*, Verdi's *Aida*, *La forza del destino*, and *Il trovatore*, Lortzing's *Der Waffenschmied* and *Undine*, Eugen d'Albert's *Tiefland*, Charles Gounod's *Faust*, Ambroise Thomas's *Mignon*, Ruggero Leoncavallo's *I pagliacci*, Pietro Mascagni's *Cavalleria rusticana*, and Giacomo Puccini's *La bohème*.

After the new opera house opened in 1966, all opera activity shifted there. The first complete season opened on September 24, 1966, with Wagner's *Der fliegende Holländer*. Other works in the repertory included Verdi's *La forza del destino*, Puccini's *Madama Butterfly*, Bedřich Smetana's *Prodaná nevěsta* (The Bartered Bride), and the world premiere of the commissioned opera *Eli* by Nelly Sachs and Walter Steffens. Well-known artists like Wolfgang Windgassen and Teresa Zylis-Gara sang in Dortmund at the beginning of their career, and other guest stars like Giulietta Simionato, Tatiana Troyanos, Anja Silja, and Ingrid Bjoner also performed in the new house. Now guest singers are invited only when necessary. There is a permanent ensemble of 11 men and 13 women.

Dortmund was characterized as a conservative and traditional opera house presenting the standard works of Mozart, Wagner, Puccini, and Strauss, until John Dew arrived as Intendant in 1995. Dew felt that opera is not a museum and wanted to experiment. Slowly, he is changing the Dortmund operatic landscape. He introduced modern, experimental, even radical productions, but the problem was that an audience which had only seen traditional staging stayed away from the theater when "different" works were mounted, so the pace of change was slowed. Dew's specialty is French grand opera and those works are represented in the repertory, especially Halévy's *La Juive*, which has been in the repertory every year since his arrival. The opera, which takes place during the Middle Ages, has a timeless message — to reject anti–Semitism, intolerance, hate, and prejudice. The radically stark production — where the stage is bare for almost the entire opera — makes the condemnation to death of Rachael much stronger — when a black curtain rises to reveal concentration camp ovens. The visual impact is overwhelming. The only negative of this admirable undertaking is that the musical impact is anti-climactic — the opera is cut mercilessly. The 4½ hour work is presented in 2½ hours, making it sound more like "the best melodies from *La Juive*" for anyone familiar with it. Maybe in the future the conservative Dortmund audience, which can sit through an uncut six-hour Wagner opera, will be able to listen to uncut French grand opera as well. Other recent repertory operas include Wagner's *Die Walküre*, *Parsifal*, and *Der fliegende Holländer*, Hector Berlioz's *Les Troyens*, Karl Goldmark's *Die Königin von Saba*, Giacomo Puccini's *Tosca*, Weber's *Der Freischütz*, Humperdinck's *Hänsel und Gretel*, and Otto Nicolai's *Die lustigen Weiber von Windsor*.

Theater Dormund

The theater is a large, modern "shell" building covered with an elliptical concrete roof resting on three points with an underneath area of glass. The two-tier auditorium has steeply graded seating areas, with black and red plaid fabric seats. The arms of the tiers are split into boxes, stacked one behind the other. The dark wood walls contrast with the white on the tiers and seat frames. The auditorium accommodates 1,160.

Practical Information. Theater Dortmund, Kuhstraße 12, 44137 Dortmund. Tel: 49 231 502-2426, Fax: 49 231 502-6252. When visiting the Theater Dortmund stay at the Holiday Inn Römischer Kaiser, Olpe 2, 44135 Dortmund. Tel: 49 231 54 32 00 or 1 800 465 4329, Fax: 49 231 57 43 54. The Holiday Inn Römischer Kaiser is centrally located only a few blocks from the opera house. The hotel can assist with opera tickets and schedule.

COMPANY STAFF

Intendanten. John Dew (1995–present), Horst Fechner (1985–85), Dieter Geske (1983–85), Paul Hager (1975–83), Dieter Geske (1974–75), Wilhelm Schüchter (1965–74), Hermann Schaffner (1962–65), Paul Walter Jacob (1950–62), Herbert Junker (1947–50), Willem Hoenselaers (1945–47), Peter Hoenselaers (1937–44), Georg Hartmann (1935–37), Bruno Bergmann (1933–35), Richard Gsell 1927–33), Karl Schäffer (1922–27), Johannes Maurach (1919–22), Hans Bollmann (1913–19), Alois Hoffmann (1907–13), Hans Gelling (1904–07).

Bibliography. E. Elschner (ed.), *75 Jahre Städtisches Theater in Dortmund 1904–79* (Dortmund, 1979). A. Mämpel, *Das Dortmunder Theater* 2 Vol. (Dortmund, 1935). Interview with Bernhard Helmich, Chefdramaturg, December 1995.

Thanks to the administration, Theater Dortmund.

DRESDEN

Sächsische Staatsoper Dresden (Semperoper)

The third Semperoper opened its doors on February 13, 1985, with Carl Maria von Weber's *Der Freischütz* with all the important Communist Party members in attendance. The world premiere of Siegfried Matthus's *Judith* had been planned for the reopening, but when Intendant Harry Kupfer left in 1983 for the Komische Oper in East Berlin, he took *Judith* with him. The opera house was meticulously rebuilt according to Gottfried Semper's original plans. The second Semperoper had been destroyed during the night of February 13-14, 1945. This opera house had been inaugurated on February 2, 1878, with Carl Maria von Weber's *Jubel-Ouvertüre* and Goethe's *Iphigenie auf Tauride* (with the first operatic performance, Ludwig van Beethoven's *Fidelio*, taking place two days later). Fire had damaged the original Semperoper on September 21, 1869. The identical inaugural program that opened the first house also opened the second on April 12, 1841— Weber's *Jubel-Ouvertüre* and Johann Wolfgang Goethe's *Iphigenie auf Tauride* (with the first operatic performance, Weber's *Euryanthe*, taking place the next evening). Semper designed both opera houses.

The first theater performances date back to 1324, and as early as 1482 there is evidence of the existence of a *Hofcantorei*, the precursor of the *Staatskapelle*. The history of opera and ballet dates to the early 17th century with the world premiere on October 31, 1617, of Heinrich Schütz's *Apollo und die neun Musen*, a "singballet." A decade later, on April 23, 1627, the first opera with a German text, Schütz's *Dafne*, had its premiere at the Hartenfels Castle in Torgau. It was composed for the marriage of the Saxon Elector's daughter to the Landgrave of Hesse-Darmstadt. On November 3, 1662, Giovanni Andrea Bontempi's *Il Paride*, the first Italian opera written for Dresden, was presented. Italian opera was favored at the court. One had to wait until the 19th century before German opera emerged on its own right in Dresden.

On August 1, 1664, the first stone for Dresden's first opera house, the Kurfürstlicher Opernhaus am Taschenberg, was laid. The opera house was inaugurated on January 27, 1667, with Giovanni Andrea Moneglia's *Il Teseo*. Constructed by Wolf Casper von Klengel in Baroque style, the 2,000-seat theater was connected to the palace by a passageway. Outstanding Italian singers were hired for the productions. Another of Moneglia's works, *Dafne* was introduced on September 3, 1671, followed by *Io* on January 16, 1673. When Augustus the Strong of Saxony adopted Catholicism in 1697, in his bid for the Polish Throne (becoming August II, King of Poland), the opera house was subsequently converted to a Catholic court church in 1707. The Redoutensaal of the castle was then used as a temporary performance venue. Here the world premiere of Antonio Lotti's *Giove in Argo* was staged on October 25, 1717, ushering in the second period of Italian court opera in Dresden. The first stone was laid for the new court opera house at the Zwinger on September 9, 1718. Designed by Matthäus Daniel Pöppelmann, the opera house was the largest and most modern German opera house of the time. Lotti's *Giove in Argo* inaugurated the new house on September 3, 1719. Lotti's *Ascanio* was staged on September 7, 1719, and his *Teofane* was world premiered on September 13, 1719. Works by Georg Friedrich Händel, Georg Philipp Telemann, and Carl Heinrich Graun graced the stage. Johann Adolf Hasse's *Cleofide* was introduced in 1731, ushering in a grand era of Italian Baroque opera. The opera house witnessed several world premieres of Hasse's operas, including *Tito Vespasiano*, *Lucio Papirio*, *Arminio*, *Demofoonte*, *Attilio Regolo*, *Solimano*, *Olympiade*, and *Siroe*. In 1769, Johann Gottlieb Naumann's *La clemenza di Tito* received its world premiere and was the last opera to be premiered in the house. It was closed soon thereafter and in 1782-83 converted by J.G.

Benedikt into a Redoutenhaus. Meanwhile, two brothers, Angelo and Pietro Mingotti, directors of an Italian opera society, built a three balcony, wooden theater which Paolo Scalabrini's *Argenide* inaugurated on July 7, 1746. Opera performances in Mingotti's Theater took place four times a week, and was the first theater open to the public in Dresden. This opera house burned to the ground on January 29, 1748, and was not rebuilt. The next opera house, known as the "kleines Hoftheater" (small court theater) was built by Julius Heinrich Schwarze between the Zwinger, the castle, and the Elbe. Constructed of wood and holding 350 seats, the opera house opened on May 23, 1755, with Baldassare Galuppi's *Arcadia in Brento*. It was erected for performances of Italian opera and German plays. Stone replaced the wood in 1761. Fifteen years later, on May 22, 1776, the Theater auf dem Linckeschen Bade was inaugurated. This public theater hosted both opera and drama, including Italian and French operas performed in German. Here the first performance in Dresden of Wolfgang Amadeus Mozart's *Die Entführung aus dem Serail* took place in 1785, followed by *Die Zauberflöte* on August 7, 1793. The court opera witnessed Domenico Cimarosa's *Il matrimonio segreto* in 1792, which quickly became the most popular opera in the repertory. The last opera to grace the stage was Albert Lortzing's *Der Wildschütz* on September 24, 1858.

After the turn of the century, Naumann's last opera, *Acis e Galatea,* received its premiere, followed by Francesco Morlacchi's *Raul de Crequi*, and his *Il barbiere di Siviglia*. Meanwhile, German opera began to take root with the *Uraufführung* of Ferdinando Paër's *Sargino* and his *Leonora*. A Dresden novelty was Weber's *Abu Hassan* on July 15, 1814. Weber arrived in Dresden in 1817, and was named music director and leader of the "Deutsche Oper," which opened on January 30, 1817, with Etienne Nicolas Méhul's *Joseph en Egypte*. Inspired while conducting German operas in Dresden, Weber wrote a German national opera, *Der Freischütz*, which (ironically) premiered in Berlin. Weber contributed immeasurably to the German opera movement by introducing German culture, folk songs, and dances into his operas. He was also the first German composer to employ the leitmotiv method, and gave greater dramatic significance to the recitative and more importance to the orchestra. Even the egotistical Wagner conceded that the road from Weber led directly to him. Weber equalized a repertory which favored Italian works by presenting in 1817 five French operas, including Méhul's *Helena*, Adrien Boieldieu's *Jean de Paris*, and Luigi Cherubini's *Lodoïska*. Three years later, more non–Italian works graced the stage, Grétry's *Richard, Coeur de Lion* and Giacomo Meyerbeer's *Emma di Resburgo* and *Wirt und Gast*. At the same time, Weber expanded the existing Italian repertory with the Dresden premieres of Gioachino Rossini's *Gazza ladra* and *L'italiana in Algeri* in 1819, and the repertory in general with world premieres of Heinrich Marschner's *Heinrich IV und d'Aubigne*, Joseph Rastrelli's *Die neugierigen Frauen*, Morlacch's *La giovento di Enrico V*, Carl Gottlieb Reißiger's *Didone Abbandonata*, Marschner's *Der Holzdieb*, and Reißiger's *Die Felsenmühle von Etaliers* and *Turandot*.

That same year, 1835, architect Semper was invited to Dresden for advice about erecting a statue to King Frederic Augustus. During his visit, he conceived of the idea to erect a new court theater, the first Semperoper, also known as the "Großes Königliche Hoftheater." Here his architectural principals of "radial" were born. Although rococo style was in fashion during this period, the opera house was constructed in a noble but somber Neo-Renaissance mode and became a model for other opera houses. After the opera house opened in 1841, Mozart's *Don Giovanni*, Beethoven's *Fidelio*, Vincenzo Bellini's *I Capuleti e i Montecchi* and *I Puritani*, and Meyerbeer's *Les Huguenots* all graced the stage. The following season saw the world premieres of Richard Wagner's *Rienzi, Der fliegende Holländer* (which survived only four performances) and *Tannhäuser*. Other world premieres included Marschner's *Kaiser Adolph von Nassau* and Reißiger's *Schiffbruch der Medusa*. Three years earlier, Wagner had been appointed *Kapellmeister*, a post he held for six years. In 1849 he joined the uprising and was forced to flee to Switzerland. The last opera performance to take place in the first Semperoper was Meyerbeer's *Les Huguenots* on September 19, 1869, before the building was consumed by fire.

The first stone for the second Semperoper was laid on February 17, 1871, and until its completion seven years later, performances took place in a temporary theater, which witnessed the world premiere of Edmund Kretschmer's *Die Folkunger* in 1874. The opera house was considered an architectural masterpiece when it opened in 1878, with its two grand staircases, each with its own carriage entrance and door that made it unnecessary to provide a separate staircase for the court, since one of the two staircases could be closed off. The royal boxes were placed in prominent locations, an important touch, since the opera house was more a social gathering place than a cultural oasis during the 19th century. In 1872, Ernst von Schuch was appointed music director and raised the standard of the orchestra to a high artistic level and created a singers's ensemble. On March 12, 1882, Ödön Mihalovich's *Hagbart und Signe* was the first world premiere offered in the new opera house. Wilhelm Kienzl's *Urvasi* followed in 1886, the same year as the first complete Ring Cycle of Wagner was mounted. Meanwhile the world premieres continued with Felix Draeseke's *Herrat*, and the three operas that comprised the opera trilogy of August Bungert's *Homerische Welt*: *Odysseus Heimkehr, Kirke*, and *Nausikaa*. The turn of the century brought the first of nine world premieres of Richard Strauss's operas: *Feuersnot* on November 21, 1901. His other premieres included *Salome, Elektra, Der Rosenkavalier, Intermezzo, Die Aegyptische Helena, Arabella, Die schweigsame Frau*, and *Daphne*.

Meanwhile, the National Socialist Party of Adolf Hitler had been voted into power and all Jews were expelled. Both Intendant Alfred Reucker and Fritz Busch, who had been appointed *Kapellmeister* in 1922, were forced out. Karl Böhm, having no problems working with the Nazis, was named musical director in 1933. Two years later, when *Die schweigsame Frau* was introduced, both Hitler and Goebbels boycotted the performance — the librettist, Stefan Zweig, was Jewish. After the fourth performance, the opera was officially banned. Despite the fact that World War II was raging all around, the Semperoper continued hosting performances until August 31, 1944, when the final performance at the opera house, Weber's *Der Freischütz*, took place. Six months later, bombs reduced the structure to rubble.

Forty years passed before Dresden rebuilt their opera house. After it reopened in 1985, there was a lot to be desired in the quality of the singing and sets. So many millions of German Marks had been spent on the rebuilding that not much money was left to hire good singers or construct proper scenery. Operas were performed with ensemble singers who should have been retired and were staged with old-fashioned, tiresome sets. All that has changed since the arrival of Christoph Albrecht as Intendant and a substantial amount of money from the government — around 80 million DM to 110 million DM annually, and Albrecht feels the large amounts of money flowing to Dresden is money well spent, since around 40% of the audience are tourists and with the funds, he can built it into an important house. In fact, in only a few years, he has elevated the Semperoper from a provincial quality house to one of almost international level. He has built a good ensemble, and hired dynamic directors. Productions range from innovative to avant-garde, from timeless to outrageous. Sets are often defined by geometric shapes and creative lighting, like the ones for *Tristan und Isolde* and *La clemenza di Tito*, but at times they are atrocious, like Verdi's *Nabucco* which updated the Hebrews from the Temple of Solomon era in 586 B.C. to a formal champagne party in a ghetto during the Nazi era, with Babylonian (German) soldiers crashing through the set with tanks. The production was surprising since Albrecht stated that he did not like provocation for the sake of it. He also believes that the opera should tell a good story, so that when the audience leaves, it continues to think about the performance. Around 25 operas are in repertory every season and Albrecht's goal is that one quarter of those are from the second half of the 20th century — but it is difficult to sell out the house with such programming. He feels some of the most successful productions have been Bernd Alois Zimmermann's *Die Soldaten,* Strauss's *Capriccio,* and Wagner's *Tristan und Isolde.* Recent repertory includes Aribert Reimann's *Lear,* Georg Friedrich Händel's *Belsazar,* Weber's *Der Freischütz,* Leoš Janáček's *Jenůfa,* Verdi's *Un ballo in maschera* and *Aida,* Strauss's *Friedenstag, Der Rosenkavalier, Die Frau ohne Schatten,* and *Die schweigsame Frau,* Bedřich Smetana's *Prodaná nevěsta* (The Bartered Bride), Giacomo Puccini's *Tosca* and *La bohème,* and Mozart's *Die Zauberflöte, Le nozze di Figaro* and *Così fan tutte.*

During the last two weeks in May, the Dresdener Musik Festspiele takes place, showcasing primarily early works and modern operas. Recent offerings include Jacopo Peri's *Euridice,* Luigi Rossi's *Orfeo,* Giovanni Andrea Bontempi's *Dafne,* Siegfried Matthus's *Farinelli,* and Strauss's *Friedenstag.*

Semperoper

After bombs gutted the opera house on February 13, 1945, more than 30 years passed before a new foundation stone was laid on June 1977. Reconstruction was a long, expensive and painstaking task, taking the combined effort of 274 people a little under eight years, including 56 painters. When the Semperoper reopened, it appeared exactly as it did over a century earlier, with the exception that the family circle and proscenium boxes were used for stage lights, reducing the seating from 1,700 and 300 standees to 1,284 plus 39 standees.

The large Neo-Renaissance structure offers a gently curved facade, punctuated with arched windows and doors, which alternate with Corinthian columns and pilasters. The protruding main entrance appears inspired by an ancient temple. The four-tiered, horseshoe-shaped, ivory and gold auditorium holds a mixture of sea-green and red seats. Statues inhabit niches on the sides of the proscenium arch. A mural above the proscenium arch, by James Marshall, shows Poetic Justic with Fury and Cosmos, formed from Opera and Drama, on the side. Ferdinand Keller created the curtain design of the allegory of Fantasia being united with Poetry on the left and Music on the right. Portraits of famous poets decorate the upper frieze, and the lower frieze holds portraits of great composers. The ceiling shows the four European theater nations in 1878: Germany, France, England and Greece. A magnificent, 258-bulb, two-ton chandelier illuminates the auditorium.

Practical Information. Sächsische Staatsoper Dresden, Theaterplatz 2, 01067 Dresden. Tel: 49 351 491 10, Fax: 49 351 491 1691. When visiting the Sächsische Staatsoper Dresden, stay at the Dresden Hilton, An der Frauenkirche 5, 8012 Dresden. Tel: 49 351 484 10 or 1 800 445 8667, Fax: 49 351 484 1700. It is centrally located only a couple of minutes from the opera house. The hotel can assist with opera tickets and schedule.

COMPANY STAFF AND PREMIERES

Intendanten. Christoph Albrecht (1992–present). **Kapellmeister:** Hans Vonk (1985–89), Herbert Blomstedt (1975–85), Kurt Sanderling (1964–67), Otmar Suitner (1960–64), Lovro von Matacic (1956–58), Franz Konwitschny (1953–55), Rodulf Kempe (1949–53), Joseph Keilberth (1945–50), Karl Elmendorff (1943–45), Karl Böhm (1934–42), Fritz Busch (1922–33), Frtiz Reiner (1914–21), Ernst von Schuch (1872–1914), Franz Wüllner (1877–82), Julius Rietz (1860–77), Karl August Krebs (1850–72), Richard Wagner (1843–49),

Semperoper (Dresden, Germany).

Carl Gottlieb Reißiger (1826–59), Heinrich Marschner (1824–26), Carl Maria von Weber (1817–26), Francesco Morlacchi (1810–41), Ferinando Paër (1804–07), Johann Gottlieb Naumann (1776–1801), Johann Adolf Hasse (1733–63), Jahan David Heinichen (1717–29), Antonio Lotti (1717–19), Johann Christoph Schmidt (1696–1728), Nikolaus Adam Strungk (1688–96), Christoph Bernhard (1681–92), Carlo Pallavicino (1685–88), Vincenzo Albrici (1666–80), Heinrich Schütz (1615–72), Michael Praetorius (1613–15), Rogier Michael (1587–1615), Antonio Scandello (1568–80), Mattheus le Maistre (1554–68), Johann Walter (1548–54)

World Premieres. G.A. Bontempi's *Il Paride*, November 3, 1662; G.A. Bontempi's *Daphne*, September 3, 1671; G.A. Bontempi's *Io*, January 16, 1673; C. Pallavicini's *La Gerusalemme Liberata*, February 2, 1687; A. Lotti's *Giove in Argo*, October 25, 1717; A. Lotti's *Ascanio*, 1718; A. Lotti's *Teofane*, September 13, 1719; J.A. Hasse's *Cleofide*, September 13, 1731; J.A. Hasse's *Tito Vespasiano*, 1735; J.A. Hasse's *Lucio Papirio*, 1742; J.A. Hasse's *Arminio*, 1745; *Demofoonte*, 1748; J.A. Hasse's *Attilio Regolo*, January 12, 1750; J.A. Hasse's *Solimano*, 1753; J.A. Hasse's *Olympiade*, February 16, 1756; J.A. Hasse's *Siroe*, August 3, 1763; J.G. Naumann's *La clemenza di Tito*, February 1, 1769; J.G. Naumann's *Osiride*, October 27, 1781; J.G. Naumann's *La dama soldato*, March 30, 1791; J.G. Naumann's *Aci e Galatea*, April 25, 1801; F. Paër's *Sargino*, May 23, 1803; F. Paër's *Leonora*, October 3, 1804; F. Morlacchi's *Raul de Crequi*, June 2, 1811; F. Morlacchi's *Il barbiere di Siviglia*, April 27, 1816; H. Marschner's *Heinrich IV und d'Aubigne*, July 19, 1820; J. Rastrelli's *Die neugierigen Frauen*, April 4, 1821; F. Morlacch's *La giovento di Enrico V*, September 18, 1823; C.G. Reißiger's *Didone Abbandonata*, January 31, 1824; H. Marschner's *Der Holzdieb*, February 22, 1825; C.G. Reißiger's *Die Felsenmühle von Etaliers* April 10, 1831; C.G. Reißiger's *Turandot*, January 22, 1835; R. Wagner's *Rienzi*, October 20, 1842; R. Wagner's *Der fliegende Holländer*, January 2, 1843; R. Wagner's *Tannhäuser*, October 19, 1845; H. Marschner's *Kaiser Adolph von Nassau*, January 5, 1845; C.G. Reißiger's *Schiffbruch der Medusa*, August 16, 1846. August Pabst's *Die letzten Tage von Pompeji*, August 17, 1851; A. Rubinstein's *Feramors*, February 24, 1863: E. Kretschmer's *Die Folkunger* March 21, 1874; Ö. Mihalovich's *Hagbart und Signe*, March 12, 1882; W. Kienzl's *Urvasi*, February 20, 1886; F. Draeseke's *Herrat*, March 10, 1892; A. Bungert's *Homerische Welt: Odysseus Heimkehr*, December 12, 1896, *Kirke*, January 29, 1898, *Nausikaa*, March 20, 1901; A. Bungert's *Odysseus Tod*, October 30, 1903; I. Paderewski's *Manru*, May 29,

Semperoper auditorium (Dresden, Germany).

1901; R. Strauss's *Feuersnot*, November 21, 1901; L. Blech's *Alpenkönig und Menschenfeind*, October 1, 1903; R. Strauss's *Salome*, December 9, 1905; M. von Schilling's *Moloch*, December 8, 1906; R. Strauss's *Elektra*, January 25, 1909; *Der Rosenkavalier*, January 26, 1911; E. von Dohnány's *Tante Simone*, January 22, 1913; P. Claudel's *Mariä Verkündigung*, October 5, 1913; E. Künneke's *Coeur As*, October 31, 1913; J. Brandts-Buy's *Le carillon*, December 4, 1913; W. Ferrari's *L'amore medico*, December 4, 1913; K. F. von Kaskel's *Die Schmiedin von Kent*, January 29, 1916; E. d'Albert's *Die toten Augen*, March 5, 1916; J. Brandts-Buy's *Die Schneider von Schönau*, April 1, 1916; J. Brandts-Buy's *Der Eroberer*, January 14, 1918; H. Kaun's *Der Fremde*, February 24, 1920; P. Graener's *Schirin und Gertraude*, April 28, 1920; L. Fall's *Der goldene Vogel*, May 21, 1920; J. G. Mraczek's *Ikdar*, January 24, 1921; J. Brandts-Buy's *Der Mann im Mond*, June 18, 1922; R. Strauss's *Intermezzo*, November 4, 1924; K. Striegler's *Hand und Herz*, December 9, 1924; F. Busoni's *Doktor Faust*, May 21, 1925; Kurt Weill's *Der Protagonist*, March 27, 1926; P. Hindemith's *Cardillac*, November 9, 1926; O. Schoeck's *Penthesilea*, January 8, 1927; P. Graener's *Hanneles Himmelfahrt*, February 17, 1927; R. Strauss's *Die Aegyptische Helena*, June 6,

1928; H. Kaminski's *Jürg Jenatsch*, April 27, 1929; O. Schoeck's *Vom Fischer un syner Fru*, October 3, 1930; E.N. von Reznicek's *Spiel oder Ernst?* November 11, 1930; M. Lothar's *Lord Spleen*, November 11, 1930; K. Striegler's *Dagmar*, March 18, 1932; E. d'Albert's *Mister Wu*, September 29, 1932; R. Strauss's *Arabella*, July 1, 1933; M. Lothar's *Münchhausen*, December 6, 1933; R. Wagner-Régeny's *Der Günstling*, February 20, 1935; R. Strauss's *Die schweigsame Frau*, June 24, 1935; R. Heger's *Der vorlorene Sohn*, March 31, 1936; O. Schoeck's *Massimilla Doni*, March 2, 1937; R. Mohaupt's *Die Wirtin von Pink*, February 10, 1938; R. Strauss's *Daphne*, October 15, 1938; H. Sutermeister's *Romeo und Julia*, April 13, 1940; C. Orff's *L'Orfeo* (after Monteverdi) October 4, 1940; H. Sutermeister's *Die Zauberinsel*, October 31, 1942; J. Haas's *Die Hochzeit des Jobs*, July 2, 1944; B. Blacher's *Die Flut*, March 4, 1947; R. Oboussier's *Amphitrion*, March 13, 1951; F.F. Finke's *Der Zauberfisch*, June 3, 1960; R. Hanell's *Dorian Gray*, June 9, 1962; K.R. Griesbach's *Der Schwarz, der Weiße und die Frau*, December 8, 1963; K. Friedrich's *Tartuffe*, February 3, 1964; U. Zimmermann's *Die weiße Rose*, June 17, 1967; R. Kunad's *Maitre Pathelin*, April 30, 1969; U. Zimmermann's *Levins Mühle*, March 27, 1973; U. Zimmermann's *Der Schuhu und die fliegende Prinzessin*, December 30, 1976; R. Kunad's *Vincent*, February 22, 1979; G. Schedi's *Der Schweinehirt*, May 2, 1981; K.H. Schrödl's *Der Kontrabaß*, February 8, 1984; G. Schedl's *Die Tür*, February 8, 1984; S. Matthus's *Un Weise von Liebe und Tod des Cornets Christoph Rilke*, February 16, 1985; T. Heyn & R. Oehme's *Marsyas oder Der Preis sei nichts drittes*, January 28, 1989; E. Mayer's *Der goldene Topf*, May 20, 1989; J.P. Ostendorf's *Die Erzählung der Magd Zerline*, 1997; M. Pintscher's *Thomas Chatterton* May 25, 1998.

Bibliography. Winfried Höntsch, *Opernmetropole Dresden* (Leipzig, 1996). *Semperoper: Theater journal der Sächsischen Staatsoper Dresden* (1995–1998). *Sächsische Staatskapelle Dresden* (Berlin (DDR), 1985). *Unser Opernhaus: Führer durch die Semperoper Dresden* (Dresden, 1989). Interview with Christoph Albrecht, Intendant, June 1995.

Thanks to Martina Miesler, Sächsische Staatsoper Dresden, and Norbert Lessing.

DÜSSELDORF/DUISBURG

Deutsche Oper am Rhein

The Oper am Rhein reopened the Opernhaus Düsseldorf with Richard Strauss's *Elektra* on September 29, 1956, under the baton of Karl Böhm. Astrid Varnay sang the title role. The original Opernhaus Düsseldorf, designed by Ernst Giese, was opened in 1875. Completely restored in 1906, the building was partially destroyed in 1943, but was quickly repaired, opening in January 1944. The opera house was rebuilt by architects Paul Bonatz, Ernst Huhn, and Julius Schulte-Frohlinde between 1954 and 1955.

The Oper am Rhein opened in the Theater der Stadt Duisburg with Giuseppe Verdi's *Falstaff* on September 30, 1956. Under the baton of Arthur Grüber, *Falstaff* featured Otto Wiener in the title role. The Stadttheater Duisburg was constructed in 1912 and destroyed in 1942. Architect Dülfer rebuilt the theater in the early 1950s.

The newly formed opera company, Oper am Rhein, was a theater partnership between the two industrial cities of Düsseldorf and Duisburg with the goal to establish a financially viable opera and ballet company in both cities at the Opernhaus Düsseldorf and Theater der Stadt Duisburg. It is the largest opera company in Germany.

The company's inaugural season offered a varied repertory which included Carl Orff's *Bernauerin*, Albert Lortzing's *Der Wildschütz*, Richard Wagner's *Parsifal*, Johann Strauß's *Die Fledermaus*, Wolfgang Amadeus Mozart's *Die Zauberflöte*, Leoš Janáček's *Věc Makropulos* (The Makropulos Affair), Verdi's *Don Carlo*, Gaetano Donizetti's *Don Pasquale*, and Giselher Klebe's *Die Räuber*. The second season, which opened with Wagner's *Die Meistersinger von Nürnberg*, featured the premiere of a new version of Ernst Křenek's *Karl V*,

the first German performances of Rolf Liebermann's *Die Schule der Frauen* and Heinrich Sutermeister's *Titus Feuerfuchs*, and the European premiere of Křenek's *Der Glockenturm* on December 2, 1958, with the composer on the podium. The avant-garde was represented by the world premiere of Klebe's *Die tödlichen Wünche* on June 14, 1959. Hermann Juch was the first Intendant. During the 1959-60 season, the entire Ring Cycle was staged, featuring Varnay, Hans Hopf, Otto Wiener, and Josef Greindl, along with the first German staged performance of Dmitry Shostakovich's *Ledi Makbet Mtsenskovo uyezda* (Lady Macbeth of the Mtsensk District) on November 14, 1959. Other lesser known works included Alexander Borodin's *Prince Igor* and Gottfried von Einem's *Dantons Tod*. The rarities continued the following season with Gerhard Wimberger's *La battaglia oder Der rote Federbusch*, Ruggero Leoncavallo's *Edipo Re*, Werner Egk's *Der Revisor*, Ferruccio Busoni's *Doktor Faust*, Hugh Wolf's *Der Corregidor*, and the world premiere of Peter Ronnefeld's *Die Ameise* on October 21, 1961, conducted by the composer. Among the novelties during the 1962-63 season were Shostakovich's *Nos* (The Nose), the first German performance of Frank Martin's *Der Herr von Pourceaugnac* on January 5, 1964, and Hans Werner Henze's *Prinz von Homburg* directed by the composer. Gerry de Groot, Elisabeth Schwarzenberg, Herold Kraus, Fritz Ollendorff, and Ingrid Paller were some of the artists performing with the company. During Juch's tenure, which ended in 1964 with Antonín Dvořák's *Rusalka*, a repertory of 58 works had been created.

Juch's successor, Grischa Barfuss, began his

reign with Mozart's *Idomeneo*. His offerings were varied and wide ranging, from early operas like Claudio Monteverdi's *L'incoronazione di Poppea*, Francesco Cavalli's *L'Ormindo*, and Emilio de Cavalieris *Rappresentazione di anima e di corpo*, to a new Ring Cycle, to the world premiere of Krzysztof Penderecki's *Lukas-Passion* on June 7, 1969. Twentieth century works continued to play an important role, with the first West German performances of Arnold Schönberg's *Moses und Aron* on March 23, 1968, and Dallapiccola's *Ulisse* on January 10, 1970. In addition, Luigi Dallapiccola's *Il prigioniero*, Paul Hindemith's *Cardillac* and *Mathis der Maler*, Janáček's *Z Mrtvého Domu* (From the House of the Dead) and *Příhody Lišky Bystroušky* (The Cunning Little Vixen), Béla Bartók's *A Kékszakállú herceg vára* (Duke Bluebeard's Castle), Bernd Alois Zimmermann's *Die Soldaten*, Igor Stravinsky's *The Rake's Progress*, Rudolf Kelterborn's *Ein Engel kommt nach Babylon*, Arthur Honegger's *Jeanne d'Arc au bûcher*, Aribert Reimann's *Lear*, Hans Werner Herzog's *Boulevard Solitude* graced the stage. French operas were also offered, like Hector Berlioz's *La Damnation de Faust*, Claude Debussy's *Pelléas et Mélisande*, and Francis Poulenc's *Les dialogues des Carmélites*.

In 1986, Kurt Horres replaced Barfuss as Intendant and the repertory encompassed both the known (classic operas of Mozart, Verdi, Wagner, and Strauss) and the unknown works, especially those unjustly forgotten, and contemporary pieces. The already wide-ranging repertory continued to be broadened. In addition, only 25% of the productions were traditionally staged. Horres believed that a message which is relevant for today's audience should be incorporated into the production, so most productions are experimental, with a surprisingly high public acceptance — around 88%. Horres also offered the world premiere of Giselher Klebes's *Gervaise Macquart* on November 10, 1995. One of the most successful productions of Horres's tenure was Franz Schreker's *Die Gezeichneten*. The opera, a mark of the consciousness of the time, was written in neoromantic tradition. Set as a symbol of the Nazi era, "Die Gezeichneten" (the marked ones) were doomed because they were deformed or marked as Jews. Their dreams could only end in death. This production was so well-received that it was performed at the Théâtre Royal de la Monnaie (Brussels) and during the Wiener Festwochen.

Horres, on the other hand, felt his biggest failure was his Ring Cycle. "They did not accept it, partly because they believed I was more of a Mozart-lover than a Wagner traditionalist." A good example of a traditional opera placed in an experimental production was Verdi's *Aida*. Set in a museum of Egyptian artifacts and mummies, the opera opened with time going backwards and the mummies becoming the characters in the opera. At the end, the characters were rewrapped and again became mummies in the museum. Tobias Richter took the helm in 1996 and continued with the experimental productions, some which work and some which do not. A new production of *Tristan und Isolde* under his tenure, inspired by the movie *Potemkin*, attempted to give a fresh perspective to the opera, but was a confusing and an irrelevant affair. The doomed lovers were dressed in identical sailor outfits, and before the opera began, a pantomime of soldiers passing a rose back and forth and then all being shot took place, which drew impolite comments from the usually well-mannered German audience. There was also unrelated stage activity that distracted from the work. The singing, with the exception of the American soprano Linda Watson, who was a solid Isolde, was mediocre to poor. Other operas offered better singing.

The comprehensive permanent ensemble has around 90 soloists, 70 dancers, and 82 chorus singers, and the opera budget (for production only) is 16 million DM. There are close to 400 performances a season (including ballet). Recent repertory includes Georg Friedrich Händel's *Tamerlano*, Albert Lortzing's *Zar und Zimmermann*, Alfredo Catalini's *La Wally*, Giorgio Battistelli's *Prova d'orchestra*, Verdi's *Rigoletto*, *Il trovatore*, and *Aida*, Strauss's *Der Rosenkavalier* and *Salome*, Mozart's *Così fan tutte*, *Le nozze di Figaro*, *Don Giovanni*, *Die Zauberflöte*, and *La finta giardiniera*, Wagner's *Der Ring des Nibelungen*, *Parsifal*, and *Tristan und Isolde*, Giacomo Puccini's *Turandot*, *Madama Butterfly*, and *La bohème*, Jules Massenet's *Manon*, Beethoven's *Fidelio*, and Weber's *Der Freischütz*.

Opernhaus Düsseldorf

The modern rectangular exterior of the opera house exhibits a whitish stone, block-like facade, punctuated with elongated rectangular windows and crowned by masks of Comedy and

Top: Opernhaus (Düsseldorf, Germany); *bottom:* Opernhaus auditorium (Düsseldorf, Germany).

Tragedy and musical instruments. It belies the traditional auditorium inside. Inspired by early 19th-century Italian houses, the three-tiered room sweeps around in a horseshoe shape. Mauve velvet seats complement the cream-colored parapets which hold the only lighting — three-bulb fixtures. The gray-colored proscenium arch, embellished by wreaths and leaves across the top, frames a charcoal velvet curtain. The dome shaped ceiling and mauve walls with gold rectangular tracing bordered with cream define the space. There are 1,342 seats.

Theater der Stadt Duisburg

The Neoclassical facade of the whitish, concrete theater offers a stately portico of six massive Ionic columns, topped by a relief pediment. This contrasts with the plain, functional, 1950s two-tiered auditorium of lilac seats, dark wood walls, plain, white parapets, red velvet curtain, and a curved, acoustic-striped ceiling.

Practical Information. (Düsseldorf): Deutsche Oper am Rhein, Henrich-Heine-Allee 16a, 41203 Düsseldorf. Tel: 49 211 890 80, Fax: 49 211 32 90 51. When visiting the Deutsche Oper am Rhein Düsseldorf, stay at the Hotel Breidenbacher Hof, Adenauer Allee 36, 40213 Düsseldorf. Tel: 49 211 13030 or 1 800 223 6800, Fax: 49 211 130 3830. The Hotel Breidenbacher Hof is centrally located only a couple of blocks from the opera house. The Hotel Breidenbacher Hof can assist with opera tickets and schedule. (**Duisburg**): Deutsche Oper am Rhein, Neckarstraße 1, 47051 Duisburg. Tel: 49 203 300 90, Fax: 49 203 300 9200. If visiting the Oper am Rhein Duisburg, stay at the Ibis Hotel, Mercatorstraße 15/Hauptbahnhof, 47051 Duisburg. Tel: 49 203 30 00 50, Fax: 49 203 34 00 88. The Ibis is next to the train station and near the opera house. The hotel can assist with tickets and reservations.

COMPANY STAFF

Intendanten. Tobias Richter (1996–present), Kurt Horres (1986–96), Grischa Barfuss (1964–85), Hermann Juch (1956–64).

Theater der Stadt (Duisburg, Germany).

Bibliography. G. Barfuss, *Deutsche Oper am Rhein: Almanach für Theaterfreunde Spielzeit 1970/71* (Düsseldorf, 1970). H. Schaffner & H. Redottée, *Duisburger Theatergeschichte, I. Tel. 1848–1921* (Duisburg, 1963). Interview with Kurt Horres, former Intendant, June 1995. Additional information supplied by the company.

Thanks to Benedikt Holtbernd, Karen Iakini, Eckert-Schweizer, and Eva Bucht, Deutsche Oper am Rhein, and Welf Eberling and Frank Pechmann.

--- **ESSEN**

Aalto-Theater

Richard Wagner's *Die Meistersinger von Nürnberg* inaugurated the Aalto Theater, Essen's newest opera house, on October 2, 1988. The Finnish architect Alvar Aalto had designed the theater before his death in 1976.

The city's first opera house, designed by Heinrich Seeling in a classic style, was inaugurated on September 16, 1892, with Lessing's *Minna von Barnhelm.* Constructed and paid for by Friedrich Grillo, a wealthy businessman, the Grillo Theater hosted a full inaugural season, with 14 operas on the boards. The next season saw the first Wagner work enter the repertory, *Lohengrin.* After the dawn of the 20th century, Essen witnessed Wagner's *Die Meistersinger von Nürnberg* for the first time on November 24, 1901. The opera was so popular that it was repeated 24 times during the next couple of seasons. That same year Adolphe Adam's *Postillon de Lonjumeau* with Heinrich Bötel as the Postillon was presented. The first Essen performance of Richard Strauss's *Der Rosenkavalier* took place on December 18, 1913, followed by Wagner's *Parsifal* in 1920. It also hosted several premieres including Alfred Rahlwes's *Madame Potiphar* in 1907, Max Weydert's *Enoch Arden* in 1909, Arthur Honegger's *Antigone* in 1928, and Franz Schmidt's *Notre Dame* in 1915. The Grillo was destroyed on March 26, 1944.

After the war, opera was given in performance venues in the nearby towns of Steele and Werden until the Grillo, also known as the Städtische Bühnen, was rebuilt, opening on December 29, 1950, with Wagner's *Die Meistersinger von Nürnberg.* Architects Seidenstikker and Dorsch designed the structure. The premieres of Hermann Reutter's *Die Brücke von San Luis Rey* and Giselher Klebe's *Die Ermordung Cäsars* were given in 1954 and 1959 respectively, and several contemporary German operas were also staged, including Ernst Křenek's *Karl V,* Alban Berg's *Lulu,* Luigi Dallapiccola's *Il prigioniero* and Bohuslav Martinů's *Mirandolina.* During the early 1980s the repertory offered Wagner's *Tristan und Isolde,* Verdi's *Falstaff,* Kurt Weill's *Der Aufstieg und Fall der Stadt Mahagonny,* Gioachino Rossini's *La Cenerentola,* and Bedřich Smetana's *Prodaná nevěsta* (The Bartered Bride).

After the opening of the Aalto Theater, all opera activity shifted there. The initial seasons saw Charles Gounod's *Mireille,* Klebe's *Die Fastnachtsberichte,* Pyotr Il'yich Tchaikovsky's *Pikovaya dama* (The Queen of Spades), Siegfried Matthus's *Graf Mirabeau,* and Giuseppe Verdi's *Don Carlo,* among others. During the mid–1990s Ludwig van Beethoven's *Fidelio,* Verdi's *La traviata* and *Aida,* Giacomo Puccini's *La bohème* and *Tosca,* and Jacques Offenbach's *Les contes d'Hoffmann* graced the stage. In 1997, Stefan Soltesz took over the running of the opera. He places equal emphasis on the musical and scenic aspects of the work, and is interested in well-balanced, solid productions, not star vehicles. He has no particular philosophy but is open to all types of productions, from traditional to contemporary, although traditional stagings predominate. A production of Mozart's *Le nozze di Figaro* was mounted in the traditional vein but cleverly realized and with good, solid singing. There is a fixed ensemble of 22 singers, with guest artists as needed. Soltesz is expanding the repertory with an emphasis on Strauss operas which have included *Die Frau ohne Schatten, Arabella,* and *Daphne.* Other recent offerings are Verdi's *Rigoletto,* Donizetti's *Viva la Mamma,* Benjamin Britten's *Peter Grimes,* Händel's *Giulio Cesare,* Mozart's *Die Zauberflöte,* Georges Bizet's *Carmen,* Puccini's *Madama Butterfly,* and Francis Poulenc's *Les dialogues des Carmélites.*

Aalto-Theater

Alvar Aalto won the architectural competition for the design of the new opera house in 1959.

Aalto-Theater (Essen, Germany).

Construction, however, did not begin until 1983, seven years after his death. The architect's widow supervised the construction, which lasted five years. The theater opened in 1988.

The opera house is a large, geometrically-shaped, white structure punctuated with large rectangular windows. The fan-shaped auditorium holds three tiers of reinforced concrete which undulate around the room. The sparkling white parapets contrast with the deep blue walls, embellished with clusters of geometric lines. Royal blue cloth seats, trimmed with black leather fill the asymmetrically-shaped orchestra level and tiers. Acoustic panel ceiling holds rows of spot lights. There are 1,125 seats.

Practical Information. Aalto-Theater, Rodlandstraße 10, 45128 Essen. Tel: 49 201 812 20,

Fax: 49 201 812 2105. When visiting the Aalto-Theater, stay at the Sheraton Essen Hotel, Huyssenallee 55, Essen 45128; Tel: 49 201 10070 or 1 800 325 3535, Fax: 49 201 100 7777. The Sheraton Essen Hotel is centrally located and only a few blocks from the opera house. The hotel can assist with opera tickets and schedule.

COMPANY STAFF

Opernintendant. (**Aalto Theater**): Stefan Soltesz (1997–present), Wolf-Dieter Hauschild (1992–97), Manfred Schnabel (1988–92).

Bibliography. F. Feldens, *75 Jahre Städtische Bühnen Essen 1892–1967* (Essen, 1967). Interview with Stefan Soltesz, June 1998.

Thanks to Anna Linoli, Aalto-Theater, and Melanie Stockmann.

—————— FLENSBURG

Stadttheater
(Musiktheater der Schleswig-Holsteinischen)

Friedrich von Schiller's *Die Zauberflöte* inaugurated the 601-seat Stadttheater, originally called the Landestheater, on September 22, 1894. The city architect Fielitz designed the opera house in Neoclassical style. It is one of the few opera houses in Germany that survived both wars unscathed.

In the early 1970s the three cities of Flensburg, Rendsburg, and Schleswig formed the Schleswig-Holsteinische Landestheater and Giuseppe Verdi's *Un ballo in maschera* opened the new opera season of this union. The repertory remains relatively conservative with operas of Richard Strauss, Verdi, Albert Lortzing, Mozart, Richard Wagner, and Gaetano Donizetti dominating. Operettas also play an important role in the schedule, with works from Franz Lehár and Jacques Offenbach, among others.

Practical Information. Stadttheater, Rathausstraße 22, 2390 Flensburg. If visiting, contact the German National Tourist Office, 747 Third Avenue, 33rd Floor, New York, NY 10017. Tel: 212-308-3300.

—————— FRANKFURT

Oper Frankfurt/Alte Oper

Oper Frankfurt opened its new home, the Städtische Bühnen, on December 23, 1951, with Richard Wagner's *Die Meistersinger von Nürnberg*. The Städtische Bühnen was part of the new performing arts complex, designed by Otto Apel and Hannsgeorg Beckert. The previous opera house, the Frankfurter Opernhaus, renamed the Alte Oper after World War II, was destroyed by bombs on March 22, 1944. Wolfgang Amadeus Mozart's *Don Giovanni* had inaugurated the theater on October 20, 1880. The Alte Oper reopened on August 28, 1981, as a Musik- und Kongreßzentrum.

Johann Theile's *Adam und Eva* or *Der erschaffene, gefallene und aufgerichtete Mensch*, performed on June 4, 1698, was the first opera seen in Frankfurt. Singspiele, opera buffa, and opéra comique dominated the repertory during the 18th century. Frankfurt's first theater, the Städtisches Comödienhaus, opened in 1782 on the Paradeplatz. Works by Wolfgang Amadeus Mozart dominated the repertory. Other works like Ferdinando Paër's *Camilla*, Peter von Winter's *Das unterbrochene Opferfest*, and Joseph Weigl's *Corsar* also graced the stage. The premiere of Carl Maria von Weber's *Silvana* took place in 1810, followed by Louis Spohr's *Zemire und Azor* nine years later. By the mid–1850s the city had outgrown the Städtisches Comödienhaus and the Senate voted to enlarge it. Architect Rudolf Heinrich Burnitz was commissioned to perform the work but nothing happened. There was a proposal to construct a new theater in 1862, but the marching of Prussian troops on Frankfurt four years later forced a postponement. On December 14, 1869, Oberbürgermeister Daniel Heinrich Mumm von Schwarzenstein submitted a proposal for a new theater. Meanwhile, several wealthy people grew impatient and offered the municipality of Frankfurt the funds to erect the Frankfurter Opernhaus. All they requested was a box of their choice, for which they would pay the subscription. The offer was accepted and the city donated some land at Rahmhof and contributed additional money. Architects Otto Brückwald of Altenburg, Gédéon Bordiau of Brussels, Johann Heinrich Strack of Berlin, Rudolf Heinrich Burnitz of Frankfurt, and Gustav Gugitz of Vienna were invited to submit drawings. When Gugitz withdrew for health reasons, Richard Lucae of Berlin replaced him. Lucae's drawings were selected on October 27, 1871. Two years later, the site was moved from Rahmhof to the area near Bockenheimer Warte and Lucae prepared new plans. Then on November 26, 1877, soon after the work began, he died and Albrecht Becker and Eduard Giesenberg completed the project.

Kaiser Wilhelm I, Crown Prince Friedrich Wilhelm, Prince Heinrich, and Prince Bernhard von Weimer attended the inauguration of Frankfurt's new opera house in 1880. A year after opening, the premiere of Karl Reinthaler's *Das Käthchen von Heilbronn* graced the stage. After the turn of the century, the opera house became a showplace for introducing contemporary operas, including Engelbert Humperdinck's *Dornröschen*, Julius Bittner's *Die rote Gred*, Franz Schreker's *Der ferne Klang* and *Die Gezeichneten*, Frederick Delius's *Fennimore und Gerda*, with the composer present, and Paul Hindemith's controversial opera about nuns and sexuality, *Sancta Susanna*. Clemens Krauss was named Intendant on September 1, 1924, and the novelties continued: Simon Bucharoff's *Sakahra*, Bernhard Sekles's *Die zehn Küsse*, Eugen d'Albert's *Der Golem*, Arnold Schönberg's *Von heute auf morgen*, Wilhelm Grosz's *Achtung Aufnahme*, and George Antheil's *Transatlantik* with the composer present. Even Adolf Hitler's rise to power did not stop the world premieres with Werner Egk's *Zaubergeige* and *Columbus*, Hermann Reutter's *Doktor Johannes Faust* and *Odysseus*, and Carl Orff's *Carmina burana* and *Die Kluge* on the boards. During the night of March 22, 1944, the Alte Oper was destroyed during a bombing raid. Only the facade and grand foyer remained standing.

After the war, the company was renamed Oper Frankfurt and emphasized the "classical modern" works of Arnold Schönberg, Alban Berg, Béla Bartók, Sergey Prokofiev, and Leoš Janáček, among others. On February 27, 1972, Hans Werner Henze directed his *Der junge Lord*, and three years later, his *Bassariden*. Alois Zimmermann's *Die Soldaten* was on the boards in 1981. They presented concert versions of infrequently performed operas like Wagner's *Rienzi*, Gioachino Rossini's *Guillaume Tell*, Fromental Halévy's *La Juive*, and Giacomo Meyerbeer's *L'Africaine*. Although the company's philosophy of giving each ingredient in the performance equal weight — voices, music, scenery, and drama can lead to original and creative productions — in reality, it has often resulted in disasters — empty houses and severe financial difficulties. One such example was a double bill of Arnold Schönberg's *Pierre Lunaire* and Leoš Janáček's *Zápisník Zmizelého* (The Diary of the Young Man Who Disappeared). No more than 300 people were in the theater and the principal artist was so dreadful, even having a coughing fit in the middle of her singing, that half of those present left at intermission. More mainstream works (and more satisfying productions) are currently on the schedule, like Rossini's *Il barbiere di Siviglia*, Weber's *Der Freischütz*, Giacomo Puccini's *La bohème*, Camille Saint Saëns's *Samson et Dalila*, and Franz Léhar's *Die lustige Witwe*, along with the contemporary pieces like Leoš Janáček's *Z Mrtvého Domu* (From the House of the Dead) and *Jenůfa*, and Luciano Berio's *La vera storia*.

Alte Oper

The rebuilding of the Frankfurter Opernhaus did not begin until 1971. Taking almost ten years to complete, the facade was reconstructed following Lucae's original plans. The inside was redesigned as a music and convention center by the architectural group of Braun, Schlockermann, and Professeur Keilholz. This multifunction interior better justified the enormous rebuilding expense.

The Alte Oper, faced with Savonnières stone, kept its Neoclassical facade, fused with Florentine Renaissance. The allegorical figures Rhein and Main by Emil Hundrieser embellish the main pediment and DEM WAHREN SCHOENEN GUTEN (To the true, beautiful, and good) is carved on the facade, amid Corinthian columns and pilasters, rounded arches and lavish carvings. There are four statues by Gustav Herold representing Poetry, Dance, Comedy, and Tragedy. Inside is a state-of-the-art Music-and-Congress Center with modern exhibition halls and three auditoriums: Großer Saal (2,012 seats), Mozart Saal (676 seats), and Hindemith Saal (304 seats). It hosts one opera a year.

Städtische Bühnen

The opera house (Großes Haus) was built on the site of a destroyed playhouse and is part of a complex which includes a Schauspielhaus (playhouse) and Kammerspiel (experimental theater). It was damaged by arson on November 12, 1987, the fire having been set by an unemployed East German who believed the building to be a bank (as so many glass buildings in Frankfurt are). The Oper Frankfurt performed in the Schauspielhaus until the mid-1990s, when the repaired opera house reopened.

The Städtische Bühnen (city stages) is a

Alte Oper (Frankfurt, Germany).

large, modern, glass-concrete-and-steel complex with a block-long glass facade. The three theaters are connected through a long foyer. Before the fire, the auditorium was red and black. The restored auditorium is several shades of blue — royal blue seats, indigo blue walls, cobalt blue parapets, and a midnight blue ceiling with clusters of spotlights forming a lyre. There are three horseshoe-shaped tiers with a row of recessed lights under each level. Architect Toyo Ito designed the blue space. The room seats 1,375.

Practical Information. Oper Frankfurt, Untermainanlage 11, 6000 Frankfurt. Tel: 49 69 2123 7338, Fax: 49 69 212 37222. Alte Oper, Opernplatz, 60075 Frankfurt am Main. Tel: 49 69 134-0400, Fax: 49 69 134-0379. When visiting the Oper Frankfurt or Alte Oper stay at the Frankfurt Intercontinental, Wilhelm-Leuschner Straße 43, 60329 Frankfurt am Main. Tel: 49 69 26050 or 1 800 327 0200, Fax 49 69 252-467. The Frankfurt Intercontinental is centrally located and near the opera houses. The hotel can assist with opera tickets and schedule.

COMPANY STAFF AND PREMIERES

Intendanten. Martin Steinhoff, Gary Bertini, Michael Gielen, Christoph von Dohnanyi, Harry Buckwitz, Hans Meissner, Josef Turnau, Clemens Krauss, Ernst Lert, Karl Zeiß, Robert Volkner, Paul Jensen, Emil Claar.

Premieres. (Alte Oper): C. Reinthaler's *Das Käthchen von Heilbronn*, December 8, 1881; E. Humperdinck's *Dornröschen*, November 12, 1902; J. Bittner's *Die rote Gred*, October 26, 1907; F. Schreker's *Der ferne Klang*, August 18, 1912; F. Schreker's *Das Spielwerk und die Prinzessin*, March 15, 1913; F. Schreker's *Die Gezeichneten* April 25, 1918; F. Delius's *Fennimore und Gerda*, October 21, 1919; F. Schreker's *Der Schatzgräber* January 21, 1920; R. Stephan's *Die ersten Menschen*, July 1, 1920; P. Hindemith's *Sancta Susanna*, March 26, 1922; E. Křenek's *Der Sprung*

Städtische Bühnen (Frankfurt, Germany).

über dem Schatten, July 9, 1924; S. Bucharoff's *Sakahra*, November 8, 1924; B. Sekles's *Die zehn Küsse*, February 25, 1926; E. d'Albert' *Der Golem*, November 14, 1926; A. Schönberg's *Von heute auf morgen*, February 1, 1930; W. Grosz's *Achtung Aufnahme*, March 23, 1930; H. Antheil's *Transatlantik*, May 25, 1930; M. Pfugmacher's *Prinz Eugen, der edle Ritter*, January 31, 1934; H. Dransmann's *Münchhausens letzte Lüge*, May 18, 1934; W. Egk's *Die Zaubergeige*, May 22, 1935; H. Reutter's *Doktor Johannes Faust*, May 26, 1936; C. Orff's *Carmina burana*, June 8, 1937; W. Egk's *Columbus*, January 13, 1942; H. Reutter's *Odysseus*, September 7, 1942; C. Orff's *Die Kluge*, February 20, 1943.

Bibliography. Albert Richard Mohr, *Das Frankfurter Opernhaus 1880–1980* (Frankfurt, 1980). Horst Reber and Heinrich Heym, *Das Frankfurter Opernhaus: 1880–1944* (Frankfurt, 1971).

Thanks to Frau Oreskovic, Opera Frankfurt, and Nicholas Craxton and Beate König.

— FREIBURG

Städtische Bühnen

Richard Wagner's *Die Meistersinger von Nürnburg* inaugurated the Städtische Bühnen, previously called the Stadttheater, on December 30, 1949. The first Freiburger Stadttheater was completely demolished on November 27, 1944, during bombing raids. Inaugurated on October 8, 1910, with Carl Maria von Weber's *Jubel-Ouvertüre*, Friedrich von Schiller's *Wallensteins Lager*, and the festival scene from *Die Meistersinger*, the Stadttheater had been designed by Heinrich Seeling in Jugendstil.

As early as 1513, there existed a *Vereins von Meistersängern* in Freiburg, giving the city a musical history that dates back almost five centuries. The 1970s saw an introduction of the avant-garde into the repertory with the world premiere of Franz Schreker's *Christophorus* on October 1, 1978, as well as the staging of Paul Dessau's *Puntila* on October 13, 1977, followed by his *Leonce und Lena* two years later. That same season also witnessed the world premiere of Arghyris

Kounadi's *Die Baßgeige* on January 13, 1979, and three years later, Jost Meier's *Das Sennentuntschi* was seen for the first time. Meanwhile Richard Strauss's *Elektra* and *Salome* were given as well as Wagner's Ring Cycle. Recent repertory includes Gaetano Donizetti's *Don Pasquale*, Sergey Prokofiev's *Lyubov'k tryom apel'sinam* (The Love for Three Oranges), Mozart's *Le nozze di Figaro*, and Strauss's *Salome*.

Practical Information. Städtische Bühnen, Bertoldstraße 46, 7800 Freiburg. Tel: 49 761 34874. If visiting, contact the German National Tourist Office, 747 Third Avenue, 33rd Floor, New York, NY 10017. Tel: 212-308-3300.

COMPANY STAFF

Intendant. Hans Ammann.
Bibliography. H.R. Müller, *Ein Deutsches Stadttheater Freiburg 1866–1966* (Freiburg, 1966).

GELSENKIRCHEN

Musiktheater im Revier

William Shakespeare's *A Midsummer Night's Dream* inaugurated the Musiktheater im Revier on December 15, 1959. The architectural team of Werner Ruhnau, Ortwin Rave, and Max von Hausen designed the theater in modern style. The previous theater had been destroyed during bombing raids in 1944-45.

The end of the 1800s saw the first operettas performed and after the turn of the century, opera graced the stage, including Friedrich von Flotow's *Alessandro Stradella* on December 15, 1913. In 1922, a contract with Dortmund was made where that city brought opera to Gelsenkirchen, and in the 1930s Münster brought opera to the Gelsenkirchen. Finally on October 16, 1935, the Stadttheater opened in its own right with Johann Wolfgang Goethe's *Egmont*. One of the last performances to take place before the theater was destroyed was Ludwig van Beethoven's *Fidelio* in 1944.

After the war, Albert Lortzing's *Der Waffenschmied*, Giacomo Puccini's *Madama Butterfly*, and Carl Maria von Weber's *Der Freischütz* were offered, and at the end of the 1960s, a noteworthy production of Sergey Prokofiev's *Voyna i mir* (War and Peace) graced the stage. During this time, some well-known artists appeared, including Marilyn Horne, Manfred Schenk, Birgit Nilsson and Grace Bumbry. Recent repertory includes Lortzing's *Regina* and *Der Wildschütz*, Jacques Offenbach's *Les contes d'Hoffmann*, Giuseppe Verdi's *Don Carlo*, and Alban Berg's *Lulu*.

Practical Information. Musiktheater im Revier, Kennedyplatz, 45881 Gelsenkirchen. Tel: 49 209 40970, Fax: 49 209 409-7250. If visiting, contact the German National Tourist Office, 747 Third Avenue, 33rd Floor, New York, NY 10017. Tel: 212-308-3300.

COMPANY STAFF

Intendant. Ludwig Baum.
Bibliography. H. Jahn & J. Loskill (ed.), *Musiktheater: Bühnen in Gelsenkirchen* (Gelsenkirchen, 1979).

GERA

Bühnen der Stadt Gera

On October 18, 1902, the Gera Theater, designed by Heinrich Seeling in Jugendstil, opened. The first permanent theater was erected in 1787 on today's Puschkinplatz, where operas by Wolfgang Amadeus Mozart were staged. Different theaters were constructed during the 19th century. After World War I, permanent opera and operetta ensembles were established, and during the 1920s operas by Igor Stravinsky, Kurt Weill, and Béla Bartók, among others, were staged at the former "Fürstliche Theater Gera" then renamed the Reußisches Theater. (Russian Theater—Gera is located in the former DDR.)

After World War II, Mozart's *Le nozze di Figaro* reopened the opera season on September 15, 1945. Opera shares the stage with plays, ballets, concerts and even puppets. Both the standard repertory, including Richard Strauss's *Der Rosenkavalier* and Richard Wagner's *Der fliegende Holländer* and the unusual, like Schmidt's *Notre Dame* and Geißlers Kleist's *Der zerbrochene Krug* grace the stage. Recent offerings include Giuseppe Verdi's *Don Carlo* and *Un ballo in maschera*, Wagner's *Tannhäuser*, and Mozart's *Die Entführung aus dem Serail*.

Practical Information. Bühnen der Stadt Gera, Küchengartenallee 2, 07548 Gera. Tel: 49 365 6940, Fax: 49 365 694132. If visiting, contact the German National Tourist Office, 747 Third Avenue, 33rd Floor, New York, NY 10017. Tel: 212-308-3300.

COMPANY STAFF

Intendant. Michael Schindhelm; **Opernintendant:** Hubert Kross.

Bibliography. *Fünf Sparten in einem Haus*, *Orpheus* (Berlin, May 1993).

───── GIEßEN

Stadttheater

Geißlers Kleist's *Der zerbrochene Krug* and Friedrich von Schiller's *Wallensteins Lager* inaugurated the Stadttheater on July 27, 1907. The Geißen architect Hans Meyer, working together with Ferdinand Fellner and Hermann Helmer, designed the Stadttheater in Jugendstil with classic elements. Although the theater was heavily damaged on December 6, 1944, it was rebuilt and reopened on November 18, 1951, with Richard Wagner's *Tannhäuser*.

During the 1977-78 season Gian Carlo Menotti traveled to Gießen to direct his opera, *The Consul*. Menotti's connection to Geißen remained and he returned in 1981 for the European premiere of his *La Loca* on April 26, 1981. Recent offerings include Jules Massenet's *Werther*, Giacomo Puccini's *La bohème*, Franz Lehár's *Das Land des Lächelns*, Gaetano Donizetti's *L'elisir d'amore*, and Alban Berg's *Wozzeck*.

Practical Information. Stadttheater Gießen, Berliner Platz, 35356 Gießen. Tel: 49 641 795760, Fax: 49 641 79 57 80. If visiting, contact the German National Tourist Office, 747 Third Avenue, 33rd Floor, New York, NY 10017. Tel: 212-308-3300.

COMPANY STAFF

Intendant. Guy Montavon.

───── HAGEN

Theater Hagen

Richard Strauss's *Der Rosenkavalier* reopened the Theater Hagen, also known as the Städtische Bühne, on September 5, 1949. The previous theater, the Hagener Theater, was destroyed during bombing raids between January and April 1945. Inaugurated on October 5, 1911, with Friedrich von Schiller's *Wallensteins Lager*, the original theater had been designed by Ernst Vetterlein in Jugendstil.

The Hagener Theater hosted its first opera performance the evening after the inaugural, when Richard Wagner's *Die Meistersinger von Nürnberg* was staged on October 6, 1911. Only in 1919 could the theater boast of its own opera ensemble. Two of its noteworthy "Cycles" were *Musiktheater des Ostens* (Music Theater of the East) with works by Leoš Janáček, Sergey Prokofiev, Modest Mussorgsky, Bedřich Smetana, Zoltán Kodály, Jaromir Weinberger, Pyotr Il'yich Tchaikovsky, Jakov Gotovac, Stanisław Moniuszko, and *Shakespeare auf dem Musiktheater* (Shakespeare in Opera) with works like Giuseppe Verdi's *Macbeth* and *Falstaff*. During the 1970s Hagen witnessed contemporary operas like Isang Yun's *Träume*, the German premiere of Aarre Merikanto's *Juha*, and (West) German premiere of Siegfried Matthus's *Die letzte Schuß*. Recent offerings include Wagner's *Tannhäuser*, Mozart's *Die Zauberflöte*, Puccini's *Tosca*, Verdi's *Un ballo in maschera*.

Practical Information. Theater Hagen, El-
berstraß 65, 58095 Hagen. Tel: 49 2331 207-
3210. If visiting, contact the German National
Tourist Office, 747 Third Avenue, 33rd Floor,
New York, NY 10017. Tel: 212-308-3300.

COMPANY STAFF

Intendant. Peter Pietzch.

HAMBURG

Hamburgische Staatsoper

Wolfgang Amadeus Mozart's *Die Zauberflöte* inaugurated the Hamburgische Staatsoper on October 15, 1955, with Germany's President Theodor Heuß in attendance. The structure was designed by Gerhard Weber. The previous opera house had been damaged by fire on August 3, 1942.

Johann Theile's *Adam und Eva* or *Der erschaffene, gefallene und aufgerichtete Mensch* inaugurated the first public opera house in Germany, the Opern-Theatrum, on January 2, 1678. The Italian builder Sartorio constructed the oblong and gabled wooden structure between Jungfernstieg and the corner of Gänsemarkt and the Colonnaden. It was a self-supporting operation. Singspiele, by the local composers Johann Wolfgang Franck, Nikolaus Adam Strungk, and Theile, were the primary fare, with subjects based on biblical and allegorical themes. In 1694, Reinhard Keiser ushered in the first golden age of opera in Hamburg, composing more than 100 operas during the next 40 years. Among his most popular works were *Mahmuth II* (1696), *Ismene* (1699), *Störtebecker und Gödje Michel* (1701), *Ottavia* (1705), *Die Leipziger Messe* (1710), *L'inganno fedele* (1714) and *Der Hamburger Jahrmarkt* (1725). He was appointed Intendant in 1703 and during his tenure, Georg Friedrich Händel joined the orchestra, playing the violin and harpsichord. Händel's first opera, *Almira*, was premiered in Hamburg on January 8, 1705, followed by *Nero* and *Rodrigo*. During the same time, composer, conductor, and singer Johann Mattheson saw his operas staged, but not without some real-life excitement. As legend has it, on December 5, 1704, Mattheson was conducting a performance of his *Cleopatra* while Händel played second violin. Mattheson also sang on stage during one act with Händel taking over the conducting. When Mattheson returned, Händel refused to hand over the baton and a duel took place. It was only the breaking of Mattheson's sword on a big button on Händel's clothes that saved his life (or so the story goes). The resident company disbanded in 1738, because of financial mismanagement, lack of public interest, and clerical attacks. Traveling comedy troupes performed in the Opern-Theatrum until 1763, when it was demolished.

The Ackermannsche Commödienhaus, named after its founder Konrad Ernst Ackermann, opened on July 31, 1765. Located on the site of the demolished Opern-Theatrum, it offered 1,600 seats. One of the first ticket subscription systems in theater was established by the company's director, Friedrich Ludwig Schröder. The theater was renamed Deutsches Nationaltheater in 1767, hosting Singspiele by Johann Adam Hiller and Christian Weiße. Two decades later, the first Mozart work graced the stage, *Die Entführung aus dem Serail*, followed by *Don Giovanni*, *Le nozze di Figaro* and *Die Zauberflöte*. Among the other works hosted were Ludwig van Beethoven's *Fidelio*, Gioachino Rossini's *Il barbiere di Siviglia*, and Carl Maria von Weber's *Der Freischütz*. The Deutsches Nationaltheater became the Hamburgisches Stadttheater in 1809 and then the Hamburgisches Deutsches Stadttheater two years later. When Napoleon occupied Hamburg, it was known as Théâtre du Gänsemarkt. After more than fifty years, the theater was "retired." The cornerstone for the Neue Stadt-Theater was laid on May 16, 1826, and just under a year later, on May 3, 1827, the New City Theater was opened with Johann Wolfgang Goethe's *Egmont* with music by Beethoven. Designed by Carl Friedrich Schinkel, the brick building was located on the site of the current Staatsoper on Dammtorstraße. The 2,800-seat auditorium held three box tiers topped by a gallery and was lit by a 64-oil-lamp chandelier. Among the works gracing the stage during the first few decades were Louis Spohr's *Jessonda*,

Beethoven's *Fidelio*, Gasparo Spontini conducting his *La vestale*, and Friedrich von Flotow conducting the world premiere of his *Alessandro Stradella* on December 30, 1844. That same year, the German premiere of Giuseppe Verdi's *Nabucco* was staged. Other performances of note were Richard Wagner leading his *Rienzi* and Charles Gounod conducting his *Faust*.

The theater's technical facilities were updated in 1873-74, with Martin Haller supervising the work. Richard Wagner's *Lohengrin* reopened the theater on September 16, 1874. That same year Bernhard Pollini became Intendant, ushering in a second golden era of opera. Operas of Verdi and Wagner played an important role in the repertory, starting with Verdi's *Aida* in 1876 and Wagner's Ring Cycle in 1878. He also mounted the first German performances of Verdi's *Otello* and Pyotr Il'yich Tchaikovsky's *Eugene Onegin*. Opera reached its highest level when Gustav Mahler was appointed *Kapellmeister* in 1891. During his final season (1896-97), he conducted 13 new productions. His final work, before going to Vienna, was Beethoven's *Fidelio*. Pollini died in November and Hamburg's most glorious opera era came to an end. After the turn of the century, the works of Richard Strauss were popular, and contemporary operas like Paul Hindemith's *Sancta Susanna*, Igor Stravinsky's *L'histoire du soldat*, Leoš Janáček's *Jenůfa* were on the boards, alongside the world premieres of Leo Blech's *Versiegelt* on November 4, 1908, Erich Wolfgang Korngold's *Die tote Stadt* on December 4, 1920, and Ottorino Respighi's *La campana Sommersa* on November 18, 1927. Enrico Caruso and Lotte Lehmann, among other famous singers, performed in the Hansestadt.

After World War I, the political unrest in Germany entered the opera house on November 6, 1918, when during the third act of Wagner's *Tannhäuser*, armed revolutionary workers and soldiers stormed the theater, ordering the patrons to leave. A decade later, Adolf Hitler seized power, but fortunately for the Hamburg Oper, the Nazis believed a first-rate opera house in Hamburg was good propaganda, so they practiced a hands-off policy except for forcing all the talented Jewish artists to flee. It was elevated to Staatsoper (state opera) and Karl Böhm and Oscar Fritz Schuh were put in artistic control. For the 260th anniversary celebration on June 23, 1938, Hitler, Paul Joseph Goebbels, and Joachim von Ribbentrop attended a performance of Wagner's *Die Meistersinger von Nürnberg*. Four years later the opera house lay in ruins, a victim of Hitler's ambitions.

The provisional opera house opened on January 9, 1946, with Mozart's *Le nozze di Figaro*, and on October 15, 1949, Richard Strauss's *Der Rosenkavalier* reopened the theater after its seating capacity was doubled. Günther Rennert, the first Intendant, introduced the concept of Musiktheater, and placed contemporary works at the forefront of the repertory. During Rolf Liebermann's tenure, the focus changed to commissioning new works — Hans Werner Henze's *Prinz von Homburg* (1960), Walter Goehr's *Arden muß sterben* (1967), Humphrey Searle's *Hamlet* (1968), Krzysztof Penderecki's *Diably z Loudun* (The Devils of Loudun) (1969), Mauricio Kagel's *Staatstheater* (1972), and Walter Steffens's *Unter dem Milchwald* (1973). The leading artists of the time performed with the company — including Birgit Nilsson, Leonie Rysanek, Montserrat Caballé, Plácido Domingo, and Luciano Pavarotti. Few superstars perform now in Hamburg — the company cannot afford their fees.

The quality of the production depends on two factors — when it was originally premiered and who is singing. Known for innovative and controversial concepts, the Hamburg Oper originated the famous Ruth Berghaus production of *Tristan und Isolde*. Although there were many moments of genius and brilliance, the idea suffered from overabundance — too much activity and movement — that distracted from the music and superb singing, especially by Sabine Haas (Isolde) — and provoked boos at the end of both the first and second acts. On the other hand, an "old" *Elektra* staging was so heavy and uninspired that it sunk from its own weight. Other recent repertory offerings include Mozart's *Die Zauberflöte*, Verdi's *Macbeth*, *Falstaff*, and *La traviata*, Benjamin Britten's *Peter Grimes*, and Leoš Janáček's *Jenůfa*, Wagner's *Der fliegende Holländer*, *Der Ring des Nibelungen*, and *Lohengrin*, and Rossini's *Il barbiere di Siviglia*.

Hamburgische Staatsoper

The auditorium of the opera house was destroyed by fire ignited from bombs during the night of August 3, 1942, but the stage area was not damaged. So after the war, the stage was divided

Hamburgische Staatsoper (Hamburg, Germany).

in two — half stayed the stage area and the other half was transformed into a 606-seat auditorium. The seating capacity was increased to 1,226 in 1949, and in the early 1950s a new opera house was built around the existing stage.

The Hamburgische Staatsoper is a stark, modern geometric structure of glass and concrete. The glass facade is bordered with turquoise and is supported by gold-colored poles. Although the new opera house was built around the existing stage, it bears no resemblance to the previous Staatsoper. The auditorium holds four tiers and is decorated in several colors — red seats, yellow-tinted tiers, green walls, midnight blue velvet curtain, plain black proscenium arch, and dark woods — that do not harmonize. Two tiers protrude on the sides, divided into shoebox-like sections. There are 1,675 seats.

Practical Information. Hamburgische Staatsoper, Große Theaterstraße 34, 20354 Hamburg. Tel: 49 40 35680, Fax: 49 40 356 8456. When visiting the Hamburgische Staatsoper, stay at the Kempinski Hotel Atlantic Hamburg, An der Alster 72–79, 20099 Hamburg. Tel: 49 40 28880 or 1 800 223 6800, Fax: 49 40 247129. The Kempinski Hotel Atlantic Hamburg is on the banks of Lake Alster and convenient to the opera house. The hotel can assist with opera tickets and schedule.

COMPANY STAFF AND PREMIERES

Intendanten (since 1921). Peter Ruzicka & Gerd Albrecht (1988–present), Rolf Liebermann (1985–88), Kurt Horres (1984–85), Christoph von Dohnányi (1977–84), August Everding (1973–77), Rolf Liebermann (1959–73), Heinz Tietjen (1956–59), Günther Rennert (1946–56), Albert Ruch (1945–46), Alfred Noller 1940–45), Heinrich Strohm (1933–40), Albert Ruch (1931–33), Leopold Sachse (1921–31).

World Premieres (since 1982). J.P. Ostendorf's *William Ratcliff*, September 15, 1982 (Opera stabile); A. Schönberg's *Ein Überlebender aus Warschau*, December 4, 1983 (first stage performance); U. Zimmermann's *Weisse Rose*, February 27, 1986 (Opera stabile); A. Kounadis's *Der Sandmann*, February 7, 1987 (Opera stabile); J. Tal's *Der Garten*, May 29, 1988 (Opera stabile); D. Schnebel's *Vergänglichkeit*, May 12, 1991; W. Rihm's *Die Eroberung*, February 9, 1992; A. Schnittke's *Faust*, June 22, 1995.

Bibliography. Max Busch & Peter Dannenberg (eds.), *Die Hamburgische Staatsoper 1678–1945: Bürgeroper, Stadt-Theater, Staatsoper* (Zurich, 1988). Max Busch & Peter Dannenberg (eds.), *Die Hamburgische Staatsoper 1945–1988* (Zurich, 1989). G. Jaacks (ed.), *300 Jahre Oper in Hamburg* (Hamburg, 1977). K. Stephenson, *Hamburgische Oper zwischen Barock und Romantik* (Hamburg, 1948). Joachim Henzel, *Geschichte der Hamburger Oper, 1678–1978* (Hamburg, 1978); Rolf Liebermann, *Opernjahre: Erlebnisse und Erfahrungen* (Bern, 1977). *Thanks to Susanne Semmroth.*

HANNOVER

Niedersächsische Staatstheater

Richard Strauss's *Der Rosenkavalier* inaugurated the Niedersächsische Staatstheater on November 30, 1950. Werner Kallmorgen designed the theater. The previous opera house, Königlisches Hoftheater, renamed the Städtisches Opernhaus in 1921, had been destroyed on June 26, 1943, during a bombing raid. The Royal Court Theater had been inaugurated on August 1, 1852, with a Festspiele *Kunst und Natur*, music by Heinrich Marschner, and Johann Wolfgang Goethe's *Torquato Tasso*. The first opera performance, Wolfgang Amadeus Mozart's *Le nozze di Figaro*, took place on September 5, 1852. The architect was Georg Ludwig Friedrich Laves.

On January 30, 1689, the first Hofoper, located in the Leineschloß (castle), was inaugurated with Agostino Steffani's *Enrico Leone*. The Baroque theater offered 1,300 seats and the population at the time was only 11,000. Other operas by Steffani followed — *La superbia d'Alessandro*, *Orlando generoso*, *Le rivali concordi*, *La libertà contenta*, *I trionfi del Fato*, and *Briseide*. The last performance in the castle opera house, before a 71 year hiatus, took place in 1697. In the meantime, Georg Friedrich Händel became *Hofkapellmeister* in 1710, but because the city did not have an opera ensemble at the time, he left two years later for London. The castle theater reopened in 1769 and German Singspiele conquered Hannover. The last performance in the Baroque structure took place on June 27, 1852. Two years later, the theater was torn down. Between 1815 and 1835, more than 80 different operas by 27 composers were performed in the Hoftheater. The most popular composers were Gioachino Rossini (eleven operas, including *Guillaume Tell*, *Mosè*, *La donna del lago*, and *Tancredi*), Ferdinando Paër (eight operas including *Achille*, *Camilla*, and *Griselda*), Daniel Auber (seven operas, including *La muette di Portici*, *Fra Diavolo*, and *Lestocq)*, Wolfgang Amadeus Mozart

(six works, including *Die Zauberflöte*, *Don Giovanni*, and *Die Entführung aus dem Serail*), Adrien Boïeldieu (six works, including *Jean de Paris*, *La Dame Blanche*, and *Le Calife de Bagdad*), and Joseph Weigl (five works including *Die Uniform*, *Nächtigall und Rabe*, and *Das Dörfchen im Gebirge*). Counted among the other operas were Giacomo Meyerbeer's *Robert le Diable*, Gasparo Spontini's *La vestale*, Louis Spohr's *Faust*, and Vincenzo Bellini's *Norma*. Meanwhile, the composer Heinrich Marschner became *Hofkapellmeister* in 1831, and the first Hannover performance of his *Hans Heiling* took place on September 30, 1833. Other works of his offered were *Der Vampyr*, *Des Falkners Braut*, and *Der Templer und die Jüdin*.

The first discussions about constructing a new opera house began in 1816, which led two years later to the establishment of an Aktiengesellschaft (joint stock company) to improve the financial position of the theater. Finally, in 1843, King Ernst August commissioned Laves, his chief court builder, with the planning of a new opera house. Two years later, construction began and after seven years of work, the 1,800-seat Königlische Hoftheater was opened in 1852. When the kingdom of Hannover became another province of Prussia in 1866, the theater was placed under the control of Berlin. This situation, which except for a short interlude, lasted until 1921, at which time the city took over the running of the opera house and the theater was renamed the Städtisches Opernhaus (city opera house). During this time, the contemporary works of Richard Wagner, Giuseppe Verdi, Giacomo Puccini, and Strauss were staged fairly soon after their premieres. In 1924, the era of Rudolf Krasselt began, which lasted until 1943. He broadened the repertory by introducing more than 90 operas, including ten world premieres. Among the repertory favorites receiving their first Hannover hearing were Puccini's

Niedersächsische Staatstheater (Hannover, Germany).

Gianni Schicchi, Turandot, Manon Lescaut, and *La fanciulla del West*, Francesco Cilea's *Adriana Lecouvreur*, Amilcare Ponchielli's *La gioconda*, Umberto Giordano's *Fedora*, and Verdi's *Don Carlo, Simon Boccanegra, Macbeth*, and *La forza del destino*. Twentieth century works were also prominent, with Paul Hindemith's *Cardillac*, Hans Pfitzner's *Palestrina* and *Das Christ-Elflein*, Werner Egk's *Die Zaubergeige*, Carl Orff's *Carmina burana*, Julius Bittner's *Der Musikant*, Franz Schreker's *Der ferne Klang* and *Die Gezeichneten*, Ermanno Wolf-Ferrari's *Sly* and *I quattro rusteghi*, and Ernst Křenek's *Leben des Orest* among them. Other novelties included Eugen d'Albert's *Mr. Wu*, Julius Weismann's *Die pfiffige Magd*, Jacov Gotovac's *Morana* and *Ero, der Schelm*, Giordano's *Il Re*, and Strauss's *Capriccio, Intermezzo, Die Frau ohne Schatten*, and *Die Aegyptische Helena*. After the destruction of the opera house in 1943, performances continued on August 12, 1943, until the autumn of 1944, in the still-standing gallery of the Herrenhausen.

After the war, opera resumed in the Herrenhausen on May 11, 1945, with Pietro Mascagni's *Cavalleria rusticana* and Ruggero Leoncavallo's *I pagliacci*. The reconstructed opera house reopened at the end of 1950, although construction work continued into the following year. There was a problem with the acoustics. The 1950s saw works like Leoš Janáček's *Z Mrtvého Domu* (From the House of the Dead), Egk's *Der Revisor*, Alban Berg's *Wozzeck*, Claude Debussy's *Pelléas et Mélisande*, Rolf Liebermann's *Die Schule der Frauen*, Giordano's *Andrea Chénier*, Luigi Dallapiccola's *Il volo di notte*, and Gottfried von Einem's *Dantons Tod*, along with the repertory favorites. The 1960s and 1970s continued with similar diversity, including Janáček's *Kát'a Kabanová* and *Příhody Lišky Bystroušky*, Antonín Dvořák's *Rusalka*, Béla Bartók's *A Kékszakállú herceg vára* (Duke Bluebeard's Castle), Gaetano Donizetti's *Viva la mamma*, and Křenek's *Die Vertrauenssache*. During the mid–1980s, the opera house was closed for renovation, reopening on November 23, 1985, with Arnold Schönberg's *Moses und Aron*. On January 29, 1989, in celebration of the 300th anniversary of opera in Hannover, a new production of Agostino Steffani's *Enrico Leone* was mounted. The first performance in Hannover of Schönberg's *Gurrelieder* took place on September 10, 1993, followed by a staging of Aribert Reimann's *Das Schloß* on January 29, 1994, and the Hannover premiere of Henze's *König Hirsch* in September 1996. In April 1997, the opera house was closed for renovation. Performances continued at various venues around the city.

There is a permanent ensemble that offers a large and varied repertory in diverse production styles from modern to traditional. There are usually five to six new productions a season. A repertory opera plays two seasons and then is "retired" for a couple of seasons before it is brought back, since the audience is local and subscription based. The budget is 80 million DM. A production of Puccini's *Tosca* production was so traditional that the staging for the end of Act II was modeled on Hohenstein's original poster for the world premiere in Rome. The production and voice quality was comparable to that of a very good regional opera company in the United States, except the sets looked "inexpensive." The ensemble singers were good, although a couple of them needed time to get their voices up to speed. Recent repertory includes d'Albert's *Tiefland*, Albert Lortzing's *Zar und Zimmermann*, John Corigliono's *Ghosts of Versailles*, Verdi's *Nabucco, Rigoletto, La traviata,* and *Falstaff,* Künneke's *Der Vetteraus Dingsda,* György Ligeti's *Le grand macabre,* Strauss's *Ariadne auf Naxos* and *Der Rosenkavalier,* and Puccini's *La bohème* and *Madama Butterfly.*

Opernhaus Hannover

In November 1949, the city decided to rebuild the destroyed opera house, and chose the plans of Kallmorgen. After 10 months of construction, the opera house opened in 1950. In December 1983, the state of Niedersachsen and the capital city Hannover concluded that there was a dire need to renovate the auditorium. With a gala evening of opera on July 5, 1984, a "good-by" was said to the old hall. Renovation work began the next day according to drawings by Dieter Oesterien. The theater was again closed after the 1996 season until 1999 for additional work. During that

time, performances took place at the Theater am Aegi.

The opera house is a massive, stately structure, with two wings, built in a Neoclassic style with Renaissance inspiration . The three-level facade offers Doric columns, Ionic pilasters, a balustrade, statues, arches and windows. A lyre, flanked by griffins, rests on top of the unadorned tympanum of the pediment. Underneath, ERNESTUS AUGUSTUS CONDIDIT ARTA ET MUSIS MDCCCXXXXV is written in gold letters across the facade. The auditorium is a modern, three-tier, semi-circular room with dark wood walls and orange-and-brown plaid fabric seats. The sides of the three tiers are staggered. Rows of copper rectangles holding a glass rectangular light in each center embellish the parapets. Plain proscenium frames a brown curtain. The light fixtures are a collection of small glass cylinders. There are 1,207 seats.

Practical Information. Niedersächsische Staatstheater, Opernplatz 1, 30159 Hannover. Tel: 49 511 1681, Fax: 49 511 363-2536. When visiting the Niedersächsische Staatstheater, stay at the Maritim Stadthotel Hannover, Hildesheimerstraße 34-40, 30169 Hannover. Tel: 49 511 98940, Fax: 49 511 989 4901. The Maritim Stadthotel Hannover is centrally located and convenient to the opera house. The hotel can assist with tickets and schedule.

COMPANY STAFF AND PREMIERES

Intendanten. Hans-Peter Lehmann (1980–present), Günter Roth (1972–79), Reinhard Lehmann (1965–72), Kurt Ehrhardt (1943–65).

World Premieres. J. Mraczek's *Herrn Dürers Bild*, January 29, 1927; I. Lilien's *Beatrys*, April 14, 1928; W. Braunfels's *Prinzessin Brambilla*, September 16, 1931; G. Vollerthun's *Der Freikorporal*, November 10, 1931; K. Stiegler's *Die Schmiede*, April 29, 1933; H. Grimm's *Blondin im Glück*, October 6, 1934; M. Peters's *Der Sohn der Sonne*, March 3, 1936; W. Kempff's *Die Fasnacht von Rottweil*, November 27, 1937; G. Vollerthun's *Das königkiche Opfer*, May 16, 1942; E. Wolf-Ferrari's *Der Kuckuck von Theben*, June 5, 1943; M. Peter's *Luzifer,* August 31, 1947; H.W. Henze's *Boulevard Solitude,* February 17, 1952; Meyerowitz's *Die Doppelgängerin*, January 29, 1967; De la Motte's *Der Aufsichtsrat*, February 1, 1970; Einfeldt's *Palast-Hotel Thanatos*; Klebe's *Rendezvous,* October 7, 1977; Koerppen's *Ein Abenteuer auf dem Friedhof*, February 3, 1980; Müller-Siemens's *Genoveva oder Die weiße Hirschkuh* (first staged performance), February 3, 1980; Hespos's *Spot*, June 3, 1980; Goldberg & Hoppe's *Zurück vom Ring*, February 19, 1993; Thoma's *Draußen vor der Tür*, January 30, 1994; Kirchner's *Inferno d'amore*, March 12, 1995. **German Premieres:** B. Britten's *Albert Herring*, June 11, 1950; G. Donizetti's *Il campanello*, April 17, 1956; G.B. Pergolesi's *Lo frate'n-namorato*, March 24, 1959; F.J. Haydn's *Il mondo della luna*, October 4, 1959; B. Smetana's *Tajemství*, February 25, 1969; F.J. Haydn's *Armida*, July 6, 1969; G. von Einem's *Jesu Hochzeit*, November 26, 1980.

Bibliography. Sabine Hammer (ed.), *Oper in Hannover: 300 Jahr Wandel im Musiktheater einer Stadt* (Hannover, 1990). K.H. Streibung (ed.), *100 Jahre Opernhaus 1852–1952* (Hannover, 1952). R. Rosendahl, *Geschichte der Hoftheater in Hannover und Braunschweig* (Hannover, 1927).

Thanks to Barbara Krüger, Niedersächsische Staatstheater.

HEIDELBERG

Städtische Bühnen Theater der Stadt

Friedrich von Schiller's *Braut von Messina* inaugurated the Heidelberg Theater on October 31, 1853. Architect Lendorf was responsible for the Neoclassical style building. The auditorium, however, was redecorated in Art Deco between 1924 and 1925, with Richard Wagner's *Die Meistersinger von Nürnberg* reopening the opera house on September 25, 1925. At the end of the 1970s Giuseppe Verdi's *Falstaff* was staged. The repertory spans works from the Baroque to the classical with operas from the 19th century dominant. Recent offerings include Giuseppe Verdi's *Il trovatore*, Gioachino Rossini's *Il barbiere di Siviglia*, Richard Strauss's *Arabella*, and Ludwig van Beethoven's *Fidelio*.

Practical Information. Städtische Bühnen Theater der Stadt, Friedrichstraße 5 69117 Heidelberg. Tel: 49 6221 583 502, Fax: 49 6221 583 599. If visiting, contact the German National Tourist Office, 747 Third Avenue, 33rd Floor, New York, NY 10017. Tel: 212-308-3300.

COMPANY STAFF

Intendant. Volkmar Clauss.

HILDESHEIM

Stadttheater

Lessing's *Nathan der Weise* opened the rebuilt Stadttheater on September 10, 1949. The previous Stadttheater had been destroyed on March 22, 1945. Designed by Max Littmann, it had been inaugurated on October 2, 1909, with Friedrich von Schiller's *Jungfrau von Orleans*.

After the reopening of the theater until the 1960s, operetta and spoken drama were the main offerings. The 1960s witnessed an increase in operatic performances with Giacomo Puccini's *Madama Butterfly*, Giuseppe Verdi's *Otello* and *Un ballo in maschera*, Ludwig van Beethoven's *Fidelio*, Bedřich Smetana's *Prodaná nevěsta* (The Bartered Bride), and Richard Wagner's *Der fliegende Holländer* on the boards. A few seasons later, a successful production of Verdi's *Nabucco* graced the stage, along with several musicals — *Cats, Hello Dolly!, Kiss Me Kate*, among them. Recent offerings include Sergey Prokofiev's *Lyubov'k tryom apel'sinam* (The Love for Three Oranges), Igor Stravinsky's *L'histoire du soldat*, Wagner's *Der fliegende Holländer*, and Georg Friedrich Händel's *Alcina*.

Practical Information. Stadttheater, Theaterstraße 6, 31141 Hildesheim. Tel: 49 5121 33164. If visiting, contact the German National Tourist Office, 747 Third Avenue, 33rd Floor, New York, NY 10017. Tel: 212-308-3300.

COMPANY STAFF

Intendant. Martin Kreutzberg.

—————— HOF

Städtebundtheater

Wolfgang Amadeus Mozart's *Don Giovanni* inaugurated the Städtebundtheater on September 23, 1994. The modern structure was designed by the Munich architects Auer and Weber, who submitted the winning drawings in the 1987 architectural competition. The cornerstone for the new theater was laid on July 6, 1991.

The previous theater was opened on June 11, 1930, with Richard Wagner's *Die Meistersinger von Nürnburg*. It had been a private theater which city architect Wörner reconstructed. After World War II, an opera ensemble was established which presented Giuseppe Verdi's *La traviata* on October 4, 1948. More opera performances followed, including Heinrich Marscher's *Hans Heiling*, Charles Gounod's *Faust*, Jacques Offenbach's *Les contes d'Hoffmann*, and Pyotr Il'yich Tchaikovsky's *Eugene Onegin*. During the early 1980s, works like Ludwig van Beethoven's *Fidelio* and Giacomo Puccini's *Gianni Schicchi* were in the repertory. When Reinhold Röttger became the director in 1985, he reduced the number of musicals from eight to two and presented more interesting operas like Paul Hindemith's *Cardillac*, Claude Debussy's *Pelléas et Mélisande*, Igor Stravinsky's *The Rake's Progress*, among others. Recent repertory includes Mozart's *Die Zauberflöte*, Jules Massenet's *Werther*, and Franz Schubert's *Fierrabras*.

Practical Information. Städtebundtheater, Kulmbacherstraße 5, 95028 Hof. Tel: 49 9281 70700. If visiting, contact the German National Tourist Office, 747 Third Avenue, 33rd Floor, New York, NY 10017. Tel: 212-308-3300.

COMPANY STAFF

Intendanten. Reinhold Röttger (1985–present), Gerd Nienstedt (1981–85), Günther Pentzold (1981), Horst Gnekow (1978–80), Toni Graschberger (1974–78), Hannes Keppler (1963–74), Hanns Jessen (1951–63), Ulrich Lauterback (1948–51).

—————— KAISERSLAUTERN

Pfalztheater

Ludwig van Beethoven's *Fidelio* inaugurated the 750-seat Pfalztheater on September 30, 1950. The building, which earlier had served as a movie house, was converted into a theater by the builder Albert. The previous theater, known as the old Stadttheater, had been destroyed on August 14, 1944. Inaugurated on June 20, 1862, the theater was built through the generosity of a culture-loving citizen named Andreas Müller, who paid the construction bills and the costs of the first few artistic seasons. Damaged by fire and rebuilt several times, the theater was taken over by the city in 1897. There were joint productions with Zweibrücken.

After the Pfalztheater opened in 1950, musicals, like *My Fair Lady*, *Hello Dolly!*, *Man from La Mancha*, *Silk Stockings*, and the like were the primary fare. A few operas are also staged each season. Recent offerings include Carl Maria von Weber's *Oberon*, Giacomo Puccini's *Madama Butterfly*, and Richard Wagner's *Der fliegende Holländer* and *Die Meistersinger von Nürnberg*.

Practical Information. Pfalztheater, Willy Brandt Platz 4-5, 67657 Kaiserslautern. Tel: 49 631 36750, Fax: 49 631 3675 235. If visiting, contact the German National Tourist Office, 747 Third Floor, New York, NY 10017. Tel: 212-308-3300.

COMPANY STAFF

Intendant. Pavel Fieber.

KARLSRUHE

Badisches Staatstheater

Wolfgang Amadeus Mozart's *Die Zauberflöte* inaugurated the 1,002-seat Badisches Staatstheater on August 8, 1975. Helmut Bätzner designed the modern, concrete structure. The previous theater, the Großherzogliche Hoftheater, later renamed Badisches Landestheater, was destroyed during a bombing raid the night of September 26-27, 1944. Designed by Heinrich Hübsch with a classic facade, the 2000-seat theater opened on May 17, 1853, with Friedrich von Schiller's *Jungfrau con Orleans.*

As early as the 1600s, there were reports of Singspiele, mythological scenes, and ballet performances in Karlsruhe. On January 13, 1719, the east wing of the castle was designated an opera house and opened with *Celindo.* In 1774 Christoph Willibald Gluck arrived in the city, improving its musical offerings. In 1806, the Grand Duke Karl Friedrich commissioned his builder Friedrich Weinbrenner to construct a new theater, which opened on November 9, 1808, with two Singspiele, Spindler's *Fest der Weihe* and *Triumph mütterlicher Liebe.* Two years later, Ferdinando Paër's *Achille* inaugurated the first regular season on November 9, 1810. Johann Wolfgang Goethe visited the theater in 1815 and Niccolò Paganini gave a violin concert there in 1829. During a performance of the ballet *Der artesische Brunnen* on February 28, 1847, the drapery in the royal box caught fire, which quickly engulfed the entire house, killing 63 spectators.

The first musical event in the new theater, which opened in 1853, was Ludwig van Beethoven's Ninth Symphony. A decade later, Richard Wagner conducted two concerts from his own works. The theater was nicknamed "Little Bayreuth" due to the strong Wagner tradition that took root during this era. Hermann Levi conducted Wagner's *Die Meistersinger von Nürnberg* in 1868. Hector Berlioz's *Les Troyens* received its first complete Karlsruhe production on December 6, 1890, with Felix Mottl on the podium. Richard Strauss conducted his own works during a Richard Strauss Festival Week in 1924, and Hans Pfitzner led his *Palestrina* on January 11, 1924. The theater hosted its final performance, Mozart's *Le nozze di Figaro,* on July 9, 1944. Bombs destroyed it a couple of months later. After World War II, the Städtisches Konzerthaus was reconstructed into an opera house and opened on October 14, 1953, with Mozart's *Die Zauberflöte.* During this time the company staged the Italian premiere of Carl Orff's *Die Kluge* at Teatro la Fenice in Venice, and a couple of performances of Alban Berg's *Lulu* in Lisbon. Mozart's *Così fan tutte* on June 29, 1975, was the final performance in the city concert house.

After the new opera house opened, a festival called "Händel-Tage des Badischen Staatstheater" (Händel Days at the Bad State Theater) took place in 1977, with the staging of several of Georg Friedrich Händel's works. The following year saw the German premiere of a Giovanni Paisiello work. Another novelty was mounted in 1983, Max von Schilling's *Mona Lisa.* The beginning of the 1990s witnessed Giuseppe Verdi's *Nabucco,* Albert Lortzing's *Zar und Zimmermann,* Claude Debussy's *Pelléas et Mélisande,* Wagner's *Tannhäuser,* and Strauss's *Capriccio* and *Ariadne auf Naxos.* The high point was the world premiere of Helge Jörns's *Zufall der Liebe.* Recent offerings include Giacomo Puccini's *Madama Butterfly,* Mozart's *Don Giovanni,* Ernst Křenek's *Jonny spielt auf,* Gaetano Donizetti's *Lucia di Lammermoor,* and Wagner's *Die Meistersinger von Nürnberg.*

Practical Information. Badisches Staatstheater, Baumeisterstraße 11, 76137 Karlsruhe. Tel: 49 721 380-300. If visiting the Badisches Staatstheater, contact The German National Tourist Office, 747 Third Avenue, 33rd Floor, New York, NY 10017. Tel: 212-308-3300.

COMPANY STAFF

Intendanten. Günter Könemann (1977–present), Hans-George Rudolph (1963–77), Waldemar Leitgeb (1962–63), Paul Rose (1953–62), Heinz Wolfgang Wolff (1949–53), Heinrich Köhler Helffrich (1948–49), Hanns Schulz-Dornburg (1948), Erwin Hahn (1946–47), Erich Weidner (1946), Hans Herbert Michels (1945–46).

Bibliography. H.G. Rudolph, *Badisches Staatstheater Karlsruhe: Festschrift sur Eröffnung des Neuen Hauses am Ettlinger Tor 1975* (Karlsruhe, 1975). G. Haass, *Geschichte des ehemaligen Großherzoglich Badischen Hoftheaters Karlsruhe 1806–52* (Karlsruhe, 1932).

KASSEL

Stadttheater

The premiere of Rudolf Wagner-Régney's *Prometheus* inaugurated the 953-seat Stadttheater on September 12, 1959. Paul Bode and Ernst Brundig designed the modern structure. The previous theater was severely damaged during World War II and demolished in 1950. Albert Lortzing's *Undine* opened this earlier theater on August 26, 1909.

The first opera performance in Kassel dates back to 1701. The Landgraf Friedrich II contributed much to the development of Italian opera by engaging leading musicians and artists of the time for the Hoftheater. The Hoftheater was established between 1766 and 1769, when a former Prinzenpalais was converted into a modern Court Theater. Wolfgang Amadeus Mozart's *Die Zauberflöte* and *La clemenza di Tito* were seen in 1793 and 1794, followed by *Le nozze di Figaro* three years later and *Idomeneo* in 1802. Louis Spohr became *Hofkapellmeister* in 1822 and opera flourished. Five of his operas received their premieres here: *Jessonda* (July 28, 1823), *Der Berggeist* (March 24, 1825), *Pietro von Abano* (October 13, 1827), *Der Alchymist* (July 28, 1830), and *Die Kreuzfahrer* (January 1, 1845). In 1843, Richard Wagner's *Der fliegende Holländer* was staged in Kassel not long after its world premiere in Dresden. Between 1883 and 1885 Gustav Mahler was music director in Kassel.

A new theater opened after the turn of the century but it was a difficult time. There was a high turnover among the theater's directors making any kind of artistic continuity difficult. After the theater was demolished and the current theater opened in 1959, the opera part of the repertory improved. There was (and still is) a strong emphasis on Mozart, Wagner, Giuseppe Verdi, Giacomo Puccini, and Richard Strauss works. The first Kassel performance of Strauss's *Die Frau ohne Schatten* took place in 1962 followed by an impressive Ring Cycle between 1970 and 1973. The 1980s witnessed several world premieres, including Peter Michael Hamel's *Ein Menschentraum* on June 27, 1981, Walter Haupt's *Marat* on June 9, 1984, and his *Pier Paolo* on May 23, 1987, Wilhelm Dieter Siebert's *Liebe, Tod, und Tango* on October 12, 1986, and Josef Tal's *Der Turum* on September 19, 1987. The end of the 1980s and beginning of the 1990s saw Lortzing's *Der Waffenschmied*, Wagner's *Lohengrin*, Mozart's *Don Giovanni* and *La clemenza di Tito*, and some novelties like Wolfgang von Schweinitz's *Patmos*, Dominick Argento's *The Aspern Papers*, and Paul Lincke's *Frau Luna*. More recent offerings include Wagner's *Das Rheingold*, *Die Walküre*, Vincenzo Bellini's *Norma*, Mozart's *Die Zauberflöte* and *Don Giovanni*, Lortzing's *Zar und Zimmermann*, and Leoš Janáček's *Jenůfa*.

Practical Information. Stadttheater, Friedrichsplatz 15, 34117 Kassel. Tel: 49 561 109-4222, Fax: 49 561 109-4204. If visiting, contact the German National Tourist Office, 747 Third Avenue, 33rd Floor, New York, NY 10017. Tel: 212-308-3300.

COMPANY STAFF

Intendant. Michael Leinert.

Bibliography. *Theater in Kassel: Aus der Geschichte des Staatstheaters Kassel* (Kassel, 1959). H.J. Schaefer, *475 Jahre Orchestra in Kassel: Abriß einer Entwick-*

KIEL

Bühnen der Landeshauptstadt Kiel

Beethoven's *Fidelio* reopened the Bühnen der Landeshauptstadt Kiel, originally known as Neues Stadttheater, and later as Opernhaus am Kleinen Kiel, in 1953 during Kieler Woche. Architects Hansen and Widmann were responsible for the construction. The previous theater, destroyed during World War II, had been inaugurated on October 1, 1907, with Ludwig van Beethoven's *Fidelio*, the overture to Richard Wagner's *Parsifal*, and the prologue to Ernst von Wildenbruch's *Der Kunst ein Haus*. Constructed between 1905 and 1907, the theater was designed by the Berlin architect Heinrich Seeling.

The first opera performance venue in Kiel

dates back to 1764 when a Ballhaus was converted to an "Opern-and Komödienhaus." Torn down in 1840, it was replaced by the Altes Stadttheater. Here Carl Maria von Weber's *Oberon* was given on February 2, 1845. Works by Wolfgang Amadeus Mozart and Albert Lortzing dominated the stage during the directorship of L.F. Witt (1857–73), who refused to present Wagner operas. When the helm passed to Richard Jesse in 1876, Kiel saw its first Wagner operas — *Lohengrin* and *Der fliegende Holländer*. One of the first conductors in the Neues Stadttheater was Leon Jessel, who was also the composer of the successful operetta, *Schwarzwaldmädel*.

The end of the 1960s and beginning of the 1970s witnessed several performances of "New Music" from composers like John Cage, Karlheinz Stockhausen, and Mauricio Kagel. Beginning with the 1971-72 season, there were 13 world premieres at the opera house during the next decade. The mid–1980s saw operas like Jacques Offenbach's *Les contes d'Hoffmann*, Albert Lortzing's *Zar und Zimmermann*, Richard Strauss's *Arabella*, Giuseppe Verdi's *Otello*, Giacomo Puccini's *Tosca*, Eugen d'Albert's *Tiefland*, Gioachino Rossini's *Il barbiere di Siviglia*, and Friedrich von Flotow's *Martha*. The Kieler Opernhaus has a resident ensemble which perform all the operas. During Kieler Woche, unusual and experimental productions are staged. Recent offerings include Otto Nicolai's *Die lustigen Weiber von Windsor*, Wagner's *Die Walküre*, Eric Wolfgang Korngold's *Die tote Stadt*, and Wolfgang Amadeus Mozart's *Idomeneo*.

Opernhaus am Kleinen Kiel

The opera house was first damaged during World War II on June 30, 1941, and again on December 13, 1943. It was totally destroyed with another aerial bombing attack in 1944. Between 1950 and 1953, the theater was reconstructed. It is a large, severe-looking, red brick structure which holds a three-tier auditorium. There are 869 seats.

Practical Information. Bühnen der Landeshauptstadt Kiel, Rathausplatz 4, 24103 Kiel. Tel: 49 431 901 2880, Fax: 49 431 901 2838. If visiting the Bühnen der Landeshauptstadt Kiel, contact the German National Tourist Office, 747 Third Avenue, 33rd Floor, New York, NY 10017. Tel: 212-308-3300.

COMPANY STAFF

Intendanten. Walter Gugerbauer (General Music Director), Peter Dannenberg, Volker Clauß, Horst Fechner, Claus Henneberg, Joachim Klaiber, Hans-Georg Rudolph, Rudolf Meyer, Alfred Noller, Paul Belker, Wolfram Humperdinck, Hans Schulz-Dornburg, Ernst Maritin, Hans Brockmann, Kurt Elvenspoek, Max Alberty, Carl Alving, Anton Otto, Franz Gottschied.

Bibliography. R. Meyer & H. Niederauer, *Festschrift zum 50 jährigen Bestehen des Hauses am Kleinen Kiel* (Kiel, 1957).

Thanks to Hans-Joachim Weiherich.

KOBLENZ

Stadttheater

Wolfgang Amadeus Mozart's *Die Entführung aus dem Serail* inaugurated the Stadttheater on November 23, 1787. Peter Joseph Krahe designed the house in early Rhein classical style. The theater was damaged on November 6, 1944, but repaired after the war and reopened on June 1, 1946, with Lessing's *Nathan der Weise*.

After the City Theater opened in 1787, it hosted Mozart operas, like *Le nozze di Figaro* and *Die Zauberflöte*. In 1846, Gaetano Donizetti's *La fille du régiment* was staged and was so successful that it was repeated 17 times. Henriette Sontag, who was born in Koblenz, gave a concert in her native city in 1851, and sang the title role in Carl Maria von Weber's *Euryanthe*. The 1854-55 season witnessed Richard Wagner's *Tannhäuser*. The city of Koblenz took over the theater in 1867 and updated and renovated the building. It reopened on November 23, 1869, with Ludwig van Beethoven's *Fidelio* with Queen Augusta present. Four years later, Wagner's *Lohengrin* graced the stage. Near the end of the century the city saw Wagner's *Die Meistersinger von Nürnberg*, and in 1924, the complete Ring Cycle was staged. The 150th anniversary was celebrated with a performance of Mozart's *Die Entführung aus dem Serail*.

Johann Strauß's *Eine Nacht in Venedig* was given in 1950, followed by Wagner's *Tristan und Isolde* in 1966, Giuseppe Verdi's *Aida* in 1971, and Richard Strauss's *Der Rosenkavalier* the next year. Recent offerings include Paul Hindemith's *Cardillac*, Johann Strauß's *Die Fledermaus*, Donizetti's *Lucia di Lammermoor*, and Mozart's *Die Entführung aus dem Serail*.

Practical Information. Stadttheater (Theater der Stadt), Clemensstraße 1, 56068 Koblenz. Tel: 49 261 129 2801, Fax: 49 261 129-2800. If visiting, contact the German National Tourist Office, 747 Third Avenue, 33rd Floor, New York, NY 10017. Tel: 212-308-3300.

COMPANY STAFF

Intendanten. Hannes Houska (1975–present), Heinz Wolfgang Wolff (1955–75), Otto Kraus (1949–55), Bruno Schoenfeld (1945–49), Hanns Kämmel (1939–44), Fritz Richard Werkhäuser (1937–38), Hans Press (1933–37), Bruno Schoenfeld (1931–33), Richard Jost (1928–30), Herbert Maisch (1926–28), Ludwig Meinecke (1920–26).

Bibliography. F.R. Werkhäuser (ed.), *150 Jahre Theater der Stadt Koblenz* (Koblenz, 1937).

KREFELD/MÖNCHENGLADBACH
Vereinigte Städtische Bühnen

Krefeld

Richard Wagner's *Lohengrin* inaugurated the Vereinigte Städtische Bühnen on October 7, 1952. Eugen Bertrand designed the modern structure. Fire destroyed the previous theater on June 23, 1943. It had opened on October 2, 1886, with Weber's *Der Freischütz*.

Opera in Krefeld dates back to the 1799 when works from Karl Ditters von Dittersdorf, Giovanni Paisiello, André Grétry, Antonio Salieri, and Wolfgang Amadeus Mozart, including *Die Zauberflöte*, *Le nozze di Figaro*, and *Die Entführung aus dem Serail* were offered in a stone theater erected in 1780 by the city master building Martin Leydel. In 1824, the "Thomala'schen Theatertruppe" brought Carl Maria von Weber's *Der Freischütz*. Michael Rump constructed a new theater in 1825 on Rheinstraße which hosted opera until it was closed by the fire marshals in 1886. It was reconstructed, reopening in 1886. The theater offered 900 places. Opera continued until fire gutted it in 1943. After World War II, the first operatic performances took place in the Ricarda-Huch-School in 1946. When the new theater opened, opera activity moved to its new home.

Mönchengladbach

Richard Wagner's *Die Meistersinger von Nürnberg* inaugurated the Vereinigte Städtische Bühnen on September 10, 1959. Paul Stohrer designed the modern glass and concrete building.

The first theater, Kaiser Friedrich Halle, was originally constructed as a concert hall between 1901 and 1903, but also served as a theater until 1959. Architects Friedrich-Wilhelm Werz and Paul Huber were responsible for the project. In this hall, the first Mönchengladbach performance of Ludwig van Beethoven's *Fidelio* took place in 1904. On September 15, 1923, Richard Wagner's *Tristan und Isolde* was given followed by his *Siegfried*, Richard Strauss's *Salome*, Eugen d'Albert's *Tiefland* Georges Bizet's *Carmen*, Gaetano Donizetti's *Pasquale*, and Erich Wolfgang Korngold's *Die tote Stadt*. Severe financial problems followed this outstanding opera season. In 1929, the theater merged with the Theater der Stadt Rheydt until the formation of the Vereinigte Städtische Bühnen in 1951. Until the establishment of the Vereinigte Städtische Bühnen, there were occasional guest performances but nothing of note.

Krefeld/Mönchengladbach

After the joining with Krefeld, an interesting opera repertory was developed with the world premiere of Richard Rodney's *Am Abrund* on December 1, 1963, and the German premiere of Stanisław Moniuszko's *Straszny dwór* (The Haunted Manor) on February 7, 1971. Other works included Gian Carlo Menotti's *The Consul*, Igor Stravinsky's *The Rake's Progress*, Werner Egk's *Peer Gynt*, Humphrey Searle's *Aus dem Tagebuch eines Irren*, Benjamin Britten's *A Midsummer Night's Dream*, Krzysztof Penderecki's *Diably z*

Loudun (The Devils of Loudun), Mauricio Kagel's *Kantrimusik*, and Bernd Alois Zimmermann's *König Ubu*. In addition, the 1970s and 1980s saw Strauss Cycles and Mozart cycles. Recent offerings include Johann Strauß's *Die Fledermauß* and Benjamin Britten's *Albert Herring*.

Practical Information. Vereinigte Städtische Bühnen, Theaterplatz 3, 47798 Krefeld; Tel: 49 2151 8050, Fax: 49 2151 28295. If visiting, contact the German National Tourist Office, 747 Third Avenue, 33rd Floor, New York, NY 10017. Tel: 212-308-3300.

COMPANY STAFF

Intendant. Jens Pesel.

LEIPZIG

Oper Leipzig

The Opernhaus Leipzig opened on October 9, 1960, with Richard Wagner's *Die Meistersinger von Nürnberg*. Taking four years to complete, the theater was designed by Kunz Nierade and Kurt Hemmerling. The previous opera house, the Neuer Theater am Augustusplatz had been destroyed during the night of December 3–4, 1943.

Two hundred and fifty years earlier, in 1693, the first opera house opened in the city. The Elector of Saxony had granted Nicolaus Adam Strungk the rights to run the theater. During the next 27 years, more than 100 operas were given, and when Georg Philipp Telemann took over the directorship around 1701, his works played an important role in the repertory. In 1720, the opera house saw its final performance and was then transformed into an orphanage until it was torn down in 1729. Opera continued despite the lack of a principal venue, and beginning in 1744, traveling Italian troupes of Angelo and Pietro Mingotti visited, raising the popularity of Italian opera. During the second half of the century, Singspiel was favored beginning with an offering of H.G. Koch's *Der Teufel ist los*. Works of Karl Ditters von Dittersdorf and Wolfgang Amadeus Mozart were also popular.

In the beginning of the 1760s the art-loving businessman Gottlieb Benedict Zehmisch gave his hometown a new theater. Named after its location, the Theater auf der Ranstädter Bastei was built by Georg Rudolf Fäsch and modeled after the small court theater in Dresden. The 1,186-seat theater, offering an orchestra level and four balconies, opened with Koch's *Die verwandelten Weiber* on October 6, 1776. Johann Wolfgang von Goethe (a student in Leipzig at the time) was in the audience. In 1783, P. Bondini's opera troupe offered Mozart's *Die Entführung aus dem Serail*.

When the Leipziger Stadttheater was established under the direction of K. T. Künster in 1817, the opera house was remodeled by Friedrich Weinbrenner, who introduced classical elements into the theater's basic form. The stage, however, remained small, making productions of works from Giacomo Meyerbeer complicated. Besides Mozart, those of Carl Maria von Weber were popular and in 1826 his *Oberon* was staged with the composer on the podium. Heinrich Marschner's *Der Vampyr* received its world premiere in 1828, followed by his *Templer und die Jüdin* the next year. From that year until 1832, the theater was known as the Sächsisches Hoftheater. The next composer to make his mark in Leipzig was Albert Lortzing with eight of his operas produced, including the world premieres of *Zar und Zimmermann* on December 22, 1837, and *Der Wildschütz* on December 31, 1842. Robert Schumann's *Genoveva* was introduced eight years later. Then in 1853, Leipzig saw the first operas of its hometown son Richard Wagner performed, *Tannhäuser*, and in 1878, the first outside of Bayreuth *Der Ring des Niberlungen* was staged. Eight years later, Gustav Mahler began a two year conducting stint.

On January 28, 1868, a new theater, the Neuer Theater am Augustplatz, was opened. Constructed between 1865 and 1867 and designed by Carl Ferdinand Langhans, the building combined late classical and Renaissance elements. The auditorium held four tiers accommodating 2,000 people. Beginning in 1912, the theater offered exclusively opera. That same year, the opera, which had been run on the leaseholder system, appointed its first general director, Max Martersteig. Discussions about the changeover actually began as early as 1850, and during the 1870s and 1880s bills were brought before the city council about placing the theater under city administration, but they were turned down because the city representatives feared the financial consequences. After Martersteig took the helm, classical and experimental operas found favor. In 1924, when Gustav Brecher was hired as the music director of the opera, the city became an arena for contemporary works, witnessing the world premieres of Ernst Křenek's *Jonny spielt auf* in 1927 followed by his *Leben des Orest* in 1930, and Kurt Weill's *Der Aufstieg und Fall der Stadt Mahagonny* the same year. Weill's work caused a scandal. The opera was disrupted by hecklers and debates followed in the city council with the opera subsequently disappearing from the repertory. When the Nazis seized power, Brecher was denounced as a Jew and removed as music director. Nazi policy in Leipzig was to continue with premieres and in 1943, the world premiere of Carl Orff's *Catulli Carmina* was given on November 6, 1943. Less than a month later, the opera house was destroyed. Wagner's *Die Walküre* had been the last production. The Drei Linden Theater became the temporary opera venue until a new house could be constructed. Opera began again on July 20, 1945, with Ludwig van Beethoven's *Fidelio*. More novelties graced the stage, including Boris Blacher's *Nachtschwalbe* in 1948.

In 1960, the new opera house opened and the Intendant, Joachim Herz, was an influential figure. During his reign, the first German performance of Sergey Prokofiev's *Voyna i mir* (War and Peace) took place, and he offered numerous works by Mozart, Richard Strauss, Giacomo Meyerbeer, Richard Wagner, Leoš Janáček, and Dmitri Shostakovich. In the contemporary vein, Alan Bush's *Guayana Johnny*, Robert Hanell's *Griechische Hochzeit* conducted by the composer, and Fritz Geissler's *Der zerbrochene Krug* and *Der Schatten* graced the stage. A new Ring Cycle was mounted between 1973 and 1976. In 1989, in the course of democratization, the centralized management of the Leipzig theaters was abolished and on March 1, 1990, the composer Udo Zimmermann became the new Intendant. To recall the glorious era of 20th-century opera in Leipzig, Zimmermann revived Křenek's *Jonny spielt auf*, Ferruccio Busoni's *Doktor Faust*, and György Ligeti's *Le grand macabre*. On the other side, to recognize composers connected to Leipzig from the 18th century, Georg Philipp Telemann's *Don Quichotte auf der Hochzeit des Comacho* and Johann Adam Hiller's *Die Jagd* were staged.

The repertory exhibits a variety of works. In keeping with Zimmermann's interest in the 20th century — Janáček's *Kát'a Kabanová*, Carey Blyton's *Dracula*, Hans Werner Henze's *Elegy for Young Lovers*, Béla Bartók's *A Kékszakállú herceg vára* (Duke Bluebeard's Castle), Arnold Schönberg's *Erwartung*, and Shostakovich's *Nos* (The Nose) have been presented, along with Pyotr Il'yich Tchaikovsky's *Eugene Onegin* and Lortzing's *Zar und Zimmermann*, among others. A production of Wagner's *Der fliegende Holländer* was realistic and very Germanic. The sensation of being on a boat deck, complete with mast, lines, and the like, was well conveyed, and the Dutchman's boat rose eerily behind Daland. The Spinning scene was set during a "Kaffee Klatsch." The quality of singing and acting was good, especially Florian Cerny as the Dutchman, whose tortured interpretation showed depth of character. Recent offerings include Wagner's *Tristan und Isolde*, Mozart's *Die Zauberflöte*, and Georges Bizet's *Carmen*.

Opernhaus Leipzig

Three architectural competitions took place between 1950 and 1952, since satisfactory designs were not submitted during the first two competitions. Finally Nierade and Hemmerling were commissioned with the project. Due to the Communist ideology of the time, a rigidly symmetrical, heavily ornamented, almost bombastic structure resulted. In December 1955, the ruins of the New Theater were removed and on January 2, 1956, construction on the new opera house began.

The massive building of grayish stone exhibits severe lines with golden framed windows. Basic decorations of Comedy and Tragedy masks, a cornucopia of fruit, and peace doves embellish the structure. A double-level "portico" with fluted columns and square pillars lines the front of the theater. The single-tier auditorium is rectangular in shape and holds golden textured seats. Single side boxes protrude from the light-wood covered walls on each side. The parapets are textured white and the proscenium arch is plain. Rows of squares of varying shades of yellow, gold, and maroon embellish the ceiling from which hang rows of glass-ball fixtures. The Stalin-era influence permeates the space — it lacks the warmth and intimacy of the city's previous opera houses. There are 1,700 seats.

Opernhaus Leipzig (Leipzig, Germany).

Practical Information. Oper Leipzig, Augustplatz, 04109 Leipzig. Tel: 49 341 126-1261, Fax: 49 341 126-1300. When visiting the Oper Leipzig, stay at the Hotel Inter-Continental Leipzig, Gerberstraße 15, 04105 Leipzig. Tel: 49 341 9880 or 1 800 327 0200, Fax: 49 341 988-1299. The Hotel Inter-Continental Leipzig is a centrally-located establishment close to the opera house. The hotel can assist with opera tickets and schedule.

COMPANY STAFF AND PREMIERES

Intendanten. Udo Zimmermann (1990–present), Gert Bahner & Günter Lohse (1976–89), Joachim Herz (1959–76).

World Premieres. (Important) H. Marschner's *Der Vampyr*, March 29, 1828; A. Lortzing's *Zar und Zimmermann*, December 22, 1837; R. Schumann's *Genoveva*, June 25, 1850; E. Křenek's *Jonny spielt auf*, February 10, 1927; K. Weill's *Der Augstieg und Fall der Stadt Mahagonny*, March 9, 1930; C. Orff's *Catulli Carmina*, November 6, 1943. A. Schlünz's *Matka*, February 27, 1991.

Bibliography. Fritz Hennenberg, *Oper Leipzig: 300 Jahre Leipziger Oper 1693–1993* (Leipzig, 1993). Thomas Topfstedt, *Oper Leipzig: Das Gebäude* (Leipzig, 1993). K. Kayser & H. Michael, *Leipziger Theater 1965: Herausgegeben aus Anlaß des 800 jährigen Bestehens der Stadt Leipzig* (Leipzig, 1965).

Thanks to M. Ernst, Oper Leipzig, and Gerhard Mitrovits.

LÜBECK

Bühnen der Hansestadt

Lübeck's theater was opened on October 1, 1908, with the overture to Richard Wagner's *Die Meistersinger von Nürnberg*, Johann Wolfgang Goethe's *Die Geschwister*, and Friedrich von Schiller's *Demetrius*. The first opera performance, Wagner's *Lohengrin*, took place on October 5, 1908. Martin Dülfer designed the theater in Jugendstil.

The first theater in Lübeck dates back to 1753 when traveling theater troupes presented shows. A permanent ensemble was established in 1800. The theater built in 1753 was torn down and a new one constructed in 1857. This theater was closed in 1905 for not having sufficient fire safety measures. The first opera of note took place after the current theater opened in 1908 when tenor Karl Erb assayed the titled role in Wagner's *Lohengrin*. The theater also hosted baritone Jaro Prohaska. Counted among the conductors were Wilhelm Furtwängler and Hermann Abendroth. Works of Wagner were well represented in the repertory. After World War II, especially during the late 1960s and 1970s, musicals played a dominant role in the schedule. Recent offerings include Verdi's *La traviata*, Mozart's *Le nozze di Figaro*, Jacques Offenbach's *Les contes d'Hoffmann*.

Practical Information. Bühnen der Hansestadt, Fischergrube 5-21, 23539 Lübeck. Tel: 49 451 122-4212, Fax: 49 451 122 4277. If visiting, contact the German National Tourist Office, 747 Third Avenue, 33rd Floor, New York, NY 10017. Tel: 212-308-3300.

COMPANY STAFF

Intendant. Dietrich von Oertzen.

LÜNEBURG

Stadttheater

William Shakespeare's *As You Like It* inaugurated the Stadttheater on October 8, 1961. Originally constructed as a movie theater, the Lüneburg architect Homann was responsible for the transformation.

In 1822, the Kaulitzsche Gesellschaftshaus became the "Stadttheater" and with a permanent ensemble staged opera and operetta. Johann Strauß and Albert Lortzing guest conducted there. The theater was destroyed by fire in 1921. Next the cinema house owner August Greune converted his movie house into a theater, which hosted, among others, opera performances given by the Hamburger Oper. The theater established a permanent ensemble and the 1970s saw many operettas including those by Johann Strauß, Franz Lehár, and Karl Millöcker. The 1980s saw more Wolfgang Amadeus Mozart works like *Die Entführung aus dem Serail* and *Bastien und Bastienne*, and Gaetano Donizetti's *L'elisir d'amore* and *Viva la Mamma*. Recent repertory includes Puccini's *Tosca*, Mozart's *Die Entführung aus dem Serail*, and Strauß's *Die Fledermaus*.

Practical Information. Stadttheater, An der Reeperbahnen 3, 21335 Lüneburg. Tel: 49 4131 42100. If visiting, contact the German National Tourist Office, 747 Third Avenue, 33rd Floor, New York, NY 10017. Tel: 212-308-3300.

COMPANY STAFF

Intendant. Jan Aust.

MAGDEBURG

Theater der Landeshauptstadt

The opera house in Magdeburg burned to the ground on May 20, 1990. Although arson was suspected, no one was ever charged with the crime. Until a new opera house is built, the company performs in several locations: the Kaserne on Jerichower Platz, the Campus Theater, and at the university.

When the city was part of the German Democratic Republic (DDR), the repertory was limited. Since the city has been freed and Max Hoffmann appointed the theater's director, the repertory has expanded to include Hector Berlioz's *Les Trojans*, Udo Zimmermann's *Weiße Rose*, and the first stage performance of Berthold Goldschmidt's *Beatrice Cenci*. Other offerings include Richard Wagner's *Die Meistersinger von Nürnberg*, Carl Maria von Weber's *Der Freischütz*, and Wolfgang Amadeus Mozart's *Die Entführung aus dem Serail*. Recent offerings include Richard Strauss's *Der Rosenkavalier*, Mozart's *Don Giovanni*, and Gian Carlo Menotti's *The Telephone*.

Practical Information. Theater der Landeshauptstadt, Postfach 1240, 39002 Magdeburg. Tel: 49 391 540-6500. If visiting, contact the

German National Tourist Office, 747 Third Avenue, 33rd Floor, New York, NY 10017. Tel: 212-308-3300.

MAINZ

Staatstheater

The Staatstheater, previously known as the Städtische Bühnen, was opened on November 24, 1951, with a ballet performance. The architect was Richard Jörg. The previous theater had been destroyed in 1942. Carl Maria von Weber's *Jubel-Ouvertüre* and Wolfgang Amadeus Mozart's *La clemenza di Tito* had inaugurated that theater on September 21, 1833. Georg Moller designed the building in classical style.

Opera history dates back to 1789 when on May 23 of that year Mozart's *Don Giovanni* was performed (in German). The company performed in England, France and Belgium during the 1840s. Well-known composers like Hans Pfitzner and Konradin Kreutzer were connected with Mainz's musical life. In 1982, Alban Berg's *Wozzeck* was offered with László Anderkó in the title role. Recent repertory includes Mozart's *Die Zauberflöte*, Vincenzo Bellini's *Anna Bolena*, Giuseppe Verdi's *Luisa Miller*, and Jacques Offenbach's *Les contes d'Hoffmann*.

Practical Information. Staatstheater, Gutenbergplatz 7, 55116 Mainz. Tel: 49 6131 285-1222. If visiting, contact the German National Tourist Office, 747 Third Avenue, 33rd Floor, New York, NY 10017. Tel: 212-308-3300.

MANNHEIM

Nationaltheater

Carl Maria von Weber's *Der Freischütz* inaugurated the Nationaltheater on January 13, 1957. Gerhard Weber designed the 1,200 seat, modern glass-and-concrete building. The previous Nationaltheater, also known as the Comödien- und Redoutenhaus, was destroyed on September 5, 1943, during a bombing raid on the city. Opened in 1777, the theater resulted from the reconstruction of an old Zeug- und Schütthauses by architect Lorenzo Quaglio.

The year following the opening of the theater in 1777, a permanent ensemble was established. Opera, however did not arrive until 1821, during the tenure of Carl von Luxburg. Heinrich Marschner's *Hans Heiling* was offered and then Albert Lortzing brought his *Undine*. The first Richard Wagner opera appeared in 1855, *Tannhäuser*, followed four years later by *Lohengrin*, and in 1869 by *Die Meistersinger von Nürnberg*. Wagner, himself, arrived in Mannheim in 1871 to direct a concert of his own works as well as those of Ludwig van Beethoven and Wolfgang Amadeus Mozart. To this day, Wagner works play a role in the repertory. On June 7, 1896, the world premiere of Hugo Wolf's *Corregidor* was given, followed by the introduction of Egon Wellesz's *Alkestis* on March 20, 1924. During the 1930s the operas of Richard Strauss, Giuseppe Verdi, and Wagner dominated the repertory. Meanwhile, there were exchanges of performances between Mannheim and Karlsruhe. Karlsruhe brought Hector Berlioz's *Les Trojans* and Mannheim performed Léo Delibes's *Lakmé* in Karlsruhe. The company also took a complete Ring Cycle to Baden-Baden after World War I.

Only a few hours after a performance of Weber's *Der Freischütz* in September 1943, the opera house was destroyed. A temporary performance venue was found in the Schauburg Kino and soon after the war ended, performances of Gioachino Rossini's *Il barbiere di Siviglia* and Beethoven's *Fidelio* were given. More operas followed, including Mozart's *Don Giovanni*, Verdi's *Il trovatore* and *Otello*, Strauss's *Ariadne auf Naxos* and *Elektra*, Pietro Mascagni's *Cavalleria rusticana*, and Ruggero Leoncavallo's *I pagliacci*. In 1953, contemporary works arrived with Werner Egk's *Columbus* followed by Egk and Boris Blacher's *Abstrakter Oper Nummer Eins*. The latter work provoked a scandal. The next years witnessed Blacher's *Preußisches Märchen*, Paul Hindemith's *Mathias der Maler* and *Cardillac*, Frank Martin's *Zaubertrank*, Carl Orff's *Carmina burana* and *Catulli Carmina*, Igor Stravinsky's *Oedipus Rex*, and Ernst Křenek's *Pallas Athene weint*.

The year following the opening of the new house (1958), Wagner's *Tristan und Isolde* graced the stage. The commitment to contemporary works continued with Hindemith conducting the premiere of his *Das lange Weinachtsmahl*. In addition, Günther Bialas's *Hero und Leander* and Giselher Klebe's *Der jüngste Tag* were on the boards. During the 1986-87 season, Wolfgang Rihm's *Hamletmaschine* was staged, followed four seasons later by Detlev Müller-Siemens's *Die Menschen*. There is a permanent ensemble of 36 soloists. Guest artists appear at special gala evenings. Recent repertory includes Verdi's *Don Carlo* and *Il trovatore*, Puccini's *Tosca* and *La bohème*, Wagner's *Der fliegende Holländer* and *Parsifal*, and Kurt Weill's *Der Aufstieg und Fall der Stadt Mahagonny*.

Practical Information. Nationaltheater, am Goetheplatz, 68161 Mannheim. Tel: 49 621 168-0138, Fax: 49 621 168-0385. When visiting the Nationaltheater, contact the German National Tourist Office, 747 Third Avenue, 33rd Floor, New York, NY 10017. Tel: 212-308-3300.

COMPANY STAFF

Intendanten. (important) Ulrich Schwab, Klaus Schultz, Arnold Petersen, Michael Hampe, Ernst Dietz Hans Schüler, Richard Payer, Richard Dornseiff, Erich Kronen, Carl Onno Eisenbart, Fredrich Brandenburg, Herbert Maisch, Francesco Sioli, Ferdinand Grepori, Carl Hagemann, August Bassermann, Philipp Jacob Düringer, Carl von Luxburg, Wolfgang Heribert von Dalbert.

Bibliography. K. Heinz & H. Schönfeldt, *200 Jahre Nationaltheater Mannheim: Geschichte und Jubiläum* (Mannheim, 1980). *Das Nationaltheater Mannheim: 1779–1970* (Mannheim, 1970). E. L. Stahl, *Das Mannheimer Nationaltheater: Ein Jahrhundert deutscher Theaterkultur im Reich* (Berlin, 1940).

MEININGEN

Das Meininger Theater
(Südthüringisches Staatstheater)

On December 17, 1909, the Meininger Theater, originally called the Hoftheater, was inaugurated with Friedrich von Schiller's *Wallensteins Lager*. The Meininger court builder Behlert designed the new theater in a classic style. Fire had destroyed the previous Hoftheater on March 5, 1908. This theater had been inaugurated on December 17, 1831, with Daniel Auber's *Fra Diavolo*.

After the theater opened, there were annual seasons of opera and drama performances. When Duke Georg II succeeded as duke of Sachsen-Meiningen, he personally took over the direction of the theater. In 1880, the duke invited Hans von Bülow to become the director of the Hofkapelle. Other important appointments followed, including Richard Strauss, who arrived in 1885, Fritz Steinbach, Wilhelm Berger, and Max Reger. Drama played the primary role in the Hoftheater, but works of Richard Wagner and Strauss received prominent positions.

After World War II, Meininger was one of the first German theaters to stage a performance, Gerhart Hauptmann's *Die Versunkene Glocke*. The works of Strauss and Wagner continued to be an important part of the repertory during the German Democratic Republic (DDR) era. Since the union of the two Germanys, the repertory has expanded considerably. On April 26, 1996, it hosted the first staged performance of Franz Schubert's *Der Graf von Gleichen*. Recent repertory includes Giuseppe Verdi's *Aida*,

Wagner's *Tannhäuser* and *Der fliegende Holländer*, Johann Strauß's *Eine Nacht in Venedig*, Ludwig van Beethoven's *Fidelio*.

Practical Information. Das Meininger Theater, Bernhardstraße 5, 98617 Meiningen. Tel: 49 3693 451-0, Fax: 49 49 3693 452-2285. If visiting, contact the German National Tourist

Office, 747 Third Avenue, 33rd Floor, New York, NY 10017. Tel: 212-308-3300.

COMPANY STAFF

Intendant. Ulrich Burkhardt.
Bibliography. Das Meininger Theater— Südthüringisches Staatstheater (Meiningen, 1994).

MUNICH

Staatstheater am Gärtnerplatz

On June 19, 1948, the Staatstheater am Gärtnerplatz, previously known as the Königlicher Theater am Gärtnerplatz, as well as the Gärtnerplatztheater, reopened with Johann Strauß's *Eine Nacht in Venedig*. The building had been severely damaged during the war. The original theater, called the Actien-Volkstheater, was inaugurated on November 4, 1865, with a festival show, including allegorical Festspiele *Was wir wollen* and *Eine musikalische Soirée in der Vorstadt*, and excerpts from *Le nozze di Figaro*. The theater was designed by Franz Michael Reiffenstuel.

Eight years after opening, the theater was renamed the Königlicher Theater am Gärtnerplatz and became the third court stage in Bavaria. It was primarily a home for operetta, and many world premieres of the genre were mounted in the house. Strauß's *Die Fledermaus* was first heard in the theater on July 10, 1875, followed by the world premiere of Richard Genée's *Die letzten Mohikaner* on September 10, 1878. Karl Millöcker's *Der Bettelstudent* had its first performance at the theater on February 15, 1883. Two years later, Millöcker conducted some works at the opera house. The world premiere of Alfred Zamara's *Der Doppelgänger* took place on September 16, 1886, with the first performance in Munich of Arthur Sullivan's *Mikado* occurring that same year. The following year, Herman Zumpe's *Farinelli* received its world premiere on March 19, 1887, followed by Josef Krägel's *Die Zuaven* on May 28, 1889. Munich first saw Jacques Offenbach's *Les contes d'Hoffmann* on November 16, 1889. Some of the artists appearing at the Königlicher Theater am Gärtnerplatz were Adolf Brakl, Eduard Brummer, Konrad Dreher, Analie Schönchen, Joseph Benz, and Elise Bach.

After the turn of the century, Richard Weinhöppl's *Das Gespenst Matschatsch* was world pre-

miered on January 18, 1905, and by 1907, Strauß's *Die Fledermaus* had received 300 performances. Franz Lehár's *Die lustige Witwe* achieved 300 performances the next year. The *Uraufführung* of Wilhelm Mauke's *Der Tugendprinz* took place on April 23, 1910, and that of Richard Trunk's *Herzdame* on May 5, 1917. A decade later, Richard Tauber was a guest artist in Strauß's *Zigeunerbaron* and in 1928, Munich saw its first Ernst Křenek's *Jonny spielt auf*. Lehár conducted the first Munich performance of his *Das Land des Lächelns* with Tauber as Sou Chong. The theater came under the control of the Free State of Bavaria on April 8, 1937, and the next year, Johannes Heersters made his debut as Graf Danilo in Lehár's *Die lustige Witwe*. In 1939, Karl Valentin appeared as Frosch in Strauß's *Die Fledermauß*.

After the war, operetta was performed in the Theater an der Schornstraße. The opening night took place on December 7, 1945, with excerpts from a variety of pieces. The following year the world premieres continued, including Karlheinz Gutheim's *Helene wenig fromm*. After the company moved back to Gärtnerplatz, Edmund Nick's *Das Halsband der Königin* graced the stage for the first time ever. At the beginning of the 1950s a folk opera from Oscar Straus, *Bozena*, was premiered on May 16, 1952. A decade later, the first German performance of Nikokay Rimsky-Korsakov's *Snegurochka* (The Snow Maiden) was staged on March 14, 1962, signaling a turn toward operatic performances. A folk opera from Mark Lothar was world premiered on February 8, 1968, after which the theater was closed for renovations. It reopened on September 10, 1969, with Jean-Philippe Rameau's *Platée*. The German premiere of Dmitry Shostakovich's *Nos* (The Nose) was given on February 18, 1971, and the first staging of Carl Orff's *Die Bernauerin* took place on April 28,

1976. During the 1980s, the *Uraufführung* of Wilfried Hiller's *Der Goggolori* was offered on February 3, 1985, followed by Werner Egk's *Die Zaubergeige* on October 29, 1989. The 1990s saw a continuation of premieres with Paul Engel's *Daniel* on February 16, 1994, and the first Munich performance of Boris Blacher's *Preußisches Märchen* on October 22, 1995. The theater offers a mixture of opera, light opera, operetta, and musicals.

The production quality varies. Some are imaginative and others are uninspired. One production of *Les contes d'Hoffmann* fell into the latter category and the quality of the ensemble singing was mediocre. All operas are sung in German. The problem was a lack of nuance and tone coloration from the orchestra and the voices. But it is a *Volkstheater*, opera for the people, and cannot be compared to the quality at the Bayerische Staatsoper.

Staatstheater am Gärtnerplatz

The theater is a large, white structure, with a facade of arched windows, Doric columns that form a portico, a pediment embellished with music motifs and crowned by a Muse statue. The Biedermeier style auditorium holds four tiers in a lyre shape. Dark marble Muses draped with golden cloth flank the center royal box. Raspberry velvet seats contrast with the gold-trimmed red curtain, and music motifs, putti, and flower-filled vases decorate the dome ceiling. There are 932 seats.

Practical Information. Staatstheater am Gärtnerplatz, Gärtnerplatz, 80455 Munich. Tel: 49 89 202 411, Fax: 49 89 266 499. When visiting the Staatstheater am Gärtnerplatz stay at the Hotel Rafael, Neuturmstraße 1, 80331 München. Tel: 49 89 29 09 80, Fax: 49 89 22-25-39. The Hotel Rafael is centrally located and only steps from the opera house. The hotel can assist with opera tickets and schedule.

COMPANY STAFF

Intendanten. Klaus Schultz, (1997–present), Hellmuth Matiasek (1983–96), Kurt Pscherer (1964–83), Arno Assmann (1959–63), Willy Duvoisin (1955–58), Curth Hurrle (1946–52).

Bibliography. Thomas Siedhoff (ed.), *125 Jahre Gärtnerplatztheater: Vom Actien-Volkstheater zu Münchens anderer Oper* (Munich, 1990). *Staatstheater am Gärtnerplatz: 13 Jahre Gärtnerplatztheater, 13 Jahre Intendanz, Hellmuth Matiasek* (Munich, 1996). *Thanks to Helga Dowideit, Staatstheater am Gärtnerplatz.*

Bayerische Staatsoper–Cuvilliéstheater

Richard Strauss's *Die Frau ohne Schatten* opened the third Nationaltheater on November 21, 1963. Gerhard Graubner and Karl Fischer were responsible for the project. The previous opera house, the Hof- und Nationaltheater, had been destroyed during a bombing raid on October 4, 1943. It was opened on January 2, 1825, with a ballet, *Cinderella*, and was a reconstruction of the original opera house which had burned to the ground only two years earlier, on January 14, 1823. The first Hof- und Nationaltheater was inaugurated on October 12, 1818, with Albert Klebe and Ferdinand Fränzl's *Die Weihe*. Karl von Fischer designed the structure. Fischer died in 1820, so when the theater was consumed by fire, Leo von Klenze was responsible for the building which followed Fischer's original plans, but incorporating some of his own ideas.

Back in 1651, Elector Maximilian I celebrated the marriage of his son, Ferdinand Maria to Henriette Adelaide of Savoy with a *commedia cantata*. Two years later, in 1653, the new Italian style opera arrived in Munich when Giovanni Battista Maccioni's *L'arpa festante* was performed in the Herkulessaal der Residenz, a chamber theater that Elector Ferdinand Maria had constructed. Around the same time, Ferdinand Maria built Germany's first detached opera house, Opernhaus am Salvatorplatz. Dubbed the "oat box" since it was a converted old grain storage house, the theater was a Baroque jewel inside. Pietro Zambonini's *La ninfa ritrosa* opened with house in 1654. After renovations, the theater reopened with Johann Kaspar von Kerll's *Oronte* in 1657. The first documented German-language opera took place in 1681, Veit Weinberger's *Lisimen und Calliste*. Italian opera, however, dominated for almost a century. Beginning in 1688, Agostino Steffani wrote six operas for the court, including *Servio Tullio* and *Niobe*. Another theater, the Altes Residenztheater, better known as the Cuvilliéstheater after its architect François

Staatstheater am Gärtnerplatz (Munich, Germany).

Cuvilliés, was opened on October 12, 1753, with Giovanni Battista Ferrandini's *Catone in Utica*. Here the world premiere of Wolfgang Amadeus Mozart's *Idomeneo* took place on January 29, 1781. *Opera buffa* found a home in the Redouten-haus on Prannerstraße where Mozart's *La finta giardiniera* was premiered on January 13, 1775, in the presence of the composer, and Carl Maria von Weber's *Abu Hassan* on June 4, 1811. Munich also hosted other Mozart works: *Don Giovanni,*

Die Entführung aus dem Serail, and *Die Zauberflöte.*

Discussion about building an opera house to replace the aging Opernhaus am Salvatorplatz (torn down in 1802) began in 1792, but nothing was done until Duke Max IV Joseph (later King Max I Joseph), impressed with Paris's Théâtre de l'Odéon while on a trip to the city, commanded a similar theater built on the palace grounds. The cost was 800,000 gold ducats with King Max I Joseph, himself, laying the cornerstone. After the Hof- und Nationaltheater opened in 1818, most of Munich's operatic activity took place there. The works of Gioachino Rossini were especially popular with no fewer than 15 gracing the stage, including *L'italiana in Algeri, La Cenerentola, Otello, Elisabetta, regina d'Inghilterra,* and the German premieres of *Eduardo e Cristina, Tovaldo e Dorliska,* and *Semiramide.* The king paid most of the rebuilding costs after fire ravaged the first opera house. The year the opera house reopened, 1825, King Ludwig I ascended to the throne. He closed the Volkstheater at Isartor and disbanded Italian opera, helping pave the way for local talent. Opera reached new heights in 1836 when Franz Lachner was appointed general music director. A composer in his own right, he premiered his *Catharina Cornaro* in 1841, and although his works were popular at the time, they have since fallen into obscurity. He introduced many new works to Munich, those of Charles Gounod, Giacomo Meyerbeer, Gaetano Donizetti, Albert Lortzing, Daniel Auber, Louis Spohr, Heinrich Marschner, Fromental Halévy, Friedrich von Flotow, and Giuseppe Verdi. Verdi's *Ernani* was premiered on April 13, 1848. He also conducted the Munich premiere of *Tannhäuser* on August 12, 1855, and *Lohengrin* on February 28, 1858. Later he distanced himself from Wagner, taking leave in 1865 and resigning his post in 1868. With the ascent to the throne of King Ludwig II, Wagner received royal patronage that led to the world premieres at the opera house of *Tristan und Isolde* (June 10, 1865), *Die Meistersinger von Nürnberg* (June 21, 1868), *Das Rheingold* (September 22, 1869), and *Die Walküre* (June 26, 1870). Although *Siegfried* and *Götterdämmerung* were introduced at Bayreuth, the entire Ring Cycle took place at the Hof- und Nationaltheater in November 1878. After Wagner's death, *Die Feen* was premiered on June 29, 1888.

With the dawn of the 1900s, a Mozart renaissance took place in the Cuvilliéstheater, called "the site of the stylistically correct Mozart performances," and the Prinzregenten Theater was opened (see Prinzregenten entry). Novelties continued at the Hof-und Nationaltheater with Ermanno Wolf-Ferrari's *Le donne curiose, I quattro rusteghi,* and *Il segreto di Susanna,* Hans Pfitzner's *Das Christelflein* and *Palestrina* and Erich Wolfgang Korngold's *Violanta* and *Der Ring des Polykrates,* among others. Strauss's operas played a prominent role on the schedule, but *Salome* and *Elektra* shocked the middle-class audience. Renowned artists sang with the company, including Enrico Caruso, Karl Erb, and Maria Ivogün in her debut in 1913 as Mimi in Giacomo Puccini's *La bohème.* When the era of royalty ended in 1918, Hof was dropped from the theater's name.

The Nationaltheater continued to be a showcase for contemporary music after World War I, with *Uraufführungen* of both major and long-forgotten works, including Hugo Röhr's *Coeur Dame,* Jaromir Weinberger's *Die geliebte Stimme,* Gian Francesco Malipiero's *Torneo notturno,* and Pfitzner's *Das Herz.* By 1933, the Nazis were in power and they eliminated all Jewish artists and anyone else who disagreed with them. Both Intendant Clemens von Franckenstein and Generalmusikdirektor Hans Knappertsbusch had to flee. Then Clemens Krauss, more to the Nazis's taste, assumed both posts and mounted the world premieres of Strauss's *Der Friedenstag* and *Capriccio,* and Karl Orff's *Der Mond.* The Third Reich had planned to give Munich a new, 3,000-seat opera house, located near the Hauptbahnhof and designed by Waldemar Brinkmann, but the project never materialized. The Nationaltheater was destroyed during the war.

Opera resumed on November 15, 1945, at the Prinzregenten-Theater with Beethoven's *Fidelio.* Mozart's *Le nozze di Figaro* reopened the Cuvilliéstheater on June 12, 1958. His works dominated at the Cuvilliéstheater, which also introduced Heinrich Sutermeister's *Seraphine oder Die stumme Apothekerin* and *Le Roi Bérenger,* and Günter Bialas's *Die Geschichte von Aucassin und Nicolette.* The Nationaltheater reopened in 1963, with ex–King Umberto of Italy, ex–Queen Soraya, and Begum Aga Khan, along with Europe's most prominent families in attendance. Around a week later, the Bayerische Staatsoper continued in its role of introducing contemporary German operas, with

Werner Egk's *Die Verlobung in San Domingo*, Aribert Reimann's *Lear* and *Troades*, Giuseppe Sinopoli's *Lou Salomé*, and Volker David Kirchner's *Belshazar* on the boards. During the 20th century, the company has mounted more than five dozen world premieres.

The Bavarian State Opera presents the quintessential productions of Strauss operas, from a rich, glittery *Die Liebe der Danae*, to a straightforward, Japanese-inspired *Die Frau ohne Schatten*, with lavish costumes and eye-catching special effects. The singing is high quality and the conducting exceptional. Other productions have been experimental, even avant-garde. One was the staging of Hector Berlioz's *La Damnation de Faust*, which in the American rating system could be classified as "x-rated." The Bayerische Staatsoper offers more than 30 operas a year at the Nationaltheater, in addition to performances at the Cuvilliéstheater and the Prinzregenten-Theater. Recent repertory included Strauss's *Salome, Ariadne auf Naxos, Der Rosenkavalier*, Verdi's *Simon Boccanegra, La traviata, Il trovatore, Aida*, and *Nabucco*, Wagner's *Tristan und Isolde, Götterdämmerung, Siegfried, Parsifal, Die Meistersinger von Nürnberg*, Mozart's *Die Zauberflöte, Le nozze di Figaro, Così fan tutte*, Benjamin Britten's *Peter Grimes*, and Henze's *Der junge Lord*, among others.

Nationaltheater

A decade after the opera house was destroyed, the citizens of Munich formed the Friends of the Nationaltheater in 1953, starting an annual lottery to raise money for reconstruction. They raised around $5 million, and the Freistaat Bayern paid the remaining $15 million needed. Reconstruction began in 1958, and lasted five years.

The Neoclassical Nationaltheater offers a massive portico formed by eight huge Corinthian columns supporting an unadorned pediment. The auditorium holds five ivory and gold tiers which curve around in a horseshoe-shape. The pink one of the space and rose-colored orchestra seats contrast with the sky-blue proscenium and royal box seats, and blue-hued ceiling. Heavy Corinthian columns flank the proscenium boxes, and large caryatids guard the royal box. The room is poorly balanced, fusing the delicate with the massive in an uneven harmony. There are 2,120 seats.

Cuvilliéstheater

Although the Cuvilliéstheater, or altes Residenztheater theater, was also destroyed during the war, its interior had been dismantled and stored. When the theater reopened in 1958, the original decor was restored to the gold, ivory, and raspberry-colored, rococo-style auditorium. Four intricately ornamented tiers curve around the space, which contains a red-and gold-crowned royal box in the center, surrounded by cherubs and goddesses. Electrified crystal chandeliers light the silk-lined auditorium. Horn-blowing cherubs embellish the marble gray proscenium arch. The theater has 442 seats.

Practical Information. Bayerische Staatsoper, Max-Joseph-Platz 2, 80539 Munich. Tel: 49 89 218-501, Fax: 49 89 218-51003. When visiting the Bayerische Staatsoper stay at the Hotel Rafael, Neuturmstraße 1, 80331 Munchen. Tel: 49 89 29 09 80, Fax: 49 89 22-25-39. The Hotel Rafael is centrally located and only steps from the opera house. The hotel can assist with opera tickets and schedule.

COMPANY STAFF AND PREMIERES

Intendanten. Peter Jonas (1993–present), Wolfgang Sawallisch (1982–93), August Everding (1977–82), Wolfgang Sawallisch (1976–77), Günther Rennert (1967–76), Rudolf Hartmann (1952–67), Georg Hartmann (1947–52), Clemens Krauss (1937–44), Oskar Walleck (1934–37), Clemens von Franckenstein (1924–34), Karl Zeiß (1920–24), Clemens von Franckenstein (1912–18), Albert von Speidel (1905–12), Ernst von Possart (1893–1905), Karl von Perfall (1867–93), Wilhelm Schmitt (1860–67), August von Frays (1857–60), Franz von Dingelstedt (1851–57), August von Frays (1844–51), Eduard Yrsch (1842–44), Theodor von Küstner (1833–42), Johann Nep. von Poißl (1824–33), Karl August Delamotte (1811–1821), Josef Marius Babo (1799–1810).

World Premieres. (1900–1998): A. Gentili's *Weihnachten*, December 29, 1900; M. Zenger's *Eros und Psyche*, January 11, 1901; S. Wagner's *Herzog Wildfang*, March 23, 1901; J.M. Weber's *Die neue Mamsell*, November 21, 1901; K. von Kaskel's *Der Dusle und das Babeli*, February 11, 1903; E. Wolf-Ferrari's *Le donne curiose*, November 27, 1903; R. Hugo's *Das Vaterunser*, June 14, 1904; E. Wolf-Ferrari's *I quattro rusteghi*, March 19, 1906; H. Pfitzner's *Das Christelflein*, December 11, 1906; A. Beer-Wallbrunn's *Don Quijote, der sinnreiche Junker von der Mancha*, Janaury 1, 1908; E. Wolf-Ferrari's *Il segreto di Sussana*, December 4, 1909; W. Mauke's *Fanfreluche*, April 27, 1912; P. von Klenau's *Sulamith*, November 16, 1913; E. Korngold's *Der Ring des*

Nationaltheater (Munich, Germany).

Polykrates, March 28, 1916; E. Korngold's *Violanta,* March 28, 1916; H. Pfitzner's *Palestrina,* June 12, 1917; W. Courvoisier's *Lanzelot und Elaine,* November 3, 1917; P. Graener's *Theophano,* June 5, 1918; W. Mauke's *Die letzte Maske,* March 6, 1920; F. Schreker's *Das Spielwerk,* October 30, 1920; W. Braunfels's *Die Vögel,* November 30, 1920; W. Courvoisier's *Die Krähen,* April 28, 1921; W. Braunfels's *Don Gil von den grünen,* November 15, 1924; G. Vollerthun's *Island-Saga,* January 17, 1925; H. Röhr's *Coeur-Dame,* January 15, 1927; E. Wolf-Ferrari's *La veste di cielo,* April 21, 1927; A. Coates's *Samuel Pepys,* December 21, 1929; A. Piechler's *Der weiße Pfau,* April 10, 1930; J. Weismann's *Die Gespenstersonate,* December 19, 1930; J. Weinberger's *Die geliebte Stimme,* February 28, 1931; G.F. Malipiero's *Torneo notturno* (Komödie des Todes), May 15, 1931; H. Pfitzner's *Das Herz,* November 12, 1931; R. Heger's *Bettler Namenlos,* April 8, 1932; V. Giannini's *Lucedia,* October 20, 1934; K.A. Fischer's *Eulenspiegel,* April 9, 1935; R. Strauss's *Friedenstag,* July 24, 1938; C. Orff's *Der Mond,* February 5, 1939; R. Strauss's *Capriccio,* October 28, 1942; H. Sutermeister's *Seraphine oder Die stumme Apothekerin,* February 25, 1960 (Cuvilliéstheater); W. Egk's *Die Verlobung in San Domingo,* November 27, 1963; M. Spoliansky's *Wie lernt man Liebe…,* March 5, 1967; J. Cikker's *Das Spiel von Liebe und Tod,* August 1, 1969; G. Bialas's *Die Geschichte von Aucassin und Nicolette,* December 12, 1969 (Cuvilliéstheater); W. Haupt's *Sümtome,* December 15, 1970; I. Yun's *Sim Tjong,* August 1, 1972; J. Tal's *Die Versuchung,* July 26, 1976; A. Reimann's *Lear,* July 9, 1978; W. Hiller's *An diesem heutigen Tage,* July 15, 1979 (Marstalltheater); W. Hiller's *Ijob,* July 15, 1979 (Marstalltheater); B. Lorentzen's *Eine wundersame Liebesgeschichte für Sopran, Tenor, Bariton,* December 2, 1979; W. Haupt's *Neurosen-Kavalier,* March 13, 1980 (Marstalltheater); R. Anton's *"der siebte,"* March 13, 1980 (Marstalltheater); G. Sinopoli's *Lou Salomé,* May 10, 1981; R. Febel's *Euridice,* November 10, 1983 (Marstalltheater); H. Sutermeister's *Le Roi Bérenger,* July 22, 1985 (Cuvilliéstheater); V.D. Kirchner's *Belshazar,* January 25, 1986; A. Reimann's *Troades,* July 7, 1986; A. Ruppert's *Der letzte Orpheus,* November 29, 1989 (Marstalltheater); V. Heyn's *Geisterbahn,* May 16, 1990 (Marstalltheater); R. Platz's *Dunkles Haus,* June 6, 1991 (Marstalltheater); K.Penderecki's *Ubu Rex,* July 6, 1991; S. Oswell & F. Hummel, *Laokoon,* February 21, 1992 (Marstalltheater); H.J. Hespos's *"augen der wörter,"* April 30, 1992 (Marstalltheater); F. Schreker's *Drei phantastische Geschichten,* November 12, 1992; T. Jelde's *Hans und Grete,* December 16, 1993

(Marstalltheater); H.J. von Bose's *Der ganz normale Wahsinn: "Liebe, Haß, Sehnsucht, Tod*, June 24, 1994 (Marstalltheater); E. Mayer's *Sansibar*, July 18, 1994 (Cuvilliéstheater); A. Askin's *Trommeln im Licht*, December 31, 1994; W. Osborne's *Beeb and Bab*, January 4, 1995; H.J. von Bose's *Schlarchthof 5*, July 1, 1996, Henze's *Venus und Adonis*, January 11, 1997, Trojahn's *Was Ihr Wollt*, May 17, 1998 (Cuvilliéstheater).

Bibliography. Hans Zehetmair and Jürgen Schläder (ed.), *Nationaltheater: Die Bayerische Staatsoper* (Munich, 1992). *The Munich National Theater: From Royal Court Theatre to the Bavarian State Opera* (Munich, 1991). *Jahrbücher der Bayerischen Staatsoper 1989–1996* (Munich, 1989–1995).

Thanks to Bianca Mundt and Franziska Hunke, Bayerische Staatsoper.

Prinzregenten-Theater

On November 10, 1996, the "new" Prinzregenten-Theater opened with a gala production of Richard Wagner's *Tristan und Isolde*, signaling a renewal of operatic activity at the theater. Lorin Maazel conducted the Bayerische Rundfunk Orchestra for the occasion. The theater was named after the Prinzregent, since he "restored reason" to the throne, after the excesses of his nephew "mad" King Ludwig II.

The Prinzregenten-Theater was first inaugurated on August 21, 1901, with Wagner's *Die Meistersinger von Nürnburg*, launching Munich's first Wagner festival, to the displeasure of Cosima Wagner, who wanted a monopoly of Wagner's works at Bayreuth. The first festival, in addition to the inaugural opera, offered *Tannhäuser*, *Tristan und Isolde*, and *Lohengrin*. The theater, a copy of Bayreuth's Festspielhaus, was also built as a Festspielhaus devoted to presenting Wagner's works. After World War I, the theater was converted into a *Volksbühne* (people's stage), and offered spoken drama. When the National Socialists seized power, it became a Nazi propaganda tool known as the "Cultural Center for the German Worker." The motto was *Kraft durch Freude* (Strength through Joy). The posters proclaimed *Das Theater des Volkes ist Dein Theater* (The Theater of the People is Your Theater.)

The Prinzregenten-Theater received a new lease on life after World War II. With the Nationaltheater in ruins, the Bayerische Staatsoper moved in, calling the Prinzregenten-Theater home for 17 years. The Staatsoper opened in their new venue with Ludwig van Beethoven's *Fidelio* on November 15, 1945, under the musical direction of Bertil Wetzelsberger, with Hans Hotter, Franz Klarwein, and Helena Braun. The rest of the season offered Giacomo Puccini's *La bohème*, Eugen d'Albert's *Tiefland*, Carl Maria von Weber's *Der Freischütz*, and Bedřich Smetana's *Prodaná nevěsta* (The Bartered Bride). During its seasons

in residence, the operas of Wagner, Wolfgang Amadeus Mozart, Richard Strauss, and contemporary works dominated. In addition to two world premieres, Henri Tomasi's *Don Juan de Manara* on March 29, 1956, and Paul Hindemith's *Die Harmonie der Welt* on August 11, 1957, it hosted the first Munich performances of Arthur Honegger's *Johanna auf dem Scheiterhaufen* on January 22, 1953, Werner Egk's *Irischer Legende* on March 22, 1957, and *Columbus* on May 3, 1960, Alban Berg's *Wozzeck* May 29, 1957, and Orff's *Oedipus der Tyrann* on March 23, 1961.

Once the Bayerische Staatsoper moved back to the Nationaltheater in November 1963, the opera house experienced a decline in fortunes. The authorities condemned the building as unsafe and closed it, and so it remained for almost a quarter of a century. When it was reopened in 1988, it did not have the capabilities to host opera, thus its second overhaul. Now it offers two operas a year. Recently productions include Claudio Monteverdi's *L'incoronazione di Poppea* and Engelbert Humperdinck's *Hänsel und Gretel*.

Practical Information. Prinzregenten-Theater, Prinzregentenplatz 12, 81675 Munich. Tel: 49 89 29 16 14, Fax: 49 89 21 85 28 13. When visiting the Prinzregenten-Theater stay at the Hotel Rafael, Neuturmstraße 1, 80331 München. Tel: 49 89 29 09 80, Fax: 49 89 22-25-39. The Hotel Rafael is centrally located and convenient to the Prinzregenten-Theater. The hotel can assist with opera tickets and schedule.

COMPANY STAFF AND PREMIERES

General Musikdirektors (1946–1963). Georg Solti (1946–51), Rudolf Kempe (1952–54), Ferenc Fricsay (1956–58), Joseph Keilberth (1959–63).

World Premieres. H. Tomasi's *Don Juan de Manara*, March 29, 1956; P. Hindemith's *Die Harmonie der Welt*, August 11, 1957.

Prinzregenten-Theater (Munich, Germany).

Bibliography. Klaus Jürgen Seidel (ed.), *Das Prinzregenten-Theater in München* (Nurenburg, 1984). Hans Zehetmair and Jürgen Schläder (ed.), *Nationaltheater: Die Bayerische Staatsoper* (Munich, 1992).
Thanks to Manfred Mayer, Prinzregenten-Theater.

MÜNSTER

Städtische Bühnen

Wolfgang Amadeus Mozart's *Die Zauberflöte* inaugurated the Städtische Bühnen on February 4, 1956. The architects responsible for the unusual, modern building were Deilmann, von Hausen, Rave, and Ruhnau. The previous theater, the Lortzing-Theater was damaged by fire during the night of July 9-10, 1941. Bombs eventually wrecked it. Albert Lortzing's *Zar und Zimmermann* had inaugurated the theater on November 11, 1895.

Münster opened its first permanent theater, the 500-seat Komödienhaus, on October 12, 1775. It boasted a royal box and two galleries for the aristocracy and military. Traveling troupes provided the entertainment, which included opera.

In 1818, a new theater opened which offered the world premiere of Albert Lortzing's first opera, *Ali Pascha* on February 1, 1828. A lyrical play, *Hochfeuer,* and an oratorio, *Die Himmelfahrt Jesu Christi,* followed. The theater, however, found itself frequently in financial difficulties. It was closed in 1882 for reasons of fire safety. The Lortzing-Theater opened in 1895, and was named in honor of Lortzing, for the time he spent in Münster. In 1922, the city took over the running of the theater, and the stage saw mainly drama. After the war, performances took place in the reception room of the town hall, but opera only entered the repertory near the end of the 1940s. Works of Giuseppe Verdi, Wolfgang Amadeus Mozart, along with

Richard Strauss's *Elektra*, Carl Orff's *Die Kluge* and the world premiere of Hans Brehme's *Der versiegelte Bürgermeister*, were in evidence.

After the Städtische Bühnen opened in 1956, several modern works were offered from Ernst Křenek, Giselher Klebe, and Wolfgang Fortner. The end of the 1970s and early 1980s continued with the modern repertory, including the world premiere of Dieter Schönbach's (after Alessandro Scarlatti) *Come Santo Francesco*, and Hans Ulrich Engelmann's *Der Fall von Damm* and *Die Mauer*. Recent repertory includes Giacomo Puccini's *Tosca*, Mozart's *Le nozze di Figaro*, Verdi's *La forza* *del destino*, and Leoš Janáček's *Z Mrtvého Domu* (From the House of the Dead).

Practical Information. Städtische Bühnen, Neubrückenstraße 63, 48127 Münster. Tel: 49 251 590-9100, Fax: 49 251 590-9202. If visiting, contact the German National Tourist Office, 747 Third Avenue, 33rd Floor, New York, NY 10017. Tel: 212-308-3300.

COMPANY STAFF

Intendant. Thomas Bockelmann.

--- NÜRNBERG

Städtische Bühnen

The Städtische Bühnen, also known as the Nürnberger Opernhaus, was opened on September 1, 1905, with a Festspiel *Im neuen Haus* by the mayor of the city, and the last scene from Richard Wagner's *Die Meistersinger von Nürnberg*. Heinrich Seeling was the architect.

Three days after the inauguration of the new opera house, a complete production of *Die Meistersinger von Nürnberg* was staged. In addition to the standard repertory, the works of Richard Strauss, Giacomo Puccini, Pietro Mascagni, Engelbert Humperdinck, Wilhelm Kienzl, and Hans Pfitzner graced the stage. Of special note were Felix Mottl conducting *Tristan und Isolde*, the 1913 production of *Parsifal*, a mounting of the complete Ring Cycle, and Jacques Offenbach's *La belle Hélène*. After World War I, full opera seasons were mounted. The repertory offered more than two dozen German operas, at least a half a dozen Italian operas, and a few French, Russian or Slavic works. Included among the German works were Wagner's *Tristan und Isolde*, *Tannhäuser*, *Lohengrin*, and *Der Ring des Nibelungen*, Albert Lortzing's *Undine*, *Zar und Zimmermann*, and *Der Waffenschmied*, Mozart's *Die Entführung aus dem Serail*, Erich Wolfgang Korngold's *Die tote Stadt*, Eugen d'Albert's *Tiefland*, Pfitzner's *Palestrina*, Strauss's *Der Rosenkavalier*, *Die Frau ohne Schatten*, and *Salome*, Friedrich von Flotow's *Martha* and *Alessandro Stradella*, Carl Maria von Weber's *Der Freischütz*, and Ernst Křenek's *Jonny spielt auf*. The operas of Giuseppe Verdi played a commanding role among the Italian works offered, including *Il trovatore*, *Aida*, *La forza del destino*, *Otello*, *Rigoletto*, and *Un ballo in maschera*, as well as Giacomo Puccini's *La bohème*, *Turandot*, and *Tosca*, Domenico Cimarosa's *Il matrimonio segreto*, Pietro Mascagni's *Cavalleria rusticana*, Ruggero Leoncavallo's *I pagliacci*, Mozart's *Don Giovanni* and *Così fan tutte*, and Ermanno Wolf-Ferrari's *I quattro rusteghi*. On the French side, Giacomo Meyerbeer's *La Juive* and *L'Africaine*, Georges Bizet's *Carmen* and *Les pêcheurs de perles*, Adolphe Adam's *Le Postillon de Longjumeau*, Daniel Auber's *Fra Diavolo*, Adrien Boïeldieu's *La Dame Blanche*, Charles Gounod's *Faust*, and Ambroise Thomas's *Mignon* graced the stage. Leoš Janáček's *Jenůfa*, Alexander Borodin's *Prince Igor*, and Modest Mussorgsky's *Sorochintsy Fair* were among the Russian and Slavic operas. In the fall of 1944, after a performance of Wagner's *Götterdämmerung*, the opera house was closed. Although it was damaged in 1945, it was useable and opera performances began almost immediately after the war, with Mozart's *Die Zauberflöte* on October 29, 1945. Engelbert Humperdinck's *Hänsel und Gretel*, Verdi's *Un ballo in maschera*, Mascagni's *Cavalleria rusticana*, and Mozart's *Die Entführung aus dem Serail* completed the season. By the 1950s the repertory had more than a dozen offerings, including novelties like Gian Carlo Menotti's *The Consul*, Carl Orff's *Der Mond* and *Die Kluge*, Bedřich Smetana's *Prodaná nevěsta* (The Bartered Bride), Werner Egk's *Peer Gynt*, Franz Lehner's *Die schlaue Susanna*, Igor Stravinsky's *Oedipus Rex*, and Joseph Haas's *Tobias Wunderlich*.

Städtische Bühnen (Nürnberg, Germany).

The productions are avant-garde, experimental to the point of absurdity. One production of Strauss's *Elektra* had Elektra crawling around the stage on all fours, wolves were on the sides and top of the proscenium, and a four-foot-high, pink-and-white penis was stationed in a prominent position for the entire opera. The production was irritating, and appeared to be the work of a self-indulgent director expressing his personal vision of the opera which had no relationship to anything else.

Recent repertory included Alban Berg's *Wozzeck*, Gioachino Rossini's *Il barbiere di Siviglia*, Sergey Prokofiev's *Ognennïy angel*, Fromental Halévy's *La Juive*, Carl Maria von Weber's *Der Freischütz*, Arnold Schönberg's *Moses und Aron*, Wolfgang Rihm's *Die Eroberung von Mexico*, Christoph Willibald Gluck's *Iphigénie en Tauride*, and Mozart's *Don Giovanni*.

Nürnberger Opernhaus

The initial building of the opera house took four years, lasting from 1901 to 1905. It was reconstructed in 1935 by Paul Schulze-Naumburg.

The opera house exterior, in the "Gründerzeit" style, has remained essentially unaltered since its construction. The 1995-renovated auditorium holds three tiers in a horseshoe configuration. The white-gray parapets are ornamented with gilded musical motifs and medallions. Rose colored columns with gilded Corinthian capitals support the tiers. The proscenium arch, embellished with gilded decorations, is bordered in gold. Deep coral velvet seats match similarly colored walls. There are 1061 seats, many of which have very poor sight-lines.

Practical Information. Städtische Bühnen, Richard Wagner Platz 2-10, 90443 Nürnberg. Tel: 49 911 231 3808, Fax: 49 911 231-3534. When visiting the Städtische Bühnen, stay at the Maritim Hotel Nürnberg, Nürnberg. Tel: 49 911 236-3824, Fax: 49 911 236-3823. Centrally located, Maritim Hotel Nürnberg is very near the opera house. The hotel can assist with tickets and schedule.

COMPANY STAFF

Intendanten. Lew Bogdan, Burkhard Mauer, Hans Gierster, Karl Pschigode, Walter Bruno Iltz, Willy Hanke, Johannes Maurach, Willy Stuhlfeld, Alois Federler, Richard Balder.

Bibliography. F. Bröger (ed.), *50 Jahre Opernhaus: Städtische Bühnen Nürnberg-Fürth* (Nürnberg, 1955). Peter Kertz & Ingeborg Strößenreuther, *Bibliographie zur Theatergeschichte Nürnbergs* (Nürnberg, 1964). Jürgen Söllner, *Nürnberger Theater: Das Opernhaus* (Nürnberg, 1986). Robert Plank (ed.), *Festschrift anläßlich der Wiedereröffnung des Nürnberg Opernhauses, September 1935* (Nürnberg, 1935).
Thanks to Gabriele Nutz, Städtische Bühnen Nürnberg.

Pocket Opera Company

The Pocket Opera Company was founded in the 1970s. One of its purposes has been to make modern Italian music theater better known in Germany. To this end, the company recently presented the world premiere of Alessandro Melchiorre's chamber opera *Unreported Inbound Palermo*, which dealt with a 1980 plane crash in Italy. It was a co-production with the Teatro Comunale, Bologna. Additional commissioned works include one from composer Andrea Molino on the topic of "Advertisement and Communication," and another from composer Ivan Fedele.

Practical Information. Pocket Opera Company, Gertrudstraße 21, 90429 Nürnberg. Tel: 49 911 32 90 47, Fax: 49 911 31 46 06. If visiting, contact the German National Tourist Office, 747 Third Avenue, 33rd Floor, New York, NY 10017. Tel: 212-308-3300.

COMPANY STAFF

Künstlerischer Leiter (artistic director). Beat Wyrsch.

Bibliography. Adrian Mai, *Streiflicht-Ein neuer Schwerpunkt der Pocket Opera Company*, *Orpheus* (Berlin, May 1998).

OLDENBURG

Oldenburgisches Staatstheater

The 861-seat Staatstheater, designed in Neoclassical style by P. Zimmer, opened in 1893. The first theater in the city was founded in 1833 and an ensemble from Bremen offered opera performances. Another theater opened on October 8, 1881, but survived only a decade before fire claimed it. Two years later, in 1893, the present theater opened and in 1929 offered Alban Berg's

Wozzeck. Ludwig Leopold became *General-musikdirektor* in 1936 and five years later, a festival was held commemorating opera in the city. The first operas given after the war were Richard Strauss's *Salome* and Benjamin Britten's *Peter Grimes.* The late 1960s and early 1970s saw Giacomo Puccini's *Turandot,* Berg's *Lulu,* Paul Dessau's *Die Verurteilung des Lukullus,* Claude Debussy's *Pelléas et Mélisande,* and Igor Stravinsky's *Solovey* (The Nightingale) and *Mavra,* among others. Recent repertory includes Puccini's *La bohème,* Gaetano Donizetti's *Don Pasquale,* Johann Strauß's *Die Fledermauß.*

Practical Information. Oldenburgisches Staatstheater, Theaterwall 19, 26122 Oldenburg. Tel: 49 441 222-5111, Fax: 49 441 222-5222. If visiting, contact the German National Tourist Office, 747 Third Avenue, 33rd Floor, New York, NY 10017. Tel: 212-308-3300.

COMPANY STAFF

Intendant. Stephan Mettin.
Bibliography. H. Schmidt (ed.), *Hoftheater, Landestheater, Staatstheater: Beiträge zur Geschichte des Oldenburgischen Theaters 1833–1933* (Oldenburg, 1983).

Städtische Bühnen

Calderon's *Über allem Zauber der Liebe* inaugurated the Städtische Bühnen on September 9, 1950. The previous theater was first damaged in 1942 and then totally destroyed on March 25, 1945. It had been inaugurated on September 29, 1909, with William Shakespeare's *Julius Caesar.* Friedrich Lehmann designed the theater in Jugendstil.

The first director of the theater "revered" Richard Wagner and frequently staged his operas. In addition, rarities also found their way into the repertory, like Umberto Giordano's *La cena delle beffe,* Kaun's *Menandra,* and Carter's *Der weiße Vogel.* During the Nazi era, Wagner operas dominated the repertory with *Die Meistersinger von Nürnberg, Tannhäuser,* and *Der Ring des Nibelungen.* After the war, opera performances continued in the Blumenhalle with Wolfgang Amadeus Mozart's *Die Entführung aus dem Serail*

and Emmerich Kálmán's *Gräfin Mariza.* When the new opera house opened, new productions graced the stage. During the 1980s there was an emphasis on contemporary works, among them Mauricio Kagel's *Aus Deutschland* staged in 1982. Recent repertory includes Benjamin Britten's *Albert Herring,* Modest Mussorgsky's *Boris Godunov,* and Carl Maria von Weber's *Der Freischütz.*

Practical Information. Städtische Bühnen, Domhof 10-11, 49074 Osnabrück. Tel: 49 541 323 3331, Fax: 49 541 323-5297. If visiting, contact the German National Tourist Office, 747 Third Avenue, 33rd Floor, New York, NY 10017. Tel: 212-308-3300.

COMPANY STAFF

Intendant. Jean-François Monnard.

Südostbayerisches Städtetheater

The Fürstbischöfliche Opernhaus was inaugurated on November 1, 1783, with Anton Schweitzer's *Alceste.* The court architect Johann Georg Hagenauer converted a former Ballhaus into an early classical style theater. The beginning of the 1960s saw major restoration to the building, which was reopened on November 11, 1961, with Domenico Cimarosa's *Il matrimonio segreto.*

The first opera performance took place on April 12, 1773, when Antonio Salieri's *La fiera di Venezia* graced the stage. Giovanni Paisiello's *Il re Teodoro in Venezia* followed in 1785. The next season saw Wolfgang Amadeus Mozart's *Die Entführung aus dem Serail* followed by *Le nozze di Figaro* and *Die Zauberflöte.* The 1800s was a difficult time for the house with almost 50 directors during an 80 year period. In 1848, the city saw Ludwig van Beethoven's *Fidelio*, but five years later operetta replaced opera in the repertory with works by Jacques Offenbach and Franz von Suppé. The dawn of the new century saw the return of opera with Richard Wagner's *Die Walküre* on the boards in 1933.

The Südostbayerisches Städtetheater was established in 1952 with the joining of Passau with Landshut. After the restoration of the theater, regular opera seasons began, with works like Giuseppe Verdi's *Il trovatore* and *La forza del destino*, and Umberto Giordano's *Andrea Chénier*. The 1970s welcomed contemporary opera including Humphrey Searles *Tagesbuch eines Irren*, Mauricio Kagel's *Staatstheater*, Bruno Maderna's *Satyricon*, and Karl Amadeus Hartmann's *Simplicius Simplicissimus*. Igor Stravinsky's *The Rake's Progress* ushered in the 1980s. Recent repertory includes Mozart's *Entführung aus dem Serail* and Giacomo Puccini's *Tosca*.

Practical Information. Südostbayerisches Städtetheater Passau: Schäfferstraße 2, 94032 Passau. Tel: 49 851 929-1910, Fax 49 851 929-1920. Südostbayerisches Städtetheater Landshut: Ländtorplatz 2-5, 84028 Landshut. Tel: 49 871 922 080, Fax: 49 871 922-0834. If you visit the Südostbayerisches Städtetheater in Passau or Landshut, contact the German National Tourist Office, 747 Third Avenue, 33rd Floor, New York, NY 10017. Tel: 212-308-3300.

COMPANY STAFF

Intendanten. Johannes Reitmeier (1996–present), Klaus Schlette (1970–96), Ludwig Bender (1967–70), Willy Meyer-Fürst (1961–67), Eric Wildhägen (1949–61), Richard Rückert (1949), Peter Hauser (1946–48).
Bibliography. G. Schäffer, *Fürstbischöfliches Opernhaus zu Passau* (Munich, 1971).

PFORZHEIM

Stadttheater

A new, modern Stadttheater (City Theater), also called the Großes Haus, finally opened to host opera in Pforzheim, after several decades of delay. The geometrically-shaped structure is gray and silver, set on its own plaza. Vertical stripes of orange, yellow, green, blue, and purple are the building's only embellishment. Opera had been performed since 1948 in a large hall of a school which had been converted into an interim theater by architect Turnhalle. William Shakespeare's *A Midsummer Night's Dream* had inaugurated the structure. The previous theater was destroyed on February 23, 1945, during a bombing raid.

The 1980s saw a range of operas from the Baroque to the contemporary, including Georg Friedrich Händel's *Il mondo della luna* and *Giulio Caesar*, Christoph Willibald Gluck's *Orfeo ed Eu-*ridice, Albert Lortzing's *Undine*, Giuseppe Verdi's *Rigoletto*, Carlo Orff's *Die Kluge*, Jacques Ibert's *Angelique*, Igor Stravinsky's *The Rake's Progress*, and Benjamin Britten's *Albert Herring*. During the 1990s, works like Richard Strauss's *Der Rosenkavalier* and Franz Lehár's *Die lustige Witwe* graced the stage. Recent offerings include Verdi's *Luisa Miller* and Bedřich Smetana's *Prodaná nevěsta* (The Bartered Bride).

Practical Information. Stadttheater, am Waisenhausplatz 5, 75172 Pforzheim. Tel: 49 7231 392 440. If visiting, contact the German National Tourist Office, 747 Third Avenue, 33rd Floor, New York, NY 10017. Tel: 212-308-3300.

COMPANY STAFF

Intendant. Manfred Berben.

REGENSBURG

Städtische Bühnen

Giacomo Meyerbeer's *Les Huguenots* inaugurated the Städtische Bühnen, originally known as the Stadttheater, on October 12, 1852. Emanuel d'Herigoyen designed the 540 seat theater in Neo-Baroque style. The previous theater had burned to the ground on July 18, 1849.

Stadttheater Pforzheim (Pforzheim, Germany).

The inaugural season also offered Giuseppe Verdi's *Ernani*, Vincenzo Bellini's *I Capuletti e i Montecchi*, Albert Lortzing's *Der Waffenschmied*, Gaetano Donizetti's *La fille du régiment*, Wolfgang Amadeus Mozart's *Le nozze di Figaro*, and Gioachino Rossini's *Il barbiere di Siviglia*. In 1857, a permanent opera ensemble was formed with six women and nine men. The turn of the century brought the first performance in the city of Richard Wagner's *Die Walküre*, followed by a complete Ring Cycle. In 1905, Giacomo Puccini's *La bohème* entered the repertory followed four years later by Richard Strauss's *Salome*. Financial problems caused a suspension of homegrown opera in the 1920s with the Munich Opera visiting instead. The city of Regensburg took over the theater in 1933 and a new opera ensemble was founded with opera prominent in the repertory. The early 1950s saw Engelbert Humperdinck's *Hänsel und Gretel*. The beginning of the 1980s welcomed Verdi's *Otello*, Wagner's *Rienzi*, Ermanno Wolf-Ferrari's *I quattro rusteghi*, Alban Berg's *Wozzeck*, and Donizetti's *Lucia di Lammermoor*. Recent repertory includes Bedřich Smetana's *Prodaná nevěsta* (The Bartered Bride), Verdi's *Nabucco*, Rossini's *Il barbiere di Siviglia*, and Franz Lehár's *Die lustige Witwe*.

Practical Information. Städtische Bühnen, Bismarckplatz 7, 93047 Regensburg. Tel: 49 941 507 1870, Fax: 49 941 507 4429. When visiting the Städtische Bühnen contact the German National Tourist Office, 747 Third Avenue, 33rd Floor, New York, NY 10017. Tel: 212-308-3300.

COMPANY STAFF

Intendant. Marietheres List.

SAARBRÜCKEN

Saarländisches Staatstheater

Wolfgang Amadeus Mozart's *Die Zauberflöte* inaugurated the Staatstheater on March 8, 1948. Heinz Petrall was the architect. The previous Staatstheater was destroyed in 1942, rebuilt, and destroyed again during the winter of 1944-45. The theater had been inaugurated on October 9,

1938, with Richard Wagner's *Der fliegende Holländer*. The Berlin architect Paul Baumgartner designed the structure.

After the war, Georg Friedrich Händel's *Orpheus und Eurydike* initiated opera performances on May 9, 1946, on a side stage of the destroyed house. A flood in 1947 damaged this temporary venue. After the Staatstheater reopened several operas were staged, including Giuseppe Verdi's *Nabucco*, *Simon Boccanegra*, *Otello*, and *Don Carlos*, Richard Strauss's *Elektra*, Wagner's *Der fliegende Holländer*, Alexander Borodin's *Prince Igor*. Recent repertory includes Mozart's *Die Zau-* *berflöte*, Pyotr Il'yich Tchaikovsky's *Eugene Onegin*, and Ludwig van Beethoven's *Fidelio*.

Practical Information. Saarländisches Staatstheater, Schillenplatz 1, 66111 Saarbrücken. Tel: 49 681 32204, Fax: 49 681 309-2325. If visiting, contact the German National Tourist Office, 747 Third Avenue, 33rd Floor, New York, NY 10017. Tel: 212-308-3300.

COMPANY STAFF

Intendant. Helmut Beckamp.

———— STUTTGART

Württembergisches Staatstheater

The Württembergisches Staatstheater, also known as the Großes Haus, was inaugurated on September 15, 1912, with a Festspiele of Wolfgang Goethe's *Faust*, the festival scene from Richard Wagner's *Die Meistersinger von Nürnberg*, Friedrich von Schiller's *Glocke*, and a scene from Niccolò Jommelli's *Vologesco*. Max Littmann designed the building in Neoclassic style.

Opera dates back to 1698 when the Stuttgarter Hofoper (Stuttgart Court Opera) was established by Johann Sigmund Kusser. He had been Kapellmeister in Hamburg and Braunschweig. On August 30, 1750, Carl Heinrich Graun's *Artaserse* inaugurated Stuttgart's first opera house, a reconstruction of the Lusthaus, erected by Georg Beer between 1584 and 1593. The city experienced a "golden age" of opera during this time with the appointment in 1753 of Jommelli as Hofkapellmeister. This was the same year that he composed *Fetone* for the Duke Carl Eugene's birthday, which premiered on February 11, 1753. Two other operas by Jommelli had already been staged in 1751—*Merope* and *Didone abbandonata*. He remained in Stuttgart until 1771 and during that time more than a dozen of his operas were performed. After the turn of the century, the opera house was enlarged in 1811, and reconstructed in 1883. Nine years later, Joachim Gans Edler von Pulitz was appointed director. During the night of January 19-20, 1902, the opera house burned to the ground, but a temporary theater was ready by October 1902. On the initiative of von Pulitz, two opera houses were constructed in

its place. The first one, the Kleines Haus, opened on October 25, 1912, with Richard Strauss conducting the world premiere of the original version of his *Ariadne auf Naxos*, with Maria Jeritza, Hermann Jadlowker, and Margarethe Siems. The world premiere of Alexander Zemlinsky's *Florentinische Tragödie* followed on December 6, 1917. This opera house was destroyed in 1944 and rebuilt as a playhouse. The second opera house, the Großes Haus, also opened in 1912. Max von Schillings was appointed Hofkapellmeister and during his tenure, more than 45 world premieres took place, including his own opera, *Mona Lisa*, on September 26, 1915, and the novelty, Siegfried Wagner's *An allem ist Hütschen schuld*. Albert Kehm was appointed Intendant in 1920. Modern works continued to be an important part of the repertory, with the premieres of Ture Rangström's *Die Kronbraut*, Paul Hindemith's *Mörder, Hoffnung der Frauen* and *Das Nusch-Nuschi*, Egon Wellesz's *Sherz, List und Rache*, Paul Höffer's *Der falsche Woldemar*, and Paul August von Klenau's *Rembrandt van Rijin*. Stuttgart also hosted the first German performances of Giuseppe Verdi's *Les vêpres siciliennes* and Antonín Dvořák's *Rusalka*. Works from Kurt Weill and Ernst Křenek, and the Stuttgart composers Reutter and Hugo Herrmann were also on the boards. With the rise of National Socialism in 1933, Kelm was forced out. That same year the 50th anniversary of Wagner's death was commemorated with a special Wagner cycle. Under the Nazis, world premieres by Hans Pfitzner and Carl Orff graced the stage, along with

Nico Dostal's *Flucht ins Glück*, and the German premiere of Alfredo Casella's *Favola d'Orfeo*.

Kehm returned after World War II, and first presented *Tage der zeitgenössischen Musik* (Days of Contemporary Music). Alongside the classical repertory, 57 contemporary operas were staged, including both world and German premieres — Hindemith's *Mathis der Mahler* (1946), Carl Orff's *Bernauerin*, *Comoedia de Christi resurrectione* (1957), *Oedipus der Tyrann* (1959), and *Ludus de nato infante mirificus*, Werner Ergk's *Der Revisor* (1957), Francis Burt's *Volpone* (1960), Igor Stravinsky's *The Rake's Progress* (1951), Orff's *Trionfi* (1953), Kurt Weill's *Lost in the Stars* (1962), Ján Cikker's *Auferstehung* (1964) and *Das Spiel von Liebe und Tod* (1969), Hans Werner Henze's *Junger Lord* (1965), Krzysztof Penderecki's *Lost Paradise* (1979), and Henze's *Pollicino* (1981). Well-known directors like Wieland Wagner, Götz Friedrich, Günther Rennert, and Jean-Pierre Ponnelle have staged productions in Stuttgart, including Wolfgang Fortner's *Bluthochzeit* and Krzysztof Penderecki's *Diably z Loudun* (The Devils of Loudun), and Wagner's *Der Ring des Nibelungen*. The 1990s brought Luigi Nono's *Intolleranza 1960* (1992), Violeta Dinescu's *Eréndira* (1992), Hans Zender's *Don Quichotte de la Mancha* (1993), Rolf Riehm's *Schweigen der Sirenen* (1994), Wolfgang Rihm's *Séraphin* (1996), Nono's *Al gran sole carico d'amore* (1998), and controversial productions, including Ruth Berghaus's staging of Verdi's *La traviata* and *Macbeth*, and Weill's *Der Aufstieg und Faller Stadt Mahagonny*. A complete Ring Cycle will be staged in 2000 in an unusual manner — each opera will feature a different cast and production team.

Both before and after the war, established artists performed in Stuttgart, including Karl Aagard Oestvig, who sang in Schillings's *Mona Lisa*, Theodor Scheidl, who launched his international career from the city, Gerhard Stolze, Peter Hoffmann, Martha Mödl, Anja Silja, and Fritz Wunderlich, to mention only a few. Guest artists perform along with members of the permanent ensemble, which currently includes some talented American singers, like Catherine Nagelstad, who sang the title role in a clever, modern production of Georg Friedrich Händel's *Alcina*. The Baroque opera was made relevant for today by updating it to a love triangle, emphasizing the universal problems of lovers and the subsequent heartbreak. It worked well, although not all updates are so successful. Another production, Karol Szymanowski's *Król Roger*, presented

in a timeless setting, rendered the psychological opera — the multi-levels of the universal struggle of the creative process and search for spiritual strength — relevant for all time. The essence of the work was captured with the intelligent staging, and good singing and acting by the fixed ensemble cast.

In the early 1990s, the then Intendant Wolfgang Gönnenwein ran over budget by approximately 5 million DM, causing a scandal, a trial, and the abolishment of the all powerful Intendant position. Now there are separate positions for each art form — an opera director (Opernintendant), ballet director, and theater director and each has his own budget and is responsible to account for it. Essentially, all the funding comes from the government. There are around five new productions each year with a total schedule of 20 operas per season. Recent offerings include Ludwig van Beethoven's *Fidelio*, Wolfgang Amadeus Mozart's *Die Entführung aus dem Serail* and *Die Zauberflöte*, Giacomo Puccini's *Tosca* and *La bohème*, Verdi's *Simon Boccanegra* and *Falstaff*, Dmitry Shostakovich's *Ledi Makbet Mtsenskovo uyezda* (Lady Macbeth of the Mtsensk District), Henry Purcell's *King Arthur*, Alban Berg's *Lulu*, Modest Mussorgsky's *Boris Godunov*, Rossini's *L'italiana in Algeri*, Ruggero Leoncavallo's *I pagliacci*, Pietro Mascagni's *Cavalleria rusticana*, and Richard Wagner's *Die Meistersinger von Nürnberg*.

Württembergisches Staatstheater

The majestic, tending toward bombastic, facade of the Staatstheater is sand-colored concrete and gently curved. Six pairs of massive Ionic columns flank arched windows and doors with masks of Comedy and Tragedy. Ten statues crown the structure. The silver and gray U-shaped auditorium holds three tiers, with heavily decorated parapets displaying masks. Golden orange silk and dark wood paneling cover the walls. The ornate proscenium arch frames a deep purple curtain, matched by purple drapes that adorn each of the three royal boxes, a center one and two proscenium boxes, which are all topped by a silver crown. The seats are golden cloth in dark wooden frames, of which there are 1,426.

Practical Information. Württembergisches Staatstheater, Oberer Schloßgarten 6, 70173 Stuttgart. Tel: 49 711 20320, Fax: 49 711 203-2389.

Württembergisches Staatstheater (Stuttgart, Germany).

When visiting the Württembergisches Staatstheater, stay at the Hotel Inter-Continental Stuttgart, Willy-Brandt-Straße 30, 70173 Stuttgart. Tel: 49 711 20200 or 1 800 327-0200, Fax 49 711 202012. The Hotel Inter-Continental Stuttgart is conveniently located next to the Schloßgarten Park and close to the opera house. The hotel can assist with opera tickets and schedule.

COMPANY STAFF

Intendanten. Klaus Zehelein (1992–present), Wolfgang Gönnenwein (1985–91), Hans Peter Doll (1972–85), Walter Erich Schäfer (1949–72), Bertil Wetzelsberger (1946–49), Albert Kelm (1945–46), Gustav Deharde (1937–45), Otto Krauß (1933–37), Albert Kelm (1920–33), Victor Stephany (1919–20), Joachim zu Putlitz (1912–19).

Bibliography. R. Krauss, *Das Stuttgarter Hoftheater* (Stuttgart, 1908). *Festschrift der Württembergischen Staatstheater* (Stuttgart, 1962). Kurt Honolka, *Dreitausend Mal Musik: Stars und Premieren in Stuttgart und anderswo* (Stuttgat, 1978). W.E. Schäfer, *Die Stuttgarter Staatsoper 1950–1972* (Pfullingen, 1972).

Thanks to Anne-Marie Schwinger, Staatstheater Stuttgart, and Gerald Etter and Nicholas Craxton.

TRIER

Theater der Stadt

Ludwig van Beethoven's *Fidelio* inaugurated the Theater der Stadt on September 27, 1964. Gerhard Graubner and Hans Schneider designed the modern, 622-seat structure. The previous Theater der Stadt was destroyed in December 1944. Originally constructed in 1802, the theater was expanded and renovated several times before its demise during World War II.

During the first theater's existence, there were more than 60 directors, of which Heinz Tietjen was the best known and survived the longest tenure (1907 to 1922). The best known of the guest singers was Francisco d'Andrade, who assayed the title role of Wolfgang Amadeus Mozart's *Don Giovanni*. After World War II, opera was performed in the Treviris-Festsaal and then in the Bischof-Korum-Haus, until the new opera house opened in 1964. Recent repertory includes Mozart's *Le nozze di Figaro*, Pietro Mascagni's *Cavalleria rusticana*, and Ruggero Leoncavallo's *I pagliacci*.

Practical Information. Theater der Stadt, am Augustinerhof, 54224 Trier. Tel: 49 651 718 3464, Fax: 49 651 718 3466. If visiting, contact the German National Tourist Office, 747 Third Avenue, 33rd Floor, New York, NY 10017. Tel: 212-308-3300.

COMPANY STAFF

Intendant. Reinhard Petersen.

ULM

Ulmer Theater

Bertolt Brecht's *Leben des Galilei* inaugurated the Ulmer Theater on October 3, 1969. Fritz Schäfer designed the modern, 815-seat structure. The previous Ulmer Theater, constructed in 1782, was destroyed on December 17, 1944. The theater hosted as its first opera production Wolfgang Amadeus Mozart's *Die Entführung aus dem Serail* on April 26, 1792. During the 1800s, the orchestra was made up of military musicians which ended only after World War I. After the dawn of the 20th century, works like Richard Wagner's *Tannhäuser* and *Die Walküre*, Charles Gounod's *Faust*, Eugen d'Albert's *Tiefland*, and Carl Maria von Weber's *Der Freischütz* were on the boards. In 1928 the city took over the theater, which previously had been in private hands. The following year, Herbert von Karajan was hired as Opernkapellmeister, one of his early stepping stones to an international career. After World War II, a temporary performance venue was used, and offered mainly Mozart works. When the new theater opened in 1969, the "grander" operas like Richard Strauss's *Der Rosenkavalier*, Wagner's *Der fliegende Holländer*, Giuseppe Verdi's *Aida* and *Otello* could again be staged. The 1980s saw contemporary works grace the stage, including the commissioned opera, *Das Ende des Kreises* by Bruno Liberda and Michael Beretti. Recent repertory includes Gaetano *Don Pasquale* and Ludwig van Beethoven's *Fidelio*.

Practical Information. Ulmer Theater, Olgastraße 73, 89073 Ulm/Donau; Tel: 49 731 161 4444, Fax: 49 711 161 1619. If visiting, contact the German National Tourist Office, 747 Third Avenue, 33rd Floor, New York, NY 10017. Tel: 212-308-3300.

WEIMAR

Deutsches Nationaltheater

The rebuilt Deutsches Nationaltheater reopened on August 28, 1948, with Johann Wolfgang Goethe's *Faust*. The previous theater, originally called the Hoftheater, and renamed the Landestheater in Weimar in 1918, and Deutsches Nationaltheater Weimar the following year, had been destroyed by bombs on February 9, 1945. It was inaugurated on January 11, 1909, with a festive celebration. Heilmann & Littmann designed the structure.

Back in 1696, the first opera was staged in the Wilhelmsburg, and in 1779, the first Komödienhaus, built by A. Hauptmann, opened on January 7, 1780, with a masked ball. Iffland's *Die Jager*, under the direction of Goethe, inaugurated the transformation of the Komödienhaus into a Hoftheater on May 7, 1791. Three years later, on January 16, 1794, the first performance at the Hoftheater of Wolfgang Amadeus Mozart's *Die*

Zauberflöte took place. The work received 82 performances. Other Mozart pieces, Singspiele, and opera were staged. By 1819, the operas from Christoph Willibald Gluck, Carl Maria von Weber, and Gioachino Rossini had gained favor. The former Komödienhaus burned to the ground on March 22, 1825, and a second Comedy House was constructed by Herr Steiner on the same location. It opened on September 3, 1825, with Rossini's *Semiramide*. In 1842, Franz Liszt became associated with the theater and brought the music of Hector Berlioz and especially Richard Wagner to production. On February 16, 1849, the first performance in Weimar of Wagner's *Tannhäuser* took place followed by the world premiere of his *Lohengrin* on August 28, 1850. In 1889, Richard Strauss was hired as Kapellmeister and he concentrated on modern, novel productions of Gluck and Wagner operas. On December 23, 1893, the world premiere of Engelbert Humperdinck's *Hänsel und Gretel* was presented under Strauss's tenure. He left the following year. Goethe's *Iphigenie auf Tauris* on February 16, 1907, was the final performance in the Komödienhaus before it was torn down.

In 1907, construction began on the new theater, which was inaugurated two years later. In 1918 Ernst Hardt took over the direction, offering contemporary works, including those of Igor Stravinsky and Arnold Schöenberg. Since the reopening of the new opera house in 1948, opera, ballet, concerts, and drama all share the stage. Works from Mozart, Wagner, Rossini, Weber, Giuseppe Verdi, Giacomo Puccini, and Strauss dominate the repertory—*Arabella, Parsifal, Lohengrin, Die Walküre, Tristan und Isolde, La traviata, Aida, Un ballo in maschera, La forza del destino, Die Entführung aus dem Serail, Don Carlo, Le nozze di Figaro, Don Giovanni, Il barbiere di Siviglia, Tosca,* and *Turandot.* Other offerings included Jules Massenet's *Werther,* Daniel Auber's *Fra Diavolo,* Georg Friedrich Händel's *Alcina,* and Adolphe Adam's *Le Postillon de Longjumeau,* and among the novelties one finds Ján Cikker's *Coriolanus,* Grothe's *Das Wirtshaus im Spessart,* Joseph Haas's *Die Hochzeit des Jobs,* Friedrich von Flotow's *Die unverhoffte Heirat oder Witwe bietet mehr,* Boris Blacher's *Die Flut,* and Heinrich Sutermiester's *Romeo und Julia.* The budget is close to 40 million DM and more than 400 people work in the theater. There is a permanent ensemble of singers.

A production of Verdi's *Rigoletto* was an updated, modern, symbolic reinterpretation. Rigoletto was not a hunchback and Maddelena, not Sparafucile, killed Gilda after she crossed the threshold — a red neon light shaped as a door frame. Gilda had crossed the same symbolic threshold before the Duke raped her. Everyone in the court dressed like the Duke — in cream-colored tailcoats, his servants in midnight-blue velvet outfits, and carried knives. Everyone else was attired in yellow. There appeared to be Mafia overtones to the production, of stereotyping Italians as gangsters. Recent repertory includes Albert Lortzing's *Zar und Zimmerman,* Giacomo Puccini's *Madama Butterfly,* Strauss's *Ariadne auf Naxos,* and Jacque Offenbach's *Les contes d'Hoffmann.*

Deutsches Nationaltheater

From the declaration of "total war" in 1944 until the theater was destroyed by bombs in 1945, it was used by Siemens-Halske to produce equipment for the war effort. The Soviet military authority helped rebuild the theater in 1948. It was reconstructed between 1973 and 1975, with the renovation of the auditorium and modernization of the stage machinery.

The classic, off-white stone building offers a portico formed by six large Doric columns which support a balcony. Ionic pilasters flank long, rectangular windows which punctuate a facade ornamented with garlands and wreathes. The modern, rectangular-shaped auditorium holds two tiers with white, sculpted parapets. The first tier stretches across the orchestra, the second is shaped like an arch, thrusting down on the sides. The seats are an orange-maroon plaid fabric, and the plain, black proscenium arch frames a gray curtain. The walls are covered with a light-colored wood. Sculpted geometric shapes embellish the ceiling. There are 859 seats.

Practical Information. Deutsches Nationaltheater, 99401 Weimar. Tel: 49 3643 755-334, Fax: 49 3643 755 307. When visiting the Deutsches Nationaltheater, contact the German National Tourist Office, 747 Third Avenue, 33rd Floor, New York, NY 10017. Tel: 212-308-3300.

COMPANY STAFF AND PREMIERES

Intendanten. Günther Beelitz (1993–present), Fritz Wendrich (1987–92), Gert Beinemann (1973–87), Otto Lang (1958–73), Karl Kayser (1950–58),

Deutsches Nationaltheater (Weimar, Germany).

Hans-Robert Dortfeldt (1946–50), Hans Viehweg (1945–46), Hans Severus Ziegler (1936–45), Ernst Nobbe (1933–36), Ranz Ulbrich (1924–33), Ernst Hardt (1919–24), Carl von Schirach (1909–18), Hiiippolyt von Vignau (1895–1908), Hans Bronsart von Schellendorf (1887–95), August von Loën (1867–87), Franz von Dingelstedt (1857–67), Karl Olivier Freiherr von Beaulieu-Marconnay (1854–57), Karl Emil von Spiegel (1828–47).

World Premieres. (Since 1945) Böckmann's *Doktor Eisenbart*, September 4, 1954; Bush's *Die Männer von Blackmoor*, November 18, 1956; Forest's *Die Blumen von Hiroshima*, June 24, 1967; Geißler's *Das Chagrindleder*, May 19, 1981; Gerster's *Der fröhliche Sünder*, March 9, 1963; Griesbach's *Marike Weiden*, October 7, 1960; Günther's *Macette*, September 12, 1979; Günther's *Der erklärte Weiberfeind*, August 28, 1981; Hanell's *Fiesta*, May 28, 1974; Link's *Pluft, das Geisterlein*, October 26, 1980; Matthus's *Omphale*, September 27, 1976; Rosenfeld's *Der mantel*, July 4, 1978; Zimmermann's *Lewins Mühle*, March 28, 1973; Hanell's *Babettes grüner Schmetterling*, October 6, 1982; Xennakis's *Kraanerg*, March 17, 1995; Hintzenstern's *Hochland oder Der Nachhall*, September 10, 1995.

Thanks to Hedi Strempel, Deutsches Nationaltheater.

WIESBADEN

Hessisches Staatstheater

The Hessisches Staatstheater was inaugurated on October 16, 1894, with the overture and Act II of Richard Wagner's *Tannhäuser*. The opera house was designed by Ferdinand Fellner and Hermann Helmer.

Opera performances date back to the second half of the 18th century when the Komödienhaus, under the direction of Berner, mounted 32 French and Italian opera between 1765 and 1795. Among the offerings were Wolfgang Amadeus Mozart's *Bastien und Bastienne* and Karl Ditters von Dittersdorf's *Doktor und Apotheker*. A new theater was inaugurated on June 11, 1810, which hosted Mozart's *Die Entführung aus dem Serail*, followed by *La clemenza di Tito*, *Die Zauberflöte* and *Don Giovanni*. Another theater was opened on June 26, 1827, with Gaspare Spontini's *La vestale*. The building served as Wiesbaden's opera house for 67 years and witnessed all the great works of the 19th century, including Gaetano Donizetti, Fromental Halévy, Giacomo Meyerbeer, and Daniel Auber, whose *La muette di Portici* was mounted in 1838, 1848, and again in 1982. Ludwig Schindelmeisser conducted Wagner's *Lohengrin*, which appeared for the first time on July 2, 1853, and *Rienzi* and *Der fliegende Holländer* entered the repertory the next year.

Two years after the opening of the Hessisches Staatstheater, by decree of Kaiser Wilhelm II, a May Festival was established, which continued with little interruption until 1914. It resumed again between 1928 and 1939, and has again been taking place since 1950. In the first year of the festival Hans Richter conducted Wagner's *Die Meistersinger von Nürnberg* and three years later, in 1897, the first performance in Wiesbaden of Wagner's *Tristan und Isolde* took place with Lilli Lehmann and Paul Kalisch, and the Wiesbaden premiere of Wagner's *Parsifal* was mounted in 1914. One of the most popular operas in the festival was Carl Maria von Weber's *Oberon*, which by 1914 had been performed 200 times. Enrico Caruso sang in Giuseppe Verdi's *Rigoletto* in 1908, and Leo Slezak in Verdi's *Aida*, Wagner's *Tannhäuser*, and Halévy's *La Juive*. Max von Schillings conducted his opera *Mona Lisa* and Richard Strauss his *Salome*. Between the wars, the festival witnessed works by Schillings, Eugen d'Albert, Hans Pfitzner, and Erich Wolfgang Korngold, among others. During this same period, several contemporary works were staged, like Franz Schreker's *Der Schatzgräber*, Ferruccio Busoni's *Arlecchino*, and Maurice Ravel's *L'heure espagnole*. Otto Klemperer's conducting helped raise the musical level to a high point. A low point followed with the theater's strong ties to Nazism between 1933 and 1943, including the renaming of the theater to Preußisches Staatstheater.

After the theater reopened in 1947, works of contemporary composers graced the stage, including Paul Hindemith, Gian Carlo Menotti, Boris Blacher, and Igor Stravinsky. The tenure of Claus Helmut Drese was particularly successful. His debut opera was Georges Bizet's *Carmen*, followed by Anja Silja in the title role of Strauss's *Sa-*

lome. He concentrated on operas by Mozart, Verdi, Giacomo Puccini, and Strauss, as well as contemporary pieces by Stravinsky and Bohuslav Martinů. During the 1985-86 season, the complete *Der Ring des Nibelungen* was mounted and the beginning of the 1990s saw several world premieres.

There is a very specific philosophy that governs the opera house. As the head dramaturg of the theater put it, "we believe that to 'earn' our money there should be a 'message' in our works." Their productions, however, are not experimental — in fact the double-bill of Pietro Mascagni's *Cavalleria rusticana* and Ruggero Leoncavallo's *I pagliacci* were conventionally staged (set-wise that is) but unconventionally executed: Tonio's prologue was sung *before Cavalleria rusticana*, because in both, opera "society" impassively watches someone die and "society" blindly accepted it. In the *Cav* opera, society was judged guilty for Turiddu's death because the law of honor demanded the fight. "Another example is Strauss's *Elektra*. Is revenge the right answer, the correct solution? And because Elektra only lives for revenge, is she just as guilty? The philosophy is to question: should society blindly accept these solutions or should they question them, even carrying their questioning to Germany's ultimate horror: the Final Solution — the killing of 6 million Jews, while German society never questioned, but blindly accepted it, even willingly participated." Opera in Wiesbaden is not necessarily for entertainment, but to give the audience something to think about, to leave the theater asking the right questions. Productions mirror society. They are not trying to be provocative, but provoke questions about how the theme of the opera applies to life. The directors they hire must have this opinion and philosophy. The singers are all permanent employees of the theater with an occasional guest artist. Although the singing is mediocre, the intriguing productions somewhat compensate. The repertory is eclectic with pieces as diverse as Albert Lortzing's *Zar und Zimmermann*, Béla Bartók's *A Kékszakállú herceg vára* (Duke Bluebeard's Castle), Ambroise Thomas's *Hamlet*, Puccini's *Madama Butterfly*, and Wagner's *Tristan und Isolde* sharing the stage. Recent offerings include Korngold's *Die tote Stadt*, Verdi's *Aida*, and Puccini's *La bohème*.

The Internationale Maifestspiele, which takes place every year in the Hessischen Staatstheater, offers international artists and productions in an eclectic mix of works. A recent festival presented Puccini's *Tosca* with Aprile Milo, Luis Lima, and Carlo Guelfi; Verdi's *Rigoletto* with Joan Pons, Patrizia Ciofi, Ramon Vargas; Giovanni Paisiello's *Il re Teodoro in Venezia* from Opéra de Montpellier, and Benjamin Britten's *The Rape of Lucretia* from Euro-Oper.

Hessisches Staatstheater

On March 18, 1923, the opera house was damaged by fire, but was quickly repaired, reopening on December 20 of the same year with Wagner's *Lohengrin*. It was partially destroyed during bombing raids in 1944 and 1945. Rudolf Dörr was responsible for the rebuilding with Joseph Huber executing the ceiling painting. The theater reopened on September 17, 1947, with Wolfgang Amadeus Mozart's *Die Zauberflöte*. The house was restructured between 1975 and 1978, with Wolfgang Lenz in charge of the refurbishing of the auditorium. The opera house reopened on May 13, 1978, with Wagner's *Die Meistersinger von Nürnberg*.

The majestic facade of the opera house boasts a six column portico which supports an allegorically-inspired relief pediment. Sculptures of figures evoking Apollo, Muses, and griffins embellish the facade. The Neo-Baroque style auditorium, overflowing with reliefs and sculptures, holds three gold-and-ivory ornamented tiers, proscenium boxes, and a center royal box topped with a golden crown. Fleur-de-lis medallions, putti, and ivory-colored caryatids embellish the space. The seats are a deep red plush blending with the deep red silk wallcovering. Portraits of well-known composers and writers decorate the allegorically-inspired ceiling. There are 1041 seats.

Practical Information. Hessisches Staatstheater, Christian-Zeis Straße, 6200 Wiesbaden. Tel: 49 611 132 269, Fax: 49 611 132 337. When visiting the Hessisches Staatstheater, stay at the Hotel Nassauer Hof, Kaiser-Friedrich-Platz 3/4, 65183 Wiesbaden. Tel: 49 611 1330 or 1 800 223 6800, Fax: 49 611 133 632. The Nassauer Hof is

Hessisches Staatstheater (Wiesbaden, Germany).

only a couple of blocks from the opera house. The hotel can assist with tickets and schedule.

COMPANY STAFF AND PREMIERES

Intendanten. Achim Thorwald (1996–present), Arnold Petersen (1994–96), Claus Leininger (1986–94), Christoph Groszer (1978–86), Peter Ebert (1975–78), Alfred Erich Sistig (1968–75), Claus Helmut Drese (1962–68), Friedrich Schramm (1953–26), Heinrich Köhler-Helffrich (1949–53), Otto Henning (1946–49), Max Spilcker (1943–44), Carl von Schirach (1933–43), Max Berg-Ehlert (1932–33), Paul Bekker (1926–32), Carl Hagemann (1920–26), Ernst Legal (1918–20), Kurt von Mutzenbecher (1903–18), Georg von Hülsen (1894–1903).

World Premieres. V.D. Kirshner's *Die Trau-ung* April 27, 1975; V.D. Kirshner's *Das kalte Herz* April 25, 1981; G. Salvatore's *Lektionen der Finsternis* May 6, 1990; F.F. Weyh's *Der schwere Gang der Zeuginnen von M.* February 6, 1991; H. Gefors's *Der Park* April 25, 1992; J. Kalitzke's *Bericht vom Tod des Musikers* May 9, 1992; J. MacMillan's *Busqueda* May 9, 1993; **German Premieres:** A. Ayckbourn's *In Gedanken* December 20, 1986; E. Bond's *Restauration* January 24, 1987; J. Sobol's *Das Jerusalem Syndrom* April 4, 1991.

Bibliography. Rudolf Cyperrek, Otto Laux, Hans-Peter Scholz, *Hessisches Staatstheater Wiesbaden: Geschichte eines Theatergebäudes 1860–1978* (Wiesbaden, 1978). *Hessisches Staatstheater Wiesbaden* (Wiesbaden, 1994). Interview with head dramaturg.

Thanks to Eleonore Ryschka, Hessisches Staatstheater, and Karl Nüser.

WÜRZBURG

Stadttheater

On December 4, 1966, Richard Wagner's *Die Meistersinger von Nürnburg* inaugurated the new Stadttheater. It was designed by Hans Joachim Budeit. The previous theater had been destroyed by bombs on March 16, 1945.

Back in 1773, the Fürstbischof Adam Friedrich von Seinsheim had a theater built in the White Room of the Residenz. The Würzburg Theater opened on August 3, 1804, with an English comedy, *Still Water Is Deep*. Constructed between July 1803 and August 1804 from a 1750-built cloister of the Holy Anna, the building was designed by Balthasar Neumann. Opera was offered soon after the theater's inauguration. The works of Wolfgang Amadeus Mozart were favored, like *Don Giovanni* and *Die Entführung aus dem Serail*. Soon the Hoftheater (Court Theater) became a Provinztheater (Provincial Theater) and experienced financial problems.

In 1833, Wagner was the Chordirektor, and presented part of his early opera, *Die Feen*, in concert form. A decade later, the theater became a Stadttheater (City Theater) when the city purchased it from the widow Julie von Münchhausen, on February 7, 1843, for 60,500 Gulden. During this time, French grand opera, especially works of Giacomo Meyerbeer, was very popular, next to the usual German and Italian repertory. Of note were Heinrich Marschner's *Hans Heiling*, and Ludwig van Beethoven's *Fidelio*. A Mozart Festival began in 1921 when Rudolf Bertram was the director and during the festival Mozart's *La finta giardiniera* was performed. Richard Strauss directed his *Ariadne auf Naxos* in Würzburg on April 15, 1926. After the war, performances took place in a high school auditorium on Wittelsbacherplatz. One found in the repertory Eugen d'Albert's *Tiefland* and *Die toten Augen*, Adolphe Adam's *Le Postillon de Longjumeau*, Georges Bizet's *Carmen*, Gaetano Donizetti's *Don Pasquale* and *Lucia di Lammermoor*, Friedrich von Flotow's *Martha*, Joseph Haas's *Die Hochzeit des Jobs* and *Tobias Wunderlich*, Georg Friedrich Händel's *Giulio Cesare*, Franz Lehner's *Die schlaue Susanne*, Albert Lortzing's *Der Waffenschmied*, *Undine*, and *Zar und Zimmermann*, Gioachino Rossini's *Il barbiere di Siviglia*, Daniel Auber's *Fra Diavolo*, and Wagner's *Der fliegende Holländer*.

After the opening of the new theater, many modern works entered the repertory — Werner Egk's *Der Revisor*, Paul Hindemith's *Mathis der Maler* and *Cardillac*, Hans Werner Henze's *Der junge Lord* and *Elegy for Young Lovers*, Leoš Janáček's *Kát'a Kabanová*, *Jenůfa*, and *Příhody Lišky Bystroušky* (The Cunning Little Vixen), Alban Berg's *Wozzeck*, and Igor Stravinsky's *The Rake's Progress*. The theater also hosted the German premieres of Lorenzo Ferrero's *Salvatore Guiliano* and Mozart's *Ascanio in Alba*, and the European premiere of Philip Glass's *The Juniper Tree*. There is a permanent ensemble and the budget is 22 million DM, which comes from the city and the region, and requires the company to travel to Schweinfurt, Fulda, and Aschaffenburg, where there is no permanent ensemble.

The season schedule includes a couple of premieres, usually of an 18th-century opera and a contemporary piece. Many works are light opera and operetta. One production of Otto Nicolai's *Die lustigen Weiber von Windsor* was zany and amusing. Updated and performed in contemporary attire, it was good entertainment, although hardly great opera-operetta. Nonetheless, for a provincial house, it was cleverly executed. Recent offerings include Claude Debussy's *Pelléas et Mélisande*, Wagner's *Lohengrin*, and Lortzing's *Zar und Zimmermann*.

Stadttheater, Würzburg

The Stadttheater is a modern, rectangular building with a facade of glass and metal. A sculpture called *Wurfel* (cube) is displayed in front of the structure. The single tier auditorium has light wood walls, silver-toned ceiling, green seats, a plain black proscenium arch. The room is practically square with only a slight curve in the tier to "soften" the lines. There are 744 seats.

Practical Information. Stadttheater, Theaterstraße 21, 8700 Würzburg. Tel: 49 931 39080. When visiting the Stadttheater, contact the German National Tourist Office, 747 Third Avenue, 33rd Floor, New York, NY 10017. Tel: 212-308-3300.

COMPANY STAFF

Intendanten. Tebbe Harms Kleen (1988–present), Achim Thorwald (1985–88), Joachim von Groeling (1970–85), Herbert Decker (1965–70), Hans Scherer (1946–65), Helmut Ebbs (1941–44), Otto Reimann (1936–41), Eugen Keller (1930–36), Paul Smolny (1927–30), Heinrich Strohm (1925–27), Rudolf Bertram (1920–25), Willy Stuhlfeld (1914–20), Otto Reimann (1906–14), Heinrich Hagin (1904–06), Heinrich Adolphi (1899–1903), Eduard Reimann (1870–98).

Thanks to Renata Freyeisen.

Stadttheater (Würzburg, Germany).

WUPPERTAL

Wuppertaler Bühnen

Paul Hindemith's *Mathis der Maler* inaugurated the Wuppertaler Bühnen on October 14, 1956. The previous theater, the Barmer Theater, was destroyed in 1943. Richard Wagner's *Tannhäuser* had inaugurated the building on September 30, 1905. It was designed by C. Moritz in Jugendstil.

Opera was included in the repertory performed at the Barmer Theater, until its destruction during World War II. After the war, a temporary performance venue was found in city hall until the new theater was reopened. During the 1970s forgotten Baroque opera was brought to light. Recent repertory includes Verdi's *La travi-ata*, Pietro Mascagni's *Cavalleria rusticana*, Ruggero Leoncavallo's *I pagliacci*, and Jacques Offenbach's *Les contes d'Hoffmann*.

Practical Information. Wuppertaler Bühnen, Spinnstraße 4, 42283 Wuppertal. Tel: 49 202 5631, 49 202 563 8077. If visiting, contact the German National Tourist Office, 747 Third Avenue, 33rd Floor, New York, NY 10017. Tel: 212-308-3300.

COMPANY STAFF

Intendant. Peter Gülke (chief conductor).

Other German Companies

Other German opera companies are noted below by name, address, telephone, recent repertory, and general director (as available).

Landestheater Altenburg. Theaterplatz 19, 06429 Altenburg. Tel: 49 3447 5850, Fax: 49 3447 585186. **Recent Repertory:** Carmen, Die Entführung aus dem Serail, Die Fledermaus, Zar und Zimmermann, Boccaccio. **Intendant:** Georg Mittendrein.

Eduard Von Winterstein Theater Annaberg-Buchholz. Ernst Thalmannstraß 67, 09456 Annaberg-Buchholz. Tel: 49 3733 14070, Fax: 49 3733 140-7150. **Recent Repertory:** Così fan tutte, Prodaná nevěsta (The Bartered Bride). **Intendant:** Hans-Hermann Krug.

Deutsch-Sorbisches Volkstheater. Seminarstraße 12, 02625 Bautzen. Tel: 49 3591-5840. **Recent Repertory:** Carmen, Der Freischütz, Die Fledermaus. **Intendant:** Jörg Liljeberg.

Metropol-Theater. Friedrichstraße 101-102, 10117 Berlin. Tel: 49 30 203 640, Fax: 49 30 208-4236. **Recent Repertory:** Der Bettelstudent, Die lustige Witwe, Das Land des Lächelns. **Intendant:** Werner Seiferth.

Brandenburger Theater. Grabenstraß 14, 14776 Brandenburg. **Recent Repertory:** L'heure espagnole, I pagliacci, Così fan tutte. **Intendant:** Michael Muhr.

Opernhaus Chemnitz. Theaterplatz 2, 09111 Chemnitz. Tel: 49 371 488 4662, Fax: 49 371 488 4697. **Recent Repertory:** Martha, La bohème, Tannhäuser, Hänsel und Gretel, Die Meistersinger von Nürnberg. **Intendant:** Rolf Stiska.

Staatstheater Cottbus. Karl Liebknechtstraße 136, 03046 Cottbus. Tel: 49 355 782 4161. **Recent Repertory:** Der fliegende Holländer, Fidelio, Die Zauberflöte, Le nozze di Figaro, La traviata, Der Freischütz. **Intendant:** Martin Schüler (opera director).

Landestheater Dessau. Friedensplatz 1a, 06844 Dessau. Tel: 49 340 25110, Fax: 49 340 251-1213. **Recent Repertory:** Tiefland, La bohème, Luisa Miller, Die lustigen Weiber von Windsor.

Staatsoperette Dresden. Pirnaer Landestraße 131, 01257 Dresden. Tel: 49 351 207-9937. **Recent Repertory:** Der Vetter aus Dingsda, Zar und Zimmermann, Der Bettelstudent, Die lustige Witwe, Der Zigeunerbaron. **Intendant:** Fritz Wendrich.

Theater an der Rott Eggenfelden. Pfarrkirchenerstraße 70, 84307 Eggenfelden. Tel: 49 8721 8181, Fax: 49 8721 10174. **Intendant:** Adi Fischer.

Landestheater Eisenach. Leninplatz 47, 99817 Eisenach. Tel: 49 3691-2560. **Recent Repertory:** Madama Butterfly, Così fan tutte, Der Bettelstudent. **Intendant:** Günter Müller.

Städtische Bühnen Erfurt. Dalsbergsweg 2, 99084 Erfurt. Tel: 49 361 562 6267. **Recent Repertory:** Die lustige Witwe, Tannhäuser, Prodaná nevěsta (The Bartered Bride), Fidelio, Die Fledermaus. **Intendant:** Dietrich Taube.

Kammeroper Frankfurt. Nordenstraße 60, 60318 Frankfurt. Tel: 49 691 556-189.

Stadttheater Freiburg. Borngasse 1, 09599

Freiburg. Tel: 49 3731 35820. **Recent Repertory:** Der Freischütz, Le nozze di Figaro, Der fliegende Holländer. **Intendant:** Christa Girbarth.

Europera Musiktheater der Stadt Görlitz. Demianiplatz 2, 02826 Görlitz. Tel: 49 3581-474747. **Recent Repertory:** Zar und Zimmermann, Der Freischütz, Der Bettelstudent, Werther, I pagliacci, L'heure espagnole. **Intendant:** Wolfgang Schaller.

Theater Griefswald. Anklamerstraße 106, 17489 Griefswald. Tel: 49 3834-899-375. **Recent Repertory:** Jenůfa, Tosca, Hänsel und Gretel, Die Fledermaus. **Intendant:** Dieter Wagner.

Volkstheater Halberstadt/Nordharzer Städtebundtheater. Spiegelstraße 20 A, 38820 Halberstadt. Tel: 49 3941 24202, Fax: 49 3941 44 26 52. **Recent Repertory:** Der Waffenschmied, La traviata, Eine Nacht in Venedig, Tosca, Undine, Don Giovanni. **Intendant:** Gero Hammer.

Opernhaus Halle. Universitätsring 24, 06108 Halle. Tel: 49 345 202 6458, Fax: 49 345 511 0102. **Recent Repertory:** Don Giovanni, Madama Butterfly, Tosca, Die Zauberflöte, Der Freischütz, Il barbiere di Siviglia, Aida. **Intendant:** Klaus Froboese.

Operettahaus Hamburg. Spielbudenplatz 1, 20359 Hamburg. Tel: 49 40 2707 5270, Fax: 49 40 31 11 72 52. **Recent Repertory:** Cats. **Intendant:** Gunter Irmier.

Musikalische Komödie Leipzig. (Haus Dreilinden) Dreilindenstraße, 04177 Leipzig. Tel: 49 341 12610. **Recent Repertory:** La Périchole and Der Zigeunerbaron. **Intendant:** Monika Geppert.

Theater im Pfalzbau Ludwigshafen. Berlinerstraße 30, 67059 Ludwigshafen. Tel: 49 621 504-2558. **Recent Repertory:** Stabat Mater (Rossini). **Intendant:** Michael Haensel.

Neuburger Kammeroper. Willstätterstraß 18, 85055 Ingolstadt. Tel: 49 841 56663. **Intendanten:** Heinrich Wladarsch, Anton Sprenzel, Horst Vladar.

Landestheater Mecklenburg. Postfach 1342, 17223, Neustrelitz. Tel: 49 3981 2770. **Recent Repertory:** Fidelio, Weiner Blut, Prodaná nevěsta (The Bartered Bride). **Intendant:** Manfred Straube.

Theater Nordhausen/Loh-Orchester Sondershausen. Käthe Kollwitzstraße 15, 99734 Nordhausen. Tel: 49 3631 983 452, Fax: 49 3631 6260 166. **Recent Repertory:** La traviata, Wiener Blut, Rigoletto. **Intendant:** Christoph Nix.

Vogtland Theater Plauen. Theaterplatz, 08523 Plauen. Tel: 49 3741 291-2431, Fax: 49 3741 291-2446. **Recent Repertory:** Le nozze di Figaro, Der Freischütz. **Intendant:** Dieter Roth.

Hans-Otto-Theater Potsdam. Berlinerstraße 271, 14467 Potsdam. Tel: 49 331-98110, Fax: 49 331 981-1280. **Recent Repertory:** Fräulein Julie (Antonio Bibalo), La voix humaine. **Intendant:** Stephan Märkl.

Landesbühnen Sachsen. Meissner Straße 152, 01445 Radebeul. Tel: 49 381 2440. **Recent Repertory:** Zar und Zimmermann, Tannhäuser, Così fan tutte, La traviata, Le nozze di Figaro. **Intendant:** Manfred Straube.

Volksteater Rostock. Patriotischer Weg 33, 18057 Rostock. Tel: 49 381 2440. **Recent Repertory:** Zar und Zimmermann, Tannhäuser, Così fan tutte, La traviata, Le nozze di Figaro. **Intendant:** Manfred Straube.

Thüringer Landestheater Rudolstadt. Anger 1, 07392 Rudolstadt. Tel: 49 3672-4500, Fax: 49 3672 22226. **Recent Repertory:** Così fan tutte, Madama Butterfly. **Intendant:** Peter Pachi.

Rudolstädter Festspiele. Thüringer Landestheater, 07407 Rudolstadt. Tel: 49 3672 22766, Fax: 49 3672 22226. **Recent Repertory:** Wahnopfer and Schwarzschwanenreich (Siegfried Wagner), Die Schwarze Spinni (Judith Weir). **Intendant:** Peter Pachi.

Schleswig-Holsteinisches Landestheater. Lollfuss 53, 24837 Schleswig. Tel: 49 4621 25989. **Recent Repertory:** Die Zauberflöte, Don Pasquale, Wiener Blut. **Intendant:** Horst Mesalla.

Bayerische Kammeroper Schwanfeld. Wengertspfad 2, 97523 Schwanfeld. Tel: 49 93 848 772, Fax: 49 93 848 678. **Intendant:** Blagoy Apostolov.

Mecklenburgisches Staatstheater Schwerin. Alter Garten, 19055 Schwerin. Tel: 49 385 53000. **Recent Repertory:** Das Land des Lächelns, Così fan Tutte, Die Lustige Witwe. **Intendant:** Joachim Kümmritz.

Theater der Altmark Stendal/Landestheater Sachsen-Anhalt Nord. Moltkestraße 32, Stendal. Tel: 49 39576 21 29 77, Fax: 49 39576 21 20 64. **Intendant:** Goswin Moniac.

Theater Stralsund. Olof Palme Platz, 18439 Stralsund. Tel: 49 3831 295-491, Fax: 49 3831 295-496. **Recent Repertory:** Hänsel und Gretel, West Side Story. **Intendant (conductor):** Daniel Kleiner.

Elbe-Saale Bühnen Wittenberg. Thomas Müntserstraß 14-15, 16515 Wittenberg. Tel: 49 3491-82113. **Recent Repertory:** Zar und Zimmermann, Albert Herring, La Bohème. **Intendant:** Helmut Bläss.

Zwickaur Theater. Postfach 308, 08004 Zwickau. Tel: 49 375 212 168. **Recent Repertory:** Rigoletto, Il barbiere di Siviglia. **Intendant:** Horst-Dieter Brand.

Iceland

REYKJAVÍK

Íslenska Óperan

In March 1979, Ruggero Leoncavallo's *I pagliacci*, performed in the Háskola Bió, inaugurated the Íslenska Óperan. Iceland's best-known soprano, Olöf Kolbrún Hardardóttir, was Nedda and Gardar Cortes conducted. Cortes is also an Icelandic tenor who founded the company to establish an operatic tradition in Iceland as well as to give Icelandic singers an opportunity to perform in their own country. The company's home is the Gamla Bió, a former movie palace which dates from November 2, 1906. The theater, designed by Einar Erlendsson, was transformed into an opera house by architect Stefan Benediktsson from money received from the estate of Sigurlidi Kristjánsson and Helga Jónsdóttir.

The first staged performance of opera in Iceland occurred in 1950, when a visiting Swedish company presented Wolfgang Amadeus Mozart's *Le nozze di Figaro*. Homegrown opera performances began the following year at the Pjódleikhúsinu (National Theater), featuring Icelandic singers Stefán Islandi and Gudmundur Jónsson in Giuseppe Verdi's *Rigoletto*. Verdi's *La traviata* followed in 1953, and his *Il trovatore* a decade later. Other standard repertory works, like Mozart's *Die Zauberflöte*, *Le nozze di Figaro*, and *Così fan tutte*, Giacomo Puccini's *Madama Butterfly*, *La bohème*, and *Tosca*, Gioachino Rossini's *Il barbiere di Siviglia*, Gaetano Donizetti's *Don Pasquale*, Jacques Offenbach's *Les contes d'Hoffmann*, and Georges Bizet's *Carmen*, played alongside less frequently performed pieces like Christoph Willibald Gluck's *Orfeo ed Euridice*, Bedřich Smetana's *Prodaná nevěsta* (The Bartered Bride), and two Icelandic operas, Jón Ásgeirsson's *Prymskvida*, and Atli Heimir Sveinsson's *Silkitromman*. Iceland's most famous tenor, Kristján Jóhannsson, has performed in Puccini's *La bohème* and Verdi's *Un ballo in maschera*. Although the Pjódleikhúsinu witnessed many opera performances, it also hosted plays and ballets and only hired actors and dancers on a permanent basis, not singers. There was a need to establish a permanent opera company, the Íslenska Óperan.

After the inaugural opera, there was a three year hiatus in productions while the Gamla Bió, the movie theater purchased in 1980 with the money the company inherited, was converted into an opera house. On January 9, 1982, Johann Strauß's *Der Zigeunerbaron* inaugurated the Gamla Bió, the company's new home. Cortes compares his company to the Folksoperan in Stockholm (see Folksopera entry), where opera is distilled to its essence — Verdi's *Aida* was performed with eight singers. The repertory is dominated by the popular works like Mozart's *Die Zauberflöte*, *Le nozze di Figaro*, and *Don Giovanni*, Verdi's *La traviata*, *Il trovatore*, *Aida*, *Otello*, and *Rigoletto*, Donizetti's *Lucia di Lammermoor*, Rossini's *Il barbiere di Siviglia*, Bizet's *Carmen*, and Puccini's *Madama Butterfly* and *Tosca*. He is trying to educate the Icelandic population about opera, since there is no operatic heritage and opera arrived only a few decades ago. When Gian Carlo Menotti's *The Medium* and *The Telephone* were staged, it was a disaster. In the future, however, he hopes to expand the repertory and stage works like Benjamin Britten's *Peter Grimes* and Leoš Janáček's *Jenůfa*. The productions are traditional. Cortes feels that there is no sense in doing "something weird" if the audience has never seen a traditional production of the opera. Most of the singers come from the Reykjavik School of Singing that Cortes established. Cortes and Hardardóttir also still perform. They were Canio and Nedda in the 1990 production of Leoncavallo's *I pagliacci*, Alfredo and Violetta in Verdi's *La traviata*, and Tamino and Pamina in Mozart's *Die Zauberflöte*. Cortes attracted established directors, like John Copely for Pyotr Il'yich Tchaikovsky's *Eugene Onegin* and Francesco Zambello for Rossini's *Il barbiere di Siviglia*. There is no set run for any opera and subscriptions are only possible for the opening week-end. An opera always opens on a Saturday. It plays Sunday as well and then the following Friday, Saturday, and Sunday. It runs every week-end until not enough tickets are sold to make it profitable to continue, since 44 percent of their three-quarters of a million dollar budget comes from box office. Six percent is from private sources and the remaining half comes from the government. Recent offerings include Mozart's *Così fan tutte* and Donizetti's *L'elisir d'amore.*

Every other year the Reykjavik Arts Festival takes place in June. This is the company's platform for presenting new and less-known works and more daring productions. In fact, the company's first world premiere, Jan Ásgeirsson's *Galdra-Loftur,* took place on June 1, 1996, during the Reykjavik Arts Festival, conducted by Cortes and directed by Halldór Laxness. The second, Leifur Thórarinsson's *The Mariaglass,* was given as part of the company's regular season, on March 14, 1998.

Gamla Bió

On September 13, 1925, work began to transform the Gamla Bió into a movie theater, which hosted its first film on August 2, 1927. Films like *Appassionata, The Bells of St. Mary's, Valley of Decision, The White Cliffs of Dover, Meet Me in St. Louis, Notorious, The Stranger,* and *30 Seconds Over Tokyo* were popular features. In 1980, its life as a cinema ended and it was converted into an opera house.

The Gamla Bió is sandwiched between two buildings, with its classically-inspired gray-and-white facade in sharp contrast to the neighboring structures. Incorporating elements from the 18th-century Italian opera house, the facade offers GAMLA BIÓ etched in the center, flanked by pairs of fluted Ionic pilasters, and street-level arches. A pediment crowns the theater. The rectangular-shaped auditorium is a mixture of Bauhaus and Jugendstil that successfully captures an "opera house" atmosphere. A single balcony, with a light blue, ivory, and gold colored parapet, undulates across the room. The cloth pink seats match the pink walls. Gilded, green pilasters connected by graceful arches and bordered by a fret embellish the walls. Gilded candelabras

are affixed to the pilasters. A maroon-and-salmon-colored patterned carpet covers the floor and a zig-zag pattern in muted shades of beige and brown decorate the ceiling. There are 479 seats.

Practical Information. Íslenska Óperan, Ingólfsstræti, 121 Reykjavík. Tel: 354-552-7033, Fax: 354-522-7384. Listahátíd í Reykjavík (Reykjavík Arts Festival), Lækjargata 3b, 121 Reykjavík. Tel 354-561-2444, Fax 354-562-2350. When visiting the Íslenska Óperan or Listahátíd í Reykjavík, stay at the Hotel Borg, Pósthússtræti 11, 121 Reykjavík. Tel: 354-551-1440. It is a traditional hotel overlooking the main square and close to the opera house. The hotel can help with opera tickets and schedule.

COMPANY STAFF, WORLD PREMIERES, AND REPERTORY

General Director. Gardar Cortes (1979–present).

World Premieres. J. Ásgeirsson's *Galdra-Loftur,* June 1, 1996; L. Thórarinsson's *The Mariaglass,* March 14, 1998.

Repertory. **1979:** I pagliacci. **1982:** Der Zigeunerbaron, Let's Make an Opera, Die Zauberflöte. **1983:** Mikado, La traviata, The Medium, The Telephone. **1984:** Il barbiere di Siviglia, Noyes Fludde, Carmen. **1985:** Die Fledermaus. **1986:** Il trovatore. **1987:** Aida. **1988:** Let's Make an Opera, Don Giovanni, Les contes d'Hoffmann. **1989:** Le nozze di Figaro, Tosca. **1990:** Carmina Burana, Pagliacci, Rigoletto. **1991:** Die Zauberflöte. **1992:** Otello, Lucia di Lammermoor. **1993:** Czárdásfürstin, Eugene Onegin. **1994:** The Ring Cycle (condensed version of 5 hours). **1995:** La traviata, Carmina burana, Madama Butterfly. **1996:** Hänsel und Gretel, Galdra-Loftur. **1997:** Die lustige Witwe. **1998:** Così fan tutte, L'elisir d'amore, The Mariaglass, Carmen Negra.

Bibliography. Interviews with Gardar Cortes, general director, and Olöf Kolbrún Hardardóttir, chief administrator, February 1997. Additional information supplied by the company.

Thanks to Gunnar Eklund, Icelandair, for providing transportation to Iceland, and Einar Gustavsson, Iceland Tourist Office, New York, for providing accommodations.

Gamla Bio (Reykjavík, Iceland).

Ireland

————————————————————— DUBLIN

Opera Ireland

Opera Ireland, originally formed as the Dublin Grand Opera Society, was established in 1941. Opera was first heard in Dublin as early as 1705 when Henry Purcell's *The Island Princess* was given in Smock Alley. Italian opera was produced by Antonio Minelli's troupe in 1761, including Scolari's *La cascina* on December 19. Over time, works by Giovanni Paisiello and Pasquale Anfossi, among others, were staged and Christoph Willi-

bald Gluck's *Orfeo ed Euridice* was first performed in 1784. During most of the 19th century, the Theatre Royal hosted the opera seasons, with artists like Giovanni Battista Rubini, Giuditta Grisi, and Pauline Viadot gracing the stage. When the Gaiety Theatre opened in 1871, opera activity shifted there, with traveling troupes like Carl Rosa Company and Colonel Mapleson Company mounting productions. Between 1928 and 1938, the newly founded Irish Opera Society used it as their performance venue.

After the Dublin Grand Opera Society was founded, it offered a winter and spring season, with two operas performed in each season. The 1970s and 1980s witnessed Gaetano Donizetti's *La favorita*, Giuseppe Verdi's *Don Carlo* and *Simon Boccanegra*, Amilcare Ponchielli's *La gioconda*, Claude Debussy's *Pelléas et Mélisande*, Francesco Cilea's *Adriana Lecouvreur*, and a novelty, Licinio Refice's *Cecilia*. In the mid–1990s, Charles Gounod's *Faust*, Giacomo Puccini's *La bohème* and *Tosca*, and Gioachino Rossini's *La Cenerentola* were on the boards. Recent repertory includes Franz Lehár's *Die lustige Witwe*, Pyotr Il'yich Tchaikovsky's *Eugene Onegin*, Jacques

Offenbach's *Les contes d'Hoffmann*, and Giuseppe Verdi's *Falstaff*.

Practical Information. Opera Ireland, John Player House, 276-288 South Circular Road, Dublin 8. Tel: 353 1 453 5519, Fax 353 1 453 5521. When visiting Dublin, stay at the Westbury Hotel, Grafton Street, Dublin 2. Tel: 353 1 679 1122, Fax: 353 1 679 7078. It is centrally located and convenient to the opera house.

COMPANY STAFF

General Manager. David Collopy.
Bibliography. T. Walsh, *Opera in Old Dublin: 1819–1838* (Dublin, 1952). T. Walsh, *Opera in Dublin: 1705–1797* (Dublin, 1973).

--- WEXFORD

Wexford Festival Opera

Michael Balfe's *The Rose of Castille* inaugurated the Wexford Festival in the 500-seat Theatre Royal on October 21, 1951. A tiny Georgian theater, the Royal was built in the 1700s. The inaugural season offered four performances of this opera.

The idea for the festival was planted in 1950 by Sir Compton Mackenzie, founder of *Gramophone* magazine. When addressing a meeting of the gramophone society, he suggested that hearing live opera would be preferable to listening to recordings. The next year, a local doctor, Tom Walsh, along with another physician Des French, and hotel owner Eugene McCarthy launched the first Wexford Festival. Walsh, acting as the artistic director, imported singers from Italy — Fiorenza Cossotto, Afro Poli, Graziella Sicutti — who joined with their counterparts from Ireland and the United Kingdom — Janet Baker, Heather Harper, Geraint Evans — to perform in works from the bel canto repertory — Vincenzo Bellini, Gioachino Rossini, and Gaetano Donizetti. But the operas performed were the lesser known ones, like Rossini's *Le Comte Ory*, and Donizetti's *Lucrezia Borgia* and *Anna Bolena*. This was very successful. When popular repertory was staged, like Giuseppe Verdi's *La traviata* and Donizetti's *Lucia di Lammermoor*, they were not as successful and not repeated. A repertory developed with predominately unusual and neglected Italian works,

with some French and German ones, during the first half of the 1960s. The neglected French repertory included Jules Massenet's *Don Quichotte*, *Thaïs*, *Hérodiade*, *Grisélidis*, and *Le Jongleur de Notre Dame*, Charles Gounod's *Mireille* and *Roméo et Juliette*, and Georges Bizet's *La jolie fille de Perth* and *Les pêcheurs de perles*. The German repertory explored Peter Cornelius's *Der Barbier von Baghdad*, Eugen d'Albert's *Tiefland*, Carl Maria von Weber's *Oberon*, and Albert Lortzing's *Der Wildschütz*. When Brian Dickie took the reins, he changed the festival's direction, introducing modern works, like those of Benjamin Britten, Sergey Prokofiev (*Igroki*, The Gamblers), and Leoš Janáček (*Kát'a Kabanová*). The season, which had expanded to two works by the second season, was again increased to three operas. When Elaine Padmore was appointed artistic director in 1982, she introduced some obscure operas, including Heinrich Marschner's *Hans Heiling* and *Der Templer und die Jüdin* (one of her favorite composers), Antonín Dvořák's *The Devil and Kate*, Giuseppe Gazzaniga's *Don Giovanni*, and Ferruccio Busoni's *Turandot*. Nicolas Maw's *The Rising of the Moon* welcomed the 1990s, but it was not well-received, mainly for political reasons. The 1992 season included Pietro Mascagni's *Il piccolo Marat*, Stephen Storace's *Gli Equivoci*, and Heinrich Marschner's *Der Vampyr*, followed by Pyotr Il'yich Tchaikovsky's *Cherevichki*, Giovanni

Paisiello's *Il barbiere di Siviglia*, and Ferdinand Hérold's *Zampa* in 1993. The Wexford Festival is dedicated to rare and unusual works performed by unknown artists. The three-opera schedule is described as "one for the heart, one for the head, and one for fun."

Practical Information. Wexford Festival, Theatre Royal, High Street, Wexford. Tel: 353 453 22144, Fax 353 453 24289. The Festival can supply lodging information.

Managing Director. Jerome Hynes (1988–present). **Artistic Directors:** Elaine Padmore (1982–1994), Adrian Slack (1979–82), Thomson Smillie (1973–78), Brian Dickie (1965–73), Tom Walsh (1951–65).

Bibliography. Kevin Lewis, *Memories of Wexford Festival Opera* (Wexford, 1984). John O'Hagen, *The Ecomonic and Social Contribution of the Wexford Festival* (Wexford, 1989).

Other Irish Companies

Other companies in Ireland are noted below by name address, telephone, fax, repertory, and general director (as available).

Irish Operatic Repertory Company. Kinlay House, Shandon, Cork. Tel: 353 21 506 133, Fax: 353 21 506 017. **Director:** John O'Flynn.

Opera Theatre Company Dublin. 18 St. Andrew Street, Dublin 2. Tel: 353 1 679 4962, Fax: 353 1 679 4963. **Recent Repertory:** Flavio, Life on the Moon. **Director:** James Conway.

Humewood Opera Festival. Hilltown, Dunboyne, Co. Meath; Tel: 353 1 8255395.

Italy

—————————————————————— ASCOLI PICENO

Teatro Ventidio Basso

Giuseppe Verdi's *Ernani* and Vincenzo Bellini's *I Puritani* were given the honor of inaugurating the Teatro Ventidio Basso in November 1846. For this occasion, it has been written that the celebrated singer Anna De La Grange received 10,000 lira in gold. Architect Giovanni Battista Carducci designed the structure.

The previous theater in Ascoli Piceno was of wood and occupied a place in the Arengo Palace. In 1839, the *consiglio comunale* decided that a new theater should be built on a different site in the city, since the old one no longer served the needs of the growing populace. The first stone for the new Teatro Ventidio Basso was laid on March 1, 1841. The theater was named in honor of the Ascolanese hero that Pompeo Magno raised to the level of Consul for his heroic deeds.

At the Ventidio Basso, Pietro Mascagni conducted in 1886 and 1896, Alberto Franchetti in 1902, and Riccardo Zandonai in 1922.

In November 1971, there were several seismic shocks which damaged the theater. It was repaired and reopened, but it was not sufficient and the

theater was forced to close for a 14-year major overhaul. The last season before closure witnessed Gaetano Donizetti's *Don Pasquale* and Verdi's *Il trovatore*. The work was completed and on October 15, 1994, Verdi's *La traviata* with Giusy Devinu and Giuseppe Sabatini reopened the opera house. Gioachino Rossini's *Il barbiere di Siviglia* followed seven days later with Donizetti's *Lucia di Lammermoor* gracing the stage in December. Other operas on the boards included Giacomo Puccini's *La bohème*, Verdi's *Rigoletto* and *Il trovatore*, and Pietro Mascagni's *L'amico Fritz*. The repertory is exclusively Italian. One recent exception was Wolfgang Amadeus Mozart's *Der Schauspieldirektor*. The Ascoli Piceno celebrated its 150th anniversary in 1996 with a novelty, Giacinto Cornacchioli's *Diana Schernita*, Rossini's *La Cenerentola*, and Domenico Cimarosa's *I Traci amanti* on the boards. It is a "teatri di tradizione of the Marche region." Recent productions include Donizetti's *Lucia di Lammermoor* and *L'elisir d'amore*, Puccini's *Madama Butterfly* and *Tosca*, Cimarosa's *Il maestro di Cappella*, and Verdi's *Aida*.

Teatro Ventidio Basso

The original plans for the theater were executed by the architect Ireneo Aleandri with the engineer Luigi Mazzoni overseeing the construction, assisted by Ignazio Colucci. But there were many obstacles to the construction and differences of opinion in the realization of the project, so Aleandri left the project and Carducci took over.

A plain grayish white stone facade of Neoclassic inspiration offers five archways separated by Ionic columns as entrances to the building. The horseshoe shaped auditorium radiates in gold and plush red, with four tiers topped by a loggione.

Practical Information. *Teatro* Ventidio Basso, Via del Trivio 44, Ascoli Piceno. Tel: 39 736 298311. If visiting contact the Italian Government Travel Offices (ENIT), 630 Fifth Avenue, New York, NY 10011. Tel: 212-245-4822.

BIBLIOGRAPHY

Bibliography. Luca Luna, *Teatro Ventidio Basso, Città di Ascoli Piceno* (Ascoli Piceno, 1996).

Thanks to Giuseppe Merciai and Ada Gentile, Teatro Ventidio Basso.

—————— BARI

Teatro Petruzzelli (Teatro di Tradizione)

The Teatro Petruzzelli was inaugurated on February 14, 1903, with Giacomo Meyerbeer's *Les Huguenots*. Other works on the schedule for the inaugural season included Umberto Giordano's *Andrea Chénier*, Giuseppe Verdi's *Il trovatore* and *Aida*, and the premiere of a work by a composer from Apulia, P. la Rotella entitled *Dea*. Angelo Messeni was responsible for the construction.

During the successive seasons, all the major operas were performed, including Gioachino Rossini's *Il barbiere di Siviglia*, Pietro Mascagni's *Cavalleria rusticana*, Giacomo Puccini's *La bohème* and *Tosca*, Verdi's *La traviata*, Gaetano Donizetti's *Linda di Chamounix*, Ambroise Thomas's *Mignon*, Jules Massenet's *La Navarraise* and *Manon*, Ruggero Leoncavallo's *I pagliacci*, Francesco Cilea's *Adriana Lecouvreur*, Giordano's *Fedora*, and especially works from Giovanni Paisiello, *Pirro* and *Elfrida* (since he was from Taranto, Apulia). Other works of interest included Antonio Carlos Gomes's *Il Guarnay*, Massenet's *Werther*, *Hérodiade*, and Daniel Auber's *Fra Diavolo*. Mascagni was one of the most popular composers at the Petruzzelli with 116 performances of his *Cavalleria rusticana* between 1903 and 1926. The opera house also welcomed operas by Richard Wagner and those from the Russian repertory. Some of the better known artists who performed there included Lina Bruna Rasa as Desdemona in Verdi's *Otello*, and Florica Cristoforeanu, Mina Horne, Beniamo Gigli, Tito Schipa, Toti dal Monte, and Giacomo Lausri-Volpi Lauri Volpi. The contemporary repertory was not neglected with performances during the 1950s and 1960s of Gian Carlo Menotti's *The Telephone* and Nino Rota's *Il cappello di paglia di Firenze*, among others. Niccolò Piccinni's *Ifigenia in Tauride* was unearthed for the first performance in modern times on December 6, 1986. Other operas offered during the 1980s included Rossini's *Il turco in Italia*, Wolfgang Amadeus Mozart's *Die Zauberflöte*, Verdi's *Rigoletto*, and Puccini's *Madama Butterfly*. Fire destroyed the opera house in 1991.

Teatro Petruzzelli

The Petruzzelli was constructed between 1877 and 1903 by the Petruzzelli family which invested much of their wealth in the theater and received permission from the commune to have the theater named after them. Fire destroyed the theater in 1991, leaving only the exterior. Ferdinando Pinto, the ex–theater manager, was found guilty of arson. There has been a long delay in reconstructing the opera house due to problems between the Comune, which owns the land, and the Petruzelli family, which owns the theater.

The facade of the opera house, which survived the blaze displays statues of Verdi,

Rossini, and Vincenzo Bellini, and is embellished with "Apollo crowning the Muses." The original auditorium, holding four tiers and a gallery, was inspired by Teatro di San Carlo (Naples), Teatro alla Scala (Milan), and Palais Garnier (Paris). There were 2,252 seats.

Practical Information. Teatro Petruzzelli, Via Cognetti 26, 70121 Bari. Tel: 39 80 524 1741, Fax: 39 80 521 0527.

BIBLIOGRAPHY

Bibliography. Information supplied by the theater administration.

BATIGNANO

Musica nel Chiostro (Summer Festival)

The Musica nel Chiostro was inaugurated in 1974 with Henry Purcell's *Dido and Aeneas*. Founded by Adam Pollock, a Brit who "dropped out" of London society in the late 1960s headed for Italy, the Musica nel Choistro takes place in a monastery (*chiostro*) which Adam purchased in an advanced state of disrepair. Pollock decided to produce opera, using all the available spaces — the courtyard, olive groves, and gardens — as stages. The concept of opera in one's home which is far away from everything, with gardens to stroll in, stems from Glyndebourne, but the attire is definitely informal.

The first season had no funding, but by the second year, the community and province of Grosetto were impressed enough to offer financial assistance. Five years later, the region of Tuscany also provided funds, and the company was established as a permanent fixture in the area. The audience is a mixture of Germans, British, and Italians.

The repertory from the beginning has been different from other opera establishments in Italy. Concentrating on obscure works from the Baroque era and modern works, the young company boasts an impressive number of world premieres and first performances in modern times of several operas, including Antonio Salieri's *La grotta di trofonio*, Johann Sebastian Bach's *Temistocle*, Francesco Provenzale's *Schiavo di sua moglie*, and Antonio Cesti's *Le disgrazie d'amore*. His preference in the modern repertory concentrates on British composers, like Michael Tippett's *King Priam* and Benjamin Brittens's *The Turn of the Screw*. The company has also hosted Italian premieres, like Leonard Bernstein's *Candide*, and Georg Friedrich Händel's *Flavio*, *Tamerlano*, and *Tolomeo*. The schedule is determined by what operas will work well in the spaces available.

Pollock has three basic tenets for running the company: progressive opera, which means that instead of changing scenery to move the opera's location, he moves the audience from one place to another around the chiostro; operas not often seen; and the casting of young, up-and-coming singers, willing to perform without fees. In fact, no one at Musica nel Chiostro receives any wages, although they get airfare and expenses. Everyone does everything, from cleaning toilets to being the prima donna. The season's budget is around $50,000 of which 25% is from box office, 25% from the Comune and Provincia di Grosetto, 25% from the Regione Toscana, and 25% from private sources in England. Pollock has no plans to expand from his current schedule of two operas a season.

The production of Alessandro Stradella's *Salomè* was definitely "progressive." The first act took place in the olive grove where a pond had been built for the production, so John the Baptist could baptize his followers. The rest of the work took place in the chiostro's courtyard, transformed to Herod's palace by metal platforms and neon lights that formed Hebrew letters. The production was blunt and direct, at times, extreme. The singing was impressive, and the acting stark and raw.

In such a shoe-string operation, one would expect some interesting tales, and there are many. A few years ago, during a performance, a ferocious thunderstorm stuck, interrupting the performance. First the chairs were moved under an arcade. Then the power went out, so the audience held candles and the village boys came by with

Chiostro courtyard, set for *Salomè* (Batignano, Italy).

their motorbikes, lighting the show with their headlights. The festival retains some of the rustic atmosphere present when Pollock purchased the chiostro, when there was not even any running water. Now the kids who work in the opera sleep in tents in the garden.

Practical Information. Musica nel Chiostro, Santa Croce, 58041 Batignano. Tel: 39 564-38096, Fax: 39 564 38085. When visiting the Musica nel Chiostro, stay at the Bastiani Grand Hotel, Via Gioberti 64, Grosetto. Tel: 39 564 20047, Fax 39 564 29321. It is centrally located and as convenient to the Musica nel Chiostro as possible. The hotel can assist with tickets and make arrangements to get to the festival.

COMPANY STAFF, PREMIERES, AND REPERTORY

Artistic Director. Adam Pollock (1974–present)
World Premieres. S. Oliver's *The Garden,* summer 1977; S. Oliver's *Euridice,* summer 1981; S. Oliver's *The Beauty and the Beast,* summer 1984;

Oliver's *Mario and the Magician,* summer 1988; Dove's *L'Augellin Belverde,* summer 1994; Amendola's *I giganti della montagna,* summer 1995.

Opera Repertory. **1974:** Dido and Aeneas. **1975:** L'Ormindo. **1976:** Tamerlano. **1977:** Tandredi e Clorinda, The Garden, La serva padrona. **1978:** Dido and Aeneas. **1979:** Orontea, Il ballo delle ingrate, Tandredi e Clorinda. **1980:** Tolomeo, The Chemist. **1981:** La finta semplice, Zaide. **1982:** Platea. **1983:** The Turn of the Screw, La Dori. **1984:** The Beauty and the Beast, Apollo and Dafne, La Zingara, Apollo e Giacinto. **1985:** Flavio, La grotta di trofonio. **1986:** Il ritorno di Ulisse in Patria, Il Re Teodoro in Venezia. **1987:** Leonora. **1988:** Temistocle, Mario and the Magician, BATA-CLAN. **1989:** Lo schiavo di sua moglia, Rodelinda. **1990:** King Priam, L'aio nell'imbarazzo. **1991:** The Goose of Cairo, Zaide. **1992:** Euridice, Orlando. **1993:** Le disgrazie d'amore, Candide. **1994:** L'Augellin Belverde, Don Giovanni. **1995:** I giganti della montagna, La calisto. **1996:** Salomè ovvero San Giovanni Battista, A Sensible Man (Stephen Oliver).

Bibliography. Program from Musica nel Chiostro, Batignano 1996. Interview with Adam Pollock, artistic director, July 1996.

Thanks to the administration of Musica nel Chiostro.

BERGAMO

Teatro Donizetti
(Teatro di Tradizione)

The Teatro Donizetti, originally named Teatro Riccardi, was inaugurated on August 24, 1791, with *Didone abbandonata*, the music by various composers. Luigia Todi led the cast and the first violinist, G.B. Rovelli, conducted, as was the custom at that time. Originally named Teatro Riccardi after the gentleman who built it, Bortolo Riccardi, the building was designed by G. Francesco Lucchini.

First performances in Bergamo included a wide range of events, from masquerades and tournaments to comedies and operas. Often they took place in Teatri Provvisionali (Provisional Theaters) so called because they were temporary wooden theaters which were pulled down at the end of the seasons and rebuilt the following season, with the material stored in special warehouses. They were erected in an area called the Fiera (Fair Grounds), and it was on the same location that Riccardi decided to build a permanent structure. But there was one major obstacle, city regulations prohibited the erection of any buildings not of a temporary nature on the Fiera. His construction caused much controversy, but he was strong-willed and ultimately won.

As early as 1784, Riccardi's half-finished theater hosted a musical opera, Giuseppe Sarti's *Medonte re di Epiro* with cloth and wood covers serving as a temporary roof. Riccardi's theater, which still had not been officially named (since it still was not completed) was referred to as either Teatro Nuovo al Prato di Fiera, Teatro Nuovo, or Teatro di Fiera. Two years later, in 1786, *Didone abbandonata* was staged, with music by composers other than those who wrote the music for the 1791 presentation. Domenico Cimarosa's *I due supposti conti ossia lo sposo senza moglie* and *Alessandro nelle Indie*, featuring Gasparo Pacchiarotti as the bel canto star, were staged in 1788. The opera house was completed and inaugurated in 1791. The theater featured a small portico in front of the plastered facade. The elliptically-shaped auditorium held three tiers of boxes topped by a loggia. The Riccardi hosted three seasons: spring, summer, and the Fair, until fire destroyed it on January 11,

1797. Four nights earlier, fire devoured the city's other theater, Teatro della Cittadella, located in the Città Alta (high city). Both fires were suspicious. Nonetheless, Riccardi decided to rebuild his theater, this time entirely of brick. Lucchini again designed the structure, which was more imposing than the first theater. The burnt-out Cittadella was replaced as well, with a new structure called Teatro Cerri. But the city imposed a curious restriction. The boxes had to be devoid of any ornamentation or elements that would distinguish one box from another to prevent competition amongst the owners of the boxes. There were 74 boxes on three tiers topped by a loggia. It was inaugurated in 1798 and remained active until 1807. The programming included both comic works and serious works. The wooden theater disappeared in 1818.

A few years before the Teatro Cerri ceased to operate, a third theater, Teatro della Società was constructed. The nobility and families living in the high city were tired of the vicissitudes, fires, and hardships involving Bergamo's other theaters, so they formed a Società to build a theater in the Città Alta that would give prestige to all of Bergamo. On March 3, 1803, the "project " was agreed upon and Leopoldo Pollack was chosen as the architect. Construction began between 1804 and 1805, with the inauguration of the theater taking place on December 26, 1808, the opening of the Carnival season. Beautiful decorations, the work of Vincenzo Bonomini, Lattanzio Querena, and Francesco Pirovani, ornamented the parapets in front of the three levels of boxes and loggia, lending an air of aristocratic elegance to the place. Besides operas, the theater offered a place to play billiards, games, and to eat. The Teatro Società hosted grand opera and the *cantanti* of the era, including several works by Donizetti and Giovanni Simone Mayr. In 1816, the Emperor of Austria Franz I paid a visit followed in 1824 by the Viceroy Ranieri of Italy. The nobility strove to make their theater not only the most important in Bergamo, but beyond, leading to fierce competition between the Teatro Riccardi and the Teatro della Società.

But the Riccardi reigned supreme, with the Teatro Società (subsequently called Teatro Sociale) in second position. After many vicissitudes, the theater suffered progressive decline.

Three petite theaters arose as well to accommodate companies which needed only a small space. They were Teatrino di Rosate and Teatro di S. Cassiano in the Città Alta (high city), and Teatro della Fenice in the Città Bassa (low city).

The turn of the century also saw the arrival of the well-known German composer Giovanni Simone Mayr in Bergamo and the presentation of his *L'equivoco* at the Riccardi in 1801. Mayr settled in Bergamo and played an important role in the musical life of the city, and especially with Bergamo's own son, Gaetano Donizetti. More of Mayr's works were presented at the Riccardi, including *L'Elisa*, *Labino e Carlotta*, *Il venditor d'aceto*, and *Ginevra di Scozia*. For Carnival 1804, his *dramma per musica*, *Lodoïska*, was given at the Teatro Cerri.

Six years before Bartolomeo Merelli took over the running of Teatro alla Scala (Milan) in 1836, he became director of the Teatro Riccardo. That same year, 1830, Vincenzo Bellini visited to stage his *La straniera* followed in 1831 by *Norma*. Merelli also staged numerous works of Donizetti beginning in 1837. Three years later, the Bergamo composer was honored in the theater while attending a performance of his *L'esule di Roma*, with Domenico Donzelli, Eugenia Tadolini, and Ignazio Marini. Donizetti returned to Bergamo a year before his death, just after the Riccardi hosted his *Maris di Rohan*. Giuseppe Verdi paid a visit in 1844 to oversee his *Ernani*, with triumphant results. A performance of Verdi's *I Lombardi alla prima Crociata* in 1847 struck a patriotic chord. The Austrians had controlled the city since 1814 and its inhabitants were growing more intolerant of their presence. At the end of the famous "O Signore dal tetto natio" chorus, a seemingly endless ovation followed, symbolically expressing their desire for freedom. Verdi returned to direct his *Rigoletto* at the Riccardi, which was the first performance in the Lombardy region, and not successful, a result of a mediocre performance. The Riccardi hosted several well-known singers of the era, including several from Bergamo itself: Giuditta Pasta, Giuditta Grisi, Giuseppina Strepponi, Domenico Reina, Erminia Frezzolini, Carlo Guasco, Napoleone Moriani, Angelica Ortolani, and Giovan Battista Rubini, among others. (Busts of the latter two singers are on display in the theater's entrance hall.)

A cholera epidemic closed the opera house for the 1848 and 1849 Fiera seasons, and for a while, the building served as a military hospital. Finally in 1859, Bergamo was free from its Austrian rulers and the dream of Italy as a united sovereign power under King Victor Emmanuel II had become a reality. To celebrate the king's visit to Bergamo, the Riccardi hosted a concert on August 12. In 1879, Giovannina Lucca took over the directorship of the Riccardi and introduced to Italy Giacomo Meyerbeer's *Étoile du Nord*. During her reign, Donizetti's unfinished work, *Il Duca d'Alba*, received a hearing, with Maestro Matteo Salvi completing the missing sections. During the last decade of the century, after the building had passed to a partnership composed of citizens who purchased shares in the theater, Richard Wagner works were heard for the first time.

For the centenary of Donizetti's birth in 1897, the Teatro Riccardi was renamed Teatro Gaetano Donizetti, and a monumental sculpture of the composer, executed by Francesco Jerace, was unveiled, which dominates a small man-made pond in the gardens next to the opera house. (The theater acquired the nickname "Il nostro Massimo.") As the 20th century dawned, traditional works of the era, like Giacomo Puccini's *La bohème*, *Manon Lescaut* and *Tosca*, Pietro Mascagni's *Cavalleria rusticana*, Ruggero Leoncavallo's *I pagliacci*, and Umberto Giordano's *Fedora* and *Andrea Chénier* were mounted, alongside the then new form of entertainment, film. Even during World War I, opera continued to grace the stage, including the world premiere of *Liacle*, an opera by the Bergamo-born composer, Edoardo Berlendis. Fine talent entertained the Bergamo populace, including Beniamino Gigli, Toti dal Monte, Mercedes Capsir, Rosetta Pampanini, Claudia Muzio, Riccardo Stracciari, and Nazareno de Anglis. On the podium, one found Tullio Serafin, Leopoldo Mugnone, Franco Capuana, among others.

In 1938, the ownership of the theater was transferred from the boxholders to the City Council, and an adventurous policy to support new works and stage unpublished works called Teatro delle Novità (Theater of Innovation) was born. It lasted until 1973. As a prelude to this new enterprise, Giannandrea Gavazzeni's *Paolo e Virginia* was introduced during the 1935 season. All told, by the end of this project, 77 new works had been performed in Bergamo between 1937 and 1973, including Vieri Tosatti's *Il sistema della dolcezza* in 1957, and several Donizetti works: *Rita, o Le mari battu, Maria di Rohan, Maria Stuarda, L'ajo nell'imbarazzo, Marin Faliero, Roberto Devereux, Il giovedì grasso, Belisario, Lucrezia Borgia,* and *Parisiana.* The concluding work in this program was a reworking of *Poliuto,* known as *Les martyrs,* in 1975.

During World War II, opera continued, although on a reduced scale, with the orchestra and singers from La Scala, who had to be evacuated from Milan. It was after the war, for the centennial celebrations for Donizetti's death, that the beginning of a Donizetti renaissance took root. Old works were unearthed that had been long forgotten or rarely ever performed and were brought to light again. Counted among them were Donizetti's *Poliuto, Betly, Il campanello,* and surprisingly enough, *Anna Bolena.* The building was closed from 1958 to 1964 for much needed expansion and modernization. Architects Luciano Galmozzi and Peiro Pizzigoni, together with engineer Eugenio Mandelli, were responsible for the project. Donizetti's *Lucia di Lammermoor* reopened the Teatro Donizetti on October 10, 1964. Two years later, Adolfo Camozzo was appointed artistic director, followed by Riccardo Allorto in 1977. Meanwhile, Teatro Donizetti was included in the category of Teatro di Tradizione in 1968.

The birth of the festival *Donizetti e il suo tempo* (Donizetti and his time) in 1981 led to the blossoming of the seeds planted during the centenary to uncover the obscure, lost, and rarely seen works of Donizetti. It opened with Donizetti's *La favorita* (Italian version) and a decade later was staged in the original French version, *La favorite.* The festival now takes place every other year. Some of the first decade unearthings included *I pazzi per progetto* (1982), *Sancia di Castiglia* (1984), *Torquato Tasso* (1986), *Fausta* (1987), *Gianni di Parigi* (1988), *Elisabetta al castello di Kenilworth* (1989), and *L'assedio di Calais* (1990). Since during the festival years Donizetti works are showcased, the non-festival opera seasons tend to exclude the maestro's operas. Recent offerings included Puccini's *La bohème,* Verdi's *Rigoletto, La forza del destino,* and *I vespri siciliani,* Bellini's *I Puritani,* Gioachino Rossini's *Il barbiere di Siviglia,* Amilcare Ponchielli's *La gioconda,* Wolfgang Amadeus Mozart's *Così fan tutte,* and Franz Lehár's *Die lustige Witwe.* Productions are shared through the Associazione Lirica e Concertistica.

The same *Così fan tutte* production which played at the Teatro Donizetti also was produced at the Teatro Fraschini (Pavia), Teatro Grande (Brescia), Teatro Sociale (Como), and Teatro Ponchielli (Cremona). The *Così* was a clever, light, and innovative production, with young, up-and-coming singers, a majority of whom were Italian. In 1998, Bergamo celebrated the bicentennial of Donizetti's birth with a season devoted exclusively to the master: *Adelia, Don Pasquale,* and *Lucia di Lammermoor.*

Teatro Donizetti (Teatro Riccardo)

For the centennial of Donizetti's birth, the facade was reconstructed to the appearance it has today (aside from a few minor details). Pietro Via was the architect in charge. TEATRO GAETANO DONIZETTI, etched in the stucco facade, identifies an unusual peach-tinted and cement-block building. The names of Donizetti's operas — LINDA D'CHAMOUNIX, DON PASQUALE, SEBASTIANO, FAVORITA, LUCIA DI LAMMERMOOR — are written above each of the five facade windows, framed by engaged Ionic columns and crowned by a lunette. Masks of Comedy and Tragedy and lyres embellish the facade.

A bronze bust of Donizetti greets one on entering the theater. Plush red seats accentuate the gray/pink color scheme of the auditorium. The balustrades of all five tiers are painted with chiaroscuro style putti and wreaths simulating stucco. Deep red valences decorate the boxes and massive gilded Corinthian columns flank the proscenium boxes, painted a deep green in faux-marble style. The Bergamo seal rests high above the stage. Angels ornament the proscenium arch. There are 1,154 seats.

Practical Information. Teatro Donizetti, Piazza Cavour 15, 24121 Bergamo. Tel: 39 35 416 0613, Fax: 39 35 233-488. When visiting the Teatro Donizetti stay at the Excelsior Hotel San Marco, Piazzale Republic 6, Bergamo. Tel: 39 35 366 163, Fax 39 35 223 201. It is conveniently located only a few blocks from the opera house. The hotel can assist with tickets and schedules.

COMPANY STAFF AND SELECT REPERTORY

Direttori Artistici. (since 1966). Riccardo Allorto 1977–present), Adolfo Camozzo (1966–77).

Teatro Donizetti (Bergamo, Italy).

Total Number Performances of Donizetti's Operas in Italy Between 1830 and 1849. L'elisir d'amore 434, Lucia di Lammermoor 356, Gemma di Vergy 317, Il furioso 232, Lucrezia Borgia 223, Roberto Devereux 171, Marin Faliero 163, Torquato Tasso 160, Anna Bolena 159, Parisina 133, Linda di Chamounix 129, La figlia del reggimento 124, Don Pasquale 111, Belisario 110, Olivo e Pasquale 107, L'ajo nel'imbarazzo 96, Maria di Rohan 42, Il campanello 33, Maria de Rudenz 30, Maria Padilla 28, Pia de'Tolemei 13, Poliuto 4.

Mayr's Works at the Teatro Riccardo. Elisa, Labino e Carlotta, Il venditor d'aceto (1803); Elisa (1808); Alonso e Cora (1809); Cantata per Napoleone (1810); Ginevra di Scozia, Cantata per la lascita del Re di Roma (1811); Adelasia e Aleramo (1812); La rosa bianca e la rosa rossa (1815); Ginevra di Scozia (1820); Accademia per il Pio Istituto (1822); Cantata L'armonia (1825).

Mayr's Works at the Teatro della Società. L'amor coniugale (1812); L'amor non ha ritegno (1813); La roccia di Frauenstein (1814); Alfredo il grande (1819); Medea in Corinto (1821); La rosa bianca e la rosa rossa (1822); L'amor coniugale (1831).

Bibliography. *L'opera teatrale di Gaetano Donizetti* (Atti del Convegno Internazionale di Studio 1992). Ermanno Comuzio, *Il Teatro Donizetti* (Bergamo, 1995). Ermanno Comuzio & Andreina Moretti, *Bergamo durante gli anni di Giovanni Simone Mayr* (Quaderno dello spettacolo: stagione lirica autunnale 1995). Egidio Saracino, *Invito all'ascolto di Donizetti* (Milan, 1984).

Thanks to Tatiana Debelli and Andreina Moretti, Teatro Donizetti.

BOLOGNA

Teatro Comunale (Ente Autonomo Lirico)

The Teatro Comunale, originally known as the Nuovo Teatro Pubblico di Bologna was inaugurated on May 14, 1763, with Christoph Willibald Gluck's *Il trionfo di Clelia*, a work especially commissioned for the occasion. Antonio Galli Bibiena, from the well-known family of architects and set designers, was commissioned to erect the new opera house and construct the elaborate sets for the opening production, which required no fewer than twelve set changes.

As early as February 1610, opera was documented in Bologna. *L'Andromeda*, the work of the local composer Girolamo Giacobbi, was given at the Teatro del Pubblico. Opera continued at the Teatro Formagliari, which opened in 1636. Seventeen years later, the Teatro Malvezzi was inaugurated. Gradually it became the favorite gathering place for the aristocracy, obscuring the prestige of the Teatro Formagliari. In 1697, the Malvezzi was enlarged and renovated by Bibiena. The opera house enjoyed an illustrious career until the night of February 19, 1745, when fire devoured the structure. It was decided that the city needed a new, even more illustrious theater and commissioned Bibiena to design and build one.

Despite some disagreement about the merits of the inaugural opera, *Il trionfo di Clelia*, it enjoyed twenty-eight performances during May and June of 1763. Gluck operas were prominent in the repertory with his *Orfeo ed Euridice* in 1771 and *Alceste* in 1778. Another popular composer of the decade was Pasquale Anfossi, with *La finta giardiniera* and *L'avaro* in 1776 and *Il matrimonio per inganno* in 1779. His work was heard again in 1792 when *Zenobia di Palmira* was staged. During this time, it was not uncommon for the operas to be the work of several composers, like *Vologeso re di'parti* and *Didone abbandonata*. The first decade also witnessed other *prime assolute* including Gregorio Sciroli's *Alessandro nell'Indie*, Niccolò Jommelli's *Ezio*, Josef Mysliweczek's *La nitteti*, Vincenzo Manfredini's *Armida*, and Tommaso Traetta's *L'isola disabitata* mounted for the occasion of the Archduchess of Austria Maria Carolina's passage through Bologna.

As the 1700s drew to a close and into the early part of the 1800s, the Nuovo Teatro Pubblico hosted works like Sebastiano Nasolini's *Merope*, *La morte di Cleopatra*, *La vendetta di Nino*, Niccolò Antonio Zingarelli's *Apelle e Campaspe*, *Il conte di Saldagna*, *Giulietta e Romeo* and one opera, *Alzira*, by both composers. As the decade progressed, Ferdinando Paër, Giovanni Paisiello, and Giovanni Simon Mayr works dominated the schedule. It is interesting to note that performances of works by Luigi Cherubini or Gaspare Spontini were not listed and, as was the case in almost all Italian opera houses, no operas of Wolfgang Amadeus Mozart, Ludwig van Beethoven, and Carl Maria von Weber were staged. In 1814, Gioachino Rossini entered the repertory and quickly eclipsed everyone, with twenty works in the repertory between 1814 and 1833: *L'italiana in Algeri*, *Tancredi*, *Aureliano in Palmira*, *La gazza ladra*, *La Cenerentola*, *Il barbiere di Siviglia*, *L'inganno felice*, *La donna del lago*, *Mosè in Egitto*, *Il turco in Italia*, *Elisabetta regina d'Inghilterra*, *Semiramide*, *Sigismondo*, *Otello ossia Il moro Venezia*, *L'assedio di Corinto*, *Zelmira*, *Torvaldo e Dorliska*, *Il serto votivo*, *Eduardo e Cristina*, *Matilde di Chabran*. Rossini's works opened a new chapter in the history of melodrama as well as the fortunes of the Comunale.

Meanwhile, Gaetano Donizetti had become a strong presence, and by the mid–1830s had usurped Rossini's dominant position with *Anna*

Bolena, L'esule di Roma, Fausta, L'elisir d'amore, Il furioso nell'isola Parisina, Belisario, Marino Faliero, Lucia di Lammermoor, Torquato Tasso, Gemma di Vergy, Roberto Devereux, L'ajo nell'imbarazzo, Lucrezia Borgia (until 1852 as *Eustorgia da Romano*), *La regina di Golconda, Le convenienze teatrali, Maria di Rohan, Linda di Chamounix, Maria de Rudenz, Maria Padilla, La fille du régiment, Don Pasquale, Il campanello, Poliuto, La favorita,* and *Don Sebastiano re di Portogallo* in the repertory. In the middle of the 20th century, the first Bologna performances of *Il duca d'Alba* and *Rita* took place. His works encompassed all three genres — *buffo, semiserio,* and *serio.* The last great Italian composer before Verdi came on the scene was, of course, Vincenzo Bellini. Seven of his ten operas received their Bologna premiere between 1830 and 1837. *Il pirata* was staged three years after its La Scala *prima,* followed by *La straniera, I Capuleti e i Montecchi* and *Norma,* with all three operas dominating the 1833 season. *La sonnambula, I Puritani e i Cavalieri,* and *Beatrice di Tenda* completed the Bellini works. Other composers popular then, but whose works did not stand the test of time, include Giovanni Pacini (*La sposa fedele, Il falegame di Livonia, Federico II, re di Prussia ossis il barone di Dolsheim Saffo, Bondelmonte, Lidia di Bruxelles*), Federico Ricci (*La prigione di Edimburgo*), and Luigi Ricci (*Chiara di Rosembergh, L'orfanella di Ginevra, Un'avventura di Scaramuccia, Chi dura vince, Eran due ed or son tre, Il nuovo Figaro, Il birraio di Preston*). Meanwhile, the first works of Giacomo Meyerbeer to be heard at the (Nuovo) Pubblico were his Italian operas, beginning in 1820 with *Semiramide riconosciuta,* followed four years later by *Margherita d'Anjou* and *Il crociato in Egitto* in 1826. His French operas reached Bologna in the mid–1840s with *Robert le Diable.* After a fourteen year hiatus, *Le Prophète* was heard in 1860, then *Les Huguenots, L'Africaine,* and *Dinorah.* The taste of the public was very fickle, and practically every decade new composers and different works were in vogue. The Italian public of the mid–19th century could afford to be — they lived during a time of unparalleled operatic development and when a substantial part of the standard repertory of today was composed.

In 1843, the greatest Italian composer of the 19th century and probably of all times, Giuseppe Verdi, burst on the scene with 32 performances of *Nabucco* (originally called Nabucodonosor).

Thirty stagings of *Ernani* followed, and the operatic stage was permanently altered. The tremendous success enjoyed by Rossini was repeated. The works from his "galley years" followed —*I due Foscari, I Lombardi alla prima Crociata, Attila, Macbeth,* and *Luisa Miller,* before the trio arrived that ensured Verdi's immortality —*La traviata, Il trovatore,* and *Rigoletto* (as Viscardello). Verdi operas took the lion's share of numerous opera seasons. *I vespri siciliani* (Giovanna di Guzman), *Aroldo, Un ballo in maschera, La battaglia di Lagnano, Simon Boccanegra, Don Carlo, La forza del destino, Aida, Otello,* and *Falstaff* all graced the stage — most of Verdi's works were mounted at the Comunale. Mid-century, French operas received some attention, especially during the 1846-47 season with both *Robert le Diable* and Daniel Auber's *La muette de Portici* in the schedule. The first musical director at the opera house was Angelo Mariani (1860–1872), who ushered in an impressive period which lasted almost half a century. He brought technical perfection to the orchestra and chorus, quality singers, and "appropriate dignity" to the productions. He concentrated on the melodramatic works from the Italian, French, and German repertory including Verdi's *Un ballo in maschera, Simon Boccanegra, La forza del destino, Don Carlos* (Italian premiere of the French version), Fromental Halévy's *La Juive,* Gounod's *Faust,* and a Meyerbeer "celebration" in the fall of 1869 with *Le Prophète, Les Huguenots,* and *Roberto le Diable.* Théophile Gautier stated that "the immense trilogy (three Meyerbeer works) corresponded to the three phases of the human experience."

Mariani's introduction of the operas of Richard Wagner in Italy with the Italian premiere of *Lohengrin* on November 1, 1871, was significant. Enrico Panzacchi described the event like this: "Around eight o'clock an eager crowd, serious and solemn, had filled the theater. Many carried a huge book under their arm. Even the ladies entered their boxes, sitting silently with solemn expectation and a composed deportment. The orchestra, boxes, proscenium boxes were all overflowing with people, everyone at their seat. The men almost all wore white tie and top hat, the women were attired with the most elegant low-cut gowns.... In the loggione, some rude murmurings, laughter, and a shout: *viva Verdi, viva Rossini!* But it lasted only a moment." Verdi came and noted the Wagnerian score in his impressions. Hans von Bülow came, expressing above all his enthusiasm for Mariani and the tenor Italo Campanini. Critics, musicians, impresari, and the just curious arrived from all over Italy. The Comune decided to confer an honorary citizenship on Wagner. In his letter of thanks, he noted that it was only possible to present a work so out of the ordinary where there was liberty. The presentation also led to much debate in the streets, cafes, salons, the clubs, and the family. Everywhere, it seemed, an indescribable "disorder" was born, with its own epilogue — new dissent the following year with the Italian premiere of *Tannhäuser*. Marino Mancinelli took over the directorship of the theater and brought Wagner's *Rienzi* to the stage in 1876. Although that opera never returned, Wagner, together with Cosima, arrived on December 4, 1876, and watched the performance from a box. The third Italian premiere of a Wagner work took place the following year with *Der fliegende Holländer*. The entire *Der Ring des Nibelungen* was mounted in 1883. Arrigo Boïto had arrived at the Comunale for the performance of his *Mefistofele* on October 4, 1875, seven months after its disastrous premier at La Scala. It was, however, well received in Bologna and traveled to other Italian theaters.

Mancinelli died suddenly while in the United States and the Comunale invited Franco Faccio to replace him. Faccio was on the podium for Verdi's *Messa di Requiem* which featured Teresa Stolz, Giuseppina Pasqua, Enrico Barbacini, and Ormondo Maini. That fall saw the world premiere of Gaetano Coronaro's *La creola* on November 24, 1878. The following season, the brother of the deceased Marino Mancinelli, Luigi Mancinelli, was appointed to lead the opera house and another outstanding chapter in the Comunale's history unfolded, with Verdi, Wagner and several French operas on the boards — Ambroise Thomas's *Hamlet* and *Mignon*, Gounod's *Roméo et Juliette*, Auber's *Fra diavolo*, Meyerbeer's *Dinorah*, and a German work, Karl Goldmark's *Die Königin von Saba,* with the composer in attendance. World premieres were also in evidence with Giulio Mascanzoni's *Cloe*, Stefano Gobatti's *Cordelia*, and John Urich's *Flora Mac-Donald*. Mancinelli left his post suddenly in 1886 and Giuseppe Martucci was invited to replace him. In the fall of 1894 a 27-year-old Arturo Toscanini arrived, who prepared three works that were new for Bologna — Verdi's *Falstaff*, Alberto Franchetti's *Cristoforo Colombo*,

and the *prima esecuzione assoluta* of Natale Canti's *Savitri*. *Falstaff* was not as well received in Bologna as in the other Italian cities. It appeared as though the Bolognese expected music which was more overflowing, more stirring — in other words, more "Verdian." Toscanini delivered spirited, pure, impeccable interpretations. He returned in 1896, and again in 1904, 1905, and 1906. After Toscanini, Mancinelli was considered the most famous conductor in Italy, and he returned to Bologna for an illustrious 1907 season which included a revival of Wagner's *Tristan und Isolde*, the Italian premiere of Pyotr Il'yich Tchaikovsky's *Yolanda*, and the world premiere of his own *Paolo e Francesca* in 1907.

Despite the outbreak of World War I, the 1914-15 opera season took place, with Meyerbeer's *L'Africaine*, Rossini's *Il barbiere di Siviglia*, Alfredo Catalini's *Loreley*, *L'elisir d'amore*, and *Don Pasquale*, and the world premiere of Ugo Fleres' *L'elisir di vita*. In May 1915, Pietro Mascagni conducted two performances of *Mosè* before war forced a reduction. In 1916, for the benefit of the war orphans, five performances of *La bohème* and nine of *Tosca* were offered. Two operas were mounted in 1917, *Lucrezia Borgia*, and Giacomo Puccini's *La rondine*. By 1918, the opera season was back in full swing with Rossini's *Stabat Mater* and *Il barbiere di Siviglia*, Donizetti's *Don Pasquale*, Verdi's *Aida*, *Rigoletto*, and *La traviata*, Gounod's *Faust*, Bellini's *La sonnambula*, and Massenet's *Werther*.

On the night of November 27-28, 1931, a fire destroyed the stage of the Comunale, closing it until November 14, 1935, when Bellini's *Norma* with Gino Marinuzzi on the podium and Gina Cigna in the title role, reopened the repaired theater. Next came Mascagni's infamous *Nerone* with tenor Aureliano Pertile and Mascagni himself conducting, followed by Verdi's *Don Carlo*, featuring tenor Francesco Merli, bass Tancredi Pasero, baritone Mario Basiola, bass Duilio Baronti, and Cigna Emma as Elisabetta. Three performances of Wagner's *Götterdämmerung* completed the fall 1935 season. Despite the Second World War, the Comunale maintained a full opera season during the first years, including the first presentation at the theater of Rossini's *Il conte Ory* in commemoration of the 150th anniversary of the composers birth. No operas saw the stage in 1943 and only two performances of Domenico Cimarosa's *Il matrimonio segreto* were given in 1944. With the return of peace in April 1945, the enormity of the devastation caused by the war became apparent and the past glories at the Comunale were difficult to attain again.

Meanwhile, the Ente Autonomo, founded in 1942, took over the administration of the theater and the position of sovrintendante was created. (The sovrintendante is a political appointee whose primary job is to find the money for the theater.) The artistic director chooses the programming, but since the sovrintendante appoints the artistic director, usually for a period of four years, the sovrintendante can exert his or her artistic preferences by the appointment. The mayor of the city is also in the honorary position of being the actual head (president) of the theater. The theater is financed through contributions from the state, region, and city governments, private sponsors, box office receipts, and other earned income sources, like production rentals.

The Comunale's history extends back more than 200 years, from the papal government to the domination of Napoleon, from Austrian rule to the national liberty in 1859, from the Resistance of World War II to the proclamation of the Italian Republic, and over the two plus centuries, the opera house has grown and changed with the times. It is one of the most adventurous opera houses in terms of both repertory and production style in Italy. (Bologna has a population of only 400,000.) The *cartellone* is chosen to represent all the different periods, from the 1600s through the 20th century. The type of production one sees depends upon its origin. A 1995 *Wozzeck* from the Nederlandse Opera was modern and clever in its simplicity, and pin-point accurate in its German characterizations (although many empty seats were in evidence), a 1997 *I Puritani* co-production with Barcelona's Teatro La Zarzuela offered traditional sets, with a few modern touches, and many historical inaccuracies in the depiction of the Puritans. Another 1997 production, Benjamin Britten's *Turn of the Screw*, originating at the Comunale was fluid and precise in its spellbinding recreation of Henry James's story. There is no resident company, but different artists of high caliber are brought in for each production.

Teatro Comunale

The foundation for the Comunale was laid in 1756, under the direction of Bibiena, and assisted by Michelangelo Galletti. Controversy fol-lowed almost immediately, and Bibiena had to modify his original plans. When the Teatro Comunale opened in 1763, many essential services were missing which, during the course of the century were added, and especially after the opening of the Teatro del Corso in 1805, which gave the Public Theater much competition. The stage's current appearance dates from 1931, when Armando Villa restructured it after a fire. Four years later, Umberto Ricci reworked the portico and main facade to its current appearance. It is one of Italy's most beautiful opera houses.

A soft-peach-colored arcade wraps around the theater's facade on two sides, contrasting with the off-white exterior above it. Bronze reliefs of Verdi and Wagner are in the entrance lobby. The horseshoe-shaped auditorium of ivory and gold holds five tiers — four box tiers topped by a balconata. The boxes have similar balustrades, with each appearing as a separate balcony. Gilded masks of Comedy and Tragedy are on the proscenium arch which frames a rich green curtain that matches the green velvet seats. The symbol of Bologna called Effigie decorates the curtain. The flat ceiling is painted as a dome with allegorical figures. The opera house seats around 1,000.

Practical Information. Teatro Comunale, Largo Respighi 1, 40126 Bologna. Tel: 39 51 52 99 99, Fax: 39 51 52 99 34. When visiting the Teatro Comunale, stay at the Grand Hotel Baglioni, Via Indipendenza 8, 40121 Bologna. Tel 39 51 22 54 45 or 1-800-223-6800, Fax 39 51 234-840. It is in the heart of Bologna, near the opera house. The hotel can assist with tickets and schedules.

COMPANY STAFF, PREMIERES, AND REPERTORY

Sovrintendante. Felicia Bottino (1995–present), Sergio Escobar, Carlo Fontana, Carlo Maria Badini, Carlo Alberto Cappelli, Pino Donati, Riccardo Nielsen.

Direttori Artistici. Gianni Tangucci (1995–present), Gioacchino Lanza Tomasi, Luigi Ferrari, Valentino Bucchi.

World Premieres. C.W. Gluck's *Il trionfo di Clelia*, May 14, 1763. G. Sciroli's *Alessandro nell'Indie*, May 31, 1764; N. Jommelli's *Ezio*, January 31, 1768; T. Traetta's *L'isola disabitata*, April 1768; J. Mysliweczek's *La nitteti*, April 29, 1770; V. Manfredini's *Armida*, June 1770; F. Gnecco's *L'amore in musica*, April 1805; P. Generali's *Clato*, 1816-1817; F. Sampieri's *Gl'illinesi*, May 7, 1823; V. Trento's *Giulio Sabino nel suo castello di Langres*, May 1, 1824;

Teatro Comunale (Bologna, Italy).

G. Tadolini's *Moctar Gran Visir di Adrianopoli*, May–June 1824; G. Mililotti's *Lo sposo di Provincia*, January 14, 1829; P. Torrigiani's *La Sibilla*, October 22, 1842; L. Badia's *Gismonda di Mendrisio*, February 10, 1846; F. Campana's *Mazeppa*, November 6, 1850; L. Badia's *Il cavaliere nero*, October 28, 1854; G. Pacini's *Lidia di Bruxelles* (also called Lidia di Brabante), October 21, 1858; C. Pedrotti's *Mazeppa*, December 3, 1861; C. Dall'Argine's *Il barbiere di Siviglia*, November 11, 1868; E. Vera's *Valeria*, March 16, 1869; C. Pinsuti's *Il mercante di Venezia*, November 8, 1873; S. Gobatti's *I goti*, November 30, 1873; C. Dall'Olio's *Ettore Fieramosca*, November 6, 1875; S. Gobatti's *Luce*, November 26, 1875; G. Cimino's *La Catalana*, December 7, 1876; G. Ruiz's *Wallenstein*, December 4, 1877; G. Coronaro's *La creola*, November 24, 1878; G. Mascanzoni's *Cloe*, November 15, 1879; S. Gobatti's *Cordelia*, December 6, 1881; J. Urich's *Flora Mac-Donald*, December 6, 1882; F. Clementi's *La pellegrina*, November 16, 1890; F. Clementi's *Vandea*, November 21, 1893; N. Canti's *Savitri*, December 1, 1894; G. Orefice's *Consuelo*, November 27, 1895; V. Gnecchi's *Cassandra*, December 5, 1905; L. Mancinelli's *Paolo e Francesca*, November 11, 1907; F.B. Pratella's *Rosellina dei Vergoni*, December 4, 1909; O. Respighi's *Semirama,* November 20, 1910; A. Lozzi's *L'elisir di vita*, November 21, 1914; G. Guerrini's *Nemici*, January 19, 1921; F. Alfano's *La leggenda di Sakuntala*, December 10, 1921; A. Gandino's *Imelda*, December 10, 1936; F.B. Pratella's *Fabiano*, December 7, 1939; L.F. Trecate's *Buricchio*, November 5, 1948; G. Guerrini's *L'arcangelo*, November 26, 1949; L. Chailly's *Il canto del Cigno*, November 16, 1957; V. Tosatti's *L'isola del tesoro*, November 20, 1958; L. Liviabella's *Antigone*, May 28, 1960; F. Testi's *La brocca rotta*, May 30, 1997. **First Performance In Italy:** F. Paër's *Sargino ossia L'allievo dell'amore*, June 1811. G. Meyerbeer's *L'Africaine*, November 4, 1865. G. Verdi's *Don Carlos*, October 26, 1867. R. Wagner's *Lohengrin*, November 1, 1871. R. Wagner's *Tannhäuser*, November 7, 1872. R. Wagner's *Der fliegende Holländer*, November 14, 1877. Tchaikovsky's *Iolanta*, November 23, 1907; G. Puccini's *La rondine*, June 5, 1917. A. Honegger & J.F. Ibert's *L'aiglon*, November 16, 1956.

Opera Repertory. **1763:** Il trionfo di Clelia, La reggia de'fati. **1764:** Alessandro nell'Indie. **1768:** Ezio, L'isola disabitata. **1770:** Il gran cidde, Ecuba, La nitteti, Armida. **1771:** Orfeo ed Euridice, Aristo e Temira. **1772:** Didone abbandonata. **1774:** Vologeso re di'Parti. **1776:** La finta giardiniera (Anfossi), L'avaro. **1778:** Alceste. **1779:** La scuola de'gelosi, Il matrimonio per inganno. **1787:** Il barone a forza ossia Il trionfo di bacco. **1788:** Li tre Orfei. **1792:** Zenobia di Palmira. **1785:** Apelle e Campaspe. **1796:** Merope, Ines de Castro. **1797:** Alzira, La morte de Cleopatra. **1799:** Il valore, la verità, il merito, Marte

Teatro Comunale auditorium (Bologna, Italy).

e la fortuna. **1802:** Il nuova podestà o le nozze di Lauretta, L'inganno per amore, Antigona. **1803:** La vendetta di Nino, La vergine del sole, La selvaggia nel Messico. **1804:** Il conte di Saldagna, Lodoïska. **1805:** Filandro e Carolina, L'amore in musica. **1807:** Giulietta e Romeo, Le nozze campestri, I due gemelli. **1808:** Il principe di Taranto, Il Re Teodoro in Venezia, Il testamento ossia seicentomila franchi, Il fantatico in Berlina, Ginevra di Scozia. **1809:** La locanda dei vagabondi. **1809:** Le gelosie villane, Giannina e Bernardone, Traiano in Dacia, Artemisia. **1811:** Sargino ossia L'allievo dell'amore, Griselda ossia La virtù in cimento, Zilia. **1812:** Adelasia ed Aleramo, Attila. **1814:** Tancredi, L'italiana in Algeri. **1815-16:** Pamela nubile, Elisa, La pianella perduta, La gelosie di Giorgio. **1816-1817:** Clato. **1817:** Tancredi, La morte di Mitridate, La vestale (Pucitta). **1820:** Semiramide riconosciuta, Aureliano in Palmira. **1821:** Arminio ossia L'eroe germano, Maria Stuarda, regina di Scozia, Ginevra di Scozia, La Cenerentola, Emma di Resburgo, La sposa fedele, Il barbiere di Siviglia. **1821-1822:** La gazza ladra. **1822:** L'italiana in Algeri, Ser Marcantonio, L'inganno felice, Mosè in Egitto, Alzira, La donna del lago. **1823:** Giannina e Bernarone, Annibale in Bitinia, Gl'illinesi, Il venditore d'aceto, La scelta dello sposo, La Cenerentola. **1823-1824:** Pietro Il grande Kzar delle Russie ossia Il falegname di Livonia. **1824:** La dama soldato, La locanda dei vagabondi, Giulio Sabino nel suo castello di Langres, Moctar Gran Visir di Adrianopoli, Margherita d'Anjou, La capanna russa. **1824-1825:** Tebaldo e Isolina. **1825:** Andronico, Amalia e Palmer, La Cenerentola, Il turco in Italia, Il Re Teodoro, Elisabetta Regina d'Inghilterra, Semiramide. **1826:** Clotilde, Le glosie villane, Il crociato in Egitto, Il torneo, La pastorella feudataria. Otello ossia Il Moro di Venezia, Il barbiere di Siviglia, Ser Marcantonio, Semiramide, Pompeo in Siria, Donna Caritea Regina di Spagna, Sigismondo, Il falegname di Livonia. **1828:** Clotilde, L'italiana in Algeri, L'assedio di Corinto, Zelmira, Otello, Tornaldo e Dorliska. **1829:** Lo sposo di Provincia, Il barbiere di Siviglia, Il serto votivo, Il voto di jefte, Giulietta e Romeo, Otello ossia Il moro di Venezia, Semiramide, Tancredi, La Cenerentola. **1830:** L'italiana in Algeri, Ginevra di Scozia, La contessina ossia Il finto pascià, Il parata, La donna del lago. **1831:** Donna Caritea, regina di Spagna, Eduardo e Cristina, Otella ossia Il moro di Venezia, Semiramide, L'esule di Roma. **1832:** La straniera, I normanni a Parigi, Anna Bolena, La gazza ldara, I Capuleti e i Montecchi, Tancredi. **1833:** Matilde di Chabran, L'orfanella di Ginevra, Edoardo in Iscozia, La straniera, Norma, I Capuleti e i Montecchi. **1834:** Otello ossia Il moro di Venezia, La sonnambula, Norma, I Capuleti e i Montecchi, Fausta, Anna Bolena, Tebaldo e Isolina. **1835:** Chiara di Rosembergh, L'elisir d'amore, Il furioso nell'isola di S. Domingo, Un'avventura di

Scaramuccia, Il barbiere di Siviglia, Zulma, La pazza per amore. **1836:** La sonnambula, Danao re d'Argo, Ines de Castro, Norma, Parisina, Belisario, I Puritani, Clotilde. **1837:** Marino Faliero, Lucia di Lammermoor, I Puritani, Torquato Tasso, L'elisir d'amore, Beatrice di Tenda, La straniera. **1838:** Gemma di Bergy, Ines di Castro, La sonnambula, Iginia d'asti, Roberto Devereux, Norma, Beatrice di Tenda, Belisario, Emma e Ruggero. **1839:** La prigione di Edimburgo, Il barbiere di Siviglia, L'ajo nell'imbarazzo, Gemma di Vergy, Norma, Federico II, re di Prussia ossia Il barone di Dolsheim, Elena da Feltra, Beatrice di Tenda, Lucia di Lammermoor, Anna Bolena. **1840:** L'elisir d'amore, La Cenerentola, La sonnambula, Chi dura vince, La nina pazza, Rodolfo di Sterlinga, Il giuramento, I due Figaro ossia Il soggetto di una commedia. **1841:** Gemma di Vergy, La sonnambula, Eran due ed or son tre, Chi dura vince, Don Desiderio, Lucrezia Borgia (Eustorgia da Romano), I Puritani, Antonio Foscarini. **1842:** Chiara di Rosemberg, L'elisir d'amore, Chi dura vince, La regina di Golconda, Il nuovo Figaro, Saffo, La sibilla, Lucrezia Borgia (Eustorgia da Romano). **1843:** Giovanna, prima regina di Napoli, Marino Faliero, Le convenienze teatrali, Nabucco (Nabucodonosor), Roberto Devereus, Lucia di Lammermoor, Il pirata, Chi dura vince. **1844:** Il ritorno di Columella di Padova, La prova di un'opera seria, Maria di Rohan, Ernani, Lucrezia Borgia (Eustorgia da Romano), Linda di Chamounix. **1845:** L'elisir d'amore, I due Foscari, I Lombardi alla prima crociata, Ernani, Maria de Rudenz. **1846:** La vestale (Mercadante), Gismonda di Mendrisio, Attila, Luida Strozzi, La sonnambula, Norma, Robert le Diable. **1847:** La muette de Portici, Maria Padilla, Ernani, Gusmano il buono ossia L'assedio di tarifa. **1848:** La pazza per amore, Il ventaglio, I masnadieri, Gennaro Annese, Lucia di Lammermoor, La fille du régiment. **1849:** Don Pasquale, L'elisir d'amore, Leonora, Il templario, Macbeth, La Vestale (Mercadante). **1850:** Un'avventura di Scaramuccia, I due Foscari, Bondelmonte, Macbeth, Luisa Miller, Mazeppa, Lucrezia Borgia, Linda di Chamounix. **1851:** Un duello alla montagnola di Bologna ovvero Tutti amanti, Eran due ed or son tre, Il campanello, Lucia Miller, Poliuto, Ernani, La vestale, Crispino e la comare. **1852:** Fiorina o La fanciulla di Glaris, La prova di un'opera seria, Poliuto, Norma, I Puritani, Lucrezia Borgia (Eustorgia), Rigoletto (Viscardello). **1853:** La sonnambula. **1854:** La zingara, Lucia di Lammermoor, Luisa Miller, Il cavaliere nero, Caterina Howard, Il barbiere di Siviglia, Tancredi. **1855:** Il birraio di Preston, Nabucco, I masnadieri, Il trovatore, La traviata as (Violetta), Lida di Granata. **1856:** Luisa Miller, Rigoletto (Viscardello), I due Foscari, Mosè, Francesca da Rimini, Giovanna di Guzman, Otello ossia il moro di Venezia. **1857:** I Capuleti e i Montecchi, Etra l'astrologa, Bondelmonte, Lucia di Lammermoor, La traviata (Violetta), Aroldo, Attila, La

sorrentina, Pipelè ossia Il portinaio di Parigi. **1858:** Crispino e la comare, Don Procopio, Semiramide, Lidia di Bruxelles, La traviata (Violetta). **1859:** Robert le Diable (Roberto di Normandia), La muette de Protici, Amina o Due nozze in una sera, Vittore Pisani, La favorita, La lega Lombarda, Le precauzioni ossia Il carnevale di Venezia. **1860:** L'ajo nell'imbarazzo, Il campanello, Tutti in maschera, I Lombardi, Un ballo in amschera, La favorita, Le Prophète, La battaglia di Legnano. **1861:** Rigoletto, Ernani, Simon Boccanegra, Marta, Les Huguenots, Mazeppa. **1862:** La sonnambula, I fidenzati, Macbeth, Norma, Nabucco, Il trovatore. **1863:** Poliuto, Rigoletto, Un ballo in maschera. **1864:** Faust, Ernani, La traviata, Guglielmo Tell, Il barbiere di Siviglia. **1865:** Don Pasquale, Linda di Chamounix, Jone, L'Africaine, L'eroe delle asturie. **1867:** Norma, Don Carlos, Un ballo in maschera. **1868:** La favorita, Don Sebastiano re di Portogallo, Il giuramento, La Juive, Zampa, Il barbiere di Siviglia (Dall'Argine), La favorita, Alda, Lucia di Lammermoor. **1869:** Faust, Valeria, Messa Solenne (Rossini), Le Prophète, Un ballo in maschera, Les Huguenots, Otello ossia Il moro di Venezia, Robert le Diable. **1870:** Dinorah, La forza del destino, Macbeth. **1871:** Ruy Blas, Faust, Lohengrin. **1872:** Mosè, Tannhäuser, Norma. **1873:** Guglielmo Tell, Il mercante di Venezia, Lucrezia Borgia, I goti. **1874:** Ruy Blas. **1875:** Mefistofele, Les Huguenots, Ettore Fieramosca, Luce. **1876:** L'Africaine, Dolores, Rienzi, Ruy Blas, La catalana. **1877:** Aida, La favorita, Der fliegende Holländer, Wallenstein. **1878:** Messa di Requiem (Verdi), Le Roi de Lahore, Don Carlo, La creola. **1879:** Die Königin von Saba, Mignon, Cloe, Faust. **1880:** La favorita, Roméo et Juliette, Aida, Mefistofele, Cordelia. **1882:** La gioconda, Faust, Lohengrin, Flora MacDonald. **1883:** Das Rheingold, Die Walküre, Siegfried, Götterdammerung, Hamlet, Jone, Fra Diavolo, Ruy Blas. **1884:** Isora di Provenza, Tannhäuser, Mefistofele. **1885:** Die Königin von Saba, La traviata, Le Villi, Dinorah, Linda di Chamounix. **1886:** Hérodiade, Un ballo in maschera, Carmen, Lohengrin, La Juive. **1888:** Carmen, Asrael, I Puritani, Les pêcheurs de perles, Tristan und Isolde, Il matrimonio segreto, Alceste, Otello. **1889:** William Ratcliff, Lohengrin. **1890:** Faust, La pellegrina. **1892:** La Juive, Les Huguenots. **1893:** Manon Lescaut, Vandea. **1894:** Falstaff, Savitri, Cristoforo Colombo. **1895:** Faust (Schumann, concert form), Manon Lescaut, Consuelo. **1896:** La bohème, Le Villi. **1897:** Die Walküre, Norma. **1898:** Götterdämmerung, Orfeo ed Euridice. **1899:** Andrea Chénier, Samson et Dalila. **1900:** Iris, Tosca. **1901:** Manon, Mefistofele, La traviata, Rigoletto, Parisina—Emigranti. **1902:** Lohengrin, Germania. **1903:** Adriana Lecouvreur. **1904:** Die Meistersinger von Nürnberg, Dinorah. **1905:** Siegfried, Madama Butterfly, Hänsel und Gretel, Cassandra. **1906:** Das Rheingold, La Damnation de Faust. **1907:** Stabat

Mater (Rossini), Il battista, Tristan und Isolde, Paolo e Francesca, Iolanta. **1908:** Die Walküre, La Wally, Aida. Götterdämmerung, Mefistofele, Rosellina dei Vergoni. **1910:** La favola d'Orfeo, Tannhäuser, Norma, Semirama. **1911:** Salome, Arianna e Barbablù, Il matrimonio segreto, Boris Godunov. **1912:** Tristan und Isolde, Isabeau, Don Carlo. **1913:** Messa di Requiem (Verdi), Lohengrin, L'amore dei tre re, I Lombardi. **1914:** Parsifal, L'Africaine, Il barbiere di Siviglia, L'elisir di vita, Loreley. **1915:** L'elisir d'amore, Don Pasquale, Mosè. **1916:** La bohème, Tosca. **1917:** Lucrezia Borgia, La rondine. **1918:** Stabat Mater (Rossini), Il barbiere di Siviglia, Don Pasquale, Aida, Faust, La sonnambula, La traviata, Werther, Rigoletto. **1919:** Francesca da Rimini, Mefistofele. **1920:** Lohengrin, Otello, Manon Lescaut, Dejanice, Iris. **1921:** Rigoletto, Nemici, Aida, Andrea Chénier, Il tabarro, Gianni Schicchi, Tristan und Isolde, La Cenerentola, Loreley, Carmen, La leggenda di Sakuntala, Il barbiere di Siviglia. **1922:** Les Huguenots, Rigoletto, Tannhäuser, Isabeau, Il barbiere di Siviglia, La traviata, Andrea Chénier. **1923:** Die Walküre, Falstaff, Il piccolo Marat, Francesca da Rimini. **1924:** Nerone, Das Rheingold, La favorita, Luisa, Andrea Chénier, La bohème. **1925:** Lucia di Lammermoor, La traviata, Manon, La cena delle beffe, Tosca. **1926:** Lohengrin, Tristan und Isolde, Il trovatore, Guglielmo Tell, Floriana. **1927:** Tosca, Turandot, Boris Godunov, Mefistofele, Conchita, La gioconda, Salome, Cavalleria rusticana, Isabeau. **1928:** La favola d'Orfeo, Carmen, Götterdämmerung, I quattro rusteghi, Risurrezione, La fanciulla del West, Otello. **1929:** Siegfried, Otello, Manon Lescaut, La campana sommersa, Francesca da Rimini, La traviata. **1931:** Parsifal, La bohème, La wally, La forza del destino. **1935:** Norma, Nerone, Don Carlo, Götterdämmerung. **1936:** Messa di Requiem (Verdi), La fiamma, Die Meistersinger von Nürnberg, Don Pasquale, Aida, Lucia di Lammermoor, Die Walküre, Tosca, Imelda. **1937:** L'elisir d'amore, La bohème, Falstaff, Tristan und Isolde, Mefistofele, Ginevra degli Almieri, La farsa amorosa, Mignon. **1938:** Madama Butterfly, Simon Boccanegra, Tannhäuser, Faust, L'amico Fritz, La monacella della fontana, La gioconda. **1939:** Un ballo in maschera, Turandot, Andrea Chénier, Manon Lescaut, Rigoletto, Carmen, La traviata, Fabiano. **1940:** Maria Egiziaca, Otello, Palla de'mozzi, Il trovatore, Le nozze di Figaro, La fanciulla del West, Siegfried. **1942:** Die Walküre, La forza del destino, Adriana Lecouvreur, La bohème, Giocondo e il suo re, Il conte Ory, L'arlesiana. **1944:** Il matrimonio segreto. **1945:** Rigoletto, La traviata, Cavalleria rusticana, Pagliacci, Madama Butterfly. **1946:** Nabucco, La sonnambula, Lohengrin, Così fan tutte. **1947:** Pelléas et Mélisande, Fidelio, Aida, Die Entführung aus dem Serail, La traviata, Tannhäuser, La fanciulla del West, Belfagor. **1948:** Francesca da Rimini, Werther, Un ballo in maschera, Buricchio, Don Pasquale,

Boris Godunov. **1949:** Norma, Tristan und Isolde, Il barbiere di Siviglia, Rigoletto. L'arcangelo, La bohème Der Freischütz. **1950:** La traviata, Il trovatore, Torneo notturno, Salome, Falstaff, Fedora, Aida, Turandot. **1951:** Messa di Requiem (Verdi), La bohème, La traviata, Madama Butterfly, L'amico Fritz, Tosca, Die Walküre, Risurrezione, Faust, L'amore dei tre re, Samson et Dalila, Manon, Maria Egisiaca, Amelia al ballo, Il fratello innamorato. **1952:** Lohengrin, L'elisir d'amore, Simon Boccanegra, I cavalieri di Ekebù, Mefistofele, Don Quichotte, Siegfried. **1953:** Der fliegende Holländer, Manon Lescaut, Don Giovanni, The Medium, Gianni Schicchi, Don Carlo, Fra'Gherardo, Tristan und Isolde. **1954:** Boris Godunov, Lucia di Lammermoor, Cavalleria rusticana, Carmina Burana, Thaïs, I quattro rusteghi, Das Rheingold, Khovanshchina, Werther, Madama Butterfly, La forza del destino, Le nozze di Figaro, Giulietta e Romeo, Götterdämmerung. **1956:** Un ballo in maschera, L'aiglon, Il barbiere di Siviglia, Adriana Lecouvreur, Otello, Prince Igor. **1957:** Nabucco, La Guerra, Il canto del Cigno, Allamistakeo, La bohème, Pikovaya dama (Queen of Spades), Siegfried, Guglielmo Tell, Faust. **1958:** Il trovatore, La fanciulla del West, L'isola del tesoro, Die Zauberflöte, Die Meistersinger von Nürnberg, Aida. **1959:** Il trovatore, Cavalleria rusticana, Pagliacci, Il barbiere di Siviglia, Turandot, La forza del destino, Lohengrin, Carmen, Andrea Chénier, Il duca d'Alba. **1960:** Antigone, Rita, Turandot, La traviata, Macbeth Boris Godunov. **1961:** Francesca da Rimini, Tosca, Rigoletto, Un ballo in maschera, Norma, Manon Lescaut, Les contes d'Hoffmann. **1962:** Rigoletto, Tristan und Isolde, Prodaná nevěsta (The Bartered Bride), Don Carlo, La bohème, Aida, Don Giovanni, Il segreto di Susanna, Il maestro di cappella, Lucrezia Romana, Isabeau, La bohème. Tannhäuser, Luisa Miller. **1963:** Lyubov k tryom apel'sinam (The Love for Three Oranges), La traviata, Otello, Il trovatore. **1964:** Messa di Requiem (Verdi), La forza del destino, Madama Butterfly, La forza del destino, Falstaff. **1965:** Otello, Il matrimonio segreto, Parisina d'Este, Der fliegende Holländer, Falstaff, L'heure espagnole, Il teatro dei pupi, La pluce d'oro, Der Rosenkavalier, Ernani, Falstaff, Lucia di Lammermoor, Il barbiere di Siviglia. **1966:** Simon Boccanegra, Il canto di natale, Hänsel und Gretel, La bohème, Pelléas et Mélisande, Lohengrin, Manon, A Kékszakállú herceg vára (Duke Bluebeard's Castle), Il prigioniero, Adriana Lecouvreur, Three Penny Opera, Il turco in Italia, Il tamburo di panno, Il cordovano, Il trovatore. **1967:** I due Foscari, Norma, Carmen, Arlecchino, Il ballo delle ingrate, Das Rheingold, Die Walküre, Les contes d'Hoffmann, Barbe-Bleue, La fanciulla del West, Rigoletto. **1968:** Siegfried, L'italiana in Algeri, Kát'a Kabanová, Macbeth, Allez-Hop, Cambiale di matrimonio, Il Signor Bruschino ossia il figlio per azzardo, Aida, Pia de' Tolomei, Erwartung, Oedipus

Rex, Mosè, Katerina Izmaylova, La bohème. **1969:** Lucia di Lammermoor, Manon Lescaut, Elektra, La sonnambula, Don Carlo, Sorochintsy Fair, I Puritani, Götterdämmerung, Wozzeck, Turandot. **1970:** Mosè, Řecké pašija (The Greek Passion), Rita, Il giovedí grasso, Rigoletto, La forza del destino, La Cenerentola, La bohème, Tannhäuser, Mavra, Giovanni Sebastiano, Così fan tutte, Blood Wedding, La traviata. **1971:** Falstaff, Pikovaya dama (Queen of Spades), Die Meistersinger von Nürnberg, La rondine, La forza del destino, La traviata, Il pozzo e il pendolo, Il Capitan Spavento, La faccrica illuminata, L'elisir d'amore, Tosca. **1972:** Tosca, Il coccodrillo, Rusalka, Le convenienze e inconvenienze teatrali, Cavalleria rusticana, I pagliacci, Il conte Ory, Don Giovanni, Otello, Tosca, Macbeth. **1973:** Eugene Onegin, Madama Butterfly, Der fliegende Holländer, La fille du régiment, Der Freischütz, L'histoire du soldat, Billy Budd, Ognenniy angel (The Fiery Angel). **1974:** Macbeth, La favorita, Jenůfa, Madama Butterfly, La traviata, La fille du régiment, La donna del lago. **1975:** La traviata, The Golden Cockerel, Lud Ghidia, Faust, Tristan und Isolde, Ognenniy angel, Il barbiere di Siviglia (Paisiello), Macbeth, Carmen. **1976:** Beatrice di Tenda, Maria Stuarda, Faust, Le nozze di Figaro, Tristan und Isolde, The Night of Christmas. **1977:** Oberto conte di San Bonifacio, Le nozze di Figaro, Beatrice di Tenda, Il barbiere di Siviglia (Rossini), Medea, Faust, Carmen, Die Fledermaus. **1978:** Orfeo ed Euridice, Il barbiere di Siviglia, Fedora, Z Mrtvého Domu (The House of the Dead), Boris Godunov, Rake's Progress, Rigoletto, Parsifal. **1979:** Die Fledermaus, Nos (The Nose), Oberto conte di San Bonifacio, La sonnambula, Anna Bolena, Turandot, The grand macabre, Fedora, Così fan tutte. **1980:** La sonnambula, Otello, Parsifal, Les pêcheurs de perles, Don Pasquale, Turandot, The grand macabre, Khovanshchina. **1981:** Abu Hassan, Adina ovvero Il califfo di Bagdad, Otello, Lakmé, Die Entführung aus dem Serail, Aida. **1982:** Khovanshchina, Tosca, Adriana Lecouvreur, Don Giovanni, Die Zauberflöte, La damnation de Faust. **1983:** La bohème, Aida, La Cenerentola, Tosca, Il matrimonio segreto, Pikovaya dama (Queen of Spades), La forza del destino, Tristan und Isolde. **1984:** Don Giovanni, Simon Boccanegra, Manon Lescaut, Lucrezia Borgia, Armide. **1985:** Die lustige Witwe, Attila, Madama Butterfly, Doktor Faust, Faust, Der Freischütz, Tosca. **1986:** I vespri siciliani, Die Entführung aus dem Serail, Salome, La pietra del paragone. **1987:** Lucia di Lammermoor, Madama Butterfly, Tosca, Das Rheingold, Falstaff. **1988:** La clemenza di Tito, Il Signor Bruschino, Don Carlo, Adriana Lecouvreur, La Grand Duchesse de Gerolstein, Madama Butterfly, I Puritani, Die Walküre, La maschere. **1989:** Achille (Teatro delle Celebrazioni), Un ballo in maschera, La fille du régiment, La fanciulla del West, Boris Godunov, Don Carlo, Manon, Giovanna d'Arco, I Capuleti e i Montecchi. **1990:** Il viaggio, Siegfried, La bohème, Intermezzo, Rigoletto, Don Giovanni. **1991:** Eugene Onegin, Pollicino, Un ballo in maschera, Mosè, Capriccio, Die Zauberflöte, Werther. **1992:** Tancredi, La serva padrona, Il maestro di cappella, Roberto Devereux, Francesca da Rimini, Luisa Miller, La Cenerentola, Götterdämmerung. **1993:** L'incoronazione di Poppea, Amor rende sagace, Simon Boccanegra, Adriana Lecouvreur, Rigoletto, Histoire du soldat, Les noces, Il tabarro, Suor Angelica, Gianni Schicchi. **1994:** L'Italiana in Algeri, Maria Stuarda, Věc Makropulos (The Makropulos Case), I Lombardi, Barbablu. **1995:** Serse, Macbeth, Carmen, Norma, Der Rosenkavalier, Wozzeck. **1996:** La molinara ossia L'amor contrastato, Anna Bolena, Madama Butterfly, Fedora, Tristan und Isolde, Otello. **1997:** Le nozze di Figaro, I Puritani, The Turn of the Screw, Linda di Chamounix, La brocca rotta, Cavalleria rusticana, Turandot. **1998:** Simon Boccanegra, Il campiello, Don Carlo, Don Pasquale, Don Giovanni.

Bibliography. Lamberto Trezzini, ed. *Due secoli di vita musicale: Storia del Teatro Comunale di Bologna* 3 vols. (Bologna, 1987). Renzo Giacomelli, *Il teatro comunale di Bologna (1763–1963)* (Bologna, 1965). Interview with Michele d'Agostino, capo Ufficio Stampa e Pubbliche Relazioni, December 1995.

Thanks to Michele d'Agostino, Teatro Comunale, and Pier Luigi Magrini.

BRESCIA

Teatro Grande (Teatro di Tradizione)

The Teatro Grande (originally called Teatro Nuovo) was inaugurated on December 27, 1810, with Giovanni Simone Mayr's *Il sacrificio di Ifigenia*. Fashioned out of the old theater, the Teatro Grande was an impressive reconstruction. Luigi Canonicarose was responsible for the work.

Although musical history in Brescia dates back to 1562, it was not until 1619, when the Accademia degli Erranti was founded that musical activities began in earnest. The Accademia had a long history of "grand" programs, but the structural precursors to the Teatro Grande had more humble beginnings. In 1664, an impresario called Antonio Barzino performed musical works in a room in the Accademia degli Erranti, which had been converted into a tiny theater with three boxes on a large column of wood: one box for the Venezian Vice-Chancelor, one for the citizens' Authority, and one for the Regency of the Academy. The members of the Erranti society took armchairs from their homes for themselves and their families to sit on in the boxes. The stage, where the musicians and artists were seated, was on the same level as the orchestra section. It continued this way for around a half a century, until a "real" theater was built in 1709, but so reduced in size to keep down the cost that thirty years later, the Academy had to enlarge it. There were four box tiers (even the loggione was divided into boxes) with 29 boxes on each level which curved around the room without interruption by either doors or the royal box (which did not yet exist). In addition, there were also four proscenium boxes. The orchestra section was opened to the middle classes, and the stage was raised and separated by a curtain. The lighting, like before, was by candles and oil lamps, and the theater was heated with warming pans.

Brescia was open to new works in the field of opera and between 1800 and 1971, hosted 328 novelties. It was also quick to host many operas of the important Italian composers of the 1800s. First came Gioachino Rossini in 1814 with *Aureliano in Palmira*. Five years later *La Cenerentola* arrived, followed by *Edoardo e Cristina* in 1820, *La gazza ladra* in 1821, *Ciro di Babilonia* in 1822, *La donna del lago* in 1824, *Tancredi* in 1825, *Otello ossia Il moro di Venezia* in 1827, *Mosè in Egitto* in 1830, *L'assedio di Corinto* in 1831, *Matilde Shabran ossia Bellezza e cuor di ferro* in 1835, and *Il turco in Italia* in 1840. During the 1820s and 1830s, the lesser important Italian composers were not forgotten, with several operas by the Luigi & Federico Ricci, Carlo Coccia, Giovanni Pacini, and Saverio Mercandante including his *I Normandi a Parigi* and *Elisa e Claudio ossia L'amore protetto dell'amicizia*. In 1826, Giacomo Meyerbeer's Italian opera *Il crociato in Egitto* was mounted. Meyerbeer's better known and more successful French operas, like *Robert le Diable,* first took center stage in 1843, and *Les Huguenots* in 1877. Fro-

mental Halévy's *La Juive* arrived in 1861, followed three years later by Charles Gounod's *Faust.* Both offerings for the 1871 Fair season were French — *Robert le Diable* and *La Juive.* Vincenzo Bellini's works began appearing in 1829 with the staging of *Il pirata*, followed by *La straniera* (1831), *Norma* (1834), *La sonnambula* (1835), and *I Capuleti ed i Montecchi* in 1836. Five years earlier, in 1831, Gaetano Donizetti's *Olivo e Pasquale* was first staged in Brescia. His works made a strong showing, among them: *Anna Bolena* (1834), *Belisario* (1837), *Roberto Devereaux* (1838), *Torquato Tasso* (1839), *Furioso all'Isola di S. Domingo* (1840), *Fausta* (1840), *Parisina* (1841), *Lucia di Lammermoor, Marin Faliero, Lucrezia Borgia,* and *Gemma di Vergy*, all in 1843, *La fille du régiment* (1844), and for the 1850 Fair season, both works were Donizetti operas, *Poliuto* and *Roberto Devereux.* In 1844, the first of many Giuseppe Verdi operas, *Ernani,* arrived at the Grande. The next year offered *I Lombardi alla prima crociata*, followed by *I due Foscari* (1846), *Attila* (1847), *Macbeth* (1848), *I masnadieri* (1850), *Giovanna d'arco* (1856), *La traviata* (1857), *Il trovatore* (1857), and *Aida* (1875). Three of Verdi's operas rank in the top five of the most performed operas in Brescia since 1893: *Aida, Rigoletto,* and *La traviata,* although the first performance of *Nabucco* did not take place until 1946, and *Macbeth* was not seen until 1969.

One of the many highlights at the Teatro Grande included Arturo Toscanini conducting Bellini's *I Puritani* and Verdi's *La traviata,* among others, early in his career. But Brescia is probably best known as the place where on May 28, 1904, a revised *Madama Butterfly* (subsequently known as the Brescia-version and the version almost always performed) found success, after its failure three months earlier at La Scala. Meanwhile, Puccini's first and second operas, *Le Ville* and *Edgar,* received their Brescia premiere in 1890 and 1892 respectively. Richard Wagner's *Tannhäuser* first was seen in the Grande in 1897. Even during the Second World War, the Grande kept its doors open. It was after the war, however, with many of the major opera houses in Italy damaged that the Grand offered some especially memorable seasons, with artists like Maria Callas, Renata Tebaldi, Giulietta Simionato, Magda Olivero, Gianna Pederzini, Mario del Monaco, and Nicola Rossi Lementi. With the formation of the *Enti Lirici* and the *Teatro di Tradizione*, difficult times befell some Teatri di Tradizione, including the

Teatro Grande. Although the Teatro Grande has not been able to again reach the heights of those great years after World War II, it is firmly established as a Teatro di Tradizione. Although George Gershwin's *Porgy and Bess* was presented in 1972, the repertory is predominately standard Italian fare. Recent repertory includes Verdi's *Falstaff*, Donizetti's *Don Pasquale*, Wolfgang Amadeus Mozart's *Le nozze di Figaro*, and Puccini's *Manon Lescaut*.

Teatro Grande (Teatro Nuovo)

The imposing Teatro Grande is lined with Ionic columns of alternating bands of white and dark golden marble and crowned by a balustrade. Three banks of wide marble steps lead into the Hall of Statues, so called because it is home to 16 legendary Greek figures. The auditorium glitters with gold, and rococo-style decorations embellish the ivory-colored parapets. Horseshoe in shape, the five tiers (four of boxes topped by a gallery) curve around plush red orchestra seats, which match the rich red stage curtain decorated with gold. Allegorical figures of Tragedy, Comedy, Music and Dance inhabit the ornately frescoed ceiling, complemented by chiaroscuro gilded medallions depicting various Roman and Greek gods.

Practical Information. Teatro Brescia, Corso Zanardelli, 25100 Brescia. Tel: 39 30 377-1643, Fax 39 30 377-1647. When visiting the Teatro Grande, stay at the Master, via Apollonio 72, Brescia. Tel: 39 030 399 037, 39 030 370 1331. The hotel, located in a quiet section, can assist with tickets and schedules.

COMPANY STAFF, PREMIERES, AND REPERTORY

Direttore Artistico. Giuseppe Morandi
Premieres. M. Portogallo's *L'inganno poco dura*, Carnival 1801. Orlandi's *Il Podestà di Chioggia*, Carnival 1802. V. Lavigna's *La musta per amore* and M. di Capua's *Furberia e Puntiglio* Carnival 1804. B. de Dominicis's *Romolo e Numa*, Fair 1805. C. Guglielmini's *La scelta dello sposo*, Fair 1806. B. Neri's *I Saccenti alla Moda*, Carnival 1808. C. Mellara's *I Gauri*, Fair 1811. F. Grazioli's *La festa della riconoscenza ossia Il pellegrino bianco*, Carnival 1823. L. M. Viviani's *L'eroe Francese*, Fair 1826. M. Gnecco's *La prova di un'opera seria*, Carnival 1828. R. Manna's *Jacopo di Valenza*, Fair 1833. C. Quaranta's *Ettore Fieramosca*, Carnival 1842. Peruzzini's *Il Borgomastro di Scheidam*, Spring 1846. Palomba's *Paolo e Virginia*, Spring 1847. A. Randeg-

ger's *Bianca Cappello*, Carnival 1854. Petrali's *Giorgio Bary*, Carnival 1857. L. Vicini's *Anelda di Salerno*, Carnival 1866. V. Marchi's *Il cantore di Venezia*, Carnival 1868. G. Libani's *Il conte Verde*, Carnival 1880. M. Zafred's *Amleto*, Carnival 1973; L. Manenti's *La galla*, Carnival 1974; G. Malipiero's *Uno dei dieci*, Carnival 1974; G. Facchinetti's *La finta luna*, Fall 1989.

Opera Repertory. **1800:** La pianella, La morte di Mitridate. **1801:** L'inganno poco dura, Pirro Re di Epiro. **1802:** Il podestà di Chioggia. **1803:** L'Andromaca. **1803:** La Griselda. **1804:** La muta per amore. **1805:** Romolo e Numia. **1806:** La scelta dello sposo, La capriccisoa corretta, La calzolaia. **1807:** L'avaro e il ritratto, Le convenienze teatrali **1808:** Orfeo ed Euridice. (1809–1810 Theater closed to construct new theater.) **1811:** Il sacrificio di Ifigenia, I Gauri, Aspasia e Clearco. **1812:** Traiano in Dacia. **1813:** Li pretendenti delusi, Fingallo e Comalla. **1814:** Ser Marcantonio, Aureliano in Palmira. **1815:** La vestale (Pacini). **1816:** Egeria, Alzira. **1817:** Teodoro, Ginevra di Scozia. **1818:** Rodrigo di Valenza. **1818:** Evellina. **1819:** La Cenerentola, Il marcato di Monfregoso. **1819:** Gli Orazi e i Curiazj. **1820:** La morte di Semiramide, Edoardo e Cristina, Aristodemo, Rodrigo di Valenza. **1821:** La gazza ladra, Arminio ossia L'eroe germano. **1822:** L'imboscata, Ciro di Babilonia. **1823:** La festa della riconoscenza ossia Il pellegrino bianco, Tebaldo ed Isolina. **1824:** Clotilde, La donna del lago, La rosa bianca e la rosa rossa. **1825:** Il Barone di Dolsheim, Clotilde, Tancredi, Aureliano in Palmira. **1826:** La sposa fedele, Il crociato in Egitto, L'eroe francese. **1827:** Elisa e Claudio ossia L'amore protetto dell'amicizia, Otello ossia Il Moro di Venezia. **1828:** La prova di un'opera seria, Caritea Regina di Spagna, Gli arabi nelle Gallie ossia Il trionfo della fede. **1829:** La prova di un'opera seria, Il pirata. **1830:** Il crociato in Egitto, Francesca da Rimini (Generali), Mosè in Egitto. **1831:** Olivo e Pasquale, La Semiramide, La straniera, L'assedio di Corinto. **1832:** Zadig e Astartea, Didone abbandonata. **1833:** Chiara di Rosembergh, Jacopo di Valenza, I Normandi a Parigi. **1834:** Un avventura di Scaramuccia, Anna Bolena, Norma. **1835:** Matilde Shabran ossia Bellezza e cuor di ferro, La sonnambula, I Capuleti ed i Montecchi. **1836:** La pazza per amore, L'orfanella di Ginevra. **1837:** La gazza ladra, Eran due ed or son tre, Belisario. **1838:** Ines de Castro, Roberto Devereux. **1839:** Il colonnello, Torquato Tasso, Beatrice di Tenda, Il bravo. **1840:** La prigione di Edimburgo, Il turco in Italia, Il furioso all'Isola di S. Domingo, Fausta. **1841:** Il nuovo Figaro, Parisina, Chiara di Rosemburgh, Anna Bolena, Elena da Feltre. **1842:** L'avaro, Chi dura vince, Ettore Fieramosca, Il tempiario, I Puritani ed i Cavalieri. **1843:** Gemma di Vergy, Robert le Diable, La fanciulla di Castel Guelfo, Il ritorno di Columella da Padova ossia il pazzo per amore, Lucia di Lammermoor,

Marin Faliero, La Cenerentola, Nabucco (Nabuccodonosor), Lucrezia Borgia. **1844:** La fille du régiment, La Regina di Golgonda, Chi dura vince, Maria di Rohan, Ernani. **1845:** I Capuletti ed i Montecchi, Saffo, La fiera di Tolobos, I ciarlatani in Spagna, I falsi monetari, Il furioso all'Isola di S. Domingo, Il barbiere di Siviglia, Il nuovo Figaro, I Lombardi alla prima Crociata, Beatrice di Tenda, L'italiana in Algeri. **1846:** Roberto Devereux, Linda di Chamounix, Robert le Diable, Il Borgomastro di Scheidam, Il ritorno di Columella da Padova ossia il pazzo per amore, I due Foscari, Ernani. **1847:** La vestale (Mercandante), Saffo, Lucrezia Borgia, I due Figaro ossia Il soggetto di una Commedia, Stabat Mater, Paolo e Virginia, Gemma di Vergy, L'aio nell'imbarazzo, Attila, I Puritani, I Lombardi. **1848:** Don Pasquale, Lucia di Lammermoor, Linda di Chamounix, Un avventura di Scaramuccia, Il barbiere di Siviglia, Gli esposti, Macbeth, Nabucco, Beatrice di Tenda, L'elisir d'amore. **1849:** Chiara di Rosembergh, La prova di un'opera seria. **1850:** Don Procopio, I masnadieri, Gemma di Vergy, Poliuto, Roberto Devereux. **1851:** Ernani, Marin Faliero, Nabucco, Linda di Chamounix, Eran due ed or son tre, I Lombardi, Macbeth. **1852:** Il fornaretto, Il barbiere di Siviglia, Lucrezia Borgia. **1853:** Luisa Miller, Polituo, Orazj e Curiazj, I due Foscari, Don Bucefalo, Lucrezia Borgia, Buondelmonte, Rigoletto, Otello (Rossini), Semiramide. **1854:** Bianca Cappello, Fiorina o la fanciulla di Glaris, Il barbiere di Siviglia, Il trovatore, La zingara, Maria di Rohan. **1855:** Robert le Diable, I due Foscari, Ernani, I falsi monetari, il campanello, il nuovo Figaro. **1856:** La testa di Bronzo, Poliuto, La favorita, Scaramuccia, I masnadieri, Giovanna d'arco, L'assedio di Leida, Mosè in Egitto, I Puritani e i Cavaliari. **1857:** La traviata, Giorgio Bary, Il trovatore, Pipelè ossia Il portinaio di Parigi, Il barbiere di Siviglia, Il ritorno di Columella da Padova ossia il pazzo per amore, Il birrajo di Preston, Ultimi giorni di Suli, I Lombardi, Rigoletto. **1858:** La traviata, Macbeth, Nabucco, Don Checco, La prova di un'opera seria, Marco Visconti, Gemma di Vergy. **1859:** Il carnovale di Venezia, Chi dura vince, Roberto Devereux, Saffo, Il trovatore, Attila. **1859:** La sonnambula, Lucia di Lammermoor, Il barbiere di Siviglia, Vittor Pisani, Norma. **1861:** La Juive, Giovanna di Flandra, Ernani, Il domino nero, Aroldo, Beatrice di Tenda. **1862:** Macbeth, Nabucco. **1863:** Un ballo in maschera, Il trovatore. **1864:** Rigoletto, Il giuramento, Maria di Rohan, Faust, Don Bucefalo, **1865:** La favorita, Lucrezia Borgia, L'assedio di Brescia, Jone, Don Sebastiano re di Protogallo. **1866:** Anelda di Salerno, Isabella d'Arragona, Lucia di Lammermoor. **1867:** La Contessa d'Amalfi, Robert le Diable, Ernani. **1868:** Il cantore di Venezia, Celinda, La favorita, Un bacio per amore, Norma, Caterina Howard. **1869:** Un ballo in maschera, La Juive, Lucrezia Borgia, I Puritani, I vespri siciliani. **1870:** Luisa Miller, La sonnambula,

Marco Visconti, Il barbiere di Siviglia, Don Giovanni, Dinorah, Crispino e la comare, L'elisir d'amore. **1871:** Linda di Chamounix, Martha, Un'avventura di Scaramuccia, Robert le Diable, La Juive. **1872:** Jone, Ruy Blas, La forza del destino, Le educande di Sorrento. **1873:** I Lombardi, Ruy Blas, Romeo e Giulietta (Marchetti), Cicco e Cola, Le precauzioni. **1874:** La notte di Natale, La sonnambula, I promessi sposi, I Goti, La favorita. **1875:** L'assedio di Layda, Isabella d'Aragona, Aida. **1876:** Un ballo in maschera, La Contessa di Mons, Diana di Chavarny, Faust, Dolores. **1877:** Marta (Pletau) La Contessa d'Amalfi, Les Huguenots. **1878:** Salvator Posa, Rigoletto, Nabucco, Mefistofile. **1879:** Il Guarany, Jolanda, Vittor Pisani, Semiramide, Anna Bolena. **1880:** Il trovatore, Il conte Verde, Papà Marin, Le educande di Sorrento, Il barbiere di Siviglia, Don Pasquale, Crispino e la comare, L'Africaine. **1881:** Macbeth, Il lago delle fate, Un ballo in maschera, La stella del nord. **1882:** I Lombardi, La Juive, Ruy Blas, Don Carlo, Il barbiere di Siviglia. Romeo e Giulietta (Marchetti) Ernani, La gioconda. **1884:** Saffo, Il giuramento, La traviata, Carmen. **1885:** Faust, Poliuto, Marion Delorme. **1886:** La forza del destino, Martha, Rigoletto, I Lituani. **1887:** La sonnambula, La traviata, Lucia di Lammermoor, Otello. **1888:** Mignon, Dinorah, Asrael. **1889:** Aida, Il trovatore, Un ballo in maschera, Mefistofile. **1890:** Le ville, Le roi de Lahore, Carmen, Cavalleria rusticana, Lohengrin, Norma. **1892:** L'Africaine, Lucrezia Borgia, Andrea del Sarto, Simon Boccanegra, Edgar, I pagliacci, Cavalleria rusticana, Falstaff, Manon Lescaut. **(By year of first performance 1893–1981): 1893:** Otello, Manon, Il malacarne. **1894:** La traviata, Il barbiere di Siviglia, Die lustigen Weiber von Windsor, Le donne curiose (Usiglio), I due soci, I Puritani. **1895:** La favorita, Samson et Dalila, L'amico Fritz, Les pêcheurs de perles, Guglielmo Ratcliff. **1896:** La bohème, Rigoletto, Andrea Chénier, Maruzza. **1897:** Manon Lescaut, Faust, Tannhäuser. **1898:** Les Huguenots, Edmea. **1899:** La gioconda, Fedora, Il trillo del diavolo, Ruy Blas. **1900:** Tosca, Lohengrin, falstaff. **1901:** Aida, Werther, Lorenza. **1902:** Iris, Ernani, Germania. **1903:** Carmen, Adriana Lecouvreur, Hamlet. **1904:** Madama Butterfly, Lucia di Lammermoor, La damnation de Faust, Chopin, I pagliacci, Zazà. **1905:** Un ballo in maschera, Hänsel und Gretel, Giovanni Gallurese, L'elisir d'amore, Mosè. **1906:** Mefistofele, Tristan und Isolde, Don Pasquale. **1907:** Thaïs, Germania, Amica, Nadeya. **1908:** La Wally. **1909:** Loreley, Guglielmo Tell, Hérodiade. **1910:** Don Carlo. **1911:** La fanciulla del West, Roméo et Juliette, Cristoforo Colombo, Salome. **1912:** Die Walküre, Isabeau, Conchita. **1913:** Le donne curiose, L'amore dei tre re, Messa da Requiem. **1914:** Parsifal. **1916:** Norma, Madama Sana-gène. **1917:** Francesca da Rimini. **1920:** Cavalleria rusticana, Suor Angelica, Gianni Schicchi, Il tabarro, Il segreto di Susanna, Lodoletta.

1921: I quattro rusteghi. 1923: Dejanice. 1924: Giulietta e Romeo. 1925: Il piccolo Marat, Boris Godunov, La cena delle beffe. 1926: Turandot, Il trovatore. 1928: Mignon, Odette. 1931: La forza del destino, Siegfried. 1933: La favola d'Orfeo. 1935: La sonnambula. 1938: La baronessa di Carini. 1939: Scherzo veneziano, La vedova scaltra. 1940: Il campiello. 1941: Anima allegra. 1942: Stellina d l'orso. 1943: L'Arlesiana. 1946: Nabucco. 1948: Così fan tutte. 1949: In terra di leggenda. 1950: Il matrimonio segreto, Donata. 1951: Fiammetta e l'avaro. 1952: The Medium, La via della finestra. 1954: Simon Boccanegra, Il maestro di musica, Osteria portoghese. 1955: Il Signor Bruschino, L'italiana in Londra. 1956: L'italiana in Algeri, Terra senza passato. 1957: The Telephone. 1959: La domanda di matrimonio. 1961: Lord Byron's Love Letters, Rita. 1962: Il rosario, Il maestro di Cappella. 1964: Luisa Miller. 1965: Pelléas et Mélisande, Prince Igor. 1966: Una donna uccisa con dolcezza. 1967: Così fan tutte. 1968: Assassinio nella cattedrale, Kát'a Kabanová. 1969: Macbeth, La Cenerentola. 1971: Fidelio, La passione Greca. 1972: Porgy and Bess, Vivi. 1973: Khovanshchina, Amleto (Zafred), Der Freischütz. 1974: Prodaná nevěsta (Bartered Bride). 1975: The Rake's Progress. 1981: La jolie fille de Perth, Maria Stuarda.

Bibliography. *Teatro Grande Brescia dal 1800 al 1972 (Brescia, 1972).*

Thanks to Luigi Fertonani, Teatro Grande, and Corrado Ambiveri.

CAGLIARI

Teatro Comunale (Ente Autonomo Lirico)

When the Teatro Comunale was inaugurated on September 2, 1993, the city had been without a proper theater since the early 1940s. The Politeama Regina Margherita, constructed in the second half of the 1800s, was destroyed by fire in 1942 and not reconstructed. The Teatro Civico was destroyed during a bombing raid in 1943. Fifty years passed before a new opera house opened.

After the war, performances took place in the auditorium of the Conservatorio di Musica and in a 2,000-seat movie theater known as the Massimo, constructed in 1947. Structural problems eventually forced its closure and the opera seasons continued in the 1,000-seat Palestrina, where Verdi's *Otello* was performed during the mid–1980s. Other works staged included Gioachino Rossini's *L'italiana in Algeri*, Verdi's *Rigoletto*, Giacomo Puccini's *Madama Butterfly*, and Wolfgang Amadeus Mozart's *Le nozze di Figaro*. After the opening of the Teatro Comunale in 1993, it hosted the first staged performance in Italy of Richard Wagner's *Die Feen* on January 12, 1998. Recent productions include Puccini's *La bohème*, Donizetti's *L'elisir d'amore*, and Benjamin Britten's *The Turn of the Screw*.

Teatro Comunale

An architectural competition was held in 1964 with 34 entries, and three years later, the designs of Luciano Galmozzi, Teresa Ginoulhaic Arslan, and Francesco Ginoulhiac were accepted. Several events delayed construction, including strikes and a layer of water discovered underneath the building site. Work finally began in 1971 but 22 years passed before the theater was completed. It is a huge modern structure of various geometric shapes, angles, and protrusions fused together. There are 1,600 seats in the main hall.

Practical Information. Teatro Comunale, Via Sant'Alexainedda 111/E, Cagliari. Tel: 39 70 40821, Fax: 39 70 408-2251. If visiting, contact the Italian Government Travel Offices (ENIT), 630 Fifth Avenue, New York, NY 10011. Tel: 212-245-4822.

COMPANY STAFF

Sovrintendente. Mauro Meli. **Direttore Artistico:** Massimo Biscardi.

Bibliography. Francesco Sforza, *Grand Teatri Italiani* (Rome, 1993). Additional information supplied by the theater.

Thanks to Cesare Salmaggi and Fausto Fontecedro.

———————————————————————————— CATANIA, SICILY

Teatro Massimo Bellini
(Teatro di Tradizione)

Vincenzo Bellini's *Norma* inaugurated the Teatro Massimo Bellini on May 31, 1890. The opera house was named after Catania's native son and renowned composer. One hundred years later, another production of *Norma* marked the Massimo Bellini's centennial celebration on May 31, 1990. Red and pink flowers in the piazza garden formed "1890–1990" for the occasion. Carlo Sada designed the theater.

Before the opening of the Massimo Bellini, opera was performed in the Teatro Comunale. When the Catanese premiere of *Norma* took place, on November 10, 1835, only two months after the composer's death, the audience was dressed in mourning clothes. The Comunale, however, suffered from structural problems, which closed the third box tier, and pointed to the need for a new theater. After the Massimo Bellini opened, it hosted celebrations which revolved around the anniversaries of Bellini's birth, death, and premiere of *Norma*. The 100th anniversary of the composer's birth took place in November 1901, marked by a production of *Norma*. Then there was a centennial celebration of the world premiere of *Norma* on December 26, 1931, with another production of the opera, featuring Fidelia Campigna, (Norma), Irene Minghini Cattaneo (Adalgisa), and Iesus de Gaviria (Pollione) under the baton of Antonio Guarnieri. Four years later, in 1935, the centennial celebration of Bellini's death featured *Beatrice di Tenda*, *Norma*, *I Capuleti e i Montecchi*, and *I Puritani*. In November 1951, for the 150th anniversary celebration of Bellini's birth, the theater presented a festival with productions of *Norma*, *Il pirata*, *I Puritani*, and *La sonnambula*. Five years later, the fall season of 1956 was of interest with the first performances in Catania of Giuseppe Verdi's *Don Carlos* and Pietro Canonica's *Medea*, and another production of *Norma* to mark the 125th anniversary of its world premiere. Also on the boards was Richard Wagner's *Die Walküre*, Umberto Giordano's *Andrea Chénier*, and Giacomo Puccini's *Madama Butterfly*.

In addition to staging all of Bellini's works, the Massimo Bellini has offered other works as diverse as Jules Massenet's *Don Quichotte* in 1928, Arthur Honegger's *Jeanne d'Arc au bûcher* in 1960, a "scandalous" *Vivì* of Franco Mannino in 1963, the Italian premiere of Nabokov's *La morte di Rasputin* also in 1963, the world premieres of Zafred's *Kean* in 1981 and Mannino's *Il ritratto di Dorian Gray* in 1982. Other noteworthy offerings included Francis Poulenc's *Les dialogues des Carmélites*, Carl Maria von Weber's *Oberon*, Richard Strauss's *Arabella*, and Mozart's *La clemenza di Tito*. Maria Callas has sung at the Massimo Bellini in *Norma*, *I Puritani*, Verdi's *La traviata*, and Donizetti's *Lucia di Lammermoor*, while Giuseppe Taddei has assayed Falstaff. Beniamino Gigli, Gina Cigna, and, of course, Giuseppe di Stefano, who was born at Motta Santa Anastasia, six miles from Catania, have all graced the stage.

In 1986, the theater became part of the Ente Autonomo Regionale. Nevertheless, the production quality has a way to go. The centennial celebration performance of *Norma* on May 31, 1990, was redeemed only by the presence of Daniel Oren, who made the orchestra sound better than any of the singers, and saved the evening, because, at the beginning of Act II, when Norma was so overcome with despair at her lover's betrayal that she wanted to kill her children, the children were busy hitting each other in a game of tag, ruining the entire Act. It was a reminder that the Teatro Massimo Bellini is still a provincial house, very much like the city in which it is located. The centennial season also witnessed the world premiere of Sylvano Bussotti's *Bozzetto siciliano*, the first performances in Catania of Pyotr Il'yich Tchaikovsky's *Eugene Onegin* and Weber's *Der Freischütz*, and the first performance at the opera house of Giovanni Battista Pergolesi's *La serva padrona*. In addition, Puccini's *La bohème*, Mascagni's *Guglielmo Ratcliff*, and Verdi's *Il trovatore* were on the boards. During the 1996-97 season the first performances in the city of Azio Corghi's *Divara* and Umberto Giordano's *Madama Sans-Gêne* took place. Recent offerings include a reinterpretation of Georg Friedrich Händel's *Rinaldo* by Corghi called *Rinaldo & C.*, Ludwig van Beethoven's

Fidelio, Strauss's *Elektra*, Puccini's *Il trittico*, Jacques Offenbach's *Les contes d'Hoffmann*, Verdi's *Rigoletto*, Mascagni's *Cavalleria rusticana*, and Bellini's *La sonnambula*.

Teatro Massimo

The Cantanese had wanted to construct a grand opera house for many years before the city council approved the architectural project of Zahra-Buda in 1812. But this opera house was not to be as Algerian pirates invaded Catania, forcing a halt in the construction, so the city could erect fortifications instead. When the city council decided to continue work on an opera house, Zahra-Buda's project was forgotten and only a description of his grandiose plans survived. It held a public competition, but there were no entries. Finally in 1874, Sada came up with a design which was approved, and construction began in 1880.

The usual legal and political battles ensued which extended the building time to a decade.

The Teatro Massimo Bellini is a masterpiece of eclectic styles, blending Neoclassical, Renaissance, and Baroque. The building stretches across the bordering streets with graceful archways. The facade displays Ionic columns and pilasters, rounded arches and lyre etched windows, cornices and friezes with lyres and masks of Tragedy and Comedy, cherubs and nymphs, and busts of composers. On the top, TEATRO BELLINI is etched in gold on white marble. The horseshoe-shaped auditorium holds four box tiers capped by a large gallery. In the center, a red-and-gold draped royal box is topped by two cherubs holding a crown. Intricately carved stucco on the parapets, executed by Andrea Stella, complements elaborate decorations on the proscenium arch. The ceiling presents the apotheosis of Bellini, surrounded by allegorical illustrations from four of his operas. There are 1,266 seats.

Practical Information. Teatro Massimo

Teatro Massimo Bellini (Catania, Italy).

Bellini, Via Perrotta 12, Catania 95131. Tel: 39 95 32 53 65, Fax: 39 95 31 18 75. If visiting the Teatro Massimo Bellini, contact the Italian Government Travel Offices (ENIT), 630 Fifth Avenue, New York, NY 10011. Tel: 212-245-4822.

COMPANY STAFF

Direttore Artistico. Piero Rattalino.
Bibliography. *Teatro Bellini Stagione Lirica*

1990 (Catania, 1990). *Sicilia Magazine: Speciale Teatro Massimo Bellini* Supplemento al N.6 di SM 1989. *31 Maggio 1890–1990: Per il centenario dell'inaugurazione* (Catania, 1990). Domenico Danzuso & Giovanni Idonea, *Cento anni di un teatro* (Catania, 1990). Domenico Danzuso & Giovanni Idonea, *Musica, Musicisti e Teatri a Catania: dal mito alla cronaca* (Palermo, n.d.).

Thanks to the Ufficio Stampa, Teatro Massimo Bellini.

COMO

Teatro Sociale
(Teatro di Tradizione)

The Teatro Sociale was inaugurated August 28, 1813, with *Adriano in Siria*. The evening was dedicated to the *"ornatissima Società dei Palchettisti"* (Society of Boxholders) which was an association of nobility, whose money made the building possible. A five-act ballet *Ghislen ed Erbinee* by Domenico Grimaldi concluded the evening. Architect Cusi was responsible for the theater's design.

In 1764, the *Società dei Palchettisti* had built a tiny theater of wood, designed by Sig. Broletto. After the turn of the century, they decided they needed a larger, more "modern" theater and commissioned Cusi to design one containing three tiers of boxes with a minimum of twenty boxes a tier, topped by a large open gallery. The noblemen's purchase of the theater's boxes paid for the structure. The repertory of the theater's early years saw works by the composers and librettist of late 1700s, and the operas of Gioachino Rossini, whose early work *Demetrio e Polibio* was staged in September 1813. Rossini's operas played an important role in the theater's repertory, and included *La Cenerentola* in 1819 and a decade later, *Tancredi* with Giuditta Pasta. Every year, the opera season began in August with two or three works which were repeated around thirty times. After the opera house underwent its first restoration, Luigi Ricci's *Un'avventura di Scaramuccia* and Vincenzo Bellini's *Norma* were staged for the reopening in 1838. Ricci's *Chiara di Rosemberg* and Graffigna's *Un lampo di fedeltà* were on the schedule in honor of the crown prince of Russia's visit and in 1852, a Carnival season began, which offered between two and five operas. Giuseppe Verdi's *Attila* was

the first of his works to be staged at the Sociale. The most popular of Verdi's operas were *Rigoletto*, first performed in 1854, *Il trovatore* (1855), *I due Foscari* (1855), *Macbeth* (1856), *La traviata* (1857), *Nabucco* (1857), and *I masnadieri* (1858). Some well-known artists interpreting his operas included Giuseppe de Sanctis (*Luisa Miller*) and Geltrude Reiz (*Un ballo in maschera*), and Carnival of 1882 saw the first performance at the Sociale of Verdi's *Aida*. Other frequently performed works included Donizetti's *Don Pasquale*, *Lucrezia Borgia*, and *Lucia di Lammermoor*, and Bellini's *Beatrice di Tenda* and *I Capuleti e i Montecchi*.

Near the end of the 1870s and 1880s, the operas of four French composers were on the schedule — Charles Gounod's *Faust*, Giacomo Meyerbeer's *Les Huguenots* and *Robert le Diable*, Georges Bizet's *Carmen*, and Daniel Auber's *Fra Diavolo*. The seasons of the 1890s were marked by the works of (then) new Italian composers. In 1891, Pietro Mascagni's *Cavalleria rusticana* and *L'amico Fritz* were staged, followed by Ruggero Leoncavallo's *I pagliacci* in 1892, and Amilcare Ponchielli's *La gioconda* in 1893. The most enthusiasm, however, was reserved for the first formances in Como of Giacomo Puccini's *Manon Lescaut* and *La bohème*. Every seat in the theater was occupied and every daily newspaper and magazine in Milan sent critics. Even Jules Massenet and Verdi sent congratulatory telegrams. The final year before the turn of the century offered Verdi's *Otello*, Perosi's *La resurrezione di Cristo*, and for the fall season, six opera and ballets in the repertory — Mascagni's *Cavalleria rusticana* and

Leoncavallo's *I pagliacci*, Ferdinando Paër's Il *maestro di Cappella*, Gastaldon's *Pater*, Benedetto Ferrari's *Cantico dei cantici*, and Marenco's *Ballo Excelsior*.

With the dawn of the 20th-century, the area around Como was industrialized, making the 19th-century opera house too small to accommodate everyone who wanted to attend a performance. This led, in 1908, to two proposals to remedy the problem: either increase the seating capacity of the theater by replacing the center boxes on the fourth tier with gallery-type seats, and adding a second gallery, or build another theater. Although the first task would have been easier and less expensive to accomplish, the boxholders would not approve the opening up of the theater to such a large public: They felt it would have destroyed the "fundamental origins of the *Palchettisti*" (elitism and exclusivity). So a new building was erected, the Politeama. Designed by Federico Frigerio, it was inaugurated on September 14, 1910, with Puccini's *La bohème*.

The early part of the 1900s saw Umberto Giordano's *Andrea Chénier* and *Fedora*, which were very popular, Richard Wagner's *Lohengrin*, Hector Berlioz's *La Damnation de Faust*, Mascagni's *Iris* and *Amica*, Massenet's *Manon*, Verdi's *Aida*, Puccini's *Madama Butterfly*, and Arrigo Boïto's *Mefistofele*. The 1913 season marked both the centennial of the birth of the Sociale and that of Verdi. Operas by Mascagni, Adriano Lualdi, Ferrari, Giordano, and Puccini played a prominent role in the centennial celebrations for the theater, and a special evening was organized devoted to Verdi's music, to commemorate the birth of Italy's greatest composer. At the same time, a marble bust of Verdi, by the sculptor G. Fontana, was unveiled. After a performance of Massenet's *Werther*, the Sociale closed because of World War I, reopening again in 1919 for the Carnival season. The centennial of the death of Bellini was commemorated during the 1935 season with a staging of his *La sonnambula*. The Sociale remained open during World War II, hosting the 40th anniversary of Verdi's death and the 50th anniversary of the world premiere of Mascagni's *L'amico Fritz*. Singers like Mafalda Favero, Giulietta Simionato, and Mario del Monaco performed, and after Teatro alla Scala was destroyed in 1943, it used the Sociale during 1943 and 1944.

After the war, Giordano attended a performance celebrating the 50th anniversary of his *Fe-dora*, with Mario Parenti on the podium, and in 1951, Beniamino Gigli sang in Puccini's *Manon Lescaut* and Tito Schipa in Francesco Cilea's *Arlesiana*. A few novelties for Como appeared in the following years, including Alfredo Casella's *La giara*, Riccardo Zandonai's *Francesca da Rimini*, Gian Carlo Menotti's *The Medium* and Virgilio Mortari's *La Scuola delle mogli*. The 100th anniversary of Puccini's birth, in 1959, was commemorated with *Turandot*. In 1966 there was a crisis within the Sociale — disinterest of the boxholders combined with the huge expense necessary for a major restoration to guarantee the stability and security of the Teatro Sociale. The predicament was caused by the public's indifference to the theater, now that they had movies and television for entertainment. This resulted in reduced profits which led to poor artistic quality of the productions. Opera was characterized by inferior performances of the standard repertory. The opera house was regarded as a museum, a testimony of the past. The theater lacked good artistic direction, one that was in touch with the present. The opera house was then closed at the end of the 1960s for restoration. When it reopened, during the 1970s, some unusual works were on the boards, like Francesco Morini's *La vindice*, Alberto Soresina's *Tre sogni*, and Roberto Hazon's *Agenzia matrimoniale*. Although the 1980s and 1990s saw additional lesser known works, like Claudio Monteverdi's *La favola d'Orfeo*, Giovanni Battista Pergolesi's *La serva padrona*, Jean-Phillipe Rameau's *Platée*, Domenico Cimarosa's *Il maestro di cappella*, Cipollini's *Piccolo Haydn*, Ferrari's *Ettore Fieramosca*, and Ugo Bottacchiari's *Severo Torelli*, the Sociale remains a conservative house, with a faithful adherence to the traditional Italian repertory with surprisingly rich stagings. The "old-fashion" stereotype of opera is alive and well in Como — singers face the audience and belt out their arias, and then break character to acknowledge the applause. With no pretense of acting and static movements, they compensate with feeling and emotion in their singing. The result is a uniquely Italian atmosphere with a dialogue between the audience and the artists, which does not and probably could not exist in any other country of the world. The Sociale shares productions with the Teatro Coccia di Novara and the Teatro Sociale di Mantova. Recent repertory includes Puccini's *La bohème*, Giordano's *Andrea Chénier*, Mozart's *Così fan tutte*, and Rossini's *La gazzetta*.

Teatro Sociale

The construction of the Teatro Sociale began in February 1812 with Francesco Bollini in charge and Innocenzo Bossi as his assistant. The *Palchettisti* wanted the theater completed by August, which was not enough time for such a large project. The haste resulted in many problems which included two unfortunate accidents with the architrave collapsing. After the second accident, the entire portico was demolished and rebuilt. The problems, however, did not end there. A few days after the theater opened, the local government sent another architect, Sig. Zanoja to inspect the safety of the building, and he found irregularities which required further rebuilding, giving credence to the saying, "haste makes waste." Finally, a year late, the theater opened in August 1813.

Six massive Corinthian columns soar in front of a classic facade of mustard-tone stucco supporting a relief pediment, with a central lyre flanked by masks of Comedy and Tragedy. The ivory and gold auditorium holds five tiers in an elliptical-shape. An allegorical mural embellishes the ceiling, with angels and cherubs holding crown wreaths and lyres, and horns evoking Apollo. A seal of Como and a clock rest high above the elaborately decorated proscenium arch which frames a deep maroon stage curtain.

Practical Information. Teatro Sociale, Via Bellini 3, 22100 Como. Tel: 39 31 27 01 71, Fax: 39 31 271-472. When visiting the Teatro Sociale, stay at the Grand Hotel di Como, Via per Cernobbio, 22100 Como. Tel: 39 31 5161, Fax 39 31 516-600. It is in a quiet location and convenient to the opera house. The hotel can assist with tickets.

BIBLIOGRAPHY

Bibliography. Donato de Carlo & Filomena Scalzo, *Teatro Sociale di Como* (Bergamo, 1988); A. Sevesc, *Gli spettacoli lirici nei Teatri comaschi (1874–1924* (Como, 1924), U. Barbaglia, A Luzzani, *Ottanta anni di vita del Teatro Sociale* (Como 1955); V Lucati, *Centocinquantanni di storia del Teatro Sociale di Como* (Como, 1963).

Thanks to La Direzione, Teatro Sociale.

COSENZA

Teatro Alfonso Rendano (Teatro di Tradizione)

The Teatro Alfonso Rendano, originally called the Teatro Comunale di Cosenza, raised its curtain for the first time on November 20, 1909, for Giuseppe Verdi's *Aida*. Arrigo Boïto's *Mefistofele* and Verdi's *Rigoletto* completed the inaugural season. In 1935, the opera house was renamed in honor of a native son, Alfonzo Rendano, a famous musician and pianist.

The first public theater, Teatro Real Ferdinando had been closed by a decree in 1853 from King Ferdinando of Bourbone to satisfy the demands of the Jesuits, who owned the school where the theater had been built. From the time the Teatro Alfonso Rendano was inaugurated until 1943, the repertory was almost exclusively Italian and the composers from the romantic and *verismo* schools — Vincenzo Bellini, Arrigo Boïto, Francesco Cilea, Gaetano Donizetti, Umberto Giordano, S. Giacomantonio, Ruggero Leoncavallo, Pietro Mascagni, Amilcare Ponchielli, Giacomo Puccini, Quintieri, Gioachino Rossini, and Verdi.

Verdi was the most popular composer followed by Puccini. The only unfamiliar works on the program were Giacomantonio's *Fior d'Alpe* during the 1913 season, and a decade later, Quintieri's *Julia*, conducted by the composer. Georges Bizet and Ambroise Thomas were the only non–Italian composers represented. Works like *Il trovatore, La favorita, Norma, La forza del destino, Andrea Chénier, La gioconda, Carmen, Mignon, Manon Lescaut, Zaza, Un ballo in maschera, Ernani, Otello,* and *La sonnambula* graced the stage. Then in 1943, after a season of Ponchielli's *La gioconda,* Rossini's *Il barbiere di Siviglia,* and Puccini's *La bohème,* the theater closed and did not open its doors for 24 years.

During part of the time, the Rendano underwent a renovation and refurbishment, reopening in 1967 with Verdi's *La traviata.* Rossini's *Il barbiere di Siviglia,* Wolfgang Amadeus Mozart's *Don Giovanni,* Verdi's *Il trovatore,* and Quintieri's *Liliadeh* also graced the stage that season. This represented an expansion of the repertory with the introduction of Mozart works into the schedule. Although the opera seasons floundered during the 1970s and early 1980s, with no seasons at all between 1972 and 1976, it made a comeback and between 1977 and 1988, the repertory was extended to include Richard Wagner, Jules Massenet, and the 18th-century composers Giovanni Paisiello and Domenico Cimarosa. Verdi and Puccini remained the most popular composers. The repertory included *Lohengrin, Nabucco, Rigoletto, La traviata, Werther, Don Carlo, Il matrimonio segreto, Tosca, Cavalleria rusticana, I pagliacci, Madama Butterfly,* and *L'Arlesiana* among others, with Giacomantonio's *La leggenda del ponte* and *Quelle Signore* the only unknown works.

By the mid–1990s one unusual work was introduced each season that included Nikolay Rimsky-Korsakov's *Motsart i Sal'yeri* (Mozart and Salieri) and Franz Schubert's *Die Zwillingsbrüder* and *Der vierjährige Posten.* A typical schedule for the mid–1990s offered Puccini's *Manon Lescaut* and *Tosca,* Verdi's *Rigoletto,* Rossini's *La scala di seta* and *Il Signor Bruschino.* Recent repertory includes Donizetti's *Lucia di Lammermoor* and *Don Pasquale,* and Puccini's *Madama Butterfly.*

Teatro Alfonso Rendano

A three-arch portico surmounted by second level of three arched windows flanked by pairs of Ionic pilasters defines the facade. TEATRO COMUNALE A. RENDANO is written across the front. The horseshoe-shaped auditorium of three-tiers and a loggione is filled with musically-inspired ornamentation of stucco and gold. Acoustic panels of aluminum are on the ceiling.

Practical Information. Teatro Alfonso Rendano, Piazza XV Marzo, 87100 Cosenza. Tel: 39 984 813229, Fax: 39 984 74165. If visiting, contact the Italian Government Travel Offices (ENIT), 630 Fifth Avenue, New York, NY 10011. Tel: 212-245-4822.

BIBLIOGRAPHY

Bibliography. Amedeo Furfaro, *Storia del Rendano* (Cosenza, 1989).
Thanks to Ufficio Stampa.

CREMONA

Teatro Comunale Amilcare Ponchielli (Teatro di Tradizione)

The Teatro Comunale Amilcare Ponchielli, originally called the Teatro Nazari after its owner, Giovanni Battista Nazari, opened on December 26, 1747, with an opera buffa. The local architect Giovanni Battista Zeist, who belonged to the architectural circle that included the famous Antonio Galli Bibiena, was entrusted with the commission.

Music in Cremona predates the construction of the Nazari, tracing back to 1670 with the construction of the Teatro Ariberti, which hosted performances until 1717. At that time, the family who owned the theater, which was in a state of disrepair, gave it to a religions order. It was transformed into a place of worship. During its existence as a theater, works like Antonio Cesti's *Il tito,* G.A. Boretti's *Marcello in Siracusa,* and *Enone gelosa* graced the stage. In 1746, a group of nobility decided to give the city a real and proper theater. Work on the opera house was begun that same year and completed before the end of the next. Constructed of wood, the Nazari boasted a U-shaped auditorium with four tiers of boxes including a royal box. The ceiling was painted and decorated by the architects Zeist and Borroni and Guerrini. It offered works like Pietro Chiarini's *Artaserse,* Baldassarre Galuppi's *Vologeso, Semiramide riconosciuta, Il filosofo di campagna,* and Niccolò Piccinni's *La buona figliola.* The world premiere of G.M. Rutini's *I matrimoni in maschera* took place. Works of Domenico Cimarosa, Luigi Cherubini, and Michelangelo Valentini's *La clemenza di Tito* were also on the boards. In 1785 the Nobile Associazione (*palchettisti* or boxholders) purchased the theater, renaming it Teatro della Società. In 1793, Cimarosa's *L'italiana in Londra* was performed. Around the same time, encores were forbidden, so as to not "tire" the singers and not prolong the show to a late hour. The theater hosted opera until fire claimed it in 1806. The *palchettisti* decided to immediately rebuild, giving the commission to one of the best-known architects of the time, Luigi Canonica. Renamed the Teatro della Concordia, it opened on October 26, 1808, with a double-bill of Ferdinando Paër's *Il principe di Taranto* and Gaetano Marinelli's *Il trionfo d'amore*, the latter commissioned for the opening. The Concordia hosted operas like Giovanni Simone Mayr's *Ginevra di Scozia*, Giovanni Paisiello's *I zingari in fiera*, Stefano Pavesi's *Elisabetta, Regina d'Inghilterra*, and Domenica Cimarosa's *Gli amanti comici*, and non-operatic events as well until it was partially destroyed by fire on January 26, 1824.

The theater was immediately restored under the direction of Faustino Rodi and Luigi Voghera, following the original plans of Canonica, and was reopened on September 9, 1824, with Gioachino Rossini's *La donna del lago*. Initially the works of Vincenzo Bellini, Rossini, the brothers Luigi and Federico Ricci, and Giuseppe Valier held the stage, but the operas were eventually replaced with works by Giacomo Meyerbeer, Saverio Mercadante, Gaetano Donizetti, and early Giuseppe Verdi, the first being *Nabucco* in 1843. The *prima assoluta* of *I promessi sposi*, composed by Ponchielli, took place in 1856 followed by his *La Savoiarda* five years later. Subsequently, Ponchielli took the post of the theater's musical director. The operas of Umberto Giordano, Jules Massenet, Charles Gounod, Giacomo Puccini, Pietro Mascagni, Richard Wagner, and Alberto Franchetti's *Germania* all entered the repertory in 1905. Also at the beginning of the 20th century, Amilcare Ponchielli was added to the theater's name, to honor their native son. Some novelties after the war included De Martino's *Il cosacco*, Renzo Rossellini's *La guerra*, and Jacopo Napoli's *Il rosario* and *Il malato immaginario*. Concerts, ballets, classic theater, and even cinema shared the stage with opera.

The Comune purchased the theater from the boxholders in 1986, and it has been designated a *Teatro di Tradizione*. Since 1989, the theater has undergone major restoration work, as well as acquiring advanced stage technology. The seasons are almost exclusively of Italian operas, with Italian casts, conductors and directors. Some

offerings include Ponchielli's *La gioconda* and *I promessi sposi*, Giacomo Puccini's *Tosca* and *Manon Lescaut*, Verdi's *Rigoletto*, *Falstaff* and *Simon Boccanegra*, Donizetti's *Don Pasquale*, Gioachino Rossini's *Il barbiere di Siviglia*, Niccolò Piccinni's *La cecchina, ossia La buona figliuola*, and Wolfgang Amadeus Mozart's *Le nozze di Figaro* and *Così fan tutte*.

Teatro Comunale Amilcare Ponchielli

The actual opera house building is the result of several constructions, reconstructions, modifications, and restorations over the past 250 years. The most important, however were the original ones, in 1747 and 1808. The rebuilding after the fire in 1806 brought several improvements to the theater with the enlargement of the stage.

The opera house displays a Grecian-style portico, which dominates the Neoclassic facade. *Sociorum Concordia Erexit a MDCCCVII* noting the Society responsible for the structure and the date of the construction, is engraved on the entablature. The horseshoe-shaped auditorium holds three tiers of boxes topped by two galleries. There is a center royal box and proscenium boxes. The rose and gold filled space radiates with the gilded stucco embellishments on the ivory-colored parapets. The seats are plush red. The curtain, dating from 1892 and executed by Antonio Rizzi has been recently restored. There are 1,249 seats.

Practical Information. Teatro Comunale Amilcare Ponchielli, Corso V. Emanuele, 52/54, 26100 Cremona. Tel: 39 372-407-273, Fax: 39 372-460-180. When visiting the Teatro Ponchielli, stay at the Continental, piazza della Libertà 25, 25100 Cremona. Tel: 39 0372 434 141, Fax: 39 0372 454 873. It is centrally located and convenient to the opera house.

BIBLIOGRAPHY

Bibliography. Francesco Maria Liborio, Elia Santoro, Sergio Carboni, Arnaldo Bassini, *Il Teatro Ponchielli di Cremona* (Cremona, 1995), and Arnaldo Bassini, *Il sipario di Antonio Rizzi* (Cremona, n.d.).

Thanks to Arnaldo Bassini, Teatro Ponchielli, and Ghiraloli Enrico.

Teatro Comunale
(Teatro di Tradizione)

The Teatro Comunale was inaugurated in September 1798 with Saverio Mercadante's *Gli Orazi e i Curiazi*. The structure was designed by Cosimo Morelli and Antonio Foschini, with Serafino Barozzi responsible for the interior decorations.

Ferrara's theatrical history goes back a few centuries to a performance of *Ercole d'Este*, a forerunner of lyric opera. In 1773, the Cardinal Legato Borghese wanted to build a new, elegant theater for the city, open to the public, with a large seating capacity. He requested the architect Morelli for drawings. Morelli proposed a bell-shaped curve, but this new idea never came into being since the funds necessary for construction did not materialize and the task of building the theater was left to his successor, Cardinal Legato Carafa. Carafa, without any hesitation, entrusted the project to the architect Giuseppe Campana. He chose the most central location in the city and expropriated the houses that were in the way, quickly beginning with the construction. Unfortunately for Carafa, some of the houses belonged to the Camera Apostolica, which was not happy about this turn of events. Carafa paid for his imprudence by quickly leaving Ferrara. By this time, the theater was almost completed, except for the roof, when in November 1786, a new cardinal, Legato Spinelli, arrived from Rome and ordered an immediate stop to the construction. He opened an inquiry as to the conduct of Campana and discovered both technical and administrative improprieties. The building was destroyed. Spinelli then entrusted two architects, Morelli and Foschini, with the project, consulting with Giuseppe Piermarini as well.

Less than 30 years after its inauguration in 1798, the building was in need of restoration. Between 1825 and 1826, Angelo Monticelli executed the work. The appearance that the theater has today was achieved during the redecoration between 1849 and 1851. The theater needed repairs and this opportunity was used to upgrade the technology to the time as well as to redecorate according to the fashion of the day. The theater was only intermittently opened to the public, primarily for grand festivals and masked balls, until it was declared unsafe in 1956 and closed. The theater received a major restoration during the 1980s.

Gisberto Morselli, the theater's current director, explained that one of his goals is to make the theater better known to the public and to get more people to go to the theater in Ferrara. There is no internal structure at the theater, no fixed orchestra, chorus, singers. Everyone who appears in the operas are guests and everything is borrowed or rented. The theater receives money from the state, thanks to Law #800 of 1962 which created the Ente Liriche. The theater hosts several different activities, besides opera. About the only well-known person with ties to the theater is the conductor Claudio Abbado, who led Wolfgang Amadeus Mozart's *Le nozze di Figaro* (1994) and *Don Giovanni* (1996), and Gioachino Rossini's *Il barbiere di Siviglia* (1995).

Morselli collaborates with the five other theaters in Emilia Romana on productions: Teatro Comunale (Bologna), Teatro Comunale (Modena), Teatro Municipale (Piacenza), Teatro Regio (Parma), and Teatro Muncipale Valle (Regia Emilia). A world premiere had been planned but was postponed for financial reasons. The opera house has also established a collaboration with various cities in Germany to bring German productions to Italy. In 1996, Richard Wagner's *Der fliegende Holländer* was a co-production with Oper Stuttgart, and the following season the Städischen Bühnen Münster's György Ligeti's *Le grand macabre* was presented. *Le grand macabre* was staged in a modern, grotesque manner, filled with Germanic symbolism. It played to a half empty theater and confused audience — the work was performed in German with no Italian supertitles and contained a lot of spoken dialogue. Although a "narrator" was present in lieu of supertitles, he "explained" little and all the Italians were baffled. Other works staged in the mid–1990s were Giacomo Puccini's *La bohème*, Gaetano

Donizetti's *Anna Bolena*, Domenico Cimarosa's *Le astuzie femminili*, Mozart's *Don Giovanni*, and Giuseppe Verdi's *La traviata*. Recent repertory includes Mozart's *La clemenza di Tito*, Verdi's *Rigoletto*, and Rossini's *L'italiana in Algeri*.

Teatro Comunale

The Teatro Comunale first received an orchestra pit in 1928, and between 1935 and 1937, the secret staircase of the Cardinals was destroyed. From 1940, German troops occupied the entire theater complex and everything which could be destroyed, was. (Germany was allied with Italy during World War II).

A classic, earth-toned building with several high arches houses the theater along with several shops. Two rows of seven rectangular windows punctuate the facade. Inside, the five-tiered, horseshoe-shaped auditorium is decorated in a ro-

mantic-inspired manner. Raspberry velvet seats match a raspberry-colored curtain. The overhang is cream and gold. Floral designs, gilded griffins and horses on a light green background embellish the parapets. There are 890 seats.

Practical Information. Teatro Comunale, Corso Martiri della Libertà 5, 44100 Ferrara. Tel: 39 532 202 312, Fax: 39 532 247 353. When visiting Teatro Comunale, stay at the Astra Hotel, Viale Cavour, 55, 44100 Ferrara. Tel: 39 532 206 088, Fax: 39 532 247 002. It is centrally located and close to the theater. The hotel can assist with tickets and schedules.

BIBLIOGRAPHY

Bibliography. Teatri Storici in Emilia Romagna (Bologna, 1982). Deanna Lenzi, *Teatro Comunale di Ferrara* (Bologna, 1977). L.N. Cittadella, *Sul Teatro Pubblico di Ferrara* (Ferrara, 1850). Interview with Gisberto Morselli, director, April 1997.

Thanks to Andrea Strocchi, Teatro Comunale.

Teatro Comunale (Ferrara, Italy).

Teatro Magnani

The Teatro Magnani was inaugurated on October 26, 1861, with Giuseppe Verdi's *Il trovatore*. The construction took a long time and was based on the original plans of Nicola Bettoli, but completed by Antonio Armarotti. Girolamo Magnani was responsible for the interior decorations.

The idea of a new theater dated back to 1812, when an association of wealthy citizens and civil servants decided to give Fidenza an opera house built around Piazza Verdi. The project was entrusted to Bettoli, who had previously designed the Teatro Ducale in Parma. Unfortunately the work did not progress very far before lack of funds forced its termination. Then in 1831, the association proposed to the Comune to take ownership to prevent further decay and to finish the building, but a decree by Maria Luiga on October 1, 1838, prevented this. Her reason was that it would incur expenses larger than the Comune would be able to sustain. Finally, on March 1848, authorization was granted but work did not begin again until 1854. At this time, Antonio Armarotti had taken over the project, but six more years would pass before the theater was completed.

The Gruppo Marchetti organizes an October season of opera at the theater, with two to three works in the repertory. The repertory is mainstream Italian operas with recent productions including Gaetano Donizetti's *L'elisir d'amore* and Verdi's *Rigoletto*.

Teatro Magnani

The theater offers a Neoclassic style facade with a portico that was a former carriage entrance. Five large windows surmounted by stucco medallions enclosed in lunettes line the second level. Above the large center window, one finds the coat of arms of the city and in the tympanum, a frieze. The auditorium, in the traditional horseshoe-shape, with three box tiers topped by a loggione, including a center royal box, and proscenium boxes. Gilded stucco decorations and dancing putti decorate the space, whose ceiling dome is a deep blue frescoe.

Practical Information. Teatro Magnani, Piazza Verdi, Fidenza. Tel: 39 521 522044. If visiting, contact the Italian Government Travel Offices (ENIT), 630 Fifth Avenue, New York, NY 10011. Tel: 212-245-4822.

BIBLIOGRAPHY

Bibliography. Various Authors, *Teatri Storici in Emilia Romagna* (Bologna, 1982). Nullo Musini, *Il Teatro Girolamo Magnani di Fidenza la sua storia nel centenario della sua inaugurazione 1861–1961.*
Thanks to the Fidenza Tourist office.

Teatro Comunale (Ente Autonomo Lirico)
Maggio Musicale Fiorentino (Spring Festival)
Teatro della Pergola

Florence is the city that gave birth to opera, and the tradition continues in the Teatro Comunale, which was inaugurated on May 8, 1961, with Giuseppe Verdi's *Don Carlo*. Architect C. Bartolini and engineer A. Giuntoli created the modern structure out of the Politeama Fiorentino Vittorio Emanuele, which had been opened on May 17, 1862, with Gaetano Donizetti's *Lucia di Lammermoor*. The Politeama was an open-air amphitheater, which had been destroyed by fire within a year after opening. Telemaco Bonaiuti designed the 6,000-seat arena, which he reconstructed after the fire.

The oldest music festival in Italy, Maggio Musicale, first opened on April 22, 1933, with Verdi's *Nabucco* in the Teatro Comunale. Founded by Vittorio Gui, it was started as a triennial event, and began offering annual festivals in 1937.

A group of men known as the *Camerata dei Bardi*, which included composers Jacopo Peri,

Giulio Caccini, Emilio de Cavalieri, and Vincenzo Galilei, offered pastorals by Emilio de'Cavalieri—*Il Satiro* and *La disperazione di Fileno*—at Carnival in 1590 as its first efforts towards this new genre of music known as opera. Cavalieri's *Il giuoco della cieca* followed in 1595 at the Palazzo Pitti. Peri's *Dafne* (considered the first "opera") was seen, most likely, two years later at the Palazzo Corsi. From it only six arias have survived. The earliest complete extant work is Peri's *Euridice*, introduced at the Palazzo Pitti on October 6, 1600. Giulio Caccini's *Euridice* followed on December 5, 1602, and the first masterpiece of this new art form, Claudio Monteverdi's *La favola d'Orfeo*, was staged shortly after its Mantua premiere. The Uffizi hosted Marco da Gagliano's *La flora* in 1628 and Francesco Cavalli's *Egisto* in 1646.

Florence's first opera house, the Teatro della Pergola, was inaugurated with Jacopo Melani's *Il potestà di Colognole* during Carnival 1656. Designed by Ferdinando Tacca and located on via della Pergola, the wooden structure was built as a private theater for Florence's aristocrats and noblemen. It had been opened by the Accademia degli Immobili, which was founded by Giovanni Carlo de' Medici. Two years after opening, Medici's *Il passo per forza* and Cavalli's *L'Hipermestra* were staged. Actually, *L'Hipermestra* was scheduled to inaugurate the Pergola, but stage machinery problems caused delays and the honor went to Melani's *Il potestà di Colognole*. In 1661, Melani's *Ercole in Tebe* celebrated the marriage of the Grand Duke Cosimo III de' Medici to Marguerite Louise d'Orleans which took place in the theater. Two years later, Giovanni Carlo de' Medici died and *Amor vuol inganno* was the last work staged before the theater was closed. Since the new Accademia head, Cosimo de' Medici, was not interested in music, the Pergola was deserted. In 1688, the situation improved when Ferdinando de' Medici took charge and hired Ferdinando Sengher to remodel the theater for his marriage to Violante Beatrice di Baviera which was to take place the following year. Giovanni Maria Pagliardi's *Il greco in Troia* was presented in honor of the occasion, but Pergola's glory was short-lived. The theater was again deserted after the festivities and the bills left unpaid. The Grand Duke Cosimo III prevented foreclosure, and reopened the opera house in 1718 with the premiere of Antonio Vivaldi's *Scanderbegh*. A second premiere, Luc Antonio Pedieri's *La fede ne' tradimenti*, followed a couple of months later. For Carnival 1719, La Pergola offered the *prima* of Pedieri's *La finta pazzia di Diana*, followed by his *Il trionfo di Solimano*, *Il trionfo della virtù*, and *Astarto*. On September 19, 1721, the theater was again closed to observe a year of mourning after the death of the Grand Duchess Marguerite Louise d'Orleans (estranged wife of Cosimo III). Antonio Vivaldi's *L'Atenaide* was introduced in 1728, with Giovanni Porta's *Il gran Tamerlano* on the boards two years later. Carnival 1736 hosted Vivaldi's *Ginevra, Principessa di Scozia*. Each season, three to four different operas were offered, sharing the stage with the occasional ballet and masked ball. Unlike the other theaters in Florence, La Pergola was not rented to visiting troupes. After the death of Gian Gastone, the last Medici, in July 1737, Duke Francesco di Lorena became the protector of the Immobili and took control of the Pergola, which was then renovated by Antonio Galli Bibiena.

By 1740, there were fourteen theaters in Florence, but only La Pergola was devoted exclusively to opera seria, which competed with gambling for the noblemen's attention. Gambling was an important source of income for the theater, so when steps were taken to abolish gambling in 1748, profits plummeted but opera concentration improved. Despite the number of operas Florence witnessed during the 18th century, it was not considered one of the major opera centers in Italy.

During the 19th century, the Pergola hosted several *prime assolute*, including Giuseppe Persiani's *Danao re d'Arco* on June 16, 1827, Donizetti's *Parisina d'Este* on March 17, 1833, *Rosmonda d'Inghilterra* on February 27, 1834, Salvatore Cammarano's *Bondelmonte* on June 18, 1845, Carlo Romani's *Un duello alla montagnola di Bologna ovvero Tutti amanti*, on January 20, 1847, Luigi Ricci's *Il birraio de Preston* on February 4, 1847, Salvatore Auteri Manzocchi's *Dolores* on February 23, 1875, Pietro Mascagni's *I Rantzau* in 1892, and, of course, the most famous premiere, written for the theater and commemorated with a plaque on the facade was Verdi's *Macbeth* on March 14, 1847. It was a success and Verdi received 38 curtain calls. Italian premieres also played a role with Donizetti's *Marino Faliero* in 1837, Giacomo Meyerbeer's *Robert le Diable* on December 26, 1840, Meyerbeer's *Les Huguenots* on December 26, 1841, Meyerbeer's *Le Prophète* on December 26, 1852, and Daniel Auber's *Fra Diavolo* on December 29, 1866, all on the schedule. Most of the operatic fare, however, were the popular works of the time. (The Teatro Pagliano hosted the Italian premiere of Meyerbeer's *Dinorah* on March 29, 1867.)

Meanwhile, after the Politeama Vittorio Emanuele opened in the 1860s, it became the focus of the cultural life of the city, especially after 1882 when the open-air structure was covered. The Politeama was reopened with Giuseppe Verdi's *Nabucco*. In 1896, Mascagni moved to the Politeama (from the Pergola) where for 14 years he conducted. There was, however, no regular opera season and the occasional opera performance shared the stage with the circus, baby contests, and gymnastic demonstrations. Only in 1928, with the formation of the *Stabile Orchestrale Fiorentina*, subsequently renamed Orchestra del Maggio Musicale Fiorentino, and directed by Gui Gatti, did opera have a secure place in Florence. The orchestra formation also planted the seeds which sprouted the Maggio Musicale.

The Maggio Musicale Fiorentino began in 1933, with the stated objectives to produce contemporary works and rediscover forgotten masterpieces, presenting them in musically authentic versions. Within the first few decades, under the leadership of Gui Gatti, the Maggio Musicale attained both goals. It gained a reputation for presenting important *prime assolute*, including Gian Francesco Malipiero's *Deserto tentato* and *Antonio e Cleopatra*, Vito Frazzi's *Re Lear* and *Don Chisciotte*, Luigi Dallapiccola's *Il prigioniero*, and Ildebrando Pizzetti's *Vanna Lupa*— and for unearthing works that had fallen into oblivion, including Cavalli's *Didone*, on June 21, 1952, Da Gagliano's *Dafne*, on June 17, 1965, Peri's *Euridice*, and Tommaso Traetta's *Antigone*, on May 12, 1962.

Productions emphasize the visual aspects of the opera, presented in an innovative and controversial manner, like Giacomo Puccini's *Tosca*, set in 1943 Rome during the Nazi occupation, and Richard Wagner's *Das Rheingold*, with the Rhine maidens stark naked (symbolizing their innocence) when the curtain was raised. Festivals often have themes, like "Rossini Renaissance," "early Verdi," "historic 20th century," and "early Romanticism." Maggio Musicale has mounted many Italian premieres, among them Sergey Prokofiev's *Voyna i mir* (War and Peace, May 26, 1953), Henry Purcell's *Dido and Aeneas* (May 15, 1959), Jean-Philippe Rameau's *Castor et Pollux* (April 27, 1935) and *Ines galantes* (June 26, 1963), Maurice Ravel's *Les enfant et sortilèges* (May 2, 1939),

Gaspare Spontini's *Olimpia* (May 14, 1950), Igor Stravinsky's *Edipo re* (May 22, 1937), and Lully's *Armide* (May 11, 1950). Leading artists of the times have graced the festival stage. The inaugural season heard Carlo Galeffi, Alessandro Dolci, and Tancredi Pasero in Verdi's *Nabucco*, Rosa Ponselle and Ebe Stignani in Spontini's *La vestale*, and Ezio Pinza, Giacomo Lauri-Volpe, and Mercedes Capsir in Vincenzo Bellini's *I Puritani*. Maria Callas's first appearance was in Bellini's *Norma* on November 30, 1948, followed by her first Violetta in 1951. She returned for Gioacchino Rossini's *Armida* and Maria Luigi Cherubini's *Médée*. The 53° Maggio Musicale (1990) featured Luciano Pavarotti as Manrico in Verdi's *Il trovatore*. Other operas presented during the 1990 festival were Nikolai Rimsky-Korsakov's *Skazaniye o nevidimom grade Kitezhe* (The Legend of the Invisible City of Kitezh), Mozart's *Don Giovanni*, Donizetti's *Parisina*, Verdi's *Il trovatore*, and Kurt Weill's *Aufstieg und Fall der Stadt Mahagonny*. Counted among recent offerings are Dmitry Shostakovich's *Ledi Makbet Mtsenskovo uyezda* (Lady Macbeth of the Mtsensk District), Alban Berg's *Wozzeck*, Puccini's *La bohème*, and Rossini's *Le Comte Ory* (Teatro della Pergola). The festival attracts top conductors and Bruno Walter, Claudio Abbado, Wolfgang Sawallisch, Lorin Maazel, Riccardo Muti, and Zubin Meta have all been welcomed at the Maggio Musicale.

The Teatro Comunale offers opera outside of the Maggio Musicale, and the early 1990s saw Verdi's *Rigoletto*, Arrigo Boïto's *Mefistofele*, and Leoš Janáček's *Kát'a Kabanová*. Recent repertory includes Donizetti's *L'elisir d'amore*, Rimsky-Korsakov's *Skazka o Tsare Saltane* (The Tale of Tsar Saltan), and Puccini's *La fanciulla del West*.

Teatro Comunale

Vittorio Emanuele II first proposed a new theater, and the Societá Anonima del Regio Politeama Fiorentino "Vittorio Emanuele II" adopted a constitution on May 25, 1861, recommending the construction of a 6,000-seat amphitheater. The result was the Politeama Fiorentino Vittorio Emanuele, a horseshoe-shaped, open-air arena with stone gallery seats. Fire erupted during a gala ball the following year, killing several ball-goers and gutting the stage and part of the auditorium. The theater was rebuilt, reopening on April 7,

Teatro della Pergola (Florence, Italy).

1864. In 1910, the Società Italiana Anonima Teatrale took over its management until 1929, when the city of Florence acquired the opera house. It was renamed Teatro Comunale the following year, and became the Ente Autonomo del Teatro Comunale in 1933. Damaged during a bombing raid on May 1, 1944, the Comunale remained closed until 1947. Near the end of the 1950s, the Comunale suffered from "stability problems," forcing its closure on January 9, 1958. The reconstruction gave the theater its current appearance.

The Teatro Comunale, which has retained its original oblong form, is a spacious building with an unpretentious facade of arched windows, Ionic pilasters, and gold fleurs-de-lis on the glass door transoms. The starkly modern auditorium holds a single tier of boxes and two large amphitheater-like semicircular galleries. A sea of plush red seats complements the dark-and-light-gray proscenium arch, plain white parapets, and warm wood paneling. Starlike lights in a sky-like dome brighten the space. The Comunale accommodates 2,000.

Teatro della Pergola

La Pergola received the appearance it has today during an 1857 remodeling. Currently it hosts theatrical productions, except during Maggio Musicale when opera graces the stage. Teatro della Pergola's orange-coral stucco façade, displaying a plaque commemorating the world premiere of Verdi's *Macbeth*, is lined with shuttered windows, wooden doors, and wrought-iron electrified "gas" lights. The auditorium holds three tiers of boxes, topped by a gallery, that wrap around plush red velvet orchestra seats. In the center, ivory and white pilasters flank the royal box. Golden scrolls and angels embellish the parapets. La Pergola seats 1,000.

Practical Information. Teatro Comunale di Firenze, via Solferino 15, 50123 Florence. Tel: 39 55 211 158, Fax 39 55 239-6954. Teatro della Pergola, via della Pergola 32, Florence. When visiting the Teatro Comunale di Firenze, Maggio Musicale, or Teatro della Pergola, stay at the Grand Hotel Villa Medici, via Il Prato 42, 50123 Florence. Tel: 39 55 238-1331 or 1-800-223-6800,

Teatro della Pergola auditorium (Florence, Italy).

Fax 39 55 238 1336. The Grand Hotel Villa Medici is centrally located and near the opera houses. The hotel can assist with opera schedules and tickets.

COMPANY STAFF AND WORLD PREMIERES

Sovrintendente (select). Francesco Ernani, Massimo Bogianckino, Giorgio Vidusso, Remigio Paone, Pariso Votto, Mario Labroca, Vittorio Gui. **Direttori Artistici:** Cesare Mazzonis, Bruno Bartoletti, Luciano Alrettori, Roman Vlad, Francesco Siciliani, Guido Gatti.

World Premieres. (since 1928) Pizzetti's *Orseolo,* May 4, 1935; G.F. Malipiero's *Deserto tentato,* May 8, 1937; G.F. Malipiero's *Antonio e Cleopatra,* May 4, 1938; Anonimo's *Vergini savie e vergini folli,* May 21, 1938; O. Vecchi's *Amfiparnaso,* May 21, 1938; V. Frazzi's *Re Lear,* April 29, 1939; L. Dallapiccola's *Volo di notte,* May 18, 1940 (Pergola); F. Alfano's *Don Juan de Manara,* May 28, 1941; I. Pizzetti's *Vanna Lupa,* May 4, 1949; L. Dallapiccola *Il prigioniero* (first staged-performance) May 20, 1950; I. Pizzetti's *Ifigenia* (first staged performance) May 9, 1951; V. Frazzi's *Don Chisciotte,* April 27, 1952; V. Bucchi's *Il contrabbasso,* May 20, 1954; M. Castelnuovo-Tedesco's *Aucassin ed Nicolette,* June 2, 1952; G.F. Malipiero's *Venere prigioniera,* May 14, 1957; G.F. Malipiero's *Figliol prodigo,* May 14, 1957; L. Chailly's *Il mantello,* May 11, 1960; V. Bucchi's *notte in paradiso* (first staged performance), May 11, 1960; M. Castelnuovo-Tedesco's *Mercante di Venezia,* May 25, 1961; Testi's *Celestina,* May 28, 1963; A. Schönberg's *Mano felice,* May 31, 1964; S. Sciarrino's *Aspern,* June 8, 1978; F. Vacchi's *Girotondo* June 16, 1982.

Bibliography. Rodolfo Tommasi, *Il Teatro Comunale di Firenze: presenza e linguaggio* (Florence, 1987). *Il Maggio Musicale Fiorentino* (Florence, n.d.). Leonardo Pinzauti, *Il Maggio Musicale Fiorention* (Florence, 1967).

Thanks to Aldo Cerboneschi, Teatro Comunale, and Rolando Fallini.

Teatro Carlo Felice
(Ente Autonomo Lirico)

On October 18, 1991, Verdi's *Il trovatore* inaugurated the Teatro Carlo Felice, the second Teatro Carlo Felice on the site. Architects Ignazio Gardella, Aldo Rossi, and Angelo Sibilla were responsible for the project. The first opera house had been destroyed in a fire-bombing of the city on August 8, 1943. The building, however, was patched together and reopened August 1, 1948, with Giuseppe Verdi's *Aida*, conducted by Tulio Serafin. The patchwork began to fall apart and in 1960, the theater was abandoned. Vincenzo Bellini's *Bianca e Fernando* inaugurated the original Teatro Carlo Felice on April 7, 1828, with Adelaide Tosi, Giovanni David, and Antonio Tamburini creating the principal roles. An *apposita cantata* by Gaetano Donizetti preceded the opera, given in honor of the royal family, who were in attendance. A ballet, *Gli adoratori del fuoco*, choreographed by Giovanni Galzerani, was also staged, as was the custom at that time. The Carlo Felice, designed by Carlo Barabino, was located on the border of the medieval and new sections of the city.

Genoa was already hosting performances in the 1500s. The shows took place in inns, where traveling troupes stopped and offered a variety of entertainment in exchange for room and board. The origins of the Teatro Falcone, one of the oldest public theaters in Italy and the first to host opera in Genoa, are traced to the remodeling of an inn known as the Hostaria sub signo falconis (Hostelry under the Sign of the Falcon) which was given to the city by the Adorno family. Here the works of Alessandro Stradella and Carlo Goldini, among others, took center stage. Melodrama was also very popular.

During the 1700s, a more modern structure, the 1,500-seat Teatro S. Agostino was erected. It soon became the focal point of operatic activity in the city, although the Falcone continued to host opera as well. In January 1814, Rossini's *Tancredi* was staged there and three years later the Falcone hosted Rossini's *Il barbiere di Siviglia*. There were other theaters in Genoa: Teatro delle Vigne, Teatro Campetto, and Teatro di S. Francesco d'Albaro,

which in September 1814 hosted Rossini's *L'italiana in Algeri*. None of these theaters, however, were considered of sufficient magnitude for a city the size of Genoa, and inadequate to welcome the opera explosion of the 19th century. Meanwhile, architect Andrea Tagliafichi had submitted plans in 1799 for a new theater with boxes. After being discussed for 26 years, it was set aside in 1825. Meanwhile, on December 24, 1824, the Eccellentissima Direzione dei Teatri (The Most Excellent Theater Management Committee) was formed and charged with providing the city with a first-rate opera house and four years later the Teatro Carlo Felice, named after King Carlo Felice, was opened.

Performances at the Carlo Felice began on December 26, and were divided into three seasons—Carnival, Spring, and Autumn. Tradition dictated that theaters of a certain level, like that of the Carlo Felice, open with a novelty, and included Achille Peri's *I fidanzati*. Unpublished operas comprised a good percentage of these novelties. The repertory during the first years were characterized by a predominance of Bellini and Rossini operas. In 1828, the opera house hosted *Il barbiere di Siviglia*, *L'assedio di Corinto* and *Otello ossia Il moro di Venezia*. The following year saw *Semiramide* and *La Cenerentola*, and in 1830, *Zelmira*, *La gazza ladra*, *Tancredi*, *Il conte Ory*, *L'inganno felice*, *L'italiana in Algeri* and *Mosè in Egitto* were all mounted. One of the most authoritative interpreters of Rossini at the Carlo Felice was Luigi Gilberto Duprez.

The connection between Giuseppe Verdi and Genoa was very strong. The reasons were put very well in a letter from Verdi addressed to Gino Monaldi: "You probably wonder why I've chosen Genoa instead of Milan as my usual residence? It is not that I love the sea or the desire to watch it from my window; you know I do not love the sea, and because of my aversion, I never went to America, and refused to go to Cairo for the production of *Aida*. I chose Genova to keep myself a little distant from the musical world and all the people of that world who believe themselves to be my lord." Verdi wintered in Genoa for many years, living in several different places, one of which was the apartment in the Palazzo of the Marchese Sauli in Carignano, where Angelo Mariani also resided. Mariani was the director and chief conductor at the Carlo Felice from 1852 until his death in 1873. From 1841, the year in which Verdi's *Oberto, conte di S. Bontifacio* was first mounted in the opera house, hardly a season passed without at least one Verdi opera on the boards. During the 1850s, his works dominated the repertory. Although none of his works were ever world premiered, many were performed there not long after their introduction. Verdi was made an honorary citizen of Genova as a "European celebrity" and for Italian glory on April 24, 1867.

For the 400th anniversary (1892) of Christoforo Colombus's discovery of America (Columbus came from Genoa), the mayor of Genoa asked Verdi to write an opera for the celebration, but Verdi did not accept the offer. He supported the composer Alberto Franchetti for the commission, and on October 6, 1892, the world premiere of Alberto Franchetti's *Cristoforo Colombo* was staged in honor of Genoa's famous native son. The opera house, however, served as more than just a stage for opera. It became the city landmark and a magnet for the Risorgimento, which looked for the smallest excuse to disrupt performances. One such occasion arose during Verdi's *Luisa Miller*, sung by the Austrian artist Sofia Cruvelli. The performance was interrupted with whistles and protests that led to the arrest of several spectators, including Nino Bixio. Drama, including an appearance by Sarah Bernhardt, also graced the stage, along with entertainment ranging from circus acrobatics to snake charmers.

French opera was very popular at the Carlo Felice, especially the works of Giacomo Meyerbeer, followed by Jules Massenet and Ambroise Thomas, and Charles Gounod's *Faust*. It even hosted the Italian premiere of Fromental Halévy's *La Juive*. But when Georges Bizet's *Carmen* arrived in Genoa in 1881, it was first seen at the Teatro Paginini. Claude Debussy's *Pelléas et Mélisande*, although programmed during the 1910 season, was not actually staged until 1965.

As the end of the 19th century approached, the Carlo Felice welcomed a new generation of Italian composers — Giacomo Puccini, Mascagni, Ruggero Leoncavallo, Umberto Giordano, and Francesco Cilea, and a new type of music — from the *verismo* and *giovine* schools. Puccini's *Le Villi* was heard in 1887, and *Manon Lescaut* in 1894. Mascagni arrived in 1891 with *Cavalleria rusticana* which was favorably received, where as his *Le maschere*, heard on January 17, 1901, as part of six simultaneous premieres, was a disaster. Leoncavallo's *I pagliacci* was first heard in 1893, followed three years later by Giordano's *Andrea Chénier*. Like most Italian theaters, the Carlo Felice was slow to present operas of Wolfgang Amadesu Mozart. *Don Giovanni* arrived only in 1867 and was a colossal failure, and *Die Zauberflöte* was not staged until 1953. The Politeama Genovese hosted the first appearance of a Richard Wagner work in Genoa, *Lohengrin* in 1880, and Richard Strauss conducted the Italian premiere of his *Arabella* in 1936. A quarter of a century earlier, his *Salome* had been staged for the first time. It was Arturo Toscanini who began what could be characterized as a Wagner-Strauss cult in Genoa. Toscanini's initial appearance was in 1891, and he stayed until 1894. Igor Stravinsky's *Solovey* (The Nightingale) was first performed in 1937. Unfortunately, the fascist government blocked works by Arnold Schönberg and Alban Berg, whose *Wozzeck* not mounted until 1970 and *Lulu* not until 1982 (for a different reason). Many great singers of the era, like Beniamino Gigli, Aureliano Pertile, Mariano Stabile, Enrico Caruso, Titta Ruffa, Toti dal Monte, Gilda dalla Rizza, Margherita Carosio, and Gina Cigna sang at the opera house.

The outbreak of World War I had a negative impact on the theater's activities. Between the wars, in 1936, the impresario-management of the opera house came to an end with the appointment of the first Sovrintendente, Corrado Marchi. That same year, Mascagni's *Nerone* was mounted and the first performance in Genoa of Mozart's *Le nozze di Figaro*, along with the world premiere of Gian Francesco Malipiero's *Giulio Cesare*, took place. Ludwig van Beethoven's *Fidelio* received its Genevese premiere the following year. During the Second World War, performances continued until May 9, 1942, when after a performance of Mascagni's *Cavalleria Rusticana* and Leoncavallo's *I pagliacci*, it closed. Since Genoa was a major seaport, it played an important tactical role from a military viewpoint that resulted in heavy bombing raids on the city. The opera house first sustained heavy damage between October and November of 1942. The damage was repaired and its artistic activities continued until August 8, 1943, when a fire bombing destroyed the building. After the war, the theater reopened in 1948, and Maria Callas appeared in Puccini's *Turandot*, opposite Mario del Monaco. Other well-known artists included Margherita Carosio, Gina Cigna, Renata Tebaldi, Ferruccio Tagliavini, Galliano Masini, Pia Tassinari. Between 1945 and 1970, Celestina Lanfranco led the theater. Under her tenure during the 1950s, there were some outstanding seasons, especially 1954, which offered Rossini's *Guglielmo Tell*, Puccini's *Tosca*, Verdi's *La forza del destino*, Bizet's *Djamileh*, Adriano Lualdi's *La granceola*, Gian Carlo Menotti's *Amahl and the Night Visitors*, and Wagner's *Die Meistersinger von Nürnberg*. After the theater had to be abandoned in 1960, opera activity moved to the Teatro Margherita, a glorious theater dating from the 1800s in which Toscanini conducted. The Margherita had subsequently been converted into a movie house, so it had to be transformed again into an opera house. Novelties were on the boards with Luigi Cherubini's *Médée* (1969), Francesco Cavalli's *Giasone* (1972), Sergey Prokofiev's *Ognenniy angel* (The Fiery Angel) (1973), and Luigi Dallapiccola's *Il volo di notte* (1975) among them.

When the Teatro Carlo Felice finally reopened on October 18, 1991, Italian opera dominated the repertory — Verdi's *Don Carlo, Nabucco, Simon Boccanegra* and *Aida*, Alfredo Catalani's *Loreley*, Rossini's *L'assedio di Corinto* and *Il barbiere di Siviglia*, Donizetti's *Il duca d'Alba* and *Roberto Devereux*, Puccini' *Turandot* and *Tosca*, Mozart's *Don Giovanni*, and Bellini's *Norma* — with established singers like Ghena Dimitrova, Marilyn Zschau, Kristian Johannsson, Raina Kavaivanska, Daniela Dessì, and Ferruccio Furlanetto. Recent offering include Benjamin Britten's *Peter Grimes*, Hans Werner Henze's *Venus und Adonis*, Donizetti's *Adelia*, Verdi's *Rigoletto* and *Macbeth*, Rossini's *Il barbiere di Siviglia*, Ponchielli's *La gioconda*, and Donizetti's *Don Pasquale*.

Teatro Carlo Felice

The struggle to rebuild the opera house began immediately after World War II and lasted almost half a century. Antonio Chessa submitted plans in 1950 and was declared the winner on October 16, 1951, but nothing happened. He sued the Municipality in 1959, demanding construction begin with two months, but lost. Carlos Scarpa next submitted plans but he died unexpectedly. Finally, architects Ignazio Gardella, Aldo Rossi, and Angelo Sibilla finished the project. The cornerstone was laid on April 7, 1987, and the opera house was completed in time to host a *stagione dell'inaugurazione* to celebrate the 500th anniversary of Columbus's discovery of America. The cost was $150 million.

The new Carlo Felice Theatre retained its original Neoclassic exterior. The façade offers an imposing hexastyle portico. On the pronao is a Latin inscription: *REGE CAROLO FELICI DUCE NOSTRO ORDO GENUENSIS SATAGENTE HECTORE YENNEO REGIO GUBERNATORE CONSULUIT NE URBI TOT INSIGNIBUS MONUMENTIS INSTRUCTAE TEATRUM SPECTABILIUS DEESSET — MDCCCXXVII* (During the reign of Carlo Felice, our leader, the Civic Corps of Genoa, under the vigil guidance of Ettore d'Yenne, the royal governor, decreed that the city, with many excellent buildings, should have a spectacular theater — 1827). The auditorium looks like an outdoor Genovese piazza — the integration of the artistic environment with the city. It is a post-modern hall with an expansive, raked orchestra, side boxes which appear as white balconies flanked by green shutters, a galleria, and two slivers of a second balcony. Gray marble streaked with blue and white cover the side walls which imitate the exterior of a building. Tiny spotlights which look like twinkling stars shine from the white-tinted ceiling. There are 2,000 seats.

Practical Information. Teatro Carlo Felice, Passo al Teatro 4, 16121 Genoa. Tel: 39 10 53811, Fax: 39 10 538-1233. If you visit, stay at the City Hotel, via San Sebastiano 6, 16123 Genoa. Tel 39 10 5545 or 1 800 528 1234, Fax 39 10 586 301. It is centrally located and only steps from the opera house. The hotel can assist with opera schedule and tickets.

COMPANY STAFF, WORLD PREMIERES, AND VERDI'S OPERAS

Sovrintendente. Nicola Costa.

Direttore Artistico: Niccolò Parente (1992–present).

World Premieres (select). V. Bellini's *Bianca e Fernando* (reworking of *Bianca e Gernando*), April 7, 1828; G. Donizetti's *Alina, Regina di Golconda*,

Teatro Carlo Felice (Genoa, Italy).

May 12, 1828; F. Morlacchi's *Cristoforo Colombo,* June 21, 1828; A. Peri's *Tancreda,* December 26, 1847; A. Peri's *I fidanzati,* February 7, 1856; A. C. Gomes's *Salvator Rosa,* 1874; A. Franchetti's *Cristoforo Colombo,* October 6, 1892; G.F. Malipiero's *Giulio Cesare,* 1936.

Verdi's Operas. (Date of first performance in Genoa and of world premiere) *Oberto, conte di S. Bonifacio,* **January 9, 1841** (Teatro alla Scala, Milan, **November 17, 1839**). *Nabucco,* **April 17, 1843** (Teatro alla Scala, Milan, **March 9, 1842**). *Ernani,* **June 13, 1844** (Teatro la Fenice, Venice, **March 9, 1844**). *I Lombardi alla prima crociata,* **January 13, 1844** (Teatro alla Scala, Milan, **February 11, 1843**). *I due Foscari,* **April 12, 1845** (Teatro Argentina, Rome, **November 3, 1844**). *Giovanna d'Arco,* **December 26, 1845** (Teatro alla Scala, Milan, **February 15, 1845**). *Attila,* **January 9, 1847** (Teatro la Fenice, Venice, **March 17, 1846**). *Macbeth,* **May 13, 1848** (Teatro la Pergola, Florence, **March 14, 1847**). *I masnadieri,* **January 25, 1849** (Queen's Theatre, London, **July 22, 1847**). *La battaglia di legnano,* **June 12, 1850** (Teatro Argentina, Rome, **January 27, 1849**). *Luisa Miller,* **December 26, 1850** (Teatro di San Carlo, Naples, **December 8, 1849**). *Rigoletto,* **December 26, 1852** (Teatro la Fenice, Venice, **March 11, 1851**). *Il trovatore,* **December 26,** 1853 (Teatro Apollo, Rome **January 19, 1853**). *La traviata,* **January 17, 1855** (Teatro la Fenice, Venice, **March 6, 1853**). *I vespri siciliani* as Giovanna de guzman, **May 22, 1856** (Teatro Ducale, Parma, **December 26, 1855**). *Aroldo,* **March 19, 1859,** (Teatro Nuovo, Rimini, August 16, 1857). *Simon Boccanegra,* **December 26, 1859** (Teatro la Fenice, Venice, **March 12, 1857**). *Un ballo in maschera,* **April 1, 1861** (Teatro Apollo, Rome, **February 12, 1859**). *La forza del destino,* **April 3, 1866** (Teatro Imperiale, Saint Petersburg, **November 10, 1862**). *Aida,* **December 26, 1875** (Teatro dell'Opera, Cairo, **December 24, 1871**). *Don Carlo,* **December 26, 1887** (Teatro alla Scala, Milan, **January 10, 1884**). *Otello,* **November 24, 1888** (Teatro alla Scala, Milan, **February 5, 1887**). *Falstaff,* **April 6, 1893** (Teatro alla Scala, Milan, **February 9, 1893**). *Un giorno di regno* (Teatro Politeama, Genoa) **September 12, 1980** (Teatro alla Scala, Milan, **September 5, 1840**).

Bibliography. Roberto Iovino, *Il Carlo Felice, due volti di un teatro* (Genova, 1991). Iovino, et al., *I palcoscenici della lirica-dal Falcone al Carlo Felice* (Genova, 1991). Giovanni Monleone, *Storia di un Teatro: il Carlo Felice* (Genova, 1979). Monleone, *I 100 anni del Carlo Felice (1828–1928)* (Genova, 1928). Edilio Frassoni, *Due secoli di lirica a Genova (1772–1900) (1901–1960),* 2 Vols. (Genova, 1980).

Frassoni, *Teatro Comunale dell'Opera di Genova* (Genova, 1973). M. Bottaro, M. Patternostro, *Storia del Teatro a Genova* (Genova, 1982). A. Brocca, *Il teatro Carlo Felice dal 7 aprile 1828 al 27 febbraio 1898* (Genova, 1898). G. B. Vallebona, *Il Teatro Carlo Felice: Cronistoria di un secolo, 1828–1928* (Genova, 1928). Karyl Lynn Zietz, "Rebirth in Genoa," *Opera News*, May 1993.

Thanks to the Ufficio Stampa, Teatro Carlo Felice, and Corrado Ambiveri.

— JESI

Teatro Comunale G.B. Pergolesi
(Teatro di Tradizione)

The Teatro Comunale, originally called the Teatro della Concordia, opened in 1798 with two works attributed to Domenico Cimarosa, *Il principe spazzacamino* and *La capricciosa corretta*. Anna Guidarini, mother of Gioachino Rossini, was the lead soprano. Francesco Maria Ciaraffoni, with the collaboration of Giovanni Grilli, were responsible for the design, which was modified by the State architect Cosimo Morelli, who enlarged the elliptical curve of the auditorium.

Early records indicate that in Carnival 1715, Francesco Gasparini's *Flavio Anicio Olibio* was performed, and in 1727, Giuseppe Maria Orlandini's *Nino* was staged. The first real theater built in Jesi dates to 1731. Called Teatro del Leone (Theater of the Lion), it was so named to pay homage to the civil crest of Jesi. The Jesian architect Domenico Valeri built and decorated the theater at his own expense. He subsequently sold the boxes for a handsome profit and in 1753 tried to build another theater at his own expense, but these efforts did not bear fruit. Few records survived to indicate programming as Giovanni Annibaldi pointed out in his 1882 published history of the Teatro Pergolesi, but there are some indications that in 1732 two melodramas, *Amore e fortuna* and *Nel perdono la vendetta* (with no names of the librettists or composers known), were given to celebrate the holiday of Saint Settimio. For Carnival two years later, Gaetano Maria Schiassi's *Alessandro nelle Indie* was staged. During the theater's existence, twice a year, for Carnival and during the September fair, musical works, primarily *drammi giocosi* from the Neapolitan school, were offered. Both comic and tragic plays were also staged. The Teatro del Leone survived until 1892, when a sudden fire destroyed it. The Leone was not rebuilt.

Around a century earlier, in 1790, the nobility had wanted to construct a larger theater than the Leone to offer both musical and dramatic fare. The initial estimated cost was 16.000 scudi, to be paid by the sale of the boxes. But the bill came to 24.000 scudi, so the initial price of the boxes was raised and four gentlemen — Signori Baldassini, Franciolini, Mosconi, and Ripanti — paid the difference. La Concordia opened its doors for the first time in 1798. Popular works of the era, like Felice Alessandri's *Il vecchio geloso*, Giuseppe Gazzaniga's *La moglie capricciosa*, Pietro Alessandro Guglielmi's *Le due Gemelle*, Antonio Salieri's *La scuola dei gelosi*, Domenico Cimarosa's *L'amor costante* and *Il ritorno di Don Calandrino*, Giovanni Paisiello's *Le due contesse* and *L'amore ingegnoso* were on the boards. The last year of the 18th century was marked by a celebration on May 21, 1799, given in honor of Napoleon Bonaparte. For the occasion, Nicola Zingarelli composed a cantata for two voices with choral and orchestral accompaniment. In 1804, Valentino Fioravanti's *Le contadine villane* was presented. A novelty took the stage in 1808, *Chi troppo abbraccia niente stringe*, with composer unknown, and a decade later Nicola Vaccai's *La feudataria*, followed by Vincenzo Bellini's *La straniera* in 1833, were presented. The Concordia saw its first Gaetano Donizetti work in the fall of 1842 when *Roberto Devereux* was mounted. Works by Gioachino Rossini, Giovanni Pacini, and early Verdi operas — *Nabucco*, *I Lombardi alla prima Crociata*, *Ernani*, and *I due Foscari* — graced the stage in the 1840s with singers like Marietta Albini Vellani, Luigi Salandri, Amalia Zacconi Brutti, Lorenzo Biacchi, Luigi Stegher, and Niccola Morigi brought life to the works.

For the 1850 season, Verdi's *Macbeth* and Giovanni Pacini's *Buondelmonte* were mounted. Two years later, Timoteo Pacini's *Imelda De'*

Lambertazzi was staged. The 1854 *cartellone* saw Verdi's *Luisa Miller* and Timoteo Pasini's *Giovanni Grey*, and the 1856 Carnival presented Saverio Meradante's *Il giuramento* and Carlo Pedrotti's *Fiorina*. The September 1868 season presented a 20 year old, Jesian Niccolina Favi Campora, and baritone Francesco Crescia in Verdi's *Un ballo in maschera* and *La traviata*. In 1875, Gaspare Spontini's *La vestale* was given in celebration of the 100th anniversary of Spontini's birth, an "adopted" Jesi native. (Although Spontini was born in Majolati, he grew up in Jesi.) A few years later, in 1880, another famous Jesian composer, Giovanni Battista Pergolesi, was honored for the 170th anniversary of his birth, with the renaming of the Teatro della Concordia to the Teatro G.B. Pergolesi. In celebration of this occasion, his *Stabat Mater*, under the baton of Nicola Mancini, was given. The new name however, did not become official until on September 30, 1883, when all the co-owners of the theater, the administration, and related associations had signed the documents. After the destruction of the Teatro Leone in 1892, operettas graced the stage along with operas, including *I granatieri*, which had replaced the originally scheduled *Norma*.

When the 20th century arrived, Cinematography Lumière was projected in the Pergolesi in October 1900. The situation changed three years later when Puccini's *La bohème* returned to the stage. Puccini's *Manon Lescaut* was on the boards in 1908, with Tina Desana in the title role. In 1910, the bicentennial of the birth of Pergolesi was celebrated with another production of *Stabat Mater* on October 2, 1910. During the same period, the traditional opera season returned with Hector Berlioz's *La damnation de Faust*, featuring José Palet, Ramon Blanchard, Alfieri, and Desana. For the 100th anniversary of Verdi's birth, the 1913 fall season offered several performances of his *La forza del destino*. The 1919 season included the Brescia version of Puccini's *Madama Butterfly* and *La bohème*. Verdi's *Aida* reopened the opera house in 1927, after a two year closure for repairs. The following season (1928) hosted Giordano's *Fedora* and Pietro Mascagni's *L'Amico Fritz*. At the end of the season, the Società Teatrale, made up of the theater's original box holders, was dissolved and on March 13, 1929, the ownership of the Pergolesi Theater was passed to the Comune.

The theater reopened in 1931, hosting the Compagnia dell'Opera Lirica Italiana which mounted Mascagni's *Cavalleria rusticana*, Ruggero Leoncavallo's *I pagliacci*, and Verdi's *Rigoletto* and *La traviata*. The same traveling company returned the following season with Puccini's *Madama Butterfly*, Mascagni's *L'Amico Fritz* and *Cavalleria rusticana*, Verdi's *La traviata*, Donizetti's *Lucia di Lammermoor*, and a novelty for Jesi, Francesco Cilea's *Adriana Lecouvreur*. When the Fascists were in power, works of Pergolesi and Spontini were staged, conducted by the well-known composer Riccardo Zandonai. During World War II the theater remained open until 1943, mounting Mascagni's *Cavalleria rusticana*, Leoncavallo's *I pagliacci*, Puccini's *Turandot*, and Verdi's *Rigoletto*. The Pergolesi reopened its doors in 1947 with Puccini's *Tosca* and Giordani's *Andrea Chénier*. In celebration of the centennial of Puccini's birth, *Tosca* was repeated in 1958. For the 250th anniversary of Pergolesi's birth in 1960, the first (and only) Festival Internazionale dell'Opera da Camera (International Festival of Chamber Opera) took place. Opening on September 1, the music of Pergolesi, Bach, Georg Friedrich Händel, and Mozart was offered by the Camerata Accademica of the Mozarteum in Salzburg. This was followed by performances of Antonio Vivaldi's *La senna festeggiante*, Henry Purcell's *Dido and Aeneas* (production from Festival de Musique di Aix-en-Provence), and Donizetti's *Don Pasquale*, with Italo Tajo in the title role. Probably the high point of the festival was a Franco Zeffirelli production of Pergolesi's *Lo frate innamorato*, conducted by Bruno Bartoletti. The rest of the season consisted of standard fare, Puccini's *Turandot* with Margherita Casals Mantovani, Gino Sinimberghi, and Vera Montananri with Ottavio Ziino on the podium and Puccini's *La bohème* with Mafalda Micheluzzi, Antonio Galiè and Attilo D'Orazi, with Giuseppe Ruisi conducting.

In 1968, the Teatro G.B. Pergolesi was recognized as a "Teatro di Tradizione." This helped stabilize its financial position, permitting more modern and contemporary fare, like the world premiere of Berto Boccosi's *La lettera scarlatta* on September 26, 1968, followed by a second world premiere, Fernando Squadroni's *Calandrino & C.* on September 25, 1969. *Calandrino & C.* was paired with *Le notti della Paura* by Franco Mannino. Seasons consisting of both contemporary and little known fare was mixed with traditional works, including a triple bill of Fernando Squadroni's *Un treno*, Mannino's *La stirpe di Davide*, and Jacopo Napoli's *Il barone Avaro* in 1970. The following year offered Puccini's *Suor Angelica*, Alfredo Strano's *Sulla via Maestra*, and Nuccio Fiorda's *Margot* on another triple bill. In 1972, Mannino's *VIVT* joined Puccini's *Tosca*, Giordano's *Andrea Chénier*, and Verdi's *La traviata* in the *cartellone*. These unusual works continued until the mid–1970s. The 1980s and 1990s saw the unearthing of obscure works by Jesi's "own" composers, Spontini's *Teseo Riconosciuto* and Pergolesi's *Il prigionier superbo*, along with the standard Italian repertory. Artistic director Angelo Cavallaro enjoys discovering obscure works and presenting the *prima esecuzione moderna* (first modern presentation) of an opera. Besides Pergolesi's *Il prigionier superbo*, the 1996 season opened with Nicola Vaccai's *Giulietta e Romeo*. Recent works include Pergolesi's *La serva padrona* and George Gershwin's *Blue Monday*.

Teatro Comunale G.B. Pergolesi (Teatro della Concordia)

The French occupied Jesi when an accord between the nobility of Jesi and the Pelate Governor Mons was reached on February 23, 1790, which paved the way for the construction of the Teatro della Concordia. It is one of the few opera houses from the late 1700s which has never been destroyed by fire, bombs, or anything else.

TEATRO PERGOLESI in large letters identifies the long rectangular building of Neoclassic design faced with earth-colored Roman brick. The three-story facade boasts a ground-floor exterior of marble, punctuated by a series of nine arched portals, Neoclassic windows, and a small balcony. The 750-seat auditorium is elliptical in shape and intimate in scale, with four tiers of boxes, the highest serving as the loggione (amphitheater). Glittering with gold stucco on ivory-hued wood, and filled with plush red seats, the room displays a dome ceiling of "Apollo's Tale" painted by Felice Giani. The curtain portrays "The entrance of the Emperor Federico II of Svenia in Jesi in 1220."

Practical Information. Teatro Comunale G.B. Pergolesi, Piazza della Repubblica 9, 60035 Jesi. Tel: 39 731 538 355, Fax 39 731 538 356. If visiting, contact the Italian Government Travel Offices (ENIT), 630 Fifth Avenue, New York, NY 10011. Tel: 212-245-4822.

COMPANY STAFF AND REPERTORY

Direttori Artistici. Angelo Cavallaro (1995–present), Giorgio Merighi, Filippo Zigante.

Repertory *(beginning in 1968).* **1968:** Otello, Lucia di Lammermoor, La lettera scarlatta, Il barbiere di Siviglia. **1969:** Mefistofele, Madama Butterfly, Calandrino & C., La notti della paura, La bohème. **1970:** Norma, Un treno, La stirpe di Davide, Il Barone Avaro, L'elisir d'amore, Adriana Lecouvreur. **1971:** La forza del destino, Don Pasquale, Rigoletto, Sulla Via Maestra, Margot, Suor Angelica. **1972:** Tosca, Andrea Chénier, La traviata, VIVT. **1973:** Il trovatore, Madama Butterfly, Uno sguardo dal ponte, Il barbiere di Siviglia. **1974:** La vestale, Turandot, The Old Man and the Thief, Nabucco. **1975:** Carmen, La Bohème, Un amore asfissiante. **1976:** La traviata, Così fan tutte, Rigoletto. **1977:** Falstaff, Madama Butterfly, Un ballo in maschera. **1978:** Don Carlo, Il barbiere di Siviglia, Tosca. **1979:** Don Pasquale, La bohème, Il trovatore. **1980:** Attila, La Cenerentola, Lucia di Lammermoor. **1981:** L'Italiana in Algeri, Rigoletto, Andrea Chénier. **1982:** L'assedio di Corinto, La traviata, Cavalleria rusticana, I pagliacci. **1983:** Fernando Cortez, Madama Butterfly. **1984:** Il pirata, Norma, Don Pasquale. **1985:** Otello, Rigoletto, Il barbiere di Siviglia. **1986:** La vestale, La traviata, La bohème. **1987:** Tosca, Turandot, L'elisir d'amore. **1988:** Don Giovanni, Fedora, Carmen. **1989:** Werther, Don Carlo, La sonnambula. **1990:** Macbeth, Messa da Requiem, Adriana Lecouvreur, Il matrimonio segreto. **1991:** Aida, Requiem (Mozart), Le nozze di Figaro, Il barbiere di Siviglia. **1992:** Rigoletto, Tosca, Suor Angelica, Mese Mariano (Giordano). **1993:** La bohème, La Wally, La traviata. **1994:** Andrea Chénier, Madama Butterfly, Il cavaliere dell'intelletto, Otello. **1995:** Teseo Riconosciuto, Lucia di Lammermoor, Carmen. **1996:** Il trovatore, Manon Lescaut, The Little Chimney Sweeper (children's opera by Britten). **1997:** Il prigioniero superbo, La serva padrona, Otello, Blue Monday, Cavalleria rusticana.

Bibliography. *La storia sconosciuta del Teatro Pergolesi di Jesi* from *L'architettura teatrale delle Marche* (Jesi, n.d.). B. Tosi, *Il Teatro Pergolesi 20 anni dopo* and *Cronologia 1968–1988* from *Teatro Comunale G.B. Pergolesi*, Ufficio Stampa (Jesi, 1988). Programs of the *Teatro Comunale G.B. Pergolesi*, Ufficio Stampa (Jesi, 1994, 1995, 1996, 1997). Additional articles provided by the company. Interview with Angelo Cavallero, artistic director, November 1997.

Thanks to Davide Annachini, Teatro Jesi.

Teatro Politeama Greco
(Teatro di Tradizione)

The Politeama Greco, originally called the Politeama Principe di Napoli, was inaugurated on November 15, 1884, with Giuseppe Verdi's *Aida*, conducted by Carlo Lovati. Constructed by Donato Greco with help from his engineer brother Oronzo Greco, the structure was located on then called Regio Udienza (today XXV Lugio).

For almost three decades, the theater hosted operatic works by Verdi, Gaetano Donizetti, Vincenzo Bellini, Gioachino Rossini, Umberto Giordano, Giacomo Meyerbeer, Giacomo Puccini, Arrigo Boito, Pietro Mascagni, Ruggero Leoncavallo, Francesco Cilia, and Georges Bizet, along with operettas and drama. The Politeama was then closed and transformed into a "real" opera house, with orchestra level, box tiers, and stage. The hall was beautified with gilded stucco, velvet, and mirrors, and the ceiling and proscenium arch were embellished with allegorical figures and portraits of great Italian composers, the work of Sig. Palmieri. Heating, electricity, and sanitary and anti-incendiary devices were also installed. Additional seats were added for a total seating capacity of 1,500. The theater reopened for the spring opera season in 1913. More work was done in 1926 to honor the famous Lecce tenor, Tito Schipa.

In 1969, the Politeama Greco was recognized as a Teatro di Tradizione. Three operas from the mainstream repertory in traditional productions are offered every season and have included Giacomo Puccini's *Manon Lescaut*, George Bizet's *Carmen*, and Verdi's *Falstaff*. Recent offerings include Vincenzo Bellini's *I Puritani* and Umberto Giordano's *Fedora*.

Practical Information. Teatro Politeama Greco, Via XXV Luglio, 73100 Lecce; Tel: 39 832 241 468. If visiting, contact the Italian Government Travel Offices (ENIT), 630 Fifth Avenue, New York, NY 10011. Tel: 212-245-4822.

BIBLIOGRAPHY

Bibliography. Information supplied by the company.

Thanks to Roberto Errico.

Comitato Estate Livornese
(Teatro di Tradizione)

The Comitato Estate Livornese (CEL) has three missions: to celebrate and make better known, especially outside of Italy, famous composers, librettists, singers, and conductors who originated from Livorno; to explore the lesser known works of Pietro Mascagni and other composers from the Tuscany region, and to examine and bring to the stage works from the *verismo* school. To this end, in commemoration of the fiftieth anniversary of the death of Magcagni and the centennial of the *prima assoluta* of his *Guglielmo Ratcliff*, the work was staged during the 1995 season, as well as brought to the Bonn Opera, Germany. The 1996 project was of Christoph Willibald Gluck's *Orfeo ed Euridice* (in concert form), because the librettist of this work, Ranieri de Calzabigi, was from Livorno. The other celebration in 1996 was that of the 100th anniversary of the birth of the great Livornesse tenor Galliano Masini.

Opera has been in Livorno since 1658. The first work was *Eurillo* by Margaritoni. The CEL was founded in 1931. Every season witnesses at least one opera from the *verismo* school, and since 1988, one by Mascagni as well: 1988: *Iris*; 1989: *Il piccolo Marat*; 1990: *Cavalleria rusticana*; 1991: *Amico Fritz*; 1992: *I Rantzau*; 1993: *Cavalleria rusticana*; 1994: *Lodoletta*; 1995: *Guglielmo Ratcliff*, and 1996: *Silvano*. Other *verismo* school operas have included *La Wally*, *Il tabarro*, and *Pagliacci*.

The CEL presented its first world premiere in 1990 with Marco Tutino's *La lupa*. The productions are traditional with a cast of both young, up-and-coming singers and established artists. The production of *Guglielmo Ratcliff* was an exception to the traditional vein, since it was a co-production with Bonn, where Gian-Carlo del Monaco, the son of the Italian singer Mario del Monaco, is the artistic director. Gian-Carlo del Monaco had been a frequent guest in Livorno.

The number of productions has grown quickly since 1994, from two, to three in 1995, and six in 1996. The rapid growth had been made possible through co-productions, primarily with the opera houses in Lucca, Mantova, Cosenza, Pisa, and Jesi. There is both state and city funding of the CEL.

Teatro La Gran Guardia

Unlike most other cities in Italy, Livorno's great opera house, which was destroyed during the Second World War, has not been rebuilt, although it is currently under reconstruction. The company had performed at the Teatro Goldoni, inaugurated in 1847, and currently performs in the Teatro La Gran Guardia, inaugurated in 1955. It is a multipurpose theater which also hosts cinema. The auditorium holds an orchestra and one balcony.

Practical Information. Comitato Estate Livornese, Via Goldini 83, 57125 Livorno. Tel: 39 586 889-111, Fax: 39 586 899-920. When visiting the Comitato Estate Livornese, stay at the Hotel Città, Via di Franco 32, 57100 Livorno. Tel: 39 586 883-495, Fax 39 586 890-196. It is centrally located and near the theater. The hotel can assist with tickets and schedule.

BIBLIOGRAPHY

Bibliography. Program from *Guglielmo Ratcliff*, Ufficio Stampa (Livorno, 1995). Interviews with Alberto Paloscia, artistic director, and Fuluvo Venturi. Additional information supplied by the company.

Thanks to Antonella Peruffo, Comitato Estate Livornese, and Roberto Romani.

Teatro La Gran Guardia (Livorno, Italy).

LUCCA

Teatro del Giglio
(Teatro di Tradizione)

The Teatro del Giglio, originally called Teatro Pubblico, was inaugurated on January 14, 1675, with two works, Niccolò Berengani's *L'Attila in Capua* and Niccolò Minato's *Seiano*. The theater, based on the plans of Francesco Buonamici, was brought to fruition by architect Maria Giovanni Padreddio.

The birth of the Teatro Pubblico took place during a period when the most important theater activity was held in the *teatri di corte* (court theaters), which were in the salons of the grand palaces belonging to the princes and dukes. In Lucca, there were two such theaters, one in the Palazzo Pretorio, known as the Sala del Podestà, and the other in the Palazzo de' Borghi. Although these rooms were adapted for theatrical use, the increase in the needs of the population required the construction of a public theater. On August 19, 1672, the Consiglio of the Repubblica of Lucca decreed that a citizen's commission study the feasibility of constructing a theater on the site of an old Convent of the Jesuit, next to the church of San Geralamo.

After the Pubblico opened in 1675, it enjoyed only thirteen seasons before the carelessness of the verger caused a fire which destroyed the structure on February 16, 1688. Only the perimeter walls remained standing. The theater was rebuilt, based on the original plans, four years later. The auditorium held three levels of boxes or better described as little rooms rising on columns of stone. All the boxes were decorated in the same modest manner, except the center box, which was ornamented to reflect its illustrious visitors, the gentlemen of the governing body. The Luccese painter Angelo Livoratti decorated the walls. The opera house hosted two opera seasons — Carnival and a fall season — to coincide with the Festival of Santa Croce. Rehearsals occupied the stage during the summer. The artistic activity of the theater assumed such importance in the life of the city during the 18th century that the governor was persuaded to create an additional office, the *Cura sopra il Teatro*, responsible for its maintenance and administration, which remained in existence until 1799. Without proper maintenance, the Pubblico fell into a state of disrepair which led to the designing of a new structure by Giovanni Lazzarini. Construction began in 1817, ending two years later. Maria Luisa Bourbon, then sovereign of Lucca, had the honor of inaugurating the new theater and selecting its name from among the follow choices: Teatro San Luigi (the Saint of her name day), Teatro Alfieri (after the Italian playwright), or Teatro Giglio (flower on the coat of arms of the House of Bourbon). Teatro Giglio was chosen and the name stuck.

The theater became the property of the state on September 22, 1819. The Marchese Antonio Mazzarosaand was responsible for its maintenance. During the 1800s Gioachino Rossini, Gaetano Donizetti, Vincenzo Bellini, Giuseppe Verdi, and, near the end of the century, Pietro Mascagni were the composers whose works predominated the repertory. Here Rossini's *Guglielmo Tell* (the Italian version of *Guillaume Tell* which was given its world premiere at the Salle le Peletier in Paris on August 3, 1829), had its Italian premiere on September 17, 1831. Verdi and Donizetti were guests at the theater, leading productions of their works. It was closed in 1917 during World War I, to be used as a military warehouse. Reopening in 1919, the composers mostly in repertory were Giacomo Puccini, Alfredo Catalani, and Luporini. (Puccini grew up in Lucca.) In March 1983, artistic activity was stopped because the theater did not meet the safety standards of the day. Seven months later, it was reopened, and on February 20, 1985, it became a Teatro di Tradizione.

Giacomo Zani, former artistic director, explained that due to the limited seating capacity of the theater (750), to guarantee its financial stability, a popular repertory is followed, with the exception that one production be a less well-known piece, "to serve the art." Some examples are Alfredo Catalani's *Edmea*, Rossini's *Aureliano in Palmira*, and George Gershwin's *Porgy and Bess*. Recent offerings include Verdi's *Rigoletto*, Vincenzo Bellini's *Norma*, and Puccini's *La rondine*.

Teatro del Giglio, Lucca (Teatro Pubblico)

The Teatro del Giglio is a Neoclassic building overlooking the Piazza del Giglio. The three-level facade holds six Corinthian pilasters which alternate with five rectangular windows, topped by bas-reliefs and crowned by a pediment. The coat-of-arms of the city decorates the tympanum. There is a porte cochere on the street level. The horseshoe-shaped auditorium rises four levels (three box tiers toped by a gallery) with a center royal box and proscenium boxes. It is painted in beige with delicate green and rose colors decorating the floral trim.

Practical Information. Teatro del Giglio, Piazza del Giglio, 55100 Lucca. Tel: 39 583 47521. When visiting the Teatro del Giglio, stay at L'Universo, Piazza del Giglio 1, Lucca. Tel: 39 0583 493-678, Fax: 39 0583 954-854. Located in the historic center of the city, it is next to the opera house.

BIBLIOGRAPHY

Direttore Artistico. Luciano Albert
Bibliography. Gilberto Bedini (ed.), *Il Teatro del Giglio a Lucca, L'architettura di Giovanni e Cesare Lazzarini* (Lucca, 1991).
Thanks to Lia Borelli, Teatro Giglio.

LUGO

Teatro Rossini

The Teatro Rossini, originally called Teatro Comunale, was inaugurated in 1761 with *Catone in Utica*, a work by an unknown composer with libretto from Pietro Metastasio. The opera house was designed by Farncesco Ambrogio Petrocchi and modeled after the Teatro of Medicina. Antonio Galli Bibiena executed the inside decorations.

Some of the earliest records indicate opera was performed in 1641, when the Teatro Pavaglione hosted Giovanni Battista Guarini's *Il pastor fido*. The performance space was actually a Roman amphitheater seating 4800 (which still hosts opera during the summer with productions from Macerata's Sferisterio.) By the mid–1700s, the need for an indoor performance venue became obvious and the Comunale was erected. Renamed Teatro Rossini in 1859 (Gioachino Rossini's father came from Lugo) it hosted several of Rossini's works, including *Tancredi, L'italiana in Algeri, La gazza ladra, La Cenerentola, Il turco in Italia, Il barbiere in Siviglia, Adelaide di Borgogna, La donna del lago, Semiramide, Otello ossia Il Moro di Venezia, Eduoardo e Cristina, Matilde di Shabran*, and *Mosè in Egitto*. Over the years, the Rossini has staged works by Domenico Cimarosa, Simone Mayr, Saverio Mercadante, Giovanni Pacini, Gaetano Donizetti, Giuseppe Verdi, and Giacomo Meyerbeer. During the 1845 season, Verdi's works were introduced — *I Lombardi alla prima crociata* and *I due Foscari*. The first Puccini work staged was *Manon Lescaut* in 1896, followed by *La bohème* three years later.

Due to the small space of the theater (it seats only 448) it evolved into a showcase for 17th- and 18th-century *opera seria* by Claudio Monteverdi to Christoph Willibald Gluck, and 18th- and 19th-century *opera buffa* and *opera giocosa* including composers like Giambattista Pergolesi, Cimarosa, and Giovanni Paisiello, among others. This choice (or limitation) of works has led to some unusual fare, like the first performance in the 20th-century of the theater's inaugural work, Vinci's *Cantone in Utica*, Baldassare Galuppi's *Il mondo della luna*, Donizetti's *Le convenienze ed inconvenienze teatrali, I pazzi per progetto*, and *Betly, ossia La capanna svizzera*, Ferdinando Paër's *Achille*, Antonio Salier's *La locandiera*, and Niccolò Jommelli's *Didone abbandonata*. The 20th-century pieces include Raffaello de Banfield's *Una lettera d'amore di Lord Byron* and Felice Lattuada's *Le preziòse ridicole*.

Teatro Rossini (Teatro Comunale)

A site in the area of Orto dei Padri del Carmine, next to the building of the College of the SS Petronio and Prospero, within the confines of the peripheral wall, was chosen for the construction of the Teatro Comunale. In 1763, two years after the theater opened, it was turned over to the Comunità. The first restoration work took place in 1812. Seven years later, Leandro Marconi modified the curve of the boxes, added the loggione, and changed the opening of the proscenium arch, among other changes.

After the World War I, it was converted into

a movie theater, and major detrimental alterations were made to the theater that eventually led during the 1950s to its closing. A group called Pro Loco di Lugo restored the building in 1970.

Practical Information. Teatro Rossini, Piazza Cavour, 48022 Lugo. Tel: 39 545 33037, Fax 39 545 32859. If visiting, contact the Italian Government Travel Offices (ENIT), 630 Fifth Avenue, New York, NY 10011. Tel: 212-245-4822.

BIBLIOGRAPHY

Bibliography. Various Authors, *Teatri Sotrici in Emilia Romagna* (Bologna, 1982).

―――――――――――― MACERATA

Macerata Opera–Lo Sferisterio
(Teatro di Tradizione, Summer Festival)

On September 5, 1829, the Sferisterio was inaugurated with a month-long celebration which included ballgames, tournaments on horseback, medieval jousts, bull fighting, and of course, the requisite fireworks. The Sferisterio began its new life as host to a summer opera festival in 1967. Giuseppe Verdi's *Otello* featuring Mario del Monaco in the title role inaugurated the Macerata opera in 1967. Carlo Perucci, a former baritone, founded the company and was its first artistic director. Ireneo Aleandri was the architect of the Sferisterio.

There had been opera performances back in 1921, due to the superb acoustics of the Sferisterio. Count Pier Alberto of Macerata arranged performances of Verdi's *Aida* in a season which lasted from July 27 to August 15. Amilcare Ponchielli's *La gioconda* followed in 1922. Despite a successful concert given by the famous Italian tenor Beniamino Gigli in 1927, opera did not reappear until 1967.

The early years were marked by traditional productions with outstanding casts, like Giacomo Puccini's *Turandot* in 1970 with Birgit Nilsson and Franco Corelli, Gaetano Donizetti's *Lucia di Lammermoor* with Luciano Pavarotti and Renata Scotto, and Arrigo Boïto's *Mefistofele* with Cesare Siepi and Magda Olivero, under the baton of Nello Santi. In 1977, Macerata ventured into new territory with the staging of Ildebrando Pizzetti's *Assassino nella cattedrale*. The 1980s ushered in a broadening of the repertory from almost exclusively Italian fare (the only exceptions had been *Carmen* and *Lohengrin*) to include several foreign works—Modest Mussorgsky's *Khovanshchina*, Richard Strauss's *Elektra*, Leonard Bernstein's *West Side Story*, Wolfgang Mozart's *Die Zauberflöte*, and Richard Wagner's *Tannhäuser*. The experiment was not successful and the repertory returned to primarily standard Italian fare, with the exception of Roberto de Simone's *La gatta Cenerentola* in 1989. The problem was financial. Outside of the popular repertory, only around 1,600 spectators came, enough to fill most Italian opera houses but filled only a half or a third of the Sferisterio (depending on the opera's set).

The stage measures 270 feet in length, but only 30 feet deep, lending itself to creative staging. One was the 1996 symbolic interpretation by Hugo de Ana of Puccini's *Turandot*. In Act I, a single sphere, which turned bright orange with Turandot's appearance, was on the stage. Turandot was standing on top of a world inside the sphere, her regal attire and superior height contrasting with her hovering, plain black-clad subjects. In Act II, the ball split into three: she is no longer the only one with her own world. By Act III, she was on the same level as Calaf and her subjects and dressed in the same plain, black attire. With a strong cast (Alessandra Marc, Vladimir Bogachov, and Daniela Dessì), it was a feast for the ears and well as the eyes.

Sferisterio has also seen its share of problems and controversy. In 1995, tenor Fabio Armiliato, singing Cavaradossi in Puccini's *Tosca,* was injured when a real bullet escaped from one of the rifles. The usual lawsuits followed. The next season, Verdi's *Attila* was on the boards, in celebration of the 150th anniversary of its world premiere. The production was updated by director Hanning Brockhaus to the tyranny of the Nazi era to make it more meaningful to today's society, but it primarily caused a revolt among three principals, Carlo Colombara (Attila), Maria Guleghina

(Odabella), and Renato Bruson (Ezio), who disassociated themselves from the production "out of respect for the public and for Verdi." They wore their own, traditional costumes, and boycotted most of the rehearsals, which showed in the tepid and sloppy performance. Brockhaus lamented the "star system," stating that those singers had a vision of opera from a hundred years ago. There was also a problem with the execution. To fill the huge stage, slides of war destruction, fire and death were projected, that also fell on the singers, so a compromise was reached and the slides were not projected during the arias. Due to the monumental size of the projection, the effect could have been awesome, but the mixing of ancient weapons of destruction with modern ones, and primitive garb with that of decadent 20th-century Germany, diminished the effect, despite the message that tyranny in any time is destructive.

In 1996, the Associazone Arena Sferisterio was created to raise money privately. This followed a new federal law in Italy that gives the initiative to the opera companies to raise money privately, up to 40% or their budget. Previously, opera was totally supported through funding from the federal, state, and city governments.

Sferisterio

On May 9, 1820, a project was approved for creating a playing field for *pallone a bracciale* (or from the Greek *sphaera*, hence sfera) a type of ballgame popular in the region from the 15th century to the mid 19th century. One hundred of Macerata's wealthiest families formed the Società Fondatrice di Macerata to build the Sferisterio, paying for its construction and becoming the owners. A competition was held with architects Spata, Casella, and Ausuttoni, and the engineer Salvatore Innocenzi plans submitting plans. The Spata and Innocenzi were chosen but the Società made a few design changes which Spata would not accept so he dropped out. Innocenzi accepted them, but before the first stone was laid, problems began. One of the major ones was the number of boxes necessary to accommodate all the founding members. Soon there was a falling out between Innocenzi and the Società and new design submissions from other architects were called for. The project was awarded to Aleandri in 1823. In 1966, the arena underwent a restructuring to convert it to a proper open-air theater. The seating capacity ranges from 3,000 to 5,000 (depending upon the set). The Macerata Opera does something very admirable — they do not sell seats or side boxes if the view of the stage is obstructed.

The Sferisterio is a Neoclassic structure of earth-tone brick, gently curved on one side with the front and rear of the building straight, against the massive straight playing wall (now the stage area). Crowned by the seal of the Comune of

Sferisterio (Macerata, Italy).

Sferisterio "auditorium" (Macerata, Italy).

Macerata, the multi-arched facade is dedicated to the hundred original founders: *AD ORNAMENTO DELLA CITTÀ A DILETTO PUBBLICO LA GENEROSITÀ DI CENTO CONSORTI EDIFICO MDCCCXXIX.* The exterior resembles an amphitheater with a long series of arches that run along two superimposed levels. Inside the open-air structure, a wide hemicycle, are two tiers of 52 boxes in an open-sided gallery setting, divided by large Doric columns which support a roof terrace lined with a balustrade. In the center is a "magistrate" box, set underneath a soaring arch embellished with Doric pilasters.

Teatro Lauro Rossi

Teatro Lauro Rossi was designed by Antonio Bibiena and inaugurated in 1774, with a work by Metastasio. It was restructured in 1989, and began staging opera the next year, with Mozart's *Così fan tutte* as its first offering. Donizetti's *Don Pasquale* followed in 1991, but after the 1993 season production of Mozart's *Le nozze di Figaro*, there was a hiatus of five years. Giorgio Battistelli's *Giacomo*

mio, salviamoci, an opera commissioned to celebrate the bicentennial of the birth of the poet Giacomo Leopardi, was world premiered on July 11, 1998.

A tiny jewel of a theater, the Lauro Rossi holds a horseshoe-shaped auditorium with three tiers topped by a gallery. The *sala* is decorated with delicately carved balustrades and embellished with stucco ornamentation and imitation marble.

Practical Information. Macerata Opera, Via Santa Maria della Porta 65, 62100 Macerata. Tel: 39 733 230-735, Fax: 39 733 261-499. Teatro Lauro Rossi, Piazza della Libertì 21, Macerata. Tel: 256 306. If visiting Macerata, contact the Azienda Promozione Turistica, Via Garibaldi 87, Macerata. Tel: 39 733 231-547, Fax: 39 733 230 449. There are few hotel rooms in Macerata.

REPERTORY

Opera Repertory. (Sferisterio) **1921:** Aida. **1922:** La gioconda. **1967:** Otello, Madama Butterfly. **1968:** Carmen, Tosca. **1969:** Aida, Cavalleria rusticana, La forza del destino. **1970:** Turandot, La traviata, Andrea Chénier. **1971:** Lucia di Lammermoor, Il trovatore, Lohengrin, Messa da Requiem (Verdi)

1972: Mefistofele, La gioconda, Madama Butterfly, La resurrezione di Cristo. **1973:** Tosca, Messa da Requiem (Verdi), Aida. **1974:** Rigoletto, Pagliacci, Cavalleria rusticana, Carmen. **1975:** Rigoletto, Lucia di Lammermoor, Un ballo in maschera. **1976:** La traviata, Falstaff, Aida. **1977:** Il trovatore, La bohème, Assassino nella cattedrale. **1978:** La traviata, Simon Boccanegra, Madama Butterfly. **1979:** Tosca, Norma, Carmen, La bohème. **1980:** Rigoletto, Otello, Khovanshchina, Il barbiere di Siviglia. **1981:** Elektra, West Side Story, Pagliacci, Cavalleria rusticana, Nabucco, Die Zauberflöte, La forza del destino. **1982:** Tannhäuser, Norma, Carmen, La bohème, Aida. **1983:** Tosca, Don Carlos. **1984:** La traviata, Madama Butterfly, La bohème, Il barbiere di Siviglia. **1985:** Rigoletto, Lucia di Lammermoor, Aida. **1986:** Turandot, Il trovatore, I pagliacci, Cavalleria rusticana. **1987:** La traviata, Manon, Manon Lescaut. **1988:** Tosca, Macbeth, Carmen. **1989:** La gatta Cenerentola (De Simone), Aida. **1990:** Messa da Requiem (Verdi), Il trovatore, La bohème. **1991:** Don Giovanni, Messa da Requiem (Mozart), Madama Butterfly. **1992:** La traviata, La sonnambula. **1993:** Rigoletto, Lucia di Lammermoor. **1994:** L'elisir d'amore, Carmen, La bohème. **1995:** Tosca, La traviata, Samson et Dalila. **1996:** Turandot, Attila, L'elisir d'amore, La traviata. **1997:** Faust, Nabucco, Lucia di Lammermoor. 1998: Turandot, Falstaff, Carmen.

Opera Repertory. (Teatro Lauro Rossi) 1990: Così fan tutte. **1991:** Don Pasquale, Così fan tutte. **1992:** La scala di seta, L'occasione fa il ladro, La cambiale di matrimonio, Il Signor Bruschino. **1993:** Le nozze di Figaro. **1998:** Giacomo mio, salviamoci!

Bibliography. Libero Paci, *Lo Sferisterio: Una Attrezzatura culturale* (Macerata). *L'Opera* (Milan, Luglio/Agosto 1997, N. 110). Additional information supplied by the Macerata Opera and the Associazione Arena Sferisterio.

Thanks to Daniela Boari, Franziska Kurth, and Marco Spada, Macerata Opera, and the Associazione Arena Sferisterio.

MANTUA

Teatro Sociale
(Teatro di Tradizione)

The Teatro Sociale was inaugurated the evening of December 26, 1822, with a gala performance. Luigi Canonica designed the opera house.

As early as 1607, opera was offered in the court of Mantua when Claudio Monteverdi's *La favola d'Orfeo* was performed. The following year, Monteverdi composed *Arianna*, which was staged on June 2, 1608. More than two centuries later, in 1817, a society was formed to construct a new theater. The members, as their first task, chose Canonica as the architect. He submitted not one but two projects, the more majestic of which was chosen. The expense was estimated at 290,983 Lire. The following year, 1818, the houses located on the site chosen for the new structure were demolished and work began on the theater. The building was opened four years later. The Teatro Sociale was named a Teatro di Tradizione in 1967. There are co-productions with Teatro G.B. Pergolesi (Jesi) and CEL Teatro di Livorno (Livorno). Recent repertory includes Verdi's *Otello*, Donizetti's *Lucia di Lammermoor*, Bellini's *Norma*.

Teatro Sociale

The Teatro Sociale is a Neoclassic building with a facade of six Ionic columns supporting a peristyle, statues of Melpomene and Talia (the work of Antonio Spazzi), and the inscription AERE SOCIALI ANNO MDCCCXXII. The auditorium originally held five tiers of boxes, 27 boxes to a tier. The top two levels have since been transformed into a gallery and the loggione. The interior pictures were executed by Tranquillo Orsi. Girolamo Staffieri was responsible for the stucco and the gilding done by Anselmo Berazzi.

Practical Information. Teatro Sociale, Piazza Folengo 4, 46100 Mantova. Tel: & Fax: 39 376 362 739. If visiting contact the Italian Government Travel Offices (ENIT), 630 Fifth Avenue, New York, NY 10011. Tel: 212-245-4822.

MARTINA FRANCA

Festival della Valle d'Itria (Summer Festival)

The Festival della Valle d'Itria was founded in 1975 by Paolo Grassi to establish a different type of summer music festival in his native city. (Grassi, a former sovrintendente at Teatro alla Scala, also founded the Piccolo Teatro in Milan.) The inaugural season offered Christoph Willibald Gluck's *Orfeo ed Euridice* and Gioachino Rossini's *Petite Messe Solennelle*.

The festival has resurrected bel canto style Italian melodrama from the period of Claudio Monteverdi (1567–1643) to the mid–19th century, although the repertory sometimes reaches outside this time period. There is an emphasis on the composers from the Neapolitan era. A specific philosophy guides the festival — operas are performed uncut with the certified original text, and sung in the stylistically correct, interpretative vocal technique of the bel canto era. With this philosophy, the festival has presented the first contemporary performances of the uncut editions of Gaetano Donizetti's *Roberto Devereux*, and several Vincenzo Bellini operas — *I Capuleti e i Montecchi*, *I Puritani*, *La straniera*, and *Il pirata*, and the world premiere of the original version of *Norma* (Norma is a mezzo-soprano and Adalgisa a soprano), Giovanni Paisiello's *Il barbiere di Siviglia* and Gioachino Rossini's *Il barbiere di Siviglia*, the first contemporary performances of Tommaso Traetta's *Ifigenia in Taurdie* and Rossini's *Adelaide di Borgogna*, and the first modern performance of the Italian edition of Daniel Auber's *Fra diavolo*. Long-forgotten scores in their uncut version, like Mercadante's *Il giuramento* and Cimarosa's *La astuzie femminilli* have been presented, along with neglected first versions, like the 1847 version of Giuseppe Verdi's *Macbeth*, and the French edition from 1837 of Donizetti's *Lucia di Lammermoor* (as Lucie de Lammermoor). Although from a scholarly point of view this can be interesting, from a listener's point of view, it can be very boring. There are exceptions, but usually there is a good reason why operas are cut, certain versions are not staged, or why the works have fallen into oblivion.

Practical Information. Festival della Valle d'Itria, Centro Artistico Musicale "Paolo Grassi," Palazzo Ducale, 74015 Martina Franca. Tel: 39 80 707-191. If visiting, contact the Italian Government Travel Offices (ENIT), 630 Fifth Avenue, New York, NY 10011. Tel: 212-245-4822.

COMPANY STAFF AND REPERTORY

Direttori Artistici. Rodolfo Celletti, Paolo Grassi.

Opera Repertory. **1975:** Orfeo ed Euridice, Petite Messe Solennelle (Rossini). **1976:** Tancredi, Missa Papae Marcelli (Palestrina), Stabat Mater (Pergolesi). **1977:** Antigone (Traetta), Norma. **1978:** Nina ossia la pazza per amore. **1979:** Maria Stuarda. **1980:** I Capuleti e i Montecchi, Le serve rivali, Salve Regina, Stabat Mater (Pergolesi). **1981:** Il cappello di paglia, Fra Diavolo, Messa di Requiem (Paisiello). **1982:** Il barbiere di Siviglia (Paisiello), Il barbiere di Siviglia (Rossini), Turandot (Busoni), La Resurrezione (Händel). **1983:** Martha, La straniera, La morte d'Abele, Beatus Vir/Dixit. **1984:** Il giuramento, La astuzie femminili, Adelaide di Borgogna, Requiem pro defunctis. **1985:** I Puritani, La serva padrona, Aci e Galatea, Stabat Mater (Haydn). **1986:** Ifigenia in Tauride, Semiramide, Messa in Re maggiore. **1987:** Il pirata, Attila, Stabat Mater (Rossini). **1988:** L'incoronazione di Poppea, Maria di Rohan, Juditha Triumphans, La creazione. **1989:** Giulio Cesare in Egitto, La favorita, Messa in C minore, Guglielmo d'Aquitania, Petite Messe Solennelle (Rossini). **1990:** Cecchina, ossia La buona figliola, Il bravo, Piramo e Tisbe, Les pêcheurs de perles, Il cunto de li cunti ovvero Il passatempo dei bambini. **1991:** Farnace, Ernani, Endimione e Cintia, Lakmé, Grande Messa K.427 (Mozart). **1992:** Roméo et Juliette, Il matrimonio segreto. **1993:** Lucregia Borgia, La pietra del paragone. **1995:** Caritea Regina di Spagnal, Médée, Messa di Gloria (Mascagni). **1997:** Macbeth, Lucie de Lammermoor (Paris version), Armida imaginaria. **1998:** Il trovatore as Le trouvère, Il fortunato inganno.

Bibliography. Various authors, *Festival della Valle d'Itria 1991* (Martina Franca, 1991).

Teatro Vittorio Emanuele (Ente Autonomo Regionale)

The Teatro Vittorio Emanuele, originally called Real Teatro Santa Elisabetta, was inaugurated on January 18, 1852, with Antonio Laudamo's *Il trionfo della pace* and Gaetano Donizetti's *Marin Faliero*, titled as Il Pascià di Scutari by the royal censors to avoid any anti–Bourbon allusion. The date was chosen to celebrate the 42nd birthday of Ferdinando II. The Neapolitan architect, Pietro Valente, was entrusted with the commission for the structure.

The opera house opened during politically troubled times and there was a *Comitato Rivoluzionario* (Revolutionary Committee) of Messina which was secretly fighting the throne. For the inauguration of the new opera house, named for the mother of Ferdinando II, King of the Two Sicilies, the Revolutionary Committee asked the citizens to abstain from participating in the festivities, but the plea fell on deaf ears. The Messinesians did not want to miss such a grand event.

The opera house immediately became a central meeting place in the city and soon a cafe, restaurant, billiard room, a small reading room, and a *Circolo della Borsa* were added, but there was also a full season of opera, with as many as eight offerings during the 1852/53 season, which included four Verdi operas—*Ernani, Nabucco, I Lombardi alla prima crociata*, and *Macbeth*—Donizetti's *Poliuto*, and the first performance at the opera house of G. Battista's *Ermelinda*. World premieres were also on the boards with three mounted before 1860—G. Miceli's *Zoe*, A. Laudame's *Caterina Howard*, and G. Longo's *Ezzelino III*. Established artists of the era, like Emma Albani, Francesco Cherubini, and Antonietta Pozzoni, graced the stage and eminent personages were welcomed to the theater, among them Vittorio Emanuele II, Umberto I and Queen Margherita, Vittorio Emanuele III, and even the Czar of Russia, Constantine.

After the liberation of Sicily in 1860, the *consiglio comunale* (municipal council) changed the theater's name in honor of the new king of Italy, Vittorio Emanuele II. Full seasons of opera continued as well as concerts, ballet, drama, and even magicians with trained dogs, "wonder" children, and ghosts. Fittingly, the opera which opened the first season under "liberated" Italy on December 15, 1860, was Verdi's *La battaglia di Legnano*. Salvatore Mercandante's *Eleonora* followed on January 1. Two other Verdi works, along with operas from Gioachino Rossini, Vincenzo Bellini and Donizetti among others, were in the repertory. Although the repertory was mainly standard Italian fare, a season of French operetta, with works by Jacques Offenbach, including *Barbe-bleue, Orphée aux enfers, La belle Hélène*, and *La Grand Duchesse de Gérolstein*, and Charles Lecocq's *La fille de Madame Angot* took place in 1876. Ten years earlier, French grand opera had graced the stage with Giacomo Meyerbeer's *Les Huguenots*, followed in 1868 by Charles Gounod's *Faust*, Meyerbeer's *Robert le Diable* and Fromental Halévy's *La Juive* in 1878, Meyerbeer's *L'Africaine* the next year, and his *Le Prophète* in 1882. Of the world premieres which graced the stage — P. Sorace's *Eleonora da Romano*, S. Aspa's *Piero di Calais*, R. Trimarchi's *Rita Ferrant*, and two operas by R. Casalina none stood the test of time. One of the more popular operas of the time, but hardly seen today was Filippo Marchetti's *Ruy Blas*, offered in ten different seasons. By comparison Donizetti's *Lucia di Lammermoor* was seen in twelve, or only two more, as was Verdi's *Rigoletto*. During the more than half a century that the theater survived before being damaged by an earthquake, Verdi works dominated the repertory, with some of his most popular works like *La traviata* seen in more than one third of the total season offered, and *Il trovatore* in more than a quarter. Only when the 20th century dawned did composers from the *verismo* school replace Verdi in popularity.

On December 28, 1908, four hours after the curtain had fallen on Verdi's *Aida*, the earthquake struck. Although the theater was "spared" in relation to the other structures, it sustained sufficient damage to render it unsafe and was closed for more than seven decades. Only on January 7, 1986, was the opera house officially reopened with Verdi's *Aida*. (A concert had been given by the London Philharmonia Orchestra, with Giuseppe Sinopoli on the podium, on April 24, 1985, but the theater was immediately closed again for completion of the restoration work.)

The seasons offer around six productions of almost exclusively Italian fare, but ranging from 1700s to the 20th century. Recent productions include Giacomo Puccini's *Madama Butterfly*, Donizetti's *L'elisir d'amore*, Rossini's *La gazza ladra*, Bellini's *Norma*, Ermanno Wolf-Ferreri's *Il segreto di Susanna*, Gian Carlo Menotti's *The Telephone*, and in the Sala Laudamo, G.B. Pergolesi's *Livietta e tracollo* and G.B. Martini's *Don Chisciotte*.

Teatro Vittorio Emanuele (Real Teatro Santa Elisabetta)

The local architects were very unhappy that the commission for the opera house went to an "outsider," a Neapolitan, and their protest delayed construction for a few years. When the theater was finally completed in 1852, it was a dignified, almost elegant structure. After the 1908 earthquake, seventy-eight years passed before the theater was reopened with Tito Varisco the architect in charge of the reconstruction.

Following Neoclassical principles, the Teatro Vittorio Emanuele offered three principal entrances, with another two on the sides, and a three-arch portico topped by a terrazzo. The facade incorporated three orders. The horseshoe-shaped auditorium overflowed with red velvet, white Carrara marble floors, and wood and gold *zecchino* walls decorations, except the proscenium area had walls of Taormina marble. The auditorium accommodates around 1,000.

Practical Information. Teatro Vittorio Emanuele, Via Pozzoleone, 98122 Messina. Tel: 39 90 5722111, Fax: 39 90 343-629. If visiting, contact the Italian Government Travel Offices (ENIT), 630 Fifth Avenue, New York, NY 10011. Tel: 212-245-4822.

WORLD PREMIERES AND OPERA REPERTORY

World Premieres. G. Miceli's *Zoe*, February 6, 1856; A. Laudame's *Caterina Howard*, March 16, 1859; G. Longo's *Ezzelino III*, February 13, 1860; P. Sorace's *Eleonora da Romano*, September 7, 1871. S. Aspa's *Piero di Calais*, March 6, 1872; R. Trimarchi's *Rita Ferrant*, March 8, 1898; R. Casalaina's *Aretusa*, February 9, 1904; R. Casalaina's *Attollite Portas*, February 23, 1906.

Opera Repertory. (Teatro Santa Elisabetta) **1852:** Marin Faliero as Il Pascia di Scutari, Orazj e Curiazj, Don Pasquale, Maria d'Inghilterra, Poliuto. **1853:** Ermelinda, I Lombardi, Ernani, Il barbiere di Siviglia, Macbeth, Nabucco, Rigoletto as Viscardello. **1854:** Crispino e la comare, Saffo, Il pirata. **1855:** Lucrezia Borgia, Eleonora, Il trovatore, Don Checco, Parisina, Otello (Rossini), Rigoletto as Viscardello. **1856:** Il barbiere di Siviglia, Zoe, Ernani, La traviata, Gemma di Vergy, L'assedio di Leida, La sonnambula, Luisa Miller, Lucia di Lammermoor. **1857:** Macbeth, Elena di Tolosa, Poliuto, Il trovatore, Il barbiere di Siviglia, Marco Visconti. **1858:** Il birraio di Preston, I Puritani, I due Foscari, La favorita as Elda, Norma, La traviata, Roberto di Piccardia. **1859:** La vestale, Ernani, Caterina Howard, Nabucco, Lucia di Lammermoor, Linda di Chamounix, Il trovatore, Don Pasquale. **1860:** Simon Boccanegra, Le precauzioni, Ezzelino III, L'elisir d'amore, La straniera, La traviata, I due Foscari. (Real Teatro Vittorio Emanuele) **1860:** La battaglia di Legnano. **1861:** Eleonora, Norma, La Cenerentola, Roberto Devereux, Il barbiere di Siviglia, Luisa Miller, Pipelet, La traviata, Norma, Ernani. **1862:** Il trovatore, Crispino e la comare, Don Pasquale, Nabucco, La traviata. **1863:** Lucia di Lammermoor, Vittor Pisani, Macbeth, Un ballo in maschera, Poliuto, La traviata, Tutti in maschera, Lucrezia Borgia, Il barbiere di Siviglia, L'ebreo. **1864:** Beatrice di Tenda, La sonnambula, Martha, I Puritani, Jone, Il barbiere di Siviglia, Norma, Il trovatore. **1865:** I Lombardi, I vespri siciliani, La sonnambula, Ester, Rigoletto, La favorita, Lucrezia Borgia, I due Foscari. **1866:** Les Huguenots, Don Pasquale, Aroldo, Lucia di Lammermoor. **1867:** Ernani, Linda di Chamounix, Macbeth, La traviata, L'elisir di'amore, Un ballo in maschera, Don Procopio, La Contessa d'Amalfi. **1868:** Gemma di Vergy, Crispino e la comare, La traviata, Il comino nero, Poliuto, Faust. **1869:** Un'avventura di Scaramuccia, Il barbiere di Siviglia, Rigoletto, Linda di Chamounix, Mosè in Egitto, Un ballo in maschera, La sonnambula. **1870:** Saffo, Alina, Regina di Golconda, Nabucco, La muette de Portici, Guillaume Tell, Martha. **1871:** Anna Bolena, Lucia di Lammermoor, La fille du régiment, Lucrezia Borgia, Eleonora da Romano, Ruy Blas, La favorita. **1872:** Roberto Devereux, Le educande di Sorrento, Il barbiere di Siviglia, Piero di Calais, Rigoletto, Faust, Macbeth. **1873:** Il trovatore, Papa Martin, L'elisir di'amore. **1874:** Lucrezia Borgia, Ruy Blas, Norma, Un ballo in maschera, La Contessa d'Amalfi, La forza del destino, Mosè in Egitto, Don Pasquale. **1875:** Faust, Don Bucefalo. **1876:** Les brigades Crispino e la comare, La Grand Duchesse de Gérolstein, Una follia a Roma. **1876:** Barbebleue, La fille de Madame Angol, La loterie de Vienne, Orphée aux enfers, La Grand Duchesse de Gérolstein, La belle Hélène, Les brigades, La fête de Piedgrotte. **1876:** Ruy Blas, Jone. **1877:** Norma, Aida. **1878:** La sonnambula, La traviata, La forza del destino, Il guarnay, Robert le Diable, La Juive, Ruy Blas. **1879:** Rigoletto, Un ballo in maschera, Don Carlos, Lucia di Lammermoor, I Puritani, L'Africaine, I promessi sposi (Petrella). **1880:** Luisa Miller, Faust, Ernani, La favorita, Lucia di Lammermoor, Norma, Il trovatore. **1882:** Ruy Blas, Il trovatore, La traviata, Aida, Rigoletto, Ernani, L'elisir d'amore, Le Prophète. **1883:** Maria di Rohan, Lucrezia Borgia, L'Africaine, La favorita, Ernani, La forza del destino. **1884:** Il trovatore, I Lombardi, La traviata, Dinorah, Norma, La sonnambula. **1885:** Le roi de Lahore, Faust, Ruy Blas, Isabella d'Aragona, Ernani, Rigoletto, La forza del destino, Un ballo in maschera. **1886:** La traviata, La gioconda, Lucia di Lammermoor, La sonnambula, Faust. **1887:** Mefistofele, L'ebreo, Ernani, Maria di Rohan, Jone, Il trovatore, La gioconda. **1888:** Carmen, Les Huguenots, Otello, I Puritani, Poliuto. **1889:** Rigoletto, Mignon, Ruy Blas, Aida, Il trovatore. **1890:** La forza del destino, Ernani, Lohengrin, Norma, Hamlet, Les Huguenots. **1891:** Il trovatore, Faust, Cavalleria rusticana, Lucia di Lammermoor, Ruy Blas. **1892:** La sonnambula, Simon Boccanegra, L'étoile du Nord, Il birichino, Cavalleria rusticana. **1893:** Un ballo in maschera, I pagliacci, Manon Lescaut, La favorita. **1894:** Carmen, Macbeth, Mefistofele, Cavalleria rusticana. **1895:** I vespri siciliani, I promessi sposi, Cavalleria rusticana, I pagliacci, La traviata, Il trovatore, La Wally. **1896:** Ernani, Maruzza, Ruit-Hora, Rigoletto, Otello, La forza del destino. **1897:** La bohème,

I due Foscari, La traviata, Lucia di Lammermoor, Carmen. **1898:** Cavalleria rusticana, I pagliacci, Il piccolo Haydn, Andrea Chénier, Rita Ferrant, La forza del destino. **1899:** Ruy Blas, Il trovatore, La gioconda, Faust, Cavalleria rusticana, Lucrezia Borgia, Aida, La bohème. **1900:** Il barbiere di Siviglia, Rigoletto, La traviata, Manon Lescaut, L'Africaine, La sonnambula, Cavalleria rusticana, Tosca, Linda di Chamounix. **1901:** Lucia di Lammermoor, Luisa Miller, La traviata, Rigoletto, Manon. **1902:** Tosca, La traviata, Ruy Blas, La bohème, Fedora, Norma, Germania, Il trovatore. **1903:** La gioconda, Aida, Adriana Lecouvreur, Andrea Chénier. **1904:** Fedora, Carmen, Aretusa, Tosca, Mignon. **1905:** LaCabrera, Cavalleria rusticana, La sonnambula, Adriana Le couvreur, L'elisir d'amore, Manuel Menendez, Un ballo in maschera, Manon Lescaut. **1906:** Mefistofele, La traviata, Loreley, Don Pasquale, Attollite Portas, Lucia di Lammermoor, La bohème, Il barbiere di Siviglia, Linda di Chamounix, Zaza, Manon. **1907:** Carmen, Cavalleria rusticana, Il maestro di cappella, La navarrese, I pagliacci, Tosca, Fedora, Les pêcheurs de perles. **1908:** La sonnambula, Gloria, L'amico Fritz, I pagliacci, Madama Butterfly, Aida. **1997:** Madama Butterfly, L'elisir d'amore. **1998:** The Telephone, Il segreto di Susanna, La gazza ladra, Norma. (Sala Laudamo) **1998:** Livietta e Tracollo, Il Don Chischiotte.

Bibliography. N. Scaglione, *La vita del Teatro Vittorio Emanuele* (Messina, 1933). G. Donato, *Il Teatro Vittorio Emanuele di Messina, storie e vita musicale* (Messina, 1979). G. Uccello, *Lo spettacolo nei secoli a Messina* (Palermo, 1986). G. Molonia, *L'archivio storico del Teatro Vittoria Emanuele*, 2 Vol. (Messina, 1990).

Thanks to Sig. Pustorino, Teatro di Messina.

MILAN

Teatro alla Scala (Ente Autonomo Lirico)

Teatro alla Scala reopened on May 11, 1946, with Arturo Toscanini conducting music by Giuseppe Verdi, Gioachino Rossini, Arrigo Boïto and Giacomo Puccini. Verdi's *Nabucco* inaugurated the regular opera season on December 26, 1946. Bombs had destroyed the original opera house on August 16, 1943. Luigi Secchi rebuilt La Scala following the original architectural plans of Giuseppe Piermarini. Antonio Salieri's *Europe riconosciuta* and two ballets, *Pafio e Mirra* and *Apollo placato* had inaugurated the Teatro alla Scala on August 3, 1778, with Maria Balducci,

Francesca Lebrun Danzi and the celebrated *castrato* Gasparo Pachiarotti in the (opera) cast. The Archduke Ferdinando, accompanied by his wife, the Archduchess Maria Ricciarda Beatrice d'Este attended the opening and on the program, their names overshadowed the opera title. The composer's name was not even mentioned. Piermarini designed the original opera house.

Milan's first theater dates back to 1598 when the Salone Margherita, built in honor of Princess Margherita of Austria, opened in the Ducal Palace. The first opera performance, Francesco

Manelli's *Andromeda*, took place in 1644. More opera graced the stage when the Teatrino della Commedia was converted into an opera house in 1686. Then flames engulfed the Salone Margherita in 1708. The Teatro Regio Ducale was built to replace the Salone Margherita, opening with Francesco Gasparini's *Costantino* on December 26, 1717. This magnificent theater featured long seasons from November to August, with works by Johann Hasse, Niccolò Piccinni, and Alessandro Scarlatti, among others. Here Christoph Willibald Gluck's *Artaserse* was premiered in 1741, followed by Wolfgang Amadeus Mozart's *Mitridate, Rè di Ponto* on December 26, 1770, *Ascanio in Alba* on October 17, 1771, and *Lucio Silla* on December 26, 1772. Fire engulfed the opera house during Carnival on the night of February 25, 1776. Two theaters were constructed to take its place. The first one, called the Teatro la Canobbiano, was reserved for the court, and the second one, which would become Teatro alla Scala, would be open to the public. Within months, Maria Theresa, Empress of Austria and Duchess of Milan, granted permission for La Scala to be built on the site of a demolished church, Santa Maria alla Scala. Construction began on August 15, 1776. The ancient bas-relief of Pilade was uncovered during the excavation and was interpreted as a good omen. Maria Theresa bragged, "*S'alza già il nuovo teatro, destinato offuscare la celebrità dei più famosi d'Italia.*" (A new theater is being built that will obscure the glory of the most famous theaters in Italy.) Initially the opera house was called Il nuovo Regio Ducale Teatro di Santa Maria della Scala after Regina della Scala, the wife of Duke Barnabò Visconti who had constructed the church. Since the name was a mouthful, it was shortened to Teatro alla Scala.

Gluck was offered the commission to compose the inaugural work for Teatro alla Scala but declined, so the task fell to Salieri. Four years after the inauguration, on September 14, 1782, Giuseppe Sarti's *I due litiganti* graced the stage for the first time, and within the first 150 years, La Scala would premiere around 350 operas. In 1788, two independent impresarios, Gaetano Maldonati and Francesco Benedetti Ricci, took over managing the opera house and published the theater's first regular season program, with works by Sarti, Giovanni Paisiello, Domenico Cimarosa, and Niccolò Antonio Zingarelli in the repertory. Orchestra seats back then were uncomfortable wooden benches reserved for the military and the servants of the rich. Most of those seated there were drunk and noisy, overpowering the singers. Instead of applause, they hit their sticks against the benches. The "public," seated in the galleries, showered the stage with paper instead of applauding. This deportment was disruptive to the performers and performances so the management passed by-laws governing behavior: displaying disapproval of a performance either during or after was forbidden; applauding "in a manner which did not represent the true worth of the performance" was forbidden; encores were forbidden; calling singers back onto the stage more than once was forbidden. When the French arrived on May 14, 1796, they defaced the boxes, and removed the family coats-of-arms from them, calling the coats-of-arms "relics from an age of barbarity and slavery." La Scala then witnessed the coronation of Napoleon as king of Italy. When the Austrians returned, so did the family coats-of-arms, and the boxes were restored to their previous splendor. The Austrian rulers offered good programming and inexpensive tickets to the opera house, to distract the rebellious population from patriotic or terrorist activities.

After the dawn of the 19th century, La Scala hosted the world premieres of the most famous composers of the time, beginning with Gioachino Rossini's *La pietra del paragone, Aureliano in Palmira, Il turco in Italia, La gazza ladra,* and *Bianca e Falliero,* which opened the 1819 season. Saverio Mercadante's *Elisa e Claudio* followed in 1821 and *Il giuramento* in 1837. Meanwhile, when Domenico Barbaia took over as impresario in 1826, he commissioned Vincenzo Bellini to write three operas, and the premieres of *Il pirata, La straniera* and *Norma* were on the boards. Ironically, the premiere of *Norma* was a disaster. As the story goes, Marchesa Bianchi was in love with Bellini, but Bellini did not have the same sentiments. As a scorned woman, Bianchi paid spectators to yell, whistle, hiss, and boo during the first performance. Fortunately for Bellini, she did not have enough money to pay for the uproar to continue. Several of Gaetano Donizetti works also received their *prime assolute—Chiara e Serafina, Ugo, conte di Parigi, Lucrezia Borgia, Gemma di Vergy, Gianni di Parigi* (revised version) and *Maria Padilla.*

La Scala did not host all the important premieres and artists in Milan. On May 12, 1832, Donizetti's *L'elisir d'amore* was introduced at the

Teatro della Cannobiana. This was the opera house built for the court when La Scala was constructed for the public. Salieri's *Fiera di Venezia* inaugurated the 2,000-seat theater in 1779, which was also designed by Piermarini. In 1894, Sonzogno bought the theater and renamed it Teatro Lirico, which was opened with Samara's *La martire*. Here Enrico Caruso made his Milan debut in the world premiere of Cilea's *L'Arlesiana* on November 27, 1897. The next year Umberto Giordano's *Fedora* was introduced on November 17, followed by Leoncavallo's *Zazà* on November 10, 1900, and *Adriana Lecouvreur* on November 26, 1902. The Lirico was reconstructed by Achille Sfondrini. Recently it hosted the world premiere of Azio Corghi's *Blimunda* on May 20, 1990, and the Italian premiere of Fabio Vacchi's *La Station thermale* on March 19, 1995. Two other theaters in Milan hosted opera as well — the Teatro Carcano and Teatro dal Verme. The Carcano was inaugurated in September 1803, with Vincenzo Federici's *Zaira* and saw the world premieres of Donizetti's *Anna Bolena* on December 26, 1830, and Bellini's *La sonnambula* March 6, 1831. Recently, the theater has hosted ballet performances. The Dal Verme opened in 1872 with Giacomo Meyerbeer's *Les Huguenots* and hosted the world premieres of Puccini's first opera *Le Villi* on May 31, 1884, Ruggero Leoncavallo's *I pagliacci* on May 21, 1892, and Riccardo Zandonai's *Conchita* in 1911. It now serves as a movie house.

Bartolomeo Merelli had taken over La Scala in 1836, and presented Verdi's first opera, *Oberto, conte di San Bonifacio*, on November 17, 1839. He then commissioned Verdi to write three more operas. *Un giorno di regno* was premiered on September 5, 1840, and was not well received. Verdi refused to compose any more and Merelli returned the contract. Then, as the story goes, he met Verdi and gave him the libretto for what would become *Nabucco*. *Nabucco* was introduced on March 9, 1842, with Giuseppina Strepponi (his future wife) as Abigaille. The opera received 65 performances, a record still unbroken in the annals of La Scala, and *Va, pensiero sull'ali dorate* (Fly, thought, on wings of gold) became the unofficial national anthem of the Risorgimento. *I Lombardi alla prima crociata* was introduced next, followed by *Giovanna d'Arco* in 1845. After *Giovanna d'Arco*, Verdi's association with La Scala ended until the revised version of his *Simon Boccanegra* was presented in 1881. Near the end of his career, he re-

turned to La Scala for the world premieres of his two final operas, *Otello* and *Falstaff*. On January 27, 1901, Scala shut its doors and thousands gathered outside the Grand Hotel, where the world's greatest Italian opera composer had died of a stroke at the age of eighty-eight. A few days later, Toscanini conducted a concert of Verdi's music, with Enrico Caruso singing.

The world premiere of Giovanni Peruzzini's *Jone* took place on January 26, 1858, followed a decade later by Boïto's *Mefistofele* on March 5, 1868. There were violent protests between Boïto's admirers and his enemies during the performance, and when the demonstrations disrupted the second performance as well, Milan's chief of police ordered the opera withdrawn from the repertory. On the other hand, the world premiere of Amilcare Ponchielli's *La gioconda* took place on April 8, 1876, without incident. The introduction of several of Puccini's operas came next, with *Edgar* gracing the stage in 1889. Although it was a disaster, it was mild in comparison to the hostile reaction *Madama Butterfly* received. Puccini did not live to see his only La Scala triumph, *Turandot*, which was completed by Franco Alfano. Toscanini conducted the premiere and when he came to where Puccini had stopped composing, he put down his baton, turned to the audience, and said, *"Qui finisce l'opera, perché a questo punto il maestro è morto"* (Here the opera ends, because at this point the composer died) and left the podium.

When Toscanini was appointed permanent conductor at La Scala in 1898, he ushered in another golden era with several world and Italian premieres. In fact, Toscannini had three separate tenures at La Scala, 1898–1903, 1906–1908, and 1920–1929. The world premieres included Alfredo Catalani's *La Wally* on January 20, 1892, Leoncavallo's *I Medici* in 1893, Giordano's *Andrea Chénier* on March 28, 1896, Alberto Franchetti's *Germania* on March 11, 1902, Giordano's *Siberia* on December 19, 1903, Mascagni's *Parisina* on December 15, 1913, Italo Montemezzi's *L'amore dei tre Re* on April 10, 1913, Ildebrando Pizzetti's *Fedra* on March 20, 1915, Montemezzi's *La nave* on November 3, 1918, and Zandonai's *Cavalieri di Ekebù*, March 7, 1925, among others. La Scala also hosted the first Italian performances of Richard Strauss's *Salome*, *Elektra*, and *Der Rosenkavalier*, Claude Debussy's *Pelléas et Mélisande*, and Pyotr Il'yich Tchaikovsky's *Eugene Onegin*. World War I closed the opera house. It reopened on December 26, 1921, with Toscanini conducting Verdi's *Falstaff*. During his last tenure, Toscannini turned La Scala into a "shrine of opera," until his legendary clashes with Italian dictator Benito Mussolini forced his resignation in 1929. Six years later, Mascagni's *Nerone*, which glorified Mussolini and fascism, was premiered, but there was no glory for La Scala.

During the 1920s and 1930s La Scala welcomed the great voices of the era, including Lauri Vopli, Toti dal Monte, Beniamo Gigli, and Gina Cigna. One of the most memorable events was after World War II, when Maria Callas made her debut in Verdi's *Aida*, substituting for Renata Tebaldi. She captivated La Scala's audiences for a decade. Among the other famous voices after the war were Franco Corelli, Tito Gobbi, Mario del Monaco, Giulietta Simionato, Cesare Siepi, Gabriella, and Tucci. The opera world's great artists continue to sing at La Scala.

World premieres after the opera house was rebuilt included Ildebrando Pizzetti's *L'oro*, Giorgio Federico Ghedini's *Baccanti*, Goffredo Petrassi's *Il Cordovano*, Mario Peragallo's *La gita in campagna*, Francis Poulenc's *Dialogues des Carmélites*, Pizzetti's *Assassinio nella cattedrale*, Renzo Rossellini's *La leggenda del ritorno*, Karlheinz Stockhausen's *Donnerstag aus Licht*, *Samstag aus Licht*, and *Montag aus Licht*, Giacomo Manzoni's *Doktor Faustus*, and Luciano Berio's *Outis*. A smaller venue for chamber opera, La Piccola Scala, was inaugurated on December 26, 1955, with Cimarosa's *Il matrimonio segreto*. The theater hosted its first world premiere, Ghedini's *L'ipocrita felice* on March 10, 1956. Riccardo Malipiero's *La donna è mobile* followed on February 22, 1957, Mortari's *La scuola delle mogli* on March 17, 1959, Nino Rota's *La notte di un nevrastenico* on February 8, 1960, Bruno Bettinelli's *Count Down* and Gino Negri's *Pubblicità ninfa gentile* on March 26, 1970, Angelo Paccagnini's *La misura, il mistero* on November 12, 1970, and Sylvano Bussotti's *Le Racine* on December 9, 1980. Small-scale works are now presented in the Nuovo Piccolo Teatro, which hosted Aldo Clementi's *Carillon* in October 1998.

At times, La Scala has been plagued with political infighting, inadequate budgets, traditional repertory, and union problems. One crisis occurred in 1974-75 when there was no money and the unions squeezed. A difficult fight followed, resulting in the *sovrintendente*, Paolo Grassi, requesting a reform of the *enti lirici* and a special law to define the role of theater. When Carlo Fontana took over, the contributions from the state had been drastically cut and the amount of earned money had to be increased, which it was, from raising ticket prices to increasing rentals of scenery, and the number of sponsors. La Scala's budget at the beginning of his reign was $100 million, of which 64% came from government subsidies, 20% from ticket sales, and the rest from sponsors, advertising recordings, radio and television rights. For an Italian opera house to earn 36% of its budget is unusual. The commercialization of Milan's great opera house has come at a price, creeping into the productions and the atmosphere. From Verdi's *Nabucco* in 1987, presented with flawless precision and exacting interpretation, to Verdi's *Falstaff* in 1995, which was a good, solid production, but nothing overwhelming, to Charles Gounod's *Faust* in 1997, which lost its soul somewhere during the trip, La Scala is recreating the days when one went to the opera to see and be seen, when the audience (except for the *loggione*) was dominated by wealthy tourists and corporate sponsors. It is drifting towards becoming like the Metropolitan Opera (New York), a very expensive opera museum, with a few exceptions. Fortunately, it has not yet wandered too far off the path. Its recent offerings includes Nino Rota's *Il cappello di paglia di Firenze*, Mozart's *Die Zauberflöte*, Verdi's *Falstaff*, *Macbeth*, and *La traviata*, Donizetti's *Lucia di Lammermoor*, *Linda di Chamounix*, *L'elisir d'amore*, and *Lucrezia Borgia*, Modest Mussorgsky's *Khovanschchina*, Carl Maria von Weber's *Der Freischütz*, and Puccini's *Manon Lescaut*.

Teatro alla Scala

In 1921, the descendants of the *palchettisti* surrendered their boxes (for a price) to the municipality and Teatro alla Scala became an *Ente Autonomo* (autonomous corporation). World War II caught up with La Scala on August 16, 1943, when bombs destroyed the opera house. Only the outer shell and stage area survived. The sets and costumes for more than one hundred operas were also lost. After the war, a two percent amusement tax imposed in the Lombardy region (of which Milan was the capital), combined with part of the gate money from football matches, helped pay for

Teatro alla Scala (Milan, Italy).

the reconstruction of the opera house. La Scala gave birth to a daughter known as La Piccola Scala in 1955, that was designed by Piero Portaluppi. The 500-seat theater, adjoining La Scala, was built primarily as a home for 16th-, 17th-, and 20th-century chamber works.

The Teatro alla Scala is a Neoclassic building with a severe facade of soft copper-colored stucco embellished with white-and-salmon-tinted-stone Corinthian pilasters and attached columns that flank Empire windows. A balustrade crowns the structure along with a pediment displaying a chariot relief. The rusticated, arched ground level was the former carriage entrance. The exquisitely proportioned, horseshoe-shaped auditorium holds four tiers of boxes topped by two galleries, and a center royal box. Filled with cherubs, griffins, and caryatids, the gold, ivory, and red space is illuminated by a Bohemian crystal chandelier, complemented by clusters of white glass globes on the parapets. There are approximately 2,800 seats.

The mystique of La Scala begins before the performance, when the center chandelier and light clusters on the tiers dim, but the box and gallery lights are still shining. As those lights fade, a magic ripples through the auditorium as the curtain rises. Then you know why La Scala is still one of the world's great opera houses.

Practical Information. Teatro alla Scala, Via Filodrammatici 2, 20121 Milan. Tel: 39 2 88791, Fax: 39 2 887 9331. When visiting Teatro alla Scala, stay at the Four Seasons, Via Gesù 8, 20121 Milan. Tel 39 2 77088 or 1-800 332-3442, Fax 39 2 7708-5004. It is centrally located and close to La Scala. The Four Seasons can assist with schedules and tickets.

COMPANY STAFF AND WORLD PREMIERES

Sovrintendente. (since 1972) Carlo Fontana (1990–present), Carlo Maria Badini (1983–90), Paolo Grassi (1972–82). **Direttori Artistici:** Paolo Arcà (1997–present), Roman Vlad (1994–96), Alberto Zedda (1991–93), Cesare Mazzonis (1988–90), Cesare Perucci, Francesco Siciliani (consulente). **Direttori Musicali:** Riccardo Muti (1980–present), Claudio Abbado (1972–79).

World Premieres. A. Salieri's *Europa riconosciuta*, August 3, 1778; P. Anfossi's *Cleopatra*, January 1779; Bianchi's *L'olimpiade*, December 26, 1781; G. Sarti's *Fra i due litiganti il terzo gode*, September 14, 1782; D. Cimarosa's *La circe*, December 26, 1782; D. Cimarosa's *I due baroni di Rocca Azzurra*, April 1786; N.A. Zingarelli's *Ifigenia in Aulide*, January 27, 1787; F. Paër's *Rossana*, January 31, 1795; G. Gazzaniga's *La vendemmia*, November 4, 1796; S. Mayr's *Amor non ha ritegno*, May 18, 1804; Lavigna's *L'impostore avvilito*, September 11, 1804; S. Mayr's *Eraldo ed Emma*, January 8, 1805: S. Pavesi's *Il trionfo di Emilia*, February 9, 1805; Gnecco's *La prova di un opera seria*, August 16, 1805; Mosca's *L'italiana in Algeri*, August 16, 1808; P. Generali's *Chi non risica non rosica*, May 18, 1811; Mosca's *I pretendenti delusi*, September 7, 1811; S. Pavesi's *Tancredi*, January 18, 1812; P. Generali's *La vedova stravagante*, March 30, 1812; Orlandi's *Il cicisbeo burlato*, May 2, 1812; Mosca's *La bestie in Uomini*, August 17, 1812; G. Rossini's *La pietra del paragone*, September 26, 1812; S. Mayr's *Tamerlano*, December 26, 1812; G. Rossini's *Aureliano in Palmira*, December 26, 1813; G. Rossini's *Il turco in Italia*, August 14, 1814; Soliva's *La testa di bronzo*, September 3, 1816; G. Rossini's *La gazza ladra*, May 31, 1817; Gyrowetz's *Il finto Stanislao*, August 5, 1818; G. Rossini's *Bianca e Falliero, ossia Il consiglio dei tre*, December 26, 1819; G. Meyerbeer's *Margherita d'Anjou*, November 14, 1820; S. Mayr's *Fedra*, December 26, 1820; S. Mercadante's *Elisa e Claudio*, October 30, 1821; G. Meyerbeer's *L'eluse di Granata*, March 12, 1822; G. Donizetti's *Chiara e Serafina ossia I pirati*, October 26, 1822; S. Mercadante's *Amleto*, December 26, 1822; G. Pacini's *La vestale*, February 6, 1823; V. Bellini's *La straniera*, February 14, 1829; V. Bellini's *Il pirata*, October 27, 1827; V. Bellini's *Norma*, December 26, 1831; G. Donizetti's *Ugo, conte di Parigi*, March 13, 1832; G. Donizetti's *Lucrezia Borgia*, December 26, 1833; G. Donizetti's *Gemma di Vergy*, December 26, 1834; S. Mercandante's *Il giuramento*, March 11, 1837; S. Mercadante's *Il bravo*, March 9, 1839; G. Donizetti's *Gianni di Parigi* (revised), September 10, 1839; G. Verdi's *Oberto, conte di San Bonifacio* November 17, 1839; G. Verdi's *Un giorno di regno*, September 5, 1840; G. Donizetti's *Maria Padilla*, December 26, 1841; G. Verdi's *Nabucco*, March 9, 1842; G. Verdi's *I Lombardi alla prima crociata*, February 11, 1843; G. Verdi's *Giovanna d'Arco*, February 15, 1845; A. Boïto's *Mefistofele*, March 5, 1868; C. Gomes's *Il guarany*, March 19, 1870; A. Ponchielli's *La gioconda*, April 8, 1876; A. Ponchielli's *Il figliuol prodigo*, December 26, 1880; G. Verdi's *Simon Boccanegra* (revised version), March 24, 1881; A. Catalani's *Dejanice*, March 17, 1883; G. Verdi's *Otello*, February 5, 1887; G. Puccini's *Edgar*, April 21, 1889; A. Catalini's *La Wally*, January 20, 1890; G. Verdi's *Falstaff*, February 9, 1893; P. Mascagni's *Guglielmo Ratcliff*, February 16, 1895; U. Giordano's *Andrea Chénier*, March 28, 1896; P. Mascagni's *Le maschere*, January 17, 1901; A. Franchetti's *Germania*, March 11, 1902; A. Smareglia's *Oceana*, January 22, 1903; U. Giordano's *Siberia*, December 19, 1903; G. Puccini's *Madama Butterfly*, February 17, 1904; A. Franchetti's *La figlio di Iorio*, March 29, 1906; I. Montemezzi's *L'amore dei tre Re*, April 10, 1913; P. Mascagni's *Parisina*, December 15, 1913; I. Pizzetti's *Fedra*, March 20, 1915; I Pizzetti's *Debora e Jaele*, December 16, 1922; A. Boïto's *Nerone*, May 1, 1924; R. Zandonai's *I cavalieri di Ekebu*, March 7, 1925; G. Puccini's *Turandot*, April 25, 1926; E. Wolf-Ferrari's *Sly*, December 29, 1927; O. Respighi's *Lucrezia*, February 24, 1937; I. Pizzetti's *L'oro*, January 2, 1947; G.F. Ghedini's *La baccanti*, February 21, 1948; R. Bianchi's *Gli incatenati*, May 7, 1948; G.C. Sonzogno's *Regina Uliva*, March 17, 1949; G. Petrassi's *Il Cordovano*, May 12, 1949; L. Ferrari-Trecate's *L'orso re*, February 8, 1950; G. F. Malipiero's *L'allegra brigata*, May 4, 1950; J.J. Castro's *Proserpina e lo straniero*, March 17, 1952; J. Napoli's *Mas'Aniello*, March 25, 1953; V. Mortari's *La figlia del diavolo*, March 24, 1954; M. Peragallo's *La gita in campagna*, March 24, 1954; D. Milhaud's *David*, January 2, 1955; V. Tosatti's *Il guidizio universale*, April 2, 1955; F. Lattuada's *Caino*, January 10, 1957; F. Poulenc's *Les dialogues des Carmélites*, January 26, 1957; L. Chailly's *Una domanda di matrimonio*, May 22, 1957; I. Pizzetti's *Assassinio nella cattedrale*, March 1, 1958; I. Pizzetti's *Il calzare d'argento*, March 23, 1961; G. Turchi's *Il buon soldato Svejk*, April 5, 1962; M. De Falla's *Atlantida*, June 16, 1962; I. Pizzetti's *Clitennestra*, March 1, 1965; R. Rossellini's *La leggenda del ritorno*, March 10, 1966; K. Stockhausen's *Donnerstag aus Licht*, March 15, 1981; S. Sciarrino's *Lohengrin*, January 15, 1983; K. Stockhausen's *Samstag aus Licht*, May 25, 1984; F. Donatoni's *Atem*, February 16, 1985; F. Testi's *Riccardo III*, January 27, 1987; F. Mannino's *Il principe felice*, July 7, 1987; K. Stockhausen's *Montag aus Licht*, May 7, 1988; G. Manzonis *Doktor Faustus*, May 16, 1989, L. Berio's *Outis*, October 2, 1996.

World Premieres. **Rossini Operas:** *La pietra del paragone*, September 26, 1812; *Aureliano in Palmira*, December 26, 1813; *Il turco in Italia*, August 14, 1814; *La gazza ladra*, May 31, 1817; *Bianca e Falliero, ossia Il consiglio dei tre*, December 26, 1819. **Bellini Operas:** *Il pirata*, October 27, 1827; *La straniera*, February 14, 1829; *Norma*, December 26, 1831. **Donizetti Operas:** *Chiara e Serafina ossia I pirati*, October 26, 1822; *Ugo, conte di Parigi*, March 13, 1832; *Lucrezia Borgia*, December 26, 1833; *Gemma di Vergy*, December 26, 1834; *Gianni di Parigi* (revised), September 10, 1839; *Maria Padilla*, December 26, 1841. **Verdi Operas:** *Oberto, conte di San Bonifacio*, November 17, 1839; *Un giorno di regno* September 5, 1840; *Nabucco*, March 9, 1842; *I Lombardi alla prima crociata*, February 11, 1843; *Giovanna d'Arco*, February 15, 1845; *Simon Boccanegra* (revised version), March 24, 1881; *Otello*, February 5, 1887;

Falstaff, February 9, 1893. **Puccini Operas:** *Edgar*, April 21, 1889; *Madama Butterfly*, February 17, 1904, *Turandot*, April 25, 1926.

Bibliography. Luigi Ferrari, *La Scala: Breve storia attraverso due secoli* (Milan, 1981). Guido Vergani, "Carlo Fontana," *Vogue Teatro alla Scala 1946–1996* (Milan, 1996). Carlo Mezzadri (ed.), *Teatro alla Scala* (Milan, 1976). *Teatro alla Scala: Bimestrale di informazione musicale e culturale del Tearo alla Scala* (Milan, 1995–1996). Giampiero Tintori, *Duecento anni di Teatro alla Scala — Opere, Baletti, Concerti — 1778–1977* (Milan, 1979). Luigi Lorenzo Secchi, *Il Teatro alla Scala: 1778–1978* (Milan, 1977). Giorgio Lotti & Raul Radice, *La Scala: From Backstage to Performance — The Life of the Most Famous Opera House in The World* (New York, 1979) Programs from *Teatro alla Scala: 1975–1997* (Milan, 1975–1997). L. Arruga, *La Scala* (Milan, 1975). Sergio Segalini's *La Scala* (Paris, 1989); F. Armani (ed.), *La Scala, 1946–66* (Milan, 1967).

Thanks to Paolo Klun & Paola Calvatti, Teatro alla Scala, and Vincenzo Finizzola & Andrea Filippi.

MODENA

Teatro Comunale
(Teatro di Tradizione)

On October 2, 1841, Alessandro Gandini's *Adelaide di Borgogna al Castello di Canossa*, an opera commission for the occasion from the Modenese composer, inaugurated the Teatro Comunale with the principal roles created by Erminia Frezzolini Poggi, Antonio Poggi, and Domenico Donzelli. A ballet entitled *Rebecca* followed the opera. Francesco Vandelli designed the building.

Modena's operatic history dates back almost four centuries and unfolded in several opera houses. In 1539, the first recorded performance took place, a *comedia* staged before an audience of invited guests in a barn-like room in a structure known as La Spelta. (Theater in the 16th century was still a private affair.) In 1643, six years after the first public theater opened in Venice, Modena inaugurated the Teatro Valentini. Constructed primarily of wood, with the architecture vaguely resembling that of a classic amphitheater, it was destroyed by fire on January 20, 1681, after a performance by Giuseppe Tortorici's company. Reconstruction began in February 1682, but a boundary dispute between the Valentini family and the Rangoni family held up construction until November 18, 1683. It then acquired a new owner, the Marquis Fontanelli and opened for the 1685 Carnival season, offering Carlo Pallavicino's *Il vespasiano*. As the Teatro Fontanelli, it hosted only eleven operas, which included three world premieres — Domenico Gabrielli's *Flavio Cuniberto*, Antonio Giannettini's *L'ingresso alla gioventù di Claudio Nerone*, and Gaetano Boni's *Il figlio delle selve*.

Two more theaters were built during the 17th century, the Teatro di Corte and the Teatro Ducale di Piazza. The latter was erected by Francesco I d'Este and opened in 1656. Designed by Gaspare Vigarani, it included elegantly decorated proscenium boxes flanked by Corinthian columns, six side boxes split between two tiers, and bleacher benches in the back of the room. Francesco Manelli's *Andromeda* inaugurated the theater. The Ducale di Piazza also hosted the first world premieres in Modena: Prospero Mazzi's *Il prencipe Corsaro* in 1674 and Filippo Acciajuoli's *Il girello* in 1675. Other operas of note included Benedetto Ferrari's *Erodilda*, Marcantonio Cesti's *La schiava fortunata*, Pier Francesco Cavalli's *Il ciro*, Giovanni Legrenzi's *Germanico sul reno*, Giandomenico Freschi's *Helena Rapita* and Carlo Pallavicino's *Bassiano*. Although the final opera staged took place in 1710, Clemente Monari's *Atlanta* performed by a local academy, the theater had fallen into disuse back in 1685, after the staging of Giacomo Antonio Perti's *Oreste in Argo* and Marcantonio Ziani's *Alcibiade*. In 1769, the Ducale di Piazza was demolished.

The existence of the Teatro di Corte was first noted in 1669, but work on it was probably begun as early as 1634, and was most likely based on a design of the Roman architect Bartolomeo Avanzini. It was a tiny, family theater. Francesco II then constructed a larger theater (for the family) and commissioned Tommaso Bezzi for the project. This theater was opened on March 13, 1686, with Giovanni Battista Rosselli-Genesini's *L'Eritrea*. It was very active, with productions by the students of the Collegio dei Nobili, including Giuseppe Tricarico's *Endimione*, Giacomo Antonio Perti's *L'Apollo geloso*, and Pietro Pulli's *Il carnevale e la pazzia.* The Seven Years' War forced the court to leave and the theater was closed. When the court returned in 1749, the theater was enlarged, based on the designs of Antonio Cugini. After this reconstruction, it was opened to the public in 1750. Several world premieres took place, including Gian Marco Rutini's *La nitteti,* Michele Mortellari's *Armida,* Ferdinando Bertoni's *Creonte,* D. Bortnianski's *Quinto Fabio,* Francesco Bianchi's *Erifile* and *Enea nel Lazio,* and Giovanni Paisiello's *Artaserse* and *Alessandro nelle Indie.* In 1796, during the first Napoleonic period, the Teatro di Corte was renamed the Teatro Nazionale, and when Napoleon was crowned King of Italy, it was renamed Teatro Regio. In 1806, it hosted a novelty, Sebastiano Nasolini's *Archille e Patroclo.* With the arrival of the Austrian rulers, the theater reacquired its birth name (Teatro di Corte) in 1814, and eight works by the local composer Antonio Gandini were introduced: *Erminia, Il ruggero, Antigono, Il disertore, Demetrio, Zaira, Isabella di Lara, Maria di Brabante.* The last novelty mounted was Temistocle Solera's *La fanciulla di Castel Guelfo* in 1842.

Meanwhile, the Teatro Fontanelli had again changed hands and name. Fontanelli sold the structure to Count Teodoro Rangoni for 65,000 Modenese lire on July 29, 1705. Theatrical activity began again in the now-named Teatro Rangoni with *Il trionfo d'amore nè tradimenti* in the autumn of 1705. The Rangione introduced Paisiello's *Madama l'umorista* and *Il Demetrio,* and staged several of his works like *Il Re Teodoro, Il fanatico in Berlina, Il Pirro, La mulinara, Il Demofonte,* and *Gli zingari in fiera.* Around the middle of the century, more novelties graced the stage, including Girolamo Abos's *Tito Manlio* and Giuseppe Scolari's *Il finto cavaliero,* Antonio Pio's *Demofoonte,* Francesco Sirotti's *La zenobia,* Antonio Maria Giuliani's *Guerra in pace,* and Giuseppe Giordani's *La vestale.* As the century drew to a close, an amusing novelty, Giuseppe Gazzanigo's *Il divorzio senza matrimonio* (Divorce without Marriage) was mounted. In 1807, after 102 years, Teatro Rangoni was passed to a society of boxholders who managed the theater for a decade. Three years later, poor quality singing of a performance of Valentino Fioravanti's *Amore e dispetto* was met with such protests that the performance was stopped and the theater remained shut for 23 days. The boxholders then gave the building to Duke Francesco IV, who in turn gave it to the Comune, which at the same time returned the boxes to their original owners. This led to a type of joint ownership between a public corporation and private citizens and the theater's name was again changed to Teatro Comunale via di Emilia to reflect the ownership arrangement. In 1825, Antonio Gabussi's *I furbi al cimento* was the last world premiere to grace the stage. After the new Teatro Comunale opened in 1841, the Teatro Comunale via di Emilia was known as the Comunale Vecchio (old Comunale). The structure, which closed its doors in 1859, offered five tiers of boxes which rose in horseshoe-shape, interrupted by a center royal box on the 2nd and 3rd levels, and by an entrance door on the orchestra level.

On December 26, 1713, another theater had been inaugurated, the Teatro Molza. Built on the initiative of Nicolò Molza, it opened for carnival with Francesco Gasparini's *La fede tradita e vendicata.* Under the direction of Antonio Maria Bononcini, several operas were offered, including the *prima assoluta* of Gaetano Maria Schiassi's *La Zanina finta contessa.* The final opera at the Molza, Giuseppe Scarlatti's *Pompeo in Armenia,* took place in 1749.

The latter part of 1700s counted Giuseppe Sarti, Paisiello, Domenico Cimarosa, as the most favored composers. Although today's audience is familiar with only one of Cimarosa's operas, *Il matrimonio segreto,* he wrote many. Some of those staged in Modena's theaters included *Gli amanti comici, Il matrimonio segreto, L'olimpiade, Cajo Mario, Giannina e Bernardone, Il convito, Le trame deluse, Il Demetrio, Il credulo deluso, La villanella riconosciuta,* and *Le astuzie femminili.* Sarti's works seen in Modena included *Cleomene, Il Medonte Re d'Epiro, Idalide, Tra i due litiganti il terzo gode,* and *Le gelosie villane.* After the turn of the century, the works of Ferdinando Paër were frequently represented, including *La Loncanda dei vagabondi, Il principe di Taranto, La griselda, La virtù al cimento, Agnese,* and *Sofonisba.*

The arrival of Gioachino Rossini's operas in the repertory in 1813, followed by Gaetano Donizetti and Vincenzo Bellini, soon displaced the Italian masters of the 1600s and 1700s, placing most in oblivion. Even composers who were popular during the 1800s, like Saverio Mercadante, Giovanni Pacini, Errico Petrella, and Luigi and Federico Ricci are almost all but forgotten today. The first Rossini work on the boards, *Demetrio e Polibio,* was at the Teatro di via Emilia in 1813, followed by *Tancredi* the next year. For Carnival 1814-15 *L'inganno felice* was staged, then *L'italiana in Algeri*. At the same time, Rossini works were staged at the Teatro di Corte with *Tancredi* in 1815 followed by *L'italiana in Algeri*. The latter was also repeated for the Lent season at the Via Emilia Theater. Eventually around half of Rossini's works were staged in Modena, among them: *Il barbiere di Siviglia, Il turco in Italia, Ciro in Babilonia, La Cenerentola, La pietra di paragone, Aureliano in Palmira, La gazza ladra, L'inganno felice, Matilde di Shabran, Semiramide, Ricciardo e Zoraide, Aureliano in Palmira, Mosè in Egitto,* and *Otello ossia Il Moro di Venezia*. Giacomo Meyerbeer's *Il crociato in Egitto* was first staged in Modena in 1826. Four years later, Donizetti's *L'ajo nell'imbarazzo* was presented, followed by *Gli esiliati in Siberia, Olivo e Pasquale, Settimio, L'elisir d'amore, Il furioso dell'isola di Santo Domingo, Anna Bolena, Gemma di Vergy, Lucia di Lammermoor,* and *Belisario*. Bellini's operas first entered the repertory in 1832, including *Il pirata, La straniera, Norma, La sonnambula, Beatrice di Tenda,* and *I Puritani*.

Before proceeding to the new Teatro Comunale, a note about the Italian audience of the time. They are probably best described in an 1834 letter from the German composer Otto Nicolai, whose opera inaugurated the Carnival season in 1847-48 with *Il templario*, to his father (reprinted in *L'opera nel teatri di Modena*): "It appears trivial to me the way the Italian family listened to its own operas. The family has taken a box which they consider like a room to receive visitors, and only from time to time listen "in passing" to a little music. The noise in the auditorium is such that one struggles to hear the music. And this is the custom in all Italy. Even more, the opera is composed in two acts and between which a dance is presented that has nothing to do with the opera, and that lasts around an hour, such that after the ballet, one has forgotten the first act of the opera. Often an act of one opera is given with one of another act of a different opera making a *pasticcio* (mess). In fact, to an Italian, it is not important to bring away any impression: he/she wants to hear sound, watch the stage and people which moves them, and pass the time to amuse themselves...." The famous French composer Hector Berlioz was equally harsh in his judgment of the Italian audience writing that "they have no interest in the poetic aspect of the music, and are ready

to consume a new opera like a plate of macaroni and cheese." Actually, even a decade after World War II one could still smell the odor of stewed meat, salami, and cakes lightly emanating from the corridors of the boxes.

After the Teatro Comunale opened in 1841, it hosted a two month inaugural season with three more operas — Mercadante's *Il bravo*, Bellini's *Beatrice di Tenda*, and Angelo Catelani's *Carattaco*. Two years later Giuseppe Verdi's works first entered the repertory with *Nabucco* (as Nabucodonosor) followed by *Ernani, I Lombardi alla prima crociata, I due Foscari, I masnadieri, Luisa Miller, Macbeth, Il corsaro, Il trovatore, Attila, La traviata* (as Violetta), *I vespri siciliani, Un ballo in maschera, Rigoletto* (as Viscardello). With rare exception, the repertory was almost entirely Italian, except for some French grand operas like Meyerbeer's *Robert le Diable* and *Les Huguenots*. The royal censors forced name changes to operas like *Rigoletto* (Viscardello), *La traviata* (Violetto), *Lucrezia Borgia* (Eustorgia da Romano), and Giuseppe Apolloni's *L'ebreo* (Lida di Granata).

The 1859 spring opera season opened with Verdi's *Aroldo* on May 9 and for three evenings it played to an empty theater. The impresario, facing bankruptcy, fled and the theater was closed. The following month, Francesco V left Modena forever, ending the ducal period, and the Comunale was renamed the Municipale. Meanwhile, two other theaters had opened in Modena, the Arena-Teatro Goldini in 1860, and the Teatro Aliprandi two years later. The Goldini was conceived as an outdoor arena and constructed of wood. Later it was rebuilt in stone and covered with a roof of sheet iron. Between 1867 and 1888, there were twenty-four seasons of opera, alternating with the Teatro Municipale and the Teatro Aliprandi. The Teatro Aliprandi was named after the impresario Achille Aliprandi, and built on the ruins of the Teatro di Corte. Smaller in scale than the Comunale, the Aliprandi held three tiers, supported by columns. During its 19-year existence, it hosted three world premieres: Isidoro Rossi's *Mimi* (1872), Gaetano Mazzoli's *Adela d'Asturia* (1877), and Ottavio Buzzino's *L'orfanella di Gand* (1880). Fire devoured the structure the evening of March 17, 1881, a half hour before the curtain was to rise on a production of Pietro Cossa's drama, *Nerone*.

French grand opera continued in popularity at the Municipale with Charles Gounod's *Faust* (1876-77), Fromental Halévy's *La Juive* (1877-78),

Meyerbeer's *L'Africaine* (1880-81) and *Le Prophète* (1891-92). The 1882-83 was a "devil" season with *Roberto le Diable* and Arrigo Boïto's *Mefistofele* in the *cartellone*.

Another theater, the Teatro Storchi, opened in the spring of 1889, with Emilio Usiglio's *Le donne curiose*, conducted by the composer. The Storchi hosted opera for seventy years. Built by a wealthy businessman and art-lover, it was the site of several *prime assolute* including Edoardo Poggi's *Irnerio* (1899), Andrea Ferretto's *Zingari* (1900), and three works by Luigi Gazzotti in 1921 and 1922. The 1919-20 Carnival Season hosted twelve productions: *Aida, Lucia di Lammermoor, Il barbiere di Siviglia, Werther, La fanciulla del West, Loreley, La Cenerentola, Rigoletto, Fra diavolo, L'elisir d'amore, Il barbiere di Siviglia, Una partita a scacchi*. The 1959 spring season, which offered *L'elisir d'amore, La traviata, Alba di gloria*, and *Lucia di Lammermoor* was the final opera season at the Storchi. The theater is still extant and presents dramatic fare.

The seasons between 1896 and 1908 featured operas by Umberto Giordano, Giacomo Puccini, Franco Alfano, Pietro Mascagni, Ruggero Leoncavallo, Italo Montemezzi, Francesco Cilea, Riccardo Zandonai, and Alberto Franchetti, French opera and even the occasional Wagner work. In 1917, Verdi's forgotten *Oberto* was on the boards. The Comune of Modena took over the administration of the opera house beginning with the 1956-57 season and changed the name back to Teatro Comunale. The *Associazione Teatri Emilia-Romagna* was founded in 1964 and there are co-productions with the Teatro Municipale Valli di Reggio Emilia, Teatro Municipale di Piacenza, Teatro Comunale di Ferrara, Teatro Alighiera di Ravenna, Teatro Regio di Parma, and Teatro Comunale di Bologna. The 1961 season offered some novelties — the Modena premiere of Donizetti's *Rita*, the first modern performance of Franz Joseph Haydn's *Lo speziale*, and Hector Berlioz's *Le damnation de Faust*. More unusual works for Modena followed — Sergey Prokofiev's *L'yubov' k tryom apel'sinam* (Love for Three Oranges), Modena premiere of Wolfgang Amadeus Mozart's *Così fan tutte*, Nikolay Rimsky-Korsakov's *Zolotoy petushok* (The Golden Cockerel), Giorgio F. Ghedini's *La pulce d'oro*, Manuel de Falla's *El retablo de Maese Pedro*, Maurica Ravel's *L'heure espagnole*, and Arnold Schönberg's *Pierrot Lunaire*, among others. Recent offerings include Bellini's *Norma* and *I Puritani*, Donizetti's *Il campanello dello speziale* and *Betly*, Verdi's *La traviata*, Mozart's *Le nozze di Figaro*, and Benjamin Britten's *The Turn of the Screw*.

Teatro Comunale (Teatro Municipale)

Discussions began in 1838 about construction of the Teatro Comunale, to respond to the growing theatrical needs and increasing population of the city. The architect Vandelli incorporated ideas into his design of the Comunale which he got from visiting the theaters at Piacenza, Mantova, and La Scala of Milano. Twelve houses were demolished to make room for the opera house. Work was begun in May 1838, and continued for four years.

The Teatro Comunale is a dark-yellow stucco-covered building of Neoclassic design. The facade holds four Doric columns surrounded by an ashlar portico. Above are four Ionic pilasters flanking three of the nine rectangular windows which punctuate the front. Apollo holding a torch with a mask of Tragedy, and musical instruments crowns the building. The horseshoe-shaped auditorium, decorated in red, gold, and ivory, holds five tiers — three box tiers, a gallery and loggione. There are approximately 1,000 seats.

Practical Information. Teatro Comunale, Via Fonteroso 8, 41100 Modena. Tel: 39 59 224-443, Fax 39 59 214-775. If visiting, contact the Italian Government Travel Offices (ENIT), 630 Fifth Avenue, New York, NY 10011. Tel: 212-245-4822.

WORLD PREMIERES AND REPERTORY

World Premieres (*except Teatro Comunale, Municipale*). P. Mazzi's *Il Prencipe Corsaro*, Teatro Ducale di Piazza, 1674; F. Acciajuoli's *Il girello*, Teatro Ducale di Piazza, 1674; Bonocini's *I primi voli dell'aquila austriaca dal sogno imperiale alla gloria*, Teatro Ducale di Piazza, 1677; (unknown) *L'eritrea*, Teatro di Corte, 1686; D. Gabrielli's *Flavio Cuniberto*, Teatro Fontanelli 1688; A. Giannettini's *L'ingresso alla gioventù di Claudio Nerone*, Teatro Fontanelli, 1691-92; G. Boni's *Il figlio delle selve*, Teatro Fontanelli, 1700; G.M. Schiassi's *La Zanina finta contessa*, Teatro Molza, 1727. G. Abos's *Tito Manlio*, Teatro Rangoni, 1753; G. Latilla's *Antigona*,

Teatro Comunale (Modena, Italy).

Teatro di Corte, 1753; G. Scolari's *Il finto cavaliero*, Teatro Rangoni, 1760; G.B. Lampugnani's *La scuola delle cantatrici*, Teatro Rangoni, 1760; G.M. Rutini's *Gli sposi in maschera*, Teatro Rangoni, 1765; G. Paisiello and P. Guglielmi's *Madama l'umorista*, Teatro Rangoni, 1765; G. Paisiello's *Il Demetrio*, Teatro Rangoni, 1765; G.M. Rutini's *La nitteti*, Teatro di Corte, 1769; G. Paisiello's *Artaserse*, Teatro di Corte, 1771; G. Piasiello's *Alessandro nelle Indie*, Teatro di Corte, 1773; M. Mortellari's *Armida*, Teatro di Corte, 1775; F. Bertoni's *Creonte*, Teatro di Corte, 1776; D. Bortnianski's *Quinto Fabio*, Teatro di Corte, 1778; G. Calegari's *La Zenobia*, Teatro di Corte, 1779; F. Bianchi's *Erifile*, Teatro di Corte, 1781: A. Pio's

Demofoonte, Teatro Rangoni, 1782; F. Sirotti's *La zenobia*, Teatro Rangoni, 1783; A.M. Giuliani's *Guerra in pace*, Teatro Rangoni, 1784; G. Giordani's *La vestale*, Teatro Rangoni, 1785; F. Bianchi's *Enea nel Lazio*, Teatro di Corte, 1785-86; G. Gazzanigo's *Il divorzio senza matrimonio*, Teatro Rangoni, 1794; S. Nasolini's *Archille e Patroclo*, Teatro di Corte, 1806; S. Pavesi's *La fiera di Brindisi*, Teatro Rangoni, 1814; A. Gandini's *Erminia*, Teatro di Corte, 1818; A. Gandini's *Il ruggero*, Teatro di Corte, 1820; A. Gandini's *Antigono*, Teatro di Corte, 1824; A. Gabussi's *I furbi al cimento*, Teatro Comunale di via Emilia, 1825; A. Gandini's *Il disertore*, Teatro di Corte, 1826; A. Gandini's *Demetrio*, Teatro di Corte, 1829; A. Gandini's *Zaira*, Teatro di Corte, 1829; A. Gandini's *Isabella di Lara*, Teatro di Corte, 1830; A. Gandini's *Maria di Brabante*, Teatro di Corte, 1833; T. Solera's *La fanciulla di Castel Guelfo*, Teatro di Corte, 1842; I. Rossi's *Mimi*, Teatro Aliprandi, 1872; G. Mazzoli's *Adela d'Asturia*, Teatro Aliprandi, 1877; O. Buzzino's *L'orfanella di Gand*, Teatro Aliprandi, 1880; E. Poggi's *Irnerio*, Teatro Storchi, 1899; A. Ferretto's *Zingari*, Teatro Storchi, 1900; L. Gazzotti's *Lo zingaro cieco*, Teatro Storchi, 1921; L. Gazzotti's *La procella*, Teatro Storchi, 1922; L. Gazzotti's *Il campanaro di camalò*, Teatro Storchi, 1922. **(Teatro Comunale)**: A. Gandini's *Adelaide di Borgogna al Castello di Canossa*, 1841; A. Catelani's *Carattaco*, 1841; N. Perelli's *Galeotto Manfredi*, 1843; A. Mammi's *Zaira*, 1845; G. Carlotti's *Rita*, 1853; **(Teatro Municipale)**: Achille e Peri's *Orfano e Diavolo*, 1871; A. Giovanini's *Irene*, 1872; C.Pedrotti's *Olema*, 1872; G. Verdi's *Don Carlo* (5 acts without ballet, Edizione di Modena); E. Bertini's *Roncisval*, 1891; A.F. Carbonieri's *Edith*, 1912; Q. Azzolini's *Wanda*, 1937; G. Valentini's *Mi-kel*, 1941; Q. Azzolini's *Rossana*, 1950.

Repertory. (Teatro Ducale di Piazza): 1656: Andromeda. **1658:** Erodilda. **1674:** La schiava fortunata, Il prencipe Corsaro. **1675:** Il ciro, Il girello. **1677:** Germanico sul reno. **1681:** Helena Rapita. **1683:** Bassiano. **1685:** Oreste in Argo, Alcibiade. **1710:** Atlanta. **(Teatro Fontanelli): 1685:** Il vespasiano. **1686:** Il trespolo tutore balordo, i due germani rivali. **1688:** Flavio Cuniberto. **1689:** Mauritio. **1690:** Eteocle e Polinice. **1691:** L'inganno scoperto per vendetta. **1692:** L'ingresso alla gioventù di Claudio Nerone. **1697:** Giustino. **1700-1701:** Il figlio delle selve, La ninfa bizzarra. **1703:** La Semiramide. **(Teatro Rangoni): 1705:** Il trionfo d'amore nè tradimenti. **1707:** Il trionfo dell'umiltà. **1713:** La ninfa Apollo, Il Principe Selvaggio. **1716:** L'Atlanta, Dorinda in Arcadia. **1720:** Nino. **1735-36:** La Semiramide riconosciuta. **1740:** Un matrimonio disgraziato. **1741:** La clemenza di Tito (Leo), Il conte immaginario, La finata cameriera. **1744:** La zanina maga per amore. **1746:** Il pandolfo. **1751-52:** Caio Mario. **1753-54:** Tito Manlio, L'Antigono, Le astuzie amorose. **1755:** La zenobia, Lo speziale. **1755-56:** Le

virtuose ridicole, Le pescatrici, Il mondo alla roversa. **1758:** Il filosofo di campagna, Le nozze. **1758-59:** Il mercato di malmantile, La conversazione. **1759-60:** La calamita de'cuori, Il ritorno da Londra, Gli uccellatori. **1760:** Il finto cavaliero, Il ciarlatano. **1760-61:** La scuola delle cantatrici. **1761-62:** Il signore dottore, L'amante di tutte. **1762-63:** Il viaggiatore, I tre amanti ridicoli. **1763-64:** Le contadine bizzarre, L'arcadia in Brenta, La moglie in calzoni. **1764-65:** Il nuovo norlando, Gli sposi in maschera, Madama l'umorista, Il demetrio. **1765:** Le vicende della sorte. **1766-67:** L'olimpiade, Il trionfo di Camillo. **1767-68:** Il ratto della sposa, Il matrimonio per concorso. **1768:** La straniera riconosciuta, Il ratto della sposa, L'amore senza malizia. **1769:** Il calzolajo di Strasburgo. **1770:** Cleomene. **1781-82:** Perseo, La nitteti. **1782:** Il convito, Gli amanti canuti. **1782-83:** Deemofonte, La zenobia. **1784:** Giulio Babino. **1784:** Piramo e Tisbe, Guerra in pace. Artaserse. **1784-85:** L'olimpiade, Il Medonte Re d'Epiro. L'infanta supposta. **1785:** La vestale, Enea nel lazio. **1786:** Idalide. **1786-87:** Ezio, Alessandro nelle Indie. **1787:** Il Demofonte. **1787:** Gianna e Bernardone, Gli amanti alla prova, Tra i due litiganti il terzo gode. **1787:** La secchia rapita. **1787-88:** Il Pirro. **1788:** Catone in Utica. **1788-89:** Alciade e Telesia, Una cosa rara. **1789:** Enea e Lavinia. **1789-90:** La mulinara, Le trame deluse, Le gelosie villane. **1790:** Artaserse. **1780-91:** La scuffiara, L'Antigono. **1791:** Il credulo deluso, La bella pescatrice. **1791-92:** La pastorella nobile. **1792:** Il Pirro. **1792-93:** L'Ezio, Il Deemofonte. **1793:** La vendetta di Nino. **1793-94:** Il fanatico in Berlina, Il divorzio senza matrimonio. **1794:** Cajo Mario. **1794-95:** Il matrimonio segreto, La dama soldato. **1795:** L'olimpiade. **1795-96:** La Cleopatra. **1796-97:** La virtuosa bizzarra, La capricciosa corretta. **1797:** Il matrimonio segreto, Gli amanti comici. **1797-98:** La donna di genio volubile. **1798-99:** Il Re Teodoro, La vera somiglianza, La moglie capricciosa. **1799:** Zulema. **1799-1800:** L'impresario burlato, Gli zingari in fiera. **1801:** Le trame deluse. **1802:** I due gemelli, La sposa in contrasto, L'avaro deluso. **1803:** Il matrimonio segreto, La donna di genio volubile. La muta per amore. **1803-04:** La villanella riconsciuta. **1804:** La locanda dei vagabondi, Giannina e Bernadone. **1804-05:** Il ciabattino incivilito. **1807:** La prova di un'opera seria. **(Teatro di Via Emilia): 1807-08:** La vedova contrastata, La convenienze teatrali. **1808:** Il ritorno di Serse. **1809:** L'avaro. **1809:** Il principe di Taranto. **1809-10:** La Grisdelda, La virtù al cimento, Le cantatrici villane. **1810:** La burla fortunata, L'incantesimo senza magia, Omar Re di Termagene. **1810-11:** Amore e dispetto, L'innocenza premiata. **1811-12:** Il corradino, La guerra aperta. **1812-13:** Ser Marcantonio. **1813:** Demetrio e Polibio, Omar Re Di Termagene, Agnese. **1814:** L'amor marinaro, Tancredi. **1814-15:** La fiera di Brindinsi, L'inganno felice, Adelina. **1815:** L'italiana in Algeri. **1816:** I tre pretendenti, Agnese di Fitzhenry, Cecchina suonatrice di Ghironda. **1816:** Ginevra di Scozia, L'italiana in Algeri, La cameriera astuta. **(Teatro Comunale di Via Emilia): 1816-17:** Alzira, Sofonisba. **1817:** Evelina. **1817-18:** Il barbiere di Siviglia, Gli originali, Il turco in Italia. **1818:** Trajano in Dacia, Ciro in Babilonia. **1818-19:** La Cenerentola, Le astuzie femminili, Gli originali, Carolina e Filandro. **1819:** La pietra di paragone, Il filosofo immaginario. **1819:** La rosa bianca e la rosa rossa, I baccanali di Roma. **1819-20:** La Clotilde, Il servo padrone. **1820:** Aureliano in Palmira. **1820-21:** La gazza ladra, Il turco in Italia, Gli originali, Adelina. **1821:** Elizabetta Regina D'Inghilterra. **1821-22:** La gioventù di Enrico V°, L'italiana in Algeri, Il barbiere di Siviglia. **1822:** Eduardo e Cristina. **1822-23:** La sposa fedele, La Cenerentola, Il matrimonio segreto. **1823:** Annibale in Bitinia, Gli Illinesi. **1823-24:** Elisa e Claudio, L'inganno felice, Il Barone di Dolsheim. **1824:** Moctar Gran Visir di Adrianopoli, Giulio Sabino in Langres. **1824-25:** Matilde di Shabran, La capanna moscovita, Il finto sordo, I furbi al cimento. **1825:** La Cenerentola, Semiramide. **1826:** Il crociato in Egitto, Il barbiere di Siviglia. **1827:** Ricciardo e Zoraide, Aureliano in Palmira. **1828:** L'italiana in Algeri, Torvaldo e Dorliska. **1829:** Giulietta e Romeo, Il barbiere di Siviglia. **1830:** Gli arabi nelle Gallie, L'ajo nell'imbarazzo. **1830-31:** Elisa e Claudio, Gli esiliati in Siberia. **1831-32:** Olivo e Pasquale, La Cenerentola, Il turco in Italia. **1832:** I pirata, Matilde di Shabran. **1832-33:** La straniera, Mosè in Egitto, La calzolaja. **1833:** Settimio. **1833-34:** Chiara di Rosenberg, L'elisir d'amore. **1834:** Norma, Il furioso dell'isola di Santa Domingo, Il nuovo Figaro, Chiara di Rosenberg. **1835:** Gli arabi nelle Gallie, Otello ossia Il Moro di Venezia. **1835-36:** La pazza per amore, La Cenerentola, Il barbiere di Siviglia. **1836:** La sonnambula, Ines di Castro. **1836-37:** Anna Bolena, La straniera, Un'avventura di Scaramuccia. **1837:** Norma, Beatrice di Tenda, Anna Bolena, Il pirata. **1837-38:** La pazza per amore, Il turco in Italia, Chiara di Rosenberg, Un'avventura di Scaramuccia. **1838:** Gemma di Vergy, Beatrice di Tenda. **1838-39:** Lucia di Lammermoor, Norma. **1839-40:** Marin Faliero, I Puritani. **1840-41:** Emma d'Antiochia, Belisario, Beatrice di Tenda, Il campanello delle speziale. **(Teatro Molza): 1713-14:** Le fede tradita e Vendicata. **1714:** Il Radamisto. **1716:** L'enigma disciolto, Lucio vera. **1717:** Fernando. **1718:** L'eudamia, Alessandro severo. **1719:** L'Arsace, Li veri amici. **1720:** Il Conte d'Altamura, La partenope. **1721:** Il finto chimico, Il solimano. **1727:** Gli inganni amorosi scoperti in villa. **1727-28:** La Zanina finta contessa. **1730:** Il savio delirante, Albumazar. **1733:** Idaspe. **1738-39:** Il Bajazette, Artaserse. **1740-41:** Ezio, Didone abbandonata. **1742:** La clemenza di Tito. **1744:** L'arsace. **1748:** La maestra. **1749:** Pompeo in Armenia. **(Teatro di Corte): 1686:** L'eritrea. **1697:** Amore fra gl'impossibili. **1698:**

Endimione. **1700:** Il dittatore romano. **1701:** Demetrio. **1708:** L'Apollo geloso. **1728:** La Zanina finta contessa. **1738:** Il Carnevale e La Pazzia. **1750:** Vologeso Re dei Parti, Cajo marzio Coriolano. **1751:** Demetrio. **1753:** Merope, Antigona. **1763:** La Baronessa Maritata, La buona figliuola. **1764:** I francesi brillanti, Il ciarlone. **1767:** Amor industrioso. **1768-69:** La clemenza di Tito, L'Antigono. **1769:** Le nozze disturbate, L'Olandese in Italia, La contadina in corte. **1769-70:** La nitteti, Adriano in Siria. **1770:** La schiava riconosciuta. **1770-71:** Il Demetrio, La Semiramide riconosciuta. **1771-72:** Artaserse, Ezio. **1772:** Calandrano, L'astratto. **1772-73:** Scipione in Cartagena, Ipermestra. **1773:** L'amore soldato. **1773-74:** Alessandro nelle Indie, Demofoonte. **1774:** L'isola d'Alcina, L'innocente fortunata, La contessina. **1774-75:** Cajo Mario, L'adriano in Siria. **1775-76:** Armida, Creonte. **1776:** Il geloso in cimento, L'avaro. **1776-77:** L'isola di Calipso, Farnace. **1777:** La vera Costanza, Il Marchese Tulipano. **1777-78:** Antigono, L'Ezio. **1778:** Le gelosie villane, Il curioso indiscreto. **1778-79:** Quinto fabio, La zenobia. **1779:** La discordia fortunata, La vendemmia. **1779-80:** Demetrio, Il Medonte Re d'Epiro. **1781:** Erifile, La scuola dei gelosi, L'albergatrice vivace. **1783:** Li viaggiatori felici. **(Teatro Nazionale): 1800:** Le donne cambiate, L'intrigo della lettera, Il fanatico in Berlina. **1801:** La serva padrona. **1803:** Il pirro, Teseo a stige. **(Teatro Regio): 1806:** Achille e Patroclo, Giulietta e Romeo. **1807:** Teresa e Wilk, Il vanditore d'aceto, La Cleopatra. **1809:** Saulle. **1811:** Giulietta e Romeo. **(Teatro di Corte): 1815:** Tandredi. **1816:** L'italiana in Algeri. **1817:** La contessa di colle ombroso. **1818:** Erminia. **1819:** Erminia. **1820:** Ruggero. **1822:** Ruggero. **1824:** Antigono. **1825:** Antigono, Erminia. **1826:** Il disertore, **1827:** Eduardo e Cristina. **1828:** Demetrio. **1829:** Ginevra di Scozia, Saira. **1830:** Zaira, Isabella di Lara. **1831:** Zadig ed Astartea, I concorrenti al matrimonio, Giuletta e Romeo. **1832:** L'orfanella di Ginevra, Il barbiere di Siviglia, L'inganno felice. **1833:** Maria di Brabante, La straniera. **1834:** La sonnambula, Tebaldo e Isolina. **1835:** I Capuleti e i Montecchi, Donna Caritea Regina di Spagna. **1837:** La Clotilde, I Puritani. **1838:** Belisario, Roberto Devereux. **1839:** Roberto Devereux, Il giuramento. **1842:** La Regina di Golconda, La fanciulla di Castel Guelfo, Un'avventura di Scaramucca. **1843:** Don Pasquale, La fille du régiment. **1844:** I falsi monetari, Il Borgomeasto di Schiedam. **1845:** Linda di Chamounix, Il turco in Italia. **(Teatro Aliprandi): 1863:** Il ritorno di Columella dagli studi di Padova, Don Procopio, La traviata, Il trovatore, Norma, La precauzioni, Il birraio di Preston, Il campanello dello speziale. **1864:** Norma, Gemma di Vergy, tutti in maschera, Il barbiere di Siviglia. **1865:** Crispino e la comare, Pepelè, Le precauzioni, Don Pasquale, I falsi monetari, Mimì. **1866:** Lucia di Lammermoor, Roberto di Normandia, Il trovatore,

Beatrice di Tenda. **1867:** Luisa Miller, Poliuto. **1868:** I masnadieri, Ernani. **1869:** Vittor Pisani, Rigoletto, Crispino e la comare, Il menestrello, Il matrimonio segreto, Il furioso dell'isola di Santo Domingo. **1870:** L'elisir di'amore. **1871-72:** I Capuleti e i Montechhi. **1872:** La sonnambula, Linda di Chamounix. **1873:** I Lombardi, Norma, Don Checco, Il barbiere di Siviglia. **1874:** Un ballo in maschera, Il trovatore, Macbeth, I promessi sposi, La sonnambula, Eran due or son tre. **1875:** Il barbiere di Siviglia, Le precauzioni, Rigoletto. **1876:** Renani, L'ebreo. **1877:** La sonnambula, Lucia di Lammermoor, Adela d'asturia, Pipelè, Semiramide, Norma. **1878:** La traviata, La Cenerentola, L'italiana in Algeri, La sonnambula, I Capuleti e i Montecchi. **1879:** Il barbiere di Siviglia, La favorita. **1880:** Esmeralda, Crispino e la comare, L'orfanella di Gand, Lucia di Lammermoor. **(Arena-Teatro Goldini):** **1867:** Il barbiere di Siviglia, Il ritorno di Columella dagli studi di Padova, Pipelè. **1869:** La Contessa d'Amalfi, Roberto Devereux, Nabucco. **1870:** Otello, Saffo. **1871:** Il birraio di Preston, Le educande di Sorrento, Norma. **1872:** Pipelè, Chiara di Rosenberg, Il barbiere di Siviglia. **1873:** La statua di carne, Il trovatore, Il barbiere di Siviglia. **1976:** Don Checco, Pipelè, Cicco e Cola. **1877:** Chi dura vince, Don Pasquale. **1878:** Papà Martin, Martha, Attila. **1880:** La sonnambula. **1881:** La educande di Sorrento, Pipelè, L'elisir d'amore, La sonnambula. **1882:** Faust, Fiorina. **1885:** Lucia di Lammermoor, Ernani, Il barbiere di Siviglia. **1887:** La favorita, Fra Diavolo. **1888:** L'elisir d'amore, Il barbiere di Siviglia. **(Teatro Storchi):** **1889:** Le donne curiose (Usiglio), Don Pasquale. **1890:** Norma. **1891:** Il trovatore, La sonnambula, Poliuto. **1892:** La favorita, La traviata, Lucia di Lammermoor. **1893:** Cavalleria rusticana, I pagliacci. **1895:** Lohengrin. **1896:** Il barbiere di Siviglia, Ruy Blas. **1897:** La Cenerentola, Fra Diavolo, Papà Martin, Napoli di carnivale. **1898:** La bohème, Il maestro di cappella, La sonnambula, Rigoletto. **1898-99:** Manon Lescaut, La bohème, La traviata. **1899:** Il matrimonio segreto, Crispino e la comare, Don Pasquale, La forza del destino, Irnerio, Il barbiere di Siviglia, Luisa Miller, Il trovatore. **1900:** Un ballo in maschera, Zingari, Dal sogno alla vita, Lucia di Lammermoor. **1901:** Lucia di Lammermoor, Crispino e la comare, La favorita, 1901, La traviata, Ordinanza. **1902:** Il trovatore, Ernani, Ruy Blas, Un ballo in maschera, Poliuto, Il trovatore, Il barbiere di Siviglia. **1903:** Norma, Il barbiere di Siviglia, Il trovatore, Norma. **1904:** La bohème, La gioconda, L'elisir d'amore, Il barbiere di Siviglia, Lucia di Lammermoor, Matelda, Hazil. **1905:** Don Pasquale, Magnon. **1906:** I Puritani, La traviata. **1907:** Rigoletto, Un ballo in maschera, Velve. **1908:** Cavalleria rusticana, I pagliacci, Sarrona, L'amica, Ernani, Nabucco. **1909:** Mognon, Virginia, La favorita, Carmen. **1909-10:** La traviata, La nave rossa, Il trovatore. **1910:** Jone, Andrea Chénier. **1911:** Rigoletto, Madama Butterfly, La

traviata. **1912:** Norma, Ernani, Il barbiere di Siviglia, Don Pasquale. **1913:** Carmen, Lohengrin, Tosca, Cavalleria rusticana, I pagliacci. **1914:** Werther, Aida, La bohème. 1915: Il barbiere di Siviglia, Cavalleria rusticana, I pagliacci. **1916:** Mefistofele, Isabeau, I Puritani, Werther. **1917:** Magnon, Carmen, Il barbiere di Siviglia. **1917-18:** Cavalleria rusticana, Rigoletto, La traviata, La gioconda, Lucia di Lammermoor. **1918:** Faust, Maedama Butterfly, La favorita, Tosca, La bohème. **1918-19:** Andrea Chénier, Manon, Un ballo in maschera, Fra diavolo, Wally. **1919-20:** Aida, Lucia di Lammermoor, Il barbiere di Siviglia, Werther, La fanciulla del West, Loreley. **1920:** La Cenerentola, Rigoletto, Fra diavolo, L'elisir d'amore, Il barbiere di Siviglia, Una partita a scacchi. **1920-21:** La traviata, La forza del destino, Manon Lescaut, Lo singaro cieco. **1921:** L'amico Fritz. **1922:** Madama Butterfly, Suona la ritirata, Otello, La procella, Il campanaro di Camaló. **1922:** Il barbiere di Siviglia, Rigoletto. **1924:** Il trovatore, Cavalleria rusticana, I pagliacci, Carmen. **1925:** Il barbiere di Siviglia, Ernani, Tosca. **1926:** Lucia di Lammermoor. **1927:** La favorita, Il barbiere di Siviglia, Madama Butterfly, Aida, Rigoletto. **1928:** La sonnambula, L'elisir d'amore, Madama Butterfly, Don Pasquale, Il matrimonio segreto, La traviata, Il barbiere di Siviglia, La bohème, La traviata, Tosca, Fra diavolo, L'amico Fritz, Crispino d la comare, La sonnambula, Madama Butterfly, L'elisir d'amore. **1929:** Andrea Chénier, La bohème, Iris, Carmen, Manon Lescaut. **1930:** La traviata, Madama Butterfly, Aida, Norma, Don Pasquale. **1931:** L'elisir d'amore, La via della finestra, La traviata, Il barbiere di Siviglia, I quattro rusteghi, Lucia di Lammermoor, Cavalleria rusticana, I pagliacci, La bohème, La Cenerentola, Rigoletto. **1932:** Lohengrin, Il barbiere di Siviglia, Il trovatore, Fedora, Cavalleria rusticana, I pagliacci, Rigoletto, Madama Butterfly, Lucia di Lammermoor. **1933:** La forza del destino, Il barbiere di Siviglia, Ernani. **1936:** La bohème. **1937:** Rigoletto. **1938:** Cavalleria rusticana, I pagliacci, La traviata, Il trovatore. **1939:** Tosca. **1940:** La bohème, La traviata. **1941:** Madama Butterfly, Lucia di Lammermoor. **1942:** Andrea Chénier, Il trovatore. **1943:** Rigoletto, Cavalleri rusticana, I pagliacci, La bohème. **1946:** Madama Butterfly. **1952:** Il trovatore. **1957:** Cavalleria rusticana, I pagliacci, Lucia di Lammermoor, Il barbiere di Siviglia, Ave Maria, Madama Butterfly. **1959:** L'elisir d'amore, La traviata, Alba di gloria, Lucia di Lammermoor. **(Teatro Comunale):** **1841:** Adelaide di Borgogna al Castello di Canossa, Il bravo, Beatrice di Tenda, Carattaco. **1841-42:** La prigione di Edimburgo, Chi dura vince, Il barbiere di Siviglia. **1842:** I Normanni a Parigi, Beldario, Marin Faliero, L'elisir di'amore. **1842-43:** La vestale (Mercandante), Il giuramento, Galeotto Manfredi. **1843-44:** Nabucodonosor (Nabucco), Corrado d'Altamura. **1844-45:** Ernani, Zaira. **1845:** Il ritorno di Columella degli studi di Padova. **1845-46:** I Lombardi alla prima crociata, Nabucco. **1846-47:** Lucia di Lammermoor, Saffo. **1847:** I due Foscari, Maria Rohan. **1847-48:** Il Templario, Beatrice di Tenda, I Lombardi alla prima crociata, Il barbiere di Siviglia. **1848-49:** I masnadieri, I Puritani, Ernani. **1849-50:** Poliuto, I due Foscari, Bondemonte. **1850:** Luisa Miller, Attila. **1850-51:** Macbeth, Gemma di Vergy, Medea. **1851:** Lucia di Lammermoor, Ernani, Caterina Howard, Allan Cameron, La prova di un'opera seria, Don Procopio, Il campanello dello speziale. **1851-52:** La Regina di Cipro, Nabucco, La sonnambula, I masnadieri, Il barbiere di Siviglia. **1852:** Norma, Luigi V°, **1852-53:** Il corsaro, Lucrezia Borgia as Eustorgia da Romano, Robert le Diable. **1853:** Rigoletto as Viscardello, Robert le Diable, Linda di Chamounix. **1853:** Crispino e la comare, Rita (Carlotti), Il campanello dello speziale. **1853-54:** Il trovatore, Il giuramento, La sonnambula. **1854:** Don Crescendo, Il birraio di Preston, Mosè in Egitto, Rigoletto (as Viscardello). **1854-55:** Attila, Lorenzino de' Medici, Bondelmonte. **1855:** La traviata (as Violetto), Il trovatore. **1855-56:** Leonora, Don Pasqulae, I falsi monetari. **1856-57:** I due Foscari, La sonnambula, I fidanzati. **1857:** Pipelè, Crispino e la comare. **1857-58:** L'assedio di Leida, Ernani. **1858:** Il profeta, Il trovatore. **1858-59:** L'ebreo (Lida di Granata), La straniera, Poliuto. **1859:** Aroldo, Il mantello, Eran due or son tre. **1859-60:** I Lombardi, La traviata. **(Teatro Municipale):** 1860-61: I vespri siciliani, Ernani, Otello ossia Il Moro di Venezia. **1861:** Ernani, Norma. **1861-62:** Isabella d'Aragona, Un ballo in maschera. **1862:** Poliuto, Jone. **1862-63:** Lucrezia Borgia, Rigoletto. **1863:** Norma, Poliuto. **1863-64:** La favorita, Il trovatore. **1864:** L'ebreo. **1864-65:** Un ballo in maschera, Norma, Werther (Gentile). **1865:** La sonnambula. **1865-66:** Faust, Linda di Chamounix, Martha. **1866-67:** Aroldo, Maria di Rohan, I due Foscari. **1867-68:** Guglielmo Tell, Les Huguenots. **1868:** Ernani. **1868-69:** Lucia di Lammermoor, Dinorah. **1869-70:** Giovanna d'Arco, Irene, Un ballo in maschera. **1870-71:** La Contessa d'Amalfi, Orfano e diavolo, Rigoletto. **1871:** Reginella, La traviata. **1872:** Ruy Blas, Olema. **1872-73:** Giovanna di Napoli, La Duchessa di Guisa, Un ballo in maschera. **1873:** Il trovatore, La statua di carne. **1873-74:** Poluito, La favorita. **1874:** La sonnambula, Norma. **1874-75:** Ruy Blas, Macbeth, Il trovatore. **1875-76:** Salvator Rosa, Lucrezia Borgia, La traviata, Un ballo in maschera. **1876-77:** La forza del destino, Faust. **1877-78:** La Juive, Ernani, Jone. **1878:** La traviata, Martha. **1878-79:** Don Sebastiano, Rigoletto, Roderigo di Spagna. **1879-80:** I vespri siciliani, Ruy Blas, Il trovatore. **1880:** L'avaro, La sonnambula. **1880-81:** L'Africaine, Aida. **1881-82:** I Lombardi, Norma, Saffo. **1882-83:** Mefistofele, Roberto le Diable. **1883:** Luisa Miller. **1883-84:** La gioconda, Rigoletto, Les Huguenots. **1884-85:** Le roi de Lahore, La creola, La traviata.

1885-86: Il guarnay, Ruy Blas, Aida. **1886-87:** Don Carlo, I Puritani, Les Huguenots. **1887-88:** Nabucco, Otello, Ernani. **1888-89:** Simon Boccanegra, Un ballo in maschera, Fosca. **1889-90:** Dinorah, Lohengrin. **1890:** La favorita. **1890-91:** Carmen, Mignon, Roncisval. **1891-92:** La gioconda, Le prophète, Cavalleria rusticana. **1892-93:** Aida, Mefistofele. **1893-94:** Rigoletto, Manon Lescaut, Faust. **1894-95:** L'Africaine, Lucia di Lammermoor, Falstaff. **1895-96:** Otello, La traviata, L'étoile du Nord, Ernani. **1896-97:** I Puritani, La bohème, La gioconda. **1897-98:** Manon, Carmen, Cavalleria rusticana, I pagliacci. **1900:** L'amico Fritz, Andrea Chénier. **1900-01:** Tosca, Norma, Lohengrin. **1901-02:** Guglielmo Tell, Il barbiere di Siviglia, A basso porto, Les Huguenots. **1902-03:** Aida, Mefistofele, La favorita. **1903-04:** Adriana Lecouvreur, Manon, Siberia, Cavalleria rusticana, I pagliacci. **1904-05:** Tännhauser, Iris, Germania. **1905:** Andrea Chénier, Fedora. **1905-06:** I Lombardi, Hänsel und Gretel, Il Guarnay. **1906-07:** La Damnation de Faust, Werther, Benvenuto Cellini. **1907-08:** Madama Butterfly, La forza del destino, Giovanni Gallurese, Rigoletto. **1908-09:** Loreley, Il battista, La gioconda. **1909-10:** La wally, La bohème, Thaïs. **1910-11:** Samson et Dalila, Iris, Aida, Resurrezione. **1911:** Il matrimonio segreto. **1911-12:** Mefistofele, La fanciulla del West, Edith. **1912-13:** Die Walküre, Lucia di Lammermoor, Otello. **1913:** Le donne curiose. **1913-14:** Tristan und Isolde, Un ballo in maschera, Edmea, Lorenza. **1914-15:** Francesca da Rimini, La wally, Il trovatore, Manon Lescaut. **1923-24:** Dejanice, Andrea Chénier, Aida. **1924:** La traviata. **1924-25:** Lohengrin, Giuletta e Romeo, Guglielmo Tell, Madama Butterfly, Boris Godunov. **1925-26:** La cena delle beffe, Francesca da Rimini, Mefistofele, Falstaff, Manon Lescaut. **1926:** Norma. **1926-27:** I quattro rusteghi, Iris, La gioconda, Turandot. **1927:** Il matrimonio segreto. **1927-28:** Siegfried, Otello, Manon, Il piccolo Marat. **1928-29:** Loreley, Cavalleria rusticana, La bohème, La forza del destino. **1929-30:** La Wally, La fanciulla del West, Rigoletto, Fedora, Mignon. **1930:** Madama Butterfly. **1931:** I misteri gaudiosi, Il barbiere di Siviglia, Il matrimonio segreto. **1931-32:** Guglielmo Ratcliff, Mefistofele, Turandot, Otello, Tosca, Lucia di Lammermoor. **1932-33:** Boris Godunov, Carmen, Un ballo in maschera, Manon Lescaut. **1933-34:** Manon, La Baronessa di Carini, I Puritani, Andrea Chénier. **1934:** Tristan und Isolde, La gioconda. **1935:** Orfeo, Aida, L'amico Fritz, Un ballo in maschera. **1936:** Lucia di Lammermoor, Il barbiere di Siviglia, Cavalleria rusticana, I pagliacci. **1936-37:** Les pêcheur de perles, Lohengrin, Il trovatore. **1937:** Manon, Tosca, Wanda, Otello, Madama Butterfly, Faust, La bohème, Maria d'Alessandria. **1938:** La fanciulla del West, Rigoletto, La forza del destino, Cecilia. **1939-40:** Turandot, La traviata, Adriana Lecouvreur. **1940:** La bohème. **1941:** Manon Lescaut, Aida, Il campiello, Mi-Kel. **1942:** Mefistofele, Cavalleria rusticana, I pagliacci, Ernani, Il segreto di Susanna, Notturno Romantico, Rigoletto, La bohème, La traviata. **1943:** La Wally, Siberia, Il barbiere di Sivigila, Madama Butterfly, L'amico Fritz. **1944:** Rigoletto, La bohème, Tosca. **1945:** Il barbiere di Sivigila, Madama Butterfly, Cavalleria rusticana, I pagliacci, La traviata, La bohème, Rigoletto, Andrea Chénier. **1946:** Rigoletto, Cavalleria rusticana, I pagliacci. **1946-47:** Aida, La gioconda, Manon. **1947:** Lucia di Lammermoor, Tosca, Madama Butterfly, La bohème, Cavalleria rusitcana, Il trovatore, Tosca. **1948:** Madama Butterfly, L'elisir d'amore, Il barbiere di Sivigila. **1949:** Andrea Chénier, Werther, La traviata, Faust, Ghirlino, Turandot, Il trovatore, I misteri gaudiosi, Maria Egiziaca. **1950:** Manon Lescaut, Guglielmo Tell, Fedora, Carmen, Rigoletto, Donata, Rossana. **1950-51:** Mignon, Cavalleria rusticana, L'amico Fritz, La bohème, Lohengrin, Rossana, Messa di Requiem. **1951-52:** La forza del destino, Madama Butterfly, Iris, Manon, L'Arlesiana, Tristan und Isolde. **1952-53:** Turandot, La traviata, Otello, Boris Godunov, Tempo di carnivale, Don Pasquale, Un ballo in maschera. **1953:** La bohème. **1953-54:** La gioconda, Tosca, Norma, L'elisir d'amore, Ave maria, I pagliacci, Rigoletto. **1954:** Manon, Il re, Cavalleria rusticana, La scala di seta, Il campanello dello speziale, Don Pasquale, L'elisir d'amore. **1955:** Andrea Chénier, Il trovatore, Madama Butterfly, Carmen, Loreley. **1955-56:** Otello, Aida, La bohème, The Medium, Cavalleria rusticana, Werther. **(Teatro Comunale): 1956-57:** Prince Igor, Samson et Dalila, La traviata, Mefistofele, Tosca, The Telephone, I pagliacci. **1957:** La bohème. **1958:** Pikovaya dama, Manon Lescaut, Lucia di Lammermoor, Il trovatore. **1959:** Die Meistersinger, Madama Butterfly, La sonnambula, Rigoletto, Faust. **1959-60:** Il Duca d'Alba, Lohengrin, Il barbiere di Siviglia, Nabucco. **1961:** Un ballo in maschera, Falstaff, Le damnation de Faust, Turandot, Turandot, Carmen, Rita, Lo speziale. **1961:** La bohème. **1962:** La traviata, La forza del destino, La bohème. **1962-63:** I Puritani, Lucia di Lammermoor, Il trovatore, L'yubov' k tryom apel'sinam (Love for Three Oranges). **1963-64:** Otello, Cavalleria rusticana, I pagliacci, Ernani, Così fan tutte, Zolotoy petushok, (The Golden Cockerel). **1964-65:** Don Giovanni, Rigoletto, La traviata, La pulce d'oro, El Retablo di Maese Pedro, L'heure espagnole. **1966:** Simon Boccanegra, La bohème, Boris Godunov, Pelléas et Mélisande, Manon, Le nozze di Figaro, La guerra, Una lettera d'amore di Lord Byron. **1967:** Un ballo in maschera, Nabucco, L'elisir d'amore, L'histoire du Soldat, Pierrot Lunaire, Il figliuol prodigo venere prigioniera, Lucia di Lammermoor, Die Walküre. **1967-68:** La bohème, La serva padrona, Il maestro di cappella, Adriana Lecouvreur, Assassinio nella cattedrale, Macbeth, Allez hop, Partita a pugni, Il barbiere di Siviglia.

1969: Manon Lescaut, Madama Butterfly, La sonnambula, Un quarto di vita, Il matrimonio segreto, Don Carlo, Rigoletto. **1970:** Aida, Prodaná nevěsta (The Bartered Bride), Didone and Aeneas, La voix humane, Il cordovano, Mosè, Il dottore di vetro, Rigoletto, La favorita. **1971:** La traviata, Tosca, I Puritani, Katerina Izmaylova, Don Pasquale, La forza del destino, Il pozzo e il pendolo, La fabbrica illuminata, Capitan spavento. **1972:** Norma, Porgy and Bess. Otello, Il barbiere di Siviglia, Rusalka, Francesca di Rimini, La bohème, Don Giovanni. **1973:** Un ballo in maschera, Carmen, Eugene Onegin, Attila, Der Freischütz, La fille du régiment, Bastien und Bastienne, Il maestro di cappella, La serva padrona. **1974:** I Lombardi, Jenůfa, Werther, Madama Butterfly, Die Zauberflöte, Billy Budd, La traviata. **1975:** I masnadieri, Fidelio, Così fan tutte, Lucia di Lammermoor, La bohème, Werther. **1975-76:** La Wally, Ognennïy angel (The Fiery Angel), Luisa Miller, Tosca, Khovanshchina, Il barbiere di Siviglia (Paisiello), Tristan und Isolde. **1976-77:** Die Entführung aus dem Serail, Simon Boccanegra, Il trovatore, Anna Bolena, Beatrice di Tenda, Per Massimiliano Robespierre. **1977:** Messa da Requiem. **1977-78:** Rigoletto, Ernani, Oberto conte di San Bonifacio, The Beggar's Opera, Don Pasquale, Madama Butterfly. **1978-79:** Nabucco, Nos (The Nose), La bohème, La Cenerentola, L'histoire du Soldat, La sonnambula, Anna Bolena. **1979-80:** La traviata, Albert Herring, La vestale, Giovanni d'Arco, Parsifal, Lucia di Lammermoor. **1980-81:** I Capuleti e i Montecchi, Mosè, Don Pasquale, Alzira, Manon Lescaut, La belle Hélèn, Lakmè. **1981-82:** L'elisir d'amore, Aida, Don Carlo, Khovanshchina, Věc Makropulos (The Makropulos Affair), Norma. **1982-83:** Pelléas et Mélisande, Czárdásfürstin, Otello, La Cerentola, Die Walküre, Un ballo in maschera, Il matrimonio segreto. **1983-84:** L'italiana in Algeri, Nabucco, Salome, Il trovatore, Pikovaya dama (Queen of Spades), Madama Butterfly. **1984-85:** Ernani, Die lustige Witwe, Rinaldo, Lucia di Lammermoor, Semiramide. **1985-86:** La traviata, Eugene Onegin, Torquato Tasso, Andrea Chénier, Dido and Aeneas, Madama Butterfly, La bohème. **1986-87:** Falstaff, Anna Bolena, Il turco in Italia, Rigoletto, Adriana Lecouvreur, Boris Godunov. **1987-88:** Porgy and Bess, Werther, Le nozze di Figaro, Tosca, Il Signor Bruschino, Les contes d'Hoffmanns, La forza del destino.

Bibliography. Giuseppe Gherpelli, *L'Opera nei teatri di Modena* (Modena, 1988). Arturo Rabetti, *Modena d'una volta* (Modena, n.d.). Rovatti-Sossaj, *Cronache modenesi* (Modena, n.d.). Vincenzo Tardini, *I teatri di Modena* (vol I, (Modena, 1902). Lodovico Vedriani, *Storia di Modena* (Bologna, 1967). Silvo d'Amico, *Enciclopedia dello spettacolo* (Roma, 1954). Alessandro Gandini, *Cronistoria dei teatri di Modena 1539–1873* (Bologna, 1969). *Thanks to La Direzione, Teatro Comunale.*

Teatro di San Carlo
(Ente Autonomo Lirico)

On January 12, 1817, King Ferdinand's birthday, the Teatro di San Carlo, originally called Reale Teatro di San Carlo, reopened its doors with a work written for the occasion, Johannes Simon Mayr's *Il sogno di Partenope.* Fire had destroyed the first opera house on February 12, 1816. Antonio Niccolini was entrusted with the project. The first Teatro di San Carlo, named after the king's patron saint, had been inaugurated with Domenico Sarro's *Achille in Sciro* on November 4, 1737. Giovanni Antonio Medrano designed and Angelo Carasale built the original theater.

Opera in Naples dates back to 1650, when Francesco Cavalli's *Didone* was performed privately in the Palazzo Reale. The first public performance of an opera was Francesco Cirillo's *L'Orontea, regina d'Egitto,* presented on April 3, 1654, in the Teatro di San Bartolomeo. However, it was Alessandro Scarlatti's move to Naples in 1682 that transformed the city into an important operatic center, where his operas flourished in the Neapolitan school, which he founded. When the San Bartolomeo premiered Giambattista Pergolesi's *La serva padrona* on August 28, 1733, the theater witnessed the beginning of an important tradition in Italian opera — opera buffa. During the early 1700s three more theaters opened before the Teatro di San Carlo was built — Teatro dei Fiorentini (1709–1820), Teatro Pace (1724–1749), and Teatro Nuovo (1724–1828). Naples welcomed another opera house in 1779, Teatro del Fondo, which presented mainly opera buffa. Renamed Teatro Mercadante a century later, it is still in use today.

On March 4, 1737, Charles III commissioned a new royal theater, what would become the Teatro di San Carlo, to replace the Teatro di San Bartolomeo. It was completed in less than nine months at a cost of 100,000 ducats. The inaugural season hosted, in addition to Sarro's *Achille in Sciro,* Leonardo Leo's *L'Olimpiade* and Leonardo Vinci's *Artaserse.* The early years saw works by Pietro Auletta, Johann Adolph Hasse, Giovanni Alberto Ristori, Niccolò Porpora, David Perez, Gaetano Latilla, Egidio Romualdo Duni,

and Gennaro Manna. By the mid–1750s works by Gioacchino Cocchi, Niccolò Jommelli, Tommaso Traetti, Niccolò Piccinni, and Giovanni Paisiello had entered the repertory. Naples also attracted foreign composers like Christoph Willibald Gluck, Franz Joseph Haydn, and Johann Christian Bach. On May 30, 1770, Jommelli's *Armida abbandonata* was premiered, followed by the *prima* of Niccolò Zingarelli's *Montezuma* on August 13, 1781. Other Zingarelli works presented *Gli Orazi, Giulietta e Romeo, Ines de Castro, Montezuma, Il trionfo di Davide,* and *L'oracolo sannita.*

Teatro di San Carlo's golden age started when impresario Domenico Barbaia, who was also running Teatro alla Scala in Milan, took the helm. He presented the Italian premieres of Gaspare Spontini's *La vestale* in 1811 and Gluck's *Iphigénie en Aulide* in 1812. Mayr was commissioned to write an opera, and *Medea in Corinto,* was premiered on November 28, 1813. Other Mayr operas included *Adelasia ed Aleramo, Alonso e Cora, Atalia, Elisa, Mennone e Zemira, Il trionfo dell'amicizia, Ginevra di Scozia, Lodoïska, I misteri eleusini,* and *Il sogno di Partenope.* Barbaia also commissioned Vincenzo Bellini to write an opera, and the *prima assoluta* of *Bianca e Fernando* took place on May 30 in 1826. Of Bellini's ten works, only *Adelson e Salvini* (introduced at the Reale Conservatorio in Naples on January 12, 1825) and *Zaira* have not been staged at the San Carlo. Barbaia's biggest coup was getting Gioachino Rossini to be the house composer. His first opera, *Elisabetta regina d'Inghilterra,* was introduced on October 4, 1815, *Armida* (November 11, 1817), *Mosè in Egitto* (March 5, 1818), *Riccardo e Zoraide* (December 3, 1818), *Ermione* (March 27, 1819), *La donna del lago* (October 24, 1819), *Maometto II* (December 3, 1820), and *Zelmira* (February 16, 1822). Around 30 of the Pesaro composer's works have graced the San Carlo stage. Additional Rossini operas were introduced at the other Neapolitan theaters — *La gazzetta* (September 26, 1816, Teatro dei Fiorentini) and *Otello, ossia Il moro di Venezia* (December 4, 1816, Teatro del Fondo). Gaetano Donizetti followed Rossini, arriving in

Naples in 1822, and serving as director of the San Carlo from 1827 to 1838. The Bergamo maestro composed more than a dozen operas for San Carlo and the other Neapolitan theaters — *La zingara*, May 12, 1822 (Nuovo); *La lettera anonima*, June 29, 1822 (Fondo); *Alfredo il Grande* July 2, 1823; *Il fortunato inganno*, September 3, 1823 (Nuovo); *Elvida*, July 6, 1826; *Il borgomastro di Sardaam*, August 19, 1827 (Fondo); *L'esule di Roma*, January 1, 1828; *Il castello di Kenilworth*, July 6, 1829; *Francesca di Foix*, May 30, 1831; *Fausta*, January 12, 1832; *Sancia di Castiglia*, November 4, 1832; *Maria Stuarda* (as Buondelmonte), October 18, 1834; *Lucia di Lammermoor*, September 26, 1835; *Il campanello*, June 1, 1836; *L'assedio di Calais*, November 19, 1836; *Roberto Devereux*, October 29, 1837, and *Caterina Cornaro*, January 12, 1844. A total of 49 of the 70 operas which Donizetti composed were staged at the San Carlo.

Saverio Mercadante succeeded Donizetti as director of the opera house, and 29 of his works were staged at the San Carlo, including *L'apoteosi d'Ercole*, *Didone abbandonata*, *Medea*, *Leonora*, *Pelagio*, *Il proscritto*, *Il bravo*, *I briganti*, *Le due illustri rivali*, *Elena da Feltre*, *Elisa e Claudio*, *Virginia*, *Zaira*, *Violetta*, and *La vestale*. Mercadante's music was soon overshadowed by that of Verdi, so when Verdi came to Naples, Mercadante played a leading role in the unfavorable reception accorded Verdi's *Oberto*, and the *prima assoluta* of *Alzira* on August 12, 1845. The world premiere of Verdi's *Luisa Miller* December 8, 1849, almost ended in disaster because San Carlo did not have the money to pay his fee. Verdi felt that his contract was broken and tried to cancel the opening — and just for threatening, he was essentially placed under house arrest. More problems occurred after he was commissioned to write *Un ballo in maschera*. Originally called *Gustavo III* then *Una vendetta in domino*, the opera was rejected by the censors, partly because Mercadante was composing *Il reggente*, an opera on the same subject. Verdi was given a new libretto and title, *Adelia degli Ademari*, but he refused to present the opera as the censors demanded and *Un ballo in maschera* was introduced at Rome's Teatro Apollo. Verdi works, however, dominated the stage during the second half of the 19th century, with only *Un giorno di regno* and *Jerusalem* not in the repertory. After the unification of Italy in 1860, some of the glory faded. The world's most famous Neapolitan

tenor, Enrico Caruso, sang only one season (1901-1902) in Donizetti's *L'elisir d'amore* and Jules Massenet's *Manon*, and the Neapolitan composer Ruggero Leoncavallo experienced his greatest success, *I pagliacci*, in Milan, although the San Carlo has hosted seven of his operas — *La bohème*, *Edipo re*, *I medici*, *I pagliacci*, *Rolando di Berlino*, *Zazà*, and *Zingari*.

In 1880, the first Wagner opera, *Lohengrin*, graced the stage, followed by *Die Walküre*, and *Tannhäuser*. In the 1900s, *Götterdämmerung*, *Tristan und Isolde*, *Die Meistersinger von Nürnberg*, *Parsifal*, *Das Rheingold*, *Siegfried*, and *Der fliegende Höllander* were mounted. Many well-known conductors like Arturo Toscanini, Leopoldo Mugnone, Eduardo Vitale, Ettore Panizza, Vittorio Gui, and Gino Marinuzzi, appeared at the San Carlo, and Richard Strauss led the Italian premiere of his *Salome* in 1908. The world premiere of Riccardo Zandonai's *Francesca da Rimini* took place on January 15, 1921, with his *I cavalieri di Ekebù*, *Conchita*, *La farsa amorosa*, *Giuliano*, *Giulietta e Romeo*, *Una partita*, and *La via della finestra* also gracing the stage. Ildebrando Pizzetti's *Fedra* was introduced on April 16, 1924, and three years later, the Teatro San Carlo became an Ente Autonomo. Franco Alfano's *L'ultimo Lord* was premiered on April 19, 1930, and his *Cyrano di Bergerac*, *Il dottor Antonio*, *La leggenda di Sakuntala*, *Resurrezione*, and *L'ultimo Lord* were all on the boards at the San Carlo. All of Giacomo Puccini's works, except *Edgar*, have been staged. Most of the greatest singers of the era were at the San Carlo, including Tito Schipa, Beniamino Gigli, and Toti dal Monte. After World War II, the opera house hosted Renata Tebaldi in her debut (Violetta) in Verdi's *La traviata* on February 21, 1948, and Maria Callas (Abigaille) in Verdi's *Nabucco*, who opened the 1949-50 season. Twenty operas were on the schedule during that season, including lesser known and contemporary Italian works like Leoncavallo's *Zazà*, Alfano's *Il Sottor Antonio*, Enrico Petretta's *I promessi sposi*, Alfredo Sangiorgi's *La bardana*, Alban Berg's *Wozzeck*, Licinio Refice's *Margherita di Cortona* (composer conducted), and Pizzetti's *Vanna Lupa* (composer conducted). The 1950s continued offering unusual and rarely-staged Italian works from the Baroque to the 20th century with Francesco Cilea's *Gloria*, Carlo Jachino's *Giocondo e il suo re*, Refice's *Cecilia*, Jacopo Napoli's *I pescatori*, Mario Persico's *La locandiera*, Spontini's *Fernando Cortez*, Terenzio

Gargiulo's *Maria Antonietta*, Albert Roussel's *Padmavati*, Pizzetti's *Assassinio nella cattedrale*, *Debora e Jaele* and *La figlia di Jorio*, Guido Pannain's *Madama Bovary*, Verdi's *Giovanna d'Arco*, Franco Mannino's *Vivì*, Mascagni's *Le maschere*, Barbara Giuranna's *Mayerling*, and Umberto Giordano's *Fedora*. German contemporary works also played a role with Carl Orff's *Der Mond* and *Carmina Burana*, Paul Hindemith's *Neues vom Tage*, Gottfried von Einem's *Der Prozeß*, Arnold Schönberg's *Von Heute auf Morgen*, Kurt Weill's *Der Protagonist*, and Hans Werner Henze's *Boulevard Solitude*, as well as Ottorino Respighi's *Belfagor*, Nicolay Rimsky-Korsakov's *Mozart e Salieri*, Béla Bartók's *A Kékszakállú herceg vára* (Duke Bluebeard's Castle), Manuella de Falla's *La vita breve*, Igor Stravinsky's *Mavra*, and Bedřich Smetana's *Dalibor* (original edition). The same trend continued during the 1960s, 1970s, and early 1980s with Pizzetti's *Fedra*, *Clitennestra*, and *Il calzare d'argento*, Enzo de Bellis's *Il faro*, Zandonai's *Francesca da Rimini*, Nino Rota's *Aladino e la lampada magica* and *Torquemada*, Donizetti's *Rita* and *Maria di Rohan*, Dino Milella's *Una storia d'altri tempi*, Bellini's *Beatrice di Tenda*, Adriano Lualdi's *La grançeola*, Giorgio Federico Ghedini's *Re Hassan*, Daniel Auber's *Fra Diavolo*, Stravinsky's *Solovey* (The Nightingale), Renzo Rossellini's *Uno sguardo dal ponte*, Rimsky-Korsakov's *Sadko*, Rossini's *Zelmira*, Luigi Dallapiccola's *Job* and *Il prigioniero*, Napoli's *Il barone Avaro*, Giulio Viozzi's *Allamistakeo*, Leoncavallo's *Edipo Re*, Jan Meyerowitz's *Il mulatto*, Alfredo Strano's *Sulla via maestra*, Ghedini's *La pulce d'oro*, Otello Calbi's *Il ritorno*, Nicolò Jommelli's *La schiava liberata*, and Pergolesi's *Il flaminio*. By the mid–1980s and through the 1990s, the number of operas on the scheduled had been decreased to around ten with a more mainstream repertory. Works like Verdi's *Falstaff* and *Simon Boccanegra*, Giordano's *Andrea Chénier*, Puccini's *La bohème*, Rossini's *Il barbiere di Siviglia*, and Jules Massenet's *Don Quichotte* in the late 1980s and Verdi's *Un ballo in maschera*, Wolfgang Amadeus Mozart's *Don Giovanni*, Cimarosa's *Il maestro di cappella* and *Il matrimonio segreto*, Francis Poulenc's *La voix humaine*, Gian Carlo Menotti's *The Telephone*, Charles Gounod's *Faust*, Richard Strauss's *Der Rosenkavalier* and Pergolesi's *Il flaminio* in the 1990s were on the schedule.

As the 20th century draws to a close, one of the company's missions is to rediscover the music of the 1700s, incorporating one or two works from that era into the schedule every season. Emphasis is also placed on the forgotten operas of famous composers like Verdi's *Giovanna d'Arco*, Rossini's *L'assedio di Corinto*, Arrigo Boïto's *Nerone*, Donizetti's *Roberto Devereux* and *Caterina Coraro*. There are few contemporary operas currently on the schedule. The productions are almost always traditional and set in the period in which the composer wrote the opera. The press office stressed that there is no avant-garde and no updating of productions. A recent production of *Nabucco* confirmed this. It was traditional, if bordering on old-fashioned, but capturing the essence of Verdi's work. The only problem was, it glossed over some of the pivotal moments in the opera. Although the government pays almost all of the 30 billion Lire budget, the company hopes that the new tax law passed in 1998, which allows tax deductions for contributions will increase the amount of private donation. Recent repertory includes Donizetti's *L'elisir d'amore* and *Roberto Devereux*, Wagner's *Tannhäuser*, Verdi's *Macbeth* and *Aida*, Gluck's *Orfeo ed Euridice*, Mascagni's *L'amico Fritz*, and Gioachino Rossini's *Il Turco in Italia*.

Teatro di San Carlo

After fire destroyed the San Carlo in 1816, it was rebuilt in six months, following Medrano's original plans. Camillo Guerra and Gennaro Maldarelli were responsible for the royal blue and gold interior decor. Red replaced the royal blue after the unification of Italy. An orchestra pit was created in 1872. The opera house was slightly damaged in October 1943 during a British bombing raid, but was repaired by December. The Allied forces kept the theater open during the Italian campaign. During the subsequent occupation of Italy, almost two million troops visited the opera house. It was closed in 1989 for structural problems which have been solved. It is one of the world's most beautiful opera houses.

San Carlo's Neoclassic facade is inscribed with the names of famous Italian composers and writers. Fourteen Ionic columns form a second level portico, and friezes adorn the five-arched, rusticated stone, former carriage entrance. Four tiers of boxes topped by a galleria and loggione soar in gold, ivory, and red splendor around the auditorium. Intricately carved allegorical figures and scrolls decorate the parapets. A large crown tops the center royal box, flanked by two gilded winged maidens holding red velvet drapes. San Carlo accommodates around 1,444.

Practical Information. Teatro di San Carlo, Via San Carlo 98F, 80133 Naples. Tel: 39 81 797 2301, Fax: 39 81 797 2306. When visiting the Teatro di San Carlo or the archives, stay at the Grand Hotel Vesuvio, via Partenope, 45, 80121 Napoli. Tel: 39 81 764 0044 or 1-800-223-6800, Fax: 39 81 589 0380. The Grand Hotel Vesuvio, with a view of the Bay of Naples, is conveniently located near the opera house and can assist with schedules and opera tickets.

COMPANY STAFF, WORLD PREMIERES, AND REPERTORY

Sovrintendente. Francesco Canessa. **Direttore Artistico:** Filippo Zigante.

World Premieres (Teatro di San Carlo). Rossini Operas: *Elisabetta regina d'Inghilterra*, October 4, 1815; *Armida*, November 11, 1817, *Mosè in Egitto*, March 5, 1818; *Riccardo e Zoraide*, December 3, 1818; *Ermione*, on March 27, 1819; *La donna del lago*, October 24, 1819; *Maometto II*, December 3, 1820; *Zelmira*, February 16, 1822. **Bellini Operas:** *Bianca e Fernando*, May 30, 1826. **Donizetti Operas:** *Alfredo il Grande*, July 2, 1823; *Elvida*, July 6, 1826; *L'esule di Roma o Il proscritto*, January 1, 1828; *Il paria*, January 12, 1829; *Elisabetta al castello di Kenilworth o Il castello di Kenilworth*, July 6, 1829; *Il diluvio universale*, February 28, 1830; *Imelda de' Lambertazzi*, September 5, 1830; *Francesca di Foix*, May 30, 1831; *Fausta*, January 12, 1832; *Sancia di Castiglia*, November 4, 1832; *Maria Stuarda*, (as Buondelmonte), October 18, 1834; *Lucia di Lammermoor*, September 26, 1835; *L'assedio di Calais*, November 19, 1836; *Roberto Devereux*, October 29, 1837; *Caterina Cornaro*, January 12, 1844; *Poliuto*, November 30, 1848; *Gabriella di Vergy* (3 act version), Novem-ber 29, 1869. **Verdi Operas:** *Alzira*, August 12, 1845; *Luisa Miller*, December 8, 1849.

Repertory. First hundred years (1737–1837): **1737-38:** Achille in Sciro, L'Olimpiade, Artaserse. **1738-39:** Le nozze di Amore e Psiche (festa teatrale), Demetrio, La locandiera, La clemenza di Tito (Hasse & Palella), Temistocle, Semiramide riconosciuta. **1739-40:** Partenope, Adriano in Siria, Le nozze di Teti e Peleo (festa teatrale), Il trionfo di Camilla. **1740-41:** Siroe Re di Persia, Tiridate, Alceste in Ebuda. **1741-42:** Ezio, Demofoonte, Ciro riconosciuto. **1742-43:** Andromaca, Issipile, Alessandro nelle Indie. **1743-44:** Artaserse, L'Olimpiade, Didone. **1744-45:** Semiramide riconosciuta, Antigona, Achille in Sciro. **1745-46:** Il Tigrane,

Lucio Vero, Ipermestra, Catone in Utica. **1746-47:** Lucio Papirio dittatore, Caio Fabrizio, Arianna e Teseo. **1747-48:** Eumene, Siroe, Il sogno di Olimpia, Adiano in Siria, Merope. **1748-49:** Siface, Ezio, Demetrio, Artaserse, **1749-50:** Zenobia, Alessandro nelle Indie, L'Olimpiade, Demofoonte. **1750-51:** L'olimpiade, Ciro riconosciuto, Antigono, Semiramide riconosciuta. **1751-52:** Tito Manlio, Farnace, Ipermestra, Attalo re di Bitinia. **1752-53:** Sesostri re d'Egitto, La clemenza di Tito (Gluck), Lucio Vero, Didone abbandonata. **1753-54:** L'eroe cinese, Ricimero Re de'Goti, Ifigenia in Aulide, Alessandro nelle Indie. **1754-55:** Arsace, Adriano in Siria, Issipile, Caio Mario. **1755-56:** Antigona in Tebe, Merope, Demetrio, La disfatta di Dario. **1756-57:** Antigono, Solimano, Zenobia, L'incendio di Troia. **1757-58:** Farnace, Nitteti, Temistocle, Arianna e Teseo. **1758-59:** Ezio, Demofoonte, Siroe, La clemenza di Tito (Hasse). **1759-60:** Adiano in Siria, Achille in Sciro, Ciro riconosciuto, Artaserse. **1760-61:** Il trionfo di Camilla, Astrea placata, Caio Fabrizio, Zenobia, Attilio Regolo, Cantata per il giorno natalizio di Re Carlo III. **1761-62:** Andromaca, Catone in Utica, Ipermestra, Cantata per il giorno natalizio di Re Ferdinando IV, Cantata per il giorno natalizio di Re Carlo III, Alessandro nelle Indie. **1762-63:** Sesostri Re d'Egitto, Artaserse, Antigone, Demetrio, Cantata per il giorno natalizio di Re Ferdinando IV, Cantata per il giorno natalizio di Re Carlo III, Clelia. **1763-64:** Armida, L'Olimpiade, Issipile, Cantata per il giorno natalizio di Re Ferdinando IV, Cantata per il giorno natalizio di Re Carlo III, Didone abbandonata. **1764-65:** Nitteti, Lucio Vero, Catone in Utica, Cantata per il giorno natalizio di Re Ferdinando IV, Cantata per il giorno natalizio di Re Carlo III, Caio Mario. **1765-66:** Il re pastore, Creso, Romolo ed ersilia, Cantata per il giorno natalizio di Re Ferdinando IV, Cantata per il giorno natalizio di Re Carlo III, Arianna e Teseo. **1766-67:** Antigone, Il gran Cid, Lucio Vero, Cantata per il giorno natalizio di Re Ferdinando IV, Alessandro nelle Indie, Cantata per il giorno natalizio di Re Carlo III, Belleronfonte. **1767-68:** Semiramide (Bertoni), Lucio Papirio dittatore, Partenope (festa teatrale) Farnace, Zenobia, Cantata per il giorno natalizio di Re Ferdinando IV, Cantata per il giorno natalizio di Re Carlo III, Alceste in Ebuda. **1768-69:** Alessandro nelle Indie, Peleo (festa teatrale), Cantata per il giorno natalizio di Re Ferdinando IV, Cantata per il giorno natalizio della Regina, Ipermestra, Artaserse, L'Olimpiade. **1769-70:** Demetrio, Zenobia, Cantata per il giorno natalizio della Regina, Merope, Adriano in Siria, Cantata per il giorno natalizio di Re Carlo III, Didone abbandonata. **1770-71:** Armida abbandonata, Cantata per il giorno natalizio della Regina, Antigono, Demofoonte, Eumene. **1771-72:** Ifigenia in Tauride, Armida abbandonata, Cantata per il giorno natalizio della Regina, Nitteti, Ezio, Cantata per il giorno natalizio di Re Ferdinando IV, Il Ruggiero, Didone abbandonata. **1772-73:** La clemenza di Tito (Anfossi), Archille in Sciro, Ipermestra, Arianna e Teseo. **1773-74:** Il trionfo di Clelia, Cantata per il giorno natalizio di della Regina, Romolo ed Ersilia, Adriano in Siria, Alessandro nelle Indie. **1774-75:** Olimpiade, Cantata per il giorno natalizio di della Regina, Artaserse, Orfeo ed Euridice, Cantata per il giorno natalizio di Re Ferdinando IV, Demofoonte. **1775-76:** Ezio, Il Natale di Apollo, Antigono, Nitteti, Cantata per il giorno natalizio di Re Ferdinando IV, Didone abbandonata. **1776-77:** Vologeso, Semiramide riconosciuta, Creso, Arianna e Teseo. **1777-78:** Ricimero, La disfatta di Dario, Ifigenia in Tauride, Cantata per il giorno natalizio di Re Ferdinando IV, Cantata per il giorno natalizio di Re Carlo III,

Bellerofonte. **1778-79:** Calliroe, Cantata per il giorno natalizio della Regina, Il re pastore, L'Olimpiade, Cantata per il giorno natalizio di Re Ferdinando IV, Ifigenia in Aulide, Cantata per il giorno natalizio di Re Carlo III. **1779-80:** Medonte, Cantata per il giorno della Regina, Demetrio Creso in Media, Cantata per il giorno natalizio di Re Ferdinando IV, Il gran Cid. **1780-81:** Ipermestra, Armida abbandonata, Amore e Psiche, Arbace. **1781-82:** Antigone, Montezuma, La Zemira, Il Farnace,. **1782-83:** Calipso, l'eroe cinese, La Zulima, La Nitteti. **1783-84:** Medonte, Oreste, La felicità dell'Anfrisio, Artaserse, Adone e Venere. **1784-85:** Caio Mario, Artenice, Catone in Utica, Antigono. **1785-86:** Ifigenia in Aulide, Lucio Vero, Enea e Lacinia, Olimpiade. **1786-87:** Pallade, Olimpia, Giulio Sabino, Mesenzio re d'Etruria, Pirro Giunone e Lucina, L distruzione di Gerusalemme. **1787-88:** Laocoonte, Scipione Africano, Arianatte, Fedra, Debora e Sisara. **1788-89:** Didone abbandonata, Enea e Lavinia, Rinaldo, Catone in Utica, Debora e Sisara. **1789-90:** Ademira, Ricimero, Una cosa rara, Alessandro nelle Indie, Pirro, La distruzione di Gerusalemme. **1790-91:** Zenobia in Palmira, La disfatta di Dario, La vendetta di Nino, Pizarro elle Indie. **1791-92:** Lucio Papirio, Briseide, Antigone, Alessandro nelle Indie, Gionata. **1792-93:** Medonte, Arminio, Elfrida, Ercole al Termedonte, Sofronia e Olindo. **1793 94:** Olimpiade, Attalo re di Bitinia, Giasone e Medea, Elvira. **1794-95:** Ines de Castro, Ero e Leandro, Didone abbandonata, La morte di Semiramide, Debora e Sisara. **1795-96:** Il trionfo di Camilla, Arsinoe, Gli Orazi, Lucio Papirio. **1796:** Apelle e Campaspe. **1797-98:** Artemisia regina di Caria, Consalvo di Cordova, Andromace, Antigono, Gionata Maccabeo. **1798-99:** La morte di Cleopatra, La vendetta di Medea, Ippolito, Micaboro in Jucatan, Il disinganno. **1800:** Ginevra ed Ariodante. **1801-1802:** Scipione in Cartagine, Sesostri. **1802-03:** Siface e Sofonisba, Armida e Rinaldo, Gonzalvo, La reggia del destino, Ginevra ed Ariodante. **1803-04:** Piramo e Tisbe, Asteria e Teseo, Obeide ed Atamare, Andromaca. **1804-05:** Peribea e Telamone, Ginevra di Scozia, Ifigenia in Aulide, Ciro. **1805-06:** Andromeda, Gonzalvo, L'oracolo sannita, Paride, Il trionfo di Davide. **1806-07:** Merope, Ines di Castro, Licurgo, Artemisia, Il trionfo di Tomiri,

Teatro di San Carlo (Naples, Italy).

Elisa, Climene, L'albergatrice scaltra. **1807-08:** Aristodemo, Gli Orazi e i Curiazi, Penelope, I Pitagorici, Edipo a Colono, Traiano. **1808-09:** Argete, Giulietta e Romeo, Giulio Sabino, La chioma di Berenice, La clemenza di Tito, Aristodemo. **1809-10:** Il Natale di Alcide, Annibale in Capua, I misteri Eleusini, Bajazet, Cesare in Egitto. **1810-11:** Marco Ilbino in Siria, Adelasia ed Aleramo, Odoardo e Cristina, La conquista del Messico, La prova di un-opera seria. **1811-12:** L'oracolo di Delfo, La vestale, La giardiniera abruzzese, Pirro, L'oro non compra amore, Il salto di Leucade, La dama soldato. **1812-13:** Ifigenia in Aulide, I Manlii, Ecuba, Zaira, Gaulo ed Oitona, Nefte, I riti di Efeso. **1813-14:** Marco Curzio, I Manlii, I riti di Efeso, La vestale, Il califfo di Bagdad, Medea in Corinto, L'Africano generoso, I Baccanali di Roma, Diana ed Endimione, Partenope, Donna Caritea regina di Spagna. **1814:** La donzella di Raab, Medea in Corinto, I Manlii, La vestale, Donna Caritea regina di Spagna, Ginevra di Scozia, Arianna in Lasso, I pretendenti delusi, La gioventù di Enrico V, Alonso e Cora, Il califfo di Bagdad, Le nozze di Figaro, L'oracolo di Cuma, Sargino, La morte di Semiramide. **1815-16:** Elisabetta regina d'Inghilterra, Medea in Corinto, Alonso e Cora, Gli Otazi e i Curiazi, Sargino, Il trionfo di Alessandro, Ginevra di Scozia. **1817-18:** Il sogno di Partenope, Otello (Rossini), Gabriella di Vergy, Sargino, Aganadeca, Elisabetta regina d'Inghilterra, Paolo e Virginia, Alonso e Cora, Mennone e Zemira, La testa di bronzo, Medea in Corinto, Gli Orazi e i Curiazi, Ifigenia in Tauride, Edipo a Colono, Maometto II, Armida, Baodicea, Mosè in Egitto. **1818-19:** Tancredi, La vestale, Traiano, Berenice in Siria, Gabriella di Vergy, Lodoïska, Armida, Griselda, Ricciardo e Zoraide, Alzira, Otello (Rossini), Mosè in Egitto, Ermione. **1819-20:** Il trionfo dell'amicizia, Elisabetta regina d'Inghilterra, Ricciardo e Zoraide, Gabriella di Vergy, Otello (Rossini), Armida, Ulisse nell'isola di Circe, La gazza ladra, L'Apoteosi di Ercole, Ginevra di Scozia, La donna del lago, Castore e Polluce, Fernando Cortez, Mosè in Egitto, Ciro in Babilonia. **1820-21:** La gazza ladra, Sofonisba, Nina pazza per amore, Otello (Rossini), Elisabetta regina d'Inghilterra, Gianni da Parigi, Solimano II, La donna del lago, Il califfo di Bagdad, Gabriella di Vergy, Anacreonte in Samo, Torvaldo e Dorliska, Il barone di Dolsheim, Maometto II, Adelaide di Baviera, Il barbiere di Siviglia, Mosè in Egitto. **1821-22:** La donna selvaggia, Il sacrificio di Epito, Elisabetta regina d'Inghilterra, Il barbiere di Siviglia, Elena ed Olfredo, Valmiro e Zaida, La donna del lago, La riconoscenza, La sposa indiana, Ricciardo e Zoraide, Matilde di Shabran as Bellezza e cuor di ferro, La gazza ladra, Zelmira, Atalia. **1822-23:** Anco Marzio, Elisabetta regina d'Inghilterra, Otello (Rossini), Argene e Alsindo, Gabriella di Vergy, Solimano II, La Cenerentola, La gazza ladra, Elisabetta in Derbyshire, Ines d'Almeida, Elena ed Olfredo, I

cavalieri del nodo, La capricciosa pentita, Armida, Arminio, Mosè in Egitto, Gli Sciti. **1823-24:** La donna del lago, Aristea, La vestale, Alfredo il Grande, Argia, Adelina, Rodrigo, Costanzo ed Almeriska, Medea in Corinto, Otello (Rossini), Il barbiere di Siviglia, La Cenerentola, Il falegname di Livonia, Ricciardo e Zoraide, Semiramide, La fondazione di Partenope, La gazza ladra, Fedrico II re di Prussia, Le nozze dei Sanniti, Elisabetta regina d'Inghilterra, Sansone. **1824-25:** Semiramide, La vestale, Isolina, Zelmira, La Cenerentola, Tancredi, Ginevra di Scozia, Alessandro nelle Indie, Berenice in Roma, Tamerlano, L'inganno felice, Il disertore, Zadig ed Astartea, Mosè in Egitto. **1825-26:** Semiramide, Ricciardo e Zoraide, Bianca e Falliero, Elisabetta regina d'Inghilterra, L'inganno felice, Maometto II, Amazilia, Inno con ballo, Didone abbandonata, Il matrimonio segreto, Francesca da Rimini (Carlini), La donna del lago, Gli Italici e gli Indiani, L'ultimo giorno di Pompei, Il barbiere di Siviglia, Ipermestra, La shiava di Bagdad, Tazia. **1826-27:** Semiramide, Il solitario ed Elodia, Argia, Bianca e Gernando, Amazilia, Elvida, Alahor in Granata, L'ultimo giorno di Pompei, Zelmira e Zamori, Rlisabetta regina d'Inghilterra, Il crociato in Egitto as Il cavaliere Armando d'Orville, Meleagro, La donna del lago, Olimpia, Medea in Corinto, Niobe, Zelmira, Tancredi, Gabriella di Vergy, Otello (Rossini), Giuditta, Mosè in Egitto, La dama bianca, Nina pazza per amore. **1827-28:** Gli arabi nelle Gallie, Elisabetta regina d'Inghilterra, Ricciardo e Zoraide, La Cenerentola, Margherita regina d'Inghilterra, La donna del lago, L'ultimo giorno di Pompei, L'esule di Roma, Ulisse in Itaca, Zadig ed Astartea. Semiramide, Il pirata, ALexi, Bianca e Gernando, Giovanni d'Arco (Vaccai). **1828-29:** L'assedio di Corinto, Il pirata, Bianca e Gernando, Giovanna d'Arco (Vaccai), Priamo alla tenda di Achille, Il barbiere di Siviglia, Gianni di Calasi, L'esule di Roma, L'ultimo giorno di Pompei, Il paria, Malvina, Il matrimonio segreto, Il giovedì grasso, Saul, Mosè. **1829-30:** L'esule di Roma, Elisabetta regina d'Inghilterra, Gli arabi nelle Gallie, la vestale, Biance e Gernando, Il castello di Kenilworth, La prova di un'opera seria, Teresa Navagero, L'annunzio felice, Margherita regina d'Inghilterra, La donna del lago, Il contestabile di Chester, L'ultimo giorno di Pompei, Il barbiere di Siviglia, L'ofano della selva, I portoghesi in Goa, I pazzi per progetto, Il diluvio universale. **1830-31:** L'assedio di Corinto, Gli arabi nelle Gallie, Amazilia, La Cenerentola, Costanza ed Oringaldo, Bianca e Falliero, Il barbiere di Siviglia, Il castello di Kenilworth, La straniera, Il ritorno desiderato, Semiramide, Imelda dei Lambertazzi, Otello (Rossini), Leonilda, I pazzi per progetto, La donna del lago, Il conte Ory, Zelmira, La pubblica esultanza, L'inganno felice, Il contestabile di Chester, Matilde di Shabran (Corradino), Francesca da Rimini. **1831-32:** Imelda dei Lambertazzi, La straniera, I pazzi per progetto,

Eduardo in Scozia, La donna del lago, Francesca di Foix, Elisabetta regina d'Inghilterra, L'assedio di Corinto, Il Constestabile di Chester, Zaira, Otello (Rossini), Semiramide, Le convenienza ed inconvenienze teatrali, Il barbiere di Siviglia, I Capuleti e in Montecchi, Fausta, Amazilia, Argene, Achille in Sciro. **1832-33:** I Capuleti e i Montecchi, Bianca e Falliero, Ricciardo e Zoriade, Matilde di Shabran (Corradino), Zelmira, Otello (Rossini), Il barbiere diSiviglia, La prova di un'opera seria, Anna Bolena, La Cenerentola, Fausta, La gazza ladra, L'esule di Roma, Il matrimonio segreto, Sancia di Castiglia, Gli arabi nella Gallie, Semiramide, Il felice imeneo, Clato, Gli Elvezi, Il Contestabile di Chester. **1833-34:** Guglielmo Tell, Otello (Rossini), La Cenerenta, Semiramide, I Capuleti e i Montecchi, Anna Bolena, Ferdinando duca di Valenza, Elisabetta regina d'Inghilterra, La sonnambula, Norma, Il Contestabile di Chester, Chiara di Rosemberg, L'esule di Roma, La prova di un'opera seria, La gazza ladra, Irene, Gli Aragonesi in Napoli, Zampa, La figlia dell'arciere, Il matrimonio segreto, Il barbiere di Siviglia. **1834-35:** I Normanni a Parigi, L'esule di Roma, Don Giovanni, Parisina, Anna Bolena, Caterina di Guisa, L'elisir d'amore, La donna del lago, I

Capuleti e i Montecchi, Elisabetta regina d'Inghiterra, Maria Stuarda (Buondelmonte), Il pirata, Beatrice di Tenda, Tancredi, La sonnambula, Norma, L'assedio di Corinto, Amelia, Ruggiero, Ines de Castro, Mosè in Egitto, La straniera. **1835-36:** Emma d'Antiochia, Torquato Tasso, Alfonzo d'Aragona, Eduardo in Scozia, Semiramide, Beatrice di Tenda, Marfa, I Capuleti e i Montecchi, Ivanhoe, Danao re di Argo, Parisina, Lucia di Lammermoor, Norma, Lara, Palmira, Eufemio da Messina, Otivo e Pasquale, Il bravo, Il furioso all'isola di San Domingo. **1836-37:** Manfredi trovatore, Norma, I Capuleti e i Montecchi, Parisina, L'assedio di Corinto, Isabella degli Abenanti, Chiara di Rosemberg, L'assedio di Calais, La pazza per amore, I Puritani, Odda di Bernaver, La straniera.

Bibliography. Carlo Marinelli Roscioni, *Il Teatro di San Carlo: La Cronologia 1737—1987* Vol. I (Napoli, 1988). Various authors, *Il Teatro di San Carlo* Vol. II (Napoli, 1988). *Centi anni di vita del Teatro di San Carlo, 1848–1948* (Napoli, 1948). *Cronache del Teatro di S. Carlo, 1948–1968* (Milano, 1969).

Thanks to Antonio Loreto, Teatro di San Carlo.

Teatro Coccia
(Teatro di Tradizione)

The "new" Teatro Coccia was inaugurated the evening of December 22, 1888, with Giacomo Meyerbeer's *Les Huguenots*. The performance was not enthusiastically received. The next offering of the inaugural season, Giuseppe Verdi's *Aida*, opened on January 12, 1889, and was even less fortunate. Everyone criticized the dark staging, and kept calling for "Luce, luce, luce." (Light, light, light.) The final opera of the inaugural season was Verdi's *La forza del destino*. The Teatro Coccia had been born as the Teatro Civico (also called Teatro Nuovo and later Teatro Antico) and inaugurated with *Medonte Re d'Epiro* in the spring of 1779. G. Vigorè was responsible for the project. After a complete restoration with Giuseppe Oliverio in charge of the project, it reopened as the "new" Teatro Coccia.

As early as 1695 a *dramma per musica*, *Antemio in Roma*, was staged. The next documented work, *Il filosofo di campagna*, a melodrama, was presented in a "theater" in the Petazzi house in 1757. Other offerings included *La cascina*, *Le serve*

rivali, *L'amore arrigiano*, *La locanda*, and *La moda*. Since Novara did not have a "permanent" theater, a variety of places were temporarily converted for the shows. Two distinct genere of opera held the stage in Novara during the 1700s —*opera seria*, which included *melodramma* and *dramma per musica*, and *opera comica*, which included *Intermezzo*, *opera buffa*, *commedia e musica*, and *dramma eroicocomico*. Opera comica was the favorite, as G. Bustico wrote in his 1922-published *Il teatro antico a Novara (1695–1873)*, "(Giambattista) Pergolesi, (Pasquale) Anfossi, (Domenico) Cimarosa, (Giovanni) Paisiello, (Alessandro) Guglielmi, and (Niccolò) Piccini are now the greatest and most applauded composers."

The Teatro Civico opened in 1779 and a decade later Pietro Carlo Guglielmi's *Enea e Lavinia*, and two "heroic" dances, *Nozze di Ciro e Cassandane* and *I soldati volontair* were staged in honor of the marriage of Prince Vittorio Emanuele of Savoy to the Princess Maria Teresa of Austria. *Le gelosie fortunate* was mounted in 1790, followed by Cimarosa's *Il matrimonio segreto*, Paisiello's *Il barbiere di Siviglia*, *I raggiri della serva*, *Il sedicente filosofo*, *l'amante anonimo*, *I pretendenti delusi*, and *Amore tutto vince*. On August 15, 1808, Napoleon's birthday was celebrated with the presentation of F. Dussak Cormundi's *Cantico*, a musical cantata. The theater was closed in 1812, and by 1814, Novara was under the domination of the House of Savoy, and a grandiose opera *Incoronazione ed innalzamento al trono della Svezia dell'infante Gustavo* (The Coronation and Ascent to the Throne of Sweden of the Infant Gustaf) reopened the theater. In 1822, a visit by King Carlo Felici was commemorated with a performance of Rossini's *Il barbiere di Siviglia*. More Rossini works, *Matilde di Shabran*, *Semiramide*, *Torvaldo e Dorliska*, *Il conte Ory*, and *Aureliano in Palmira*, along with Carlo Coccia's *Evellina*, Saverio Mercadante's *Elisa e Claudio*, Giovanni Pacini's *Il barone di Dolsheim* and *Gli arabi nelle Gallie*, Filippo Celli's *La secchia rapita*, Francesco Morlacchi's *Gianni di Parigi* graced the stage during the decade. The 1830s saw Vincenzo Bellini's *I Capuleti e i Montecchi*, *La straniera*, *La sonnambula*, *Norma*, Rossini's *Riccardo e Zoraide*, *Tancredi*, *La donna del lago*, Donizetti's *Anna Bolena*, *Parisina*, *Belisaro*, *Il furioso*, *Gemma di Vergy*, and *Lucia di Lammermoor*, Mercadante's *Il giuramento*, and Coccia's *Carlotta e Werter*, among others.

Around this time, the role of the impresario was created in the running of the theater. He took care of all the administration aspects, as well as organizing the seasons, hiring the singers, commissioning the scenery, costumes, music, libretto, and collecting entrance fees and renting empty boxes for the season. Considering how expensive it was to mount an opera, the impresario tried to limit and economize on the orchestra, chorus, and dancers, so out-of-tune choristers were hidden among the good ones, bad and good violinists were mixed together, and beautiful ballerinas concealed the ugly ones. If then the impresario did not attain the success he expected, he recovered the shortfall by fining the artists. Some amusing examples: a Signora Parodi was fined on January 4, 1892, Lire. 5.00 for not having taken off a black corset during the performance as ordered by the administration; two days later Parodi was fined L. 2.00 for poor behavior on stage, and on January 27 she was fined for having fought in the theater with Signora Traversi.

The other phenomenon born around the same time was that of the claque. Composed of a group of supporters, they were employed to applaud their singer, not only after the aria but also with the singer's first stage entrance. The promoters, impresarios, and directors of the theater all found the claques useful to assure the success of their presentations.

By the middle of the century, the economy of the theater was not flourishing, and the Novara public had become very critical and made their dissatisfaction vocally known. They whistled and cackled incessantly. The management finally had their fill of this behavior and in January 1850 posted the following rules on the entrance door:

One is not able to enter without being properly dressed.

One is not able to smoke.

One is not able to give signs of approval or disapproval excessively noisy [the public were forbidden to whistle, yell, shout, and cackle].

It is forbidden to repeat parts of an opera or ballet without the authorization of the director of the performance.

It is forbidden to call the artists outside of the intermissions.

Servants are not permitted to enter the orchestra with livery.

In 1855, a second theater was inaugurated in Novara. Called Teatro Sociale, it was designed by Paolo Rivolta and became the home for minor companies and young, rising talent. Within a few years, the Sociale gave serious competition to the Teatro Nuovo by staging a comedy on the same night as opera was given the Nuovo. This led to the renaming of the Teatro Nuovo to Teatro Antico (Ancient Theater) and both theaters slid into mediocrity. This gave birth to the idea to construct a new "modern" theater. Then on April 13, 1873, the Carlo Coccia, maestro of the Cappella of the Duomo in Novara, died. Less than three months later, the Società decided to changed the name of the Teatro Antico to Teatro Coccia, to honor their deceased master. In 1874, the Teatro Sociale requested that the two theaters merge into one large theater. Things had not been going well and the Coccia closed for the entire year, opening only for carnival with Charles Gounod's *Faust* and Donizetti's *Lucrezia Borgia* on the boards. The seasons continued until 1885, when after Gounod's *Faust* and Verdi's *Aida*, the Coccia was closed for a complete overhaul. When it reopened in 1888, it was so superior to the Teatro Sociale, now called the Teatro Municipale, that it reigned supreme. Five years later the Municipale was renovated.

The repertory at the Coccia featured primarily Italian fare with some French works, with the exception of the 1894-95 season, which opened with Fromental Halévy, *La Juive* and closed with *Les Huguenots*. Also during the last decade, a fair number of works that did not survive the test of time were mounted — P. Floridia's *Maruzza*, E. Sarria's *La camoana dell'eremitaggio*, A.S. De Ferrari's *Pipelet*, A. Cagnoni's *Papa Martin*, C. Pedrotti's *Tutti in maschera*, and S. Falchi's *Il trillo del diavolo*. The first Wagner operas were heard in this decade — *Lohengrin*, interpreted by Y. Schuber, V. Falconis, M. Cavallini, G. VIttoria, L. Iribarne, with P. Sormani on the podium, and *Tannhäuser* with R. D'Arone, O. Cosentini, G. Polesi, M. Faccenda, M. Fiori, L. Minoz, conducted by A. Palminteril.

The Teatro Coccia continued to hold a predominate role in the cultural life of the city as it ushered in the 20th century, but due to the high cost of the productions, only one or at most two seasons were possible every year. The rest of the time the theater's shutters remained closed. The works of Pietro Mascagni, Ruggero Leoncavallo, Alberto Franchietti, Giuseppe Verdi, and Giacomo Puccini were now in favor.

A third theater, the Teatro Faraggiana, opened in Novara on April 2, 1905. Designed by Oliverio, the theater was inaugurated with Donizetti's *La sonnambula*. It was erected by Senator Faraggiana who did not like the other boxholders at the Coccia and built the theater for himself!

During World War I, life remained normal in Novara, and the Coccia kept its doors open, but a different type of crisis stuck — that of the growing popularity of cinema. In the spring of 1914, opera was forced to share the stage with cinema. The *Corriere* (newspaper) expressed its indignation, "Poor Coccia, destined to the most pure expression of art, to what have you been reduced...." At the same time, stage lighting became more innovative with lights creating spatial illusions and special effects. Between the two world wars, Leoncavallo, Mascagni, Umberto Giordano, and Puccini were the composers of choice and although Verdi operas were often staged, they were viewed as

"old." Other works included Riccardo Zandonai's *Francesca da Rimini*, Arrigo Boïto's *Mefistofele*, Modest Mussorgsky's *Boris Godunov* and Jules Massenet's *Thais*, and on January 20, 1929, E. Trentinaglia's *Rosmunda* received its world premiere. The Coccia remained opened during World War II, offering seven operas during both the 1940-41 and 1941-42 seasons, including forgotten works like L. S. Colonna's *Sagre Ampezzane*, A. Lualdi's *Le furie di arlecchino* and G. Garau's *La guardia innamorata*, which increased to ten standard works for the 1943-44 season. After the war, popular Italian operas prevailed with some novelties like F. Mannino's *Vivì*, V. Cinque's *Pierrot innamorato*, S. Allegra's *Medico suo malgrado*, S. Massaron's *La prima notte* and *La mamma dei gatti*, F. Ferrari's *I mantici*, U. Bottachiari's *L'ombra*, and the infrequently performed Verdi opera, *La battaglia di Legnano*. After the 1985 season which included Puccini's *Manon Lescaut*, Donizetti's *La sonnambula*, and Verdi's *Il trovatore*, the Coccia was closed for another restoration. After it reopened, works like Puccini's *La bohème*, Verdi's *Nabucco*, and Rossini's *L'italiana in Algeri* were on the boards. Recent offerings include Verdi's *Il trovatore*, Rossini's *La Cenerentola*, and Wolfgang Amadeus Mozart's *Così fan tutte*.

Teatro Civico (Teatro Nuovo, Teatro Antico)

Construction began in 1777 on the Teatro Civico, also known as the Teatro Nuovo (New Theater), and located on one side of the piazza Rivarola. It was completed in two years. The Galliari brothers were responsible for the interior decor and stage curtain.

The Teatro Nuovo was small with a short, squat exterior. The auditorium held silk upholstered boxes, and wood carved orchestra seats, covered with brocade. Gilded wood itaglio decorated the proscenium arch. The floor was an oakwood. A huge central chandelier with torches of oil lamps illuminated the room. By the beginning of the 1800s the theater was dirty and "indelicate" so in 1830 the box holders decided to restore the theater at their own expense.. They contacted architect Luigi Canonica of Milan who presented two projects, but then had to withdraw for reasons of health. The job went to A. Agnelli who reworked Canonica's ideas.

Teatro Coccia (New)

Actually, two renovation projects were submitted — one by Erminio Andreoni for the restoration of the Teatro Sociale, and another by Oliverio for the restoration of the Teatro Coccia. Oliverio's project was chosen, and in February, 1886, the theater's owners removed everything of value from their boxes, including furniture and lighting fixtures, and on March 9, 1886, work began, which lasted two years.

Solid Doric columns line the peristyle of the Teatro Coccia. A classic-style building of soft yellowish tint, the theater stretches the length of the Piazza Martiri della Libertà. Ionic pilasters flank the rectangular windows which punctuate the long facade. The original outside balcony was enclosed with glass, contrasting the modern with the classic. Four gilded tiers sweep around the auditorium in an elliptical form, three box tiers topped by a gallery. The theater seats 1,200.

Practical Information. Teatro Coccia, Via Fratelli Rosselli 4, Novara. Tel: 39 321 620-400. (Comune di Novara-Assessorato per La Cultura) Fax: 39 321-370-561. If visiting, contact the Italian Government Travel Offices (ENIT), 630 Fifth Avenue, New York, NY 10011. Tel: 212-245-4822.

REPERTORY

Opera Repertory. **1779:** Medonte. **1779-80:** Il matrimonio per inganno, L'italiana in Londra. **1780:** L'Avaro, La scuola dei Gelosi. **1780-81:** La virtuoso alla moda, L'Avaro. **1781-82:** L'albergatrice vivace, I contrattempi. **1782-83** Gli amanti canuti, Il convito. **1783:** La frascatana, Giannina e Bernardone, Epponina. **1784-85:** La villanella rapita, Le astuzie di Bettina. **1785-86:** Il geloso in Cimento, La ballerina amante, L'impostore punito, Il barbiere di Siviglia (Paisiello). **1786-87:** I due baroni di rocca azzura, Fra i due litiganti il terzo gode. **1787-88:** I due castellani burlati. **1788-89:** I due supposti conti, I fratelli Pappamosca. **1789:** Enea e Lavinia. **1789-90:** La gelosie fortunate, La cuffiara. **1790-91:** Il bertoldo. **1791:** Bella pescatrice. **1794:** Il servo astuto. **1795-96:** La molinara, La gelosie villane. **1797:** La virtuosa bizzarra, Le due gemelle, La cuffiara. **1798:** La pastorella nobile, Il matrimonio segreto, Il barbiere di Siviglia (Paisiello). **1801:** Licenza. **1805-06:** Licenza. **1807:** La virtù al cimento, La capricciosa pentita, Il venditore di aceto. **1807-08:** L'amico dell'uomo, Le cantatrici villane, Lo sposo contrastato. **1808:** La ferita mortale risanta dal matrimonio, Cantico. **1808-09:** Te Deum. **1809-10:** Il matrimonio segreto. **1810:** I raggi della serva, Carolina e Filan-dro, Il sedicente filosofo, Ercole ed Anteo. **1811:** L'amante anonimo. **1811-1812:** Amore tutto vince. **1812:** I pretendenti delusi, Amore e Dispetto. **1818:** Incoronazione ed innalzamento al trono di Svezia dell'Infante Gustavo. **1822:** Il barbiere di Siviglia. **1826-27:** Evellina. **1827-28:** Elisa e Claudio. **1828:** Matilde di Shabran, Semiramide. **1828-29:** Il Barone di Dolsheim, La secchia rapita. **1829:** Torvaldo e Dorliska, Il conte Ory, Gianni di Parigi. **1829-30:** Gli Arabi nelle Gallie, Aureliano in Palmira. **1830-31:** Il falegname di Livonia, I Capuletti e i Montecchi, La Ssposa fedele. **1832-33:** La straniera, Semiramide. **1833:** Gli Arabi nelle Gallie, Carlotta e Werter, La gabbia dei matti, Il barbiere di Siviglia, Riccardo e Zoraide, Anna Bolena, Chiara di Rosemberg. **1833-34:** I normanni a Parigi, Tancredi, L'elisir d'amore, Il nuovo Figaro, Torquato Tasso, Il furioso. **1834-35:** Anna Bolena, Norma. **1835:** La pazza per amore, Il barbiere di Siviglia, Il giovedi grasso. **1835-36:** La sonnambula, I capuletti e i Montecchi. **1836:** Olivo e Pasquale, Eran due ed or son tre. **1836-37:** Parisina. **1837:** Matilde di Shabran, La sonnambula, L'italiana in Algeri. **1837-38:** Belisario, Caterina di Guisa. **1838:** Un'avventura di scarmuccia, L'organa di Ginevra, Lucia di Lammermoor, Eran due ed or son tre. Il furioso. **1838-39:** Il giuramento, I Capuletti e i Montecchi. **1839:** Gemma di Vergy, Norma, L'elisir d'amore. Gariella di Vergy, Il conte Ory. **1839-40:** Roberto Devereux, Semiramide, La donna del lago. La sposa velata. 1840: Clotide, Il barbiere di Siviglia, I Capuletti e i Montecchi. **1840-41:** Beatrice di Tenda, Emma d'Antiochia, Semiramide. **1841:** Chi dura vince, Odie e amore. **1841-42:** Il brabo, I Puritani. **1842:** Il giuramento, Chiara di Rosemberg, L'elisir d'amore. **1843:** La pazza per amore, Il furioso, La prigione di Edimburgo, Gemma di Vergy. **1843-44:** Lucrezia Borgia, Marin Fliero. **1844:** Il nuovo Figaro, Columella, La pazza per amore, L'aio nell'imbarazzo, Il giuramento. **1844-45:** Nabucco, La marescialla d'Ancre. **1845:** La fille du règiment, Il borgomastro di Schiedam, L'elisir d'amore, Lucinda di Roccaforts, Lucia di Lammermoor, Gemma di Vergy. **1845-46:** Ernani, I falsi monetari, Il campanello, La vestale (Mercadente). **1846:** Il Puritani e i Cavalieri, La contesse villane. **1846-47:** I Lombardi, Otello (Rossini). **1847:** La Cenerentola, Ascanio il gioielliere. **1847-48:** I due foscari, Lucrezia Borgia, Maria di Rohan. **1848-49:** Ernani, Attila. **1849:** Fausta, Don Pasquale. **1849-50:** Don Pedro di Portogallo, I due foscari. **1850:** La gazza ladra, Il barbiere di Siviglia, Torquato Tasso, Linda di Chamounix, La prova di un'opera seria. **1850-51:** I masnadieri, Poliuto, Attila. **1851:** Ila regina di leone, L'elisir d'amore. **1851-52:** La Favorite, Saffo, Anna Bolena. **1852:** Nabucco, Crispino e la comare. **1852-53:** Il reggente, Il corsaro, La sonnambula. **1853:** Saul, Luisa Miller, Elena da feltre. **1854:** Don Bucefalo, Un'avventura di scarmuccia, Crispino e la comare, I Lombardi, Il birraio di

Preston, I falsi monetari. **1854-55:** Il trovatore, Maria di Rohan, I due Foscari, Rigoletto, Riorina. **1855-56:** Macbeth, Carlo Magno, Ernani. **1856:** Ernani. **1856-57:** La traviata, Il diavolo ossia Il conte di S. Germano. **1857-58:** Don Sebastiano, Lucia di Lammermoor, La sonnambula, il trovatore. **1858-59:** I Capuletti e i Montecchi, Belisario, Rigoletto, I Lombardi. **1859-60:** L'ebreo, La traviata, Semiramide. **1860-61:** Mosè in Egitto, Roberto Devereux, Attila. **1861:** Il barbiere di Siviglia, Chiara di Rosemberg. **1861-62:** Robert le Diable, Il bravo, Il campanello, Nabucco. **1862-63:** La regina di Cipro, Lucrezia Borgia, I due Foscari. **1863:** Linda Di Chamounix, Pipelet. **1863-64:** Vittor Pisano, La favorite, Un'avventur di carnevale. **1864:** Luisa Miller, L'ebreo. **1864-65:** Un ballo in maschera, I Capuletti e i Montecchi, Il templario, I domino nero, Il trovatore. **1865-66:** Jone, La straniera. **1867:** I falsi monetari, Columella, L'elisir d'amore. **1867-68:** Marta, La traviat **1868-69:** La Contessa d'Amalfi, Un ballo in maschera. **1869-70:** I Lombardi, I Puritani, Norma. **1870-71:** Aroldo, La vestale (Mercadante), Macbeth. **1871-72:** Jone, Il trovatore, Gemma di Vergy. **1872-73:** Ruy Blas (Marchetti), Nabucco, Luisa Miller. **1873-74:** La favorite, Rigoletto, Tripilla. **1874-75:** Faust, Lucrezia Borgia. **1875-76:** I promessi sposi, Saffo, Gismonda di Sorrento. **1876-77:** Il fornaretto, Lucia di Lammermoor, Maria di Rohan. **1877-78:** La muette de Portici, Ruy Blas (Marchetti, Davide Rizio. **1878-79:** La forza del destino, Faust, I due Foscari. **1879-80:** Robert le Diable, Dinorah, La favorite. **1880-81:** Salvator rosa, un ballo in maschera. **1881-82:** La forza del destino, Ernani. **1882-83:** Le precauzioni, Don Pasquale. **1883-84:** L'Africaine, Arrigo II, La favorite. **1884-85:** Aida, Faust. **1888-89:** Les Huguenots, Aida, La forza del destino. **1889-90:** Carmen, La gioconda, La favorite. **1890:** Rigoletto. **1890-91:** Otello, Ernani. **1891-92:** Mefistofele, Cavalleria rusticana, La traviata. **1892-93:** Lohengrin, Mignon. **1893-94:** Manon Lescaut, La favorite, Edmea. **1894:** Il trovatore, un ballo in maschera, Il barbiere di Siviglia. **1894-95:** La Juive, La sonnambula, Les Huguenots. **1895:** I pagliacci. **1895-96:** Tannhäuser, La gioconda, Loreley. **1896:** Carmen. **1896-97:** La bohème, Maruzza, Faust, Lucia di Lammermoor. **1897-98:** Fra Diavolo, Don Pasquale, Il barbiere di Siviglia, Crispino e la Comare, La campana delleremitaggio, L'elisir d'amore, Pipelet, La fille du règiment. **1898:** Papà Martin. **1899:** Manon, Marta, Tutti in maschera. **1899-00:** La bohème, Aida, Il trillo del diavolo. **1900:** Cavalleria rusticana, Pagliacci. **1900-01:** Tosca, Otello. **1901:** I Lombardi. **1901-02:** Andrea Chénier, Mefistofele. **1902:** La resurezione. **1902-03:** Germania, Il trovatore, Manon Lescaut. **1903:** La favorite. **1903-04:** Adriana Lecouvreur, Fedora, Zaza. **1904:** Nerina. **1904-05:** Lohengrin, La bohème, Madre, La traviata. **1905:** L'amico Fritz. **1905-06:** Iris, Poliuto, Tosca, Giovanni Gallurese.

1906-07: Falstaff, Madama Butterfly, Rigoletto. **1907-08:** L'Africaine, La Wally, Un ballo in maschera, Lucia di Lammermoor. **1908:** Fedora. **1908-09:** Carmen, Andrea Chénier, Silvano, La navarrese. **1909:** Don Pasquale. **1909-10:** La gioconda, Loreley. **1910:** Ernani, Rigoletto. **1910-11:** Aida, Faust, Risurrezione. **1911:** La traviata, Il matrimonio segreto, La bohème. **1911-12:** Siberia, Manon, Isabeau. **1912-13:** La fanciulla del west, La forza del destino, La traviata. **1913:** La donne curiose. **1913-14:** La Damnation de Faust, La favorite, Thaïs, Saffo. **1914:** Orma. **1914-15:** Un ballo in maschera, Tosca, La gioconda, La traviata. **1915:** Don Pasquale, Cavalleria rusticana, I pagliacci. **1915-16:** Madama Buterfly, Otello, Edmea, La bohème. **1916:** Il barbiere di Siviglia, Fedora, Lucia di Lammermorr. **1916-17:** Carmen, Andrea Chénier, Cavalleria rusticana, Pagliacci. isabeau. **1918-19:** La traviata, Rigoletto, Manon Lescaut, Il trovatore, La Wally, La bohème. **1919:** La sonnambula, Lucia di Lammermoor, Don Pasquale, Il barbiere di Siviglia, L'elisir d'amore. **1919-20:** Aida, Tosca, Lohengrin, La traviata. **1920:** Werther, Cavalleria rusticana, I pagliacci, Sulle rive del Danubio, Antigone, La Cenerentola. **1921:** Don Pasquale. **1921-22:** Rigoletto, Andrea Chénier, La fanciulla del west, La traviata, La bohème, **1922:** Madama Butterfly, Manon Lescaut. **1922-23:** Mefistofele, Manon, Carmen, Tosca, Cavalleria rusticana, I pagliacci. **1923:** La resurrezione di Lazzaro. **1923-24:** La gioconda, Iris, Mignon, Lodoletta, La bohème. **1924:** Il barbiere di Siviglia. **1942-25:** Otello, La Wally, Il trovatore, Die Walküre, Tosca, Norma. **1925:** Madama Butterfly. **1925-26:** Francesca da Rimini (Zandonai), Un ballo in maschera, Loreley, Il piccolo Marat. **1925-26:** La forza del destino. **1926:** Rigoletto, Il barbiere di Siviglia. **1926-27:** Andrea Chénier, Turandot, Ernani, La traviata, Anima allegra. **1927:** La bohème, Fedora, Madama Butterfly. **1927-28:** Mefistofele, Aida, Segreto di Susanna, Suor Angelica, Gianni Schicchi, Boris Godunov. **1928:** Il matrimonio segreto, L'elisir d'amore, Don Pasquale, La serva padrona. **1928-29:** Lohengrin, La traviata, Thaïs, Rosmunda, Guillaume Tell. **1929:** Madama Butterfly, Il barbiere di Siviglia. **1929-30:** Samson et Dalila, Rigoletto, Manon Lescaut, Germania, Il trovatore. **1930:** I quattro rusteghi. **1930-31:** Turandot, Lucia di Lammermoor, Otello, Pittori Fiammingh, Un astuzia di Colombina, La bohème, Rigoletto. **1931:** Il matrimonio segreto. **1931-32:** La gioconda, Andrea Chénier, La traviata. **1932:** Beatrice Cenci, Pinotta, Cavalleria rusticana. **1932-33:** Boris Godunov, Carmen, La bohème, La forza del destino. **1933:** Papà Martin. **1933-34:** Manon Lescaut, La traviata, Lohengrin, La cena delle beffe, Lucia di Lammermoor, Isabeau, Tosca, I Puritani. **1934:** La bohème. **1934-35:** Rigoletto, Madama Butterfly, Aida, L'amico Fritz. **1935:** Il barbiere di Siviglia. **1935-36:** Un ballo in maschera, Adriana

Lecouvreur, Tristan und Isolde, Le furie di Arlecchio, Maria Egiziaca, La favola di Orfeo, Lucia di Lammermoor. **1936-37:** Tosca, Rigoletto. **1937:** La traviata, Don Pasquale. **1937-38:** Mefistofele, La bohème, La gioconda, Il piccolo Marat. **1938-39:** La forza del destino, La Wally, Cavalleria rusticana, Notturno romantico, Madama Butterfly, Turandot. **1939-40:** Otello, Manon, Baldo, La traviata, La fanciulla del West. **1940-41:** Rigoletto, Fedora, Tosca, Lucia di Lammermoor, Francesca da Rimini, Sagre Ampezzane, Zanetto. **1941-42:** Andrea Chénier, Cavalleria rusticana, I pagliacci, Il segreto di Sussana, Le furie di Arlecchino, La guardia innamorata, Manon Lescaut. **1942:** Madama Butterfly. **1942-43:** Rigoletto, L'elisir d'amore, La traviata. **1943-44:** Rigoletto, La bohème, Tosca, Un ballo in maschera, Il barbiere di Siviglia, Carmen, Turandot, Madama Butterfly, Werther, Il trovatore, La traviata, L'amico Fritz. **1944-45:** Don Pasquale, Tosca. **1945:** La traviata. **1947:** La bohème. **1948-49:** Aida, Turandot, Tosca. **1949-50:** Andrea Chénier, Carmen, Rigoletto, Tosca. **1950:** L'italiana in Londra, Osteria dei Proteghesi. **1950-51:** Il trovatore, Madama Butterfly, Adriana Lecouvreur, Faust, La traviata. **1951-52:** La bohème, Otello, La gioconda, Cavalleria rusticana, I pagliacci. **1952:** Bastien und Bastienne. **1952-53:** La sonnambula, Un ballo in maschera, Tosca, La traviata. **1953:** L'amico Fritz, Lucia di Lammermoor, La bohème. **1953-54:** La forza del destino, Madama Butterfly, Cavalleria rusticana, I pagliacci, Rigoletto, Tosca. **1956-57:** Madama Butterfly, Lucia di Lammermoor, La bohème, Manon. **1957-58:** Manon Lescaut, Andrea Chénier, Don Pasquale. **1958-59:** La traviata, Tosca, Il barbiere di Siviglia. **1959-60:** Lohengrin, Cavalleria rusticana, I pagliacci, Carmen, Il trovatore. **1960-61:** La traviata, Rigoletto, Turandot. **1961-62:** Vivì, L'amico Fritz, Nabucco. **1962-63:** Un ballo in maschera, Madama Butterfly, Novella, Cavalleria rusticana, La bohème, Il barbiere di Siviglia. **1963-64:** Tosca, La traviata, Aida, Agenzia matrimoniale, Bathassar. **1964-65:** Otello, Cavalleria rusicana. **1965-66:** Il barbiere di Siviglia, Lucia di Lammermoor. **1966:** Così fan tutte. **1966-67:** Madama Butterfly, Carmen, Rigoletto. **1968-69:** Tosca, La traviata, Il Signor Bruschino, Il telefono, Il barbiere di Siviglia. **1972:** Aida. Pierrot innamorato, Medico suo malgrado, La bohème. **1976-77:** Madama Butterfly, Rigoletto. **1978:** Carmen, La prima notte, La mamma dei gatti, I mantici, La traviata. **1979:** Tosca, Lucia di Lammermoor, Il trovatore. **1980:** Don Carlo, Andrea Chénier, I pagliacci, L'ombra. **1981:** Il matrimonio segreto, Il barbiere di Siviglia, Madama Butterfly, La battaglia, Carmen. **1982:** La bohème, Rigoletto, Norma. **1983:** Un ballo in maschera, L'elisir d'amore, La traviata. **1984:** Nabucco, Don Pasquale, Tosca. **1985:** Manon Lescaut, La sonnambula, Il trovatore.

Bibliography. Silvia Raimondi, *Oltre Il Velario: Fantasmi di palcoscenico al Teatro Coccia di Novara*, Silvana Editoriale (Milan, 1993). Maria Teresa Castoldi & Valeria Piasentà, *Dal Mito alla Scena: Luoghi, tempi e committenze dello spettacolo a Novara*, Istituto Geografico de Agostini (Novara, 1989). E. Andreoni, *Relazione del comm. G. Lucca sui progetti del Nuovo Teatro di Novara* (Novara, 1882). G. Bustico, *Il Teatro Antico a Novara* (1695–1873) (Novara, 1922). G. Brunetti, P. Carbone, L. Paolini, *Teatro di Novara, il rispetto della storia* in *Modula 137*; (December 1987.)

Thanks to Maria Laura Tomea, director, Musei, Comune di Novara-Assessorato per La Cultura.

PADUA

Teatro Comunale "Giuseppe Verdi"

The Teatro Comunale "Giuseppe Verdi," originally called Il Teatro Nuovo, was inaugurated on June 11, 1751, with Baldassarre Galuppi's *Artaserse*, written especially for the occasion. The theater was the result of the efforts of a group of nobility which had formed *Nobile Società del Teatro Nuovo* three years earlier to promote the construction of a new theater. Antonio Cugini designed the structure and Giovanni Gloria directed the building work.

Padua's first theater dates back to 1642. Located in the Palazzo del Capitanio, it hosted Domenica Gabrieli's *Maurizio* in May 1691, the first confirmed account of a *melodrammatico* presentation. Fire claimed the theater on April 7, 1777. Padua had other theaters, but it was Teatro degli Obizzi, constructed in 1652, that would "compete" with the new theater.

The year after the Teatro Nuovo opened, Domenico Scarlatti was commissioned to write a new opera, *Demetrio*, which was well-received. Meanwhile the composer of the inaugural opera, Galuppi, wrote several more works for the Nuovo —*Demofonte, Solimano, Demetrio, Muzio Scevola, Arianna e Teseo.* Between 1793 and 1800, several new works graced the stage, works of

Giuseppe Sarti, Felice Alessandri, Sig. Fabrizi, Ferdinando Paër, and Sig. Montellari. Napoleon Bonaparte visited the theater during this period. After the dawn of the 1800s, the first works of Gioachino Rossini entered the repertory in 1811 and the opera house hosted several well-known artists, like Signore Soltz and Pandolfini, and Signor Brambilla. In 1818, Giuditta Pasta sang in Padua for the first time, and during Carnival 1841-42, Francesco Malipiero's *Giovanno, prima regina di Napoli* was world premiered. The house closed between 1846 and 1847 for restructuring. Performances then continued until 1876 when the theater had to shut its doors due to several cracks in the ceiling. Verdi's *Aida* reopened the opera house in 1884 and the composer, himself, was invited to attend the reopening, but Verdi declined, citing old age, health and posed the question "What would I do?" In 1880, Richard Wagner's *Lohengrin* was presented, followed a decade later by Verdi's *Otello* and Pietro Mascagni's *Cavalleria rusticana* in 1891. Austrian bombs damaged the theater in 1918. It reopened on December 21, 1920, with Arrigo Boïto's *Mefistofele* with Vittorio Emanuele III, King of Italy, in attendance. The repertory focused on the well-known operas until the theater was closed for World War II. It reopened immediately after the war.

The comune took over the opera season in 1973, mounting for the rest of the 1970s the following repertory. Verdi's *I due Foscari*, Giacomo Puccini's *Madama Butterfly* and *Tosca* for 1973; Puccini's *Turandot*, Umberto Giordano's *Fedora*, and Verdi's *Rigoletto* for 1974; Verdi's *Luisa Miller* and *La traviata*, and Rossini's *Il barbiere di Siviglia* for 1975; Verdi's *Il trovatore*, Mascagni's *Il piccolo Marat*, and Ermanno Wolf-Ferrari's *I quattro rusteghi* in 1976; Verdi's *Un ballo in maschera*, Puccini's *La bohème*, Wolfgang Amadeus Mozart's *Don Giovanni* in 1977; Rossini's *La Cenerentola*, George Bizet's *Carmen*, Mascagni's *Cavalleria rusticana*, and Ruggero Leoncavallo's *I pagliacci* in 1978, and Verdi's *Otello*, Gaetano Donizetti's *Lucia di Lammermoor* and *Don Pasquale* in 1979. That same year witnessed the birth of the Asso-

ciazione Teatri Antichi del Veneto, whose headquarters since 1988 have been in Padua. A recent schedule offers unusual works, like Hector Berlioz's *Roméo et Juliette*, George Gershwin's *Porgy and Bess*, and Giovanni Paisiello's *Il Re Teodoro in Venezia*.

Teatro Comunale "Giuseppe Verdi"

A site in the San Nicolò district was selected for the opera house and work commenced in 1749. Two and a half years later, the theater opened. The horseshoe-shaped auditorium offered four tiers of boxes, with 29 boxes to a tier, and a loggione for the servants. The orchestra level held 250 stools and a separate standing area. The theater has undergone numerous restorations and renovations. Of note were the new facade and new auditorium by Giuseppe Jappelli begun January 6, 1846, and completed following year; a curtain painted by Vincenzo Gazzotto that depicted "The Entrance of the Carroccio in Padua" unveiled in 1856, the reconstruction by Achille Sfondrini between 1882 and 1884, and the work to repair the destruction caused by Austrian bombs on December 29, 1917, that destroyed the frescoes on the dome ceiling, damaged the orchestra area and the dividing walls of the boxes as well as the proscenium arch. The 1990s saw additional work to bring the theater up to fire safety code.

Practical Information. Teatro Comunale "Giuseppe Verdi," Viale Codalunga 4/H, Padua. Tel: 39 49 875-8269. If visiting the Teatro Comunale "Giuseppe Verdi," contact the Italian Government Travel Offices (ENIT), 630 Fifth Avenue, New York, NY 10011. Tel: 212-245-4822.

BIBLIOGRAPHY

Bibliography. *Il Teatro Comunale "Giuseppe Verdi" di Padova* (Padua, 1998). *Teatro Comunale "G. Verdi"* (Padua, 1996). *Indagine Storica sul Teatro Comunale "Verdi"* (Padua, 1980).

Thanks to Sig. Bertinelli, Teatro Comunale, "Giuseppe Verdi."

PALERMO, SICILY

Teatro Massimo–Politeama Garibaldi
(Ente Autonomo Lirico)

Giuseppe Verdi's *Falstaff* inaugurated the Teatro Massimo on May 16, 1897. The evening commenced at 9 pm with the arrival of Maestro Leopoldo Mugnone at the podium and the playing of the royal march. Giovanni Battista Filippo Basile, who had died six years before the completion of the theater, had designed the Massimo thirty-two years earlier, in 1865. The work was completed by his son, Ernesto Basile. The long delay in building the Massimo led to the construction of the Politeama Garibaldi, inaugurated on June 7, 1874, with Bellini's *I Capuletti e i Montecchi*. The theater was designed by Giuseppe Damiani Almeyda.

Some of the first operas heard in Palermo date back to the 1650s with Francesco Cavalli's *Giasone* given at the Teatro della Misericordia and his *Serse* at the Teatro dello Spasimo, the latter to celebrate the inauguration of the Accademia di Musicia. The Spasimo itself goes back to the late 1500s, having been established in a church where the "Madonna dello Spasimo" had been witnessed. The birth of Alessandro Scarlatti in 1660 in Palermo lead to many of his works being staged there, beginning with *Il Pompeo* in 1690.

Opera came more into its own with the inauguration of the Teatro di Santa Cecilia on October 28, 1693, with the work of a local composer, Ignazio Pollice's *L'innocenza pentita*. In 1726, a 500-seat wooden structure known as Teatro Santa Lucia (also referred to as Teatro della Corte del Pretore in one book) was constructed to host *opera buffa*. In 1809, the building was enlarged to 700 seats and renamed Teatro Carolino, after the consort of Ferdinand I of Bourbon, Queen Maria Carolina. The Carolina enjoyed a full, year-round schedule, if the historians' records are accurate. One highlight during the 1826-27 season was Gaetano Donizetti conducting the world premiere of his *Alahor in Granata* on January 7, 1826, with Antonio Tamburini in the title role. The Irishman Michael Balfe was the lead baritone during the 1829-30 season and also saw the staging of his first complete opera *I rivali di se stesso*. The repertory concentrated, however, on works by Dom-

enico Cimarosa, Giovanni Simone Mayr, Gioachino Rossini, Donizetti, and Vincenzo Bellini. Censorship was a problem, and one found Bellini's *I Puritani* as Elvira ed Arturo, Verdi's *Ernani* as Elvira d'Aragona, *Attila* as Gli Unni di Romani, and *Giovanni d'Arco* as Orietto di Lesbo. In May 1848 the parliment of Sicily renamed the Carolino, Real Teatro Bellini, but it hosted fewer and fewer operas over the years. After World War I it was converted into a movie house, and then fire claimed it in 1964.

Meanwhile, Palermo had finally opened its new, long-awaited opera house, Teatro Massimo, but the inaugural season was short — only two additional works were in the program: Amilcare Ponchielli's *La gioconda* and Giacomo Puccini's *La bohème*. *La gioconda* featured a young, little-known young tenor as Enzio — Enrico Caruso. The following season saw seventeen performances of Jules Massenet's *La Roi de Lahore* and then money problems ensured, resulting in the closure of the theater. The diligence of impresario Signor Laganà reopened the Massimo, which he guided from 1901 to 1905. Current works of the era, especially of the *verismo* school — Ruggero Leoncavallo's *Zazà*, Pietro Mascagni's *Iris*, Puccini's *Tosca*, Umberto Giordano's *Fedora*, Francesco Cilea's *Adriana Lecouvreur*, and Alberto Franchetti's *Germania* — and operas never seen before in Palermo — Camille Saint-Saëns' *Samson et Dalila* and Richard Wagner's *Tannhäuser* — were prominent in the schedule. Well-known singers of the time sang at the Massimo, including Gemma Bellicioni in Verdi's *La traviata*, Amelia Pinto in Ponchielli's *La gioconda* and Wagner's *Tannhäuser*, and Mario Sammarco and Titta Ruffo in Verdi's *Rigoletto*.

Ignazio Florio took over the management of the opera house in 1906, guiding it until 1919, and then after a few year absence, returned again in 1923 staying until 1926. During his tenures at the helm, several works new for Palermo, especially "foreign" operas, like Wagner's *Die Walküre*, *Siegfried*, *Götterdammerung*. *Tristan und Isolde*, and *Parsifal*, Hector Berlioz's *Le damnation de*

Faust, Richard Strauss's *Salome*, Engelbett Humperdinck's *Hänsel und Gretel*, Jacques Offenbach's *Les contes d'Hoffmann*, Massenet's *Thaïs*, as well as the contemporary works of Italian composers, including Giordano's *Madame Sans-Géne*, *La cena delle beffe*, and *Siberia*, Alfredo Catalini's *Wally* and *Dejanice*, Mascagni's *Isabeau*, *Amica*, and *Lodoletta*, Gaspare Spontini's *La vestale*, Zandonai's *Conchita*, and Ermanno Wolf-Ferrari's *I quattro rusteghi* and *Il segreto di Susanna* were prominent in the *cartellone*. World premieres were also in evidence with Stefano Donaudy's *Sperduti nel buio*, Riccardo Storti's *Venezia*, Giordano's *Mese mariano*, and Leoncavallo's *Mimì Pinson*, (a revised version of his *La bohème*, first performances in 1897 at La Fenice in Venice). The 1918 season was special regards casting, with a 19-year-old Toti dal Monte and 28-year-old Beniamino Gigli appearing together in Mascagni's *Lodoletta*, and Gigli also interpreting Des Grieux in Puccini's *Manon Lescaut*. Other illustrious singers at the Massimo included Tito Schipa in Donizetti's *La sonnambula*, Verdi's *La traviata* and *Rigoletto*, and Puccini's *Tosca* and *Madama Butterfly*, and Ezio Pinza as Colline in Puccini's *La bohème*. Gigli returned in 1935 for Giordano's *Andrea Chénier*, Puccini's *Manon Lescaut*, and Bellini's *La pirata*. Several first presentations of operas at the Massino were conducted by the composers themselves: Puccini led his *Rondine* and *Il trittico*, Zandonai his *Francesca da Rimini* and *Giulietta e Romeo*, and Gino Marinuzzi his *Palla de'Mozzi*.

The Massimo was very elitist with a rigid "pecking order" of the boxes. The first level of boxes was reserved for the military and government officials, the second (and most desirable level) for aristocrats, the third for the rich borghese, the remaining orchestra and loggione for the other classes. The orchestra and loggione were frequented by a diverse public whose interest was either the opera itself—a new opera or a long awaited revival—or a particular singer. Until 1936, the theater was managed by private individuals and companies. That year, the figure of the sovrintendente was born with the transformation of the Massimo into an Ente Autonomo and the financing secured by public funds. The first to assume the newly created position was Maestro Cardenio Botti, and in his first season a novelty for Palermo was offered, Licinio Refice's *Cecilia*. Monte returned to sing in Rossini's *Il barbiere di Siviglia*, and Francesco Merli and Iva

Pacetti appeared in Verdi's *Otello*. Verdi's *I vespri siciliani* inaugurated the next season, which saw the return of Schipa for Donizetti's *L'elisir d'amore*. The composer Franco Alfano took the helm in 1940 and offered Giuseppe Mulè's *La Zolfara*, an opera by a Sicilian composer. The following season saw Signor Raccuglia succeeded Alfano, but the hostilities of World War II forced a suspension of activities. The Massimo escaped almost unscathed. A small bomb ripped through the stage roof and exploded on the ground level but caused little damage.

The 50th anniversary of the birth of the theater was celebrated during the 1946/47 season with a repeat of the inaugural season operas—Verdi's *Falstaff*, Ponchielli's *La gioconda* and Puccini's *La bohème*—among other works. An opera season was also given at the Politeama Garibaldi (see below). With the 1949 season, the Italian premiere of Karol Szymanowski's *Król Roger* (King Roger) took place, as well as several Palermo premieres—Ambroise Thomas's *Hamlet*, Jean Françaix's *Le diable boiteux*, Alfred Casella's *La favola di Orfeo*, and Elisabeth Lutyens' *The Pit*. That same season witnessed a rare singing treat, Maria Callas as Brunhilde in *Die Walküre*. Callas returned two years later to assay the title role in Bellini's *Norma*, and Renata Tebaldi arrived in 1953 for Margherita in Arrigo Boïto's *Mefistofele*. Also in 1953, the Massimo received a new sovrintendente, Maestro Cuccia, who initiated a program to revive unjustly forgotten operas of the past like Bellini's *Beatrice di Tenda*, *Il pirata*, and *I Capuleti e i Montecchi*, which received its first performance in the 20th century, and Verdi's *Giovanna d'Arco*. Works by Wolfgang Amadeus Mozart, which had been ignored not only in Palermo, but in almost every Italian opera house, finally had a hearing—*Don Giovanni*, *Der Schauspieldirektor*, and *La finta semplice*, as did Strauss's *Elektra*. At the same time lesser known contemporary works were staged, including Alfano's *Cyrano de Bergerac* and Vincenzo Tommasini's *Il tenore sconfitto*, and several world premieres (between 1955 and 1969)—Nino Rota's *Il cappello di paglia di Firenze*, Michele Lizzi's *Pantea* and *L'amore di Galatea*, Giuseppe Savagnone's *Né tempo né luogo*, Franco Mannino's *Il diavolo in giardino* and *Luisella*, and Angelo Musco's *Il gattopardo*. The last three seasons of the 1960s also witnessed breadth and depth (for an Italian house), especially in the introduction of foreign works, which included Béla Bartók's *A Kékszakállú herceg vára* (Duke Bluebeard's Castle), Carl Orff's *Carmina burana*, Alexander Borodin's *Prince Igor*, Bedřich Smetana's *Prodaná nevěsta* (The Bartered Bride), Massenet's *Don Quichotte*, Françis Poulenc's *La voix humaine*, and Maurice Ravel's *L'heure espagnole*. The Italian part of the schedule mixed early works like Giovanni Paisiello's *Don Chisciotte della mancia*, Claudio Monteverdi's *La favola d'Orfeo* and *L'incoronazione di Poppea*, and Rossini's *Il conte Ory* and *Il Signor Bruschino* with contemporary ones — Goffredo Petrassi's *Il cordovano*, Giorgio Federico Ghedini's *Billy Budd*, Ildebrando Pizzetti's *Ifigenia*, Gianfrancesco Malipiero's *Sette canzoni*, Luigi Dallapiccola's *Il volo di notte*, and Orazio Fiume's *Il tamburo di panno*.

Since its opening in 1897, the Massimo has hosted 4,450 performances of 308 different titles. Then in January 1974, its history came to an abrupt halt. After a concert performance of Verdi's *Nabucco* the Massimo was closed, declared unsafe and all performances were transferred to the Politeama Garibaldi. As the story goes, the Mafia wanted to control the reconstruction, and the politicians did not want to be controlled by the Mafia, so they closed the theater. Before its closure, many legendary voices of the era sang at the Massimo during its last decades like Franco Corelli, Magda Olivero, Mirella Freni, Victoria de Los Angeles, Mario del Monaco, Joan Sutherland, Giuseppe di Stefano, Luciano Pavarotti, Cesare Siepi, and Giuseppe Taddei. Several of these artists worked at the Massimo at the beginning their careers, as did the renown conductors Riccardo Muti and Claudio Abbado and prominent directors such as Luchino Visconti, Franco Zeffirelli, and Peter Hall. This is part of the Massimo's philosophy — to find promising young singers, directors and conductors. It is primarily from necessity, since it is difficult to lure established artists to Palermo for several weeks at a time, the period required, since each opera is repeated many times.

On May 12, 1997, after twenty-three years and 100 billion LIT in renovation costs, the city finally reopened their opera house with Claudio Abbado, a native son, conducting a concert which began with *Va'pensiero* from Verdi's *Nabucco*. But, only the orchestra level and two box tiers were completed, the tickets to the "event" were exorbitant, and the theater was closed immediately thereafter, causing speculation that this pre-opening was purely political. Even a group of students protested the "show." But the reopening was also a happy occasion. As one of the local papers *Il Mediterraneo* put it, "The hope is that (the opening) signals a disinfection from the Mafia." Finally in April 1998, Verdi's *Aida* inaugurated the first opera season at the Massimo since 1974, followed by Richard Struass' *Der Rosenkavalier* and Richard Wagner's *Tannhäuser*.

Politeama Garibaldi

Although the Politeama had been originally constructed to host variety shows, opera also graced the stage until the Massimo opened. One coup of the Garibaldi was the arrival of Arturo Toscanni for the 1892-93 season, when he conducted several works, including Leoncavallo's *I pagliacci*, Mascagni's *Cavalleria rusticana*, Ponchielli's *La gioconda*, Verdi's *Rigoletto*, Rossini's *Il barbiere di Siviglia*, Catalani's *Loreley*, Richard Wagner's *Die fliegende Holländer* and Bellini's *Norma*. The Politeama also attracted some of the best singers, among them, Francesco Tamagno and Nellie Melba.

Once the Massimo finally opened, the Politeama's twenty-three years of opera activity came to a halt. The Politeama then hosted an assortment of entertainment — until the Massimo was closed in 1974, and the regular opera seasons were transferred back to the Garibaldi. Unusual pieces, like Gomes' *Il guarany* occupied the stage during the first "transferred" season. In 1975, the artistic direction was entrusted to a committee which included Girolamo Arrigo, Delogu, Gavazzeni, Petrassi, and Santi, and more unusual operas were staged for the first time in Palermo — Niccolò Piccinni's *La cecchina, ossia La buona figliola*, Pyotr Il'yich Tchaikovsky's *Eugene Onegin*, Christoph Willibald Gluck's *Iphigénie en Tauride*, Luigi Dallapiccola's *Il prigioniero*, and Gino Negri's *Pubblicità ninfa gentile*. In 1977, Arrigo was named sole artistic director and Ubaldo Mirabelli the new sovrintendente. A new course of activity was initiated that saw an increase in the productions, and a renewed interest in the staging of forgotten operas and those never before seen in Palermo that last into the next decade. Again, many foreign operas, rarely seen in any Italian opera house graced the stage, like Igor Stravinsky's *The Rake's*

Progress, Georges Bizet's *Le docteur miracle*, Sergey Prokofiev's *Ognenniy angel* (The Fiery Angel) and *War and Peace*, George Gershwin's *Porgy and Bess*, Strauss's *Ariadne auf Naxos*, Benjamin Britten's *Turn of the Screw* and *The Rape of Lucretia*, Leoš Janáček's *Jenůfa*, Ernst Křenek's *Jonny spielt auf*, and Tchaikovsky's *Pikovaya dama* (Queen of Spades). More Mozart works made its way onto the Palermo stage with *Idomeneo* and *La clemenza di Tito* on the boards, along with Georg Friedrich Händel's *Alcina*. Among the Italian novelties was the Italian premiere of Vittorio Rieti's *Don Perlimplin*, Gianfrancesco Malipiero's *La favola del figlio cambiato*, Alfredo Casella's *La donna serpente*, Luciano Chailly's *L'idiota*, Franco Mannino's *Il ritratto di Dorian Gray*, and Ottorino Respighi's *Semirama*. There was one world premiere, Barbara Giuranna's *Hosanna*, introduced on May 30, 1978.

The quality of the performances at the Politeama during its final full season before the reopening of the Massimo offered a schedule of Italian operas from the standard repertory. Gone was the adventurous offerings found earlier at Politeama and the Massimo. A new production of Verdi's *Falstaff* proved disappointing with unimaginative sets, routine staging and exaggerated movements, taken to excess, to express comedy. The old-fashion and conservative way of thinking prevalent in Sicily carried over to the operatic stage, which took on a museum quality. The cast of young, Italian singers produced a good sound, symmetrically balanced, but needed much prompting and the orchestra overpowered. The production of Mozart's *Così fan tutte*, borrowed from Teatro Donizetti (Bergamo) although more interesting than that of *Falstaff*, worked better in Bergamo (see Teatro Donizetti entry). The singing, however, especially of the men, was of questionable quality. It should be added, however, that the acoustics of the Politeama were not created nor well-suited for opera. The final repertory before reopening of the Massimo included Charles Gounod's *Roméo et Juliette*, Johann Strauß's *Die Fledermaus*, Giordano's *Fedora*, Marco Tutino's *La Lupa*, and Puccini's *Gianni Schicchi*.

Teatro Massimo

The first discussions about construction of the Massimo took place in 1851. An architectural competition was announced in 1864 and Basile was declared the winner. He received 25,000 lire, but the comune decided that insufficient funds had been allotted and annulled the results of the competition. The controversy surrounding the cancellation continued for five years, when Basile resubmitted a more economical project which was limited to the bare essentials to allow performances. Finally on January 12, 1875, with the mayor of Palermo, Emanuele Notarbartolo in attendance, the first stone was laid. A medallion commemorates this historic day. Work had finally begun, but hopes for a new opera house soon were premature. In 1881, an overzealous engineer from the Municipal Technical Office found excessive expense in the roof and construction of the auditorium and the stage. Construction was suspended, and the commission to Basile was revoked. There was even talk about giving the commission to Alessandro Antonelli. Bureaucratic wrangling held up the project for nine years, until 1889. Then the bureaucracy wanted the building completed for the Exposition of 1891. This was all too much for poor Basile, who died on January 16, 1891. Four days later, Basile's son Ernesto was nominated to complete his father's project.

The enormous building of local Tufaceous stone mixes several styles—a Grecian-style portico of fluted Corinthian columns with a Roman rotunda, defined by Neocloassic lines and a touch of Art Noveau in a fusion of various geometric shapes. Corinthian-Italian fluted, engaged columns ring the building, alternating with arched windows. There is an inscription—*L'Arte rinnova i popoli e ne rivela la vita. Vano delle scene il diletto ove non miri a preparare l'avvenire.* (Art renews the people and tells about their life. If entertainment does not prepare for the future, the performances are in vain.) The horseshoe-shaped auditorium holds five gilded tiers topped by a gallery. Festoons of flowers and fruit, musical motifs and putti fill the space. Gilded caryatid Muses with headpieces of lights flank the center royal box. The chairs are a deep rose-colored velvet, and the dome ceiling is divided into twelve panels representing the twelve signs of the zodiac, called The Triumph of Music. There are 1,316 seats.

Politeama Garibaldi

On the sidewalk in front of the Politeama Garibaldi is a somber reminder of the presence of

Top: Teatro Massimo (Palermo, Sicily); *bottom:* Politeama Garibaldi (Palermo, Sicily).

the Mafia. Police-like outlines of bodies in a variety of colors are drawn on the sidewalk, commemorating all the people killed by the Mafia. Hints of Spanish influence are revealed in the facade of the politeama. The building is semi-circular in shape, the front-half circled by fluted Doric columns on the lower level with fluted Ionic columns encircling above. A triumphant arch defines the principal entrance crowned by a four horse-drawn chariot. A relief of putti with musical instruments extends across the arch, flanked by musical motifs. The unusual interior takes on a U shape but with the ends curving toward each other on the two lower box tiers, which hold red velvet seats. Open wood-bench seating prevails on the upper levels, an area illuminated by wrought-iron candelabras. A huge bust of Garibaldi rests above the proscenium arch. Above the stage, flanked by white marble Muses, is a recessed arcade. There are 1,860 seats.

Teatro di Vedura

In 1957, the Teatro di Vedura, located in the park surrounding the Villa Castelnuova, opened. Verdi's *Otello*, with Mario del Monaco, inaugurated the newly created summer festival. The Verdura, formed in the last decades of the 18th century, is an open-air theater surrounded by lush green vegetation. A mixture of opera, operetta, and musicals are staged, including *West Side Story*, *Chorus Line*, *Die lustige Witwe*, and *Il paese dei campanelli*, among others. Recent offerings include Franz Lehár's *Die lustige Witwe*.

Practical Information. Teatro Massimo, Piazza Verdi, 90138 Palermo. Tel: 39 91 605-3111, Fax: 39 91 605-3324. Politeama Garibaldi, Piazza Ruggero Settimo, Palermo. Tel: 39 91 605-3315. If attending performances at either the Teatro Massimo or Politeama Garibaldi, stay at the Astoria Palace Hotel, Via Montepellegrino 62. 39 91 637 1820; Fax 39 91 637-2178. It is centrally located and convenient to the opera houses.

COMPANY STAFF, WORLD PREMIERES, AND REPERTORY

Sovrintendentes. Cardenio Botti, Franco Alfano, Sig. Racciglia, Maestro Cuccia, Leopoldo de Simone, Ubaldo Mirabelli, Attilio Orlando. **Direttori Artistici :** Giralamo Arrigo, Marco Betta.

World Premieres. G. Marinuzzi's *Barberina*, May 5, 1903; S. Donaudy's *Sperduti nel buio*, April 27, 1907; Riccardo Storti's *Venezia*, 1908; U. Giordano's *Mese mariano*, March 7, 1910; R. Leoncavallo's *Mimì Pinson* (revised La bohème), April 14, 1913; G. Savagnone's *Millesima seconda*, February 5, 1949; N. Rota's *Il cappello di paglia di Firenze*, April 21, 1955; M. Lizzi's *Pantea*, April 14, 1956; G. Savagnone's *Né tempo né luogo*, March 7, 1961; F. Mannino's *Il diavolo in giardino*, February 28, 1963. M. Lizzi's *L'amore di Galatea*, March 12, 1964; A. Musco's *Il gattopardo* December 19, 1967; F. Franco Mannino's *Luisella*, February 28, 1969, Barbara Giuranna's *Hosanna*, May 30, 1978. **First Performance In Italy:** K. Szymanowsky's *Król Roger* (King Roger) April 19, 1949; E. Chabrier's *L'étoile*, April 30, 1970; V. Rieti's *Don Perlimplin*, March 2, 1979.

Repertory (By year of first performance in Palermo). **1874:** Armida. **1898:** Le Roi de Lahore. **1901:** Iris, Tosca. **1902:** Fedora, Zazà. **1903:** Barberina. **1904:** Adriana Lecouvreur, Aretusa, Samson et Dalila. **1904:** Tannhäuser. **1905:** Germania. **1906:** La damnation de Faust, Siberia, Die Walküre. **1907:** Sperduti nel buio, La Wally. **1908:** Alceste, Hänsel und Gretel, Thaïs. **1909:** Tristan und Isolde. **1910:** Amica. **1911:** Götterdämmerung. **1911:** Vita brettona. **1912:** La baronessa di Carini, Il battista. **1913:** La fanciulla del West, Isabeau. **1914:** Conchita, Parsifal, Radda, Salome. **1915:** Les contes d'Hoffmann. **1919:** Il segreto di Susanna. **1920:** La rondine. **1921:** Francesca da Rimini. **1922:** Gianni Schicchi, Giulietta e Romeo, Il piccolo Marat, Suor Angelica, Il tabarro. **1923:** Sigfried. **1924:** I compagnacci. **1925:** Dejanice, I quattro rusteghi. **1926:** La cena delle beffe. **1928:** Turandot. **1930:** Dafni. **1931:** Boris Godunov. **1932:** Der Rosenkavalier. **1932:** Palla de'mozzi, Risurrezione. **1934:** Galatea. **1936:** Cecilia. 1937: Liolà, La vedova scaltra. **1938:** Il combattimento di Tancredi e Clorinda, Il gobbo del Califfo. **1939:** Donata, Fra Gherardo. **1940:** L'Arlesiana, Fidelio. **1941:** l'intrusa, Zanetto, La zolfara. **1942:** Il campiello, La via della finestra. **1943:** Amahl and the Night Visitors. **1947:** L'amore dei tre re. **1948:** Fedra. **1949:** Hamlet, Le diable boiteux, La favola di Orfeo, The Pit, Król Roger (King Roger). **1951:** Giuditta, Terra santa. **1952:** Amelia al ballo. **1953:** Cyrano de Bergerac, Don Giovanni. **1954:** Elektra. **1955:** Il cappello di paglia di Firenze, Giovanna d'Arco, Der Schauspieldirektor. **1956:** La finta semplice, La grançeola, Pantea, Persefone, Il tenore sconfitto. **1957:** La guerra. **1958:** La domanda di matrimonio, L'enfant et les sortilèges, The Old Maid and the Thief. **1959:** Hin und zurück, Ivan The Terrible, Die Entführung aus dem Serail, El retablo de Maese Pedro. **1960:** Pelléas et Mélisande. **1961:** Allamistakeo, Die Zauberflöte. **1962:** Assassinio nella cattedrale, Lord Byron's Love Letter. **1963:** Il diavolo in giardino, Der Freischütz, Khovanschchina. **1964:** L'amore di Galatea, Le campane, Dialogues des

Carmélites, Emperor Jones. **1965:** Arlecchinata, Partita a pugni, Wozzeck. **1966:** Arlecchino, O Le finestre, Rita, La scala di seta. **1967:** Don Chisciotte della mancia, Il conte Ory, Il gattopardo, La leggenda del ritorno, Prince Igor, Sette canzoni, Prodaná nevěsta (The Bartered Bride), Il volo di notte. **1968:** A Kékszakállú herceg vára (Duke Bluebeard's Castle), Don Quichotte, L'heure espagnole, Ifigenia, L'incoronazione di Poppea, Il Signor Bruschino, Il tamburo di panno, La vita breve. **1969:** Billy Budd (Ghedini), Carmina burana, Il cordovano, 2=pochi, 3=troppi, Orfeo, La voix humaine. **1970:** L'étoile, Il governatore, Das Rheingold. **1971:** Laudes evangelii, La sagra del signore della nave. **1972:** Filomela e L'infatuato, L'histoire du soldat, Laborintus secondo, Uno dei dieci. **1974:** L'uomo più importante, Le rossignol. **1975:** La cecchina, ossia La buona figliola, Eugene Onegin, Iphigénie en Tauride, Il prigioniero, Pubblicità ninfa gentile. **1976:** Der Zar lässt sich photographieren. **1977:** The Rake's Progress, Le docteur miracle. **1978:** Ognennïy angel (The Fiery Angel), Hosanna, Porgy and Bess. **1979:** Ariadne auf Naxos, Turn of the Screw, Jenůfa, Don Perlimplin. **1980:** La favola del figlio cambiato, Beggar's Opera. **1981:** La clemenza di Tito, L'idiota. **1982:** La donna serpente. **1983:** Idomeneo, Il ritratto di Dorian Gray, The Rape of Lucretia. **1984:** The Consul, Pikovaya dama (Queen of Spades). **1985:** Alcina. **1986:** Voyna i mir (War and Peace). **1987:** Jonny spielt auf, Semirama.

Bibliography. Ottavio Tiby and Iganzio Ciotti, *I Cinquant'anni del Teatro Massimo (1897–1947)* (Palermo, 1947). Ciotti, *La Vita Artistica del Teatro Massimo di Palermo (1897–1937)* (Palermo, 1938). Tiby, *Il Real Teatro Carolino e L'800 Musicale Palermitano* (Florence, 1962). Corrado Martinez, *Il Teatro Massimo: 40 Anni di Attività Artistica dalla Costituzione dell'Ente Autonomo (1936–1975)* (Palermo, 1980). A.M. Fundario, *Il concorso per il Teatro Massimo di Palermo* (Palermo, 1984). L. Maniscalco Basile, *Storia del Teatro Massimo di Palermo* (Rome, 1984). *L'Opera a Palermo dal 1653 al 1987* (Palermo, 1988). Maria Adele Rubino, *Il Teatro Massino di Palermo* (Palermo, 1988). G. Pirrone, *Il Teatro Massimo di G.B. Basile di Palermo* (Rome, 1984). Newspapers: *Il Mediterraneo*, May 11, 1997; *Gazzetta del Sud*, May 12, 1997; *Giornale di Sicilia*, May 12 and 13, 1997.

Thanks to Lauro Oddo, Teatro Massimo; Matteo Corrao, and Vincenzo Gabriele.

—————— PARMA

Teatro Regio
(Teatro di Tradizione)

Vincenzo Bellini's *Zaira* and the ballet *Oreste* inaugurated the Teatro Regio di Parma, originally called Il Nuovo Teatro Ducale, on May 16, 1829. The opening night audience was not enthusiastic about *Zaira* and gave it a hostile reception. The Regio was designed by Nicola Bettòli and modeled after Teatro alla Scala.

In 1617, Ranuccio Farnese commissioned the construction of the Teatro Farnese. Designed by Gian Battista Aleotti, the Farnese was opened in 1628 with *Mercurio e Marte*, with music by Claudio Monteverdi and text by Claudio Archillini. Monteverdi's *Gli amori di Diana e di Endimione* was staged a short time later. The theater, however, was primarily used for wedding celebrations. On October 6, 1732, the Farnese hosted its final performance. Ranuccio Farnese's heir, Ranuccio II, built three theaters in Parma: Teatro della Rocchetta, opened in 1674 and demolished in 1822, Teatrino di Corte, opened in 1689 and demolished in 1832, and the Teatro Ducale, opened in 1688 with Antonio Giannettini's *Teseo in Atene*.

The Teatro Ducale, designed by the Court architect Stefano Lolli, was constructed where the central post office is now located. Built of wood, the auditorium held four tiers topped by a gallery, and a center ducale box. It accommodated 1,200. In 1738, Giambattista Pergolesi's *La serva padrona* was staged, and fifty years later, Giovanni Paisiello's *Il barbiere di Siviglia* was presented. In 1789, the Ducale witnessed the first opera by Parma-born composer Ferdinando Paër, *La locanda dei vagabondi*. Several of Paër's operas were introduced in the Ducale, including *Agnese*. Gioacchino Rossini arrived in Parma in 1814. Some of his operas, like *Tancredi* and *La Cenerentola*, were accepted by the critical Parma audience, and others like *L'italiana in Algeri* and *Il turco in Italia* were not appreciated. His *Il barbiere di Siviglia* was both: it started successfully but ended up a failure. It was difficult to gauge the reception a performance would receive at Teatro Ducale. But despite the unpredictable behavior of the audience, almost every important artist of the era appeared on its stage.

For the inauguration of the Nuovo Teatro Ducale (New Ducal Theater later Teatro Regio) Rossini was invited to compose an opera, but he declined and the task fell to Bellini. Despite the cool reception given to *Zaire*, contrary to what has been written, *Zaire* received seven more performances before sinking into oblivion. Four additional operas graced the stage during the inaugural season: Luigi Ricci's *Colombo*, and Rossini's *Mosè e Faraone*, *Semiramide*, and *Il barbiere di Siviglia*. During the first few years, Rossini operas dominated the stage, but soon works by Bellini and Gaetano Donizetti eclipsed Rossini and dominated until Giuseppe Verdi entered the scene. Verdi was born at Le Roncole, less than thirty miles from Parma, so the city adopted him as its native son, with his operas playing a dominant role in the Regio's repertory. Every one of Verdi's 27 operas has been staged, including *Jérusalem*. On April 17, 1843, *Nabucco* as Nabucodonosor was the first of Verdi's works to be offered, which was directed by the composer. It enjoyed 23 performances. He returned to direct *Aida* in April 1872. A half of century after the Regio opened, almost a quarter of all the performances had been of Verdi operas. Parma operagoers had taken it upon themselves to learn each note and word of every Verdi opera. It was a problem for any director, singer, or conductor who did not.

Amilcare Ponchielli came to Parma in 1885 to direct his *La gioconda*, and the Parma premiere of his *Marion Delorme* was staged the following year. Umberto Giordano led the opening of his *Andrea Chénier* on December 26, 1896. Although Giacomo Puccini was in Parma for *La bohème* in 1898, it was not well received, and Pietro Mascagni's *Amica* was laughed off the stage in 1908. Meanwhile, Stefano Gobatti attended his *I goti* in 1874, and four years later, Primo Bandini conducted his *Euremio da Messina*. To celebrate the centennial of Verdi's birth in 1913, the Regio programmed only Verdi operas — *Oberto, conte di San Bonifacio*, *Nabucco*, *Un ballo in maschera*, *Aida*, *Falstaff*, *Don Carlo*, and *Messa da Requiem*. A celebration of the 50th anniversary of Verdi's death took place in 1951 with performances of *Ernani*. *Don Carlo*, *La battaglia di Legnano*, and *Falstaff*. Another Verdi Festival took place in September 1990, with *Alzira*, *Il trovatore*, and *Le trouvère* on the boards.

The Regio was not damaged by World War II and hosted performances during the war years. An earthquake on November 9, 1983, however, closed the theater for the season and forced the cancellation of Ludwig van Beethoven's *Fidelio* and Richard Strauss's *Salome*. The remainder of the season was held at the Teatro Ducale. The Regio officially reopened with Verdi's *I due Foscari* on January 8, 1985. The season included a novelty for Parma, Charles Gounod's *Roméo et Juliette*. The 1986-87 season was adventurous with three novelties for Parma — Nino Rota, *Il cappello di paglia di Firenze*, Christoph Willibald Gluck's *Orfeo ed Euridice*, and Antonio Salieri's *Falstaff ossia Le tre burle*.

Between 1829 and 1979, of the ten most performed operas at the Regio, five were by Verdi — *Aida* (189), *Il trovatore* (177), *Rigoletto* (164), *Ernani* (102), and *La traviata* (92). Donizetti held second place with *Lucia di Lammermoor* (122) and *La favorita* (90), followed closely by Bellini with *Norma* (119) and *La sonnambula* (99). The surprise was to find Wagner's *Lohengrin* (105) in the top ten. The Regio's audience is notorious for showing its displeasure at substandard performances and singers. The practice goes back to the Teatro Ducale when in 1816 Alberico Curioni, a tenor in Vincenzo Federici's *Zaira*, was loudly hissed and booed. The tenor yelled obscenities at the audience, and bedlam erupted. Only after the tenor's arrest and the replacement of the opera with a ballet was order restored. An impresario suffered a similar fate two years later when the opening night of the 1818 season was a failure. The opera house was closed and the impresario sent to jail for "offending the public sensibilities." Many operas have also experienced premature conclusions like Antonio Marchisio's *Piccarda Donati* in 1860 which had its final curtain fall after the second act, and Carlo Pedrotti's *Fiorina* suffered a similar fate the next year, but here the curtain was brought down *during* the second act. On February 11, 1907, the public protest of Antonio Pagura's *L'apostata* was so vociferous that it was interrupted during the first act and the audience received their money back. More recently, the 1989/90 season experienced two premature curtains, with one opera lasting only a half an hour. The audience knows how much every singer is paid, and the higher the fee, the more ruthless is their reaction to a bad note. No singer survives a bad night at the Regio.

The press office explained the situation like

this, "Teatro Regio realizes it needs to be the best because the audience are all experts. There is a tremendous pressure to be exceptional, but, of course, we do not always succeed."

The repertory concentrates on the operas of Verdi with a mixture of contemporary and traditional production styles. Verdi's *Simon Boccanegra* was a recreation of the historic first performance, but another of Verdi's opera received a modern, high tech rendering. Some productions of Wolfgang Amadeus Mozart works have been very modern, but the press office made it clear that avant-garde has no place in Parma. Recent repertory includes Verdi's *Un giorno di regno*, *Un ballo in maschera*, and *Don Carlo*, Engelbert Humperdinck's *Hänsel und Gretel*, and Rossini's *L'italiana in Algeri*.

Teatro Regio

The Teatro Regio, until 1849 called Nuovo Teatro Ducale, was conceived by the Imperial Princess and Archduchess of Austria, Marie Louise, who was also the Duchess of Parma. She chose Bettòli as the architect and Gian Battista Borghesi and Paolo Toschi for the interior decoration. Eight years passed before the opera house was finished.

The Teatro Regio is a deep yellow stucco structure with a severe, Neoclassic facade, punctuated by five Empire windows, and an Ionic-column-supported portico. Masks of Comedy and Tragedy embellish the tympanum. An elliptically-shaped auditorium of red, ivory, and gold holds four box tiers topped by a gallery. In the middle is the ducal box, adorned with a gold-and-maroon drapery and topped by the crown of the Holy Roman Empire. Medallions of composers and gilded horn-blowing cherubs embellish the parapets. The red velvet seats match the red velvet curtain. The auditorium seats 1,244.

Practical Information. Teatro Regio, via Garibaldi 16/A, 43100 Parma, Italy. Tel: 39 521-218-678; Fax 39 521-206-156. When visiting the Teatro Regio or the archives, stay at the Park Hotel Stendhal, via Bodoni 3, 43100 Parma, Italy. Tel: 39 521 208 057, Fax: 39 521 285 655. It is centrally located and near the Teatro Regio. The hotel can assist with schedules and tickets.

COMPANY STAFF, PREMIERES, AND REPERTORY

Direttore. Gian Piero Rubiconi.
World Premieres. L. Ricci's *Il nuovo Figaro* February 15, 1832. G. Sanelli's *Luisa Strozzi* May 27, 1846. G. Belledi's *Ubu Re* December 2, 1982; F. Battiato's *Genesi* April 26, 1987. **Italian Premieres:** G. Donizetti's *Maria di Rohan* May 1, 1844 (Teatro Ducale). G. Verdi's *I vespri siciliani* (as Giovanna di Guzman) December 26, 1855.

Repertory. **1829:** Zaira, Mosè e Farone, Semiramide, Il barbiere di Siviglia, Colombo, Giulietta e Romeo (Vaccai). **1830:** Tancredi, Bianca e Faliero, ovvero Il consiglio dei tre, Il turco in Italia, Elisa e Claudio, La Cenerentola, Clotilde, Il barbiere di Siviglia, La prova di un'opera seria, Zadig e Astartea. **1831:** Olivo e Pasquale, Gli arabi alle Gallie, La schiava di Bagdad, Marilde di Shabran ossia Bellezza e cuor di ferro, Il conte Ory, L'acquisto per raggiro, L'organella di Ginevra, Giannina e Bernardone, Elisa e Claudio, La straniera. **1832:** La regina di Golconda, Il nuovo Figaro, Il barone di Dolsheim, La gazza ladra, L'inganno felice, Torwaldo e Dorliska, Chiara di Rosembergh. **1833:** Il segreto, Anna Bolena. **1834:** Il Cid, Norma, L'elisir d'amore, Il furioso, La prova di un'opera seria, Il barbiere di Siviglia, Chiara di Rosembergh, l'inganno Felice, Elisa e Claudio, Norma. **1835:** I Capuleti e i Montecchi, Il barbiere di Siviglia, La sonnambula, I Puritani. **1836:** La Cenerentola, Gemma di Vergy, Il pirata. **1837:** Lucia di Lammermoor, Un'avventura di Scaramuccia, La nina pizza, La sonnambula, L'elisir d'amore, Torquato Tasso, Beatrice di Tenda. **1838:** Otello (Rossini), Belisario, Il furioso, Gli esposti, ossia Eran due ed or son tre, Marino Faliero, Ines di Castro (Persiani). **1839:** Il Giuramento, La prigione d'Edimburgo, L'elisir d'amore, La Cenerentola, Il barbiere di Siviglia, La sonnambula, Lucrezia Borgia. **1840:** Roberto Devereux, Norma, I due Figaro, L'elisir d'amore, Beatrice di Tenda, Il barbiere di Siviglia, Parisina. **1841:** Belisario, Elena da Feltre, Fausta, Lucia di Lammermoor. **1842:** La vestale (Mercadante), Lucrezia Borgia, Chi dura vince, L'elisir d'amore, La regina di Golconda, Stabat Mater (Rossini), Saffo. **1843:** Anna Bolena, Il templario, Ester d'Engaddi, Nabucodonosor (Nabucco), La vestale (Mercadante), Robert le Diable. **1844:** Beatrice di Renda, Il reggente, I Lombardi, Maria di Rohan, Il ritorno di Columella, Il barbiere di Siviglia, La Cenerentola, Betly, L'elisir d'amore, Ernani. **1845:** Lucia di Lammermoor, Caterina Cornaro, I due Foscari, Linda di Chamounix. **1846:** Saul, Il reggente, Alzira, I Lombardi, Nabucco (Nabucodonosor), Luisa Strozzi, La cantante, Il ritorno di Columella da Padova, La fille du régiment, Attila. **1847:** Ernani, Il brabo, Gemma di Vergy, La straniere, I monetari falsi, Ovvero Eutichio e Sinforosa, Ricciarda, Il campanello, La sonnambula, Il

Teatro Regio (Parma, Italy).

ritorno di Columella da Padova. **1848:** Orazi e curiazi, Leonora, I masnadieri, Il barbiere di Siviglia. **1849:** I masnadieri, Chi dura vince, Torquato Tasso, Macbeth. **1850:** Linda di Chamounix, Il barbiere di Siviglia, Il giuramento, I Lombardi, I Puritani, Don Procopio, La prova di un'opera seria, Crispino e la comare, Luisa Miller. **1851:** Ernani, Il barbiere di Siviglia, Elmina, Lucrezia Borgia, Il domino nero, Il fornaretto, I due Foscari, I due sergenti, Gemma di Vergy, Poliuto. **1852:** Don Crescendo, Norma, Tancredi, Luigi V, La Cenerentola, Il barbiere di Siviglia, Attila, Funerali e danze, Elena di Taranto, Rigoletto. **1853:** La favorita, Nabucco (Nabucodonosor), Le prophète. **1854:** L'italiana in Algeri, Il trovatore,

L'abbazia di Kelso, Poliuto, Luisa Miller. **1855:** La traviata (Violetta), Il trovatore, Micaela, Buondelmonte, Giovanni Giscala, I Lombardi, I vespri siciliani (Giovanna di Guzman). **1856:** Rigoletto, Maria di Rohan, La traviata. **1857:** Mosè, Il trovatore, Gusmano il prode, Corrado di Altamura, La tradita, Aroldo. **1858:** Pia de'Tolomei, I due Foscari, Il conte di Leicester, Lucia di Lammermoor, Beatrice di Tenda, Don Pasquale, Giovanna d'Arco. **1859:** I masnadieri, Gemma di Vergy, Nabucco, Il saltimbanco, Tutti in maschera, Semiramide. **1860:** Don Bucefalo, La battaglia di Legnano, Norma, Piccarda Donati, La sonnambula, I Puritani, Un ballo in maschera. **1861:** Fiorina, Ernani, La fille du régiment, Il barbiere di Siviglia, Guglielmo Shakespeare, L'ebreo, Poliuto, Les Huguenots. **1862:** Macbeth, Vittore Pisani, Ginevra di Scozia, Guerra in Quattro, Linda di Chamounix, Rigoletto, La locandiera, Norma. **1863:** Isabella d'Aragona, Il trovatore, Attila, Beatrice Cenci, Faust. **1864:** Lucrezia Borgia, La sonnambula, Roberto le Diable, Norma, Guglielmo Tell. **1865:** La gioconda, Lucia di Lammermoor, Don Sebastiano, Il barbiere di Siviglia, Pipelè ossia Il portinaio di Parigi, Il birrajo di Preston, Le Precauzioni ovvero il Carnevale di Venezia, Tutti in Maschera, La sonnambula, L'elisir d'amore, L'Africaine. **1866:** Niccolò de'Lapi, Rigoletto, La juive. **1867:** Roberto le Diable, Un ballo in maschera, Norma, I vespri siciliani. **1868:** La favorita, Jone, Don Carlo. **1869:** La favorita, Il menestrello, Linda di Chamounix, Martha. **1870:** Don Pasquale, La sonnambula, La contessa d'Amalfi, Il fornaretto, Les Huguenots, Lucrezia Borgia, Arianna e Bacco, Norma, Crispino e la comare, Le educande di Sorrento, I falsi monetari ovvero Don Eutichio e Sinforosa, Un matrimonio civile, Chi dura vince, I Lombardi. **1871:** Rigoletto, Un ballo in maschera, La contessa d'amalfi, Ruy Blas, Marco Visconti. **1872:** Il trovatore, Poliuto, Aida. **1872:** Don Sebastiano, Romeo e Giulietta (Marchetti). **1873:** Jone, Nabucco, Marcellina, La forza del destino, Faust, Stabat Mater (Rossini) I promessi sposi. **1874:** Ruy Blas, I goti, La contessa di Mons. **1875:** La favorita, Il conte Verde, Dolores. **1876:** Lucia di Lammermoor, I due Foscari, La regina di Castiglia, Romilda dei Bardi, Messa da Requiem (Verdi), Diana di Chaverny. **1877:** Il trovatore, Jone, La traviata. **1878:** Un ballo in maschera, Euremio da Messina, Dinorah, Roderigo di Spagna, La favorita, Il Guarany. **1879:** Rigoletto, La sonnambula, Dinorah, Stabat Mater (Rossini), Ruy Blas, Le donne curiose, I falsi monetari, Robert le Diable. **1880:** Niccolò dei Lapi, Aida. **1881:** Macbeth Polituo, L'Africaine. **1882:** Ernani, Salvator Rosa, Carmen, Il trovatore, La Reine de Chypre. **1883:** Stella, Lucia di Lammermoor, Lohengrin. **1884:** Attila, Les Huguenots, Amazilia, Mignon. **1885:** La bella fanciulla di Perth, Rigoletto, La favorita, La gioconda. **1886:** Aida, Marion Delorme, Faust, Mefistofele. **1887:** Dinorah, Fausta, Rigoletto, Otello, Le roi de Lahore. **1888:** La forza del destino, Il barbiere di Siviglia, Lohengrin. **1889:** Faust, La gioconda, Don Carlo. **1890:** Aida, Ernani, Sieba. **1891:** Les pêcheur de perles, Cavalleria rusticana, Mefistofele, Carmen. **1892:** L'amico Fritz, La favorita, Rigoletto, Otello. **1894:** Otello. **1895:** Manon Lescaut, Il trovatore, La favorita, Les Huguenots. **1896:** Aida, Falstaff, Andrea Chénier. **1897:** Samson et Dalila, Manon, Cavalleria rusticana, I pagliacci. **1898:** Lohengrin, La bohème, Un ballo in maschera, Mefistofele. **1899:** La resurrezione di Lazzaro, Otello, I Puritani, La traviata, Norma. **1900:** Dinorah, Tannhäuser, Guglielmo Tell, Il trovatore, Aida. **1901:** Iris, Tosca, Le preziose, Tosca, Andrea Chénier. **1902:** Mignon, Samson et Dalila, Fedora, Cavalleria rusticana, I vespri siciliani. **1903:** Il trovatore, Lohengrin, La sonnambula, La gioconda, Severo Torelli, La forza del destino. **1904:** La bohème, les Huguenots, Faust, Lucia di Lammermoor. **1905:** Germania, Manon Lescaut, Mefistofele, Siberia. **1906:** Werther, La Damnation de Faust, Benvenuto Cellini (Tubi), Die Walküre. **1907:** Aida, La Wally, L'apostata, Germania, Loreley, Rigoletto, Andrea Chénier. **1908:** Amica, L'amico Fritz, Tristan und Isolde, La sonnambula, La fata delle bambole, Rose Rosse, La Damnation de Faust, Lohengrin. **1909:** Madama Butterfly, Manon, Norma, Sigfried. **1910:** Loreley, Maria Rohan, Lucia di Lammermoor, Il barbiere di Siviglia, La fille du régiment, Die Meistersinger von Nürnberg. **1911:** Hérodiad, Norma, La gioconda, Salome, Boris Godunov. **1912:** Carmen, Rigoletto, Mefistofele, Judith (Furlotti). **1913:** Le donne curiose, Oberto, Conte di San Bonifacio, Nabucco, Un ballo in maschera, Aida, Falstaff, Don Carlo, Messa di Requiem (Verdi). **1914:** Cercando la via, Il barbiere di Siviglia, Otello, Manon Lescaut. **1915:** L'elisir d'amore, Don Pasquale, Il barbiere di Siviglia, Andrea Chénier. **1916:** La favorita, Isabeau, Aida, Il trovatore, Il barbiere di Siviglia. **1917:** Rigoletto. **1919:** Aida. **1920:** Loreley, Francesca da Rimini, Fedra, Lohengrin, La Cenerentola, La samaritana. **1921:** I quattro rusteghi, Dejanice. **1922:** La gioconda, Mefistofele, Tannhäuser, Otello, La Wally, Les Huguenots. **1923:** Giulietta e Romeo (Zandonai), Il trovatore, Manon Lescaut, Falstaff, Madama Butterfly, Parsifal. **1924:** Carmen, Guglielmo Tell, Le donne curiose, La forza del destino, Il carillon magico, Cavalleria rusticana, Judith, Die Walküre. **1925:** La traviata, La damnation de Faust, Il piccolo Marat, Aida, Manon, La bohème, Il trittico di Pierrot, Tristan und Isolde. **1926:** Norma, La leggenda di Natale, Il maestro di cappella, un ballo in maschera, Cavalleria rusticana, Faust, Samson et Dalila, Otello. **1927:** Iris, Lohengrin, Andrea Chénier, Lucia di Lammermoor, Turandot, Carmen, Sigfried. **1928:** La sonnambula, Tosca, Rigoletto, Francesca da Rimini, Boris Godunov, La gioconda. **1929:** Werther, Manon Lescaut, Aida, Salome, Falstaff, Lohengrin. **1930:** Guglielmo Tell, Manon, Turandot, Il trovatore, Hänsel und Gretel. **1931:** Faust, Rigoletto, La fanciulla del West. **1932:** Lucia di Lammermoor, Norma, La bohème, Mefistofele, La froza del destino, Adriana Lecouvreur, Die Walküre. **1933:** La traviata, Aida, Mignon, La gioconda, Lohengrin, L'elisir d'amore, Il trovatore, Otello. **1934:** Un ballo in maschera, Madama Butterfly, La cena delle beffe, I Puritani, La favorita, Fra Gherardo. **1935:** Lohengrin, Rigoletto, Turandot, La bohème, I quattro rusteghi. **1936:** Andrea Chénier, Le astuzie di Bertoldo, Carmen, Aida, Francesca da Rimini, Maria Egiziaca, Gianni Schicchi, Messa da Requiem (Verdi), Simon Boccanegra. **1937:** Lucia di Lammermoor, La farsa amorosa, Tristan und Isolde, Tosca, La samaritana. **1938:** La fanciulla del West, Rigoletto, Mefistofele, Morrurno romantico, Il salice d'oro, Il barbiere di Siviglia, Fiorella, Otello, Il trovatore, La bohème. **1939:** La sonnambula, Madama Butterfly, La traviata, Il piccolo Marat, La forza del destino. **1940:** Faust, Cleopatra, Cavalleria rusticana, Fedora, Rosa rossa, Aida, Il barbiere di Siviglia. **1941:** La traviata, Luisa Miller, Rigoletto, Il trovatore, Falstaff, Madama Butterfly, L'amico Fritz, Il barbiere di Siviglia, La bohème, Un ballo in maschera. **1942:** Lohengrin, Il campiello, Ghirlino, Tosca, Andrea Chénier, Rigoletto, Ariodante. **1943:** Minnie la candida, La forza del destino, Il barbiere di Siviglia, L'elisir d'amore, Werther, L'Arlesiana, Lo straniero, Il segreto di Susanna, Aida, Antigone, La traviata, La bohème, Cavalleria rusticana, Otello. **1944:** Rigoletto, Madama Butterfly, Manon Lescaut, La bohème, Aida, La traviata, Il barbiere di Siviglia. **1945:** Manon, Madama Butterfly, Il trovatore, La bohème, L'amico Fritz, La traviata, Andrea Chénier, Tosca, Turandot. **1946:** Faust, La traviata, Carmen, Cavalleria rusticana, I pagliacci, Lohengrin, Norma, Il barbiere di Siviglia, La bohème, Lucia di Lammermoor. **1947:** Un ballo in maschera, Adriana Lecouvreur, Manon, Il trovatore, Raggio di Sole, La sonnambula, La bohème, Tosca, Rigoletto, Madama Butterfly. **1948:** La traviata, L'amico Fritz, La gioconda, Mefistofele, Die Meistersinger von Nürnberg, Werther, L'elisir d'amore, Nabucco. **1949:** Manon Lescaut, Buricchio, Aida, La traviata, Andrea Chénier, I misteri grandiosi, La terra santa, Cavalleria rusticana, I pagliacci, La forza del destino, Rigoletto, Fedora, Madama Butterfly. **1950:** Carmen, L'elisir d'amore, Cyrano di Bergerac, Il trovatore, Don Giovanni, Aida, La sonnambula, Turandot. **1951:** L'arlesiana, Lohengrin, Rigoletto, Manon, La forza del destino, Ernani, Don Carlo, La battaglia di Legnano, Falstaff, Andrea Chénier. **1952:** La traviata, Lucia di Lammermoor, La bohème, Amelia al ballo, Cavalleria rusticana, Carmen, La favorita. **1953:** Il trovatore, La serva padrona, L'italiana in Londra, l'osteria portoghese, Madama Butterfly, Faust, Un ballo in maschera, La capanna dello zio Tom, Die Walküre. **1954:** The Consul, Rigoletto, Aida, Norma, Otello. **1955:** Macbeth, La sonnam-

bula, Madama Butterfly, Un ballo in maschera, In terra di leggenda, La gioconda, Boris Godunov. **1956:** Werther, Otello, La figlia di Iorio, Tosca, La forza del destino, Samson et Dalila. **1957:** Prince Igor, Il trovatore, La bohème, Andrea Chénier, La traviata, La filgia del diavolo, Cavalleria rusticana, Simon Boccanegra. **1958:** Faust, Pikovaya dama (Queen of Spades), Lucia di Lammermoor, The Medium, I pagliacci, Carmen, Manon, Nabucco. **1959:** Turandot, Rigoletto, Die Zauberflöte, Les pêcheurs de perles, Aida. **1960:** La forza del destino, Madama Butterfly, Il maestro di Cappella, Lord Byron's Love Letter, Procedura penale, I Puritani, Falstaff. **1961:** Il trovatore, La sonnambula, Un ballo in maschera, Arlecchinata, Orfeo Anno Domini MCMXLVII, Rita, Don Carlo. **1962:** La Clementina, Quaturo, Agenzia matrimoniale, La traviata, Fidelio, La bohème, Luisa Miller. **1963:** Tosca, Uno sguardo dal ponte, La forza del destino, Emiral, Tannhäuser, Le nozze di Figaro, Suor Angelica, Messa da Requiem (Verdi), Macbeth, Il finto Stanislao (Un giorno di regno), Ernani. **1964:** Manon, L'elisir d'amore, Lucia di Lammermoor, The Golden Cockeral, Giulio Cesare, Tre amanti ridicoli, Un ballo in maschera. **1965:** Il matrimonio segreto, Rigoletto, Andrea Chénier, Die Walküre, Parisina d'Este, Simon Boccanegra. **1966:** La bohème, Otello, Il trovatore, Pelléas et Mélisande, Le nozze di Figaro, The Old Maid and the Thief, Un domanda di matrimonio, I due Foscari. **1967:** Il barbiere di Siviglia, Il trovatore, Così fan tutte, Madama Butterfly, Un donna uccisa con dolcezza, Tosca, Salome, Il lupo, La forza del destino. **1968:** La traviata, L'italiana in Algeri, Assassinio nella cattedrale, La serva padrona, Il maestro di cappella, Sigfried, Adriana Lecouvreur, Don Pasquale. **1969:** I pagliacci, Cavalleria rusticana, Stiffelio, Lucia di lammermoor, Manon Lescaut, Un quarto di vita, Sorochintsy Fair, The Greek Passion, Aida. **1970:** Rigoletto, Prodaná nevĕsta (The Bartered Bride), Didone ed Enea, La voix humaine, Midnight Summer's Dream, Turandot, A kékszakállú herceg vára (Duke Bluebeard's Castle), The Marvelous Mandarin, La favorita Il cordovano, Il dottore di vetro, Falstaff. **1971:** Madama Butterfly, Il trovatore, Die Meistersinger von Nürnberg, I Puritani, Fidelio, Norma. **1972:** Otello, Don Pasquale, La bohème, Il corsaro, Rusalka, Hin und zurück, Turn of the Screw, He Who Says Yes — He Who Says No, Francesca da Rimini, Don Giovanni, Un ballo in maschera. **1973:** Lucia di Lammermoor, Eugene Onegin, La Cenerentola, Attila, Der Freischütz, Carmen, Khovanshchina, I Lombardi. **1974:** Rigoletto, Macbeth, Leonora ossia l'amore coniugale, Die Zauberflöte, Werther, Billy Budd, I masnadieri. **1975:** La bohème, Le nozze di Figaro, Fidelio, L'elisir d'amore, Tristan und Isolde, Il barbiere di Siviglia, Luisa Miller. **1976:** La Wally, Ognennÿi angel (Fiery Angel), Tosca, Halka, Khovanshchina, Il mondo della luna, Il barbiere di Siviglia, Ovvero, La inutile precauzione (Paisiello), La peri, Per Massimiliano Robespierre, Simon Boccanegra. **1977:** Il trovatore, Anna Bolena, Die Entführung aus dem Serail, Ernani. **1978:** Madama Butterfly, Rigoletto, Oberto conte di San Bonifacio, The Beggar's Opera, Don Pasquale, Nabucco. **1979:** La bohème, Nos (The Nose), La Cenerentola, L'histoire du soldat, La sonnambula, La traviata. **1980:** La vestale (Spontini), Giovanna d'Arco, L'arcadia in Brenta, Lucia di Lammermoor, Messa da Reqiem (Verdi), Manon, Les pêcheurs de perles, Macbeth. **1981:** Adriana Lecouvreur, Alzira, Manon, Werther, La belle Hélène, Lo frate 'nnamorato. **1982:** Don Carlo, Thaïs, Norma, The Makropolous Affair, La favorita, Ubu Re, Maria Padilla. **1983:** Otello, Die Walküre, Un ballo in maschera, Il barbiere di Siviglia, Attila, Don Pasquale. **1984:** Nabucco, La fille du régiment, Carmen, Il barbiere di Siviglia. **1985:** I due Foscari, Tosca, Rinaldo, Samson et Dalila, Semiramide, Roméo et Juliette. **1986:** Jerusalem, Eugene Onegin, Faust, Lucia di Lammermoor, Cavalleria rusticana, Pagliacci, Falstaff. **1987:** Falstaff ossia le tre burle (Salieri), Il cappello di paglia di Firenze, Rigoletto, Orfeo ed Euridice, Genesi. **1988:** Aida, L'elisir d'amore, La fille du régiment, Les contes d'Hoffmann. **1989:** Un ballo in maschera, Turandot, Don Giovanni, La bohème, Wozzeck, La donna del lago. **1990:** La traviata, La fanciulla del West, Ernani, Werther, La Cenerentola. **1991:** Alzira, Eugene Onegin, Manon, Luisa Miller. **1992:** Madama Butterfly, L'elisir d'amore, Don Quichotte. **1993:** Tosca, Don Pasquale, La sonnambula, Boris Godunov. **1994:** Rigoletto, I Capuleti e i Montecchi, Don Giovanni, Falstaff. **1995:** Werther, Il barbiere di Siviglia, Messa da Requiem (Verdi), Die Fledermaus, Die Zauberflöte, La bohème. **1996:** La Cenerentola, Der fliegende Holländer, I quattro rusteghi, Simon Boccanegra, Il cavaliere dell'intelletto, L'Arlesiana. **1997:** La traviata, Amelia al ballo/Cavalleria rusticana, Die Entführung aus dem Serail, Un giorno di regno. **1998:** Messa da Requiem (Verdi), Hänsel und Gretel, L'italiana in Algeri, Don Carlo.

Bibliography. *Teatro Regio di Città Parma Cronologia degli Spettacoli Lirici 1829/1879* (Parma, 1981); *Teatro Regio di Città Parma Cronologia degli Spettacoli Lirici 1879/1929* (Parma, 1980); *Teatro Regio di Città Parma Cronologia degli Spettacoli Lirici 1929/1979* (Parma 1979); *Teatro Regio di Città Parma Cronologia degli Spettacoli Lirici 1979/1989* (Parma, 1989); *Teatro Regio di Città Parma Cronologia degli Spettacoli Lirici Indici 1829–1979* (Parma, 1982). Maurizio Corradi-Cervi, *Il Teatro Regio* (Parma, 1962)

Thanks to Claudio del Monte, Teatro Regio, and Roberta Cenci, Archivio Storico e Museo, Città di Parma.

PESARO

Rossini Festival-Teatro Rossini (Summer Festival)

The first Rossini Festival was inaugurated with Gioachino Rossini's *La gazza ladra* on August 28, 1980, in the Teatro Rossini. One hundred and six-two years earlier, on June 10th, the Teatro Nuovo (later renamed Teatro Rossini on August 26, 1854) had been inaugurated with the same opera, which Rossini had conducted. The inaugural season of the festival also offered Rossini's *L'inganno felice* in the Auditorium Pedrotti, the festival's other performing venue.

Gianfranco Moretti and Francesco Sorlini were the primary forces behind the creation of the festival, founded to rescue Rossini's more obscure works, and to utilize in September the abundant supply of beach hotels Pesaro has to offer, after the summer crowds had returned to work. Moretti explained that no other major composer has so many unknown pieces, and that of the approximately three dozen works Rossini created, only a handfull are known. The goal of the festival is to present all of Rossini's operas, especially the many still unknown *opere serie*. It performs the critical editions of the maestro's operas, and to this end has unearthed such obscure pieces as *Bianca e Falliero*, *Ermione*, *Armida*, *Ricciardo e Zoraide*, and the once popular *Otello*, until Giuseppe Verdi composed his interpretation.

But after a few years of the festival, it was apparent that it could not grow, due to the limited seating available in the two performing halls: Teatro Rossini offers 860 seats and Auditorium Pedrotti only 500. So in 1988, the Palasport, the town's sport arena, was transformed into another performance venue, called Palafestival, which offered 1,500 additional seats. Lacking air-conditioning and offering the acoustics of, well, a sport's arena, the "palace" hosted only short one-act operas like *L'occasione fa il ladro* and *Il Signor Bruschino*. But after a generous and wealthy Rossini-lover paid for air-conditioning and acoustic panels, critical editions of Rossini's longer and more demanding works graced the enormous stage of the Palafestival, like *Semiramide* which required two hours and twenty minutes just to get through the first act. (Comfort was not a priority item: the seats are hard, molded-fiberglass.) This has all been possible due to the maestro himself who left all of his money to the Comune of Pesaro, which, in turn, created the Accademia Rossiniana and the Fondazione Rossini. The function of the latter is to publish and produce critical editions of all the maestros works.

Not only does the festival, officially an Ente Lirico (foundation or corporation), endeavor to revive the long dead works of the maestro and insert them to the current repertory, but also to promote their execution elsewhere in Italy and abroad. To this end, the U.S. stage premiere of *Bianco e Falliero* took place at the Greater Miami Opera the year following its 1986 Pesaro revival, and *Ermione*, resuscitated at the festival in 1987, arrived at Opera/Omaha (Omaha, Nebraska) in 1992, and in concert form that same year at the San Francisco Opera, which has also recently staged Rossini's *Otello* and *Guillaume Tell* in memorable productions.

Although the festival is devoted to Rossini, occasionally works of other composers are in the program. The 1980 season offered both Rossini's *Stabat Mater* and Giambattista Pergolesi's *Stabat Mater*, the 1983 season presented Antonio Vivaldi's *Dixit Dominus*, and the 1989 season offered Wofgang Amadeus Mozart's *Requiem in Re Min. K 626*. In 1992, to celebrate the bicentennial of Rossini's birth, a special *Messa di Gloria* took place on February 29, two hundred years to the day after the maestro's birth.

The casts range from promising young singers, many of whom have since become international artists, to bel canto specialists. Samuel Ramey was a frequent guest, especially in the early 1980s, but continued to sing in Pesaro through 1992, as did Chris Merritt. Marilyn Horne appeared for three seasons in the mid–1980s, and June Anderson sang Desdemona to Merritt's Otello in the 1988 season's *Otello ossia Il Moro di Venezia* and Zoraide to William Matteuzzi's Ricardo two years later in *Ricciardo e Zoraide*. Jennifer Larmore made her first appearance at the festival in *L'italiana in Algeri* in 1994. On the Italian side Daniela Dessì, Katia Ricciarelli (a regular until 1989), Ruggero Raimondi, Ferruccio Furlanetto, Cecilia Bartoli, and Mariella Devia have all sung in Pesaro. In fact, in the 1989 *La*

gazza ladra with Ricciarelli, Furlanetto, and Ramey, a real thieving magpie joined the cast at the end of the performance. Two years earlier, Montserrat Caballé joined Marilyn Horne and Chris Merritt in *Ermione*, conducted by Gustav Kuhn. Riccardo Chailly led *Otello ossia Il Moro di Venezia* the following year. To celebrate the bicentennial of Rossini's birth, *Il viaggio a Reims* was staged, with a cast that included Cheryl Studer, Chris Merritt, Samuel Ramey, Ruggero Raimondi, among others, with Claudio Abbado on the podium.

Musical history in Pesaro predates, by around three-and-a-half centuries, the Rossini Festival. In fact, it began in 1637 with the inauguration of the Teatro del Sole on February 23, 1637, with the Pesaro composer, Giovanni Ondedei's *Asmondo*, a tragedy with *intermezzi* of dancing and singing. After Rossini died, a *Pompe Funebri Rossiniani* was presented, offering *Semiramide*, *Otello*, and Teresa Stolz as soprano soloist in *Stabat Mater*. All those happening are well chronicled in Carlo Cinelli's *Le Memorie Cronistoriche del Teatro di Pesaro dal 1637—1897*. On January 23, 1887, the opera house was illuminated by electricity for the first time. On the *cartollone* was *Il barbiere di Siviglia*, Giacomo Meyerbeer's *Dinorah*, and *Le Comte Ory*. Nine years later, the *prima* of Pietro Mascagni's *Zanetto* took place. The 1897 Carnival season offered Pietro Mascagni's *Guglielmo Ratcliff* and Georges Bizet's *Les pêcheurs de perles*. The Rossni was then closed, reopening with the arrival of the 20th century, with Edmond Audran's *La mascotte* and Vincenzo Valente's *I granatieri*, performed by an operetta company called E. Vitale. In fact, there was as strong presence of operetta in the repertory until the opera house was closed again in 1966. A variety of visiting operetta companies, among them U. Checchi & C., Pietro Lombardi & C., Pericle Palombi, Enrico Dezan, Raffaele Trengi, Angiolo, De Rois-Gandosio, and a group from the Palermo presented works by Oscar Straus, Johann Strauß, Emmerich Kálmán, Franz von Suppé, Romeo Dionesi, Charles Lecocq, Robert Planquette, Franz Lehár, Edmond Audran, such as *D'Artagnan*, *Le petit duc*, *Boccaccio*, *La fille de Madame Angot*, *Les Cloches de Corneville*, *Die lustige Witwe*, *Walzertraum*, *La Poupée*, *Czárdásfürstin*, and *Der Graf von Luxembourg*. Opera as also on the boards and besides the standard Italian repertory of Verdi, Giacomo Puccini, Gaetano Donizetti, and, of course,

Rossini, French opera, such as Jules Massenet's *Manon* (1905) and *Werther* (1908), and Ambroise Thomas's *Mignon* (1910), and German pieces, like Richard Strauss's *Salome* (1911) and Richard Wagner's *Lohengrin* (1920) graced the stage. In 1921, a special concert in memory of Enrico Caruso was held, with arias from Verdi's *Il trovatore*, Giordano's *Andrea Chénier*, and Puccini's *La fanciulla del West*, among others.

Riccardo Zandonai was a student of Pietro Mascagni at the Conservatory in Pesaro, and afterwards, he became the director and orchestra conductor of the Conservatory. During his tenure, he conducted many of his own operas, which appeared frequently on the opera house stage, among them *Giuliano*, *I cavalieri di Ekebù*, *Giulietta e Romeo*, *Francesca da Rimini*, *La farsa amorosa*, and the introduction of *La via della finestra* in 1919. Other less-known works were also staged, like Alfredo Soffredini's *Il piccolo Haydn*, Carlo Pedrotti's *Tutti in maschera*, Arnaldo Carloni's *Lezione amorosa*, and Giovanni Battista Polleri's *Cristoforo Colombo fanciullo*. On the occasion of the 150th anniversary of Rossini's birth, the Rossini Conservatory of Music and Rossini Foundation offered the maestro's *La gazza ladra* and *Le Comte Ory*, along with Arrigo Boito's *Mefistofele*. On a darker note, there was a celebration to mark the XXIII anniversary of the founding of the Fighting Fascists. The 1950s also saw some forgotten and unusual works like Pino Donati's *Corradino lo Svevo*, Adriano Lualdi's *Le furie di Arlecchino*, and Gaspare Spontini's *Milton*. The 160th anniversary celebration of Rossini's birth brought *Stabat Mater*, *Il barbiere di Siviglia*, and *Guglielmo Tell* to the stage. The 1960 season presaged the Rossini Festival with *La cambiale di matrimonio*, *Il Signor Bruschino*, *L'italiana in Algeri*, and *Il barbiere di Siviglia* which continued three years later with the staging of one of his more obscure operas, *Adina ovvero Il califfo di Bagdad*. In 1966, the theater was declared unsafe and closed. Large cracks were found in the walls, beams crumbled when pressed, and water was discovered in the subsoil. Fourteen years pasted before the Teatro Rossini reopened on April 6, 1980, with a concert by Luciano Pavarotti.

The Rossini Festival has produced some bizarre interpretations of Rossini's operas, like the 1992 production of *Il barbiere di Siviglia* which featured Dr. Bartolo as Dr. Strangelove, who spent most of his time operating on a statuesque cadaver, planted in the middle of the stage, surrounded by heavy drapes and oppressive furniture. The festival's press officer explained the production like this: "Rossini's original intent was a relatively serious piece. It is the directors who have imposed the slapstick on the opera." The work was repeated in the 1997 season, with the same director, Luigi Squarzina, and although the cadaver was absent, there was still the appearance of the macabre: the presence of skulls on a table, tossed like baseballs. In fact, it combined the gruesome with the ridiculous: Figaro rubbed Rosina's feet, servants rolled on the floor, breaking in through the window instead of the customary ladder, and the storm scene had no people.

Monumental productions take place in the Palafestival, and immense they are, at least the 1997 *Moïse et Pharaon*. With a budget of $800,000 for four performances, at $200,000 a performance, it was marred by excessive, irrelevant, and gratuitous activities and that distracted from the work itself, and demonstrated that British director Graham Vick knew of no other way to depict the Hebrews than to make then into stereotypical, Eastern European ghetto Jews, performing religious rituals. The opera, however, concerns Israelites, not orthodox Jews, and the updating was inappropriate, serving no purpose. Adding to the absurdity was that the Egyptians were dressed in space-age costumes. And huge mummies dropped from the ceiling to crush the Egyptian soldier, who then drowned in the "Red Sea." The Rossini festival offers the unusual and the different.

Teatro Rossini (Teatro Nuovo)

The Teatro Rossini was created in the early 1800s from the restructuring of the 1637-built Teatro del Sole. Pietro Ghinelli was responsible for the design. The laying of the cornerstone took place on April 25, 1816. Two years later, the Teatro Nuovo was inaugurated.

The theater of light mustard-tinted stone displays a Neoclassic facade with the main entrance marked by an arch order, topped by Doric pilasters flanking a window and crowned with scrolls. The horseshoe-shaped gold and ivory auditorium offers four box tiers topped by a *loggione*. Cherubs, bouquets of flowers and wreaths ornament the parapets. Ceiling decorations are

Teatro Rossini (Pesaro, Italy).

allegorical showing Apollo and the nine Muses, the work of Samoggia and Dalpane, and restored by Carlo Ferretti and Werther Bettini in 1980. There are 860 seats.

Auditorium Pedrotti

Auditorium Pedrotti dates back to 1892. Restored in 1995, it is a large classical Italianate building of peach-colored stone and white-framed Palladium windows. A pair of Corinthian columns flank the main entrance and the piano nobile exhibits a fine balcony. The shoe-box-shaped auditorium holds red velvet seats and a single tier, supported by delicate Corinthian columns. There are 500 seats.

Practical Information. Teatro Rossini, Via Rossini 37, 61100 Pesaro. Tel: 39 721 34473, Fax: 39 721 30979. If attending the Rossini Festival, stay at the Hotel Savoy, Viale Repubblica, 22, 61100 Pesaro. Tel 39 721 67440; Fax 39 721 64429. It is centrally located and close to the per-

formance venues. The hotel can assist with tickets and schedule.

COMPANY STAFF AND REPERTORY

Sovrintendente. Gianfranco Mariotti. **Direttore Artistico:** Luigi Ferrari.

Repertory (1901–1960). **1901:** La bohème. **1902:** La bohème, Rigoletto, La gioconda. **1903:** La gioconda, Faust. **1905:** Ernani, Manon. **1906:** Manon, Lucia di Lammermoor, La forza del destino, Il barbiere di Siviglia, Tosca. **1907:** La traviata. **1908:** Lucia di Lammermoor, La sonnambula, Il barbiere di Siviglia, Werther. **1909:** Werther, L'amico Fritz, Adriana Lecouvreur, Don Pasquale, La cena delle beffe. **1910:** Mignon, Aura, L'elisir d'amore, Cavalleria rusticana, Lucia di Lammermoor, Il barbiere di Siviglia, Carmen. **1911:** Salome, Il matrimonio segreto. **1912:** Andrea Chénier, Un ballo in maschera, La cena delle beffe. **1913:** La bohème, La favorita, Il barbiere di Siviglia. **1914:** Carmen, Il trovatore, Norma, Francesca da Rimini, Werther. **1915:** Lucia di Lammermoor. **1916:** L'occasione fa il ladro. **1918:** Cavalleria rusticana, I pagliacci, La bohème, Don Pasquale. **1919:** La cena delle beffe,

Rigoletto, La Wally, La via della finestra, Andrea Chénier. **1920:** Madama Butterfly, Lohengrin, La Cenerentola, Il barbiere di Siviglia, Fedora, Iris. **1921:** Manon, La fanciulla del West, Lodoletta, Mefistofele. **1922:** La traviata, Tosca, Giulietta e Romeo. **1923:** Aida, La gioconda, Ernani, La grazia. **1924:** Rigoletto, Manon Lescaut, Francesca da Rimini, La traviata, La Wally. **1925:** Lucia di Lammermoor, Lorely, I cavalieri di Ekebù. **1926:** La fanciulla del West, Francesco d'assisi, La Sulamita. **1927:** Francesca da Rimini, Tosca, Cavalleria rusticana. **1928:** Giuliano, L'italiana in Algeri, L'amico Fritz, Lucia di Lammermoor. **1929:** Il piccolo Haydn. **1930:** I quattro rusteghi, La Cenerentola, Madama Butterfly, Tutti in maschera, Lezione amorosa, La sonnambula, L'amico Fritz. Francesca da Rimini, Il piccolo Haydn. **1932:** Francesca da Rimini, Il piccolo Haydn, Cristoforo Colombo fanciullo. **1934:** Guglielmo Tell, Il barbiere di Siviglia. **1935:** La bohème, La sonnambula. **1936:** La farsa amorosa, Turandot, La serva padrona. **1937:** La traviata, Tosca, La via della finestra. **1938:** La bohème, Norma, Suor Angelica, Astuzie d'amore. **1939:** La favorita, I pagialcci, Manon, Tosca. **1940:** Francesca da Rimini, Manon Lescaut. **1941:** La gazza ladra, La traviata, Il segreto di Sussanna, Hänsel und Gretel. **1942:** La gazza ladra, Il conte Ory, Mefistofele. **1943:** Madama Butterfly, Fedora. **1945:** Il barbiere di Siviglia, Rigoletto. **1946:** Madama Butterfly, La bohème, Don Pasquale. **1947:** La traviata, Il barbiere di Siviglia, Carmen, Werther, Francesca da Rimini, Tosca. **1948:** Il trovatore, La traviata, Adriana Lecouvreur, Cavalleria rusticana, Pagliacci, Rigoletto, Il barbiere di Siviglia, Andrea Chénier. **1949:** Risurrezione, Aida, Il piccolo Haydn, Cristoforo Colombo fanciullo, Manon, La bohème, L'Arlesiana. **1950:** Ave Maria, Cavalleria rusticana, La fanciulla del West, Rigoletto, Corradino lo Svevo, Le furie di Arlecchino, Madama Butterfly. **1951:** La traviata, Tosca, La bohème, Milton, La serva padrona, Cavalleria rusticana, I pagliacci, Madama Butterfly. **1953:** Il barbiere di Siviglia, Madama Butterfly. **1954:** I cavalieri di Ekebù, Cavalleria rusticana, Pagliacci. 1955: La forza del destino, Tosca. **1956:** La Cenerentola, Il barbiere di Siviglia, Rigoletto. **1957:** Madama Butterfly. **1959:** Lucia di Lammermoor, Il barbiere di Siviglia. **1960:** La cambiale di matrimonio, Il Signor Bruschino, L'italiana in Al-geri, Il barbiere di Siviglia. **1963:** Il barbiere di Siviglia, Adina ovvero Il califfo di Bagdad. **1964:** L'amico Fritz, Madama Butterfly. **1965:** La bohème, Tosca, L'elisir d'amore, Orfeo ed Euridice, Otello, Ossia il Moro di Venezia. **1965:** Madama Butterfly, La traviata, Il segreto di Susanna, Cavalleria rusticana, Il maestro di cappella, Il telefono, Il Signor Bruschino. **Rossini Festival: 1980:** La gazza ladra, L'inganna felice. **1981:** L'italiana in Algeri, La gazza ladra, Stabat Mater, La donna del lago. **1982:** Edipo a Colono, Tancredi, Stabat Mater (Pergolesi), Stabat Mater (Rossini), L'italiana in Algeri. **1983:** La donna del lago, Mosé in Egitto, Il turco in Italia, Dixit Dominus (Vivaldi), Stabat Mater (Rossini). **1984:** Stabat Mater (Vivaldi), Le Comte Ory, Il viaggio a Reims, Petite Messe Solennelle. **1985:** Mosé in Egitto, Il Signor Bruschino, Maometto II. **1986:** Il turco in Italia, Bianca e Falliero ossia Il consiglio dei tre, Le Comte Ory. **1987:** L'occasione fa il ladro, Ermione, Stabat Mater (Rossini), Petite Messe Solennelle. **1988:** Otello ossia Il Moro di Venezia, La scala di seta, Il Signor Bruschino. **1989:** La gazza ladra, L'occasione fa il ladro ossia Il cambio della valigia, Giovanna d'Arco (Cantata, Rossini) Bianca e Falliero ossia Il consiglio dei tre, Requiem in Re Min. K 626 (Mozart). **1990:** Ricciardo e Zoraide, La scala di seta, Atelier Nadar. **1991:** Tancredi, Otello, Ossia il Moro di Venezia, Die Schuldigkeit des ersten Gebots, La cambiale di matrimonio. **1992:** Messa di Gloria, Semiramide, La scala di seta, Il viaggio a Reims, Il barbiere di Siviglia. **1993:** Armida, Maometto II, Di tanti palpiti. **1994:** L'inganno felice, Semiramide, L'italiana in Algeri, Stabat Mater (Rossini). **1995:** Guillaume Tell, La cambiale di matrimonio, Edipo a Colono. Messa di Gloria, Zelmira. **1996:** Matilde di Shabran, L'occasione fa il ladro, Ricciardo e Zoraide. **1997:** Moïse et Pharaon, Il Signor Bruschino, Petite Messe Solennelle, Il barbiere di Siviglia. **1998:** Otello (Rossini), Isabella, La Cenerentola.

Bibliography. Gilberto Calcagnini, *Il Teatro Rossini di Pesaro fra spettacolo e cronaca 1898–1966.* Antonio Brancati, *Vicende architettoniche e struttutali del Teatro Rossini di Pesaro* (Pesaro, 1985). Karyl Lynn Zietz, *Rossini on the Beach, Opera News* May 1993.

Thanks to Simona Barabesi, Rossini Festival; and F. Artegiani, and Marcucci Pinoli.

PIACENZA

Teatro Municipale (Teatro di Tradizione)

The world premiere of Giovanni Simone Mayr's *Zamori* inaugurated the Teatro Municipale on October 10, 1804. Fireworks marked the festive occasion which lasted to well past midnight. Lotario Tomba designed the structure.

By 1641, Piacenza had developed a taste for

musical performances, hosting the ballet *La vittoria d'Amore* with music by Claudio Monteverdi. Three years later, a theater was erected, Teatro Gotica, which survived until 1720. Another theater, Teatro Saline, had been constructed in 1595. It was so named because there were salt deposits under the building. Although this theater lasted until 1804, by the mid–1700s it was in a terrible state of disrepair. A third theater, Teatro Cittadella (also called Teatro Ducale della Cittadella) was erected in the first half of the 17th century which succumbed to fire on December 24, 1798.

After the Municipale opened, the principal opera season took place during carnival, followed by a spring season and the traditional *fiera d'agosta* (end of summer holiday) season. The early 1800s saw Domenica Cimarosa's *Il matrimonio segreto*, *Gli Orazi e i Curiazi* and *Giannina e Bernardone*, Ferdinando Paër's *Griselda* and *La Camilla*, Giovanni Simone Mayr's *L'equivoco*, *Lodoïska*, *Che originali* and *Ginevra di Scozia*, and Giuseppe Nicolini's *Il trionfo del bel sesso* and *Traiano in Dacia* (Nicolini was from Piacenza.) The works of F. Orlandi, Valentino Fioravanti, G. Farinelli, Stefano Pavesi were also frequently on the boards. The 1815-16 Carnival season brought the first opera from Gioachino Rossini, *L'Italiana in Algeri*. Also offered were Cimarosa's *Il matrimonio segreto* and Pavesi's *San Marcantonio*. Rossini's *Il turco in Italian* appeared during the 1816 summer season, along with Cimarosa's *Gli amanti comici*. Many Rossini operas — *Tancredi*, *Il barbiere di Siviglia*, *La Cenerentola*, *Mosè in Egitto*, *Otello*, *La pietra del paragone*, *L'inganno felice*, *La donna del lago*, *La gazza ladra*, *Edoardo e Cristina*, *Aureliano in Palmira*, *Ciro in Babilonia*, and *Demetrio e Polibio* — graced the stage. The Municipale also introduced several Nicolini operas, including *La feudataria*, *Vitikindo*, and *Il trionfo di Manlio*. The 1830s saw a surge of operas by Gaetano Donizetti and Vincenzo Bellini enter the repertory. The year Bellini died (1835), three of his operas, *La sonnambula*, *Norma*, and *La straniera* were in the *cartellone*. His *Il pirata* had been mounted the previous season, and *Beatrice di Tenda* was seen in 1836. Both Donizetti's well-known and less-known works, like *Anna Bolena*, *L'elisir d'amore*, *Parisina*, *Belisario*, *Gemma di Vergy*, *Olivo e Pasquale*, and *Il furioso all'isola di S. Domingo* graced the stage. Operas of two other contemporary composers, Saverio Mercadante and Luigi Ricci were also mounted.

As the second half of the century began,

Giuseppe Verdi works were firmly entrenched in the repertory, opening every carnival season for the decade: *Attila* (1849-50), *I masnadieri* (1850-51), *Luisa Miller* (1851-52), *Il corsaro* (1852-53), *Rigoletto* (1853-54), *Il trovatore* (1854-55), *Macbeth* (1855-56), *La traviata* (1856-57), *Aroldo* (1858-59). (There was no 1857-58 carnival season.) Up to the present, Verdi has been the composer most performed and most acclaimed at the Municipale.

On December 26, 1863, the Municipale hosted the world premiere of Amilcare Ponchielli's *Roderico Re dei Goti*. Ponchielli had been the director of the Municipale Band of Piacenza. His more memorable *La gioconda* was offered in 1885. The opera house closely followed the operas from the *verismo* school, perhaps, influenced by the librettist Luigi Illica who lived in Piacenza. Among his *verismo* libretti were Puccini's *La bohème*, *Tosca*, and *Madama Butterfly* (with Giuseppe Giacosa), Mascagni's *Iris* and *Isabeau*, Giordani's *Andrea Chénier* and *Siberia*, Catalini's *La Wally*, and Alberto Franchetti's *Germania*. Within two years of its world premiere in Rome, Pietro Mascagni's *Cavalleria rusticana* reached the Municipale and was triumphantly received; less welcome was Giacomo Puccini's *Le Villi* in 1893. Other works included Puccini's *Manon Lescaut*, Ruggero Leoncavallo's *I pagliacci*, and Catalini's *Loreley*. Mascagni directed his *I piccolo Marat* for Carnival 1922-23. Noteworthy French and German works were also staged, including Charles Gounod's *Faust*, Georges Bizet's *Carmen* and *Les pêcheur de perles*, Berlioz's *Le damnation de Faust*, Giacomo Meyerbeer's *L'Africaine*, Richard Wagner's *Lohengrin*, *Tristan und Isolde*, and *Tannhäuser* and even Karl Goldmark's *Die Königin von Saba*. During the 20th century the opera house hosted the world premieres of several operas, including A. Zanella's *La sulamita*, L. Ferrari Trecate's *Ciottolino*, Zanaboni's *Myrica*, L. Gorgni's *Il sacrifizio*, R. Rossi's *I commediante alla corte di Francia*, and G. Zanaboni's *Casello 83*.

The repertory of the 1990s is almost exclusively Italian with two known operas and one lesser known work, sometimes from a famous composer, like Verdi's *I Lombardi alla prima crociata* or (a best forgotten) Donizetti's *Linda di Chamounix*. Most are co-productions with Teatro Comunale di Modena or Teatro Comunale di Bologna. Despite the promising offerings, the performances can be disappointing, lacking the professionalism seen in the larger houses, with (some) singers breaking character to acknowledge applause. But the co-productions can be interesting. Donizetti's *Linda di Chamounix* flowed seemlessly from location to location by creative use of screens, and a couple of props to suggest the place. With the exception of the title role, sung by Mariella Devia, who possesses a world-class voice and "brought the house down" with her performance, all the other singers were mediocre, with one hapless tenor being literally booed off the stage at his curtain call. Recent works include Puccini's *Manon Lescaut*, Verdi's *I masnadieri*, and Rossini's *L'italiana in Algeri*.

Teatro Municipale

At the dawn of the 19th century, Piacenza needed a new theater. On April 4, 1802, Pietro La Boubée submitted the first drawings, which were inspired by Giuseppe Piermarini's La Scala (Milan), only 45 miles to the north. Within a few months, problems arose and Boubée withdrew his project. The work went to the Piacenzese architect Tomba. The interior design was the work of Signor Bracciologna and Signor Antonini.

The Neoclassic facade of today was added in 1830, from a design left by Tomba and modified by Alessandro Sanquirico. Similar in color to La Scala's, it has a center portico of four off-white Ionic columns supporting a pediment, complemented by four engaged Ionic columns. The tympanum, bordered by dentils, displays the crest of Piacenza. There is a double arcade topped by a balcony with a balustrade. The auditorium is a three-quarter ellipse, with four tiers and a loggia. There is a large central royal box. The original color scheme was ivory and gold, with blue silk in all boxes. In 1856, pink silk replaced the blue, with green valences. This color scheme remains today. The seats are a deep plush red. Gilded designs decorate the tiers, and gilded pilasters embellish the proscenium boxes. An allegorically inspired painting ornaments the ceiling dome. There are approximately 1,000 seats.

Practical Information. Teatro Municipale, Via Verdi 41, Piacenza. Tel: 39 523 492-251, Fax 39 523 492-253. When visiting the Teatro Municipale or archives, stay at the Grande Albergo

Teatro Municipale (Piacenza, Italy).

Teatro Municipale auditorium (Piacenza, Italy).

Roma, Via Cittadella, 14, Piacenza. Tel: 39 523 323-201, Fax 39 523 330-548. The Grande Albergo Roma is where the artists stay when they perform at the Municipale. It is centrally located and can assist with tickets, schedules, and archival visits.

WORLD PREMIERES

World Premieres. G.S. Mayr's *Zamori ossia l'eroe delle Indie*, September 9, 1804; G. Nicolini's *La feudataria* January 18, 1812. G. Nicolini's *Vitikindo* February 6, 1813; G. Nicolini's *Il trionfo di Manlio* March 2, 1833. A. Costamagna's *È pazza* May 1837. F. Besanzoni's *Ruy Blas*, 1843. A. Buzzi's *L'indovino* February 22, 1862. A. Ponchielli's *Roderico Re dei Goti*, December 26, 1863. F.G. Piazzano's *Carlo il temerario* February 28, 1867. L. Chessi's *La contessa di Medina* April 21, 1867. G. Marcarini's *Francesca da Rimini* February 2, 1870. E. Guindani's *Agnese* February 27,

1878. S. Auteri-Manzocchi's *Stella* May 22, 1880. G. Bolzoni's *Jella* July 30, 1881. L. Romaniello's *Alda* January 30, 1896. A. Zanella's *La sulamita* February 11, 1926. L. Ferrari Trecate's *Ciottolino* May 14, 1927. G. Pallastrelli's *Prezzemolina* May 29, 1927. F. Morini's *La Vindice* May 22, 1946. G. Zanaboni's *Myrica* February 2, 1949. G. Zanaboni's *La regina delle nevi* February 10, 1955. L. Gorgni's *Il sacrifizio* on March 16, 1957. R. Rossi's *I commediante alla corte di Francia* January 12 1960. L. Gorgni's *Poi sarà l'alba* January 14, 1961. G. Zanaboni's *Casello 83* January 5, 1963.

Bibliography. Maria Giovanna Forlani, *Il teatro Municipale di Piacenza (1804–1984)* (Piacanza, 1985); Various Authors, *Teatri Sotrici in Emilia Romagna* (Bologna, 1982); *La Storia del Teatro Municipale di Piacenza* (Piacenza, 1994). A. Rapetti, *Cronologia degli spettacoli in Piacenza dal 1230 al 1890* (Piacenza, V.T.P., 1943). *La curiosa storia del teatro delle Saline in Libertà* (1951).

Thanks to Paolo Baldini, Teatro Municipale, and Elena Prati.

PISA

Teatro Verdi
(Teatro di Tradizione)

The Teatro Verdi, originally called Regio Teatro Nuovo, was inaugurated on November 12, 1867, with Gioachino Rossini's *Guglielmo Tell* featuring Amelia Colombo, Remigio Bartolini,

Vincenzo Quintili Leoni. The idea to build another theater arose (Pisa already had two theaters, Teatro Rossi and the Politeama) because Pisa wanted a spacious opera house "similar to the Teatro Pergola in Florence." The architect was Andrea Scala of Venice.

The Teatro Rossi was constructed in 1770 by the noble family Prini and designed by architect, Oreste Cacconi with four tiers of boxes, twenty boxes on each tier. Niccolò Piccinni's *L'astratto, ovvero il giocator fortunato* inaugurated the theater in 1773. A quarter of a century later, in 1798, it passed to the Costanti Academy and in 1822 to Ravvivati Academy. Nicola Vaccai's *Giulietta e Romeo* graced the stage in 1831 to celebrate the visit of the Bey of Algeria. Vincenzo Bellini's *La straniera* was presented the next year, but was not well received. A local music critic called the voices "ugly," and pandemonium broke out among the spectators because of the poor quality of the singing. The police were called to quell the riot, and several rioters were arrested. Mediocre executions of Gaetano Donizetti's *L'elisir d'amore* in 1833 necessitated the police being called in again to break-up disturbances. Then on January 23, 1838, the world premiere of Luigi Casamorata's *Iginia d'Asti* took place, followed by Jozef Poniatowski's *Don Deserio* on December 26, 1840. The flooding of the Po River in 1867 caused the closing of Teatro Rossi for three years, to repair water damage to the orchestra level. Although Bellini's *Norma* reopened the theater in 1870, its doors remained open a scant two years before major structural work caused its closing again. The name, Teatro Rossi, was assumed in 1878 to honor the author from Livorno, Ernesto Rossi, and to indicate a change in direction. (It was previously known as the Teatro Ravvivati from its association with the Ravvivati Academy.) It became primarily a home for drama, although opera made an occasional appearance until 1929, when Rossini's *Il barbiere di Siviglia* was the last opera. Three years later the Società, which owned the building, went bankrupt, which led to its sale at a public auction. It changed hands a few times before it closed its shutters reopening only in 1946.

The Politeama Pisano was inaugurated in 1865 by Luigi Ricci's *Crispino e la comare*. Designed by Florido Galli, it was immense, seating more than 2,000. It hosted not only opera but operetta, and in the 20th century, cinema. During its rather uneventful opera career, which saw mainly works by Rossini, Bellini, Donizetti, and Giuseppe Verdi, there were two noteworthy events: Pietro Mascagni conducting his *Lodoletta* in 1931, and returning the next year to lead his *Pinotta* and *Cavalleria rusticana*. It was destroyed in a bombing raid on May 31, 1942, and not rebuilt.

After the Regio Teatro Nuovo opened in 1867, the Società (boxholders who owned the theater) supported four seasons of opera during the first half of the century—Carnival, Lent, Spring, and Fall. Then in 1876, an 18-year-old Giacomo Puccini walked from Lucca (12 miles away) to attended a performance of Verdi's *Aida* at the Regio that played a pivotal role in his life. He was so fascinated by the work that after the performance he decided to devote his life to writing opera (or so legend goes). Twenty-one years later, in 1887, the first performance in Pisa of his *Le Villi* took place. During the 1894 Lent opera season, a 27-year-old Arturo Toscanini conducted Puccini's *Manon Lescaut* and Verdi's *Otello*. The following year Verdi's *Falstaff* and Alberto Franchetti's *Cristoforo Colombo* graced the stage. Already acclaimed as one of the world's great conductors, Toscanini was so successful that these two seasons were repeated. Puccini even came to hear his *Manon Lescaut* and Verdi telegraphed his compliments to the maestro. The Pisa premiere of Pietro Mascagni's *Cavalleria rusticana* took place in 1891, followed by his *L'amico Fritz* in 1906. Baritone Titta Ruffo, a resident of Pisa, made his Pisa debut in 1901 in Verdi's *Otello*.

The Regio Teatro Nuovo changed its name to Teatro Verdi in 1904, in honor of Giuseppe Verdi, who had died three years earlier. The Società del Teatro dissolved itself in 1935, and the Verdi passed to the Comune of Pisa. At the same time, the 4th and 5th box tiers were transformed into a galleria and loggione. This also improved the acoustics. Ottorino Respighi came that same year to conduct his *La fiamma*, followed by the arrival of Riccardo Zandonai to lead his *La farsa amorosa* in 1936. He was again on the podium in 1939, conducting his better known opera *Francesca da Rimini*. Beniamino Gigli visited Teatro Verdi in 1939 for Giordani's *Andrea Chénier*, and legend has it that as soon as he saw the opera house, he exclaimed, "This is a theater designed for my voice." Tito Schipa sang in Donizetti's *L'elisir d'amore* in 1942; the next year, Mario del Monaco appeared in Puccini's *Manon Lescaut* and Mascagni's *Cavalleria rusticana*, and Giuseppe di Stefano's performed in Georges Bizet's *Les pêcheur de perles* in 1947, returning in 1953 for *La bohème*. In 1950, Maria Callas sang Tosca, and her Cavaradossi was tenor Galliano Masini. The intermission between the first and second acts was unusually long. Apparently Masini had not yet been paid, so he marched to Callas's dressing room and asked if she had received her fee. Upon hearing that she had, he exclaimed, "If they do not pay me now as well, they will not be able to shoot Cavaradossi this evening." Someone pulled out his check book, but Masini wanted cash, and until he cashed the check, the second act of the opera could not go on.

In 1961, Teatro Verdi was recognized as a "teatro di tradizione" and received some financial benefit. There was a major restoration between 1985–89 under the direction of architect Massino Carmassi. During the closure of the Verdi, opera took place at the Teatro Tenda (Tent Theater). Actually a theater of canvas, The Tenda usually hosted rock concerts. The world premiere of Roberto de Simone's *Mistero e processo di Giovanna d'Arco* reopened the Teatro Verdi on October 26, 1989. It was not until the end of the 1980s that the operas of Wolfgang Amadeus Mozart reached Pisa, with *Le nozze di Figaro* and *Così fan tutte* on the boards. The 1990s offered his *Idomeneo* and *Die Zauberflöte*. By the mid–1990s, the repertory had expanded and works from the 17th century through the 20th century graced the stage. The 1996 season included Gluck's *Orfeo ed Euridice*, Puccini's *Manon Lescaut*, Monteverdi's *Il ritorno di Ulisse in patria*, and Rossini's *Il Signor Bruschino* and *La scala di seta*. The 1997 season concentrated on the 20th century with the world premiere of Manfred Gurlit's *Wozzeck* and Ildebrando Pizzetti's *L'assassinio nella cattedrale*. The singers are mainly young, up-and-coming, and willing to stay for the long rehearsal times, allowing in-depth preparation. Recent repertory includes George Gershwin's *Blue Monday*, Mascagni's *Cavalleria rusticana*, Bellini's *Norma*, and Puccini's

Madama Butterfly. There are plans to showcase operas inspired by Shakespeare, including Verdi's *Macbeth*, Zandonai's *Giulietta e Romeo*, and Ambroise Thomas's *Amleto*.

Teatro Verdi

Construction of the Teatro Verdi, then called the Teatro Nuovo (New Theater) began in 1865. The money came from the sale of the boxes to members of the Società. There were 119 boxes for sale. After fifteen months of construction, the theater was ready, despite a controversy which arose between the architect Scala and the engineer, Ranieri Simonelli, resulting in the dismissal of Scala and Simonelli finishing the project. Signor Bernasconi was responsible for the interior decorations of the auditorium, and Signor Quadri executed the stucco.

TEATRO COMUNALE G. VERDI, in large letters, stretches across the facade. There is a dentil-bordered pediment above it. Pilasaters alternating with arched indentures embellish the facade. The auditorium, ovoid in shape, holds 120 boxes divided among five tiers, including a center royal box. The tiers are decorated with gold and ocher colored stucco. There are plush velvet chairs of yellow ocher. The theater accommodates 900.

Practical Information. Teatro Verdi, Via Palestro 40, 56127 Pisa. Tel: 39 50 94 11 11, Fax 39 50 94 12 18. If visiting the Teatro Verdi, contact the Italian Government Travel Offices (ENIT), 630 Fifth Avenue, New York, NY 10011. Tel: 212-245-4822.

COMPANY STAFF

Direttore Artistico. Claudio Proietti.
Bibliography. Giampaolo Testi, *Quattro "puntate" per una piccola storia del Teatro Verdi in Pisa* (Pisa, 1990). Gino dell'Ira, *I teatri di Pisa (1773–1986)* (Pisa, 1987). Adami Giocomo, *I cento anni del Teatro Verdi (1867–1967)* (Pisa, 1967). Massimo Carmassi, *Il restauro del Teatro Verdi di Pisa* (Pisa, 1994). Fabrizio Sainati, *Teatro Rossi: Lo Splendore e L'Abbandono* (Pisa, 1997).

Thanks to Maria Beatrice Meucci, Teatro Verdi.

RAVENNA

Teatro Comunale Dante Alighieri (Teatro di Tradizione) *Ravenna Festival* (Summer Festival)

The Teatro Comunale Dante Alighieri (named after the famous Italian poet from Ravenna) was inaugurated on May 15, 1852, with Giacomo Meyerbeer's *Robert le Diable*, Giovanni Pacini's *Medea*, and two ballets, *La Zingara* and *La finta sonnambula*. Designed by Tommaso e Giambattista Meduna, the theater resembled Teatro La Fenice in Venice, the Meduna brothers' previous commission.

Ravenna offered, as early as 1556, a permanent place for performances in the room of the Palazzo Comunale (now the Sala del Consiglio or Council Room) where a wooden stage for the "Comedia" was built. Various rooms in the Palazzo Apostolico also were periodically adapted for public shows between 1615 and 1841. In 1702, the stage in the Sala del Palazzo Comunale was destroyed, and it was decided to construct a new public theater, the Teatro Comunitativo. Designed by Giacomo Anziani, it opened in 1724, in the Borghetto part of the city. The exterior was unremarkable, but inside, there were 97 boxes subdivided into 4 tiers, with an elegant Baroque decor. Fifty-six of its boxes had been purchased by the nobility, city, private citizens, and the church, with the nobility owning more than half. Between 1779 and 1782, the theater was enlarged. It was closed in 1857, destined for other usages. An interesting comparison to the Alighieri, where private citizens owned almost two-thirds of the boxes, with the nobility purchasing less than one third.

After opening in 1852, the Alighieri hosted many contemporary Italian operas by minor composers, among them Giovanni Pacini, Carlo Pedrotti, Luigi & Federico Ricci, Filippo Marchetti, Errico Petrella, and Achille Peri. Ravenna, possibly more than other cities, followed the latest fashion in opera and wanted the composers of the day. For this reason, the early masters of Italian opera vanished at times from the *cartellone*. Gioachino Rossini's works had already vanished from the Ravenna stage by the late 1840s, with the exception of *Il barbiere di Siviglia*, which was mounted in 1858, 1875, and 1878. By 1860, Vincenzo Bellini's works were nowhere to be found in the Alighieri repertory, except for a single *Norma*, staged in 1866. Until 1870, Donizetti's works were the most often in the repertory. Then only *Linda di Chamounix* (1875), *Lucia di Lammermoor* (1879), and *Don Pasquale* (1894) were on the boards. However, if one looks at the approximately 300 operas mounted between 1802–1902, half in the Comunitativo and half in the Alighieri, a third belonged to Giuseppe Verdi, (40), then Gaetano Donizetti (37) and Gioachino Rossini (28). Bellini followed (15), then another five to ten titles each were the work of Valentino Fioravanti, Domenico Cimarosa, Guglielmi, Giovanni Simone Mayr, Pacini, Gnecco, Saverio Mercadante, Ricci, Meyerbeer, and Petrella. An oligarchy of composers ruled the repertory at both of Ravenna's opera houses.

A French opera, however, had inaugurated the Alighieri, and the 1870s witnessed more of Meyerbeer's works — *Les Huguenots, Dinorah*, and *L'Africaine*. Other French operas followed, Charles Gounod's *Faust*, Georges Bizet's *Carmen*, and Ambroise Thomas's *Mignon*. Even German works, Richard Wagner's *Lohengrin*, and Friedrich von Flotow's *Martha* entered the repertory. At the end of the century, works from the *verismo* school were on the boards with Pietro Mascagni's *Cavalleria rusticana* and Ruggero Leoncavallo's *Pagliacci* in the spring of 1893, and Giacomo Puccini's *Manon Lescaut* and *La bohème* in 1895 and 1897 respectively. The repertory of the Ravenna Festival is just the opposite, filled with unusual and rarely performed works.

Ravenna Festival

The Ravenna Festival is a recent arrival in Ravenna, established in 1980 by Maria Cristina Mazzavillani Muti, the wife of renown conductor and artistic director of Teatro alla Scala, Riccardo Muti. Of course, with those connections, the festival attracted the top symphony orchestras, ensembles, and soloists from around Europe. Opera is not always in that league and it plays only a small role in the festival, which presents more than two dozen events. The repertory of the early 1990s offered rarely-performed operas, including Antonio Salieri's *Les Danaïdes*, Christoph Willibald Gluck's *La danza*, Luigi Cherubini's *Lodoïska*, and Donizetti's *Poliuto*. By the mid to late 1990s, there was more familiar fare, like Mascagni's *Cavalleria rusticana*, Modest Mussorgsky's *Boris Godunov*, and Verdi's *Attila*. If the productions will be staged at Teatro alla Scala, Muti conducts. Many works are by guest companies like the Marinsky Theater of St. Petersburg produced Mussorgsky's *Boris Godunov*.

A production of Verdi's *Attila* began with an effective pantomine during the overture, but the quality of the cast of mixed nationalities was average, except for Roberto Sanduzzi, and the technical aspects of lighting and stage effects were not as polished as one would have hoped. The sets, however, were monumental, of the kind seen frequently in larger Italian houses — symmetrical, geometric blocks, symbolically locating the action. The audience at the Ravenna Festival operas is unusual for Italy — they are quiet, sitting on their hands and not voicing any opinion, positive or negative. The uniquely Italian atmosphere was absent, most likely because a majority are foreigners.

Teatro Comunale "Dante Alighieri

The old Comunitativo opened in 1724. Although it was enlarged in 1782, it had become inadequate for the "dignity" of the city, and the requirements of the spectators. Around 1830, Ignazio Sarti was officially commissioned to prepare a project for remodeling and enlarging the Comunitativo, as well as increase security against fire. This would have given the city an almost new theater without major expense. Then something unusual happened. Passing over the "authorities" the first stone for a new theater, the "Alighieri" was laid on September 1840, with a buried slab of marble indicating that the architects were the Meduna brothers from Venice: SI POSERO LE FONDAMENTA DI QUESTO TEATRO NEL MDCC-CXL PER GLI ARCHITETTI TOMMASO E

GIAMBATTISTA MEDUNA VENEZIANI (One lays the foundation of this theater in 1840 by Venetian architects Tommaso and Giambattista Meduna.) Giving the commission to the Meduna brothers caused controversy with the feeling that if a new theater were to be built, there should have been an open architectural competition. The Meduna brothers arrived in Ravenna in 1839 and began work on July 9. The opera house was not inaugurated until 1852.

The Neoclassic facade of the Alighieri bears a resemblance to that of La Fenice — the four column portico, statues in niches, and Palladium-inspired windows. But there are differences. The Alighieri has Ionic columns, four statues, and is a buttery yellow color. La Fenice has Corinthian columns, has two statues, and is whitish in color. The horseshoe-shaped auditorium holds five tiers — three box tiers topped by two galleries. Gilded stucco music motifs, interspersed with clusters of Muses and angels, decorate the tiers. The seats are raspberry red, contrasting with the blue valences decorating the boxes. Above the proscenium arch are two angles flanking a gilded crest of Ravenna. There are 830 seats.

Practical Information. Teatro Comunale "Dante Alighieri, Via Mariani 2, 48100 Ravenna. Tel: 39 544 32577, Fax: 39 544 36303. Ravenna Festival, Via Corrado Ricci, 48100 Ravenna. Tel: 39 544 39585, Fax 39 544 34309. If visiting Ravenna, stay at the Bisanzio, Via Salara 30, 48100 Ravenna. Tel 39 544 217111, Fax: 39 544 32539. It is ideally located near the opera house. The hotel can assist with tickets and schedule.

COMPANY STAFF AND REPERTORY

Sovrintendente. Mario Salvagiani.
Ravenna Festival Repertory. **1980:** Turandot. **1981:** Otello. **1982:** Adriana Lecouvreur, Aida. **1983:** Aida, La bohème, La forza del destino. **1984:** Manon Lescaut, Simon Boccanegra, Il trovatore. **1985:** La fanciulla del West, Rigoletto, Cavalleria rusticana, Pagliacci. **1986:** Die Zauberflöte, Madama Butterfly, Lucia di Lammermoor. **1987:** Carmen, Messa Solenne (Rossini). **1988:** Messa di Requiem (Verdi), Turandot, Le maschere. **1989:** Don Carlo, La traviata, Falstaff. **1990:** Les Danaïdes, La danza. **1991:** Lodoïska, La muette de Portici. **1992:** Poliuto, Il matrimonio segreto, Stabat Mater (Rossini). **1994:** Norma, Il combattimento di Tancredi e Clorinda, Don Chisciotte, Purgatorio di Dante, Messa da Requiem (Verdi). **1995:** Nabucco (concert), Inferno di Dante,

Teatro Comunale "Dante Alighieri" (Ravenna, Italy).

A Midsummer Night Dream. **1996:** Così fan tutte, Cavalleria rusticana. **1997:** Attila, Boris Godunov.

  Bibliography. Paolo Fabbri & Nullo Pirazzoli, *Il Teatro Alighieri: Un'opera Veneziana a Ravenna* (Ravenna, 1988). Various authors, *Teatri Storici in Emilia Romagna* (Bologna, 1982). Giovanni Oliva (ed.), *Ravenna Festival 1996 & 1997*, (Ravenna, 1996 & 1997).

Thanks to Fabio Ricci & Giovanni Trabalza, Ravenna Festival; and Donatella Fabbri and Fabio Laghi.

Teatro Comunale "Dante Alighieri" auditorium (Ravenna, Italy).

REGGIO EMILIA

Teatro Municipale Valli
(Teatro di Tradizione)

On April 21, 1857, for the opening of the 1857 *stagione di fiera*, the Teatro Municipale Valli, originally called the Teatro Municipale, was inaugurated with the world premiere of Achille Peri's *Vittor Pisani*. (Peri was from Reggio Emilia.) Gaetano Donizetti's *Anna Bolena*, Vincenzo Bellini's *Norma*, and Giuseppe Verdi's *Simon Boccanegra* were also on the schedule for the Municipale's first season. The opera house was designed by Cesare Costa. Valli was added to the theater's name in 1980, in honor of Romolo Valli, a popular Italian actor.

Reggio Emilia can trace its musical roots to the 17th century, when the Teatro della Comunità was established in 1637, created by adding boxes to the large room in the Palazzo Grande del Comune known as the Sala delle Commedie. (Today the Palazzo is known as del Monte di Pietà.) It was used both for entertainment and for betting on the game of *pallone*. The newly constructed boxes were distributed to the city's residents. Gaspare Vigarani was responsible for the conversion project. More work was done in 1675 when the community constructed a box for the Duke, and five years later, an arch, for a performance of *La Tullia superba*.

A new theater, the Teatro di Cittadella, opened on November 4, 1722, with *Ifigenia*, a play by Jean Baptiste Racine. Musical works also graced the stage, including the world premieres of Nicola Porpora's *Didone abbandonata* (1725) and Antonio Vivaldi's *Siroe re di Persia* (1727). In 1738 a Ducal decree saw the theater repaired, but fire reduced it to ashes on March 6, 1740. Shortly thereafter, reconstruction began, financed by the sale of boxes. Ready in time for the Fair Season it opened on April 29, 1741, with a *prima assoluta*, Pietro Pulli's *Vologeso re de' Parti*, and a ballet. Christoph Willibald Gluck's *Demofoonte* was staged in 1743 before a five-year hiatus. Performances resumed in 1748 with Pietro Auletta's *Orazio* and the world premiere of Giuseppe d'Avossa's *Lo scolaro alla moda*. Giovan Battista Lampugnani's *Il gran Tamerlano* followed. Popular opera subjects during the 1700s included *Alessandro nell'Indie* with Leonardo Vinci's *Alessandro nell'Indie* (1733), Giuseppe Scarlatti's *Alessandro nell'Indie* (1753), and Tommaso Traetta's *Alessandro nell'Indie* (1762); *L'Ezio* with Niccolò Conforto's *L'Ezio* (1754) and Giovanbattista Pescetti *L'Ezio* (1764), and *Demofoonte* with Gluck's *Demofoonte*, Niccolò Piccinni's *Demofoonte* (1761), and Aniolo Tarchi's *Demofoonte* (1787).

The opera season was held every year during *fiera* (fair) and *carnevale* (carnival). Among the works gracing the stage were Baldassarre Galuppi's *Lucia Papirio*, Giuseppe Gazaniga's *La locanda*, Giovanni Marco Rutini's *L'olandese in Italia*, Pasquale Anfossi's *Gli amanti canuti*, Giuseppppe Sarti's *Le gelosie villane*, Pasquale Anfossi's *Li viaggiatori felici*, and Francesco Zannetti's *Le cognate in contesa*. Near the end of the 1700s and the beginning of the 1800s, the public favored Domenico Cimarosa's *Il matrimonio segreto*, *L'italiana in Londra*, *Il convito*, *Giannina e Bernardone*, and *L'impresario in angustie*, Giovanni Paisiello's *La frascatana*, *Le nozze disturbate*, *Il barbiere di Siviglia ovvero La precauzione inutile*, and *La molinara ossia L'amor in contrasto*, Nicola Zingarelli's *Giulietta e Romeo* and *Ines de Castro*, and Giuseppe Farinelli's *Attila*. In 1816, Gioachino Rossini's works began entering the repertory with *Aureliano in Palmira*, and soon became a dominate presence at the Cittadella — *L'italiana in Algeri* (1817), *Sigismondo* (1819), *La Cenerentola* and *Eduardo e Cristina* (1820), *Il barbiere di Siviglia* and *Otello ossia Il moro di Venezia* (1821), *L'italiana in Algeri*, *Il turco in Italia*, and *La Cenerentola* (1822), *La gazza ladra* (1823), *La pietra del paragone* and *Zelmira* (1824), *La donna del lago* (1825), *L'inganno felice* and *Torvaldo e Dorlisca* (1826), *Mosè in Egitto* (1827) *Bianca e Faliero* (1830), *Il Tancredi* and *La Matilde di Schabran* (1831). The beginning of the 1830s witnessed the operas of Bellini and Donizetti take prominent positions in the repertory, including *La straniera* (1831), *Olivio e Pasquale* and *Gli esiliati in Siberia* (1832), *Il pirata* (1833), *Anna Bolena* (1834),

L'elisir d'amore, *Il furioso all'isola di S. Domingo* and *Norma* (1835), *La sonnambula* (1838) and *Lucia di Lammermoor* (1839). Luigi Ricci was another popular composer with *Il nuovo Figaro*, *Chiara di Rosenberg*, and *Eran due ora sono tre* having been staged. Bellini and Donizetti dominated the repertory through the 1840s until Giuseppe Verdi entered the picture, with *Macbeth*, *Nabucco*, *I due Foscari*, *Ernani*, and *I masnadieri* on the boards. Also in the 1840s, two world premieres of Peri took place, *Il solitario* (May 8, 1841) and *Dirce* (May 20, 1843). Fire destroyed the Teatro di Cittadella in the early morning houses of April 21, 1851, after a rehearsal, earlier in the evening, of Peri's *La Tancreda*. Since the Fair was about to open, and it appeared impossible to hold a Fair without a theater, the city council voted on April 23, 1851, to construct a temporary theater based on a design submitted by Pietro Marchelli. By May 4, 1851, enthusiasm for the project had vanished and the fair was held without the usual opera performances.

On January 10, 1852, the Teatro Comunale Filo-Drammatico, a small, temporary theater based on the designs of Engineer Taganit, was inaugurated with Angelo Villanis's *Regina di Leone*. Giuseppe Mazza's *La prova d'un'opera seria* followed 21 days later. Verdi's *Rigoletto* was actually the preferred inaugural opera, but the minister scorned the opera, calling it immoral and prohibiting its staging. Noted singers of the day who performed in the Comunale Filo-Drammatico, included Maria Piccolomini, Settimio Malvezzi, Giovan Battista Bencich, Virginia Boccabadati, Carlo Baucardé, Geatano Fiori, Noemi de Roissi, Carlo Negrini, and Giovanni Guicciardi. The theater hosted several Reggio Emilia premieres — Verdi's *Luisa Miller* (1852), Donizetti's *Poliuto* (1853), Verdi's *Il trovatore*, Verdi's *Rigoletto* as Viscardello (1854), Verdi's *Giovanna d'Arco*, Enrico Petrella's *Marco Visconti* (1855), and Giuseppe Apolloni's *L'ebreo* (as Lida di Granata, 1856) — and the world premiere of Peri's *Orfano e diavolo* (December 27, 1854).

Verdi arrived in Reggio Emilia on May 10, 1857, a month after the Municipale had opened, to supervise his *Simon Boccanegra*, recently introduced at the Teatro La Fenice (Venice). He began immediately working, but it soon became obvious that the preparations could not be hurried, and another opera on the program, Bellini's *Norma*, was staged first. Verdi had arranged for

the principal artists, which included Luigia Ben-
dazzi, tenor Pietro Mongini, baritone Leone Gi-
raldoni, and bass Gian Battista Cornago. The
opening night of Verdi's *Simon Boccanegra* was
sold-out. The prologue was well-received, with
much applause, but the first half of Act I was met
with silence. Then technical difficulties prevented
the curtain from rising on the second half of the
act. Verdi leaped on stage, yelling "pull on it" to
the stagehand. When the stage technician replied,
"What is this pull?" Verdi retorted, "Go to the
devil." (As legend has it.) His *La traviata* (as Violetta) was more successful. Donizetti works were
also well represented at the Municipale with
twelve of them staged in the second half of the
1800, from the inaugural season's *Anna Bolena*, to
L'elisir d'amore, *La favorita* (as Elda), *Gemma di
Vergy*, *Poliuto*, *Linda di Chamounix*, *Don Sebastiano*, *Lucrezia Borgia*, *Lucia di Lammermoor*,
Belisario, *Maria di Rohan*, and *Marin Faliero*. His
Don Pasquale, *La fille du régiment* and *Rita* were
not staged until the second half of the 20th cen-
tury. The Municipale also hosted operas by lesser-
known composers, such as Nicola de Giosa's *Don
Checco*, Giovanni Pacini's *Il saltimbanco*, Peri's
Giuditta, Giuseppe Sinico's *Moschettieri*, Carlo
Pedrotti's *Tutti in maschera*, Domenico Lucilla's
L'eroe delle Asturie, Antonio Cagnoni's *Michele
Perrin* and *Don Bucefalo*, Valentino Fioravanti's
Don Procopio, and Serafino Amedeo de Ferrari's *Il
menestrello*.

French grand opera entered into the repertory with Charles Gounod's *Faust* on May 8, 1869,
followed by Giacomo Meyerbeer's *L'Africaine*, *Les
Huguenots* and *Robert le Diable*. Fromental Halévy's
masterpeice's *La Juive* premiered at the Municipale in 1884 and was repeated for carnival 1892-
93. The Italian repertory, however, dominated
with both Verdi and Donizetti works, and long-
forgotten pieces like Ferruccio Ferrari's *Maria
Menzikoff*, Ciro Pinsutti's *Il mercante di Venezia*,
Petrella's *Jone*, Pacini's *Saffo*, and Giovanni Mag-
nanini's *Giorgione*. The turn of the century saw
the Municipale premiere of Richard Wagner's *Lohengrin* on January 3, 1900, followed by *Tannhäuser*, *Die Walküre*, and *Tristan und Isolde*.

Meanwhile, another theater, Arena del Sole,
had opened in the city on June 29, 1892, with an
operetta *Le donne guerriere*, and a ballet, *Il re delle
tenebre*. It was located where the Piazza del Tri-
colore is today. Its musical offerings, however,
were not particularly noteworthy.

The Municipale was closed after the 1924-25
Carnival Seasons, for reconstruction. It had been
judged unsafe. Thirteen years passed before the
theater reopened with the Reggio Emilia premiere
of Italo Montemezzi's *L'amore dei tre re*. It hosted
several well-known artists like Magda Olivero as
Violetta in Verdi's *La traviata* (1940), Giulietta
Simionato as Suzuki in Giacomo Puccini's *Madama
Butterfly* (1941), and Tito Schipa as Nemorino in
Donizetti's *L'elisir d'amore* (1942), and Giuseppe
di Stefano in Jules Massenet's *Manon* (1946). In
1957, there was a special season for the centennial
celebration of the Municipale — Puccini's *La bohème*, Verdi's *Falstaff*, Wagner's *Die Walküre*,
Verdi's *Nabucco*, and Modest Mussorgsky's *Khovanshchina*. During the late 1960s and early 1970s,
the repertory became more adventurous with the
presentation of both new and long-forgotten Italian operas, like Gian Francesco's Malipiero's *Il
figiuol prodigo* and *Venere prigioniera*, Giambattista Pergolesi's *La serva padrona*, Ildebrando
Pizzetti's *Assassinio nella cattedrale*, and Luigi Dallapiccola's *Job*, as well as broadened with foreign
works like Richard Strauss's *Salome*, Leoš Janáček's *Kát'a Kabanová*, Bedřich Smetana's *Prodaná nevěsta* (The Bartered Bride), and Béla
Bartók's *A Kékszakállú herceg vára* (Duke Bluebeard's Castle) among others. The repertory in
the 1990s is still primarily Italian, with two popular works and one lesser known opera. Recent
offerings include Pacini's *Saffo*, Verdi's *Rigoletto*,
and Bellini's *I Capuleti e i Montecchi*.

Teatro Municipale Valli

The municipality held an architectural competition for the design of the opera house with
four submissions: Marchelli, Nicola Bettòli,
Francesco Vandelli, and Costa. The outcome was
based on politics, not on the best design. Marchelli was preferred by the community; Costa was
favored by the council and officially named the architect of the new theater. Work began during
the summer of 1852 and lasted for five years.

The Teatro Municipale Valli is a monumental Neoclassical structure with striking features.
The Palladian-inspired facade holds twelve Doric
columns which form a portico, above which fourteen Ionic pilasters alternate with thirteen classic
rectangular windows. Fourteen statues representing (from right to left, Sound, Comedy, Caprice,

Teatro Municipale Valli (Reggio Emilia, Italy).

Dance, Jest, Fable, Pleasure, Instruction, Truth, Virtue, Drama, Glory, Vice, Tragedy) line the facade. Bernardino Catelani was responsible for the decorative layout and the allegorical themes of the statues. The horseshoe-shaped auditorium holds five tiers. Gilded stucco decorations embellish the ivory-colored parapets. There are 106 boxes on four tiers, plus the center former ducal box, and the galleria. The ceiling, decorated by Domenico Pellizi, is divided into four themes: Melodrama with Metastasio, Pergolesi, and Bellini; Tragedy with Alfieri, Monti, and Maffei; Choreography with Viganò alluding to his *Le creature di Prometheo*, and Comedy with Nota and Cecchi. Alfonso Chierici did the stage curtain which depicts the "Genius of Italy descending from Olympus" with allegorical figures representing both the figurative arts and performing arts (Music, Tragedy, Comedy.) The seats are plush red. The hall accommodates 1,100.

Practical Information. Teatro Municipale Valli, Piazza Martiri 7, 42100 Reggio Emilia. Tel: 39 552 458811, Fax: 39 552 458822. If visiting, contact the Italian Government Travel Offices (ENIT), 630 Fifth Avenue, New York, NY 10011. Tel: 212-245-4822.

WORLD PREMIERES AND REPERTORY

World Premieres. (1645–1887) *L'innocente giustificato* (tragicommedia), Carnival 1645; *I contraposti amorosi ovvero I rotti inganni* (pastorale), Fair 1648; *Amor non inteso* (opera scenica) Fair 1688; F. Ballarotti's *Ottaviano in Sicilia*, Fair 1692; C. Pollarolo's *Almansorre in Alimena*, Fair 1696; C.F. Pollaroli's *L'Oreste in Sparta*, Fair 1697; C.F. Pollaroli's *L'enigma*, Fair 1698, *L'Ulisse sconosciuto in Itaca*, Fair 1698; F. Ballarotti's *La caduta de decemviri*, Fair 1699; A. Gianettini's *Tito Manlio*, Fair 1701; C. Monari's *I rivali generosi*, Fair 1710; S. A. Fiorè's *Il trionfo di Camilla*, Fair 1713; F. Gasparini's *L'Eumene*, Fair 1714; F. Gasparini's *Il tartaro nella Cina*, Fair 1715; A. Lotti's *Il Ciro*, Fair 1716; A. Bononcini's *La conquista del vello d'oro*, Fair 1717; G. Orlandini's *Le Amazoni vinte da Ercole*, Fair 1718: G.M. Capelli's *Nino*, Fair 1720; N. Porpora's *Didone abbandonata*, Fair 1725; V. Chiocchetti's *L'Andromaca*, Fair 1726; A. Vivaldi's *Siroe re di Persia*, Fair 1727; P. Pulli's *Vologeso re de'Parti*, Fair 1741; B. Galuppi's *Lucio Papirio*, Fair 1730; G. d'Avossa's *Lo scolaro alla moda*, Carnival 1748; G. Scarlatti's *Alessandro nell'Indie* May 12, 1753; N. Conforto's *L'Ezio* April 29, 1754; G. Cocchi's *Artaserse*, April 29, 1755; G.B. Pescetti's *Il Solimano*, April 29, 1756; T. Traetti's *La Nitteti*, April 30, 1757; A. Ferradini's *L'Antigono*, April 29, 1758; N. Piccinni's *Il Demofoonte*, May 10, 1761; T. Traetta's *Alessandro nell'Indie*, April 29, 1762;

P. Anfossi's *Montezuma*, May 29, 1776; (?) D. Cimarosa's *Attilio Regolo*, Carnival 1797; S. Nasolini's *Timoleone*, Fair 1798; *La morte di Decio* (cantata), Carnival 1799; A. Savj's *Il ritorno d'Alberto signor d'Este* (cantata) July 27, 1814; L. Savi's *Luigia e Leandro ossia L'amante prigioniero*, February 13, 1825; G. Sangiorgio's *Il contestabile di Chester*, September 26, 1839; A. Peri's *Il solitario*, May 8, 1841; A. Peri's *Dirce*, May 20, 1843; A. Peri's *Orfano e diavolo*, December 27, 1854; A. Peri's *Vittor Pisani*, April 21, 1857; A. Franchetti's *Asrael*, February 11, 1887.

Repertory. **1645:** Santo Alessio. **1648:** La finta Passa. **1668:** Il Giasone, Antioco, La Dori. **1670:** Artemisia. **1671:** Argia. **1674:** Le fortune di Rodope e Damira, L'Orontea. **1676:** La Stratonica overo Né stati o qualitade amor osserva, Il Girello. **1677:** Floridea regina di Cipro, Nel tacere giammi si trova fallo overo Fingendo si scopre il vero. **1679:** Tullia

Teatro Municipale Valle auditorium (Reggio Emilia, Italy).

superba, Gli amori sagaci. **1681:** L'onor vindicato o sia l'armisia gran dinastessa di Tauris. **1684:** La calma fra le tempeste overo Il prencipe Roberto fra le sciagure felice. **1685:** L'Anagilde over Il Rodrigo. **1686:** Alba soggiogata da Romani. **1687:** D'Odoacre. **1689:** Clearco in Negroponte. **1692:** Ottaviano in Sicilia. **1696:** Almansorre in Alimena. **1697:** L'Oreste in Sparta. **1698:** L'enigma, L'Ulisse sconosciuto in Itaca. **1699:** La caduta de decemviri. **1700:** L'odio padre d'amore. **1701:** Tito Manlio. **1710:** I rivali generosi. **1712:** La virtù trionfante dell'inganno. **1713:** Il trionfo di Camilla. **1714:** L'Eumene. **1715:** Il tartaro nella Cina. **1716:** Il Ciro. **1717:** Amici rivali, La conquista del vello d'oro. **1718:** Le Amazoni vinte da Ercole. **1719:** Il Bajazet. **1720:** Nino. **1723:** Mitridate Eupatore. **1725:** Didone abbandonata. **1726:** L'Andromaca. **1727:** Imeneo in Atene, Siroe re di Persia. **1729:** Parsa per musica. **1730:** Lucio Vero. **1732:** Amore e gelosia, Il regno posposto ad amore. **1733:** Alessandro nell'Indie. **1739:** Il Demetrio. **1741:** Vologesco re de'Parti. **1743:** Demofoonte. **1748:** Oraio, Il gran Tamerlano. **1749:** Madama Ciana. **1750:** Il Farnaspe. **1751:** Lucio Papirio. **1752:** Didone abbandonata. **1753:** Alessandro nell'Indie. **1754:** L'Ezio. **1755:** Artaserse. **1756:** Il Solimano. **1757:** La Nitteti. **1758:** L'Antigono. **1759:** La clemenza de Tito. **1760:** Il filosofo di campagna, Il Demetrio. **1761:** Il Demofoonte. **1762:** Alessandro nell'Indie. **1763:** La baronessa riconosciuta. **1764:** L'Ezio. **1765:** Gli sposi in maschera. **1766:** La cascina (intermezzo). **1767:** Il mercato di Malmantile, La donna stravagante. **1768:** La straniera riconosciuta. **1769:** La nozze disturbate. **1770:** L'olandese in Italia, La contadine bizzarre, La schiava riconosciuta, La nozze. **1771:** L'amante di tutte, L'amore senza malizia. **1772:** Lo sposo burlato (intermezzo), Calandrano, La locanda, L'astratto ovvero Il giocator fortunato. **1773:** La locanda, Amore artigiano, L'inimico delle donne. **1774:** La fininte gemelle, Li filisofi immaginari, L'isola d'Alcina. **1775:** L'amore in musica, La frascatana. **1776:** Il geloso in cemento, La villanella incostante, Montezuma. **1777:** L'avaro, Il marchese Tulipano, La vera costanza. **1778:** Le gelosie villane. **1779:** L'isola d'amore. La vendemmia, La discordia fortunata. **1781:** Il cavaliere magnifico, L'albergatrice, La scuola de'gelosi. **1782:** Il fanatico per la musica, L'italiana in Londra. Il convito, Gli amanti canuti. **1783:** L'italiana in Londra, La vendemmia., Il vecchio geloso, Li viaggiatoi felici. **1784**: Giannina e Bernardone, Le cognate in contesa, Giulio Sabino. **1785**: La statua matematica, Il matrimonio in commedia, Medonte. **1786**: La finta principessa ossia Li due fratelli Pappamosca, I pretendenti delusi o sia Tra due litiganti il terzo gode, Idalide. **1787**: Il due supposti conti ossia Lo sposo senza moglie, I due castellani burlati, Il Demofoonte. **1788**: Il barbiere di Siviglia, Catone in Utica. **1789**: Gli amante prova, L'impresario in angustie, Don Giovanni Tenorio o sia Il convitato di pertra, Enea e Lavinia. **1790**: L'italiana in Londra, I due baroni di Roccazzurra, La morte d'Abele, L'Artaserse. **1791**: La morte di Cesare, La Virginia, Giulio Sabino, La bella pescatrice, Il credulo deluso. **1792**: I singari in fiera, Il capriccio drammirico, Don Giovanni Tenorio, Il Pirro. **1793**: Le gelosie villane, Le cendemmie, Le astuzie amorose, La vendetta di Mino. **1794**: Il Cajo Mario. **1795**: Le feste d'Iside, Il conte di Saldagna. **1796**: La molinara ossia L'amor in contrasto, Giulietta e Romeo. La moglie caprissiosa, Il re Teodoro. **1797**: Attilio Regolo, Il matrimomio segreto. **1798**: Il Pigmalione (cantata), Timoleone, Il matrimonio segreto, La donna di genio volubile. **1799**: La morte di Decio (cantata). **1800**: Gli Orazj e i Curiazj. **1801**: Il ritorno di Serse. **1802**: L'Annetta, La muta ossia Il medico per forza, L'impresario in angustie, Zaira ossia Il trionfo della religione, Zaira ossia Il trionfo della religione. **1803**: La Merope. **1804**: La cantatrici villane, L'impresario in angustie, Ginevra di Scozia, L'impresario, Che originali. **1805**: La Virginia. **1806**: Il furbo contro il furbo, L'Andromaca. **1807**: La morte di Oloferne ossia Il trionfo di Giuditta (oratorio in musica), Lodöiska, Pignalione. **1808**: Ines de Castro, I Cherusci, La vendetta di Nino, Il Pigmalione (cantata). **1809**: Il Mitridate. **1810**: Trajano in Dacia, La prova di un'opera seria, La scelta dello sposo, I due prigionieri o La burla fortunata, Sisara e Debora, Fingallo e Comala. **1811**: I riti d'Efeso, Ser Marcantonio. **1812**: La guerra aperta fossia Astuzia contro astuzia, Le concenienze teatrali, Pamele, Adelasia e Aleramo. **1813**: Artemisia. 1814: Ser Marcantonio, I riti cherusci, L'adelina, l'inganno felice, Il ritorno d'Alberto signor d'Este. **1815**: I quattro rivali in amore, Amori ed armi, La prova di un'opera seria, Attila. **1816**: L'amor marinaro, Il convitato di pietra, Le lagrime d'una vedova, L'apre musicale. Aureliano in Palmira. **1817**: L'italiana in Algeri, La capricciosa pentita, Carlo Magno. **1818**: I baccanali di Roma. **1819**: Sigismondo. **1820**: La Cenerentola, Il Corradino ossia Il trionfo delle belle, Che originali, Eduardo e Cristina. **1821**: Il barbiere di Siviglia, Il finto sordo, Il filosofo, Otello (Rossini), Costantino. **1822**: L'italiana in Algeri, Il turco in Italia, Clotide, Tebaldo e Isolina, La Cenerentola, L'Adelina. **1823**: La principessa per ripiego, La gazza ladra, Aminta ed Argira, Odoardo primo re d'Inghilterra. **1824**: L'ajo in imbarazzo, La pietra del paragone, La burla fortunata, Zelmira, I misteri eleusini. **1825**: Elisa e

Claudio, La sposa fedele, L'Adelina, Luigia e Leandro ossia L'amante prigioniero, La donna del lago. **1826**: Ser Marcantonio, L'inganno felice, Torvaldo e Dorlisca, Il crociato in Egitto. **1827**: La sposa fedele, Roberto capo degli assassini, Le cantatrici villane, Mosé in Egitto. **1828**: Gli arabi nelle Gallie. **1829**: La Cenerentola, La Clotilde, I baccanali di Roma. **1830**: Il barbiere di Siviglia, Il turco in Italia, Corradino, Caritea regina di Spagna, Bianca e Faliero. **1831**: Il Tancredi. La Matilde di Schabran, La straniera. **1832**: Olivo e Pasquale, Gli esiliati in Siberia. **1833**: Il pirata. **1834**: Chiara di Rossembergh, Elisa e Claudio, Anna Bolena. **1835**: Il nuovo Figaro, L'elisir d'amore, Il furioso all'isola di S. Domingo, Chiara di Rossembergh, Uggero il danese, Semiramide, Norma. **1836**: Nina pazza per amore, Il barbiere di Siviglia, Eran due ora sono tre, Norma, I Capuleti ed i Montecchi. **1837**: Il furioso all'isola di S. Domingo, Un'avventura di Scaramuccia, Norma, Anna Bolena, Maria Stuarda, Il barbiere di Siviglia. **1838**: La schiava di Bagdad, Il barbiere di Siviglia, La sonnambula, La Cenerentola, Marino Faliero, Parisina. **1839**: La gazza ladra, L'elisir d'amore, Lucia di Lammermoor, La Cenerentola, Elema da Feltre, Lucia di Lammermoor. **1840**: Il contestabile di Chester (beginning December 1839) Il barone di Dolsheim, Torquato Tasso, Gemma di Vergy, La straniera, La sonnambula. **1841**: Il Belisario, Beatrice di Tenda, Roberto Devereux, Gemma di Vergy, Il solitario. **1842**: Norma, La Fausta, La sonnambula, Il giuramento, Saffo. **1843**: Nina pazza per amore, L'elisir d'amore, Otello (Rossini), L'ajo in imbarazzo, Lucia di Lammermoor, Dirce. **1844**: I Puritani, Torquato Tasso, Chi dura vince Maria di Roham, Beatrice di Tenda. **1845**: Le fille du regiment, Le prigioni di Edimburgo, Gemma di Vergy, Il barbiere di Siviglia, Il ritorno di Columella da Padova, La Betly, Lorenzino de Medici, I due Foscari, Ernani. **1846**: Nabucco, La sonnambula, Ester d'Engaddi, Attila, Ernani. **1847**: Linda di Chamounix, Il Columella, Eustorgia da Romanom I lombardi alla prima crociata, Beatrice di Tenda. **1848**: Giovanna di Napoli, Macbeth, Lucia di Lammermoor, Gennaro Annese. **1849**: I falsi monetari, Don Pasquale. **1850**: I masnadieri, I due Foscari, I lombardi alla prima crociata, Il Bondelmonte. **1851**: Maria de Rudenz, I due Foscari, Imelda de Lambertazzi. **1852**: La regina di Leone, La prova di un'opera seria, Luisa Miller, Ernani, La nuova pianella, Petly. **1853**: Don Procopio, Crispino e la comare, Polituo, Il trovatore, Don Pasquale. **1854**: I masnadieri, Il furioso all'isola di S. Domingo, Tancreda, Rigoletto (as Viscardello), I Puritani. **1855**: Orfano e diavolo, Il Belisario, I due foscari, Giovanna d'Arco, Il trovatore, Marco Visconti. **1856**: Fiorina, Il birrajo di Preston, Lida di Granata, Lucrezia Borgia (as Eustorgia da Romano). **1857**: Beatrice di Tenda, Il domino nero, Il barbiere di Siviglia. **Teatro Municipale** (By date of first performance): **1857**:

Vittor Pisani, Anna Bolena, Norma, Simon Boccanegra, Don Checco. **1858:** La traviata (as Violetta), L'elisir d'amore, La favorita (as Elda), Il trovatore, Gemma di Vergy. **1859:** Il saltimbanco, La sonnambula, Poliuto, Il lombardi. **1860:** Giuditta, Ernani, I due Foscari. **1861:** I moschettieri, I Puritani, Un ballo in maschera, Linda di Chamounix. **1862:** Tutti in maschera, Il barbiere di Siviglia, Don Sebastiano, Aroldo, Lucrezia Borgia. **1863:** L'eroe delle asturie, La forza del destino, Martha. **1864:** I vespri siciliani, Michele Perrin. **1865:** Crispino e la comare, Don Bucefalo, Marin Faliero, Don Procopio, Attila, I masnadieri. **1866:** Robert le Diable. **1867:** Il giuramento, Dinorah, La vestale. **1868:** Beatrice di Tenda, Tancreda, La muette de Portici, Maria di Rohan. **1869:** I Capuleti e i Montecchi, Faust, Isabella d'Aragona. **1870:** Belisario, La schiava, Ruy Blas, L'italiana in Algeri. **1871:** Il Menestrello, Macbeth, L'ebreo. **1872:** La Contessa di Amalfi, L'Africaine. **1873:** Les Huguenots. **1874:** Don Carlo. **1875:** Jone, Amore e Vendetta. **1876:** Cuor di Marinaro. **1877:** Maria Menzikoff. **1878:** Il mercante di Venezia, Il guarany. **1879:** Stabat Mater, Nabucco. **1880:** Saffo. **1881:** Giorgione. **1882:** Il conte di Chatillon. **1883:** Luisa Miller. **1884:** La Juive, I promessi sposi. **1885:** La fata del nord, Aida. **1886:** La Gioconda, Salvator, Guglielmo Tell, Carmen. **1887:** Asrael. **1888:** Mefistofele. **1892:** Mignon. **1893:** Trecce nere, I pagliacci, Cavalleria rusticana. **1896:** Sabat Mater. **1897:** Manon Lescaut, Andrea Chénier. **1898:** Manon, La bohème. **1900:** Lohengrin. **1903:** A basso porto, Severo Torelli, Otello. **1904:** Tosca, Germania. **1905:** Samson et Dalila, Fedora. **1907:** Siberia, Le fate bianche. **1908:** La Wally. **1910:** Patria, Madama Butterfly. **1911:** Werther. **1913:** Tannhäuser. **1914:** Die Walküre, La damnation de Faust. **1915:** La nave rossa. **1920:** La Cenerentola, Una partita a scacchi (First performance in Italy), Dejanice. **1921:** La fanciulla del West, Tristan und Isolde. **1922:** Il segreto di Susanna. **1925:** Francesca da Rimini. **1938:** L'amore dei tre re. **1939:** Turandot. **1940:** L'amico Fritz. **1941:** L'Arlesiana, Notturno romantico. **1941:**

La morte di frine. **1942:** La vedova Scaltra. **1948:** Raggio di Sole. **1949:** Ghirlino, Maria Egiziaca, I misteri Gaudiosi. **1950:** David. **1951:** Resurrezione. Messa da Requiem. **1952:** Boris Godunov, Manuela. **1953:** Donata. **1954:** Paganetta. **1955:** The Medium, La pietra nel pozzo. **1956:** La caverna di Salamanca, La finta semplice. **1957:** Khovanshchina. **1958:** Suor Angelia, Il tabarro, Gianni Schicchi. **1961:** Lo speziale, Rita. **1962:** Fidelio. **1963:** Lyubov'k tryom apel'sinam (The Love for Three Oranges), Le nozze di Figaro, Zolotoy petushok (The Golden Cockerel). **1964:** Così fan tutte. **1965:** Don Giovanni, Der fliegende Holländer, Prince Igor. **1966:** Pelléas et Mélisande. **1967:** Salome, Il figiuol prodigo, Venere prigioniera. **1968:** La serva padrona, Assassinio nella cattedrale, Kát'a Kabanová, Siegfried, I sette peccati (Ballet), Allez-hop!, Parita a Pagni, Il Signor Bruschino. **1969:** Un quarto di vita, Il matrimonio segreto, The Fair at Sorochinsk, Job. **1970:** Prodaná nevĕsta (The Bartered Bride), Řecké pašije (The Greek Passion), Dido and Aeneas, La voix humaine, Akékszakállú herceg vára (Duke Bluebeard's Castle), Il dottore di vetro, Il cordovano, Pikovaya dama (Queen of Spades). **1971:** Hänsel und Gretel, Katerina Ismailova, Ledi Makbet Mtsenskovo Uyezda (Lady Macbeth of the Mtsensk District), Il capitan spavento, Il pozzo e il pendolo, La fabbrica illuminata. **1972:** Porgy and Bess, Rusalka. **1973:** Eugene Onegin, Die Freischutz, Bastien, Bastienne. **1974:** Jenůfa, Leonora, Die Zauberflöte, Billy Budd, Il barbiere di Siviglia (Paisiello), Ognennïy angel (The Fiery Angel). **1975:** The World of the Moon, Halka.

Bibliography. Sergio Romagnoli and Elvira Garbero, *Teatro A Reggio Emilia: Vol I Dal Rinascimento alla Rivoluzione Francese; Vol II Dalla Restaurazione al Secondo Novecento* (Florence, 1980). Paolo Fabbri & Roberto Verti, *Due secoli di teatro per musica a Reggio Emilia: Repertorio cronologico delle opere e dei balli 1645–1857* (Reggio Emilia, 1987). Giannino Degani e Mara Grotti, *Opere in musica: 1857–1976* (Four Volumes, Reggio Emilia, 1976).

Thanks to Susi Davóli, Teatro Municipale Valli.

ROME

Teatro dell'Opera (Ente Autonomo Lirico)

On November 27, 1880, Gioachino Rossini's *Semiramide* inaugurated the Teatro dell'Opera (originally called Teatro Costanzi) with King Umberto I and Queen Margherita in attendance. Achille Sfondrini designed the new opera house, which was paid for by Domenico Costanzi, a wealthy builder. After Rome acquired the theater

in 1926, it reopened as the Teatro Reale dell'Opera with Arrigo Boïto's *Nerone* on February 27, 1928. Marcello Piacentini was responsible for the renovation.

In 1600, Emilio de Cavalieri's *Rappresentazione di anima e di corpo* was the first "opera" given in Rome. Agostino Agazzari's *Eumelio* was offered in 1606, followed by Filippo Vitali's *Aretusa* in 1620. Twelve years later, (1632) the 3,000-seat Palazzo Barberini opened with Stefano Landi's *Sant' Alessio*. Pope Clement IX then granted Count Giacomo d'Alibert permission to build Rome's first public opera house, Teatro Torre di Nona (commonly called Teatro Torinona), which was inaugurated in 1670 with Francesco Cavalli's *Scipione Africano*. The next pope disapproved of opera and closed the theater. Although the Torinona reopened in 1690, Pope Innocent XII had it demolished in 1697. Another theater, Teatro Caprinaca, opened as a private theater in 1679, but admitted the public starting in 1695. (Teatro Caprinaca's last opera, Giuseppe Verdi's *Ernani*, was staged in 1881.) Count d'Alibert's son constructed the Teatro delle Dame in 1717 for *opera seria*. Ten years later, Domenico Valle built the Teatro Valle, which hosted several world premieres — Rossini's *Demetrio e Polibio* (May 18, 1812), *Tovaldo e Dorliska* (December 26, 1815), and *La Cenerentola ossia La bontà in trionfo* (January 25, 1817); Donizetti's *L'ajo nell'imbarazzo* (February 4, 1824), *Olivo e Pasquale*, (January 7, 1827), and *Torquato Tasso* (September 9, 1833). It eventually became a playhouse. Teatro Argentina, built by Duke Sforza-Cesarini, was the largest of the three opera houses built during this era. Domenico Sarro's *Berenice* inaugurated the Argentina in 1732. The world premiere of Rossini's *Il barbiere di Siviglia* took place on February 20, 1816, with a hostile reception. Giovanni Paisiello's *Il barbiere di Siviglia* was still a favorite, and the audience resented Rossini's work on the same subject. The following year, Rossini's *Adelaide di Borgogna* was introduced on December 27, 1817, followed by Gaetano Donizetti's *Zoraide in Granata* (January 28, 1822), Verdi's *I due Foscari* (November 3, 1844), and *La battaglia di Legnano* (January 27, 1849). The Teatro Torinona was rebuilt in 1733, hosting performances until fire destroyed it in 1781. It was again reconstructed and renamed Teatro Apollo. The Apollo was refurbished in 1821, reopening with Rossini's *Mathilde di Shabran*, conducted by Nicolò Paganini. Donizetti's *Adelia* was introduced at the Apollo on February 11, 1841, followed by Verdi's *Il trovatore* on January 19, 1853. The opera house benefitted from Verdi's Neapolitan problems, (see Teatro di San Carlo entry) and presented the world premiere of his *Un ballo in maschera* (set in Boston) on February 17, 1859. (None of the audience knew anything about the city of Boston, so the incongruity of the opera taking place in the Puritan city was irrelevant.) The Apollo was demolished in 1879. for the construction of a Tiber River embankment.

In 1877, Costanzi first presented his concept for a new theater, a politeama "for the people" with seats for 3,000. No one liked his proposal and it was abandoned. After the razing of the Teatro Apollo, there was a need for a new royal theater, and a compromise was reached. It would be a "national" theater with the aristocrats in the first three box tiers and the working classes in the two large top galleries. After the Teatro Costanzi opened in 1880, Cencio Jacovacci became its first impresario. Under his tenure, two world premieres took place, Alessandro Orsini's *I Burgravi* on December 10, 1881, personally supervised by the composer, and Ferdinando Caronna Pellegrino's *Fayel* on June 10, 1882. The following year Edoardo Sonzogno took over the running of the opera house and held a competition for one-act operas, which Pietro Mascagni's *Cavalleria rusticana* won in 1890. It was introduced on May 17, 1890, and regarded as the Teatro Costanzi's first important *novità assoluta*. More world premieres followed — Stanislao Gastaldon's *Mala Pasqua*, Nicola Spinelli's *Labilia*, and Vincenzo Ferroni's *Rudello*. The next year, Mascagni conducted the premiere of his *L'amico Fritz* on October 31, 1891, but was not well-received. The tradition of pairing his *Cavalleria rusticana* with Ruggero Leoncavallo's *I pagliacci* was born at Costanzi in 1893.

Meanwhile, impresario Guglielmo Canori had taken over the management of the opera house, to which he brought Teatro alla Scala's world premiere production of Verdi's *Otello* in April 1887. Six years later, on April 15, 1893, La Scala's *prima assoluta* production of Verdi's *Falstaff* was staged at the Teatro Costanzi, and Verdi came as well. When the curtain fell on Act II, King Umberto I and Queen Margherita invited Verdi to their royal box where Verdi was enthusiastically applauded by the audience. On November 27, 1894, the world premiere of Pietro Vallini's *Il voto* took place, followed by Giacomo Setaccioli's *La sorella di Mark* (May 6, 1896), Mascagni's *Iris* (November 22, 1898), and Pietro Floridia's *La colonia libera* (May 7, 1899). Meanwhile, Costanzi had died on October 8, 1898, and his son Enrico took over the running of the opera house. The next important *novità assoluta*, Giacomo Puccini's *Tosca*, took place on January 14,

1900, with Leopoldo Mugnone conducting. Mascagni's *Le maschere* graced the stage for the first time on January 17, 1901. Nine years later the world premiere of Leoncavallo's *Majà* took place with Mascagni conducting, followed by Vincenzo Tommasini's *Uguale fortuna*, Alberto Gasco's *La leggenda delle sette torri*, and Domenico Monleone's *Arabesca*. Mascagni also conducted the world premiere of his *Lodoletta* on April 30, 1917, and his *Il piccolo Marat* on May 2, 1921, and Riccardo Zandonai conducted the first performance of his *Giulietta e Romeo* on February 14, 1922. The last world premiere to grace the stage at the Costanzi was Guido Laccetti's *Carnasciali* (February 13, 1925). At this point, the Teatro Costanzi had hosted around four dozen *novità assolute* during its 45 years of existence.

Meanwhile, outstanding artists of the era were performing on the stage of the Teatro Costanzi. Titta Ruffo made his debut in 1898 as the King's Herald in Richard Wagner's *Lohengrin*; Enrico Caruso made his debut the following year as Osaka in *Iris*, and on December 26, 1916, Beniamino Gigli, after whom the piazza in front of the opera house is named, made his debut as Faust in Boïto's *Mefistofele*. In 1917, Camille Saint-Saëns directed his *Samson et Dalila* with a company of French artists, and Ezio Pinza first appeared at the Costanzi in Jules Massenet's *Manon* on January 3, 1920.

Costanzi's son died on June 24, 1907, and the theater was sold to the Società Teatrale Internazionale (STIN) on July 29, 1908. The STIN then experienced money problems and sold the opera house to the city of Rome. The city closed the building for two years to convert one gallery into a box tier, install better stage machinery, hang a giant chandelier, and relocate the main entrance to via Viminale, the main thoroughfare. The theater's name was changed to Teatro Reale dell'Opera. The Teatro Reale dell'Opera had the support of Mussolini, so it thrived during the Fascist era, hosting, on the average, a premiere a year. Several composers came to dell'Opera to conduct their works, including Alfredo Casella for his *La donna serpente* on March 17, 1932; Zandonai for his *La farsa amorosa* on February 22, 1933; Ottorino Respighi for his *La fiamma* on January 23, 1934, and Giuseppe Savagnone for his *Il drago rosso* on March 28, 1935.

The acclaimed Russian bass Feodor Chaliapin made his debut on April 18, 1929, in Modest Mussorgsky's *Boris Godunov*. Many of Italy's renowned artists returned to their homeland during World War II, bringing prestige to dell'Opera. But Tullio Serafin, who was the director of the house at that time, staged the Italian premiere of Alban Berg's *Wozzeck* on November 3, 1942, an opera banned by the Nazis, who called it "depraved" and its composer a "degenerate." Serafin left Dell'Opera shortly thereafter.

The decades following the war saw important artists including Maria Callas, Tito Gobbi, Giuseppe di Stefano, and Mario del Monaco perform at the opera house, and since 1960, more than two dozen additional world premieres have been staged, in addition to numerous Italian premieres. Dell'Opera does not have as illustrious singers as in the past, but occasionally some grace the stage. The quality of the production depends upon the caliber of singers, conductors, and directors hired for the particular opera and can range from outstanding to disasterous. Recent repertory covers a broad spectrum of works from Georg Friedrich Händel's *Giulio Cesare* to George Gershwin's *Porgy and Bess*, including Ottorino Respighi's *La fiamma*, Wolfgang Amadeus Mozart's *Le nozze di Figaro*, Donizetti's *La favorite* and *La fille du régiment*, Verdi's *Nabucco* and *La traviata*, and Richard Wagner's *Parsifal*.

Teatro dell'Opera

The foundation for Teatro Costanzi was poured in 1879, and the theater was opened the following November. It acquired its current appearance after the city of Rome purchased the building on May 20, 1926.

The Teatro dell'Opera is a pretentious building of travertine stone, characteristic of Mussolini's architectural tastes. The severe lines of the whitish stone block facade are interrupted by elongated rectangular windows. A bronze bas-relief of the Muses crowns the building and TEATRO DELL'OPERA is inscribed on the portico. The gold and rose auditorium, adorned with lavish gilded frescoes of Muses and scrolls, holds four tiers of boxes topped by a gallery and a royal box. The opera house seats 2,112.

Terme di Caracalla

In 1937, the Teatro dell'Opera experimented with open-air opera at the Terme di Caracalla.

Teatro dell'Opera (Rome, Italy).

The response was overwhelming, and an annual summer season was started. The operas, given by the singers, conductors, orchestra, and chorus of the Opera di Roma, took place during July and August on a stage reputed to be the world's largest. These performances were stopped in the 1990s due to the damage caused to the archeological site.

Practical Information. Teatro dell'Opera, Piazza Beniamo Gigli 8, 00184 Rome. Tel: 39 6 481 601, Fax: 39 6 488 1253. When visiting the Teatro dell'Opera, stay at Le Grand Hotel, Via Vittorio Emanuele Orlando 3, 00185 Rome. Tel 39 6 47091 or 1 800 325 3535, Fax 39 6 474 7307. It is close to the Teatro dell'Opera. Le Grand Hotel can assist with schedules and opera tickets.

COMPANY STAFF AND
WORLD PREMIERES

Sovrintendente. Alberto Antignani.
World Premieres. Teatro dell'Opera: G. Mulè's *Dafni*, March 14, 1928; F. Casavola's *Il Gobbo del Califfo*, May 4, 1929; I. Pizzetti's *Lo Straniero*, April 29, 1930; F. Casavola's *Il castello nel bosco*, January 24, 1931; M. Persico's *La bisbetica domata*, February 12, 1931; E. Wolf-Ferrari's *La vedova scaltra*, March 5, 1931; R. Riccitelli's *Madonna Oretta*, February 3, 1932; A. Casella's *La donna serpente*, March 17, 1932; R. Zandonai's *La farsa amorosa*, February 22, 1933; E. Carabella's *Volti la lanterna*, January 3, 1934; O. Respighi's *La fiamma*, January 23, 1934; L. Refice's *Cecilia*, February 15, 1934; A. Bizzelli's *Madonna*, April 11, 1934; G. Guerrini's *La vigna*, March 7, 1935; C. Guarino's *Balilla*, March 7, 1935; G. Savagnone's *Il drago rosso*, March 28, 1935; F. Alfano's *Cyrano di Bergerac*, January 22, 1936; A. Bizzelli's *Il dottor Oss*, April 25, 1936; R. P. Mangiagalli's *Notturno romantico*, April 25, 1936; A. Lualdi's *Lumawig e la Saetta*, January 23, 1937; M. Pergallo's *Ginevra degli Almieri*, February 13, 1937; A. Ghislanzoni's *Re Lear*, April 24, 1937; F. Vittadini's *Caracciolo*, February 8, 1939; G. Mulè's *La Zolfara*, February 25, 1939; L. Rocca's *Monte Ivnor*, December 23, 1939; G.F. Malipiero's *Ecuba*, January 11, 1941; M. Persico's *La Locandiera*, March 17. 1941; G. Piccioli's *La tarantola*, January 3, 1942; G. F. Malipiero's *I capricci di Callot*, October 24, 1942; R. Caetani's *I'isola del sole*, January 30, 1943; A. Casella's *La rosa del sogno*, March 16, 1943;

R. Rossellini's *Racconto d'inverno*, April 22, 1947; F. Casavola's *Salammbò*, April 27, 1948; F. Alfano's *Il dottor Antonio*, April 30, 1949; B. Rigacci's *Ecuba*, March 31, 1951; A. Lualdi's *La luna dei Caraibi*, January 29, 1953; G. Guerrini's *Enea*, March 11, 1953; P. Canonica's *Medea*, May 12, 1953; A. Veretti's *Burlesca*, January 29, 1955; I. Pizzetti's *La Pisanella*, February 24, 1955; G. Marinuzzi's *Le accenture di Pinocchio*, May 26, 1956; V. Bucchi's *Mirandolina*, March 12, 1957; J. Napoli's *Il tesoro*, February 26, 1958; M. Zafred's *Amleto*, January 9, 1961; R. Rossellini's *Uno squardo dal ponte*, March 11, 1961; F. Mannino's *La stirpe di Davide*, April 19, 1962; O. Fiume's *Il tamburo di panno*, April 19, 1961; V. Tosatti's *La fiera delle meraviglie*, January 30, 1963;

F. Mannino's *Il quadro delle meraviglie*, April 24, 1963; V. Mortari's *Il contratto*, April 18, 1964; M. Zafred's *Wallenstein*, March 18, 1965; L. Chailly's *L'idiota*, February 18, 1970; L. Ferrero's *Marilyn*, February 23, 1980; L. Ferrero's *Salvatore Giuliano*, January 25, 1986; Sylvano Bussotti's *Fedra*, April 19, 1988; L. Ferrero's *Charlotte Corday*, February 21, 1989.

Bibliography. *Il Teatro dell'Opera di Roma* (Rome, 1990). Iole Tognelli (ed.), *Cinquant'anni del Teatro dell'Opera* (Rome, 1979). Vittorio Frajese, *Dal Costanzi all-Opera: Cronache, Documenti, Recensioni*, 4 vol. (Rome, 1978). Matteo Incagliati, *Il Teatro Costanzi (1880-1907)* (Rome, 1907). Mario Rinaldi, *Due secoli di musica al Teatro Argentina*, 3 vol. (Florence, 1978).

ROVIGO

Teatro Sociale
(Teatro di Tradizione)

Pietro Mascagni's *Iris*, conducted by the composer, inaugurated the Teatro Sociale on October 21, 1904. Designed by Daniele Donghi and paid for by the Comune of Rovigo, Cassa di Risparmio, and Società del Teatro, the Teatro Sociale was the second opera house to rest on the site. The original Teatro Sociale, known as the Teatro della Società, was destroyed by fire during the night of January 21 and 22, 1902. The first theater had been inaugurated on April 16, 1819, with Pietro Generali's *Adelaide di Borgogna*, a work written especially for the occasion, and interpreted by Violante Camporesi, Claudio Bondoldi, and Giuseppe Fioravanti. Sante Baseggio was the architect with Nicolò Pellandi responsible for the interior decorations.

The Teatro della Società was built due to the efforts of Antonio Roncali, who had obtained the authorization from the Austrian governor for its construction. The cost was 1.20000 Austrian lire. It held a large orchestra section and five box tiers with exquisitely decorated parapets. In 1823, the opera house featured Luigi Boccabadati in Gioachino Rossini's *Zelmira*. Nine years later, Vincenzo Negrini appeared on stage, followed by Sebastinano Ronconi in 1839 and Domenico Cosselli in 1841. The 1858 season offered Gaetano Donizetti's *La favorita*, Giuseppe Verdi's *Il trovatore* and *I vespri siciliani* (as Giovanna di Guzman).

After the fire and reconstruction, the Sociale hosted international artists, usually early in their careers. Two of them made their debuts at the opera house — Beniamino Gigli (Enzo Grimaldo) in Amilcare Ponchielli's *La gioconda* in 1914 and Renata Tebaldi (Elena) in Arrigo Boïto's *Mefistofele* in 1944. Gigli returned for Donizetti's *Lucia di Lammermoor* in 1939 and for Verdi's *Il trovatore* two years later. Tebaldi came back in 1948 for Umberto Giordano's *Andrea Chénier*. Other stars during the first half of the 20th century included Toti dal Monte in Gioachino Rossini's *Il barbiere di Siviglia*; Mario del Monaco in Mascagni's *Cavalleria rusticana*, Giacomo Puccini's *Madama Butterfly*, and Giordano's *Andrea Chénier* with Tebaldi; Cesare Siepi in Verdi's *Rigoletto*, and Maria Callas for Verdi's *Aida*. The repertory was mainstream Italian with the occasional French work, like Jules Massenet's *Werther*.

During the second half of the 20th century, the world-class artists continued — Franco Corelli in Georges Bizet's *Carmen* and Verdi's *Aida*; Magda Olivero in Puccini's *Madama Butterfly*, Verdi's *La traviata*, Riccardo Zandonai's *Francesca da Rimini*, and Renzo Rossellini's *La guerra*; Giuletta Simionato in Massenet's *Werther*; Alfredo Kraus in Charles Gounod's *Faust*; Ruggero Raimondi in *Faust*; Mariella Devia in Verdi's *Rigoletto*; Katia Ricciarelli in several operas including Giordano's *Fedora*, and Donizetti's *Anna Bolena* and *Lucrezia Borgia*, and Luciano Pavarotti in Verdi's *Rigoletto*.

Since 1964 the Teatro Sociale has been managed by the Comune Rovigo and the singers are no longer "star" quality. The following year contemporary works entered the repertory with Ildebrando Pizzetti's *Assassinio nella cattedrale*, followed by Rossellini's *La guerra* in 1966 and Rossellini's *Uno sguardo dal ponte* the next year. Béla Bartók's *A Kékszakállú herceg vára* (Duke Bluebeard's Castle) was mounted in 1972. Two decades later, the first modern production of Rossini's *Sigismondo* took place. Recent repertory includes Jacques Offenbach's *Les contes d'Hoffmann*, Donizetti's *La fille du régiment*, Puccini's *Madama Butterfly*, and George Gershwin's *Porgy and Bess*.

Practical Information. Teatro Sociale, Piazza Garibaldi 14, Rovigo. Tel 39 425 27853, Fax: 39 425 29212. When visiting the Teatro Sociale, stay at the Hotel Cristallo, viale Porta Adige 1, 45100 Rovigo. Tel: 39 0425 30701, Fax: 39 0425 31083. Located near the train station and opera house, the hotel can assist with tickets and schedules.

BIBLIOGRAPHY

Bibliography. Information supplied by the theater.

Thanks to La Sergretaria, Teatro Sociale, and Walter Marcheselli.

——— SAN GIMIGNANO

Festival Internazionale di San Gimignano (Summer Festival)

Opera in the Piazza in San Gimignano dates back to 1929. Giuseppe Verdi's *Il trovatore* with Lina Savi, Giomi Ruttisi, Aldo Lamperi, Gino Lulli, and Enrico Cantini, inaugurated the festival. The first season presented one additional Verdi opera, *Rigoletto*, with Renata Villani, Galliano Masini, Lulli, and Cantini. Vincenzo Marini conducted both works.

The second season also offered two operas, Gaetano Donizetti's *Lucia di Lammermoor*, and Umberto Giordano's *Andrea Chénier*. Although 1931 saw four works enter into the repertory, a permanent expansion of the offerings did not take permanent root until a few years later. Operetta was occasionally given as well, especially during the 1949 season, and the operas were essentially limited to mainstream Italian repertory, with a dominance of Verdi and Puccini operas, and some works from the late 1800s including Pietro Mascagni's *Cavalleria rusticana*, and Ruggero Leoncavallo's *I pagliacci*. Recently, works as diverse as Claudio Monteverdi's *L'incoronazione di Poppea* and Igor Stravinsky's *L'histoire du Soldat* have been presented. The festival has also expanded, offering concert works, jazz, pop, plays, and even cinema.

With artificial barriers and the hasty placement of seats, the Piazza of the Duomo becomes an open-air opera house, with the buildings surrounding the square serving as the walls, and even including an arch. The ceiling is the sky, often speckled with stars. Yellow and blue lights illuminate the soaring towers of the adjacent buildings, and a cooling wind sweeps across the piazza. The only negative is the air is filled with cigarette smoke from the predominately Italian audience. The musicians enter in front of the audience, and the opera begins. Some are fully-staged works, others are presented in concert form that capture the musical essence of the work. Different companies from around Italy are invited each summer. The Accademia dei Leggeri has staged Gian Carlo Menotti's *The Telephone* and Ermanno Wolf-Ferrari's *Il segreto di Susanna*, and the Accademia dei Concordi mounted Stravinsky's *L'histoire du soldat*. In 1996, the CEL-Teatro di Livorno staged Puccini's *Tosca* and Leoncavallo's *I pagliacci*. The latter works was in concert form, with Italian singers unknown outside of Italy. Recent offerings include Puccini's *Gianni Schicchi*, Francesco Cilea's *Gloria*, Georg Friedrich Händel's *Tamerlano*, and Verdi's *Il trovatore*.

Practical Information. Festival Internazionale di San Gimignano, Sala Consiliare, Comune di San Gimignano, San Gimignano. Tel: 39 55 219 851 or 39 577 940340. When visiting the Festival Internazionale di San Gimignano, stay at the Hotel L'Antico Pozzo, Via S. Matteo 87, San

Madama Butterfly, Tosca. **1937:** La bohème, La traviata, Cavalleria rusticana, Baronessa di Carini. **1938:** La giocanda, Monacella della Fontana, I pagliacci, Maristella. **1939:** Fedora, Un ballo in maschera. **1946:** Toaca, La traviata. **1948:** Madama Butterfly, Il trovatore. **1949:** Andrea Chénier. **1950:** Fedora. **1951:** Il barbiere di Siviglia, La traviata. **1952:** Cavalleria rusticana, Suor Angelica, Lohengrin. **1953:** Il trovatore. **1954:** Manon Lescaut. **1955:** Un ballo in maschera. **1956:** Tosca. **1957:** Madama Butterfly, Andrea Chénier. **1958:** Il barbiere di Siviglia, Il trovatore. **1959:** Otello. **1960:** Il trovatore. **1961:** Cavalleria rusticana, I pagliacci, Rigoletto. **1962:** La traviata, Norma. **1963:** Un ballo in maschera, Lucia di Lammermoor. **1964:** L'elisir d'amore, Otello. **1965:** Ernani, La bohème. **1966:** Il trovatore, Rigoletto. **1967:** Andrea Chénier, Madama Butterfly. **1968:** La traviata. **1969:** Il barbiere di Siviglia, Rigoletto. **1970:** Cavalleria rusticana, I pagliacci, Pierrot Innamorato, Medico suo malgrado. **1971:** La traviata, La bohème. **1972:** Madama Butterfly. **1973:** Il trovatore, Lucia di Lammermoor. **1974:** La bohème, Tosca. **1975:** Un ballo in maschera. **1976:** Turandot. **1977:** Rigoletto, Madama Butterfly. **1978:** Il trovatore, L'elisir d'amore. **1979:** Lucia di Lammermoor, La traviata. **1980:** La bohème, **1981:** Cavalleria rusicana, I pagliacci. **1982:** Il barbiere di Siviglia. **1983:** La sonnambula, La serva padrona. **1984:** Rigoletto. **1985:** Tosca. **1986:** Nabucco. **1987:** Lucia di Lammermoor. **1988:** La forza del destino. **1989:** Il barbiere di Siviglia, Così fan tutte. **1990:** Andrea Chénier, Le nozze di Figaro. **1991:** Madama Butterfly. **1992:** Don Giovanni. **1993:** Rigoletto, L'incoronazione di Poppea. **1994:** La Cenerentola. **1995:** L'elisir d'amore. **1996:** The Telephone, Il segreto di Susanna, Tosca, I pagliacci, Histoire du Soldat. **1997:** Gianni Schicchi, Gloria, Tamerlano, Messa da Requiem, Il trovatore.

Bibliography. Program from Festival Internazionale di San Gimignano: *Miti del '900,* 62a Stagione Lirica (San Gimignano, 1996).

Thanks to Patrizia Russi.

Piazza of Festival Internazionale di San Gimignano (San Gimignano, Italy).

Gimignano. Tel: 39 577 942014, Fax 39 577 942 117. It is in the center of the old town and close to the piazza. The hotel can assist with tickets and schedules.

REPERTORY

Opera Repertory. **1929:** Il trovatore, Rigoletto. **1930:** Lucia di Lammermoor, Andrea Chénier. **1931:** Cavalleria rusticana, I pagliacci, La bohème, Ernani, La traviata, Rigoletto, Il barbiere di Siviglia. **1932:** La bohème, Rigoletto, Ernani. **1933:** Cavalleria rusticana, I pagliacci. **1935:** Norma, Rigoloeet. **1936:**

Ente Concerti "Marialisa de Carolis" (Teatro di Tradizione)

The Politeama Verdi, originally called the Teatro Verdi, was inaugurated with Luigi Canepa's *Riccardo III* in December 1884. Cesare Sacuto was in charge of the construction.

The opera chronicle in Sassari began in 1830 with the inauguration of the Teatro Civico. The small theater hosted many unknown works which the public surprisingly appreciated. Gaetano Donzetti was a popular composer at the time and his lesser known works, like *Belisario*, *Gemma di Vergy*, and *Parisina d'Este* graced the stage. The public also welcomed Laura Rossi's *I falsi monetari*, Giacomo Ferrari's *Il portinaio di Parigi*, Saverio Mercadante's *Elisa e Claudio*, and Gioachino Rossini's *Matilde di Shabran* along side the more familiar like Rossini's *Il barbiere di Siviglia*, Giuseppe Verdi's *Rigoletto*, and Giacomo Meyerbeer's *Dinorah*.

When the Teatro Verdi opened in 1884, operatic activities shifted there, although there are indications that opera continued to be mooted in the Civico as well. At the beginning of the 1900s, Luigi Canepa founded the Istituto Musicale, but there was no much enthusiasm for opera and Giacomo Puccini's *Tosca* was performed in a reduced score for mandolin. Then Marialisa de Carolis, a pianist and conductor, moved to Sassari and founded the Ente Concerti, a merging of the Società dei Concerti and the Circolo Filarmonico Sassarese. The organization became a Teatro di Tradizione in 1967.

Some of the international artists which have appeared in Sassari included Luciano Pavarotti, Carlo Bergonzi, Perruccio Tagliavini, Niccola Rossi Lemeni, Karia Ricciarelli, Mariella Devia, Teresa Berganza, and Leo Nucci. Wolfgang Amadeus Mozart's *Così fan tutte*, Puccini's *Tosca*, and Jacques Offenbach's *Les contes d'Hoffmann* are some of the recent offerings.

Politeama Verdi

In 1878, the city demolished the Castel Aragonese to construct a new theater on the site. Five years passed before the first stone was laid, in 1883, but things proceeded rapidly after that with the theater completed by the following year. It held three box tiers and two galleries. The parapets and proscenium arch were decorated with floral patterns. After the arrival of cinema, the theater presented movies, and during one of the shows, a fire started which destroyed the theater. When it was rebuilt, it was modified to be adaptable for projecting movies. It was opened in 1926 after three years of work. The auditorium holds two box tiers, with a galleria and loggione. There are 1,100 seats.

Practical Information. Ente Concerti "Marialisa de Carolis," Viale Umberto 72, 07100 Sassari. Tel: 39 79 232 579, Fax 39 79 231 209. If visiting, contact the Italian Government Travel Offices (ENIT), 630 Fifth Avenue, New York, NY 10011. Tel: 212-245-4822.

BIBLIOGRAPHY

Bibliography. Information supplied by the company.

Teatro Comunale Chiabrera

Teatro Chiabrera was inaugurated on October 10, 1853, with Giuseppe Verdi's *Attila*. Designed by Carlo Falconieri, the theater took three years to build. Two thirds of the cost was paid by the boxholders and one third by the commune.

There was only one opera season, which took place during Carnival. The theater was managed by an impresario and subsidized by the commune. The repertory included both Italian and foreign works with singers like Sigorne Gruitz and Caruzzi, Tito Schipa, and Toti del Monte. In 1883, the commune became the owner of the theater, but 27 years later, in 1910, it stopped its subsidies and associations like Amici dell'arte and Amici della musica were formed to continue the seasons. Between 1954 and 1963, the theater was closed for restoration, and four years after reopening, the commune took over its management in 1967. The theater began collaboration with the Teatro dell'Opera Giocosa for its opera seasons in 1987 and several rarities were staged — Gaetano Donizetti's *Torquato Tasso*, *L'esule di Roma*, and *Il furioso all'Isola di San Domingo*, Gioachino Rossini's *Torlando e Dorliska*, *Ciro in Babilonia*, *La Gazzetta*, and *Aureliano in Palmira*, and works by Carlo Coccia, Giovanni Pacini, Giovanni Paisiello, Nicola Antonio Manfroce, and Giuseppe Appolloni. Artists like Daniella Dessì, Serra, and Gasdia have appeared on the Comunale's stage. An operetta season of three works was begun in 1996, in addition to the short opera season of two works. Recent offerings include Puccini's *Tosca* and Wolfgang Amadeus Mozart's *Le nozze di Figaro*.

Teatro Comunale Chiabrera

The facade exhibits a portico supported by four Doric marble columns. Above are four Ionic columns of marble and cement supporting a triangular pediment. The auditorium originally held three box tiers and a galleria, but after the 1950 restoration, the box tiers were transformed into balconies. The fresco dome ceiling shows figures and medallions. The theater offers 700 places.

Practical Information. Teatro Comunale Chiabrera, Piazza Diaz 2, Savona. Tel & Fax: 39 19 821 490. If visiting, contact the Italian Government Travel Offices (ENIT), 630 Fifth Avenue, New York, NY 10011. Tel: 212-245-4822.

COMPANY STAFF

Direttore. Roberto Bosi.
Bibliography. Information supplied by the theater.

SPOLETO

Festival dei Due Mondi (Summer Festival)

On June 5, 1958, Gian Carlo Menotti's dream of the Festival dei Due Mondi was realized. With opera as the festival's foundation, Spoleto offered Giuseppe Verdi's *Macbeth* in the Teatro Nuovo, directed by (a young) Luchino Visconti and conducted by (a young) Thomas Schippers. Four more operas were on the schedule for the inaugural season, two from the 1700s — Domenico Cimarosa's *Il maestro di cappella* and Giambattista Pergolesi's *Lo frate 'nnammorato*, and two by contemporary composers — Valentino Bucchi's *Il giuoco del barone* (costumes by Franco Zeffirelli) and Lee Hoiby's *The Scarf*. This would become indicative of eclectic opera repertory at the Festival dei Due Mondi. Menotti founded the festival to showcase the arts and discover new, young talent.

Documentation exists showing musical activities dating back to 1636 with a performance of Bernardino Campello's *Gerusalemme captiva*. Three years later, Ottavio Castelli's *Il favorito del principe* was given, either in the Palazzo Comunale or in a room in the prince's palace. Spoleto was one of the first cities in Italy and the first in Umbria to open a public theater. Two decrees gave evidence of this fact. The theater, constructed of wood and known both as the Teatro di Piazza del Duomo and Teatro della Rosa, was alluded to in 1667 regarding the opening of boxes to the public, and again in 1674, having been described as a theater with four tiers of boxes. It is presumed that this theater was located where the Teatro Caio Melisso stands today. "Modernized" in 1749, it reopened as the Nuovo Teatro di Spoleto with Nicolò Jommelli's *Ipermestra* in 1751. According to the custom of the time, the inaugural program also offered a ballet and another *dramma per musica*. The theater hosted illustrious guests, including Gioachino Rossini, who visited it on two separate occasions. One time he watched an opera from the box of Signore Gonfaloniere, commenting after the performance, "I give my best congratulations to the orchestra (consisting of all local talent) and my condolences for the singers." On another occasion, the composer from Pesaro slipped, unnoticed, into the theater during a rehearsal of his *L'italiana in Algeri* and substituted for the contrabass player, playing his part at the end of the opera to the entertainment of the public.

By the mid–1800s, the theater had outlived its usefulness. But only after the opening of the Teatro Nuovo on August 3, 1864, with Filippo Sangiorgi's *Guisemberga da Spoleto*, could the performances transfer out of the Di Spoleto. By 1880, on the same location as the Di Spoleto, a new, masonry theater was constructed, called the Teatro Caio Melisso. With two theaters hosting operatic activities, artists like Isabella Galletti, Rosina Stolts, Gemma Bellincioni, Riccardo Stracciari, Elbira de Hidalgo, Conchita Supervia, Tito Schipa, and Beniamino Gigli could be heard in Spoleto.

The existence of the two theaters, Teatro Nuovo and Teatro Caio Melisso, made Spoleto a good place to establish a festival. Francis Menotti, Gian Carlo Menotti's adopted son, explained why Spoleto was selected, "Art is not entertainment, but an offspring of society. Artists are important in the community and essential in its development. Gian Carlo was looking for a ancient, quiet town with a theater that needed him. Spoleto was forgotten and on the verge of bankruptcy, an ideal match. He went to the mayor of the town and said, 'You need money. If I establish a festival here, it will give the town money, plenty of it.'" Menotti made the necessary arrangements with town and brought in the money. By employing unknown artists, the festival was both affordable and able to do the unusual, the experimental, the avant-garde. Menotti searched for creative people, especially from film and stage, to mount the operas: Louis Malle (Richard Strauss's *Der Rosenkavalier*), Roman Polanski (Alban Berg's *Lulu*), Ken Russell (Giacomo Puccini's *Madama Butterfly*), Günther Kramer (Strauss's *Elektra*, Berg's *Wozzeck*, Leoš Janáček's *Jenůfa*), Patrice Chéreau (Rossini's *L'italiana in Algeri*) who went on to mount the controversial centennial *Ring Cycle* at Bayreuth, (see Bayreuth entry), and Schippers and Visconti (Verdi's *Macbeth*, Gaetano Donizett's *Duca d'Alba*, Strauss's *Salome*, Verdi's *La traviata*, and Puccini's *Manon Lescaut.*)

The repertory offered the new, the unusual, and the long forgotten — Sergey Prokofiev's *Ognenniy angel* (The Fiery Angel) and *Lyubov' k tryom apel'sinam* (The Love for Three Oranges), Hans Werner Henze's *Der Prinz von Homburg*, Rossini's *Il conte Ory*, Igor Stravinsky's *L'histoire du Soldat*, Donizetti's *Il furioso all'isola di San Domingo*, Luciano Chailly's *Markheim*, Stanley Hollingsworth's *The Mother*, Saverio Mercadante's *Il giuramento*, Dmitry Shostakovich's *Ledi Makbet Mtsenskovo uyezda* (Lady Macbeth of the Mtsensk District), Samuel Barber's *Antony and Cleopatra*, Alberto Bruni Tedeschi's *Paolino, la giusta causa e una buona ragione*, Philip Glass's *Hydrogen Jukebox*, Wolfgang Amadeus Mozart's *Apollo et Hyacinthus* and Erich Wolfgang Korngold's *Die tote Stadt*. After the festival was on firm footing, Menotti added his own operas to the repertory: *Vanessa*, *The Saint of Bleecker Street*,

Gian Carlo Menotti and Francis Menotti (*foreground*) at news conference, Festival dei Due Mondi (Spoleto, Italy).

The Medium, Tamu-Tamu, The Consul, The Old Maid and the Thief, The Telephone, The Lie of Martin, The Egg, The Last Savage, Juana, la Loca, Maria Golovin, The Saint of Bleeker Street, Goya, and *Amahl and the Night Visitors.* Francis described Gian Carlo's music like this: "The heart of Menotti's music is American. He is an Italian composer who writes American music about American themes."

In Italy, the festival is unique — it is the only one "free from political pressure," as Francis explained, "and that was the original idea, to avoid having the festival aligned with any party. Every year the politicians want to get hold of the Festival, but the Italians like the fact that it is a (politically) free festival. It also encompasses all the arts, and these productions are not seen anywhere else. We rarely repeat productions." Francis continued, "The festival is also atypical in that there are no stars but, instead, it is interested in finding and making stars. Many internationally known artists came to Spoleto unknown and soon became known." Francis characterized the festival as "spontaneous and full of surprises." Premieres and unusual works continue to be important.

There was much criticism when Francis took charge of the festival in 1996, which he felt was politically motivated. Not much has changed since 1996, because Francis is more interested in the artists and avoids bureaucracy (as much as possible). It is the only festival in Europe with young Americans making up the chorus and orchestra. The budget is $10 million, funded through public and private means on a 50%-50% basis.

Teatro Lirico Sperimentale

Opera continues after the festival closes in the Teatro Lirico Sperimentale "Adriano Belli." Begun in 1947 by the musicologist Adriano Belli, the theater celebrated its 50th anniversary in 1996 and offered an interesting program — Verdi's *Falstaff*, Nino Rota's *La notte di un nevrastenico*, Puccini's *Suor Angelica*, Rossini's *L'inganno felice*, and the world premiere of Helmut Öhring's *Dokumentation I* on August 31, 1996. The opera was the winner of the second edition of the Concorso Internationale Orpheus for new chamber musical theater works. Two singers who went on to international careers had been associated with the Teatro Lirico Sperimentale — Franco Corelli and Anna Moffo.

Teatro Nuovo

The Teatro Nuovo (New Theater) was build between 1854 and 1864, based on the designs of Ireneo Aleandri. Located in the area of the old church of the Monastery of Sant'Andrea, it was built on the ruins of a Roman building. Restored in 1933, the theater had suffered deterioration from hosting too many overcrowded masked balls during carnival.

The classic stone building of deep golden yellow is dominated by two levels of arch-trios. Pairs of Ionic pilasters flank the upper arches, and medallions of Rossini, Vittoria Alfiere, Carlo Goldini, and Pietro Metastasio decorate the ones of the former carriage entrance. The five-tiered, ivory and gold auditorium sweeps around in the traditional horseshoe-shape. Putti with bows and arrows, nymphs playing the harp, and faces and masks of Comedy and Tragedy embellish the tiers. The box walls are covered in reddish golden silk fabric. Deep-maroon velvet seats match the golden-fringed, deep-maroon velvet stage curtain. Clusters of Muses with horns evoking Apollo in chiaroscuro style embellish the proscenium. There are approximately 900 seats.

Teatro Caio Melisso

The Teatro Caio Melisso was named for one of the Spoletian writers from the time of Augusto, who had directed the Imperial Library at the Portico d'Ottavia. Designed by Giovanni Montiroli, the theater was completed in 1880.

Its facade of tan stone faces the Piazza del Duomo. It is simple and without architectural design. Three box tiers topped by a loggione fill the small, red, ivory and gold auditorium. Roberto Luca restored the auditorium and preserved the original decorations which showed the Apotheosis of Caio Melisso. There are approximately 500 seats.

Practical Information. Festival dei Due Mondi, c/o Teatro Nuovo, 06049 Spoleto. Tel: 39 743 44097, 39 743 220355. Teatro Lirico Sperimentale, Piazza Bovio, 06049 Spoleto. Tel: 39 743 221-645, Fax 39 743 222-930. If visiting the Festival dei Due Mondi or Teatro Lirico Sperimentale, contact Azienda di Promozione Turistica di Spoleto, Piazza della Libertà, Spoleto. Tel: 39 743 220-311, Fax 39 743 46241.

COMPANY STAFF, WORLD PREMIERES AND REPERTORY

Direttori Artistici. Francis Menotti (1996–present), Gian Carlo Menotti (1958–1996).

World Premieres. S. Oliver's *The Garden*, summer 1977; S. Oliver's *Euridice*, summer 1981; S. Oliver's *The Beauty and the Beast*, summer 1984; Oliver's *Mario and the Magician*, summer 1988; Dove's *L'Augellin Belverde*, summer 1994; Amendola's *I giganti della montagna*, summer 1995.

Repertory. **1958:** Macbeth, Il giuoco del barone, Il maestro di cappella, The scarf, Lo frate 'nnammorato, L'arlesienne. **1959:** Il duca d'Alba, Ognennïy angel (The Fiery Angel). **1960:** La bohème, Der Prinz von Homburg. **1961:** Vanessa*, Salome. **1962:** Lyubov' k tryom apel'sinam (The Love for Three Oranges), Carmen, Il conte Ory. **1963:** La traviata, The Mother, Il Signor Bruschino. **1964:** Der Rosenkavalier. **1965:** Otello, Partita a pugni, L'histoire du Soldat. **1966:** Pelléas et Mélisande, Messa da Requiem (Verdi). **1967:** Don Giovanni, Il furioso all'isola di San Domingo, Markheim. **1968:** Tristan und Isolde, The Saint of Bleecker Street*. **1969:** L'italiana in Algeri, The Medium*, El retablo de Maese Pedro. **1970:** Il giuramento, The Medium*. **1971:** Boris Godunov. **1972:** Der Aufsteig und Fall der Stadt Mahagonny, The Consul*. **1973:** Manon Lescaut, Dafne. **1974:** Lulu, Manon Lescaut, Tamu-Tamu*, A Letter for Queen Victoria, Prima la musica poi le parole. **1975:** Don Pasquale, The Old Maid and the Thief*, The Telephone*, Le Docteur Miracle. **1976:** Pikovaya dama (Queen of Spades), Paolino, la giusta causa e una buona ragione, Der Kaiser von Atlantis, The Rape of Lucretia. **1977:** Napoli millionaria, Maria Golovin*, Così fan tutte. **1978:** La Cenerentola, Falstaff, Così fan tutte, The Lie of Martin,* The Egg?* **1979:** La sonnambula, L'incoronzaione di Poppea. **1980:** Ledi Makbet Mtsenskovo uyezda (Lady Macbeth of the Mtsensk District), L'erismena. **1981:** Die lustige Witwe, The Medium*, L'ivrogne corrige. **1982:** Der fliegnde Holländer, La colombe, Juana, la Loca*. **1983:** Madama Butterfly, Antony and Cleopatra. **1984:** Ariadne auf Naxos, L'Ormindo, The Last Savage*.

Teatro Nuovo (Spoleto, Italy).

1985: La fanciulla del West, Il barbiere di Siviglia, Kun Opera of Nanking, Chuan Opera of the Sichuan. **1986:** The Saint of Bleecker Street*, Platée. **1987:** Parsifal, Montezuma, La notte, Die Gespenstersonate. **1988:** Jenůfa, Antigone, Hänsel und Gretel. **1989:** Les contes d'Hoffmann, Sarah, Salome. **1990:** Le nozze di Figaro, Elektra, Hydrogen Jukebox. **1991:** Goya*, Le nozze di Figaro, Apollo et Hyacinthus. **1992:** Il duca d'Alba, Die Meistersinger von Nürnberg. **1993:** Il trittico, The Rake's Progress. **1994:** Les Mamelles de Tirésias, Wozzeck. **1995:** Carmen, Nos (The Nose) **1996:** Semele, Eugene Onegin, Spiritus Mundi, Amahl and the Night Visitors*. **1997:** Semele, Die Tote Stadt. **1998:** The Consul*, Die Entführung aus dem Serail, Příhody Lišky Bystroušky (The Cunning Little Vixen) (* Indicates operas by Menotti.)

Bibliography. Associazione Festival dei Due Mondi, *Spoleto Trent'anni di Festival: 1958–1987 Gli spettacoli, Gli Autori, I Partecipanti* (Spoletto, 1988). Associazione Festival dei Due Mondi, *Spoleto Trentasei Anni di Festival: Aggiornamento 1988–1993* (Rome, 1994). Various authors, *Spoleto Festival 1996* (Spoleto, 1996). Various authors, *25° Spoleto Festival* (Spoleto, 1982). Interviews with Gian Carlo Menotti and Francis Menotti, July 1996.
Thanks to Carmelita Celi, Festival dei Due Mondi.

TORRE DEL LAGO

Puccini Festival (Summer Festival)

On August 24, 1930, Giacomo Puccini's *La bohème* inaugurated the Puccini Festival in a temporary theater erected in the Piazzale Puccini, a piazza in front of the composer's house on the shores of Lake Massaciuccoli. The stage was supported by piles fixed in the water, and the audience sat on benches located around the square. A group known as the Carro di Tespi Lirico produced the opera, conducted by Pietro Mascagni and directed by Giovacchino Forzano. The cast included Rosetta Pampanini, Margherita Carosio, Angelo Minghetti, and Luigi Montesanto.

In 1924, before Giacomo Puccini had left Torre del Lago for treatment of his throat cancer at a clinic in Brussels (Belgium), he said to Forzano, "I always come here first and then I take the boat to go fishing. But one time I would like to come here first and listen to one of my operas performed in the open air." With this, the seeds for the Puccini Festival at Torre del Lago were planted. Although Puccini never returned from Brussels (he suffered a fatal heart attack at the clinic), within six years after his death, the festival was founded.

The primary purpose of the festival is the presentation, examination, and perpetuation of the works of Puccini in a theater near the maestro's house, where he composed many of the operas. But after the Fascist took power, only one Festival took place, in 1937, and that was in concert-form, with Lucia Albanese as one of the soloists. Then *La fanciulla del West* was staged to commemorate the 25th anniversary of the composer's death, a production from the Teatro dell'Opera in Rome. The 1950s saw some of Puccini's best loved works — *Madama Butterfly, Tosca,* and *La bohème* on the schedule. In 1971, the festival became an annual summer event.

Puccini composed ten operas — *Le Villi, Edgar, Manon Lescaut, La bohème, Tosca, Madama Butterfly, La fanciulla del West, La rondine, Il trittico* (*Il tabarro, Suor Angelica, Gianni Schicchi*), and *Turandot,* of which five or six are well-known. Since the same works were offered season after season, it became necessary to expand the repertory, including the works of other composers, but limited to contemporaries of Puccini. *Gianni Schicchi* was paired with Maurice Ravel's *L'heure espagnole,* and Umberto Giordani's *Andrea Chénier* was included in the 1997 program, along side *Tosca* and *Madama Butterfly.* Even Richard Strauss's *Salome* was mounted one summer as an experiment (not repeated.) Puccini's rarely performed *Le Villi* and *Edgar* were mounted in 1991 and 1992 respectively. The more recent festivals have had themes: 1996 was French, with *La bohème* and *Manon Lescaut* in the *cartellone*; 1997 was dedicated to composers who were contemporaries of Puccini, and included Giordani's *Andrea Chénier* and a concert performance of Strauss's *Elektra*; 1998 was dedicated to Arturo Toscanini and Enrico Caruso. The festival has also expanded to include ballets and smaller scale operas in alternate venues, like Benjamin Britten's *Turn of the Screw* at the Villa Orlando.

Famous names from the opera stage have been welcomed at the festival. Among the male artists — Beniamino Gigli, Ferruccio Tagliavini, Giuseppe di Stefano, Gianni Raimondo, Franco Corelli, Luciano Pavarotti, Ingvar Wixell, Tito Gobbi, who made his debut in *Tosca,* and Mario del Monaco, who concluded his career with *Il tabarro* — and the female artists — Magda Olivero, Antonietta Stella, Clara Petrella, Katia Ricciarelli, Fiorenza Cossotto, Eva Marton, and Ghena Dimitrova. Conductors like Nello Santi, Giuseppe Sinopoli, and Daniel Oren have also appeared at the festival.

Opera at Torre del Lago is a large-scale presentation (although small in comparison to the Arena di Verona) of Puccini's works. For the 1996 *La bohème,* massive, realistic sets, changed for each act, were erected on the huge stage, and recreated entire Parisian neighborhoods, complete with chimneys which belched smoke. (The primary purpose was to chase away the bugs.) Only the Act III winter scene needed some imagination, since it was 85°F with high humidity. The sets looked imported directly from Hollywood, and the director-team came from Italian cinema. Some productions are more "discrete," like the *Manon Lescaut*, which used abstract and symbolic means to show locations. The drawback to such large-scale-production festivals is the inability to experiment. Whenever a production has deviated from the tried and true, it has been a financial catastrophe. Nevertheless, the concept of spectacular Hollywood-like productions of opera outdoors works in this setting, marred only by heavy cigarette smoke (even during the performance), and talking (since the audience attracted equate opera with watching a sporting event.) By necessity, the singers must have strong voices, which carry a great distance, and the predominately Italian cast for *La bohème* of Denia Massola Gavazzeni, Salvatore Fisichella, Rosemary Musoleno, and Dalibor Jenis was no exception. Younger singers are cast in the smaller roles.

Artistic director Angelo Cavallaro explained that the Puccini Festival must earn around 60% of its budget from ticket sales, and less than 10% comes from private sources. The remainder is from federal, regional, and provincial governments. By contrast, the usual percentage of earnings from ticket sales is between 15–20%. Also, unlike most other Italian summer festivals (except the Arena di Verona), the Puccini Festival draws a large foreign crowd, mainly Germans, Austrians, French, British, Americans, and Japanese. This combination makes it a financial disaster when a performance is rained out, which requires the refund of four thousand tickets — these visitors do not stay for rainchecks. Although the festival was founded in 1930, by 1996, only 42 seasons had taken place, mainly for financial reasons, (although political factors and World War II had also played a role). For that reason, on September 15, 1990, the Puccini Festival Foundation was founded to control the financial aspects of the festival and ensure its continuity through the next century. One of the festival's goals, not yet realized, is to construct a large, permanent theater in a natural environment, one that would be open-air, but could also be closed in case of rain, to continue experiencing Puccini's music in an environment which inspired Puccini to write them.

The University of Firenze and University of London are working on this project which is being funded by the wealthy Caprona family who are donating land and money for the theater's construction. It will be built in a piecemeal fashion, with the stage constructed first, then the orchestra level, and finally the balconies, so as to not interrupt any seasons. If and when this project is completed, with an indoor space, then there would be an expansion to a winter season as well. And a "real" theater would prevent some of the disasters which have befallen productions, like the ferocious thunderstorm which swept across the lake with such force during a 1995 performance of *Madama Butterfly* that it blew all the scenery from the stage into the orchestra pit, and there was a lot of scenery. Fortunately, no one was injured.

Teatro dei Quattromila

In 1966, the Teatro dei Quattromila (Theater of 4000) was erected on reclaimed land to the north of Puccini's house. Located by a tiny harbor where a few sailboats are moored, it faces Lake Massaciuccoli, which forms a beautiful natural setting. The entrance is along the lakeshore via a gangplank which crosses over part of the lake, and is raised when the performance begins. Unfortunately the natural beauty vanishes once one enters the theater, which is a massive conglomeration of steel poles which support 4000 (uncomfortable) green fiberglass seats and an enormous stage. The "opera house" has the atmosphere of a sports arena, with the audience dressed in everything from shorts and sneakers to black tie and formal evening gowns.

Practical Information. Puccini Festival, Festival Office, Piazzale Belvedere 4, 55048 Torre del Lago. Tel: 39 584 340-235; Fax: 39 584 350 562. If visiting the Puccini Festival, contact the Cavmare Agenzia Viaggi e Turismo, Via Matteotti, 3, 55049 Viareggio. Tel: 39 584 49775; Fax: 39 584 943 168. There are few rooms in Torre del Lago.

COMPANY STAFF

Direttori Artistici. Angelo Cavallaro, Renzo Giacchieri, Luciano Alberti.

Bibliography. Various authors, *Festival Puccini Program 1995 & 1996* (Pisa, 1995, 1996). Interview with Angelo Cavallaro, artistic director, August 1996.

Thanks to La Direzione, Fondazione Festival Pucciniano.

Teatro dei Quattromila, building set for *La Bohème* (Torre del Lago, Italy).

—————————————————————————————————— TREVISO

Teatro Comunale (Teatro di Tradizione)

The Teatro Comunale, originally called the Teatro Società was inaugurated in October 1869 during the *stagione di San Martino*, with Charles Gounod's *Faust*. Giuseppe Verdi's *La traviata* was also on the boards. Andrea Scala designed the opera house, with Signore Stella and Andreotti responsible for the decorations, and Fausto Asteo for the sculptural designs. This was the second Teatro Società. The first, originally called the Teatro d'Onigo, was destroyed by fire on October 2, 1868. Inaugurated on April 18, 1765, with Pietro Guglielmi's *Demofonte*, it was designed by Antonio Galli Bibiena and Giovanni Miazzi.

During the 17th century, the Teatro di Santa Margarita hosted performances until fire claimed it. In 1692, another theater opened, the Teatro

d'Onigo, named after Count Fiorino d'Onigo, whose last wish was to see it built. Completed shortly before his death, the theater was passed to his son Gerolamo. After 1714, performances were suspended, and the opera house was abandoned. The outlook improved when Guglielmo d'Onigo became the new owner. On March 8, 1763, he obtained permission from the Consiglio X to restore and reopen it. More than 1,000 spectators were present at the inaugural two years later. The theater had a prosperous existence with good productions and well-known artist. It hosted not only opera, but concerts, carnival balls, and various festivities and receptions. In 1836, fire destroyed a large part of the wooden structure. Restored in 1846, the theater acquired new decorations, improved facilities, and a new name,

Teatro di Società. Two years earlier the *Società dei Palchettisti* (Society of Boxholders) had formed. This society and Count d'Onigo paid the restoration costs. The count used the royal box (number 12 on the first tier) and two other boxes. Thirty-two years later, fire struck again in October 1868 and completely destroyed the structure. The fire was caused by a rocket! The theater's watchman, a certain Sig. Triaca, had a side business of making fireworks, and not having any suitable place for their construction, used the theater stage. One night, a rocket exploded which ignited a fire that spread to all the other fireworks, and within a short time, a blazing inferno engulfed the building. All that remained were the outside walls.

After the opera house was reconstructed, it ushered in a golden era. Emma Calvè made her debut in the fall of 1890 in Ambroise Thomas's *Hamlet*. Arturo Toscanini arrived in 1894 to conduct Giuseppe Verdi's *Falstaff* and Alberto Franchetti's *Cristoforo Colombo*. He returned the following year for Richard Wagner's *Tannhäuser* and Alfredo Catalani's *Loreley*. The turn of the century saw Enrico Caruso in the role of Cavaradossi in Giacomo Puccini's *Tosca*; Hipolito Lazaro in Amilcare Ponchielli's *La gioconda*; Carmen Melis and Viglione-Borghese in Puccini's *La fanciulla del West*; Elivira de Hidalgo in Gaetano Donizetti's *La fille du régiment*; Giacomo Lauri-Volpi in Umberto Giordani's *Andrea Chénier*, and several appearances by Toti dal Monte in Mascagni's *Lodoletta*, Gioachino Rossini's *Il barbiere di Siviglia*, Vincenzo Bellini's *La sonnambula*, Verdi's *La traviata*, and Puccini's *Madama Butterfly*. Conductors included Tullio Serafin, Leopoldo Mugnone, Pietro Mascagni, and Riccardo Zandonai.

Meanwhile, the commune had become co-owners with the box holders of the theater. Since the commune was an Ente Pubblico (public corporation) and the *Società dei Palchetti* (Association of Boxholders) an elite private group, controversy arose as to the management of the theater. The commune acquired the opera house from the *palchettisti* on October 26, 1931, at which time the theater acquired its current name, Teatro Comunale. The management of the theater was given to the Società Autonoma Gestione Teatri in 1940. The theater, however, by the decision of the mayor on June 26, 1944, had been sold on September 13, 1944, to a Mr. & Mrs. Venerio Monti and their sons. This arrangement did not work out and the commune invalidated the agreements, entrusting, instead, the running of the theater to the *Società Amici della Musica*, which they felt offered both the best guarantee for good economic management and artistic quality. This society managed the theater until 1957. Other people and organizations ran the theater until September 1, 1971, when the Ente Teatro Comunale di Treviso was formed to organize opera performances, as well as concerts, ballet, drama, and other cultural events. Since 1979, the Ente also collaborates with the Teatro Sociale in Rovigo on opera co-productions.

A work shop for young singers called the *Bottega* (shop), under the direction of Peter Maag, lends an element of adventure to some productions. Founded in 1989, the Bottega is an international laboratory for young singers and musicians which Peter Maag runs. Promising young talent, chosen through the Toti Dal Monte International Singing Competition, participate in productions, thereby gaining valuable stage experience.

The repertory is predominately Italian, with an occasional non-Italian work. The mid–1990s saw Verdi's *Macbeth*, Wolfgang Amadeus Mozart's *Die Zauberflöte*, Giacomo Puccini's *Tosca*, Umberto Giordano's *Fedora*, and Domenico Cimarosa's *Il matrimonio segreto*. Recent repertory includes, Jacques Offenbach's *Les contes d'Hoffmann*, Puccini's *Madama Butterfly*, Gaetano Donizetti's *La fille du régiment*, and George Gershwin's *Porgy and Bess*.

Teatro Comunale

An article of May 1836 in the *Gazzetta di Venezia* written by Tommaso Locatelli described the opera house like this: "The Teatro di Treviso is more graceful and lovely than man is able to imagine. Its charm emanates from the simplicity of design, from the suitable union of colors, and from the careful choice of ornamentation..."

On the front of the theater GUGLIELMUS HIER FIL. COMES DE VONIGO CULTU SPLENDIDIORE THEATRUM RESTITUIT AMPLIAVITQUE A. A. V. MDCCLXV IO. MIAZZI ARCHIT. is inscribed in honor of its founder, Guglielmo d'Onigo. Below five Palladium windows punctuate the stone, Neoclassic facade. Crowned by a balustrade, the facade presents three arched entranceways. The gilded and ivory horse-shoe-shaped auditorium holds four box tiers, each with 23 boxes, and a loggione. Gold stucco adorns the parapets. Carytids, rococo-designed embroidery of gilded pearl of Murano, and allegorical figures ornament the space. The seats are raspberry red. The hall accommodates 750, 700 seats and 50 standing.

Practical Information. Teatro Comunale, Corso del Popolo 31, 31100 Treviso. Tel 39 422 546-355; Fax: 39 422 52285. If you visit, stay at the Al Fogher, Viale della Repubblica 10, 3100 Treviso. Tel: 39 0422-432950, Fax: 39 0422 430391. It is conveniently located and can assist with tickets and schedules.

COMPANY STAFF

Artistic Consultant. Donato Renetti.
Bibliography. Biblioteca Comunale di Treviso, *Il Teatro Comunale nelle origini e nella storia* (Treviso, 1980). *Autunno Musicale Trevigiano* (Treviso, 1991).
Thanks to Luccio de Piccoli, Teatro Comunale, and G. Garatti.

TRIESTE

Teatro Verdi
(Ente Autonomo Lirico)

The *prima esecuzione* of Giovanni Simone Mayr's *Ginevra di Scozia* inaugurated the Teatro Verdi, originally called the Teatro Nuovo, on April 21, 1801. *Ginevra di Scozia* was selected from among several entries in a competition for the opening night production. Teresa Bertinotti, Luigi Marchesi, and Giacomo David created the roles. The building was designed by Giannantonio Selva, architect of Teatro La Fenice (Venice). Matteo Pertsch was responsible for the facade, which resembled that of Teatro alla Scala (Milan). (La Scala's architect, Giuseppe Piermarini, was Pertsch's teacher.)

Some of the first musical performances go back to the late 1600s when Pietro Rossetti's *La fidutia in Dio* was seen. The 1720s hosted a comic intermezzo, Johann Hasse's *La contadina*, and in 1730, the first "real" opera, Giuseppe Orlandini's *Serpilla e Bacocco* was given. Trieste was fortunate. Lorenzo da Ponte and his mistress lived in Trieste, so they brought several leading Mozart singers from Vienna and Prague to perform in their adopted city, including Calvesi, Baglioni, Fantozzi, Micelli, Mandini.

Trieste's first theater dates back to 1705, when the council chambers in the Palazzo di Città were fitted with a moveable stage. Located near the remains of the Teatro Romano, the new structure was named after the saint of a nearby church, San Pietro, following a Venetian tradition. Offering 800 seats, the San Pietro featured works by Domenico Cimarosa, Giambattista Pergolesi, Niccolò Piccinni, Baldassarre Galuppi, Giovanni Paisiello, Pasquale Anfossi, and Antonio Salieri. The theater's name was changed in 1760 to Cesareo Regio Teatro di San Pietro when the Austrians ruled Trieste. Works like Anfossi's *La finta giardiniera*, Salieri's *La grotta di Trofonio*, Paisiello's *Il barbiere di Siviglia* and *Nina pazza per amore*, Cimarosa's *Giannina e Bernardone, Il matrimonio segreto*, and *Gli orazi e curiazi* were popular in the latter part of the 1700s. As the 18th century drew to a close, it became apparent that the city had outgrown its theater, and the San Pietro permanently closed its doors in 1800.

After the Teatro Nuovo opened, Antonio Salieri's *Annibale in Capua*, which placed second in the inaugural competition, was staged on May 19, 1801. A grand festival concluded the first season. For the fall and carnival seasons of 1801-1802, *opera buffa* dominated the repertory, with Vittorio Trento's *Quanti casi in un sol giorno*, Cimarosa *Il credulo*, Valentino Fioravanti's *Chi la fa, chi disfa, chi la imbroglia*, and Francesco Cristiani's *La prova del melodramma*. The spring season for 1802 featured similar type works, opening on April 19 with Sebastiano Nasolini's *Semiramide* and a ballet *Baldovino da Spoleto* choreographed by Lorenzo Panzieri. The fall season offered Nasolini's *Gli opposti caratteri* and a repeat of Fioravanti's *Chi la fa, chi la disfa, chi la imbroglia*. The repertory between 1803 and 1813 emphasized *opera serie* and included the following works: Stefano Pavesi's *Fingallo e Comala* and *Ardano e Artula*, Nasolini's

Merope and *Vomisia e Mitridate*, Niccolò Zingaretti's *Giulietta e Romeo*, *Castore e Polluce*, and *Ines de Castro* (Pavesi and Giuseppe Farinelli also contributed), Giovanni Simone Mayr's *Polibete* and *Alonso e Cora*, *Lodöviska*, Vincenzo Federici's *Oreste in Tauride*, Giuseppe Nicolini's *Trajano in Dacia*, Farinelli's *Il Cid*, and Nicola Giuliani's *Armiro e Daura* and *Raoul Barbableu*. *Semi-serie* and *giocose* offered were Paisiello's *Nina pazza per amore* and Cimarosa's *Il matrimonio per raggio*. The repertory near the middle of the 1800s was similar to the repertory of most other Italian theaters — Gioachino Rossini, Vincenzo Bellini, and Gaetano Donizetti operas played major roles, but works of lesser composers, were also on the boards. The 1839 fall season witnessed Donizetti's *Lucia di Lammermoor*, *Marino Faliero*, and *Parisiana*, Nicolai Nicolai's *Enrico II*, and Mercadante's *Gabriella di Vergy*, followed in 1840 by Rossini's *Mosè in Egitto*, Bellini's *I Puritani*, Donizetti's *Lucrezia Borgia*, and Nicolai's *Il templario*. Artists like Eugenin Tadolini, Serafino Panzizi, and Napoleone Moriani interpreted the works. By the 1846 fall season, Giuseppe Verdi had eclipsed them all with *I due Foscari*, *Attila*, and *Ernani* in the *cartellone* along with Donizetti's *Lucrezia Borgia* and Ruggero Mann's *Il profeta velato*. The voices of Marietta Alboni and Antonio Ponzetti were heard. The Teatro Grande, as the Teatro Verdi was then called, had the honor of introducing two of Verdi's operas, neither of which were very successful: *Il corsaro* on October 25, 1848, and *Stiffelio* on November 16, 1850. Another world premiere, Federico Ricci's *La prigione di Edimburgo* had been presented on March 13, 1838, and an Italian premiere, that of Matteo Salvi's *Caterina Howard* was staged during carnival 1847-48.

Next, French works took the stage with the Italian premiere of Daniel Auber's *La muette de Portici* and Ambroise Thomas's *Mignon*. Rossini's French operas were also staged — *Le Comte Ory* and *Guillaume Tell*, and in the fall of 1866 Fromental Halévy's *La Juive* was seen in Trieste for the first time, along with Donizetti's *La favorite*, *Il Belisario*, and *Maria di Rohan*, and Bellini's *Norma*. The following season continued with French works with Giacomo Meyerbeer's *L'Africaine* and *Dinorah*, and Charles Gounod's *Faust*. Another *prima assoluta* took place on October 28, 1868, Lionello Ventura's *Alda*. In 1880, the management of the Teatro Comunale decreed "in view

of public security, the theater is closed for all performances," and a project for reconstruction was set forth.

Meanwhile, other theaters had opened which also hosted opera. On October 6, 1827, the Teatro Mauroner had began a career which lasted fortynine years. It saw its last opera in 1876 before it was consumed by fire. The Teatro Armonie was inaugurated in 1857. It hosted Ermanno Wolf-Ferrari's *I quattro rusteghi* in November 1902, and was demolished a decade later. The Teatro Fenice opened August 27, 1879, and was transformed into a movie house in 1912. The Teatro Politeama Rossetti opened on April 27, 1878, with Verdi's *Un ballo in maschera*, conducted by Luigi Ricci. A ballet followed, *Pietro micca* choreographed by Luigi Manzotti. The Politeama was suppose to have opened on April 22, but hostilities broke out between the Austrian police and the Politeama regarding the staging of Verdi's opera, which delayed the inauguration five days. Named after a famous citizen, politician and scholar of the early 19th century, it held a large auditorium which seated 3,200 and offered a 54-foot stage. Five years after the opening, the theater's most prestigious event took place, the staging of the complete Ring Cycle. Opera shared the stage with festivals, balls and dances. The beginning of the 20th century saw works by Richard Strauss and Arturo Toscanini on the podium. The opera season remained limited to avoid competition with the Teatro Verdi. The politeama was converted into a cinema in 1913. Between 1945 and 1947, the American and English armed forces requisitioned the theater, and the likes of Louis Armstrong and Josephine Baker graced the stage. It was closed in 1956, and reopened in 1969 as a multi-purpose performing venue.

The Teatro Nuovo has had several name changes. Originally named Nuovo (New) to distinguish it from the old Teatro San Pietro, it was rebaptized Teatro Grande in 1820 so it would stand apart from the other, less illustrious theaters which had been built in the city. Forty-one years later, when the Grande passed from private ownership to the municipality, it was renamed Teatro Comunale, and just two days after Verdi's death was announced on January 27, 1901, the Teatro Comunale was officially renamed Teatro Verdi.

Although World War I closed the theater, it remained open during the Second World War.

Between the wars, it became an Ente Autunomo in 1936. After World War II, the Teatro Verdi offered French, German, and Russian works along side the Italian fare. The 1949-1950 season presented Georges Bizet's *Carmen* and *Les pêcherus de perles*, Richard Wagner's *Tristan und Isolde*, Dmitry Shostakovich's *Sorochintsy Fair*, Cimarosa's *Il matrimonio segreto*, Donizetti's *Linda di Chamounix*, Giacomo Puccini's *Manon Lescaut*, *Il trittico*, and *La bohème*, Verdi's *Simon Boccanegra*, Umberto Giordano's *Fedora*, and Alfredo Catalani's *La Wally*. The next season was similar minus the French representation: Wagner's *Die Walküre* and *Die Meistersinger von Nürnberg*, Modest Mussorgsky's *Boris Godunov*, Verdi's *Ernani*, *La traviata*, and *Falstaff*, Riccardo Zandonai's *Francesca da Rimini*, Rossini's *La Cenerentola*, Puccini's *Tosca*, Wolf-Ferrari's *Il campiello*, and Wolfgang Amadeus Mozart's *Le nozze di Figaro*. By the 1980s, the number of operas had decreased, but the Russian and Wagner works remained, with some novelties, like the Italian premiere of Paulini-Haranyl's *Hary Janos*, Raffaelo de Banfield's *Lord Byron's Love Letter* (libretto by Tennessee Williams), and Dmitry Shostakovich's *Ledi Makbet Mtsenskovo uyezda* (Lady Macbeth of the Mtsensk District). Other works included Wagner's *Der fliegende Höllander*, Puccini's *Le Villi* and *Gianni Schicchi*, and Ottorino Respighi's *La fiamma*. During the 1980s and 1990s, more Russian and Eastern European operas entered the repertory, including Pyotr Il'yich Tchaikovsky's *Pikovaya dama* (Queen of Spades), Mussorgsky's *Khovanshchina*, Leoš Janáček's *Jenůfa*, Antonín Dvořák's *Rusalka*, Antonio Smareglia's *Pittori fiamminghi*, and Ivan Zajc's *Nikola Subic Zrinjski*.

The Verdi underwent reconstruction in 1992 which cost 36 billion LIT. Gino Pavan was architect with Rometro Venuti in charge of the project and Dino Tamburini as the engineer. It closed the theater for five years. During that time, opera performances were relocated to a former bus station renamed Sala Tripcovich, after the name of the shipping company which funded the project. The contract for the conversion to a theater was signed in May and on December 15, 1992, the inauguration took place. The exterior stucco was painted a faux marble peach color, embellished with a deep red stage curtain. Inside, 934 seats filled a black auditorium, decorated with pilasters with gilded capitals. The seasons were less adventurous. The 1996-97 season offered Verdi's *Rigoletto*,

Mozart's *Die Zauberflöte*, Puccini's *Madama Butterfly*, and Rossini's *Il barbiere di Siviglia*. The production of *Il barbiere di Siviglia* was traditional and unexciting. The young singers were average in voice quality and exhibited the old-fashion stage presence of standing and singing to the audience.

The Teatro Verdi reopened on May 16, 1997, with a VIVA VERDI concert which featured excerpts from many of the composer's operas: *Nabucco*, *Il trovatore*, *Il corsaro*, *I vespri siciliani*, *Otello*, *Macbeth*, *La forza del destino*, *Simon Boccanegra*, *Don Carlo*, *Un ballo in maschera*, and concluded with the "Gran finale secondo" from *Aida*. The repertory has improved with a mixture of French, German, and Italian works like Verdi's *Don Carlo*, Donizetti's *Don Pasquale*, Puccini's *Tosca*, Wagner's *Das Rheingold*, Alban Berg's *Wozzeck*, and Jules Massenet's *Manon*. The opera house is unusual in Italy in that it also hosts an International Festival of Operetta every summer. This activity of the Ente Lirico triestino is to rediscover the music genere. The seeds for the Festival were planted back at the end of the 1800s, when major Viennese operetta companies visited, and continued in the early 1900s with *primas* of several including *Eva* (1911, Teatro Fenice), *Moglie ideale* (1913), and *Federica* (1929, Politeama Rossetti). The festival is more than three decades old and in 1997 celebrated the reopening of the Teatro Verdi with *Die lustige Witwe*, *Czárdásfürstin*, and *Das Land der Glocken*.

Teatro Verdi

In 1798, Matteo Giuseppe Tommasini requested the Chancery of the Austrain Court for permission to construct a new theater at his own expense and rent it to the city of Trieste for 6400 fiorini, paid from the civic coffers. He reserved for himself box 7 and the right to all the boxes on the fifth tier. Although the compensation package would have eventually exceeded the expense of construction, the concession was granted. The contract was signed June 11, 1798, but a short time later, on July 4, 1798, Tommasini ceded it to Count Antonio Cassis. It was suspected that Tommasini was acting as a figurehead for the Cassis, who had applied unsuccessfully for a license to build a theater. Construction took four years to complete. The Teatro Verdi has had three

Teatro Verdi (Trieste, Italy).

owners — Tommasini-Cassis, Moisè Hierschel, who had obtained the theater from the heirs of Cassis on April 22, 1835, and a relative of Moisè, named Leone, who ceded it to the Comune for the sum of 275, 000 fiorini.

The Neoclassic Teatro Verdi displays a facade with a massive three-arch portico which extends onto the piazza. The peach and grayish-white facade is lined with engaged Ionic columns in the center and Ionic pilasters on the building's wings, and crowned by a statue of Apollo flanked by allegorical figures of Opera and Drama. The horseshoe-shaped ivory, gold, and raspberry-colored auditorium, holds five tiers and includes a large center royal box. Gilded musical symbols, masks of Comedy and Tragedy, and floral patterns decorate the parapets. Red seats complement the red valences suspended across each box. The theater seats 1,350.

Practical Information. Teatro Verdi, Piazza Verdi 1, 34121 Trieste. Tel: 39 40 672 2111. When visiting the Teatro Verdi or archives, stay at the Grand Hotel Duchi d'Aosta, Piazza Unità 2, 34121 Trieste. Tel: 39 40 760-0011, Fax 39 40

366-092. It is centrally located just steps from the Teatro Verdi. The hotel staff will assist with schedule and tickets.

COMPANY STAFF

Sovrintendente. Lorenzo Jorio, Giorgio Vidusso, Giuseppe Antonicelli. **Direttore Artistico:** Raffaelo de Banfield (1972 — present). **Impresari: (Teatro Nuovo):** Giovanni Drosso Plasterà (1801–1810). Adolfo Bassi, Giuseppe Scaramella, and Franc Schmölz (Lent 1810). Titus Dauchy (Spring 1810). Antonio Prividali (Spring-Summer 1810). Domenico Serpos and Antonio Fantoni (Fall 1810). Maurizio Chiotta, Giuseppe Scaramella, Franc Schmölz, Adolfo Bassi, and Antonio Prividali (Carnival 1811). Adolfo Bassi and Antonio Fantoni (1811–Carnival 1813). Antonio Fantoni and Paolo (Spring 1813), Antonio Fantoni (Fall 1813–1816). Adolfo Bassi (1817–1820). Theater Management (1822). Adolfo Bassi (1823). Luigi Prividali and Giuseppe Scaramella (1828). Feliciano Strepponi (1830). Theater Management (1830-Carnival/Lent 1831). Carlo Schütz (1831–Fall/Carnival/Lent 1832). Adolfo Bassi (1832–Carnival/Lent 1835). Natale Fabrici (Summer 1835–Easter 1840). Vincenzo Giaccone and son (Fall

Teatro Verdi auditorium (Trieste, Italy).

1840–Easter 1846). Natale Fabrici (Fall 1846–Easter 1849). Theater Management (Fall 1849-Easter 1850). Domenico Ronzani (Fall 1850–Easter 1855). Giovanni Battista Lasina (1855–1858). Ronzi brothers (Easter/Carnival/Lent 1858). The-ater Management (Fall 1859-Easter 1860). Angelo Tommasi (Fall 1860–Easter 1864). **(Teatro Comunale):** Carlo Raffaele Burlini (Fall 1864-Easter 1865). Angelo Tommasi (Fall 1865–Easter 1867). Luciano Marzi (Fall 1867-Carnival/Lent 1868). Carlo Gardini (Fall 1868–Easter 1872). Giovanni Battista Lasina (Fall 1872). Carlo Gardini (Fall/Carnival/Lent 1873-1874). Carlo Raffaele Burlini (Fall/Carnival/Lent 1874-1875). Giuseppe Brunello (Fall 1875). Theater Management (Car-nival/Lent 1875-1876). G.C. Dinico (Fall 1876). Giovanni Stancich (Car-nival/Lent 1876-1877). Giuseppe Brunello (Fall/Carnival/Lent 1877-1878). Dussich (Fall/Carnival/Lent 1878-1879). Vacant (Fall 1879). Carlo Zubbani (Carnival/Lent 1879-1880).

Bibliography. Giuseppe Ste-fani, *Il Teatro Verdi di Trieste: 1801–1951* (Trieste, 1951); Vito Levi, *La vita musicale a Trieste, Cronache di un cinquantennio: 1918–1968* Milano, 1968); Guido Botteri and Levi, *Il Politeama Rossetti (1878-1978)* (Trieste, 1978); Ireno Brem-ini, *Il Comunale di Trieste: 1801-1960* (Trieste, 1960). Levi, Botteri, and Ireneo Bremini, *Il Comunale di Trieste* (Udine, 1962); *Memorie del Teatro Comunale di Trieste 1801-1876 — Raccotte da un vecchio teatro-filo*; Silvio Rutteri, *Origini e vicende del Teatro Verdi*, Stagione Lirica 1948-49, Pubblicazione del Teatro Comunale Giuseppe Verdi.

Thanks to Hedy Benvenuti.

TURIN

Teatro Regio Torino (Ente Autonomo Lirico)

The new Teatro Regio Torino was inaugu-rated on April 10, 1973, with Giuseppe Verdi's *I vespri siciliani*. Carlo Mollino and Marcello Za- velani Rossi designed the structure. The previous theater had been destroyed by fire during the night of February 8, 1936. Francesco Feo's *Arsace* had inaugurated the first Teatro Regio Torino, originally called Il Regio Teatro di Torino, on December 26, 1740. The Regio had been commissioned by King Carlo Emanuele III as the new court theater. Filippo Juvarra designed the opera house which was constructed by Benedetto Alfieri.

The *teatro di corte* hosted the first operatic performances back in 1612 when Sigismondo d'India's *Zalizura* graced the stage. Operas originally presented in Venice and Naples were also offered in Turin, like Domenico Sarro's *Didone abbandonata*. The idea of building the Teatro Regio dates back to 1713, when the Duchy of Savoy was transformed into a kingdom. Work on the new opera house began in 1738, and everything proceeded so smoothly that the theater was ready within two years. It was connected to the palace by a private corridor so the king could go directly from the royal box to his private quarters. Many operas were composed specifically for the Regio, like Riccardo Broschi's *Merope*, Christoph Willibald Gluck's *Poro*, and Johann Christian Bach *Artaserse*, and composers like Johann Hasse, Niccolò Jommelli, Giovanni Paisiello, Domenico Cimarosa, Luigi Cherubini, Ferdinando Paër, Saverio Mercadante and Giovanni Pacini also composed for the theater. During the 1760s, French operas like François Philidor's *Le Sorcier* and *Tom Jones* were sung in French, which was unique in Italy at that time.

Another theater of note in the city was the Teatro Carignano. It opened in 1710 as the private theater of the Carignano family, but by 1753, the theater had fallen into such a state of disrepair that it had to be rebuilt. Principe Liugi di Carignano commissioned Benedetto Alfieri to do the job. Although fire gutted the Teatro Carignano in 1787, it was reconstructed soon thereafter. Decorated in gold, the intimate theater hosted the Italian premiere of Gaetano Donizetti's *Linda di Chamounix* on August 24, 1842.

Beginning in 1798, the Regio underwent a few name changes, reflecting the invading powers. After France invaded, the opera house was known first as Teatro Nazionale. Three years later, it assumed a French name, "Grand Théâtre des Arts", and in 1804, Teatro Imperiale. Only when the Savoys returned a decade later did the Teatro Regio regain its original name. In 1819, Giacomo Meyerbeer's *Semiramide riconosciuta* graced the stage, followed on February 11, 1840, by Carl Otto Nicolai's *Il templario*. The last two decades of the

1800s offered several world premieres—Alfredo Catalani's *Elda* (1880), Angelo Zanardini's *Isora di Provenza* (1883), *Loreley* (revision of *Elda*, February 16, 1890), Alfredo Keil's *Irene* (March 22, 1893), Gaetano Luporini's *I dispetti amorosi* (February 27, 1894), and Arturo Berutti's *Tarass Bulba* (March 9, 1895). The most famous *prime assolute* of the era were Giacomo Puccini's *Manon Lescaut*, (February 1, 1893), for which Puccini received fifty curtain calls, and *La bohème*, (February 1, 1896), when the audience was apathetic and the critics hostile, despite the conducting of Arturo Toscanini. (Toscanini was music director at the Regio between 1895 to 1898 and 1905 to 1906.) The Regio hosted the Italian premieres of Karl Goldmark's *Die Königin von Saba* on March 1, 1879, and Richard Strauss's *Salome* on December 22, 1906. The turn of the century also ushered in more world premieres—Italo Montemezzi's *Hellera* (March 17, 1909), Giocondo Fino's *La festa del grano* (February 12, 1911), Raffaele de Miero's *Morgana* (February 16, 1911), Ubaldo Pacchierotti's *Il Santo* (February 15, 1913), Riccardo Zandonai's *Francesca da Rimini* (February 19, 1914), Elmerico Francassi's *Finlandia* (March 25, 1914), Carlo Adolfo Cantù's *Ettore Fieramosca* (March 5, 1921), Adriano Lualdi's *La figlia del Re* (March 18, 1922), Giuseppe Blanc's *Il convegno dei martiri* (November 11, 1931), and *La valle degli eroi* (March 21, 1931).

World premieres were also staged at the Teatro Carignano and Teatro Vittorio Emanuele, including Franco Alfano's *Risurrezione* on November 30, 1904. These theaters hosted the Regio's opera seasons, along with Teatro della Moda, Teatro Alfieri, and Teatro Nuovo, after fire destroyed the opera house in 1936. During the 1940s and 1950s, works like Jules Massenet's *Manon* and *Werther*, Verdi's *Aida* with Maria Callas, Richard Wagner's *Lohengrin*, *Siegfried*, and *Tristan und Isolde*, Claude Debussy's *Pelléas et Mélisande*, Modest Mussorgsky's *Boris Godunov*, Carl Maria von Weber's *Der Freischütz*, Georges Bizet's *Les pêcheurs de perles*, Alexander Borodin's *Prince Igor* graced the various stages. The 1960s and until the Regio reopened in 1973, Cimarosa's *Il matrimonio segreto*, Nino Rota's *Il cappello di paglia di Firenze*, Vincenzo Bellini's *I Puritani* and *La sonnambula*, Wolfgang Amadeus Mozart's *Die Entführung aus dem Serail*, Igor Stravinsky's *The Rake's Progress*, Benjamin Britten's *Peter Grimes*, Richard Strauss's *Der Rosenkavalier*, Kurt Weill's *Der Aufstieg und Fall der Stadt Mahagonny*, and Verdi's *La forza del destino*, were on the schedule.

Sandro Fuga's *L'imperatore Jones* on April 4, 1976, was the first work premiere staged in the new opera house. Sylvano Bussotti's *Phaidra/Heliogabalus* followed on February 13, 1981, and Azio Corghi's *Gargantua* on May 2, 1984. The mid-1980s brought an innovative and naturalistic style to the contempory and foreign works, including Luigi Dallapiccola's *Ulisse* and Wagner's *Der Ring des Nibelungen*. The mainstream Italian operas remained traditional. The 1990s presented works like Mascagni's *Cavalleria rusticana*, Ruggero Leoncavallo's *I pagliacci*, Verdi's *Jérusalem*, *La forza del destino*, *Falstaff*, and *Simon Boccanegra*, Britten's *The Turn of the Screw*, Donizetti's *Il campanello*, *Lucia di Lammermoor*, and *L'elisir d'amore*, Bellini's *I Capuleti e i Montecchi*, Leoš Janáček's *Věc Makropulos* (The Makropulos Affair), Louis-Ferdinand Hérold's *La fille mal gardee*, Puccini's *La rondine* and *La bohème*, and Francesco Cilea's *Adriana Lecouvreur*. Recent offerings include Charles Gounod's *Roméo et Juliette*, Richard Strauss's *Ariadne auf Naxos*, Pyotr Il'yich Tchaikovsky's *Eugene Onegin*, Mozart's *Le nozze di Figaro*, Camille Saint-Saëns's *Samson et Dalila*, Puccini's *Turandot*, and Bellini's *La sonnambula*.

Teatro Regio

The struggle to get the opera house rebuilt after it was destroyed by fire lasted 37 years. It began with a national competition, which architects Morbelli and Morozzo won in 1937. There were changes made in 1939, 1948, 1955, and 1962, but no work was ever begun. The architects were finally released from their contract and their drawings replaced by a modern building, hidden behind Alfieri's original Baroque structure, (to prevent the clash of architectural styles). Construction finally began in 1966, and lasted seven years. In 1990, Teatro Regio Torino celebrated its 250th anniversary.

The Teatro Regio is a steel-and-red-brick structure with a glass facade, crisscrossed with metal rods. The U-shaped auditorium holds a large, steeply-raked orchestra level, with boxes

Teatro Regio facade (Turin, Italy).

circling the room. The ceiling, executed by the designer Castellano, is covered with vibrating indigo geometric patterns that fade as they approach the edges. The proscenium arch is purple and lavender, and clusters of crystal, needle-thin, rods, illuminate the auditorium with 1,762 bulbs. The auditorium accommodates 1,788.

Practical Information. Teatro Regio, Piazza Castello 215, Turin 10124. Tel: 39 11 88151, Fax: 39 11 881-5214. If visiting the Teatro Regio, stay at the Grand Hotel Sitea, via Carlo Alberto 35, 10123 Turin. Tel 39 11 517-0171, Fax: 39 11 548-090. It is centrally located and convenient to the opera house. The hotel can assist with opera schedules and tickets.

COMPANY STAFF

Sovrintendente. Giorgio Balmas. **Direttore Artistico:** Claudio Desderi.

Bibliography. *Guida al Teatro Regio Torino: 1740–1973* (Turin, 1978). *Teatro Regio Torino Stagione d'Opera 1988–1992* (Turin, 1992). *Teatro Regio Torino: Le Immagini 1986–89* (Turin, 1986–89). L. Carluccio, M. Cavallari, V. Ferrero, V. Massonis, *Il Teatro Regio di Torino* (Turin, 1970). Luciano Tamburini, *I teatri di Torino* (Turin, 1966). Marie-Thérèse Bouquet & Alberto Basso, *Storia del Teatro Regio di Torino*, 5 VOl: *Il Teatro di Corte dalle origini al 1788, Il Teatro della città dal 1788 al 1936, La scenografia, L'Architettura, Cronologie,* (Turin, 1976–1983), Aldo Brizio (ed.), *Il nuovo Teatro Regio di Torino* (Turin, 1973).

Thanks to Massimo Martino, Teatro Regio, and A. Bartolini.

VENICE

Teatro La Fenice (Ente Autonomo Lirico)

On January 29, 1996, Teatro La Fenice was destroyed by fire, the result of arson by an electrical contractor and his associates, who had been part of the renovation team. (They were behind in their work and faced stiff fines.) Gae Aulenti, Antonio Foscari, and Margherita Petranzan were the three architects in charge of the reconstruction, expected to take until the year 2000 and cost around 90,200,000,000 LIT. This will be the third Teatro La Fenice. The previous opera house was consumed by a fire on December 13, 1836, during rehearsals for the Venetian premiere of Gaetano Donizetti's *Lucia di Lammermoor.* The theater, like its symbol, a Phoenix, rose from the ashes, and reopened on December 26, 1837, with Giuseppe Lillo's *Rosmunda in Ravenna.* Designed by Tommaso and Giambattista Meduna, the theater was reconstructed following Giannantonio Selva's original plans. The first Teatro La Fenice, originally called Gran Teatro La Fenice, was inaugurated with Giovanni Paisiello's *I giuochi d'Agrigento* on May 16, 1792. La Fenice was so named to symbolize the resurrection of the Società which built the new theater after it lost ownership of the Teatro San Benedetto on June 10, 1787. Selva was the architect.

In 1624, Venice saw its first opera, Claudio Monteverdi's *Il combattimento di Tancredi e Clorinda,* at the Palazzo Mocenigo Dandolo, and Monteverdi's *Proserpina rapita* was presented in 1630 to celebrate the marriage of Giustiniana Mocenigo to Lorenzo Guistinian. Then the world's first public opera house, Teatro San Cassiano, opened on March 6, 1637, with Francesco Manelli's *Andromeda.* The opera house was named after the parish in which it was located, as was the Venetian custom. The theater offered five tiers of with 31 boxes on each. The Tron family owned the theater and rented the boxes to Venetian nobility and foreign princes. The general public was allowed entry to the hard, backless bench seats in the orchestra section. This was the second Teatro San Cassiano. The first one served as a playhouse, opened in 1556 and designed by Andrea Palladio. The theater was destroyed by fire in 1629. The (second) San Cassiano hosted the premiere of Monteverdi's *Il ritorno di Ulisse in patria* in February 1641, followed by Francesco Cavalli's *Egisto* in 1643, and his *L'Ormindo* the next year. The theater was extant until the 1800s. The success enjoyed by the Teatro San Cassiano led to the opening of several more public opera houses.

The Teatro San Giovanni e San Paolo was inaugurated with Francesco Paolo Sacrati's *Delia* on January 20, 1639. Monteverdi's *L'Adone,* his first opera for a public theater, was also staged during the inaugural season. The premiere of his *L'incoronazione di Poppea* was mounted in

1642. Considered Venice's best opera house of the time, it survived until 1748. Monteverdi's *Arianna* opened the Teatro San Moisè in 1640. Built by the San Barnaba branch of the Giustinian family, it hosted opera until 1818. Here several operas of Gioachino Rossini were introduced — *La cambiale di matrimonio* (November 3, 1810), *L'inganno felice* (January 8, 1812), *La scala di seta* (May 9, 1812), *L'occasione fa il ladro* (November 24, 1812), and *Il Signor Bruschino* (January 1813). Five years later, in 1818, it was converted into a puppet theater, known as Teatro Minerva. A store was subsequently constructed on the location. Sacrati's *La finta pazza* inaugurated the Teatro Novissimo on January 14, 1641. The wooden theater burned to the ground six years later. Antonio Cesti's *Orontea* opened the Teatro SS Apostoli in 1649, where opera was offered for 38 years. Cavalli's *Oristeo* opened the Teatro Apollinare and also offered his *La Calisto* in 1651. The theater was demolished in 1690. Castrovillari's *Pasife* opened the Teatro Salvatore in 1661, constructed by the Vendramin family. It is still extant and the oldest theater in Venice. In 1799, it became the Teatro San Luca, in 1833, Teatro Apollo, and since 1875 the Teatro Goldini. It hosted the premieres of Donizetti's *Enrico di Borgogna* (November 19, 1818) and *Un follia* (December 15, 1818). The Teatro Angelo, built on the Grand Canal by the families Capello and Marcello, was inaugurated with Freschi's *Elena rapita da Paride* in 1676. Operas graced its stage until the end of the 18th century, and included works by Antonio Vivaldi. Carlo Pallavicino's *Vespasiano* inaugurated the Teatro Giovanni Grisostomo in 1678. Designed by Tomaso Bezzi for Vincenzo Grimani, the opera house offered a golden auditorium with five tiers of 39 boxes each, trimmed with marble figurines and bas-reliefs. It was renamed Teatro Emoroniti, and since 1835, called Teatro Malibran, in honor of Maria Malibran who refused her fee, instructing the impresario to "use it for the theater." In 1699, the Teatro Fantino opened with Pignatta's *Paolo Emilio*, and survived 21 years. Although the Teatro San Samuele opened as a comedy house in 1655, operas graced the stage beginning in 1710 until its demise in 1894.

The history of La Fenice begins with the Teatro San Benedetto, constructed in 1755 and inaugurated with Gioacchino Cocchi's *Zoë*. Fire destroyed the building in 1773, but it was rebuilt, reopening in 1784 as the Teatro Venier. A short time later, there was a dispute between the Venier family, which owned the land, and the Società, which owned the theater. The Società took the case to court and lost. The Teatro Venier was renamed Teatro Rossini in 1868, in honor of the Rossini operas that it introduced — *L'italiana in Algeri* (May 22, 1813) and *Eduardo e Cristina* (April 24, 1819). The Rossini also hosted the world premieres of Giacomo Meyerbeer's *Emma di Resburgo* (June 26, 1819) and Federico and Luigi Ricci's *Crispino e la Comare* (February 28, 1850).

After La Fenice opened in 1792, the world premiere of Giovanni Simone Mayr's *Sapho* took place in 1794, followed by Domenico Cimarosa's *Gli Orazi e i Curiazi* two years later. Rossini opera's were then introduced — *Tancredi* (February 6, 1813), *Sigismondo*, (December 26, 1814), and *Semiramide*, (February 3, 1823); those of Vincenzo Bellini — *I Capuleti e i Montecchi* (March 11, 1830) and *Beatrice di Tenda* (March 16, 1833), and Donizetti — *Belisario* (February 4, 1836) and *Maria di Rudenz* (January 30, 1838). Five operas by Giuseppe Verdi received their world premiere at La Fenice. *Ernani*, introduced on March 9, 1844, was the first Verdi opera not premiered by La Scala. *Ernani* was so successful that Verdi took 50 curtain calls. When *Attila* was premiered in 1846, Austria occupied Venice. Verdi became a hero with *"Avrai tu l'universo, resti l'Italia a me"* (you will have the universe but leave Italy to me). Verdi's *Macbeth* also aroused patriotic fervor with Malcolm and Macduff's duet *"La patria tradita"* such that the final act was banned. Verdi's *Rigoletto* (then called La maledizione) did not please the Austrian censors, but there was a compromise and *Rigoletto* was given its *prima assoluta* on March 11, 1851. Verdi's *La traviata* followed two years later and according to some accounts, including Verdi's own, was not well-received. Among the reasons was the soprano who sang Violetta, Fanny Salvini-Donatelli, was a large lady, so when she died consumption, it looked ridiculous. His last Venetian premiere, *Simon Boccanegra* on March 12, 1857, was not one of the public's favorites, although the opera remained one of Verdi's. Meanwhile, Giuseppe Apolloni's *Lida di Granata* was introduced on January 23, 1855, followed by Ruggero Leoncavallo's *La bohème* on May 6, 1897, and Ermanno Wolf-Ferrari's *La Cenerentola* in 1901.

La Fenice also presented several Italian

premieres, including Ambroise Thomas's *Hamlet*, Richard Wagner's *Das Rheingold* on April 14, 1883, *Die Walküre* on April 15, 1883, *Götterdämmerung* on April 18, 1883, and Camille Saint-Saëns's *Samson et Dalila* on March 8, 1893. During this era, Enrico Caruso, Toti dal Monte, and Beniamino Gigli performed at the opera house. World War I closed the opera house, and in 1936, the descendants of the Società handed over their boxes to the municipality (for a price). In 1938, La Fenice became an *Ente Autonomo*, with Verdi's *Don Carlo* inaugurating the season. La Fenice hosted opera during World War II, and the liberation of Milan was announced during a performance of Giacomo Puccini's *Madama Butterfly* on April 26, 1945.

During the 1950s until the early 1970s, Venice hosted the Contemporary Music Festival, at which time La Fenice presented the world premiere of several 20th century operas, including Igor Stravinsky's *The Rake's Progress*, (September 11, 1951); Benjamin Britten's *Turn of the Screw*, (September 14, 1954); Serge Prokofiev's *Ognenniy angel* (The Fiery Angel) (first stage performance, September 29, 1955); and Luigi Nono's *Intolleranza 1960* in 1961. The era saw artists like Maria Callas, Renata Tebaldi, Marilyn Horne, Mirella Freni, and Luciano Pavarotti. In 1983, more than 130 years after its premiere at La Fenice, Ricci's *Crispino e la Comare* was restaged for carnival 1983. The beginning of the 1990s offered Donizett's *Don Pasquale*, Giacomo Puccini's *La bohème*, Wolfgang Amadeus Mozart's *Così fan tutte*, Verdi's *Ernani*, Richard Wagner's *Lohengrin*, and Ludwig van Beethoven's *Fidelio*. La Fenice's bicentennial celebration in 1992 included remounting the most important operas that La Fenice had introduced. Recently, La Fenice has been plagued by a small public subsidy and limited theater seating capacity, making its role as an international opera center something of the past. Since La Fenice burned down, subsequent seasons have been given in the tent-like Palafenice. Recent offerings include

Jules Massenet's *Werther*, Ludwig van Beethoven's *Fidelio*, and Puccini's *Suor Angelica*.

Teatro La Fenice

Teatro La Fenice acquired its current appearance (before the 1996 fire) from work done in the 1850s by Giambattista Medusa. Structural problems, resulting from a hasty rebuilding after the 1836 fire, became evident in 1853. After the work, Errico Petrella's *Marco Visconti* reopened the opera house on December 26, 1854.

La Fenice is a perfectly proportioned Neoclassical building. The lower level of the facade holds a tetrastyle portico with Corinthian columns, above which are a balustrade, masks of Comedy and Tragedy, and statues of Terpsichore

Teatro La Fenice (Venice, Italy).

Teatro La Fenice facade detail (Venice, Italy).

and Melpomene. SOCIETAS MDCCXCII is inscribed on the facade. The auditorium before the 1996 fire was a gold and coral horseshoe-shaped room that dazzled with its unrivaled elegance. The parapets of the three box tiers and two galleries display endless gold filigree encircling painted panels of medallions, putti, and flowers. The large center box, flanked by a pair of gilded caryatids, was topped by a golden Lion of Venice holding *PAX TIBI MARCE EVANGELISTA MEUS* (Peace to you Marco, my evangelist). A large gilded phoenix stared from the top of the proscenium arch. There were 823 seats.

Practical Information. Teatro La Fenice, Campo San Fantin 2519, 30124 Venice. Tel: 39 41 786 562, Fax 39 41 786 545. When visiting the Teatro La Fenice, stay at the Hotel Gritti Palace, Campo San Maria del Giglio 2467, 30124 Venice. Tel: 39 41 794-611 or 1-800-325-3535, Fax 39 41 520 0942. The Gritti Palace is located on the Grand Canal and close to La Fenice. The hotel can assist with opera schedules and tickets.

COMPANY STAFF AND WORLD PREMIERES

Sovrintendente. Tito Menegazzo. **Direttore Artistico**: Francesco Siciliani.

World Premieres. (Teatro la Fenice) **Rossini Operas:** *Tancredi*, February 6, 1813; *Sigismondo*, December 26, 1814; *Semiramide*, February 3, 1823. **Bellini Operas:** *I Capuleti e i Montecchi*, March 11, 1830; *Beatrice di Tenda*, March 16, 1833. **Donizetti Operas:** *Belisario*, February 4, 1836; *Maria di Rudenz*, January 30, 1838. **Verdi Operas:** *Ernani*, March 9, 1844; *Attila*, March 17, 1846; *Rigoletto*, March 11, 1851; *La traviata*, March 6, 1853; *Simon Boccanegra*, March 12, 1857.

Bibliography. Manlio Brusatin & Giuseppe Pavanello, *Il Teatro La Fenice: I Progetti * L'Architettura * Le Decorazioni* (Venice, 1987). Ufficio Stampa di Teatro La Fenice, *Gran Teatro La Fenice* (Venice, 1985). Mario Nani Mocenigo, *Il Teatro La Fenice: Notizie storiche e artistiche* (Venice, 1926). Nicola Mangini, *I Treatri di Venezia* (Milan, 1974).

Thanks to the Ufficio Stampa, Teatro La Fenice.

Teatro La Fenice auditorium before fire (Venice, Italy).

——————————————————————— VERONA

Arena di Verona
(Ente Autonomo Lirico, Summer Festival)
Teatro Filarmonico
(Regular Opera Season and Spring Festival)

The Arena of Verona, the second largest Roman amphitheater in the world, (only the Coliseum in Rome is larger) was constructed during the second or third decade of the first century A.D. to host *munera gladitoria* (gladitorial fights) and *venationes* (hunts). The arena attained operatic fame on August 10, 1913, when Giuseppe Verdi's *Aida*, conducted by Tullio Serafin, with Ester Mazzoleni (Aida), Giovanni Zenatello (Radames), and Maria Gay Zenatello (Amneris) inaugurated its first summer season in the presence of a distinguished audience which included Italo Montemezzi, Luigi Illica, Giacomo Puccini, Pietro Mascagni, Ildebrando Pizzetti, and Ric-

cardo Zandonai. Italian tenor Giovanni Zenatello organized the opera performances. The festival slowly grew into the most spectacular open-air operatic extravaganza in the world, its success attributed to the arena's phenomenal acoustics — sound reflects off the ancient stones with the same perfection as found in the famous opera houses of the 1700s.

One could say that the tradition of opera in the arena was born on November 25, 1822, when, as part of the festivities of the Congress of Vienna which Verona hosted, Gioachino Rossini wrote and conducted a piece called *La Santa Alleanza* (The Sacred Alliance), followed in 1842 by his

Stabat Mater. The use of the arena as a performance venue continued in 1856 when Pietro Lenotti's *Il casino di campagna* (a musical farce) and *La fanciulla di Grand* (a dance in seven scenes) were offered followed by Gaetano Donizetti's *Le convenienze e inconvenienze teatrali* and *I pazzi per progetto*.

After the initial *Aida* in 1913, which became the arena's trademark, (more than 350 performances since the inaugural, the second season (1914) offered Georges Bizet's *Carmen*. It was more an "Italian" Carmen than a French one, modeled on the *verismo* school interpretation with passion, vengeful rage, and tragic feeling. After World War II, there were several memorable *Carmen* productions, especially when Franco Corelli was José and Giulietta Simionato was Carmen. More and more, the *Carmen* productions became a "French Grand Opera" with the requisite ballet added, with the music borrowed from another Bizet work. The arena bent its "Italian-only" rule and offered the opera in French. After *Aida*, *Carmen* is the second most staged work with 120 performances, but claims the number one disaster. During the fourth act of a 1970s production, with Corelli and Grace Bumbry, there were numerous horses accompanying Escamillo's procession. A sudden loud sound from the orchestra pit startled one of the horses which leaped into the pit, landing on the kettle drums. Amazingly, neither man nor beast was hurt, but the best was yet to come. Maestro Gianandrea Gavazzeni put down his baton and, forgetting the acoustics of the arena, whispered "*Quel piccolo finocchio di regista*" (an Italian insult best left in Italian), causing hysterical laughter amongst the 18,000 spectators.

World War I closed the arena from 1914 to 1918, which was reopened on July 31, 1919, with Amilcare Ponchielli's *Il figliuol prodigo*. There were 17 scheduled performances of the work, and none came. *Il figliuol prodigo* was never staged again. During the 1920s, the repertory was broadened by mounting other rarely performed works—Mascagni's *Il piccolo Marat*, conducted by the composer himself for twelve performances, but never heard again in the arena; Jules Massenet's *Le Roi de Lahore*, although finely crafted, not only disappeared from the stage of the arena, but from the stages in all of Italy, and Arrigo Boïto's *Nerone* which bored the audience to the point of "polite intolerance." The 1920s also saw a schedule expansion to two operas, Verdi's *Aida* and Arrigo Boïto's *Mefistofele*. Richard Wagner's *Lohengrin*, with Ezio Pinza and Aureliano Pertile entered the repertory and was repeated in 1933, 1949, and 1963. Other Wagner entries survived only one season: *Parsifal* in 1924, *Die Meistersinger von Nürnburg* in 1931, *Tannhäuser* in 1938, and *Die Walküre* in 1950.

Before the founding of the Ente Autonomo Spettacoli Lirici in 1936, (suspended between 1940 and 1947), a variety of organizations and people managed the opera seasons: Lyrica Italica ARS 1919-20, Casa Musicale Sonzogno 1921-22, Ente Autonomo Fiera 1930-1931, Emilio Ferroni, Ciro Ragazzini, and Gianni Scalabrini 1932-33, Ente Comunale degli Spettacoli 1934-35, and Società Spettacoli 1946.

Riccardo Zandonai's *Giulietta e Romeo*, staged on August 16, 1939, was the last performance before the arena closed because of World War II. On August 1, 1946, Verdi's *Aida* with Margherita Grandi (Aida), Galliano Masini (Radames), and Elena Nicolai (Amneris) reopened the arena. Verdi's *La traviata* was also on the boards. Within a couple of years the program increased to three, then four and finally to five operas. Although the number of works each season increased, the variety of operas decreased. In fact, since the beginning of the summer opera festival in 1913, only five dozen different operas have been on the *cartellone*, and of that, less than three dozen of those were staged for more than one season. When the repertory veers from this course, many seats are empty. The arena must earn around 60% of its budget from ticket sales, so it sticks to the "tried and true," spectacular extravaganzas every season.

Success at the arena depends not only on the opera, but also on contracting the appropriate singers—big names with big voices. Some of the more successful ones go back to the earlier years: Giacomo Lauri-Volpi as Calaf in Puccini's *Turandot* in 1928; Beniamino Gigli as Lionello in Friedrich von Flotow's *Martha* in 1929; Lauri-Volpi in Giacomo Meyerbeer's *Les Huguenots* in 1933; Gigli in Ponchielli's *La gioconda* and Umberto Giordano's *Andea Chénier* in 1934; Maria Calla's debut in *La gioconda* in 1947; Richard Tucker and Renate Tebaldi, and Nicola Rossi Lemeni in *La gioconda* and Charles Gounod's *Faust*; Callas in Puccini's *Turandot* in 1948; Giulietta Simionato's debut as Rosina in *Il barbiere di Siviglia*; Magda Olivero's debut in 1951; Mario del Monico's debut in 1946 and return for four seasons in the early 1950s; Corelli's debut in 1955, returning every season until 1961, and returning again for three seasons in the early 1970s; Leontyne Price in Verdi's *Aida* in 1958 and *Il trovatore* in 1959; Plácido Domingo, Birgit Nilsson, and Montserrat Caballé debuts in 1969.

The arena has its own customs and atmosphere. An aspiring singer in the *gradinata* might serenade the crowd, and as the performance begins, anywhere from 1,000 to 10,000 candles are lighted. But it is difficult to concentrate — there are too many distractions: some people talk, even more smoke, the tired ones snore, empty bottles roll, and thousands of cameras flash, "flattening" the production. But it is the grand spectacles which are mounted in the world's largest "opera house" that are unique and they do not disappoint. The Aidas, Don Carlos, and Nabuccos are grand, with traditional, perfectly symmetrical, massive sets, and which are sometimes complemented by nature — a full moon for the queen's garden scene in Verdi's *Don Carlo* — or the just spectacular, like the Grand March in Verdi's *Aida* which includes most of the animals from the zoo and enough people to populate a small village. But opera on such a grand scale becomes a spectator sport. And then there was Rossini's *Il barbiere di Siviglia* in 1996, entrusted to the German director Tobias Richter, whose symbolic concept of Rosina arriving via an enormous cage attached to a hot-air balloon did not fly; it fact it crashed. The production was better suited for his Oper am Rhein in Düsseldorf (see Oper am Rhein entry), where he is Intendant. But Verdi's *Macbeth*, staged in 1997, by Pier-Luigi Pizzi was electrifying. Eschewing the spectacular conceptions associated with arena productions, Pizzi designed a simple, but powerful set which defined the emotional impact of Shakespeare's tragedy along the lines with Verdi's music. With no distracting scenery, and expressive and symbolic lighting (red and stark white) this Macbeth drove straight to the soul, leaving one drained from the profound experience. The impossible had been achieved: intimacy in an amphitheater seating 18,000, a distillation of the essence of the work without the usual arena clutter. Terror and horror called out from the castle which resembled the guard tower at a concentration camp. The usual harmonious balance of the arena productions gave way to a skewed equilibrium, with slanted ramps that included banquet table seating hundreds. In place of the stereotype movements and old fashion method of singing arias standing immobile, facing the audience, an intense interaction developed, gripping the singers and audience. This was the arena at its finest.

Teatro Filarmonico — Festival di Primavera

The Festival di Primavera (Festival of Spring) was begun in 1994 by the Ente Autonomo to showcase the richness of Italy's forgotten music. It takes place in the Teatro Filarmonico, which was constructed between 1719 and 1729 for the Philharmonic Academy, an old institution founded in 1543. Designed by Francesco Galli Bibiena, it was inaugurated the evening of January 6, 1732, with Antontio Vivaldi's *La fida ninfa*. Fire claimed the theater in 1749. Rebuilt, it reopened five years later with Johann Hasse's *Alessandro nell'Indie* and Davide Perez's *Lucio Vero*. The opera house hosted several premieres during the second half of the 1700s, including Tommaso Traetta's *Olimpiade* in 1758 and Domenico Cimarosa's *Giumio Bruto* in 1781. The Filarmonico was destroyed during a World War II bombing raid. It was reconstructed in 1982 by the Philharmonic Academy and Alberti Tantini.

The festivals have themes; the first three festivals dealt with "The Festival Theater and Music of the Republic of Venice. The result was Vivaldi's *La fida ninfa*, Antonio Salieri's *Les Danaides*, Vivaldi's *Il Tamerlano*, and Ferdinando Gasparo Bertoni's *Orfeo*, among others. A world premiere was included since it dealt with the Orfeo theme, Lorenzo Ferrero's *Nascita di Orfeo*, on April 19, 1996. The fourth festival looked toward the Orient in the works of the 1700s. To this end, Giovanni Paisiello's *I'idolo cinese* and Domenico Cimarosa's *I turchi amanti* (I traci amanti) received their Verona premieres, along with a concert form of Salieri's *Axur re d'Ormus* (first introduced in the 1994 festival). Unfortunately, the unknown does not attract many people, and the theater was practically empty. This was especially regrettable with the surprising richness and complexity of *Axur* and the entertaining quality of the other operas.

Teatro Filarmonico Opera Season

The Ente Autonomo Lirico inaugurated a regular opera season in 1975 with Salieri's *Falstaff, ossia le tre burle*. The repertory offered other rarely-performed and forgotten works, like Ferruccio Busoni's *Turandot*, Giuseppe Verdi's *Un giorno di regno* (Il finto Stanislao), the Italian premiere of Daniel Auber's *Manon Lescaut*, and the first performance in modern times of Antonio Vivaldi's *Catone in Utica*. New works were also presented with the world premiere of P. Arcà's *Gattabianca* on February 27, 1993.

Arena di Verona *ala* (remaining outside wall) (Verona, Italy)

Arena

The arena was constructed out of limestone from the Lessini Mountains, except the vaulting, which was a mixture of pebbles and concrete. The huge amphitheater rests on a bed of concrete that covered the entire area. Shaped like an ellipse, the arena was located just outside the most ancient wall of the city. Only on the northwest side, where a piece of the *ala*, or outside wall, still stands, one can get an idea of the original appearance of the amphitheater. The three orders of arches which formed the original outer wall corresponded to the three orders of seating inside. The simplicity of its modular plan made the measurements of the arena proportionate to each other. The two axes of the ellipse which form the amphitheater measure 75.68 meters and 44.43 meters, which converted into Roman measurements became 250 by 150 Roman feet. This established a 5 to 3 relationship between the two principal axes of the ellipse. The seating ranges from sitting on stone steps, to brown metal seats to cushy red velvet seat. The arena accommodates around 18,000.

Teatro Filarmonico

Although the Filarmonico boasts an impressive main entrance facade lined with six massive Ionic columns forming a colonnade, it is no longer used. Entrance is through a non-descript side entrance. The gold, red, and ivory auditorium holds four tiers of boxes plus a huge center royal box. The Filarmonico was one of the early theaters to benefit from improved sightlines by jutting the boxes out one in respect to the other, and then gently sloping them downward toward the stage. Gilded festoons

Arena di Verona preparing set for *Aida* (Verona, Italy).

and musical motifs embellish the parapets. The proscenium boxes are flanked by gilded Corinthian columns.

Practical Information. Arena di Verona or Teatro Filarmonico, Piazza Bra 28, 37100 Verona. Tel: 39 45 590 109: 39 45 590-201. If attending performances at either the Arena or Teatro Filarmonio, stay at the historic Hotel Gabbia d'Oro, Corso Porta Borsari 4/a, 37121 Verona. Tel 39 45 800-3060; Fax 39 45 590-293. It is a luxurious but cozy hotel with superb service, ideally located in the old city, and near the arena and Teatro Filarmonico. The Gabbia d'Oro can assist with opera schedules and tickets.

COMPANY STAFF, PREMIERES, AND REPERTORY

Sovrintendente. Gianfranco de Bosio 1993–present. Maurizio Pulica 1990–92. Francesco Ernani 1986–90. Renzo Giacchieri 1982–86. Carlo Alberto Cappelli 1971–82. Gianfranco de Bosio 1968–70. Bindo Missiroli 1957–67. Mario Tommasoli 1956. Pariso Votto 1953. Alberto Tantini 1949–52. Giovanni Zenatello 1947-48. Pino Donati 1936–1939.

Direttori Artistici: Gabriele Gandini 1996–present. Mauro Trombetta 1994–1996. Lorenzo Ferrero 1991–1994. Carlo Perucci 1986–90. Aldo Rocchi 1982–85. Pierluigi Urbini 1981. Aldo Rocchi 1978–80. Luciano Chailly 1975–77. Arrnando Gatto 1973-74. Mario Medici 1969-70. Gino Bertolaso 1946. Onofrio Zenatello 1930-31. Giovacchino Forzano 1926–28. Giovanni Zenatello 1921–22.

World Premieres. (Teatro Filarmonico since 1975) P. Arcà's *Gattabianca*, February 27, 1993; L. Ferrero's *Nascita di Orfeo*, April 19, 1996 (Festival di Primavera).

Opera Repertory. Arena di Verona, by year of first performance at the Arena: **1913:** Aida. **1914:** Carmen. **1919:** Il figliuol prodigo. **1920:** Mefistofele. **1921:** Samson et Dalila, Il piccolo Marat. **1922:** I pagliacci, Lohengrin. **1923:** Norma, Le Roi de Lahore. **1924:** Andra Chénier, Parsifal. **1925:** La gioconda, Mosè. **1926:** Il trovatore, Nerone. **1927:** La vestale. **1928:** Turandot, Rigoletto. **1929:** Faust, Isabeau, Martha. **1930:** La forza del destino, Boris Godunov. **1931:** Guglielmo Tell, Die Meistersinger von Nürnberg. **1932:** Un ballo in maschera, L'Africaine. **1933:** Les Huguenots. **1934:** Lucia di Lammermoor. **1935:** Cavalleria rusticana, Loreley. **1936:** Otello, L'elisir d'amore. **1937:** Tosca. **1938:** Nabucco, La bohème, La favorita, Tannhäuser. **1939:**

Giulietta e Romeo. **1946:** La traviata. **1949:** La fanciulla del West. **1948:** Il barbiere di Siviglia. **1950:** Les pêcheurs de perles, Die Walküre. **1951:** Manon. **1952:** L'incantesimo. **1969:** Don Carlo. **1970:** Manon Lescaut. **1971:** Macbeth. **1972:** Ernani. **1973:** Simon Boccanegra. **1977:** Roméo et Juliette. **1978:** Madama Butterfly. **1984:** I Lombardi. **1985:** Attila. **Teatro Filarmonico: 1975:** Falstaff ossia le tre burle. **1976:** La traviata, Il barbiere di Siviglia, Così fan tutte. **1977:** Rigoletto, Tosca, Prima la musica poi le parole, Manon, Una domanda di matrimonio, Norma. **1978:** I Capuleti e i Montecchi, Don Pasquale, La bohème, Werther, Orlando furioso. **1979:** Adriana Lecouvreur, Simon Boccanegra, Orlando furioso, Le nozze di Figaro. **1980:** Lucia di Lammermoor, Bastien e Bastienne, Turandot (Busoni), Francesca da Rimini. **1981:** Risurrezione (Alfano), Falstaff ossia le tre burle (Salieri), La voix humaine, Sette canzoni, L'elisir d'amore, Andrea Chénier. **1982:** La sonnambula, Il barbiere di Siviglia, Il sacrificio di Lucrezia, La traviata, Madama Butterfly. **1983:** Falstaff, I Capuleti e i Montecchi, Giulietta e Romeo. **1984:** Manon Lescaut, Carmina Burana, Manon Lescaut (Auber), Catone in Utica (Vivaldi). **1985:** Orfeo ed Euridice, Un giorno di regno (Il finto Stanislao), Carmina Burana. **1986:** L'amico Fritz, Fedora, Giulietta e Romeo, Orfeo ed Euridice, Luisa Miller. **1987:** Bertoldo, Bertoldino e Cacasenno, Rigoletto, Die Zauberflöte. La bohème, I quattro rusteghi, Prince Igor. **1988:** Lucia di Lammermoor, L'italiana in Algeri, Tosca, Giovanna d'Arco. **1989:** Così fan tutte, I pagliacci, Don Pasquale, Adriana Lecouvreur. **1990:** Otello, Die lustige Witwe, Il barbiere di Siviglia, Cirano. **1991:** L'amore dei tre re, Die Zauberflöte, Madama Butterfly. **1992:** Guglielmo Tell, Il trovatore, Maria Stuarda, Transitus animae. **1993:** Loreley, Gattabianca, La sonnambula. **1994:** Lucia di Lammermoor, Le nozze di Figaro. **1995:** Les contes d'Hoffmann, Die lustige Witwe. **1996:** Die Fledermaus, Les dialogues des Carmélites, L'elisir d'amore. **Festival Di Primavera: Teatro Filarmonico: 1994:** Il Tamerlano, Axur re d'Ormus, Teresa e Claudio, L'inganno felice. **1995:** La fida ninfa, Rimini addio, La finta semplice, L'amfiparnaso, Il ballo delle ingrate. **1996:** Nascita di Orfeo, Les Dandaides, Orfeo. **1997:** L'idolo cinese, I turchi amanti, Axur re d'Ormus.

Bibliography. Roberto Pasini, Remo Schiavo, *The Verona Arena: The Largest Opera House in the World* (Verona, 1995). Filippo Coarelli, Lanfranco Franzoni, *The Verona Arena: Twenty Centuries of History* (Verona, 1972). Various authors, *Arena di Verona 70°, 74°, 75°, Festivals dell'Opera Lirica* (Verona, 1992, 1996, 1997). *21° Stagione Lirica e di Balletto, Teatro Filarmonico* (Verona, 1995). *IV° Festival di Primivera* (Verona, 1997). *Arena di Verona dal 1913 al 1977 tra musica e cronaca* (Verona, 1977). *Cinquant'anni di melodrama all'Arena di Verona* (Verona, 1964).

Thanks to Annalisa Masselli and Caterina Barboni, Arena di Verona, and Feltre Silvana.

VICENZA

Teatro Olimpico

The Teatro Olimpico was inaugurated on March 3, 1585, with Sophocles's *Oedipus the King*. It was originally built as a venue for Classical drama. Andrea Palladio was the original architect, and upon his death, Vincenzo Scamozzi took over. This was Palladio's final project.

The theaters hosts mainly concerts and plays, with one opera offered a season. Some recent works include Wolfgang Amadeus Mozart's *Mitridate, re di Ponte,* and *Le nozze di Figaro,* Francesco Cavalli's *Calisto,* and Christoph Willibald Gluck's *Paride ed Elena.*

Teatro Olimpico

Behind the exterior of an old fortress, construction began on the Teatro Olimpico on February 28, 1580. It was a reinterpretation of the classic Roman theater with an elliptical auditorium replacing the customary hemishpere shape. In 1653, the walls were decorated with *trompe l'oeil* and friezes by Maffei. In 1750 the stage wall was ornamented with tabernacles, carytids, columns, and sculptures of academicians. A balustrade was also added above the colonnade, embellished with a row of statues. Cassetti was responsible for this work. The capacity is 496.

Practical Information. Teatro Olimpico, Piazza Matteotti, 36100 Vicenza. Tel: 39 444 32 37 81, Fax: 39 444 54 66 19. If visiting, contact the Italian Government Travel Offices (ENIT), 630 Fifth Avenue, New York, NY 10011. Tel: 212-245-4822.

Other Italian Opera Houses

Other opera houses in Italy are noted below by name, address, telephone, fax, and recent repertory.

Teatro Fraschini. Corso Strada Nuova, 136, Pavia. Tel: 39 382-3711, Fax: 39 382-371-2271. **Direttore Artistico:** Fiorenzo Grassi. **Recent Repertory:** La frascatana (Paisiello), Falstaff, Le nozze di Figaro, Don Pasquale, Il trovatore. When visiting

the Teatro Fraschini, stay at the Albergo Ariston Pavia, Via Scopoli 10/D, 27100 Pavia. Tel: 39 0382 34334, Fax: 39 0382 25667. Centrally situated, the Ariston is near the opera house.

Taormina Arte. (Summer Festival) Comitato Taormina Arte, Via Pirandello 31, 98039 Taormina. Tel: 39 942 21141, Fax: 39 942 23348. **Recent Repertory:** Lohengrin, Elektra, Norma, Salome.

Luxembourg
LUXEMBOURG

Théâtre Municipal

The Municipal Theater opened on April 15, 1964, with Maurice Ravel's *Boléro*, orchestral works, and a ballet. The Grand Duchess Charlotte, Prince Félix, the heir-apparent Grand Duke Jean and his consort, the Grand Duchess Joséphine-Charlotte were in attendance. Designed by Alain Bourbonnais, the theater was constructed as a birthday gift to celebrate the 1000th birthday of the founding of Luxembourg. The inaugural celebration continued a few days later with a production of Giuseppe Verdi's *Aida*.

From the 1600s, traveling French and German troupes provided theatrical entertainment to the inhabitants. Following the French Revolution, buildings constructed specifically as theaters came into being. On June 4, 1825, there was a notice in the newspaper that the opera-and-drama troupe of M. Jolibois from Thionville, France, would make its debut in Luxembourg, but it never arrived. Instead, a German troupe from Cologne, under the direction of Herr Hanzen, arrived on July 24, 1825. Scattered among the dramatic fare offered during their sojourn were some operas, including Carl Maria von Weber's *Der Freischütz* and Wolfgang Amadeus Mozart's *Die Zauberflöte*. In 1826, the Cologne troupe returned, repeating their *Die Zauberflöte* and *Der Freischütz* productions, as well as a parody of the latter opera, called *Staberl in der Wolfsschlucht*. The troupe never returned again to Luxembourg. In 1829, the St. Edme Troupe performed Verdi's *Les vêpres siciliennes*. Three years later Daniel Auber's *Fra Diavolo* graced the stage and in 1833, Herr Eisenhut's Troupe offered Joseph Weigl's *Die*

Schweizerfamilie and Lolie's *Das Geheimnis*. The year 1845 saw a lot of operatic activity. Director M. Nolte offered Vincenzo Bellini's *Norma* on May 25, which received a good review except the chorus was called "*schlect*" (bad). On May 29, Auber's *Fra diavolo* was mounted followed by Adolphe Adam's *Der Postillon von Lonjumeau* on June 10, Adrien Boildieu's *Jean de Paris* on June 29, and on July 1 by Albert Lortzing's *Zar und Zimmermann*. A substantial opera season continued in 1847 with Giacomo Meyerbeer's *Robert le Diable*, Gaetano Donzetti's *La fille du régiment*, Lortzing's *Der Waffenschmied*, Mozart's *Don Giovanni* and *Die Zauberflöte*, Friedrich von Flotow's *Alessandro Stradella*, Auber's *La muette di Portici*, V. Thonard's *Aschenbrödel*, and Bellini's *La sonnambula*. Luxembourg hosted more Bellini in 1849 — *I Capulei e i Montecchi* and *Norma*, as well as Auber's *Fra Diavolo* and Mozart's *Die Zauberflöte*. Opera continued during the 1850s including Flotow's *Martha*.

Luxembourg has no indigenous opera tradition, and it does not have its own opera company. The Municipal is a presenting organization: opera is staged by visiting companies, primarily from Germany and Poland. In 1995, Jeannot Comes, director of the Théâtre Municipal took advantage of the fact that Luxembourg was designated the Cultural Capital of Europe to create the first homegrown opera production — a world premiere of Mikis Theodorakis's *Electra* on May 2, 1995. There was a large cast composed of mainly Greek, Russian, and Polish artists, and included three mezzo sopranos, Eva Revides, Oksana Prudnik, and Wita Nikolajenko alternating in the title role; two sopranos, Martha Arapi and Joanna Cortes sharing the role of Chrysothemis; two tenors Vanghelis Hatzissimos and Slyvester Kostecki sharing the role of Egysthe; two mezzo sopranos Lina Tentzeri and Eva Werka sharing the role of Clytemnestre; two baritones Panajotis Athanassopoulos and Zbigniew Marcias sharing the role of Oreste; two tenors Stamatis Beris and Piotr Friebe sharing the role of Pylade, and basses Frangiskos Voutsinos and Bogdan Kurowski sharing the role of Pedagogue with the orchestra, chorus, and ballet from the Teatr Wielki, Pozan. The future is geared toward a more adventurous programming of modern opera and ballet.

One of Comes's goals is for the Municipal to regularly produce its own operas, starting with small productions. He is building a company in steps as money becomes available. Originally money from private sources was prohibited, when public money was plentiful. Recently, with less public money available, private donations and sponsorships are allowed. Donations, however, still make up only a small percentage (3.5%) of the budget. The state contributes only slightly more, 4%, with the rest coming from the city. Since half of the population of Luxembourg is composed of foreigners from the European Union, the audience spans a wide spectrum requiring the works presented to have a broad appeal. Recent offerings include Weber's *Oberon*, Benatzky's *Im weißen Rößl*, and Verdi's *La forza del destino*.

Théâtre Municipal

On December 20, 1958, an architectural competition was announced to design the new theater and on November 30, 1959, Bourbonnais received the commission to build it. Soon Bourbonnais grew unhappy with all the demands made upon his project from the builders, and in 1962 amidst much criticism, packed his bags and left town. Architect Josy Kons took over and directed the construction, which was completed in time for the April 1964 inauguration. It is the only theater in Luxembourg.

The Municipal is a long rectangular building. Many small windows of various sizes and shapes punctuate a facade of stones of a variety of textures and dimensions. The style of the building is Egyptian — the small windows of strange shapes to keep out the light and heat — but this is not appropriate for Luxembourg's cool, wet, climate. The auditorium has a 1960s look, fusing several colors — orange seats, olive-green carpet,

Théâtre Municipal (Luxembourg City, Luxembourg).

and red velvet curtain with dark wood walls and a plain black parapet that "zig-zags" on the single balcony. There are 888 seats for opera performances.

Practical Information. Théâtre Municipal, Rond-Point R. Schuman, 2525 Luxembourg. Tel: 32 41 21 47 20, Fax: 32 41 21 02 01. When visiting the Théâtre Municipal, stay at the Hôtel Sofitel, 6, rue du Fort Niedergrünewald, 2015 Luxembourg. Tel: 352 43 77 61, Fax 352 43 86 58. It is in a quiet location near the opera house. The hotel can assist with opera tickets and schedule.

COMPANY STAFF, PREMIERES, AND REPERTORY

Directeur. Jeannot Comes.
World Premieres. M. Theodorakis's *Electra* May 2, 1995. C. Kerger's *Drago* (children's opera) May 26, 1995.
Repertory. **1988-89:** Orpheus und Euridice (*Croatian National Theater, Zagrab*), Prodaná nevěsta (The Bartered Bride) (*Janáček Opera, Brno*), Rigoletto (*Badisches Staatstheater, Karlsruhe*), Der fliegende Holländer (*Nationaltheater Mannheim*), Albert Herring (*Badisches Staatstheater, Karlsruhe*), Pikovaya dama (Queen of Spades) (*Nationaloper Warsaw, Theatr Wielki*). **1989-90:** Aida (*Nationaltheater Mannheim*), Le nozze di Figaro (*Saarländisches Staatstheater, Saarbrücken*), Salome (*Nationaloper Zagreb*), Lucia di Lammermoor (*Badisches Staatstheater Karlsruhe*), Prince Igor (*Nationaloper Warschau, Theatr Wielki*), La bohème (*Badisches Staatstheater Karlsruhe*). **1990-91:** Madama Butterfly (*Badisches Staatstheater Karlsruhe*), Fidelio (*Nationaltheater Mannheim*), Les contes d'Hoffmann (*Saar-

ländisches Staatstheater, Saarbrücken*), Halka (*Nationaloper Warschau, Theatr Wielki*), Don Giovanni (*Nationaltheater* Prague), Die Entführung aus dem Serail (*Badisches Staatstheater Karlsruhe*). **1991-92:** Dimitrij (*Janáček Opera Brno*), Il tabarro, Suor Angelica, Gianni Schicchi (*Nationaltheater, Mannheim*), Il barbiere di Siviglia (*Badisches Staatstheater Karlsruhe*), Macbeth (*Nationaloper Warschau, Theatr Wielki*), Tannhäuser (*Badisches Staatstheater Karlsruhe*), Die lustigen Weiber von Windsor (*Nationaltheater Mannheim*). **1992-93:** Die Zauberflöte, Rusalka, Lohengrin, Cavalleria rusticana, Der Bajazzo, Norma, Il trovatore. **1993-94:** Nabucco, (*Nationaloper Warschau, Theatr Wielki*), La traviata, (*National Theater Brünn*), Lakmé (*Opéra Royal de Wallonie*), Così fan tutte (*Badisches Staatstheater Karlsruhe*), Orfeo ed Euridice (*Nationaltheater Mannheim*), Lulu (*Saarländisches Staatstheater, Saarbrücken*). **1994-95:** Carmen (*Saarländisches Staatstheater, Saarbrücken*), Straszny dwór (The Haunted Manor) (*Nationaloper Warschau, Theatr Wielki*), Maria Stuarda (*Badisches Staatstheater Karlsruhe*), Dalibor (*Janáček Opera, Brno*), Electra (Theodorakis), Madama Butterfly (*Nationaltheater Mannheim*), Parsifal *Saarländisches Staatstheater, Saarbrücken*), Aida (*Nationaloper Warschau, Theatr Wielki*). **1995-96:** Die Zauberflöte (*National Theater Mannheim*), Turandot (*Nationaltheater Brünn*), Prince Igor (*Théâtre Marinski, Théâtre de Kirov*), Tosca (*Teatr Wielki Posen*), Wozzeck (*Saarländisches Staatstheater, (Saarbrücken*), Rigoletto (*Teatr Wielki Warsaw*).

Bibliography. Théâtre Municipal Luxembourg 1964–1989 (Luxembourg, 1989); Joseph Hunt, *Theater in Luxemburg von den Anfängen bis zum heimatlichen Theater 1885* (Luxembourg, 1989); *Electra — Théâtre Municipal, Luxembourg*, (Luxembourg, 1995); Interview with Jeannot Comes, directeur, Théâtre Municipal, Luxembourg, November 1995.

Thanks to the Administration, Théâtre Municipal.

Monaco

— MONTE CARLO

Opéra de Monte-Carlo

On January 25, 1879, Monte Carlo's opera house, Salle Garnier, was inaugurated a variety of works, performed by baritone Jules Diaz de Soria, soprano Marie Miolan-Carvalho, tenor Joseph Victor Capoul, and actress Sarah Bernhardt. Designed by Charles Garnier, architect of the Théâtre National de l'Opéra de Paris Palais Garnier (see Opéra de Paris Palais Garnier entry), the theater is a miniature of the Paris opera house.

On February 8, 1879, Jean-Robert Plan-

quette's *Le Chevalier Gaston*, was the first opera staged in the new theater. Three additional operas graced the stage the first season, which was under the directorship of Jules Cohen. Adelina Patti performed in all five operas scheduled during the 1881 season and the Greek tenor Ernest Nicolini appeared with her in four of the five works. (They eventually married). In 1885, conductor Jules Étienne Pasdeloup was imported from Paris with high expectations, but he presented opera excerpts in costume instead of full-length operas, resulting in much protest. The next season, full-length operas were back in the repertory—and Pasdeloup was back in Paris. Then Charles III died and his son, Albert I, took over. Albert's second wife, the American Alice Heine, was an opera lover and her involvement with the Salle Garnier in combination with Raoul Gunsbourg's appointment as director brought a golden age of opera to Monte Carlo. Gunsbourg's tenure lasted around six decades with almost four dozen world premieres gracing the stage. He presented the first staged performance of Hector Berlioz's *La damnation de Faust* on February 18, 1893, and the world premieres of de Montgomery's *Aréthuse* on February 10, 1894, César Franck's *Hulda* on March 4, 1894 and his *Ghisèle* (finished by Franck's colleagues) on April 6, 1896, (the Franck works were posthumous), and Isidore de Lara's *Messaline* on March 21, 1899, with Francesco Tamagno creating the role of Hélion. Tamagno first appeared at Salle Garnier in the title role of Giuseppe Verdi's *Otello* on January 20, 1894. Tamagno became Salle Garnier's leading attraction, and mindful of his position, raised his fees until they accounted for 20% of the opera budget. Nevertheless, there was a rumor that he resold his house seats at scalper's prices.

As the sun was setting on Tamagno's career, the sun rose on Enrico Caruso's. After the dawn of the 20th century, he appeared as Rodolfo with Nellie Melba as Mimi in Giacomo Puccini's *La bohème* on February 1, 4, and 8, 1902, and as the Duke opposite Melba's Gilda in Verdi's *Rigoletto* on February 12, 1902. That same year the first of several operas of Jules Massenet was introduced, *Le jongleur de Notre Dame* on February 18, 1902, followed by *Chérubin* on February 14, 1905, *Thérèse* on February 7, 1907, *Don Quichotte* on February 19, 1910, with Feodor Chaliapin in the title role, *Roma* in 1912, *Cléopâtre* in 1914, and *Amadis* in 1924, (the last two after Massenet's death). Chaliapin made his final appearance in 1937, in the title role of Modest Mussorgsky's *Boris Godunov*. Additional French composers, and a few Italian ones, had their works introduced by Gunsbourg at the Salle Garnier—Camille Saint-Saëns's *Hélène* on February 18, 1904, with Melba as Hélène, Pietro Mascagni's *Amica* on March 16, 1905, with the composer conducting and Geraldine Farrar creating the title role, Saint-Saëns' *Ancêtre* on February 24, 1906, with Farrar as Mar-

garita, Georges Bizet's *Don Procopio* on March 10, 1906, and Xavier Leroux's *Théodora* on March 19, 1907. Titta Ruffo made his first appearance at the opera house in 1908, returning for many seasons. In 1909, the company managed to stage Richard Wagner's *Der Ring des Nibelungen* on Salle Garnier's toy-sized stage, along with 14 other operas, which included the premiere of Gunsbourg's *Le vieil Aigle*, Gabrielle Ferrari's *Le Cobzar*, and Philippe Bellenot's *Naristé*. Saint-Saëns's *Déjanire* was first on the boards in 1910, followed by Gabriel Fauré's *Pénélope* on March 4, 1913, André Messager's *Béatrice* in 1914, Puccini's *La rondine* on March 27, 1917, Maurice Ravel's *L'Enfant et les Sortilèges* on March 21, 1925, and Arthur Honegger's *L'Aiglon* on March 11, 1937.

With the end of Gunsbourg's reign, so ended Salle Garnier's role as an international opera house. The prohibitive cost of presenting world premieres combined with the five-digit figures of today's international-circuit singers have placed Gunsbourg-style productions beyond the reach of a small house. Opéra de Monte-Carlo continues with a more limited repertory. To celebrate its centennial in 1979, the company staged Puccini's *Turandot*, Saint-Saëns's *Samson et Dalila*, Wagner's *Die Walküre*, Verdi's *Don Carlos*, and Massenet's *Don Quichotte*.

Although the current director, John Mordler, is trying to restore Opéra de Monte-Carlo to its past glory—that of an international opera house—it is uphill battle. He is staging operas which had their world premiere in Monte-Carlo, like Massenet's *Don Quichotte* and Puccini's *La rondine*, in new productions. He is also commissioning new works, like Sergio Rendino's *Un segreto d'importanza*, and is seeking to find "forgotten" works, like Ambroise Thomas's *Hamlet*. There is a spring festival in which Baroque works are revived in modern performances, and the occasional contemporary opera, like Gian Carlo Menotti's *The Consul*, is offered. One major problem, however, is the small size of the theater. The company loses money with each performance and the government no longer makes up the losses. Mordler has succeeded in improving the quality of performances from that of a provincial theater to which it had fallen after World War II, to that of a mid-sized regional company. The casts, all guest artists, are a combination of established and up-and-coming singers. The productions are traditional (sometimes unimaginative), because the audience is very conservative, but he tries to add a contemporary vision. Mordler avoids what he calls "zany" productions." He believes that the music and story must be respected. Recent productions include Verdi's *Simon Boccanegra* and *Un ballo in maschera*, Wagner's *Tirstan und Isolde*, Umberto Giordano's *Andrea Chénier*, and Gioachino Rossini's *Il turco in Italia.*

Salle Garnier

In April 1878, Prince Charles and the Société des Bains de Mer decided that Monte Carlo needed an opera house. Four hundred skilled laborers were imported from Italy and construction began on May 9, 1878. Eight months and sixteen days later, Salle Garnier was completed.

The exterior of Salle Garnier was a miniature replica of the Palais Garnier, and the interior, like the exterior is from the *Belle Époque*. The facade of the Salle Garnier is dominated by three enormous arcaded windows, with two sculptures on either side of the balcony, and lyres woven with antique masks, in a frieze of blue, red, green, purple. Two fenestrated pilasters soar into minarets to more than 115 feet high. The ornate auditorium is bathed in crimson, yellow ocher, gold, and bronze with finely carved moldings, caryatids, garlands, sculptures, and paintings. The names of composers circle the room. Four allegorical paintings embellish the high-vaulted ceiling. The auditorium accommodates 524.

Practical Information. Opéra de Monte-Carlo, Casino de Monte-Carlo, Place du Casino, BP 139, 98007 Monaco. Tel: 33 92 16 23 18, Fax: 33 93 30 07 57. When visiting Opéra de Monte-Carlo, stay at the Hotel de Paris, Place du Casino, 98007 Monaco. Tel: 33 92 16 30 00, Fax 33 33 92 16 38 50. It is adjacent to the opera house. The hotel can assist with opera tickets and schedule.

COMPANY STAFF AND WORLD PREMIERES

Directeur Général. John Mordler (1984–present).

World Premieres. (1951–1984): Luciano Chailly's

Salle Garnier facade detail (Monte-Carlo, Monaco).

La riva delle Sirti, March 1, 1959; Jean-Jacques Grunenwald's *Sardanapale*, April 25, 1961; Bruno Gillet's *Il Viscounte Dimezzato*, November 19, 1961; Renzo Rossellini's *L'avventuriero*, February 2, 1968; Jean Anouilh's *Madama de....*, April 28, 1970.

Bibliography. Thomas Walsh, *Monte Carlo Opera: 1879–1909* (Dublin, 1975). Joelle Castallan, *Spécial Monte-Carlo: Centenaire de la Salle Garnier: 1879–1979* (Paris, 1979). Interview with John Mordler, June 1995, directeur général.

Thanks to Michel Arène & Liliane Duchene, Opèra de Monte-Carlo, and G. Bigi.

The Netherlands

AMSTERDAM

De Nederlandse Opera and Het Muziektheater

The world premiere of Otto Ketting's *Ithaka* inaugurated both De Nederlandse Opera and Het Muziektheater on September 23, 1986. De Nederlandse Opera was an outgrowth of De Nederlandse Operastichting, born on November 17, 1965, with Richard Strauss's *Der Rosenkavalier*. After many unsuccessful attempts, Amsterdam finally had an opera house and a permanent opera company. The theater was designed by Cees Dam.

The first opera performed in Amsterdam dates back to December 31, 1680, when Pietro Ziani's *Le fatiche d'Ercole per Deianira* inaugurated a theater on the Leidsegracht. Carolus Hacquart's *De Triomfeerende Min*, written to celebrate the Peace of Nijmegen, followed. There were unsuccessful attempts by Hendrik Anders and Servaas de Kunink to develop Dutch opera. Visiting companies from Germany, France, and Italy performed the French and Italian repertories at the Stadsschouwburg theater on Keizergracht, until fire destroyed it during a performance of Pierre-Alexandre Monsigny's *Le Déserteur* in 1772. The Hollandsch Opera-Gezelschap under the directorship of Johannes George de Groot began regular opera seasons on October 16, 1886, with Charles Gounod's *Faust* in the Parkschouwburg in Amsterdam. Ten additional operas were staged the first year, including Albert Lortzing's *Zar und Zimmermann*, Fromental Halévy's *La Juive*, Victor Massé's *Les noces de Jeannette*, Georges Bizet's *Carmen*, and Karl Millöllcker's *Der Betterstudent*. The next season saw Giuseppe Verdi's *Il trovatore*, *La traviata*, and *Otello*, Ambroise Thomas's *Mignon* and *Hamlet*, Aimè Maillart's *Les dragons de Villars*, and Gaetano Donizetti's *La favorite* enter the repertory. In 1888, company premieres included Giacomo Meyerbeer's *Les Huguenots*,

Cornelis van der Linden's *Catharina en Lambert*, and Ludwig van Beethoven's *Fidelio*. The company changed its name in 1890 to Nederlandsche Opera with de Groot still at the helm, and Léo Delibes's *Lakmé*, Rossini's *Guillaume Tell*, and Daniel Auber's *La muette de Portici* were new additions to the schedule. In 1891, a second company called Hoogduitsche Opera van Amsterdam under the direction of Ludwig Schwarz presented an opera season at the Paleis voor Volksvlijt, including works like Vincenzo Bellini's *Norma*, Victor Ernst Nessler's *Der Trompeter von Säkkingen*, and Wolfgang Amadeus Mozart's *Don Giovanni* and *Die Zauberflöte*. In 1893, conductor Henri Viotta founded the Wagnervereeniging and on May 19th, Richard Wagner's *Siegfried* was given at Amsterdam's Paleis voor Volksvlijt. The next year, *Die Walküre* joined *Siegfried* in the repertory, which was mounted at Amsterdam's Stadsschouwburg. In 1896, *Die Meistersinger von Nürnberg* and *Tristan und Isolde* were maestro Viotta's offerings. That same year, the Nederlandsche Opera, now under the direction of Cornelis van der Linden (since 1894) offered a season of more than twenty operas, including Engelbert Humperdinck's *Hänsel und Gretel*, Karl Dibbern's *Erik Jensen*, Ignaz Brüll's *Das goldene Kreuz*, Pietro Mascagni's *Cavalleria rusticana* and Wilhelm Kienzl's *Der Evangelimann*. The Wagnervereeniging staged the remaining two Ring operas, *Das Rheingold* and *Götterdämmerung* on February 11, 1899, and May 29, 1902, respectively. The final performances under the baton of Viotta took place in 1918, when *Die Walküre* and *Parsifal* were presented at the Stadsschouwburg. The Wagnervereeniging, however, continued mounting productions until 1959.

On September 28, 1897, the Italiaansche Opera inaugurated their first season with Amilcare Ponchielli's *La gioconda*, not in Amsterdam, but in Wetenschappen at the Gebouw voor Kunsten. The company performed at the Paleis voor Volksvlijt in Amsterdam during February and March of 1898, staging Mascagni's *Cavalleria rusticana* and *Guglielmo Ratcliff*, Vincenzo Bellini's *Norma*, and Gounod's *Faust*. Initially under the direction of Vincenzo Morghen and Machiel de Hondt, the company became the sole responsibility of De Hondt after the first season. The Italiaansche Opera performed fairly regularly until 1925. Their final season offered eleven different operas in Amsterdam, using two performance venues, the Stadsschouwburg and Hollandsche Schouwburg. The season included Giacomo Puccini's *Manon Lescaut*, *Madama Butterfly*, and *La bohème*, Umberto Giordano's *Andrea Chénier* Ruggero Leoncavallo's *I pagliacci*, Francesco Cilea's *Adriana Lecouvreur*, and Donizetti's *Don Pasquale* among others. Another Italian company, known as the Italiaansche Opera, N.V., initially under the leadership of Catharina de Hondt-Verhallen, continued the Italian seasons when the previous company ceased operations. The company's first Amsterdam production took place on October 30, 1925, at the Stadsschouwburg with Verdi's *La traviata*, followed by *Il trovatore*. The season, most of which was performed in Wetenschappen, closed in Amsterdam in February 1926 with Puccini's *Manon Lescaut*. The company offered Italian seasons every year until the Nazi occupation of Holland.

Opera continued during World War II, first offered by The Nederlandsche Operastichting under the leadership of Johannes den Hertog, who staged two seasons, opening in Amsterdam on January 10, 1940, with Jacques Offenbach's *Les contes d'Hoffmann* performed at the Stadsschouburg, then by the Gemeentelijk Theater Bedrijf afdeling Opera, with den Hertog still at the helm. The company presented five more seasons, including Verdi's *Rigoletto* and *La traviata*, Puccini's *Gianni Schicchi*, *Tosca*, and *La bohème*, Johan Wagenaar's *De Doge van Venetië*, Carl Maria von Weber's *Der Freischütz*, and Charles Gounod's *Faust* among others. After the war, De Nederlandsche Opera gevestigd te Amsterdam, under Paul Cronheim, began producing opera in Dutch at the Stadsschouwburg. The company opened on September 17, 1946, with Verdi's *La traviata*, followed by *Rigoletto* and *Don Carlo*, Wolfgang Amadeus Mozart's *Die Entführung aus dem Serail*, Puccini's *Tosca* and *Madama Butterfly*, Ruggero Leoncavallo's *I pagliacci*, Pietro Mascagni's *Cavalleria rusticana*, Jacques Offenbach's *Les contes d'Hoffmann*, and Bizet's *Carmen*. The company's last performance was Puccini's *Madama Butterfly* on March 12, 1965.

After the demise of De Nederlandsche Opera gevestigd te Amsterdam, the De Nederlandse Operastichting, (precursor of the De Nederlandse Opera) began performances in the fall of 1965. Nine works were on the boards, ranging from Franz Joseph Haydn's *Le pescatrici* to the world premiere of Peter Schat's *Labyrint*, and included Alban Berg's *Wozzeck*, Jules Massenet's *Manon*, and Verdi's *Don Carlo* among others. There was a strong emphasis on world premieres with 15 mounted, among which were Ton de Kruijf's *Spinoza*, Bruno Maderna's *Satyricon*, Ketting's *Dummies*, Schat's *Houndini* and *Aap verslaat de Knekelgeest*. With the opening of Het Muziektheater in 1986 and the name change to De Nederlandse Opera, the company has achieved international status and acclaim. Promoting Dutch opera and commissioning works for Het Muziektheater continues to be a priority and have included Louis Andriessen's *De Materie*, Theo Loevendie's *Gassir*, Alfred Schnittke's *Life with an Idiot*, Parsm Vir's *Snatched by the Gods* and his *Broken Strings*, Schat's *Symposion*, and Guus Janssen's *Noach*. Operas are staged in original and imaginative ways, and the company is considered one of the leading houses in Europe in terms of creativity. A different approach to Wagner's *Der fliegende Holländer*— it was set "under water" with a plentiful supply of undersea creatures inhabiting the stage.

Although works of Mozart, Verdi, and Wagner form the main focus, works from Claudio Monteverdi's *Il ritorno di Ulisse in patria* to Arnold Schönberg's *Die glückliche Hand* can be found on the boards. There have been lesser know works like Alfredo Catalani's *La Wally*, and Hector Berlioz's *La damnation de Faust* and *Benvenuto Cellini*, and several early operas like Christoph Willibald Gluck's *Orfeo ed Euridice* and *Iphigénie en Tauride*, and Monteverdi's *Il combattimento di Tancredi e Clorinda* in the repertory. There is an emphasis on 20th-century works, among which Ferruccio Busoni's *Doktor Faust*, Leoš Janáček's *Kát'a Kabanová*, John Adams's *Nixon in China*, Bela Bartok's *A Kékszakállú herceg vára* (Duke Bluebeard's

Castle), Sergei Prokofiev's *Ognennï angel* (Fiery Angel), Schönberg's *Von heute auf Morgen*, Claude Debussy's *Pelléas et Mélisande*, and Francis Poulenc's *Les dialogues des Carmélites* have been staged.

The company does not mount "star vehicles," but prefers to bring together as a team the best singers, conductor, and designer for each production. International artists usually appear only when they are trying out new roles. The company receives a large government subsidy but must earn at least 18% box office to retain the subsidy. They have built up a subscription base of 75%, but money is getting tighter, so they began to look for private sponsors in 1993. A recent season offered Louis Andriessen's *Rosa, A Horse Drama*, Francis Poulenc's *Les dialogues des Carmélites*, Igor Stravinsky's *Oedipus Rex*, Berg's *Wozzeck*, Verdi's *La traviata*, Puccini's *Tosca*, Wagner's *Der Ring des Nibelungen*, and Mozart's *Così fan tutte*.

Het Muziektheater

The construction of Het Muziektheater is closely intertwined with that of the building of the new city hall. In 1955, architects Berghoef and Vegter were commissioned to design a new city hall to be located at the Waterlooplein and the next year, B. Bijvoet was commissioned to design an opera house to be located at the Frederiksplein, but no further action was taken. In 1968 another competition was held to design a new city hall that Wilhelm Holzbauer won. Then the site of the proposed opera house was moved, and Bijvoet and another architect, G. Holt, were commissioned to prepare new opera house designs. But Amsterdam had a large budget deficit and was forbidden to construct any new buildings. In 1979, Bijvoet died and Dam took his place. Then the two buildings were combined at Waterlooplein.

Het Muziektheater (Amsterdam, Netherlands).

Construction began in 1982 and four years later, Het Muziektheater opened.

Het Muziektheater is a modern brick and natural stone structure, with white Carrara marble, and a curved glass facade. A red velvet transition room leads into a semicircular auditorium with two white-rimmed copper-colored tiers. Bright red velvet seats complement maroon walls and an open dark-colored ceiling which holds hundreds of light bulbs suspended on rods. Het Muziektheater seats 1,600.

Practical Information. De Nederlandse Opera, Het Muziektheater, Waterlooplein 22, 1011 PG Amsterdam. Tel: 31 20 551-8922, Fax: 31 20 551-8311. When visiting De Nederlandse Opera, stay at the Amsterdam Marriott, Stadhouderskade 19-21, Amsterdam. Tel: 31 20 607-5555 or 1-800-228-9290, Fax 31 20 833-834. It is in the center of town and convenient to the opera house. The hotel can assist with opera tickets and schedules.

COMPANY STAFF, WORLD PREMIERES, AND REPERTORY

Intendant. De Nederlandse Opera: Pierre Audi (1988–present), Jan van Vlijmen (1986–88). De Nederlandse Operastichting: Hans de Roo (1973–86), Maurice Huisman (1964–73).

World Premieres. De Nederlandse Operastichting: P. Schat's *Labyrint*, June 23, 1966; M. Mengelberg, L. Andriessen, R. de Leeuw, J. van Vlijmen, and P. Schat's *Reconstructie*, June 9, 1969; T. de Kruijf's *Spinoza*, June 15, 1971; B. Maderna's *Satyricon*, March 16, 1973; H. Knox's *Dorian Gray*, March 30, 1974; O. Ketting's *Dummies*, November 14, 1974; J. Stokkermans's *De Engel van Amsterdam*, October 9, 1975; V. Ullmann's *Der Kaiser von Atlantis*, December 16, 1975; J. van Vlijmen & R. de Leeuw's *Axel*, June 10, 1977; P. Schat's *Houndini*, September 29, 1977; H. Henkemans's *Winter Cruise*, January 27, 1979; J. van Gilse's *Thijl*, June 5, 1980, P. Schat's *Aap verslaat de Knekelgeest*, June 7, 1980; P. Glass's *Satyagraha*, September 5, 1980; T. Loevendie's *Naima*, June 7, 1985. De Nederlandse Opera: O. Ketting's *Ithaka*, September 23, 1986; L. Andriessen's *De Materie*, June 1, 1989; T. Loevendie's *Gassir*, June 3, 1991; A. Schnittke's *Life with an Idiot*, April 13, 1992; P. Vir's *Snatched by the Gods* May 11, 1992; P. Vir's *Broken Strings*, May 11, 1992; P. Schat's *Symposion* April 29, 1994; G. Janssen's *Noach* June 17, 1994.

Repertory. De Nederlandse Opera: **1986-87:** Ithaka, Falstaff, Eugene Onegin, Der Kreidekreis, L'heure espagnole, El retablo de maese Pedro, Re-

nard, Where the Wild Things Are, Boris Godunov, Der Rosenkavalier, Il barbiere di Siviglia, Doktor Faust, Madama Butterfly, Die Fledermaus. **1987-88:** Tristan und Isolde, Don Carlos, Don Pasquale, Cendrillon, Don Giovanni, Salone, Kát'a Kabanová, Die Entführung aus dem Serail, Nixon in China. **1988-89:** A Kékszakállú herceg vára (Duke Bluebeard's Castle), Die Zauberflöte, Madama Butterfly, Ariadne auf Naxos, La damnation de Faust, Il barbiere di Siviglia, L'heure espagnole, El retablo de maese Pedro, Simon Boccanegra, De materie. **1989-90:** Boris Godunov, Ariane et Barbe-Bleue, Don Pasquale, Orfeo ed Euridice, Così fan tutte, Hänsel und Gretel, Le Comte Ory, Salome, Ognennï angel (Fiery Angel). **1990-91:** Parsifal, Die Entführung aus dem Serail, Il ritorno di Ulisse in patria, Die glückliche Hand, Benvenuto Cellini, Iphigénie en Tauride, Die Fledermaus, A Kékszakállú herceg vára (Duke Bluebeard's Castle), Idomeneo, Gassir the Hero, Il combattimento di Tancredi e Clorinda. **1991-92:** Mazeppa, Fidelio, Luisa Miller, Il barbiere di Siviglia, Hyperion, Les brigands, Die Frau ohne Schatten, Mitridate, Re di Ponto, Life with an Idiot, La damnation de Faust, Broken Strings, Snatched by the Gode, Don Giovanni. **1992-93:** Samson et Dalila, Les brigands, Così fan tutte, La bohème, Punch and Judy, Der fliegende Holländer, Il ritorno di Ulisse in patria, A Midsummer Night's Dream, La Wally, Le nozze di Figaro, Il comvattimento di Tancredi e Clorinda, Gassir the Hero, Pelléas et Mélisande. **1993-94:** Parsifal, Orfeo ed Euridice, L'incoronazione di Poppea, La traviata, Il re Pastore, Wozzeck, Il barbiere di Siviglia, Salome, Symposium, Falstaff, Noach. **1994-95:** Ledi Makbet Mtsenskovo uyezda (Lady Macbeth of the Mtsensk District), La nozze di Figaro, Rosa A Horse Drama, Die Fledermaus, L'italiana in Algeri, Mazeppa, Erwartung, Die glückliche Hand, Von heute auf Morgen, L'Orfeo, Die Meistersinger von Nürnberg. **1995-96:** Moses und Aron, Der fliegende Holländer, Die Zauberflöte, Werther, Die Frau ohne Schatten, L'incoronazione di Poppea, La bohème, Pelléas et Mélisande, Otello. **1996-97:** Elektra, Nos (The Nose), La favola d'Orfeo, Rigoletto, Don Gionvanni, Parsifal, Luisa Miller, Il re pastore, Eugene Onegin, Jenůfa. **1997-98:** Das Rheingold, La traviata, Così fan tutte, Dialogues des Carmélites, Die Walküre, Oedipus Rex, Wozzeck, Tosca, Siegfried, Rosa A Horse Drama, Götterdämmerung.

Bibliography. Annalen van de Opera Gezelschappen in Nederland: 1886–1995 (Amsterdam, 1996). Een noodzakelijke luxe: 15 jaar Nederlandse Operastichting-1971–1986 (Amsterdam, 1987). Openingsprogramma Het Muziektheater *De Nederlandse Opera (Amsterdam, 1986). Het Muziektheater (Amsterdam, 1989). Het Muziektheater (Amsterdam, 1989). Overzicht produkties per seizoen: 1965–1994.

Thanks to Peter de Caluwe, De Nederlandse Opera, and Rupprecht Queitsch.

ENSCHEDE

De National Reisopera (Touring Company)

The National Reisopera, originally called Opera Forum, opened in 1955 with Wolfgang Amadeus Mozart's *Le nozze di Figaro*. For more than three decades, Opera Forum, a traveling opera company, staged well-known operas with traditional productions to build an audience. They brought works like Gioachino Rossini's *Il barbiere di Siviglia*, Gaetano Donizetti's *Don Pasquale*, Pietro Mascagni's *Cavalleria rusticana*, Ruggero Leoncavallo's *I pagliacci*, Jacques Offenbach's *Les contes d'Hoffmann*, Modest Mussorgsky's *Boris Godunov*, Bedřich Smetana's *Prodaná nevěsta* (The Bartered Bride), Georges Bizet's *Carmen* and *Les pêcheurs de perles*, Richard Wagner's *Der fliegende Holländer*, *Lohengrin*, and *Tannhäuser*, and a strong presence of Giuseppe Verdi with *La traviata*, *Rigoletto*, *Il trovatore*, *Don Carlos*, *La forza del destino*, *Nabucco*, and *Stiffelio*, Giacomo Puccini with *La bohème*, *Madama Butterfly*, *Tosca*, *Manon Lescaut*, *Il trittico*, and Mozart with *Così fan tutte*, *Don Giovanni*, *Die Zauberflöte*, *Die Entführung aus dem Serail*, and *La clemenza di Tito*, to more than a dozen cities around The Netherlands. The company also mounted an occasional 20th-century work like Leoš Janáček's *Kát'a Kabanová*, Eugen d'Albert's *Tiefland*, Alban Berg's *Wozzeck*, George Gershwin's *Porgy and Bess*, and Claude Debussy's *Pelléas et Mélidande*, and some early pieces, like Domenico Cimarosa's *Il matrimonio segreto* and Giambattista Pergolesi's *La serva padrona*.

In 1993, the company reorganized, reopening the following season as The National Reisopera under the leadership of Louwrens Langevoort. Their repertory became more diversified and dynamic, even presenting their first premiere, the Netherland's premiere of Bohuslav's Martinů's *L'arbore di Diana*. Recent titles include Antonín Dvořák's *Rusalka*, Verdi's *Macbeth*, Charles Gounod's *Faust*, Christoph Willibald Gluck's *Orfeo ed Euridice*, and Kurt Weill's *Der Aufstieg und Fall der Stadt Mahagonny*. These works are performed in Twentse Schouwburg Entschede, De Harmonie Leeuwarden, Stadsschouwburg Groningen, Stadsschouwburg Eindhoven, Stadsschouwburg Arnhem, Rotterdamse Schouwburg, Stadss-chouwburg Heerlen, Stadsschouwburg Amsterdam, AT&T Danstheater Den Haag, Theater aan het Vrijthof Maastricht, Theater aan de Parade's Hertogenbosch, Chassé Theater Breda, De Maaspoort Venlo, Stadsschouwburg Nijmegen, Stadsschouwburg Tilburg, and Stadsschouwburg Utrecht.

Practical Information. De National Reisopera, Perikwer 97, 7512 DP Enschede. Tel: 31 53 487-8500, Fax: 31 53 432-1882. When visiting the Reisopera contact The Netherlands Board of Tourism, 355 Lexington Ave, New York, NY 10017. Tel: 212-370-7360.

COMPANY STAFF, PREMIERES AND REPERTORY

Intendent. De National Reisopera: Louwrens Langevoort (1994–present). **Opera Forum:** Hans Bal (1992-93), Peter Westerhout (1985–92), Peter van de Braak (1983–85), Hans de Roo (1982-1983), Gustav Fülleborn (1965–82), Paul Pella (1955–65).

Netherlands Premiere. De National Reisopera: V. Martín y Soler's *L'arbore di Diana*.

Repertory. Opera Forum: **1955-56:** Le nozze di Figaro, Les pêcheurs de perles, Il barbiere di Siviglia, Don Pasquale, Il matrimonio segreto. **1956-57:** Rigoletto, La bohème, Così fan tutte. **1957-58:** Madama Butterfly, Don Giovanni, La traviata, La serva padrona. **1958-59:** Die Zauberflöte, Tosca, Die lustigen Weiber von Windsor, Victoria und Ihr Husar. **1959-60:** Kát'a Kabanová, Tiefland, Der Wildschütz, Cavalleria rusticana, I pagliacci, Ein Nacht in Venedig. **1960-61:** Carmen, Die Entführung aus dem Serail, La bohème, Der Zigeunerbaron. **1961-62:** Manon Lescaut, Le nozze di Figaro, Les contes d'Hoffmann, Der letzte Walzer. **1962-63:** Die Fledermaus, Prodaná nevěsta (The Bartered Bride), Il trovatore, Der Rosenkavalier. **1963-64:** Il tabarro, Gianni Schicchi, Martha, Don Carlos, Der Vogelhändler. **1964-65:** Der fliegende Holländer, Les pêcheurs de perles, Die Zauberflöte, Im weissen Rössl. **1965-66:** Tannhäuser, Don Giovanni, Don Pasquale, Nabucco, Oh, mijn Papa. **1966-67:** Così fan tutte, Die Meistersinger con Nürnberg, Il barbiere di Siviglia, Der Freischütz. **1967-68:** Fidelio, Le nozze di Figaro, La traviata, Die Blume von Hawaii. **1968-69:** Boris Godunov, Die Schule der Frauen, La forza del destino, Die lustige Witwe. **1969-70:** Madama Butterfly, Lohengrin, Der

Bettelstudent, Un ballo in maschera. **1970-71:** Wozzeck, Die Fledermaus, Zar und Zimmermann, La bohème. **1971-72:** Die Zauberflöte, Porgy and Bess, Las des Lächelns, Der Revisor. **1972-73:** My Fair Lady, Der Zigeunerbaron, Rigoletto, Prodaná nevěsta (The Bartered Bride). **1973-74:** Les contes d'Hoffmann, Die Csárdásfürstin, Cavalleria rusticana, I pagliacci, Il barbiere di Siviglia. **1974-75:** Orfeo ed Euridice, Jenůfa, Der Zarewitsch, Eine Frau von Heute, Die beiden Blinden, Tosca, The Good Soldier Schweik. **1975-76:** Die Entführung aus dem Serail, Falstaff, Les pêcheurs de perles, Il matrimonio segreto, Eine Nacht in Venedig, La voix humaine, Die sieben Todsünden. **1976-77:** Don Giovanni, Don Carlos, Die lustige Witwe, L'elisir d'amore, Carmen. **1977:** Die Zirkusprinzessin, Aida, Viva la mamma, Faust, Maria Golovin. **1978-79:** Der Graf von Luxemburg, Turandot, Così fan tutte, Il trovatore, Don Pasquale. **1979-80:** Gräfin Mariza, Fidelio, Le nozze di Figaro, Rigoletto, Madama Butterfly. **1980-81:** Die Fledermaus, Otello, Il barbiere di Siviglia, Die Zauberflöte. **1981-82:** Der vogelhändler, Die Entführung aus dem Serail, Simon Boccanegra, La bohème. **1981-82:** Ein Walzertraum, Don Giovanni, Lucia di Lammermoor, Die lustigen Weiber von Windsor. **1983-84:** Wiener Blut, Les pêcheurs de perles, Tosca, La Cenerentola, Nabucco, Albert Herring. **1984-85:** Madama Butterfly, Nabucco, Ariadne auf Naxos, Les contes d'Hoffmann, Eine Nacht in Venedig, Le nozze di Figaro, Der

Schuhu und die fliegende Prinzessin. **1985-86:** La traviata, Pelléas et Mélidande, Die Csardasfürstin, L'italiana in Algeri, Eugene Onegin. **1986-87:** Der Zigeunerbaron, Rigoletto, The Rape of Lucretia, Così fan tutte, Manon Lescaut, La traviata. **1987-88:** Die lustige Witwe, Un ballo in maschera, La finta semplice, Suor Angelica, Gianni Schicchi, L'elisir d'amore, La clemenza di Tito, L'italiana in Algeri, Jenůfa (concert). **1988-89:** Die Fledermaus, Fidelio, Rigoletto, La bohème, Die Entführung aus dem Serail, Prodaná nevěsta (The Bartered Bride), Kát'a Kabanová (concert). **1989-90:** Il barbiere di Siviglia, Il trovatore, Carmen, Don Giovanni, L'elisir d'amore. **1990-91:** Der Freischütz, Orphée aux enfers, Falstaff, Die Zauberflöte, La finta semplice, Die Entführung aus dem Serail, Don Giovanni, Così fan tutte. Přihody Lišky Bystroušky (Cunning Little Vixen) (concert). **1991-92:** Die Zauberflöte, La clemenza di Tito, Tosca, Pelléas et Mélisande, Orphée aux enfers. **1992-93:** Les pêcheurs de perles, Stiffelio, Wozzeck, Madama Butterfly. **De National Reisopera: 1994-95:** Candide, Rusalka, Macbeth, Faust. **1995-96:** Orfeo ed Euridice, Le nozze di Figaro, La forza del destino, Der Aufstieg und Fall der Stadt Mahagonny, L'arbore di Diana.

Bibliography. National Reisopera (Entschede, 1995). *Annalen van de Opera Gezelschappen in Nederland: 1886–1995* (Amsterdam, 1996). Additional information supplied by the company.

Thanks to the Administration, De National Reisopera.

Opera Zuid (Touring Company)

Wolfgang Amadeus Mozart's *Le nozze di Figaro* inaugurated Opera Zuid on February 23, 1991 in Kerkrade. Established in 1990 with British director Aidan Lang at the helm as a touring company to complement the more traditional traveling company Opera Forum (now De National Reisopera), Opera Zuid stages clever, off-beat productions, their trademark. Lang's philosphy is that opera is about vivid experiences and should be good theater as well, and that the audience should be moved by the production. In choosing the repertory, Lang picks operas that he can do well in an intelligent and interesting way with the financial means the company has at its disposal. He balances the known operas with the unknown operas in the schedule. The company does not have the financial means to do 19th-century operas, but does many 20th-century

works. Half of the 10 million Dutch Gilder budget, over a two year period, comes from the government. The remainder is contributed by various provences and cities. Young, up-and-coming singers who are good actors are hired, along with the occasional experienced artist. Rehearsals last four to six weeks. There is an interesting arrangement with the theaters. The theater takes all the risk and pays the opera company 27,000 Gilders for each performance. The Rotterdamse Schouwburg in Rotterdam is the best place to see the company. It also tours to these other theaters: Stadsschouwburg Eindhoven, Stadsschouwburg Arnhem, Stadsschouwburg Heerlen, De Maaspoort Venlo, Chassé Theater Breda, Theater aan de Parades Hertogenbosch, Theater aan het Vrijthof Maastricht, and De Stadsschouwburg Sittard.

Rotterdamse Schouwburg

The Rotterdamse Schouwburg opened on April 15, 1988. Designed by Wim Quist, the building was called *de kist van Quist* (Quist's Box) by the Rotterdam residents, since it is box-like in shape. The modern, square-shaped auditorium holds two tiers. The parapets are concrete in the back, and red panels on the side. A plain gray proscenium arch frames a deep red curtain. The seats are gray fabric. There are are 895 places.

Practical Information. Opera Zuid, Wilhelminasingel 97, 6221 Maastricht. Tel: 31 43 321 0166, Fax: 31 43 325-7655. When visiting Opera Zuid in Rotterdam, stay at the Rotterdam Hilton, 10 Weena, 3012 CM Rotterdam. Tel: 31 10 414-4044 or 1-800-445-8667, Fax 31 10 411-8884. It is a deluxe hotel, with excellent service, in the center of the city, a few blocks from the opera house. The hotel can assist with opera tickets and schedules.

COMPANY STAFF AND REPERTORY

Artistic Director. Aidan Lang.

Repertory. **1991:** Le nozze di Figaro, Werther. **1992:** La traviata, Iphigénie en Tauride. **1993:** Il barbiere di Siviglia, Ariadne auf Naxos, L'Etoile. **1994:** Falstaff, La bohème. **1995:** Příhody Lišky Bystroušky (Cunning Little Vixen), L'elisir d'amore, Lyubov' k tryom apel'sinam (The Love for Three Oranges). **1996:** Don Giovanni, Tosca. **1997:** Hänsel und Gretel, I pagliacci, Cavalleria rusticana, La finta giardiniera. **1998:** Julietta (Martinů), Madama Butterfly.

Bibliography. Stichting Opera Ziud, *Opera Zuid* (Maastricht, 1994). Season programs 1991–1998. Additional information supplied by the company. Interview with Aidan Lang, artistic director, November 1995.

Thanks to Marijne Thomas, Opera Zuid, and Matthieu Roest.

Rotterdamse Schouwburg (Rotterdamse, Schouburg).

Other Dutch Companies

Other small companies in the Netherlands are noted below by name, address, telephone, and general director.

Hoodfdstad Operette. Kloveniersburgwal 87-89, 1011 KA Amsterdam; Tel: 31 20 623 9531,

Fax: 31 20 623 2587. **General Director:** J.J. Montagna.

Operalab. Postbus 95256, 1090 HG Amsterdam; Tel: 31 20 692 8246, Fax: 31 20 663 5040. **Artistic Director:** Muriele Lucie Clément.

New Zealand

───────── AUCKLAND

Opera New Zealand

Opera New Zealand, originally known as Auckland Opera, officially changed its name on November 1995, to reflect its hoped for future operatic role in the country. The plan, known as Opera 2000, 1460 days of challenge, growth, and celebration, expresses the company's desire to expand its scope of activities and recognition. The company attracted New Zealander superstar Kiri Te Kanawa as Donna Elvira for their 1996 season production of Wolfgang Amadeus Mozart's *Don Giovanni* in the Aotea Centre. Other productions include Donizetti's *Lucia di Lammermoor*, Giacomo Puccini's *Tosca*, and Igor Stravinsky's *Les noces*.

Practical Information. Opera New Zealand, P.O. Box 77066, Mt Albert, Auckland. Tel: 64 9 846 7433, Fax: 64 9 846 7141. If visiting, contact the New Zealand Tourism Board, 501 Santa Monica Blvd. #300, Santa Monica, CA 90401. Tel: 310-395-7480, ext 209, Fax: 310-395-5453.

───────────

COMPANY STAFF

General Manager. Stephen Morrison.
Bibliography. Information supplied by the company.

Thanks to Michael Harrison.

───────── DUNEDIN

Opera Otago,
Dunedin Opera Company

The Dunedin Opera Company was formed in 1956 and in 1996 celebrated its 40th anniversary. In 1987, the company staged the New Zealand premiere of Georges Bizet's *Les pêcheurs de perles*. The repertory is mainstream and includes operetta and Gilbert & Sullivan works. All its general directors have been from New Zealand, which is a company policy. The company stages two to three works each season in the Trust Bank Theatre in South Dunedin. Originally, a movie house known as the Mayfair Theatre, the building is a small community theater with 400 seats, and is the company's permanent home. Recent productions include Jacques Offenbach's *Orphée aux enfers* and Franz Lehár's *Die lustige Witwe*.

Practical Information. Opera Otago, Dunedin Opera Company, Trust Bank Theatre, 100 King Edward Street, Dunedin. Tel: 64 3 455-4962. If visiting, contact the New Zealand Tourism Board, 501 Santa Monica Blvd. #300, Santa Monica, CA 90401. Tel: 310-395-7480, ext 209, Fax: 310-395-5453.

───────────

COMPANY STAFF

Chairman. Ian Page.
Bibliography. Information supplied by the company.

Thanks to David Wood, Opera Otago, Dunedin Opera Company.

WELLINGTON

Wellington City Opera

Giacomo Puccini's *Tosca* inaugurated the Wellington City Opera in August 1984. It was created from the De La Tour Opera Company, whose director became the deputy chairman of the Wellington City Opera. That same year, the National Opera of New Zealand ceased to exist, and the concept of professional touring opera in New Zealand died.

The company moved into its permanent home, the State Opera House, for its second season, which offered Gioachino Rossini's *Il barbiere di Siviglia*. By 1986, the season increased to two productions, Georges Bizet's *Les pêcheurs de perles* and Giuseppe Verdi's *Rigoletto*. The follow year, the company mounted a co-production with Dunedin, Gaetano Donizetti's *La fille du régiment*, which for New Zealand, was a less familiar work. By 1988, the company received its first Arts Council support and began presenting the operas in the original language with subtitles. The first work sung in French was the 1993 mounting of Bizet's *Les pêcheurs de perles*. The singers are New Zealand artists, like Peter Baille, Malvina Major, Richard Greager, and Barry Mora. The repertory is primarily standard Italian fare, with the occasional French, German, or English work. In fact, 1989 was a French season with both offerings French — Bizet's *Carmen* and Charles Gounod's *Faust*. There have been some unusual stagings, like Papagena pushed a tea trolley in Mozart's *Die Zauberflöte* and Guglielmo dropped cricket paraphernalia all over the stage in Mozart's *Così fan tutte*. There were also some un-planned comic moments like Les Dorizac (Pedrillo) lost his wig in Mozart's *Die Entführung aus dem Serail*. Seasons increased, on alternating years, to three offerings. Recent productions include Verdi's *Rigoletto* and Rossini's *Il barbiere di Siviglia*.

Practical Information. Wellington City Opera, Top Floor, State Opera House, 109 Manners Street, Wellington. Tel: 64 4 384 4434, Fax: 64 4 384 3333. If visiting, contact the New Zealand Tourism Board, 501 Santa Monica Blvd. #300, Santa Monica, CA 90401. Tel: 310-395-7480, ext 209, Fax: 310-395-5453.

COMPANY STAFF, PREMIERES, AND REPERTORY

General Manager. Patricia Hurley.

New Zealand Premier. Benjamin Britten's *Peter Grimes*, 1995.

Repertory. **1984:** Tosca. **1985:** Il barbiere di Siviglia. **1986:** Les pêcheurs de perles, Rigoletto. **1987:** La traviata, La fille du régiment. **1988:** Die Entführung aus dem Serail, Lucia di Lammermoor. **1989:** Carmen, Faust. **1990:** Die Fledermaus, Madama Butterfly. **1991:** Die Zauberflöte, Il trovatore, La bohème. **1992:** Così fan tutte, Tosca. **1993:** La traviata, Les pêcheurs de perles, Die lustige Witwe. **1994:** Un ballo in maschera, Turandot. **1995:** Le nozze di Figaro, Peter Grimes, and Hänsel und Gretel.

Bibliography. Adrienne Simpson, *Taking Stock: A Personal Reflection*, (Wellington, 1995). Additional information supplied by the company.

Thanks to Michael Gould, Wellington City Opera.

Other New Zealand Companies

Other companies in New Zealand are noted below by name, address, telephone, theater, recent repertory, and general director (as available).

Canterbury Regional Opera Trust. P.O. Box 176, Christchurch 1. Tel and Fax: 64 3 366 9932. **General Manager:** Angela Gorton.

Northern Ireland

BELFAST

Opera Northern Ireland

Opera Northern Ireland celebrated its 10th anniversary in 1995, which was exactly a century since opera became an annual event in Belfast. It was the opening of the Grand Opera House in 1895 that paved the way for the Carl Rosa Company to provide opera performances yearly until World War II. After the war, Sadler's Wells Opera Company visited.

The first local opera group was established in 1950 by Havelock Nelson. It was an amateur company known as the Studio Opera Group. A more professional homegrown opera group took root with the formation of the Grand Opera Society in 1957. Professional singers, both local and guests, worked with an amateur chorus to produce opera. The Society appointed a full-time administrator in 1969, changing its name to North Ireland Opera Trust. Different performance venues were used — churches, movie theaters and the like, until the renovation of the 1,000-seat Grand Opera House was completed in 1980. With that, the company had a permanent home.

In 1984, the North Ireland Opera Trust merged with the Studio Opera Group, giving birth to Opera Northern Ireland. During the company's first decade, it staged, among other works, Richard Strauss's *Ariadne auf Naxos*, Charles Gounod's *Faust*, Wolfgang Amadeus Mozart's *Die Zauberflöte* and *Le nozze di Figaro*, and Ludwig van Beethoven's *Fidelio*. To celebrate its 10th anniversary, the Irish premiere of Leoš Janáček's *Příhody Lišky Bystroušky* (The Cunning Little Vixen) was mounted. The company promotes Irish singers and musicians. The budget is in excess of $1 million of which 65% is provided by the Arts Council of Northern Ireland, 18% is from ticket sales, and 17% is private sponsorship.

Practical Information. Opera Northern Ireland, 185 Stranmillis Road, Belfast, BT9 5DU Northern Ireland. Tel: 44 1232 381 241, Fax 44 1232 682 709. If visiting, contact the company about accommodations.

COMPANY STAFF

Artistic Director. Stephen Barlow.

STRANGFORD LOUGH

Castleward Opera (Summer Festival)

In 1985, Castleward Opera was founded by Ian Urwin and Jack Smith, two of Ulster's best known singers. Situated on the shore of Stangford Lough, Castleward Opera was created to provide a stage for young local singers, instrumentalists, and technicians to develop their talents. The midsummer opera company was modeled on Glyndebourne (see Glyndebourne entry) where the audience is invited to attend in formal attire and the intermission lasts 1½ hours to have supper. Supported by local businesses and organizations, the festival has seen as visitors the former prime minister John Major and his wife, and the Duchess of Kent. Recently it staged Richard Strauss's *Ariadne auf Naxos* and Giacomo Puccini's *La bohème*.

Practical Information. Castleward Opera, 61 Marlborough Park North, Belfast BT9 6HL, Northern Ireland. Tel: 44 1232 661 090. If visiting, contact the company about accommodations.

COMPANY STAFF

Artistic Directors. Ian Urwin and Jack Smith.

Norway

—————————————————————————— OSLO

Den Norske Opera

Eugen d'Albert's *Tiefland*, performed in Norwegian, inaugurated Den Norske Opera in February, 1959. Staged in the Folksteater, a converted movie house constructed during the 1930s, the opera was the sole offering for the inaugural season. The Norwegian soprano Kirsten Flagstad was the company's first general director and selected the work since it was the opera in which she had made her operatic debut in 1913 at the National Theater in Oslo.

Although Norway has had a permanent opera company for only a few decades, opera was first heard back in 1749. The occasion was the visit of King Fredrik V of Denmark/Norway. The Kapellmeister of the opera company which entertained the king was Christoph Willibald Gluck. During the next two centuries, attempts were made to establish a permanent company but the efforts never came to fruition. Although the National Theater in Christiania, (the name of Oslo until 1905) which opened in 1899, had hosted opera including Giacomo Puccini's *Tosca*, Giuseppe Verdi's *Aida*, and Henry Purcell's *Dido and Aeneas*, and singers like Aagaard Østvig, Gina Oselio, and Kaia Eide Norena, that did not hasten the founding of a permanent opera company. Nonetheless, around 170 operas and Norwegian Singspiele were staged by private companies and foreign troupes.

The reason for the late arrival of a permanent opera company in Norway can be traced to the country's history. Between 1380 and 1814, Norway was part of Denmark, and from 1814 to 1905, joined to Sweden. The dominating powers did not feel that the Norwegians had any need for their own opera house. When Norway was part of the Danish union, they could frequent Det Kongelige Teater in Copenhagen, and when Norway became part of Sweden, they could go the Kungliga Teater in Stockholm. Of course such logic was impractical.

At the end of the 1940s, the Norwegian Opera Society was established and the Norwegian Opera came into being by a vote of the Storting (Norwegian National Assembly) in November 1957. Odd Grüner-Hegge took over the running of the company during its second year and brought a mainstream repertory to the stage with three composers, Verdi, Puccini, and Wolfgang Amadeus Mozart, dominating the schedule. Works during the first five seasons included Verd's *Otello*, *Rigoletto*, and *Aida*, Puccini's *Madama Butterfly*, *La bohème*, and *Gianni Schicchi*, and Mozart's *Die Zauberflöte* and *Don Giovanni*. Richard Wagner works entered the repertory in 1966 with the mounting of *Tannhäuser* followed four years later by *Der fliegende Holländer* and in 1972 by *Die Walküre*. Oslo also hosted Verdi's *La traviata*, *Il trovatore*, and *Falstaff*, Puccini's *Tosca* and *Il tabarro*, and Mozart's *Le nozze di Figaro* and *Così fan tutte*. By the first decade, 48 productions had been staged, including French, British, and Slavic works by composers from both the 17th and 20th centuries — Claudio Monteverdi and Gluck to Luigi Dallapiccola and Igor Stravinsky. A new production of Modest Mussorgsky's *Boris Godunov* celebrated the company's 25th birthday. Recently Norwegian premieres of Verdi's *Simon Boccanegra*, Richard Strauss's *Elektra*, Wagner's *Parsifal*, Leoš Janáček's *Věc Makropulos*, and Puccini's *Turandot* have been presented. The company mounted a complete Ring Cycle during the 1995-96 season, with a cast composed of 50% Norwegian singers.

In a country lacking an operatic tradition, the lack of Norwegian operas is not surprising. Although Edvard Grieg and Bjørnstjerne Bjørnson collaborated on an opera during the 1870s, it was never completed. Another Norwegian composer, Ole Olsen wrote several operas around the turn of the century but they all faded into oblivion. More recently, however, Norwegian Opera has been more successful. Arne Eggen's *Olav Liljekrans*, first performed in 1940 at the National Theater, was revived in 1960. Eight years later saw the premiere of Geirr Tveitt's *Jeppe*, followed in 1971 by Edvard Fliflet Bræin's *Anne Pedersdotter*, and his *Der geschäftige Herr Vielgeschrey* in 1975. Two years earlier, Alfred Janson's *Et fjelleventyr* (A Mountain Fairytale) was seen for the first time in 1973, as was Hallvard Johnsen's *Legend of Svein and Maria*. In 1985, the Norwegian National Opera commissioned five operas from Norwegian composers, of which three have been premiered — Oddvar S. Kvam's *In the Thirteenth Hour* (1987), Antonio Bibalo's *Macbeth* (1990), and Johan Kvandal's *Mysteries* on January 15, 1994, for the Norsk Festival held in conjunction with the Winter Olympics. Tveitt's *Jeppe*, Bræin's *Anne Pedersdotter*, and Bibalo's *Macbeth* were revived for that same 1994 Norsk Festival.

From the company's initial budget of 1.5 million Norwegian Krone with a 24 musician orchestra, ten singers, and 9 dancers, the company has grown to a budget in excess of 170 million Norwegian Krone of which 90% comes from the federal government and 10% box office. There is a permanent staff of 425 of which there are 22 ensemble singers, a 72 musician orchestra, and a chorus of 42. The ensemble singers play an important role in introducing the standard repertory to the Norwegian audience. There is the occasional guest artist, like the Italian Giorgio Tieppo imported for Calaf in Puccini's *Turandot*, although he sounded inferior to most of the Norwegian/Scandanavian cast. Some Norwegian singers, like Ragnhild Heiland Sørensen, have gone on to international careers.

The production style ranges from traditional to modern. Most directors come from theater background and emphasize a music-theater approach. The philosophy is two-fold: introduce works to the Norwegian audience that are standard repertory pieces elsewhere, like Puccini's *Turandot*, which only received its Norway premier in November 1995 — and make the operas relevant for today. Around ten operas are in repertory each season, with 3-4 new productions. To this end, the results are sometimes strange. *Turandot* was devoid of anything oriental. A guillotine takes center stage with Ping, Pang, and Pong, attired in black tailcoats and white-and-black striped "skirts." Calaf wore a tattered hunter's outfit with such a long coat that he and everyone else kept stepping on it. Turandot was wrapped in a tight clinging dress and her entourage, composed of lesbian guards, sported black leather outfits. The director's (from the Komische Oper, Berlin) intent was to make a social statement — Turandot was an outcast — to make the opera relevant for today's society, but it distracted from the music, and left the audience with a confused impression of the opera. It was, however, an adventurous national premiere. Recent offerings include Mozart's *Idomeneo* and *Die Zauberflöte*, Verdi's *Un ballo in maschera*, Strauss's *Salome*, and Rossini's *Il barbiere di siviglia*.

Folksteater

The Folksteater is an Art Deco building, whose entrance is through a passageway marked OPERAEN in white neon letters. The glass-and-brass doors which lead into the opera house have DEN NORSKE OPERA in gold letters, with brass and white-glass torches affixed above. The striking red, white, and black auditorium holds a single tier in a rectangular space. The red velvet seats contrast with the black walls and parapet. An art deco chandelier hangs from a white dome ceiling. Huge acoustic panels extend out from the proscenium arch. There are 1,100 seats.

Practical Information. Den Norske Opera, Storgaten 23, 0184 Oslo. Tel: 47 22 42 94 75, Fax: 47 22 42 57 05. When visiting Den Norske Opera stay at the Radisson SAS Scandinavia Hotel Oslo, Holbergsgate 30, 0166 Oslo. Tel: 47 22 11 3000, Fax 47 22 11 3017. It has views of the city and is convenient to the opera house. The hotel can help with opera tickets and schedule.

COMPANY STAFF AND PREMIERES

Operasjef. Bjorn Simensen, Sven Olof Eliasson.
World Premieres of Norwegian Operas. G. Tveitt's *Jeppe* (1968); E. F. Bræin's *Anne Pedersdotter* (1971); A. Janson's *Et fjelleventyr* (A Mountain Fairytale) (1973); H. Johnsen's *Legend of Svein and Maria* (1973); E. F. Bræin's *Der geschäftige Herr Vielgeschrey* (1975); O. S. Kvam's *In the Thirteenth Hour* (1987); A. Bibalo's *Macbeth* (1990); J. Kvandal's *Mysteries* (1994).

Bibliography. *The Norwegian National Opera* (Oslo, 1993). *Nytt Opera Hus i Oslo* (Oslo, 1995). *Nytt operabygg i Oslo* (Oslo, 1994). Oyvind Anker, *Christiana Theater's Repertoire, 1827–1899* (Oslo, 1956). Interview with Sven Olof Eliasson, former general director, November 1995.

Thanks to Hege Lunde, Den Norske Opera, and Frank Fiskers.

Folksteater entrance (Oslo, Norway).

Other Norwegian Houses

Other opera houses in Norway are noted below by name, address, telephone, recent repertory, and director (as available).

Bergen International Festival. Box 183, 5001 Bergen. Tel; 47 55 96 26 03, Fax: 47 55 21 06 40. **Recent Repertory:** Orfeo ed Euridice.

Opera Vest. Georgernes Verft 3, 5011 Bergen. Tel: 47 55 23 13 30, Fax: 47 55 23 13 33. **Artistic Director:** Stein Olav Henrichsen.

Opera Bergen. Komedienbakken 9, 5010 Bergen. Tel: 47 55 32 38 56, Fax: 47 55 32 24 35. **Recent Repertory:** King Arthur (Purcell), Manon Lescaut, Macbeth, Lyubov'k tryom apel'sinam (The

Love for Three Oranges). **Artistic Director:** Anne Randinr Överby.

Operean I Kristiansund. King Olav V Gt. 1, 6500 Kristiansund. Tel: 47 71 677 733, Fax: 47 71 676 657. **General Director:** Tor Andreas Dyrseth.

Trondheim Opera. Festivalkontoret, Kongsgardsgatan 2, 7013 Trondheim. Tel and Fax: 47 73 52 56 65.

Portugal

— LISBON

Teatro Nacional De São Carlos

On June 30, 1793, Domenico Cimarosa's *La ballerina amante* inaugurated the Teatro Nacional de São Carlos, formally called the Real Theatre de S. Carlos. The opera, performed by a cast of *castrati*, was joined on the program by a heroic-dramatic ballet, *A felicidade lusitana*, choreographed by Gaetano Gioia with music by António Leal Moreira. Named São Carlos in honor of Princess Carlotta Joaquina, the theater immediately became the center of Italian operatic activity in the capital. Architect José da Costa y Silva modeled the building after the Teatro di San Carlo in Naples. The original opera house still stands today.

During the last decades of the 16th century into the 17th century Spanish "comedy" was a popular form of entertainment, given by Spanish companies. These comedies were not only singing accompanied by instruments, but true "opera lyrica." It is alleged that the only complete copy of the first Spanish opera, Juan Hidalgo's *Celos aun dei aire matan*, is in Portugal. In 1713, Zarzuela was given in Lisbon. The piece, thought to have been written by the Portuguese Luiz da Costa e Faria, was entitled *En poder da harmonia*. During Carnival in 1733, the Royal Palace in Lisbon hosted the *La pazienza di Socrate* (sung in Italian) by Portuguese composer Francisco Antonio d'Almeida. That same year, the first opera with a Portuguese text, A.J. da Silva's *La Vida de Don Quichote de la Mancha* was presented. D'Almeida's *La finta pazza* was given in 1735, and his *La spinalba* in four years later. In 1736, Caldara's *Demetrio* and Gaetano Maria Schiassi, *Alessandro nelle Indie, Eurene,* and *Artaserse* were staged.

David Perez's *Alessandro nell'Indie*, with sets designed by Giovanni Carlo Bibiena, inaugurated the Teatro Paço da Ribeira in 1755. The theater was destroyed only months later when an earthquake struck Lisbon. Opera continued as popular form of court entertainment in the palace of Salvaterra before the opening of the São Carlos. Between 1761 and 1776 no fewer than 64 operas were produced at the palace. Then there was a sharp reduction in operatic activity during the next sixteen year period, from 1777 and 1792, when only 28 operas were offered. This was primarily caused by financial considerations. André Grétry's *Richard, Coeur de Lion*, a novelty in the court, graced the stage along with the usual fare of Italian *opera buffa* and *burlette* by Giovanni Paisiello, Cimarosa, and Pietro Alessandro Guglielmi, among others. In 1792, all court operatic activity ceased.

Two years before the last opera was given in the palace, the Teatro da Rua dos Condes reopened for Italian operatic activity. At the same time, Queen Maria I ascended the throne and the Royal Charter of 1771 concerning the removal of the stigma attached to those women working in the theater was annulled. This gave rise to the famous Italian *castrati*, who became the first public idols of São Carlos — Domenico Caporalini (a "prima donna buffa") and Girolamo Crescentini (a specialist in *opera seria*). Only when the ban was lifted with the rise of Angelica Catalani was the supremacy of these two *castrati* threatened. Other popular singers of the day were Elisabetta Gafforini, Domenico Mombelli, and Giuseppe Naldi.

In addition to the inaugural opera, the first season at the São Carlos offered Giuseppe Sarti's *Fra i due litiganti, Il terzo gode*, Leal Moreira's *Saloia Namorada* (sung in Portuguese) and two operas by Giovanni Paisiello. The next season witnessed Vicente Martín y Soler's *Una cosa rara*, and works by Cimarosa, Antonio Salieri, Niccolò Jommelli, and Ferdinando Paër among others. The direction and inspection of the new opera house fell to the police headquarters, which, in turn, hired impresarios to run the opera house, the first being Francesco Antonio Lodi. The theater was run by these private impresario until 1854, when the Chancellor of the Exchequer, Fontes Pereira de Melo paid off the construction loans from the merchant bourgeoisie and the government and took control of the opera house.

In 1801, Christoph Willibald Gluck's *Orfeo ed Euridice* was on the boards for the first time, followed five years later by Wolfgang Amadeus Mozart's *La clemenza di Tito*. Mozart's opera had little success and thirty years passed before another of his works was offered, *Don Giovanni* in 1839. (It was 1953 before Lisbon saw its first *Die Zauberflöte* and its first *Così fan tutte* did not arrive until 1958.) In 1815, Gioachino Rossini's *L'italiana in Algeri* and *Tancredi* were staged, and Gaetano Donizetti's *Zoraida di Granata* was first offered in 1825. The following year, on June 22, 1826, Rossini's *Adina ossia il Califfo di Bagdad*, which had been commissioned in 1818 by the son of Pina Manique, received it world premiere. The delay in presentation was apparently the result of a disagreement between Rossini, who wanted additional money for writing an Overture, and Manique, who felt the Overture was an integral part of the score. Saverio Mercadante's *Adriano in Siria* and *Gabriella di Vergy*, both written for São Carlos, were staged soon thereafter. A Civil War caused the closing of the opera house between 1828 and 1834. It reopened on January 6, 1834, with Donizetti's *L'elisir d'amore*. Donizetti and Vincenzo Bellini were both favorites at the São Carlos, with *Anna Bolena*, *Il pirata*, *La sonnambula*, *Norma*, and *I Capuleti ed i Montecchi* being staged in rapid succession. Rossini's *Mosè in Egitto* and *Guillaume Tell* received hearings in 1836. Giacomo Meyerbeer's *Robert le Diable* and Daniel Auber's *La muette de Portici* were also popular. Nine years after the theater reopened, Giuseppe Verdi's *Nabucco*, his first work at São Carlos, arrived. That same year saw the debut in Lisbon of Enrico Tamberlick in Donizetti's *Gemma di Vergy*. In 1871, when Verdi's *Don Carlo*, was mounted, it was not well received, at least not the final act. The complete opera was performed only on the first night, despite the audience hissing and whistling during the last act. On subsequent nights, the management eliminated the act altogether. Six years later Verdi's *Aida* graced the stage. The opera was so outstanding and profitable for the theater that the manage-

ment replaced other operas on the program with it. Bad move. The audience vociferously protested, forcing a premature curtain mid-way through the performance. The patrons not only disrupted Verdi operas, but also Rossini's *Stabat Mater*. Apparently the performance was so horrendous (as the legend has it) that the viewers, besides shouting insults at the singers, broke their seats and threw the pieces on the stage.

Bellini's *I Puritani* and Ruggero Leoncavallo's *I pagliacci* welcomed the São Carlos into the 20th century. The performance of *I pagliacci* was particularly amusing. It seems that the donkey which pulled the cart believed that he should also sing and on the last notes of Act I, let out a piercing bray. A repeat of *I pagliacci* six years later was more successful — Leoncavallo arrived in Lisbon to personally conduct the opera on March 26, 1906. Meanwhile, three years earlier, Enrico Caruso sang in Umberto Giordano's *Fedora*, Giacomo Puccini's *Tosca*, and Verdi's *Aida*. Lisbon saw its first *La damnation de Faust* by Hector Berlioz in 1908, and Tito Ruffo sang in Ambroise Thomas's *Hamlet*. That same year the first *Der Ring des Nibelungen* was given in German. The opera house was closed between 1934 and 1940 for repairs and when it reopened with the premiere of Rui Coelho's *Dom Joao IV*, it had acquired a new name, Teatro Nacional de São Carlo. In 1943, Hitler sent the Berlin Opera to Lisbon. Richard Wagner's *Tristan und Isolde*, sung in German, was presented on June 5th and 8th.

The repertory was slowly enlarged after the war with lesser known works and 20th century pieces like Riccardo Zandonai's *Francesca da Rimini*, Ildebrando Pizzetti's *Assassinio nella cattedrale* and *La figlia di Jorio*, Francis Poulenc's *La voix humaine* and *Les dialogues des Carmélites*, Maurice Ravel's *L'heure espagnole*, Alban Berg's *Wozzeck*, Gian Carlo Menotti's *Amelia al ballo*, *The Consul*, and *The Medium*, Bedřich Smetana's *Prodaná nevěsta* (The Bartered Bride), Ottorino Respighi's *Maris Egiziaca*, Ermanno Wolf-Ferrari's *I quattro rusteghi*, Carl Maria von Weber's *Euryante*, Modest Mussorgsky's *Khovanshchina*, Pyotr Il'yich Tchaikovsky's *Pikovaya dama* (The Queen of Spades), Claude Debussy's *Pelléas et Mélisande*, Leoš Janáček's *Jenůfa*, Franco Alfano's *Resurrezione*, Antonín Dvořák's *Rusalka*, Arthur Honegger's *Jeanne d'Arc au bûcher*, Hector Berlioz's *Les Troyens*, and Paul Dukas's *Ariane et Barbe Bleue*. In March 1958, Maria Callas interpreted Violetta in Verdi's *La traviata*. In 1964, the first resident professional soloists performed in Verdi's *Don Carlo* and the repertory continued to grow with Arnold Schönberg's *Erwartung*, Claude Monteverdi's *L'incoronazione di Poppea*, Berg's *Lulu*, Igor Stravinsky's *The Rake's Progress*, Luigi Dallapiccola's *Il prigionero*, and Hans Werner Henze's *Elegy for Young Lovers*, among others. Many of the opera world's important artists have appeared on the stage of the São Carlos, including Birgit Nilsson, Regina Resnick, Tito Gobbi, Mario del Monaco, and Franco Corelli.

As the century draws to a close, the opera house continues to expand its offerings with first performances in Portugal of Igor Stravinsky's *Perséphone*, *Renard*, and *Solovey*, (The Nightingale) along side two repertory favorites, Verdi's *La travaita* and Puccini's *Il trittico*. Productions are simple, but clever, with young, dynamic singers, as was seen with the Portuguese premiere of Franz Joseph Haydn's *L'isola disabitata*. Recent repertory includes Nicolay Rimsky-Korsakov's *Sadko*, Claudio Monteverdi's *Il ritorno di Ulisse in patria*, and a Portuguese opera, Pinho Vargas's *Os Dias Levantados*.

Teatro Nacional De São Carlos

Since the earthquake of November 1755 destroyed the Teatro Paço da Ribeira, the city had been bereft of a luxurious theater. No suitable house remained in Lisbon where opera could be properly performed, although other theaters — Salitre, Bairro Alto, and Rua dos Condos — existed. It was the influence of Police Chief Diogo Inácio Pina Manique, who wanted Lisbon to have an elegant theater, that led to the establishment of the São Carlos. Ground was broken for the theater on December 8, 1792, which was inaugurated less than seven months later, although the behind-the-scenes areas (changing-rooms, storage space, rooms for scenery) were not yet completed. The theater was financed by members of the merchant bourgeoisie — wealthy traders in soap, diamonds, and tobacco — who advanced the necessary funds to build an aristocratic theater. They included Jacinto Fernandes Bandeira, Joao Pereira Caldes, António Francisco Machado, António José Ferreira Sola, Anselmo José da Cruz Sobral, and

Teatro Nacional de São Carlos facade details (Lisbon, Portugal).

Joaquim Pedro Quintela, who gave the land in exchange for a private box with direct street access.

The Neoclassic facade of the opera house is divided into three levels. On the street level is a colonnade of rustic stone with three front arches, above which is a terrace with a ballustrade barrier. Along the building's facade are four attached-Doric columns that flank three Palladium-like windows topped by friezes representing cornucopia with the caduceus of Mercury in the middle. A clock rests on the top level. The Baroque style of the auditorium contrasts with the austere Neoclassic facade. Five tiers curve in a horseshoe-shape around the room. A bronze hue permeates the hall. Light-chocolate-colored velvet seats match a similarly colored stage curtain flanked by pairs of tan-toned Corinthian columns. Medallions embellish the tiers. The center royal box has gilded maidens growing out of the flanking pillars. The ceiling is intricately decorated with musical themes. There are 1,148 seats.

Practical Information. Teatro Nacional de São Carlos, Rua Serpa Pinto n°9, 1200 Lisbon.

Tel: 351 1 346-5914, Fax: 351 1 347-1738. When visiting the Teatro Nacional de São Carlos, stay at the Alfa Lisboa Hotel, Avenida Columbano Bordalo Pinheiro, 1070 Lisbon. Tel: 351 1 726-2121, Fax: 351 1 726-3031. It has views of the city, and is convenient to the opera. They can assist with opera tickets and schedules.

COMPANY STAFF

Artistic Director. Paulo Ferreira de Castro.
Bibliography. Joel Costa, *S. Carlos: As Cenas e as Vozes* (Lisbon, 1995). Augusto Seabra, *Ir a S. Carlos* (Lisbon, 1993). Alberto Basso, ed., *Storia dell'Opera Vol. II* (Turin, 1977). Rui Vieira Nery, Paulo Ferreira de Castro, *History of Music* (Lisbon, 1991). Joachim José Marques, *Cronologia da opera em Portugal* (Lisbon, 1947). Francisco da Fonseca Benevies, *O Real Theatro de S.Carlos de Lisboa: Memorias, 1883–1902* (Lisbon, 1902). João de Freitas Branco et al., *O Theatro de San Carlo: 1793–1956* (Lisbon, 1956).

Thanks to José Sasportes, Embassy of Portugal, Washington D.C.; Paula Vilafanha, Teatro Nacional de São Carlos, and Rolf Kettmann.

VILA RÉAL

Casa de Mateus (Summer Festival)

The festival began as an educational undertaking in 1979 by Count Fernando de Sousa Botelho Albuquerque. Six years later, a music festival was added to the enterprise which takes place in a relatively remote mountainous area 70 miles north-east of Oporto. The operas are performed in a local church, and have included Domenico Cimaroso's *Il maestro di capella.* Selections of overtures and arias are offered as well on the program, and those from Wolfgang Amadeus Mozart's *Le nozze di Figaro* and *Don Giovanni,* and Gioachino Rossini's *Il barbiere di Siviglia* have been presented. The festival has even attracted some "big names" like Ileana Cotrubas and Katia Ricciarelli, who have given recitals.

Practical Information. Casa de Mateus, 5000 Vila Réal; Tel: 351 59 323 121, Fax: 351 59 326 533. Contact the Casa de Mateus regarding accommodations in local houses, under the Manor House Tourism plan.

COMPANY STAFF

Artistic Director. Adriano Jordao.
Bibliography. Tom Higgens, *Shine On, Opera Now* (London, January-February 1997).

Other Portuguese Opera Houses

Other opera houses in Portugal are noted below by name, address, telephone, and manager.

Ópera de Câmara do Real Theatro de Queluz.

Quinta da Alagoa 12-A, 2775 Carcavelos. Tel: 351 456 6139, Fax: 351 456 2310. Manager: Mario Mont'Alvema.

Scotland

————————————————————— EDINBURGH

Edinburgh International Festival

Giuseppe Verdi's *Macbeth* in a production from Glyndebourne and Gustav Mahler's *Das Lied von der Erde* with Bruno Walter conducting the Vienna Philharmonic inaugurated the Edinburgh International in 1947. Conceived the previous year by Rudolf Bing, then artistic director of Glyndebourne, and Audrey Christie, wife of Sir John Christie, Glyndebourne's founders, the Festival was dominated by the Glyndebourne Festival Opera until 1955.

However, three years earlier, in 1952, the first foreign opera company, the Hamburgische Staatsoper, arrived at the festival, offering several works, including Richard Strauss's *Salome*. The company returned four years later and again in 1968, when they presented Strauss's *Elektra* and Richard Wagner's *Der fliegende Holländer*. In 1957, Maria Callas assayed the title role in Vincenzo Bellini's *La sonnambula*, receiving an enthusiastic response, which, however, was not reciprocated as Miss Callas left before her last scheduled appearance. Also worthy of mention was Magda Olivero in Francesco Cilea's *Adriana Lecouvreur* in 1963, and a decade later, Janet Baker in Hector Berlioz's *Les Trojans*. The end of the 1950s saw the Württembergisches Staatstheater (Stuttgart, 1958), followed by the Operan (Stockholm, 1959). The 1960s witnessed the Royal Opera, Covent Garden staging Gaetano Donizetti's *Lucia di Lammermoor* with Joan Sutherland, the Belgrade Opera, Teatro di San Carlo (Naples), Prague National Theater, Bayerische Staatsoper (Munich), the Holland Festival Opera, the Scottish Opera, and Teatro Comunale (Florence). The 1970s welcomed the Oper Frankfurt for the first time, along with the Deutsche Oper (Berlin), Teatro Massimo (Palermo), Deutsche Oper am Rhein (Düsseldorf), Hungarian State Opera, and a return of the Operan with Leoš Janáček's *Jenůfa* and Strauss's *Elektra* with Elisabeth Söderström and Birgit Nilsson. The smaller, less conventional companies visited in the 1980s, like the Folksoperan (Stockholm) importing Verdi's *Aida* with 12-member chorus, and the Opera Theater of St. Louis.

Since the early 1970s, the festival has staged its own productions as well. In 1973, Mozart's *Don Giovanni* and *Le nozze di Figaro*, with Daniel Baremboïm on the podium, was on the boards, and four seasons later, Plácido Domingo and Teresa Berganza were featured in Georges Bizet's *Carmen*. The Festival has also been the scene of almost two dozen British premieres during the first three decades, including Paul Hindemith's *Mathis der Maler*, Igor Stravinsky's *The Rake's Progress* and *Mavra*, Manuel de Falla's *La vida breve*, Sergey Prokofiev's *Lyubov' k tryom apel'sinam* (The Love for Three Oranges) and *Igroki* (The Gamblers), Ján Cikker's *Vzkriesenie* (Resurrection), Leoš Janáček's *Z Mrtvého Domu* (From the House of the Dead), Udo Zimmermann's *Die Soldaten*, and Lars Johan Werle's *The Vision of Thérèse*.

According to press office, the aims of the festival are three: to offer to all sectors of the public the opportunity to experience and enjoy the arts; to reflect an international culture in the productions to Scottish audiences, and to reflect a Scottish culture in the productions to the international audiences. The audience is 60% Scottish, 25% from the rest of the United Kingdom, and 15% overseas. The public sector funding of 38% comes from the city of Edinburgh Council and the Scottish Arts Council, 33% from ticket sales, 24% from sponsorship and donations, making it one of the most successful organizations in the United Kingdom for private funding of the arts, which is a new concept, and 5% from other sources. The festival takes place during a three-week period at the end of the summer.

Festivals often have a theme. One was devoted to the operas of Verdi which had librettos based on the plays of Friedrich Schiller. A staging of Schiller's play *The Robbers*, along with readings of other plays which Verdi adapted for the operatic stage, were also presented. In this vein, the Royal Opera, Covent Garden staged *Don Carlos* (original 5-act, French version) with Karita Mattila, Thomas Hanson, Ferruccio Furlanetto, Kurt Rydl, and Bernard Haitink on the podium,

I masnadieri with Dmitri Hvorostovsky as Francesco, *Giovanna d'arco*, and *Luisa Miller*. The second operatic focus of that festival involved Bedřich Smetana's works, including *Dalibor* and *Libuše*, which were presented by the Scottish Opera. Recent festivals included Verdi's *Macbeth*, Strauss's *Ariadne auf Naxos*, Jean-Philippe Rameau's *Platée*, and *La verbena de la Paloma*.

Edinburgh Festival Theatre

On November 7, 1892, The Empire Palace Theatre was opened. Owned by Edward Moss, the managing director of the Edinburgh Empire Palace Ltd., the theater was designed by Frank Matcham, a Victorian architect. It was lavishly decorated with nymphs, cherubs, and elephants with Nubian riders. The green, cream, and gold auditorium held four tiers and accommodated 3,000. On May 9, 1911, the illusionist Lafayette accidentally ignited a stage-drape. The resulting fire killed him and seven other people. The safety curtain prevented any casualties in the audience. The stage was rebuilt within three months, and on October 1, 1928, *Show Boat* opened the redesigned and reconstructed Empire Theatre with the Milburn brothers responsible for the project. Between 1928 and 1963, it hosted opera, musicals, variety shows, and even ice shows. During this time, the theater was completely rebuilt around the shell of the existing auditorium, reopening on June 18, 1944, as the Edinburgh Festival Theater. Colin Ross, Law & Dunbar-Nasmith were responsible for the transformation of the Empire Theater into the Festival Theatre. The cost was £24 million, the majority of which was paid by the public sector with £5 million raised privately. After the theater's reconstruction, from 1946 to 1963, it was one of the principal venues for the Edinburgh International Festival, including the hosting of a Royal Opera production of Wagner's *Tristan und Isolde* in 1953, conducted by Sir John Barbirolli. Between 1963 and 1991, it was turned into a bingo hall, with the marvelous acoustics reverberating with the calling of numbers, instead of glorious voices. After another reconstruction, it was once again the main performance venue for the festival. The City of Edinburgh Council owns the building, which is leased and operated by the Edinburgh Festival Theatre Trust. The theatre receives an annual operating grant of around £300,000.

A striking glass facade and new lobbies were added on to the original auditorium. The structure finds the glass hung from black steel and side concrete supports. The auditorium is a restoration of the Empire's 1928 hall, a blending of Art Nouveau, Beaux-Arts, Neoclassicism. There are two tiers of deep rose mohair seats, with proscenium boxes on each side. Silver gilted ornamentation decorates the proscenium arch.

Practical Information. Edinburgh

Edinburgh Festival Theater (Edinburgh, Scotland).

Festival Theatre, 13-29 Nicolson Street, Edinburgh EH8 9FT. Tel: 44 131 529-6000, Fax: 44 131 662 1199. Edinburgh International Festival, 21 Market Street, Edinburgh EH1 1BW. Tel: 44 131 226 4001, Fax: 44 131 225 1173. When visiting the Edinburgh Festival or Edinburgh Festival Theatre, stay at the Carlton Highland, North Bridge, Edinburgh EH1 1SD. Tel: 44 131 556 7277, Fax: 44 131 556 2691. It is in the heart of the city and close to the festival theater. The Carlton Highland can assist with tickets and schedule.

COMPANY STAFF AND PREMIERES

Director. Brian McMaster
British Premieres. P. Hindemith's *Mathis der Maler*, August 29, 1952; I. Stravinsky's *The Rake's Progress*, August 25, 1953; I. Stravinsky's *Mavra*, August 21, 1956; I. Stravinsky's *Oedipus Rex* (first staged performance), August 25, 1956; M. de Falla's *La vida breve*, September 9, 1958; K.B. Blomdahl's *Aniara*, September 3, 1959; F. Poulenc's *La voix humaine*, August 30, 1960; S. Prokofiev's *Lyubov' k tryom apel'sinam* (The Love for Three Oranges), August 23, 1962; S. Prokofiev's *Igroki* (The Gamblers), August 28, 1962; J. Cikker's *Vzkriesenie* (Resurrection), 1964; L. Janáček's *Z Mrtvého Domu* (From the House of the Dead), August 28, 1964; F. J. Haydn's *Le pescatrici*, 1965; R. Strauss's *Intermezzo*, September 2, 1965; G. F. Malpiero's *Sette canzoni*, 1969; A. Reimann's *Melusine*, 1971; U. Zimmermann's *Die Soldaten*, August 12, 1972; S. Szokolay's *Vérnász* (Blood Wedding), 1973; L. Johan Werle's *The Vision of Thérèse*, 1974; R. Orr's *Hermiston*, 1975; T. Musgrave's *Mary Queen of Scots*, 1977.

Edinburgh Festival Theater auditorium (Edinburgh, Scotland).

Bibliography. George Bruce, *Festival in the North: The Story of the Edinburgh Festival* (London, 1975). Additional information supplied by the theater.

Thanks to Fiona Duff, Festival Theatre, and Franco Galgani.

GLASGOW

Scottish Opera

In June 1962, the Scottish Opera's first production, Giacomo Puccini's *Madama Butterfly*, was offered at the King's Theatre in Glasgow. Claude Debussy's *Pelléas et Mélisande* completed the inaugural season. Sir Alexander Gibson founded the company.

Opera goes back to 1867, when Giuseppe Verdi's *Il trovatore* was presented on December 9, 1867, by Madame Florence Lancia's Grand English Opera Company at the Bayliss's Coliseum Theatre and Opera House. It was the first theater on Hope Street, located on the site where the

Theatre Royal (Glasgow, Scotland).

decade later, Eric Chrisholm founded the Glasgow Grand Opera Company, a local amateur opera company, which staged Mozart's *Idomeneo* in 1933 and Hector Berlioz's *Les Troyens* in 1935, as well as Arrigo Boïto's *Mefistofele* and Édouard Lalo's *Le Roi d'Ys*.

After the Scottish Opera was established in 1962, the second season saw the schedule increased to four operas with Verdi's *Otello*, Wolfgang Amadeus Mozart's *Die Entführung aus dem Serail*, and a double-bill of Luigi Dallapiccola's *Il volo di notte* and Maurice Ravel's *L'heure espagnole*. During the early years, other 20th century works were mounted, including Igor Stravinsky's *The Rake's Progress* and *L'histoire du soldat*, Benjamin Britten's *Albert Herring, Peter Grimes,* and *The Turn of the Screw,* and Hans Werner Henze's *Elegy for Young Lovers*. In May 1969, Berlioz's *Les Troyens* was staged. The 1970s brought the complete *Der Ring des Nibelungen* with the mounting of *Siegfried. Das Rheingold, Die Walküre,* and *Götterdämmerung* had already graced the stage during the 1960s. Novelties entered the repertory with Orr's *Hermiston,* Hamilton's *The Catiline Conspiracy,* Nikolay Rimsky-Korsakov's *Zolotoy petushok* (The Golden Cockerel), Wilson's *Confessions of a Justified Sinner,* Theo Musgrave's *Mary Queen of Scots,* Harper's *Fanny Robin* and Holst's *Savitiri*. The company also rediscovered forgotten early operas like Pier Francesco Cavalli's *L'egisto,* Christoph Willibald Gluck's *Orfeo ed Euridice,* and Henry Purcell's *Dido and Aeneas.*

In 1974, the Scottish Opera purchased the Theatre Royal and entrusted Derek Sugden with the renovation of the building. Johann Strauß's *Die Fledermaus* welcomed the company into its new home in October 1975. American conductor John Mauceri was appointed music director in

Theatre Royal now stands. George Bell had designed the structure, which opened on November 28, 1867, with a play, *The Sea of Ice*. Two years later, the name was changed to Theatre Royal by charter granted by Queen Victoria, and the theater came under the management of Mister Glover and Mister Francis, presenting in June 1869, Jacques Offenbach's *The Grand Duchess of Gerolstein*. The Carl Rosa Company staged opera there. Fire devoured the theater on February 2, 1879. The theater was rebuilt, designed by the London architect Charles Phipps, reopening on October 26, 1880, with *As You Like it*. It survived only 15 years before fire again destroyed it. Phipps again designed the replacement theater, which opened in September 1895. A

1986, and his first offering was Georges Bizet's *Carmen*. Interesting works under his tenure included Igor Stravinsky's *Oedipus Rex* and *Petrushka*, Leoš Janáček's *Z Mrtvého Domu* (From the House of the Dead) and *Jenůfa*, Britten's *Death in Venice*, Béla Bartók's *A Kékszakállú herceg vára* (Duke Bluebeard's Castle), Judith Weir's *The Vanishing Bridegroom*, Marc Blitzstein's *Regina*, and Kurt Weill's *Street Scene*. The last opera that Mauceri conducted was Janáček's *Věc Makropulos* (The Makropoulos Affair). In 1993, Richard Armstrong replaced Maurceri, conducting Verdi's *I due Foscari* as his first work with the company, followed by Janáček's *Kát'a Kabanová*, Britten's *Peter Grimes*, and Wagner's *Tristan und Isolde* among others. The mid–1990s witnessed more novelties — Schnittke's *Life with an Idiot*, Antonín Dvořák's *The Jacobin*, and James MacMillan's *Inés de Castro*.

The company is known for its radical, avant-garde productions, but some are in bad taste with disastrous results. One such was a new production of Camille Saint-Saëns's *Samson et Dalila*. Director/designed Antony McDonald lacked a unified concept, setting each act as though it were in a different opera, and mixing costumes from B.C. with those during the World War II era. In Act I, updated to a ghetto in 1930s Europe, the Israelites became a sterotyped Eastern European ghetto. Their back and forth prayer movement was ridiculed, and they were blindfolded. The Philistines doned Nazi-like uniforms with black leather boots. The second act could have come from a recent Dresden production of *Tristan und Isolde*, a bare stage except for a few geometric shapes, with Samson and Dalila dressed in "timeless, flowing" attire. Act III saw the Philistine women in formal gowns, and the men with orange fox, hinting at 1920s decadent Germany with Nazi undercurrents, and performing gratuitous, pagan rituals — like petting pigs. At the end, Samson's hair was not cut, but his side-curls were. The total disregard of time chronology, absurd mixture of costumes, excessive and irrelevant actions which distracted from the music and singing, and the sterotyping of a religious group made this an offensive production of a self-indulgent director. Although the underlying message was one of tolerance, its misguided approach promoted intolerance. Recent repertory includes Pyotr Il'yich Tchaikovsky's *Pikovaya dama* (The Queen of Spades), Strauss's *Ariadne auf Naxos*, Verdi's *La traviata* and *Rigoletto*, Vincenzo Bellini's *Norma*, and Mozart's *Così fan tutte*.

Theatre Royal

In 1956, the Theatre Royal was sold to Scottish Television for conversion into a studio complex, but in 1972, a feasibility study was

Theatre Royal auditorium proscenium boxes (Glasgow, Scotland).

commission concerning the building's conversion into Glasgow's Opera House with the opera company purchasing the building two years later.

It is a massive structure with a plain facade of deep yellow that extends a city block. The interior has endured several color changes over the course of its existence, from turquoise, rose, and ivory, to blue, cherry red, and off-white, to the current brown, ivory, and deep maroon, acquired in 1974. Earthy tones permeate the space of the three-tier, lyre-shaped auditorium. Pairs of lamps are suspended from the intricately decorated, ivory-colored parapets. Proscenium boxes are on either side. Fluted, Corinthian columns support the tiers, and flowers, garlands, streamers, and putti decorate the space. The ceiling is a lovely turquoise with floating putti in a variety of ornamentation. The brown velvet curtain, trimmed with gold, matches the brown seats. The theater accommodates around 1,500.

Practical Information. Scottish Opera, 39 Elmbank Crescent, Glasgow G2 4PT. Tel: 44 141 248-4567, Fax: 44 141 221 8812. Theatre Royal, 282 Hope Street, Glasgow G2 3QA Scotland. Tel: 44 141 332-900. When visiting the Scottish Opera, contact the British Tourist Authority, 40 West 57th Street, New York, NY 10019, 212-581-4700.

COMPANY STAFF

General Directors. Ruth Mackenzie (1997–present), Richard Jarman (1991–1997), Richard Mantle (1985–1990). **Music Directors:** Richard Armstrong (1993–present), John Mauceri (1985–1993).

Bibliography. C. Wilson, *Scottish Opera: The First Ten Years* (Glasgow, 1973). H. G. Farmer, *A History of Music in Scotland* (London, 1970). Additional information supplied by the company.

Thanks to Jacqueline Killeen, Scottish Opera.

Other Scottish Companies

Other small companies in Scotland are noted below by name, address, telephone, fax, recent repertory, and general director (as available).

Scottish Early Music Consort. 22 Falkland Street. Glasgow G12 9 PR. Tel and Fax: 44 141 334 9229. **Recent Repertory:** Early opera. **Artistic Director:** Warwick Edwards.

Spain

BARCELONA

Gran Teatre del Liceu

Vincenzo Bellini's *I Puritani* inaugurated the Gran Teatre del Liceu, previously known as the Teatro del Liceo, on April 20, 1862. Designed by Josep Oriol Mestres, the opera house went up in flames on January 31, 1994. Only the facade and the Art Deco style *Circulo* (Liceu Circle-a private club) survived. Architects Ignancio Sola Morales Rubió, Luís Dilmé, and Xavier Fabré were entrusted with the reconstruction. This was the second time Del Liceu had burned. The first Gran Teatre del Liceu had opened on April 4, 1847, with a program which included almost everything except opera — a symphony by the Catalan composer Gomis; a drama in verse, *Don Fernando, el de Antequera*, by Ventura de la Vega; a ballet, *Ron-*

deña, and a cantata, *Il Regio Imene*, written by Joan Cortada with music by Marià Obiols. Miquel Garriga i Roca was commissioned to design the Liceu in 1845, but Mestres took over the next year. Fire consumed this theater in April 1861.

The Teatro de la Santa Cruz, Barcelona's first theater, dates from 1579. Built near Las Atarazanas by La Rambla, the theater hosted its first opera, Antonio Caldara's *Il più bel nome*, on August 7, 1708. It was the only opera house in the city for more than a century and during its tenure, witnessed many premieres. In 1760, Durán's *Antigono*, the first opera by a Catalan composer, graced the stage, and works by other Catalan composers such as Carles Baguer, Domènec Ter-radellas, Ferran Sors, Ramon Carnicer, Mateu Ferrer, and Antoni Rovira, were introduced here. Visiting Italian troupes staged opera and Christoph Willibald Gluck's *Orfeo ed Euridice*, was presented in celebration of Carlos III's saint's day in 1780. Vicenc Cuyàs's *La Fattuchiera* was premiered in 1838.

Meanwhile, the year before, the Dominican Convent of Montesión was requisitioned as barracks for the Battalion of the National Militia. Three officers and a theatrical designer — Pere Vives, Josep M. Grau, Francesc Planas, and Josep Planella — formed the *Sociedad Filodramática de Montesión* and the Teatro Montesión was born. It hosted Bellini's *Norma* on February 3, 1838, along with several other Italian operas. Eight years later, the nuns demanded their convent back, and the Philharmonic Society of Montesión lost its performance space. The group then changed its name to *Liceo Filarmónico Dramático Barcelonés*, and three board members — Joaquim de Gispert, Manuel Gibert, and Manuel Girona — demanded compensation, receiving land at the junction of La Rambla and Calle de San Pablo. Here the cornerstone for the Teatro del Liceo was laid on April 11, 1846. Although Barcelona had only 174,000 residents, Gispert had visions of an immense opera house, which he funded with the sale of stock in a newly formed *Sociedad del Teatro* and the purchase of permanent season tickets. The Teatro de la Santa Cruz did not like the competition with the Teatro Montesión and changed its name to Teatro Principal. Although it was damaged by fire in 1787, 1915, 1924, and 1933, it was restored after each calamity and exists today as a movie house. The rivalry between the Teatro Montesión and Teatro Principal was nothing in comparison to the competition between the Principal and the new Teatro del Liceo. Known as the war of the *liceístas* and the *cruzados*, the rivalry was actually a struggle between the elder, merchant, and landed aristocracy of the Santa Cruz (Principal) and the younger, industrial bourgeoisie of the Liceo.

Gaetano Donizetti's *Anna Bolena* was the first opera presented at the Teatro del Liceo. A tradition was begun during the second season (1848) of staging Spanish or Catalan operas and included José Antonio Cappa's *Giovanna di Castiglia* in 1848 and Nicolas Guañabens's *Arnaldo d'Erill* in 1859. The works, however, were performed in Italian. Because of the competition between the Liceo and the Principal, there were 23 local premieres in less than three years. Then the administrations of the two theaters merged, with Santiago Figueras as the director. Fire gutted the Liceu in 1861.

The first season in the rebuilt Liceo, that lasted from April to June, witnessed eleven different operas. The second season offered the Barcelona premiere of Giacomo Meyerbeer's *Le Prophète* which ushered in an era of French operas. Operas by Catalan composers continued with Francesc Sánchez i Gavagnach's *Rahabba* in 1867, Obiols's *Editta di Belcourt* and Felip Pedrell's *L'ultimo Abenzerraggio* in 1874, Pedrell's *Quasimodo* in 1875, and Antoni Nicolau's *Constanza* in 1879. Two years later, the first Catalan opera sung in Catalan, Joan Goula's *A la voreta del mar*, was premiered at the Teatro Principal. The Principal also hosted the Barcelona premiere of Richard Wagner's *Lohengrin* on May 17, 1882. The Catalan tenor Francesc Viñas made his debut in the title role and was the first to sing a Wagner opera in Catalan.

Del Liceo had become a center of political intrigue that resulted in Santiago Salvador Franch hurling two bombs from the fifth balcony on opening night of the season, November 7, 1893, during the second act of Gioachino Rossini's *Guillaume Tell*, with Leopoldo Mugnone on the podium. Twenty people were killed with dozens more wounded.

The world premieres continued with Tomás Breton's *Garín* (1892) Pedrell's *Els Pirineus*, called "a kind of Catalan *Parsifal*," (1902), Enric Morera's *Bruniselda* and *Empòrium* (1905), Jaume Pahissa's *Gal la Placídia* (1913), Amadeu Vives's *Balada de Carnaval* (1920), and Joaquim Cassadó's *Il monaco nero*, (1920) conducted by the composer. Leading artists of the period performed at the opera house, including Adelina Patti, Feodor Chaliapin, Enrico Caruso, Tita Ruffo, and Tito Schipa. Barcelona-born Maria Barrientos made her debut in 1899 in Meyerbeer's *L'Africaine*. During the civil war, the Liceo continued offering performances but the repertory was limited. World War II, however, closed the opera house, with the last performance taking place on January 22, 1939. Georges Bizet's *Carmen*, advertised for January 24, 1939, was canceled. Generalissimo Franco had entered Barcelona. After the war, Carles Suriñach Wrokona's *El mozo que casó con mujer brava* and Xavier Montsalvatge's *El gato con botas* were introduced and three Barcelona-born artists have achieved international recognition: Victoria de Los Angeles, Montserrat Caballé, and José Carreras. They performed regularly at del Liceo, along with other international circuit singers like Leonie Rysanek, Eva Marton, Mirella Freni, Nicolai Ghiaurov, Pilar Lorengar, and Plácido Domingo. In December 1980, the descendants of the original shareholders relinquished their seating rights under a reorganization plan, which established a consortium comprised of representative from the Barcelona City council, the Ministry of Culture, the Diputació of Barcelona, the Generalitat of Catalunya, and the Association of Opera Box Owners of the Gran Theatre del Liceu. The 1980s also marked the first time the Liceu had received public subsidies.

Barcelona traditionally opened the season with operas having a Spanish connection. Two openings of note were Manuel de Falla's *Atlàntida* in 1961, featuring de los Angeles, and Leonardo Balada's *Cristobal Colón* on September 19, 1987. The latter opera was commissioned by the Spanish government to commemorate the 500th anniversary of Columbus's arrival in America. Productions can be powerful and evocative, like the company's chilling-realistic staging of Leoš Janáček's *Jenůfa*, which demonstrated that despite its traditional bent, contemporary operas executed with equal emphasis on the dramatic and musical elements are impressive. The Liceu continued its opera seasons during the reconstruction of the theater at the Palau de la Musica, offering works like Richard Wagner's *Die Walküre*, Hector Berlioz's *La damnation de Faust*, Donizetti's *La favorita* and *L'elisir d'amore*, and Pyotr Il'yich Tchaikovsky's *Eugene Onegin*.

Gran Teatre del Liceu

Calamity struck shortly after 7:00 p.m. on April 9, 1861. The curtain was about to go up on Tomas Rubi's play *Fortuna contra fortuna* when fire broke out in the fourth-floor wardrobe area. Only the foyer, staircases, and entrance hall were spared. The theater was immediately rebuilt, funded through the sale of shares to Catalonia's

Gran Teatre del Liceu before fire (Barcelona, Spain).

rising bourgeoisie. A new opera house was joined to the surviving sections, and one year after the fire, the rebuilt Teatro del Liceo opened. (When Catalan became the official language of Catalonia in 1977, the Gran Teatro del Liceo became Gran Teatre del Liceu.)

After the 1994 conflagration, authorization was immediately granted to rebuild, and at the same time, to demolish several buildings on either side of the Liceu to allow for a much needed enlargement of the structure (its size has doubled from approximately 16,000 square yards to 31,930 square yards) and an up-dating of technical facilities. The new building kept the "soul" of the old Liceu (despite the 50% reduction in the number of private boxes) but planted inside one of the most modern opera houses in the world. The project cost 9,765 million pesetas.

The facade of the opera house mixes Neoclassical and Oriental elements in a unique manner. Inscriptions pay homage to *Mozart*, *Rossini*, *Calderón* and *Moratín*. The red and gold, Neo-Renaissance-style auditorium offers five tiers of boxes and balconies in a horseshoe-shape. The lamps are the original gas lamps, which have been turned upside down to accommodate electric light bulbs. The proscenium arch depicts operatic scenes. The auditorium accommodates 3,000.

Practical Information. Gran Teatre del Liceu, Rambla dels Caputxins 61,E-09001. Tel: 34 93 318-9122, Fax: 34 93 412 1198. When visiting Gran Teatre del Liceu, stay at the Husa Palace, Gran Via Cortes Catalanas 668, 08010 Barcelona. Tel: 34 93 318-5200, Fax: 34 93 318-0148. It is in the center of the city and convenient to the opera. The hotel can assist with opera tickets and schedules.

COMPANY STAFF

General Director. Josep Caminal i Badia.
Bibliography. Antoni Sàbat, *Gran Teatro del Liceo-The Grand Liceo Theatre* (Barcelona, 1979). *Cien años del Liceo: 1847–1947* (Barcelona, 1948). *Arquitecturas para la musica: VI Muestra Internacional de Arquitectura bienal de Venecia 1996* (Madrid, 1996). José Subirá, *La ópera en los teatros de Barcelona Vol. I, II* (Barcelona, 1960). Marcos Jesus Bertran, *El gran Teatre del Liceu de Barcelona: 1837–1930* (Barcelona, 1931).

Thanks to Juan Romero de Terreros, Embassy of Spain, Washington D.C.

Teatro Arriaga de Bilbao

Bilboa is experiencing a resurgence. Their $100 million Guggenheim Museum Bilbao recently opened and soon a new Palacio de Congresos y de la Música which includes a 2,220-seat Teatro de Opera opens. Designed by Federico Soriano and M. Dolores Palacios, the building resembles a gigantic boat. Nonetheless, while awaiting its new performance venue, the city still boasts an impressive opera season which unfolds at the Teatro Coliseo Albia with no fewer than seven works on the boards. The repertory concentrates on the 19th century with operas like Charles Gounod's *Romeo et Juliette*, Georges Bizet's *Carmen*, Giuseppe Verdi's *Nabucco*, and Gaetano Donizetti's *Roberto Devereux* and *Linda di Chamounix*, and popular early works including Wolfgang Amadeus Mozart's *Don Giovanni* and Domenico Cimarosa's *Il matrimonio segreto*. There have been forays into German territory with Richard Wagner's *Der fliegende Holländer* and Ludwig van Beethoven's *Fidelio*, and the *verismo* school with Pietro Mascagni's *Cavalleria rusticana* (paired with Giacomo Puccini's *Suor Angelica*). The artists are often internationally known like Sharon Sweet and Dolora Zajick in Vincenzo Bellini's *Norma*, and Zajick and Fabio Armiliato in *Cavalleria rusticana*, and Niel Schicoff, Barbara de Malo and Paolo Gavaneli in Verdi's *Ernani*. Other repertory favorites offered include Verdi's *Il trovatore* and *Luisa Miller*, Puccini's *Madama Butterfly*, and Mozart's *Così fan tutte*.

The city's previous opera house was the Teatro Arriaga, which opened in 1890 and closed in 1986, because of extensive deterioration in the interior structure of the building. Designed by Francisco Hurtado de Saracho, the Arriago was a beautiful testimony to Bilboa's architecture of the end of the 19th century.

Practical Information. Teatro Colisea

Albia, Rodriguez Arias 3-1°, Bilboa. Tel: 34 94 415-5490, Fax: 34 94 415-2200. When visiting the Teatro Colisea Albia, stay at the Hotel Lopez de Haro, 2 Obispo Orueta, Bilboa. Tel: 34 94 423-5500, Fax: 34 94 423-4500.

COMPANY STAFF
Director. Mikel Viar Bilbao.
Bibliography. *Arquitecturas para la musica: VI Muestra Internacional de Arquitectura bienal de Venecia 1996.*

Thanks to Juan Romero de Terreros, Embassy of Spain, Washington D.C.

MADRID

Teatro Real

The Teatro Real was inaugurated on November 19, 1850, with Gaetano Donizetti's *La favorita* and in 1925, was closed. Finally, more than seven decades later, its doors were reopened on October 11, 1997, with Manuel de Falla's *La vida breve* and the ballet *El sombrero de tres picos*. The gala opening night audience included the royal family. A week later, the world premiere of Anton Garcia Abril's *Divinas palabras* took place on October 18, 1997. The opera, commissioned for this special occasion, featured Plácido Domingo, a native of Madrid. Antonio López Aguado and Custodio Moreno were the architects of the original building. Francisco Rodríguez de Partearroyo was in charge of the restructuring.

Opera came to Madrid back in 1635, performed in private Royal theaters. King Philip IV enjoyed his opera in the Palacio Real Buen Retiro. After the turn of the century, the Teatro de los Caños del Peral hosted Italian opera in 1703 and 1708, performed by a traveling company. Italian opera flourished during the reign of King Philip V. He even brought the great *castrato* Farinelli to Spain. Opera was also heard at the Teatro del Príncipe.

In the 1800s the Teatro del Real Palacio and the new Teatro Real, constructed on the location of the old Teatro de los Caños del Peral, were home to Italian opera. Works by Donizetti, Gioachino Rossini, and Vincenzo Bellini graced the stage of the new opera house. Operas by Giuseppe Verdi were especially popular. Verdi even traveled to Madrid for the Spanish premiere of his *La forza del destino* on February 21, 1863. Then in 1925, the impressive operatic career of the Teatro Real came to an end. After a performance of Giacomo Puccini's *La bohème* the opera house was closed. Spring water had destroyed its foundation. Now 73 years later, it has resumed its role

as the city's foremost opera house. There were, however, some behind the scene intrigue before the inaugural. Richard Wagner's *Parsifal* was originally scheduled for the reopening, featuring, of course, Domingo with Lorin Maazel conducting. This, however, was planned by the artistic director Stéphane Lissner who had the misfortune of being appointed by a different political party than the one in power for the inaugural. Lissner was fired and his plans annulled.

The inaugural season offered nine operas. In addition to Abril's *Divinas palabras* and Falla's *La vida breve*, there was a mixture of contemporary works and standard fare — Benjamin Britten's *Peter Grimes*, George Gershwin's *Porgy and Bess*, Leoš Janáček's *Příhody Lišky Bystroušky* (The Cunning Little Vixen), Puccini's *Turandot*, Wolfgang Amadeus Mozart's *Le nozze di Figaro*, Donizetti's *L'elisir d'amore*, and Verdi's *Un ballo in maschera*. Artists included Jane Eaglen, Thomas Allen, Willard White, Cynthia Haymon, William Cochran, Carlos Alvarez, and Carlos Chausson, among others.

Teatro Real

The work on the Teatro Real began in 1818, but was not completed for more than 30 years. Every imaginable delay was experienced during its construction. After opening in 1850, it was modified several times, in 1884 by architect De La Concha, in 1926 by architect Flores, and in 1941, by architects Moya and Méndez. In 1965, José Manuel González Valcárcel was put in charge of the building's rehabilitation as a Sala Conciertos (Concert Hall), but leaving open the possibility for a return to its roots as an opera house. On October 13, 1966, the building reopened as a concert hall with Ludwig van Bee-thoven's *Ninth Symphony* under the baton of Frübeck de Burgos.

Two decades later, on January 14, 1986, the announcement was made of the reconversion of the Teatro Real into an opera house. It took more than a decade and cost $140 million. The story behind it sounds like an opera in itself. Changes in political climate and parties caused several delays, along with a revolving door of architects, joining and leaving the project, with one suffering a fatal heart attack on the stage. The result is an exterior that juxtaposes incompatible styles, but had no adverse effect on the interior.

The opera house is a massive structure of gray granite, with three levels of attached gilded columns. The first level is of the Doric order, the second level of Ionic order, and the Corinthian order reigns on top. There are additional Neoclassic features, like the roof-top balustrade and street level arcade, imposed on the severe structure. The horseshoe-shaped auditorium holds five gilded tiers and a center royal box. There are plush red seats. There are 1,640 places.

Practical Information. Teatro Real, Madrid. Tel: 34 91 516-0660, Fax: 34 91 558-8787. When visiting El Teatro Real, stay at the Hotel Ritz, Plaza de la Lealtad 5, 28014. Tel: 34 91 521-2857; Fax: 34 91 532-8776. It is in the center of the city and convenient to the opera. The Ritz can assist with opera tickets and schedules.

Teatro Real (Madrid, Spain).

Muestra Internacional de Arquitectura bienal de Venecia 1996 (Madrid, 1996). José Subirá, *Historia y anecdotario del Teatro Real* (Madrid, 1949). José Subirá, *El teatro del Real Palacio* (Madrid, 1950). Gaspar Gómez de la Serna, *Gracias y desgracias del Teatro Real* (Madrid, 1975). M. Muñoz, *Historia del Teatro Real* (Madrid, 1946).

Thanks to Juan Romero de Terreros, Embassy of Spain, Washington D.C.

COMPANY STAFF

Director. Juan Cambreleng.
Bibliography. *Arquitecturas para la musica: VI*

Teatro de la Zarzuela

In the middle of the 19th century, composers Joaquin Gastambide, Rafael Hernando, and Francisco Asenjo Barbieri, joined together, creating another style of Spanish music — the zarzuela — which could be likened to a Spanish operetta. Its birth took place on March 21, 1849, with the premiere of Hernando's *Colegialas y Soldados* at the Teatro Comedia. Later that year, on December 24, 1849, Gastambide's *La Mansajera* was staged, followed by Barbieri's *Gloria y Peluca* on

March 9, 1850. Zarzuela had mass appeal and was very popular. Jerónimo de la Gandara was commissioned to design the Teatro de la Zarzuela, with the support of the Spanish Music Society (*La españa Musical*). Gandara's design was inspired by the Teatro alla Scala (Milano). José Maria Gallart was responsible for part of the exterior.

In November 1909, fire destroyed most of the theater. Only the exterior walls and interior framework remained standing. The following year, Cesáreo Iradier was in charge of the reconstruction. The theater was remodeled in 1956 by Vallejo and Dampiere, when they removed Iradier's decorations. Meanwhile, the Asociación Amigos de la Opera de Madrid, bemoaning the absence of opera in the nation's capital (see Teatro Real Madrid entry), organized opera seasons at the Teatro de la Zarzuela. Giacomo Puccini's *Tosca* initiated the first season in 1964. Other operas on the boards included Puccini's *La bohème*, Gioachino Rossini's *La Cenerentola*, Giuseppe Verdi's *Il trovatore*, Wolfgang Amadeus Mozart's *Don Giovanni*, and Charles Gounod's *Faust*. To reflect the theater's new, albeit temporary, role as the city's theater for Zarzuela and opera, it was renamed Teatro Lírico Nacional la Zarzuela.

In the mid–1980s, the opera seasons were impressive with international stars, some trying out new roles on stage — Monserrat Caballé assayed her first staged Sieglinde (Richard Wagner's *Die Walküre*); José Carreras his first Canio (Ruggero Leoncavallo's *I pagliacci*); Ruggero Raimondi the title role in Modest Mussorgsky's *Boris Godunov*; Agnes Baltsa in Rossini's *La Cenerentola*, and Plácido Domingo in Puccini's *La bohème*. By the mid–1990s, as the Teatro Real was about to reopen, the quality of opera was not so impressive. A production of Donizetti's *La fille du régiment* was poorly sung and clothed in a traditional and unimaginative production — surprisingly enough, a co-production with Opéra de Monte-Carlo, Grand Théâtre de Genève, and Deutsche Oper am Rhein (Düsseldorf-Duisburg). The theater was ready to revert to its roots, original name, and forte, zarzuela. Recent offerings include Federico Chueca's *El chaleco blanco* and *La gran via*, Tomás Bretón's *Los amantes de teruel*, Francisco Asenjo Barbieri's *El barberillo de Lavapies*, and Amadeo Vives's *Doña Francisquita*.

Teatro de la Zarzuela

The Teatro de la Zarzuela is a large structure sandwiched between two apartment buildings. Its peach-colored facade is ornamented with white

Teatro de la Zarzuela facade details (Madrid, Spain).

stucco music motif decorations and statues of the Muses. The horseshoe-shaped auditorium holds three gilded tiers that end with three levels of proscenium boxes. Deep rose-colored seats blend with a deep, rich maroon curtain. The gilded proscenium arch is covered with a grill-like pattern, the center of which holds a lyre embellished by a festive wreath. There are 1,242 seats.

Practical Information. Teatro de la Zarzuela, Jovellanos 4, 28014 Madrid. Tel: 34 91 524-5400, Fax: 34 91 523-3059. When visiting the Teatro de la Zarzuela, stay at the Hotel Ritz, Plaza de la Lealtad 5, 28014. Tel: 34 91 521-2857; Fax:

34 91 532-8776. It is in the center of the city and convenient to the opera. The Ritz can assist with opera tickets and schedules.

COMPANY STAFF

Director. Emilio Sagi.

Bibliography. José Subirá, *Historia y anecdotario del Teatro Real* (Madrid, 1949). Gaspar Gómez de la Serna, *Gracias y desgracias del Teatro Real* (Madrid, 1975). M. Muñoz, *Historia del Teatro Real* (Madrid, 1946). Additional information supplied by the Spanish National Tourist Office.

Thanks to Angel Barreda, Teatro de la Zarzuela.

SANTANDER

Festival Internacional de Santander (Summer Festival)

Santander, along with Bilbao and Seville, has received a new performing arts venue. The Palacio de Festivales was inaugurated in 1991. Designed by Javier Sáenz de Oiza, the Festival Palace hosts visiting opera companies from around the world during its festival. It has offered works like Benjamin Britten's *Turn of the Screw*, Giuseppe Verdi's *Nabucco*, Giacomo Puccini's *La bohème*, and Richard Wagner's *Der fliegende Holländer*. International artists like Samuel Ramey, Mirella Freni, Hildegard Behrens, Carol Vaness, and Matti Salminen have performed there. Recent offerings include Verdi's *Don Carlo*, staged in commemoration of the 400th anniversary of the death of Phillip II.

Practical Information. Festival Interna-

cional de Santander, Palacio de Festivales de Cantabria, Calle Gamazo, S/N, 39004 Santander. Tel: 34 42 21 05 08, Fax: 34 42 31 47 67. When visiting the Festival Internacional de Santander, stay at the Hotel Real, Perez Galdos 28, 39005 Santander. Tel: 34 42 27 25 50, Fax: 34 42 27 45 73. It is a comfortable hotel convenient to the festival venues.

COMPANY STAFF

Director. José Luis Ocejo.

Bibliography. *Arquitecturas para la musica: VI Muestra Internacional de Arquitectura bienal de Venecia 1996.*

Thanks to Juan Romero de Terreros, Embassy of Spain, Washington D.C.

SEVILLE

Teatro de la Maestranza

When Seville opened its new opera house, Teatro de la Maestranza on May 10, 1991, with operatic excerpts that included performances by the opera world's great Spanish singers—José Carreras, Alfredo Kraus, Montserrat Caballé, and Plácido Domingo, it was back on the international opera stage. Designed by Luis Marín de Terán and Aurelio del Pozo, the new opera house took three years to complete at a cost of $40 million.

Italian opera was a well-liked form of entertainment during the 1800s, performed frequently at the Teatro de San Fernando and the Anfiteatro. Works by Giuseppe Verdi, Gaetano Donizetti, and Gioachino Rossini among others dominated the schedule, performed by established artists. After the first world war, opera lost its popularity, but with the opening of the new theater, interest in the art form has been revived. The season offered five productions, including Richard Wagner's *Tannhäuser*, Verdi's *Nabucco*, Rossini's *L'italiana in Algeri* and *Il barbiere di Siviglia*, and Giacomo Puccini's *Turandot*. Well-known directors like Werner Herzog and Sonja Frisell, and singers like Ferruccio Furlanetto, Simon Estes, and Eva Johansson have performed in the new performance venue. The repertory is expanding with a couple of rarities scheduled — Donizetti's *Alahor in Granata* and Jules Massenet's *Le Cid*. The new opera house is a huge structure with a cylindrically shaped exterior and a Neoclassic-inspired facade. There are 1,774 seats.

Practical Information. Teatro de la Maestranza, Paseo de Colón 22, 41001 Seville. Tel: 34 95 422-6573, Fax: 34 95 422-5995. When visiting the Teatro de la Maestranza, stay at the Hotel Alfonso XIII, Calle San Fernando 2, 41004 Seville. Tel: 34 95 422-2850, Fax: 34 95 421-6033. It is convenient to the theater.

COMPANY STAFF

Director. José Luis Castro.
Bibliography. *Arquitecturas para la musica: VI Muestra Internacional de Arquitectura bienal de Venecia 1996.*

Thanks to Juan Romero de Terreros, Embassy of Spain, Washington D.C.

Other Spanish Opera Houses

Other opera houses in Spain (and islands) are noted below by name, address, telephone, recent repertory, and director (as available).

Opera Cómica de Madrid. Acuerdo 17, 1°A, 28015 Madrid. Tel: 34 1 522 0583, Fax: 34 1 522 8628. **President:** Luis Alvarez.

Teatro Principal. Carrer La Riera 2a, E-07003 Palma de Mallorca, Balearic Islands. Tel: 34 71 725 548, Fax: 34 71 725 542. **Director:** Miguel Vidal.
Teatro Campoamor Melquiades. Alvarez 20 1, E-33203 Oviedo. Tel: 34 8 5211 705, Fax: 34 8 521 2402.

Sweden

--- GÖTEBORG

Göteborgs Operan

Göteborgs Operan opened on October 1, 1994, with the inaugural festivities lasting three days. The first opera performance, Karl Birger Blomdahl's *Aniara*, took place on October 15, 1994. Jan Izikowitz designed the structure.

Before the Operan opened, opera was performed at the Stora Teatern. Inaugurated in 1859, the Stora was originally designed for touring companies. It was not until 1920 that an opera company took up residence, but many standard repertory works, like Giuseppe Verdi's *La traviata* and *Rigoletto*, and Puccini's *La bohème* and *Tosca*, did not receive their first performance in Göteborg until the beginning of the 1980s. More Göteborg premieres of standard fare followed — Georges Bizet's *Carmen* (1988), and Verdi's *Don Carlo* (1987) and *Macbeth* (1990). Also during the 1980s, Scandinavian operas, like Lars Edlund's *Flickan i Ögat*, Carl Nielsen's *Maskarade*, Aulis Sallinen's *Det Röda Strecket*, Lars Johan Werle's *Lionardo*

and *Kvinnogräl och Gudars Skymning*, and other 20th century works — Dominick Argento's *The Voyage of Edgar Allan Poe*, Igor Stravinsky's *The Rake's Progress*, Dmitry Shostakovich's *Ledi Makbet Mtsenskovo uyezda* (Lady Macbeth of the Mtsensk District), Kurt Weill's *Der Aufstieg und Fall der Stadt Mahagonny*, Gian Carlo Menotti's *The Medium*, Peter Maxwell Davies's *Lighthouse* and *Miss D* among others, were also seen for the first time in the Swedish port city.

After the Göteborgs Operan opened, the trend toward standard repertory fare continued with four additional operas and one operetta during the inaugural season — Giacomo Puccini's *Madama Butterfly*, Wolfgang Amadeus Mozart's *Don Giovanni* and *Le nozze di Figaro*, *Der fliegende Holländer* and Johann Strauß's *Die Fledermaus*. The following season (1995-96) added Leoš Janáček's *Jenůfa,* Mozart's *Così fan tutte*, a Swedish musical *Kristina från Duvemåla*, and the world premiere of Lars Johan Werle's *Äppelkriget* on February 10, 1996, to the repertory. Managing director Dag Hallberg explained that the eclectic repertory reflects their philosophy to avoid competition with the Kungliga Teater in Stockholm, but instead to complement the Stockholm opera, by showcasing Swedish composers and mounting more Swedish premieres. This philosophy is carried over in their creation of a different profile, a more "Swedish" profile if you will at the Operan, with young Swedish artists and new talent. There is a permanent ensemble of 28 singers and productions are given in both the original language (Richard Wagner's *Der fliegende Holländer*) and in Swedish, (Mozart's *Così fan tutte*). The drawback with Swedish-sung productions is if a singer gets sick, it is difficult to find a replacement. It is Hallberg's dream to work with established artists but the budget does not allow such a luxury. Since there are few Swedish conductors, the money is used to attract good conductors.

As the company builds up their repertory of traditional operas, they are produced in unusual stagings, with "acting" singers. The productions themselves reflect a good balance between the musical and dramatic aspects of the work, with an avoidance of the "old-fashion" opera style and an attempt to make the opera meaningful for today. This is important since the population of Göteborg is only around a half a million, so the opera must also appeal to the younger generation for a broader audience base. There is a long rehearsal time in carefully constructed productions. With new, superb technical facilities, much attention is given to design, lighting and special effects. There are co-productions with Malmö, Copenhagen (Denmark) and Oslo (Norway). The budget is around $40 million (230 million Swedish Krone) of which the city contributes half, the federal government a quarter and a quarters is earned from box office. The city owns the new opera house and donates it to the company. Recent offerings include Puccini's *Madama Butterfly* and *Tosca*, Jacques Offenbach's *Les contes d'Hoffmann*, and Franz Lehár's *Die lustige Witwe*.

Göteborgs Operan

Many locations were discussed for the location of the new opera house before Packhuskajen, a former fortification ground on the shores of Göta Älv, was selected. Ground was broken on June 3, 1991, and by the spring of 1994, the work had been completed and the staff moved in. Göteborgs Operan was officially opened that fall. The cost was SEK 558 million or approximately $100 million. The State paid SEK 347 million, 500 companies gave SEK 117 million, the city of Göteborg contributed SEK 28 million, eight neighboring cities SEK 63 million, and 4,000 private individuals donated SEK 3 million. The new structure is in contrast to the classic opera house in Stockholm, a product of the glorious, traditional past. The Göteborgs Operan looks toward the future.

Designed to resemble a boat, which is fitting for its location on Packhuskajen, (a wharf in the Port of Göteborg) Göteborgs Operan fuses classic colors and materials with contrasting lines in a modern design. Occupying two city blocks, the opera house was inspired by the port environment and offers a ship-like prow over the entrance colonnade. The foyer areas look like decks on a ship. The auditorium recalls the great Italian opera houses of the 18th century. Although semicircular in shape, it is shallow with a high ceiling. Illuminated by a "modern" chandelier, a large donut with two rows of halogen lamps, the hall holds three tiers and a few boxes, which create their own level. Burgundy red, cloth seats, textured blue walls which resemble the ocean, cherry-wood floors, and clinker-built balcony fronts define the space. There is a plain blue proscenium arch with acoustic side panels framing a red curtain. There are 1,301 seats.

Practical Information. Göteborgs Operan, Christina Nilssons Gata, 41104 Göteborg. Tel: 46 31 10 80 00; Fax: 46 31 10 80 30. When visiting the Göteborg Operan, stay at the Radisson SAS Park Avenue Hotel Göteborg, Kungsportsavenyn 36-38, 40016 Göteborg. Tel: 46 31 17 65 20, Fax 46 31 16 95 68. It has views of the city and is convenient to the opera house. The hotel can help with opera tickets and schedule.

COMPANY STAFF AND WORLD PREMIERES

Chefer. Göteborgs Operan: Dag Hallberg (managing director, 1995–present), Jubani Raiskinen (artistic director, 1995–present). **Stora Teatern:** Staffan Aspegren (1993–present), Gardar Cortes (1991–93), Sven-Olof Eliasson (1988–91), Eskil Hemberg (1984–87), Jackie Söderman (1980–83),

Göteborgs Operan "sea" foyer (Göteborg, Sweden).

Gösta Sjögren + Christer Irestad (1978-79), Ragner Ulfung (1977-78), Folke Abenius (1971-77), Styrbjörn Lindedal (1970-71), Bernhard Sönnerstedt (1960–70), Styrbjörn Lindedal (1958–60), Einar Hjort (1948–58), Lars Egge (1938–48), Oscar Textorius (1937-38), Harry Stangenberg (1936-37), Gustaf Bergman (1935-36), Karl Kinch (1927–35), Carl Barklind (1925–27), Gustaf Bergman (1922–25), Gunnar Kronwin (1920–22).

World Premieres. Stora Teatern: G. Nystroem's *Herr Arnes Penningar* January 6, 1961; U. Björlin's *Den Stora Teatern* February 25, 1972; W.W. Glaser's *En Naken Kung* April 6, 1973; L.J. Werle's *Flower Power* May 31, 1978; L.J. Werle's *Animalen* May 19, 1979; S.E. Johanson *Pojken med Flöjten* December 3, 1980 (Skolförest.); T. Jennefelt's *Gycklarnas Hamlet* December 2, 1990; **Göterborgs Operan:** L.J. Werle's *Äppelkriget* February 10, 1996.

Bibliography. Ingrid Arensberg, *Göteborgs Operan i Hamn* (Göteborg, 1994). *Stora Teatern: Göteborgs Musikteater* (Göteborg, n.d.). Additional information supplied by the company. Interview with Dag Hallberg, Managing Director, November 1995.

Thanks to Anita Manskog, Göteborgs Operan, and Torsten Andersson.

KARLSTAD

Musikteatern I Varmland

The Musikteatern was established in 1974, under the new cultural plan that the Swedish government had for the country—decentralizing opera and creating five regional theaters and ensembles. Karlstad, the capital of Varmland and located in the middle of Sweden with a population of 60,000, was designated to be as one of the regional theater formed. Miklos Kundler was the first general director. The inaugural season, (1974-75) took place in a "Culture House," since Karlstad's theater was undergoing a transformation from having served as a movie house for 47 years.

The Karlstad theater, designed by Axel Anderberg, the same architect that designed the Kungliga Teater in Stockholm, was inaugurated in 1893 with a musical and literary evening. The theater hosted opera, primarily given by traveling troupes, and drama. By 1937, the economic situation was such that the theater was converted into a movie house. The two-tier auditorium is delicately decorated, the work of Carl Grabow. The theater was converted back to its original function in 1974. During the transformation, a chandelier replaced the gas lighting, and the orchestra pit was enlarged, to accommodate a larger orchestra. There are approximately 400 seats. Nonetheless, the use of the theater as a cinema still welcomed the Swedish prima donna Zarah Leander, who was born in Karlstad, for the celebration of its 50th anniversary.

The repertory during the first two years offered by general director Kundler proved unpopular and he departed. In fact, no general director survived for long. This was more the result of the residents of Karlstad questioning the necessity of a theater at all in their city, than a reflection of the abilities of the former general directors. In small towns in Sweden, opera is a "forbidden" word — Music Theater is art for the masses. On July 1, 1993, another general director, Hans Hiort arrived. He previously had worked at the Folksoperan in Stockholm, which had popularized opera and was more successful than his predecessors. His repertory choices, however, for a small Swedish town, was considered daring. He opened the 94-95 season, the first he had completely

planned, with an unknown work, Riccardo Zandonai's *I cavalieri di Ekebù*. Other works offered included Richard Wagner's *Der fliegende Holländer* in an unconventional production by Wilhelm Carlsson, with Stig Tysklind in the title role, Leoš Janáček's *Jenůfa*, Johann Strauß's *Die Fledermaus*, and the musical *Les Misérables*. When Hiort joined the company, there was an ensemble of 15 permanent singers, which has since dwindled to eight, and he plans to keep it that way, to allow for guest artists. His budget is around SEK 9 million. His primary goal is to popularize opera. There are no subscriptions, but instead, discounted tickets for students and retired folks, and half-price tickets for the unemployed. The company also has an obligation to tour throughout Värmland, visiting the small towns, like Arvika, Filipstad, and Hagfors.

Practical Information. Musikteatern i Varnland, Klaraborgsgatan 3, 65226 Karlstad. Tel: 46 54 10 29 10. Fax: 46 54 10 05 33. When visiting the Musikteatern i Varmland, contact the Swedish Travel & Tourism Council, 655 Third Avenue, New York, NY 10017-5617. Tel: 212-949-2333, Fax 212-697-0835.

BIBLIOGRAPHY

Bibliography. Bernd Hoppe, *Das Musiktheater im Värmland in Karlstad, Orpheus* (Berlin, 1995).

MALMÖ

Malmö Musikteater

The Malmö Musiktheater became an independent organization, an opera company in its own right, in 1996. Four years earlier, the Malmö Musiktheater had been created under an umbrella organization known as the Malmö Musik och Teater. The opera company was originally not a separate entity, but part of and known as the Malmö Stadsteater. The Malmö Stadsteater was inaugurated on September 23, 1944, with *A Midsummer Night's Dream* by William Shakespeare. The theater was designed by the three architects who won the architectural competition: Eric Lallerstedt, Sigurd Lewerentz, and David Helldén.

The opera season usually includes a traditional opera, a contemporary opera, and an experimental work, often clad in a non-traditional

production. There is a permanent chorus of 40, an orchestra of between 60 and 70 musicians, and a small ensemble of seven principal singers. The remaining roles are filled by other Swedish singers, "before their big-break" hired on a per production basis. All operas are sung in Swedish. The rehearsal period is between 6 to 8 weeks. Young directors and set designers are brought in, as Lars Rudolfsson, artistic director explained, "to bring something new out of the art form." Box office revenue amounts to 10–15% of the budget, with some private sponsors, but the lion's share is paid by the city and state.

Rudolfsson likes to push the company in a new direction each season and strives to give meaning to the operas he stages. He believes that the audience must have something to think about when they leave the theater. All kinds and types of productions are mounted so the audience does not get accustomed to one style. His aim is to "overwhelm" the audience every year, by finding new directions and making them see things that they did not see before. Initially, the opera goers did not take too kindly to the avant-garde concepts. In fact, in 1984-85, they reacted violently to Lars Johan Werle's *En midsommarnattsdröm*, an unfamiliar, contemporary opera, complaining about almost everything, especially the music and the direction. Soon, however, the audience reactions switched and they began to appreciate the new, the different, the unusual. Some of the more obscure works mounted included Nino Rota's *Il cappello di paglia di Firenze*, Hans Gefors's *Vargen Kommer*, and Reine Jönsson's *Gunsmoke in Utopia III*. These were staged in a 204-seat, 9-row theater, called the Intima Teatern. Also a not-so-obscure work, Wolfgang Amadeus Mozart's *Die Entführung aus dem Serail*, was also performed there, in a production that converted the entire theater into the "harem"—the audience were seated on cushions on the floor, with water in the middle of the room. Some of the more mainstream operas performed since the opera company's independence included Giacomo Puccini's *Madama Butterfly*, Gioachino Rossini's *Il barbiere di Siviglia*, and Gaetano Donizetti's *Lucia di Lammermoor*. The company also created a Swedish musical, *Kristina från Duvemåla*, about Swedish emigrants that attained in Sweden the popularity that the most popular American Broadway musicals have in the United States. The company also mounts Broadway musicals, like *Hello Dolly* and *The Man of La Mancha*. Recent offerings include Mozart's *Die Zauberflöte* and *The Fiddler on the Roof*.

Malmö Stadsteater

The Malmö Stadsteater is a huge rectangular beige concrete and glass structure on "pillars" in a design resembling more the performing arts centers of the 1960s. A bronze fountain called "tragos" by Nils Sjögren is located on the marble-paved piazza in front of the theater. The auditorium is fan-shaped, amphitheater-like, with a large single balcony. The design was influenced by the demand for a "people's theater" where the performers could come into close contact with the audience and where there would be a large number of

Malmö Stadsteater (Malmö, Sweden).

inexpensive seats with good sightlines. There is a plain black proscenium arch, light-wood slats covering the parapet, and red cloth seats. The city of Malmö owns the theater. It accommodates 1,450.

Practical Information. Malmö Musikteater, Box 17520, 20010 Malmö; Malmö Stadsteater, Kalendegatan 12, Malmö. Tel: 46 40 20 85 00, Fax: 46 40 20 84 79. When visiting the Malmö Musikteater, stay at the Radisson SAS Hotel Malmö, Östergatan 10, 21125 Malmö. Tel: 46 40 23 92 00, Fax 46 40 611 2840. It is centrally located, and convenient to the opera house. The hotel can assist with opera tickets and schedule.

COMPANY STAFF AND REPERTORY

Chefer. (**Malmö Musikteater**) Lars Rudolfsson, Artistic and Managing Director; **Teaterchefer:**

(**Malmö Stadsteater**) Bengt Hall (1992–95), Lars Larsson (1989–92), Claes Sylwander (1983–89), Holger Reenberg (1980–83), Rolf Rembe (1977–80), Gösta Folke (1960–77), Lars-Levi Læstadius (1950–60), Stig Torsslow (1947–50), Sandro Malmquist (1944–47).

Repertory. (Most popular operas 1944–1994) Aida, Carmen, La traviata, Porgy and Bess, Les contes d'Hoffmann, Il trovatore, Hänsel und Gretel, Rigoletto, Die lustige Weiber von Windsor, Tosca, Le nozze di Figaro, Die Zauberflöte, La bohème, Un ballo in maschera, Madama Butterfly, Don Giovanni, A Midsummer Night Dream.

Bibliography. Henrik Sjögren, *Konst & Nöje: Malmö Stadsteater 1944–1994* (Malmö, 1994). *Malmö Stadsteater * Malmö's Municipal Theatre* (Malmö, 1995). Interview with Lars Rudolfsson, Artistic and Managing Director, November 1995.

Thanks to Malin Ekström, Malmö Musikteater, and Jukka Turku.

STOCKHOLM

Drottningholms Slottsteater

In 1754, Queen Lovisa Ulrika commissioned the first theater in Stockholm, the Drottningholm Slottsteater (palace theater), built on her summer palace grounds, on an island near Stockholm. George Greggenhoffer designed the court theater, which not only hosted plays but also housed all the actors, actresses, and their families. It survived eight years before fire broke out August 26, 1762, in the middle of a performance. As legend has it, an actress ran on stage, shouting, "fire, fire!" and fainted, but the audience thought it was part of the show. When they saw the flames, panic broke out and four people died. Ulrika commissioned Carl Frederick Adelcrantz to rebuild the theater, but she had little money to pay for it, so Adelcrantz created a masterpiece of illusion — by disguising inexpensive materials to look like the genuine article. Drottningholms Slottsteater reopened in July 1766 and hosted touring French and Italian opera troupes. In 1777, King Gustav III purchased the theater from his mother, Queen Ulrika. When an assassin's bullet ended the life of Gustav III in March 1792, it also ended the theatrical life of the Slottsteater for more than a century.

The saga continued in 1921, when on a cold winter day, an inquisitive theater historian, Agne Beijer, discovered Drottningholms Slottsteater

buried under more than a 129 years of dust (and some snow). Amazingly, its fifteen sets of scenery and Donato Stopany stage machinery, including wave, thunder, wind, and cloud machines, were still intact. The theater was reconstructed, reopening to the public on August 19, 1922. The Kungliga Teater (Swedish Royal Opera) staged some opera at the theater, but not until 1946, when the first artistic director was appointed, along with a management team, did regular seasons of opera take place. The initial season hosted Josef Martin Kraus's *Födelsedagen firad i fiskarstugan* and André Grétry's *Les deux avares*, followed by Wolfgang Amadeus Mozart's *Bastien und Bastienne* and Domenico Cimarosa's *Il matrimonio segreto* in 1947, and André Grétry's *Le tableau parlant* in 1948. Georg Friedrich Händel's *Orlando furioso* ushered in the 1950s, which saw A. Blaise's *Anette et Lubin*, Benjamin Britten's *Rape of Lucretia*, Cimarosa's *Il maestro di capella*, Georg Philipp Telemann's *Pimpinone*, Alessandro Scarlatti's *Il trionfo dell'onore*, Giambattista Pergolesi's *Il maestro di muscia*, and Christoph Willibald Gluck's *Iphigénie en Aulide* and *Orfeo ed Euridice* among others, enter the repertory. Gluck's *Le Cinesi* welcomed the 1960s along with *Iphigénie en Tauride*. His *Alceste*, Scarlatti's *L'honesta negli amori*, Henry Purcell's *Dido and Aeneas*,

Cimarosa's *L'impresario in angustie*, Händel's *Acis and Galatea*, Claudio Monteverdi's *L'Orfeo*, and Antonio Sacchini's *Oedipe à Colone* also graced the stage. In 1968, and lasting for a dozen years, the artistic concept changed from historical recreations of the operas to modern directorial productions, (contemporary concepts) with works like Purcell's *King Arthur*, Claudio Monteverdi's *L'incoronazione di Poppea*, Mozart's *Così fan tutte*, Jean-Baptiste Lully's *Le carnaval*, Jean-Phillipe Rameau's *Plateé*, and Niccolò Piccinni's *La buona figliola* on the schedule. The 1980s brought a different artistic concept, one that emphasized original instrumentation and period instruments in historically traditional productions. Additional works like Martín y Soler's *L'arbore di Diana*, Gluck's *Paride ed Elena*, and Mozart's *Idomeneo* and *La finta giardiniera* were on the boards. These two Mozart opera were repeated for the celebration of the composer's bicentennial. More obscure pieces were staged in the latter part of the 1990s, including Jacopo Peri's *Euridice* and Luigi Rossi's *Orfeo*. Recent offerings include Gluck's *Orfeo ed Euridice*, *Alceste*, and *Paride ed Helena*.

Drottningholms Slottsteater

The Drottningholms Slottsteater is a perfectly preserved 18th-century royal court theater. The plain yellow facade gives the building the appearance of a manor house. The steeply raked T-shaped auditorium is a mixture of rococo, Neoclassical, and Baroque styles. Symmetrically shaped (although fake doors were painted to achieve the effect), the ochre-colored room is made out of wood, stucco, and papier-mâché. The auditorium holds an orchestra level and six side boxes. When the king and queen attend, they sit on a pair of Louis XV fauteuils, placed front and center. Only the presence of electric bulbs hints at the 20th century. But even that has been "authenticated" with the invention of specially designed flickering electric candles. As in the 1700s, the candles remain at the same brightness before, during, and after the performance. The theater seats 454.

Practical Information. Drottningholms Slottsteater, Drottningholm Palace grounds, Stockholm. Tel: 46 8 660-8225, Fax 46 8 661-0194.

Drottningholms Slottsteater (Stockholm, Sweden).

When visiting the Drottningholms Slottsteater, stay at the SAS Strand Hotel, Nybrokajen 9, 10327 Stockholm. Tel: 46 8 678-7800, Fax 46 8 20 44 36. It is convenient to the boat for Drotningholms Slottsteater. The hotel can help with opera tickets and schedule.

COMPANY STAFF

Konstnärliga Ledare (Artistic directors). Per-Erik Öhm (1996–present), Elisabeth Söderström

(1993–1995), Arnold Östman (1980–1992), Bertil Bokstedt (1968–1979), Gustaf Hilleström (1947–1967).

Bibliography. Ture Rangström, *Drottningholms Slottsteater*The Drottningholm Court Theater* (Stockholm, 1985). *The Drottningholm Theatre Museum* (Stockholm, 1984). Gustav Hilleström, *The Drottingholm Theatre: Past and Present* (Stockholm, 1980). Agna Beijer, *Drottningholms slottsteater på Lovisa Ulrikas och Gustaf IIIs tid* (Stockholm, 1981).

Thanks to Per Forsström, Drottingholms Slottsteater.

Folkoperan

The Folksoperan (People's Opera) began as a "fringe" group in 1976. Claes Fellbom, Kerstin Nerbe, Staffan Rydén, and Arne Akerstrom founded the company to "compensate" for the elitist attitudes connected to opera. The Folksoperan, unlike some other opera companies in Sweden, does not have a fixed ensemble, but hires Swedish opera singers, who normally would have to leave Sweden to find work, for its productions. It has grown into the largest "free lance" employer in Sweden, hiring around 400 performers a year. They use a music-drama style of performance.

The first performances were commissioned by the Rijks Theatre, and the newly formed company toured hospitals with a "pocket opera"— minibus and piano. The first productions included Giambattista Pergolesi's *La serva padrona*, Gian Carlo Menotti's *The Medium*, Anthony Hopkins's *Tango for Tre*, and Engelbert Humperdinck's *Hänsel und Gretel*. In 1980, the Folksoperan established its first "home" in a small theater in Roslagsgaten Stockholm. Their first "home" production, Werner Egk's *Die Verlobung in San Domingo*, saw an audience of six and a performance group of 25 on stage! Their second production, Giacomo Puccini's *Madama Butterfly*, was more successful. The opera, staged as a serious drama and not a sentimental melodrama, was performed in a night club. The company purchased a permanent home in 1984, a run-down movie theater in Hornsgatan. Since the structure had historical significance, it qualified for government money for restoration. The Folksoperan christened their new home with Giuseppe Verdi's *Aida*. Since the opera house was a former cinema, it does not offer an orchestra pit, so the 30-musician orchestra plays (reduced scores) behind the singers, thereby bringing the singers closer to the audience, and offering a greater musical and visual impact.

Practical Information. Folkoperan, Hornsgatan 72, 11821 Stockholm. Tel: 46 8 669 0095. Fax: 46 8 84 41 46. When visiting the Folkoperan, stay at the SAS Strand Hotel, Nybrokajen 9, 10327 Stockholm. Tel: 46 8 678-7800, Fax 46 8 20 44 36. It has wonderful views, and is close to the opera house. The hotel can help with opera tickets and schedule.

COMPANY STAFF, PREMIERES, AND REPERTORY

Chefer. Staffan Rydén, Managing Director; Claes Fellbom, Artistic Director.

Premieres. L. J. Werle's *Lionardo* 1988; X. S. Qu's *Oidipus* 1993; Sagvik & Nyquist's *Vändringen till Sköldpaddsberget* (children's opera) 1993; G. Riedel's *Hernsöborna* (musical) 1994 D. Börtz's *Marie Antoninette* 1998.

Repertory. **1976–79:** La serva padrona, The Medium, La salustia, Tango for Tre, Hänsel und Gretel, Die schöne Galatea, **1980:** Die Verlobung in San Domingo. **1981:** Madama Butterfly. **1982:** Carmen. **1985:** Aida. **1986:** Die Zauberflöte. **1988:** Turandot, Lionardo. **1989:** Il barbiere di Siviglia. **1990:** Les contes d'Hoffmann. **1991:** Samson et Dalila. **1992:** Die Fledermaus, Don Carlos. **1993:** Turandot, Oidipus, Vändringen till Sköldpaddsberget. **1994:** Hemsöborna. **1995:** Otello. **1997:** Carmen, Lyubov'k tryom apel'sinam (The Love for Three Oranges). **1998:** Marie Antoninette.

Bibliography. Andy Love, *The Survival and Development of "Folkoperan"* (Glasgow, 1993). Additional information supplied by the company.

Thanks to Lars Tallent, Folkoperan.

Kungliga Teater and Operan

On September 19, 1898, excerpts from Franz Berwald's *Estrella di Soria*, Adolf Lindblad's *Frondörerna*, and a cantata by Ivar Hallström inaugurated the Kungliga Teater, also called the Operan. Axel Anderberg designed the opera house. This was the second Royal Theater. The first Kungliga Teater, also known as the Kongliga Stora Teater and the Kongliga Operan, was inaugurated on September 30, 1782, with Johann Gottlieb Naumann's *Cora och Alonzo*. It was designed by Carl Frederick Adelcrantz and is probably best known as the place where King Gustav III's was assassinated in 1792, a tragic event immortalized in Giuseppe Verdi's *Un ballo in maschera* and Daniel Auber's *Gustave III*.

In the mid–1700s, Stockholm heard opera from French and Italian companies, but when King Gustav III ascended the throne in 1771, seeds for homegrown opera were planted. The king first tried Swedish theater, but he was unhappy listening to a play in Swedish. (Swedish aristocracy, like Prussian aristocracy, used French as the language of culture.) He felt that music would soften the language, and he established Swedish opera in 1773, collaborating with Johan Wellander to write the first one, for which he commissioned Francesco Uttini to compose the music. The result was *Thetis och Pelée* which inaugurated the Kunglia Svenska Operan on January 18, 1773, in a *bollhuset* (dance hall), which had been converted into a theater. The opera received 24 performances. On November 25, 1773, Uttini's arrangement of Christoph Willibald Gluck's *Orfeo ed Euridice* was premiered, followed two years later by Uttini's *Aline, drottning av Golconda*, André Grétry's *Lucile*, Naumann's *Amphion*, Grétry's *Zémire et Azor*, and Gluck's *Iphigénie en Aulide*. Josef Martin Kraus's *Aeneas i Cartago* was scheduled to inaugurate the first Kungliga Teater, but (as the story goes) "Dido" had to leave the country with her husband to escape the creditors, so Naumann's *Cora och Alonzo* was the inaugural opera. Another Naumann opera, *Gustav Vasa*, with libretto by Gustav III, was premiered on January 19, 1786, followed by Johann Häffner's *Elektra* on December 10, 1787, Georg Volger, *Gustav Adolf och Ebba Brahe*, on January 24, 1788, (Gustav III wrote the libretto), Kraus's *Soliman den II* on September 22, 1789, and Kraus's *Aeneas i Cartago* in 1799. Interest in Swedish opera waned after Gustav's assassination, and in 1806, the doors of the opera house were shut. They reopened on May 30, 1812, with the Swedish premiere of Wolfgang Amadeus Mozart's *Die Zauberflöte*, followed by the Swedish premiere of his *Don Giovanni* on December 6, 1813. Mozart was so popular that by 1830, all of his important works had been produced.

Foreign operas dominated the repertory during most of the 19th-century. Especially popular were the French composers Giacomo Meyerbeer, Daniel Auber, and Adolphe Adam. Ludwig van Beethoven's *Fidelio* was first heard on April 14, 1832, and the operas of Giuseppe Verdi first entered the repertory on April 29, 1852, with *Macbeth*, and those of Richard Wagner on June 5, 1865, with *Rienzi*. Georges Bizet's *Carmen* arrived on March 22, 1878. Swedish works were also on the boards with Eduard Brendler's *Ryno* (completed by crown prince Oscar) in 1834, Adolf Lindblad's *Frondörerna* on May 11, 1835, Andreas Randel's *Värmländningarne* in 1846, Ivar Hallström's *Vita frun på Drottningholm* in 1847, Berwald's *Estrella di Soria* on April 9, 1862, Hallström's *Den bergtagna* in 1874, his *Vikingarna* in 1877, and Per August Ölander's *Blenda* in 1876. A second theater, Arsenalsteater, hosted the premieres of lighter operas by Domenico Cimarosa and Giovanni Paisiello, among others, until fire destroyed it in 1825. There is conflicting evidence as to when the most famous Swedish soprano of that time, Jenny Lind, made her debut, but it is believed to have been in Lindblad's *Frondörerna* on May 11, 1835. Lind left Stockholm for an international career, but returned during the 1847-48 season for Gaetano Donizetti's *La fille du Régiment*, Vincenzo Bellini's *Norma*, and Mozart's *Le nozze di Figaro*. Verdi's *Otello* and Jacques Offenbach's *Les contes d'Hoffmann* were among the final works presented before the opera house was razed in 1892.

The Nya Svenska Theater was the company's performance venue until the new opera house was completed. Here Stockholm saw its first performances of Wagner's *Die Walküre*, Verdi's *Falstaff*, Jules Massenet's *Manon*, Bedřich Smetana's *Prodaná nevěsta* (The Bartered Bride), Ruggero Leoncavallo's *I pagliacci*, and Engelbert Humperdinck's

Hänsel und Gretel among others. Fire destroyed the theater in 1925.

The new Kungliga Teater opened in 1898, and continued presenting new Swedish operas, including Wilhelm Stenhammar's *Tirfing* on September 19, 1898, Andreas Hallén's *Valdemarsskatten* in 1899, Stenhammar's *Gillet på Solhaug* on October 31, 1902, Wilhelm Peterson-Berger's *Ran* on May 20, 1903, *Arnljot* on April 13, 1910, *Domedagsprofeterna* in February 1919, and *Adils och Elisiv* on February 27, 1927. Wagner's *Der Ring des Nibelungen* was given (in Swedish) between March 14 and 20, 1907, and *Parsifal* followed a decade later. Verdi's *Un ballo in maschera* was first staged in 1927 — in the Boston version, and it was filled with inaccuracies — Gustav III was a lady's man, and his assassin, Anckarström, was his friend. It was Göran Gentele who produced an accurate, but controversial *Maskaradbalen* in 1958, set in the court of Gustav III, with the assassination of the king in the climatic moment. Three years later, Ingmar Bergman made his debut as director at Operan with Igor Stravinsky's *The Rake's Progress.*

Meanwhile, the Kungliga Teater continued introducing Swedish operas — Gunnar Frumerie's *Singoalla* on March 16, 1940, Oskar Lindberg's *Fredlös* in 1943, Heinrich Sutermeister's *Raskolnikov* on October 14, 1948, Karl-Birger Blomdahl's *Aniara* on May 31, 1959, and 100 years after the death of Berwald, *Drottningen av Golconda*, on April 1, 1968, Hilding Rosenberg's *Hus med dubbel ingång* in May 1970, Lars Johan Werle's *Tintomara* on January 18, 1973, in celebration of the bicentennial of Swedish opera, Per Nørgård's *Siddharta* on March 18, 1983, and Hans Gefors's *Christina* in October 1986.

Some of the great singers of the 20th century were Swedish and made their debut either at the Kungliga Teater or Drottningholms Slottsteater, including Jussi Björling as Ottavio in Mozart's *Don Giovanni* in 1930, Birgit Nilsson as Agathe in Weber's *Der Freischütz* in 1946, Elisabeth Söderström as Bastienne in Mozart's *Bastien und Bastienne* in 1947, and Nicolai Gedda as Chapelou in Adolphe Adam's *Le Postillon de Longjumeau* in 1952.

The Operan is veering away from operas sung in Swedish, mainly because it is difficult to locate enough singers who can sing in Swedish combined with the lack of their marketability, and the impossibility of hiring international guest artists. Comic operas are still given in Swedish, but most other works are in the original language with Swedish subtitles. The quality of the production depends on its age. The old productions are uninspiring, but the newer ones can be a challenge. The repertory is predominately standard fare, complemented by one contemporary work and sometimes a Swedish opera. The early 1990s saw Mozart's *Don Giovanni* and *Die Entführung aus dem Serail*, Giacomo Puccini's *Madama Butterfly*, Richard Wagner's *Lohengrin* and *Die Walküre*, George Bizet's *Carmen*, Gounod's *Faust*, Jacques Offenbach's *Les contes d'Hoffmann*, Dominick Argento's *The Aspern Papers*, and Sven-Erik Bäck's *Tranfjädrarna*. Recent offerings include Massenet's *Werther*, Bellini's *Norma*, Richard Strauss's *Salome*, Mozart's *Le nozze di Figaro*, Wagner's *Die fliegende Holländer*, *Tannhäuser*, and *Das Rheingold*, Puccini's *Tosca*, and Erich Wolfgang Korngold's *Die tote Stadt*.

Kungliga Teater

Both architects Magnus Isaeus and Axel Anderberg submitted plans for the second Kungliga Teater, but the 27-year-old Anderberg won the commission because his drawings were easier to execute. Bank director K. A. Wallenberg led a theater-construction-consortium, which volunteered to built the new opera house and turn it over to the state.

The Operan is a Neoclassically-inspired building with Doric columns supporting a portico, Ionic columns forming the window arches, and Corinthian columns holding statues that remained from the previous royal opera house. The red and gold auditorium holds three tiers and is circular in shape. Arabesque arches buttress the gallery. High above the proscenium arch, is a representation of Gustav III. Operan seats 1,239.

Practical Information. Operan-Kungliga Teatern, Gustav Adolfs Torg, 10322 Stockholm. Tel: 46 8 24 82 40. Fax: 46 8 11 02 42. When visiting the Operan stay at the SAS Strand Hotel, Nybrokajen 9, 10327 Stockholm. Tel: 46 8 678-7800, Fax 46 8 20 44 36. It has a wonderful view, and is near the opera house. The hotel can help with opera tickets and schedule.

Kungliga Teatern (Stockholm, Sweden).

COMPANY STAFF AND REPERTORY

Operachefer. Bengt Hall (1996–present), Eskil Hemberg (1987–1995), Lars af Malmborg (1984–87), Folke Abenius (1978–84), Bertil Bokstedt (1971–78), Görran Gentele (1963–71), Set Svanholm (1956–63), Joel Berglund (1949–56), Harald André (1939–49), John Forsell (1924–39), Karl Axel Riben (1919–24), Hans von Stedingk (1910–19), Albert Ranft (1908–10), Artur Tiel (1907–08), Axel Burén (1892–1907), Conrad Nordquist (1888–92). **Förste Direktör:** Anders Willman (1883–1888), Henrik Westin (1881–83), Erik af Edholm (1866–81), Eugène von Stedingk (1861–66), Daniel Hvasser (1860), Gunnar Olof Hyltén-Cavallius (1858–60), Knut Bonde (1852–56), Svante Schyberg (1848–52), Hugo Adolf Hamilton (1844–48), Per Westerstrand (1832–40), J. P. Törner (1832), Bernhard von Beskow (1831–32), Carl Johan Puke (1827–1831), Gustaf Lagerbielke (1823–27), Gustaf Löwenhielm (1812–18), Anders Fredrik Skjöldebrand (1810–12), Abraham Niklas Edelcrantz (1804–10), Jonne Hugo Hamilton (1798–1804), Claes Rålamb (1792–98), Gustaf Maurits Armfelt (1786–92), Carl von Fersen (1780–86), Adolf Barnekow (1776–80), Gustaf Ehrensvärd (1773–76).

Repertory. (Most popular operas 1773–1972): Carmen, Le nozze di Figaro, Die Zauberflöte, Faust, La bohème, Il barbiere di Siviglia, Cavalleria rusticana, Don Giovanni, Mignon, Aida, I pagliacci, Madama Butterfly, Tannhäuser, Lohengrin, La fille du règiment, La traviata, Tosca, Der Freischütz, Roméo et Juliette, Les contes d'Hoffmann, Rigoletto, Il trovatore, Si j'étais roi, La muette di Portici, Fra diavolo, Mefistofele, Martha, Orfeo ed Euridice, Guillaume Tell, Eugene Onegin, Samson et Dalila, Un ballo in maschera, Robert le Diable, Die Entführung aus dem Serail, Die Walküre, Les Huguenots, Gustav Vasa, Die lustige Weiber von Windsor.

Bibliography. Klas Ralk, ed., *Jubelboken Operan 200 År* (Stockholm, 1963), Ake Sällström, *Opera på Stockholmsoperan* (Stockholm, 1977), Klas Ralf, *Kungliga Teatern: Repertoar 1773–1973* (Stockholm, 1974). Additional information supplied by the company.

Thanks to Staffan Carlweitz, Operan.

Norrlands Operan

Gioachino Rossini's *L'italiana in Algeri* inaugurated the Norrlands Operan on March 21, 1975. Founded under the new cultural plan that the Swedish government had for the country by decentralizing opera and creating five regional theaters and ensembles, the Norrlands Operan was one of those formed, with Arnold Östman as the founding director. The company performs in a converted fire station. The orchestra is located under the stage and the audience sit on either side of the stage, facing each other. It one of the western world's most remote opera companies. Until 1995, the company also toured through all of northern Sweden and the Arctic Circle, setting up a theater in the gymnasiums of the small towns. The company had to bring its own stage and chairs, in addition to the sets and costumes. When the funding returns, the company will resume touring.

The company consists of a fixed ensemble of five singers performing around two operas a year. Until the mid–1990s, four to five operas/musicals were performed each year, but the combination of a budget cut and the preference of the orchestra to play symphonic works resulted in a sharp cut in the number of performances. The opera budget is around SEK 15 million or $3 million. The repertory concentrates on works from the 1600s and 1700s and the 20th century, although works from all periods have been produced. Several premieres have also been mounted. The early repertory included Christoph Willibald Gluck's *Orfeo ed Euridice* and Georg Friedrich Händel's *Lucretia*, as well as operas by Giambattista Pergolesi and Alessandro Scarlatti. Wolfgang Amadeus Mozart and Rossini works played a prominent role with *Le nozze di Figaro*, *Don Giovanni*, and *Così fan tutte* and *Il barbiere di Siviglia*, *La Cenerentola*, *L'italiana in Algeri* respectively. Other better known works included Giacomo Puccini's *La*

Norrlands Operan (Umeå, Sweden).

bohème and *Il tabarro*, Kurt Weill's *Der Aufstieg und Fall der Stadt Mahagonny*, Benjamin Britten's *The Rape of Lucretia* and *A Midsummer Night's Dream*, and Gian Carlo Menotti's *The Medium* and *Amahl and the Night Visitors*. A couple of lesser known pieces were William Walton's *The Bear* and Francis Poulenc's *La voix humaine*. Although Carl Maria von Weber's *Der Freischütz*, Jacques Offenbach's *Les contes d'Hoffmann*, Charles Gounod's *Faust*, and Giuseppe Verdi's *Falstaff*, *La traviata* and *Un ballo in maschera* have been seen in Umeå, they are infrequently performed.

Practical Information. Norrlands Operan, Vasagatan 22, 90108 Umeå. Tel: 46 90 14 10 70. Fax: 46 90 12 68 45. When visiting the Norrlands Operan, contact the Swedish Travel & Tourism Council, 655 Third Avenue, New York, NY 10017-5617. Tel: 212-949-2333, Fax 212-697-0835.

COMPANY STAFF AND PREMIERES

Chefer. Jonas Rorssell (1996–present), Per-Erik Öhrn (1986–95), Tom Lagerborg (1981–86), Paul Stempel (1978–81), Per-Erik Öhrn (1977–78), Arnold Östman (founder) (1974–77).

Premieres. E. Eyser's *Carmen 36* November 13, 1975; L. Horvath's *Ingen Rädder för Plugget Här* May 18, 1977; S.E. Johansson's *Skandal Era Majestät* May 12, 1978; B. Lindberg's *Spelet om Herodes* February 12, 1979; U. Lindh's *Voff-Historien om Alban* September 4, 1979; A. Mellnäs's *Spöket på Canterville* April 25, 1981; J. Forssell's *Hästen och Gossen* October 15, 1988. I. McQueen's *Fortonato* March 6, 1993; J. Sandström's *Bombi Bittoch Nick Carter* March 5, 1994. B. Lindman's *Grabbhalvan* October 1, 1994.

Bibliography. Claes Rosenquist, ed., *Norrlandsoperan: Tonernas teater* (Gideå, 1992). Interview with Björn Björklund, Informatör, November 1995.

Thanks to Torborg Fagerlund and Sophie Ternheim, Swedish Travel & Tourism Council, Stockholm and New York.

— VADSTENA

Vadstena-Akademien (Summer Festival)

The Vadstena Academy was founded in 1964 by Ingrid Maria Rappe to present rare early operas and newly commissioned works, and to give aspiring young singers a stage on which to perform. The operas are staged in the Vadstena Old Theater constructed in 1825 inside the walls of a monastery, and in the Castle of Vadstena, established in 1545 by King Gustav Vasa on the edge of Lake Vättern. Recent offerings include Georg Benda's *Walder* (1776), performed on instruments characteristic of the period, and Carl Unander-Scharin's *Tokfursten*.

Practical Information. Vadstena Akademien, Lastköpingsgatan, 59232 Vadstena. Tel: 46 143 122 29, Fax: 46 143 129 03. When visiting the Vadstena Akademien, contact the Vadstena Tourist Office, Tel: 46 143 151 25, Fax 46 143 151 29.

COMPANY STAFF

Artistic Director. Anders Wiklund.

Other Swedish Opera Houses

Other opera houses in Sweden are noted below by name, address, telephone, and director.

Ystadoperan. Knut den Stores gata 7, 22221 Lund. Tel: 46 46 12 96 89; Fax: 46 46 14 37 51. **Director:** Richard Bark.

Switzerland

———————————————————— BASEL

Stadttheater Basel

The new Stadttheater was inaugurated on October 3, 1975, with a "Theatermarkt" which involved 35 different performances and a large number of artist. Built between 1968 and 1975 as a modern structure in an arena-style theater, the City Theater was designed by the architectural group of Felix Schwarz, Rolf Gutmann, Frank Gloor, and Hans Schüpbach. It was the fourth Basel music theater.

The first Musiktheater, Theater auf dem Blömlein, opened on October 4, 1834, with a traditional Swiss Festival consisting of an allegorical Festspiel followed by Eduard von Schenk's *Die Krone von Cypern*. There was no fixed company, but the theater hosted traveling troupes. After a performance of Vincenzo Bellini's *I Capuleti e i Montecchi* on April 4, 1873, the theater was closed and demolished. Two years later, Wolfgang Amadeus Mozart's *Don Giovanni* inaugurated the second theater, called Theater am Steinenberg. In 1892, the "Kommission der Gesellschaft des Stadttheater" took control of the theater, hired a director, and founded a permanent ensemble. A fire destroyed the building in October 1904. After much discussion, the third Basel theater was constructed. The house, inaugurated on September 20, 1909, with Richard Wagner's *Tannhäuser*, was found to have bad sight-lines and be too large for more "intimate" works. In 1931, plans were made for restructuring but they were never done. Finally in 1963, an architectural competition was announced for a new theater. There were 47 entries. Before the theater was even completed, it hosted Karl Kraus's *Die letzten Tage der Menschheit*. The old theater was blown-up in 1975.

The new 1,015-seat Stadttheater hosted the entire Ring Cycle, and then changed its emphasis to French opera, along with works of Giuseppe Verdi, like his *Rigoletto*. The theater has a fixed ensemble of 49 soloists, a 45-member chorus, and 168 musicians. Recent offerings include Mozart's *Die Entführung aus dem Serail*, Engelbert Humperdinck's *Hänsel und Gretel*, and Leoš Janáček's *Jenůfa*.

Practical Information. Stadttheater, Elisabethenstraße 16, 4051 Basel; Tel: 41 61 271 11 30, Fax: 41 61 271 19 90. If visiting the Stadttheater, contact the Swiss National Tourist Office, 608 Fifth Avenue, New York, NY 10020; Tel: 212-757-5944.

COMPANY STAFF

Intendanten. Hans Peter Doll, Frank Baumauer, Horst Statkus, Hans Hollmann, Werner Düggelin, Adolf Zogg, Albert Wiesner, Friedrich Schramm, Gottfried Becker, Egon Neudegg, Oskar Wälterlin, Otto Henning, Ernst Lert, Leo Melitz.

Bibliography. Völker, K. *Theaterarbeit in Basel. Inszenierungen von Hans Hollmann 1968 bis 1978* (Basel, 1978). Fritz Weiss, *Das Basler Stadttheater: 1834–1934* (Basel, 1934).

———————————————————— BERN

Stadttheater Bern

On September 25, 1903, the new Stadttheater was inaugurated with Richard Wagner's *Tannhäuser*. Designed by René von Wurstemberger, the City Theater was built in the *fin des siècle* style.

In 1678, the first theater to host visiting troupes was built, known as the Ballenhaus, it witnessed Wolfgang Amadeus Mozart's *Die Zau-* berflöte in 1796. Meanwhile in 1766 a "Grand Société" was founded which built another theater called the Hôtel de Musique, that opened in 1770. In this theater, Mozart's *Don Giovanni* played in 1812, followed by Carl Maria von Weber's *Der Freischütz* in 1823 and Ludwig van Beethoven's *Fidelio* in 1836. The following year, the theater began receiving subsidies from the city, and since then regular seasons with a permanent staff have taken place. In 1850, Giuseppe Verdi's *Attila* was staged followed by Wagner's *Tannhäuser*, and on March 18, 1889, the Swiss premiere of Wagner's *Tristan und Isolde* took place. When Engelbert Humperdinck's *Hänsel und Gretel* was performed in 1895, the theater had electricity. The theater would host operas for only five more years; the last was Charles Gound's *Faust*, which took place on April 6, 1900.

In 1908, five years after the new opera house opened, Wagner's *Der Ring des Nibelungen* was mounted, and in 1911, only 10 months after its world premiere in Dresden, Richard Strauss's *Der Rosenkavalier* was staged. A new production of the Ring Cycle was given in 1912-13, and in 1917, Strauss's *Elektra* and *Ariadne auf Naxos* graced the stage. Wagner's *Parsifal* arrived in 1920 and another Ring Cycle was given during the 1931-32 season. Between 1931–33, a "Wagner Cycle" was presented with *Tannhäuser, Lohengrin, Die Meistersinger von Nürnberg, Parsifal*, and *Tristan und Isolde* on the boards. Next came a "Verdi Cycle" with *Aida, I vespri siciliani, La traviata*, and *Don Carlo*.

The 1970s saw several contemporary works in the repertory, including the Swiss premiere of Ján Cikkers's *Spiel von Liebe und Tod* and *Auferstehung*, and the premieres of Rolf Liebermann's *Penelope* and Antonio Carlos Gomez's *Lo Schiavo*. The house was closed for extensive remodeling in the early 1980s, reopening with *Tannhäuser* on October 20, 1984. Other productions included Verdi's *Il trovatore*, Mozart's *Die Entführung aus dem Serail*, Otto Nicolai's *Die lustigen Weiber von Windsor*, and Benjamin Britten's *Albert Herring*.

It is an ensemble company with 45 soloists, 35-member chorus, and orchestra of 92 musicians. Francesco Cilea's *Adriana Lecouvreur*, Jacques Offenbach's *Les contes d'Hoffmann*, and Mozart's *Le nozze di Figaro* are recent repertory offerings.

Stadttheater Bern

In 1895, discussions began regarding the construction of a new theater and von Wurstemberger was contracted in November 1897. Work began in 1899 and lasted four years. The architect designed an ornate facade for the structure, and modeled the interior on the Opéra-Comique in Paris. It is an open balcony theater with 800 seats.

Practical Information. Stadttheater Nägeligasse 1, 3000, Bern. Tel: 41 31 21 71 11, Fax: 41 31 22 39 47. If visiting the Stadttheater, stay at the Hotel Bellevue Palace, Kochergasse 3-5, 3001 Berne. Tel: 41 31 320 4545, Fax 41 31 311 4743. The hotel is close to the theater and can assist with opera schedules and tickets.

COMPANY STAFF

Intendanten. Elice Grauss, Philippe de Poros, Edgar Kelling, Wolfgang Zörner, Walter Oberer, Albert Nef, Stephan Beinl, Ekkehard Kohlund, Eugen Keller, Hans Zimmermann, Karl Lustig-Prean, Hans Kauffmann, Ludwig Peppler, Albert Kelm, Benno Koebke, Alfred Stender-Stefani, and Julius Bergmann, Georg Kiedaich.

Bibliography. Peter Tschanz, ed., *Stadttheater Bern: Unser Theater* (Bern, 1984).

GENEVA

Grand Théâtre de Genève

The Grand Théâtre de Genève, originally known as the Théâtre Municipal de Genève, reopened on December 10, 1962, with Giuseppe Verdi's *Don Carlos*. Displaying a 19th-century facade and a 20th-century auditorium, the opera house was reconstructed by architects Schopfer of Geneva and Zavelani-Rossi of Milan after a disastrous fire that destroyed the auditorium in 1951. This was the second building. Gioachino Rossini's *Guillaume Tell* had inaugurated the first Grand Théâtre de Genève on October 4, 1879. Jacques-Elysée Gosse was the architect.

In 1766, the Théâtre de Rosimond became the first theater to open in Geneva. Referred to as *La grange des étrangers* (The Barn of the Foreigners) by the inhabitants (because Geneva was a Calvinist city), it seated 800 in three tiers of boxes. It was lighted by a huge chandelier, whose candles dripped on the heads, hats, and clothes of the audience before glass trays were placed to catch the drippings. The Théâtre de Rosimond hosted only one season, 1766-1767, but offered 140 performances. The most notable event was the presentation of André Grétry's *Isabelle et*

Gertrude, his first opera and Geneva's first world premiere. The theater, built of wood, burned to the ground on the night of January 29, 1768.

The city had no theater for more than a decade, until the first stones were laid on July 2, 1782, for the Théâtre de Neuve. Designed by the architect Matthey, Théâtre de Neuve opened on October 18, 1783, with *Jeu de l'Amour et du Hasard*. The Neuve had a plain facade with three large shuttered windows flanked by six Ionic columns, and crowned by a clock. Posters hung next to the entrance doors announced the upcoming performances. The auditorium, described as sumptuous and comfortable, held a parterre and three galleries. There was a central oil-burning chandelier and seats for 940 with 160 standing. During the early years, opéra comique was the fare, with Grétry operas on the boards. Then the works of Wolfgang Amadeus Mozart entered the repertory along with Italian fare. Since the city lacked a permanent company, the theater relied on traveling troupes from Italy and Germany for its offerings, but performances were irregular because of political problems. The Théâtre de Neuve closed its doors on December 13, 1788. They were periodically reopened until October 11, 1797, when all performances were banned. The theater reopened on November 2, 1798. Five years later, in 1803, the Act of Mediation, which gave the Swiss cantons their independence, was passed and the doors of the theater were again shut, this time until 1817.

Rossini's *Guillaume Tell* was presented in Geneva soon after its Paris premiere to popular acclaim. Then in 1850, two events of note took place—Marietta Alboni performed in Gaetano Donizetti's *La favorite* and Gilbert Duprez was named director of the theater. Four years later, the first *création mondiale* in more than eight decades graced the stage, Bovy-Lysberg's *La Fille du Carillonneur*. This was followed by *La Reine de Provence*, an opera composed by two Geneva residents, and Kling's *Le dernier des Paladins* and *Le Flûtiste*. During the almost century of existence of the Théâtre de Neuve, some of the more popular works mounted include Rossini's *Il barbiere di Siviglia* and *Guillaume Tell*; Gaetano Donizetti's *Don Pasquale*, *Lucia di Lammermoor*, *L'elisir d'amore*, and *La fille du régiment*; Vincenzo Bellini's *Norma*, *La sonnambula*, and *I Capuleti e i Montecchi*; Charles Gounod's *Faust*; Verdi's *Rigoletto*, *Il trovatore*, *Un ballo in maschera*, and *La traviata*;

Wolfgang Amadeus Mozart's *Don Giovanni*, *Le nozze di Figaro*, and *Die Zauberflöte*; Richard Wagner's *Tannhäuser*; Ludwig van Beethoven's *Fidelio*, and Carl Maria von Weber's *Der Freischütz*.

As early as 1861, it had become evident that Geneva had outgrown its opera house. During Théâtre de Neuve's existence, the population of Geneva had tripled and its tastes in opera had broadened. A legacy from the Duke of Brunswick enabled Geneva to construct a luxurious new opera house, and in 1879, the Théâtre Municipal was inaugurated. The following year, the Théâtre de Neuve was demolished. After the opening, grand opera took center stage with Giacomo Meyerbeer's *Les Huguenots* and Fromental Halévy's *La Juive*. The Geneva premiere of Jules Massenet's *Hérodiade* followed, with the composer present. His *Sapho* was also staged with Massenet there to receive the applauds. His *Cendrillon* was also popular, but his *La Navarraise* was not well-received. Other Massenet operas were *Don César de Bazan*, which Massenet conducted himself, *Werther*, *Esclarmonde*, and *Thaïs*.

The Municipal hosted its first world premiere, de Grisy's *Jacques Clément*, on December 16, 1886, which received seven performance. Louis Lacombe's *Winkelried* arrived during the 1891-92 season and Geneva-born composer Emil Jacques-Delcroze saw his *Janie* staged for the first time two season later. *Janie*, although well-received, did not stand the test of time. In 1896, Audran's *Photis* was premiered, followed by Jacques-Delcroze's *Sancho*, Delaye's *A bicyclette*, Signan's *Anita*, G. de Seigneux's *Tout s'arrange*, Maurice's *Le Drapeau blanc*, and L. Aubert's *La Forêt bleue*. Other works of note were Ruggero Leoncavallo's *La bohème*, presented before Giacomo Puccini's version; Amilcare Ponchielli's *La gioconda*, performed after his death and conducted by his son; the French premiere of Umberto Giordano's *Siberia*, and Henri Rabaud's *Mârouf, Savetier du Caire*, conducted by the composer.

The theater's name was changed at the beginning of the 1910-1911 season from Théâtre Municipal de Genève to Grand Théâtre de Genève and during the 1923-24 season, Knopf's *Les baisers perdus* graced the stage for the first time. Then both the quality and number of the productions declined. Operettas dominated the repertory during World War II. After the war, the repertory expanded with the Geneva premieres of several works, including Maurice Ravel's *L'heure espagnole*,

Gabriel Fauré's *Pénélope*, Richard Strauss's *Salome*, Modest Mussorgsky's *Boris Godunov*, and Nikolai Rimsky-Korsakov's *Zolotoy petushok* (The Golden Cockerel). In 1951, fire closed the theater and eleven years would pass before it reopened. During this time, performances continued at the Casino Théâtre.

The delay in rebuilding resulted from the reconstruction proposal being turned down after a referendum. A revised proposal was then submitted, which although more expensive, was approved. When the opera house reopened, it was run as a foundation subsidized by the city of Geneva. The first season in the new theater saw more than a dozen works in the schedule including Wagner's *Tristan und Isolde*, Claude Debussy's *Pelléas et Mélisande*, Verdi's *Rigoletto*, Puccini's *Tosca*, Paul Dukas's *Ariande et Barbe Bleue*, and Charles Gounod's *Faust*. The second season hosted Mozart's *Le nozze di Figaro*, Massenet's *Manon*, Richard Strauss's *Der Rosenkavalier*, Camille Saint-Saëns's *Samson et Dalila*, and Ludwig van Beethoven's *Fidelio* among others in an equally ambition schedule. There were three novelties during the 1964-65 season — Heinrich Sutermeister's *Raskolnikov*, Benjamin Britten's *Peter Grimes*, and the *création mondiale* of Rafaello de Banfield's *Alissa*. Herbert Graf was named general director in 1965 and during his first season, the local premieres of Alban Berg's *Wozzeck*, Claudio Monteverdi's *L'incoronazione di Poppea*, and Arthur Honegger's *Jeanne d'Arc au bûcher* took place, along with the first performance ever of Darius Milhaud's *La mère coupable*. Operas continued to be added to the repertory with the first Geneva performances of Frank Martin's *La tempête*, Ernest Bloch's *Macbeth*, Carl Orff's *Der Mond*, Verdi's *Simon Boccanegra*, Rossini's *Mosè in Egitto*, Jean-Philippe Rameau's *Platée*, Britten's *The Rape of Lucretia* and *Turn of the Screw*, Berg's *Lulu*, Leoš Janáček's *Jenůfa*, Honegger's *Antigone*, and Puccini's *Turandot*, Georg Friedrich Händel's *Serses*, Sergey Prokofiev's *Lyubov'k tryom apel'sinam* (The Love for Three Oranges), Kurt Weill's *Der Aufstieg und Fall der Stadt Mahagonny*, Krzysztof Penderecki's *Diably z Loudun* (The Devils of Loudun), and Strauss's *Arabella*.

The 1980s ushered in a new era with Hugues Gall at the helm. He had been Rolf Liebermann's right-hand man in Paris, and carried Liebermann's successful formula to the Grand Théâtre during his 15-year tenure, (before leaving to run the Opéra National de Paris) — grand productions, great singers, and absorbing performances. Counted among his successes were Rossini's *L'italiana in Algeri* conceived by Ken Russell, Wagner's *Parsifal* conceived by Liebermann with Jon Vickers in the title role, Verdi's *Un ballo in maschera* with Luciano Pavarotti and Anna Tomowa-Sintow, and Donizetti's *Lucia di Lammermoor* conceived by Pier-Luigi Pizzi with June Anderson making her European debut.

In 1995, the Grand Théâtre de Genève received its first woman director, Renée Auphan, who rules more from her heart that her mind. She brought a different outlook to the season, with strong emotions and opinions about what should (and should not) happen on stage — more emphasis on the theatrical aspects of the operas — opera is first and foremost theater, theater that is true to the story and explains it. Her philosophy was evident in the *verismo* productions of Mascagni's *Cavalleria rusticana* and Leoncavallo's *I pagliacci*. The performance was a passionate and emotional affair, rendered by a well-rehearsed cast, with authentic staging (including tightrope walkers in *I pagliacci*) that followed in a logical and sensible manner the stories of the operas, with a theatrical power that never distracted from the music, but rather enhanced it. Auphan is concerned with the French repertory and women composers, and under her guidance, the theater is (very) slowly making a transition from the Italian to the French repertory, with works like Ambroise Thomas's *Hamlet* and Gounod's *Roméo et Juliette* — and French operas that are not in the standard repertory. Superstars are only occasionally seen in Geneva. The emphasis is on "theater" — the drama, acting, sets, not star vehicles. The budget is 40 million SF, and recently the company experienced financial problems, since the city's subsidy has remained the same for the past eight years, although expenses have climbed. The state, however, took over part of the city's support, and that combined with private donations from the wealthy population has helped.

The repertory spans a couple of centuries from Georg Friedrich Händel's *Serse* to Sergey Prokofiev's *Bethrothal in a Monastery*. In-between one finds Donizetti's *La fille du régiment*, Verdi's *Il trovatore*, Mozart's *Mitridate, re di Ponto*, Hector Berlioz's *La Damnation de Faust*, Puccini's *Madama Butterfly* and Jacques Offenbach's *Orphée aux Enfers*. These productions are creative and imaginative, yet remain true to the composer's intent. For a city of only 300,000 inhabitants, Geneva's opera is of international quality. Recent productions include Massenet's *Cendrillon*, Strauss's *Der Rosenkavalier*, Rossini's *Semiramide*, Mozart's *Don Giovanni*, Donizetti's *Lucia di Lammermoor*, Wagner's *Das Rheingold*, Verdi's *Macbeth*, and Tania Leòn's *Scourge of Hyacinths*.

Grand Théâtre de Genève

On morning of May 1, 1951, when the company was rehearsing Wagner's *Die Walküre*, Wotan uttered "*Herauf, wabernde Lohe, umlodre mir feurig den Fels!*" (Arise magic flame, girdle the rock with fire for me!) and a real fire erupted, caused by an oxygen tank that had been used to "improve" the fire around Brünnhilde's rock. The auditorium and stagehouse were completely destroyed. The exterior was unscathed, so the outside of the current theater dates back to 1879, with its facade, modeled after Paris's Palais Garnier. (The original architect, Gosse, was trained in Paris, and the French influence was evident.) The Belle Époque auditorium was not rebuilt, but a pragmatic auditorium replaced it.

In 1996, the stage machinery of the Grand Théâtre developed dangerous cable problems, forcing the closure of the opera house during the 1997-98 season. The company moved into an unusual performance venue, a unused power plant known as the Bâtiment des Forces Motrices which dated from 1886. The long, L-shaped, Beaux-Arts structure, designed by Théodore Turrettini and located on an island in the Rhône River, was transformed by Geneva architect Bernard Picenni, into a functional opera house seating 985. In fact, the transformation was so successful, that even after the company returned to the Grand Théâtre, operatic activity, along with concerts, ballet, and theater, continued in the former power plant.

The Grand Théâtre is a miniature Opéra de Paris with Corinthian columns, busts, statues, gargoyles, the names of composers, and the words, TRAGÉDIE — POÉSIE LYRIQUE — COMÉDIE embellishing its facade. The modern auditorium offers an orchestra level, balcony, gallery, and amphitheater in a semicircular space. Paneled with

Grand Théâtre de Genève (Geneva, Switzerland).

dark wood, the room offers red velvet seats and plain parapets. The ceiling has been transformed into a gold-and-silver, galaxy-filled sky designed by Jacek Stryjenski. The auditorium offers 1,488 seats.

Practical Information. Grand Théâtre de Genève, 11 Boulevard du Théâtre, 1211 Geneva 11. Tel: 41 22 418 30 00, Fax: 41 22 418 30 01. When visiting Grand Théâtre de Genève, stay at the Hôtel du Rhône, Quai Turrettini 1, 1211 Geneva 1. Tel: 41 22 731 98 31 or 1-800-223-6800, Fax 41 22 732 45 58. The Hôtel du Rhône is in the center of the city with views of the Rhône, and is close to the opera house. The Hôtel du Rhône can assist with opera tickets and schedule.

COMPANY STAFF AND PREMIERES

Directeur Général. Renée Auphan (1995–present), Hugues Gall (1980–1995), Jean-Claude Riber (1973–1980), Herbert Graf (1965–1973), Marcel Lamy (1962–65).

World Premieres. Grétry's *Isabelle et Gertrude*, 1767; Bovy-Lysberg's *La fille du Carillonneur*, 1853-54; N.N. *La Reine de Provence*, 1856-57; Kling's *Le dernier des Paladins*, 1863-64; Kling's *Le Flûtiste*, 1876-77; Grisy's *Jacques Clément*, 1886-87; Lacomb's *Winkelried*, 1891-92; Jaques-Dalcroze's *Janie*, 1893-94; Audran's *Photis*, 1895-96; Delaye's *A bicyclette*, 1897-98; Signan's *Anita*, 1898-99; De Seigneux & Lauber's *Tout s'arrange*, 1903-04; Maurice's *Le Drapeau blanc*, 1903-04; Deveux's *Le Mariage impromptu*, 1906-07; De Seigneux & Combe's *Yvonne*, 1907-08; Aubert's *La forêt bleue*, 1912-13; Knopf's *Les baisers perdus*, 1923-24; Jaques-Dalcroze's *Le petit roi qui pleure*, 1931-32; Chatelain's *Nuit d'Argentine*, 1933-34; Closset's *Amour des Ailes*, 1939-40; Dupérier's *La Malade imaginaire*, 1943-44; Martin's *Monsieur de Pourceaugnac*, 1962-63; Banfield's *Alissa*, 1964-65; Milhaud's *La mère coupable*, 1965-66; Liebermann's *La forêt*, April 8, 1987; Arrigo's *Il ritorno di Casanova*, April 18, 1985.

Bibliography. Roger de Candolle, *Histoire du Théâtre de Genève* (Geneva, 1978). Jean-Jacques Roth, *Grand Théâtre de Genève: Opéras-Moments d'exception* (Geneva, 1987). *Centenaire du Grand Théâtre de Genève: 1879-1979* (Geneva, 1979). *Le Grand Théâtre de Genève* (Geneva, 1995). Interview with Edouard Lambelet, Attaché de direction.

Thanks to Marie-Claire Mermoud and Isabelle Jornod, Grand Théâtre de Genève; Marco Torriani, and Stevan Bradly.

LUZERN

Luzerner Theater

The Luzerner Theater, also called the Stadttheater Luzern, was inaugurated on November 7, 1839, with Schiller's *Wilhelm Tell*. Designed by Louis Pfyffer in classic style, the theater was under construction for two years. It was run by the city of Luzern from 1839, but not until 1931 was an Intendant was hired.

The Jesuits build the first theater in 1740, the Comödienhaus. After the religious order was disbanded in 1773, the town took control of the theater. Discussions started as early as 1812 about replacing the structure, which only came to fruition in the late 1830s, opening in 1839. It was remodeled near the end of the 19th century and reopened with Goethe's *Egmont*. In 1906 a Jugendstil annex was added. Between 1968 and 1970, the theater was remodeled and updated with open balconies and holding 564 seats. It was reopened with Molière's *Die gelehrten Frauen* on March 14, 1970.

Although it is primarily a theater for spoken drama, operas do share the stage and over the years, several well-known (in Europe) singers have used it as a springboard for their careers, like Inge Borkh, Fritz Uhl, Manfred Röhrl, and Ferry Gruber. It is an ensemble company with 27 soloists, 16-member chorus, and orchestra. Since 1970, it has concentrated on less frequently staged Verdi works, like *Ernani* and the Swiss premiere of Giuseppe Verdi's *Il due Foscari*, and has also mounted other Swiss premieres, like Gian Carlo Menotti's *Help, Help, the Globolinks*, Sergey Prokofiev's *Bethrothal in a Monastery*, Gaetano Donizetti's *Maria Stuarda*, Dimitri Shostakovich's *Nos* (The Nose), Benjamin Britten's *Owen Wingrave*, and Hans-Werner Henze's *Die englische Katze*. On May 14, 1975, it hosted a world premiere, Kurt Schwertsik's *Der lange Weg zur grossen Mauer*. Among other works offered were Jacques Offenbach's *Les contes d'Hoffmann*, Wolfgang Amadeus Mozart's *Così fan tutte* and *Idomeneo*, and Verdi's *Macbeth*. Recent repertory includes Mozart's *La clemenza di Tito*, Ludwig van Beethoven's *Fidelio*, Gaetano Donizetti's *L'elisir d'amore*, and Domenico Cimarosa's *Il matrimonio segreto*.

Practical Information. Luzernertheater, Theaterstraße 2, 6002 Luzern. Tel: 41 210-6618, Fax: 41 210-3367. If visiting the Luzernertheater, contact the Swiss National Tourist Office, 608 Fifth Avenue, New York, NY 10020; Tel: 212-757-5944.

COMPANY STAFF

Intendanten. Horst Statkus, Philippe de Bros, Ulrich Meyer, Kraft-Alexander, Horst Gnekow, Walter Oberer, Ernst Dietz, Albert Wiesner, Paul Eger, Carl Schneider, Gottfried Falkenhausen.

Bibliography. André Gottrau, ed., *Luzern und sein Theater: 150 Jahre Stadttheater* (Luzern, 1989).

———— ST. GALLEN

Stadttheater St. Gallen

The Stadttheater was inaugurated on March 15, 1968 with Ludwig van Beethoven's *Fidelio*. The modern 855-seat, concrete structure, designed by Claude Paillard, was built between 1964–68.

The first opera arrived in St. Gallen in 1806 with the visit of a French troupe. In 1850, Johann Christoph Kunkler submitted plans for a new theater in a "courtly" Baroque style. Known as Theater am Bohl, it was opened with Wolfgang Amadeus Mozart's *Don Giovanni*. By the early part of the 20th century almost all of Richard Wagner's works had been staged, along with Richard Strauss's *Salome* (1910-11), *Der Rosenkavalier* (1912-13), and *Ariadne auf Naxos* (1913-14).

Discussions about a new building began at the beginning of the 1960s. When it finally opened in 1968, Christoph Groszer was at the helm. He staged a variety of operas including Mozart's *Die Zauberflöte*, *Le nozze di Figaro*, *Don Giovanni,* and *Così fan tutte*, Giuseppe Verdi's *La forza del destino*, *Il trovatore*, *Don Carlos*, Carl Orff's *Die Kluge*, Benjamin Britten's *Albert Herring*, Wagner's *Der fliegende Holländer*, Eugen d'Albert's *Tiefland*, and Maurice Ravel's *L'heure espagnole*. When Wolfgang Zörner took the reins in 1973, his first staging involved Britten's *Beggar's Opera* foiled by Verdi's *Attila*. The 1975-76 season opened with Verdi's *Aida*. Gaetano Donizetti's *Lucia di Lammermoor* arrived at the beginning of 1976, and Verdi's *Simon Boccanegra* and Charles Gounod's *Faust* graced the stage in early 1977. The *Faust* production was unusual — conceived as a catholic mystery play. The following year Mozart's *Idomeneo* and Beethoven's *Fidelio* were in the repertory. Arthur Honeggers's *Jeanne d'Arc au bûcher* was staged in 1979. Four years later, the first stage performance ever of Max Lang's *Der Alchimist* took place on April 15, 1983. The Swiss premiere of Nicolay Rimsky-Korsakov's *The Tsar's Bride* was staged in 1985, followed by another novelty, Peter Maxwell Davies's *The Lighthouse*. Meanwhile, works as varied as Christoph Willibald Gluck's *Orfeo und Euridice* and Leoš Janáček's *Jenůfa* ushered in the 1980s. Verdi's *Nabucco*, Pyotr Il'yich Tchaikovsky's *Eugene Onegin*, and Gioachino Rossini's *Il barbiere di Siviglia* among others were on the 1981-82 season schedule. Beginning with the 1984-85 season "mini-Verdi-cycles" and "mini-Italian-cycles were offered. For example, *Nabucco*, *Otello*, and *La forza del destino* played that first season, followed by Verdi's *Ernani* and *La traviata*, and Giacomo Puccini's *La bohème* two seasons later. Donizetti's *Lucia di Lammermoor*, Vincenzo Bellini's *Norma*, and Verdi's *Rigoletto* were mounted in 1989, and a rarely performed Verdi opera, *I due Foscari*, Ruggero Leoncavallo's *I pagliacci*, Puccini's *Gianni Schicchi*, and Verdi's *Il trovatore* were also given. The company offered the first performance outside of Romania of Nicolae Bretan's *Golem der Rebell* on October 19, 1990, and the world premiere of Daniel Fueter's *Stichtag* on February 7, 1998. The programming at the Stadttheater is approximately 40% opera. Recent offerings include Georges Bizet's *Carmen*, Georg Friedrich Händel's *Serses*, and Verdi's *La traviata* and *Attila*.

Practical Information. Stadttheater St. Gallen, Museumstraße 24, 9000 St. Gallen. Tel: 41 71 26 05 05, Fax: 41 71 26 05 06. If visiting the Stadttheater, contact the Swiss National Tourist Office, 608 Fifth Avenue, New York, NY 10020; Tel: 212-757-5944.

COMPANY STAFF AND WORLD PREMIERES

Intendanten. Hermann Keckeis, Glado von May, Wolfgang Zörner, Ernst Dietz, Christoph Graszer.

World Premieres (Since 1980). M. Lang's *Der Alchimist* (first stage production), April 15, 1983; D. Fueter's *Stichtag* on February 7, 1998. **Swiss Premieres:** N. Rimsky-Korsakow's *The Tsar's Bride* February 23, 1985; P. M. Davies's *The Lighthouse*, September 13, 1986; N. Bretan's *Golem der Rebell* October 19, 1990.

Bibliography. Stadttheater St. Gallen 1980 bis 1992 (St. Gallen, 1992).

Thanks to Kimberly Randall and Thomas Potter.

ZURICH

Opernhaus Zürich

On October 1, 1891, the Opernhaus Zürich, originally known as the Stadttheater, hosted Richard Wagner's *Lohengrin*. The opera house, designed by Ferdinand Fellner and Hermann Helmer, had officially opened its doors the previous day. The world premiere of Rudolf Kelterborn's *Der Kirschgarten* reopened the Opernhaus on December 1, 1984, after a major expansion and restoration.

On October 24, 1832, private shareholders founded a theater society to establish a proper Temple to the Muses. The Aktientheater was inaugurated on November 10, 1834, with Wolfgang Amadeus Mozart's *Die Zauberflöte*. Konradin Kreutzer directed his *Nachtlager von Granada* there in 1839, and Wagner, during his exile in Zurich between 1849–1858, was associated with the Aktientheater. He directed the Swiss premiere of his *Der fliegende Holländer* on April 25, 1852, as well as his *Tannhäuser*, along with Carl Maria von Weber's *Der Freischütz*, Vincenzo Bellini's *Norma*, Ludwig van Beethoven's *Fidelio*, and Mozart's *Don Giovanni* and *Die Zauberflöte*, among others. The theater hosted works for more than 55 before fire ended its existence on New Year's night 1890.

The following year the Stadttheater, owned by its subscribers and managed by the municipality, opened. It hosted the world premieres of Ferruccio Busoni's *Turandot* and *Arlecchino* on May 11, 1917, Othmar Schoeck's *Venus* in 1922, Acts I and II of Alban Berg's *Lulu* on June 2, 1937, (his widow delayed the completion of Act III, only partially written at the time of his death, for more than 40 years), and Paul Hindemith's *Mathis der Maler* on May 28, 1938. The next year Helde Gueden made her debut as Cherubino in Mozart's *Le nozze di Figaro*. After World War II, Beniamino Gigli and Kirsten Flagstad performed in Zurich, followed by Hindemith's revised *Cardillac* on June 20, 1952. The first staging of Arnold Schönberg's *Moses und Aron* took place on June 6, 1957. The *Uraufführungen* continued with Bohuslav Martinů's *Recké pašije* (*The Greek Passion*) on June 9, 1961, Paul Burkhard's *Barbasuk* on December 3, 1961, Armin Schibler's *Blackwood & Co.* on June 3, 1962, with Gwyneth Jones making her debut, Kelterborn's *Die Errettung Thebens* on June 23, 1963, Heinrich Sutermeister's *Madame Bovary* on May 26, 1967, Giselher Klebe's *Ein wahrer Held* on January 18, 1975, and Kelterborn's *Ein Engel kommt nach Babylon* on June 5, 1977.

Opernhaus Zürich was a haven for young singers to try out new roles in an acoustically sympathetic auditorium. James McCracken sang his first Giacomo Meyerbeer's *Le Prophète* there, Agnes Baltsa her first Carmen, and José Carreras his first Werther. Some productions were good, and others not so. Recently, under the tenure of Alexander Pereira, the house has changed its emphasis to star vehicles with productions that belie the composer's intent. One such production was Verdi's *La forza del destino*, staged as a play inside a play, on an almost bare stage, so the opera house could afford the big fees of the star-studded cast. Recent operas include Verdi's *Rigoletto* and *Ernani*, Giacomo Puccini's *Il trittico* and *Tosca*, Franz Schubert's *Alfonso und Estrella*, Donizetti's *Linda di Chamounix* and *Lucia di Lammermoor*, Georges Bizet's *Carmen*, Wagner's *Tristan und Isolde*, Weber's *Oberon*, Frank Martin's *La vin herbé*, Umberto Giordano's *Madama Sans-Gêne*, Mozart's *Die Zauberflöte* and *Così fan tutte*, Gioachino Rossini's *Il barbiere di Siviglia*, and Jacques Offenbach's *Les contes d'Hoffmann* and *La périchole*.

Opernhaus Zürich

After the demise of the Aktientheater, construction began on the Stadttheater Zürich. In 1925, a separate playhouse was erected, and the Stadttheater was renamed Opernhaus Zürich to reflect its new role of a theater devoted exclusively to opera, operetta, and ballet.

By the 1970s, the Opernhaus was in state of disrepair and was to be razed. An architectural competition was held for the modern theater complex that was to be constructed on the site. Architect W. Dunkel won the commission but the necessary money did not appear. Instead 61 million SF were voted by the government to reconstruct the existing opera house and enlarge it. Riots followed the voting of the renovation money. There was a police cordon around the opera house for opening night. The reopening coincided with the 150th anniversary of the first permanent theater in Zurich, the Aktientheater.

The Opernhaus Zürich is a *fin-de-siècle* building, with Teutonic inspiration. Built of white and gray stone, the facade exhibits a tetrastyle portico with busts of composers, and Corinthian pilasters support two pediments. The rococo auditorium, adorned with caryatids, cherubs, and garlands, holds three tiers with ivory and gold parapets, and plush red seats. The auditorium seats 1,238.

Practical Information. Opernhaus Zürich, Falkenstraße 1, 8008 Zurich. Tel: 41 1 268 6666, Fax: 41 1 268 6401. When visiting the Opernhaus Zürich, stay at the Hotel Europe, Dufourstraße 4, 8008 Zurich. Tel: 41 1 47 10 30, Fax: 41 1 25 10 367. It is one block from the opera house. They can assist with opera tickets and schedule.

COMPANY STAFF

Intendanten. Alexander Pereira (1991–present), Christoph Grozner (1986–1991), Claus Helmut Drese (1975–1986), Hermann Juch (1964–1975), Emil Jucker, Werner Meyer and Christian Vöchting (1962–64), Herbert Graf (1960–1962), Karl-Heinz Krahl (1956–60), Hans Zimmermann (1947–56), Karl Schmid-Bloss (1932–47), Paul Trede (1921–32), Alfred Reucker (1901–1921), Karl Skraup (1898–901), Ludwig Treutler (1896–1898), Paul Schroetter (1891–96).

Opernhaus Zurich (Zurich, Switzerland).

Bibliography. Martin Hürlimann, *Vom Stadt-theater zum Opernhaus: Züricher Theatergeschichten* (Zurich, 1980). *150 Jahre Theater in Zürich* (Zurich, 1984). Hans Erismann, *Das ging ja gut an: Geschichter und Geschichte des Opernhauses Zürich* (Zurich, 1984). *Opernhaus Zürich: Jahrbuch 1989–90.* (Zurich, 1990).

Other Swiss Companies

Other opera Companies in Switzerland are noted below by name, address, telephone, recent repertory, and general director (as available).

Opéra de Lausanne, Théâtre Municipal. CP 3972, Lausanne 1002. Tel: 41 21 310 1600, Fax: 41 21 310 1690. **Recent Repertory:** La clemenza di Tito, Fidelio, L'elisir d'amore, Idomeneo, Il matrimonio segreto. **General Director:** Dominique Meyer.

Bieler Musiktheater. Burggasse 19, 2502 Biel. Tel: 41 32 22 71 21; Fax: 41 32 22 16 14. **Recent Repertory:** Die lustige Witwe, Hänsel und Gretel, L'heure espagnole, Die schwarze spinne, **Administrator:** Mario Bettoli.

Opera Factory Zürich. Grüngasse 20, 8004 Zurich. Tel: 41 1 291 22 85, Fax: 41 1 291 67 40. **Artistic Director:** David Freeman.

Wales

Welsh National Opera
(Opera Cenedlaethol Cymru Cyf)

On April 15, 1946, in the Prince of Wales Theater, Cardiff, the first staged performances of the Welsh National Opera took place with the double bill of Pietro Mascagni's *Cavalleria rusticana* and Ruggero Leoncavallo's *I pagliacci*. Along with Charles Gounod's *Faust*, presented the following evening, those were the offerings of the inaugural season. Idloes Owen, one of the company's founders, was on the podium for Mascagni's opera and Ivor John conducted *I pagliacci* and *Faust*. A Swansea section of the Welsh National Opera was formed for western Wales in 1949.

The Welsh National Opera originated as an amateur company, run by all Welsh people that evolved into a professional organization. Its philosophy was summed up by Richard Fawkes in his 1986 history of the company, "The Welsh National Opera was the first British opera company in modern times to grow out of popular demand, and the basic belief that opera is not an elitist art form but one for anybody and everybody who enjoys a good night out at the theatre…"

Back in 1890, another Welsh National Opera existed, which toured with Joseph Parry's *Arianwen* and *Blodwen*, but it went bankrupt. During the 1920s and 1930s, the Cardiff Grand Opera Society flourished before it, too, drowned in a sea of red ink. Before World War II, the Barry Grand Opera Company along with a few other amateur companies staged occasional productions with professional singers. The first seeds for the current Welsh National Opera were planted on November 21, 1943, at a gathering at Owen's house, with Helena Hughes Brown, and John Morgan, a former singer with the Carl Rosa Opera Company. It was professional companies like the Carl Rosa, Moddy-Manners, and the British National Opera that brought grand opera to Wales before the founding of the present company.

The company took root on December 2, 1943, when 28 people, who knew Owen, met at the Cathays Methodist Chapel and established the company of amateur singers. There were two purposes: to stop the exodus of talent from Wales, and to give local singers an opportunity to perform in grand opera. It was originally called the Lyrian Grand Opera Company, but then renamed (before the meeting adjourned) Welsh National Opera. The company's first performance was on April 23, 1944, a fund-raising concert given at the Empire Theater in Cardiff. Excerpts from Carl Maria von Weber's *Der Freischütz*, Giuseppe Verdi's *Un ballo in maschera*, the overture to

Mikhail Glinka's *Ruslan and Lyudmila*, and a concert rendering of *Cavalleria rusticana* were on the program. The company's second season opened on April 28, 1947, with Georges Bizet's *Carmen*, which, in addition to repeating the first season's works, completed the repertory. In September, the company made its first appearance in Swansea, giving a Sunday concert in the Empire Theatre as part of Swansea's Civic Week. Owen and John shared the conducting chores. The third season added Verdi's *La traviata* and Giacomo Puccini's *Madama Butterfly* to the schedule. By the fourth season, 1949, the company expanded from the mainstream to mount Bedřich Smetaná's *Prodaná nevěsta* (The Bartered Bride) followed by Jacques Offenbach's *Les contes d'Hoffmann* in 1950. Two more Verdi operas, *Nabucco* and *Rigoletto* were mounted in 1952, before the company presented its first world premiere on November 9, 1953, Arwel Hughes' *Menna*. Verdi works continued to be popular with *Les vêpres siciliennes*, *I Lombardi*, *Il trovatore*, *La battaglia di Legnano*, *Macbeth*, and *Falstaff* all in the repertory before 1970.

The dawn of the 1960s witnessed another Welsh opera, Hughes's *Serch Yw'r Doctor* staged on August 1, 1960, at the Sophia Gardens Eisteddfod Pavilion in Cardiff. Meanwhile, Richard Wagner operas entered the repertory on October 1, 1962, with the staging of *Lohengrin*. Two of Gioachino Rossini's grandeur works, *Guillaume Tell* and *Mosè in Egitto* also arrived in the first part of the 1960s. The 1970s brought Verdi's *Aida*, *Simon Boccanegra*, *Otello*, *I masnadieri*, *Ernani*, and *Don Carlo*, along with Alban Berg's *Lulu* and Leoš Janáček's *Jenůfa* and *Věc Makropulos* (The Makropoulos Affair). Janáček's *Z Mrtvého Domu* (From the House of the Dead) and *Příhody Lišky Bystroušky* (The Cunning Little Vixen) followed in the early 1980s. The company staged Wagner's *Tristan und Isolde* for the first time in 1979 followed by the Ring Cycle in the early 1980s. The schedule also offered a couple of rarities like Bohuslav Martinů's *Řecké pašije* (The Greek Passion) and Antonín Dvořák's *Jakobín*. Worthy of mention are the company's world premieres: Grace Williams's *The Parlour* on May 5, 1966, Alun Hoddinott's *The Beach of Fales* on March 26, 1974, William Mathias's *The Servants* on September 15, 1980, and John Metcalf's *The Journey* on June 12, 1981.

The repertory spans four centuries from Claudio Monteverdi to Benjamin Britten, to provide as wide an offering as possible, as mandated by the Arts Council in their funding. The company concentrates on the Italian and German repertory, but covers all types, with recent works like Britten's *Billy Budd*, Puccini's *Tosca*, Monteverdi's *L'incoronazione di Poppea*, Mussorgsky's *Boris Godunov*, and Verdi's *La traviata*. It has gained a reputation for its interest in lesser known works like Christoph Willibald Gluck's *Iphigénie en Tauride*. Each tour offers a few popular works and one less known one. The company's two goals are to give Welsh singers a platform to launch their careers and to champion Welsh operas. There is a permanent chorus and orchestra. The productions unite a musical tradition with a sense of theater, but not always successfully. Controversial German directors like Harry Kupfer and Ruth Berghaus staged Ludwig van Beethoven's *Fidelio* and Wolfgang Amadeus Mozart's *Don Giovanni*, respectively — and caused scandals, and the 50th anniversary production of *Nabucco* was called "offensive." There is no "company" style, but a mixture of traditional, straightforward, productions with the outrageous and provocative ones — to challenge the audience. The singers are predominately young and of Welsh background with an occasional international artist performing to try out a new role in a secure environment. Projects are shaped around available talent. The quality of voices is similar to that of a middle-level regional company in the United States.

The company does not have a theater it calls home but it is planned that on St. David's Day, 2000, the Cardiff Bay Opera House will open, at which time the Welsh National Opera will have a permanent home. Anthony Freud, the general director, believes this will help the company "come of age, to reach maturity," and "provide the natural next step in development." The touring will continue in the following cities and theaters — the two principal ones being Cardiff (New Theatre) and Swansea (Grand Theater). The others are Oxford (Apollo Theatre), Plymouth (Theatre Royal), Southampton (The Mayflower), Birmingham (Hippodrome Theatre), Liverpool (Empire Theatre), Bristol (Hippodrome Theatre). It tours for 15 weeks in England and 3 weeks in Wales. The Arts Council decides where the company tours, not the company nor the finances.

New Theater (Cardiff, Wales).

Cardiff New Theatre

The New Theatre, designed by Ernst Runtz in the Edwardian style, opened in late 1906, during King Edward's reign. The cornerstone was laid on March 29, 1906. The theater experienced a bad period during the 1960s when it was converted to a bingo hall, but a group formed, known as the New Theater Society, which helped bring a renaissance to the theater during the 1970s. It underwent restoration in 1987-88.

The red brick exterior leads into a cozy, two-tier auditorium. Fluted, gilded, pillars separate the pairs of proscenium boxes, which are embellished with gilded wrought iron. The maroon velvet seats match the maroon patterned wallpaper and maroon-painted ceiling. Garland-wreath designs embellish the ivory-colored parapets. A spider-like chandelier with glass globes illuminates the space.

Grand Theatre (Swansea, Wales).

Swansea Grand Theatre

Adelina Patti laid the cornerstone for the Grand Theater, which opened on July 26, 1897. William Hope was the architect with H.H. Morell and R. Mouillot as the proprietors. The Grand hosted opera from the beginning of the century, when on January 29, 1900, the Carl Rosa Opera Company visited, offering *Carmen, Lohengrin, The Bohemian Girl, Faust* and *Maritana*. On February 5, 1923, the Swansea Amateur Opera Society presented six nights of the *Mikado* and *Patience.*

The theater is a Victorian jewel. The two-tier auditorium is lyre shaped with deep salmon-colored pillars supporting the balcony. Gilded acanthus leaves and putti embellish the pillars, and gilded putti and angels ornament the ivory-colored parapets. The dome ceiling holds a small crystal chandelier ringed with gilded decorations. The ceiling and walls are painted a faux-marble green. Red pillars line the side walls, their capitals serving as lamp fixtures.

Practical Information. Welsh National Opera, John Street, Cardiff CF1 4SP. Tel: 44 1222 464-666, Fax: 44 1222 483-050. When visiting the Welsh National Opera in Swansea, contact the Swansea Tourism Office, County Hall, Oystermouth Road, Swansea SA1 3SN. Tel: 44 1792 636 851, Fax: 44 1792 636 603. For Cardiff, contact the British Tourist Authority, 40 West 57th Street, New York, NY 10019, 212-581-4700.

COMPANY STAFF AND PREMIERES

General Director. Anthony Freud (1994–present). Music Directors: Carlo Rizzi (1992–present), Charles Mackerras (1987–91), Richard Armstrong (1973–86), James Lockhart (1968–73), Bryan Balkwill (1963–67), Charles Groves (1961–63).

World Premieres. 1946–1985 A. Hughes *Menna,* November 9, 1953; Grace Williams's *The Parlour,* May 5, 1966; Alun Hoddinott's *The Beach of Fales,* March 26, 1974; William Mathias's *The Servants,* September 15, 1980; John Metcalf's *The Journey,* June 12, 1981.

Bibliography. Richard Fawkes, *Welsh National Opera* (London, 1986). *Welsh National Opera: A Celebration* (Cardiff, 1995). *Opera Live: Magazine of the*

Grand Theater auditorium detail (Swansea, Wales).

Welsh National Opera, Issue One. Interviews with Dewi Savage, Isabel Murphy, and David Alden, Welsh National Opera.

Thanks to Liza Ford, Hazel Hardy, and Debbie Court, Welsh National Opera; and Jackie Thomas, Economic Development Division, City and County of Swansea.

SWANSEA VALLEY

Neath Opera Group

The Neath Opera Group was established in 1963 by Clive John and Dudley Hopkins, who staged their first opera in the tiny theater at Craig-y-Nos, Adelina Patti's former castle residence. Patti inaugurated her theater in 1891 with Giuseppe Verdi's *La traviata* (Act I, Patti as Violetta), Charles Gounod's *Faust* (garden scene, Patti as Marguerite and Ernesto Nicolini as Faust).

Patti bought the castle as a retreat, but after her death in 1919, it was used as a tuberculosis hospital and then a home for the elderly, until the Neath Opera Group began staging opera. The company successfully mixes professional soloists, a semi-professional orchestra, and an amateur chorus to stage works as Otto Nicolai's *Die lustigen Weiber von Windsor* and Georges Bizet's *Les pêcheurs de perles*. Recent offerings include Giacomo Puccini's *Tosca*.

There are also discussion between Gwyneth Jones and the current castle owners about converting it to a full-time music center, with funds from the British Lottery.

Craig-Y-Nos Theatre

The castle is a "Victorian/Edwardina country house." The small theater auditorium is embellished with delicate floral patterns, fluted Corinthian columns, and a stage curtain with a painting of Patti as Semiramide. There are 158 seats.

Practical Information. Neath Opera Group, Craig-y-Nos castle, Swansea Valley (near Abercrave on A4067)). Tel: 44 1222 464-666, Fax: 44 1222 483-050. When visiting the Neath Opera Group, contact the Swansea Tourism Office, County Hall, Oystermouth Road, Swansea SA1 3SN. Tel: 44 1792 636 851, Fax: 44 1792 636 603.

Thanks to Jackie Thomas, Economic Development Division, City and County of Swansea.

Other Welsh Companies

Other companies in Wales are noted below by name, address, telephone, fax, and general director.

Music Theatre Wales (Touring Company). 5 Llandaff, Cardiff CF1 9NF. Tel: 44 1222 230 833, Fax: 44 1222 342 046. **Artistic Director:** Michael McCarthy, Michael Rafferty.

Mid Wales Opera (Touring Company). Meifod, Powys SY22 6By. Tel: 44 1938 500 611, Fax: 44 1938 500-681. **Director:** Barbara McGuire.

Book Recommendations

The following books are the best I found on their respective subjects. They are grouped by languages, and are recommended as additions to both public and private libraries. Publisher information, as available, is included.

English

Annalen van de Opera Gezelschappen in Nederland: 1886–1995 (Amsterdam, 1996). Bilingual (Dutch and English). Published by Theater Institut Nederland.

Arensberg, Ingrid. *Göteborgs Operan i Hamn / Göteborg Opera House* (Göteborg, 1994). Bilingual (Swedish and English). Published by Byggnadskommittén för NY Musikteater.

Fawkes, Richard. *Welsh National Opera* (London, 1986). Published by Juliá MacRae Books.

Holmes, Robyn (ed.). *Through the Opera Glass* (Adelaide, 1991).

Kaldor, Andras. *Opera Houses of Europe* (Suffolk, England, 1988). Published by the Antique Collector's Guild, Market Street Industrial Park, Wappinger's Falls NY 12590; Tel: 914-297-0003; Fax 914-297-0068.

Mead, Christopher Curtis. *Charles Garnier's Paris Opera: Architectural Empathy and the Renaissance of French Classicism* (Cambridge, Massachusetts, 1991). Published by the MIT Press, 55 Hayward Street, Cambridge MA 02142-1399. Tel: 617-625-8569.

Oopperatalo Helsinki • Opera House Helsinki. Published by Kustannus Oy Projektilehti (Helsinki, 1995). (Finnish, English, German).

Pasini, Roberto, and Remo Schiavo. *The Verona Arena: The Largest Opera House in the World* (Venice, 1995). Published by Arsenale Editrice, San Polo 1789, 30125 Venice, Italy. Tel: 39 41 524-0610; Fax: 39 41 524-0865. (Originally published in Italian).

Spott, Frederic Spott. *Bayreuth: A History of the Wagner Festival* (New Haven and London, 1994). Published by Yale University Press, P.O.Box 209040, New Haven CT 06520-9040. Tel: 203-432-0964; Fax: 203-432-2394.

Walker, Hugh. *The O'Keefe Center: Thirty Years of Theatre History* (Toronto, 1991). Published by Key Porter Books.

Dutch (see also Flemish)

Annalen van de Opera Gezelschappen in Nederland: 1886–1995 (Amsterdam, 1996). Bilingual (Dutch and English). Published by Theater Institut Nederland.

Finnish

Il mari laukkonen, Pohjalaisista Carmenin: Vaasan Ooppera Historia 1956–96. (Vaara, 1995).

Oopperatalo Helsinki • Opera House Helsinki. Published by Kustannus Oy Projektilehti (Helsinki, 1995). (Finnish, English, German).

Flemish

Various authros, *De Opera van Gent: Het "Grand Théâtre" van Roelandt, Philastre en Cambon* Uitgeverij Lannoo (Ghent, 1993)

French

Le centenaire Opera. Ville de Montpellier (Toulouse, 1988).
Chabro, Philippe. *Chorégies d'Orange 1971–1994* (Avignon, 1995). Published by Actes Sud.
Le Grand Théâtre de Genève (Geneva, 1995). Published by Editions Suzanne Hurter, Cercle du Grand Théâtre de Genève.
La Monnaie • De Munt: Gerard Mortier 1981–1991 (Brussels, 1992).
Opéra de Nice Histoire d'un Centenaire 1885–1985 (Nice, 1985).
Un Théâtre d'Opéra: L'Equipe de Grand Mortier à la Monnaie (Paris, 1986). Published by Éditions Duculot.
Trois Siècles d'opera à Lyon (Lyon, 1982).

German

Die Bregenzer Festspiele Residenz Verlag (Salzburg and Vienna, 1995). Residenz Verlag, Gaisbergstraße 6, 5025 Salzburg, Austria. Tel: 43 662 64 19 86; Fax: 43 662 64 35 48.
Dreissig Jahre Deutsche Oper Berlin (Berlin, 1985).
Fuhrich, Edda, and Gisela Prossnitz. *Die Salzburger Festspiele Band I 1920–1945: Ihre Geschichte in Daten, Zeitzeugnissen und Bildern* (Salzburg and Vienna, 1990). Published by Residenz Verlag, Gaisbergstraße 6, 5025 Salzburg, Austria. Tel: 43 662 64 19 86; Fax: 43 662 64 35 48.
Hammer, Sabine (ed.). *Oper in Hannover* (Hannover, 1990). Published by Schlütersche Verlagsanstalt und Druckerei, Georgswall 4, 3000 Hannover, Germany.
Hönrsch, Winfried. *Opern Metropole Dresden* (Dresden, 1995). Published by G+B Fine Arts Verlag GmbH, Glashütter Straße 55, 01309 Dresden, Germany. Tel: 49 351 310 0052; Fax: 49 351 310 5245.
Nationaltheater: Die Bayerische Staatsoper (Munich, 1992). Published by Verlagsgruppe Bruckmann, Nymphenburger Straße 86, 80636 Munich, Germany. Tel: 49 89 125-7308; Fax: 49 89 125-7318.
Oopperatalo Helsinki • Opera House Helsinki. Published by Kustannus Oy Projektilehti (Helsinki, 1995). (Finnish, English, German).

Italian

Bedini, Gilberto (ed.). *Il Teatro del Giglio a Lucca: L'architettura di giovanni e Cesare Lazzarini* (Lucca, 1998).
Brusatin, Manlio, and Giuseppe Pavanello. *Il Teatro La Fenice: I Progetti • L'Architettura • Le Decorazioni* (Venice, 1987). Published by Albrizzi Editore.
Carmassi, Massimo. *Il Restauro del Teatro Verdi di Pisa* (Pisa, 1994). Published by Pucini Editore.
Dell 'Ira, Gino. *I Teatri di Pisa (1773–1986)* (Pisa, 1987). Published by Giardini Editori.
Fabbri, Paolo, and Roberto Verti. *Due secoli di teatro per musica a Reggio Emilia* (Reggio Emilia, 1987).
Gherpelli, Giuseppe. *L'Opera nei Teatri di Modena* (Modena, 1988). Published by Artioli Editore.
Liberio, Francesca Maria, et al. *Teatro Ponchielli di Cremona* (Cremona, 1995).
Luna, Luca. *Teatro Ventidio Basso Città di Ascoli Piceno* (Ascoli Piceno, 1996). Published by D & D Editori.
Motta, Fermo Giovanni (ed.). *Teatri delle terre di Pesaro e Urbino* (Milan, 1997). Published by Electa.
Raimondi, Silvia. *Oltre Il Velario: Fantasmi di palcoscenico al Teatro Coccia di Novara* (Milan, 1993). Published by Silvana Editoriale.
Romagnoli, Sergio, and Elvira Garbero. *Teatro a Reggio Emilia: Dal Rinascimento alla Rivoluzione Francese Vol I* (Florence, 1980). Published by Sansoni Editore.
_____, and _____. *Teatro a Reggio Emilia: Dalla Restaurazione al Secondo Novecento Vol II* (Florence, 1980). Published by Sansoni Editore.
Roscioni, Carlo Marinelli. *Il Teatro di San Carlo: La Cronologia 1737–1987 Vol. I* (Napoli, 1988). Various authors, *Il Teatro di San Carlo Vol. II* (Napoli, 1988). Published by Guida Editori.
Sainati, Fabrizio. *Teatro Rossi. Lo Splendore e L'Abbandono* (Pisa, 1997). Published by Pucini Editore.
Sforza, Francesco Sforza. *Grandi Teatri Italiani* (Rome, 1993). Published by Editalia, Edizioni d'Italia S.p.A., via di Pallacorda 7, 00186 Rome, Italy. Tel: 39 6 687-9655; Fax: 39 6 686-9561.
Trezzini, Lamberto (ed.). *Due Secoli di Vita Musicale: Storia del Teatro Comunale di Bologna 3 vols.* (Bologna, 1987). Published by Nuova Alfa Editoriale.

Portuguese

Seabra, Augusto. *Ir a S. Carlos* (Lisdon, 1993).

Swedish

Arensberg, Ingrid. *Göteborgs Operan i Hamn / Göteborg Opera House* (Göteborg, 1994). Bilingual (Swedish and English). Published by Byggnadskommittén för NY Musikteater.

Sjögren, Henrik. *Konst & Nöje: Malmö Stadsteater 1944–1994* (Malmö, 1994).

Bibliography

Books used for reference in researching specific houses are listed within the text, as part of the entries for those particular houses. Books that provided information on several houses are listed below, along with other works of interest.

Selected Works on Music, Architecture, and History

English

British and International Music Yearbook 1997 (London, 1997).
Dembsky, Stephen, et al. *International Vocabulary of Music* (New York, 1979).
Ewen, David. *Encyclopedia of the Opera* (New York, 1963).
Grout, Donald Jay. *A Short History of Opera* (New York, 1963).
Grun, Bernard. *The Timetables of History* (New York, 1979).
Harewood, Earl of. *The Definitive Kobbé's Opera Book* (New York, 1987).
Harris, Cyril (ed.). *Illustrated Dictionary of Historic Architecture* (New York, 1977).
Kaldor, Andras. *Opera Houses of Europe* (Suffolk, England, 1988).
Kennedy, Michael. *The Oxford Dictionary of Music* (New York and Oxford, 1985).
Musical America Directory 1997 (New York, 1997).
Rosenthal, Harold, and John Warrack. *The Concise Oxford Dictionary of Opera* (Oxford, 1989).
Sachs, Harvey. *Music in Fascist Italy* (New York, 1987).
Sadie, Stanley (ed.). *History of Opera* (New York and London, 1990).
_____. *The New Grove Dictionary of Music and Musicians* (Washington, D.C., and London, 1980).
_____. *The New Grove Dictionary of Opera* (New York and London, 1992).
Slonimsky, Nicolas (ed.). *Lectionary of Music* (New York, 1989).
Zietz, Karyl Lynn. *Opera! The Guide to Western Europe's Great Houses* (Santa Fe, 1991).
_____. *Opera Companies and Houses of the United States: A Comprehensive, Illustrated Reference* (Jefferson, North Carolina, and London, 1995).

German

Zöchling, Dieter. *Opernhäuser in Deutschland, Österreich und der Schweiz* (Düsseldorf, 1983).

Italian

Lo Spettacolo La Musica • Il Teatro • Il Cinema (Busto Arsizio, 1987).
Mioli, Piero. *Dizionario della Musica Italiana: La musica lirica* (1996, Milan).
Motta, Fermo Giovanni (ed.). *Teatri delle terre di Pesaro e Urbino* Electa (Milan, 1997).
Sforza, Francesco. *Grandi Teatri Italiani* (Rome, 1993).

Selected Works on Composers, Conductors, Singers

English

Becker, Heinz, and Gudrun Becker. *Giacomo Meyerbeer: A Life in Letters* (Portland, 1983).
Blaukopf, Kurt. *Mahler* (New York, 1985).
Brophy, Brigid. *Mozart the Dramatist* (New York, 1988).
Budden, Julian. *Verdi* (New York, 1987).
Chotzinoff, Samuel. *Toscanini: An Intimate Portrait* (New York, 1956).
Conati, Marcello. *Encounters with Verdi* (New York, 1984).
Cross, Milton, and David Ewen. *Milton Cross' Encyclopedia of Great Composers and Their Music, Volumes I and II* (Garden City, 1962).
Dowley, Tim. *Schumann—His Life and Times* (New York, 1982).
Gillies, Malcom. *The Bartok Companion* (London, 1993).
Glass, Philip. *Music by Philip Glass* (New York, 1987).
Greenfeld, Howard. *Caruso* (New York, 1983).
Lehmann, Lilli. *My Path Through Life* (New York, 1914).
Lehmann, Lotte. *My Many Lives* (New York, 1948).
Leinsdorf, Erich. *Cadenza* (Boston, 1976).
Lesznai, Lajos. *Bartók* (London, 1961).
Massenet, Jules. *My Recollections* (Boston, 1919).
Mordden, Ethan. *Demented* (New York, 1990).
Mountfield, David. *Tchaikovsky* (London and New York, 1990).
Murphy, Agnes. *Melba: A Biography* (New York, 1909).
Osborne, Charles. *The Complete Operas of Verdi* (New York, 1987).
_____. *The Complete Operas of Richard Strauss* (North Pomfret, Vermont, 1988).
Osborne, Richard. *Rossini* (Boston, 1986).
Phillips-Matz, Mary Jane. *Verdi: A Biography* (New York, 1993).
Pleasants, Henry. *The Great Singers* (New York, 1981).
Pugnetti, Gino. *Life and Times of Beethoven* (Milan and New York, 1967).
Sachs, Harvey. *Toscanini* (New York, 1987).
Sadie, Stanley (ed.). *Handel* (New York, 1968).
Snowman, Daniel. *Placido Domingo's Tales from the Opera* (London, 1994).
Vogel, Jaroslav. *Leoš Janáček* (New York, 1981).
Wechsberg, Joseph. *Verdi* (New York, 1974).
_____. *The Waltz Emperors* (New York, 1973).
Weinstock, Herbert. *Rossini* (New York, 1987).
_____. *Bellini: His Life and His Operas* (New York, 1971).

German

Willaschek, Wolfgang. *Mozart-Theater von Idomeneo bis zur Zauberflöte* (Stuggart, 1996).

Italian

Sara cino, Egidio (ed.). *Tutti I Libretti di Donizetti* (Milan, 1993).

Index

459